Encyclopedia of Rhetoric and Composition

GARLAND REFERENCE LIBRARY OF THE HUMANITIES (VOL. 1389)

Advisory Board

Encyclopedia of Rhetoric and Composition
Communication from Ancient Times to the Information Age

Edited by
Theresa Enos

GARLAND PUBLISHING, INC.
New York & London
1996

Library of Congress Cataloging-in-Publication Data

Encyclopedia of rhetoric and composition: communication from ancient times to
    the information age / edited by Theresa Enos
        p.   cm.
    Includes index.
    ISBN 0-8240-7200-6 (alk. paper)
      1. Rhetoric—Encyclopedias. I. Enos, Theresa.
PN172.E53 1996   95-25581
808'.003—dc20   CIP

Cover design by Larry Wolfson Design, NY

Printed on acid-free, 250-year-life paper
Manufactured in the United States of America

Contents

Preface

The *Encyclopedia of Rhetoric and Composition* is a one-volume reference work and guide, arranged in alphabetical sequence, that provides an introduction to rhetoric, including the major periods and personages, concepts and applications. Rhetoric, though the oldest and broadest of the humanities, is becoming ever more difficult to locate in a conceptual framework because it draws increasingly on disciplines like anthropology, linguistics, philosophy, and psychology. Nearly every article or book on rhetoric attempts to place it within one or another of these frameworks, although many theorists are reconceptualizing rhetoric in its own terms. The *Encyclopedia*'s entries discuss rhetoric's debts and contributions to these and other disciplines and present an overview of rhetoric in the late twentieth century.

Confining the spaciousness of rhetoric and its 2,500-year history of theory and praxis into one volume cannot completely capture rhetoric's metadisciplinary nature. I hope, however, that this *Encyclopedia of Rhetoric and Composition* can not only suggest the scope of rhetoric as it is studied in different disciplines in American higher education but also give us future direction in communicating within and across complex, multilayered discourse communities.

The *Encyclopedia*'s 467 entries (over half a million words) take four forms: brief "identifications" of a figure, term, or concept (for example, Hugh Blair, Commonplaces, *Kairos*); elaborated "notes" (for example, Exposition, Hermeneutics, Nietzsche); "essays" that explore a topic in depth (for example, Aristotle, Ethos, Feminist Rhetoric); and full "articles" that illuminate rhetoric's art and methodology (for example, Argument, Composition Studies, Invention).

The number of contributors—288—reflects the vitality of work in rhetoric in two-year colleges, liberal arts colleges, comprehensive universities, and research universities. The author of each entry either has established professional recognition by scholarship on a figure or area in rhetoric or is currently doing research, traditional or revisionist, on a specific topic.

The *Encyclopedia* is written for the student in rhetoric, for the specialist in literature or another field of study who wants to learn about one or more aspects of rhetoric, and for the specialist in rhetoric who wants to see how the discipline is evolving. In addition, I hope that the volume will provide many opportunities for those in different yet similar disciplines to form research communities, sharing scholarship.

Following each entry is a bibliography of key texts and recommended reading. Cross-references are provided as "see also" topics at the end of an entry when there is significant further discussion of the topic or a closely related topic to which the reader is directed for further reading. For complete references, a comprehensive index has been provided. Also provided is a list of contributors and entries.

I am deeply indebted to my eminent advisory board. They not only fleshed out my beginning list of topics but also suggested names of appropriate contributors. Because each advisor has published major scholarship in a particular area, I asked that each write a substantive entry. Those board members who actively participated by writing a major entry—in some cases, entries—have strengthened the *Encyclopedia*'s ethos of "authority." I particularly thank those who became editors as well as advisors and contributors, reading and evaluating many entries for coverage and accuracy: Carroll C. Arnold, Ernest G. Bormann, Stuart C. Brown, Richard Leo Enos, Richard L. Johannesen, Henry W. Johnstone, Jr., James J. Murphy, Robert L. Scott, Kathleen E. Welch, and W. Ross Winterowd.

I thank Gregory R. Glau, my editorial assistant, who created the project's computer database and kept track of all the manuscripts as they went through several copyediting stages. And I thank the interns who efficiently formatted the manuscripts: Richard McNabb, Leslie Dupont, and Roberta Binkley.

I owe special thanks to Garland's Gary Kuris, who took a chance on my undertaking the general editorship alone after two colleagues had to withdraw from the project because of the sentence of time it imposed. I have tried to live up to Gary's faith in me, to pull off what some said couldn't be done—to put the history of rhetoric into one volume. Gary offered encouragement when I needed it the most during the three years I lived with this project, coming to feel more and more as Samuel Johnson described himself while working on his *Dictionary:* a "harmless drudge."

But I have learned much about rhetoric and have greatly expanded my circle of colleagues. Especially I have learned how much I did not know about the field in which I've been working for twenty years. This endeavor has enriched me as a teacher, scholar, and editor working in the realm of rhetoric.

Theresa Enos
University of Arizona

Contributors

Don Paul Abbott
Department of Rhetoric and Communication
University of California, Davis
Renaissance Rhetoric

Valentina M. Abordonado
Department of English
University of Arizona
Gertrude Buck

Chris M. Anson
Department of English
University of Minnesota
Portfolio
Writing across the Curriculum

Dianne Armstrong
Department of English
Santa Barbara City College
Pragmatics

Carroll C. Arnold, Emeritus
Department of Communication
Pennsylvania State University
Herbert A. Wichelns
James Albert Winans

Janet M. Atwill
Department of English
University of Tennessee
Aristotle
Technê

Ken Autrey
Department of English
Francis Marion University
Demosthenes
Lysias
Fred Newton Scott

Philip Bakelaar
Department of Rhetoric and Communications
Temple University
Protest Rhetoric

James S. Baumlin
Department of English
Southwest Missouri State University
Roland Barthes
Paul de Man
Eloquence

Charles Bazerman
Department of Literature, Communication,
    and Culture
Georgia Institute of Technology
Royal Society of London

Walter H. Beale
Department of English
University of North Carolina, Greensboro
Decorum

Samuel L. Becker
Department of Communication Studies
University of Iowa
Albert Craig Baird

Daniel Bender
Department of Literature and Communications
Pace University
Copia
Imitation

James Benjamin
Department of Communication
University of Toledo
Deliberative Oratory

Beth S. Bennett
Department of Speech Communication
University of Alabama
Alcuin of York
Cassiodorus

Thomas W. Benson
Department of Speech Communication
Pennsylvania State University
Longinus
Rhetoric of Film

Stephen A. Bernhardt
Department of English
New Mexico State University
Electronic Rhetoric
Visual Rhetoric

James A. Berlin
Department of English
Purdue University
Cultural Studies
Ralph Waldo Emerson

Margie Berns
Department of English
Purdue University
Sociolinguistics

Goodwin Berquist
Department of Speech
Ohio State University
Robert T. Oliver

Don H. Bialostosky
Department of English
Pennsylvania State University
M.M. Bakhtin
Dialogics

Barbara A. Biesecker
Rhetoric Department
University of Iowa
Oratory
The Other

Susan Biesecker
Department of Rhetoric and Communication
University of Pittsburgh
Oratory

Gerald Biesecker-Mast
Department of Rhetoric and Communication
University of Pittsburgh
Oratory

Roberta Binkley
Department of English
University of Arizona
Walter J. Ong

Patricia Bizzell
Department of English
College of the Holy Cross
Discourse
Margaret Fell
Women Rhetoricians

Jane Blankenship
Department of Communication
University of Massachusetts, Amherst
Karl R. Wallace

Saralinda Blanning
Department of Humanities
Michigan Technological University
Julia Kristeva

Dennis R. Bormann
Department of Speech Communication
University of Nebraska, Lincoln
George Campbell

Ernest G. Bormann
Department of Speech-Communication
University of Minnesota
Fantasy Theme Analysis
Ghostwriting

Grant M. Boswell
Department of English
Brigham Young University
Henry Peacham

Deborah Brandt
Department of English
University of Wisconsin, Madison
Literacy

Bill Bridges
Department of English
New Mexico State University
Logology
Pentad
Terministic Screens

Glenn J. Broadhead
Department of English
College of the Redwoods
Generative Rhetoric

Dottie Broaddus
Arts and Sciences
Arizona State University West
Rhetoric of Advertising

Brenda Gabioud Brown
Department of Language and Literature
University of Science and Arts of Oklahoma
Elocution

Robert L. Brown
Department of English
University of Minnesota
Marxist Rhetoric

Stuart C. Brown
Department of English
New Mexico State University
Basic English
I.A. Richards

Barry Brummett
Department of Communication
University of Wisconsin, Milwaukee
Rhetoric of Silence

Richard Buchanan
Department of Design
Carnegie Mellon University
Richard P. McKeon

Christopher C. Burnham
Department of English
New Mexico State University
James Britton
Peter Elbow
Journal Writing
New Rhetorics

Siew C. Burroughs
Department of English
Bowling Green State University
Rhetor
Rhetorician

Gideon Burton
Department of English
University of Southern California
Jean-Jacques Rousseau

Donald E. Bushman
Department of English
University of North Carolina, Wilmington
Deduction
Example

Induction
Periodic Style

Guanjun Cai
Department of English
University of Arizona
Eight-Legged Essay

Alice Calderonello
Department of English
Bowling Green State University
Clarity

Linda T. Calendrillo
Department of English
Eastern Illinois University
Memory

Martin Camargo
Department of English
University of Missouri
Ars Dictaminis

J.L. Campbell
Department of English
Henderson State University
Speech Acts

Karlyn Kohrs Campbell
Department of Speech-Communication
University of Minnesota
Feminist Rhetoric

Robert W. Cape, Jr.
Department of Classical and
        Modern Languages
Austin College
Horace

Susan Brown Carlton
Department of English
Pacific Lutheran University
Poetics

Thomas M. Carr, Jr.
Department of Modern Languages
University of Nebraska, Lincoln
René Descartes
Port-Royalists

Michael Carter
Department of English
North Carolina State University, Raleigh
Persona
Paul Ricoeur

Vincent Casaregola
Department of English
Saint Louis University
Sir Philip Sidney
Technical Communication
Twentieth-Century Rhetoric

Richard A. Cherwitz
Department of Communication
University of Texas, Austin
Logic

James W. Chesebro
Department of Communication
Indiana State University
Dramatism

Gregory Clark
Department of English
Brigham Young University
Contextuality

Jeanne Clark
Department of English
Arizona State University
African-American Rhetoric

John M. Clark
Department of English
Bowling Green State University
Computer Applications in Rhetoric
Readability

Dana L. Cloud
Department of Speech Communication
University of Texas, Austin
Edwin Black

Richard M. Coe
Department of English
Simon Fraser University, Burnaby
Metaphor
Pre-Socratics

Herman Cohen
Department of Speech Communication
Pennsylvania State University
Belles-lettres
Speech Communication

Joseph Colavito
Department of English
Northwestern State University
Antidosis
Digressio

Exordium
Narratio
Partitio
Pathos
Peroratio
Quadrivium

James Comas
Department of English
Syracuse University
Philosophy of Rhetoric

Joseph Comprone
Arts and Sciences
Arizona State University West
Rhetoric of Advertising

Celeste Michelle Condit
Department of Speech Communication
University of Georgia
Robert L. Scott

Louise Rodriguez Connal
Department of English
University of Arizona
Comparison
Contrast
Emphasis

Ulla M. Connor
Department of English
Indiana University
Contrastive Rhetoric

Robert J. Connors
Department of English
University of New Hampshire
Edward P.J. Corbett
Henry Noble Day

Martha Cooper
Department of Communication Studies
Northern Illinois University
Michel Foucault
Persuasion

Edward P.J. Corbett
Department of English
Ohio State University
John Henry Newman

L.A. Coutant
Department of English
New Mexico State University
Baldesar Castiglione

William A. Covino
Department of English
University of Illinois at Chicago
Thomas DeQuincey
Magic
W. Ross Winterowd

Andy Crockett
Department of English
University of Arizona
Cause and Effect
Unity

Sharon Crowley
Department of English
Pennsylvania State University
Current-Traditional Rhetoric
Jacques Derrida

Timothy W. Crusius
Department of English
Southern Methodist University
James L. Kinneavy

Roger Dahood
Department of English
University of Arizona
Bede

Frank J. D'Angelo
Department of English
Arizona State University
Rhetorical Criticism

Beth Daniell
Department of English
Clemson University
Eric Havelock
Orality

Reed Way Dasenbrock
Department of English
New Mexico State University
J.L. Austin
Karl Popper

Suzanne M. Daughton
Department of Speech Communication
Southern Illinois University
Kathleen M. Hall Jamieson

Diane (Mowery) Davis
Department of English
Old Dominion University
Logocentrism

Janet B. Davis
Division of Language and Literature
Northeast Missouri State University
Eristic
Stasis Theory

Sheila Davis
The New School for Social Research, New York
Metonymy
Synecdoche

Ray D. Dearin
Department of Speech Communication
Iowa State University
Lucie Olbrechts-Tyteca
Chaïm Perelman

Stephen P. Depoe
Department of Communication
University of Cincinnati
Political Rhetoric

Michael E. Doherty, Jr.
Department of English
Bowling Green State University
Thomas Hobbes

William G. Doty
Department of Religious Studies
University of Alabama
Myth

Bernard K. Duffy
Department of Speech Communication
California Polytechnic State University,
     San Luis Obispo
Richard M. Weaver

Patricia L. Dunmire
Department of English
Carnegie Mellon University
Irony

Leslie Dupont
Department of English
University of Arizona
Lloyd F. Bitzer
Frank J. D'Angelo

Bruce L. Edwards
Department of English
Bowling Green State University
Robert E. Longacre
Kenneth L. Pike
Donald C. Stewart
Tagmemics

Lois J. Einhorn
Department of English, General Literature,
    and Rhetoric
Binghamton University
Carroll C. Arnold

Peter Elbow
Department of English
University of Massachusetts, Amherst
Speaking and Writing

Richard Leo Enos
Department of English
Texas Christian University
Cicero
Corax
Empedocles
Wilbur Samuel Howell
Henry W. Johnstone, Jr.
Rhetorica ad Herennium
Suetonius
Tisias

Elizabeth Ervin
Department of English
University of North Carolina, Wilmington
Prolegomena
Trivium

H.L. Ewbank
Department of Communication
University of Arizona
Symbolic Action

Lahcen E. Ezzaher
Department of English
University of Arizona
Arabic Rhetoric

Jeanne Fahnestock
Department of English
University of Maryland, College Park
Arrangement

Julie M. Farrar
Department of English
Saint Louis University
Evidence
Proof
Twentieth-Century Rhetoric

Thomas B. Farrell
Department of Communication Studies
Northwestern University
Commonplaces

Contingency
Phronésis

Julia Kay Ferganchick-Neufang
Department of English
University of Arizona
Description

Linda Ferreira-Buckley
Department of English
University of Texas, Austin
Nineteenth-Century Rhetoric
Pedagogy

Linda Flower
Department of English
Carnegie Mellon University
Cognitive Rhetoric

Elizabeth A. Flynn
Department of Humanities
Michigan Technological University
Julia Kristeva

Mary Foertsch
Department of English
Bentley College
Hélène Cixous
Refutatio

Dawn M. Formo
Department of English
University of Southern California
Percy Bysshe Shelley

Karen A. Foss
Department of Speech Communication
Humboldt State University
Ernesto Grassi
Jürgen Habermas

Dana L. Fox
Department of Language, Reading, and Culture
University of Arizona
Empirical Research

Roselyn L. Freedman-Baum
Department of Communications/Journalism
St. John Fisher College
Leonard Cox

Mary G. French
Department of English
New Mexico State University
Journal Writing

Richard Fulkerson
Department of English
East Texas State University
Axiology
Informal Logic
Stephen Toulmin
Warrant

John T. Gage
Department of English
University of Oregon
Enthymeme
Albert R. Kitzhaber

Lynee Lewis Gaillet
Department of English
Georgia State University
George Jardine

Robert N. Gaines
Department of Speech Communication
University of Maryland, College Park
Syllogism

Mark Gellis
Department of English
Purdue University
Edmund Burke
Joseph Priestley

Karen H. Gentry
Department of English
Clemson University
Eric Havelock

Cheryl Glenn
Department of English
Oregon State University
Aspasia

Maureen Daly Goggin
Department of English
Carnegie Mellon University
Rhetoric Society of America

W. Terrence Gordon
Department of French
Dalhousie University, Nova Scotia
Jeremy Bentham
Charles Kay Ogden

James R. Gray
Department of Education
University of California, Berkeley
The National Writing Project

Lawrence D. Green
Department of English
University of Southern California
Scholasticism

Stuart Greene
Department of English
University of Wisconsin, Madison
Protocols

Bruce E. Gronbeck
Department of Communication Studies
University of Iowa
Donald C. Bryant
Douglas W. Ehninger
Marshall McLuhan
Walter J. Ong

Alan G. Gross
Department of Rhetoric
University of Minnesota
Paradigm Shift
Rhetoric of Science

Ken Guyer
Department of English
New Mexico State University
Bertrand Russell

Anne-Marie Hall
Department of English
University of Arizona
Ethnography
Louise M. Rosenblatt

Gary Layne Hatch
Department of English
Brigham Young University
Ernest G. Bormann
Robert Zoellner

Sheri L. Helsley
Department of English
Old Dominion University
Kairos

Edwina Helton
Department of English
Miami University
Diotima

Diane L. Hendrix
Department of English
New Mexico State University
Rhetorical Question

Carl G. Herndl
Department of English
New Mexico State University
Paulo Freire
Marxist Rhetoric
Raymond Williams

Bruce Herzberg
Department of English
Bentley College
Gilbert Austin
Alexander Bain
Hugh Blair
Boethius
Erasmus
Adams Sherman Hill
David J. Hill
Peter Ramus
Thomas Sheridan

James W. Hikins
Department of Communication
Ohio State University
Logic

Russel Hirst
Department of English
University of Tennessee
Homily
Liturgy
Sir Joshua Reynolds
Sermon

David Holmes
Department of English
Pepperdine University
Nonfiction Prose

Winifred Bryan Horner
Department of English
Texas Christian University
William Edmondstoune Aytoun
Eighteenth-Century Rhetoric

Forrest Houlette
Department of English
Ball State University
H. Paul Grice
Roman Jakobson

Sue Hum
Department of English
University of Massachusetts, Dartmouth
Semiotics

Anne Hungerford
Department of English
Simon Fraser University, British Columbia
Pre-Socratics

Billie Andrew Inman
Department of English
University of Arizona
Thomas Carlyle

William F. Irmscher, Emeritus
Department of English
University of Washington
*Conference on College Composition and
 Communication*

Robert L. Ivie
Department of Speech Communication
Indiana University
Figurative Language

Martin J. Jacobi
Department of English
Clemson University
Richard M. Weaver

Debra L. Jacobs
Department of English
University of South Florida
Voice

Dale Jacquette
Department of Philosophy
Pennsylvania State University
David Hume
Willard Van Orman Quine

Richard L. Johannesen
Department of Communication Studies
Northern Illinois University
Martin Buber
Ethics
Ultimate Terms

Clifford Johnson
Department of English
University of California, Irvine
Reader-Response Criticism

Nan Johnson
Department of English
Ohio State University
Ethos
John Franklin Genung
Barrett Wendell

Ralph H. Johnson
Department of Philosophy
University of Windsor, Ontario
Fallacy

Henry W. Johnstone, Jr.
Department of Philosophy
Pennsylvania State University
Philosophical Argument

David A. Jolliffe
Department of English
DePaul University
Genre

David S. Kaufer
Department of English
Carnegie Mellon University
Irony

Phil M. Keith
Department of English
St. Cloud State University
Janice M. Lauer

George A. Kennedy
Department of Classics
University of North Carolina
Letteraturizzazione

Thomas Kent
Department of English
Iowa State University
Deconstruction
Paul Feyerabend
Ludwig Wittgenstein

M. Jimmie Killingsworth
Department of English
Texas A&M University
Discourse Community
Environmental Rhetoric

Robert L. Kindrick
Office of the Dean for Academic Affairs
University of Montana
Geoffrey de Vinsauf

James L. Kinneavy
Department of English
University of Texas, Austin
Communication Triangle
Homiletics
Pistis

John T. Kirby
Department of Classics
Purdue University
Atticism
Greek Rhetoric
The Second Sophistic

C.H. Knoblauch
Department of English
State University of New York, Albany
Ernst Cassirer

Bruce Krajewski
Department of English
Laurentian University, Ontario
Friedrich Nietzsche

Barry M. Kroll
Department of English
Lehigh University
John Dewey

Carol Dana Lanham
UCLA Center for Medieval and Renaissance
    Studies
University of California, Los Angeles
Salutatio

Richard L. Lanigan
Department of Speech Communication
Southern Illinois University
Phenomenology

Catherine Lappas
Department of English
Saint Louis University
Ferdinand de Saussure
Signified/Signifier/Signifying

Richard L. Larson
English, Herbert H. Lehman College
City University of New York
National Council of Teachers of English

Janice M. Lauer
Department of English
Purdue University
Heuristics
Topics
Richard E. Young

John Philip Lesko
Department of Applied Linguistics
University of Edinburgh
American Indian Rhetoric

Creighton Lindsay
Department of English
University of Oregon
George Payn Quackenbos

Stephen W. Littlejohn
Department of Speech Communication
Humboldt State University
Communication Theory

Yameng Liu
Department of English
Carnegie Mellon University
Confucius
Correctness

Elenore Long
Department of English
Carnegie Mellon University
Cognitive Rhetoric

Ronald F. Lunsford
Department of English
University of North Carolina, Charlotte
Noam Chomsky

William Lutz
Department of English
Rutgers University, Camden
Doublespeak

Teresa A. Lyle
Department of English
Miami University
Sappho

Arabella Lyon
Department of English
Temple University
Alfred Jules Ayer
Gottlob Frege
Logical Positivism

Chris McCloud
Department of English
Arizona State University
Sojourner Truth

Bruce McComiskey
Department of English
East Carolina University
Dissoi Logoi
Nomos

James P. McDaniel
Department of Communication Studies
University of Iowa
Oratory
The Other

Geraldine McNenny
Department of English
University of Houston, Downtown
Collaboration

Mark Lawrence McPhail
Department of Communication
University of Utah
Black English
Ideological Criticism

Steven Mailloux
Department of English and Comparative
    Literature
University of California, Irvine
Hermeneutics
Pragmatism
Reception Study

LuMing R. Mao
Department of English
Miami University
Metadiscourse

Marlene V. Meisels
Learning Skills Center
University of North Carolina, Chapel Hill
Jean Piaget

Yvonne Merrill
Department of English
University of Arizona
Christine de Pizan

David Metzger
Department of English
Old Dominion University
Biblical Rhetoric
Indian Rhetoric

Louis T. Milic, Emeritus
Department of English
Cleveland State University
Stylistics

Bernard A. Miller
Department of English
Eastern Michigan State University
Gorgias

Keith D. Miller
Department of English
Arizona State University
African-American Rhetoric
W.E.B. DuBois

Thomas P. Miller
Department of English
University of Arizona
Lord Kames
John Wilkins
John Witherspoon

Clyde Moneyhun
School of Humanities
New Mexico Highlands University
Antonio Gramsci

Aron Morgan
Department of English and Comparative
 Literature
University of California, Irvine
Medieval Rhetoric

Jean Dietz Moss
Department of English
Catholic University of America
Dialectic(s)

Roxanne Mountford
Department of Language, Literature, and
 Communication
Rensselaer Polytechnic Institute
Ars Praedicandi

Mark Mullen
Department of English and Comparative
 Literature
University of California, Irvine
Umberto Eco
Postmodernism

James J. Murphy
Department of Rhetoric and Communication
University of California, Davis
Quintilian
Omer Talon

Leonard Nathan, Emeritus
Department of Rhetoric
University of California, Berkeley
Rhetoric and Poetry

Jasper Neel
Department of English
Vanderbilt University
Poststructuralism

Gerald Nelms
Department of English
Southern Illinois University
Janet Emig
Ken Macrorie

Eugene A. Nida
American Bible Society
Kennett Square, Pennsylvania
Translation

William L. Nothstine
Portland, Oregon
Persuasion

Donovan J. Ochs
Department of Rhetoric
University of Iowa
Roman Rhetoric
Stoics

Kathryn M. Olson
Department of Communication
University of Wisconsin, Milwaukee
Dissociation

Sean Patrick O'Rourke
Department of Communication Studies
Vanderbilt University
Confirmatio
Modes of Discourse
Progymnasmata

John Paddison
Department of English
Northern Arizona University
Alasdair MacIntyre

Terry L. Papillon
Department of Foreign Languages
Virginia Polytechnic Institute and State
 University
Handbooks
Rhetorica ad Alexandrum
Socrates

Elizabeth Patnoe
Department of English
Ohio State University
Hyperbole
Narrative Theory

Amy Patterson
Department of English
Texas Christian University
Mina Shaughnessy

Cynthia Patton
Department of Rhetoric and Communication
Temple University
Protest Rhetoric

Catherine Hobbs Peaden
Department of English
University of Oklahoma
Condillac
John Locke

Richard Penticoff
Department of English
University of Idaho
Saint Augustine

Jane M. Perkins
Department of English
Iowa State University
Donald Davidson

Tarla Rai Peterson
Department of Speech Communication and
    Theater Arts
Texas A&M University
Rhetoric and Technology

James Phelan
Department of English
Ohio State University
Wayne C. Booth
Narrative Theory
Rhetoric in Fiction

Louise Wetherbee Phelps
The Writing Program
Syracuse University
Composition Studies

Daniel J. Pinti
Department of English
New Mexico State University
John of Salisbury

Ralph S. Pomeroy
Department of Rhetoric and Communication
University of California, Davis
Lord Chesterfield
Richard Whately

James E. Porter
Department of English
Purdue University
Audience
Author

Carol Poster
Department of English
University of Missouri
Demetrius
Peripatetics

George L. Pullman
Department of English
Georgia State University
Semantics

William M. Purcell
Department of Speech Communication
University of Washington
Style

Arthur Quinn
Department of Rhetoric
University of California, Berkeley
Accumulatio
Anacoluthon
Anadiplosis
Anapodoton
Anastrophe
Antanaclasis
Anthimeria
Antimetabole
Antiptosis
Antithesis
Aposiopesis
Apostrophe
Asterismos
Asyndeton
Catachresis
Chiasmus
Diacope
Diaphora
Ellipsis
Enallage
Epanalepsis
Epanorthosis
Epiphora
Epizeuxis
Figures of Speech
Gradatio
Hendiadys
Hypallage
Hyperbaton
Hyperbole

Inclusio
Isocolon
Metalepsis
Parenthesis
Periphrasis
Pleonasm
Ploce
Polyptoton
Polysyndeton
Preteritio
Repetitio
Scesis Onomaton
Syllepsis
Symploce
Tmesis
Zeugma

D.R. Ransdell
Department of English
University of Arizona
James Moffett
George of Trebizond

Lyon Rathbun
Department of Rhetoric
University of California, Berkeley
Accumuatio
Anacoluthon
Anadiplosis
Anapodoton
Anastrophe
Antanaclasis
Anthimeria
Antimetabole
Antiptosis
Antithesis
Aposiopesis
Apostrophe
Asterismos
Asyndeton
Catachresis
Chiasmus
Diacope
Diaphora
Ellipsis
Enallage
Epanalepsis
Epanorthosis
Epiphora
Epizeuxis
Figures of Speech
Gradatio
Hendiadys
Hypallage
Hyperbaton

Hyperbole
Inclusio
Isocolon
Metalepsis
Parenthesis
Periphrasis
Pleonasm
Ploce
Polyptoton
Polysyndeton
Preteritio
Repetitio
Scesis Onomaton
Syllepsis
Symploce
Tmesis
Zeugma

Lucinda C. Ray
Department of English
Iowa State University
Thomas S. Kuhn

John Frederick Reynolds
Department of English
City College, CUNY
Delivery

Jennifer L. Rigdon
Department of Speech Communication
Southern Illinois University
Kathleen M. Hall Jamieson

Duane H. Roen
Department of English
Arizona State University
Coherence
Cohesion
Collaboration
Discourse Analysis
Louise M. Rosenblatt

Hephzibah Roskelly
Department of English
University of North Carolina, Greensboro
Charles Sanders Peirce

J. Clarke Rountree, III
Department of Communication Arts
University of Alabama, Huntsville
Sophist

Katherine E. Rowan
Department of Communication
Purdue University
Exposition

John Paul Russo
Department of English
University of Miami
Samuel Taylor Coleridge

David Sabrio
Department of Language and Literature
Texas A&M University, Kingsville
Actio
Classification
Illustration

Muriel Saville-Troike
Department of English
University of Arizona
Anaphora

Edward Schiappa
Department of Communication
University of Minnesota
Definition
Protagoras
Rhêtorikê
Sophistic Rhetoric

Janice Schuetz
Department of Communication and
    Journalism
University of New Mexico
Wayne Brockriede

Robert L. Scott
Department of Speech-Communication
University of Minnesota
Epistemic Rhetoric

Lynda Sexson
Department of Religion
Montana State University
Biblical Rhetoric

Cady W. Short-Thompson
Department of Communication
University of Cincinnati
Political Rhetoric

Herbert W. Simons
Department of Rhetoric and Communication
Temple University
Protest Rhetoric

David Snowball
Department of Speech Communication
Augustana College
Style

J. Michael Sproule
Department of Communication Studies
San Jose State University
Propaganda

Jayme Stayer
Department of English
University of Toledo
M.M. Bakhtin
Dialogics

John Stewart
Department of Speech Communication
University of Washington
Walter R. Fisher

James F. Stratman
Technical Communication Program
University of Colorado, Denver
Legal Rhetoric

Omar Swartz
Department of Communication
Purdue University
Hermagoras
Praxis
Probability

C. Jan Swearingen
Department of English
University of Texas, Arlington
Plato

Bernadette Takano
Department of English
University of Oklahoma
Condillac

Victor E. Taylor
Department of English
Syracuse University
Hans-Georg Gadamer

Nathaniel Teich
Department of English
University of Oregon
Rogerian Rhetoric

David M. Timmerman
Department of Humanities
Indiana University, Kokomo
Epideictic Oratory

Barbara Toth
Department of English

Bowling Green State University
Kenneth L. Pike

Judith S. Trent
Department of Communication
University of Cincinnati
Political Rhetoric

John Trimbur
Department of English
Worcester Polytechnic Institute
Social Construction

Lynn Quitman Troyka
Department of English
Queensborough Community College
City University of New York
Basic Writing

H. Lewis Ulman
Department of English
Ohio State University
Adam Smith

Clifford Vaida
Department of English
Ohio State University
Immanuel Kant

Richard E. Vatz
Department of Speech and Mass
    Communication
Towson State University
Rhetoric and Psychiatry

Rex L. Veeder
Department of English
St. Cloud State University
Ann E. Berthoff

Donald Phillip Verene
Department of Philosophy
Emory University
Giambattista Vico

Victor J. Vitanza
Department of English
University of Texas, Arlington
Historiographies of Rhetoric
Logocentrism

William A. Wallace
Department of English
University of Maryland, College Park
Telos

Arthur E. Walzer
Department of Rhetoric
University of Minnesota
Purpose

Barbara Warnick
Department of Speech Communication
University of Washington
Fénelon
Bernard Lamy
Scottish Enlightenment

John Warnock
Department of English
University of Arizona
William E. Coles, Jr.
Expressionism
James Moffett
Process/Product

Tilly Warnock
Department of English
University of Arizona
Kenneth Burke
Identification

Duane F. Watson
Department of Religion and Philosophy
Malone College
Antiphon
Ars Poetica

Sam Watson
Department of English
University of North Carolina, Charlotte
Michael Polanyi

John C. Weaver
Department of English
Purdue University
Thomas Wilson

Lee S. Weinberg
Public and International Affairs
University of Pittsburgh
Rhetoric and Psychiatry

Irwin Weiser
Department of English
Purdue University
Linguistics

Kathleen E. Welch
Department of English
University of Oklahoma
Isocrates

Jennifer Welsh
Department of English
University of Southern California
Matthew Arnold

Joseph W. Wenzel
Department of Speech Communication
University of Illinois
Marie Hochmuth Nichols

Charles Arthur Willard
Department of Communication
University of Louisville
Argument

David Cratis Williams
Division of Language and Literature
Northeast Missouri State University
Consubstantiality

Theodore Otto Windt, Jr.
Department of Communication
University of Pittsburgh
Hoyt Hopewell Hudson
Everett Lee Hunt

W. Ross Winterowd
Department of Rhetoric, Linguistics, and
    Literature
University of Southern California
Grammar
E.D. Hirsch, Jr.

Cecil Wooten
Department of Classics
University of North Carolina
George A. Kennedy

George E. Yoos
Department of Philosophy
St. Cloud State University
Logos

Richard E. Young
Department of English
Carnegie Mellon University
Invention

Pat Youngdahl
Department of English
University of Arizona
Identification
Pulpit Oratory
Religious Rhetoric

Ning Yu
Department of English
University of Arizona
Imagery

James P. Zappen
Department of Language, Literature, and
    Communication
Rensselaer Polytechnic Institute
Francis Bacon

David Zarefsky
School of Speech
Northwestern University
Speech Communication Association

Heping Zhao
Department of English and Comparative
    Literature
California State University, Fullerton
Chinese Rhetoric

Accumulatio

Stringing together words, phrases, or clauses that say essentially the same thing. The author of *Rhetorica ad Herennium* used accumulatio in explaining, "He [the defendant] is the betrayer of his own self-respect, and the waylayer of the self-respect of others; covetous, intemperate, irascible, arrogant; disloyal to his parents, ungrateful to his friends" (I.xl). Repetition, the essence of accumulatio, can be used to amplify a contention, as in the above quotation, or to make an audience more comfortable with an unfamiliar idea by allowing them to dwell on it. Shakespeare achieves the latter effect humorously in *Henry IV, Part 2* when Shallow answers Falstaff, "I will not excuse you; you shall not be excus'd; excuses shall not be admitted; there is no excuse shall serve you; you shall not be excus'd" (5.1.5).

Arthur Quinn and Lyon Rathbun
University of California, Berkeley

Actio

Latin word for "action" or "doing"; effective use of physical gestures when delivering a speech. *Actio* is the Latin term for the effective delivery of a speech. Quintilian writes in Book 3 of *Institutio Oratoria* that *actio* is synonymous with *pronuntiatio*, or delivery. The latter term is the fifth part of the art of oratory; the first four are *inventio* (invention or discovery), *dispositio* (arrangement or organization), *elocutio* (style), and *memoria* (memorizing the speech). Later in *Institutio Oratoria*, however, Quintilian, citing Cicero, distinguishes between *actio* and *pronuntiatio,* the former referring to physical gestures, the latter to the voice. Quintilian concludes, nevertheless, that whichever term

one uses, the delivery of a speech has a "powerful effect in oratory" (Book 11).

Before Quintilian, Aristotle and Cicero discussed the importance of delivering speeches effectively. In Book 3 of the *Rhetoric,* Aristotle considers delivery "of the greatest importance." And in *De oratore,* Cicero asserts that delivery "is the dominant factor in oratory," repeating the story that Demosthenes, when asked what was of utmost concern in oratory, said that delivery was first, second, and third in importance (Book 3).

Eighteenth-century rhetoricians continued to assign *actio* an important place in oratory. Hugh Blair (1718–1800) in *Lectures on Rhetoric and Belles Lettres* (1783) devotes lecture number thirty-three to the delivery of a speech. He discusses the loudness of the voice, distinctness of articulation, and the slowness and appropriateness of pronunciation; he further mentions emphases, pauses, tones, and gestures (II.206–10).

In the earlier nineteenth century, Richard Whately (1787–1863) considered *actio* so important that he devoted all of Part 4 of *Elements of Rhetoric* (1828) to this subject. In the table of contents, Part 4 is titled "Of Elocution, or Delivery." Later in the century, however, the growing split between spoken and written rhetoric became more apparent. For example, Alexander Bain (1818–1903), in *English Composition and Rhetoric* (1866), devotes less than one page (of the 343-page book) to the topic of *actio,* noting only that the "Demeanor of the Speaker includes certain points affecting the orator's success" (256). By "demeanor," Bain refers to the speaker's "tone and manner in general" (256).

In the twentieth century, with the rift ever widening between speech departments and

English departments in most schools and colleges in the United States, *actio* and delivery of speeches now receive comparatively little attention. The end of this century and the beginning of the next may witness a revival of interest in *actio* and delivery of speeches as a result of the recently renewed emphasis on the "whole language" approach, that is, the integration of reading, writing, speaking, and listening. The English Coalition Conference, meeting in 1987 under the aegis of the National Council of Teachers of English, passed several resolutions, one of which reads, in part, "The ability to communicate their [students'] views in oral and written form . . . is also indispensable to citizens in a democracy."

David Sabrio
Texas A&M University, Kingsville

Bibliography

Aristotle. *The Art of Rhetoric.* Trans. John Henry Freese. Cambridge, MA: Harvard UP, 1926.

Bain, Alexander. *English Composition and Rhetoric. A Manual.* 1866. New York: Appleton, 1876.

Blair, Hugh. *Lectures on Rhetoric and Belles Lettres.* 1783. Ed. Harold F. Harding. Vol. 1. Carbondale: Southern Illinois UP, 1965.

Cicero. *De Oratore.* Trans. E.W. Sutton. Cambridge, MA: Harvard UP, 1942.

Corbett, Edward P.J. *Classical Rhetoric for the Modern Student.* 3rd ed. New York: Oxford UP, 1990.

Lloyd-Jones, Richard, and Andrea Lunsford, eds. *The English Coalition Conference: Democracy through Language.* Urbana, IL: National Council of Teachers of English, 1989.

Parker, William Riley. "Where Do English Departments Come From?" *College English* 28 (1967): 339–51.

Quintilian. *Institutio Oratoria.* Trans. H.E. Butler. Cambridge, MA: Harvard UP, 1920.

Whately, Richard. *Elements of Rhetoric.* 1828. Ed. Douglas Ehninger. Carbondale: Southern Illinois UP, 1963.

See also DELIVERY; MEMORY

Advertising, Rhetoric of

Symbol systems represented in aural, visual, and verbal advertising texts. Advertising rhetoric has been the subject of analysis in several disciplines throughout the twentieth century. This essay reviews representative areas of cultural and literary theory as they have informed current rhetorical perspectives on advertising in several academic disciplines.

Current theory from a variety of language-oriented disciplines encourages rhetorical applications, including the conscious merging of ideological analysis and textual criticism, to the field of advertising text perhaps more than to any other field. This fact is supported by work in several related disciplines, all of which have in one way or another carried out rhetorical analyses of text.

Recently, the modern and classical language disciplines have been strongly influenced by the work of literary theorists such as the American Stanley Fish, the Russian Mikhail Bakhtin, and feminists Jane Tomkins in America and Julia Kristeva and Hélène Cixous in France. These theorists have broadened the range and critical-ideological perspective on the entire notion of textuality and, more pointedly, on the cultural areas from which the texts subjected to serious consideration are drawn. The disciplines of speech and communication have also broadened their approaches from a traditional study of political discourse to include a far broader range of cultural texts and media. They have also broadened their methodological perspectives to include theorists traditionally associated with the social sciences and humanities.

Finally, historical applications of rhetorical theory, as in recent work on the cultural contexts surrounding the Greek sophists, have been broadened to include analysis of texts drawn from the so-called "low" as well as "high" cultures. In fact, in the different disciplines in which rhetorical theory and analysis have been carried out, distinctions between low and high culture have been effectively blurred if not totally eliminated. Also, as the range of texts subject to historical analysis have expanded, so has the range of study broadened to focus on far more complex socially constructed contexts, rather than simply the texts themselves. The texts become windows opened to new social realities.

These areas traditionally marked out for rhetorical theory and analysis have recently been collectively influenced by two fields of inquiry: composition and cultural studies. In both fields rhetoric has become a favored methodology, a means of connecting political and literary theory to the practice of analyzing and teaching literacy and culture. Composition, with its focus on increasing the writing skills of students, has used classical and modern rhetoric to develop theory-based pedagogies in which rhetorical analysis of culture supports critical writing. Cultural studies, which now exert significant influence on composition studies, have from the 1960s brought together neo-Marxist and new social theory and criticism drawn from a broad range of cultural contexts, including those influenced by mass media.

This collection of traditional academic disciplines and emerging fields of inquiry has created a strong foundation for theoretically informed, critically acute, and pedagogically useful work on the rhetoric of advertising. The rest of this article will describe and summarize work in two specific areas within the larger fields of cultural studies and literary theory. These areas contribute directly to rhetorical theory and practice as they apply to advertising.

Fantasy Theme Theory and the Rhetoric of Advertising

Ernest G. Bormann's fantasy theme theory provides an effective methodology for analyzing advertising, inasmuch as it combines several elements of cultural criticism including social construction of truth and reality, examination of cultural myths, dramatization of those myths in everyday life and language, and investigation of personal feelings and values that are bound to cultural myths and that make possible persuasive communication. According to Bormann, a fantasy theme is something that happened to a group in the past or a dream of what the group might do in the future. A fantasy theme "chains out," or becomes dramatized, developing within the group a common culture in which values and attitudes are tested and legitimized. Personal feelings and values fuse with symbols and images that sustain a sense of group or communal identity, impel individuals to action, and provide a social reality. A rhetorical vision, or composite drama, constructed from fantasy themes that chain out into dramas contains motives that impel group members to act in a certain way and to ignore contradictions based on logic or prior knowledge. An example of rhetorical vision is the perception of unspoiled frontier, ready to be conquered, used, or escaped into, that appears in many automobile and cigarette advertisements. These advertisements proceed by populating space with symbolic characters, actions, or gestures that complete the fantasy vision.

In practice, fantasy theme theory connected with rhetorical methods of criticism provides a powerful tool, enabling critics, theorists, and teachers to interpret the symbol systems repre-

sented in aural, visual, and verbal advertising texts. These systems, viewed from the fantasy theme perspective and subjected to rhetorical analysis, are effectively associated with underlying social, psychological, and ideological patterns embedded in contemporary, electronically reproduced mass culture. Rhetoric and fantasy theme theory can be combined with ideologically sensitive theory and criticism such as feminist critique (which is capable of adding perceptions of stereotyped representations of the sexes to the critical approach) or with theories such as those drawn from the work of philosopher and constructionist Michel Foucault (which are capable of intensifying critical perceptions of the hegemonic control that visual, aural, and verbal language has on the consumers of advertisements) to produce methods that have powerful critical and pedagogical implications.

Kenneth Burke and Mikhail Bakhtin: Literary Rhetoric and Advertising Text

Much contemporary cultural criticism had its origins in works by literary critics and rhetorical theorists who earlier broadened the base from which criticism drew its theory. Two of these theorists and critics, the American Kenneth Burke and the Russian Mikhail Bakhtin, working in very different cultural contexts, are perfect examples of how literary, critical, and historical methods can be transformed into powerful tools of cultural interpretation. Burke, working from a more confined modernist critical perspective on "high" culture and literature in the 1920s, and influenced by the social and cultural upheavals of the 1930s and 1940s, generated in those decades and the 1950s and 1960s a set of powerful rhetorical analyses of a wide range of cultural artifacts, ranging from Hitler's *Mein Kampf* to the slogans of advertising and the lyrics of popular songs. The scope of Burke's critical methodology is best represented in his dramatistic theory (embodied in a critical apparatus he called the "Pentad"), which applies a basic formula for human action within cultural contexts to the dynamic of social-psychological interaction embedded in particular texts.

Bakhtin, a classicist who based his later work on earlier studies of classical and folk traditions in the novel, developed two seminal theoretical concepts that are becoming central to rhetorical analyses of text from sociocultural perspectives. The first of those concepts is Bakhtin's notion of *heteroglossic* text. Such texts are marked by the bringing together of different linguistic registers and fields and by the mixing of different social-political and ideological frameworks and languages in texts that are unified by themes that cross those linguistic and ideological boundaries. The point of the critical-interpretive act, then, is to learn to read complex texts as dynamic social entities within which the voices of different passages interact with one another in ways that reveal deeper social, political, and psychological processes.

The second concept important to the rhetoric of advertising is embodied in the "carnival" metaphor that Bakhtin uses to represent the dynamic and unpredictable ways in which the language of text interacts with the social classes and groupings of its readers. The social carnival surrounding textual reception must, for Bakhtin, be part of the critical-interpretive act. The interpreter cannot look for one-to-one relationships between the structure of a text and the readers, for texts themselves are heteroglossic and the readers are constructed out of many contending and overlapping communities of belief, education, political leaning, occupation, and the like.

Burke's dramatism and Bakhtin's heteroglossic sense of the carnivalesque provide the culturally attuned critic and teacher of advertising rhetoric with the broad critical base necessary to go beyond surface analysis of the contents of cotemporary advertising. Once beyond that surface, the latent complexities of advertising reveal themselves to critic, teacher, and student; these revealed complexities can then become a conscious part of the meaning we take from the rhetoric of advertising.

Dorothy Broaddus and Joseph Comprone
Arizona State University

Bibliography

Andrews, James R. *The Practice of Rhetorical Criticism*. 2nd ed. New York: Longman, 1990.

Bakhtin, M.M. *The Dialogic Imagination: Four Essays*. Trans. Caryl Emerson and Michael Holquist. Ed. Michael Holquist. Austin: U of Texas P, 1981.

———. *Rabelais and His World*. Trans. Helene Iswolsky. Cambridge, MA: Harvard UP, 1968.

———. *Speech Genres and Other Late Essays*. Trans. Vern W. McGee. Ed. Caryl Emerson and Michael Holquist. Austin: U of Texas P, 1986.

Bizzell, Patricia, and Bruce Herzberg, eds. *The Rhetorical Tradition: Readings from Classical Times to the Present*. Boston: Bedford, 1990.

Bormann, Ernest G. "A Fantasy Theme Analysis of the Television Coverage of the Hostage Release and the Reagan Inaugural." *Quarterly Journal of Speech* 68 (1982): 133–45.

———. "Fantasy and Rhetorical Vision: The Rhetorical Criticism of Social Reality." *Quarterly Journal of Speech* 58 (1972): 396–407.

———. *The Force of Fantasy: Restoring the American Dream*. Carbondale: Southern Illinois UP, 1985.

Burke, Kenneth. *A Grammar of Motives*. Cleveland: World, 1962.

———. *Language as Symbolic Action: Essays on Life, Literature and Method*. Berkeley: U of California P, 1966.

———. *A Rhetoric of Motives*. Berkeley: U of California P, 1941.

Comprone, Joseph J. *From Experience to Expression*. 2nd ed. Boston: Houghton, 1981.

D'Angelo, Frank. "Advertising in the Composition Class." *Journal of English Teaching Techniques* 12 (1982): 31–37.

Foucault, Michel. *The Order of Things: An Archaeology of the Human Sciences*. New York: Pantheon, 1971.

Fox, Richard Wightman, and T.J. Jackson Lears, eds. *The Culture of Consumption: Critical Essays in American History, 1880–1980*. New York: Pantheon, 1983.

Gitlin, Todd. *Inside Prime Time*. New York: Pantheon, 1985.

Hall, Stuart, et al., eds. *Culture, Media, Language: Working Papers in Cultural Studies, 1972–79*. London: Hutchinson, 1980.

Hart, Roderick P. *Modern Rhetorical Criticism*. Glenview, IL: Scott, 1990.

Jameson, Fredric. *Postmodernism, or The Cultural Logic of Late Capitalism*. Durham, NC: Duke UP, 1991.

Jamieson, Kathleen Hall, and Karlyn Kohrs Campbell. *The Interplay of Influence: Mass Media and Their Publics in News, Advertising, Politics*. 2nd ed. Belmont, CA: Wadsworth, 1988.

Jarrett, Susan C. *Rereading the Sophists*. Carbondale: Southern Illinois UP, 1991.

Marchand, Roland. *Advertising the American Dream: Making Way for Modernity, 1920–1940*. Berkeley: U of California P, 1985.

Morson, Gary Saul, ed. *Bakhtin: Essays and Dialogues on His Work*. Chicago: U of Chicago P, 1986.

Williams, Raymond. "Advertising: The Magic System." *Problems in Materialism and Culture: Selected Essays*. London: NLB, 1980.

Williamson, Judith. *Decoding Advertisements: Ideology and Meaning in Advertising*. London: Marion Boyars, 1978.

See also FANTASY-THEME ANALYSIS

African-American Rhetoric

History of the oral and written languages of African-Americans. Many of the sermons, speeches, autobiographies, poems, novels, plays, songs, and polemics (as well as the theoretical discourse) of African-Americans serve as complex responses to the oppression they experienced as slaves and second-class citizens of the United States.

Often legally prohibited from learning to read and write, illiterate slaves developed robust oral traditions, passing down spirituals, sermons, and folktales from one generation to the next. Without this cultural and rhetorical process, African-Americans as a group might not have survived at all. With it, they produced such orators as Sojourner Truth, whose illiteracy did not interfere with her eloquence or leadership.

This oral culture has persisted throughout the twentieth century. Martin Luther King, Jr., was nurtured by a folk pulpit tradition developed by slaves and continued by others, including King's father, who began sermonizing when he could barely read and write. In the younger King's final, incandescent speech, "I've Been to the Mountaintop," he adapted the slaves' religious world view as he wrote a garbage workers' strike into the biblical story of the Exodus.

Jesse Jackson delivered a variation of a sermon originally given at least as early as the 1860s. The gospel music of Thomas Dorsey, Mahalia Jackson, and James Cleveland sprang from the folk music of spirituals and blues. In some respects, rap music derives from and resembles folk sermons. An example of the process of folk composition, "We Shall Overcome," began as a hymn around the turn of the century, became a labor song in Charleston during the 1940s, and evolved into a national and international civil rights anthem during the 1960s and afterward.

Related to oral traditions is autobiography, the most significant genre of African-American writing. Scores of slave narratives (sometimes transcribed and framed by whites) sold in extremely large numbers, persuading thousands of Northerners of the shocking brutality and hypocrisy of slavery. Frederick Douglass wrote three of the most thoughtful slave narratives, masterfully transmuting his personal traumas as a slave into a call for radical social change. In her narrative, Harriet Jacobs explains her owner's sexual advances and the travails of her escape. Again, personal experience serves as a powerful vehicle for political protest.

A vigorous African-American autobiographical tradition persists in the twentieth century, when almost every important African-American literary and political figure—from W.E.B. DuBois and Booker T. Washington to James Baldwin and JoAnn Robinson—has written autobiographically. These works often intertwine personal revelation with analysis of racial exploitation, accommodation, and resistance. Two of the most brilliant of these works, *All God's Dangers* by Nate Shaw and *The Autobiography of Malcolm X* by Malcolm X, are as-told-to autobiographies recorded and transcribed by others.

African-American women writers, such as Anne Moody, Maya Angelou, Audre Lorde, and bell hooks, use autobiographical forms as means of defining themselves and, in hooks's words, of "talking back" to challenge established rules of speech and conduct for black women. Mapping a terrain where the private and the social intersect, these writers insist that only here is radical change possible.

Gerda Lerner, Henry Louis Gates, Jr., and other contemporary editors are compiling documentary histories, journals, and writings by and about African-American women, who have often been neglected or misrepresented. Based on misplaced or suppressed records or on oral testimonies (including those from court proceedings), some of these works chronicle the lives of public figures, such as Harriet Tubman and Sojourner Truth, but many record little-known women, whose stories typically reveal a pattern of survival and resistance.

Drawing from oral testimony that she collected as a folklorist, Zora Neale Hurston, in her 1937 novel *Their Eyes Were Watching God*, showcases a female protagonist who learns to shed conventional straitjackets of race and sex, reenvisioning herself and her community. Through other fictional re-creations of women's stories, such contemporary writers as Toni Morrison and Alice Walker (who resurrected Hurston's work) are likewise rewriting oral testimony and diaries. They are, in Walker's words, "in search" of their "mothers' gardens."

For them, as for Douglass, Jacobs, DuBois, Hurston, and Malcolm X before them, self-definition becomes a prerequisite to social change. Like their predecessors, King, Walker, Morrison, and Angelou have become role models and mentors for other African-Americans who want to reenvision their lives, tell their stories, and transform the world.

Jeanne Clark and Keith D. Miller
Arizona State University

Bibliography

Andrews, William. *To Tell a Free Story: The First Century of Afro-American Autobiography, 1760–1845.* Urbana: U of Illinois P, 1986.

Douglass, Frederick. *Narrative of the Life of Frederick Douglass.* 1845. New York: Doubleday, 1963.

Gates, Henry Louis, Jr. *The Signifying Monkey.* New York: Oxford, 1988.

hooks, bell. *Talking Back: Thinking Feminist, Thinking Black.* Boston: South End, 1989.

Jacobs, Harriet. *Incidents in the Life of a Slave Girl.* New York: Schomburg Library of Nineteenth-Century Women Writers, 1990.

King, Martin Luther, Jr. *A Testament of Hope.* Ed. James Washington. New York: Harper, 1986.

Lerner, Gerda. *Black Women in White America: A Documentary History.* New York: Vintage, 1992.

Lorde, Audre. *Sister Outsider: Essays and Speeches.* Freedom, CA: Crossing, 1984.

Shaw, Nate (with Theodore Rosengarten). *All God's Dangers.* New York: Random, 1984.

Walker, Alice. *In Search of Our Mothers' Gardens: Womanist Prose.* San Diego: Harcourt, 1983.

Alcuin of York (735–804)

A lifelong deacon, born in Northumbria, became the dominant educational force in Charlemagne's Frankish empire. His self-penned epitaph reads: *Alchuine nomen erat, sophiam mihi semper amanti*—Alcuin was my name, my love always wisdom." Although he was educated at York, a leading center of learning for both ecclesiastical and classical studies, and spent most of his life there, Alcuin's influence was greatest as *magister* of Charlemagne's palace school in Aachen and afterwards at the abbey of Saint-Martin-de-Tours. In Aachen he composed the rhetorical treatise *Disputatio de rhetorica et de virtutibus*, a work derived from the Ciceronian tradition and labeled "a work of popularization" (Howell 33).

Alcuin first began teaching in 768 at the cathedral school of York. Ten years later he was given the position of headmaster. There, as a bibliophile, he acquired many Christian and secular works, especially Virgil, occasionally traveling to the continent to buy books or to meet with other scholars. On one of those sojourns, in 781, Alcuin met with Charlemagne, who offered him the position of head of the palace school.

Charlemagne apparently recognized in Alcuin the type of teacher and scholar he admired, believing that under Alcuin's direction the Frankish court could become a major center of learning. Certainly, during the fourteen years that Alcuin served in that position, from 782 to 796, Aachen attracted visitors from all over Europe, and notable scholars and dignitaries, as well as Charlemagne himself and his family, became students of Alcuin's. The curriculum Alcuin established was developed from the liberal arts tradition: the *trivium*—grammar, rhetoric, and dialectic—and the *quadrivium*—music, astronomy, arithmetic, and geometry. But the overall program was decidedly ecclesiastical. Among Alcuin's most significant scholarly efforts were revisions of the Vulgate and of the Gregorian sacramentary. He was also active in theological controversies of the era and represented Charlemagne's iconoclastic views at the Council of Frankfurt in 794.

Alcuin's chief contribution to the rhetorical tradition was his textbook on rhetoric and the virtues (794), a fictionalized dialogue between Charlemagne and Alcuin. The work is primarily a compendium of Ciceronian rhetorical doctrine, especially Cicero's *De inventione* and Julius Victor's *Ars rhetorica*. What is original in the work is that which he supplied or adapted from rhetorical doctrine for ecclesiastical purposes, such as applying epideictic terms to a homily. Most important, he changed the purpose of the virtues—prudence, justice, courage, and temperance—from Ciceronian use as topics for invention to moral themes or goals in public questions for the responsible sovereign and his subjects (Howell 63–64).

In reward for his service to Charlemagne, in 796 Alcuin was given charge of the monks at Saint-Martin-de-Tours. There he continued to teach and more frequently to write for himself. He wrote numerous letters to bishops, kings, and even Pope Leo III, sharing with them his moral counsel. When he died on May 19, 804, he had good reason to believe that he had served his age well, if not greatly advancing learning, then certainly protecting it.

Beth S. Bennett
University of Alabama

Bibliography

Alcuin: The Bishops, Kings, and Saints of York. Ed. Peter Godman. Oxford: Clarendon, 1982.

Alcuin. *Disputatio de rhetorica et de virtutibus sapientissimi regis Karli et Albini Magistri. Rhetores latini minores.* Ed. Carolus Halm. Leipzig, 1863. Rpt. Dubuque, IA, n.d., 523–50.

Alcuin. *Grammatica. Patrologia Latina.* Ed. J.P. Migne. Paris: Garnier Fraters, vol. 101, cols. 849–902.

Alcuin. *The Rhetoric of Alcuin and Charlemagne.* Trans. Wilbur Samuel Howell. New York: Russell and Russell, 1941, 1965.

Allott, Stephen. *Alcuin of York, c. 732–804.* York: Wm. Sessions, 1974.

Duckett, Eleanor Shipley. *Alcuin, Friend of Charlemagne. His World and His Work.* New York: Macmillan, 1951.

Wallach, Luitpold. *Alcuin and Charlemagne: Studies in Carolingian History and Literature.* Cornell Studies in Classical Philology, No. 32. Ithaca, NY: Cornell UP, 1959.

American Indian Rhetoric

Language craftsmanship of the American Indian, from the oral traditions of tribal culture to the modern mainstream contributions of Native Americans. Both traditional and mainstream American Indian rhetoric reflect the oral traditions of Native American tribal culture.

The traditional literature of the American Indian was originally composed orally and passed on orally from generation to generation. Tribal literature has been transcribed and translated into English only in recent times. In these transcriptions and translations, which are but pale shadows of the original compositions, we see great beauty and superb language craftsmanship, a tribute to the verbal eloquence of the Native American. Traditional American Indian rhetoric comprises the mythology, tales, songs, poetry, and oratory of tribal cultures. There is a long history of traditional American Indian rhetoric, and this history is continuing, although much of the traditional literature composed today is in English. Furthermore, many modern American Indian writers are choosing to write not in the traditional tribal genres but in the mainstream genres of American literature. Mainstream American Indian rhetoric is composed of English works written by American Indians in American literature genres such as biography, fiction, history, and poetry (Velie 6–7).

The traditional rhetoric of each tribe had—and still does have—its own local color and unique features, as a result of varying literary tastes from tribe to tribe. Alanson Skinner, a collector of Indian narratives, recorded that the Sioux particularly relished war stories (Velie 11). Vine Deloria, a Sioux Indian, explains the military traditions of her tribe:

> The Sioux, my own people, have a great tradition of conflict. We were the only nation ever to annihilate the United States Cavalry three times in succession. And when we find no one else to quarrel with, we often fight each other. . . . During one twenty-year period in the last century the Sioux fought over an area from La Crosse, Wisconsin, to Sheridan, Wyoming, against the Crow, Arapaho, Cheyenne, Mandan, Arikara, Hidatsa, Ponca, Iowa, Pawnee, Otoe, Omaha, Winnebago, Chippewa, Cree, Assiniboine, Sac and Fox, Potowatomi, Ute, and Gros Ventre. (Velie 6–7)

Other tribes had different literary tastes. For example, the Ojibways preferred tales about sex, the Menominis stories dealing with the supernatural (Velie 11).

Taboos, customs, and prohibitions governed storytelling. Sacred narratives, such as origin myths and stories about cultural heroes, were told on winter nights only. The Kiowas told stories about Saynday, a trickster who warned, "Always tell my stories in the winter, when the outdoors work is finished / Always tell my stories at night, when the day's work is finished." Violators of this taboo risked having their noses cut off by Saynday. Other tribes had similar taboos and prohibitions: Cheyennes who told their sacred myths in daytime would become hunchbacked; the Arapaho winter storytelling season ended in spring when, after a rain, bugs could be seen swimming in the puddles. Only when snakes were underground did the Winnebagos tell their trickster tales (Velie 11).

The narrator of a myth or tale was not just a narrator but also an actor, a performer. Dramatizing the narrative was just as important as the actual words of the story; accordingly, the performer mimicked characters' voices and added gestures and facial expressions. Tales and myths were a vital part of daily life in tribal culture. Tales (more contemporary and secular than myths) in anecdotal form taught tribal beliefs, values, standards, and prohibitions, lending authority to, and giving rationale for, unwritten behavior codes. Myths (more ancient and sacred than tales) transported tribal audiences through strange, fantastic realms, such as the multiple worlds and monster-inhabited domains of Navaho mythology.

According to Navaho mythology, ancient earth was inhabited by evil monsters illicitly sired by the Sun God and other deities, making the earth unfavorable for humans or civilization. But the Sun God's evil offspring were doomed, for the twin brothers Monster Slayer and Child-of-the-Water were destined to free the earth from the power of these horrible creatures. Ironically, the twins were also the Sun God's children, born to Changing Woman after her sanctioned mating with the Sun God. Only with great sorrow and reluctance did the Sun God give the twins the power to destroy the monsters, for the Sun God loved his evil offspring, horrible though they were. The twins fulfilled their destiny, killing the evil monsters and making the earth safe for human habitation. Today, Navaho land contains many remnants of the ancient battle between the twins and their evil brethren: gigantic monster carcasses transformed into mountains; heads and body parts of decapitated and mutilated monsters transformed into mountain peaks and rock formations; the spilt blood hardened into stone. It is said that Cliff Monster, when killed by Monster Slayer, was transformed into a massive rock formation, today known as Shiprock, in Arizona; from a distance, this huge rock formation resembles a winged monster. Nearby lava fields are believed to be the dried, coagulated blood of the slain Cliff Monster. These gruesome remnants of battle testify to the ancient conflict between the twins and the horrible children of the Sun God (Reichard 21–22, 26–27, 58). The Navaho's interpretation of geological phenomena illustrates the importance of mythology in tribal culture. For the Navaho and for other tribes, mythology provided an explanation of natural phenomena, such as the fantastic geological formations of the Southwest.

Oratory was as important as mythology in American Indian tribal culture. Generally speaking, the American Indian was a powerful orator, a fact evident in the many examples of eloquent speeches that have been transcribed. The greater the oratorical skills of a tribal chief, the greater his power in the tribe. Great respect was afforded those with oratorical skills, and we see in the speeches of the American Indian great powers of verbal expression. Oratorical skills were especially valuable at tribal ceremonies; whole days were devoted to reciting tribal history, the history of whites on the North American continent, and the history of tribal relationships with the white man. These speeches were displays of oratorical abilities, an important part of tribal ceremonies (Turner 236–37).

Composition of songs and poetry was another opportunity for the Indian to demonstrate oral abilities. Songs and poetry were composed on many topics relating to daily life—tribal relationships, nature, the earth, love, war, illness, religious beliefs. There were songs and poems to relate the earth's origin, to prepare warriors for battle, to make enemy tribes peaceful, to ensure a bountiful harvest, to extol courage and bravery in the hunt or in battle, to celebrate the earth's rebirth in the spring, and to express joy or mourning. The Chippewa song "I can charm the man" supposedly caused the hearer to fall in love with the singer, and the song "If I am beaten" expressed with slow voice rhythm and rapid drum beat all of the excitement and suspense of gambling in the moccasin game. Traditional American Indian poetry anticipates the obscurity, surrealism, and metaphysical abstractions of much of today's modern poetry. Today American Indians are still composing much poetry; there are more Indian poets publishing their work than Indian novelists, short story writers, or authors in other mainstream American literature genres (Velie 79, 211–12).

The first mainstream literature publication by an Indian was Samson Occom's "A Sermon Preached at the Funeral of Moses Paul, American Indian," published in 1772. In 1768 Occom wrote a biographical memoir, but this was not published until some time later. The first published Indian novelist was a Cherokee, John Rollin Ridge, also known as Yellow Bird, who wrote a fictional account of Hispanic folk hero Joaquin Murieta. Simon Pokagon's *Queen of the Woods*, published in 1899, was the first novel about Indians written by an Indian. Early in the twentieth century, Charles Eastman, a Sioux, became known for his autobiography and tribal tales. Alexander Posey, a Creek, gained recognition for his poetry and political satire. But until the 1960s, Americans were by and large unfamiliar with Indian works in mainstream American literature genres, because most of the works were of poor literary quality. There were a few exceptions, however, such as Flathead novelist D'Arcy McNickle's *The Surrounded* (1936), *Runner in the Sun* (1954), and *Wind from an Enemy Sky* (1978). It was in the 1960s, however, that the renaissance in American Indian literature began, with the publication in 1968 of Kiowa novelist N. Scott Momaday's *House Made of Dawn*, which subsequently received the Pulitzer prize in 1969. James Welch, a Blackfeet Gros Ventre, was another writer of the renaissance with his novels *Winter in the Blood* (1974), *The Death of Jim Loney* (1979), and *Fools Crow* (1986). Successful novelists of the eighties include Gerald Vizenor, Leslie Silko, and Louise Erdrich, who have had their novels reviewed in the *New York Times Book Review* and who have also been successful as poets (Velie 7–8).

The stereotype of the Indian as a grunting, monosyllabic savage could not be further from the truth. Quite the contrary—we see eloquence of speech in the oral traditions of the American Indian and superb literary quality in modern American Indian mainstream contributions, which rank with the best works in American literature. In the traditional and mainstream works of the American Indian, we see fantastic flights of imagination, lucidity, practicality, metaphysical abstractions, surrealism, entertainment, and more. The American Indian has been composing traditional works for public performance at tribal gatherings for thousands of years. Traditional literature is today composed mainly in English; the traditional genres remain, nonetheless, and together with the blossoming and flowering of the renaissance in American Indian literature, a long history of language craftsmanship is continuing.

John Philip Lesko
University of Edinburgh

Bibliography

Allen, Paula Gunn, ed. *Studies in American Indian Literature: Critical Essays and Course Designs.* New York: Modern Language Assn., 1983.

Reichard, Gladys A. *Navaho Religion: A Study of Symbolism.* 2nd ed. Princeton: Princeton UP, 1974.

Turner, Frederick W. *The Portable North American Indian Reader.* New York: Viking, 1974.

Velie, Alan R., ed. *American Indian Literature: An Anthology.* Norman: U of Oklahoma P, 1991.

Anacoluthon

Completing a sentence with a construction that presupposes a different beginning. Shakespeare used anacoluthon in "They who brought me in my master's hate, I live to look upon their tragedy" (*Richard III* 3.2.57). Anacoluthon is common in spoken language when a speaker begins a sentence in a way that implies a certain logical resolution and then ends it differently. Consequently, anacoluthon is often found in interior monologues: "I suppose she was pious because no man would look at her twice I hope Ill never be like her a wonder she didnt want us to cover our faces but she was a welleducated woman certainly and her gabby talk . . ." (Joyce, *Ulysses*).

Arthur Quinn and Lyon Rathbun
University of California, Berkeley

Anadiplosis

The repetition of the last word of one line or clause to begin the next. Albert Camus used anadiplosis in "To me, it's a tragedy. A tragedy, everyone knows what that is. It leaves you defenseless" (*L'Etranger*). Anadiplosis can infuse emotional force into a passage: "Both princes and population groaned in vain; in vain did the King's brother, in vain did the King himself clasp Madame to his bosom" (Bossuet, *Oraison funebre de la duchesse d' Orléans*). In dialogue anadiplosis serves to link replies together, as shown in this passage from *King Lear:* "Cornwall: Fetch forth the stocks! As I have life and honor, there shall he sit till noon. Regan: Till noon? Till night, my lord, and all night too!" Anadiplosis can also express the premises of a syllogism, as Richard III does in exclaiming, "Come! I have learn'd that fearful commenting is leaden servitor to dull delay; delay leads impotent and snail-pac'd beggary. Then fiery expedition be my wing" (*Richard III* 4.3.51).

When used to string together a series of clauses, anadiplosis can produce either a catalogue or gradatio (q.v.). Paul demonstrates this use of anadiplosis in writing, "More than that, we rejoice in our suffering, knowing that suffering produces endurance, endurance produces character, and character produces hope, and hope does not disappoint us, because God's love has been poured into our hearts through the Holy Spirit which has been given to us" (Romans 5.3–5).

Arthur Quinn and Lyon Rathbun
University of California, Berkeley

Anaphora

From Greek *ana-* "on, up" + *pherein* "to carry": the repetition of the same word or phrase in several successive clauses. More traditional usage within rhetoric restricts the term only to repetition which occurs sequentially in *clause-initial* positions. Analysts in the more recent fields of discourse analysis, pragmatics, and theoretical linguistics maintain strong interests in phenomena that are given this label but have developed divergent concepts of its identity and scope.

Recognition of repetition as a specific rhetorical device dates back to the classical period, when analysts ascribed to it functions of force and emphasis. Application to textual analysis has persisted from the focus on its function in speeches by Greek orators, to the hermeneutic explication of biblical texts, to the stylistic analysis of literary figures. Dickens, for instance, might be characterized as using anaphora in conveying a penchant for "tidiness," Joyce as extending anaphora to whole sentences in presenting a stream of consciousness, and Orwell as exaggerating anaphora in creating images of political intimidation and oppression. Critical discourse analysis incorporates this tradition by relating the use of anaphora in spoken and written text to the enactment of socially constituted power and to the exercise of dominance.

In the field of discourse analysis, however, the term *anaphora* is used to designate any linguistic element that has the same referent as an element that precedes it. This referential tie may be within the same clause, in sequential clauses, or over a greater distance: That is, anaphora involves reference to any element that has already been established in the discourse. The anaphoric element may be an exact repetition ("In the beginning was *the Word,* and *the Word* was with God"); it may be a synonym or paraphrase (*Mary* eloped with Bill. *The woman* is a fool); it may be a personal pronoun substituted for a prior noun or noun phrase (*All candidates* think *they* can win); it may be a demonstrative (Mary was concerned about her own *welfare,* as well as *that* of others); it may be an epithet (I invited *John* to dinner, but I can't stand *the idiot*); or it may be a form of *do* or *do it* substituted for a prior predicate (Bill accused Tom of *stealing his wallet,* but Tom didn't *do it*). Even a linguistic "zero" may signal anaphora (*John* wants 0 [John] to go; cf. John wants *him* [someone else] to go). This list is not exhaustive for English, and types of anaphoric structures differ among languages. Of particular interest to discourse analysts is how anaphora contributes to cohesion within text, and how distance between referential ties is related to patterns of overall rhetorical organization.

The term *cataphora* is sometimes used for "forward anaphora," in which the element precedes the term it refers to (Because *it* receives so little rain, *Death Valley* is a desert). A closely related discourse phenomenon is *exophoric* reference, where the primary referent is not explicitly stated but is evident from context (*That* is unacceptable). Exophoric reference is much more common in spoken than in written text, where less nonlinguistic context is available for interpretation.

In pragmatics, the analysis of anaphora is further extended to include the effect of presuppositions on the interpretation of elements not traditionally recognized as anaphoric. For example, in "Did you see the car?" use of the definite article indicates that the referent has already been introduced in the discourse (text or context) and thus has an anaphoric function.

Linguists have been primarily interested in different types of anaphora in relation to the "scope" over which they apply, and as they function to signal clause relationships and carry other grammatical information. Most theoretical developments since the 1970s that apply to coreference have focused on universal syntactic constraints within the binding theory proposed by Noam Chomsky. Essentially, the theory (derived from logic) claims that a reflexive anaphor must occur within the same clause (or binding domain) as its antecedent referent, as in "*John* kicked *himself.*" On the other hand, a pronoun like *he, she, him,* or *her* cannot be coreferential with any noun or noun phrase in the same clause; in "John kicked him," *him* could not be coreferential with *John.* This is presented as a general linguistic principle that applies to all languages in the world, although the scope of a binding domain may vary

Muriel Saville-Troike
University of Arizona

Bibliography

Aoun, Joseph. *A Grammar of Anaphora.* Cambridge, MA: MIT P, 1985.

Chomsky, Noam. *Some Concepts and Consequences of the Theory of Government and Binding.* Cambridge, MA: MIT P, 1982.

Fox, Barbara A. *Discourse Structure and Anaphora: Written and Conversational English*. Cambridge: Cambridge UP, 1987.

Halliday, M.A.K., and Ruqaiya Hasan. *Language, Context, and Text: Aspects of Language in a Social-Semiotic Perspective*. Oxford: Oxford UP, 1985.

Jespersen, Otto. *A Modern English Grammar: On Historical Principles*. London: Allen & Unwin, 1913.

Levinson, Stephen C. *Pragmatics*. Cambridge: Cambridge UP, 1983.

Nash, Walter. *Rhetoric: The Wit of Persuasion*. Oxford: Basil Blackwell, 1989.

van Dijk, Teun A. "Principles of Critical Discourse Analysis." *Discourse & Society* 4 (1993): 249–83.

Vickers, Brian. *In Defence of Rhetoric*. Oxford: Clarendon, 1988.

Anapodoton

Also anantapodoton; a kind of ellipsis (q.v.) in which an entire clause, usually the second member of a correlative expression, is left unstated. When Jefferson writes "That to secure rights, Governments are instituted among Men, deriving their just powers from the governed," it is obvious from what he has already written that he intends the reader to supply "We hold self-evident . . ." Likewise, when Caligula states, "Would that the Roman people had a single neck," the unstated concluding clause is self-evident.

Arthur Quinn and Lyon Rathbun
University of California, Berkeley

Anastrophe

"To turn upside down"; reversal of the usual order of words. "In my years lusty, many a deed doughty did I" (Puttenham); "Figures pedantical" (Shakespeare, *Love's Labor's Lost* 5.2.407). Whereas hyperbaton (q.v.) emphasizes the displacement of a single element, the anastrophe emphasizes the reversal of two elements. Sometimes the anastrophe can be used to unstring conventional meanings, as Eliot does in "Time present and time past / Are both perhaps present in time future, / And time future contained in time past" ("Burnt Norton," *Four Quartets*). More typically, the anastrophe is used to draw attention to, and emphasize, the words that have been re-

versed: "Are you good men and true?" (*Much Ado About Nothing* 3.3.1). Verbs can be reversed with their related nouns or adjectives as easily as nouns and adjectives. Cervantes is reversing verb and predicate adjective in "For if he like a madman lived, / At least he like a wise one died."

Arthur Quinn and Lyon Rathbun
University of California, Berkeley

Antanaclasis

"Reflection, bending back"; repetition of the same word in two contrasting senses to create a pun: "Your argument is sound, nothing but sound" (Benjamin Franklin); "The long cigarette that's long on flavor" (ad for Pall Mall cigarettes). Antanaclasis is frequent in aphorisms: "O mortal man, think mortal thoughts!" (Euripides); "True eloquence takes no heed of eloquence, true morality takes no heed of morality" (Pascal). The antanaclasis often appears in dialogue, where a speaker takes up the words of the interlocutor and changes their meaning to the speaker's own advantage. Shakespeare often uses antanaclasis in that way, as when Armado declares, "By the North Pole, I challenge thee." Costard replies, "I will not fight with a pole, like a Northern man. I'll slash; I'll do it by the sword" (*Love's Labor's Lost* 5.2.699).

Arthur Quinn and Lyon Rathbun
University of California, Berkeley

Anthimeria

The substitution of one part of speech for another. A form of enallage (q.v.), anthimeria is found in many of Shakespeare's most memorable lines: "Report That I am sudden sick. Quick and return!" (*Antony & Cleopatra* 1.3.4); "I'll unhair thy head!" (2.5.64). "His complexion is perfect gallows" (*The Tempest* 1.1.32). In these lines Shakespeare has used an adjective as an adverb, a noun as a verb, and a noun as an adjective. Many notable lines of modern poetry are also the result of anthimeria: "The hot of him is purest in the heart" (Stevens); "he sang his didn't he danced his did" (Cummings); "O dark dark dark. They all go into the dark. / The vacant interstellar spaces, the vacant into the vacant" (Eliot).

Arthur Quinn and Lyon Rathbun
University of California, Berkeley

A

Antidosis

Written c. 353 B.C.E. by Isocrates (436–338 B.C.E.) concerning rhetorical and educational theory and the composition of the public man. Composed long after *Against the Sophists*, *Antidosis* provides a glimpse into Isocrates' theories regarding education and rhetoric. Eminent among his discussions, according to Bizzell and Herzberg, is "a long panegyric on the civilizing powers of the *logos*" (45). The logos, according to Isocrates, would be exercised via interdisciplinary training through the *trivium* and rhetorical studies, though he cautions: "I hold that men who wish to do some good in the world must banish utterly from their interests all vain speculations and all activities which have no bearing on our lives" (51). Thus, if trained and used properly, "by the best of conventional morality," the logos will form the foundation of successful oratorical training and the effective orator (45). The logos, in fact, favorably influences the other aspects of persuasion; "the power to speak well and think right will reward the man who approaches the art of discourse with a love of wisdom and love of honor" (52). These dual "loves" lead the orator to seek out, study, and use "examples which are the most illustrious and the most edifying; and, habituating himself to contemplate and appraise such examples, he will feel their influence not only in the preparation of a given discourse, but in all actions in his life" (52).

These theories offer some inkling of the not-yet-formed Roman notions about rhetoric and the training and composition of the orator. Susan Jarratt notes that Isocrates, among other sophists, took great care in developing a "model of the public intellectual" (98), individuals formed by contact with a multitude of disciplines but who did "not allow their minds to be dried up by these barren subtleties, nor to be stranded on the speculations of the ancient sophists" (51). The public intellectual, for Isocrates, is thus public in the sense that he or she is formed by information in the public domain and uses that information to serve and advance the society.

The connection between education and rhetorical theory that Isocrates espouses can thus be conceptualized by studying good models, emulating them in action, and using them in discourse. The rhetor thereby constructs an eminent public persona. This persona will allow the rhetor to "establish a most honorable name among his fellow citizens" (52).

Joseph Colavito
Northwestern State University

Bibliography

Bizzell, Patricia, and Bruce Herzberg, eds. *The Rhetorical Tradition: Readings from Classical Times to the Present*. Boston: Bedford, 1990.

Guthrie, W.K.C. *The Sophists*. Cambridge: Cambridge UP, 1971.

Isocrates. "Antidosis." *The Rhetorical Tradition: Readings from Classical Times to the Present*. Ed. Patricia Bizzell and Bruce Herzberg. Boston: Bedford, 1990.

———. *On the Peace. Aereopagiticus. Against the Sophists. Antidosis. Panathenaicus.* Trans. George Norlin. Cambridge, MA: Harvard UP, 1929.

Jaeger, Werner. "The Rhetoric of Isocrates and Its Cultural Ideal." *The Province of Rhetoric*. Ed. Joseph Schwartz and John A. Rycenga. New York: Ronald, 1965.

Jarratt, Susan. *Rereading the Sophists: Classical Rhetoric Refigured*. Carbondale: Southern Illinois UP, 1991.

Antimetabole

Inverting the order of repeated words. Kennedy used antimetabole in his famous phrase "Ask not what your country can do for you, ask what you can do for your country." A striking way to contrast ideas while sharpening their sense, antimetabole is an elegant means of creating an antithesis. "The sabbath was made for man, and not man for the sabbath" (Mark 2:27); "Ye have not chosen me, but I have chosen you" (John 15:16); "Circumstances rule men; men do not rule circumstances" (Herodotus); "I wasted time, and now doth time waste me" (*Richard II* 5.5.49). As these examples demonstrate, antimetabole turns a sentence spatially around a center, allowing it to become a self-contained expression of memorable thought: "If a man will begin with certainties, he shall end in doubts; but if he will be content to begin with doubts he shall end in certainties" (Bacon).

Arthur Quinn and Lyon Rathbun
University of California, Berkeley

Antiphon (c. 480–411 B.C.E.)

An early Attic orator from Athens. He taught rhetoric and, although rarely appearing in court himself, worked as a legal advisor and *logographos*, one composing speeches for others to use in court. Main sources of his life include Thucydides 8 (chapters 68 and 90) and

Plutarch's *Moralia 10, Vitae X Oratorum* (chapter 1).

When the Four Hundred overthrew democracy in Athens during the war with Sparta (411 B.C.E.) in what is known as the oligarchic conspiracy, Antiphon led the extremists against the moderates who followed Theramenes and Aristocrates. When dissension grew in the ranks of the Four Hundred, Antiphon and a small band went to negotiate peace with Sparta, hoping to obtain support for the extremists. Negotiations failed, and the regime of the Four Hundred fell. Antiphon was tried, condemned, and executed as a traitor.

Antiphon's written legacy consists of several speeches. Sixty were circulated under Antiphon's name in antiquity, of which at least thirty-five were genuine. Some survive only as fragments, including the magnificent speech Antiphon delivered in his own defense at his trial. Several complete speeches survive. Three were written for clients to deliver during trials: *On the Choreutes* (c. 419), *Against the Stepmother* (c. 416) (possibly a rhetorical exercise), and *On the Murder of Herodes* (c. 414). The other speeches, the three *Tetralogies*, were written during the third quarter of the fifth century as rhetorical exercises outlining how speeches should be composed for both the prosecution and defense. All three pertain to homicide: the first to murder, the second to manslaughter, and the third to homicide in self-defense. The *Tetralogies* are not based on real cases, but are rather models of judicial oratory. Each contains the prosecutor's opening speech, the defense's first speech, the prosecutor's second speech, and the defendant's second and closing speech.

Antiphon's speeches were written according to the standards of fifth-century rhetoric. They often lack a developed narrative, for that element of arrangement, deriving from Tisias of Sicily, had not yet reached Athens. His speeches, especially the *Tetralogies*, rely mainly on argument from probability (that is, artificial proofs like character and divine law) rather than inartificial proofs (like the evidence of witnesses or human laws). When evidence is used in proof, it is not integrated well with arguments from probability. Other avenues of proof are not systematically explored. For example, the ethos of the speaker and arguments from pathos are underdeveloped.

Antiphon's influence includes establishment of the standard structure of the court speech: an introduction describing the circumstances of the case, a narration of facts, arguments, and proofs, and a peroration. Also, prior to Antiphon there was no convention of prose style in the Attic dialect. Antiphon was one of the first to exhibit periodic style more befitting rhetorical argument than the running style of narrative. To accomplish this he employed antithesis in thought and word, as well as balanced clauses that correspond even to the number of syllables.

Duane F. Watson
Malone College

Bibliography

Caizzi, Fernanda D. *Antiphontis Tetralogiae*. Milan: Istituto Editoriale Cisalpino, 1969.

Edwards, M., and S. Usher. *Greek Orators–I. Antiphon & Lysias*. Chicago: Bolchazy Carducci, 1985.

Kennedy, George A. *The Art of Persuasion in Greece*. Princeton: Princeton UP, 1963. 129–33.

Maidment, K.J. *Minor Attic Orators*. 2 vols. Loeb Classical Library. Cambridge, MA: Harvard UP, 1941.

Antiptosis

"Exchange of case." Whereas the hendiadys (q.v.) adds an *and* between the old and new nouns, the antiptosis adds an *of*. The glorious kingdom becomes "the kingdom of glory" rather than "the kingdom and the glory." The following three examples show how substituting the preposition *of* rather than the conjunction *and* adds weight to the word being emphasized: "Why are thou so far from helping me, and from the words of my roaring?" (Psalm 22:1); "And above all these things put on charity, which is the bond of perfectness" (Colossians 1:17); "The King's name is a tower of strength" (*Richard III* 5.3.12).

Arthur Quinn and Lyon Rathbun
University of California, Berkeley

Antithesis

The conjoining or contrasting of ideas. "A man should be mourned at his birth, not at his death" (Montesquieu). Where the number of repetitions in the accumulatio (q.v.) is seemingly arbitrary and open, the antithesis conveys a sense of completeness with only two terms. Amos depicts the absoluteness of divine judgment, asking, "Shall not the day of the Lord be darkness, and not light? even very dark, and no brightness in it?" (Amos 5:20). Because the negative presentation of its opposite makes the principal idea more striking, antithesis is a powerful vehicle for emphasis: "All things were made by Him, and without Him was not anything made" (John 1:3).

Arthur Quinn and Lyon Rathbun
University of California, Berkeley

Aposiopesis

"To become silent"; a form of ellipsis (q.v.) in which a narrator or character either breaks off discourse or radically changes its direction. King Lear conveys his rage, stating, "I will have revenge on you both that all the world shall—I will do such things—What they are yet, I know not; but they shall be the terrors of the earth!" (2.4.282). Aposiopesis can be used to express hesitation or distractedness as well as deep emotion. The figure occurs frequently in interior monologues where the stream of words is not cut off so much as fragmented. Thus Joyce writes, "All quiet on Howth now. The distant hills seem. Where we. The rhododendrons. I am a fool perhaps. . . . Where I come in. All that old hill has seen. Names change: thats all. lovers: yum, yum" (*Ulysses* 308). Aposiopesis is sometimes difficult to distinguish from the anacoluthon (q.v.).

Arthur Quinn and Lyon Rathbun
University of California, Berkeley

Apostrophe

G. apostrophein, "to turn away"; when an orator abruptly breaks to address another person or personified thing either present or absent. Mark Antony uses apostrophe when he turns from the assassins to address Caesar's corpse: "That I did love thee, Caesar, O, 'tis true / If then thy spirit look upon us now, / Shall it not grieve thee dearer than thy death / To see thy Antony making his peace / Shaking the bloody fingers of thy foes, / Most noble! in the presence of thy corpse?" (*Julius Caesar* 3.1.194). As this quote demonstrates, apostrophe can be used to amplify a speech with heightened feeling. When addressed to some personified thing, an apostrophe can raise the tone of discourse. In "Ode to the West Wind," P.B. Shelley writes: "O wild West Wind, thou breath of Autumn's being / Thou from whose unseen presence the leaves dead / Are driven, like ghosts from an enchanter feeling / . . . / Wild Spirit, thou art moving everywhere." Quintilian notes that "apostrophe—which consists in the diversion of our address from the judge—is wonderfully stirring, whether we attack our adversary . . . or turn to

make some invocation." More prosaically, apostrophe can be used to communicate something to a third party who is overhearing a conversation. Thus, at the beginning of Molière's *Don Juan*, Sganafrelle scolds his own master while pretending to be addressing someone else: "I'm not speaking to you. . . . I'm speaking to the master I mentioned before."

Arthur Quinn and Lyon Rathbun
University of California, Berkeley

Arabic Rhetoric

The translation of classical Greek philosophical texts into Arabic as well as the commentaries written by medieval Muslim philosophers such as Al-Farabi, Avicenna, and Averroes constitute a considerable contribution to the rhetorical and philosophical tradition in the West. This note sketches some of the aspects of the transmission of Greek philosophy into Arabic during the medieval period, paying special attention to the importance of the medieval Muslim commentaries on Aristotle's work and the significant implications they should have when included in the canon of Western rhetoric.

When the Arabs first marched on the Roman Empire, c. 560 C.E., they conquered Syria, Egypt, North Africa, some parts of Asia Minor, and the southern Roman provinces. Under the Omayyads, who were centered in Damascus, the Arabs in 664 C.E. continued their conquest, sweeping over North Africa until they reached the Atlantic. They crossed the Mediterranean Sea, conquered Spain, and moved northward until they reached the plains of France around 732 C.E.

When the Abbasids came to power in the ninth century C.E., they established their dynasty in Baghdad. In less than fifty years, it became the center for a worldwide culture. After a troubled period of wars, the Arabs devoted their time and wealth to the study of various branches of knowledge under Harun Al-Rashid and his son Al-Mamun, whose empire was a good place for a fruitful dialogue between East and West: The cultural diversity the empire hosted was, as Landau puts it, "nicely moulded into an amalgam that was truly Arab" (53). Following the Prophet's tradition, which urges Muslims to "seek knowledge even unto China," Muslim scholars in effect sought knowledge from the neighboring cultures of the Mediterranean. During the reign of Harun Al-Rashid, who entertained good diplomatic relations with

Charlemagne, exchanging gifts and embassies with the European monarch, the Muslim empire was open to the West in the sense that the Abbasid Caliph's palace in Baghdad was turned into a house of learning in which scientists, theologians, musicians, and poets made tremendous contributions in the arts, letters, and science.

Harun Al-Rashid's son and successor Al-Mamun continued his father's work by establishing in Baghdad the famous *Bayt al-Hikma* (House of Wisdom), which combined a library, an academy, and a translation department. Hence Greek cultural influence was important during the reign of Al-Mamun; as a result, many Greek philosophical and scientific texts were translated into Arabic. Thus, through Baghdad, into North Africa and Spain flowed a Greek culture that was to awaken the European Renaissance. Also during this period, the Arabic culture assimilated other foreign cultures in addition to the Greek language and civilization, namely, those of the Persians, the Latins, the Andalusians, and the North Africans. In effect, the Islamic texts in astronomy, theology, mathematics, and medicine made the names of Avicenna, Averroes, Al-Farabi, and Ibn Hazm appear in the works of medieval and Renaissance scholars such as Roger Bacon and Thomas Aquinas.

In the department of translation (*bayt attarjama*), numerous books were translated from Greek, Persian, Syriac, Hebrew, Aramaic, and Ethiopian into the Arabic language. Music, art, architecture, grammar, mathematics, medicine, astronomy, chemistry, and several other branches of learning were studied and cultivated in this "House of Wisdom." Nearly all of the philosophical works of Aristotle, together with the Neo-Platonic commentaries on them, were translated into Arabic.

Since the Prophet's death in 632 C.E., Muslim philosophers had started to raise profound philosophical questions about the relationship of humans with God in the light of the teachings of the Koran and the tradition left by the Prophet. How can a Muslim kill another Muslim? What is it that makes a true believer? Other puzzling questions arose about the apparent contradiction between a perfect God and an imperfect world, and the position human beings hold between predestination and free will. These concerns, however, never shook the Muslim philosophers' faith in God; still they were worth asking, so as to produce a synthesis of the truths of religion and other truths arrived at through scientific investigation and philosophical reasoning.

In addition to the koranic tenets that needed to be explained and interpreted, poetry was an important part of the intellectual concerns of Muslim philosophers. From the ninth century onward, Islamic philosophy was interested in the question of the position that poetry should have in the hierarchy of knowledge. Al-Farabi, Avicenna, Averroes, and other Muslim philosophers apparently demonstrated dissatisfaction with what was known about the rules of poetry in Arabic culture, and one can argue that their discovery of Aristotle's *Poetics* seemed to have prompted them to undertake commentaries on Aristotle's treatise in which they evinced, to use Butterworth's terms, "a desire to redirect Arabic poetry itself, to turn it away from frivolous, irresponsible, even voluptuous and dissolute concerns and to make it serve moral goals" (1986: xi). Because of the pleasure it gives through the imaginative representations set forth by the poet and because of the delight it offers in its measured lines of rhymed verse, poetry can be a powerful persuasive tool, eventually shaping opinions. Muslim commentators of Greek texts like the *Poetics* therefore set the goal for themselves of drawing universal principles of poetry.

Thus, from the ninth century C.E. until the eleventh century, Muslim translators and commentators, many of whom were Neo-Platonists or Neo-Pythagorians, were seriously involved in the transmission of Greek thought into Arabic. Some, like Al-Kindi, took upon themselves the task of translating directly from the Greek works in philosophy, medicine, and astrology, and writing commentaries on them. In fact, Al-Kindi was the first Muslim philosopher to translate Aristotle's work directly from Greek and Syriac; he wrote commentaries on it in the first half of the tenth century. Other philosophers, such as Al-Farabi and Averroes, based their commentaries and treatises on translations already available to them in Arabic.

In general, Muslim philosophers worked closely with Greek commentators such as Themistius and John the Grammarian, with whom they engaged in an academic debate over Aristotle's works as well as the commentaries of Alexander of Aphrodisias, a well-known Aristotelian commentator at that time. Al-Farabi (870–950 C.E.), known in Arabic as "the second teacher" after Aristotle, and Avicenna (Ibn Sina) were among the major figures in Islamic philosophy in the ninth century C.E. who earned excellent reputations in medieval academic circles. Al-Farabi's first major contribution to Muslim philosophy was his classification of Aristotle's works into two categories. In the first he put the *Categoriae*, the *Organon, Analytica Priora, Analytica Posteriora, Topica, Sophistica, Rhetorica,* and *Poetica*. In the second he put Aristotle's eight books on physical matters and also included the three books on *Metaphysics, Ethics,* and *Politics*. In addition, Al-Farabi devoted a whole series of commentaries to the *Organon*.

Besides doing important work in philosophy and medicine, Avicenna (980–1034 C.E.) produced scholarly commentaries on Greek texts, among which the most valuable is his commentary on Aristotle's *Poetics*.

Right after Al-Farabi and Avicenna came Averroes (1126–1198 C.E.), whose several commentaries on Aristotle's work made him a well-known Muslim philosopher in the Middle Ages. Averroes composed three types of commentary. First, he composed short commentaries or summaries that often included additional material to help readers relate the philosophical discussion to contemporary theological and legal matters. Second, he wrote middle commentaries, longer than the short ones, that tended to come closest to the primary text itself. And third, he produced large commentaries that dealt at considerable length with the primary text but showed frequent diversions to discuss related issues.

The noted translators of that period, Hunayn Ibn Ishaq, his son Ishaq, and Ibn Al-Bitriq, translated most of Aristotle's works. Plato's *Republic* was also translated into Arabic during this period. The Muslim chronicler Ibn Nadim paid a tribute to these translators by referring to them as "the encyclopedists."

In the twelfth century, most Latin translations from the Greek came through the Norman kingdom of Sicily. Yet the school of translation in Toledo, Spain, was another important center in the West actively involved in the rendering into Latin of the Arabic translations and commentaries. Hermannus Alemannus did most of the translations of the Arabic commentaries by Averroes and Al-Farabi on Aristotle's *Poetics* and *Rhetoric* into Latin between 1243 and 1256.

Lahcen E. Ezzaher
University of Arizona

Bibliography

Badawi, Abdurrahaman. "Averroes Face Au Texte Qu'il Commente." *Multiple Averroes. Ouvrage publié avec le concours du CNRS*. Paris: Les Belles Lettres, 1978.

———. *La transmission de la philosophie grecque au monde arabe*. Paris: Vrin, 1968.

Butterworth, Charles E., ed. *Averroes' Middle Commentaries on Aristotle's* Categories *and* De Interpretatione. Princeton: Princeton UP, 1983.

———. *Averroes' Middle Commentary on Aristotle's* Poetics. Princeton: Princeton UP, 1986.

———. *Averroes' Three Short Commentaries on Aristotle's "Topics," "Rhetoric," and "Poetics."* Albany: State U of New York P, 1977.

Cantarino, Vicente. *Arabic Poetics in the Golden Age*. Leiden: Brill, 1975.

Consacrés aux premieres traductions arabes d'oeuvres grecques. *Byzantion* 29–30 (1959–1960): 425–36.

Dahiyat, Ismail M. *Avicenna's Commentary on the* Poetics *of Aristotle*. Leiden: Brill, 1974.

Faqih, Irfan. *Glimpses of Islamic History*. Lahore: Kazi, 1979.

Jum'a, Mohamed Lotfi. *The History of Muslim Philosophers in the East and the West*. Cairo: Al-Maktaba Al-'Ilmiyya, 1927.

Kemal, Selim. *The Poetics of Alfarabi and Avicenna*. Leiden: Brill, 1991.

Landau, Rom. *Islam and the Arabs*. New York: Macmillan, 1959.

Langhade, J., and M. Grignaschi, eds. *Al-Farabi: Deux ouvrages inédits sur la rhétorique*. Beyrouth: Dar El-Machreq, 1971.

Leaman, Oliver. *Averroes and His Philosophy*. Oxford: Clarendon, 1988.

Peters, F.E. *Aristoteles Arabus: The Oriental Translation and Commentaries on the Aristotelian Corpus*. Leiden: Brill, 1968.

Walzer, Richard. *Greek into Arabic*. Oxford: Bruno Cassirer, 1962.

Argument

(1) A *process* of controversy, dispute, inference, and critique; (2) a dialectical or dialogical *procedure* used in discussion and debate; (3) a logi-

cal *product,* a serial predication, an utterance; a textual object open to analysis and critique; a linguistically explicable claim supported by a reason. (To logicians, *logical product* means a conjunction, a proposition of the form *p&q.*)

In popular parlance the term *argument* suggests a disagreeable confrontation. American journalists, for instance, use it interchangeably with such terms as *altercation, quarrel,* and even *fight.* In academic parlance, however, the term has more agreeable connotations. Social scientists study "argument" as a valuable empirical occurrence that takes any number of forms in thought, conversations, small groups, organizations, legal proceedings, and mass communication. Humanists treat argumentation as a pedagogically valuable discipline and study arguments as instances of rational discourse. Rhetorical scholars use "argument" to label a variety of processes—including creative invention, public reason-giving and influence, symbolic enactment, and the joint creation of situations and identities. And logicians construe arguments as serial predications, as linguistic or linguistically explicable sets of premises and conclusions.

These diverse scholarly interests fall roughly into three categories—*process, procedure,* and *product.* Joseph W. Wenzel introduced these rubrics to distinguish the critical norms derived from rhetoric, dialectic, and logic, but the labels will serve here to cluster the various uses of argument with the scholarly interests that drive them. The term *process* suggests action and change—that arguments are inferential moves, processes of reasoning from data to claims, or differently, that arguments are *rhetorical* processes of invention and reason-giving, or that arguments are emergent social processes, *interactions* that evolve over time as arguers adjust to one another. Argument-as-process is thus synonymous or closely allied with such terms as *reasoning* and *justification, arguing* or *making arguments,* and with *polemic, dispute, controversy, conflict,* and *dissensus.*

The idea of *procedure* distinguishes debates and discussions from other forms of dissensual conversation (say quarrels) by emphasizing that argument is governed by rules— by implicit conversational norms, explicit codes of conduct, professional and disciplinary norms, and by constraints negotiated in specific contexts. Arguers thus differ from other social actors by virtue of their self-conscious agreement on rules, by their roles as advocates, and by their reciprocally acknowledged relations to one another as disputants. Argument-as-procedure thus evokes such closely allied terms as *debate, dialogue, dialectic,* and *discussion.* And the idea of argument as *product* suggests argument's historical association with logic. Arguments-as-products are textual objects, discursive units of proof composed of claims on someone's attention and belief linked explicitly or implicitly to justifications or warrants. Arguments in this sense are distinguishable components of discourse, claims backed by reasons.

Argument-as-process is often studied by researchers interested in the organization and coherence of discourse in general. Taking naturally occurring talk as primary data, these studies see argument as a phenomenon that flares up and simmers down in social interaction. Interactions become arguments when overt opposition is present. As opposition can be manifested in many ways, and may spark a diverse array of utterances and actions, the main empirical question has been why the process is coherent. That is, how do arguers make sense of it? How do they know they are *arguing*? Why are their claims and counterclaims mutually intelligible *as* claims and counterclaims?

One answer is that opposition per se is a kind of relationship or co-orientation in which interactants, taking one another's perspectives, see themselves as arguing, as engaged in a reciprocal process in which their utterances mesh as claims and counterclaims (Willard 1987). Drawing upon their cognitive repertoires, naive social actors impute argumentative intentions to one another and then frame their ongoing behavior according to scripts and plans generally appropriate to arguments (Benoit). Another answer is that opposition is itself interpreted by arguers in terms of broader principles of language comprehension and discourse coherence. Barbara J. O'Keefe and Pamela Benoit, for instance, argue that argumentative competence is a special case of one's general knowledge about language, conversational structure, and interaction. Even very young children know how to make assertions, requests, directives, and promises, how to express approval and disapproval, how to take turns in conversations, and how to take the perspectives of others and to acknowledge and respond appropriately to others' utterances. So "in producing arguments children call on their general conversational skills" (173). Their arguments are processes of managing or resolving opposition governed by general principles of discourse coherence (turn-taking, perspective-taking, speaking appropriately, and so forth).

The theoretical perspective that has most extensively studied argument in order to understand discourse coherence is *conversation analysis,* which in the argumentation field has received its most detailed theoretical and empirical treatment in the work of Scott Jacobs and Sally Jackson. Conversation, in this view, is a process of "coordinating plans and negotiating meanings," a goal-directed problem-solving process "whereby people generate and infer means to achieve ends according to principles of cooperative action and practical reasoning" (164–65). At a purely conventional level, conversation is based on a tacit rule system that prefers agreement. Communicative acts are *significant gestures,* in George Herbert Mead's terms. They find their completion in conventionally preferred responses: questions imply answers; requests imply that wishes be granted. Disagreements arise when preferred responses are withheld; arguments, at this simplest level, are processes of conversational repair. Conversations, however, are not simply linear, sequential progressions of *adjacency pairs*—naturally coupled speech acts such as *question-answer, offer-accept/decline, request-grant/refuse.* There may be many coherent replies—to, say, a question—that are not literal or direct *answers.* Nor do conversations get their coherence exclusively from the felicity conditions of speech acts. Ordinary language philosophers see felicity conditions as purely conventional intentions one communicates by performing an act. In *promising,* for instance, one enters an institution of public obligations and rules. One is presumptively *able* to fulfill the promise, one is presumptively *sincere,* and one presumptively means to be understood as entering the institution of *promising.* But Jackson and Jacobs report "empirical anomalies" following such an exclusively conventional account, for people do not characteristically decipher and respond to one another's utterances by labeling them as speech-act types. They respond to what they perceive to be a communicator's goals and plans. There is thus a conversational presumption that when speakers refer to the felicity conditions of particular act types, they have strategically selected conventional means to achieve a goal. This presumption—that as a rule, the behavior of other people is strategic and goal-directed—allows conversationalists to make sense of one another's actions, to produce messages with intelligible implications for one another, and to respond coherently and appropriately to one another. Within the framework of this presumption, arguers strategically adapt conversational conventions to fit their intentions and plans. Arguments emerge as conversationalists project, avoid, produce, or resolve disagreement; they are communicative acts organized and interpreted in terms of mutual perceptions of clashing intentions.

In contrast to the largely descriptive focus of research centered on argument-as-process, most approaches to argument-as-procedure are normatively focused—that is, less concerned with explaining discourse coherence than with identifying optimal ways in which disagreements are or might be disciplined. The term *discipline* suggests, first, that argument is a *public* process. Stephen Toulmin, Richard Rieke, and Allan Janik, for instance, use the rubric *reasoning* to designate an interpersonal and social process of thinking and speaking, where thinking and speaking about the justification of beliefs and claims are understood to be equivalent, or virtually so. Argument in this view is a mode of private or public inference—the difference between private and public being a matter of candor (arguers may conceal their intentions) or a matter of skill (arguers may differ in their ability to translate intentions to performance). Reasoning, in this scheme, is a way of putting ideas to the test of public standards. The study of reasoning thus focuses on principles of soundness: how claims are supported by reasons, how reasons are justified and opened to criticism, and on the principles by which some arguments are better and others worse.

The idea of discipline also suggests that arguments are to some degree self-regulating—that quite apart from any formal rules arguers may follow, context-specific standards of adequacy and fairness emerge as arguments unfold. The presence of opponents obliges arguers to frame their behavior around the expectation of critique and to adjust their actions to the ongoing moves and perceived expectations of others. As arguers hold one another to the procedural implications of their respective positions and ways of arguing, they develop a complementary relationship, a mutual awareness of ground rules. Douglas Ehninger calls this emergent reciprocity *argu-*

ment as method. The method, in this view, lies in opposition per se—in each arguer's awareness of being engaged with another person in a process of attack and defense. The result is a relationship of circumstantially equal power in which mutual obligations and opportunities emerge.

And the idea of argument-as-disciplined-procedure suggests that arguments are sometimes governed by explicit rules and professional canons. Debates, for instance, are characteristically more formalized than ordinary conversations. They follow explicit rules that define speaking time, speaker order, and speaker roles. And they usually require rebuttals in which audiences expect debaters to clash with one other, to explicitly address or refute one another's claims. Parliamentary procedures further elaborate debate formalities by defining in detail all correct ways of adjudicating competing procedural claims and by prohibiting as many foreseeable infractions as possible. The most elaborate apparatus is the code of conduct proposed by the Pragma-Dialectical theory of the Amsterdam School (Eemeren and Grootendorst 1984, 1992). The code is a normative apparatus—meant for arguers who jointly intend to resolve a dispute and who hope to behave reasonably in the process. Argumentative discussions, in this view, require much agreement and cooperation. The arguers must agree on a common definition of their disagreement, on rules that will govern their dispute, and on the standards for adjudicating the dispute. And after the argumentation stage of their discussion has been completed, they must agree on the results. Argumentation, in this scheme, is a series of complex speech acts by which arguers *externalize* their opinions, turn them into verbal claims, test them against one another, and submit them to arbitration by a rational judge. The code of conduct thus consists of rules for the performance of speech acts. It defines, for instance, which acts are permissible (or not) and indispensable (or not) at given stages of an argumentative discussion. It specifies in detail the conditions for making correct moves in the exchange. Incorrect moves, in this theory, are called *fallacies*—meaning any speech acts that hinder the resolution of disputes.

The preceding views of process and procedure focus on what Daniel J. O'Keefe calls *arguments₂*—interactions marked by extended, overt disagreement. They emphasize processes that differ markedly from what he calls *arguments₁*, or arguments-as-products. Arguments₂ are interactions people *have* or *engage in*. Arguments₁ are things people *make* and *utter*; they are complexes of claims and reasons conveyed by the speech-act *making an argument*. This distinction arose from a controversy about the nature of arguments₁. Some writers challenge the very idea of seeing arguments as *things* (Brockriede). Others claim that since arguers may use any or all of the communication vehicles available to them, any communication in an argument₂, verbal or nonverbal, logical or aesthetic, may be germane to explanations of the meaning and coherence of the process of arguing (Willard). Arguing that these criticisms obscure the distinction between argument₁ and argument₂, O'Keefe advocates defining arguments₁ by their paradigm cases. A paradigm case definition emphasizes the most commonly accepted, least controversial examples, which in the case of arguments₁ "are ones involving a linguistically explicable claim and one or more linguistically explicable reasons" (17). Arguments in this sense are discursive units of proof, serial predications, claims backed by reasons, premises, and conclusions. They are textual objects. They are found in or can be replicated in written documents. They are thus open to criticism, to the analysis of their logical and procedural soundness, and to the assessment of the soundness of their *warrants* (the premises from which one reasons) and of the validity of their *conclusions* (the degree to which their premises logically entail their conclusions).

O'Keefe's paradigm case is the most often quoted definition in the argumentation field, but it has not generated a consensus about how best to explicate arguments₁. The paradigm case strategy emphasizes the most clear-cut features of argument, features about which there is already a consensus, but it does not rule out borderline cases. Borderline cases arise because texts are often open to an indefinite number of interpretations. To determine the meanings of claims, the argument analyst may need to speculate about intentions—what particular people mean to be saying in real contexts. Since any number of variables may operate beneath the surface of situated speech to affect the meanings of statements, and since arguers employ a diverse array of behaviors during arguments₂, the range of phenomena that might be functionally relevant structural features of arguments₁ is significantly widened. And since the analyst's conjectures about

A

the meanings of, say, nonverbal cues, the arguers' relationship, and context-specific understandings may themselves be open to objections—the participants, for instance, might object that they are being misunderstood—the nature of arguments₁ becomes increasingly fuzzy. That fuzziness might be seen as a predicament, a distressing obstacle to the achievement of a concrete definition of arguments₁. But Barbara O'Keefe and Pamela Benoit propose that fuzziness is best seen as a fact to be explained. Given the diversity of actions that may happen in arguments₂, "attending solely to paradigm cases can blind the analyst to the operation of multiple attributes and processes" (161).

The debate about the range of phenomena that are functionally relevant to arguments₁ reflects a long-standing tension between logic and persuasion. That tension, briefly put, is that the degree to which logic is said to be independent of the human frailties that drive persuasion might also be the degree to which logic is irrelevant to human discourse. That tension perhaps originated with Plato's distinction between perfection and imperfection—a pristine, impersonal logic exemplifying the former, the mundane facts of persuasion the latter. But the tension is sharpest in Aristotle's *Rhetoric,* where a view of logical form is tied to matters of human belief, feeling, and context. Rhetorical argument, Aristotle says, proceeds either by *induction*—that is, arguing from examples, from a number of similar cases to a general conclusion—or by *deduction.* And it is in his explanation of deduction that the merger of logic and psychology is most explicit. He called rhetorical deductions *enthymemes*—a term that many translators believe meant "in the mind."

Aristotle calls the enthymeme a *rhetorical syllogism,* thereby subordinating his explanation of the forms and materials of rhetorical proof to a central distinction in his larger philosophical system, that between form and matter. The enthymeme takes the form of the deductive syllogism while its premises, or materials, are the ordinary opinions of audiences. Syllogistic form is a matter of the arrangement of premises and the distribution of terms within and among premises. The classic illustration is a syllogism not found in Aristotle: *Major Premise: All humans are mortal; Minor Premise: Socrates is human; Conclusion: Socrates is mortal.* This reasoning starts with a general, universally true statement (the major premise); it then fits a specific case into the universal (the minor premise); and finally it draws an inevitable conclusion. The syllogism's *validity* (its logical soundness) comes from the arrangement of its terms: The minor term ("Socrates") must fit into the major term ("human") to validly conclude that Socrates shares the universal attribute of the class (mortality). Aristotle's rhetorical syllogism may also be formally valid or fallacious, but it differs from the demonstrative scientific syllogism in three respects. First, its substance, or matter—the content of its premises—are probabilities, not certainties. Second, rhetoric is a cooperative process; persuasion cannot occur unless the listener actively participates in the process, so the premises of enthymemes must consist of probabilities believed by audiences. And third, these premises need not be fully stated, or in some cases stated at all: The orator, Aristotle says, should not waste time saying what is obvious; the listeners will supply the missing parts.

Few modern scholars doubt that rhetoric and discourse are dependent on mutual accommodation and cooperation. Lloyd F. Bitzer's portrait of Aristotle's enthymeme is widely accepted: Rhetorical proof is a joint creation of speaker and listener; persuaders *ask for* premises from audiences. Nor would many scholars dispute the claim that ordinary speech capitalizes on the ability and willingness of listeners to supply meanings and ideas left unsaid. Nonetheless, if there is a consensus about Aristotle's picture of argumentative form, it is about Wayne Brockriede's claim that the syllogism is a poor basis for understanding arguments₁. The syllogism, Brockriede argues, is a closed system; it involves no inferential leaps. There is nothing in the conclusion of a properly formed syllogism that does not also appear in its major and minor premises. Since rhetorical proof cannot proceed in a closed system, since all its premises are open to doubt, uncertainty, dispute, multiple interpretations, and situation-specific interpretations, the criteria for defining a properly formed syllogism are irrelevant to the criteria appropriate to judging properly formed arguments.

The most familiar alternative to the syllogism is Stephen Toulmin's functional model (see Figure 1), which shifts the emphasis from form to the functions that statements serve in the process of reasoning:

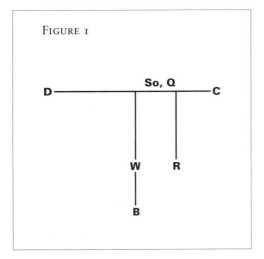

FIGURE I

If one knows, to use Toulmin's example, that everyone born in Bermuda is a British citizen and that Harry was born in Bermuda, one's conclusion that Harry is a British citizen is explicable by noticing the functions of each element of the argument. That Harry was born in Bermuda is the *data* (the answer to the question "What do you have to go on?"); that he is a British citizen is a claim on someone's attention and belief. The movement from data to claim is an inferential leap licensed by a *warrant* (the answer to the question "How do you get there?"), namely that everyone born in Bermuda is a British citizen. The *backing* for this "inference license" might be a quotation of the British Nationality Acts, which confer British citizenship on people born in Bermuda. The *reservation* might be that Harry's parents were aliens, or that Harry has become a naturalized citizen of another country. The *qualifier* for the claim is thus: *Unless* Harry's parents were aliens or he has become a citizen of another country, Harry is presumably a British subject.

Toulmin's layout is a widely accepted pedagogical device, and for some an adequate portrayal of the nature of arguments$_1$. Nonetheless, some scholars continue to question whether naturally occurring discourse can be faithfully reduced to linear, depersonalized, decontextualized, and entirely linguistic form (Gilbert 1993). Others claim that the layout is not genuinely different from the syllogism, that it lacks a principled basis for distinguishing data and warrants, and that warrants, backing, reservations, and data may themselves be claims issuing from different arguments. Thus, in laying out the details of complex arguments, the analyst may create an unmanageably detailed filigree of crisscrossing lines (Hample 1977).

David Zarefsky has pointed out that many disputes about the nature of arguments$_1$ stem from differences in the analysts' points of view. Some scholars focus chiefly on the process of rhetorical invention, in which arguers draw on their cognitive repertoires to fit claims and reasons together. Others focus on the translation of intentions into performance. Others focus on messages. And still others focus on the reasoning by which listeners process the messages they hear. These foci may capture different facets of the process of argument, but they also illustrate how different scholarly interests yield different and sometimes conflicting empirical claims. For instance, some scholars see messages as impersonal texts open to many possible interpretations. Others see texts as empirical records of situated-action. And still others see messages and texts as evidence of a speaker's beliefs and knowledge about communication (B. O'Keefe 1988). What might or might not count as arguments$_1$ is up to the analyst in the first case, up to the participants in the second, and a matter of distinguishing expressive, conventional, and rhetorical messages in the third. Invention and listening, to take another instance, are both cognitive processes, but speakers and listeners may have different goals and situated motives. A listener may process an arguer's claims as data for a different argument—for instance as evidence about the arguer's credibility. In such empirical cases, analysts such as Dale Hample, who hold that arguments have no existence except in the cognitive processes of arguers, might plot differences among many arguments$_1$ and produce an empirical picture that differs from those of analysts who focus on texts of messages.

Given these differences in scholarly interests, the diversity of behavior associated with arguments, and the range of phenomena that might be functionally relevant to them, no consensus about how best to characterize arguments$_1$ is likely. A consensus, indeed, may be quite unlikely in light of another obstacle, namely, a shift in how scholars think about rationality. The idea of *rationality*—of reason and reasonableness—is the argumentation field's most enduring concern. But the range of phenomena thought to be relevant to rationality has expanded, thanks to developments in psychology and to an increasing interest by scholars in many fields in the social grounds of knowledge. Some historical details will clarify these developments.

Reason, Aristotle held, is the most distinctively human attribute, and therefore the highest ideal toward which humans should strive. It is not an absence of emotion, but a virtue that governs, or disciplines, or keeps in proper proportion the lower, more animallike appetites and passions. Aristotle's dialectic thus blended process and procedure. The process was a matter of question and answer, argument and counterargument; the procedure was a matter of the disputants' virtues, civility, and respect for truth. The result was a disciplined form of social interaction.

The rhetorical theories of the Enlightenment transformed Aristotle's vision of rationality. Following the faculty psychology then in vogue, these theories divided the human mind into discrete functions or domains. They depicted reason and emotion as dichotomies, indeed hostile forces contending for supremacy, and thus stipulated a distinction between rational and irrational beliefs—a difference in kind between beliefs arising from logical reason (conviction) and beliefs excited by emotional appeals (persuasion). This *conviction-persuasion dualism* influenced many theories in the nineteenth century. The sociology of knowledge, for instance, described social life as so irrational that science had to be nonsocial. This exemption sparked a debate that waxed and waned for more than a century, and the degree to which scientific knowledge is socially grounded is still a matter of controversy. Argumentation likewise arose as an academic discipline by laying claim to the conviction side of the dualism, but it took on the more difficult task of describing the grounds of rationality in practical and political discourse. The earliest theorists saw the dualism as a fact of nature (Baker). Rationality, in this view, was a pristine state of grace to be achieved by following strictly defined rules. Argumentation was to be a pedagogy of rules—its goal being to instill in students habits of conduct that would, among other things, keep thought and speech uncontaminated by emotion.

This strong version of the dualism weakened as the faculty psychology behind it passed from favor. By 1917, for instance, Mary Yost argued that psychologists were abandoning dualism in favor of more holistic views of mind. Logic and emotion are interdependent cognitive processes, Yost argued. They cannot be separated or seen as hostile forces. There is no such thing—in the human mind—as pristine logic. In response to this new holism, the argumentation textbooks hedged: Argumentation was to study the *primarily rational* or *essentially logical* part of rhetoric—appeals addressed "primarily" to the reason; "psychological appeals" were distinctly secondary (Winans and Utterback 1930).

The new holism did not mean that logic and emotion were scientifically indistinguishable. Modern attitude theory, for instance, describes affective and cognitive elements as open to conscious balancing. Behavior, in this view, issues from *decisions* people make. One creates behavioral intentions by *weighing* the expectations of others against one's own desires, and one's desires against one's predictions of outcomes. Other theories still focus on the emotions as contaminants of logic—the idea being that although human thought takes logical form, its premises may be corrupted. *Wishful thinking,* for instance, distorts perceptions of probability; and an innate drive for cognitive consistency may lead some people to describe invalid syllogisms as valid when they agree with the syllogisms' conclusions.

Today many argumentation theorists defend the conviction-persuasion duality, not as a psychological fact but as a normative goal—thus reviving Aristotle's vision of rationality as a virtue-governed balance of reason and passion. Informal logicians, for instance, focus on an array of procedural flaws and rule violations, as well as wishful thinking, suppression of evidence, biases, ad hominem (personal) attacks, emotional appeals, and many other factors as contaminations of reason in ordinary discourse. J. Anthony Blair and Ralph Johnson thus use *fallacy theory* as a pedagogical device for protecting discourse from the worst excesses of persuasion. Toulmin, Rieke, and Janik, on the other hand, see rationality as the manner in which an advocate "handles and responds to the offering of reasons for and against claims." Rationality is one's "openness" to argument—one acknowledges the force of counterclaims or feels obliged to reply to one's interlocutors (13). Its antonyms thus include dogmatism, closemindedness, zealousness, and an unwillingness to risk one's ideas in the public marketplace.

Together, the concepts of argument and rationality have a long historical association with the idea of knowledge; and both ideas have changed as broader theories of knowledge (or epistemologies) have changed. The earliest philosophies, for instance, took a view that modern scholars call *foundationalism*. The idea—roughly—was that justification is a process of finding or presenting grounds for claims. Knowledge claims have a basis, a standing, in knowledge systems. Their reliability comes from their footing in those systems. Systematic philosophies such as Aristotle's and Kant's assumed that human knowledge directly reflects the orderly, determinate, and holistic nature of reality itself. Aristotle thus arranged all departments of knowledge in an authoritative hierarchy. All knowledge claims are thus grounded in particular systems, that are themselves grounded upon still higher order systems. Rationality consists of letting the system do its work—that is, reasoning in compliance with the system's internal laws. In the least scientific domains, where rhetoric's concern for probabilities is paramount, arguments were thought to be best grounded in the practical disciplines: The political orator, Aristotle said, must know the facts of statecraft, diplomacy, law, economics, and politics.

Despite the demise of systematic philosophy, the idea of grounded knowledge remains a central concept in the argumentation field. For instance, in many of the definitions surveyed above, the act of *warranting* is virtually definitive of the act of arguing. Claims become arguments when they are linked to reasons —when they are justified by appeal to something beyond themselves. In the simplest case, claims are authorized by other claims, their evidence or warrants. Sanctioned claims, however, may themselves need backing—perhaps confirmation by further reasoning, or the endorsement of expert authority, or an appeal to the state of consensus in expert fields.

The idea that knowledge claims are grounded in the discourses in which they function is a common claim of *epistemic* theories of argument. These theories emphasize, to one degree or another, the social grounds of knowledge, that speech and writing, and therefore ideas, take their meaning and coherence from the human practices that spawn them, and that these practices are constituted in social worlds that are, to one degree or another, coherent wholes. Epistemic theories focus on such units of analysis as groups, disciplines, professions, rhetorical communities, knowledge systems, thought systems, social systems, institutions, and—to use Michel Foucault's terms—*enunciative regularities, discursive formations,* or more simply, *discourses.*

These units of analysis differ in their determinism—the degree to which various theorists suppose that human action is coerced by the social formation—but they share the view that the grounding of claims can be analyzed by considering their fit within particular judgmental systems. In the argumentation field, a common term for such local systems is *argument fields*.

The idea of argument fields originated in Ludwig Wittgenstein's *Philosophical Investigations*, which warned analysts to avoid "the danger of wanting to find an expression's meaning by contemplating the expression itself" (601). Knowledge and language do not form a homogeneous whole, Wittgenstein argued. They are divided into manifold *forms of life* or *language games*, within which expressions take meaning from their functions and uses, and claims are grounded in the particulars of local practices. The builder, Wittgenstein says, speaks of blocks, pillars, slabs, and beams in a language game that is "complete in itself." Whether Wittgenstein intended this view to justify an epistemological relativism is a matter of controversy. He likely did not intend to evoke the most extreme kind of relativism—*complete unintelligibility*. The idea of a game "complete in itself" does not dictate that if one is immersed in one game, one will find other games, even very alien ones, incomprehensible. Nor did Wittgenstein likely intend to evoke another of *relativism's* meanings–*incomparability*—for, while the builder, the electrician, and the plumber work within their own forms of life, they are also able to coordinate their activities.

Nonetheless, proposition 12e in the *Investigations* seems to limit in a fundamental way the analyst's liberty to generalize across forms of life: "If you do not keep the multiplicity of language games in view, you will perhaps be inclined to ask questions like: 'What is a question?'" This proposition, and others like it, squared with the truism in the social sciences that there are empirical differences between the beliefs and practices of groups, cultures, societies, nations, and religions. Few social scientists take such differences to mean that all beliefs and practices are on a moral par or that the knowledge claims of competing groups cannot be compared or adjudicated. Many indeed treat *relativity* or *pluralism* simply as constraints on the scope of permissible scientific generalizations. Nonetheless, the idea of the language game also filtered into a developing literary genre that is often loosely called *social theory*.

A

This genre is a hybrid field. Its scholars include philosophers and humanists in many fields, as well as political scientists, sociologists, social psychologists, and a variety of communication specialists. An organizing problematic in social theory is to understand what Jürgen Habermas calls *the force of the better argument*; and a central question in this problematic is whether the grounds for the appraisal of claims are to any degree universal or whether they are strictly local (peculiar, that is, to particular language games). Thus many debates in the field of social theory have resembled the philosophical stand-off between *absolutism* (the belief that there is a single, holistic, unchanging, universal knowledge) and *relativism* (a label for any number of sometimes quite different theories that emphasize differences).

With the aim of charting a middle course between absolutism and relativism, Wittgenstein's student, Stephen Toulmin, coined the expression *field of argument* in *The Uses of Argument,* in which he proposed that some standards of judgment and verification are *field-dependent,* while some standards of argument validity are *field-invariant.* As a unit of analysis, the argument field is meant to explain and assess the trustworthiness of claims. In *Human Understanding,* Toulmin divides knowledge into *rational enterprises*—meaning academic fields or subject matters—and arrays those enterprises along a hierarchy of *compactness.* Compact disciplines (for example, atomic physics) are marked by substantial agreement about what does and does not count as knowledge. Their standards for verifying claims and adjudicating disputes have been subjected to a continuing, reflective scrutiny, so the claims they authorize are proportionately trustworthy. Most academic fields, however, lack this compactness. They are diffuse or would-be disciplines, characterized to different degrees by competing schools of thought and less agreement about judgmental standards. Freudians and behaviorists, for instance, may see their respective paradigms as defining the whole of psychology, but they talk about different phenomena: Freudians speak of id, ego, and superego; behaviorists speak of conditioned responses and reinforcement. They use different research methods and focus on different problems, and they thus lack a common language in which to plot their differences. They cannot develop, let alone adjudicate, disputes. Schools of thought such as Freudianism and behaviorism are thus provincial discourses whose knowledge claims

may be controversial or even incomprehensible when viewed from other perspectives.

Aside from explaining the grounds of knowledge claims, another reaction to the idea of argument fields has been a concern for the state of public discourse. G. Thomas Goodnight argues that the public sphere—meaning the time and space for public discourse—has been "steadily eroded by the elevation of the personal and technical groundings of argument" (223). In the personal sphere, people are not citizens; their grounds of judgment are matters of taste and lifestyle; and their privacy dilutes their civic responsibility. One reason for this retreat to privacy is that the epistemic authority of expert fields has devitalized the public sphere. Technical specialism and the disciplinary control of knowledge have disenfranchised the public by depriving it of the general knowledge needed to govern a democracy and by using modes of argument that favor specialism or expertise. By this reasoning the rationale for argumentation and critical thinking pedagogies is mass enfranchisement—an empowerment of the citizenry.

A different approach (Willard 1987) is to say that experts, public decision-makers, and ordinary citizens share a common predicament: No individual can grasp all the subdivisions of knowledge; in respect to complex issues, everyone is to some degree authority-dependent. As many public issues are partly or wholly technical, specialism and expertise are to some degree indispensable. And as public issues often touch upon multiple subjects, public decision-makers are often forced to adjudicate disputes among experts—often by reducing the trustworthiness of public knowledge claims to mere prestige of particular fields and experts and interpreting the implications of expert testimony in terms of slogans and political agendas. In this view, the onus for improving public argument is on the expert fields. The study of argumentation may serve this goal by focusing on the interplay between competing specialists' claims in public life and on the nature and epistemic effects of discourse across field boundaries. Fields are rarely complete in themselves. They exchange ideas and methods, address problems whose complexity overlaps field boundaries, and cooperate in interdisciplinary projects. They thus grapple with the problem of distinguishing the trustworthiness of imported ideas from the authority of the exporting field. So one focus of study is on how ideas are imported and exported and on how opinion changes in the border fields move inward toward the larger field's center, sometimes causing further evolutionary development in the field's ideas, at other times sparking revolutionary changes.

Considered historically, the various approaches to argument as a social and institutional process have evolved from the argumentation field's earliest focus on the solitary thinker. They developed in part from the view that arguments-as-products are quasi-logical, that they are addressed to particular audiences in concrete situations, and are thus valid insofar as they spark audience adherence (Perelman and Olbrechts-Tyteca). Rationality, in this view, is a matter of pragmatic justification (McKerrow), of proceeding appropriately within conventional constraints. And the critical question is the degree to which judgmental and veridical conventions are local or universal—field-dependent or field-invariant—or how the rationalities of particular audiences compare to idealized abstractions such as Perelman and Olbrechts-Tyteca's universal audience. But whether questions of this sort will define the future directions of the argumentation field is open to doubt. There is little consensus about how best to describe the universal audience, and there is empirical evidence that fields cooperate on specific topics and projects in concrete contexts. Border-spanning discourse is thus often based on regional and sometimes temporary achievements of common ground. Case studies of such interfield cooperation may undercut such abstract distinctions as inside versus outside and local versus universal—or lead argument scholars to regard them as rhetorical stances (Lyne). If field-invariance is a rhetorical achievement, then it is endemic to contexts, subjects, and audiences. Argumentation scholars may thus turn increasingly to social scientific and rhetorical case studies.

Charles Arthur Willard
University of Louisville

Bibliography

Baker, George Pierce. *Principles in Argumentation*. Waltham: Ginn, 1895.

Barthe, Else M., and Erik C.W. Krabbe. *From Axiom to Dialogue*. Berlin: de Gruyter, 1982.

Benoit, Pamela. "Characteristics of Arguing From a Social Actor's Perspective." *Readings in Argumentation*. Ed. William L. Benoit, Dale Hample, and Pamela J. Benoit. Berlin: Foris, 1992. 165–83.

Bitzer, Lloyd F. "Aristotle's Enthymeme Revisited." *Quarterly Journal of Speech* 45 (1959): 399–408.

Brockriede, Wayne E. "Where Is Argument?" *Journal of the American Forensic Association* 11 (1975): 179–82.

Ducrot, Oswald, and Jean-Claude Anscombre. *L'Argumentation dans la Langue*. Brussels: Mardaga, 1986.

Eemeren, Frans H. van, and Rob Grootendorst. *Argumentation, Communication, and Fallacies*. Hillsdale: Erlbaum, 1992.

———. *Speech Acts in Argumentative Discussions*. Dordrecht: Foris, 1984.

Eemeren, Frans H. van, Rob Grootendorst, J. Anthony Blair, and Charles Arthur Willard, eds. *Argumentation: Across the Lines of Discipline*. Dordrecht: Foris, 1987.

———. *Argumentation Illuminated*. Dordrecht: Foris, 1992.

Ehninger, Douglas. "Argument as Method: Its Nature, Its Limitations, and Its Uses." *Speech Monographs* 37 (1970): 101–10.

Gilbert, Michael. "Multi-Modal Argumentation." *Philosophy of the Social Sciences* 24 (1993): 159–77.

Goodnight, G. Thomas. "The Personal, Technical, and Public Spheres of Argument: A Speculative Inquiry into the Art of Public Deliberation." *Journal of the American Forensic Association* 18 (1982): 214–27.

Grize, Jean-Blaise. *De la Logique à L'Argumentation*. Gèneva: Droz, 1982.

Hample, Dale. "A Third Perspective on Argument." *Philosophy and Rhetoric* 14 (1985): 1–22.

———. "The Toulmin Model and the Syllogism." *Journal of the American Forensic Association* 14 (1977): 1–9.

Jackson, Sally A., and Scott Jacobs. "Structure of Conversational Argument: Pragmatic Bases for the Enthymeme." *Quarterly Journal of Speech* 66 (1980): 251–65.

Jacobs, Scott, and Sally Jackson. "Building a Model of Conversational Argument." *Rethinking Communication Vol. 2: Paradigm Exemplars*. Ed. Brenda Dervin, Lawrence Grossberg, Barbara J. O'Keefe, and Ellen Wartella. Newbury Park, CA: Sage, 1989. 153–71.

A

Johnson, R.H., and J.A. Blair. *Logical Self-Defense*. 2nd ed. Toronto: McGraw-Hill Reyerson, 1983.

Lyne, John. "Bio-Rhetorics." *The Rhetorical Turn*. Ed. Herbert W. Simons. Chicago: U of Chicago P. 35–57.

Maier, Robert, ed. *Norms in Argumentation*. Dordrecht: Foris, 1989.

McKerrow, Raymie. "The Centrality of Justification: Principles of Warranted Assertability." *Argumentation Theory and the Rhetoric of Assent*. Ed. David Cratis Williams and Michael David Hazen. Tuscaloosa: U of Alabama P, 1990. 17–32.

O'Keefe, Barbara J. "The Logic of Message Design." *Communication Monographs* 55 (1988): 80–103.

O'Keefe, Barbara J., and Pamela Benoit. "Children's Arguments." *Advances in Argumentation Theory and Research*. Ed. J. Robert Cox and Charles Arthur Willard. Carbondale: Southern Illinois UP, 1982. 154–83.

O'Keefe, Daniel J. "The Concepts of Argument and Arguing." *Advances in Argumentation Theory and Research*. Ed. J. Robert Cox and Charles Arthur Willard. Carbondale: Southern Illinois UP, 1982. 3–23.

Perelman, Chaïm, and Lucie Olbrechts-Tyteca. *The New Rhetoric: A Treatise on Argumentation*. Notre Dame, IN: Notre Dame UP, 1969.

Plantin, Christian. *Essais sur L'Argumentation*. Paris: Editions Kimé, 1990.

Toulmin, Stephen E. *Human Understanding*. Princeton: Princeton UP, 1972.

———. *The Uses of Argument*. Cambridge: Cambridge UP, 1958.

Toulmin, Stephen E., Richard Rieke, and Allan Janik. *An Introduction to Reasoning*. New York: Macmillan, 1979.

Wenzel, Joseph W. "Perspectives on Argument." *Readings in Argumentation*. Ed. William L. Benoit, Dale Hample, and Pamela J. Benoit. Berlin: Foris, 1992. 121–43.

Willard, Charles Arthur. *Argumentation and the Social Grounds of Knowledge*. Tuscaloosa: U of Alabama P, 1983.

———. *A Theory of Argumentation*. Tuscaloosa: U of Alabama P, 1987.

Winans, James A., and William E. Utterback. *Argumentation*. New York: Century, 1930.

Wittgenstein, Ludwig. *Philosophical Investigations*. Oxford: Oxford UP, 1953.

Yost, Mary. "Argument from the Point of View of Sociology." *Quarterly Journal of Public Speaking* 3 (1917): 109–27.

Zarefsky, David. "Process, Product, or Point of View?" *Proceedings of the [First] SCA/AFA Conference on Argumentation*. Ed. Jack Rhodes and Sara Newell. Annandale, VA: Speech Communication Assn., 1980. 228–38.

See also ENTHYMEME; FALLACY; PERSUASION

Aristotle

Fourth-century B.C.E. philosopher. Perhaps no single figure has had as much influence on rhetoric's disciplinary character as Aristotle. He was born in 384 in Stagira in Chalcidice, a much-disputed territory in northern Greece, bordering on Macedonia. His father, Nicomachus, was a member of the sacred medical cult of the Asclepiads and court physician to the Macedonian king Amyntas III. Nicomachus died in Aristotle's youth, and in 367 Aristotle was sent by his guardian to Athens. Tradition has it that Aristotle left for Athens expressly to study at Plato's Academy. His departure, however, also coincided with Amyntas's death and the political turmoil concerning the heir to the throne. Historians generally agree that Aristotle's identification with the royal court placed him in some danger. Thus, it is likely that Aristotle left Chalcidice as much to escape personal harm as to pursue his education.

At the time Aristotle arrived in Athens, Plato was in Sicily, assisting a relative of the tyrant Dionysius II in drafting a constitution reflecting Greek philosophical ideals. Plato and his Academy were heavily involved in the politics of Athens and surrounding territories. Although Aristotle's political alliances would differ from Plato's, Aristotle shared the assumption that the philosopher's best function was to advise rulers of state. The belief that the purpose of learning was to prepare one for political leadership was also shared by Isocrates, who led the Academy's rival school. Philodemus reports that Aristotle began lecturing on rhetoric some ten years after his arrival at the Academy, and Diogenes Laertius echoes Philodemus' report that Aristotle began his lectures because "it would be a base and shameful thing to remain silent" while Isocrates spoke out.

Aristotle and Isocrates differed sharply in their conceptions of rhetoric and philosophy. Isocrates made no distinction between his art of discourse and the knowledge that he called *philosophia*. Aristotle, on the other hand, made careful distinctions among metaphysics, physics, ethics, and rhetoric. Fragments of Aristotle's exoteric (popular) treatise *Protrepticus* are an early statement of the Academy's goals, apparently designed to distinguish them sharply from the objectives of Isocrates' school. At the same time, Isocrates and Aristotle shared significant characteristics. Both envisioned themselves as advisers to a ruling class, and both advocated submitting Athens to the rule of Philip of Macedon, actively working, albeit in different ways, in Philip's behalf. Perhaps the easiest way to distinguish between the two is to view Isocrates as a teacher and rhetor who depended largely on the circulation of written speeches for his political influence. Aristotle, on the other hand, was a philosopher who compiled rhetorical doctrines and gave rhetoric a formal disciplinary account. His political influence, however, resided largely in his personal counsel.

Aristotle left the Academy after Plato's death in 348–47. It is frequently suggested that Aristotle departed in anger over Plato's appointment of his nephew Speusippus to lead the school. It is more likely, however, that Aristotle left Athens to escape reprisals prompted by the ventures of Philip of Macedon into Greece. Philip had ravaged the Greek city of Olynthus, and Athens grew sharply divided between two factions: One party sought to maintain the peace made with Philip in 356 and another, led largely by Demosthenes, urged Athens to wage war against Macedonia. As anti-Macedonian sentiment grew, so did the precariousness of Aristotle's position in Athens. Aristotle left Athens for the court of the tyrant Hermias in Assos, a district in Asia Minor that was of significant military importance to Philip. It is generally agreed that Aristotle went to Assos as an emissary for Philip, for a secret agreement was eventually made between Hermias and Philip that shifted Assos' alliance from Persia to Macedonia. During his stay in Assos, Aristotle married Hermias' niece and adopted daughter, Pythias. Aristotle left Assos in 345–44, and, after a brief stay in Mytilene, on the island of Lesbos, he returned to Macedonia in 343–42.

Although Aristotle is frequently identified as the tutor to Philip's son Alexander, historians concur that Aristotle was likely only one of many tutors. There is significant speculation that during this period Aristotle was being groomed to return to Athens to aid in influencing the Academy to shift its allegiance to Philip. After Philip's murder in 336, Alexander quickly subdued revolts in Athens and attempted to resume a policy of peace and friendship with Athens. Aristotle returned to Athens in 335 with the full support of the Macedonian king. A sacred grove dedicated to Apollo was assigned to Aristotle for his school. With elaborate facilities and an extraordinary library, Aristotle's Lyceum soon became distinguished for the breadth of its studies, which encompassed philosophical dialectic, ethics, and politics, all the known natural sciences, as well as rhetoric. Eventually the "Peripatetic" school, so named for the covered colonnades where lectures were held, became the seat of Hellenistic learning, educating the sons of the ruling classes throughout the Hellenistic world.

Aristotle's fortunes continued to be tied to the fortunes of Macedonia. Alexander's death in 323 and the accompanying demise of his empire rekindled Athenian hatred toward Macedonia. Diogenes Laertius reports that Aristotle had been formally charged with sacrilege. Before he could be tried, Aristotle turned over the Lyceum to his longtime assistant Theophrastus and left Athens for the last time. He made his home on the island of Euboea, in the town of Chalcis, which was not only secure Macedonian territory but also his mother's homeland. He died only one year later, in 322.

Aristotelian Corpus and Philosophy

Like Plato, Aristotle presented his philosophy in dialogue form. Only a few fragments of these dialogues have survived, however, and our knowledge of Aristotelian philosophy is based on a corpus of texts that are generally considered to be some combination of notes and records of lectures. The corpus as we know it was edited and organized by Andronicus Rhodius, a first-century B.C.E. philosopher of the surviving Peripatetic school at Athens. Scholars speculate that Andronicus' edition may include the thought of successive Peripatetic philosophers, and it is certain that many surviving texts were excluded from his edition.

Aristotelian thought has so permeated two millennia of intellectual inquiry that philosophical, ethical, and political theories continue to define themselves by their convergence with or divergence from Aristotle. Ironically, this use of Aristotle's thought has frequently transformed a corpus of inquiry into dogma. Though textual traditions are responsible for many of the contradictions found in the corpus, it is important to bear in mind that the surviving corpus is a record of inquiry, not a closed system of knowledge. There is, however, relative consistency in two areas of Aristotle's thought: the teleological system and the taxonomy of knowledge.

Throughout the Aristotelian corpus, inquiry is described in terms of causality, purpose, and ends. For this reason Aristotle's philosophy is often described as "teleological," from the Greek word *telos*, meaning "end." Aristotle insists, however, that there are many types of causes. We are most familiar with his four causes: final, material, efficient, and formal. In the *Physics* he explains that all things come into being for an end, and that end is a final cause. Health, for example, is the final cause of the art of medicine. A material cause is "that out of which" something comes into being. Thus, bronze is the material cause of the statue, and silver is the material cause of the bowl. The source responsible for change or movement is called the efficient cause. Consequently, while health may be a final cause of the art of medicine, the doctor is the efficient cause of health. Finally, the shape, archetype, or what Aristotle refers to as the "definition of the essence" of something is the formal cause. One example of formal causality reveals the influence of Plato's theory of forms, for Aristotle describes the formal cause of a musical scale as the arithmetic ratio of 2:1. Elsewhere, however, formal causality bears a closer resemblance to the kind of definition described in Aristotle's logical treatises. Aristotle's conceptions of potentiality and actuality are closely related to these perspectives on causality. Potentiality (*dunamis*) refers to the capacity of something to act (or develop) and to be acted upon. Actuality (*energeia*) describes the movement toward "fulfillment" (*entelecheia*). Aristotle explains in the *Physics* that the house is a potentiality in the process of building, which includes the art of house-building as well as building materials. Once the house is complete, the potentiality for building is no longer there. Thus, actuality is the process by which a potentiality is fulfilled.

Another important and relatively consistent dimension of Aristotle's thought is the epistomological taxonomy. The three domains of the theoretical (*epistêmê*), the practical (*praxis*), and the productive (*poesis*) are demarcated according to their relationship to the key components of Aristotle's teleological system. Each domain of knowledge is distinguished by its relationship to a *telos*, or end. Theoretical knowledge is concerned with first (or formal) principles and ends. Theoretical knowledge is the highest knowledge, an essential constituent of true wisdom; it encompasses the study of metaphysics, the natural sciences, and mathematics. In the *Nicomachean Ethics*, Aristotle describes theoretical knowledge as the "belief about things that are universal and necessary" (1140.b.31). The most decisive characteristic of theoretical knowledge is that it is pursued for no practical or economic end. In the *Metaphysics*, Aristotle asserts that theoretical knowledge is pursued only by those who already have "almost all the necessities of life and the things that make for comfort and recreation" (982.b.23). Practical knowledge, in contrast, is expressly concerned with action and human behavior. In the *Nicomachean Ethics*, it is defined as "a reasoned and true state of capacity to act with regard to human goods" (1040.b.20). The end of practical knowledge is to bring about *eudaimonia*, variously translated as "happiness" or "the good life." The study of ethics and politics is subsumed under practical knowledge.

Finally, productive knowledge is identified with *technê*, or art, and thus concerned with "making." Examples of productive knowledge within the corpus include the arts of medicine, architecture, military strategy, seafaring, poetics, and rhetoric. Aristotle explains in the *Nicomachean Ethics* that art is "identical with a state of capacity to make, involving a true course of reasoning" (1140.a.9–10). Productive knowledge is always concerned with what can be otherwise, "with contriving and considering how something may come into being which is capable of either being or not being" (1140.a.12–13). Like nature's processes, the production associated with art is teleological—or purposive. The "making" associated with *technê* is distinct from the teleological movements of nature because art's origin is "in the maker and not in the thing made." Thus, productive knowledge is always implicated in some form of exchange. The first principles of art are in the maker or producer, and art's *telos* is in the user or receiver of the artistic construct. In contrast to both theoretical and practical knowledge, the ends of productive knowledge are always "outside itself," residing not in the "product" but rather in the use made of the artistic construct by a receiver or audience.

Aristotle's Conception of Rhetoric and Rhetorical Treatises

The *Rhetoric* was not Aristotle's only treatise on the subject. A compilation of rhetorical precepts known as the *Synagoge Technon* is mentioned by Cicero, and a lost dialogue on rhetoric titled *Gryllus* was written early in Aristotle's career. Our earliest surviving text of the *Rhetoric* is dated in the tenth century. Despite our dependence on Aristotle's *Rhetoric* for both rhetorical precepts and our sense of rhetoric's disciplinary character, Aristotle would hardly have characterized himself as a rhetor or rhetorician. In response to the popularity of Isocrates' school, fourth-century curricula had to include studies in rhetoric. In his translation of Aristotle's *Rhetoric* George Kennedy points out that parts of the text appear to be drawn from other areas of Aristotle's inquiry, psychology in particular, and much of this material is not adapted to the needs of rhetors. Thus Kennedy concludes that parts of the *Rhetoric* are addressed to students of dialectic, who likely had little interest in rhetoric. At the same time, Aristotle's *Rhetoric* remains of critical importance as one of the most comprehensive treatments of the subject. The text is a singular synthesis of systematized rhetorical precepts and discussions of rhetoric's ethical, epistemological, and disciplinary character.

The *Rhetoric* is an exhaustive collection of rhetorical precepts, encompassing discourse classification, invention, modes of proof, arrangement, and style. Aristotle's teleological system appears in various forms throughout the text. For example, Aristotle classified discourse according to its particular *telos*. Deliberative rhetoric is concerned with exhortation or dissuasion toward the *telos* of the advantageous or the harmful; judicial or forensic discourse is concerned with accusation or defense toward the *telos* of the just or the unjust; and demonstrative or epideictic discourse is concerned with praise and blame to the end of establishing either the honorable or the shameful.

Aristotle also provides one of the more complete treatments of rhetorical invention. The *Rhetoric* defines three kinds of topics: the *koina,* common topics, and special topics. These are distinguished by the extent to which they are applicable to many subjects and contexts or specific to a particular subject and context. The widely applicable are the three *koina*: possible/impossible, past and future fact, and degree of magnitude or importance.

The twenty-eight common *topoi* vary in specificity. For the most part, however, they are *not* restricted to particular subjects and contexts. For this reason many scholars have accorded them an inventional, or heuristic, function. Debates persist, however, concerning the role of the twenty-eight *topoi*. Scholars question whether they serve to facilitate judgment or to provide proof or elaboration for a thesis already in hand. Special topics, *idia* in Greek, include material specific to particular contexts, like the assembly, and types of proof, such as appeals to emotions.

The classification of types of proof is another significant contribution of Aristotle's *Rhetoric*. Proofs are first divided according to whether they are nonartistic (*atechnic*) or artistic (*technic*). Rhetoric is primarily concerned with the invention of artistic proofs. The three major types of artistic proofs are those based on character (ethos), reason (logos), and emotion (pathos). Aristotle's treatment of logical proof remains an important dimension of studies in rhetoric. Students, scholars, and rhetors alike continue to refer to Aristotle's discussion of probable argumentation and the enthymeme. The character and function of the enthymeme is subject to various interpretations. Some maintain that its role is primarily postjudgment proof, while others argue that it also serves as a heuristic. What is quite clear is that Aristotle carefully distinguished the probable reasoning associated with the rhetorical enthymeme from the more rigorous reasoning identified with the dialectical syllogism.

Book III of the *Rhetoric* contains a discussion of arrangement and style. Aristotle describes the two essential parts of a speech as statement and proof, but a discussion of introductions, narrations, and conclusions is also included. Principles discussed under the heading of style include an analysis of metaphor and a treatment of such qualities of style as appropriateness, concreteness, and vividness.

Aristotle's statements concerning rhetoric's epistemological and ethical character have been the subject of centuries of debate. The most recent commentary on the *Rhetoric,* by William M.A. Grimaldi, maintains that rhetoric's province encompasses both philosophy and ethics. His interpretation contrasts with the nineteenth-century commentary by Edward Meredith Cope, which maintains that rhetoric is more closely identified with politics and ethics than philosophy, and thus rhetoric falls into Aristotle's category of practical knowledge. Despite efforts to transform rhetoric into philosophy and ethics, Aristotle's characterization of rhetoric is consistent with his treatment of productive knowledge, which is carefully distinguished from theoretical and practical knowledge. Teleological principles appear throughout Aristotle's discussion of rhetoric. For example, the capacity of productive knowledge to deal with the indeterminate—or what can be "otherwise"—is directly applied to the art of rhetoric, for Aristotle insists that the subjects of rhetoric must "present us with alternative possibilities" (1357.a.5). If rhetoric is classified as productive knowledge, then it is a uniquely contingent kind of knowledge, subject neither to the epistemological requirements of theoretical knowledge, nor to the ethical constraints of practical knowledge.

Janet M. Atwill
University of Tennessee

Bibliography

Barnes, Jonathan, ed. *The Complete Works of Aristotle*. Rev. ed. 2 vols. Bollingen Series 71. Princeton: Princeton UP, 1984.

Black, Deborah L. *Logic and Aristotle's Rhetoric and Poetics in Medieval Arabic Philosophy*. Leiden: Brill, 1990.

Chroust, Anton-Hermann. *Aristotle: New Light on His Life and on Some of His Lost Works*. Notre Dame, IN: Notre Dame UP, 1973.

Cope, Edward M. *An Introduction to Aristotle's* Rhetoric. London: Macmillan, 1867.

———. *The* Rhetoric *of Aristotle with a Commentary*. Ed. John Sandys. 3 vols. Cambridge: Cambridge UP, 1877.

Edel, Abraham. *Aristotle and His Philosophy*. Chapel Hill: U of North Carolina P, 1982.

Erickson, Keith. *Aristotle: The Classical Heritage of Rhetoric*. Metuchen: Scarecrow, 1974.

Grimaldi, William M.A., S.J. *Aristotle, Rhetoric I: A Commentary*. New York: Fordham UP, 1980.

———. *Studies in the Philosophy of Aristotle's* Rhetoric. Wiesbaden: Franz Steiner Verlag GMBH, 1972.

Kennedy, George. *On Rhetoric: A Theory of Civic Discourse*. Oxford: Oxford UP, 1991.

Arnold, Carroll C. (b. 1912)

Distinguished scholar and teacher of public speaking. Carroll C. Arnold was born on April 29, 1912, in Lake Park, Iowa. He earned his M.A. and Ph.D. degrees in Speech Communication from the University of Iowa, where A. Craig Baird served as his mentor.

Dr. Arnold's scholarship both historically and topically spans the field. He wrote his dissertation on the nineteenth-century British orator Benjamin Disraeli and published his first book on the subject of small-group discussion. He has written articles on the classical concept of logos, the Pennsylvania Ratification Debates of the Constitution, speech as action, and many other topics. Rhetorical theory serves as his anchor, but just as rhetorical theory covers a multitude of topics, so does Dr. Arnold's research. He is clearly a humanistic, pragmatic, eclectic scholar and a generalist who examines rhetoric wherever it occurs in order to better understand public communication.

His publications include eight books and approximately fifty research articles and chapters in books. His *Handbook of Rhetorical and Communication Theory* (Boston: Allyn and Bacon, 1984), coedited with John Waite Bowers, is a selectively encyclopedic reference work about rhetorical and communication theory. Professor Arnold is currently revising his popular textbook, *Public Speaking as a Liberal Art* (Boston: Allyn and Bacon) for a seventh edition (6th ed. 1990). The book is coauthored with John F. Wilson and most recently with Molly Meijer Wertheimer. His *Criticism of Oral Rhetoric* (Columbus, OH: Charles E. Merrill, 1974) explains how to do speech criticism and how *speech* criticism differs from *literary* criticism.

Dr. Arnold's article "Oral Rhetoric, Rhetoric, and Literature," published in the first volume of *Philosophy and Rhetoric* (1968), received the James A. Winans Award for Distinguished Scholarship in Rhetoric and Public Address (1969). In addition to the Winans Award, Dr. Arnold has earned numerous other accolades. He received the Distinguished Scholar Award in 1992 from the Speech Communication Association. The award recognizes "a select group of individuals" who have "a career of outstanding contributions devoted to improving the understanding of human communication."

Carroll Arnold was a co-founder and associate editor of *Philosophy and Rhetoric* (1968–76) and is a member of the journal's editorial board (1976–present). In addition, he has served as editor for *Speech Monographs* (1966–1968), editor for the Rhetoric/Communication Series for the University of South Carolina Press (1984–1991), editorial board member for *Rhetorica,* associate editor for *Quarterly Journal of Speech, Speech Monographs, Today's Speech,* and *Communication Quarterly* for various periods since 1950. In 1964 he served as president of the Eastern Communication Association.

Professor Arnold has left an indelible impact on scores of students in his seventeen years of teaching at Cornell University and his fourteen years of teaching at Pennsylvania State University. Since retiring and earning the title of professor emeritus in July of 1977, he has been a visiting professor at seven universities, including the University of Delaware, where he served as DuPont Distinguished Visiting Professor (1978), and the University of Iowa, where he held the first A. Craig Baird Distinguished Visiting Professorship (1979).

The College of Liberal Arts of the Pennsylvania State University honored him in 1975 with a Distinguished Teaching Award and in 1984 with an Emeritus Distinction Award. At the 1992 Speech Communication Association Convention, Dr. Arnold received the Lifetime Teaching Excellence Award for "a lifetime of dedication to distinguished teaching." In 1977 he received the Speech Communication Association's Distinguished Service Award. The encomium that accompanied the award said, "We confer this award on him for being 'Teacher to Our Profession.'"

Lois J. Einhorn
Binghamton University

Bibliography

Arnold, Carroll C. *Criticism of Oral Rhetoric.* Columbus, OH: Charles E. Merrill, 1974.
———. "Introduction." *The Realm of Rhetoric.* Chaïm Perelman. U of Notre Dame, 1982.
———. "On Analysis of *Logos.* A Methodological Inquiry." *Quarterly Journal of Speech* 56 (1970): 22–32. Written with Rodney B. Douglass.
———. "Oral Rhetoric, Rhetoric, and Literature." *Philosophy and Rhetoric* 1 (1968): 191–210.
———. "Rhetoric in America Since 1900." *Re-establishing the Speech Profession.*
Ed. R.T. Oliver and M.G. Bauer. Eastern Communication Assn., 1959. 3–7.
———. "Rhetorical and Communication Studies: Two Worlds or One?" *Western Speech* 34 (1972): 75–81.
———. "Some Preliminaries to English-Speech Collaboration in the Study of Rhetoric." *Rhetoric: Theories for Application.* Ed. Robert M. Gorrell. Urbana: National Council of Teachers of English, 1967. 30–36.
———, and John Waite Bowers. *Handbook of Rhetorical and Communication Theory.* Boston: Allyn, 1984.
———, John F. Wilson, and Molly Meijer Wertheimer. *Public Speaking as a Liberal Art.* 6th ed. Boston: Allyn, 1990.

Arnold, Matthew (1822–1888)

Nineteenth-century literary critic. Matthew Arnold's importance to rhetoric lies in the combined influence of his work as a poet, school inspector, and literary critic. During the nineteenth century, rhetoric was reduced to the handbook tradition of Blair and Campbell and became largely peripheral to the social concerns of the era. Arnold's writings reflect the increasing division between morally didactic literature and the utilitarian stylistic concerns of what was known as rhetoric. His views influenced many later critics, such as Trilling, Williams, Leavis, and Eliot.

Son of a prominent educational reformer, Arnold became a school inspector at the age of twenty-eight and held the position for thirty-five years. He published numerous collections of poetry and, in his later career, several major works of literary criticism and theory including *Essays in Criticism* (1865), *Culture and Anarchy* (1869), and *Literature and Dogma* (1873). Arnold represents both the ideal, aesthetic poet of Oxford and the man who talked "to more working-class children than any other poet who has ever lived" (Honan 218). While he worked within the realm of educational policy, however, his theoretical works remained separated from practical concerns.

In the Romantic era, the imagination was often viewed as the preeminent mental faculty. Arnold acknowledged the superiority of the creative impulse over the critical faculty, but he saw criticism as creative in itself and admired the critical works of otherwise "imaginative" writers such as Wordsworth and Goethe. More important, however, criticism was necessary to interpret, analyze, and organize the world before creative works could prosper within it. In establishing this intellectual environment, critics should, according to Arnold, maintain a disinterested objectivity and distance from the partisan, practical, and political concerns they observe.

Arnold's views on criticism are often described as "moral," yet he argues for an inner, ideal morality, not a practical morality that affects actions in the social sphere. Criticism's function, as he states repeatedly in his works, is to know "the best that is known and thought in the world and thus to establish a current of fresh and true ideas" (Hoctor 28). The ultimate goal of this criticism is to lead the mind toward an inner perfection. By dwelling upon what is most perfect in the world, the mind will become perfect itself. Rhetorically, Arnold located this perfection in the use of style. In his lectures on Homer, Arnold argued that the "grand" style, which emphasized austerity, severity, and simplicity, was the expression of the nobility of the poet's character and would in turn elevate the mind of the critic. Inherent in this style is the choice of a suitably serious and morally profound subject, or 'touchstone', in Arnold's terminology.

In *Culture and Anarchy,* the term *culture* takes the place of *criticism* as Arnold continues to espouse the inward perfection created by literature. He claims that the three classes of society (aristocracy, middle class, and working class) are unable to sustain culture's mission "to formulate and uphold literary standards and to foster the vitality of language against the prevailing philistinism of the majority culture" (Goodheart 452). Arnold thus perpetuates the theories of taste presented by Hugh Blair in the late eighteenth century. Culture, like Blair's taste, is a quality belonging to a select portion of society— critics; the "practical man" is unfit for this type of contemplation. Arnold's ideal morality of the critical enterprise is maintained apart from his actual work in the schools and therefore models the split between the utilitarian and aesthetic roles of language that pervades rhetoric in the nineteenth century.

Jennifer Welsh
University of Southern California

Bibliography

Anderson, Warren D. *Matthew Arnold and the Classical Tradition.* Ann Arbor: U of Michigan P, 1965.

Arnold, Matthew. *Culture and Anarchy and Friendship's Garland.* New York: Macmillan, 1883.

———. "The Function of Criticism at the Present Time." *Matthew Arnold's Essays in Criticism: First Series.* Ed. Sister T. Marion Hoctor, S.S.J. Chicago: U of Chicago P, 1964.

DeLaura, David J. "Arnold and Literary Criticism: (1) Critical Ideas." *Matthew Arnold.* Ed. Kenneth Allot. Athens: U of Ohio P, 1976.

Goodheart, Eugene. "Arnold at the Present Time." *Critical Inquiry* 9/3 (1982–83): 451–68.

Hoctor, Sister Thomas Marion, S.S.J. *Matthew Arnold's Essays in Criticism: First Series.* Chicago: U of Chicago P, 1964.

Honan, Park. *Matthew Arnold: A Life.* New York: McGraw, 1981.

Leavis, F.R. "Revaluations, XI: Arnold as Critic." *Scrutiny* 7 (1938): 319–32.

Arrangement

Greek, ταξισ [*taxis*]; Latin, *dispositio.* One of the five parts of the full art of rhetoric; the art of dividing a discourse into its parts and the inclusion, omission, or ordering of those parts according to the rhetor's needs and situation and the constraints of the chosen genre. The full art of rhetoric, developed by the first century B.C.E. in the *Rhetorica ad Herennium,* has five "parts" or "canons" representing phases in the orator's development of a speech: invention, arrangement, style, memory, and delivery. The speaker following these five parts frames the best available arguments or appeals, arranges them in an order effective for the given audience and situation, expresses them in appropriate and forceful language, commits the sections to memory, and delivers them with apt intonation and gesture. Over the centuries each of these five parts became the subject of further elaboration in separate treatises. Invention and style have received the most attention, and even memory and delivery have had their arts and eras. Compared with the other four, however, arrangement has received little independent treatment.

A theory of arrangement requires a rationale for partitioning a discourse and reasons for disposing the parts in a particular order. These needs are interdependent, both requiring assumptions about textual features (What constitutes a "part" of a text?) and about human psychology (What effect is this part likely to have?). Inevitably generalizing, rhetorical theory and pedagogy have identified certain fixed arrangements based on recurrent rhetorical situations, like the courtroom defense, and on default assumptions about how people are persuaded; the student of rhetoric learns the fixed form and then how to adapt it to an immediate rhetorical situation. Arrangement, therefore, is that topic in rhetorical theory in which the fixed features that define a type of discourse intersect with the rhetor's immediate needs. That makes it crucial, but difficult to isolate from matter and manner. Like Poland between Germany and Russia, arrangement has always been invaded by its stronger neighbors, the first and third canons, so that discussions of arrangement frequently become discussions of invention and style.

Yet it could be argued that arrangement was the first of the arts of rhetoric and that when its founders produced the first handbooks in the fifth century B.C.E., they stipulated the divisions and arrangement of forensic speeches. We know that not from the handbooks themselves, which are lost, but from complaints about them in works by Plato and Aristotle. In the *Phaedrus,* for example, Socrates lists the then well-known parts of a courtroom speech: introduction, statement of facts supported by the evidence of witnesses, indirect evidence, arguments from probability, supplementary proof, refutation, subsidiary refutation, and recapitulation (§266–67). Socrates makes it clear, however, that such naming of parts is not true rhetoric, which should be based on an understanding of what moves the soul; the traditional lore evidently listed parts but neglected reasons. Socrates' own dialectical method of invention, and by default, arrangement, requires first defining the subject of inquiry and then dividing it into species. This "philosophical," or academic, method of arrangement, which seems to focus on the demands of the subject and not the needs of the discussants, still rivals the rhetorical perspective. It is the ancestor of our textbook advice about "outlining." Nevertheless, the evidence that the earliest art of rhetoric was primarily an art of arrangement suggests strongly the pedagogical power of arrangement advice. To learn how to produce discourse quickly, one begins with naming of parts.

By the middle of the fourth century B.C.E., two full treatises demonstrate the fixed place of arrangement in rhetorical theory: Anaximenes' *Rhetorica ad Alexandrum* and Aristotle's *Rhetoric*. Both attempt to adapt the arrangement of the typical forensic speech to other speech situations, but while Anaximenes is more prescriptive and detailed, Aristotle dismisses extensive subdivisions. He prefers instead a radical simplicity requiring only two parts to a persuasive speech: the statement and the proof, a reduction typical of geometrical demonstration or dialectical discussion. Despite this preference, Aristotle concedes that at most a speech may have four parts: the *prooemium* (introduction), the *prothesis* (statement of the facts of the case), the *pistis* (proof), and the *epilogue* (summary and conclusion). Aristotle gives advice on each part that is sometimes adapted to the type of speech, sometimes common across speech situations (III.xiii–ix). For example, though Aristotle observes that the *prooemium* in an epideictic speech can begin with praise or blame of the audience, all openings must make the audience well disposed and attentive. Aristotle briefly suggests that audiences pay attention if they are convinced the subject concerns themselves, or something great, marvelous, or pleasurable. These observations constitute both a rationale for including this section of the speech and also invention heuristics for speakers constructing the exigence of their discourse in a *prooemium*. Such observations are the substance of arrangement theory.

In later rhetorical manuals, Aristotle's four essential parts expand to six in a fixed order that has been a heuristic device for centuries: *exordium, narratio, partitio, confirmatio, refutatio,* and *peroratio.* (Occasional treatises even recommend a seventh part, a *digressio*, just after the narration or between the proof and the peroration.) Each part has its prescribed persuasive function. The exordium predisposes the audience to the speaker and topic. The narration reprises the facts of the case; in courtroom speeches, the prosecution and defense give versions of events that support their respective cases. The partition identifies the precise point at issue and predicts the parts of the argument to come in what we would now call metadiscourse. The confirmation gives the supporting arguments, and the refutation attacks the opposition. These two sections switch places depending on whether the speaker accuses or defends. Finally the peroration summarizes the case and makes a final appeal to the audience's emotions. This sequence of six parts represents the naturally persuasive order of the typical forensic speech. In Cicero's account, this structure brackets the logical core of an argument with emotional and ethical appeals (*De Partitione Oratoria* viii.27). Advice about other speech types of special circumstances is always given as an adaptation of this order. A deliberative speech can dispense with an exordium (iv.13), or an epideictic speech can omit the narration (*Rhetorica ad Herennium* III.vii). It would, in fact, be difficult to exaggerate the importance of this arrangement paradigm. The classical art of memory requires this sequencing. The very organization of the manuals depends on the six-part division, and their advice on invention and amplification is part-specific: Certain devices are best in the narration, others in the peroration.

Quintilian's *Institutio Oratoria* (first century C.E.) provides the most complete picture of the intricacies of arrangement advice in a fully elaborated rhetorical theory. To begin with, invention and arrangement in the classical system are inextricable. Though Quintilian ostensibly devotes Book VII to arrangement, which he compares to generalship in war, he in fact gives arrangement advice throughout Books III through VI, devoted to invention strategies for the six parts of the oration. For example, in IV.v.4., Quintilian recommends sometimes eliminating the partition because, without its predictive power, the arguer can appear to discover points spontaneously; the rhetor gains one kind of advantage by including the partition, another by leaving it out.

Quintilian's advice on arranging the proof is organized according to the stases; a rhetor has to determine whether the issue concerns fact, definition, quality, or a point of law to know where to begin, and must even identify the precise subdivision in each stasis. For example, in the first stasis, when both the act and the doer are under debate, natural order recommends that the prosecution first prove that the act was committed before showing it was committed by the accused, *unless* evidence of the accused's guilt is plentiful, in which case the order is reversed. The defense, on the other hand, always begins by denying the act (VII.ii.15–16). In the second stasis, definition, there is an invariable order: first establish the definition and then apply it (VII.iii.19).

Quintilian disclaims the possibility of giving arrangement advice to cover every case. Instead, the circumstances of each will suggest a structure that should appear as naturally articulated as the human body, a comparison that perhaps begins the tradition of "organic form." Given the case

sensitivity of arrangement, the best pedagogical method, according to Quintilian, has the teacher "demonstrate daily in one kind of case after another what is the natural order and connexion of the parts" (VII.x.8).

Despite such gestures to the demands of situation, the lore of arrangement, whether in classical texts or Renaissance recapitulations, contains the same themes and even the same standard variations over the centuries. Advice on where to put the rhetor's main claim, for eample, remains consistent for two thousand years. A proposition that is well known or uncontroversial can be stated at once, with support to follow. A claim that is unfamiliar or unacceptable should be postponed or only implied. Cicero's *De Inventione* and the *Rhetorica ad Herennium* (both from the first century B.C.E.) give detailed advice on how to postpone, to open indirectly by "insinuation." The latter introduces distinctions that are carried on for centuries by advising adaptation of the exordium to the kind of case—honorable, difficult, mean, ambiguous, obscure—and the state of the audience—bored, hostile, or apparently convinced by the opposition.

Advice on how to order the arguments in the *confirmatio* and *refutatio*, also repeated for centuries, depends on their supposed "strength," a quality judged relative either to the audience or to some logical principle. One scenario of persuasion recommends that the strongest arguments should come first, on the assumption that they will stun the audience into agreement. The opposite counsel advises placing the weaker arguments first and building to climax with the strongest; that was Quintilian's advice to the defense. (Modern communication researchers have also studied the relative merits of "primacy" and "recency.") The compromise to this contradictory advice was the so-called "Nestorian" order, which, mimicking Nestor's disposition of his forces in the *Iliad* (such military metaphors abound in discussions of arrangement), puts the strongest arguments in the beginning and the end and the weaker in the middle.

New insights on the traditional advice for ordering arguments are found in Chaïm Perelman and Lucie Olbrechts-Tyteca's *New Rhetoric* (1958). The Belgians point out, for example, that though speakers necessarily adapt to their situation, that situation is not static but is changed by the order of elements in the argument (491). They also claim that arguments have no strength independent of their position in a text: "In fact, an argument will often appear strong only because preceding arguments have laid the ground for it" (500). They therefore recommend any order which *confers* the greatest strength. Most important, the authors of *The New Rhetoric* point out that "the order adopted can itself be a matter for the hearer to reflect upon, and can, in this way, directly affect the result of the argumentation" (502). Awareness of a principle of order can come from something external to the speech (that is, chronological order or the highly conventional organizational patterns within disciplinary genres). Or speakers can, with deliberate reference, create an audience's consciousness of their own ordering or of the ordering of another's speech (as Demosthenes did in *On the Crown*). An audience's appreciation of the overall order or, "form" (in, the Belgians claim, the gestalt sense of that word) makes it possible for some arguments to be understood by implication; recognizing the overall form, the audience supplies what is missing. The speaker who arranges arguments according to an external order recognized by the audience strengthens their force; their arrangement "will not seem a device" (504).

Though rhetorical theorists over the centuries have necessarily played off fixed forms against the pressure of circumstance, there is an inevitable tendency in the manuals and pedagogical tradition for arrangement advice to become fixed rather than contingent. This tendency is demonstrated forcibly in the rhetorical exercises known as the *progymnasmata* and in the tradition of defining literary genres according to the nature and order of their typical parts. The *progymnasmatic* exercises developed to practice the separate skills needed in the six parts in the oration (for example, retelling of a fable was good practice for later construction of the forensic narration). But, eventually, these separate exercises became ends in themselves and even separate genres, and they were taught as exercises in filling in a paradigm. A case in point is the treatment of epideictic in Aristotle and in Aphthonius' *Progymnasmata*. In the *Rhetoric* (I.ix), Aristotle discusses generally the special topics of epideictic rhetoric, the virtues, the deeds, and the background details that increase the probability of a favorable character portrait. Aphthonius, on the other hand, prescribes specifically the "heads" of an encomium, the subject's class, nation, city, ancestors, parents, upbringing, habits, art, and deeds of soul, body, and fortune (Matsen et al. 276). Aristotle's general invention advice thus solidifies into a particular genre defined by its precise arrangement of prescribed components.

The entire project of defining and imitating genres, in antiquity and beyond, depends on identifying crucial parts and their ideal sequence. In the medieval *Ars dictaminis,* for example, aspiring letter writers were advised to fill in the fixed parts of a paradigm: the salutation, securing of good will, narration, petition, and conclusion (Murphy 7). Even modern business and technical writing texts teach genres as predictable formats. Pedagogy that emphasizes arrangement can freeze the forms and reduce sensitivity to the immediate rhetorical situation. But since a chosen genre also to some extent creates a situation, and since prescribing the parts is likely to stimulate rather than stifle invention, especially for beginners, the gains of a pedagogy of arrangement probably outweigh the liabilities.

Though *dispositio* concerns primarily the organization of an entire text, there is a parallel tradition in rhetoric of *compositio,* the arrangement of words into cola and periods into longer sections, a switch from the global to the local level. Arrangement at this level was more important to eighteenth-century rhetorical theorists, but even they could find much to build on in the classical tradition. The enthymeme and syllogism can be described as small-scale schemes of arrangement, but more important for rhetorical persuasion is the epicheireme, defined in the *Ad Herennium* as the method of arranging individual arguments (ILL.ix.16). The *epicheireme* has five parts: the proposition, the reason, the proof of the reason, the embellishment, and the resume, a development corresponding roughly to a paragraph. Proposition and reason alone would give us an enthymeme; adding the proof of the reason expands the base to a syllogism or to the claim, data, and warrant of the Toulmin model. But most important, adding embellishment gives us the rhetorical dimension of this arrangement, the slot for meeting the audience's need to have an argument illustrated, expanded, and given presence.

Twentieth-century rhetoricians no longer focus on arrangement, but they pursue similar issues under the rubric of "form," part of genre theory and analysis. They are less interested in descriptions based on the six parts of the oration than they are in describing clusters of strategies typical of more precisely defined discourse types. Presidential inaugural addresses, scientific research reports, and even academic articles have been the objects of intense genre analysis, identifying, among other features, the typical sequencing of sections. In all these studies, however, the basic constituents of classical arrangement theory remain, and the methods are not far from those of the fifth century B.C.E. originators of rhetoric: to derive the ideal pattern of a type of discourse and then to show how that pattern is adapted to particular circumstances.

Jeanne Fahnestock
University of Maryland

Bibliography

Aristotle. *On Rhetoric*. Trans. George A. Kennedy. Oxford: Oxford UP, 1991.

Campbell, Karlyn Kohrs, and Kathleen Hall Jamieson, eds. *Form and Genre: Shaping Rhetorical Action*. Annandale, VA: Speech Communication Assn., 1978.

Cicero. *De Inventione*. Trans. H.M. Hubbell. Rpt. Cambridge, MA: Harvard UP, 1976.

———. *De Partitione Oratoria*. Trans. H. Rackham. Rpt. Cambridge, MA: Harvard UP, 1992.

———. *Rhetorica ad Herennium*. Trans. H. Caplan. Rpt. Cambridge, MA: Harvard UP, 1981.

Corbett, Edward P.J. *Classical Rhetoric for the Modern Student*. 3rd ed. New York: Oxford UP, 1990.

Matsen, Patricia P., Philip Rollinson, and Marion Sousa, eds. *Readings from Classical Rhetoric*. Carbondale: Southern Illinois UP, 1990.

Miller, Carolyn R. "Genre as Social Action." *Quarterly Journal of Speech* 70 (1984): 151–67.

Murphy, James J. *Three Medieval Rhetorical Arts*. Berkeley: U of California P, 1971.

———, ed. *Demosthenes' On the Crown: A Critical Case Study of a Masterpiece of Ancient Oratory*. Trans. John J. Keaney. Davis, CA: Hermagoras, 1983.

Perelman, Chaïm, and Lucie Olbrechts-Tyteca. *The New Rhetoric: A Treatise on Argumentation*. Trans. John Wilkinson and Purcell Weaver. Notre Dame, IN: U of Notre Dame P, 1969.

Plato. *Phaedrus and Letters VII and VIII*. Trans. Walter Hamilton. Rpt. Penguin, 1981.

Quintilian. *Institutio Oratoria*. Vols. I–IV. Rpt. Trans. H.E. Butler. Cambridge, MA: Harvard UP, 1977.

Simons, Herbert W., and Aram A. Aghazarian. *Form, Genre, and the Study of Political Discourse*. Columbia: U of South Carolina P, 1986.

Ars Dictaminis

The medieval art of composing letters and other prose documents. The terms *ars dictaminis* ("art of prose composition") and *ars dictandi* ("art of composing in prose") were used more or less interchangeably, from the twelfth century on, to designate the system of rules for composing prose documents as well as for a treatise in which those rules were set forth and illustrated. There is some preference, however, for *ars dictaminis* as the term for the discipline and *ars dictandi* (plural *artes dictandi*) for the textbook, and that distinction will be observed here. The term *dictamen* actually designated composition in general, and for that reason most *artes dictandi* begin by distinguishing the different sorts of composition—prose, metrical, rhythmical, and sometimes even "prosimetrical"—before specifying *dictamen prosaicum* as their own proper subject. As part of the technical term *ars dictaminis*, *dictamen* always refers exclusively to prose composition and particularly to the composition of letters and legal documents.

The *ars dictaminis* was developed as a simple and efficient method of training clerks in the practical writing tasks that they would have to perform in the chanceries, courts, or communal governments where they sought employment as secretaries, notaries, and the like. Thus the typical *ars dictandi* provides a relatively small set of concisely formulated rules, which are then copiously illustrated with examples appropriate for a wide range of situations. With few exceptions, the discipline remained pragmatic rather than literary throughout the four centuries of its history, and it consistently emphasized concrete examples over abstract theory.

The earliest teachers of the *ars dictaminis* sought to reduce to a system letter-writing practices that had already been in use for centuries. Taking the six-part Ciceronian oration as their model, they divided the typical letter into five parts: (1) the greeting (*salutatio*), (2) the securing of good will (*captatio benevolentiae*), (3) the statement of facts (*narratio*), (4) the request for action (*petitio*), and (5) the summation (*conclusio*). The choice of such a structure indicates that the public, official letter rather than the private, familiar letter was perceived as the paradigm of the genre. Indeed, when public speeches were added to the repertoire of the *dictator* (the person trained in the *ars dictaminis*), they were constructed in much the same way as the letters.

The *salutatio* and the *captatio benevolentiae* normally receive detailed treatment in an *ars dictandi*, whereas the last three parts often merit only a few sentences each. Many textbooks also include remarks on epistolary style, in particular the *cursus*, a system of prescribed rhythmical clause endings, and the *distinctiones* (*comma, colon,* and *periodus*), the constituents of a well-constructed sentence. The *Rhetorica ad Herennium* provided the *dictatores* with other topics that can be considered the common property of medieval stylistics, such as the vices and virtues of style and the "colors" of rhetoric. Brevity and variety of expression are frequently recommended. Besides the full range of letters from official to familiar, an *ars dictandi* might also provide instruction in the preparation of some of the more common legal documents. A very common supplement to the standard *ars dictandi* was a collection of model letters (*dictamina*), usually divided into ecclesiastical and secular letters, each paired with a model reply and organized by sender and receiver in descending order of rank.

In the history of the *ars dictaminis*, Italy, particularly Bologna, plays the leading role. Beginning around 1100, the increased use of secular clerks in Italian chanceries created a demand for more streamlined training in the skills of literacy than the grammar-dominated curriculum of the cathedral schools could provide. Alberic of Monte Cassino was apparently the first medieval teacher to discuss letters in a treatise on rhetoric, late in the eleventh century; the textbooks of Adalbert of Samaria, Hugh of Bologna, and other teachers active in northern Italy, during the first half of the twelfth century, would set the pattern for the emerging discipline. Many of the early *dictatores* taught at Bologna, where the *ars dictaminis* became an important part of the university curriculum and developed strong ties to the flourishing study of law.

By the mid twelfth century, the *ars dictaminis* had been carried beyond the Alps into France and Germany. In France it took firm root in the schools of the Loire valley, where the grammar curriculum, with its emphasis on the study of Latin poetry, was especially prominent. The French grammar masters began to produce *artes dictandi* that contrasted with their Italian predecessors in their predilection for a complex, obscure, "manneristic" style, their copious quotations from ancient authors,

and the use of grammatical rather than rhetorical terminology. The French teachers also seem to have been the first to incorporate treatments of privileges and other documents on a regular basis and to formulate a set of rules for the *cursus* as an integral part of the *ars dictaminis*. Finally, their treatises tended to reduce theory to a minimum while expanding the collections of model letters, documents, proverbs, and salutations to unprecedented dimensions.

The new direction given to the *ars dictaminis* in France was transmitted to England, to Germany, and even to Italy. In several works written in the 1190s, the Bolognese *dictator* Boncompagno took arms against the French invaders, who he claimed were corrupting the plain, easily understood style proper to letters and misaligning the *ars dictaminis*, whose true domain is practical rhetoric, with the literary concerns of the grammarians. Bene of Florence also acknowledged the rivalry, devoting an entire section of his encyclopedic *Candelabrum* to the French *dictamen*. The French influence in Italy, however, was neither deep nor long lasting. Guido Faba includes a long catalog of figures in his *Summa dictaminis*, but his model letters (*Dictamina rhetorica*) exhibit an extremely plain style. By the mid thirteenth century, the Italian manuals had clearly regained a mastery that they would not again relinquish. In fact, the works of the thirteenth-century Italians, particularly the *artes dictandi* of Guido Faba, Thomas of Capua, and Lawrence of Aquilegia, together with the letter collections of Peter of Vinea and Richard of Pofi, shaped the future course of the *ars dictaminis* throughout Europe. These treatises were already being imitated in Spain and Germany during the thirteenth century, and they were the chief source for the manuals produced in England during the late fourteenth and early fifteenth centuries.

Thirteenth-century Italy produced the first vernacular *artes dictandi*. Textbooks in Latin ranged from Bene of Florence's *Candelabrum* and Boncompagno's *Rhetorica antiqua*, rivaled in their comprehensiveness only by Bernard of Bologna's *Summa dictaminum* among earlier treatises, to numerous short tracts that specialize in a single type of document, among them Boncompagno's entertaining love-letter manual, the *Rota Veneris*. Sister disciplines also developed: The art of composing speeches (*ars arengandi*) remained ancillary to the *ars dictaminis,* strengthening its ties to classical rhetoric, while the notary's art (*ars notariae*) gradually detached itself and flourished in direct association with the law schools rather than the arts faculty.

The later history of the *ars dictaminis* in Italy is bound up with the origins of humanism. As a professional literate class whose employment as lawyers, notaries, and secretaries involved them directly in civic government, the *dictatores* saw themselves as the descendants of those Romans whose education was crowned by training in rhetoric. The reintroduction of training in deliberative oratory is one sign of this self-consciousness. The fact that in fourteenth-century Bologna John of Bonandrea and his successors lectured on the *ars dictaminis* as well as on the *Rhetorica ad Herennium* is another. As imitation of classical Latin style increased, the use of the *dictamen* became correspondingly restricted. It continued to be employed in official letters well into the fifteenth century, by which time it had long since been replaced by humanist style in the private letters of the *dictatores.*

Martin Camargo
University of Missouri

Bibliography

Camargo, Martin. *Ars dictaminis, Ars dictandi.* Typologie des sources du moyen âge occidental, 60. Turnhout, Belgium: Brepols, 1991.

Faulhaber, Charles B. "Letter-Writer's Rhetoric: The *Summa dictaminis* of Guido Faba." *Medieval Eloquence: Studies in the Theory and Practice of Medieval Rhetoric.* Ed. James J. Murphy. Berkeley: U of California P, 1978. 85–111.

Murphy, James J. "*Ars dictaminis*: The Art of Letter-Writing." *Rhetoric in the Middle Ages.* Berkeley: U of California P, 1974. 194–268.

Patt, William D. "The Early *Ars dictaminis* as Response to a Changing Society." *Viator* 9 (1978): 133–55.

Witt, Ronald. "Boncompagno and the Defense of Rhetoric." *Journal of Medieval and Renaissance Studies* 16 (1986): 1–31.

———. "Medieval *Ars Dictaminis* and the Beginnings of Humanism: A New Construction of the Problem." *Renaissance Quarterly* 35 (1982): 1–35.

Ars Poetica

A letter on poetry by the Roman poet Horace. Originally entitled *Epistula ad Pisones,* Quintilian already referred to it by its current name (*Epistula ad Tryphonem* 2; cf. *Institutio oratoria* 8.3.60). It is a verse-epistle, being the first known poem on poetics in epistolary form, and comprises *Epistulae* 2.3 of Horace's *Epistles.* Piso and his two sons were the recipients, but they cannot be positively identified. Porphyrio (third century C.E.) identifies Piso as the consul of 15 B.C.E., Lucius Calpurnius Piso (48 B.C.E.–32 C.E.), whose sons may have been named Lucius and Gaius. Date of composition is disputed, but 14–8 B.C.E. covers the typical estimates.

Although it bears the title *ars,* the work is not a comprehensive, systematic treatment of poetry intended as a handbook for poets. Horace was a master of lyric poetry, but the *Ars* only mentions it and says very little about Latin poetry in general. Instead, as was typical of the Aristotelian tradition dominant at the time, discussion of epic and drama predominate. Thus the focus is on plot, characterization, style, and imitation of life. Comedy and tragedy are discussed, particularly in regard to pathos. Other topics include imitation, unity, propriety, polished style, coinage of new words, training and criticism of the poet, and the benefits of poetry for humanity (underscoring moral responsibility). Humor is sprinkled throughout.

Porphyrio asserts that the *Ars* draws its main precepts from the poetics of Neoptolemus of Parium (third century B.C.E.). Although that is disputed, many scholars agree, and also conclude that the *Ars* draws its structure from Neoptolemus as well. Both Neoptolemus and the *Ars* emphasize unity, large-scale poetry, and poetry's twofold functions of entertaining and being useful. These topics are common to rhetoric and prose of the time, a fact making dependence unconvincing to other scholars. In any case, Neoptolemus could be an intermediary source explaining the links between the *Ars* and Aristotle's *Poetics,* links that cannot be explained by direct literary dependence.

The structure of the *Ars* is informal, alternating between prescriptive passages and set pieces. Unity is derived by repetition and interweaving of themes. Larger structural patterns are allusive, but the poetics of Neoptolemus may provide guidance. Neoptolemus divided discussion into three main sections: *poema* (form, genres and their component parts, and small poems); *poesis* (poetry as a whole, especially subject matter and large-scale poems); and *poeta* (the poet). Since this structure is common to Hellenistic works on poetry, the issue of dependence will continue to be debated. Even those postulating this dependence disagree on how to structure the *Ars.* One prominent scheme is introduction (ll.1–40), *poema* (ll.41–118), *poesis* (ll.119–294), and *poeta* (ll.295–476).

Whatever its shortcomings, the *Ars* is the most comprehensive treatment of poetry in extant Latin literature and has Aristotle's *Poetics* as its Greek counterpart. Through the *Ars,* Horace is doing for poetry what Cicero did for prose in providing general Greek classical theories and models in Latin for study and imitation.

Duane F. Watson
Malone College

Bibliography

Brink, C.O. *Horace on Poetry.* 3 vols. Cambridge: Cambridge UP, 1963–1982.

Fraenkel, Eduard. *Horace.* Oxford: Oxford UP, 1957.

Kiessling, A., and R. Heinze. *Horaz. III. Briefe.* 6th ed. Berlin: Weidmann, 1959.

Rudd, Niall. *Epistles Book II and Epistle to the Pisones* ('Ars Poetica'). Cambridge: Cambridge UP, 1989.

Russell, D.A. *"Ars Poetica." Horace.* Ed. C.D.N. Costa. London: Routledge, 1973. 113–34.

See also Horace

Ars praedicandi

Formalized guidelines for preparing and delivering sermons that have served ministers of mainline churches throughout much of the history of Christianity. *Ars praedicandi,* or art of preaching, come down through history either as published handbooks or as published lectures. Today published in the form of book-length preaching manuals not unlike college composition textbooks, the art of preaching is one of the most vital and long-lived rhetorical genres in North America.

Throughout the history of the *ars praedicandi,* the writers of preaching manuals have been influenced by or have been involved in the writing of secular rhetorics. Beginning with St. Augustine's *On Christian Doctrine,* preaching manuals have been influenced by the secular rhetorical theories of the age. St. Augustine adapted Ciceronian rhetoric to the task of preaching, thus reversing the trends in the early church against the use of secular rhetoric. St. Augustine argued, "While the faculty of eloquence, which is of great value in urging either evil or justice, is, in itself indifferent, why should it not be obtained for the uses of the good in the service of truth . . . ?" St. Augustine and others, notably Martin Luther, urged preachers to study the art of rhetoric in school. Thereafter, many rhetoricians wrote both secular and sacred rhetorics, including François Fénelon, George Campbell, and Hugh Blair, while most preaching manuals up to the early twentieth century exhibit significant influence by classical and Enlightenment rhetorical theories. Thus, whatever else might be said about the art of preaching, it has been an academic, classically influenced rhetorical genre throughout its history.

Until the nineteenth century, the dominant elements in preaching manuals were considerations of arrangement and style. Classifications of style, in fact, are the main element that St. Augustine borrows from Cicero. Associating particular sacred purposes with particular rhetorical styles (for example, the plain style for instruction), is an enduring feature of the art of preaching. In the twentieth century, some preaching manuals are organized around a particular rhetorical style—for instance, narrative preaching, which is an extension of Cicero's plain style. Throughout the tradition, authors of preaching manuals have argued that the arrangement of a sermon is critical to its effectiveness. Medieval preaching manuals, which introduced "thematic preaching," advised preachers on the divisions and subdivisions of their sermons, influencing a style of preaching that Roger Bacon dismissed as "endless divisions and quibblings, in which there is neither sublimity of style nor depth of wisdom." In the eighteenth century, the arrangement of the sermon was simplified to two parts—explication and application. This trend, along with the introduction of psychology to aid ministers in their development of sermons, endures in many twentieth-century preaching manuals. In the late twentieth century, the art of preaching has begun to shed its ethnocentrism, with new preaching manuals and scholarship focusing on feminist sermons, the black preaching tradition, and Jewish preaching practices.

Roxanne D. Mountford
Rensselaer Polytechnic Institute

Bibliography

Baxter, Batsell B. *The Heart of the Yale Lectures*. New York: Macmillan, 1947.

Herr, Alan F. *The Elizabethan Sermon: A Survey and Bibliography*, 1940. Rpt. New York: Octagon, 1969.

Hirst, Russel. *Rhetorical Invention in the Conservative Tradition in American Protestant Homiletic Theory, 1850–1900*. Diss. Rensselaer Polytechnic Institute, 1990.

Horner, Winifred Bryan, ed. *The Present State of Scholarship in Historical and Contemporary Rhetoric*. Columbia: U of Missouri P, 1990.

Lischer, Richard, ed. *Theories of Preaching: Selected Readings in the Homiletical Tradition*. Durham, NC: Labyrinth, 1987.

Moss, Beverly J. *The Black Sermon as a Literacy Event*. Diss. U of Illinois at Chicago, 1988.

Mountford, Roxanne. *The Feminization of the* Ars Praedicandi. Diss. Ohio State U, 1991.

Murphy, James Jerome. *Medieval Rhetoric: A Select Bibliography*. Toronto Medieval Bibliographies, 3. 2d ed. Toronto: U of Toronto P, 1989.

———. *Rhetoric in the Middle Ages: A History of Rhetorical Theory from Saint Augustine to the Renaissance*. Berkeley: U of California P, 1974.

Thompson, William, and William Toohey, eds. *Recent Homiletical Thought: A Bibliography, 1935–65*. Nashville, TN: Abingdon, 1967.

Aspasia of Miletus

Milesian intellectual who emigrated to Athens, joined Pericles' brain trust as rhetorician. In the fifth century B.C.E., Aspasia emigrated from Miletus, a far-eastern Greek colony renowned for its literacy and moral philosophy, and arrived in Athens brilliantly educated. The great statesman Pericles (fl. 442 B.C.E.) linked himself with her.

We know about Aspasia exactly the way we know about Socrates: from secondary sources. Her reputation as both a rhetorician and philosopher was memorialized by Plato (437–328 B.C.E.), Xenophon (fl. 450 B.C.E.), Cicero (100–43 B.C.E.), Athenaeus (fl. 200 C.E.), and Plutarch (46–c. 120 C.E.). The best-known source of information about Aspasia is Plutarch's *Lives of the Noble Grecians and Romans* (100 C.E.), an account written several hundred years after her death, which confirms all earlier mentions of her:

> That she was a Milesian by birth, the daughter of Axiochus, is a thing acknowledged. And they say it was in emulation of [beautiful, charming, sagacious] Thargelia, a courtesan of the old Ionian times, that she made her addresses to men of great power. . . . Aspasia, some say, was courted and caressed by Pericles upon account of her knowledge and skill in politics. Socrates himself would sometimes go to visit her, and some of his acquaintances with him; and those who frequented her company would carry their wives with them to listen to her. Her occupation was anything but creditable, her house being a home for young courtesans. . . . [I]n Plato's Menexenus . . . she had the repute of being resorted to by many of the Athenians for instruction in the art of speaking. Pericles's inclination for her seems, however, to have rather proceeded from the passion of love. He . . . took Aspasia, and loved her with wonderful affection; every day, both as he went out and as he came in from the market-place, he saluted and kissed her. (200–201)

By every historical account, Aspasia distinguished herself by her rhetorical accomplishments, her sexual attachment to Pericles, and her public participation in political affairs. Aspasia opened an academy for young women of good families that soon became a popular salon for the most influential men of the day. Within that circle the assertively intelligent Aspasia made contributions to rhetoric that have paradoxically been enumerated by men and often attributed to men, in particular, to Socrates and Pericles.

According to several ancient authors, Socrates deeply respected Aspasia's thinking and admired her rhetorical prowess. In Xenophon's *Memorabilia,* for instance, Socrates quotes Aspasia regarding the "art of catching friends." And in Xenophon's *Oeconomicus,* Socrates ascribes to Aspasia the marital advice he gives to Critobulus: "There's nothing like investigation. I will introduce Aspasia to you, and she will explain the whole matter [of good wives] to you with more knowledge than I possess" (III.15). Athenaeus calls Aspasia "clever . . . to be sure, . . . Socrates' teacher in rhetoric" (V.29). In the *Menexenus* the Platonic Socrates agrees that were the council chamber to elect him to make the recitation over the dead (the *Epitaphios*) he "should be able to make the speech . . . for she [Aspasia] who is my instructor is by no means weak in the art of rhetoric; on the contrary, she has turned out many fine orators, and amongst them one who surpassed all other Greeks, Pericles" (235–36). Plato's *Menexenus* contains Plato's version of Socrates' version of Aspasia's version of Pericles' Funeral Oration, which Socrates pronounces as the work of Aspasia:

> I was listening only yesterday to Aspasia going through a funeral speech. . . . [S]he rehearsed to me the speech in the form it should take, extemporizing in part, while other parts of it she had previously prepared, . . . at the time when she was composing the funeral oration which Pericles delivered. (236b)

Several centuries later, Philostratus (fl. 250 C.E.) wrote in his *Epistle* 73 that Aspasia "sharpened the tongue of Pericles in imitation of Gorgias," echoing Plato.

As logography (the written composition of speech) was commonly the province of rhetoricians, Aspasia, the rhetorician most closely associated with Pericles, no doubt supplied Pericles with speeches that established him as a persuasive speaker and a respected citizen-orator. Few women participated in the intellectual life of ancient Greece; the influential Aspasia is a striking exception.

Cheryl Glenn
Oregon State University

Bibliography

Athenaeus. *The Deipnosophists*. Trans. Charles Burton Gulick. Cambridge: Harvard UP, 1967.

Bloedow, Edmund F. "Aspasia and the 'Mystery' of the Menexenos." *Wiener Studien (Zeitschrift fur Klassiche Philologie und Patristic) Neu Folge* 9 (1975): 32–48.

Courtney, William. "Sappho and Aspasia." *Fortnightly Review* 97 (1912): 488–95.

Plato. *Timaeus, Critias, Cleitophon, Menexenus, Epistles*. Trans. R.G. Bury. 1929. London: Heinemann-Loeb, 1981.

Plutarch. *The Lives of the Noble Grecians and Romans*. Trans. John Dryden. Rev. Arthur Hugh Clough. New York: Modern Library, 1932.

Waithe, Mary Ellen, ed. *A History of Women Philosophers, Vol. I/600 B.C.–500 A.D.* Dordrecht: Martinus Nijhoff, 1987.

Xenophon. *Memorabilia and Oeconomicus*. Trans. E.C. Marchant. Cambridge, MA: Harvard UP, 1988.

Asterismos

"Marking with stars"; addition of a logically unnecessary word at the beginning of a phrase, or a phrase at the beginning of a sentence, to emphasize what follows. Pascal states, "All human evil comes from this, man's being unable to sit still in a room." The pronoun *this* interrupts the flow of thought and draws attention to what follows. Beaumarchais is using *that* as an asterismos in "Drinking when we are not thirsty and making love at all seasons, Madam: That is all there is to distinguish us from other Animals." In the Bible the most frequent asterismos is *behold*: "Behold, the Lord God said . . ." In contemporary sports interviews, *hey* is frequently used as an asterismos: "Hey, that game was . . ."

Arthur Quinn and Lyon Rathbun
University of California, Berkeley

Asyndeton

The omission of expected conjunctions between words, phrases, or clauses. Spinoza omitted the conjunction between words in describing peace as a "disposition for benevolence, confidence, justice." Lincoln was omitting the conjunction between phrases in "The government of the people, by the people, for the people shall not perish from this earth." In Caesar's famous declaration, "I came, I saw, I conquered," the omission occurs between complete clauses. Asyndeton can speed up the sentence, as in the Caesar example, or it can suggest the essential unity of the items, as in the Lincoln and Spinoza examples. Omitting conjunctions can also be used to evoke a sense of disorder, as Marie-Claire Blais demonstrates: "There had been so many funerals since grandmother Antoinette reigned over her household, little black deaths, in winter, disappearances of children, of babies, who had only lived a few months, mysterious disappearances of adolescents in autumn, in spring" (*Une Saison dans la vie d'Emmanuel* 28).

Arthur Quinn and Lyon Rathbun
University of California, Berkeley

Atticism

Appropriated in Latin as a loan-word from Greek (*attikismos*); in its simplest sense, used to describe an attribute of written language akin to, if not identical with, elegance (Quintilian 1.8.8), and the redolence of the genuine flavor of things Athenian (Quintilian 6.3.107). Its more common application, however, was in the expression of a literary preference, among post-classical critics, for what they perceived as a simple and pure style of language—particularly in oratory—as opposed to the defective style of "Asianism." The latter term was used, by contrast, to designate (perceived) excesses both of emotional expression and of stylistic floridity. As Kennedy (1963:330) points out, this valorization of a "pure" style—as evinced in the "best" prose of Athens of the classical period—is an archaizing gesture that links Atticism closely with notions of classicism and the canonization of literary genres. Moreover, certain authors and works within those genres were singled out for particular praise; thus the quintessentially Attic author would be someone like Lysias.

Asianism, insofar as it is an historically recognizable phenomenon, had its own roots in the training offered during the postclassical period at the rhetorical schools of Asia Minor (in cities such as Pergamum) and on the island of Rhodes. Because of this, the objection to Asianism, particularly in Rome, may have had to do with the suspicion and deprecation of all things Eastern as being proverbially associated with luxury, softness, decadence, excess, and intemperance. Greek-speaking contributors to the debate over Atticism included Dionysius of Halicarnassus and Caecilius of Calacte; the latter's work unfortunately survives only in fragmentary form.

Greek Atticism, then, was primarily a written phenomenon characterized by strict adherence to a carefully circumscribed vocabulary and to a collection of syntactical patterns favored by the canonical authors of the fifth and fourth centuries B.C.E. On the Roman side, however, the discussion is not merely concerned with the scrutiny of antique literary models: It is heavily inflected by heated debate over the characteristics appropriate to spoken oratory in the contemporary civic arena. Here the principal name is Cicero himself, who, in the *Brutus* and *Orator* defends his own oratorical style against charges of Asianism. (It would be interesting to be able to inspect the oratory of C.

Licinius Caluus, who was touted as a paragon of pure Attic style, and of Q. Hortensius Hortalus, whose style was notoriously Asianic, but we know of their work only from oblique references in Cicero and other writers.)

The concern for Atticism in the writing of Greek continued well into the Byzantine period. In this respect it was comparable to the "Ciceronianism" sometimes insisted upon in the European Renaissance—the slavish devotion to a Latin prose style that closely approximated that of Cicero and that attempted to use (whenever possible) vocabulary attested in the extant works of Cicero.

John T. Kirby
Purdue University

Bibliography

Castorina, Emanuele. *L'atticismo nell'evoluzione del pensiero di Cicerone*. Catania, 1952.

Douglas, A.E. "M. Calidius and the Atticists." *Classical Quarterly* 5 (1955): 241–47.

Kennedy, George A. *The Art of Persuasion in Greece*. Princeton: Princeton UP, 1963.

———. *The Art of Rhetoric in the Roman World*. Princeton: Princeton UP, 1972.

Leeman, A.D. *Orationis ratio*. Amsterdam, 1963.

Norden, Eduard. *Die antike Kunstprosa*. 1898. 2 vols. 3rd ed. Leipzig, 1915.

Radermacher, Ludwig. "Über die Anfänge der Atticismus." *Rheinisches Museum* 54 (1899): 351–74.

Schmid, Wilhelm. *Der Atticismus in seinen Haupter tretern von Dionysius von Halikarnass bis auf den zweiten Philostratus*. 5 vols. Stuttgart: Kohlhammer, 1887–1897.

Wilamowitz-Moellendorf, Ulrich von. "Asianismus und Atticismus." *Hermes* 35 (1900): 1–50.

Wooten, Cecil W. "Le développement du style asiatique pendant l'époque hellénistique." *Revue des études grecques* 88 (1975): 94–104.

See also CICERO; GREEK RHETORIC; LYSIAS; QUINTILIAN

Audience

Usually refers to the person(s) to whom the rhetor addresses an oral or written discourse. Audience has been an important concern of rhetoric since the fifth century B.C.E., and the injunction to "consider audience" is one of the oldest and most common suggestions to writers and speakers.

Rhetoric has established audience as a significant component of its art: Rhetors must in some way contemplate the needs of their audiences when they give a speech or write a text. *How* rhetors should attend to audience is a matter of some debate, but theorists generally agree that rhetors should be responsive to audience differences; they cannot ignore audience, nor can they treat audience simply as a generic entity.

Numerous fields claim audience as a concern: the mass media areas of film, theater, radio, television, and journalism; areas related to speech communication and oral contexts, such as oral interpretation and debate; and disciplines that apply theories from these domains, such as law, politics, psychology, and advertising. Practitioners in these fields develop audience analysis techniques suitable for their particular areas of inquiry (for example, for jury selection or for product marketing). Audience and its related construct, the reader, are also important in the fields of rhetoric and composition, literary theory, and education and reading.

Given the multidisciplinary nature of the subject, this article limits itself to addressing two main questions in general rhetoric theory: What does "audience" refer to? How should the rhetor "consider" audience? It treats these questions by tracking several key developments: classical and other traditional approaches that constitute the historical basis for much contemporary written and speech communication theory; modern theories pertaining specifically to audience for written discourse, principally in the fields of rhetoric and composition and in literary theory; and postmodern theories (especially the view of audience as community), which challenge traditional models.

Issues and Disciplinary Perspectives

In rhetoric theory, audience is a problematic concept from a number of perspectives. First is the problem of what "audience" refers to. "Audience" and terms related to it (like "reader" and "listener") have proven to be slippery notions. Meanings can vary from context to context. Audience is treated as the concrete flesh-and-blood entity external to a written or spoken text ("people"); as an extratextual abstraction to which texts appeal for their authority (as in Perelman's "universal audience"); and as a property of a given text or set of texts (as in the reader-response critics' notion of the "implied reader").

Audience is located in different places: in the writer's or speaker's imagination, in the text, and in the assembly hall. Audiences are characterized in terms of demographic characteristics, social or psychological stereotypes, and argumentative or stylistic properties.

Audience terms are easily confused. For instance, the terms *audience* and *reader* are sometimes used interchangeably to refer simply to the flesh-and-blood persons who read a piece of writing (what reader-response critics call the "real reader"). The terms can also, however, signify important differences. One common distinction views *reader* as referring to a person's written or oral response to a piece of writing: *Reader* signifies the person-in-the-act-of-reading (and responding to) a written work. *Audience* refers to the prior idea or imaginative construction that the writer-in-the-act-of-producing a text creates and then embodies in the written discourse itself. In short, it is often but not always the case that *reader* (or *listener*) refers to flesh-and-blood people and that *audience* refers to an abstract construct in the rhetor's imagination or in the composed text. Other audience constructs include culture, community (also speech community and discourse community), forum, receiver (or decoder), user (in computer contexts), consumer (in marketing contexts), and interlocutor (the last applying to the engaged, active audience of dialectic).

Such distinctions often correspond to how different fields define their focus of inquiry. Rhetoric and composition theorists focus on activities of the writer and so tend to be more interested in *audience,* conceived as an abstract entity. Their research examines how writers analyze audiences and how written texts embody audience values, expectations, and assumptions. Literary critics and reading researchers focus more on the hermeneutics of reception, on how *readers* make meaning. Communication research has tended toward the view of audience as real people, for instance exploring how different media (television, radio, performance) affect audiences as receivers.

Second is the question of how (sometimes even whether) to conduct audience analysis. Through the history of rhetoric, the dominant view of audience is a common-sense one based on an oral communication model: Audience refers to the physically present listeners of a speech or the flesh-and-blood readers of a text. In other words, audience = real people. Though some have questioned whether a speech model is adequate for written contexts, such a model might seem to make sense for predominantly oral cultures (like fifth-century B.C.E. Greece) and for certain face-to-face oral situations. But even in oral situations where the audience is physically present, theorists have wondered what difference that makes to the art of rhetoric: What does it mean to address an audience as "real people"? Theorists have approached this problem by observing that rhetors construct texts to address or appeal to certain qualities of audiences. (George Campbell, for instance, suggests that rhetors use language to appeal to general psychological faculties; Chaïm Perelman insists that the important qualities are audience beliefs and values.) Though deceptively simple, the real audience construct does not offer much practical help to the rhetor. The rhetor often has to contend, first, with the absence of audience: The writer or speaker in the act of preparing a text or producing a speech must *imagine* an audience whenever one has not yet physically convened. Second, even when the audience has physically convened, the rhetor must decide which audience qualities to address or appeal to, invoking some strategy for assessing those qualities.

Not everyone even agrees that direct consideration or analysis of audience is helpful. Some have doubted whether the art of rhetoric can adequately address the problem of the seemingly infinite diversity of audiences. When in the composing process should concern for audience begin? Is audience a component of invention—that is, should audience influence one's approach to the subject—or does the rhetor "adapt" or redesign writing or speech to suit the audience later? Some view audience analysis with considerable suspicion (as potential manipulation), and ask whether it is ethical to consider audience. For most rhetoricians, however, the ethical mandate works the other way: an ethical rhetoric *must* consider audience.

Classical Rhetoric and the Linear Model
Classical rhetoric imagines audience as a collected body of flesh-and-blood listeners assembled on a specified occasion to hear a speech. Aristotle's rhetoric imagines this assemblage as either a voting audience, such as the Athenian assembly, or as passive spectators. Similarly, Cicero distinguishes between the jurists and civic leaders to whom the orator spoke *ad senatum* and the public mass audience that the orator addressed *ad populum*.

Both Plato and Aristotle accept that rhetors will be addressing different classes of listeners and that rhetoric must therefore acknowledge audience differences. In Book 2 of *Rhetoric,* Aristotle develops an extensive typology of audiences: He considers the various emotional states of listeners (such as anger, shame, pity, and envy) and links these with various character types. Aristotle's typology distinguishes his male listeners according to age, fortune, and birth—the demographic variables that Aristotle viewed as most significant to understanding the Athenian public audience. Though Aristotle acknowledges the importance of audience differences, he does not much consider how such features might influence the rhetor's decisions about the content or construction of the speech. The extensive discussion of audience character in Book 2 is not explicitly or consistently connected to strategies for invention, arrangement, or style. Later Roman rhetorics, such as *Rhetorica ad Herennium* and *De inventione,* further this gap between audience character and formal features of speech construction, generally ignoring concern for audience character.

Aristotle's *Rhetoric* identifies two important audience types: the passive spectator audience (θεωρός) of the epideictic and the more active audience, the judge (κριτήσ) who renders a decision, as in a democratic gathering. In *Organon,* Aristotle characterizes a third type of audience: the interlocutor, the worthy opponent with whom the rhetor engages in dialectic. From one perspective (that of New Rhetoric), the term *audience* can be seen to apply generally to all these particular types. But the more common perspective sees audience as associated exclusively with "public audience" and, increasingly in later rhetorics, with "passive spectators," the mass public that later emerges as the unitary construct of the "general audience," "general reader," or "consumer." In concert with Plato, Aristotle encourages this treatment of audience in creating a privileged status for the intelligent and philosophical individual listener with whom one engages in face-to-face dialectic (considered a superior form of discourse for arriving at truth or knowledge). This division becomes the basis, eventually, for the general audience construct and the linear communication model, which conjoin to assume that the rhetorical situation involves a knowledgeable rhetor already in possession of truth or knowledge and an ignorant audience who must be persuaded to accept that truth. The rhetor might need to learn *about* the audience in order to persuade them, but the rhetor does not need to learn *from* audience. (Aristotle does observe that the rhetor relies on audience opinion in the construction of enthymemes. Yet the enthymemic premise is not invested with any authority as knowledge; it may simply be a belief.) The rhetor is the privileged entity who discovers truth and knowledge through a process prior to rhetoric (dialectic); rhetoric is the art of persuading the audience to accept that preestablished truth or providing them with the necessary knowledge. The rhetor is the authority; the audience is the receiver of the rhetor's wisdom.

George Campbell and the General Audience Construct

In *The Philosophy of Rhetoric* (1776), George Campbell provides a comprehensive discussion of audience character, but also views audience primarily as a subordinate collective. The rhetor's concern for audience is purely managerial: The rhetor must understand how language can be used to elicit various audience responses but need not look to audience for any substantive contribution.

Campbell's rhetoric provides a thorough treatment of how the rhetor should "adapt" the speech to suit the audience. In seeing rhetoric as an adaptive art, Campbell implies that invention—the construction of content, knowledge, or truth—is prior to rhetoric: The art of rhetoric involves adapting given material for suitable consumption by the audience, imagined as flesh-and-blood people. Developing his audience theory from David Hume's faculty psychology, Campbell says that the orator must appeal to the audience's four mental faculties: understanding, imagination, passion, and will. Campbell discusses how various stylistic strategies can trigger the desired responses. For instance, he suggests that the rhetor use the principle of resemblance, stimulating the imagination by presenting a known entity in a new way. To aid audience memory, the orator follows the principles of coherence and order and makes use of repetition. To invoke passion, the rhetor develops vivacity, appealing to the audience's senses by using concrete, vivid imagery. In short, rhetoric is the art of knowing which sorts of stylistic and organizational strategies will trigger the mental faculties so as to evoke the desired audience response. While Campbell acknowledges that

"the characters of audience may be infinitely diversified" (1.8), he does not say much about how the rhetor handles the problem of diverse audiences. His implied conclusion seems to be that rhetoric cannot hope to deal with audience diversity; rather, it should describe "men in general," the mental faculties assumed to be common to all audiences.

Composition pedagogy of the late nineteenth and early twentieth centuries borrowed many of Campbell's principles—in particular, the static abstractions of coherence, unity, and emphasis—but, over time, the principles came to develop their own independent significance. The psychological theory justifying the textual theory was left out, and the textual (or formal) principles became universalized. In the formalist composition pedagogies of the twentieth century, audience is thus treated generically and implicitly, the assumption being that the rhetor meets the needs of the general audience not by any supplementary form of audience analysis but by adhering to recommended stylistic and organizational conventions. The construct of the general literate reader receives further support from E.D. Hirsch's cultural literacy program (*Cultural Literacy*, 1987), which argues the need to develop a base of shared knowledge common to all readers of a given culture. The assumption, again, is that rhetoric (and the educational process in general) cannot practically accommodate difference, and so it should focus its attention only or mainly on what is common or shared among audiences. In short, rhetoric should address the needs of the *one* rather than the *many*.

Also promoting the managerial view of rhetoric was the emergence, in 1949, of the influential Shannon-Weaver model of communication. This model, based on a telecommunications metaphor, views the written or spoken text as a physical medium, like a telephone wire, for conveying the rhetor's ideas to the audience (characterized as a "receiver"). Though admitting the possibility of "feedback," the model principally assumes a one-way, linear flow of information: The rhetor has data, the rhetor "encodes" the data and sends it via some medium, and the audience (or "decoder") receives the data (which may be somewhat distorted by "noise" in the medium). The Shannon-Weaver model became the basis for much research in speech communication and a common discourse model in the field of technical writing.

Expressivism and the Distrust of Audience

Expressivist rhetoric, which has its roots in Romantic theories of art and writing and receives its strongest theoretical support from literary studies, has traditionally been distrustful of the art of rhetoric in general and the concept of audience in particular. According to M.H. Abrams, nineteenth-century English Romanticism is historically responsible for establishing the critical interest in the author and for thereby displacing concern for audience (*The Mirror and the Lamp*, 1953). Concurring, Wayne Booth notes that nineteenth-century poetic theory establishes what would evolve into a central principle of twentieth-century aesthetics: "True art ignores the audience. . . . True artists write only for themselves" (*The Rhetoric of Fiction*, 89). The principal focus of literary criticism became either "the text itself" or the internal operation of the ingenius mind of the poet or author, as evident in the literary text. Indifference or scorn toward audience became an acceptable ethos for the modern writer.

Such aesthetic principles influenced later expressivist composition pedagogy, which persists in its distrust of rhetoric and audience. E.B. White in *The Elements of Style* warns writers that their "concern for the reader must be pure. . . . The whole duty of a writer is to please and satisfy himself, and the true writer always plays to an audience of one [himself]" (71). The view of audience that warrants this position is a limited one: The audience is imagined as the general public, as a mass flesh-and-blood readership of largely ignorant real people with suspect tastes. Audience is imagined as a market— and the appeal to market values threatens the integrity, accuracy, and truth of the writer's message. Considering audience is characterized as an unethical or at least suspect activity threatening, not enhancing, the quality of a discourse.

A somewhat less dire warning is issued by Peter Elbow in "Closing My Eyes as I Speak: An Argument for Ignoring Audience" (*College English*, 1987). Elbow cautions writers and writing teachers against overemphasis on audience, because such concern can interfere with the spontaneity of the composing process and the integrity of the writer.

Twentieth-century New Rhetoric and the Revival of Audience

Two twentieth-century developments help reestablish the importance of audience: the New Rhetoric and reader-response criticism.

In the 1950s and 1960s, an eclectic group of theorists in philosophy, speech communication, English, and composition revived principles from classical rhetoric theory (mainly those of Aristotle) and integrated them with insights from modern philosophy, linguistics, and psychology to develop what became known as the New Rhetoric. New Rhetoric treatises of particular importance to audience theory include Stephen Toulmin's *The Uses of Argument* (1958) and, especially, Chaïm Perelman and L. Olbrechts-Tyteca's *The New Rhetoric* (1959). The key concept in Perelman and Tyteca's comprehensive argumentative theory is the "universal audience": a set of ideal respondents to whose beliefs and standards for argumentation rhetors appeal in order to persuade their actual local audiences (who will resemble the universal audience in some, but not all, respects, and who will be inclined to its presumptions).

Instead of focusing on the formal or aesthetic features of a spoken or written text, New Rhetoric theory focuses on discourse as action: Writing or speech is perceived in terms of its capacity to do something for people—inform them, persuade them, enlighten them, change them, amuse them, or inspire them. The New Rhetoric challenges the classical division between dialectic and rhetoric, seeing rhetoric as referring to all sorts of discourse, whether philosophical, academic, professional, or public in nature—and so seeing audience considerations as applicable to all discourse types. The New Rhetoric recognizes situation (or context) as the basic principle of communication and revives invention as an indispensable component of rhetoric. In so doing, it establishes audience and audience analysis as important to the rhetorical process and vital to invention. Perelman's and Toulmin's theories especially establish audience belief as the basis for all rhetorical activity (which covers most written and spoken discourse), and as the starting point for the construction of arguments. Later, theorists applied the insights of New Rhetoric theory specifically to composition theory and instruction. James Kinneavy's *Theory of Discourse* (1971) and its sequel, *Aims and Audiences in Writing* (1976), offers a comprehensive discourse theory establishing the primacy of aim, audience, and situation. (Situation is defined differently by different theorists, but it generally refers to the purpose, audience, and setting for a given discourse, whether spoken or written.)

Despite reviving the importance of audience, much of New Rhetoric theory still presumes a linear and managerial model, with the writer as originator-author of meaning and with the audience as a passive agent that is acted upon. Although linked with the New Rhetoric, Kenneth Burke anticipates later social rhetorics in his questioning of this managerial model. Burke (*A Rhetoric of Motives*) views persuasion as not simply one way, but as a "moralizing process" by which rhetors are also changed as they work to achieve identification with audience (39). Burke views this process in theological terms, as "consubstantiality" (one in being). Burke reconfigures persuasion not as a linear progression—a writer producing a text in order to induce change in the reader—but as a cooperative activity. While audience and audience analysis per se are not a significant interest for Burke, he suggests an alternative construct that later rhetorics would develop. In *Rhetoric: Discovery and Change* (1970), Young, Becker, and Pike elaborate the notion of rhetoric as a cooperative activity between writer and reader and construct it into an entire writing pedagogy, offering a Rogerian rhetoric based on the principles of cooperation and the "assumption of similarity" as an alternative to what they perceive as the essential agonism of classical rhetoric. *Rhetoric: Discovery and Change* also promotes audience analysis as a strategy for writing. Such work emerging out of the New Rhetoric challenges the presumed authority of the rhetor-as-author/originator and blends the notions of rhetor and audience, anticipating later collaborative and dialogic visions of the rhetor-audience relationship.

Reader-Response Criticism and the Complexity of Audience Role

As a literary critical movement, reader-response criticism acknowledges the key role that audience plays in the construction of textual meaning and the multiple ways that audience can be constructed (for example, as a textual construct, as "real reader" reactions to literary works, or as the reading conventions of an interpretive community). Reader-response criticism challenges the emphasis of formalist and Romantic approaches to literary analysis and complicates literary hermeneutics by admitting the reliance of any text on its reader.

Reader-response criticism refers to the work of an eclectic group of critics, including Louise Rosenblatt, Wolfgang Iser, Judith Fetterley, David Bleich, Steven Mailloux, Stanley Fish, and Jonathan Culler, who share the assumption that the reader (variously defined) plays a prominent role in determining the meanings of a literary text (see

Tompkins). Some reader-response critics (such as Iser) examine how reader and textual schema intersect to produce meaning. Those associated with the *Rezeptionsästhetik* responses to literary works are shaped by attitudes and beliefs of different communities in different historical eras. Feminist criticism—which some view as a development of reader-response criticism, others as a fundamental rejection of its male-centeredness—establishes sex as an important, if not the most important, audience variable. Feminist theory interprets texts by revealing how they embody masculine or feminine attitudes. Such theory also points out that the concerns, perspectives, and values of female readers may be quite different from those of male readers. Feminist research argues that traditional rhetorical principles and strategies—for instance, various attempts to conventionalize rules for valid argumentation—may be arbitrarily biased toward masculine values and habits, assuming "maleness" as a reading norm.

Reader-response criticism has generated a profuse vocabulary for distinguishing various sorts of reading presences. Wolfgang Iser develops the notion of the "implied reader." Walter Ong ("The Writer's Audience") argues for the importance of the fictional audience, that is, the reader type that any written text assumes, which provides a role that real readers (flesh-and-blood people) can adopt or reject. Stanley Fish (*Is There a Text in This Class?*, 1980) sees reading behavior as guided by the conventions of the "interpretive community," the collective of readers that develops reading conventions within a given discipline or field (such as literary criticism) and, thus, directs how meaning is to be constituted through the interpretive act.

Though reader-response critics have been primarily interested in literary hermeneutics, their insights about readers and reading have been applied to nonliterary texts and to composition instruction—most notably, by Douglas Park, Lisa Ede, and Andrea Lunsford. Park ("Meanings of 'Audience'") observes that discussions of audience in composition tend to diverge in two directions: some view the audience as "out there," as a group of flesh-and-blood people; others take an "in there" view, imagining audience as a construct of a given text. Ede and Lunsford ("Audience Addressed/Audience Invoked") offer a dynamic view of the role of the audience in the composing process: describing how the writer-in-the-act-of-writing coordinates different writer-reader roles, both invoking audience (that is, constructing textual roles) and addressing the audiences "out there."

Generally, reader-response theory sees the real reader or listener construct as by itself insufficient as a basis for a theory of discourse reception or production because real readers and listeners are never purely "outside" texts; they interact with texts, engage them, adapt to them, and sometimes change them. The "real reader" is not a static person apart from the text. Reader-response theory calls special attention, then, to the reader or listener roles provided by texts and to how these roles shape or direct audience reactions.

The Discourse Community and the Neosophistic Notion of Audience

Perhaps the most significant development in audience theory has been the reconceptualization of audience according to postmodern notions of community. The theory of community starts with the proposition that the rhetor's use of speech or writing is not original, but is guided by the conventions of various communities whose discourse patterns influence discourse production, and even construct the very identity of the rhetor. This model of course challenges the view of the rhetor as absolute authority bringing knowledge to the audience. Rather than viewing the rhetor as an author-originator, this theory emphasizes that the rhetor is a "borrower" of texts, one who constructs texts out of the community intertext. This notion is also neosophistic insofar as it does not suppose that truth and knowledge are the intellectual property of the rhetor, who discovers this truth or knowledge through some intellectual activity prior to rhetorical acts. Rather, truth and knowledge are probable, local, and contingent—their source of authority is *nomos* rather than logos—and they are constructed *through* rhetorical acts which are always social and contextual, collaborative and dialectic: Writer and audience contribute. Such an interactive model recalls Aristotle's theory of dialectic more than his theory of rhetoric.

The notion of audience as community provides a mediating ground between the idea of a universal audience (whether its universal character derives from a general theory of cognition or faculty psychology, like George Campbell's rhetoric, or argumentative premises, like Chaïm Perelman's) and an ad hoc approach that sees all readers as distinct, and therefore despairs of rhetoric's providing much helpful guidance on the subject. The community metaphor offers a way to characterize audiences generally, while at the same time accommodating differences between and within communities. It authorizes the idea of difference and suggests strategies by which the rhetor can acquire knowledge about and achieve identification with audiences.

Some, however, have viewed community theory, and communities, as potentially constraining, even threatening to individual human rights and identity. Communities can be potentially oppressive and hegemonic. They can stifle genuine inquiry, and they can marginalize or exclude those who do not conform to community standards. From that perspective, some view the role of the rhetor as one of resistance to rather than cooperation with the community. While agreeing that any given community might construct itself in such a manner, others argue that (a) actual communities can be positive insofar as they provide the rhetor with a means of achieving identity; and (b) the issue is not whether communities are good or bad so much as to what degree the community metaphor proves helpful to the rhetor.

Communities are described in various ways: (1) From the realist perspective, the community is perceived as a group (in the sociological sense) of individuals whose speech practices are guided by a common set of conventions. Research on speech communities often starts with the premise that the community preexists its discourse. (2) Postmodern theory sees the community as constructed *by* its discourse. The postmodern notion defines community not as an a priori group but rather as constituted by its discursive relations. Prominent postmodern community constructs include Thomas Kuhn's paradigm, Stanley Fish's interpretive community, and Michel Foucault's discursive formation. James Porter develops a postmodern theory of community, offering Foucault's discursive formation as a model appropriate to developing a rhetorical theory of audience (*Audience and Rhetoric*). The postmodern sense of community conceives of audience as a structure embodied in the sets of texts that define a given discourse community, as a discursive field, or even a kind of communal implied reader. (3) Yet others imagine community in a more material form as the physical setting or place of "publication" (forum), as an established setting in which discourse takes place. As Douglas Park ("Analyzing Audiences") points out, no audience ever exists unless there is some social purpose and physical site for its assemblage. It is this site that influences (some say determines) the nature of the rhetor-audience relationship, establishing the identities of both rhetor and audience as well as the form of their relationship.

Community theory has developed in several distinct realms of study, most importantly in professional writing and computer-mediated communication.

Professional writing theory and pedagogy, itself influenced by the New Rhetoric, has developed audience constructs based on research in the workplace (for example, the organizational audience, the managerial reader, corporate culture). In *Audience Analysis for Technical Writing* (1969), Thomas Pearsall revives a strategy from Aristotle by creating an audience typology for technical writing contexts. His characterizations—layman, executive, expert, technician, and operator—became widely used as an audience guide for technical writing. In *Designing Technical Reports: Writing for Audiences in Organizations* (1976), J.C. Mathes and Dwight Stevenson recognize the problem of the multiple audience and provide a discussion of the many audience levels involved in technical and business communication. Their treatment recognizes the presence of multiple audiences, anticipating later studies that focus on the construct of the organizational audience. More recent work in professional writing promotes specific tactics for evaluating both the "readability" and the "usability" of written documents. Writing across the curriculum (WAC) research—which is related to but is more academically directed than professional writing studies—looks at disciplinary discourse, both spoken and written, to understand what discourse conventions are present in various academic and professional communities, with the aim of familiarizing community conventions and thereby encouraging writer and speaker socialization.

Developments in computer-mediated communication—or the use of various forms of computer technology for writing, storing, and distributing electronic texts—raise new audience issues. As a human design, computer technology has embedded in its structure an ideology: It promotes certain options (while excluding others) and assumes certain ideal relationships between itself and its users and between users. As a writing tool, the computer influences the consciousness and practice of both writers and readers and changes how writers produce documents and how readers read them. The dynamic of electronic mail has proven particularly interesting. Though E-mail appears on the computer screen as print, the ease and rapidity of its distribution gives it the spontaneous, immediate feel of face-to-face discourse (only without the faces). As users bring their expectations from conventional print and oral media, they struggle to develop new writing and speaking styles for this medium as well as to learn its new conventions. When users post messages to electronic discussion groups, the rhetorical dynamic is further complicated. Writers sometimes address a group as if they were speaking to an assembled multitude; other times they respond to an individual in a personal way, though the posting may be distributed to all members of the group. Sometimes postings resemble spontaneous conversation, other times formal academic publications. New electronic communities frequently begin their on-line conferences by carefully establishing some guidelines about discursive relations. Since there are no well-established conventions for discourse in this medium, participants have to clarify their understandings about rhetor-audience roles in order to avoid possible miscommunications. Studies in hypertext and hypermedia point out how in these media readers contribute actively to textual construction in making their own navigation decisions. In the realm of interactive hypertext, the unitary notions of "text" and "author" are further eroded, as is any notion of the audience as a passive receiver.

James E. Porter
Purdue University

Bibliography

Campbell, George. *Philosophy of Rhetoric.* Ed. Lloyd Bitzer. Carbondale: U of Illinois P, 1988.

Ede, Lisa, and Andrea Lunsford. "Audience Addressed/Audience Invoked: The Role of Audience in Composition Theory and Pedagogy." *College Composition and Communication* 35 (1984): 155–71.

Kirsch, Gesa, and Duane H. Roen, eds. *A Sense of Audience in Written Communication.* Newbury Park, CA: Sage, 1990.

Ong, Walter, S.J. "The Writer's Audience Is Always a Fiction." *PMLA* 90 (1975): 9–21.

Park, Douglas. "Analyzing Audiences." *College Composition and Communication* 37 (1986): 478–88.

———. "The Meanings of 'Audience.'" *College English* 44 (1982): 247–57.

Porter, James E. *Audience and Rhetoric: An Archaeological Composition of the Discourse Community.* Englewood Cliffs, NJ: Prentice Hall, 1992.

Tompkins, Jane P., ed. *Reader-Response Criticism: From Formalism to Post-Structuralism.* Baltimore: Johns Hopkins UP, 1980.

Augustine, Saint, Bishop of Hippo (354–430 c.e.)

Medieval religious figure whose voluminous output of sermons, letters, and treatises not only helped establish the character of Catholic doctrine during his own era but also helped determine the significant approaches to theological questions for later generations and ensured that a substantial portion of the classical pagan approach to literary education would be appropriated for Christian purposes.

Saint Augustine was born Aurelius Augustinus at Thagaste, near Carthage, in what is now modern Algeria. His father was "a burgess of slender means," but Augustine was able to receive advanced education in Madaura and Carthage through the sacrifices of his parents and the patronage of a wealthy townsman, Romanianus. Augustine's literary abilities flourished, and upon completing his education he taught school at both Thagaste and Carthage for some nine years. Seeking pupils less rowdy than those found in the provinces, Augustine sailed for Rome in 383. A year later he was appointed professor of rhetoric at Milan. While at Milan he converted to Christianity and was baptized by Ambrose, Milan's learned and powerful bishop. In 388 he returned to Africa and soon after founded a monastery at Hippo. In 395 he was appointed Bishop of Hippo and held that office for the rest of his life.

Augustine's major rhetorical work, *De doctrina Christiana (On Christian Doctrine)*, helped transform classical canons of invention and expression. His major theological treatise, *De Trinitate (On the Trinity)*, in theorizing a critical epistemological and psychological function for tropes, provided grounds for later writers to argue for the significance of poetic language.

While passages on rhetoric and philosophy of language are scattered through a number of Augustine's works, among them, *De ordine, De magistro, Confessions, De catechizandis rudibus, De Trinitate, and De dialectica,* his most comprehensive treatment of rhetorical principles and methods is offered in *De doctrina Christiana*. The treatise can be divided both conceptually and biographically into two sections. The first, comprising Books One, Two, and most of Three, was written in 396 or 397; the second, comprising the rest of Book Three and Book Four, was written in 426 or 427, near the end of Augustine's life. Books One through Three discuss matters concerning the discovery of God's Word in Scripture. Book Four outlines how an understanding of Scripture should then be used to instruct, please, and persuade the faithful. For the Christian whose office is to profess the faith, the Bible is the first place one goes to gather material for rhetorical occasions, that is, for invention. This makes invention for homiletic occasions radically different from invention for rhetorical occasions (law court, legislature, ceremonial event) in the classical, civic-oriented tradition. Not only does the Bible provide a set of *topoi* (topics) for discourse different from those listed in the pagan handbooks, it also transforms the principal task of invention from selecting topics based on rhetorical situations to interpreting the truth of sacred texts—that is, from analytics to hermeneutics. Interpretation is necessary because the words of Scripture are often obscure in meaning. Before the material of Scripture can be used for rhetorical purposes, its meaning must first be determined.

Augustine begins his discussion of interpretation in Book One by drawing a distinction between things (*res*) and signs (*signa*). Things exist prior to signs; signs exist (in human use) only for "bringing forth and transferring to another mind the action of the mind in the person who makes the sign" (*De doctrina* 35). The signs humans use may be mere fallen shadows of the divine Word, but their highest use is in seeking their original source, the primary substance from which all things proceed, God. Thus, Book One of *De doctrina* expounds some of the cardinal tenets of Catholic Christianity on the assumption that methods of scriptural exegesis and homiletical expression can be effective only if knowledge of God and His Word is firmly established. In discovering knowledge of God, an interpreter of Scripture should be guided by the truth that "the end of the Law and of all the sacred Scriptures is the love of a Being which is to be enjoyed. . ." (*De doctrina* 30). Scripture may often be obscure. The exact nature of things to which scriptural signs refer may frequently be uncertain. So where there is uncertainty about the meaning of a scriptural passage, the exegete should advance an interpretation that builds up charity (love of God, neighbor, and oneself for God's sake).

Having established the basis for sound doctrine through knowledge of First Things and the principle of charity in Book One, Augustine takes up in Books Two and Three specific problems in interpreting the textual source of doctrine, the Bible. Book Two discusses how to go about interpreting scriptural signs that might be misconstrued through ignorance of things. Augustine elaborates on some of the information and tools needed for overcoming ignorance of things, among them knowledge of languages (for accurate translations); general knowledge of worldly things like history, natural history, and the mechanical arts; accurate texts of Scripture; and so forth. Book Three concerns how an exegete should interpret ambiguous signs in Scripture, presenting a number of strategies for overcoming ambiguity and obscurity. Despite the difficulties that figural language presents to an interpreter, Augustine defends its presence in Scripture. He asserts that all tropes found in the rhetorical handbooks are also found in Scripture, and thus he defends the Bible against secular charges of rhetorical vulgarity, an opinion that he himself had held as a young man.

In Book Four Augustine takes up more traditional rhetorical issues when considering how a Christian should go about professing the truths discovered in Scripture. He says that he will not provide a handbook of rhetorical rules because they can be found elsewhere. Moreover, he claims that eloquence is better learned through imitating eloquent speakers and diligent practice than through memorizing lists of rules. What he does provide is a discussion of some principles that should guide Christians who profess the faith through the rhetorical means of sermons, letters, and treatises. He first asserts the necessary relationship between wisdom (by which he means knowledge of sacred things) and eloquence, saying that while one can know and convey truth without possessing eloquence, one will, if eloquent, be more effective not just at teaching the faithful what they should do but also at actually moving them to do what should be done.

He proceeds to a discussion of style and adapts the Ciceronian precepts for Christian purposes. Cicero had linked the use of stylistic registers to the relative weight of a subject being considered. Small matters, like monetary disputes, should be addressed in a plain style. Great matters, like issues of life and death or affairs of state, should be treated in a grand style. Intermediate matters should be treated in a moderate style. Augustine notes that for Christians all matters are equally significant because they concern man's eternal welfare, so one's use of different stylistic registers should be linked to one's rhetorical purpose. A pastor should use a plain style for instructing the faithful, a moderate style for delighting an audience and making it more receptive or sympathetic to sacred teachings, and a grand style for moving the faithful to action. Although Augustine says that a preacher's chief homiletical purpose is instruction, he acknowledges that few people will act based on instruction alone; most must be moved to act through the psychological and rhetorical means employed in the grand style. At the end of Book Four, he takes up the topic of ethos and, in a departure from Aristotelian doctrine, links credibility more to the rhetor's actual character and behavior than to a discursive persona.

Augustine's discussion of discovery and expression in the *De doctrina* must be seen in light of his philosophy of language and its place in a larger Christian theology. His theology perpetuates the assumption of many classical philosophers that realities (ideas in Plato, substances in Aristotle, God in Augustine) exist prior to and independent of human knowledge of them. But within that philosophical tradition, the capability of human language to represent reality accurately is variously conceived. In Aristotle, for instance, theories of language use (demonstration, exploration, argumentation, deception) are tied to the degree of reality being referred to. Language can accurately represent substances, and through the science of demonstration, humans can discourse with certainty on them. Human affairs, existing more in the realm of accident than of substance, cannot be represented with certainty, and discourse upon them must be handled through the art of rhetoric.

Augustine, on the other hand, says that however hard humans might try to bridge it, an eternal gulf exists between the reality of God and our knowledge of and means of communicating about Him. Augustine's explorations of divine ontology in *De Trinitate* are wholly circumscribed by his realization that language cannot completely or transparently represent the transcendent reality of God's nature. This position is akin to Plato's views on the imperfect human representation of transcendent Ideas. What distinguishes Augustine and his Christian philosophy of language from

Plato and other secular philosophies is the theological significance he attributes to tropes. As St. Paul says (1 Cor. 13.12), humans can know God only *per speculum in aenigmate*, traditionally translated "through a glass, darkly." As a former professor of rhetoric, Augustine knows that an enigma is a trope, a species of "obscure allegory." Since it is only indirectly, through likeness and analogy, that humans can represent knowledge of divinity, tropes function as the best linguistic means of conveying this knowledge. Furthermore, obscure tropes serve a psychological as well as epistemological function for Augustine: "No one doubts that things are perceived more readily through similitudes and that what is sought with difficulty is discovered with more pleasure" (*De doctrina* 38). The work necessary to understand the obscurity of figural language (*signa*) raises a hunger for pursuing truth (*res*) and fights the arrogance of pride. And, as verbal ornaments, tropes arouse a listener's or reader's pleasure and make one more receptive to sacred teachings. In this way tropes are an essential psychological means of turning humans toward God.

The *De doctrina Christiana* by itself or in combination with Augustine's other writings does not offer a theory of rhetoric or a manual of rhetorical precepts as extensive as those written by, say, Aristotle or Cicero. But his writings were essential for ensuring that the teachings of those and other figures in the classical tradition of rhetoric were passed on to later generations as the Roman empire and its educational institutions crumbled in the fifth century. Augustine defends the use of secular knowledge and arts as "gold and silver, which [pagans] did not institute themselves but dug up from certain mines of divine Providence" (*De doctrina* 75). Without the authority of this defense, it is open to question whether rhetoric and other secular liberal arts would have survived the attacks of Church fathers like Jerome, who saw their proponents as fallen pagans and their precepts as perversions of sacred truth.

The specific rhetorical principles Augustine advocated became a basis for many of the medieval handbooks on preaching, the *ars praedicandi*, as well as for a later homiletical tradition called Sacred Rhetoric. That tradition emphasized the importance of moving the will to action and of the role emotion and a grand, eloquent style play in achieving that end. During the Renaissance and early modern periods in particular, the tradition served as a primary alternative to Protestant homiletical theories emphasizing instruction and plain style. In addition, there is an as-yet-unexplored connection between that tradition and the rise of Romanticism during the eighteenth and nineteenth centuries as an alternative to an increasingly powerful scientific empiricism. Finally, Augustine's elevation of figural obscurities to a central epistemological and psychological role served as grounds for poets such as Dante, and later, the Romantics and their twentieth-century heirs, modernist writers and the New Critics, to privilege the status and function of literary language over other forms of language use.

Richard Penticoff
University of Idaho

Bibliography

Augustine, Saint. *On Christian Doctrine* [*De doctrina Christiana*]. Trans. D.W. Robertson, Jr. Indianapolis: Bobbs, 1958.

———. *The Trinity* [*De Trinitate*]. Trans. Stephen McKenna. The Fathers of the Church 45. Washington, D.C.: Catholic U of America P, 1963.

Brown, Peter. *Augustine of Hippo: A Biography*. Berkeley: U of California P, 1969.

Colish, Marcia L. "Augustine: The Expression of the Word." *The Mirror of Language: A Study in the Medieval Theory of Knowledge*. Rev. ed. Lincoln: U of Nebraska P, 1983. 7–54.

Fortin, Ernest L. "Augustine and the Problem of Christian Rhetoric." *Augustinian Studies* 5 (1974): 85–100.

Harrison, Carol. *Beauty and Revelation in the Thought of Saint Augustine*. Oxford: Clarendon, 1992.

Marrou, Henri-Irénée. *Saint Augustin et la fin de la culture antique*. 4th ed. Paris: Éditions E. De Boccard, 1958.

Meagher, Robert E. *An Introduction to Augustine*. New York: New York UP, 1978.

Press, Gerald A. "The Content and Argument of Augustine's De Doctrina Christiana." *Augustiniana* 31 (1981): 165–82.

Sullivan, Sister Therese. *Augustini De doctrina Christiana Liber Quartus*. Catholic University of America Patristic Studies 23. Washington, D.C.: Catholic U of America P, 1930.

See also ARS PRAEDICANDI; MEDIEVAL RHETORIC; ROMAN RHETORIC

Austin, Gilbert (1753–1837)

Irish clergyman and teacher; graduate of Trinity, Dublin. Like his more famous countryman, Thomas Sheridan, Austin devoted himself to elocution. Austin's *Chironomia* (1806) is the most extensive and important work on elocution of the period.

Dictionaries and grammar books first appeared in Britain and France in the eighteenth century, a manifestation of an unprecedented general interest in the origins and proper use of language. Propriety and correctness became watchwords—even causes of popular dispute—among both writers and speakers. Those who sought a leading role in public life (such as clergymen, teachers, or actors) made great efforts to learn the "standard" dialect—the dialect, that is, of the urban aristocracy. There was soon a ravenous market for pronouncing dictionaries, hard-word dictionaries, error-hunting grammars, and tracts on elocution, while educational reformers worked to make "proper" English part of the curriculum.

The greatest champion of the elocution movement was Irish actor Thomas Sheridan, who argued for the revival of elocution in a number of works on oratory, education, and reading, in the introduction to his pronouncing dictionary, and in a series of popular lectures. Also influential were a group of Edinburgh intellectuals, the Select Society, who worked to reform Scottish education by introducing composition in English and practice in English speech delivery. The Select Society included David Hume, Hugh Blair, Lord Kames, and Edinburgh's professor of rhetoric Adam Smith.

Courses in delivery or elocution soon became a standard part of the college curriculum, and a large number of treatises and textbooks on proper delivery were published through the eighteenth and nineteenth centuries. The most notable of these is Austin's *Chironomia*. Here Austin restates Sheridan's call for more education in English, repeats long-standing complaints about dull preaching, and produces a monumental compilation of quotations from the classics on every aspect of nonverbal communication. He also presents an elaborate system of notation for posture, gesture, facial expression, and movement, analyzing nonverbal communication in greater detail than had ever been done before. He hoped that his system would make it possible to record and study the actions of successful orators, without which the record of their words would be incomplete. Moreover, speeches could be choreographed with these notations, so that students could be taught proper action.

Austin illustrates his system with extensive drawings showing proper gestures and expressions. The system proved too cumbersome for practical use, but his idea of analyzing nonverbal performance is standard practice today. In his remarks on articulation, pronunciation, pause, pitch, tone, and other vocal qualities, Austin identifies the concerns of modern speech instruction and offers much advice that is now quite standard. Many nineteenth-century speech textbooks in Europe and the United States are based on Austin's work. The elocution movement may in many ways be regarded as the origin of modern instruction in speech and, to some extent, English composition as well.

Bruce Herzberg
Bentley College

Bibliography

Mohrmann, G.P. "The Real *Chironomia*." *Southern Speech Journal* 34 (1968): 17–27.
Robb, Mary Margaret, and Lester Thonssen. "Introduction." *Chironomia, or, a Treatise on Rhetorical Delivery. 1806.* Carbondale: Southern Illinois UP, 1966.

See also ELOCUTION; SHERIDAN, THOMAS

Austin, J.L. (1911–1960)

English ordinary-language philosopher and founder of speech act theory. J.L. Austin's work in philosophy had a number of concerns, but the aspect of his philosophy most influential for rhetoric is what became known after his death as "speech-act theory." The key text in Austin's work in this direction is the posthumously published *How to Do Things with Words,* a collection of the William James Lectures he gave at Harvard in 1955. Austin's central insight into language was that the approach to language dominant in philosophy since Plato was one-sided in its focus on how language refers to and represents the world. Words do things as well as refer to things, and a full theory of language needs to explain what words do and how we do things with them.

Austin's analysis begins by defining what he called the "performative," a sentence that performs an action rather than describing one. Such sentences include "I bet you," "I do" (at a marriage ceremony) and "I declare war" (when said by a head of state). Austin initially defined this class of sentence in opposition to "constative" sentences such as "Jack and Joe made a bet," "Jack and Jill got married," or "Great Britain declared war on Nazi Germany yesterday." Constative sentences are either true or false, while performatives either achieve their goal or do not. This distinction has been widely influential, and Austin's term *performative* now has a life of its own as roughly a (more positive) synonym for *rhetoric*. But as *How to Do Things with Words* shows, Austin came to think that this distinction was a crude one that didn't stand up to sustained examination.

First, Austin saw that he was analyzing utterances, not sentences, since exactly the same words—the same sentence—can have remarkably different effects in differing contexts. All sentences have performative aspects inasmuch as they all do something, and what they do depends upon the context in which they are uttered. Utterances thus cannot be categorized as either constative or performative; they are constative and performative simultaneously. This led Austin to decide that the class of utterances that are actions was not limited to that of explicit performatives: All utterances are acts or speech acts. In making an utterance, one performs an act, or, as Austin went on to say, three different acts simultaneously: the locutionary, the illocutionary, and the perlocutionary. The constative and the performative provide the basis for the first two of these, but the perlocutionary is new to the analysis. The locutionary is the act *of* saying something, the illocutionary the act I perform *in* saying those words, and the perlocutionary the act I achieve *by* saying those words. In saying to a group of children that a car is coming down the street, I state something and perform a locutionary act, but, more important, in stating that fact I warn them to be careful (thus performing an illocutionary act). And by stating that fact I (hope to) alarm them if they are in the road (thus performing a perlocutionary act).

For rhetoricians, the importance of Austin's work is not so much the details of his analysis, which have been disputed, revised, and elaborated by subsequent "speech-act theorists" such as John Searle and by the movement in linguistics known as pragmatics. Far more important is the broad notion of language implicit in the analysis. Language is a mode of acting in the world, not just a mode of reflecting on it. To say, as Austin does, that to speak is to act is to adopt a deeply rhetorical vision of language.

Reed Way Dasenbrock
New Mexico State University

Bibliography

Austin, J.L. *How to Do Things with Words.* Ed. J.O Urmson and Marina Sbisa. 1962. Cambridge, MA: Harvard UP, 1975.

———. *Philosophical Papers.* 2nd ed. Ed. J.O. Urmson and G.J. Warnock. Oxford: Clarendon P, 1970.

———. *Sense and Sensibilia.* Ed. G.J. Warnock. London: Oxford UP, 1962.

Dasenbrock, Reed Way. "J.L. Austin and the Articulation of a New Rhetoric." *College Composition and Communication* 38 (1986): 291–305.

Grice, Paul. *Studies in the Ways of Words.* Cambridge, MA: Harvard UP, 1989.

Leech, Geoffrey. *Principles of Pragmatics.* London: Longman, 1983.

Searle, John. *Speech Acts: An Essay in the Philosophy of Language.* Cambridge: Cambridge UP, 1969.

See also SPEECH ACTS

Author

Commonly, the individual who publishes writing and who is, in that sense, a professional writer. In legal, literary, and rhetorical theory, *author* has a more complicated and problematic status. Legal, literary, and rhetorical theories provide distinctive—and yet at the same time intersecting and complementary—perspectives on *author*. It is helpful to examine the concept conjoining the three disciplinary perspectives, as most published treatments do.

From the legal perspective, the author is the person (or persons) assigned intellectual credit for a produced work, who "owns" the text as intellectual property (the publisher typically owns the work as legal, or physical, property). Intellectual property becomes complicated when the author is a group of writers or editors, or a conglomeration (for example, a corporation or government can function as author), or when derivative forms of a text are produced. Copyright law and other fair-use conventions help define authorship and provide direction to writers who copy, distribute, or otherwise use authors' published work. (Copyright law aims to balance the rights of authors to receive credit for their labors with the rights of society to benefit from the free exchange of ideas and information.) Disciplinary citation practices have developed as ethical procedures for acknowledging intellectual property rights.

Literary and rhetorical theories have been less interested in issues of ownership, focusing more on the relationship of author to text with the aim of developing theories and practices for producing text (in the case of rhetoric) or for interpreting it (in the case of literary theory). In literary and rhetorical theory, *author* becomes entangled with text-based principles such as ethos, persona, and voice; with other agent constructs such as writer and professional writer, poet, and novelist; and with postmodern issues of identity, subject formation, authority, and presence.

In the Romantic tradition of literary criticism, as it evolved in the twentieth century, the *author* was not simply any published writer, but a special writer whose works were thought to have achieved a superior value as aesthetic objets d'art—and which could thus be assigned canonical status. From this perspective, not all writers, not even all published writers, deserve the title. In literary criticism, *author* (along with text, or work) has long been a foundational principle: Indeed, much criticism still presupposes the existence of the author as the unifying presence of the literary work.

Various strands of contemporary criticism challenge the status of *author* as a foundational concept or as a unified (or unifying), authoritative voice, emphasizing instead the writer as scribe, compiler, or commentator (rather than as originator or creator). This perspective recalls an earlier, Christian and medieval notion of writer-as-instrument (of an ultimate originating Author, that is, God). The principle of intertextuality raises questions about the "originality" of any piece of writing. If all writing is a process of social meaning making, then writers are not original creators so much as collaborators and participants in a wide-area textual discussion. Social rhetorics view the writer as a discussant rather than a solitary voice of inspired genius, noting how writers are themselves constructed, by texts as well as by audiences.

The *author* is a fairly recent concept historically—born perhaps in the case of Donaldson versus Becket (1774)—with significant connections to social and technological developments and to economic history. Most acknowledge that the modern conception of *author* was influenced by the printing press (a technological means of standardizing, and thereby stabilizing, texts), but that it did not fully emerge until ownership of texts became a legal issue in the eighteenth century. The notion developed out of an emerging laissez-faire capitalism that argues the need to credit individuals for their labor in order to motivate labor, whether those individuals are authors seeking monetary capital, or, later, in the case of student writers, capital in the form of grades and course credit.

In conventional literary theory, the *author* concept stabilizes the text, invests it with a unifying central authority, and provides stability among a series of texts (the corpus) produced under the same signature. Poststructuralism views such a move as an effort to maintain control of text and textual meaning (and thereby to control knowledge and garner intellectual power), and as an effort to inhibit conflict, contradiction, and revolution. Such a move valorizes the lone individual voice: a male voice according to feminist theorists, and a Western logocentric one according to cultural critics. From another quarter, *author* comes under critique for presupposing a linear (or "information transfers") model of communication: The author is someone in possession of knowledge or insight (meaning), who installs that meaning in a text, the instrument that "carries" meaning to the reader.

Other contemporary developments further challenge conventional notions of authorship. Feminist theory encourages writing practices promoting a plurality of voices (rather than consistency of a dominant voice), a dialogic rather than monologic model. In rhetoric and composition, collaboration research has challenged "the myth of the solitary writers" (Lunsford and Ede 73), establishing how frequent and typical collaborative writing is and suggesting social alternatives to the predominant individual models of discourse production. Developing computer writing technologies have exposed the inadequacies of conventional notions of authorship—particularly problematic in electronic publishing, where standard print notions of text have proved inadequate to account for the fluidity of "electronic text." In interactive hypertext, where users can construct their own documents based on the reading paths they choose, the conventional boundaries between author and audience are further eroded, as each user actively contributes to textual construction. It remains to be seen whether the concept of author has outlived its usefulness—is it dead, as Roland Barthes has claimed?—or whether the concept can survive (though no doubt in an extensively revised form) the challenges of postmodern theory and practice. Certainly in rhetoric theory, and increasingly in literary theory, the "writer" has supplanted the "author."

James E. Porter
Purdue University

Bibliography

Barthes, Roland. "The Death of the Author." *Image—Music—Text*. Trans. Stephen Heath. New York: Hill and Wang, 1977. 142–48.

Foucault, Michel. "What Is an Author?" *The Foucault Reader*. Ed. Paul Rabinow. New York: Pantheon, 1984. 101–20.

Lunsford, Andrea, and Lisa Ede. *Singular Texts, Plural Authors*. Carbondale: Southern Illinois UP, 1990. See esp. Chapter 3, "The Concept of Authorship: Explorations and (Dis)Closures" (72–102).

Porter, James E. "Intellectual Property and the Construction of Authorship." *Cardozo Arts & Entertainment Law Journal* 10.2 (1992).

———. "Selected Bibliography: The Concept of 'Author' in Rhetoric and Literary Theory." *Rhetoric Society Quarterly* 23 (1993): 71–75.

Woodmansee, Martha. "The Genius and the Copyright: Economic and Legal Conditions of the Emergence of the Author." *Eighteenth-Century Studies* 17 (1984): 425–48.

See also PERSONA

Axiology

The general study of the theory of value and evaluation. The term *axiology* was apparently first used by the French philosopher Paul Lapie in *Logic of the Will* (1902). "Syllabus of Axiology" (*Grundriss der Axiologie*) was the title of Part 5 of Eduard von Hartmann's *System of Philosophy in Outline* (1908). The first use of the term in English was by W.M. Urban in *Valuation* (1909). The term derives from the Greek *axios* (value or worth) and *logos* (account, reason, theory).

As a major division of philosophy, axiology, dealing with "the good," is a companion to epistemology, and metaphysics, which deal respectively with "the true" and "the real." Axiology includes the more specific studies of the morally good (ethics) and the beautiful (aesthetics). Many philosophers prefer the phrase "value theory" to the term *axiology*.

Bahm surveys what he regards as the four major axiological viewpoints: Hedonism (which locates intrinsic value in pleasant feelings), Voluntarism (which locates intrinsic value in satisfaction of desire), Romanticism (which locates intrinsic value in desire itself and sees apathy as evil), and Anandism (which locates intrinsic good in feeling contented, at one with the universe, *nirvana*) (57–64).

Several speech rhetoric scholars have used the term, but it was not introduced into composition until Fulkerson's 1990 paper "Composition Theory in the Eighties: Axiological Consensus and Paradigmatic Diversity."

Clearly, value judgments pervade composition. It is axiomatic that the goal of teaching composition is to enable students to produce "good" writing. And from the initial decision that it is good to be able to read and write, to decisions about what sorts of classroom activities are useful in promoting those abilities, to the writer's decisions about whether one introduction or one word is better than another, to peer and teacher assessment of writing—value judgments are constantly being made. The task of an axiological perspective is to articulate the principles by which value judgments and value choices are or ought to be made.

When Fulkerson asserted that, in the decade of the nineties, composition teachers and theorists were approaching "axiological consensus," he meant specifically that they were coming to agree upon an answer to the question "What constitutes good writing?" He argued that a decade earlier the field was deeply divided among allegiances to several often conflicting theories of what made writing good. He identified four such theories, the expressive, the mimetic, the formalist, and the rhetorical, and argued that in the eighties the field had essentially agreed that good writing was to be defined contextually as writing that achieved the writer's goals within a rhetorical situation.

For those who study axiology, it has become traditional to distinguish between instrumental (or means) values and ultimate (or ends or intrinsic) values. The rhetorical perspective of what makes writing good suggests that good writing is an instrumental rather than an intrinsic value in that it produces effects on readers, effects that are themselves valued by the writer. That is, a well-written paper is seen not as a good-in-itself but as a means to some other desired goal, broadly defined as persuasion or communication.

Conceivably, the other three textual axiologies Fulkerson identified considered well-written papers not as instrumental but as intrinsic goods. For a formalist, a paper was good because it had the desired form, irrespective of any end achieved. The same reasoning applied mutatis mutandis to expressivism and mimeticism.

In addition to these "textual values," however, there is a much broader sense in which axiological theory might apply to composition. In this perspective, teaching writing is also necessarily teaching a way of seeing the world and a way of acting in the world. Proponents of what has been called in speech an "axiological" approach to rhetoric maintain that to teach discourse necessarily means teaching not just the values of texts but also values beyond texts (Eubanks 1978).

The argument goes as follows: Whenever one teaches discourse (or learns to discourse), one is not just teaching (or learning) the features of good discourse but also a view about what is responsible intellectual life. Among the extratextual value questions addressed in the writing classroom are the following:

1. Which topics are worth discussing and which are trivial?
2. Do writers have a responsibility to become informed about the topics they address?
3. Does one have a responsibility to provide evidence or logical support for claims?
4. Is it acceptable to engage in fallacious or emotive or propagandistic attempts to communicate?
5. What constitutes fair and accurate use of other texts?
6. Can one equally well argue for any side of any issue? (for instance, proracism or pro-Hitler?)
7. Do writers have a responsibility to further social justice?

Ralph Eubanks and Virgil Baker have argued that the modern world suffers from "axiological impotence" (341), and that a major (if not the major) function of rhetorical education should be to help alleviate the crisis in values and valuation. For them, and others, Western rhetoric has always asked and answered key value questions, such as what is preferable or what is just within the civic and cultural arena. And it is no less important for it to do so today. Rhetoric, says Eubanks, is "applied axiology" (215).

Modern compositionists tend to accept as axiomatic the notion that neither language nor a perspective can be value neutral, so that the writer is enmeshed in value issues even prior to beginning to write. Garko and Cissna have described the situation as follows:

> Two distinct positions can be identified regarding the relationship between communication and values. The "axiological" perspective holds that values and communication are inherently linked. The "positivist" view implies that values and communication have or ought to have nothing to do with one another.

On this issue contemporary composition is militantly antipositivist. As the postmodern aphorism goes, we are "always already" situated; we cannot escape to some neutral and external observation post. Or to put it another way, there is no view without a preexistent viewpoint. Hence the formulation that all teaching is ideological, and that teachers should at least become conscious of their own ideological presuppositions.

But that raises another axiological issue. Are all ideologies created equal? Is there no way to make reasoned choices among them? And is a writing teacher justified in (1) focusing the class on the study of ideology and (2) requiring students to agree with the teacher's viewpoint? Some teachers identify themselves as Marxists, and their writing classes focus overtly on critique of the dominant ideology of the economically privileged; such teachers explicitly commit themselves to a "liberatory" or "radical" pedagogy. Other teachers, however, maintain that it is not the goal of rhetoric courses to teach students what to say, only how to say well what they choose.

Both views make axiological commitments, but they are of contrasting sorts. It is impossible to teach rhetoric (or for that matter any field) without axiological presuppositions, yet the presuppositions are themselves value judgments, and there seems to be no way of adjudicating between contrary and conflicting sets of commitments. This is the axiological paradox.

Richard Fulkerson
East Texas State University

Bibliography

Bahm, Archie. *Axiology: The Science of Values.* Abbrev. ed. Albuquerque, NM: World Books, 1984.

Eubanks, Ralph T. "Axiological Issues in Rhetorical Inquiry." *The Rhetoric of Western Thought.* 2nd ed. Ed. James L. Golden, Goodwin F. Berquist, and William E. Coleman. Dubuque, IA: Kendall/Hunt, 1978. 211–16.

Eubanks, Ralph T., and Virgil Baker. "Toward an Axiology of Rhetoric." *Quarterly Journal of Speech* 47 (1962): 157–68. Rpt. *Contemporary Theories of Rhetoric: Selected Readings.* Ed. Richard L. Johannesen. New York: Harper, 1971. 340–56.

Fulkerson, Richard. "Composition Theory in the Eighties: Axiological Consensus and Paradigmatic Diversity." *College Composition and Communication* 53 (1990): 409–29.

Garko, Michael G., and Kenneth N. Cissna. "An Axiological Reinterpretation of I.A. Richards' Theory of Communication and Its Application to the Study of Compliance-Gaining." *Southern Speech Communication Journal* 53 (1988): 121–39.

Morris, Van Cleve, and Young Pai. "Axiology: What Is Good?" *Philosophy and the American School.* 2nd ed. Boston: Houghton, 1976. 204–99.

Ayer, Alfred Jules (1910–1989)

British philosopher associated with logical positivism, studied at Oxford and University of Vienna. Of his twenty-one books, the first, *Language, Truth, and Logic* (1936), is most influential in and relevant to rhetorical concerns. In it, he divided propositions into categories of meaningfulness, developed a principle of verification, and limited philosophy to the logic of science.

Influenced by British empiricism and logical positivism, Ayer rejected the meaningfulness of metaphysical statements and began his thinking with Hume's division of genuine propositions into two types: those concerning "relations of ideas" (logic and mathematics) and those concerning "matters of fact" (empirical). Logical propositions make no assertion about the world, but are meaningful by their form—that is, by our agreement to express relationships in a specific form. The literal meaning of empirical propositions (empirical hypotheses), on the other hand, is never certain, and consequently their probability must be verified. Ayer's principle of verification posits that empirical statements could not count as meaningful, true or false, without supporting observations. He conceived philosophy as sharing the logic of the sciences.

Ayer also is recognized for his development of an emotive theory of ethics that separates value statements in ethics from claims to truth and argues that there is no moral knowledge. He characterized ethics as emotive, simply expressions of a speaker's position, which may evoke a similar response in the listener.

Arabella Lyon
Temple University

Bibliography

Ayer, A.J. *Language, Truth, and Logic.* 2nd ed. London: Victor Gollancz, 1936.

Gower, Barry. *Logical Positivism in Perspective: Essays on Language, Truth, and Logic.* Totowa, NJ: Barnes and Noble, 1987.

Quine, W.V.O. "Two Dogmas of Empiricism." *From a Logical Point of View.* Cambridge, MA: Harvard UP, 1953. 20–46.

See also LOGICAL POSITIVISM

Aytoun, Edward Edmondstoune (1813–1865)

First Professor of English Literature at the University of Edinburgh from 1845–1865. The tradition of belles-lettres was already well established when Aytoun assumed the chair of rhetoric and belles-lettres at Edinburgh in 1845. In his lectures he maintained "the utter worthlessness of the art" of rhetoric and criticized the "artificiality of the system" that was encumbered with rules in such number "that were we to observe them all, our speech would degenerate into a tissue of woven sophistry." In his introductory lecture, he stated: "I would much rather sit in this chair as Professor of English Language and Literature than as Professor of Rhetoric and Belles Lettres." In the manuscript "I would much rather" has been erased and "I am delighted to sit in this chair" is substituted, an alteration obviously made after his title was changed. His lectures were hugely successful at the University of Edinburgh, where the townspeople flocked to hear him speak on the subject of English literature. During his tenure, attendance rose from twenty-seven to 150 students, and, largely because of his influence and popularity, the Royal Commission of 1861 recommended that the study of English literature be added to the curriculum in all of the Scottish universities.

Aytoun was a strong supporter of the Scottish system of education and took "to task people who think it beneath the dignity of a university to deal with rudimentary elements." He opposed the compulsory entrance exams that excluded the poorer Scots. He felt that the title of the chair was prejudicial to attendance, and, inasmuch as professors were customarily paid fees by their students, this was not an insignificant consideration. He believed that "many persons entertain the idea that 'Rhetoric' is a trifling art, unsatisfactory as a department of mental training, and that the term 'Belles Lettres' signifies nothing more than general, and sometimes aimless criticism." He suggested that the course would be better called "English Literature and Composition"; bowing to part of his request, the Royal Commissioners of 1858–1862 doubled his salary and renamed the chair the Regious Professorship of Rhetoric and English Literature. Thus the Scottish universities adopted English literature as an academic subject some forty or fifty years ahead of either Oxford or Cambridge.

The National Library of Scotland has a large collection of Aytoun manuscripts in their special collections. His lectures on rhetoric are a rather pedestrian review of traditional rhetoric, interspersed with his constant criticism of the ancient system. The most interesting work in the collection is his introductory lecture, in which he outlines his ideas on education, rhetoric, and the study of English literature. Aytoun, like his American contemporary, Francis Child, who was also an early professor of English literature (at Harvard), is best known in Scotland today for his collection of ballads.

Winifred Bryan Horner
Texas Christian University

Bibliography

Aytoun, William Edmondstoune. Manuscripts 4897–4928. Lectures, accounts, correspondence.

Frykman, Erik. *W.E. Aytoun, Pioneer Professor of English at Edinburgh*. Gothenburg Studies in English 17, Goteborg: Acta Universitatis Gothoburgensis, 1963.

Horner, Winifred Bryan. *Nineteenth-Century Scottish Rhetoric*. Carbondale: Southern Illinois UP, 1993.

Martin, Theodore. *Memoir of William Edmondstoune Aytoun*. Edinburgh and London: William Blackwood, 1867.

Meikle, Henry W. "The Chair of Rhetoric and Belles-Lettres in the University of Edinburgh." *University of Edinburgh Journal* 13 (1945): 89–103.

B

Bacon, Francis (1561–1626)

Lawyer, educational reformer, rhetorician, scientist, lord chancellor of England. Author of the *Advancement of Learning, Novum organum, New Atlantis,* and other scientific and literary works, Francis Bacon sought to reform the whole of human learning in his time by proposing new methods for the development and communication of knowledge. Bacon sought to replace Aristotelian and scholastic methods of knowing with a new scientific method, developed a rhetorical theory as a means of communicating knowledge thus acquired, and presented both his scientific method and his rhetoric in a paradoxical language that has inspired diverse positivist, institutional, and democratic forms of scientific rhetoric.

Bacon's scientific method and his rhetoric are both grounded in faculty psychology, a view of human nature that posits distinct capacities corresponding to each stage in the development and communication of knowledge. These faculties include understanding, reason, imagination, memory, appetite, and will. Understanding and reason work together, understanding serving to assimilate and organize past experience, reason serving to communicate and express that experience. Imagination depicts in the mind past experiences, either individually or in novel combinations. Memory stores experience as singular instances, derived from external stimuli, the raw materials for all mental processes. Appetite and will convert knowledge acquired through the other faculties into fruitful action: appetite by its attraction to apparent good, will by translating that attraction into action. Sense is not among these faculties, but it enters into the knowing process when imagination depicts in the mind experiences derived from sense and stored in memory.

Drawing upon this faculty psychology, Bacon seeks to replace traditional methods of knowing with his new scientific method. In the *Advancement of Learning,* he specifically rejects methods of knowing that he associates with Aristotle and the medieval scholastics and that he scornfully characterizes as "cobwebs of learning, admirable for the fineness of thread and work, but of no substance or profit" (6:122). Their method of induction is "utterly vicious and incompetent" because it enumerates particular instances on one side without regard for whether or not contrary instances appear on the other side (6:265). Their method of deduction, the syllogism, is equally faulty because it is based upon sequences of propositions, which in turn are based upon words, which themselves are merely popular notions of things, "grossly and variably collected out of particulars" and therefore subject to error at the very foundation (6:266).

In place of these faulty methods Bacon sets his new scientific method, often identified with the method of induction. As set forth in *Novum organum,* however, this method actually has three parts or stages, which serve as aids to sense, memory, and understanding. These stages are the compilation of natural and experimental histories, the tabulation or arrangement of the content of those histories, and the gradual development of true forms via induction. The natural and experimental histories are uninterpreted records of observations of natural phenomena, derived from sense and stored in memory. These histories, the basis of all natural philosophy, are complete records of all instances of a natural phenomenon (for example, heat), from which may be selected especially striking instances that point the way to further inquiry. The tables and arrangements of instances drawn from the histories are lists of significant instances that show their relationships (for example, instances of the presence or absence of heat or of increases or decreases of heat) and that serve as an aid to memory. The method of induction is a guide to the understanding in its search for the true form of the phenomenon under investigation, a means of identifying, through a process of exclusion, "such a nature as is always present or absent with the given nature, and always increases and decreases with it" (as heat is always associated with motion) (8:204).

Drawing again upon the faculty psychology, Bacon develops his rhetorical theory as a means of communicating the knowledge acquired by way of his scientific method. Bacon's rhetoric encompasses a variety of methods and styles of communication, including at least two different styles suitable for use at different stages in his scientific method. In the *Advancement of Learning* and its Latin translation *De augmentis scientiarum*, Bacon describes several pairs of methods of communication, including the magistral and initiative methods, the exoteric and acroamatic methods, and aphorisms and "methods" ("the arrangement and connexion and joining of the parts") (6:291). The magistral and exoteric methods and "methods" address popular audiences for the purpose of putting knowledge to use. The initiative and acroamatic methods and aphorisms, in contrast, address scientific audiences for the purpose of advancing knowledge.

In addition to these methods of communication, in the *Advancement of Learning* and *Parasceve* Bacon also describes two styles suitable for use in his scientific method: the imaginative style is addressed to the understanding and is suitable for use in the method of induction; the plain style is addressed to sense and memory and is suitable for use in the natural and experimental histories and perhaps also in the tables and arrangements of instances. The imaginative style has justification in Bacon's claim that the duty and office of rhetoric is "*to apply Reason to Imagination* for the better moving of the will" (6:297). In its figured form, this style employs the "force of eloquence and persuasion" to move the will to action (6:299). In its unfigured form, such as the aphorism, this style does not employ figures but demands that the imagination create its own figures. The imaginative style, in its unfigured form, is most suitable for use in the method of induction. The plain style has justification in Bacon's rejection of a highly figured style as the "affectionate study of eloquence and copie [copiousness] of speech," in favor of a style that omits all "orna-

ments of speech, similitudes, treasury of eloquence, and such like emptinesses" and sets things down "briefly and concisely, so that they may be nothing less than words" (6:119; 8:359). The plain style is most suitable for use in the natural and experimental histories and perhaps the tables and arrangements of instances.

Bacon presents both his scientific method and his rhetoric in a paradoxical language that has inspired positivist, institutional, and democratic forms of scientific rhetoric. Bacon's language is paradoxical because it combines tradition and innovation, engaging old mythologies and traditions to present new ideas. In *New Atlantis*, for example, Bacon engages the myth of the lost civilization of Atlantis and the biblical portrait of Solomon's temple to create an image of a scientific community dedicated to the discovery of new knowledge and its practical application for the benefit and use of humanity.

Such images have inspired diverse interpretations of Bacon's scientific method and his rhetoric. Positivist science, for example, has found in Bacon a justification for a stylistic ideal of plain prose exhibiting clearness, brevity, and appropriateness. Institutional science has found in him an ideal for the communal organization of science and a figured style suitable for use in scientific communities. Most recently, proponents of democratic science have reinterpreted Bacon's ideal of plain prose as a vehicle for broad participation in science for the purpose not of dominating nature but of addressing human wants and needs. For their literary qualities, therefore, no less than their substantive contributions to scientific method and scientific rhetoric, Bacon's writings have an enduring appeal.

James P. Zappen
Rensselaer Polytechnic Institute

Bibliography

Bacon, Francis. *The Works of Francis Bacon.* Ed. James Spedding, Robert Leslie Ellis, and Douglas Denon Heath. 15 vols. New York: Hurd, 1869.

Briggs, John C. *Francis Bacon and the Rhetoric of Nature.* Cambridge, MA: Harvard UP, 1989.

Jardine, Lisa. *Francis Bacon: Discovery and the Art of Discourse.* London: Cambridge UP, 1974.

Stephens, James. *Francis Bacon and the Style of Science.* Chicago: U of Chicago P, 1975.

Vickers, Brian. *Francis Bacon and Renaissance Prose.* London: Cambridge UP, 1968.

Wallace, Karl R. *Francis Bacon on Communication and Rhetoric.* Chapel Hill: U of North Carolina P, 1943.

Whitney, Charles. *Francis Bacon and Modernity.* New Haven: Yale UP, 1986.

Zappen, James P. "Francis Bacon and the Historiography of Scientific Rhetoric." *Rhetoric Review* 8 (1989): 74–88.

Bain, Alexander (1818–1903)

One of the pioneers of the scientific study of psychology. Bain was born and educated in Aberdeen, Scotland, and graduated from Marischal College in 1840. From 1841 to 1843 he held the chair of Moral Philosophy at Marischal, and in 1860 he became the first occupant of the chair of English and Logic at Aberdeen. In 1855 he published *The Senses and the Will* and in 1859 *The Emotions and the Will,* both of which explore the connection between psychology and physiology. These books became the standard textbooks in psychology for much of the remainder of the nineteenth century.

Bain used the rhetorical theory of fellow Scotsman George Campbell to devise a psychological approach to written composition. Bain applies his own versions of the theories of associationism and physiological psychology to composition in a rigorous and inventive way. He identifies the chief mental operations as discrimination, retentiveness, and agreement. These operations are associative, bringing ideas together through contrast, contiguity, and similarity. In *English Composition and Rhetoric: A Manual* (1866), Bain says that the key figures of speech may be classed under these same heads, suggesting that they are parallel to mental operations. That is, it is a natural function of the mind to generate metaphor, metonymy, and antithesis. Moreover, the response to such figures is stimulation of the corresponding mental function. The reader or auditor, Bain says, will be more easily instructed or moved when these basic operations are stirred up by the right kinds of images.

All behavior, Bain says in his psychology texts, is based on the desire to gain pleasure or avoid pain. The will operates by seeking out actions that will lead to the desired end. Applied to rhetoric, this idea follows Campbell's similar observation that the speaker or writer should create an image of a future state and set forth a course of action that will, depending on the argument, lead to or away from that future state.

Bain is also responsible for the decisively influential formulation of the modes of discourse—description, narration, exposition, and persuasion—and for the notion of paragraph unity and topic sentences as important features of written discourse. Through Bain's followers in the United States—Adams Sherman Hill, Barrett Wendell, John Genung, and others—these ideas became standard parts of the English composition course.

Bruce Herzberg
Bentley College

Bibliography

Crowley, Sharon. *The Methodical Memory: Invention in Current-Traditional Rhetoric.* Carbondale: Southern Illinois UP, 1990.

Johnson, Nan. *Nineteenth-Century Rhetoric in North America.* Carbondale: Southern Illinois UP, 1991.

Kitzhaber, Albert. *Rhetoric in American Colleges.* Dallas: Southern Methodist UP, 1990.

Lunsford, Andrea. "Alexander Bain's Contributions to Discourse Theory." *College English* 44 (1982): 290–300.

Mulderig, Gerald P. "Nineteenth-Century Psychology and the Shaping of Alexander Bain's English Composition and Rhetoric." *The Rhetorical Tradition and Modern Writing.* Ed. James J. Murphy. New York: Modern Language Assn., 1982.

Baird, Albert Craig (1883–1979)

One of the major figures who nurtured the renewed growth and systematic study of classical rhetoric in the first half of the twentieth century. Through his teaching and guidance of students who also became important rhetorical scholars—Carroll Arnold, Waldo Braden, Loren Reid, Norwood Brigance, and Lester Thonssen—and through his writings, he helped to make the rhetorical study of public address an important field of scholarship in the United States.

From his first teaching position at Ohio Wesleyan University in 1910–1911, through two years on the Dartmouth faculty (1911–1913), twelve at Bates (1913–1925), and forty-four at the University of Iowa (1925–1969), Baird not only popularized and improved rhetorical study but also shaped intercollegiate debate and debaters. He inaugurated international debating in 1921 when he took his Bates College students to England to argue before the Oxford Union.

Craig Baird was also influential in developing the teaching and study of group discussion in departments of speech. Strongly influenced by John Dewey and the growing belief in the scientific method that characterized the first half of the twentieth century, he saw discussion as "the art of reflective thinking and communication, usually oral, by members of a group, whose aim is the cooperative solution of a problem" (1943:9). He argued that such cooperative problem-solving is even more important than debate for the citizen and for a democracy. He introduced discussion contests into forensics tournaments, with participants judged not on the basis of "beating" the other participants but on the basis of their contributions to helping the group arrive at a wise decision. Baird published his first book on discussion, *Public Discussion and Debate,* in 1928. His most influential work on this topic, however, is *Discussion: Principles and Types,* first published in 1943.

But it was on the practice of rhetorical criticism that Craig Baird had his greatest impact. The first edition of *Speech Criticism* (1948), which he wrote with one of his first Ph.D. students, Lester Thonssen, formed the mold for rhetorical study of public address that was to last for many years. It was a mold of many dimensions, most of them—logos, pathos, ethos, and *elocutio*—derived from classical rhetorical theory. To those he added a fifth dimension, history, for he believed that one could not understand discourse, let alone judge it, without first understanding the history of the rhetor and the situation that led to the discourse.

He also saw a close relationship between rhetoric and politics. For him, democracy functions through talk; rhetorical criticism and theory are therefore essential for raising the standards and practices of politics. This interrelationship of rhetoric and politics was one of the key reasons he placed such stress on ethics. As he and Thonssen said in *Speech Criticism:*

> If politics—and, in its turn, rhetoric—is associated with the means of getting things done, it is imperative that ethics, which deals with ends and the relative values of what is achieved, be reunited with the political art. Rhetoric, as the intermediary between the will to action and the achievement of the result, must accordingly be conceived as both a political and an ethical instrument. (467)

That stress on ethics grew out of Craig Baird's unabashed idealism, a rare sort of idealism that permeated his rhetorical scholarship,

his teaching, and his life. For him, it was the most important dimension of rhetorical study.

Also related to ethics was Baird's conviction that an important purpose of rhetorical criticism is to improve the quality not only of public discourse but also of the citizen public at whom that discourse is directed. To paraphrase the cliché about art, Baird would have said that without a great audience there can be no great rhetoric.

Samuel L. Becker
University of Iowa

Bibliography

Baird, A. Craig. *Discussion: Principles and Types.* New York: McGraw, 1943.
———. *Public Discussion and Debate.* Boston: Ginn, 1928.
———. *Rhetoric: A Philosophical Inquiry.* New York: Ronald, 1965.
———, ed. *Representative American Speeches.* 22 vols. New York: Wilson, annual 1938–1959.
Reid, Loren, ed. *American Public Address: Studies in Honor of Albert Craig Baird.* Columbia: U of Missouri P, 1961.
Thonssen, Lester, and A. Craig Baird. *Speech Criticism.* New York: Ronald, 1948.

Bakhtin, M(ikhail) M(ikhailovich) (1895–1975)

Russian philosopher of discourse who wrote on consciousness, language, and literature from the 1920s to the 1960s but became widely known in the West only from the late 1960s on (see Holquist and Clark for further biography and reception history; Morson and Emerson for an extensive account of his ideas). Mikhail Bakhtin is best known for his accounts of the novel as a dialogic form and of carnival as a social and literary institution. His theory of language as essentially dialogic, consisting of utterances that respond to and anticipate other utterances, has been received by contemporary theorists of rhetoric and composition as both an alternative to rhetoric and a development of it.

Starting from Aristotelian premises, Bialostosky (1986) has proposed Bakhtin's dialogics as an alternative art to rhetoric and the other traditional verbal liberal arts, and his theory of the novel as an alternative to Booth's *Rhetoric of Fiction* (1990; see also Booth 1984). But Schuster, who from the start has taken Bakhtin as a rhetorical theorist (1985), can call him "a rhetorophilologist in the sophistic tradition" (1992). These judgments depend at least as much on how their authors understand "rhetoric" as on how they understand Bakhtin, for when Bialostosky (forthcoming) adopts a sophistic version of rhetoric from Michael Billig, he too can make a rhetorical theorist of Bakhtin.

Bakhtin himself makes several pronouncements on rhetoric in which he emphasizes its monologic one-sidedness and closure to other voices. One of his most widely quoted remarks, from notes written late in his life, contrasts the rhetorical with the dialogic: "In rhetoric there is the unconditionally innocent and the unconditionally guilty; there is complete victory and destruction of the opponent. In dialogue the destruction of the opponent also destroys that very dialogic sphere in which the word lives" (1986:150). Remarks like this may have been conditioned in part by the way in which rhetoric functioned in the official language of Soviet life when Bakhtin was writing (see Halasek) and in part by Bakhtin's lifelong dialogue with the monologic Soviet rhetorical theorist Victor Vinogradov (see Perlina and Busch).

Bakhtin also, however, develops original reinterpretations of several distinctions, topics, and practices that we can recognize as rhetorical. His image of the prose writer's discursive situation provides a vivid personification of the idea of a *topos*, or place, where diverse opinions of contending voices can be found. His attention to the signs of a writer's or speaker's response to or anticipation of other people's words similarly animates and reconceptualizes the classical rhetorical figures of thought, almost all of which enact dialogic relations (see Bialostosky 1992). He rethinks the rhetorical triangle, again animating and personifying its objectified "logos" corner, substituting a notion of the "hero" of an utterance for the naming of its "topic" (see Voloshinov 1987; Bialostosky 1983; Schuster 1985). His notion of speech genres, "relatively stable thematic, compositional, and stylistic types of utterances," expands the characterization of discourse by its inventional, dispositional, and stylistic features from the three classical rhetorical genres to the whole range of utterances from "short rejoinders of daily dialogue . . . to the multivolume novel" (1986). His account of "individual ideological development" fruitfully redescribes a rhetorical *paideia* from *imitatio* to *exercitatio*

common in European rhetorical education and influential in Continental philosophy (see Smith; Bakhtin 1981).

The implications of these and other aspects of Bakhtin's dialogic theories for composition pedagogy have not gone unnoticed. Appropriations of Bakhtin in this area have already been summarized and critiqued by Ewald, whose bibliography is the most complete to date (but see in addition Bialostosky 1991; Klancher). Like the uses of Bakhtin's work in literary criticism and theory, those in rhetoric and composition vary in both the premises of the user (social-constructionist, pragmatist, Marxist, expressivist) and the aspect of Bakhtin's work they highlight. His inquiry into "answerability" (Ewald), his focus on dialogic discourse and "individual ideological development" (Bialostosky 1991), his theories of parody, authoritative discourse, and subaltern styles (Klancher), and his notion of carnival (Miller) have all proved fruitful and controversial. Texts of disputed authorship published under the name of his collaborator V.N. Voloshinov (see Holquist and Clark; Morson and Emerson) have also informed recent arguments on language, self, culture, and writing. Not just theoretical debates but also close readings of student texts (see Ritchie and Recchio) have claimed Bakhtin as inspiration and authority.

Don H. Bialostosky
Pennsylvania State University
Jayme Stayer
University of Toledo

Bibliography

Bakhtin, M.M. *Art and Answerability: Early Philosophical Essays by M.M. Bakhtin.* Ed. Michael Holquist and Vadim Liapunov. Trans. Vadim Liapunov. Austin: U of Texas P, 1990.

———. *The Dialogic Imagination.* Ed. Michael Holquist. Trans. Michael Holquist and Caryl Emerson. Austin: U of Texas P, 1981.

———. *Problems of Dostoevsky's Poetics.* Ed. and Trans. Caryl Emerson. Minneapolis: U of Minnesota P, 1984.

———. *Rabelais and His World.* Trans. Helene Iswolsky. Bloomington: Indiana UP, 1984.

———. *Speech Genres & Other Late Essays.* Ed. Caryl Emerson and Michael Holquist. Trans. Vern W. McGee. Austin: U of Texas P, 1986.

B

Bialostosky, Don H. "Antilogics, Dialogics, and Sophistic Social Psychology: Michael Billig's Reinvention of Bakhtin from Protagorean Rhetoric." *Rhetoric, Sophistry, Pragmatism.* Ed. Stephen Mailloux. Cambridge: Cambridge UP, 1995.

———. "Bakhtin versus Chatman on Narrative: The Habilitation of the Hero," *University of Ottawa Quarterly* 53 (1983): 109–16.

———. "Booth's Rhetoric, Bakhtin's Dialogics and the Future of Novel Criticism." *Novel* 18 (1985): 209-16. Rpt. *Why the Novel Matters: A Postmodern Perplex.* Ed. Mark Spilka and Caroline McCracken-Flesher. Bloomington: Indiana UP, 1990. 22–29.

———. "Dialogics as an Art of Discourse in Literary Criticism." *PMLA* 101 (1986): 788–97.

———. "Liberal Education, Writing, and the Dialogic Self." *Contending with Words.* Ed. Patricia Harkin and John Schilb. New York: Modern Language Assn., 1991. 11–22.

———. *Wordsworth, Dialogics, and the Practice of Criticism.* Cambridge: Cambridge UP, 1992.

Billig, Michael. *Arguing and Thinking: A Rhetorical Approach to Social Psychology.* Cambridge: Cambridge UP, 1987.

Booth, Wayne C. "Introduction." *Problems of Dostoevsky's Poetics.* Ed. and trans. Caryl Emerson. Minneapolis: U of Minnesota P, 1984.

———. *The Rhetoric of Fiction.* 2nd ed. Chicago: U of Chicago P, 1983.

Busch, Robert. "Bakhtin's 'Problemy tvorchestva Dostoevskogo' and V.V. Vinogradov's 'O khudozhestvennoi proze'—A Dialogic Relationship." *Social Discourse* 3 (1990): 311–32.

Ewald, Helen Rothschild. "Waiting for Answerability: Bakhtin and Composition Studies." *College Composition and Communication* 44 (1993): 331–48.

Halasek, Kay. "Starting the Dialogue: What Can We Do about Bakhtin's Ambivalence Toward Rhetoric?" *Rhetoric Society Quarterly* 22 (1992): 1–9.

Holquist, Michael, and Katerina Clark. *Mikhail Bakhtin.* Cambridge, MA: Harvard UP, 1984.

Klancher, Jon. "Bakhtin's Rhetoric." *Reclaiming Pedagogy: The Rhetoric of the Classroom.* Ed. Patricia Donahue and Ellen Quandahl. Carbondale: Southern Illinois UP, 1989. 83–96.

Miller, Susan. *Textual Carnivals: The Politics of Composition.* Carbondale: Southern Illinois UP, 1991.

Morson, Gary Saul, and Caryl Emerson. *Mikhail Bakhtin: Creation of a Prosaics.* Palo Alto, CA: Stanford UP, 1990.

Perlina, Nina. "A Dialogue on the Dialogue: The Baxtin—Vinogradov Exchange (1924–1965)." *Slavic and East European Journal* 32 (1988): 526–41.

Recchio, Thomas E. "A Bakhtinian Reading of Student Writing." *College Composition and Communication* 42 (1991): 446–54.

Ritchie, Joy S. "Beginning Writers: Diverse Voices and Individual Identity." *College Composition and Communication* 40 (1989): 152–74.

Schuster, Charles I. "Mikhail Bakhtin as Rhetorical Theorist." *College English* 47 (1985): 594–607.

———. "Mikhail Bakhtin: Philosopher of Language." *The Philosophy of Discourse: The Rhetorical Turn in Twentieth-Century Thought.* Ed. Chip Sills and George H. Jensen. Vol. 1. Portsmouth, NH: Boynton/Cook, 1992. 164–98.

Smith, John H. *The Spirit and Its Letter: Traces of Rhetoric in Hegel's Philosophy of Bildung.* Ithaca, NY: Cornell UP, 1988.

Voloshinov, V.N. "Discourse in Life and Discourse in Art." *Freudianism: A Critical Sketch.* Trans. I.R. Titunik. Ed. Neal H. Bruss. Bloomington: Indiana UP, 1987. 93–116.

———. *Marxism and the Philosophy of Language.* Trans. L. Matejka and I.R. Titunik. Cambridge, MA: Harvard UP, 1986.

See also DIALOGICS

Barthes, Roland (1915–1980)

French critical theorist; faculty member of the Collège de France and a prolific writer (eleven books and over two hundred articles, prefaces, and contributions to miscellanies). Roland Barthes is perhaps the most influential French critic of the twentieth century. Marked by innovation and a refusal, ultimately, to identify with any of the theories he himself pioneered,

Barthes's career charts the development of European criticism through structuralism and semiotics to poststructuralism.

In the 1960s Barthes became a leading proponent of structuralism, a method premised in the linguistic theories of Ferdinand de Saussure. Following Saussure's distinction between *parole* ("speech") and *langue* ("language" as a system of rules or "codes" that precede and enable speech), Barthes sought to analyze the codes underlying discourse, outlining his own practice in "The Structuralist Activity" (*Critical Essays*, 1964). The structuralist "dissects" a text into its constituent elements and then, through a process termed "articulation," "recomposes" it *as a system of relations* among elements. The result is a redescription or "*simulacrum* of the object*" that "makes something appear which remained invisible, or . . . unintelligible. . . . The simulacrum is intellect added to object" (*Critical Essays* 215). Stated simply, the product of structural analysis is a syntax or grammatical "map" of the original.

Barthes offers a literary application in "Introduction to the Structural Analysis of Narratives" (1966) where, he argues, each "narrative is a great sentence, just as every constative [declarative] sentence is, in a way, the sketch of a little narrative" (*Semiotic Challenge* 100). The analyst thus seeks a "grammar" of narrative, attending to its distinctive "subjects" and "categories of the verb: tenses, aspects, modes, persons" (100).

While structuralists hoped to fashion a "science" of structure, one capable of articulating the *langue* or underlying "grammar" of discourse, Barthes soon came to admit the arbitrariness of all such analysis; the structuralist "map" is hardly adequate to the "territory" or original. Thus Barthes's *S/Z* (1970) marks definitively his turn from structuralist to poststructuralist thought. The five *lexias*, or "units of reading" (*S/Z* 13), he charts through Balzac's *Sarrasine* are creatively (indeed, arbitrarily) imposed upon the original; far from reconstituting its structure, *S/Z* consciously, artfully rewrites Balzac's novella. As Jonathan Culler notes, *S/Z* "is predicated upon a distinction between the readable and the writerly, between classic writing that complies with our expectations and avant-garde writing that we don't know how to read but must in effect compose in our reading" (87).

Such a distinction raises problems of authorial intention. While the "readable" text lays claim to a singular, stable, authorial meaning, the "writerly" text—and much "modernist" litera-ture is such—remains radically open to readers' changing interpretations. In "The Death of the Author" (1968), Barthes explicitly denies authorial control: A text "consists not of a line of words, releasing a single 'theological' meaning (the 'message' of the Author-God), but of a multi-dimensional space in which are married and contested several writings, none of which is original: the text is a fabric of quotations, resulting from a thousand sources of culture" (*Rustle* 52–53). Meaning belongs not to culture, however, but finally to the individual reader who "is the very space in which are inscribed, without any of them being lost, all of the citations out of which a writing is made; the unity of a text is not its origin but its destination" (*Rustle* 54).

Even as it explored the problematic relations among writers, readers, texts, and meanings, Barthes's later work became itself increasingly modernist, "writerly," and committed to *jouissance*—to a reveling in writing as a self-reflexive, self-referential activity. Thus the autobiographical *Roland Barthes by Roland Barthes* (1975) plays with the disjunction between its author's living personality and his ethos or self-representation: The author is himself rendered as a text and subject to reading.

James S. Baumlin
Southwest Missouri State University

Bibliography

Barthes, Roland. *Critical Essays*. Trans. R. Howard. Evanston: Northwestern UP, 1972 (Paris: Seuil, 1964).
———. *The Pleasure of the Text*. Trans. R. Miller. New York: Hill and Wang, 1975 (Paris: Seuil, 1973).
———. *Roland Barthes by Roland Barthes*. Trans. R. Howard. New York: Hill and Wang, 1977 (Paris: Seuil, 1975).
———. *The Rustle of Language*. Trans. R. Howard. New York: Hill and Wang, 1986.
———. *S/Z*. Trans. R. Miller. New York: Hill and Wang, 1975 (Paris: Seuil, 1970).
———. *The Semiotic Challenge*. Trans. R. Howard. New York: Hill and Wang, 1988.
Culler, Jonathan. *Roland Barthes*. New York: Oxford UP, 1983.
Lavers, Annette. *Roland Barthes: Structuralism and After*. Cambridge, MA: Harvard UP, 1982.
Wasserman, George R. *Roland Barthes*. Boston: Hall, 1981.

Basic English

A simplified system intended as an auxiliary universal language for international communication. Developed in the late 1920s by C.K. Ogden, a British linguist and psychologist, Basic maintains the grammar and vocabulary of the English language but reduces both. There are 850 basic words: 600 nouns, 150 adjectives, and 100 operative words such as *can, do, the, if,* and *very.* Eighteen verbs with standard English conjugation are used in combination with nonverbs to replace approximately 4,000 standard verbs.

Basic's vocabulary is based on the use of regular forms of English, which in combination with one another provide for the greatest possible coverage of everyday usage. Its intention is to provide access to English that then enables users to apply and extend learning of the language as individual circumstances require.

Ogden and I.A. Richards, the educator and language theorist, devoted much of their careers to advancing Basic English, or what Richards eventually labeled World English. Ogden developed its principles from Jeremy Bentham, especially Bentham's aversion to verbs. He established the Orthological Institute in England in the early 1930s to train teachers from around the world in Basic's principles and pedagogy. Richards established his own center, what would become Language Research, Inc., at Cambridge, Massachusetts, in 1941. Interest in Basic developed rapidly during World War II after Winston Churchill endorsed it as important to the war effort. George Bernard Shaw later promoted Basic in conjunction with his own call for a simplified English spelling system.

Ogden oversaw the translation of great works into Basic (including the New Testament) as well as scientific treatises and dictionaries, including work by J.B.S. Haldane translated by William Empson. Both Ogden and Richards were called upon to defend Basic against charges of cultural imperialism and oversimplification of language learning.

Richards, who first collaborated with Ogden in 1923 on *The Meaning of Meaning,* spent much of the 1930s in the United States and China developing Basic English as an educational tool to promote international understanding of literature, business, history, culture, and science. He presented Basic as a means for both native and nonnative speakers to learn and use English more effectively. As a demonstration, he published Plato's *Republic* in Basic in 1942. With numerous coauthors, he applied its principles and the concept of "learning through pictures" to the teaching of other languages, including Spanish, French, German, Hebrew, Italian, and Russian.

Rhetorically, the importance of Basic English is in what it set out to achieve rather than its success in achieving it. An attempt to provide a universal language (as opposed to an artificial language like Esperanto), Basic was designed to ensure more effective communication and international understanding by "reforming" an existing language and approaches to teaching it, to allow for rapid acquisition (rather than replacement of) the language. Its principles, based on identifying essential aspects of language and, later, on using media technology and providing contextual clues through pictures and visualization, highlight the complexities of language use and meaning-making.

Stuart C. Brown
New Mexico State University

Bibliography

Gordon, W. Terrence. *C.K. Ogden: A Bio-Bibliographic Study.* Metuchen, NJ: Scarecrow, 1990.

Ogden, C.K. *Basic English: A General Introduction with Rules and Grammar.* London: Kegan Paul, 1930.

———. *The Basic Vocabulary: A Statistical Analysis with Special Reference to Substitution and Translation.* London: Kegan Paul, 1930.

———. *The General Basic English Dictionary.* New York: Norton, 1942.

Richards, I.A. *Basic English and Its Uses.* New York: Norton, 1943.

———. *Design for Escape: World Education Through Modern Media.* New York: Harvest, 1968.

———. *So Much Nearer: Essays Toward a World English.* New York: Harcourt, 1968.

Richards, I.A., and Christine Gibson. *Learning Basic English: A Practical Handbook for English Speaking People.* New York: Norton, 1945.

———. *Techniques in Language Control.* Rowley, MA: Newbury, 1974.

Russo, John Paul. *I.A. Richards: His Life and Work.* Baltimore: Johns Hopkins UP, 1989.

Basic Writing

Until the late 1970s, the field of Basic Writing (BW) usually was called Remedial Writing. The term *remedial* has been dropped for its negative connotations. Some widely accepted alternate terms for BW include *Developmental Writing* and *Writing for Underprepared Students*.

Students in BW courses generally fall into two groups. One group consists of students newly graduated from high school, sometimes having earned average or even above-average grades in English. Yet on college placement tests, these students' scores are low; they are advised or required—depending on a college's policy—to take BW.

The second, usually larger, group fits the profile of the so-called "nontraditional student": over twenty-five years of age; a graduate from high school more than six years ago; working full-time; attending college part-time; hoping to train for a new or better job; having limited funds for books and related materials; raising a family (if a single parent, almost always the mother).

For a small but rapidly growing subset of BW students, English is not their first language. Some, though not all, have completed courses in English as a second language (ESL) by the time they take BW. Often, the instructional needs of ESL students in BW courses differ from those of native-born students linguistically as well as culturally. Inevitably, however, when ESL students are in the minority in a BW class, instruction is geared to the native-born students.

The writing of BW students can be described from two perspectives: typical behavior during the writing process and features of the writing itself.

Typical behavior during writing might include an avoidance of planning, seemingly torturous labor to get even a few sentences onto paper, and over-concern with fine tuning—such as attending to a spelling or punctuation uncertainty—long before sufficient material has been drafted or revised. Such "premature editing" prevents writers from focusing on the larger issues of developing ideas, marshaling of context and support, and arranging material effectively. This typical behavior sometimes can be so overwhelming and discouraging that BW students withdraw from class—or even from college. For BW teachers to give attention sufficiently individual to help each student to correct such self-defeating practices, BW classes must be reasonable in size. Fifteen students per teacher is the standard in the Modern Language Association's "ADE (Associated Departments of English) Guidelines for Class Size and Workload for College and University Teachers of English."

Grammatical and punctuation errors are typical of the writing of BW students. Another typical feature is a paucity of conceptual complexity, seen in a thin or illogical line of reasoning, little specific support for the points being made, or the drawing of an unrelated conclusion. The importance assigned to such features tends to vary according to the type of institution. A study of essays written by BW students at two- and four-year colleges and universities reveals that the lack of conceptual complexity, even in the absence of grammatical errors, often led to BW placement at four-year colleges and universities; at two-year colleges, however, lack of conceptual complexity by itself was rarely sufficient cause for such placement.

To teach BW effectively, teachers need background in linguistics, composition theory, and learning theory. Since the mid 1980s, a small but growing number of institutions have come to require that BW instructors have taken at least one or two graduate courses in the theory and practice of teaching BW.

Configurations of BW programs vary greatly. At some colleges, BW is a single, one-semester course. At others BW is a sequence of courses, most commonly two. The pedagogical approach, based soundly on theory and research, is "top-down," exposing BW students at all levels to the concept that writing is a process of making meaning rather than a collection of atomistic skills. In courses with a "top-down" approach, students write multiple drafts of most papers, intensive revision, and learn to be peer critics. A recent enhancement of the "top-down" approach, implemented at a growing number of colleges, integrates the processes of reading with those of writing to encourage analysis and synthesis—often through a crafted sequence of assignments. An alternative to the "top-down" approach is the "bottom-up" structure, with the lower BW level concentrating on sentence and paragraph writing and the upper BW level focusing on essay writing. This approach is widely used though increasingly considered inadequate.

At many institutions, writing labs or centers (often equipped with computers) are available for BW students, usually to support, not replace, BW classes. Instruction is usually provided by tutors supervised by a writing specialist.

Two controversies have recently engendered much spirited debate at conferences and on the pages of some journals. The first concerns the idea of eliminating BW by absorbing BW students into regular freshman English courses. Strong opinions (and passions) notwithstanding, few institutions seem to be pursuing that approach. The second concerns a "re-vision" and criticism of the work of the late Mina Shaughnessy, a key pioneer in the field of BW. Though such views receive some attention, recognition of the value of Shaughnessy's work remains intact.

Lynn Quitman Troyka
City University of New York

Bibliography

Enos, Theresa, ed. *A Sourcebook for Teachers of Basic Writing.* New York: Random, 1987.

Journal of Basic Writing. New York: Instructional Resource Center of the City University of New York.

Rose, Mike. *Lives on the Boundary.* New York: Free, 1989.

Shaughnessy, Mina. *Errors and Expectations.* New York: Oxford UP, 1977.

See also SHAUGHNESSY, MINA

Bede (672 or 673–735 c.e.)

Historian, grammarian, exegete, hagiographer, homilist, cosmographer, poet, letter writer, and computist (dealing with the reckoning of time); styled "the Venerable" from at least the ninth century. Bede (also Bæda, Beda), a monk and priest, lived from age seven at the twin monastery of Wearmouth-Jarrow in Northumbria, where an outstanding library, assembled by the abbots Benedict Biscop (628?–689) and Ceolfrith (c. 642–716), provided the foundation of his considerable learning.

Bede maintained an English tradition of Greek and Latin learning, established with the arrival at Canterbury (c. 670) of Theodore of Tarsus and Hadrian. In the eighth century, Anglo-Saxon missionaries such as Boniface first spread Bede's reputation to the Continent. Alcuin of York, who, beginning in 782 as head of Charlemagne's palace school, established English learning on the Continent, accorded

Bede equal standing with Ambrose, Augustine, Jerome, and Gregory the Great as a Doctor of the Church. Bede's *Historia Ecclesiastica Gentis Anglorum (Ecclesiastical History of the English People),* notable for its reliance on first-hand informants and otherwise verified testimony, which the author took care to cite, is one of our two main sources of early English history. The other, the *Anglo-Saxon Chronicle,* itself draws on Bede.

In every field of study Bede turned to, clarity and accuracy characterize his work. Two instructional pieces, *De Arte Metrica (On the Metrical Art)* and the later addition to *De Arte, De schematibus et tropis (On Figures and Tropes),* are of especial interest to rhetoric studies. In antiquity, discussions of metrics frequently appear in rhetorical treatises under the sections on style, but by about 500 c.e. metrics and figures had come within the province of the teachers of grammar. Bede produced *De Arte* and *De Schematibus* (Book I and Book II of a single work, as presented in the modern standard edition) in response to inadequacies of Donatus's fourth-century *Ars Grammatica.*

The Wearmouth-Jarrow community, although generally antagonistic toward pagan classical culture and suspicious of classical rhetoric for emphasizing persuasion, sometimes at the expense of truth, nevertheless acknowledged the desirability of rhetorical study for interpreting Scripture. Bede's composition of *De Schematibus,* as if an afterthought, perhaps indicates his ambivalence (for which there is otherwise ample evidence) toward rhetorical study. *De arte* first treats of the simplest units, the letters of the alphabet, progresses to matters of increasing complexity (syllables, poetic feet, quantitative meters, alternating stress rhythm), and ends with a chapter on kinds of poetry. *De Schematibus,* an introduction to frequently employed rhetorical devices, distinguishes "schemes," or embellished phrasings, from tropes, or phrasings involving figural or otherwise oblique expression, and provides illustrative examples. Near the beginning of *De Schematibus,* Bede observes that all the rhetorical devices known to classical authors first appeared in Scripture. *De Schematibus* is the first grammar to exclude pagan authors and take illustrative examples entirely from Scripture and Christian writers.

Roger Dahood
University of Arizona

Bibliography

Bede. *Bedae Venerabilis Opera*. Various eds. Corpus Christianorum Series Latina (CCSL). In progress. Turnhout, Belgium: Brepols, 1955.

———. *Bede's Ecclesiastical History of the English People*. Ed. and trans. Bertram Colgrave and R.A.B. Mynors. Oxford: Clarendon, 1969.

———. *De Arte Metrica et De Schematibus et Tropis*. Ed. C.B. Kendall and M.H. King. CCSL 123A. Turnhout, Belgium: Brepols, 1975. 59–171.

Blair, Peter Hunter. *The World of Bede*. London: Secker and Warburg, 1970. 2nd ed. Cambridge: Cambridge UP, 1990.

Brown, George Hardin. *Bede the Venerable*. Twayne's English Authors Series 443. Boston: Twayne, 1987.

Curtius, Ernst R. *European Literature and the Latin Middle Ages*. Trans. Willard R. Trask. New York: Pantheon, 1953. Rpt. New York: Harper, 1963. 438–43.

Tanenhaus, Gussie Hecht. "Bede's *De Schematibus et Tropis*—A Translation." *Quarterly Journal of Speech* 48 (1962): 237–53. Rpt. in *Readings in Medieval Rhetoric*. Ed. Joseph M. Miller et al. Bloomington: Indiana UP, 1973. 96–122.

Wallace-Hadrill, J.M. "Bibliography." *Bede's Ecclesiastical History of the English People: A Historical Commentary*. Oxford: Clarendon, 1988. 244–69.

Ward, Benedicta. *The Venerable Bede*. London: Chapman, 1990.

See also ALCUIN OF YORK; AUGUSTINE; FIGURES OF SPEECH

Belles-lettres

A movement seeking to find universal principles that could be applied to all verbal discourse. By the late seventeenth century, it was becoming clear to philosophers and other thinkers that a single set of principles and rules underlay the various fields of study that had come under their investigations. This perception was, to a considerable degree, based on the methods, assumptions, and findings of the new science of the Enlightenment. As the scientists had discovered and revealed universal laws and rules that governed the natural world, so the humanists felt that rules and laws that governed the human world could also be discovered. Early philosophical works that sought to subject human knowledge to systematic analysis, and which were later influential in rhetorical studies, were Francis Bacon's *Advancement of Learning* and *Novum Organum,* and John Locke's *Essay on Human Understanding.*

When the search for overarching laws and explanations was applied to discourse, the result was a body of writings that have come to be characterized as the *belles-lettres* movement. Under that rubric, writers of the seventeenth and eighteenth centuries undertook to formulate a set of principles that were equally applicable to almost all of the forms of verbal discourse and to some nonverbal forms as well. Perhaps most important, from the perspective of rhetoric, the writers applied the principles equally to oral and written discourse. The word *rhetoric* was used in a broad sense, and it was not limited to spoken, or even persuasive, discourse.

The works devoted to the belles-lettres range from works dedicated to the instruction of students such as Hugh Blair's *Lectures on Rhetoric and Belles Lettres* (1759) and Charles Rollin's *The Method of Teaching and Studying the Belles Lettres* (1731) to more scholarly investigations such as Edmund Burke's *Philosophical Inquiry into the Origin of Our Ideas on the Sublime and the Beautiful* (1757), Lord Kames's *Elements of Criticism* (1761), and Alexander Gerard's *Essay on Taste* (1759).

Some of the works, such as those of Blair and Rollin, were specifically directed to the study of rhetoric. In other cases the works were devoted to the general study of the "polite arts," from which implications for rhetoric could be drawn. In almost all cases, certain principles were explicated to form a basis for the critical study of the verbal arts. The strongest of the foundations for the examination of literature was that of the faculty of *taste.* How human beings come to appreciate the "beauties of nature and art" became of central concern to most of the prominent rhetorical, literary, and philosophical writers of the period. Sir Joshua Reynolds, for example, devoted much attention to a discussion of taste in his *Discourses on Art* (1769).

The treatment of taste as a prerequisite for the study of rhetoric is perhaps best exemplified in Rollin's *Method* and Blair's *Lectures*. Both authors introduce their discussions of taste early in their treatises. After an introductory section, Rollin turned to "General Reflections on Taste." Blair's second lecture, following his introduction,

B

is simply titled "Taste." From the perspective of the belletristic rhetoricians, an understanding and appreciation of taste was essential for those who would judge or perform literary works. Although the writers in the School of Taste were not unanimous in their views, they generally held to a position that taste was a product of both nature and art. We are endowed with the faculty of taste (delicacy), but we must also learn its proper use (correctness). They also held that one of the important criteria for taste was a test of time: That which men persist in admiring is therefore admirable.

The authors of the belletristic rhetorics typically dealt with matters common to various literary genres before turning to rhetoric per se. Blair, for example, devoted twenty-four lectures to preliminary matters. He wrote of genius, language, style, and criticism. He devoted ten of the remaining twenty-seven lectures to eloquence. He then treated historical writing, philosophical writing, poetry, tragedy, and comedy, using the same common bases of judgment that had been applied to rhetoric.

Rollin, after treating rhetoric in more than 350 pages, devoted the rest of his work to history, fables, and the education of youth.

The attempt by the belletrists to find a governing set of principles was carried on in the rhetoric and composition textbooks of the nineteenth century. Those works refused to draw a firm line between written and oral compositions, and they maintained that, in general, the same rules were applicable to all forms of discourse.

Herman Cohen
Pennsylvania State University

Bibliography

Bacon, Francis. *Advancement of Learning and Novum Organum*. New York: Colonial, 1899.

Blair, Hugh. *Lectures on Rhetoric and Belles Lettres*. London: William Sills, 1836.

Burke, Edmund. *A Philosophical Inquiry into the Origin of Our Ideas of the Sublime and the Beautiful*. *The Works of Edmund Burke*. New York, 1836.

Kames, Henry Home. *Elements of Criticism*. New York: A.S. Barnes, 1871.

Rollin, Charles. *The Method of Teaching and Studying the Belles Lettres, or an Introduction to Languages, Poetry, Rhetoric, Moral Philosophy, Physics &c*. London, 1810.

See also BLAIR, HUGH; KAMES, LORD

Bentham, Jeremy (1748–1832)

Chiefly associated with utilitarianism. Born in London, Bentham was educated at Westminster School and entered Queen's College, Oxford, at age twelve. The son of an attorney, he studied law and was called to the bar but never practiced law. The underpinnings of the legal system interested him deeply, however, and he published *A Fragment on Government* in 1776. This penetrating analysis of a passage from *Commentaries on the Laws of England* by Sir William Blackstone (1723–1780), though published anonymously, earned recognition for Bentham from the Earl of Shelburne and set the course for all of his later writings.

It was through the Earl that Bentham met his future editor and disciple, Etienne Dumont. The latter drafted the *Traité de législation civile et pénale* from Bentham's notes, written in French. The work was published in 1802 and translated into English as *The Theory of Legislation* (1864) by an American, Richard Hildreth.

When Bentham turned his attention to the relationship between civil and penal law, he began to focus increasingly on questions of definition and the connection between the law and the use of language. Though Bentham is best known for his ideas of utilitarianism (the greatest happiness principle) and his best-known work remains *An Introduction to the Principles of Morals and Legislation* (1789), his writings, many of which remained in manuscript form till the twentieth century, contain a great deal of linguistic observation, which drew the attention of C.K. Ogden (1889–1957).

At the core of these observations is the notion of linguistic fictions or incomplete symbols—that is, forms of expression that impute concrete qualities where none exist. This concept of fictions is a linguistic corollary of the nominalism that dominated English philosophy in Bentham's day. In language, as in the legal field, Bentham was a codifier, classifying the seventeen properties of language that favor linguistic reform.

Bentham was a profound influence on Ogden, who simplified English into the 850-word system called Basic English. The key to that simplification was the elimination of verbs, which Bentham viewed as the slippery eels of language.

Bentham's boundless interests, upon all of which he wrote prolifically, included constitutional theory, social welfare, prison reform, educational reform, and the banking system. It is to him that English owes, among other terms, *maximize, minimize, codify,* and *international.*

According to Bentham's wishes, his body was preserved, and it continues to sit on view today as an auto-icon (Bentham's term), clad in his everyday clothes, at University College, London, of which he was a founder.

W. *Terrance Gordon*
Dalhousie University

Bibliography

Atkinson, Charles Milner. *Jeremy Bentham: His Life and Work.* Westport: Greenwood, 1970.

Dinwiddy, John. *Bentham.* Oxford: Oxford UP, 1989.

Mack, Mary P. *Jeremy Bentham: An Odyssey of Ideas 1748–1792.* London: Heinemann, 1962.

Ogden, C[harles] K[ay], ed. *Bentham's Theory of Fictions.* London: Kegan Paul, 1932.

———. *The Theory of Legislation.* London: Kegan Paul, 1931.

See also BASIC ENGLISH

Berthoff, Ann E. (b. 1924)

Educator known for basing her rhetoric upon her experience as a writing teacher and addressing it to other educators. She holds degrees from Radcliffe and Cornell College and has taught writing for forty-five years. Her career includes assignments at the University of Massachusetts, Vassar, Bryn Mawr, and Haverford. She has conducted seminars, or acted as consultant, for institutions as diverse as the New England Conservatory of Music and the Lawrence Berkeley Laboratories at the University of California. She directed a National Endowment for the Humanities seminar "Philosophy and the Composing Process" at the University of Massachusetts/Boston.

Berthoff developed her rhetorical theory in response to the practical needs of writing students. Her definition of rhetoric equates rhetorical activity with the act of composing, and composing with thinking. In *Forming/Thinking/Writing,* she asserts that rhetoric is an art of clarifying and articulating relationships as the "rhetorician/composer" transforms information into meaning (137). One of the primary relationships she clarifies is the dialogue between personal conceptions and social contexts. Berthoff chooses to focus on the interaction of the composer's thinking to the composer's current and historical social contexts to clarify the means by which the composing mind integrates those contexts as the composer initiates a dialogue between insights and experiences.

Berthoff's works treat the study of rhetoric, composition, literature, science, and philosophy as integral parts of the same study. Her eclectic approach is founded on her belief that divisions between the cognitive and the affective, reason and emotion, thinking and feeling are a root cause for failure in rhetorical study and application. Her answer to rhetoric's failures is to insist that the rhetor, whether writer or reader, reflect constantly on the mind's operations in order to understand how meaning is made and, therefore, become a better composer. Thus her rhetoric is best described as a reflective rhetoric in which she identifies and enumerates the available means of making a composer aware of the operations involved in the acts of reading and writing.

A central feature of Berthoff's work is her sustained reading of individual writers and her synthesis of those readings. A short list of principal writers featured in her writings demonstrates her involvement in philosophy, literature, rhetoric, and language. The list includes I.A. Richards, Susanne Langer, Charles Peirce, Edward Sapir, Samuel Taylor Coleridge, Paulo Freire, Lev Vygotsky, and Andrew Marvell. Her work on Marvell reveals her interest in literature, and one of her tenets for the teaching of writing is that composition and literature are best taught together.

Berthoff's contributions to the field of rhetoric revolve around her insistence that we should recognize the purposeful activity of meaning-making as central to both private and public discourse. She reasons that significant public communication grows from rigorous private habits of thinking, and that the best ways to develop those habits are through the close readings of texts and the writing of well-formed texts.

Her legacy to rhetoric includes her many works that detail practical approaches to invention and analysis, using language as a heuristic. Her works in progress reveal her sustained interest in the relationship between reading and composing, including a collection of essays based on "language and its limits" and a work defining the "powers of metaphor" as a way of thinking rather than metaphor as mere figure. For Berthoff, each language act involves purposeful speculation, and all language use begins and ends in purpose.

Rex L. Veeder
St. Cloud State University

Bibliography

Berthoff, Ann E. *Forming/Thinking/Writing: The Composing Imagination.* Portsmouth, NH: Boynton/Cook, 1988.

———. *Reclaiming the Imagination: Philosophical Perspectives for Writers and Teachers of Writing.* Portsmouth, NH: Boynton/Cook, 1984.

———. *Richards on Rhetoric: Selected Essays of I.A. Richards (1929–1974).* New York: Oxford UP, 1991.

———. *The Making of Meaning: Metaphors, Models, and Maxims for Writing Teachers.* Portsmouth, NH: Boynton/Cook, 1981.

———. *The Sense of Learning.* Portsmouth, NH: Boynton/Cook, 1990.

Biblical Rhetoric

A term that implies ways of reading as much as it does a collection or library of diverse literatures ranging over the history of two millennia. Biblical canons and authoritative collections reflect the divergent views of communities of belief. The key to biblical "reading" is the notion that sacred history has its roots in language. The essential characteristic of biblical rhetoric, in these terms, is the rhetorical question, the various methods to "inquire of the LORD."

Establishing the conceptual integrity of the idea of "biblical rhetoric" requires responses to two major obstacles. One obstacle is faced by all students of ancient and early rhetorics: *rhetoric* is a term that one must import from one or more cultural traditions, including one's own, into another. The other obstacle is the Bible itself: not simply that it is a varied collection of writings (including narratives, poetry, laws, prophetic books, letters, and apocalypses), but also that there are a number of collections that warrant the term *Bible*.

In response to these obstacles, many examinations of biblical rhetoric have focused on particular readings of and responses to the Bible. The feeling is that even if "rhetoric" is potentially a curiosity for those who may have written, recorded, or compiled the Bible as a collection of texts, it certainly is not for many who have subsequently read or responded to it. Other discussions of biblical rhetoric provide what might be termed "reconstructive or revisionist readings," oral traditional, literary, postmodern and, of particular note, feminist. These readings treat the Bible as if it had been compelled to exist, so much so that its study (particularly of its unifying characteristics) affords the opportunity to examine extratextual concerns—for example, the relationships among power, knowledge, and discourse.

It may be possible to impose the classical canons of rhetoric upon the Bible. Such an exercise could reveal that the prophets emphasize arrangement and that the earliest poetic forms are stylistic wonders. What is more, the Bible as a whole melds invention and memory, inasmuch as both the locus of truth and the discovery of the divine are situated at every turn in the memory of the patriarchs and the history of the people of Israel.

At the heart of the Hebrew Scripture is the strategy of divination. *Torah*—which means "law" in the sense of ethical as well as cosmic order—may be etymologically linked to *casting*, as in the casting of lots. In these terms, ethical, social, and political order is based upon the very order of the universe, which is "discovered" in the yes/no responses provided by divination. This order is inherently textual; more particularly, it is construed as resemblances and emblems and as the act of redaction, the collecting of the biblical stories themselves. Resemblance is a poetic and prophetic principle as well as a mode of argumentation: Israel is like a wayward wife or spoiled linen; Hosea takes a wife of harlotry (Hosea 1) and Jeremiah buries his linen waist cloth (Jeremiah 13). Emblems demonstrate how the future, as divine knowledge, structures the present moment and how the present captured in sacred texts can, in turn, represent the past (the memory of a chosen people). In Jacob's blessing in Genesis 49, his sons are emblematic of the political relations among Israel's twelve tribes: "Let Dan be a viper on the road"; "Judah, a lion's whelp"; "Napthali is a spreading terebinth." Underlying each of these is the paradox of difference and resonance that might be called metaphor.

This ethical and cosmic order "cast" in language could easily be turned back on itself—accounting for the "literary artistry" of the Bible and its fundamental iconoclasm.

Artistry

There is the sacred language of resemblance, resonance, and metaphor—for example, theophorous names and paronomasia. The multiple meanings—resulting from assigning a sacred name to experience, person, or place—provide a hinge for the ancient stories of Israel and sacralize the act of interpreting them. This is most effective in biblical paronomasia—sacred punning—from Yahweh's pulling Adam (man) from Adamah (earth) to Jesus' building his church on Peter (his disciple) on petros (rock). The gendered language and repetitive parallelism of the scriptures may also invoke characteristics of sacred order: a balanced structure set in motion according to the dictates of reciprocity and resemblance.

Iconoclasm

The Hebraic legacy of a monotheistic myth engendered a rhetorical understanding of the universe grounded in iconoclasm. In part, monotheism developed out of an angry rebuttal of the neighbors' manifold and dazzling gods.

What is more, prophets could critique their own religious traditions and imperatives in polemics against ancient stories and cultic rituals. The first of the writing prophets (Amos) was so iconoclastic that he represented worship as a purifying, social critique: "I [God] spurn with loathing your pilgrim-feasts; I take no pleasure in your sacred ceremonies; Spare me the sound of your songs; I shall not listen to the strumming of your lutes. Instead let justice flow on like a river and righteousness like a never-failing torrent" (Amos 5:21–24).

Although the Christian Bible concentrates not on the origin and design of the universe as much as its own mirrored destiny, it carries forward the dominant rhetoric of the Hebrew Scriptures as a critique of political and social behavior—distending history into eschatological allegory. The parables from the sayings of Jesus are a rhetorical highlight of the New Testament—perhaps surpassing even the epistolary or gospel forms. By means of the primary rhetorical twists and turns of these spare biblical utterances, the polemical remains saturated in the cosmological: the surprise that a Samaritan might be more of a neighbor, more compassionate than a fellow Jew; the surprise and disappointment of the good son in his father's estimation of his prodigal brother. Furthermore, the Christian Bible focuses not on myth's *illo tempore* but on the mythic eschaton, the fabulous end. The so-called "little apocalypse" of Mark 13 conflates and exemplifies the rhetoric of apocalypse, turning the historical, prophetic, and mythic voices of the Hebrew scriptures into a drama of the end time. Apocalypticism—employing specific rhetorical devices such as allegory, dramatic time, and stylized esoteric visions—becomes the ultimate trope of New Testament reality.

From sacred scriptures and their interpretations, Western culture has inherited a deeply embedded rhetoric. The spare narratives and the historical encounters with the prophecies, the interpretations, redactions, and critiques of Scripture enumerate the primary qualities of biblical rhetoric.

David Metzger
Old Dominion University
Lynda Sexson
Montana State University

Bibliography

Alter, Robert. *The Art of Biblical Narrative.* Basic, 1983.

Auerbach, Erich. "Odysseus' Scar." *Mimesis.* Princeton: Princeton UP, 1953. 3–23.

Bal, Mieke. *Death and Dissymmetry.* U of Chicago P, 1988.

Burke, Kenneth. *The Rhetoric of Religion.* U of California P, 1970.

Crossan, John Dominic. *The Dark Interval: Towards a Theology of Story.* Niles, IL: Argus, 1975.

Fishbane, Michael. *Biblical Interpretation in Ancient Israel.* Oxford: Oxford UP, 1985.

Frye, Northrop. *The Great Code.* Harcourt, 1983.

———. *Words With Power.* Harcourt, 1990.

Funk, Robert. *Jesus as Precursor.* Philadelphia: Fortress, 1975.

Kinneavy, James. *Greek Rhetorical Origins of Christian Faith.* New York: Oxford UP, 1987.

Ong, Walter. *The Presence of The Word.* New Haven: Yale UP, 1967.

Sanders, James. *Canon and Community: A Guide to Canonical Criticism.* Philadelphia: Fortress, 1984.

Warner, Martin, ed. *Bible as Rhetoric.* London: Routledge, 1990.

See also HOMILETICS; HOMILY; PULPIT ORATORY; RELIGIOUS RHETORIC

Bitzer, Lloyd F. (b. 1931)

Professor of Communication Arts, University of Wisconsin, Madison; B.S. 1955 Southern Illinois University; M.A. 1957 Southern Illinois University; Ph.D. 1962 University of Iowa.

In his famous 1968 essay "The Rhetorical Situation," Lloyd F. Bitzer argues that rhetoric is inspired and conditioned by a complex set of elements that compose the rhetorical situation. Specifically, he claims that the elements of exigence, audience, and constraints inspire and determine the appropriateness of discourse. Bitzer posits that a rhetorical situation has structure and organization and exists independently of the discourse applied to it. The situation, according to Bitzer, is real, objective, "publicly observable," and historically actual (11). Situation generates a need for discourse that can inspire mediating action in an audience capable of instigating change. In Bitzer's theory, discourse presupposes the existence of situation.

Bitzer defines exigence, audience, and constraints. Exigence is "an imperfection marked by urgency" (6); it is alterable or resolvable by appropriate discourse. The audience must be able to influence and effect change within the parameters of a specific rhetorical situation and is therefore "capable of being influenced by discourse" (8). Constraints can influence the rhetor's discourse choices and the audience's reactions. Constraints are motives, belief systems, prejudices, and so forth, that act as obstacles to resolution. Although a situation in Bitzer's view exists objectively, it must be recognized as requiring discourse, or, in most circumstances, it will deteriorate.

In a 1973 article in *Philosophy and Rhetoric*, Bitzer's theory was challenged by scholar Richard E. Vatz, who argued that discourse generates situation and that the rhetor imbues any situation with meaning through discourse. According to Vatz's relativistic argument, situation can never exist before discourse.

Bitzer's later essays "Rhetoric and Public Knowledge" (1978) and "Functional Communication: A Situational Approach" (1980) develop his situational theory. "Public Knowledge" examines the nature of public representation—public as it relates to the speaker and the audience. A public worthy of representation is a group whose communication is based in a shared "set of truths and values" (83). Speaker and audience can effectively represent this public when they share these fundamental concerns. In "Functional Communication" Bitzer expands primarily on exigence and the development of situations in relation to both physical and mental environments. Although Bitzer allows that exigence can exist as an objective condition, its perceived urgency is based on the degree of interest felt by speaker and audience—areas over which these two bodies sometimes disagree. Bitzer determines that four phases of situational development exist, from initial genesis of its components—exigence, audience, and constraints—to final dissolution, at which point a situation is no longer changeable. In these two essays, Bitzer's situational theory approaches maturity.

In addition, Bitzer is a scholar of eighteenth-century rhetoric, particularly of the theories of Richard Whately and George Campbell. In "Whately's Distinction Between Inferring and Proving" (1992), Bitzer examines in depth Whately's discourse theory and the scholarly research surrounding it. Bitzer's introduction to the 1988 edition of Campbell's *Philosophy of Rhetoric* provides a lengthy historical analysis of Campbell's rhetorical theory.

Bitzer's contributions to both contemporary and eighteenth-century rhetoric are invaluable resources for modern scholars.

Leslie Dupont
University of Arizona

Bibliography

Bitzer, Lloyd F. "Functional Communication: A Situational Perspective." *Rhetoric in Transition: Studies in the Nature and Uses of Rhetoric.* Ed. Eugene E. White. University Park: Pennsylvania State UP, 1980. 21–38.

———. "Rhetoric and Public Knowledge." *Rhetoric, Philosophy and Literature: An Exploration.* Ed. Don M. Burks. West Lafayette, IN: Purdue UP, 1978. 67–93.

———. "The Rhetorical Situation." *Philosophy and Rhetoric* 1 (1968): 1–14.

———. "Whately's Distinction Between Inferring and Proving." *Philosophy and Rhetoric* 25 (1992): 311–40.

———, ed. Introduction. *The Philosophy of Rhetoric.* George Campbell. Rpt. Carbondale: Southern Illinois UP, 1988. vii–li.

Vatz, Richard E. "The Myth of the Rhetorical Situation." *Philosophy and Rhetoric* 6 (1973): 154–61.

Black, Edwin (b. 1929)

U.S. rhetorical critic. Edwin Black's rhetorical criticisms, unparalleled in their elegance and spanning almost four decades, emphasize three crucial ideas: (1) criticism is a practice that begins with text rather than method or theory; (2) style and form are meaningful, ideological, and strategic components of the rhetorical act; and (3) the critic's responsibility is to attend not only to the means of rhetoric but also to its ends. Black transformed the field of rhetoric in his critical enactment of these principles.

A native of Houston, Texas, Edwin Black studied philosophy at the University of Houston (B.A., 1951), going on to Cornell University for his M.A. (1953) and Ph.D. (1962) in rhetoric and public address, with minors in philosophy and social psychology. His university teaching career took him first to Washington University in St. Louis (1956–1961), then to the University of Pittsburgh in the English Department (1961–1967), and finally to the University of Wisconsin at Madison (1967–1994), where he retired in 1994 from the Department of Communication Arts.

Consistent in all of Black's work is the central theme that good criticism allows generalizations and methods to emerge from the critic's engagement with the text. Black insists that the critic come to the object on its own terms, "seeking to coax from the critical object its own essential form of disclosure" (1980:332).

That idea is at the center of *Rhetorical Criticism: A Study in Method* (1965), in which Black rejects the predominant method of rhetorical criticism, neo-Aristotelianism, in favor of criticism featuring the critic's experience with the text. He argues that neo-Aristotelianism, in its clinical, categorial schemata and pragmatic focus on immediate effects, cannot fathom the lasting and indirect effects of discourses that participate in historical dialogues with multiple audiences—not the least of which is the critic. Black's examination concludes that the critic "may end with a system but he should not, in our present state of knowledge, begin with one" (1965:177).

A second major contribution is the idea that style and form serve meaningful functions beyond the ornamental. As Black demonstrates in a number of articles, the rhetor's stylistic choices often reveal the discourse's ideological investments, triumphs, and shortcomings. "There are strong and multifarious links between a style and

an outlook," he writes in "The Second Persona" (119). Here Black argues that rhetorical texts not only construct the persona of the speaker but also imply an ideal auditor, a *second* persona. He analyzes the "communism as cancer" metaphor as the token of an American Right ideology that beckons auditors as members of a nation-state-as-organism. This piece remains a foundational moment in the rhetorical tradition, and in it Black's final overriding concern is clear: The art of rhetoric can be put to purposes sophistic and sinister or authentic and emancipatory. Black's lasting message, amply demonstrated in his work, is that evaluation of the ends of rhetoric, as well as its means, is a fundamental critical responsibility.

Dana L. Cloud
University of Texas

Bibliography

Black, Edwin. "A Consideration of the Rhetorical Causes of Breakdown in Discussion." *Speech Monographs* 22 (1955): 15–19.

———. "Electing Time." *Quarterly Journal of Speech* 59 (1973): 125–29.

———. "Gettysburg and Silence." *Quarterly Journal of Speech* 80 (1994): 21–36.

———. "Ideological Justifications." *Quarterly Journal of Speech* 70 (1984): 144–50.

———. "A Note on Theory and Practice in Rhetorical Criticism." *Western Journal of Speech Communication* 44 (1980): 331–36.

———. "Plato's View of Rhetoric." *Quarterly Journal of Speech* 19 (1958): 361–74.

———. *Rhetorical Criticism: A Study in Method*. 2nd ed. Madison: U of Wisconsin P, 1978.

———. "The Second Persona." *Quarterly Journal of Speech* 56 (1970): 109–19.

———. "Secrecy and Disclosure as Rhetorical Forms." *Quarterly Journal of Speech* 74 (1988): 133–50.

———. "Sentimental Style as Escapism, or the Devil with Dan'l Webster." *Form and Genre: Shaping Rhetorical Action*. Ed. Karlan Kohrs Campbell and Kathleen Hall Jamieson. Falls Church, VA: Speech Communication Assn., 1978.

Black, Edwin, and Lloyd Bitzer, eds. *The Prospect of Rhetoric*. Englewood Cliffs, NJ: Prentice, 1971.

Black English

Linguistic term used to describe the casual speech of lower-class African-Americans in particular and African-American language in general. The study of Black English, like the experience of persons of African descent in America, has been marked by conflict and controversy throughout its historical and analytical evolution. Black English is the commonly accepted linguistic term for the language of African-Americans, also labeled *Nonstandard Negro English, Negro Dialect, Negro Speech, Black English Vernacular, Black Idiom, Black Dialect, Black folk speech, Black street speech, Black Amerenglish, Ghettoese, Blackese,* and *Ebonics.*

Perspectives on the scope and significance of Black English fall under three general categories: (1) "minimalist" approaches suggest that there are few or no differences between the speech of blacks and whites; (2) "maximalist" approaches argue that Black English constitues a unique form of black speech behavior undergirded by African or creole influences; and (3) "moderate" approaches acknowledge such influences but suggest that they are basically quantitative instead of qualitative in nature. The three categories reflect the historical development of the study of Black English over time, and reflect attitudinal and cultural shifts as well as developments in linguistic theory.

In the early part of the century, Black English was seen as a deficient or unevolved form of Standard American English and, with few exceptions, was viewed negatively and uncritically. Many early considerations of Black English, such as James Harrison's 1884 description of it as "baby talk," were "simplistic and racist in nature." Minimalist interpretations offered by "dialect geographers" argued that African-American speech was no different from the speech of white Americans, although, as Hans Kurath would suggest in his 1949 *Word Geography of the Eastern United States,* "more archaic or old fashioned; not un-English, but retarded because of less schooling" (Schneider 18). This negative and demeaning depiction of Black English led to the development in the late 1950s and early 1960s of an alternative hypothesis that posited non-European influences and origins for the language of African-Americans.

The writings of creolists William Stewart and Beryl Bailey provided the foundations for this hypothesis, which was later developed and extended by scholars who used it both to refute the minimalist interpretation and to advance in

its stead a maximalist position. Joe Dillard (1973) argues that the Anglocentric bias of geographical dialectologists undermined the historical and cultural accuracy of research in Black English, emphasizing its British origins and ignoring possible African and Caribbean influences. Such influences, derived from languages that had no native speakers (pidgins) but that later evolved into primary languages of specific speech communities (creoles), were not considered by early dialectologists, who attributed differences between black and white speech to physiological and sociological factors. "The reason for the lack of study in the area of Black English seems to be that the theory of exclusively British origins is seriously challenged by the pidgin/creole theory" writes Dillard (10), whose work exemplifies the maximalist perspective.

Maximalists like Dillard argue that Black English exhibits linguistic characteristics at the syntactic level that support the creolization hypothesis and that it represents a structurally unique language, independent from Standard American English. Geneva Smitherman, for example, offers the following definition: "Black Dialect is an Africanized form of English reflecting Black America's linguistic-cultural African heritage and the conditions of servitude, oppression and life in America" (2). The maximalist interpretation has itself been challenged by linguists who contend that it is motivated more by social and political concerns than empirical evidence. Scholarship over the past two decades has continued to emphasize linguistic analysis and has resulted in conflicting perspectives and interpretations concerning the definition, significance, and scope of Black English.

The challenge to the maximalist position has been advanced by scholars who acknowledge the influences of Africanisms and creolization but remain unconvinced that Black English constitutes a unique language at the deep structural level. The maximalist position is seen as speculative in terms of its historical assessment of pidgin and creole influences and extreme in its rejection of the minimalist's emphasis on linguistic similarities. Similarly, the minimalist opposition to the creolization hypothesis tends to ignore, with some exceptions, significant quantitative differences that exist between Black English and Standard English. Moderates like Salikoko Mufwene have attempted to suggest that "the impression that either of the positions must be correct and the other one wrong is mistaken," positing instead that it is likely that both British dialectal influence and creolization have contributed to the evolution of modern Black English (Schneider 27). The moderate position has contributed significantly to theoretical perspectives that recognize social and historical influences while at the same time pursuing objective and empirically validated analyses.

Contemporary popular and scholarly attention to Black English continues to address the core issues that have influenced its original concerns: the social and political implications of black and white speech differences and the origins and influences of those differences. The 1979 Ann Arbor "Black English Case," which ruled that the city's schools "were denying Black elementary school students their civil rights by failing to teach them to speak, read, and write standard English as an alternative to the Black English that was their native dialect," brought public attention to educational inequities associated with differences between Standard and Black English (Chambers preface). Scholars continue to explore the grammatical, syntactical, and lexical influence of Africanisms on American language in general (Holloway and Vass) and African-American language in particular (Mufwene). Recent research by several linguistic scholars suggests that Black English and Standard English have undergone a process divergence that parallels and reflects the social separations of the races, yet others remain unconvinced of the evidence of such divergence and contend that there is equally compelling support for a convergence hypothesis (Butters). The ongoing debate over the status and signficance of Black English continues to raise important political and theoretical issues and contributes significantly to our understanding of American language in general, and African-American language in particular.

Mark Lawrence McPhail
University of Utah

Bibliography

Butters, Ronald. *The Death of Black English: Divergence and Convergence of White Vernaculars.* Frankfurt am Main, Germany: Verlag Peter Lang, 1989.

Chambers, John. *Black English: Educational Equity and the Law.* Ann Arbor, MI: Karoma, 1983.

Dillard, Joe. *Black English: Its History and Usage in the United States.* New York: Vintage, 1973.

Holloway, Joseph E., and Winifred K. Vass. *The African Heritage of American English.* Bloomington: Indiana UP, 1993.

Mufwene, Salikoko, ed. *Africanisms in Afro-American Language Varieties.* Athens: U of Georgia P, 1993.

Schneider, Edgar. *Earlier American Black English: Morphological and Syntactic Variables.* Tuscaloosa: U of Alabama P, 1989.

Smitherman, Geneva. *Talkin and Testifyin: The Language of Black America.* Boston: Houghton, 1977.

B

Blair, Hugh (1718–1800)

First Regius Professor of Rhetoric and Belles-Lettres at Edinburgh University. Blair was born in Edinburgh, took the M.A. from Edinburgh University in 1739, and entered the ministry in 1742. In 1758 he was appointed to the prestigious pulpit of St. Giles. He published four volumes of sermons, edited Shakespeare's works, and supervised a forty-volume edition of the English poets. As a highly placed churchman, he helped defend David Hume and Lord Kames against the charges of heresy leveled against them by the Church of Scotland.

Blair's *Lectures on Rhetoric and Belles Lettres* (1783) are directed to those who are "studying to cultivate their taste, to form their style, or to prepare themselves for public speaking or composition." Blair connects rhetoric to the leading ideas of the period: reason, human nature, taste, and moral improvement. Rhetoric seeks to persuade through appeals to reason and the passions; belles-lettres evaluates aesthetic objects on the basis of their appeals to the same faculties. Good taste is at the root of both, and human nature is the foundation of taste. Finally, the cultivation of taste leads one to the higher intellectual pleasures, including the pleasure of virtuous behavior.

In pursuing this model, Blair rejects received traditions for eloquence and style, building instead on the foundation of modern psychology. In Lecture 34, for example, he gives suggestions for self-improvement in eloquence. The first requirement of the excellent speaker is good character, so one should practice the virtues. Second, one must have knowledge of the subject of the discourse and a general familiarity with polite literature. Third comes industriousness. Fourth, good models; fifth, practice; and sixth, study of rhetorical theory. Blair warns that while the study of classical rhetoricians is "not to be neglected . . . yet I dare not say that much is to be expected from them." It is "polite" to know the ancients, but their advice is not to be heeded, a point Blair makes repeatedly. Their style does not suit modern taste, and their theory does not conform to modern science.

Blair addresses each of his subjects by finding psychological foundations, acknowledging cultural relativism, seeking a rational basis for judgments, providing illustrations from polite literature both ancient and modern, and giving judicious advice. The main subjects of the *Lectures* are taste, the sublime, and beauty (four lectures); the history and structure of language (seven lectures); figures of speech and style (six lectures); critical analysis of Addison (five lectures); the history of rhetoric (two lectures); types of speech (three lectures); organization (two lectures); pronunciation (one lecture); and belletristic genres (thirteen lectures).

Though the balance clearly tips in the direction of "polite literature," Blair develops each of his subjects from the point of view of empirical observation and psychological evaluation. George Campbell had made the connection between philosophy and rhetoric; Adam Smith and others had brought rhetoric together with belles-lettres. Now Blair brought these forces together in a persuasive and useful way. As Blair modestly acknowledges, there is little in the lectures that is original—but everything is thoroughly assimilated and elegantly presented.

In terms of his influence, Blair is the Quintilian of his time, combining in his rhetoric a theory that met with nearly universal approval and a pedagogy that won nearly universal application.

Bruce Herzberg
Bentley College

Bibliography

Bevilaqua, Vincent. "Philosophical Assumptions Underlying Hugh Blair's *Lectures on Rhetoric and Belles Lettres*." *Western Speech* 31 (1967): 150–64.

Cohen, Herman. "Hugh Blair's Theory of Taste." *Quarterly Journal of Speech* 44 (1958): 265–74. Rpt. *Readings in Rhetoric*. Ed. Lionel Crocker and Paul Carmack. Springfield, IL: Thomas, 1965.

Howell, W.S. *Eighteenth-Century British Logic and Rhetoric*. Princeton: Princeton UP, 1971.

Schmitz, Robert M. *Hugh Blair*. New York: King's Crown, 1948.

Boethius, Anicius Manlius Severinus (c. 480–524)

Served as a senator in the court of Theodoric the Great. Boethius helped educate Theodoric's family, write his official correspondence, and deliver panegyrics for the court. Theodoric, an illiterate Ostrogoth, had him executed in 524 on suspicion of plotting with the Byzantine Emperor Justin I.

Aware that Greco-Roman culture was in danger of being lost, Boethius tried to preserve what he could through his own scholarship. He aimed to translate the whole of Plato and Aristotle into Latin, a project cut short by his death. Boethius was right to think that it was necessary: Before the thirteenth century, Greek philosophy was known to Western Europe chiefly through his translations. Despite his importance to the history of rhetoric, Boethius was not particularly interested in rhetoric. He regarded himself as a philosopher. His most influential work up to the present time is his *Consolation of Philosophy*, a poignant description of the power of philosophy to help one prepare for death, written while he was in prison awaiting execution.

The most important work by Boethius on rhetoric is a treatise on logic, *De differentiis topicis* (c. 522), also known as *Topica Boetii*. Here Boethius focuses on so-called topical logic, which uses rhetorical topics or commonplaces to explore ideas. In the first three books of the treatise, Boethius analyzes and compares different classical systems of topical invention, including Aristotle's and Cicero's. In the last book, he turns to the theoretical issue implicitly raised by this borrowing of rhetorical topics for philosophical inquiry, namely, the exact boundaries between philosophy and rhetoric. Boethius holds that philosophical argument, or dialectic, deals with general questions (theses) while rhetorical argument deals with specific instances (hypotheses). Dialectic employs complete syllogisms that can be examined in dialogue with an adversary; rhetoric employs truncated syllogisms that are presented persuasively to the audience.

These distinctions subordinate rhetoric to dialectic. Rhetoric becomes a means of applying general rules of argumentation, established by dialectic, to specific cases. Rhetorical argument has no epistemological force of its own. Boethius goes even further than Aristotle in denying rhetoric a separate knowledge-generating status. Boethius thus works against the

Ciceronian tradition of classical rhetoric, an approach that treats language and knowledge as interrelated and thus affords rhetoric some parity with philosophy.

The Aristotelian approach proved attractive to later medieval scholars in the universities, which were dominated by the dialectical study of theology and law. As Boethius appears to advocate, rhetoric takes a preliminary and subordinate place in the medieval university curriculum. Book IV of *Topica Boetii* (which has not been translated into English) was often used alone as a textbook on rhetoric. The most important classical source of this work is the *Rhetorica ad Herennium*. Boethius uses its terminology and shares its emphasis on invention, barely mentioning style, memory, and delivery, and giving the reader very little sense of how rhetoric might actually be used to affect an audience. His aim is to account for rhetoric, not to explain it, treating it in a series of definitions that analyze its parts.

Bruce Herzberg
Bentley College

Bibliography

Leff, Michael. "Boethius and the History of Medieval Rhetoric." *Central States Speech Journal* 24 (1973): 134–41.

Murphy, James J. *Rhetoric in the Middle Ages*. Berkeley: U of California P, 1974: 67–71.

Patch, Howard Rollin. *The Tradition of Boethius*. New York: Oxford, 1935.

Booth, Wayne C. (b. 1921)

Rhetorical theorist, literary critic, teacher of writing. Born in American Fork, Utah. B.A., Brigham Young University, 1944; M.A., Ph.D., University of Chicago, 1947, 1950 (in English). Taught at Haverford College (1950–1953), Earlham College (1953–1962), the University of Chicago (1962–1991). Now Professor Emeritus at Chicago.

Booth's work has a remarkable coherence—remarkable given its wide range of subject matters: fictional technique, irony, metaphor, modernist philosophy, critical pluralism, teaching, the ethics of fiction. The coherence derives from his consistent rhetorical perspective, one that takes rhetoric as both a practice and a mode of analysis. As practice, it is the use of signs to effect a meeting of minds and, ultimately, a community; as a mode of analysis, it

is the effort to understand the means by which such meetings can come about. Moreover, Booth believes that rhetorical study can make a difference in our daily lives: The more we know about the workings and effects of our discourse, the more we can use it for the common good.

The Rhetoric of Fiction (1961) argues that abstract rules about fictional technique (showing is good, telling is bad) are inadequate. Booth demonstrates that different techniques create different effects and serve different purposes, and that different purposes can inform effective fiction. In attending to the relationships among techniques, effects, and purposes, Booth joins his discussion of rhetoric in fiction with a treatment of fiction as rhetoric. Along the way, he develops his most widely used terms and concepts: implied author—the image of the flesh-and-blood author created through the text; reliable narrator—one whose values and beliefs are endorsed by the implied author; unreliable narrator—one whose values and beliefs diverge from those of the implied author.

A Rhetoric of Irony (1974) analyzes how authors and readers do the complex dance of ironic communication. Booth divides irony into two main types: (1) stable, in which an author covertly signals the reader to reject the text's literal meaning and to reconstruct a new, fixed and finite, meaning; and (2) unstable, in which the author intends every reconstruction itself to be subject to further undermining. Booth's discussion of this second type is at once disappointing and fascinating, because unstable irony works against the full convergence of minds that Booth values so highly.

Modern Dogma and the Rhetoric of Assent (1974) asks how speakers are able to change listeners' minds, and under what conditions listeners should change their minds. Arguing against the fact-value split, Booth identifies multiple sources of appeals to change belief and multiple warrants for assent: logical, emotive, ethical—each of which can take different forms in different discourses. Moreover, Booth's investigation leads him to propose that we change one of our entrenched intellectual habits. Rather than doubting a new speaker until given strong reasons not to, we should assent until given warrants to doubt.

Critical Understanding (1979) applies the rhetoric of assent to literary criticism. Booth seeks a philosophically justifiable pluralism that would reduce critical warfare by valuing multiple questions and recognizing that at least two answers to the same question could be fully adequate—while also regarding some questions and answers as unproductive or inadequate. After examinations of the pluralisms of R.S. Crane, M.H. Abrams, and Kenneth Burke, Booth concludes that the philosophical quest has failed. But he argues that pluralism's potential to reduce warfare is so great that this failure is less important than pluralism's promise. So he develops a pluralism founded on a commitment to three interlocking values: vitality, justice, and, the greatest of the three, understanding.

In *The Company We Keep* (1988), Booth employs the metaphor of reading as friendship to investigate the ethical dimensions of literature. Just as some friends are good influences and others dangerous, so too with books. Booth rejects the notion that ethical judgments of works of fiction can be made by distilling their moral messages. Instead, he contends that any book extends to its readers a diverse group of invitations, and the quality of the life we live while responding to those invitations determines its ethical quality. The friendship metaphor also leads Booth to give new emphasis to the social character of reading through his attention to what he calls *coduction:* the process by which our conversations about books influence our experiences and our evaluations of our friends.

Booth's first collection of essays, *Now Don't Try to Reason with Me* (1970), shows his skills as a public speaker and especially as an ironist. The second collection, *The Vocation of a Teacher* (1988), provides a portrait of the rhetorician as teacher and an implied pedagogical program based on careful attention to the acts of reading, writing, speaking, and listening. Especially noteworthy in *Vocation* are Booth's "Teacher's Journal" and "The Idea of a University—as Seen by a Rhetorician." *The Harper and Row Rhetoric* (1984) and *The Harper and Row Reader* (1984), done with Marshall Gregory, show how Booth's general commitments as a teacher give shape to his ideas about teaching writing. His most recent offering of friendship is an edited collection, *The Art of Growing Older* (1992), representations and reflections on aging.

James Phelan
Ohio State University

Bibliography

Antczak, Frederick, ed. *Keeping Company: Rhetoric, Ethics, and Wayne C. Booth*. Columbus: Ohio State UP, 1994.

Booth, Wayne C. *The Company We Keep: An Ethics of Fiction*. Berkeley: U of California P, 1988.

———. *Critical Understanding: The Powers and Limits of Pluralism*. Chicago: U of Chicago P, 1979.

———. *The Knowledge Most Worth Having*. Chicago: U of Chicago P, 1976.

———. *Modern Dogma and the Rhetoric of Assent*. Notre Dame, IN: Notre Dame UP, 1974.

———. *Now Don't Try to Reason with Me: Essays and Ironies for a Credulous Age*. Chicago: U of Chicago P, 1970.

———. *The Rhetoric of Fiction*. 2nd ed. Chicago: U of Chicago P, 1983.

———, ed. *The Art of Growing Older*. New York: Poseidon, 1992.

———, ed. *The Vocation of a Teacher: Rhetorical Occasions, 1966–88*. Chicago: U of Chicago P, 1988.

Phelan, James. "Wayne C. Booth." *Modern American Critics since 1955*. Ed. Gregory S. Jay. *Dictionary of Literary Biography*. Vol. 67. Detroit: Gale Research, 1988. 49–66.

Bormann, Ernest G. (b. 1925)

Contributed to symbolic convergence theory and developed fantasy theme analysis. Bormann, a professor of Speech Communication at the University of Minnesota, received his B.A. from the University of South Dakota and his M.A. and Ph.D. from Iowa State University. He has taught at a number of institutions, including the University of South Dakota, Eastern Illinois University, and Florida State University. He has written books on research methods in communication studies, but he is best known for his work in symbolic convergence theory and fantasy theme analysis.

Bormann first introduced fantasy theme analysis in his 1972 article "Fantasy and Rhetorical Vision." Fantasy theme analysis grew out of his work with the small-group communication seminar at Minnesota, a project that produced a large body of data about small-group communication and dynamics. Bormann found the key to understanding that data in the work of Robert Bales. Bales's book *Personality and Interper-*

sonal Behavior describes how group fantasizing emerges within the context of small-group dynamics. The group "dramatizes" when certain messages are sent. The tempo of conversation increases. People interrupt one another or complete one another's sentences. People may blush or laugh, emerging from self-conscious roles. Members of the group begin swapping stories. Tension is released, and the members of the group feel a sense of community or common culture. In his later works, Bormann calls this process of dramatizing in small-group communication "symbolic convergence."

These dramatizing messages could take any number of forms: "a pun or other word-play, a double entendre, a figure of speech, an analogy, an anecdote, allegory, fable, or narrative" (Bormann 1985:4). The most important dramatizing message for Bormann is a narrative of characters acting out a role in a setting apart from the "here-and-now" of the group. The characters in these narratives may be real or imaginary, and their action may be set in the past or the future. The specific content of one of these dramatizing messages is called a "fantasy theme." In the process of symbolic convergence, members of a group share fantasies that have common fantasy themes. Bormann calls such recurring dramatic situations "fantasy types." The sharing of fantasy themes and fantasy types may lead to symbolic convergence and the formation of a community characterized by a group consciousness. The community then can use these fantasy themes to win new converts to the group, maintain the cohesiveness of the group, and keep the group focused on its sense of mission or vision.

Even though these fantasy themes are set apart from the "here-and-now" of the group, they reflect certain elements of group communication. By analyzing fantasy themes, the critic may be able to understand the hidden agenda or repressed problems of the group. Analysis of these narratives can also reveal how groups with no common history can create a sense of community and common culture. By identifying recurring characters, plots, and settings (fantasy types), the critic can reconstruct what Bormann calls the "rhetorical vision" of the group and can share vicariously in this vision.

In his original article, Bormann suggests that fantasy theme analysis can be used to understand small-group communication and the rhetoric of social movements and mass media. Fantasy theme analysis has also been applied to the analysis of political and religious rhetoric, marketing and advertising, and organizational behavior. Despite the popularity of fantasy theme analysis, it has received some criticism, particularly from G.P. Mohrmann (1982). Mohrmann argues that the practice of fantasy theme analysis does not follow logically from its theoretical framework and that such analysis tends to be circular. See Bormann (1982) for a response to Mohrmann.

Gary Layne Hatch
Brigham Young University

Bibliography

Bales, Robert F. *Interaction Process Analysis: A Method for the Study of Small Groups.* Cambridge, MA.: Addison-Wesley, 1950.

Bormann, Ernest G. "Fantasy and Rhetorical Vision: The Rhetorical Criticism of Social Reality." *Quarterly Journal of Speech* 58 (1972): 396–407.

———. "Fantasy and Rhetorical Vision: Ten Years Later." *Quarterly Journal of Speech* 68 (1982): 288–305.

———. *The Force of Fantasy: Restoring the American Dream.* Carbondale: Southern Illinois UP, 1985.

Cathcart, Robert. *Post-Communication: Rhetorical Analysis and Evaluation.* Indianapolis, IN: Bobbs-Merrill, 1981.

Cragan, John F., and Donald C. Shields. *Applied Communication Research: A Dramatistic Approach.* Prospect Heights, IL: Waveland, 1981.

Mohrmann, G.P. "An Essay on Fantasy Theme Criticism." *Quarterly Journal of Speech* 68 (1982): 109–32.

———. "Fantasy Theme Criticism: A Peroration." *Quarterly Journal of Speech* 68 (1982): 306–13.

See also FANTASY THEME ANALYSIS

Britton, James (1908–1994)

English linguist and educator who theorizes a developmental taxonomy of writing based on the process through which children learn language. With origins in linguistics and cognitive and developmental psychology, his taxonomy emphasizes the expressive function of language, providing linguistic and intellective raw material that can be developed for a variety of purposes. Applications involve the teaching of writing, relations between writing and learning, and writing across the curriculum.

In *Language and Learning* (1970), Britton invokes Sapir's distinction between the referential and expressive functions of language. Britton emphasizes the expressive function, as opposed to the referential, with its emphasis on transcribing material reality. The expressive function makes language personal and idiosyncratic, providing the means for individuals to connect abstract concepts with personal experience, negotiating public and private significance, and resulting in concrete understanding and learning. Additional sources for Britton's theory include Vygotsky's "inner speech," Jerome Bruner's cognitive psychology, with its emphasis on the instrumental relationship between language and learning, and Noam Chomsky's generative transformational theory of language.

In the *Development of Writing Abilities: 11–18*, an observational and empirical analysis of the writing students do in school, Britton and his colleagues focus on the two primary roles writers can play when producing language: the participant role in which writers use language to get things done and the spectator role in which writers use language to relive the past. As participants, writers shape reality to an end. As spectators, writers re-create reality.

Locating these roles at the ends of a continuum, Britton derives three categories of writing. In the participant role, writers produce *transactional* writing, in which language is used to accomplish the business of the world. Transactional writing is divided further into informative and conative writing, roughly corresponding to the traditional classifications of exposition and persuasion: Informative writing makes information available; conative writing moves an audience to some action. In each instance the writing involves a transaction between writer and reader, hence its name.

On the other end of the continuum, writers acting in the spectator role produce *poetic* writing. Poetic writing is language used as an art medium, as a verbal icon, whose purpose is to be an object that pleases or satisfies the writer. The reader's response is to share that satisfaction. In traditional terms poetic writing is literary discourse, language that "exists for *its own sake* and not as a means of achieving something else" (91).

With transactional (participant role) and poetic (spectator role) writing serving as opposite ends of the continuum, Britton establishes a third category, *expressive* writing, which mediates the two. As a functional category, expressive writing represents a mode rather than a form—its purpose is realized through creating a text rather than describing the text itself. Examples include "thinking out loud on paper" (89); notes and drafts intended for the personal and private use of writers and their collaborators; journal writing documenting or exploring immediate thoughts, feelings, and moods; and personal letters.

In the expressive mode, writers shuttle back and forth between participant and spectator roles, generating ideas, then shaping them into language that can stand on its own. With its generative function, expressive writing plays an obvious role in learning to write: "Thus, in developmental terms, the expressive is a kind of matrix from which differentiated forms of mature writing are developed" (83). In addition, as the link between the private and personal and the public and social, the language of association and connection, it is the language of learning. Writing-across-the-curriculum proponents such as Toby Fulwiler propose using expressive writing systematically in class-based journals in all disciplines as a powerful tool for improving learning.

Christopher C. Burnham
New Mexico State University

Bibliography

Britton, James. *Language and Learning.* Harmondsworth: Pelican, 1970.
———. "Shaping at the Point of Utterance." *Reinventing the Rhetorical Tradition.* Ed. Aviva Freedman and Ian Pringle. Conway, AR: L&S, 1980. 61–67.
Britton, James, et al. *The Development of Writing Abilities: 11–18.* London: Macmillan, 1975.
Burnham, Christopher. "Expressive Rhetoric: A Source Study." *Defining the New Rhetorics.* Ed. Theresa Enos and Stuart Brown. Sage Series in Written Communication. Vol. 7. Newbury Park, CA: Sage, 1993. 152–70.
Fulwiler, Toby, ed. *The Journal Book.* Portsmouth, NH: Boynton/Cook, 1987.
———. "The Personal Connection: Journal Writing Across the Curriculum." *Language Connections: Writing and Reading Across the Curriculum.* Ed. Toby Fulwiler and Art Young. Urbana, IL: National Council of Teachers of English, 1982.

Brockriede, Wayne (1922–1986)

Communication Studies scholar who viewed rhetoric as part of the epistemology of human understanding, used perspectivism as his lens for constructing theory and doing criticism, featured argument as his key term, and explained ethical stances for arguers. Brockriede classified rhetoric as one of the human sciences and focused on understanding as the rhetor's goal. His epistemology emphasizes that people are essentially rhetorical beings who "come to understandings about things through language" (1985:159). Rhetorical theorists and critics can learn about human understanding by focusing on "words about persons, words about things, or words about words" (1982:141). Brockriede's epistemology breaks down artificial barriers between behavioral science and humanistic study by showing that both types of research seek human understanding by making interpretive arguments about how people use symbols.

A perspectivist views rhetoric as a complex set of interdependent relational, actional, and situational dimensions (1968, 1985). Relational dimensions consider how interpersonal attraction, power, distance, and trust affect rhetorical transactions. Actional factors consist of ideas, issues, ideology, and attitudes. Situational attributes constitute the holistic environment in which the relations and actions occur. Since every dimension in the rhetorical event is related to everything else, Brockriede's theories present complex multidimensional frameworks for understanding rhetorical events. Each dimension is as legitimate as another, and theorists and critics can emphasize one dimension at a time within the landscape of other dimensions.

Brockriede's preferred perspective is argument. Argument means "the process whereby people reason their way from one set of problematic ideas to the choice of another" (1975:179–82). Arguers make inferences, provide rationales, offer choices among disputed options, risk confrontation, regulate uncertainty, and share a frame of reference. Argument can be a dialectical process for refining evidence and reasoning; a rhetorical process of trying to influence auditors to accept arguers' evidence, claims, and justifications; or a logical product with content that can be analyzed and dissected. Brockriede finds arguments in philosophical, theoretical, empirical, and critical research and in transactions in interpersonal, social, scientific, and aesthetic contexts. For him the ability to create and interpret arguments is essential to human understanding.

Because argument is a rhetorical process, arguers influence the "truth" of a situation and the integrity and well-being of participants. Brockriede uses the extended metaphor of rape, seduction, and love to explain arguers' attitudes and strategies in rhetorical transactions (1972:1–11). Rapist arguers try to overpower other arguers by using intimidation, threats, and sanctions and by treating them as victims to be dominated intellectually and insulted personally. Arguers adopting the attitude of seducer control their rhetorical transactions through "charm" and "deceit," trick other arguers by strategic use of fallacies, and bedazzle them with emotional proof and an attractive style and delivery. Arguers adopting the role of lovers seek power parity, risk self for the sake of compromise and understanding, and respect the ideas and concerns of other arguers. Love is the ideal ethical attitude of the arguer.

For Brockriede, rhetoric is a multidimensional humanistic method of influence in which people engage in ethical argument to reach human understanding.

Janice Schuetz
University of New Mexico

Bibliography

Brockriede, Wayne. "Arguers as Lovers." *Philosophy and Rhetoric* 5 (1972): 1–11.
———. "Arguing About Human Understanding." *Communication Monographs* 49 (1982): 137–47.
———. "Constructs, Experience, and Argument." *Quarterly Journal of Speech* 71 (1985): 151–63.
———. "Dimensions of the Concept of Rhetoric." *Quarterly Journal of Speech* 54 (1968): 1–12.
———. "Rhetorical Criticism as Argument." *Quarterly Journal of Speech* 60 (1974): 165–74.
———. "Where is Argument?" *Journal of the American Forensic Association* 12 (1975): 179–82.

Bryant, Donald Cross (1905–1987)

Professor of rhetorical theory and the history of British public address. Bryant earned his A.B. (1927), M.A. (1930), and Ph.D. in speech and English (1937) from Cornell University, studying with the founders of that fabled department of speech—Alexander Drummond, James

Albert Winans, and Herbert Wichelns. In 1929 he joined the faculty of New York State College for Teachers. From 1937 to 1958 he taught at Washington University, serving his last two years as chair of English. In 1958 he moved to the University of Iowa, teaching until his retirement in 1973. He was one of the university's first five Distinguished Carver Professors, and, after his retirement, he also served a year as the A. Craig Baird Distinguished Professor of Communication Studies.

Bryant was best known as a rhetorical scholar of eighteenth-century British literary, social, and political history. His first book, *Edmund Burke and His Literary Friends* (1939), demonstrated his lifelong devotion to Burke and his interest in relationships between rhetoric and poetic. In such concepts as "eloquence" he found key connections between the literary and the rhetorical, the aesthetic and the political. The many facets of Burke became for Bryant the many dimensions of rhetoric itself and occupied his scholarly life; at his death, he was completing volume eight of the Oxford edition of *The Writings and Speeches of Edmund Burke*.

His historical and fieldwide interests showed up regularly in the books he edited: *Papers in Rhetoric* (1940), *The Rhetorical Idiom* (1958), *A Bibliographical Guide to Research in Speech and Dramatic Art* (with others, 1963), *Essays in Rhetoric and Poetic* (1965), *Select British Speeches* (with others, 1967), and *Ancient Greek and Roman Rhetoricians* (with others, 1968).

His prime contributions to rhetorical theory appear in one of the field's most reprinted articles, "Rhetoric: Its Function and Scope" (1953). In offering two definitions of rhetoric—"the adjustment of ideas to people and people to ideas" and "the rationale of informative and suasory discourse"—Bryant captured both rhetorical process and a generic definition of rhetorical theory. His concern for process led him to a style of criticism that saw rhetorical art as accommodative; the good rhetor to Bryant identified and then overcame rhetorical problems through genius, political acumen, and technical artistry. More broadly, to Bryant conceptions of rhetoric ought to be understood theoretically, as rationales connected to practice only in part. He noted regularly the seeming lack of connection between eighteenth-century conceptions of rhetorical theory in, for instance, George Campbell and the political practices of the late eighteenth century. Theory and practice maintained an uneasy alli-

ance in most epochs of the Western world. His thinking on rhetorical theory and criticism was fully summarized in his last book, *Rhetorical Dimensions of Criticism* (1973); there he finally broke from his earlier generic separations of rhetoric, logic, and poetic, arguing that all discourse features dimensions or facets of each.

Bruce E. Gronbeck
University of Iowa

Bibliography

Bryant, Donald C., ed. *Ancient Greek and Roman Rhetoricians: A Biographical Dictionary*. Columbia, MO: Artcraft, 1968.

———. *Edmund Burke and His Literary Friends*. St. Louis, MO: Washington U Studies, 1939.

———. *Rhetorical Dimensions in Criticism*. Baton Rouge: Louisiana State UP, 1974.

———, ed. *Papers in Rhetoric*. New York: Speech Assn. of America, 1940.

———, ed. *Papers in Rhetoric and Poetic*. Iowa City: U of Iowa P, 1965.

———, ed. *The Rhetorical Idiom: Studies in Honor of Herbert Wichelns*. Rpt. New York: Russell, 1962.

Fisher, Walter R., ed. *Rhetoric: A Tradition in Transition, in Honor of Donald Cross Bryant*. East Lansing: Michigan State UP, 1974. (Includes a reprinting of "Rhetoric: Its Function and Scope" together with a *redivida*.)

Buber, [Mordekhai] Martin (1878–1965)

Existentialist philosopher born in Vienna and influenced as a student by Ludwig Feuerbach's idea of *Ich und Du* (I and thou). Buber's philosophy of dialogue emerges most clearly in his books *I and Thou, Between Man and Man,* and *The Knowledge of Man*. For Buber the fundamental fact of human existence is "man with man," person communicating with person. Meaning and a human's sense of "self" are constructed only in the realm of the "between" of relationships; the becoming of a "person" rather than a self-centered individual arises only in the "between" of dialogic relationships.

Buber describes two primary human relationships, or primary attitudes among participants in communication: I–Thou and I–It. He contrasts the I–Thou relationship, or dialogue, with the I–It relationship, or monologue. Buber's view of dialogic I–Thou communication between humans derives from his assumptions about the nature and significance of human communication with God (the Eternal Thou). Throughout his writings on dialogue, Buber emphasizes at least four crucial aspects of dialogue:

Authenticity: People are honest and straightforward in communicating all information and feelings that are relevant and legitimate for the subject at hand. But people avoid simply letting themselves go and saying everything that comes to mind regardless of consequences for others. They strive to avoid projecting a false image or "seeming" to be something they are not. Communicators minimize filters formed by inappropriate or deceptive roles, but they honestly can fulfill legitimate expectations of an appropriate role.

Inclusion: People attempt to "see the other," to "experience the other side," to "imagine the real," the reality of the other's viewpoint. Without giving up their own convictions, without yielding their own ground or sense of self, communicators imagine an event or feeling from the side of the other. They attempt to understand factually and emotionally the other's experience.

Confirmation: Communicators express nonpossessive warmth for the other person and value the other for that person's intrinsic worth as a human. People affirm their partners in dialogue as unique, even though they may oppose their partners on some matters of belief or behavior. Confirmation involves the desire to assist others to maximize their potential, and it promotes a spirit of mutual trust. But confirmation does not mean unconditional approval of every facet of the other's belief or behavior.

Presentness: Participants in dialogue give their full concentration to bringing their total and authentic beings to the encounter. They demonstrate willingness to become fully involved with each other by taking time, avoiding distractions, being communicatively accessible, and risking attachment. Participants in dialogue are not merely onlookers or observers. Dialogic persons listen receptively and attentively and respond readily and relevantly. Participants willingly reveal appropriate aspects of themselves to others and receive their reciprocal disclosures.

At the minimum, a human treated as an inanimate It in monologue simply is observed, classified, measured, or analyzed as an object, not encountered as a whole person. The communication is impersonal or nonpersonal. More frequently, in Buber's view, the I–It relationship, or monological communication, is characterized by self-centeredness, deception, pretense, artificiality, unapproachableness, seduction, domination, and exploitation. Monologic communicators manipulate others for their own selfish ends, dominate through power, and view others as objects for pleasure or things through which to profit. Monologic communicators show great concern for what others think of them, for prestige and superiority, for display of their own feelings, for display of power, and for molding others in their own image. Buber believes that some I–It relations in the form of an impersonal type of monologue often are unavoidable in human life (such as routine, perfunctory interactions or impersonal, pragmatic exchanges of information). Where understanding of each other as unique individuals is not expected or appropriate, dialogue would not be the goal. In Buber's view, I–It relations, especially in the form of exploitative monologue, become evil when they dominate a person's life and increasingly shut out dialogue.

Dialogue flowers most naturally in private, two-person, face-to-face settings that extend, even intermittently, over long periods of time. Nevertheless, dialogical and monological attitudes can manifest themselves in varying degrees and various ways in public oral and written discourse. Johannesen explores the applicability of the dialogue-monologue perspective to the understanding and evaluation of public oral and written rhetoric (57–77).

Richard L. Johannesen
Northern Illinois University

Bibliography

Buber, Martin. *Between Man and Man.* Trans. Ronald Gregor Smith. New York: Macmillan Paperback, 1965 [1936].

———. *I and Thou.* Trans. Walter Kaufmann. New York: Scribners, 1970 [1923].

———. *The Knowledge of Man.* Ed. Maurice Friedman. Trans. Maurice Friedman and Ronald Gregor Smith. New York: Harper, 1965.

Friedman, Maurice S. *Martin Buber: The Life of Dialogue.* New York: Harper Torchbooks, 1960.

Johannesen, Richard L. *Ethics in Human Communication.* 3rd ed. Prospect Heights, IL: Waveland, 1990.

Kohanski, Alexander S. *Martin Buber's Philosophy of the Interhuman.* East Brunswick, NJ: Associated U Presses, 1982.

Buck, Gertrude (1871–1922)

First American woman to receive a doctorate in rhetoric (1898), University of Michigan. Her subsequent scholarly efforts during her twenty-five years as an associate professor at Vassar College are significant for their anomalous emergence during a period that was witnessing a veritable eclipse in rhetorical theory. Her writing represents a radical departure from the principles of current traditional rhetoric; indeed, she envisioned written discourse in ways that differed markedly from the more popular, mechanistic view of writing.

In a number of periodical articles and textbooks on grammar, rhetorical theory, and composition, Buck launched an attack against the mechanistic, reductive rhetorical theories of her day, positing a remarkably modern view of language as an organic, dynamic entity. Moreover, she revealed a startlingly contemporary attitude in her appeal for reforms in grammar instruction, for a process approach to writing, and for topics that engage students in practical ways. Buck's progressive doctrine can be situated within the reform tradition that enjoyed a brief heyday at the close of the nineteenth century. That tradition emphasized self-expression, appeals to the students' own interests, and a definition of thinking and writing as constructive, social activities.

In a forceful, compelling argument against sentence diagramming, Buck's grammatical theory posited a belief that the sentence emerges first from vague, undifferentiated human thought and develops into two-branched thought—the subject (agent) and the predicate (action)—which further subdivides into clauses, phrases, and finally into words. In describing the structure of sentences, Buck consistently used organic, protoplasmic metaphors such as the ameoeba and the more highly developed structure of the tree. In other remarkably modern points about language, Buck professed the idea that language form is deeply influenced by language function, that a grammar should be descriptive rather than prescriptive, that written language has its basis in spoken language, and that children achieve a functional, unconscious mastery of grammar.

Defining rhetoric as "the science or theory of the process of communication by language," Buck argued against a disinterestedly scientific rhetorical theory. She proposed a social theory of rhetoric that involves "persuasion to the truth" and, "advantages to both the hearer and the speaker." She advised the rhetoric teacher to have students depend on their own first-hand observation as well as both inductive and de-ductive reasoning. She recommended using topics that engage students in practical ways, and she suggested that students seek the logical basis of their arguments in psychology.

Buck's composition theory advised students to write for a genuine purpose, to derive subjects from their own experience, and to write for a specific audience. She endorsed a system that replaces formal standards of evaluating writing with practical criteria for evaluating writing: for example, the reader's ability to grasp an author's ideas and the writer's ability to transmit those ideas effectively in writing.

Valentina M. Abordonado
University of Arizona

Bibliography

Allen, Virginia. "Gertrude Buck and the Emergence of Composition Instruction in the United States." *Vitae Scholasticae: Bulletin of Educational Biography 5* (1986): 141–59.

Buck, Gertrude. *A Course in Argumentative Writing.* New York: Holt, 1899.

———. "The Foundations of English Grammar Teaching." *Elementary School Teacher* 3 (1903): 480–87.

———. "Make Believe Grammar." *School Review* 17 (1909): 21–23.

———. "The Present Status of Rhetorical Theory." *Modern Language Notes* 15 (1900): 167–74.

———. "The Psychological Significance of the Parts of Speech." *Education* 18 (1898): 269–77.

———. "The Psychology of the Diagram." *School Review* 5 (1897): 470–72.

———. "Recent Tendencies in the Teaching of English Composition." *Educational Review* 22 (1901): 371–82.

———. "The Sentence Diagram." *Educational Review* 13 (1897): 250–60.

———. "What Does 'Rhetoric' Mean?" *Educational Review* 22 (1901): 197–200.

Buck, Gertrude, and Fred Newton Scott. *A Brief English Grammar.* Chicago: Scott, 1899.

Buck, Gertrude, and Elizabeth Woodbridge. *A Course in Expository Writing.* New York: Holt, 1899.

Burke, Rebecca. "Gertrude Buck's Rhetorical Theory." *Occasional Papers in the History and Theory of Composition*, No. 1. Ed. Donald C. Stewart. Manhattan, KS: Kansas State U, 1978. 1–26.

Campbell, Joann Louise. "Gertrude Buck and

the Celebration of Community: A History of Writing Instruction at Vassar College, 1897–1922." Diss. U of Texas at Austin, 1989.

Kitzhaber, Albert R. *Rhetoric in American Colleges: 1850–1900*. Dallas: Southern Methodist UP, 1990.

Mulderig, Gerald P. "Gertrude Buck's Rhetorical Theory and Modern Composition Teaching." *Rhetoric Society Quarterly* 14 (1984): 95–104.

Weir, Vickie Ricks. "Revisioning Traditions through Rhetoric: Studies in Gertrude Buck's Social Theory of Discourse." Diss. Texas Christian U, 1989.

Burke, Edmund (1729–1797)

British politician and orator, born in Dublin. His father was an Irish Protestant attorney; his mother was Catholic. Burke entered Trinity College in 1744 and received an A.B. in 1748. While at Trinity, Burke helped form a debating society called The Club. He also edited, managed, and wrote for *The Reformer*, a weekly periodical that lasted only thirteen issues. Burke moved to London in 1750 to study law, but abandoned his studies in 1755. In 1757 he married Jane Nugent. During the 1750s he published his earliest important works, including *The Vindication of Natural Society* (1754) and *A Philosophical Enquiry into the Origin of Our Ideas of the Sublime and Beautiful* (1757), which established his reputation as a man of letters.

In 1765, Burke began as private secretary to Charles Watson-Wentworth, second Marquis of Rockingham. Rockingham later helped Burke gain a seat in Parliament, where he served for almost thirty years (Wendover: 1765–1774; Bristol: 1774–1780; Malton: 1780–1794). During his career in Parliament, Burke was known for his highly dramatic speeches. He fought strenuously for reconciliation with the American colonies and the impeachment of Warren Hastings. In 1790 he published his *Reflections on the Revolution in France*. Burke left Parliament in 1794, a year in which he saw the death of both his son and his brother Richard. He died in 1797.

Besides his extensive political writings, which offer the rhetorical critic abundant material for scholarly examination, Burke is important to the study of rhetoric for two theoretical texts. The better known of these is his *Enquiry into the Origin of Our Ideas of the Sublime and Beautiful* (1757), in which he discusses the manner in which texts influence auditors. His central point is that a sense of the sublime is generated by images or impressions that suggest pain, power, or a potential threat to self-preservation (such as darkness or enormous size); a sense of the beautiful is generated by images or impressions that suggest order, pleasure, or society. As for language, Burke believed that its operation does not consist in raising in the mind of the auditor the images of the subjects described. Instead, language influences auditors by displaying or reminding them of the significance or effect of these things. Words can also influence an audience because they can be used to combine ideas and to present things known but rarely or never experienced in physical life (including God). Burke closes by making the distinction between a clear expression and a strong expression: He links the first to the understanding, to showing the subject as it is, and the other to the passions, showing the subject as it is felt.

Burke also wrote, but did not publish, "A Plan for Arguing" (see Smallwood 203–8). The "Plan" examines the credibility of the orator and outlines topics for rational and emotional appeals, dividing argumentation into categories including justice, interest (or convenience), and affection. The "Plan" demonstrates Burke's connection with the tradition of the classical rhetoricians, but is also interesting because his comments suggest that he viewed rhetorical invention as a means of generating new knowledge as well as exploring existing knowledge.

Mark Gellis
Purdue University

Bibliography

Boulton, James T. *The Language of Politics in the Age of Wilkes and Burke*. Toronto: U of Toronto P, 1963.

Chapman, Gerald W. *Edmund Burke: The Practical Imagination*. Cambridge, MA: Harvard UP, 1967.

Cone, Carl B. *Burke and the Nature of Politics*. 2 vols. Lexington: U of Kentucky P, 1957–1964.

Fussell, Paul. *The Rhetorical World of Augustan Humanism: Ethics and Imagery from Swift to Burke*. New York: Oxford UP, 1969.

Gandy, Clara I., and Peter J. Stanlis. *Edmund Burke: A Bibliography of Secondary Sources to 1982*. New York: Garland, 1983.

Reid, Christopher. *Edmund Burke and the Practice of Political Writing*. New York: St. Martin's, 1985.

Smallwood, Elizabeth Ruth. *Burke's Use of Classical Rhetoric*. Diss. Texas Tech, 1974.

B

Burke, Kenneth (1897–1993)

Major American rhetorician, literary critic, language philosopher, and poet, whose theory of language as symbolic action, developed from the 1920s through the 1990s, advocates literature as equipment for living and a dramatistic analysis of texts, defined broadly as written, oral, and situational, using the ratios among the terms of his Pentad—"act," "scene," "agent," "agency," and "purpose"—and his afterthought, "attitude."

Kenneth Burke, born in Pittsburgh, attended Ohio State University briefly, studied philosophy at Columbia University for a year, and then left in 1918, "suddenly becoming horrified at the realization of what college can do to a man of promise" (Jay 1988:56). In 1922 Burke moved to Amity Road in Andover, New Jersey, where he lived until his death in November of 1993. That rural scene, distanced from the mainstream, is appropriate for the man of words who lived a life promoting cooperation, the persuasion of people, organizations, and nations to use words not war to settle differences, and the writing of counterstatements to accepted principles of the day to help people think critically about what they are doing with words and what words are doing to them.

After leaving Columbia, Burke began educating and supporting himself and his family by writing—reviews, music, literary criticism, fiction, and poetry—researching drug addiction for the Rockefeller Foundation, translating, and working as an editorial assistant at *The Dial* from 1921 to 1929. In 1924 he published his first book, a collection of short fiction, *The White Oxen and Other Stories*. In 1931 he published his first book of criticism, *Counter-Statement,* and in 1932 he published a novel, *Towards A Better Life*. His later works of criticism include *Permanence and Change* (1935), *Attitudes toward History* (1937), *The Philosophy of Literary Form* (1941), *A Grammar of Motives* (1945), *A Rhetoric of Motives* (1950), *The Rhetoric of Religion* (1961), and *Language as Symbolic Action* (1966). He published *Book of Moments, Poems 1915–1954* in 1955 and then *Collected Poems, 1915–1967* in 1968.

The Changing Status of Burke and His Rhetoric

Although Burke acknowledged in a letter written in October of 1921 to his friend Malcolm Cowley that in him the "critical outweighs the creative" (Jay 1988:6), Burke continued to integrate the critical and the creative and to demonstrate through his creative criticism that such distinctions or binary oppositions may be useful

angles on reality in some circumstances but not in others. The terms primarily define or, to use his image, balance each other. What some readers have considered his poetic or conversational language others have regarded as jargon-ridden, confusing, and idiosyncratic. Today, however, major critics from a variety of disciplines acknowledge their debt to Burke—Wayne Booth, Clifford Geertz, Rene Girard, Frank Lentricchia, and Hayden White, among others.

Despite the many names he has been called —poet, language philosopher, monocentric, and logocentric—Kenneth Burke was primarily a rhetorician who chose *rhetoric* as his key term because, given his definition of human beings as *animal symbolicum,* it is most practical: Rhetoric is "rooted in an essential function of language itself, a function that is wholly realistic, and is continually born anew; the use of language as a symbolic means of inducing cooperation in beings that by nature respond to symbols (1950:43).

Later he explains that the need for cooperation, communication, and identification results from the fact that people are separate: "In parturition begins the centrality of the nervous system. The different nervous systems, through language and the ways of production, erect various communities of interests and insights, social communities varying in nature and scope. And out of the division and the community arises the 'universal' rhetorical situation" (1950:146).

The Dialectics of Scene and Motive

Burke, then, selects two starting points or motives for *animal symbolicum*—one is biological and the other is sociological—but the two are dialectically interrelated with language as the synthesizing third term. People are born as individuals who, collectively by nature, respond to language and have the desire to join the conversation at hand to overcome their separation through identification with others. According to Burke's definition of human beings, people are also "goaded by the spirit of hierarchy (or moved by the sense of order) and rotten with perfection" (1966:16), so that any identification or communication is likely to be brief, before the negative sets in to reintroduce hierarchy, competition, and division.

Uses and Misuses of Language as Action

In addition, language itself is a system of differences—the Upward Way and the Downward Way, the psychology of form and the psychology of information, action and motion, and biological and sociological. When people understand language as symbolic action or performance, not reference, they can *use* the differences to come to terms or to settle differences. Within the larger framework of the dialectical interrelationships among forms of the mind, forms of the world, and forms of the text, Burke understood people as able to select symbols, defined as abstractions from situations, in order to revise their words and worlds.

Burke was aware that the terministic screen he chose, "rhetoric," both focuses and limits his analysis to verbal and nonverbal acts, by human agents, in specific scenes, using language and other agencies, for particular purposes. In *Language as Symbolic Action,* he explains that "even if any given terminology is a *reflection* of reality, by its very nature as a terminology it must be a *selection* of reality; and to this extent it must function also as a *deflection* of reality" (1966: 45). To use his terms, language study was Burke's "occupational psychosis" (1935:40) which creates in him a "trained incapacity" (1935:7).

Burke also recognized the limitations of what some critics regard as his all-encompassing theory of language as symbolic action. In his introduction to *A Rhetoric of Motives,* he explains that he has "tried to show how rhetorical analysis throws light on literary texts and human relations generally" (xiv–xv); Burke turns people and situations into texts for analysis. But as he explains elsewhere, Burke grounds any analysis in specific situations: "Whatever 'free play' there may be in the esthetic enterprise, it is held down by the gravitational pull of historical necessities" (1937:57). While his terministic screen broadens the "scope and circumference" of analysis, he situates any text in a broader context, thereby denying the possibility of any totalizing or all-purpose analytical method.

Burke's Motives and His Formal and Informal Appeals

The underlying motive of Burke's rhetoric is to convince others to use language as "strategies for coping" and as "equipment for living." Burke made his own motives clear by what he says and by what he does in writing: His purpose was to persuade readers to specific attitudes and actions by identifying with them and by helping them identify with him. In a world where "anybody can do anything for any reason" (1937:355), Burke continued to calculate the gains and losses of his terms and definitions. His underlying motive to promote peace required him to analyze competition as well as

cooperation, offensive and defensive methods of language use, and situations of war and victimage. Removing specific terms, theories, arguments, or anecdotes from the context of his work as a whole can lead readers to labeling Burke as only combative, Marxist, antifeminist, or poststructuralist when, in other circumstances, he can as easily be labeled by other or opposite reductive terms.

We can track the development of Burke's rhetoric from the revision of his earliest emphasis on symbolic *form* to his interest in symbolic *action* and then to the further specification of motives, scenes, and consequences of symbolic actions. In *Counter-Statement* he argues for the rhetoric of literature and against the then-current symbolist aesthetics. He argues that form *is* appeal and that a "work has form in so far as one part of it leads a reader to anticipate another part, to be gratified by the sequence" (1931:124). Even in this early work, Burke complicates ideas about form further by arguing that linguistic forms or symbols are "patterns of experience" or "abstractions from situations" and that they have consequences in the world.

Having extricated form and appeal from then-contemporary notions of symbols and literature as removed from life, Burke developed in later works his theories of symbolic action, dramatism, identification, and god-terms. From *Counter-Statement* on, Burke assumed that all literature and language are trying to "do something": "Art is a means of communication. As such it is certainly designed to elicit a 'response' of some sort" (1941:235–36).

Later, in *A Rhetoric of Motives,* Burke further develops his notion of formal appeal and connects it with "identification," which he argues is fundamental to persuasion: "Once you grasp the trend of the form, it invites participation regardless of the subject matter. Formally, you will find yourself swinging along with the succession of antitheses, even though you may not agree with the proposition that is presented in this form" (1950:58). Burke also explored various other kinds and degrees of identification, ranging from consubstantiation, identification between a poet and a character within his poem, identification between people who share a common principle, language, property, or history.

Burke does not, however, stop with formal textual appeals. He allows readers to experience his mind at work, the starts and stops, the digressions, the reconsiderations, the contradictions, and the incoherences. In other words, he uses forms of the texts *and* forms of his own mind at work, his own thinking processes, to appeal to readers who share with him the forms of the world. Burke's texts are, in this sense, drafts, not final, seamless, polished products, with which readers can identify because of the similar actions of their own minds and words.

Now, Where Are We?

There are few final answers in Burke, but there are many ways of asking questions, methods of seeking answers, means of assessing consequences, and strategies for beginning again. Burke arouses desires and expectations that are not, in fact cannot be, fulfilled by information removed from motives and consequences. As he explains in the preface to the first edition of *Counter-Statement,* he is trying to "elucidate" a point, to handle issues "songfully" in one part and "clinically" in another, and to "trace" implications. On his continuum between "pamphleteering" and "inquiry," Burke leans in the direction of inquiry. Inquiry requires the "cult of Perhaps," the willingness to entertain alternative perspectives and to reach agreement, so that everyone says "Heads I win, tails you lose."

What distinguishes Burke's rhetoric, then, is that he enacts his theories. He persuades readers, not by appeals to authority or by logical arguments; instead, Burke invites readers to participate in the creation of meaning. Reading Burke requires a willingness to go along and to suspend certain expectations of criticism. Once people join Burke, even as recalcitrant readers, they have already accepted the terms of his argument and are convinced finally by their own experiences in making meaning. Because Burke's rhetoric is dialogic, sometimes talking to other parts of the "corporate we" named "Burke" and sometimes talking to readers and writers, past, present, and future and even to characters of his own imagination, readers cannot help but respond to him.

Another angle on Burke's rhetoric—on what he says and on what he does—is provided by the sixth and missing term in his Pentad-become-Hexad, "attitude." Burke argues that we may accurately speak of persuasion to attitude rather than of persuasion to action. He says that the operating assumption of *Attitudes toward History* is that "getting along with people is one devil of a difficult task but that, in the last analysis, we should all want to get along with people (and we do want to)" (i). In the afterword to the second edition, he redefines this underlying attitude or desire to get along: "Indeed our concern in the earlier book is with the motive of communication—and 'communication' is the most generalized statement of the principle of 'love'" (347).

Burke seems to glory in the rhetorics of the Barnyard, the Muddle, the Parlor Room, and even in the Abyss, and to enjoy the rituals of courtship, birth, religion, death, and rebirth. What seems to motivate Burke's unending conversation and to motivate the heated discussion about Burke which is still vigorously in progress is his unflagging faith in the rhetoric of the human symbolic.

From his position outside the mainstream for eight decades, Burke grew beyond being a man of promise to become the man who fulfilled expectations: He developed a rhetoric of love which is perhaps adequate to meet the challenges of the contemporary scene, characterized by a norm of frustrated expectations and violent desires, resulting from the differences and divisions in a society in which identification and love too often seem impossible acts.

Tilly Warnock
University of Arizona

Bibliography

Burke, Kenneth. *Attitudes toward History.* Berkeley: U of California P, 1937.

———. *Counter-Statement.* Berkeley: U of California P, 1931.

———. *Language as Symbolic Action.* Berkeley: U of California P, 1966.

———. *Permanence and Change.* Berkeley: U of California P, 1935.

———. *The Philosophy of Literary Form.* Berkeley: U of California P, 1941.

———. *A Rhetoric of Motives.* Berkeley: U of California P, 1950.

Jay, Paul, ed. *The Selected Correspondence of Kenneth Burke and Malcolm Cowley 1915–1981.* New York: Viking, 1988.

Lentricchia, Frank. *Criticism and Social Change.* Chicago: U of Chicago P, 1983.

White, Hayden, and Margaret Brose, eds. *Representing Kenneth Burke.* Baltimore: Johns Hopkins UP, 1982.

See also DRAMATISM; IDENTIFICATION; PENTAD; SYMBOLIC ACTION

C

Campbell, George (1719–1796)

Author of *The Philosophy of Rhetoric* (1776), an important eighteenth-century British psychological-epistemological rhetoric. Since its appearance, *The Philosophy of Rhetoric* has generally been praised by critics and is often ranked as the most important treatise among the "new" rhetorics of the Scottish Enlightenment. The book, popular in the British Isles, was also translated into German (1791) and had a great influence in America throughout the nineteenth century.

Although early commentators debated whether the work was basically a "classical" or "modern" rhetoric, recent scholarship has placed its philosophical foundations in the Enlightenment. As a minister, Campbell through his philosophical writings sought to combat epistemological and religious skepticism, and his rhetorical writings were primarily aimed at arming ministers and theologians for defending the Christian religion against atheists.

Although Campbell had sketched out some ideas on rhetoric as a minister at Banchory-Ternan (1748–1757), the body of the work consists of discourses presented to the famous Aberdeen Philosophical Society (1758–1773), of which he was a founding member. (Some of these original discourses came to light in 1982.) Campbell's discussions in this club with Thomas Reid, James Beattie, and Alexander Gerard, among others, helped mold his ideas on philosophy. Campbell and his colleagues published works that established the common-sense school of philosophy in opposition to David Hume's skeptical system.

Moreover, the group also shared a philosophical outlook, goal, and method. One goal of their society was to create a philosophy of the human mind. The method was to be Reid's slow, patient method of induction. As avowed empiricists, they wanted to apply the Baconian-Newtonian method to the study of human nature. Moral philosophy would not progress until a careful empirical study of psychology had been carried out. In his rhetoric Campbell classifies rhetoric as a branch of psychology. To understand rhetorical principles, one must know psychology; to understand psychology, one must proceed inductively in examining the faculties and powers of the mind. Hence, Campbell's purpose in the *Philosophy* is "to exhibit a tolerable sketch of the human mind . . . and . . . from the science of human nature, to ascertain . . . the radical principles of that art [that is, rhetoric]." Here, then, we see rhetoric in the service of the study of human nature or the philosophy of the mind.

The moderns, Campbell held, had made little or no improvement over the ancients in discovering the rules of composition; but a true philosophy of rhetoric would enter a "new country"—a study of the principles of human nature that explains why the "rules" work. In elucidating the relationship between the principles of rhetoric and the human mind, he employs such common eighteenth-century topics as sympathy, the association of ideas, and faculty psychology.

Aside from several chapters in Book I (which present a doctrine of evidence), the remainder of the treatise is basically a typical belletristic rhetoric of the period. Belletristic characteristics in Campbell's work are (1) his broad definition of eloquence to include poetry and all forms of imaginative literature; (2) his lack of any treatment of memory or delivery; (3) his emphasis on elocution (Books II and III treat style or verbal criticism), a canon that is common to both speakers and writers; and (4) his inclusion of topics normally treated in poetic theory, such as wit, humor, ridicule, verisimilitude, taste, and sublimity.

Campbell's famous definition of eloquence as "that art or talent by which discourse is adapted to its end" and his classification of the five ends of speaking addressed to the four faculties of the mind (the understanding, the imagination, the passions, or the will) was worked out in a theological club in the 1740s. He held to this definition in both his *Philosophy of Rhetoric* and in his posthumously published *Lectures on Pulpit Eloquence* (1807). This "expanded" definition of rhetoric (versus the classical definition of rhetoric as persuasion) had a great effect on the teaching of composition and public speaking in America well into the twentieth century.

In 1840 Campbell's *opera omnia* appeared in six volumes; in that edition the *Philosophy of Rhetoric* makes up about 16 percent of his publications.

Dennis R. Bormann
University of Nebraska (Lincoln)

Bibliography

Bevilaqua, Vincent M. "Philosophical Influences in the Development of English Rhetorical Theory: 1748 to 1783." *Proceedings of the Leeds Philosophical and Literary Society, Literary and Historical Section* 12 (1968): 191–215.

———. "Philosophical Origins of George Campbell's Philosophy of Rhetoric." *Speech Monographs* 32 (1965): 1–12.

Bormann, Dennis R. "George Campbell's *Cura Prima* on Eloquence—1758." *Quarterly Journal of Speech* 74 (1988): 35–51.

———. "Some Common Sense about Campbell, Hume, and Reid: The Extrinsic Evidence." *Quarterly Journal of Speech* 71 (1985): 395–421.

Campbell, George. *The Philosophy of Rhetoric.* Ed. Lloyd Bitzer. Carbondale: U of Southern Illinois P, 1988.

Carter, Jennifer J., and Joan H. Pittock, eds. *Aberdeen and the Enlightenment.* Aberdeen: Aberdeen UP, 1987.

Miller, Thomas. "The Formation of College English: A Survey of the Archives of Eighteenth-Century Rhetorical Theory and Practice." *Rhetoric Society Quarterly* 20 (1990): 261–86.

Rasmussen, Karen. "Inconsistency in Campbell's Rhetoric: Explanation and Implications." *Quarterly Journal of Speech* 60 (1974): 190–200.

Sher, Richard B. *Church and University in the Scottish Enlightenment: The Moderate Literati of Edinburgh.* Princeton: Princeton UP, 1985.

Ulman, H. Lewis. "Discerning Readers: British Reviewers' Responses to Campbell's Rhetoric and Related Works." *Rhetorica* 8 (1990): 65–90.

Carlyle, Thomas (1795–1881)

Born in Ecclefechan, Scotland; a rhetorical revolutionary, transforming and mixing genres and casting neoclassical rules of style to the winds, being convinced that the "mad times" in which he lived demanded new forms of expression. Destined by his Calvinist parents for the ministry, as a youth Carlyle lost faith in Christian theology and for several years floundered in skepticism. Then in 1819 he discovered German Romanticism, and between 1822 and 1830 he was the chief purveyor of German thought into Britain, publishing a biography of Schiller and essays on Goethe, Werner, Novalis, Heine, and Jean Paul F. Richter, translating Goethe's *Wilhelm Meister's Apprenticeship* and romances by Tieck, Hoffmann, and others, and reviewing a number of German plays. Imbued with Fichte's "Divine Idea of the World" and admiration for the "new criticism" in Germany, both explained in "The State of German Literature" (*Works* 26: 58, 52, 51), Carlyle stated in a letter to John Wilson, on December 19, 1829: "I have some thoughts of beginning to *prophecy* [sic], next year, if I prosper; that seems the best style, could one strike into it rightly."

The next year he began *Sartor Resartus*, in which an English editor bred on empiricism presents the life of Diogenes Teufelsdröckh, a quaint German Romantic who formulates and rhapsodically expresses his "philosophy of clothes," proclaiming Nature to be "the living garment of God." The editor deconstructs Teufelsdröckh's discourse with his running commentary on its exaggerated style and fervent lack of logic while Teufelsdröckh is deconstructing the editor's, and the British public's too common-sensical understanding of reality. A curious blend of fiction and essay, *Sartor Resartus* has been consigned by George P. Landow to the sage genre, a form in which Carlyle acts as a ventriloquist, "providing an eloquent voice for inanimate phenomena and inarticulate masses," often positions himself in opposition to his audience, and thunders forth "visionary threats" and "visionary promises" (*Elegant Jeremiahs* 42, 51, 60).

To enhance his message, Carlyle uses, in defiance of Hugh Blair's *Lectures,* words "transported" from Germany, "new-coined" words, interior parentheses, inversions, extravagant metaphors, far-fetched juxtapositions and compounds, inversions, and low, dramatic apostrophes, as when the editor exclaims to the absent Teufelsdröckh, "Thou rogue! Is it by short clothes of yellow serge, and with swineherd horns, that an infant of genius is educated?" Not desiring to be perspicuous and precise, he aims at creating in the reader a mystical wonder and a vague sense of the Infinite. With all this, *Sartor Resartus* is suffused with a whimsical humor that relates it neither to German Romance nor the Bible but to Sterne's *Tristram Shandy.*

Carlyle's second major work, *The French Revolution: A History,* was as rhetorically unconventional as the first. Reviewing it in July of 1837, J.S. Mill called it "not so much a history, as an epic poem; and notwithstanding, or even in consequence of this, the truest of histories." As Carlyle grew older, much of the drama and humor of his style disappeared, and the sagelike message became more direct and more strident.

Billie Andrew Inman
University of Arizona

Bibliography

Beirnard, Charles A. "Rebelling from the Right Side: Thomas Carlyle's Struggle against the Dominant Nineteenth-Century Rhetoric." *Studies in Scottish Literature* 22 (1987): 142–56.

Cumming, Mark. *A Disimprisoned Epic: Form and Vision in Carlyle's "French Revolution."* Philadelphia: U of Pennsylvania P, 1988.

Helmling, Steven. "The Thaumaturgic Art of Thought: Carlyle's *Sartor Resartus.*" *The Esoteric Comedies of Carlyle, Newman, and Yeats.* Cambridge: Cambridge UP, 1988. 33–95.

Landow, George P. *Elegant Jeremiahs: The Sage from Carlyle to Mailer.* Ithaca, NY: Cornell UP, 1986.

Sanders, Charles Richard, gen. ed. *The Collected Letters of Thomas and Jane Welsh Carlyle.* 15 vols. Vol. 5: January 1829–September 1831. Durham, NC: Duke UP, 1970–1987.

Seigel, Jules Paul, ed. *Thomas Carlyle: The Critical Heritage.* New York: Barnes, 1971.

Tarr, Rodger L. *Thomas Carlyle: A Bibliography of English Language Criticism 1824–1974.* Charlottesville: UP of Virginia, 1976.

———. *Thomas Carlyle: A Descriptive Bibliography.* Pittsburgh: U of Pittsburgh P, 1989.

Trail, H.D., ed. *The Works of Thomas Carlyle.* Centenary ed. 30 vols. London: Chapman and Hall, 1896–1899. [Critical edition in progress, University of California Press.]

Cassiodorus Senator, Flavius Magnus Aurelius (c. 490–c. 583)

An influential Italian politician and Christian scholar/educator. While the Goths ruled Italy, Cassiodorus held a number of official court positions. Near the age of fifty, he retired from public office to pursue religious studies in Constantinople. After returning to Italy, he took up permanent residence at Vivarium, the monastery he had founded at Scylacium (Squillace), his birthplace.

Born into a family active in Italian politics, Cassiodorus began his own political career at an early age, under the reign of the Ostrogothic king Theodoric. As a member of an Italian senatorial family, Cassiodorus had received a traditional liberal arts education that, combined with his natural talents, quickly attracted attention. His first court position was as composer of letters and public bills for Theodoric, who needed others to write for him. The most important work from Cassiodorus's political career is the *Variae* (538), compiled shortly before he left public office.

In the *Variae,* Cassiodorus collected official documents such as edicts, proclamations, and letters he had written on behalf of the barbarian kings. The collection exhibits how he transformed routine administrative letters into highly persuasive documents. The *Variae* became popular both as practical models of administrative letters and as literary models of artistically crafted letters.

About two years after completing the *Variae,* when the Gothic control of Italy was no longer secure, Cassiodorus retired from politics. He left Italy for Constantinople, where he began his work in religious studies. He is presumed to have remained there for some time, perhaps ten years or more, devoting himself to Christian scholarship.

Cassiodorus's most ambitious and influential effort was his *Expositio Psalmorum* (c. 540–548). His purpose was to make Augustine's sermons, *Enarrationes in Psalmos*, more accessible to scriptural scholars, but he produced a work that is largely original in content. The method he developed for examining each Psalm—*titulus, divisio, expositio,* and *conclusio*—and his approach to textual interpretation were used as models for scriptural exegesis until as late as the twelfth century.

Although Cassiodorus had apparently founded Vivarium on his own lands sometime before leaving Italy, it was not until after returning from Constantinople in 554 that he personally settled at the monastery. His major contribution to the rhetorical tradition, the *Institutiones* (c. 562), was written as an instructional manual on the educational program there. In Book I Cassiodorus tells how to study the Scriptures, what manuscripts were available, how to copy new manuscripts, and what heretical writers were to be avoided. In Book II he provides a brief, encyclopedic discussion of the seven liberal arts, including rhetoric. Hence, the treatise served as a guide for manuscript collections and as a compendium of the seven liberal arts. In the following centuries, the manuscripts Cassiodorus had collected and copied were widely disseminated, and later writers, such as Isidore of Seville and Hrabanus Maurus, borrowed substantially from Cassiodorus's version of rhetoric and the other liberal arts. Consequently, though the monastery at Vivarium did not survive Cassiodorus's death, much of his work prevailed for centuries.

Beth S. Bennett
University of Alabama

Bibliography

Cassiodorus Senator. *Expositio Psalmorum (In psalterium expositio)*. Ed. M. Adriaen. *Corpus Christianorum, Series Latina*. Vols. 97–98. Belgium: Turnhout, 1958.
———. *Institutiones*. Ed. Roger A.B. Mynors. Oxford: Clarendon Press, 1937.
———. *An Introduction to Divine and Human Readings*. Trans. Leslie Webber Jones. Columbia U Records of Civilization, 40. New York: Columbia UP, 1946.
———. *The Letters of Cassiodorus*. Trans. Thomas Hodgkin. London, 1886.
———. *Opera*. Ed. Maurist J. Garet. *Patrologia Latina*. Vols. 69–70. Venice, 1729 (Rouen, 1679).
———. *Variae*. Ed. Åke J. Fridh. *Corpus Cristianorum, Series Latina*. Vol. 96. Turnhout, 1973.
Murphy, James J. *Rhetoric in the Middle Ages*. Berkeley: U of California P, 1974.
O'Donnell, Joseph. *Cassiodorus*. Berkeley: U of California P, 1979.
Riché, Pierre. *Education and Culture in the Barbarian West, Sixth through Eighth Centuries*. Trans. John J. Contreni. Columbia: U of South Carolina P, 1976.

Cassirer, Ernst (1874–1945)

German Neo-Kantian philosopher whose work on the theory of "symbolic forms" helped to shape the arguments of modern semiotics, the study of signs. In *The Philosophy of Symbolic Forms* (1923–1929), *An Essay on Man* (1944), and other influential books, Cassirer elaborates a theory of knowledge as cultural artifact and a theory of culture as semiotic artifact, examining the diverse modes of symbolic action, including language, myth, science, history, art, and religion, in terms of which culture and knowledge are formed. Cassirer regards symbolic action as the essence of consciousness, where the production of meaning through the coalescence of subject and object, perceptual matter and conceptual structure, is enabled by the mediation of signs. Human experience, the substance of culture, is a web of symbolic practices and evolving meanings, a product of imaginative energies, a range of prerational, common-sense, practical, and theoretical knowledge comprising both the "everyday life" of historically situated groups of people and also their intellectual, moral, and spiritual understandings.

Cassirer is "Neo-Kantian" in accepting the "idealist" premise that a priori intellectual principles and operations account for "experience." But he promotes what he calls "anthropological philosophy," modifying Kant's "critique of reason" (which had assumed an ahistorical and restricted view of mind as discursive rationality) by appeal to the diversity of symbolic forms that emerge, interrelate, and supplant each other in the continuing production of meaning within history. Hence, although he writes extensively (as Kant had done) about science as the most fully evolved form of consciousness, he also explores alternative forms, notably language and myth, that present other dimensions of the "human spirit" through their own distinctive modes of operation.

Cassirer's intellectual values are rooted in the liberal tradition of German humanism, powerfully influenced by the philosophical idealism of Marburg (where he studied under Hermann Cohen, a great nineteenth-century authority on Kant), and importantly affected by the moral catastrophe of Nazi Germany, whose national socialism he fled in 1933. His concern for the problem of meaning is energized by broader questions about the relationship between knowledge and freedom, where the production of culture through forms of symbolic action entails a continuing process of human self-realization, a perpetual liberating of the "spirit." Cassirer explores the interpretive nature of knowing and the concrete functions of symbolization in order to explain the power of expressivity to actualize human potential and thereby realize human freedom. His work, taken together, is a systematic overview of that power: the capacity of myth to articulate an animate, passionate world in which human feelings, desires, and fears are objectified, through symbols, as responsive agencies (gods, demons) in nature itself; the capacity of language to articulate a world of "common-sense" experience, the syntactically structured universe of objects, actions, causalities, and predications that constitute ordinary life; the capacity of science to articulate an austerely rational world of abstract relationships. The symbolic practices that compose these worlds are characterized by differing principles of operation, but they have equal value as "organs of reality," producing the variety of knowledge in response to the variety of human need and aspiration.

C.H. Knoblauch
University at Albany, SUNY

Bibliography

Cassirer, Ernst. *An Essay on Man*. New Haven: Yale UP, 1944.

———. *Language and Myth*. Trans. Susanne K. Langer. New York: Dover, 1946.

———. *The Philosophy of Symbolic Forms*. 3 Vols. Trans. Ralph Manheim. New Haven: Yale UP, 1953, 1955, 1957.

Krois, John Michael. *Cassirer: Symbolic Forms and History*. New Haven: Yale UP, 1987.

Schilpp, Paul Arthur, ed. *The Philosophy of Ernst Cassirer*. New York: Tudor, 1949.

Castiglione, Baldesar (1478–1529)

A fifteenth-century Italian aristocrat who served under the dukes of Mantua, Milan, and Urbino, traveled in England, France, and Spain, and served under three popes. Castiglione's military service to his lords, as well as his own writing and travels, allowed him an intimacy with European and Italian nobility. His wife, Ippolita Torelli, died in childbirth, leaving three children. Castiglione spent his last four years in papal service at the imperial court in Madrid. He died at Toledo in 1529 from a violent fever.

Castiglione's greatest achievement was his *Il Libro del Cortegiano* (*Book of the Courtier*) which, along with Machiavelli's *Prince*, enjoyed an enduring influence over court life in all of Renaissance Europe. The book purports to be *Symposium*-like discussions, held at Urbino under the direction of Duchess Elizabetta Gonzaga and with the participation of noblemen and court ladies, concerning what qualities—talents, arts, and moral character—constitute the perfect courtier.

Castiglione's nobles engage in an epistemic rhetoric wherein the merits of noble or common birth are debated as seriously as skill in the military and the fine arts. The concept of *sprezzatura* (nonchalance) is central to this discussion, and refers to the courtier's need to make his studied accomplishments seem effortless. Much is made of the fact that these four evenings of exchange are designated as a "game" by the assembly. The dicussions of both the perfect courtier and the perfect court lady allow the participants to make oblique political and social criticisms of their peers and the many foreign and ecclesiastical influences upon them. The discussion of the court lady challenges the inherent misogyny of the period, just as the commentary on the ideal courtier allows criticism of courtiership in general—a common topic at Renaissance courts. The goal of the courtier, according to this assembly, should be to practice an aesthetic contemplation of beauty—particularly that of court ladies—while maintaining personal distance. This contemplation of beauty evokes Plato's contemplation of the Forms. Reversing Machiavelli, Castiglione's courtier becomes adviser and mentor to his prince. As is often the case with Italian Renaissance writers, an inverted political and social system is suggested, examined, and "played." Whether this game is amusement, subversive exercise, or catharsis is never clear.

Most scholarly treatments of Castiglione over the past decade are either literary or historical, although the complexity and ambiguity of his book offer a great deal to students of rhetoric. Its formal elements make the book a rich resource for examination as a model of epistemic rhetoric. Further, its investigation into the political and social effects of court life reflect the power and uses of rhetoric. Thus, the notion of the discussions as a "game" is made more complex with an understanding of the political, personal, and ecclesiastical relationships of the assembled nobility. *The Book of the Courtier* becomes a study of the uses of political rhetoric, a feature that extends its value beyond being a mere variation on Renaissance courtesy books.

L.A. Coutant
New Mexico State University

Bibliography

Castiglione, Baldesar. *The Book of the Courtier*. Trans. Charles S. Singleton. New York: Anchor, 1959.

Hanning, Robert W., and David Rosand, eds. *Castiglione, The Ideal and the Real in Renaissance Culture*. New Haven: Yale UP, 1983.

Kinney, Arthur F. *Humanist Poetics. Thought, Rhetoric and Fiction in Sixteenth-Century England*. Amherst, MA: U of Massachusetts P, 1986. 129–32.

Lanham, Richard A. "The Self as Middle Style: *Cortegiano*." *The Motives of Eloquence: Literary Rhetoric in the Renaissance*. New Haven: Yale UP, 1976. 144–64.

Rebhorn, Wayne A. *Courtly Performances. Masking and Festivity in Castiglione's "Book of the Courtier."* Detroit, MI: Wayne State UP, 1978.

Catachresis

The apparently inappropriate substitution of one word for another. When Milton speaks of "blind mouths" or Shakespeare has Hamlet declare "I will speak daggers to her," both are demonstrating the striking concentration of meaning that can be achieved with this radical form of metonymy (q.v.). Quintilian aptly called catachresis a "necessary misuse"; Miriam Joseph points out that it is often used to "secure the compression, energy, and intensity which characterize great poetry" (146). Consider cummings' arresting line, "the voice of your eyes is deeper than all roses" or Donne's "Her who still weeps with spungie eyes" or Dickinson's "And that White Sustenance—Despair." Catachresis responds to the need to name a new reality or evoke the ineffable texture of subjective experience. When Dickinson says, "I shall not live in vain / If I can ease one Life the Aching / Or cool one Pain," she uses catachresis to make her suffering bearable by turning it into memorable words that others can savor.

Arthur Quinn and Lyon Rathbun
University of California, Berkeley

Cause and Effect

Can be seen as either an absolute or contingent relationship. This Aristotelian commonplace thrives among rhetoricians and composition theorists. Building upon Plato's singular formal cause, Aristotle posited material, motor, formal, and final causalities. In reconciling faith with reason, Aquinas (1225–1274) supraordinated the final cause for its teleological, Godly dimension. Such a reconciliation forecasted later contingencies for causality, such as Spinoza's (1632–1677) divine substance.

In his system of "induction," Bacon (1561–1626) supplanted the doctrine of final cause with a method predicated on "natural law," in effect predicting the empiricism and "natural right" of John Locke and the "natural" economic laws of Adam Smith. The mechanistic universe of Newton (1642–1727) deepened the belief in an absolute causality and, paradoxically, provided a priori "laws" for empiricists to observe. Descartes (1596–1650) rejected experiential as well as probabilistic knowledge, on the other hand, favoring a priori, pure thought, a rationalist foundation based on self-evident truths and an all-knowing, metaphysical, mathematical God. Cartesianism was challenged, however, by Giambattista Vico (1668–1744) for its narrow-minded refusal to recognize the holistic, antirational properties of language. The extreme skepticism of Hume (1711–1766), moreover, discredited any notion of power and will, personal or otherwise, as agents of change, deferring all apparent cause-effect relationships to temporal or sequential conjoinings. Opposite to the scientific project in theory, Kantian, idealist, and Romantic thought, nevertheless, further center causal authority in the individual subject. Meanwhile, moral philosophy has rescued the individual ego from solipsism by positing a moral universe and virtue as an active, practical agent in an otherwise predetermined, objective world. Later, Darwinian and Freudian theory constrain individual autonomy.

Contemporary rhetoric betrays its classical and Enlightenment heritage while challenging its most basic assumptions about causality. "I think, therefore I am," may be revised as "I speak/act, therefore I am"—speech and action, in the Burkean sense, and discourse and knowledge, in the Foucauldian, being indistinguishable in terms of either cause or effect. Likewise, the causal chains supplied by syllogistic and dialectical reasoning, and the linear, sequential plot prescribed by Aristotle give way to postmodern, multicultural, and feminist (see Margaret Fell, Cixous, Kristeva) rhetorical innovations that acknowledge and invite uncertainty and multivocality while critiquing the conventional syntactical subject positions of authority and causality.

Even though essentially no new textbooks in rhetoric and writing instruction are being organized according to the modes of discourse, they still devote considerable attention to cause and effect and other strategies for amplifying or arranging evidence in argumentative as well as narrative, descriptive, and explanatory passages. Particular attention is paid to fallacies of causal logic, such as *post hoc ergo propter hoc*, the confusion of correlation with causality. Whereas comparatively older current-traditional texts have neglected the writer as conscious synthesizer of material and source of new knowledge, emphasizing instead the isolated how-to of applying cause and effect to essay arrangement, recent texts have adopted such heuristics as Burke's dramatistic pentad as a means to explore the causes or motives behind the actions of participants in any rhetorical situation.

Andy Crockett
University of Arizona

Bibliography

Barnes, Jonathan. *The Complete Works of Aristotle: The Revised Oxford Translation*. Princeton: Princeton UP, 1984.

Bizzell, Patricia, and Bruce Herzberg, eds. *The Rhetorical Tradition*. Boston: St. Martin's, 1990.

Burke, Kenneth. *Language as Symbolic Action*. Berkeley: U of California P, 1966.

Crowley, Sharon. *The Methodical Memory*. Carbondale: Southern Illinois UP, 1990.

Grassi, Ernesto. *Essays on Vico, Heidegger, and Rhetoric*. New York: Lang, 1989.

Russell, Bertrand. "On the Notion of Cause." *Mysticism and Logic*. Garden City, NY: Doubleday, 1957.

Scruton, Roger. *A Short History of Modern Philosophy*. London: Routledge, 1984.

Chesterfield, Philip Dormer Stanhope, 4th Earl of (1694–1773)

Parliamentary orator, letter writer, pamphleteer, and essayist, born in London. His early education was under the supervision of his maternal grandmother, the Marchioness of Halifax, because his father took no interest in his rearing. Up to the age of eighteen he was taught by private tutors, leaving their hands a thorough master of the French language. He then went up to Trinity Hall, Cambridge, where he remained for nearly two years; he left it in 1714, as he tells us, "an absolute pedant."

Once out of Cambridge, he made the usual grand tour of the Continent. On this tour he was befriended by the Duke and Duchess of Marlborough, then residing at Antwerp. On the news of Queen Anne's death he returned to England, where a political career was opened up for him by his kinsman General James Stanhope, who introduced him to the new king. From 1715, when he was appointed Gentleman of the Bedchamber to the Prince of Wales, until a few years before his death on March 24, 1773, he led an almost completely public life, becoming, as a *Monthly Review* writer put it, "alike distinguished in the polite, the political, and the learned circles." He eventually became an accomplished orator in both houses of Parliament, serving in the Commons from 1715 to 1722, and, upon succeeding to the earldom on the death of his father, in the House of Lords from 1726 to 1755.

Chesterfield's literary fame rests mainly on two collections of letters: the *Letters to His Son* (1774) and the *Letters to His Godson and Successor* (1890). Each is a posthumous publication never intended for the general public. The first set of letters is addressed to Chesterfield's "natural" son Philip Stanhope, beginning when he is a youngster of five living in London under his mother's care and continuing until he is thirty-three. Chesterfield had a double motive in writing these letters. On the one hand, he wanted to give his son the supervision and attentive concern that he himself missed getting from his own father; and on the other, he wanted to instruct him in the arts of worldly wisdom and the graces of a complete gentleman and political careerist. A similar double motive underlies the letters to his godson.

From a rhetorical perspective, two aspects of Chesterfield's achievement invite further study. First is the formation of his style, which appears to be an Augustan version of Quintilian's "middle style," best adapted for pleasing or conciliating the audience. Discernible variants of this style are evident in Chesterfield's letters, essays, speeches, and "Jeffrey Broadbottom" pamphlets. At present we have no comprehensive critical study of Chesterfield's discourse, oral and written, comparable to, say, Loren Reid's *Charles James Fox: A Man for the People* (1969).

Ralph S. Pomeroy
University of California, Davis

Bibliography

Coxon, Roger. *Chesterfield and His Critics.* London: Routledge, 1925.

Craig, W.H. *Life of Lord Chesterfield.* London: John Lane, 1907.

Dobrée, Bonamy, ed. *Letters of Philip Dormer Stanhope, 4th Earl of Chesterfield.* 6 vols. New York: AMS, 1932.

Scott, Temple. *Lord Chesterfield and His Letters to His Son.* Indianapolis, IN: Folcroft Library Editions, 1976.

Shellabarger, Samuel. *Lord Chesterfield and His World.* Boston: Little, 1951.

Chiasmus

"To mark with an X"; inverse repetition at the level of whole passages or entire texts; the ABBA pattern of mirror inversion. The author of Numbers is using chiasmus in writing "And the Lord said unto Moses, The man shall be surely put to death: all the congregation shall stone him with stones without the camp. And all the congregation brought him without the camp, and stoned him with stones, and he died; as the Lord commanded Moses" (15.35). Echoing the frequent use of chiasmus in the Bible, Northrope Fry uses chiasmus to structure his seminal study of the Bible, *The Great Code,* whose last four chapters invert the order of the first four chapters: Ch. 1: "Language I"; Ch. 2: "Myth I"; Ch. 3: "Metaphor I"; Ch. 4: "Topology I"; Ch. 5: Topology II; Ch. 6: "Metaphor II; Ch. 7: "Myth II"; Ch. 8: "Language II." Many well-known works, such as Shakespeare's *Hamlet* and *Tempest* and Homer's *Illiad*, are structured chiastically.

Arthur Quinn and Lyon Rathbun
University of California, Berkeley

Chinese Rhetoric

An omnipresent phenomenon in its recorded history of five millennia, much as rhetoric was in European history. The history of Chinese rhetoric has likewise been characterized by continuing changes in strict accord with the varying circumstances of social and political evolution.

Effective discourse, persuasive or otherwise, was already a central concern among ancient Chinese thinkers. *Shu Jing,* or "The Book of Documents" (admired for its "rhetorical effectiveness"), is a record of the earliest examples of the power of speech in context (Ch'en 61). "Deliberations at the royal council, memorials to the throne, records of beliefs and politics, orations and charges to feudal lords" are documented as far back as the beginning of the Xia Dynasty (2255 B.C.E.) (Ch'en 62).

The development and practice of rhetoric topped all other matters of importance in the period of Spring-Autumn and Warring States (770–221 B.C.E.), a period that later came to be known as one in which "one hundred schools of thought contended." To keep military balance and to win over other kingdoms, each of the warring powers, while engaged in fierce battles, sent counselors and diplomats to its neighbors. Known as *shuike,* or "talking visitors," such agents were essentially practitioners of political rhetoric.

Two prominent schools of discourse, Confucianism and Daoism, were the driving forces behind this vast practice of rhetoric. The former evolved from the teachings of Confucius (551–479 B.C.E.), the latter from a book titled *Dao De Jing* by Lao Zi (c. 604–517 B.C.E.). Although philosophically opposite, the two schools were both concerned with the power of language. *Lun Yu,* or "The Analects," a collection of dialogues between Confucius and his followers, records that *Yan,* or "language," was one of his favorite topics (Liu). He devised a moral code called *Li,* ethical proprieties of relationships by which all human conduct was regulated. This regulatory code defined in exact terms who one was and where one stood in respect to others in any given interaction. Knowing oneself, that is, *zhengming* ("rectifying one's name"), was in fact a rhetorical act by which the context of discourse could be correctly evaluated, an act necessary for successful communication at all levels. It helped to maintain the hierarchical social order, eliminate uncertainty, and promote stability.

Daoism, on the other hand, did not care much for man-made codes, rules, or rites. Central to its philosophy was the concept of *dao,* which some contemporary researchers consider to be the Chinese equivalent of "discourse" (Callahan). As such, the *dao* is primarily a mode of action that entails communication among the parts constituting the event. From that interpretation, Daoism as a whole can be seen, much like Confucianism, as a school of discourse. It, too, was concerned with naming, but its emphasis was on knowing through naming. To a Daoist, "language is composed of names, and knowing [the names] is having the ability to manipulate and use these names towards a desired end" (Callahan, 171). Thus, whereas a Confucianist approached discourse from the relative position of the discourser, a Daoist would do so from the perspective of the thing or event named. In their own ways, both Confucianism and Daoism considered language use their focal concern and have continued to exert their rhetorical impact on the Chinese mind up to this day.

The establishment of the first unified Chinese empire in 221 B.C.E. led to an unprecedented suppression of rhetoric. Debates and arguments, written or spoken, began to be viewed not as a means to truth but as a threat to the new social order, challenging and even endangering the ruling of the empowered few. The "great book burning and immolation of scholars" by Emperor Qin remains till this day one of the darkest moments for the lettered in Chinese history. The replacement of Qin by the Han Dynasty (206 B.C.E.) gradually resurrected writing, but oratory never regained its original vitality. Writing thereafter became the dominant form of rhetorical practice without a strong spoken counterpart.

Naturally, the need for good writing began to appear as a subject matter in books. Lu Ji (261–303), whose impact on the Chinese mind was deemed no less significant than that of Aristotle on the West, was one of the first who wrote single-subject treatises on the art of composition. Titled *Wen Fu* ("The Art of Writing"), Lu Ji's book outlines the basic principles of writing. Toward the end of the fifth century, Liu Xie (c. 465–522) wrote a fifty-chapter book on rhetoric, *Wen Xin Diao Long* ("The Enliterating of the Mind and the Carving of the Dragon"). The treatise argues that the significance of rhetoric lies in its indispensability as a tool in every facet of human existence, particularly in government and education, in practical affairs, and in self-cultivation (13–14). The treatise is composed of three major canons: typology, process, and organization. The first presents a discussion of thirty-two well-defined categories of writing, ranging from the literary to the practical. The second analyzes discourse initiation, material collection, drafting, and revision. The third investigates the relationships among words, sentences, and the entire composition, the choice of linguistic styles with respect to particular rhetorical occasions, and the various kinds of schemes and tropes appropriate for different circumstances (Zhao).

More treatises on written discourse followed over the centuries, while writing as a major rhetorical mode continued to flourish. Among the influential were *Wen Ze* ("Principles of Discourse") by Chen Kuei of the Song Dynasty (960–1279), *Wen Shuo* ("On Composition") by Chen Yi-ceng of the Yuan Dynasty (1276–1368), *Wenti Mingpian Xushuo* ("An Introduction to Discourse Forms") by Xu Shi-ceng, and *Dushu Zuowen Pu* ("A Guide to Reading and Writing") by Tang Biao of the Ming and Qing dynasties (1368–1911). The twentieth century has witnessed the publication of a few books of its own on rhetoric and composition. They are either anthologies of Chinese writings or discourse principles based on Western or Russian models.

Along with the growing interest in contrastive rhetorics, Chinese rhetoric is on its way to becoming a respectable academic endeavor in and outside of China; much, however, remains to be discovered, recovered, and established. As Karl Kao suggests, the numerous traditional sources that bear on the theory and practice of rhetoric must be carefully sifted, and a paradigm based on the nature of the Chinese language and culture constructed to facilitate the study of Chinese rhetoric.

Heping Zhao
California State University, Fullerton

Bibliography

Callahan, W.A. "Discourse and Perspective in Daoism: A Linguistic Interpretation of Ziran." *Philosophy East and West* 39 (1989): 171–89.

Ch'en, Shou-yi. *Chinese Literature: A Historical Introduction.* New York: Ronald, 1961.

Kao, Karl S.Y. "Rhetoric." *The Indiana Canon to Traditional Chinese Literature.* Ed. and comp. William H. Nienhauser, Jr. Bloomington: Indiana UP, 1986. 121–37.

Liu, Xie. *Wen Xin Diao Long* [The Literary Mind and the Carving of Dragons]. Trans. Vincent Yu-chung Shih. New York: Columbia UP, 1959.

Liu, Yameng. "Rethinking Classical Chinese Rhetoric." Paper Presented at the Conference of the International Society for the History of Rhetoric, Baltimore, MD: 1991.

Lu, Ji. "Wen Fu [The Art of Writing]." Trans. Sam Hamill. *American Poetry Review* 15.3 (1986): 23–27.

Zhao, Heping. "*Wen Xin Diao Long:* An Early Chinese Rhetoric of Written Discourse." Diss. Purdue U, 1990.

See also CONFUCIUS

Chomsky, Noam (b. 1928)

Noted American linguist. Avram Noam Chomsky was born in Philadelphia. He took his Ph.D. degree (1955) from the University of Pennsylvania, where he studied with the noted linguist and political activist Zellig Harris. He joined the faculty of the Massachusetts Institute of Technology in 1955 and now serves there as Institute Professor.

Chomsky is the originator of transformational grammar, a systematic approach to language study in which he attempts to move beyond mere description of language use to an explanation of key linguistic phenomena, among them the fact that speakers can utter, and listeners can comprehend, sentences they have never heard, that there are an infinite number of potential sentences in a human language, and that language learning seems to involve assumptions that could not have been learned from one's language environment. For example, language learners presented with a declarative sentence such as "The man who is talking is my friend" never transform it into an incorrect interrogative such as "Is the man who talking my friend?" But why not? The second sentence would seem to be a logical deduction from such a grammatical pair as "The man is my friend" and "Is the man my friend?"

Chomsky explains the curious absence of such errors by theorizing that the language learner is born knowing that transformations operate not on individual units but on structures. Thus, one might expect a grammatical structure such as "the man who is talking" to be moved, as in "My friend is the man who is talking." But the native speaker will not expect a unit within this structure, such as "is," to move by itself.

Chomsky's concept of the role that transformations play in explaining language learning has changed significantly over the years. In his early work, he envisioned a relatively simple set of lexical and phrase structure rules that produced underlying, or deep, structures and a complex set of transformations that permuted them to the various sentences possible in the language. In his more recent work, Chomsky offers a much more complicated lexicon and a greatly simplified system of transformations that are constrained by the assumptions about language structure embedded in the human brain. A constant theme of Chomsky's work is that the models he proposes are psychologically real. That is, Chomsky purports to be constructing models that reflect the actual structure of the human brain rather than metaphors that provide insight into how the brain functions.

In addition to his linguistic research, Chomsky has written numerous books and given speeches in all parts of the world on international politics and, in particular, on the role the United States has played in imperialism. He argues that all governments are designed to control their citizens and that large governments attempt to control as much of the world as they can. Chomsky's political writings explain in great detail the rhetoric used by the U.S. government to control its citizens and to keep them unaware of its real purposes in dealing with foreign governments.

Ronald F. Lunsford
University of North Carolina at Charlotte

Bibliography

Chomsky, Noam. *American Power and the New Mandarins.* New York: Pantheon, 1969.

———. *Aspects of the Theory of Syntax.* Cambridge, MA: MIT, 1965.

———. *Knowledge of Language: Its Nature, Origin, and Use.* New York: Praeger, 1986.

———. *Lectures on Government and Binding.* Dordrecht: Foris, 1981.

———. *Necessary Illusions.* Boston: South End, 1989.

———. *Reflections on Language.* New York: Pantheon, 1975.

———. *Syntactic Structures.* The Hague: Mouton, 1957.

Cook, V.J. *Chomsky's Universal Grammar.* Oxford: Blackwell, 1988.

Haley, Michael C., and Ronald F. Lunsford. *Noam Chomsky.* New York: Twayne, 1993.

Lyons, John. *Noam Chomsky.* New York: Viking, 1970.

Peck, James, ed. *The Chomsky Reader.* New York: Pantheon, 1987.

Salkie, Raphael. *The Chomsky Update.* Boston: Hyman, 1990.

Cicero, Marcus Tullius (106–43 B.C.E.)

Roman statesman, advocate, orator, and rhetorician, considered to be the most influential figure in the history of rhetoric in the West. Cicero was a prolific writer and practitioner of rhetoric; his theories about effective expression as well as his orations became standards for artistic expression. His speeches and rhetorical theory not only served as models but also say much about the social and cultural climate of the Roman Republic. Cicero's other writings in philosophy and ethics and his hundreds of personal letters to friends and influential political figures provide the most extensive amount of information for study of any individual in classical rhetoric.

Cicero was born in Arpinum, a small village about sixty miles from Rome. His family was included in the Equestrian Order and enjoyed moderate wealth. Plutarch's comments about Cicero's early education (*Vitae Parallelae: Cicero*) offer amusing accounts of his precocious ability—even at the earliest age—and his burning desire to succeed in Roman politics. Cicero had the advantage of distinguished educators; his opening passages in *De Amicitia* offer his own account of those early years, as do his retrospective comments in his *Brutus* and *Tusculanae Disputationes*. As was typical of many aspiring Romans, Cicero's early training focused on law and rhetoric with an eye toward a political career. As a young man seeking to complement his youthful education with study abroad, from 79 to 77 B.C.E. he studied ethics, philosophy, and rhetoric in Athens, Rhodes, and Asia Minor. Cicero's later works reveal that he believed this Hellenic training invaluable, and his mastery of Greek gave him access to knowledge that was beyond the limits of many of his Roman counterparts.

Shortly after his return from study abroad, Cicero began his political career and his steady rise through the *cursus honorum*, or normal course of offices for political advancement. At that time, Cicero believed that his greatest opportunity for political recognition would come when he served as *quaestor* in Sicily, Rome's oldest colony, in 75 B.C.E. Rome was then undergoing a famine, and Cicero's diligence in supplying Rome with Sicilian grain would (he believed) earn him recognition. After his office was completed, Cicero returned to Rome to discover that his diligence had gone all but unnoticed; from that point he concentrated on building his political career through his ability as an advocate.

Lacking enormous wealth, patrician status, and military brilliance, Cicero realized that his ability as an advocate could be a source of power. Recognized as brilliant in oral argument, he earned his accolades as Rome's preeminent advocate when he successfully prosecuted Gaius Verres in 70 B.C.E. for the many crimes Verres had committed as governor of Sicily. Verres' defense was represented by Quintus Hortensius Hortalus, then recognized as Rome's leading advocate. Cicero's familiarity with Sicily, his exhaustive preparation for the case, and his excellent opening arguments provided a clear victory and the recognition he had long sought. He used his career as an advocate to gain support through the successful defense of many influential *clientelae,* and through their influence established a basis of patronage that enabled him to become *consul* in 63 B.C.E., the first *novus homo,* or "new man," to be so elected in thirty years. During his consulship, Cicero successfully suppressed a reactionary conspiracy led by Catiline to overthrow the government. Cicero's orations against Catiline, the *In Catilinam,* became classic statements of the ideals of a free and just government. An ardent champion of Republicanism during a period of unrivaled duplicity and opportunism, Cicero alienated many powerful Romans and was exiled for a brief period. Upon his return, disenchanted with the sycophancy rampant in Rome, he turned from an active political career to writing. During that period, 56–44 B.C.E., Cicero wrote many of his most influential works of rhetoric.

Despite his remarks in *De Oratore* about his *"otium cum dignitatae"* (retirement with dignity) from politics, Cicero was always a visible political figure, and he gave powerful orations against those who threatened the welfare of the Republic, the *concordia ordinum.* Cicero opposed the political career and plans of his lifelong associate Caesar and even sided with Brutus in his efforts to save the Republic. His most scathing speeches were directed toward Marcus Anthony, and those orations, called the *Philippicae* because they were intended to model the speeches of Demosthenes against Philip of Macedonia, led to his death. An admirer of Cicero's uncompromising Republicanism, Augustus (then Octavius) sought to keep Cicero's name off Anthony's proscription list. Eventually, however, Anthony succeeded in having Cicero murdered and his dismembered head and hands mounted on the Rostra for public display. Anthony's taunt was that he wished to have the hands that wrote the *Philippicae.* Plutarch's account even records that Anthony's wife, Fluvia, stuck a pin in Cicero's tongue. Plutarch, in his own elegant fashion, wrote that when passersby saw this horrible sight, they viewed not the disgrace of Cicero but rather the blackness of Anthony's own soul. Augustus, according to Suetonius (*Divius Iulius*), provided the best view of Cicero: When he found his grandsons hiding the works of Cicero for fear of being "caught," he admonished them, saying that Cicero was a champion of liberty; he then returned the books to the boys so that they might learn from a true lover of Rome.

Although Cicero's works on rhetoric, collectively known as his *Rhetorica*, date back to his youth, the majority of his treatises on rhetoric were written after his consulship and return from exile. Cicero's earliest treatise, *De Inventione* (c. 86 B.C.E.), was one of the more important works on rhetoric in the Latin West through the Middle Ages. A large part of the treatise is devoted to arrangement and the ways invention is "localized" within the disposition of a rhetorical composition. In the opening passages of *De oratore*, Cicero asked his readers to ignore his *De Inventione* as nothing more than the notes of a schoolboy; its popularity endured, however, and it became one of his few treatises to survive until the eventual rediscovery of his works in the Middle Ages and Renaissance.

The *De oratore* (55 B.C.E.) is widely regarded as Cicero's major treatise on rhetoric and remains one of the more important statements on the place of rhetoric in society. Unlike his more technical treatments of the subject, in this work Cicero has his main dialogue characters, Lucius Licinius Crassus and Marcus Antonius, discuss the place of rhetoric and oratory in society. With other dialogue characters, Crassus and Antonius discuss such important topics as the place of rhetoric and philosophy in education and civic affairs, the relationship between orality and literacy, the relationship between natural talent and rigorous training, and the implications of creativity and wit in the invention of discourse. Rediscovered in the Renaissance, *De Oratore* was the next major work printed after the Gutenberg Bible. *De oratore* has since enjoyed uninterrupted popularity both for its insights into rhetoric and indirectly as a standard for humanistic education.

After *De oratore*, Cicero wrote a number of works devoted to rhetoric, some elaborations on points made in *De oratore*, and some treatises written to specific individuals on a particular subject. *Partitiones oratoriae* (50 B.C.E.) is a brief treatise on the compositional structure of discourse and a later view on the canon of arrangement. *De optimo genera oratorum* (46 B.C.E.) was intended to be the preface to his own Latin translation of Demosthenes' *On the Crown* and Aeschines' *Against Ctesiphon;* Cicero uses this work to discuss the qualifications for the best type of orator. The *Brutus* (46 B.C.E.) is an historically valuable treatise in Cicero's *Rhetorica*, for Cicero uses the work to discuss the qualifications of rhetors by mentioning scores of prominent Romans. Without this work much of what we know about rhetoric and oratory prior to Cicero would be significantly limited. Cicero's *Orator* (46 B.C.E.), written after *De oratore*, is a continued discussion of the qualifications of the ideal rhetor and largely a response to the criticism he received from his contemporaries about *De oratore*. The *Orator* makes references to prominent models, including Demosthenes, as well as extended discussions of the abstract qualities of effective expression. Although Cicero's *Topica* (44 B.C.E.) is often considered to be a treatise on the study of philosophical argument, Cicero reveals (in the process) his continued belief in the close ties between rhetoric and philosophy. Those interested in the discussion of argumentative *topoi*, particularly as it compares with Aristotle's treatment in the *Rhetoric*, will find this a valuable statement.

Although Cicero's speeches, treatises on philosophical subjects, and personal letters are not included with his *Rhetorica*, it is important to note their relationship to his rhetoric. For much of the history of rhetoric in the West, Cicero's many speeches—about fifty-eight survive in some form of completion and approximately forty-eight are known but lost—served as models of effective expression and were used to teach principles of rhetoric. Scholars today, in fact, often study Cicero's orations to illustrate his use and application of rhetoric. Cicero's *In Verrem, In Catilinam,* and *Philippicae* are illustrations of forensic, deliberative, and epideictic speeches that have been extensively studied both for their application of rhetorical principles and as cultural statements. Similarly, Cicero's philosophical works and letters often contain asides that complement topics in his *Rhetorica* or shed light on their implications. Thus, to study Cicero's *Rhetorica* requires an examination not only of his treatises but his other works as well.

Excellent editions of Cicero's *Rhetorica* and orations are available from Oxford and Teubner. Augustus S. Wilkins's edition of *De oratore* (Georg Olms, 1965) is also a distinguished example of scholarship, particularly the introduction. The Loeb Classical Library of Harvard University Press has English translations facing the Latin text and includes all the major rhetorical works and orations of Cicero. Secondary scholarship on Cicero's orations is substantial, less so on his rhetorical theory. The most recent and specific review of scholarship on Cicero's rhetoric is in *The Present State of Scholarship in Historical and Contemporary Rhetoric*, edited by Winifred B. Horner (second edition, University of Missouri Press, 1990). A comprehensive bibliography of relevant work is also included in *The Literate Mode of Cicero's Legal Rhetoric* by Richard Leo Enos (Southern Illinois University Press, 1988).

Richard Leo Enos
Texas Christian University

Bibliography

The scholarship on Cicero and his rhetoric is voluminous. The references listed here provide extensive bibliographies and commentaries on primary and secondary works. Primary works from the Loeb Classical Library series from Harvard University Press include the Latin text as well as the English translation.

Cicero. *Brutus*. Trans. G.L. Hendrickson. Loeb Classical Library. Cambridge, MA: Harvard UP, 1952.

———. *De Inventione—De Optimo Genere Oratorum—Topica*. Trans. H.M. Hubbell. Loeb Classical Library. Cambridge, MA: Harvard UP, 1949.

———. *De Oratore: I–II*. Trans. E.W. Sutton and H. Rackham. Loeb Classical Library. Rev. ed. Cambridge, MA: Harvard UP, 1948.

———. *De Oratore: III—De Fato—Paradoxa Stoicorum—De Partitione Oratoria*. Trans. H. Rackham. Loeb Classical Library. Cambridge, MA: Harvard UP, 1942.

———. *On Oratory and Orators*. Trans. J.S. Watson. Landmarks in Rhetoric and Public Address. Carbondale: Southern Illinois UP, 1986.

———. *Orator*. Trans. H.M. Hubbell. Loeb Classical Library. Cambridge, MA: Harvard UP, 1952.

Enos, Richard Leo. *The Literate Mode of Cicero's Legal Rhetoric*. Carbondale: Southern Illinois UP, 1988.

Horner, Winifred Bryan, ed. Rev. ed. *The Present State of Scholarship in Historical and Contemporary Rhetoric*. Columbia: U of Missouri P, 1990.

Kennedy, George A. *The Art of Rhetoric in the Roman World: 300 B.C.–A.D. 300*. Princeton: Princeton UP, 1972.

May, James M. *Trials of Character: The Eloquence of Ciceronian Ethos*. Chapel Hill: U of North Carolina P, 1988.

See also ROMAN RHETORIC

Cixous, Hélène (b. 1937)

French feminist writer and theorist of language, power, and relations between the sexes. She was born in Oran, Algeria, in 1937 under French colonial rule. She is now professor of English Literature at the "experimental" University of Paris–VIII at Vincennes. She helped to found this university and also began the first center for the study of women in France.

Cixous' cultural and linguistic heritage had a great impact on her later writings concerning exile, language, the nature of writing and voice, and power relations. Her father was a Sephardic Jew and had grown up speaking Spanish at home; her mother left Germany in 1933 and relocated to Algeria after Hitler's rise to power. Her mother and grandmother spoke German at home, her father, Arabic and Hebrew, but the young Hélène had to speak English at school.

The English-speaking audience came to know Cixous primarily through the translations of "The Laugh of the Medusa" ("Le Rire de la Meduse," 1975) and *The Newly Born Woman* (*La Jeune Nee*, 1975). Her first book, *The Exile of Joyce, or the Art of Replacement*, appeared in 1972. Translated later were her essays on the Brazilian novelist Clarice Lispector, Kafka, Marina Tsvetaeva, and others. She has also written more than twenty fictional works and several works for theater since 1969.

Betsy Wing, an important translator of and commentator on Cixous, has written that the English-speaking world knows Cixous primarily as a major contributor to feminist theory, specifically in "her attempts to locate the underlying structures governing language and society that contain women in a position of passivity, and her formulation of a feminine libidinal economy as a positive force to achieving freedom from those constraints" (Wing 1991:v). Wing, however, points out that theory has never been Cixous' sole metier. She has used her fictional, dramatic, and poetic texts as primary sites wherein she has struggled to decenter and set aside the limitations imposed upon women by European and Western society.

Cixous uses Lacanian psychoanalytic theory as a starting point for many productive essays in which she examines the clichés of accepted concepts of femininity that have kept women "in their place" in society. Her method is to push these concepts to the level of hyperbole, as a means of demanding that they be taken seriously and critiqued. In this way she attempts to distance her reader from the acceptance of such categories as natural or benign.

Cixous proceeded from the idea that theory and practice must be linked. This led to the development of a practice she calls "writing the body," in which she locates agency, not in a fixed identity or persona but in moments of time and space. In this way she attempts to recuperate the lost knowledge contained in women's bodies and, as an extension, in their writing. She utilizes this approach in both her theoretical and poetic works.

Mary Foertsch
Bentley College

Bibliography

Cixous, Hélène. *The Book of Promethea*. Trans. and Intro. Betsy Wing. Lincoln: U of Nebraska P, 1991.

———. "The Laugh of the Medusa." *The SIGNS Reader*. Ed. Elizabeth Abel and Emily K. Abel. Chicago: U of Chicago P, 1983. 279–97.

Cixous, Hélène, and Catherine Clement. *The Newly Born Woman*. Trans. Betsy Wing. Minneapolis: U of Minnesota P, 1986.

Conley, Verena Andermatt. *Hélène Cixous: Writing the Feminine*. Lincoln: U of Nebraska P, 1984.

Nordquist, Joan. *French Feminist Theory: Luce Irigiray and Hélène Cixous: A Bibliography*. Santa Cruz, CA: Reference and Research Services, 1990.

Clarity

Clearness of style; lucidity; without obscurity, vagueness, or ambiguity. Clarity has often been associated with other stylistic qualities such as plainness, simplicity, lack of adornment, and appropriateness. In addition to obscurity, vagueness, and ambiguity, features considered antithetical to clarity are pomposity, wordiness, and imprecison. Writers who would be "clear" are admonished to avoid jargon, to select words carefully, and to construct sentences that are compact, unified, and properly arranged.

Clarity has been consistently advocated in treatises on rhetoric or writing, beginning with those of ancients such as Aristotle, Cicero, and Quintilian, but the length and nature of such treatments vary considerably. Cicero's coverage, for example, is rather sparse, while Quintilian's is somewhat more detailed—although he devotes most of his discussion of style to ornament and embellishment. Perhaps one of the more complete discussions is housed within George Campbell's *Philosophy of Rhetoric* (1776). That work dedicates a substantial chapter in Book II to "perspicuity" (a synonym for clarity), systematically outlining the ways in which it can be violated. Because of their varying lengths and differences in content and organization, an examination of such treatments does not necessarily provide a clear, coherent sense of what clarity is or how to attain it. As with earlier works, contemporary style manuals and handbooks also differ with regard to their treatments of clarity. Some include the category "clarity" within their indexes, some do not. For those works that provide coverage, clarity can be associated with word use only or with the proper construction of sentences as well. A popular, current style manual that offers a well-argued defense for clarity and detailed strategies for its attainment is Joseph Williams's *Style: Ten Lessons in Clarity and Grace*.

Most rhetoricians and stylists recommend (and have recommended) clarity, associating its absence with sloth, lack of skill, dishonesty, sloppiness, pretention, lack of something to say, or deliberately exclusionary practices to exercise power and control. Despite the long tradition of considering clarity a laudable and attainable virtue, however, several problems, some perennial and some contemporary, have been and are associated with it. Historically, even advocates of clarity have needed to complicate their prescriptions because of the issues raised by context; suggestions to "avoid unfamiliar terminology" (unfamiliar to whom?) or to "use the proper word to designate an object" (proper under what circumstances?) are not always useful. In addition, some current theorists believe that clarity implies a correspondence theory of language, wherein words can unequivocally stand for things in a one-to-one relationship. Adherents of this view argue that meaning cannot be made fixed and determinate, and that unresolvable ambiguity permeates discourse. Finally, a number of contemporary writers have critiqued the notion of clarity on political grounds, claiming that "clear" discourse manipulates its receivers by assimilating them into the reigning order or ideology without their knowledge.

Alice Calderonello
Bowling Green State University

Bibliography

Consigny, Scott. "Transparency and Displacement: Aristotle's Concept of Rhetorical Clarity." *Rhetoric Society Quarterly* 17, 4 (1987): 413–19.

Dasenbrock, Reed. "J.L. Austin and the Articulation of a New Rhetoric." *College Composition and Communication* 38 (1987): 291–305.

Kenner, Hugh. "The Politics of Plain Style." *New York Times Book Review*. September 15, 1985: 1, 39–40.

Lanham, Richard. *Style: An Anti-Textbook*. New Haven: Yale UP, 1978.

Orwell, George. "Politics and the English Language." *Language Awareness*. 2nd ed. Ed. Paul Eschholz, Afred Rosa, and Virginia Clark. New York: St. Martin's, 1978.

Pringle, Ian. "Why Teach Style: A Review Essay." *College Composition and Communication* 34 (1983): 91–98.

Williams, Joseph. *Style: Ten Lessons in Clarity and Grace*. Glenview, IL: Scott, 1989.

Classification

A method for organizing large numbers of items into discrete categories. Classification is the act of grouping similar items into separate categories based on some principle. The fact that libraries, supermarkets, department stores, and newspaper advertisement sections use classification demonstrates that this method of organization is commonplace in everyday life.

In rhetoric, classification is one of many ways to organize an expository paragraph or essay. Whenever a writer faces the task of differentiating a number of similar items into separate groupings, the practice of classification provides an efficient framework. Classification differs significantly from division or partition. Whereas division or partition always involves one object only, which is systematically taken apart and analyzed piece by piece, classification is the act of sorting many items into separate groups based on some similarity. For instance, a single refrigerator can be partitioned into its component parts, whereas home appliances can be classified into refrigerators, washers, dryers, stoves, microwave ovens, dishwashers, and so on.

In classical rhetoric, many of the practices that writers today think of as ways to organize ideas were used as ways to discover and develop ideas. In Book 2 of the *Rhetoric*, Aristotle discusses *topoi*, or topics, which "constituted a method for probing one's subject to discover possible ways of developing that subject" (Corbett 24). Although Aristotle does not specifically mention classification as a method of developing one's ideas, he does discuss a number of other methods, such as definition, comparison, contrast, cause, effect, and others.

The *OED* credits Edmund Burke (1729–1797) as the first user of the word *classification* in English. During the eighteenth and nineteenth centuries, Aristotle's topics formed the basis for expanding the ways to organize or arrange paragraphs and essays. One of the first nineteenth-century rhetoricians to articulate the four modes of discourse—narration, description, exposition, and argument (or persuasion)—was Alexander Bain (1818–1903), in *English Composition and Rhetoric* (1866). Although Bain does not mention classification, the term began to appear as one of several methods of organizing essays, along with illustration or exemplification, comparison/contrast, cause/effect, partition, and process analysis.

While classification has been used more conventionally during most of the twentieth century as a method for organizing essays and paragraphs, classification and other traditional methods of organization since the 1960s have come to be used as tools of invention, of systematically exploring subjects in order to develop ideas for an essay. This use has helped to blur the sometimes rigid distinction between the first two parts of rhetoric, invention and arrangement. Frank D'Angelo has suggested that classification and other methods of organizing essays are systematized ways in which many human minds in the Western tradition process information.

David Sabrio
Texas A&M University, Kingsville

Bibliography

Aristotle. *The Art of Rhetoric*. Trans. John Henry Freese. Cambridge, MA: Harvard UP, 1926.

Bain, Alexander. *English Composition and Rhetoric. A Manual*. 1866. New York: Appleton, 1876.

Connors, Robert. "The Rise and Fall of the Modes of Discourse." *College Composition and Communication* 32 (1981): 444–63.

Corbett, Edward P.J. *Classical Rhetoric for the Modern Student*. 3rd ed. New York: Oxford UP, 1990.

D'Angelo, Frank J. *A Conceptual Theory of Rhetoric*. Cambridge, MA: Winthrop, 1975.

———. "Paradigms as Structural Counterparts of *Topoi*." *Linguistics, Stylistics, and the Teaching of Composition*. Ed. Donald McQuade. Akron, OH: U of Akron Dept. of English, 1979.

See also MODES OF DISCOURSE

Cognitive Rhetoric

Describes writing as a performative act, as a way of entering into rhetorical situations and discourse communities, often characterized by unique, unstable rules and expectations. The central question driving cognitive rhetoric is, How do rhetors, as goal-directed thinkers *and* as complex social beings, construct meaning and communicate with others within an immense and little-understood social context? Cognitive rhetoric contends that inquiry into this open question is itself a rhetorical act, where the rigor of one's argument comes from fine-grained analysis of observations and from tests of reliability (that is, the extent to which interpretations can be corroborated). Acknowledging the interpretive basis of its claims, cognitive rhetoric is an effort to make theory accountable to the rich and contrary data of experience.

The Nature of the Writing Process

Cognitive rhetoric emerged at the beginning of the 1970s from early research into the nature of the writing process. Janet Emig explored territory that the product-oriented current-traditional paradigm had left uncharted, asking, What are the specifiable elements in the composing process and how can we name them? What bearing do these elements in the composing process have on one another? Launching inquiry into the writing process, her work borrowed from the social sciences to introduce several research methods that have become mainstays in the repertoire of writing research, including think-aloud protocols and extensive interviews.

The basic research of the 1970s depended on observational methods and fine-grained analyses. It led to widely accepted generalizations about writing as a goal-oriented, problem-solving activity. The 1980 Hayes/Flower model described writing as organized recursively across three main processes: planning, translating text, and revising. In other studies expert-novice comparisons revealed marked group differences, in, for instance, the types of goals writers in each group tend to set for themselves, the degree to which they attend to readers' needs while planning, the strategic repertoires that each group accesses when writing, and the flexibility with which they use plans and heuristics. This research claimed that writing depends on a complex repertoire of processes, assumptions, and abilities, but that, as an activity, writing is far more teachable, critical, and empowering than the current-traditional paradigm had assumed.

The Social-Cognitive Web

What began primarily as an inquiry into the basic underlying processes involved in writing has become an effort to investigate the richly tangled web that binds cognition and context— to understand the situated cognition of different writers in different settings. Attempting to build a more inclusive social-cognitive theory of writing, cognitive rhetoric focused on the question, How does the rhetor operate as an agent and meaning-maker within the social and cultural structures, assumptions, conventions, and settings that allow and shape meaning? To address this question, researchers added ethnographic and sociolinguistic methods of discourse analysis to their methodological repertoire, and they further adapted process-tracing tools to tap writers' awareness of the contexts in which their work was situated.

Recognizing that cognitive processes do not exist in the abstract, studies in cognitive rhetoric have begun to show how writing is influenced not only by the structure of the task but also by the way individual writers represent the task to themselves, by social rules, by the ongoing interaction of people involved, and by the wider social and cultural milieu. Moving from observation to theoretical insight, cognitive rhetoric posited three general principles: that cultural and social context cues cognition; that the context is mediated by the cognition of the individual writer; and that the bounded purposes that emerge from this process are, though highly constrained, meaningful rhetorical acts.

Negotiation

Cognitive rhetoric is committed to pedagogy that speaks to the needs of individual writers, especially those student writers who traditionally have not been well served by the educational system's policies and practices. As part of an ongoing effort to refine its *praxis,* cognitive rhetoric has recently begun inquiring into the ways writers actively negotiate language, discourse conventions, social structures, and material influences. These negotiations are considered crossroads where individuals and social forces are not only active but also often in conflict. Analysis of these points of conflict works to identify discursive practices, options, goals, and constraints and their impact on literate action. This more specific line of inquiry is part of an extended effort to unravel further the ways that thinking and social context are functionally intertwined.

Elenore Long and Linda Flower
Carnegie Mellon University

Bibliography

Applebee, Arthur N. "Problems in Process Approaches: Toward a Reconceptualization of Process Instruction." *The Teaching of Writing.* Ed. David Bartholomae and Anthony Petrosky. Chicago: National Society for the Study of Education, 1985. 95–113.

Bereiter, Carl, and Marlene Scardamalia. *The Psychology of Written Composition.* Hillsdale, NJ: Erlbaum, 1987.

Bridwell, Lillian. "Revising Strategies in Twelfth Grade Students' Transactional Writing." *Research in the Teaching of English* 3 (1980): 197–222.

Britton, James, Tony Burgess, Alex Martin, and Harold Rosen. *The Development of Writing Abilities: 11–18.* London: Macmillan, 1975.

Emig, Janet. *The Composing Process of Twelfth Graders.* Urbana, IL: National Council of Teachers of English, 1971.

Flower, Linda. "Cognition, Context, and Theory Building." *College Composition and Communication* 40 (1989): 282–311.

———. "Cognitive Rhetoric: Inquiry into the Art of Inquiry." *Defining the New Rhetorics.* Ed. Theresa Enos and Stuart C. Brown. Newbury Park, CA: Sage, 1993. 171–90.

———. *The Construction of Negotiated Meaning: A Social Cognitive Theory of Writing.* Carbondale: Southern Illinois UP, 1994.

Flower, Linda, and John R. Hayes. "A Cognitive Process Theory of Writing." *College Composition and Communication* 32 (1981): 365–87.

Flower, Linda, Victoria Stein, John Ackerman, Margaret J. Kantz, Kathleen McCormick, and Wayne C. Peck. *Reading-to-Write: Exploring a Cognitive and Social Context.* New York: Oxford UP, 1990.

Freedman, Sarah W., Anne Haas Dyson, Linda Flower, and Wallace Chafe. *Research in Writing: Past, Present, and Future.* Center for the Study of Writing. Technical Report No. 1. U of California at Berkeley, 1987.

Hayes, John R., Linda Flower, Karen A. Schriver, James F. Stratman, and Linda Carey. "Cognitive Processes in Revision." *Advances in Applied Psycholinguistics: Reading, Writing and Language Processing.* Ed. Sheldon Rosenberg. Cambridge: Cambridge UP, 1987. 176–240.

Heath, Shirley B. *Ways with Words: Language, Life, and Work in Communities.* Cambridge: Cambridge UP, 1983.

Hull, Glynda, and Mike Rose. "Rethinking Remediation: Toward a Social-Cognitive Understanding of Problematic Reading and Writing." *Written Communication* 6 (1989): 139–54.

Odell, Lee, and Dixie Goswami. "Writing in a Non-Academic Setting." *Research in the Teaching of English* 16 (1983): 201–23.

Ogbu, John. "Education, Clientage, and Social Mobility: Caste and Social Change in the United States and Nigeria." *Social Inequality: Comparative and Developmental Approaches.* Ed. Gerald D. Berreman. New York: Academic, 1981. 227–306.

Perl, Sondra. "The Composing Process of Unskilled College Writers." *Research in the Teaching of English* 13 (1979): 317–36.

Rogoff, Barbara, and Jean Lave, eds. *Everyday Cognition: Its Development in Social Context.* Cambridge: Cambridge UP, 1984.

Rose, Mike, ed. *When a Writer Can't Write: Studies in Writer's Block and Other Composing-Process Problems.* New York: Guilford, 1985. 227–61.

Witte, Stephen. "Pre-Text and Composing." *College Composition and Communication* 38 (1987): 397–425.

Coherence

The logical connectedness of ideas that readers or listeners perceive in a written or oral text. While linguists consider cohesion to comprise the relationships among elements in texts themselves, coherence occurs when readers and listeners process—that is, read or listen to—those texts. The cohesion of a text does not necessarily correlate with the coherence that results when a human encounters that text. For one thing, cohesive devices can be counted. Any text has X number of such devices; it is a quantitative measure. Coherence, however, is qualitative judgment; a text that is judged to be very coherent for one person may be relatively incoherent for another. The judgment, whether explicit or implicit, depends on such factors as the reader/listener's familiarity with the topic and the genre, the reader/listener's proficiency at reading or listening, the extent to which the ideas in a text correspond to the reader/listener's experiences in the world, the kinds and quantities of explicit cohesive devices in the text, the underlying connectedness of ideas in the text, and the correspondence between the cohesive devices and the connectedness of ideas.

Take, for example, this very short text: "John repaired the truck. Linda is happy." We could insert the word *therefore* at the beginning of the second sentence to specify the relationship between the ideas in the two sentences. For some readers, that insertion would make our short text more coherent, more easily read or listened to. For other readers, the insertion may do little to affect coherence because they may readily infer that Linda is happy because John repaired the truck. If we were to insert the word *nevertheless* at the beginning of the second sentence, many readers would probably find the text less coherent because they would have difficulty understanding the semantic relationship between the two sentences. By adding another sentence to the text, though, we could once again enhance its coherence: "John repaired the truck. Nevertheless, Linda is happy. She will be able to take a nap while he takes an afternoon drive." Now we can infer that Linda wanted to spend time with John, but she will make the most of his absence by using that time alone to rest. If one idea seems to flow naturally out of the preceding ones, coherence is relatively strong. If not, it is relatively weak.

While serious scholars of texts use the terms *cohesion* and *coherence* as they are used here, some textbooks use the terms more loosely. In some cases the terms are used interchangeably. In other cases *coherence* is used to denote both concepts. The precise use of the terms, however, is less important than the understanding of how writers and speakers can make ideas flow from one to another.

Texts can be coherent at what is called the "local level" and the "global level." Local-level coherence is that which occurs within small portions of texts, usually within chunks no larger than a paragraph. A text is said to have global coherence, on the other hand, if the text hangs together as a whole.

Duane H. Roen
Arizona State University

Bibliography

Christensen, Francis. "A Generative Rhetoric of the Paragraph." *Notes Toward a New Rhetoric: Six Essays for Teachers.* New York: Harper, 1967. 52–81.

Coe, Richard M. *Toward a Grammar of Passages.* Carbondale: Southern Illinois UP, 1988.

Connor, Ulla, and Ann M. Johns. *Coherence in Writing.* Alexandria, VA: TESOL, 1990.

Fennald, James C. *Connectives of English Speech: The Correct Usage of Prepositions, Conjunctions, Relative Pronouns and Adverbs Explained and Illustrated.* New York: Funk, 1904.

Halliday, M.A.K., and Ruqaiya Hasan. *Cohesion in English.* New York: Longman, 1976.

Markels, Robin Bell. *A New Perspective on Cohesion in Expository Paragraphs.* Carbondale: Southern Illinois UP, 1984.

Tannen, Deborah, ed. *Coherence in Spoken and Written Discourse.* Norwood, NJ: Ablex, 1984.

See also COHESION

Cohesion

A semantic relationship between two elements in a written or oral text—a presupposing element and a presupposed element. The interpretation of the presupposing element depends on the presupposed element. The two elements may be words, phrases, or clauses. If they occur within adjacent sentences, they form what is called an immediate tie: "*Nick* adores Michael Jordan. *He* also likes basketball." If they are linked through an item in an intervening sentence, there is a mediated tie: "*Hanna* loves to dance. *She* attends lessons each Saturday. *She* seems to improve each week." If two cohesive elements occur in nonadjacent sentences, they form a remote tie: "*Lindsay* is eight now. That's a fun age. I wish that we could see *her* more often."

The major forms of cohesion are reference, substitution, ellipsis, lexical cohesion, and conjunction. In English, reference involves the use of personal pronouns, demonstratives, and comparatives: "*Annie* likes *books*. *She* has a bookcase filled with *them*." In substitution, one linguistic item replaces another: "I bought this *chair* at an auction of antiques. You should have seen the *one* that I couldn't afford." Ellipsis may be thought of as the omission of an item from a text or as a form of substitution in which an item is replaced by nothing, by the null set. Something is left unsaid, but it is understood: "Abby wants to use your *computer*. Hers *0* is in the shop for repair." Lexical cohesion results from the reiteration of an item, the use of a synonym, a near synonym, or a superordinate term: "Jack drives a *Mustang*. That's one hot *car*." Conjunction is simply a semantic relation in which the conjunctive element explicitly specifies how the immediately forthcoming segment of text is systematically connected with the immediately preceding segment: "Megan is only two. *Nevertheless*, she can carry on quite a conversation." There are four major kinds of conjunctive relations. In an additive relation, one segment is added to another: "Molly loves to eat lutefisk. *Furthermore*, she's a big fan of lefse." In an adversative relation, one element is placed in opposition with another: "Michael wishes that he were Norwegian. *However*, his parents are Irish." In a causal relation, one item is the cause, the other the effect: "Matthew eats Norwegian food. *Therefore*, he is healthy as a horse." In a temporal relationship, items are chronologically ordered: "Eileen flew to Oslo. *Then* she took a ship to see the fjords."

Cohesion is not the same as coherence in the text linguistics and discourse analysis literature. While cohesion comprises linguistic elements in the text itself, coherence results from a reader's interaction with a text. A text filled with cohesive elements may be relatively coherent for one reader and relatively incoherent for another.

Duane H. Roen
Arizona State University

Bibliography
Coe, Richard M. *Toward a Grammar of Passages.* Carbondale: Southern Illinois UP, 1988.
Connor, Ulla, and Ann M. Johns. *Coherence in Writing.* Alexandria, VA: TESOL, 1990.
Halliday, M.A.K., and Ruqaiya Hasan. *Cohesion in English.* New York: Longman, 1976.
Markels, Robin Bell. *A New Perspective on Cohesion in Expository Paragraphs.* Carbondale: Southern Illinois UP, 1984.
Tannen, Deborah, ed. *Coherence in Spoken and Written Discourse.* Norwood, NJ: Ablex, 1984.

Coleridge, Samuel Taylor (1772–1834)

Pamphleteer, preacher, lecturer, and matchless conversationalist (who dictated many of his later works). Coleridge was highly sensitive to the demands of rhetoric in both oral and written form and commented frequently on the matter. He recommended Aristotle's *Rhetoric* as one of those major philosophical books by means of reading which every four or five years one could ascertain whether one's mind continued to "grow." Yet his contribution to rhetoric went by other names and was grounded upon new principles.

His negative critique had been anticipated by eighteenth-century critics such as Samuel Johnson, Hugh Blair, and George Campbell. In *Biographia Literaria* (1817), Coleridge recalls his early distaste for artificial poetic diction and reiterates his support for Wordsworth's (and his own) "reformation": "He has evinced the truth of passion, and the *dramatic* propriety of those figures and metaphors in the original poets, which stript of their justifying reasons, and converted into mere artifices of connection or ornament, constitute the characteristic falsity in the poetic style of the moderns." Elsewhere "rhetorical caprices" are condemned as inorganic, though it is not the tropes and figures in themselves to which Coleridge objects so much as their dissociation from powerful thought and sincere feeling. At the same time, Coleridge rejects Wordsworth's singling out of humble and rustic life as the main source of poetic language and his denial of the essential difference between verse and prose. A poet does not copy ordinary language because the "apparent naturalness of the *representation*" is "raised and qualified by an imperceptible infusion of the author's own knowledge and talent." Poetry differs from prose chiefly by the incorporation of meter which simultaneously heightens and regulates intensity, effecting a "balance in the mind." Generally, Coleridge distinguishes three styles: verse (with meter), prose, and a third or neutral style, "the language of conversation."

The main elements of his positive contribution are creative imitation, organic form, the reconciliation of opposites, and the imagination. Delivered following his study of Kant and German philosophy and criticism, the Shakespeare lectures (1811–1813) present his mature theory combined with superb practical criticism. Whereas the form is "mechanic when on any given material we impress a pre-determined form, not necessarily arising out of the properties of the material," organic form is "innate; it shapes as it develops itself from within, and the fullness of its development is one and the same with the perfection of its outward form." The various elements of a poetic composition (image, meter, syntax, tone, thought, and feeling) must "mutually support" and "explain" one another. In the *Biographia Literaria*, he explores the nature of imagination, not seen as a part of the mind but a "strong working" of the whole mind as it "struggles" to "unify": "The poet brings the whole soul of man into activity, with the subordination of its faculties to each other, according to their relative worth and dignity." Ideally, the poet and statesman address the "all in each" of all persons.

The "Essays on Method" (published in the 1818 *Friend*) cover ground given in classical rhetoric to *dispositio* or *taxis*. In keeping with his organicist approach, he advances a theory of method as "progressive transition" or "unity with progression." A valid method "results from a balance between the passive impression received from outward things, and the internal activity of the mind in reflecting and generalizing." While impressions are collected and arranged by the understanding, the internal activity of the reason commences with an "initiative" or "leading thought" driven by a "'subtile, cementing, subterraneous' power," and as the initiative is greater in scope, so the series of transitions will embrace a larger whole "through all its ramifications": "From the first, or initiative Idea, as from a seed, successive Ideas germinate." The concept of interrelatedness and development, based upon a higher principle or "indwelling power," is fundamentally associated with the Coleridgean *natura naturans*, the active process in nature or growth into unity, of which the power of imaginative creativity and its products (symbols, poetry) are analogous.

In one educational schema, Coleridge proposes the study of "Language, Composition, Oratory, [and] Mathematics" by pupils between their twelfth and eighteenth years, with history and beginning logic introduced at fifteen. According to his *Logic* (written in the 1820s and not published in his lifetime), pupils should first learn words and grammar, then the art of arranging words and sentences, or the "logic of sentences," for which he coined the term *rhematic*. Third was "rhetoric" or "the art of declaiming persuasively," and then logic. The addition of "rhematic" to the classical trivium emphasizes the importance of sequenced learning and the developmental process; in applying the organic idea to education, he secures an intermediate landing-stage, between the study of definitions and the macrostructure, for the study of local context. The *Logic* explores the origins of language, its role in education, its relation to thought, the priority of grammar, desynonymization and "distinguishing the similar from the same," and natural and arbitrary signs. Had Coleridge found a publisher, there are indications that the work might have been called "Elements of Discourse" or "On the Power and Use of Words."

As befits someone who coined the word *marginalia*, Coleridge's insights on rhetorical subjects are scattered across his works (notebooks, table talk, letters). He gave instructions on how to prepare and deliver a lecture (letter to James Briton, February 28, 1819), arguing against reading from prepared text in favor of spontaneity as "best fitted to answer the purposes of a lecture, that is, to keep the audience awake and interested during the delivery, and to leave a sting behind, that is, a disposition to study the subject anew, under the light of a new principle."

Coleridge exerted an enormous influence on twentieth-century criticism. In *Coleridge on Imagination* (1934), which refounded Coleridgean studies, I.A. Richards translates Coleridge's metaphysics into psychological terms and shows its applicability to textual criticism; inspired by Coleridgean organicism, his *Philosophy of Rhetoric* (1936) introduces a new approach to rhetoric and metaphor. Through Richards, among others, the American "new critics" absorbed Coleridgean organicism and contextualism.

John Paul Russo
University of Miami

Bibliography

Barilli, Renato. *Rhetoric*. Trans. Giuliana Menozzi. Minneapolis: U of Minnesota P, 1989.

Bate, Walter Jackson. *Coleridge*. New York: Macmillan, 1968.

Christensen, Jerome. *Coleridge's Blessed Machine of Language*. Ithaca, NY: Cornell UP, 1981.

The Collected Works of Samuel Taylor Coleridge. Ed. Kathleen Coburn. Princeton and London: Bollingen and Routledge and Kegan Paul, 1969.

Engell, James. *The Creative Imagination: Enlightenment to Romanticism*. Cambridge, MA: Harvard UP, 1981.

Esterhammer, Angela. "Speech Acts and Living Words: On Performative Language in Coleridge's 1798 Poems." *Wordsworth Circle* 24 (1993): 79–83.

Fulford, Tim. *Coleridge's Figurative Language*. New York: St. Martin's, 1991.

Jackson, J.R. de J. Introduction. *Logic* in *Collected Works*, 1981.

McKusick, James C. *Coleridge's Philosophy of Language*. New Haven: Yale UP, 1986.

Marks, Emerson R. *Coleridge on the Language of Verse*. Princeton: Princeton UP, 1981.

Richards, I.A. *The Philosophy of Rhetoric*. New York: Oxford UP, 1936.

Smith, Olivia. *The Politics of Language, 1791–1819*. New York: Oxford UP, 1984.

Wilson, Douglas. "Two Modes of Apprehending Nature: A Gloss on the Coleridgean Symbol." *PMLA* 87 (1972): 42–52.

Coles, William E., Jr. (b. 1932)

An important teacher and theorist of composition. William E. Coles, Jr., has taught since 1974 in the Department of English at the University of Pittsburgh, where for many years he was director of composition. Before that, Professor Coles taught at the University of Connecticut (where he got his M.A. in 1955), the University of Minnesota (where he got his Ph.D. in 1968), Amherst College (during the era of the English 1–2 sequence that is associated with Theodore Baird), Case Western Reserve University, and Drexel University. For four summers (1977–1980), Professor Coles directed a National Endowment for the Humanities Summer Seminar titled "Teaching Writing: Theories and Practices." Since 1980 he has designed and taught honors writing courses for undergraduates at the University of Pittsburgh, as well as writing courses for continuing education students. He has been a consultant for a number of writing program faculties at various high schools, colleges, and universities, and he conducts workshops on writing across the curriculum.

Professor Coles has written six books and many articles concerned with teaching composition. His books are built upon sequences of writing assignments conceived of less as a series of directions for students than invitations to examine a core subject from different perspectives. Coles's later writings emphasize the ways in which these sequences may be seen as a kind of story designed to engender other stories. *Seeing through Writing* (1988), for example, presents a sequence of twelve assignments created by a shadowy teacher-persona called the Gorgon; a series of fictional sketches accompanying the assignments shows the Gorgon's students working through the issue, each in a profoundly original way.

Coles speaks frequently (as in the subtitle of *Composing*) of writing as a "self-creating process." This has led some commentators to identify him as an "expressivist." But Coles is very careful to say that the self he is concerned with is a "literary" self—the self that may be inferred from the language that has been used and not some autonomous self presumed to exist beyond language (1988:8). For Coles, as a teacher of composition, the self that matters is the one that is composed, not the self that we may take to be "expressed." Of course this composed self may be composed to mean and to matter in more than one way, as the title of one of his books, *The Plural I*, implies.

Coles's approach to teaching composition is probably best understood as literary, in the sense that he sees composition as creations which can and must be questioned in the same way we question literature. Coles sees writing and teaching writing as a matter of "style" finally—a matter of the consequences for meaning of how we choose to put language together. Thus his work stands as an abiding critique of certain aspirations to "disciplinarity" in composition. In a postmodern age, it offers a model—many models—of how to show students that it matters how language is composed.

John Warnock
University of Arizona

C

Bibliography

Coles, William E., Jr. *Composing: Writing as a Self-Creating Process*. Rochelle Park, NJ: Hayden, 1974.

———. *Composing II*. Rochelle Park, NJ: Hayden, 1981.

———. "Freshman Composition: The Circle of Unbelief." *College English* 31 (1969): 134–42.

———. "Literacy for the Eighties: An Alternative to Losing." *Literacy for Life*. Ed. R.W. Bailey and R.M. Fosheim. New York: Modern Language Assn., 1983. 248–62. Republished as "Writing as Literacy: An Alternative to Losing." *The Plural I—and After*. Portsmouth, NH: Boynton/Cook, 1988. 278–98.

———. *The Plural I: Teaching Writing*. New York: Holt, 1978. Republished with two additional essays as *The Plural I—and After*. Portsmouth, NH: Boynton/Cook, 1988.

———. *Seeing through Writing*. New York: Harper, 1988.

———. "The Sense of Nonsense as a Design for Sequential Writing Assignments." *College Composition and Communication* 21 (1970): 27–34.

———. *Teaching Composing: A Guide to Teaching Writing as a Self-Creating Process*. Rochelle Park, NJ: Hayden, 1974.

———. "The Teaching of Writing as Writing." *College English* 29 (1967): 111–16.

Coles, William E., Jr., and James Vopat. *What Makes Writing Good: A Multiperspective*. Lexington, MA: Heath, 1985.

Collaboration

Humans working together. Within the field of rhetoric and composition, interest in collaboration gained much momentum in the 1980s. In many ways this interest is a response to nineteenth-century Romanticism, which still prevails in many humanities departments at the end of the twentieth century. The Romantic view is that the inspired individual, often working alone in a dimly lit and poorly heated garret, finds the emotion and imagination to express great ideas. Complementing this view is a capitalistic view of intellectual property. That is, individuals should protect their ownership of ideas because there is profit to be had. Walter Ong, in *The Presence of the Word*, argues that such notions about individual ownership of knowledge or ideas—of individual authority—are necessary by-products of moving from an oral-aural economy of knowledge, where knowledge is "ours," to a literate one, where knowledge is "mine." Roland Barthes, in his essay "The Death of the Author," and Michel Foucault, in "What Is an Author," argue that the modern concept of individual authorship is Western and relatively recent. Martha Woodmansee, in "The Genius and the Copyright: Economic and Legal Conditions of the Emergence of the 'Author,'" illustrates how the profit motive did much to promote this modern concept.

Scholars interested in collaboration commonly draw upon social-constructionist theory, which holds that knowledge is socially constructed and therefore varies from culture to culture. (More than two millennia ago, Plato attacked the sophists for holding a similar view.) Socially constructed knowledge and discourse exist within what has been called discourse communities, language communities, or speech communities. There are, of course, many variations on the theme of social-constructionism. For example, the Soviet cognitive psychologist Lev Vygotsky argues that human activity, especially thinking and language use, is social first and subsequently individual. It is from this position that he derived his now well-known concept of the zone of proximal development, which he describes in detail in *Mind in Society*. Another Soviet theorist, Mikhail Bakhtin, argues in "Discourse in the Novel" that the language that any individual uses is filled with the thinking and the language of other people, both living and dead, whose ideas and words are swirling around in the individual language user's head. Bakhtin refers to this mixture as "heteroglossia," or "the Tower-of-Babel mixing of languages." This has occurred, Bakhtin says, since the appearance of the second human being on Earth.

From Bakhtin's position scholars argue that it is virtually impossible for anyone to claim sole ownership of ideas or words. Therefore, even when only one name appears on the byline of a written text, the nominal "author" of that text is uttering words shared with many other people. All language use, including writing, is unavoidably collaborative.

Scholars and other writers have described their own and others' versions of collaborative writing. The accounts are as varied as those who offer them, and seldom does any team of collaborators compose the same way more than once. At times collaborators work side by side in the same room, pondering each word and phrase together. At other times they may shuffle drafts back and forth several or dozens of times. Or they may each compose separate parts individually and then work together to meld those portions.

The degree to which scholars explicitly collaborate varies considerably across disciplines. In the humanities, where the Romantic concept of individual genius prevails, explicit collaboration or coauthorship is relatively rare. In other fields, however, especially ones in which various forms of empirical work occur, the practice is more common. One need only browse through journals in education, science, social science, medicine, and engineering to realize the extent to which explicit collaboration occurs in these fields.

Collaboration in the classroom also extends to the ways in which students learn. Kenneth Bruffee argues that learning collaboratively can be seen as a process of constructing or reconstructing knowledge socially, such that all facts consist of negotiated facticity. The goals of collaborative learning thus involve nurturing processes of intellectual negotiation, critical thinking, and acting in democratic ways.

Within writing classrooms, collaboration can occur in many ways. Students can coauthor written discourse. They can also respond to peers' drafts of papers. Within the context of reader-response pedagogies, such as Louise Rosenblatt's, they can share their thinking about the subject of study. With modern computer technologies, students can easily share the written word as well as the oral, through electronic conferences and multiple-user screens, among others.

Collaborative learning can also serve to build solidarity among students. At the same time, it challenges foundationalist assumptions of knowledge and traditional conceptions of the teacher's authority and role as the central power broker in the classroom. In effect, it may create a crisis of authority for both teachers and students. Thus, collaborative learning requires the rethinking of our roles as facilitators of critical thinking and education, as well as our students' repositioning as active learners and agents in their own educations.

Toward these ends Harvey Weiner offers some useful suggestions for determining clear criteria for success in the collaborative learning classroom. Among them are the stipulations that the tasks offer students opportunities for intellectual negotiation, that students have the freedom to collaborate without excessive intervention from the instructor, that tasks be written down for the benefit of metalinguistic appraisal by the group, and that consensus as well as dissent be acknowledged for purposes of examining the reasoning used to develop and shape ideas.

On the whole, collaboration is a valuable means of maximizing the student's engagement in the writing classroom. While it is not without its problematic dimensions, collaborative learning has proven its usefulness in the application of workshops, peer conferences, and collaborative projects to situations that clearly mirror circumstances students may encounter in their future careers.

Geraldine McNenny
University of Houston, Downtown
Duane H. Roen
Arizona State University

Bibliography

Bakhtin, Mikhail. "Discourse in the Novel." *The Dialogic Imagination*. Trans. and Ed. Michael Holquist. Austin: U of Texas P, 1981. 259–422.

———. *Speech Genres and Other Late Essays*. Trans. Vern W. McGee. Ed. Caryl Emerson and Michael Holquist. Austin: U of Texas P, 1986.

Berger, Peter L., and Thomas Luckman. *The Social Construction of Reality: A Treatise in the Sociology of Knowledge*. New York: Doubleday, 1966.

Bruffee, Kenneth A. "Social Construction, Language, and the Authority of Knowledge: A Bibliographical Essay." *College English* 48 (1986): 773–90.

Clark, Gregory. *Dialogue, Dialectic, and Conversation: A Social Perspective on the Function of Writing*. Carbondale: Southern Illinois UP, 1990.

Ede, Lisa, and Andrea Lunsford. *Singular Texts/Plural Authors: Perspectives on Collaborative Writing*. Carbondale: Southern Illinois UP, 1990.

Forman, Janis, ed. *New Visions of Collaborative Writing*. Portsmouth, NH: Boynton/Cook, 1992.

Foucault, Michel. "What Is an Author?" Trans. Donald F. Bouchard and Sherry Simon. *Critical Theory Since 1965*. Ed. Hazard Adams and Leroy Searle. Tallahassee: Florida State UP, 1986. 138–48.

Geertz, Clifford. *Works and Lives: The Anthropologist as Author*. Stanford, CA: Stanford UP, 1988.

Gergen, Kenneth J. *The Saturated Self: Dilemmas of Identity in Contemporary Life*. New York: Basic, 1991.

———. "The Social Constructionist Movement in Modern Psychology." *American Psychologist* 40 (1985): 266–75.

Hines, Thomas Jensen. *Collaborative Form: Studies in the Relations of the Arts*. Kent, OH: Kent State UP, 1991.

LeFevre, Karen Burke. *Invention as a Social Act*. Carbondale: Southern Illinois UP, 1987.

Mannheim, Karl. *Ideology and Utopia: An Introduction to the Sociology of Knowledge*. Trans. Louis Wirth and Edward A. Shils. New York: Harcourt, 1959.

Ong, Walter. *The Presence of the Word: Some Prolegomena for Cultural and Religious History*. New Haven: Yale UP, 1967.

Rapoport, Anatol. *Fights, Games, and Debates*. Ann Arbor: U of Michigan P, 1960.

Todorov, Tzvetan. *Mikhail Bakhtin: The Dialogical Principle*. Trans. Wlad Godgick. Minneapolis: U of Minnesota P, 1984.

Trimbur, John. "Beyond Cognition: The Voices of Inner Speech." *Rhetoric Review* 5 (1987): 211–21.

Vygotsky, Lev S. *Mind in Society*. Ed. Michael Cole, Vera John Steiner, Sylvia Scribner, and Ellen Souberman. Cambridge, MA: Harvard UP, 1978.

———. *Thought and Language*. Trans. Eugenia Hanfmann and Gertrude Vakar. Cambridge, MA: MIT P, 1962.

Weiner, Harvey S. "Collaborative Learning in the Classroom: A Guide to Evaluation." *College English* 48 (1986): 52–61.

Commonplaces

Throughout the literatures of both rhetoric and philosophy, understood to be language-constituted regions where ideational connections are made to be recalled. If, for instance, one were praising an individual, certain devices for enhancing the magnitude of deeds accomplished and virtues displayed would surely be in evidence. This is why orations as outwardly different as the economia on Helen by Gorgias and Isocrates are still recognizable creative renderings of the same figure. Closely related to topics, as conceptual lines of argument, discovery, and invention, the stylistic and compositional traits of the commonplace have managed to creep into our modern vernacular, suggesting ranges of meaning that have become fixed, codified, even clichéd.

The popular misconstrual notwithstanding, the traditional understandings of commonplaces, from both Greek and Roman theory, reveal themselves to be powerful pedagogical tools for mastering innovations of rhetorical discourse throughout a myriad of genres and institutional practices. It is this latter sense of commonplace that remains most useful and resourceful for the modern student of rhetoric. From its beginnings as a sort of flamboyant teaching practice, rhetoric has been steeped in tensions between the appropos and the creative. The notorious sophists claimed to be able to teach both in one useful art. The hypnotic stylistic enticements of Gorgias and largely unappreciated dispositional innovations of Isocrates received due censure from Plato, but not before they had established a tradition of mentoring and imitation that rewarded the appreciation and variation of stylistic conventions.

While it was Plato who questioned and temporarily silenced rhetoric's extravagant inventional claims, the real origin of commonplaces as a rhetorical technê must be found in Aristotle. In his *Topica*, and the *Rhetoric*, we find the first sustained analysis of commonplaces as an intersection of style and argument. To take just a single example, that of magnitude (*megathos*), this notion emerges at least three times in the *Rhetoric*: as a *topos* of degree where the nature of the "good" is concerned, as a line of argument in Book II, and later still as a place of magnification and embellishment. While each usage is steeped squarely within recognizable cultural norms, the variation in place and function helps to illustrate the inventional possibilities of commonplaces as well.

It was Cicero who most fully exploited the inventional power of commonplaces. Particularly in *De Inventione*, Cicero regarded disputation over unsettled issues as the very fabric of rhetoric. And within such disputation, varying angles and aspects of the common offer the most productive route to reliable civic judgment.

The modern dream of an architectonic art of rhetoric, which will invent and oversee not only arguments but entire disciples of inquiry, owes a tremendous debt to Cicero's vision of the commonplace. To the extent that the genuinely "novel" is still available to liberal inquiry, it is not likely to follow the strict ordinance of laws and codes. Perhaps the less traveled synthesis of the epistemic and the aesthetic still holds some promise for rhetorical creativity. If so, the contribution of commonplaces will continue to inform rhetorical scholarship.

Thomas B. Farrell
Northwestern University

Bibliography

Aristotle. *On Rhetoric: A Theory of Civil Discourse.* Trans. George A. Kennedy. New York: Oxford UP, 1991.

Cicero, Marcus Tullius. *De Inventione.* Trans. H.M. Hubbell. Cambridge, MA: Harvard UP, 1950.

McKeon, Richard. "Creativity and the Commonplace." *Philosophy and Rhetoric 6* (1973): 199–210.

Vickers, Brian. *In Defence of Rhetoric.* Oxford: Clarendon, 1988.

Communication Theory

(1) A systematic representation of communication or some aspect of communication developed by a scholar or team of scholars; (2) collectively, the body of systematic literature that codifies and explains aspects of communication. Communication theory throughout the twentieth century has been an interdisciplinary endeavor consisting of works from fields such as sociology, anthropology, linguistics, psychology, and philosophy. Most communication theory today is produced in the allied communication fields, including communication, speech communication, rhetoric, mass communication, journalism, broadcasting, and other kindred areas.

The primary source of ideas about communication prior to this century, dating back to ancient times, was rhetoric. Communication theory as such is a product of the twentieth century arising from the development of communication technologies, global politics and economics, progressive and pragmatic ideologies, and the rise of the social sciences. Communication theory has not replaced rhetoric, however, and a healthy intercourse between these two fields exists. The primary distinction between these rhetorical and communication literatures is methodological. Rhetorical theories tend to be based in the humanities, centered on discourse, and interpretive and critical in orientation, while communication theories tend to be based in the social sciences, centered in psychosocial processes, and scientific in orientation. The two traditions do overlap, however, as several works can be included in both bodies of literature. In fact, many European communication theorists, who rely heavily on qualitative and critical methods, clearly oppose the predominant American social scientific mode, while a growing number of communication theorists in the U.S. also eschew quantitative and experimental methods.

Communication theory as taught in most American and European universities has a strong Western bias. This may be in part because Eastern schools of thought tend not to codify and separate communication as a distinct field of study. Still, many Eastern ideas that could contribute to the study of communication have not been adequately integrated into communication theory as understood in the West. At the same time, however, Western ideas about communication are catching on in Asian countries as communication curricula are being established there.

Communication theories are of two types—general and specific. General theories present concepts and describe processes believed to apply to communication in all settings. Specific theories are designed to explain some particular type or context of communication.

General theories address a variety of topics. System theory, for example, attempts to capture the nature of communication systems, the role of information in systems, and feedback processes. Semiotics is the study of signs; the kindred field of linguistics aims to describe and explain language both as a tool of communication and as a cognitive process. Theories of discourse address the ways in which speech is used to express intentions and accomplish goals in interaction. Various theories of message production address communication traits and processes related to message generation in all contexts of communication. Theories of message reception attempt to

C

explain the cognitive processes involved in message interpretation, information organization, persuasion, and social judgment. Other general theories address the nature of interaction and the social construction of meaning, communication and culture, and societal conflict and power.

Numerous specific theories address particular aspects of communication in context. One of the more popular groups of theory, for example, deal with communication in close relationships, including patterns of interaction in relationships, the ways in which relationships develop and dissolve, and communication among friends, in marriage, and in conflict situations. Another body of theory relates to communication in group decision-making and another to communication in organizations. One of the more highly developed areas of theory involves mass communication, which deals with a wide spectrum of topics, such as the impact of media, the functions and uses of mass communication, agenda setting, and media effects.

Whether general or specific, the most fundamental building block of any theory is its concepts. A concept is a set of observations, situations, objects, or ideas believed to have something in common, given a label, and defined; a theory is basically a system of concepts. Certain rudimentary theories, called taxonomies, consist only of an organized set of concepts. Full-blown theories also include explanations, which identify and account for regularities among the concepts. Explanations can take various forms, but all rely on the principle of necessity, which is a designation of some logical force that makes one state of affairs necessary, or contingent, based upon another state of affairs. Causal necessity involves a logical relation between a cause and its effect such that the former is said to bring about the latter. Practical necessity is based on the logical relation between an act and a desired consequent such that to engage in an act is thought to lead to a desired end. Causal explanation ignores human choice while practical choice emphasizes it.

In addition to concepts and explanations, some theories also include norms or ideals. These standards establish criteria for judgment, critique, and improved performance. This aspect of theories specifies a desired state of affairs with which observed events can be compared. It can be used to measure quality, to point out the limitations of an observed set of practices, and to point out cases of social inequity and oppression.

Communication theory as a body of knowledge does not present a coherent picture of communication. Both general and specific theories vary substantially from one another in content and philosophical orientation. Metatheory attempts to explain these differences. It deals with the place of inquiry and theory in the study of communication, including the different assumptions taken by various types of theory. From the 1970s to the present time, considerable debate has been waged on how theories should be built and their uses in communication studies. This debate addresses three sets of philosophical issues—epistemology, ontology, and axiology. Issues of epistemology deal with the place of theory in generating or representing knowledge. Issues of ontology relate to the debate on the nature of human life, and axiological issues arise from the debate on the place of values in theory.

Epistemological issues revolve around what knowledge is and how it should be generated. The epistemological debate addresses such questions as the following: (1) To what extent must knowledge be based on experience? (2) To what extent must knowledge be certain? (3) By what process does knowledge arise? (4) Is knowledge best conceived in parts or wholes? (5) To what extent is knowledge explicit? Some theories tend to assume that knowledge arises from experience, that it aims to achieve certainty, that it is discovered by careful observation and analysis, and that it must be in explicit form. Other theories tend to assume that much knowledge is a priori, that it can never be certain, is often tacit, and that it is constructed in the process of theory-making rather than discovered through observation.

Ontological issues, relating to the nature of the person and social life, include questions such as the following: (1) To what extent do humans make real choices? (2) Is human behavior best explained in terms of states or traits? (3) To what extent is human experience basically individual versus social? (4) To what extent is communication contextual or situational? In this debate some theorists maintain that people do make choices and are therefore not predictable, that traits are chimerical, that human life is largely social rather than individual, and that behavior is situational rather than universal. Others, however, see human behavior as determined and predictable, traitlike, individual, and universal.

Axiological debates center on the place of values in research and theory. Such issues as the following are argued: (1) Can theory be value free? (2) To what extent does the practice of inquiry influence that which is studied? (3) To what extent should scholarship attempt to achieve social change? Value-neutral scholarship falls in line with the assumption that good research and theory is value free, that research should aim to capture reality as it is without influencing it, and that while social knowledge may be used to make social changes, the motive of the researcher or theorist should be strictly to discover reality. Value-conscious scholarship, on the other hand, denies that inquiry can ever be value free, asserts that research always intrudes on the process being studied, and accepts that scholarship can and should be used to make a better world.

The above outline of issues suggests that theories can be neatly classified according to their positions on these issues. Such is not the case. Many overlaps and shades of gray can be seen in the literature. A useful way to express the differences in theory is to identify various genres. These categories can be helpful for seeing differences and similarities among the vast number of extant theories, though their boundaries are not always sharp or the categories always distinct. At least five genres of theory are popular.

Structural and functional theories, originating from thought in sociology, linguistics, and biology, adopt a systems model of social life. In brief, these theories represent behavior as part of a system of social structures. A function is a causal relation among variables such that a change in one variable or group of variables impacts others. These theories stress synchrony, or stability over time, and therefore employ laws or principles that are considered invariant or nearly so. These theories also tend to focus on behavior that is normally out of awareness and the unintended consequences of behavior. Such theories are usually based on the assumption that the structures and functions of social life proceed in an objective world apart from the observer and that the role of the scientists is to discover the nature of those structures and functions. Under the influence of classical semiotics and structural linguistics, these theories see language as separate from reality. Recognizing the arbitrary relationship between language and events, the basic challenge for all theorizing is to represent reality accurately in language. This becomes a kind of goal-ideal against which theories can be evaluated.

One of the more prevalent structural-functional approaches to communication in relationships, groups, organizations, and communities is network theory, the idea that a system of connected individuals forms a social structure held together by communication. The nature of the network both determines and is determined by the interactions among individuals. Network theory attempts to spell out the way in which networks are formed and their effects on work efficiency, the diffusion of innovations, and other outcomes.

The second genre of communication theory consists of cognitive and behavioral theories. This group shares many of the same philosophical assumptions as the theories in the former group, including discovery methods, variable analysis, the search for universal laws, and the requirement of objective, accurate theorizing. The primary difference between these two groups is that the theories in the second genre originated in psychology and focus not on social structure but on the individual human being. These approaches are interested in the relationship among inputs, cognitive processing, and behavior. Theories with a cognitive orientation explain communication in terms of individual information processing. Most cognitive theories of communication deal with the production, processing, and reception of messages.

An example of this kind of work is the huge body of theory on message reception and information processing. This literature attempts to explain how individuals attend to, understand, and organize information in messages and how these processes lead to persuasion or change. Such theories emphasize the impact of messages on the cognitive system and the influence of cognitive processing on communication outcomes for the individual.

A number of theories adopt assumptions from both structural-functional and cognitive-behavioral traditions. Such theories look for the ways in which individual information processing is affected by and affects social interaction. Here the assumption is that a person's behavior and the situation are related. Such theories typically attempt to codify variables in the situation and show how individuals adapt or adjust to those variables in sending and receiving messages.

The third genre consists of interactional and conventional theories. For the most part, these contrast with the first two types of theory. Such theories view social life as a process of interaction, which is not always predictable. For these theories, the structure of society is an outcome of interaction, not the other way around. Social relations cannot be treated as an object outside of theory, but must be understood in terms of the meanings given them by the participants themselves. Such meanings are the products of interaction within small social groups. Theories are designed, therefore, not to represent objective reality accurately but to document the ways in which human beings create meaning in interaction with others and to capture the numerous rich and changing realities constructed in this process.

An example of interactionist theories is a popular body of literature on the social construction of reality, which shows how various cultures and groups understand their experiences differently depending upon meanings worked out in interaction. Views of self, emotions, morality, and virtually all other aspects of life are created through communication.

Closely akin to interactional models are members of the fourth genre, interpretive theories. Hailing from phenomenology and hermeneutics, these theories teach that knowledge is always a product of human experience and interpretation, and they aim to describe the process by which interpretation occurs. Most of these theories are interested not in universal structures but in the ways in which people experience reality. As such, they imagine an active mind attempting to understand human experience in whatever form it may take. A wide variety of theories can be found in this group, and they are not altogether consistent with one another. Ironically, certain classic theories of phenomenology share much with structuralism, while other branches are rather completely in line with interactionism.

For example, ethnography, or the interpretation of cultures, is an example of a field relying heavily on interpretation. Theorists of this persuasion deal with the process by which researchers come to understand the life of a culture. This process involves careful observation of details in the culture, interpretation of those details in terms of known concepts, and reinterpretation based on further observation of specifics. The key to ethnography is the active movement of the mind between generalization and observation.

The fifth genre is composed of critical theories. Critical theories are a loose gathering of ideas that find their center in a common concern regarding the quality of human social life. Most critical theories are conflict-based, and they see social structure as a struggle of forces in which dominant ideologies subvert the interests of marginalized groups. Two broad branches of critical theory are feminist and Marxist thought, and at points these merge. Numerous brands of feminist theory can be found. These theories share a common concern for the oppression of women by the dominant interests of the patriarchy. They differ in terms of their explanations for women's oppression and their proposed solutions. Marxist theories also consist of a variety of branches. Particularly popular in the communication field is cultural studies, which investigates the ways in which the practices of daily life produce cultural forms that come into conflict with one another. According to this school of thought, certain forms dominate others and thereby perpetuate dominant interests in society. Critical theories are hard to classify. They share some things in common with structuralism in that they too are searching to depict the structure of forces in society. Yet they reject the quantitative and experimental methods so often employed by functionalists and cognitivists. They employ some of the same interpretive methods used by interactionists, yet they criticize the interactional and interpretive schools for blindly perpetuating dysfunctional power relations by failing to expose them.

Theories within these five genres are developed in a variety of ways. The traditional ideal of theory development, the hypothetico-deductive method, most commonly seen in the structural-functional and cognitive traditions, revolves around four processes: (1) developing questions, (2) forming hypotheses, (3) testing hypotheses, and (4) formulating theories. The hypothesis-testing procedure is based on a set of widely shared ideas. The first is the hypothesis itself, which is a testable relationship between variables. In the variable-analytic tradition, a complex set of affairs is best understood by breaking it down into its parts and testing their relationships separately. Carefully worded hypotheses make this kind of testing possible. Operationism, which requires that terms be defined in ways that standardize their observation, is a requirement of hypothesis testing. Operationism relies on measurement, in which precise, usually numerical, indexes are employed. Measurement is evaluated in terms of validity (fidelity) and reliability (accuracy). Hypothesis testing also requires manipulation and control, made possible by the use of experimental and statistical procedures, so that extraneous influences can be accounted for.

Traditional theories developed in this way consist of generalized statements, or covering laws, that make prediction possible. Theories change when hypotheses are rejected through research and new hypotheses added to the theory's system of statements. By trial and error, then, the theorist comes to an ever-precise approximation of the actual state of affairs in the real world. A theory may change by extension as it comes to encompass more and more variables, or it may change by intension as variables are increasingly refined. This is the process of normal science, which consists of the orderly progression of knowledge. A scientific revolution occurs when the discovery of an extraordinary case brings about complete reconceptualization, and theory building must begin anew.

While it has been a powerful driving force in the development of much communication theory in the structural-functional and cognitive schools, this traditional view is rejected by many communication theorists in the other genres. Calling themselves "new paradigm" theorists, these individuals deny that complex phenomena can be understood by breaking them down into parts. They reject hypothesis testing and reliance on operational definitions. Such theorists prefer interpretive and critical methods. These theories are evaluated more in terms of their utility than their validity, and theories change as the community of theorists come to new ways of understanding.

Stephen W. Littlejohn
Humboldt State University

Bibliography

Delia, Jesse G. "Communication Research: A History." *Handbook of Communication Science.* Ed. Charles Berger and Steven Chaffee. Newbury Park, CA: Sage, 1987. 20–98.

Dervin, Brenda, Lawrence Grossberg, Barbara J. O'Keefe, and Ellen Wartella. *Rethinking Communication: Paradigm Issues.* Vols. 1–2. Newbury Park, CA: Sage, 1989.

Infante, Dominic, Andrew S. Rancer, and Deanna F. Womack. *Building Communication Theory.* 2nd ed. Prospect Heights, IL: Waveland, 1993.

Littlejohn, Stephen W. *Theories of Human Communication.* 4th ed. Belmont, CA: Wadsworth, 1992.

Communication Triangle

In rhetorical studies, the relationships among the speaker or writer, the listener or reader, the language used, and the subject matter referred to by the language. As such, the communication triangle was implicit in any communication situation, long before rhetorical theory was articulated. In Western rhetorical theory, the conscious separation of these elements was first made by the sophists and then by Plato. But the first to systematize the relationships was Aristotle, who made careful distinctions among these elements in his rhetoric (c. 343–333 B.C.E.). Aristotle used the elements of the triangle (without calling it a triangle) in his rhetorical proofs of persuasion: the ethical proof (the credibility of the speaker), the pathetic proof (the appeal to the emotions and interests of the audience), and the logical proof (the arguments about the subject matter). He also used parts of the triangle to distinguish rhetoric from science, to distinguish among the four virtues of style, to distinguish the different types of ethical proof, and the different types of logical proof (see Kinneavy, Ch. 4).

The most important modern extension and reinterpretation of these relationships can be seen in the works of Charles Sanders Peirce, whose entire philosophy, starting in 1857, was based on the triad, as he called the relationships among the I, the thou, and the it. In his later works, Peirce applied the triad of firstness, secondness, and thirdness to virtually every subject matter, including psychology, semiotics, logic, phenomenology, metaphysics, and biology.

The next important adaptation of the structure, and the first person (as far as can be determined) to draw a triangle to illustrate the relationships, was a German psychologist, Karl Büler, in an important article in 1933. He articulated for the first time expressive discourse (emphasizing the first person), rhetorical discourse (emphasizing the second person), and expository discourse (emphasizing third-person reference).

In 1946 Charles Morris in semiotics used this conceptual structure to ground the elements of modern semiotics: syntactics (the language—at the center of the triangle), semantics (the reference to the subject matter), and pragmatics (the uses made by the speaker/writer and the listener/reader of the language).

In 1951 Alan H. Gardiner used these four elements as a basis for linguistic theory in *A Theory of Speech and Language;* he also pointed out that Bühler, Durkheim, and Meillet all recognized these factors. In 1953 M.H. Abrams, in *The Mirror and the Lamp,* drew the triangle and used the four elements to differentiate theories of literary criticism. In 1960 Roman Jakobson, acknowledging Bühler as a source, again used the triangle in literary theory.

The triangle was applied to discourse theory in 1971 by James L. Kinneavy in *A Theory of Discourse.* Like Peirce, Kinneavy, in a typical structuralist technique, used the triangle at many different levels in his theory to determine the areas of language study (using Morris's semiotic theory), the subdivisions of each area, the aims of discourse, and the applications of Aristotle in rhetoric and Abrams in literary theory. Since that time, it has been used in many textbooks at the high school and college level for teaching writing.

James L. Kinneavy
University of Texas

Bibliography

Abrams, M.H. *The Mirror and the Lamp.* New York: Oxford UP, 1953.

Aristotle. *Aristotle on Rhetoric: A Theory of Civic Discourse.* Newly translated with Introduction, Notes, and Appendixes by George A. Kennedy. New York: Oxford UP, 1991.

Bühler, Karl. "*Die Axiomatik der Sprachwissenschaften.*" *Kant-Studien* 38 (1933): 19–90.

Gardiner, Alan Henderson. *A Theory of Speech and Language.* Oxford: Clarendon, 1951.

Jakobson, Roman. "Linguistics and Poetics." *Essays on the Language of Literature.* Ed. Seymour Chatman and Samuel R. Levin. Boston: Houghton, 1967. 296–322.

Kinneavy, James L. *A Theory of Discourse.* New York: Oxford UP, 1981.

Morris, Charles W. *Signs, Language and Behavior.* Englewood Cliffs, NJ: Prentice, 1946.

Peirce, Charles Sanders. *Collected Papers of Charles Sanders Peirce.* Vols. 1–6. Ed. Charles Hartshorne and Paul Weiss. Vols. 7–8. Ed. Arthur Burks. Cambridge, MA: Harvard UP, 1960.

Comparison

Used to show the similarities between things that belong to the same category. Comparison is first mentioned as a rhetorical strategy in Aristotle's *Rhetoric.* Aristotle suggests using comparison of one's position to an opponent's and mentions using comparison to illustrate the points of an argument. Comparison can also be used to restate a position in order to highlight the weakness of an opposing position in an argument or to develop a refutation of opposing arguments.

The historical point of departure for using comparison in teaching is the *Progymnasmata,* the ancient Greek sequence of assignments that remained influential throughout the Renaissance. Such modes as narration, comparison, and contrast were assigned as strategies for developing compositions. Students were told to compose narration, description, comparison, and contrast essays or orations as they moved toward composing arguments. This sequence of assignments contributed to the formation of the modern "modes of discourse," which Alexander Bain established as central to teaching writing. He believed that all writing could be classified into four modes: description, narration, argumentation, and exposition (with exposition often including classification, comparison and contrast). His emphasis on the modes of discourse maintained the classical hierarchy with argumentation at the top. Teachers and scholars began with lesser forms such as narration, description, and so forth until the students reached argumentative discourse. Since a method or mode is not generally the starting point for composing, many contemporary teachers find mode-oriented approaches to writing invalid representations of actual communication situations where more than one writing strategy is used to create an effective piece of written or oral discourse.

Comparison, as a mode of discourse, is used in various writing assignments, including evaluations of people, places, problems, or things, as well as the traditional refutation of opposing positions in an argument. Furthermore, comparison gives us methods for presenting those findings in our written discourse. Formats for comparison vary. Two approaches for presenting comparisons are the block structure and the alternate structure. In a block format, one presents elements for each person or item to be compared separately. One can also make comparisons, however, by alternating the points of comparison. In the alternate format of comparison of two cities, one could move back and forth between elements for comparison of the two cities. In order to avoid taxing the readers' or listeners' attention, one can successfully combine block and alternating comparison structures. Analogy, metaphor, and similes are other rhetorical strategies for making comparison. Analogies, the comparisons of things that are unlike one another, make the unfamiliar understandable by comparing it to something that is familiar.

Current rhetorical theories treat comparison as a mode of development that can be a useful aid in invention or arrangement. Comparison helps us to develop areas for discussion during the invention process, where contrasting the features of a topic or object can serve an exploratory function. Young, Becker, and Pike's *Rhetoric: Discovery and Change* relies on comparison to develop a "tagememic" heuristic for exploring the features of a topic. Another influential modern theory that draws on classical modes of development is James Kinneavy's *Theory of Discourse,* which treats comparison as part of the mode of classification. These works present comparison as a useful aid, or mode, in the composing process rather than an aim of composition.

Louise Rodriguez Connal
University of Arizona

Bibliography

Corbett, Edward P.J. *Classical Rhetoric for the Modern Student*, 2nd ed. New York: Oxford UP, 1971. 479.

D'Angelo, Frank J. "Aims, Modes, and Forms of Discourse." *Teaching Composition: 10 Bibliographical Essays.* 2nd ed. Ed. Gary Tate. Fort Worth: Texas Christian UP, 1987. 131–54.

Kennedy, George A. *Aristotle: A Theory of Civic Discourse: On Rhetoric.* New York: Oxford UP, 1991.

Kinneavy, James L. *A Theory of Discourse.* New York: Norton, 1980.

Young, Richard E., Alton L. Becker, and Kenneth L. Pike. *Rhetoric: Discovery and Change.* New York: Harcourt, 1970.

See also CONTRAST; MODES OF DISCOURSE

Composition Studies

The academic field that has developed since the 1960s, primarily in North American colleges and universities, to study and teach written language, emphasizing the centrality of writing and literate practices to intellectual development, learning, and critical thought; to the rhetorical construction and negotiation of knowledge, culture, and personal identity; and to democratic participation, power, and work in an "information society."

No brief definition can capture the complexity and indeterminacy of composition studies in its current stage of development. Basic questions that define a discipline—subject matter, methods, purpose, and more—remain in dispute, as suggested by the lack of consensus on a name for the field. "Composition studies" is known under many variants that express overlapping and competing conceptions of the field, each drawing its boundaries and organizing its scholarly work somewhat differently in relation to overarching interdisciplinary projects, research programs, intellectual traditions, and cognate disciplines. Probably the most well accepted designation pairs "composition" with "rhetoric," in either order: "composition and rhetoric" or "rhetoric/composition." This doublet is conveniently ambiguous regarding the meanings and relations of its constituents, which John Gage characterizes as polysemous terms ("On 'Rhetoric' and 'Composition,'" Lindemann and Tate 15–32). Only half seriously (and not exhaustively), he identifies for the two terms at least twenty-seven denotations organized into five categories and concludes that their relation must necessarily be coordinate, referencing a complex network of differences, overlaps, and linkages.

When conjoined with "composition," "rhetoric" is generally understood as the broader field of subject matter. But many who locate themselves professionally in composition studies (by belonging to organizations like "4Cs"—the Conference on College Composition and Communication—by teaching writing, graduate composition theory, or rhetoric, and by publishing in its major journals) identify their intellectual projects with a variety of broader knowledge enterprises besides or instead of rhetoric. These include, for instance, literacy, linguistics, or discourse studies; cultural studies; English; English education; and communication. Phrases that qualify or modify any of the variants (such as basic writing, advanced composition, writing in the disciplines, contrastive rhetoric, history of rhetoric, African-American rhetoric) delineate specialized areas of contemporary composition and rhetoric. In many cases, however, such as technical communication, these are not true branches but semiautonomous formations rooted partly or even primarily in disciplines and teaching practices other than college composition. College composition itself (originally "freshman English"), once isomorphic with the whole field, is now only one focus within rhetoric and composition, which has become progressively more intertwined with multiple, parallel, or transdisciplinary studies of discourse.

The names of academic fields, like place names, often reveal complex histories of influence and affiliation, as does the common use of metaphors for the interdisciplinarity of composition: colonization, immigration, separation and reunification, borrowing, and cultural exchanges. Composition studies as a contemporary discipline is conventionally dated to 1963, when calls for the revival of rhetoric (at the 1963 4Cs) and for research into composing (Richard Braddock et al., *Research in Written Composition*) sparked new scholarship in writing. In the 1970s, published research and theory began to achieve a critical mass (spurred in part by Janet Emig's exemplary case study, *The Composing Processes of Twelfth-Graders*) and to produce structures of professionalization like tenure-track appointment lines in composition, graduate programs, and sustained research programs, accompanied by new journals, increased access to publishing channels in both the humanities and the social sciences, and, in the 1980s, tenure and promotion for college faculty in composition and rhetoric. These developments were accompanied by an increasingly self-conscious and confident articulation of the process and goals of forming a new discipline.

The claims for a "new paradigm" that accompanied and drove this process obscured, however, the way that the composition revolution brought into uneasy coalition the motives, ideas, and values of at least three major traditions:

1. The *teaching tradition* in American colleges and universities, associated since the nineteenth century with practical tasks of remediating literacy crises, preparing citizens, training the work force, and otherwise serving the needs of society and of students. Its orientation to service can also be interpreted as a moral commitment to democratic literacy stretching back to Colonial times. This tradition makes undergraduate, graduate, or professional composition instruction historically and contemporaneously continuous with the teaching of English and language arts in American elementary and secondary schools. Early reformers, however, identified the teaching tradition primarily with the formalist "current-traditional rhetoric" of freshman English textbooks and classroom exercises, focused on textual products and correctness in grammar and style.

2. A revived and revised rhetorical tradition, whose renaissance was to energize development of a *new rhetoric*. From this perspective, composition is the inheritor of classical Western rhetoric as a comprehensive humanistic study of language use and an integrative system of education in the liberal arts.

3. A proposed, parallel *new science* intended to study the processes of composing, drawing on methodologies and approaches from psychology, linguistics, education, and other social sciences.

The composition revolution, while strongly motivated by pedagogical goals, viewed teaching practice as the relatively passive object that the new rhetoric and the new science were to transform or, indeed, replace through a harmonious alliance of empirical and interpretive methods (research and theory).

The amalgamation of these three traditions within modern composition studies left a dual legacy: On the one hand, the perspectival richness of what is often called an inherently "interdisciplinary" or "multimodal" discipline, and, on the other, a set of fundamental conflicts at the heart of the discipline. These new beginnings sowed in composition studies the seeds of fragmentation and discord, institutionalizing from its disparate sources what has been called the "conflict of methods" between the interpretive fields (the hermeneutical human sciences) and the empirical sciences, to which must be added the analytic-critical studies (for example, structuralism, critical social science, cultural critique) and their adaptation to pursuing scholarship as a form of political action. By appealing to such a range of intellectual traditions for key concepts and models of scholarship, reformers set a precedent for unconstrained borrowing and blending of methods and perspectives, not only from the original sources but from any other that appeared relevant. And in setting out to transform a teaching practice (not sufficiently recognized as a complex intellectual tradition in its own right) by developing and systematically applying new, rational understandings of writing and of pedagogy, the founders of composition studies built into its structure a theory/practice dichotomy that continues to haunt its discourse and practices.

From the 1960s to the present, much of the content of composition scholarship can be assimilated to the metagoal of rationally defining a discipline and legitimizing its intellectual work (and its practitioners) within the academy. This quest forms such a powerful and explicit context that almost any inquiry may be seen (or see itself) as responding, directly or indirectly, to a set of defining metaquestions and topics concerning the nature and responsibilities of the field. Theorists sought to identify or provide for composition a set of features that would demarcate, stabilize, and sustain composition studies as a knowledge enterprise. Among the features that have been proposed as essential to this project are the following: an inexhaustible topic or subject matter; relevance to broader knowledge enterprises and cultural developments; collaboration and intellectual exchange with cognate disciplines; a focused mission or purpose; methods and cross-methodological standards for evaluating scholarship and teaching; professional and institutional structures; a system for reproducing the discipline (that is, educating the next generation of scholars); and a reflexive (ironic) understanding of its own projects and discourse (thus, reflective subfields addressing the discipline itself, including historical studies, a body of criticism, sociological and rhetorical studies of the field, and so on).

Surprisingly, despite the pervasiveness of this theme in composition studies, there are still remarkably few sustained treatments that directly address or characterize the discipline globally as an intellectual domain, either historically or analytically (see Berlin, North, and Phelps for book-length works). The problem of comprehensively describing the field has most frequently been handled in an anthological or summative fashion, for example, in introductions written for graduate students like that of Lindemann and Tate, or in collections of bibliographical essays like that of Moran and Lunsford. Perhaps the most influential general characterizations are found in essays or longer works that attempt to map the schools or perspectives of the discipline (discussed below).

Initially, the drive to conceptualize and establish a new field produced strong pressures and expectations for unity. Many sought to identify or formulate frameworks to provide coherence for the remarkably diverse work that began to appear, representing differences in focus (for example, writers, readers, texts, discourse processes, discourse events, linguistic, cognitive, or social structures, material context, ideology) and, even more significantly, in methods, underlying visions, and values. The generativity of this period created a brief euphoria, in which claims for a unified theory seemed intoxicatingly persuasive, as both the instrument for seeking disciplinary status and the likely outcome of this struggle. The rapid professionalization of composition—a largely successful effort to establish the field as autonomous and intellectually viable within the academy—seemed identical with the achievement of a new conceptually unified field (see Maxine Hairston's widely cited article "The Winds of Change: Thomas Kuhn and the Revolution in the Teaching of Writing," *College Composition and Communication* 33 [1982]: 76–88).

This optimism has been tempered in the later 1980s and 1990s, despite continuing efforts by some scholars to promulgate a single paradigm (for example, cognitive rhetoric or social-epistemic rhetoric) to contain, overcome, or displace conflicting ones. Once established, the "discipline" began to crack and fissure, or more accurately to reveal the fractures that had been there all along, by virtue of its three traditions and its interdisciplinary eclecticism of ideas and methods. Subsequent consideration has discovered these traditions to be not only problematically compatible but far more complex and internally divided than was realized. (For example, the teaching tradition is not accounted for simply as the instantiation of current-traditional rhetoric; it also incorporates an enduring minority intellectual tradition, Romanticism, associated with progressive education, New Criticism, and the "expressivist" school of composition. The teaching of writing is also strongly linked, through the schools, to the social science paradigm of education research, as represented, for example, in the journal *Research in Teaching English*.) The new rhetoric has turned into "new rhetorics" (and redescribed historical rhetoric as multivariate); the new science has divided into qualitative, quantitative, and cognitive (model-building) camps, at the least. New positions have appeared that seem to fit none of these while they have influenced all (for example, feminism, deconstruction, new historicism, critical pedagogy). The apparent incompatibility and incommensurability of methods and perspectives, and the increasing contentiousness among these points of view, have become highly salient and disturbing problems for the profession.

In one useful simplification, composition studies may be understood as developing through a process of equilibration between forces of *expansion* and *differentiation*. These forces may be roughly equated with rhetoric and composition, respectively. For instance, the ancient provenance of rhetoric reconnects composition studies to European thought (particularly philosophy and poetics) and to the historical experience of rhetoric as a part of education and Western culture, while the range of cultures and contexts for language use addressed in contemporary rhetorical studies enables composition both to reconceive and escape the classroom as the sole scene of writing. (It can be argued that other fields or cross-disciplinary enterprises, such as linguistics or cognitive studies, broadly construed, have played a similarly expansive role for composition studies; it is only when these studies become rhetoricized, that is, when they begin to address discourse as event and to study symbolic activity and meaning in context, that they approach the impact of rhetoric in this respect.) Composition provides a touchstone for differentiating the discipline from others by evoking the specifically American historical practice of teaching writing and language arts, an experiment in educating for mass literacy, as a basis for framing a distinctive set of problems and moral concerns, emphasizing certain purposes, contexts, and responsibilities.

Expansion

A striking characteristic of the twentieth-century development of composition and rhetoric, and a major challenge to organizing it coherently, is the enormous expansion that has occurred in its subject matter, both denotatively (the realities that terms like *writing* refer or point to) and connotatively (what they mean). These changes understandably puzzle newcomers and outsiders, who continue to identify the teaching of writing with their memories or images of "freshman English" and the remediation of discrete skills even as they themselves are producing multimedia documents on their computers, struggling with an exponential increase in information, and negotiating new rhetorical genres. Any definition of the field must begin from and account for this augmented domain and ultimately find some principled way to navigate, if not delimit, it.

The development of composition studies has occurred during a period of extraordinary, successive transformations in both the media and technologies of communication and, relatedly, the way these (including language itself) are conceptualized in relation to information, meaning, knowledge, mind, human development, culture, societal organization, and social activity. These changes took place against a tumultuous social context for American education, including events of such massive impact as wars, generational conflict, the collapse of communism, restructuring of the global economy, the worldwide spread of increasingly interactive telecommunications, the feminist movement, civil rights, internationalization, profound and still unfolding demographic shifts, and the redefinition of American society as multicultural. While the interactions between the internally motivated development of composition and different layers of this context are myriad, complex, and not easily understood, it is clear (as noted in a pioneering intellectual history of composition studies by Nystrand et al.) that the general impact has been to enable and require composition both to widen greatly the *scope* of its subject matter beyond what is conventionally understood as "writing" and also to increase the *depth* of analysis in the form of more complex concepts of writing, teaching, and learning, and their relationship to individuals and to society. The following scenarios may give some inkling why these expansions are so comprehensive and unconstrained.

The first composition studies were undertaken in classroom settings, most often associated with "freshman English." If it is decided that to teach writing well requires an understanding of composing as a process, the first target of analysis is likely to be (and was) student writing processes and student texts, along with related teaching acts. Quickly, however, attention turns to comparing student writing with adult, or expert, practices of writing. While these comparisons may originally be confined to academic writing, they logically imply that the context for understanding student writing, and for teaching college writing, is necessarily teachers' knowledge about the entire world of adult discourse for which students are preparing. This insight (facilitated, as suggested, by the appeal to rhetoric as encompassing the whole universe of discourse) licences composition and rhetoric to study writing in any context and for any purpose that adults use it.

Such moves, once made, generate their own intellectual momentum. For example, "writing" is easily amplified to "literate practices" (that is, related verbal practices like talking about texts, electronic communication, reading, and so on) or associated with other "literacies" (for example, "information literacy," "computer literacy," and "visual" or "media literacy"). A focus on writing in actual practice invites compositionists to study and teach in contexts outside college writing classrooms: academic writing as it takes place across the curriculum; rhetorical interactions in the workplaces of business, government, the professions, and other institutions and organizations; literacy development and practices in culturally and linguistically diverse homes, in retirement homes, churches, prisons, political campaigns, and so on. Many composition theorists, believing divisions based on rhetorical context, modality, and function to be arbitrary and unenforceable, define the scope of their subject to encompass, in time, the lifespan, and in space or function, any setting for strategic language use. (This means concretely, for example, that they include speech and reading in composition research and teaching; study how writing is learned, taught, and practiced at both pre- and postcollege levels; and incorporate into writing instruction all genres of discourse.) Scholars, however, pragmatically recognize certain periods and settings (and purposes or modes of language) as historically thematic for composition while others are the traditional province of cognate disciplines like English education (reading), literature, creative writing, early childhood education, (speech) communication, or linguistics. In this sense constructing the discipline and determining its "borders" does not depend simply on the logic of subject matter but involves political negotiations of academic territory with competing fields.

Another path of expansion leads composition studies to reconceptualize "writing" from a simple translating or coding function (turning thought into intelligible, socially acceptable language forms) to include a broad variety of interactive higher-order cognitive and social functions. Suppose one asks, what does it take to be successfully literate? to write effectively? The answer has changed dramatically since the 1960s as technologically sophisticated, information-rich societies require increasingly complex skills under the rubric of "literacies." The meaning of literacy is not fixed but changes in response to the requirements and opportunities of a particular society for handling information—that is, seeking out, selecting, interpreting, and transforming meanings—through an evermore complex integration of multiple symbol systems and media. These integrations require not only technical knowledge but also creative and critical intellectual skills like categorizing, ordering, analogizing, inferring, and evaluating.

At the same time, research, together with reflections on teaching experience, reveals the indeterminate range of implied competencies and knowledge that writers must coordinate (and therefore composition teachers must study and cultivate) to accomplish intellectual and rhetorical purposes: for example, critical reasoning and logic, problem-formulation, composing techniques like drafting and revision, electronic technologies for text production and information search, content knowledge, and social knowledge about audience and rhetorical genres. It is impractical for teachers of "writing" to isolate these elements and teach them separately, or teach only a few of them.

Examining writing as a technology reveals yet another scenario of expansion. Writing as a system of inscription has been the subject of intensive analysis, for example, in Continental theories that argue for writing (over speech) as the general case for language or in sustained debates among linguists, psychologists, and classicists about the historical and developmental role of literacy in promoting critical thinking within different cultures. But while this has been going on, Western writing in the sense of an alphabetic inscription system has metamorphosed from the technologies of handwriting and print to electronic documents that mix print forms of verbal language with images and sound (language, music) in multimedia formats (film, video, photography, sound recordings, computer animation, voice mail, and so forth). Practically speaking, writing teachers are now, or will shortly be, teaching students to compose

C

in a world of telecommunications, where they conceive and inscribe ideas and manipulate information in forms that are not restricted to visual language. There is simply no way to keep separate and distinct the technologies people think of as "writing" (verbal symbols, visible language, print) from these other modes of inquiry, expression, and communication.

Achieving Disciplinarity through Order and Difference

Once these expansions take place, it is extremely hard to circumscribe either the scholarship or the teaching and service responsibilities of composition studies, which seem to diffuse and merge with those of other fields. This interpenetration between composition studies and allied disciplines takes place not only on an intellectual plane (as research and theory broaden their scope and take on increasingly general issues) but also in a panoply of professional and institutional structures. The several levels of interaction between composition and other disciplines—in scholarship, teaching, and service—both parallel and feed into one another. In writing-across-the-curriculum programs, for example, composition professionals cooperate with colleagues in other fields in a mission that is both teaching and service-oriented. In doing so they address not only the issue of teaching writing as a discipline-specific rhetoric but also the problem of teaching and learning any subject through the mediation of writing. This focus in turn broadens the scholarly interests of composition studies to include rhetorics of inquiry and forms of communication across disciplines and methodologies. All these relationships show up in the unpredictably interdisciplinary mix of faculty and courses in graduate programs preparing students for careers in rhetoric and composition studies and in the variety of programs and departments into which they are subsequently appointed.

In sum, the very expansions and importations that give intellectual depth to composition and integrate it into broader knowledge enterprises also constantly threaten its viability and autonomy by producing confusion, conflict, and a diffusion of purpose and professional identity. In response to this dilemma, scholars have constantly sought ways to order the apparent chaos of topic, methods, and values in composition and to differentiate it from other fields through a set of distinctive features or commonalities.

Scholars have adopted a number of strategies to provide order to the discipline, which may be classified as strategies of dominance, of inclusion or pluralism, and of dialogue. Probably the most common approach to organizing the discipline is "mapping." Early taxonomies (for example, those of James Moffett, James Britton, and other discourse theorists) mapped the various aims, modes, or genres of discourse, extending the nineteenth-century tradition of such classifications. James L. Kinneavy (*A Theory of Discourse*, 1980) provided the most comprehensively syntopical of these schemes, many of which had considerable impact on pedagogy. More significant to the quest for disciplinarity, however, are efforts to map composition studies itself into competing schools of thought or practice contrasting in methods, theoretical stances, pedagogical strategies, sources, and other distinguishing features.

Although much composition scholarship is argued in terms of underlying dichotomies (for example, cognitive versus social approaches to composing research, or expressionist versus new rhetorical pedagogies), the most influential maps have organized the work of the field into three or four holistic categories whose differences are traced to a primary dimension of difference such as epistemology or research method. Prominent examples include the works of James Berlin and Stephen North. Barbara Gleason and Mark Wiley ("Composition in Three Keys: Art, Nature, and Science," *Ilha do Desterro* 29 [1993]: 11–25) summarize and discuss such strategic mapping while offering their own alternative, as does Nystrand et al.

A related strategy is to organize the work of the field around key concepts, which serve as generative metaphors. Examples of such concepts, or "god terms," that have been proposed (or opposed) as organizing terms for composition include text, process, symbolic act, transaction, composing, imagination, the making of meaning, and social context. Many theoretical positions in composition may be understood as selecting one or another in a framework of discourse elements (for example, the communication triangle, or the Burkean pentad for analyzing symbolic acts) and arguing its primacy. As in the case of mapping, conceptual analysis tends to produce master narratives that advance particular values by constructing a historical progression from a simpler, less adequate paradigm for composition studies to a more complex, comprehensive one. Many recent accounts of composition studies, for instance, tend to propose or argue a historical sequence in emphasis from *text* to *mind*, or *cognition* to *social context*. Such schematic histories, however, must be understood as interested and selective interpretations, hiding many complexities and ambiguities. (For example, the notion of "social context" may be variously and conflictingly interpreted to mean cognitive construct, ideology, discourse community, a condition of dialogue or Bakhtinian "heteroglossia," and so on.)

Mapping and key concept analysis generally function as strategies of dominance in that they attempt to impose a unifying order on the discipline based on structural divisions and a hierarchy of value that have real consequences. If such analyses are accepted, they privilege certain approaches to teaching or certain directions in scholarship strongly over others, and they may devalue prior or alternate schools, perspectives, and topics in the field, even perhaps ruling some out of the discipline altogether. Strategies of inclusion or pluralism share the desire for unity but tend to be integrative and tolerant in approach. An example is the concept of multimodality advocated by Janice Lauer and others (for example, graduates of the Carnegie Mellon cognitive rhetoric program), which entails using a complement of methodologies selected and combined to fit a particular research problem. Many other arguments for the interdisciplinarity of composition (for example, by Andrea Lunsford [Lindemann and Tate]) espouse a fairly radical pluralism, dismissing problems of disparity as less important than the richness provided by a healthy diversity. Finally, some proposals for "reunifying" composition studies also express integrative impulses, but these views are not inclusively pluralistic, in that they envision a simpler unity (for example, composition and literature as "English," or writing and speech as "communication") based on a mythologized past rather than on the confused, heterogeneous sources and affiliations that now populate composition studies.

In the 1980s increasing concerns about the balkanization and apparent incoherence of research in composition studies prompted the formation of the Research Network, an annual meeting at 4Cs that has evolved into an effort to bring different modes of scholarship, and their practitioners, into contact. Speakers and workshop participants have struggled inconclusively through this forum to articulate to one another their distinctive methodological premises and moral visions, to argue the incommensurability or complementarity of their views, and to explore the possibilities for developing cross-modal standards for making critical assessments or integrating different forms of knowledge (papers from the 1988 meeting appear in the Spring 1989 issue of *Rhetoric Review;* see Bazerman et al.). These approaches, seeking neither a dominant paradigm nor an unproblematic pluralism, locate such order as composition may hope for in the ongoing dialogue itself. (They vary tonally, some scholars emphasizing cooperation and others valuing intrinsically the play and contestation of difference.)

These three strategies for navigating the differences and conflicts of composition—dominance, inclusive pluralism, and dialogue—correspond to different conceptions of disciplinarity and different values accorded to it. Strategies of dominance assume progress in the knowledge-making of composition and attempt to control its definition as a discipline, however broadly, through paradigms of ideal order. Both pluralism and dialogic strategies express a greater tolerance for looseness, fluidity, and change, characterizing composition studies as multiply mediated, transactional with many other knowledge formations, and dynamic but not progressing toward any closure. The goal of characterizing (and thus securing the viability) of composition as a discipline, however, remains important to pluralists, whereas some of those promoting dialogue, especially those who emphasize heterogeneity, diversity, and struggle as values in themselves, have begun to question the very possibility and desirability of defining composition in anything like disciplinary terms.

As recounted by Nystrand et al., the early development of composition studies coincided with a final flowering of structuralist hopes for definitively conceptualizing language, mind, human behavior, and culture. Such themes have energized certain productive research programs within composition and rhetoric (for example, the cognitive process research of Linda Flowers and John Hayes, David Bartholomae's and Patricia Bizzell's theories of discourse community as a key to literacy, social-constructivist views of writing pedagogy). But none of these frameworks have proved definitive, and each is reaching conceptual limits, encountering and indeed generating its own critique. And, even as

C

prominent scholars in composition studies pursued these notions, others (and sometimes the same ones) consistently described composition as contextualist in nature, shaped fundamentally by its emergence into a postmodern intellectual milieu characterized by themes of antifoundationalism and instabilities of meaning and structure. If composition is to be a "discipline" at all, in this view, it will not be in the traditional sense. A few scholars who identify "discipline" with a positivist notion of science or with dangers of political conformity and elitism have proposed "antidisciplinary" or "postdisciplinary" formulations for the continuing development of composition and rhetoric. Others, understanding a discipline as less an ideal than a mixed logical, pragmatic, rhetorical, and political construct, continue to seek nonessentialist ways of articulating the coherence of its different knowledge projects, teaching practices, and discourse. These views are gaining increasing currency as they parallel developments in other language studies, drawing particularly on the work of the Russian theorist M.M. Bakhtin.

There is a growing sense that, in a disciplinarity so unstable, scholars must construct the field anew and must negotiate their constructions continually with those of others to achieve some common (but always evolving) understanding of "composition studies." They do not experience themselves as simply inheriting cultural traditions as a set of engrained ideas and values but of being able to choose freely among them, from a past that is indefinitely protean and elastic. Each choice produces a different master narrative of the field and projects a different path to its future. This sense that history is not a burden, not a given, but an open field of possibilities for constantly reinventing oneself (and the past) is a very American one that appears almost unremarked in Janet Emig's article "The Tacit Tradition: The Inevitability of a Multi-Disciplinary Approach to Writing Research" (*The Web of Meaning: Essays on Writing, Teaching, Learning, and Thinking*. Ed. Dixie Goswami and Maureen Butler, 1983), originally presented at the landmark 1979 convention of the Canadian Council of Teachers of English. It gives a distinctively American cast to the postmodern sensibility of composition studies.

Some (like those who long nostalgically for reunification) construct histories on the organic model of tree diagrams, in which composition branches off or separates from a single root or master discipline (such as rhetoric), whose wholeness they constantly seek to restore. Others have written of composition in nonlinear terms, as core and margins, or as a "blurred genre" located permanently and indeterminately in the border zones between academic fields. But a better metaphor for a discipline that has been unable and increasingly unwillingly to fix its self-understanding or settle on a singular history may be the flow of a river fed by many streams, with converging and diverging tributaries and branches, a river in which composition studies is one current intermingling untraceably with others. Reconstructing precisely the history and origins of that current is meaningless in classical causal terms (as is even the notion of a "mainstream"); what is called for is something more like chaos theory, a way of identifying recurrent patterns.

It is important, and enabling to such discussions, that composition studies has in fact achieved a place in the academy—has professionalized and institutionalized itself, has established the journals, conventions, and publication channels for sustaining an internal conversation and communicating with other disciplines. Scholars who argue for antidisciplinary views of composition can do so safely because of the forums provided them by their predecessors; indeed, the very opportunity for them to make this argument presumes more stability and autonomy than they are willing to admit. But they are right that the identity of composition remains a complex and heterogeneous one, internally contentious; it does not rest on a single discourse but on a set of overlapping ones, in settings and forums that only partially coincide in their membership and communicate with difficulty. The answers now proposed for both the subject matter of composition studies (for example, expanded and blurred definitions of "writing") and its self-understanding as a field (for example, postdisciplinary, chaotic) argue that these problems may never be resolved by a definitive choice or unified framework.

Instead, composition studies may be seen as distinctive partly in this very feature. Specifically, it is a field organized by a set of tensions and oppositions that are not incidental or transitory (that is, resolved by problem-solving) but constitutive. Tensions may be identified as constitutive if they recur as underlying themes structuring and generating many specific debates, if they are irreducible and irresolvable, yet fundamental to the disciplinary project. This notion remains to be explored, but a number of candidates come to mind for constitutive tensions:

- conflicts of method, and of their underlying epistemologies and values
- the dichotomy of theory and practice
- conflicting notions of the ideal relationship and balance between the individual and culture or society, as mediated by language or literacy
- language as knowing versus language as doing, as epistemology or as symbolic action
- ethical conceptions of the disciplinary project as obligated primarily to individual students or to society

Analysis of how such differences actually constitute a field of topics, activities, problems, specific dichotomies and oppositions, and so on (as has begun to occur regarding the relationship between theory and practice) should yield deeper insights into the nature and significance of composition studies. For example, both the conflicts that generated the theory/practice tension and those that center on the relationship of persons to culture as mediated by education reflect specifically American themes (elitism versus populism, individualism versus community, conservation of culture versus innovation, cultural assimilation versus diversity).

Many schemes for unifying composition and rhetoric have attempted to discover some common ground that would identify a particular activity, topic, perspective, or motive as distinctive to the field. While this foundational hope has proven vain in the postmodern milieu, the search can be reconfigured productively as an effort to identify distinctive features as family resemblances, rather than a single common element in a set. In other words, some projects and preoccupations are prototypical in composition studies, although there are many activities of the field that range far from such prototypes; at the same time, the most extreme variants will have some features that overlap with more typical activities, in the same way that individuals in families may be identified as relatives even though they possess no single feature in common. Ultimately, what distinguishes composition studies from other disciplines is the collectivity of such similarities and distinctive features, not any one taken alone.

If one were to compile a list of such distinctive features in composition studies, the following might be considered for inclusion:

- the conception of writing as *mediating* complex dynamics (for example, various symbol systems and media, or various cognitive processes, the relationship between an individual and language/culture)
- a generalized attention to *composing* both language and action, through an inscribing medium that allows planning, self-reflection, and revision
- a *democratic,* perhaps utopian, *commitment* to literacy
- a *rhetorical (functional or strategic) perspective* on language (as distinct from, say, a formalist or structuralist one)
- a *developmental orientation* and focus on the *concrete individual,* even when the person is conceived as a nexus for heteroglossic social forces: similarly, a focus on concrete, particular discourse events or "*utterances*"
- historically special issues and concerns of earlier composition practice becoming *thematic* within an expanded subject matter: for example, within the life span of literacy, the adolescent and young adult period when language use becomes critically conscious
- *reflexivity* about the professional activities of members of the discipline
- a generalized interest in *practices,* especially reflective practice mediated by writing about an activity.

The last two features are worthy of special attention. Reflexivity is a characteristic of most contemporary disciplines, which critically examine their own methods of inquiry and genres of discourse. In composition studies this tendency is reinforced by several other factors. First, writing is the usual medium for such reflective thought, and rhetoric is understood now as the general form of inquiry in any field. Second, from its inception composition took the teaching of its subject matter (writing, rhetoric) as an object of inquiry. That is to say that composition studied critically its own professional activity, treating its members as moral agents whose activity fell within the domain of its ethi-

C

cal and intellectual, as well as practical, responsibilities. Later, the activities of teaching were studied in relation to learning and through the characteristic lenses of the field: as reading (response to writing), as rhetoric, as composing, as discourse, as meaning-making, and so on.

This duality or reflexivity in the conception of composition as a study has important consequences. First, it means that several regions of responsibility may be defined for composition beyond writing itself, corresponding to the various activities in which its members engage as professionals (that is, by virtue of their disciplinary expertise and roles). These additional regions for reflexive study include not only (1) teaching but also (2) research and theory as inquiry practices and (3) institutional and professional activities or services like teacher preparation or administration, which are central to the role of composition in higher education. Second, activities in these regions are recursively related: Each, for example, can be analyzed as a practice of composing or of rhetoric. Third, each of these activities is as subject to expansion and generalization as writing itself. Thus, for example, scholarly interests in teaching writing generalize to the study of any pedagogy, while thematizing the mediating function of writing in learning any subject, or the role of rhetoric in any field of inquiry. Similarly, an intellectual interest in the administration of writing programs generalizes to the study of institutional practices and problems like academic leadership, curriculum reform, the role of technology in organizing academic and administrative work, or assessment. Finally, each of these activities engaged in by the professional in composition studies becomes a realm of moral responsibility for the individual and the discipline.

The constitutive tensions in composition between activity and reflection, theory and practice, the academy and the quotidian or everyday world, make ethics and politics central issues. This realization has recently begun to swing attention somewhat away from the long preoccupation of composition studies with epistemology and the problem of meaning toward a greater concern for its own practitioners' actions as effective in the world and for the consequences of literacy education as empowering the symbolic and material activities of others.

Practice as Political and Ethical Action

An emphasis on "practice" is probably the single most distinctive feature of composition studies; the discipline's sense of moral purpose in teaching has pointedly shaped its intellectual curiosity and provided a reality check for its discourse and knowledge-making. (Like all other universal claims about composition studies, however, this one is disputed by scholars who argue that composition studies has advanced in large part by detaching itself from the limitations imposed by developing knowledge for the purposes of writing instruction.) But the commitment to practice, frequently framed as an ideal of democratic education for literacy, provides a question rather than a common understanding. The question is, how should that commitment be interpreted and enacted? It has, for example, at various times meant preparing students for public citizenship, transmitting the finest thoughts and expressions of high culture, teaching mastery of complex (that is, academic) writing, equipping people to contribute as workers in a high-tech society, and facilitating the development of personal identity.

On the other side, some scholars have attacked literacy education as inherently oppressive and undemocratic in practice. Much scholarship of the late 1980s and 1990s, influenced by cultural studies, powerfully reframed this political dimension of composition as a critical project undertaken by members of the discipline (acting as a collectivity of intellectuals) for resisting dominant ideologies and promoting change in the social order toward greater fairness, accounting for differences in ethnicity, gender, race, sexuality, and class. These views, sensitive to historical inequities, demographic changes signaling the coming majority of students from "minority" cultures, and the negative impact of social tensions on education, nevertheless have provoked critical response, for example, from advocates of revitalized expressivist philosophies emphasizing individual responsibility and agency. Some scholars have begun to revive ethics in contradistinction to politics as an interpretive frame for contrasting and reconciling teachers' responsibilities to students as educators with their responsibilities to society as intellectuals for transmitting culture, developing new knowledge, or promoting social change.

One result of the strong ethical and political "turn" in composition and rhetoric is to foreground the history, organization, and status of the discipline within the American academy (and schools) as one of "marginalization" or, in Susan Miller's term, *carnivalization* (*Tex-*

tual Carnivals: The Politics of Composition, Southern Illinois UP, 1991). Recent scholarship analyzes and critiques the subordination of composition studies to literature in English departments, the exploitation of part-time and non-tenure track faculty (who teach a huge proportion of writing classes in higher education, along with teaching assistants), and the relationship of these to an historical "feminization" of composition. These studies are redeemed from what sometimes appears to be self-absorption, parochialism, or self-aggrandizement by their attempt to connect academic and popular attitudes toward composition studies to its "everyday" or quotidian nature (for example, in valuing student texts or studying ordinary discourse), its longstanding commitment to active student learning and to the needs of nontraditional students, and other themes within composition scholarship and teaching (for example, in radical or critical pedagogy) that put it in tension with the academy's elitism and ivory-tower mentality, or that reflect and address conflicts or problems in the larger society.

A related political issue is the status of practitioners as intellectual and moral agents within composition studies. Many have attacked the assumption underlying the composition revolution that research and theory could ultimately rationalize and control practice. Instead, they have argued for the autonomy of teachers and their independent roles as inquirers, curriculum designers, and decision-makers, along with their students, in daily classroom interactions. These views have been promoted in part through the "teacher research" movement in the schools and in some college writing programs.

Despite the emergence of purer, nonpedagogical research, no one in the field is entirely exempt from the question "How is your work related to practice?" Initially, "practice" referred only to teaching, but it has acquired greater resonance. Like concepts of writing, practice (often "critical" or "reflective" practice, sometimes "praxis") has expanded its reference, becoming a generic term for symbolic activities and for professional and everyday activities that share with rhetoric such features as uncertainty, problem-formulation, design, artistry, strategic rather than rule-governed decision-making, and feedback. This conception helps to ensure the unique reflexivity of composition, whereby the traditional scholarly contri-butions of "research," "teaching," and "service" become both part of the object of study (along with writing in culture as a rhetorical practice that permeates all these activities) and also the occasion for ethical decisions, both individually and collectively, about purposes and effectivity. As "praxis," the notion of practice becomes infused with critical and transformative conceptions of pedagogy and scholarship.

The institutional force of composition and rhetoric within the academy is a new dimension of its "practice." Through development of interdisciplinary linkages in its scholarship and through comprehensive writing programs, sometimes established as independent units or departments, and their administrative leadership, composition studies has achieved a more significant institutional presence that enables it to play a more important role in higher education. As a result of its faculty members' experience and expertise developed in meeting the typical responsibilities of such programs (for example, teacher training, faculty development, assessment of teaching, working with faculty on transdisciplinary projects, adapting instruction for nontraditional students, reforming curriculum, developing electronic technologies for teaching and for distance learning), composition studies promises to contribute significantly to institutional reforms and reconceptualizations that are changing the landscape of higher education.

Louise Wetherbee Phelps
Syracuse University

Bibliography

Bazerman, Charles, et al. "What Are We Doing as a Research Community?" Symposium, 1988 CCCC Research Network. *Rhetoric Review* 7 (1989): 223–93.

Berlin, James A. *Rhetoric and Reality: Writing Instruction in American Colleges, 1900–1985.* Carbondale: Southern Illinois UP, 1987.

Braddock, Richard, Richard Lloyd-Jones, and Lowell Schoer. *Research in Written Composition.* Urbana, IL: National Council of Teachers of English, 1963.

CCCC Bibliography of Composition and Rhetoric. Urbana, IL: National Council of Teachers of English, 1985.

Emig, Janet. *The Composing Processes of Twelfth Graders.* Research Report No. 13. Urbana, IL: National Council of Teachers of English, 1971.

Kinneavy, James L. *A Theory of Discourse.* New York: Norton, 1980.

C

Kirsch, Gesa, and Patricia A. Sullivan, eds. *Methods and Methodology in Composition Research*. Carbondale: Southern Illinois UP, 1992.

Lauer, Janice. "Composition Studies: Dappled Discipline." *Rhetoric Review* 3 (1984): 20–29.

Lindemann, Erika, and Gary Tate, eds. *An Introduction to Composition Studies*. New York: Oxford UP, 1991.

Moran, Michael G., and Ronald Lunsford, eds. *Research in Composition and Rhetoric: A Bibliographic Sourcebook*. Westport, CT: Greenwood, 1984.

North, Stephen M. *The Making of Knowledge in Composition: Portrait of an Emerging Field*. Upper Montclair, NJ: Boynton/Cook, 1987.

Nystrand, Martin, et al. "Where Did Composition Studies Come From? An Intellectual History." *Written Communication* 10 (1993): 267–333.

Phelps, Louise Wetherbee. *Composition as a Human Science: Contributions to the Self-Understanding of a Discipline*. New York: Oxford UP, 1988.

Computer Applications in Rhetoric

Affecting every writer and reader through changing the nature and conventions of textual communication, forcing reconceptualizations of authors, audiences, authority, and ownership of texts, literatures, and writing processes. Computer technologies, in fact, influence all the professional duties of rhetoricians and writing teachers by also changing views of literacy training, writing-tool capabilities, effective writing instruction, and academic professionalism. Computer-based rhetoric, however, is still moving only unsteadily toward the states of theory and practice predicted since the late 1960s. Expectations that computers will "solve" public literacy problems more effectively than earlier writing technologies seem premature until educational institutions provide technological access and theory-based training equally to all.

The earliest commercial computers (for example, UNIVAC), huge mainframes that used punched and sorted cards for processing, were primarily conceived as tools for what computers do best—storing, retrieving, and organizing information. Though writing-study professionals foresaw classroom uses for computers by at least the late 1960s, limited access and unso-phisticated technology confined early experiments to rudimentary text-analysis programs and drill-and-practice student exercises. Major Hugh Burns of the U.S. Air Force was among the first to break this pattern by developing interactive learning aids for computer-based literacy training (c. 1979).

In the early to mid 1980s, the personal or "micro" computer gained widespread distribution, with corresponding surges in public demands for computer-based literacy and in the attention paid to electronic discourse by rhetoric and writing specialists. The evolution of computer uses in rhetoric and composition during this period was marked by efforts to establish workable writers' "help" programs. Programs such as *Writer's Workbench* and *Wandah* used then-current notions of cognition, artificial intelligence, and writing processes in hopes of creating truly interactive "expert" systems for such tasks as invention, outlining, revision, and editing. Important influences at that time included Seymour Papert, who set the stage for much of this work with his considerations of broad implications for education and society, and Helen Schwartz, an early promoter of word processors for literacy training. In addition, William Wresch and Colette Daiute did important work in computer-based methods for teaching writing, while Lillian Bridwell-Bowles and Christine Neuwirth established patterns for necessary research in writing processes through their studies of computer-based composing.

The later 1980s and early 1990s were a period of slowed but continuing growth in computer-based communication systems, as integrated systems promoting recursive models of total writing processes supplanted earlier "help" systems' emphases on singular elements. During this period, writing-study theorists (for example, Cynthia Selfe, Gail Hawisher, Billie Wahlstrom) began to question the institutional, sociopolitical, and theoretical bases of computer applications in or for rhetoric and writing. Concurrently, Dawn and Raymond Rodrigues developed important programs for computer instruction of basic writers and for teacher training while Edward Jennings and Jerome Bump gained attention by suggesting collaborative education through computer networking. Anthony Kaye and Robin Mason were among the leaders in the rapidly emerging field of on-line education.

Current theoretical consensus in computer-based rhetoric and writing sets forth three main reasons why people do or perhaps should use computers as their primary means of text-based communication: First, computer-originated texts are attractive and easy to produce. Second, electronic information-exchange is more interactive, particularly using network systems. Third, research in writing and literacy is greatly enhanced by the computer's recording capability *during* linguistic transactions.

Accumulated experiences and research in computer-based rhetoric have led theorists from the above-mentioned basic principles to certain significant and more particular hypotheses. Among these is the conclusion that audiences for electronic writing are becoming more distributed and more specialized in their interests. Proliferation of information may also lead these wider, more interactive audiences to greater selectivity and insistence on appealing writing. Moreover, concepts of textual authority and originality are rapidly evolving, forcing redefinition of *tangible, original* texts, while desktop and network publishing undercut the prestige of libraries and universities as stockpiles of knowledge.

Many theorists now describe electronic writing as more dynamic, speechlike, and representative of writers' and readers' (usually nonlinear) mental constructions of physical texts. Though this view agrees with modern cognitive theory, however, computer-produced texts also introduce new communicative limitations and suggest new criteria for effective writing. For example, symbolic "play," reminiscent of classical rhetoric, can manipulate icons, graphics, and typography in new stylistic conventions for establishing tone and context where authorial presence is minimal. Still limited to the information and paths of reference "the author" makes available, readers may know less about authorial intentionality and ethos in electronic texts (for example, networks or hypertext). In this conception, authors provide perspectives more than meaning itself.

Hypertext—interactive texts that provide readers with a variety of choices for proceeding from one "text-chunk" to the next—is just one example of the kind of theoretical polarization that has undoubtedly slowed transitions to computer-based discourse. Theorists currently debate whether hypertext is too "open" or not open enough (that is, authors still choose and provide a finite number of text-chunks and possible paths), and whether it emphasizes content over organization or the reverse. Although some postulate that hypertext silences authors by removing their power to make connections between ideas, others insist that it empowers readers *and* writers by eliminating hierarchies of knowledge. Massive hypertextual "literatures" seem likely to redefine disciplinary canons by creating a vast interconnectivity of texts.

Like those who see only the dangers of hypertext, teachers unwilling or unable to adapt to computer-based writing tools and fully integrate them into specific instructional contexts can hardly expect successful implementation. Properly utilized, computers can allow greater individualization of instruction and increased teacher/student interaction. Network-based collaborations also often lead to more student-centered, ideologically nonoppressive classes and replace emphases on individual or power-based knowledge. Some fear, however, that computers will reinforce existing power structures, that students may overly rely on computers and their limited views of processes; that over-individuation may result; and that computer programmers' ways of thinking and communicating may overinfluence those of students.

One example of productive compromise is the prevalent conclusion that most experienced writers currently mix paper-copy and electronic writing because small-screen views don't allow writers to get a feel for entire, longer texts during formatting, editing, and critical reading. Less-expert writers, many believe, may actually hinder their writing success by a too-quick transition to disk-copy only.

Computer-mediated conferencing, greatly praised because it can increase chances for interactive thinking by alleviating space and time separations of collaborators, appears to be in an equally transitional state. For greatest effectiveness, it still requires human moderation, as it creates emphatically public discourse situations, with new social demands and patterns of behavior. Newer systems of audiovisual support, however, can provide benefits of both electronic and face-to-face collaborations.

On-line courses and electronic links to libraries and databases suggest fresh approaches to professional rhetoric, writing, and writing instruction. On-line classes—utilizing mail, file, and CMC (conferencing) systems—can create new rhetorical challenges for students while increasing intellectual involvement, providing a variety of ways to read and respond to "messages." They also provide cost-effective alternatives to traditional classrooms and encourage students to see all knowledge as connected. Com-

C

puter technologies provide further services to faculty through aids to writing and publishing, in-service education, collegiality, and collaborative teaching.

Needed research in computer-based rhetoric should build upon previous work and use integrated studies, longitudinal approaches, and sample populations of varied experience. Current computer capabilities make every computer-based writing class an ideal site for ethnographic research, for which improved keystroke-analysis programs might prove particularly beneficial. Though artificial-intelligence researchers continue experimentation with computerized text translators and "Plain English" systems for interactive readability analyses—intended to lessen communicative differences—these have proved ineffective. Better understanding of human language and cognition seems prerequisite to their success.

John M. Clark
Bowling Green State University

Bibliography

Costanzo, William V. *The Electronic Text: Learning to Write, Read, and Reason with Computers.* Englewood Cliffs, NJ: Educational Technology, 1989.

Daiute, Colette. *Writing and Computers.* Menlo Park, CA: Addison-Wesley, 1985.

Gerrard, Lisa, ed. *Writing at Century's End: Essays on Computer-Assisted Composition.* New York: Random, 1987.

Handa, Carolyn, ed. *Computers and Community: Teaching Composition in the Twenty-First Century.* Portsmouth, NH: Boynton/Cook, 1990.

Hawisher, Gail E., and Paul LeBlanc, eds. *Re-Imagining Computers and Composition: Teaching and Research in the Virtual Age.* Portsmouth, NH: Boynton/Cook, 1992.

Hawisher, Gail E., and Cynthia L. Selfe, eds. *Critical Perspectives on Computers and Composition Instruction.* New York: Teachers College P, 1989.

Taylor, Robert, ed. *The Computer in Education: Tutor, Tool, Tutee.* New York: Teachers College P, 1980.

Tuman, Myron C., ed. *Literacy Online: The Promise (and Peril) of Reading and Writing with Computers.* Pittsburgh: U of Pittsburgh P, 1992.

Wresch, William. *The Computer in Composition Instruction: A Writer's Tool.* Urbana, IL: National Council of Teachers of English, 1984.

Condillac, Etienne Bonnot, Abbé de (1714–1780)

French philosopher, contemporary of Voltaire, Diderot, and Rousseau, influenced by Locke and Newton. A nonpracticing priest who early in his career participated in Paris salon society, Condillac wrote on language, psychology, aesthetics, education, economics, and history. A member of the minor nobility, he read Locke in translation as well as Voltaire's summary of Newton's work before writing his early *Essai sur l'origine des connaissances humaines* (1746), subtitled in Nugent's 1756 translation "A Supplement to Mr. Locke's Essay on the Human Understanding." In the essay he inquires into the origin of thought, proclaiming his insight that "the use of signs is the principle which unfolds all our ideas as they lye in the bud," and that "ideas are connected with signs, and it is only by this means that they are connected." He explores intellectual development before the use of articulated language in *Traité des sensations* (1754).

He formulated his educational program in the *Course of Study for the Prince of Parma* (*Cours d'Etudes,* 1769–1772) after being appointed teacher of the young Ferdinand of Parma in 1758, putting into practice his theories of language and intellectual development by stressing his method of linear analysis and the importance of signs and language for human thought. The program begins with the theory of the origins of language and thought in human emotional expression from his essay, later cited by Scottish rhetorician Hugh Blair. Condillac believed that a well-made language, beginning with the most simple ideas closest to the senses and proceeding by analogy and combination to more complex notions, was the basis for all logic and sciences. This method moved from the known to the unknown, both in discovery and communication of knowledge.

Condillac's *Cours,* first published in Paris in 1775, provides aesthetic principles as well as practical guidance on construction of language and style. His treatise "The Art of Writing" ("L'art d'écrire") defines good style as one with clarity and character—combining a sparse, direct style with the appropriate voice or emotional tone. His fundamental notion of the greatest connection of ideas (liaison des idées), allied with his analytic method, contains the germ of the art of writing. Thus Condillac leads the prince to decompose and recompose his observations and study good and bad constructions, using examples from writers such as Boileau, Bossuet, Mme. de Sévigny, and Abbé du Bos.

Condillac also believed, however, that the new in language results from deviations in order, deviations most often brought about by a great poet's use of language to set himself apart from the writing of his age. Deviation is at the heart of metaphor as well as at the origin of language. Condillac's principles are rent by this notion of deviation within order, as his principles of linearity and clarity in writing contradict his emphasis on character and emotional tone and his inclusion of schemes and tropes, including inversion. He has thus been described as both empirical and expressivist, and his major themes oppose analysis to imagination and reason to emotion.

Catherine Hobbs Peaden and Bernadette Takano
University of Oklahoma

Bibliography

Aarsleff, Hans. "Introduction." *On Language: The Diversity of Human Language Structure and Its Influence on the Mental Development of Mankind.* By Wilhelm von Humboldt. Trans. Peter Heath. Cambridge: Cambridge UP, 1988.

———. *From Locke to Saussure: Essays on the Study of Language and Intellectual History.* Minneapolis: U of Minnesota P, 1982.

Condillac, Etienne Bonnot de. *An Essay on the Origin of Human Knowledge.* Intro. James F. Stam. Rpt. 1756 ed. Trans. Thomas Nugent. New York: AMS, 1974.

———. *Oeuvres philosophiques de Condillac.* Ed. Georges Le Roy. 3 vols. Corpus General des Philosophes Francais. St. Germain and Paris: Presses Universitaires de France, 1947.

———. *Philosophical Writings of Etienne Bonnot, Abbé de Condillac.* Trans. Franklin Philip and Harlan Lane. Hillsdale, NJ: Erlbaum, 1982. [Includes *A Treatise on the Sensations* and *Logic, or the First Developments of the Art of Thinking.*]

Derrida, Jacques. *The Archeology of the Frivolous: Reading Condillac.* 1973. Trans. and Intro. John P. Leavey, Jr. Duquesne Studies, Philosophical Series 37. Pittsburgh: Duquesne UP, 1980.

Knight, Isabel F. *The Geometric Spirit: The Abbé de Condillac and the French Enlightenment.* New Haven: Yale UP, 1968.

Sgard, Jean, ed. *Condillac et les problèmes du langage.* Geneva: Editions Slatkine, 1982.

Stefanini, Jean. "Condillac et l'art d'écrire." *Au bonheur des mots: mélanges en l'honneur de Gerald Antoine.* Nancy: P.U., 1984. 593–605.

Taylor, Talbot J. *Mutual Misunderstanding: Skepticism and the Theorizing of Language and Interpretation.* Durham, NC: Duke UP, 1992. 49–70.

Conference on College Composition and Communication

The foremost professional organization for college instructors of nonfiction writing in America, identified by its familiar logo, an abstract sunburst designed by Arnold N. Fujita. "Communication" in the name originally signified a desire to include colleges that established freshman communication programs more inclusive than traditional expository writing courses. Eventually, CCCC concerned itself with other kinds of courses that included speaking and writing, technical writing, advanced composition, and cross-curricular arrangements. Yet the primary emphasis always was on teaching. The organization's administrative affiliation from the beginning with the National Council of Teachers of English—as opposed to the Modern Language Association, the chief scholarly organization of the English profession—was significant in that it gave a separate identity to an important group of college professionals largely excluded from the specialized literary and linguistic interests of MLA.

The permanent organization of CCCC dates from 1950, at which time John C. Gerber of the University of Iowa, who had led the initiative to establish a conference, served as the first chair. As early as 1948, however, members of the college section of NCTE had been demanding attention to the problems of administration, staffing, and teaching in freshman English that resulted from the vast influx of students in the colleges following World War II. An exploratory meeting on college freshman English was held in Chicago on April 1–2, 1949, on which occasion the distinguished critic and rhetorician Kenneth Burke addressed the group, delivering a speech later published in the *Journal of General Education* as "Rhetoric—Old and New" (5.202–09). One of Burke's themes was that rhetoric had been exiled and that portions of it had found refuge among various "new sciences," especially social sciences, where they were being given fresh insights. Neither he nor his listeners realized that the emerging organization of CCCC would become the agency that would restore a new and respected rhetoric in English departments during the second half of the century.

Thus, CCCC had created itself out of practical needs. Since many of the new college students attending colleges under the GI Bill were unprepared for advanced study, early discussions focused on testing, placement, remedial work, teaching methods, staffing, and maintaining uniform standards in multisection courses. The early issues of *College Composition and Communication,* the conference's quarterly journal, were essentially newsletters, devoted mainly to shop talk, a segment that continued under the heading "Staffroom Interchange" after the journal became increasingly an outlet for serious theoretical speculation and scholarly investigation.

Studies during the early 1960s began to review the state of knowledge concerning composition and revealed a dearth of substantial information concerning the composition process. Knowledge about composition was primarily anecdotal and idiosyncratic. *College Composition and Communication* was to play a major role in remedying that deficiency and establishing composition as a worthy subject for study and publication.

The influence of CCCC has continued to expand. The Rhetoric Society of America was an outgrowth of a special interest group within the organization. Further, the conference has extended its own sphere by sponsoring a monograph series titled *Studies in Rhetoric and Writing, an Annual Bibliography on Composition and Rhetoric,* regional conferences on teaching English in the two-year college, winter workshops on topics of current interest, and a job placement service.

From its inception, CCCC showed a remarkable quality of openness and inclusiveness, both to ideas and people. Minority groups were welcomed and represented on committees and task forces. Two-year college teachers were invited to participate and given formal representation on the executive committee. Members of the conference tended to favor liberal attitudes toward usage, recognition of the function of nonstandard dialects in speaking and writing, emphasis upon the total process of writing rather than the finished product only, and acknowledging the importance of free writing, prewriting, and

personal voice in the expression of ideas. The diversified membership was receptive to new approaches. The lively atmosphere of CCCC meetings has continued to attract new members and reflect the latest trends. The organization stays tuned to the new computer technology, to the complexities of second-language learning, to graduate training programs in the teaching of composition, and always, as it had from the very beginning, to maintaining professional standards and winning professional recognition in the hierarchy of higher education.

William F. Irmscher
University of Washington

Confirmatio

From the Latin, to establish or prove; in Latin rhetorical theory, the portion of an oration in which the speaker presents arguments and supporting materials to establish a fact or proposition in the minds of the audience. *Confirmatio* served Roman orators as a "place" for invention, a division of the completed speech, and one of the activities in the *progymnasmata,* the series of elementary rhetorical exercises found in the schools. It remained an identifiable concern of neoclassical Western rhetorics well into the nineteenth century, and the precepts of the classical *confirmatio* can be found today in North American textbooks on public speaking, argumentation, and composition.

Aristotle (*Rhetoric* 1414a) asserted that a speech had but two necessary parts, a statement of the case and its proof. Later rhetoricians developed more elaborate schemes, which typically involved five or six parts (arrangement). In the Latin rhetorics, the crucial portions remained proving one's case (*confirmatio*) and refuting the opposing case (*confutatio*).

As a place of invention, *confirmatio* included consideration of the types of proof, usually following the Aristotelian division into artistic and inartistic, as well as the forms of argument and the *status,* or bases, upon which those arguments were built. Quite often, as in Quintilian, writers of treatises on rhetoric admonished students to consider their arguments simultaneously as modes of proof and of refutation.

As a division of the completed speech, *confirmatio* included a consideration of the best order in which to present arguments. The *Rhetorica ad Herennium* (c. 86–82 B.C.E.) indicates two general approaches, one based on the principles of rhetoric, the other on the needs of the particular circumstances. Order based on the principles of rhetoric usually involved leading and ending with the strongest arguments and placing relatively weaker arguments in the middle. Order based upon the demands of the situation usually entailed responding to the disposition of the audience or judge, or to a strength or weakness in the opponent's case, by placing certain portions of the speech earlier or later than rule suggested. The Latin rhetoricians warned that speakers were to take great care in departing from the established principles of the art, for only experienced advocates could do so without error.

Finally, as an activity in the *progymnasmata*, *confirmatio* constituted the initial student exercise in crafting persuasive arguments. Students practiced using the *status* system to invent lines of probable argument and were required to argue orally for or against the likelihood or credibility of an historical or fictitious story, thereby practicing to persuade and dissuade on the basis of verisimilitude.

Confirmatio remained an integral part of Latin medieval and Renaissance rhetorics and was translated and transformed in the vernacular rhetorics of the seventeenth and eighteenth centuries. In the nineteenth century, the increased specialization of knowledge and the resulting diminution of the canon of invention wrote *confirmatio* out of all but the more specialized treatises on forensic and pulpit oratory.

Sean Patrick O'Rourke
Vanderbilt University

Bibliography

Anon. *Rhetorica ad Herennium*. Trans. Harry Caplan. Loeb Classical Library 403. Cambridge, MA: Harvard UP, 1954.

Cicero, Marcus Tullius. *De inventione*. Trans. H.M. Hubbell. Loeb Classical Library 386. Cambridge, MA: Harvard UP, 1976. xi–346.

Quintilianus, Marcus Fabius. *Institutio oratoria*. Trans. H.E. Butler. 4 vols. Loeb Classical Library 124–27. Cambridge, MA: Harvard UP, 1920–22.

Confucius (551–479 B.C.E.)

The classical Chinese thinker whose discourse dominated China's premodern thought for over two thousand years, including its conception of rhetoric, and continues to exert significant influence in contemporary East Asian cultural formations. His fame as a philosopher notwithstanding, the Confucius in the *Analects* and other classical texts is concerned less with philosophical topics such as destiny or human nature than with rhetorical issues of his time: for example, the style/substance relationship, the adaptation of speech to audience and to situational context, and especially the moral and political dimensions of discourse. He is keenly aware of the power of eloquence and the possibilities of both its use and abuse. This awareness gives rise to an internal tension in his conceptualization of oratory and helps to explain the frequent juxtaposition of conflicting perspectives on rhetoric in his texts. Insisting that "the realization of will depends on the employment of speech, and speech can never be made to perform its functions without the observance of its art" (Zheng 15), Confucius nevertheless distrusts overly refined and eloquent oratory. For him, "it is enough for speeches to be expressive of their meanings," and "cunning words" and "clever speeches" are as indicative of ulterior motives as they are subversive of the moral foundation of social interactions.

He detests "clever talkers" for their ability to "ruin [the audience's] virtue" and even to "overturn states and noble families." Yet he sees just as clearly the potential of putting rhetoric to good use when he finds in the "rectification of names" a key to restoring social order. "If the names are not properly defined," he points out, "the discourse will certainly go awry; and if the discourse goes awry, nothing will ever be accomplished. . . . That is why the superior men always make sure that names are so defined as to be usable in discourse and that discourse be so conducted as to produce practical effects. The superior men never take their speech lightly" (*Analects* 13:3).

In blaming the corruption of the meanings of words for the social disorder of his day and in suggesting that the first step to change the situation is necessarily the semantic clarification and stabilization of all the key terms with which social interactions are carried out, Confucius displays a profound understanding of the complex relationship among discourse, power, and politics. He is concerned above all about what the word

C

does, how it regulates social behaviors and social relations, and in what way it can be made to produce the desired perlocutionary effects within a broad social context. Just as rhetorical as these concerns is his understanding of the contingent nature of the symbolic realm, and the inventional possibilities opened up by the contingency. He calls for the "superior men" to take nothing as "necessarily so" or "of necessity not so," and to strive for what is "proper" accordingly. And yet this is balanced, again, with his caution against "advising on what cannot be changed."

Yameng Liu
Carnegie Mellon University

Bibliography

Cheng, Chung-ying. *New Dimensions of Confucian and Neo-Confucian Philosophy*. Albany: SUNY P, 1991.

Confucius. *The Analects*. Trans. D.C. Lau. London: Penguin, 1979.

Graham, A.C. *Disputers of the Tao*. La Salle, IL: Open Court, 1989.

Hall, David L., and Roger T. Ames. *Thinking through Confucius*. Albany: SUNY P, 1987.

Zheng, Ziyu. *Zhongguo Xiucixue Shigao (The History of Chinese Rhetoric: A Draft)*. Shanghai: Shanghai Education P, 1984.

See also CHINESE RHETORIC

Consubstantiality

A sharing of the same essence or substance, by which humans attain states of identification sufficient to act together cooperatively. Originally a theological term, *consubstantiality* is borrowed and secularized as a pivotal concept in the rhetorical theories of Kenneth Burke, particularly in Burke's theory of dramatism. In theology, *consubstantiality* is a Christian doctrine, which was developed in the late third and early fourth centuries to explain the simultaneous humanity and divinity of Christ; it was formally adopted by the Council of Nicaea in 325 to prohibit the belief that Christ was not fully divine but rather was a part of the created order. The doctrine posited the belief that the Father and Son were of the same substance, the same essence, thereby affirming an identity of being between them even while preserving a recognition of them as different entities.

Burke borrows the concept of consubstantiality metaphorically as a key concept in his theories of dramatism and symbolic action. Taking the theological concept of sharing the same substance yet being individuated separately, Burke applies it as an explanation of how humans are able to share sufficiently in the same ideational or communicative essence to allow for a cooperative working-together even while being individuated differently and uniquely: To be consubstantial with another is to be of the same essence, the same substance, but it is not to be identical.

Since Locke, Burke asserts, philosophy has avoided the term *substance* because of the antinomies attendant to its definition; Burke, however, views it as "doubtful whether they can ever abolish the *function* of that term, or even whether they should *want* to" (1950:21). In relation to identification, both the function of substance-thinking (essentializing) and the desire for, or necessity of, substance-thinking (a perfectionist tendency in language which Burke, again borrowing analogically, this time from Aristotle, calls "entelechy") come to a head in the concept of *consubstantiality*. That is, just as *substance* is never pure, is never itself-in-itself, so too is *consubstantiality*, as the essence or *substance* of *being identified with* or of *identification* itself, never pure. In being *consubstantial* with another, one neither becomes the other nor replaces the other; rather, there is an ambiguous merger at a *genus* level (for example, "class") in which the two *share* essence, but it is a *sharing* which is already and always paradoxically negated by *species* individuation. Just as the phrase "to be substantially the same" implies a difference within it, so too does "pure identification," or consubstantiality, submit to the "paradox of substance": Within identification "are ambiguities of substance." In being identified with B, A is "substantially one" with a person other than himself. Yet at the same time he remains unique, an individual locus of motives. Thus he is both "joined and separate, at once a distinct substance and consubstantial with another" (1950:21).

David Cratis Williams
Northeast Missouri State University

Bibliography

Burke, Kenneth. *A Grammar of Motives*. New York: Prentice, 1945. Berkeley: U of California P, 1969.

———. *A Rhetoric of Motives*. New York: Prentice, 1950. 2nd ed. Berkeley: U of California P, 1969.

Durham, Weldon B. "Kenneth Burke's Concept of Substance." *Quarterly Journal of Speech* 66 (1980): 351–64.

Contextuality

The tendency of rhetoric to locate meaning and value in the context of particular social and material situations. Rhetoric, whether theorized or practiced, whether applied to the purposes of production or interpretation of discourse, is persistently contextual. That is, its effective precepts and practices tend to be determined by what the Greeks called *kairos*—timeliness and appropriateness in a particular circumstance. From the earliest classical treatises on rhetoric to the most recent revisionist discussions, rhetoric emerges as less a stable method or discipline than an attitude toward action in social life. From well before Plato to the present, both the principles and practices of rhetoric appear to be embedded in the temporal and local conditions of particular human interactions.

Ancient Views

As opposed in epistemology and ideology as the sophists and the Platonists might have been, their separate recognitions of the essential contextuality of rhetoric seem to agree. In their theory and practice of rhetoric, the sophists concerned themselves, as Susan C. Jarratt argues, not so much with questions of transcendent truth as with the kinds of conditional and political knowledge that would determine purpose and action in the community they addressed. In his rhetorical theory and practice, Plato (427–347 B.C.E.) sought a mode of public discourse that would approach transcendent truth through, as James L. Kastely argues, an exchange of assertion and refutation that continually situates any attempt to articulate that truth in the fluidity of particular situations. In other words, the sophists used rhetoric to construct the situational knowledge they considered the most valid while Plato used it to remind those who would articulate truth that what they could articulate was not quite that, and both acknowledged in doing so the contextuality of rhetoric.

The germinal theoretical discussion of the contextuality of rhetoric is Aristotle's (384–322 B.C.E.). Contextuality is not a stated topic in *On Rhetoric,* but it may be the dominant subtext throughout. Aristotle's very definition of rhetoric, as "an ability in each [particular] case, to see the available means of persuasion," embeds rhetorical practice in the context of transient social and material situations (Kennedy 36). And Aristotle's three terms for the rhetorical means of persuasion, logos, ethos, and pathos, denote contextual categories: The shape of each, even reason, is at least partially determined by the particularities of time, place, and the people addressed. As Aristotle's most recent translator and editor, George A. Kennedy, explains, the shape of public discourse itself is particular to the public at hand: "In developed human societies . . . social and political contexts emerge that mold speech into certain conventional forms shaped by the psychology and expectations of audiences," forms that are themselves shaped by social and material contexts (7). A more direct insight into this contextuality, however, is Aristotle's description of rhetoric as, in the words of Kennedy, "a verbal, intellectual tool" rather than a discipline (10). What emerges from Kennedy's reading of Aristotle's theoretical treatise is "partly a method (like dialectic) with no necessary subject of its own but partly a practical art derived from ethics and politics on the basis of conventional uses" (12). In other words, rhetoric is, above all, a practice, and practices are embedded in context.

An insightful ancient discussion of rhetoric as a contextual practice is Cicero's *De oratore.* Here Cicero (106–43 B.C.E.) works to undermine notions of rhetoric as a discipline or method that can be mastered, or even discussed, out of the context of the circumstances of its practice. *De oratore* takes the form of a discussion of rhetoric by two masters of its practice in the Roman republic with some young and ambitious politicians. Here Cicero uses the conventions of dialogue to contrast a rendering of rhetoric as an acontextual technique, an object of expertise (presented by one master, Antonius, and sought by the eager politicians), with a rendering of rhetoric as a profoundly contextual practice (presented by the other master, Crassus, and rejected by his interlocutors) in which method and content and function cannot be disentangled. Indeed, as Crassus presents it, and as readers of *De oratore* understand Cicero to define it, rhetoric—more often termed here "eloquence"—is discourse enacted rather than conceptualized, discourse practiced in particular situations rather than theorized in principle. As such, rhetoric is rendered as a political and ethical force at a particular point in the history of a community. And there its shape and function is determined more by the social and material issues and resources that are its context than by mastery of precept that would constitute expertise in a discipline or a science of persuasive discourse.

Cicero's Crassus explains this early in Book 3, where, following a sustained dissertation on method and a review of prominent technical manuals from Antonius, he breaks what has been his relative silence:

> If you think it sufficient to have learned the rules which the writers on rhetoric have delivered, which, however, Antonius has set forth with much more grace and fullness than they are treated by them; if, I say, you are content with these qualifications, and those which you wished to be specified by me, you reduce the orator from a spacious and immense field of action into a very narrow compass. (212)

Here Crassus insists that rhetoric is not discipline but practice. In doing so, he denies not only the divisions of theory and application, and form and content, but also the division that encompasses these that is implicit in any technical discussion of rhetoric, that of expertise and citizenship.

That denial—essentially, a denial that rhetoric can be mastered as a body of precepts apart from its contextual practice—is resisted by those who are interrogating Antonius and Crassus in order to develop their own expertise. When Crassus goes on to say that a "complete orator," one he defines "as having wisdom united with eloquence" is also, necessarily, a philosopher, one whose discourse is necessarily embedded in the ethical and epistemological context of a particular time, place, and people, two of those men respond with objections (233). Cotta reminds Crassus that in their discussion Antonius had already reviewed precepts of invention and arrangement while Crassus had agreed to cover precepts of "embellishments of language," which, to this point, he has not done. Less tactfully, Sulpicius tells Crassus that he neither "desire[s] any acquaintance with your Aristotle, nor Carneades, nor any of the philosophers," and that Crassus "may either imagine that I despair of being able to acquire their knowledge or that"—Sulpicius now puts it directly—"as is really the case, I despise it." That is because Sulpicius seeks only a "degree of eloquence" circumscribed by a "narrow circle of science" (234). In response Crassus notes that these "matters which are very well known," that much is written about them in the many technical manuals, and that Sulpicius "ought to refer to those who are authors and inventors of these minute precepts" (234–35). Then he complies with their request by beginning a theoretical—and acontextual—discussion of language.

Contemporary Views

Contemporary writers on rhetoric, commenting both directly and indirectly from a variety of disciplines, have sharpened these ancient observations of rhetoric's inherent contextuality. In a commentary that addresses rhetoric indirectly, Frederic Jameson instructs literary interpreters to "always historize," a practical acknowledgment that textual meaning is "immanent" and that texts are "social functions" and "political responses" to the social and material circumstances of people in a particular time and place (9,23,86). And Steven Mailloux, addressing rhetoric directly, defines it as the "potential effectivity of trope and argument in culture" by noting that the meaning and the function of any discourse are established in the process of rhetorical exchanges (xii). Indeed, Mailloux argues that "any specific interpretation is best understood in relation to particular contexts of institutional and cultural debates." He goes on to propose the practice of a "rhetorical hermeneutic" that locates acts interpretation itself in the context of "exchanges among interpreters embedded in discourses and other social practices at specific historical moments" (57,133).

Other contemporary commentators have advanced the notion of the contextuality of rhetoric by shifting examinations of rhetorical theory and practice from the predominant orality of the ancients to the predominant textuality of the present. Susan Miller has articulated an explicitly "textual rhetoric" that is self-consciously embedded in the spaces and times of history and culture. A textual rhetoric, she suggests, "reverses oral rhetoric to place 'the public' within the written world" that constitutes both "cultural context" and "textual context" of every written discourse (42). Specifically, Miller proposes that we use this notion of a textual rhetoric "to account for a piece of writing as the result of, and as a contribution to, both cultural and textual histories beyond the immediate 'rhetorical situation' that is usually invoked for guidance when an act of writing is equated with an oral performance." Writers cannot present in writing the characters or meanings they might intend because writing works in multiple contexts, both "captur[ing] the writer's first intentions and invok[ing] a distant and unknown reader's textual experiences." Writing, from this perspective, temporarily "fictionalizes stability in the fluid instability of history and culture" (149). Consequently, for Miller,

A virtuoso performance in writing thus takes place within cultural, textual, situational, and graphic conventions that textual rhetoric addresses. The writer may allow any of these considerations to stimulate and to constrain the text, whose future revision will be inevitable. (150)

The function of this textual rhetoric is to contextualize explicitly and thus localize and relativize the meaning of a text in a way that undermines the authority of any claims to truth it might make. The effect of this function is to provoke what Mary Field Belenky and her collaborators describe epistemologically as "constructed knowing"—an understanding that "answers to all questions vary depending upon the context in which they are asked and on the frame of reference of the person doing the asking" (138). This understanding of the necessary and inherent contextuality of knowledge has two immediate consequences, and both are political. The first has to do with the authority granted by the reader to a text—readers become themselves responsible "for evaluating and continually reevaluating their assumptions about knowledge" and, in the process, skeptical of the authority claimed by expertise. For such readers, "true experts must reveal an appreciation for complexity and a sense of humility about their knowledge" (139). The second consequence has to do with the relation of knowledge and action. Belenky and her collaborators argue that this understanding of the contextuality of knowledge implicates it in action—people perceiving discourse and knowledge in this way "strive to translate their moral commitments into action, both out of a conviction that 'one must act' and out of a feeling of responsibility to the larger community in which they live" (150).

Categories and Contextuality

An exploration of contextuality in the theory and practice of rhetoric, both in the past and the present, persistently undermines the kind of categories that have always been used to make rhetoric manageable conceptually and pedagogically. A recognition of the inherent contextuality of discourse and knowledge persistently undermines the autonomy of the category of theory itself, as well as that of other important categories such as private and public and expert and citizen. Indeed, the deceptively simple statement by Kenneth Burke (1897–1993) about discursive form that undermines the categorical division of form and content can be used to intensify this recognition of the primacy of context. Form, he wrote early in this century, is "the creation of an appetite in the mind of the auditor and the adequate satisfying of that appetite" (31). It is "an arousing of and fulfillment of desires" (124); it is "a manipulation of the reader's desires using what the reader considers desirable" (146). In these statements, form and content coalesce in the particular context of the interactions of speaker and audience, reader and writer. The momentum of these statements moves them beyond the theoretical toward description of a self-conscious practice of social criticism and revision that would enact rhetoric as "a disintegrating art which converts each simplicity into a complexity, which ruins the possibility of ready hierarchies" (105). This is the consequence of a perspective that accounts more fully for rhetoric's contextuality.

Gregory Clark
Brigham Young University

Bibliography

Belenky, Mary Field, Blythe McVicker Clinchy, Nancy Rule Goldberger, and Jill Mattuck Tarule. *Women's Ways of Knowing: The Development of Self, Voice, and Mind.* New York: Basic, 1986.

Burke, Kenneth. *Counter-Statement.* Berkeley: U of California P, 1968.

Cicero, Marcus Tullius. *De oratore. Cicero on Oratory and Orators.* Trans. J.S. Watson. Intro. Ralph A. Micken. Carbondale: Southern Illinois UP, 1970.

Clark, Gregory. *Dialogue, Dialectic, and Conversation: A Social Perspective on the Function of Writing.* Carbondale: Southern Illinois UP, 1990.

Jameson, Frederic. *The Political Unconscious: Narrative and a Socially Symbolic Act.* Ithaca, NY: Cornell UP, 1981.

Jarratt, Susan C. *Rereading the Sophists: Classical Rhetoric Refigured.* Carbondale: Southern Illinois UP, 1991.

Kastely, James L. "In Defense of Plato's Gorgias." *Publications of the Modern Language Association* 106 (1991): 96–109.

Kennedy, George A., trans. *Aristotle on Rhetoric: A Theory of Civic Discourse.* New York: Oxford UP, 1991.

Mailloux, Steven. *Rhetorical Power.* Ithaca, NY: Cornell UP, 1989.

Miller, Susan. *Rescuing the Subject: A Critical Introduction to Rhetoric and the Writer.* Carbondale: Southern Illinois UP, 1989.

Contingency

Variously associated with the realm of the uncertain, the "more or less," and the probable. What is called the contingent assumes central importance for the topics and issues of rhetorical dispute. This is because, in one of his pivotal distinctions, Aristotle defined the locus of the rhetorical as that which had not been decided, that which still appeared to speakers and audiences as unsettled. His idea was that specialized sciences and logical inquiry made available reliable material and formal truth criteria for certain subjects; hence, he saw no reason for an art of persuasion and judgment in those areas. Instead, rhetoric was best addressed to those matters about which reasonable people could still expect to disagree. This area is still described by rhetoricians and philosophers under the rubric of contingency.

Even after Kant and Hegel had gotten hold of the concept of contingency, our modern vernacular of "unsettled" remained probably its best available synonym. But since Aristotle was uncustomarily ambiguous with the meaning of this concept, and very differing understandings are still available to us, it is helpful to explore some alternative construals of how contingency might relate to the practice and theory of rhetoric. An initial path through our subject can be found in the well-known distinction Aristotle makes between the realm of the probable and that of the necessary. Many commentators have observed that this distinction is as pivotal to the *Rhetoric* as the distinction between entechnic and atechnic proofs. So construed, the realm of the uncertain is simply opposed to the intractable necessities, the dead certainties of reality. Rhetoric would deal with the former, some sort of science with the latter; and that would be that.

But fortunately or not, it is not that simple. For one thing, the realm of the probable is not restricted to the attentions of rhetoric alone. Dialectic, the other universal method and craft of inquiry, also grapples with matters of general opinion, questions over which experts and philosophers may well disagree. For another thing, the whole amorphous area that eludes the closure of exact science and formal definition may offer subject matters open to widely varying characterization. So we may be uncertain whether the shadow we see on the wall is of an outside tree branch or a dangerous interloper. We may be uncertain whether abortion is morally wrong. We may not know whether to believe a charge of sexual harassment. We may not fully subscribe to the "big bang" theory of creation. We may be confused as to why dinosaurs suddenly became extinct. This widely varying array may be one reason why Aristotle offered, as part of his *Organon* of inquiry, a grammar of "moods" to describe ways of affirming and denying propositions. While he did not flesh out this theory to include every possible option, there is good reason to believe that one sense of contingency would unfold as a manner of affirming/denying propositions.

The widely held notion that propositions can be only true or false in the Aristotelian schema flies squarely in the face of the Aristotelian theory of modality. In the last passages of *De interpretatione,* we are given a rather startling array of oppositions, where propositions are concerned. Things can be true or false, predictably enough. The contradictory of something being *necessarily* true, however, is that it is not necessarily true; in other words, that it is *possibly* false. Now, of course, if a proposition is possibly false, it is possibly true as well. This is why the contradictory of the claim that something is impossible would be that it is *not* impossible; in other words, that it may be. Quite interestingly, Aristotle does not explore the teleological direction of considering that things could be *potentially* true. But this is the first place where he allows that claims may be contingently true. In fact, he explicitly allows that from the proposition that something *may* be, it follows that its truth is contingent, and that the reciprocal follows as well. First and foremost, therefore, contingency may be viewed as a manner of affirming propositions. Our second question, then: What sort of manner of affirmation or denial is included within contingency?

Here it is essential to attend to the differences between rhetoric and dialectic. While it is the case that both dialectic and rhetoric deal with matters that may or may not be the case and that both dialectic and rhetoric ask for premises from others to make their arguments, these two universal methods deal very differently with the world of uncertainty. Dialectic is speculative inquiry over generalized propositions—for instance, definitions of justice, the meaning of the good life, the best sort of political arrangement, and so forth. Rhetoric is embedded in the live options that impinge upon our practical choices as positioned subjects and actors. This may be why Aristotle explicitly works an evaluative language of the preferable into his topics of contingency: For instance, "It is contingent that it should not be," and "It is not contingent that it should not be." In rhetoric, then, the contingent is about live options for choice and action. Its materials are signs, probabilities, and examples that may reduce uncertainty when cumulated. But these would never add up to necessary truth; if they did, we would find ourselves in a nonrhetorical occasion. This second characteristic of contingency is important because it suggests that rhetoric is not some primitive mode of grappling with matters that have not yet been subjugated by science. Rather it is simply intrinsic to the human condition that some matters of judgment and action cannot be reduced to certainty.

A final characteristic of contingency brings us closest to its recognizable definition, and that is its particular *conditionality,* or circumstantiality for rendering judgments on practical civic matters. What this means is that often rhetorical judgments and arguments must rest their best evidence upon the conditions surrounding choice and action. For example, some time ago American naval forces shot down a passenger airliner from Iran, killing all persons aboard. Initially, it was claimed that the downed jet was descending toward the vessel that fired upon it, *and* that the plane was outside the proper air corridor for domestic travel. These contingencies allow the portrayal of the event as occasioning a tragic mistake. But now, suppose, as was later admitted, that none of these conditions were true, that by admission it was the naval vessel that was in Iranian waters, that the Iranian jet was actually taking off. We now have a very different construal of U.S. conduct, *depending upon* the conditions of its occurrence. To the extent that there are any truths in rhetoric worthy of the names, these are occasioned by the contingencies of deliberation and judgment.

In modern philosophy there are two strands of thought that borrow and revise the Aristotelian notion of contingency. One is the idea that even more general ethical and moral questions are grounded, if at all, in contingency. Theorists of what is called "moral luck" claim that unanticipated conditions have more to do with whether or not we have an ethical life or even justifiable political and moral arrangements than we have previously credited. Still others argue that the Aristotelian stance is too restrictive and needs to be broadened to include a sense of radical indeterminacy, what I suspect Aristotle would call "chance." There are arguments to be made on multiple sides of these questions. And regardless of the conditions, positions, and moods of the disputants, it is likely that the concept of contingency will be a durable feature of contemporary rhetorical practice and theory.

Thomas B. Farrell
Northwestern University

Bibliography

Aristotle. *De Interpretatione*. Trans. E.M. Edghill. *The Works of Aristotle*. 7th ed. Ed. W.D. Ross. Oxford: Oxford UP, 1968.

———. *On Rhetoric: A Theory of Civic Discourse*. Trans. George A. Kennedy. Oxford: Oxford UP, 1991.

Farrell, Thomas B. *Norms of Rhetorical Culture*. New Haven: Yale UP, 1993.

Kahn, Victoria. *Rhetoric, Prudence, and Skepticism in the Renaissance*. Ithaca, NY: Cornell UP, 1985.

Nussbaum, Martha C. *The Fragility of Goodness: Luck and Ethics in Greek Tragedy and Philosophy*. Cambridge: Cambridge UP, 1986.

Smith, Barbara Herrnstein. *Contingencies of Value: Alternative Perspectives for Critical Theory*. Cambridge: Harvard UP, 1988.

Waterlow, Sarah. *Passage and Possibility: A Study of Aristotle's Modal Concepts*. Oxford: Clarendon, 1982.

Contrast

Used to show the differences or distinctions between things being studied. Contrast is a function of comparison in that contrast is the result of comparing those elements that are different among things being compared. Thus, comparison along with contrast was first mentioned as a rhetorical strategy in Aristotle's *Rhetoric*. Aristotle suggests using comparison of one's position to an opponent's and mentions use of comparison of similarities and differences to illustrate the points of an argument. Rhetoricians made use of the topic of difference in order to develop arguments that would confirm or refute their positions. Comparison of similarities and differences (contrasts) can also be used to restate a position in order to highlight the weakness of an opposing position in an argument or to develop a refutation of opposing arguments.

Comparison of similarities and differences (contrasts), as a mode of discourse, is used in various writing assignments from definition or evaluations of people, places, problems, or things, as well as the traditional refutation of opposing positions in an argument. Contrast is part of the thought process that helps us make meaning through comparing differences of people, ideas, or other things being considered. As a function of thought process, contrast helps us through the invention process as we categorize things according to differences (contrasts) or similarities (comparison). Furthermore, contrast, along with comparison, gives us methods for presenting those findings in our written discourse.

Formats for contrast vary. Two approaches for presenting comparisons or contrasts are the block structure and the alternate structure. In a block format, one presents elements for each person or item to be contrasted separately. One can also, however, make contrasts by alternating the points being contrasted. In the alternate format of contrast or comparison of two cities, one could move back and forth between elements for contrast or comparison of the two cities. In order to avoid taxing readers' or listeners' attention, one can successfully combine block and alternating contrast structures.

Current rhetorical theories treat contrast as a mode of development that can be a useful aid in invention or arrangement. Contrast helps us to develop areas for discussion during the invention process, where contrasting the features of a topic or object can serve an exploratory function. An influential modern theory that draws on classical modes of development is James Kinneavy's *Theory of Discourse*, which treats contrast along with comparison as part of the mode of classification. In the works of such theorists as Kinneavy and D'Angelo, one can see that contrast and comparison can be useful as an aid in the composing process as long as one does not confuse such modes of development with the aims of composition.

Louise Rodriguez Connal
University of Arizona

Bibliography

Corbett, Edward P.J. *Classical Rhetoric for the Modern Student*. 2nd ed. New York: Oxford UP, 1971. 479.

D'Angelo, Frank J. "Aims, Modes, and Forms of Discourse." *Teaching Composition: 12 Bibliographical Essays*. Ed. Gary Tate. Fort Worth: Texas Christian UP, 1987. 131–54.

Kennedy, George A., trans. *Aristotle: A Theory of Civic Discourse: On Rhetoric*. New York: Oxford UP, 1991.

Contrastive Rhetoric

A subfield of English as a Second Language (ESL) writing research. Its beginning can be traced to 1966, when the applied linguist Robert Kaplan

at the University of Southern California published his now frequently cited article "Cultural Thought Patterns in Intercultural Education." Kaplan demonstrated that rhetorical structures of languages differ. There is a transfer from first language writing to second language, and this transfer causes interference in second-language writing. Hence, the nonnative sound of many English-as-a-second-language writers.

Kaplan's Contrastive Rhetoric

Based on samples of some six hundred ESL student writers, Kaplan drew the rhetorical structures of the first language of his sample students in the frequently reproduced diagram shown below. He also showed that their first-language rhetorical structures were evident in their second-language writing. He suggested that Anglo-European expository essays follow a linear development. In contrast, paragraph development in Semitic languages is based on a series of parallel organizations of coordinate rather than subordinate clauses. Oriental essays use an indirect approach and come to the point at the end of an essay. In

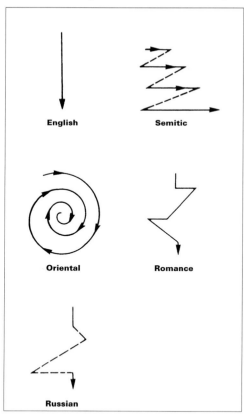

Figure 1. Diagram from Robert B. Kaplan, "Cultural Thought Patterns in Intercultural Education," Language Learning 16:15.

Romance languages and in Russian, essays contain certain digressions and extraneous material.

Kaplan was influenced by the Sapir-Whorf hypothesis of linguistic relativity (that is, that different languages affect perception and thought in different ways) and maintained that language is a cultural phenomenon; furthermore, logic and rhetoric (the basis of rhetoric being logic) are also evolved out of culture.

English rhetoric, according to Kaplan, is influenced by the Greek, Roman, and later Western thinkers. Kaplan describes the nature of English exposition as linear in the sense that a paragraph begins with a topic statement supported by examples that are related to the central theme. Although most English paragraphs are deductive in the manner described, inductive paragraph development, where the topic statement ends the paragraph, is also available for writers of English in Kaplan's theory of 1966.

Although intuitively appealing to writing teachers and popular among ESL writing researchers and graduate students in the 1970s, Kaplan's representations have been criticized a great deal. Critics have asserted that contrastive rhetoric (1) overgeneralizes terms such as *oriental* and puts in the same group languages that belong to distinct families; (2) is ethnocentric by representing the organization of English paragraphs by a straight line; (3) generalizes to the native language organization from the examination of students' L2 essays; and (4) overemphasizes cognitive factors at the expense of sociocultural factors (such as schooling) as a preferred rhetoric. Kaplan himself has modified his earlier position in a number of recent publications, calling his 1966 article a "doodles" article and suggesting, for example, that rhetorical differences do not necessarily reflect different patterns of thinking. Instead, differences may reflect different writing conventions that have been learned.

Recent Contrastive Rhetorical Research

After Kaplan's 1966 publication, much ESL writing research has been conducted in the contrastive rhetorical framework. Surveys of research on specific language contrasts (for example, Spanish/English, German/English, Thai/English, Hindi/English, Japanese/English, Chinese/English) can be found in Kaplan (1983), Connor and Kaplan, and Purves. Most findings concur with Kaplan's major thesis, namely that different languages and cultures prefer different writing styles. Differences are evident in many levels of text production: context

of writing; stages of writing process; linguistic conventions; and rhetorical patterns, that is, paragraph organizational patterns. The research of the applied linguist John Hinds is relevant here.

Hinds has shown, perhaps more convincingly than anyone else, that certain text structures are used to achieve *coherence* that allows the reader to make the right inference, and that textual patterns used to express coherence vary among languages and cultures.

Hinds has shown that writing in Japanese, Chinese, Thai, and Korean favors an inductive rather than a deductive style of presentation, or what Hinds calls "delayed introduction of purpose" (1990:98). The specifics lead up to what appears to be, and often is, the conclusion. This delayed introduction of purpose makes the writing appear incoherent to the English-speaking reader (although not to the native reader), especially since the concluding paragraph does not always constitute a conclusion in the English sense. English-speaking readers expect most essays to be organized deductively, from the general to the particular.

In addition to achieving coherence through textual structures such as the inductive, writers need to be sensitive to the different expectations of reader/writer responsibilities across cultures. In proposing a new typology of language based on "speaker and/or writer responsibility as opposed to listener and/or responsibility," Hinds has shown that with respect to coherence, for example, Japanese writing demands more of the reader, while the inference-based rhetorical form preferred in the West places the burden chiefly on the writer.

Hinds's extensive research on English and Japanese expository prose shows that English readers expect and require landmarks of coherence and unity as they read. The writer needs to provide the transitional statements. In Japanese, on the other hand, transitions may be lacking. The reader is expected to piece together sections to make a coherent text.

Text linguistic studies have been conducted to compare texts and their production in many other languages in addition to Japanese, Chinese, Thai, and Korean (see Connor and Kaplan, and Purves for studies and findings).

New Directions in Contrastive Rhetoric

In the 1990s changes are taking place in contrastive rhetorical research. A contrastive rhetoric is being defined in broader terms. Contrastive rhetoric is moving from a purely linguistic framework interested in structural analyses of written products to a framework that considers the cognitive and social aspects of the writing situation.

Influenced by trends in first-language composition research, contrastive rhetoricians are sensitive to the fact that writing is seen as a discourse process of generating, organizing, and translating ideas into text. Contrastive rhetoricians have begun examining cross-cultural differences in writing activities and processes. In addition, contrastive rhetoricians understand that the nature of writing is viewed as inherently interactive and social. Writing involves more than the generation, organization, and translation of ideas. It is considered interaction between reader and writer within a particular group, discipline, or scholarly community.

Writers' own purposes are not enough to explain decisions they make. Instead, the context situation and the reader need to be considered. Contrastive rhetoric is addressing cross-cultural components of these interactions. Research has been conducted on scientific and business writing cross-culturally, for example.

Implications of Contrastive Rhetoric for Teaching and Testing

The consequence of Kaplan's early theory was the instruction in the linear English pattern of organization in ESL writing classes. As had been the case with the theory of contrastive analysis, structures missing in the native language were considered the cause of the greatest problems in the acquisition of the target language.

More recently, the relevance for ESL teaching of contrastive rhetoric was discussed by Leki. She suggests that contrastive rhetoric has several implications for ESL teachers. First, contrastive rhetorical research helps students understand that preferences in writing styles are culturally determined. Second, students can be made aware of cultural differences in rhetoric for psychological reasons. Students can feel good about themselves when they know that their writing in English is not "bad" when it exhibits some features of their L1. Third, contrastive rhetoric helps explain why and how teachers should teach the expectations of the English audience to ESL writers.

Newer, broader definitions of contrastive rhetoric have further implications for all teachers of writing, not only for ESL teachers (Allaei and Connor). Teachers benefit from being aware of cultural differences in writing activity and understanding composing and revising behaviors of students from different cultures (see Purves). In addition, it is advantageous if teachers are sensitive to differing interactional patterns across cultures and adjust collaborative writing groups and other classroom activities accordingly.

For developers of writing tests, raters, and for those who interpret results of writing tests, contrastive rhetoric has important implications. Contrastive rhetoric informs these professionals about cross-cultural differences in appropriateness of writing topics, level and type of content, and preferred patterns of style and language.

Ulla M. Connor
Indiana University

Bibliography

Allaei, Sara, and Ulla Connor. "Exploring the Dynamics of Cross-cultural Collaboration in Writing Classrooms." *Writing Instructor* 10 (1990): 19–28.

Connor, Ulla, and Robert Kaplan, eds. *Writing across Languages and Cultures: Analysis of L2 Text*. Reading, MA: Addison-Wesley, 1987.

Hinds, John. "Contrastive Rhetoric and Second Language Learning: Notes toward a Theory of Contrastive Rhetoric." *Writing across Languages and Cultures: Issues in Contrastive Rhetoric*. Ed. A.C. Purves. Newbury Park, CA: Sage, 1988. 275–304.

———. "Cultural Thought Patterns Revisited." *Writing across Languages and Cultures: Analysis of L2 Text*. Ed. Ulla Connor and Robert Kaplan. Reading, MA: Addison, 1987. 9–22.

———. "Inductive, Deductive, Quasi-inductive: Expository Writing in Japanese, Korean, Chinese, and Thai." *Coherence in Writing: Research and Pedagogical Perspectives*. Ed. Ulla Connor and Robert Kaplan. Alexandria, VA: TESOL, 1990.

———. "Reader Versus Writer Responsibility: A New Typology." *Writing across Languages and Cultures: Analysis of L2 Text*. Ed. Ulla Connor and Robert Kaplan. Reading, MA: Addison-Wesley, 1987. 141–52.

Kaplan, Robert. "Cultural Thought Patterns in Intercultural Education." *Language Learning* 16 (1966): 1–20.

Leki, I. "Twenty-five Years of Contrastive Rhetoric: Text Analysis and Writing Pedagogies." *TESOL Quarterly* 25 (1990): 123–43.

Purves, A.C., ed. *Writing across Languages and Cultures: Issues in Contrastive Rhetoric*. Newbury Park, CA: Sage, 1988.

Scollon, R., and S.B.K. Scollon. *Narrative, Literacy and Face in Interethnic Communication*. Norwood, NJ: Ablex, 1981.

Copia

The "storehouse" of invention and style, focus of Erasmus's *De duplici copia verborum ac rerumm.* Agricultural abundance, figured in the cornucopia, offers a neat visual emblem of the rhetorical qualities prized in "copious" speech. A woven basket overflowing with grains, vegetables, and fruit, the cornucopia symbolizes a harvest that will feed a community. In terms of rhetorical practice, the cornucopia also symbolizes the variousness of that community, whose appetites range across the "difference" signified in the pointedly heterogeneous harvest gathering.

The doctrine of *copia* is hardly distinguishable from that of eloquence, except that *copia* is discussed pedagogically, in the context of training required to attain eloquence. Fittingly, the Latin *copia* can be translated into various terms, as *fullness, abundance,* and *variety.* These English translations have a central focus, however. They apply either to ample resources of diction or of invention, the guiding idea or purpose that animates an entire discourse. A copious style is able to amplify and enrich a single word or sentence by reproducing synonymous words and phrases.

An astonishing demonstration of copious style is found in Erasmus's sixteenth-century textbook on rhetoric, *On Variety of Words and Arguments.* To show that words hold potentialities of meaning that are released when varied into synonymic form, Erasmus takes the sentence "Your letter delighted me very much" and varies it into one hundred and fifty equivalent sentences. Thus, "letter" can be varied into "your words"—a personal, confidential letter—or "your message"—a letter with some valuable information or insight; "delighted" can be toned down to "pleased me" or emotionally heightened as "a feast." Although copious style may involve the enrichment of a key concept through semantic variant forms—as when a Shakespearean character praises women as "the books, the arts, the academes" of love, the larger purpose of acquiring *copia* of style is to enhance linguistic resourcefulness. Fine shades of meaning can be expressed only by selecting the finely nuanced connotations of one word over another.

The same principle of enlarging and vivifying a plain-suited concept is active in copious argument. Erasmus tells us that there is "nothing more admirable or more splendid than a speech with a rich *copia* of thoughts and words overflowing in a golden stream." And he demonstrates this by revealing how a single subject holds multiple sources of proof, not only from the logical commonplaces—of cause and effect, of greater or lesser value, of definition—but by revealing the rich particularity that inheres in every object considered circumstantially, in its unique time, place, and purpose. Thus, in his Eleventh Method for enriching argument, Erasmus explains that speech purporting to define the character of a person can be enriched by accumulating circumstantial proofs concerning the person's "family, race, country, sex, age, education, physical appearance, fortune, rank, natural disposition, desires, inclinations, previous acts and sayings. " Eloquence is not found in elegant phrasing—although that is one benefit of having verbal resources or a "storehouse"—but rather in the unfolding of propositions by which an uncertain matter emerges into the light of a probable truth. Erasmus's *De copia* is thus guided by the touchstone of rhetorical reasoning—the contingent and circumstantial. Copious speech thus expands outward, from a general statement, belief, attitude, to the dust and heat of those particular realities in which we move and have our being.

Daniel Bender
Pace University

Bibliography

Boyle, Marjorie O'Rourke. *Erasmus on Method and Theology.* Toronto: U of Toronto, 1977.

Cave, Terence. *The Cornucopian Text: Problems of Writing in the French Renaissance.* Oxford: Clarendon, 1979.

Erasmus. *On Copia of Word and Ideas.* Trans. and Ed. Donald King and H. David Rix. Milwaukee: Marquette UP, 1963.

Sloane, Thomas O. "Schoolbooks and Rhetoric: Erasmus's Copia." *Rhetorica* 9 (1991): 113–29.

See also ERASMUS

Corax (c. 490 B.C.E.–c. 440 B.C.E.)

Considered to be the "founder" of the discipline of rhetoric. Corax is credited with advancing and formalizing systems of expression in Syracuse, Sicily, and thus establishing rhetoric. The date of rhetoric's origin is set at 467–

466 B.C.E., a time in which the Syracusan tyrant Thrasybulus was deposed and democracy instated. Skepticism over the acceptance of such a precise date is evident among current scholars, particularly Edward Schiappa. While in actuality such systems had long been in evolution in Greek thought, ancient historians and Byzantine scholars consistently credit Corax with rhetoric's origin at this moment in history. The controversy over this topic is so acute that some researchers even doubt Corax's existence (Cole). It is more likely, however, that Corax did exist, and is known to us in two respects. First, he is often credited with teaching prominent rhetoricians, including Tisias, and possibly Gorgias and Lysias. Second, he is mentioned as having applied a system of probable argument to civil and forensic matters as well as the arrangement and division of rhetorical argument, ranging, by various accounts, from three to seven parts. As our knowledge of this period increases, the belief over Corax's existence and his contributions becomes correspondingly more salient.

Richard Leo Enos
Texas Christian University

Bibliography

Cole, Thomas. *The Origins of Rhetoric in Ancient Greece*. Baltimore: Johns Hopkins UP, 1991.

Enos, Richard Leo. *Greek Rhetoric before Aristotle*. Prospect Heights, IL: Waveland, 1993.

Schiappa, Edward. *Protagoras and Logos. A Study of Greek Philosophy and Rhetoric*. Columbia: U of South Carolina P, 1991.

Corbett, Edward P.J. (Patrick Joseph) (b. 1919)

American rhetorical scholar and educator, born in Jamestown, North Dakota. He attended Milwaukee, Wisconsin, schools, graduating from Marquette University High School in 1939, and matriculated at Venard College, Clark's Summit, Pennsylvania, from 1938 to 1942. He served as a radar technician in the Pacific Theatre during World War II, after which he attended the University of Chicago, attaining an M.A. degree in English Language and Literature in 1948. In 1950 he began Ph.D. work at Loyola University of Chicago, earning the Ph.D. degree in 1956 with a dissertation on "Hugh Blair: A Study of His Rhetorical Theory."

Corbett's first teaching position was at Creighton University, in Omaha, Nebraska, where he taught from 1948 to 1950 and again from 1953 through 1966. He was director of freshman English at Creighton from 1953 to 1956. In 1966 he moved to the university with which he is strongly associated, Ohio State University in Columbus, where he taught from 1966 until his retirement in 1989. At OSU he directed the freshman English program from 1966 to 1970 and became the cornerstone of the graduate program in rhetoric and composition studies that has since been recognized as one of the pioneering programs in the country.

Active in many professional organizations, Corbett was one of the founders of the Rhetoric Society of America in 1968. After many years of service to the Conference on College Composition and Communication, he was elected president of that organization in 1971. In 1974 he was appointed to the editorship of the central journal in the field of composition studies, *College Composition and Communication,* and served until 1979. During the period of Corbett's editorship, the field of composition studies really came of age, establishing itself as a mature scholarly field; Corbett was responsible for publishing nearly all of the important scholars of the decade, including Mina Shaughnessy, Janet Emig, Ann Berthoff, Donald Murray, Maxine Hairston, Frank D'Angelo, Andrea Lunsford, Linda Flower, and many others.

Corbett is best known for his scholarly work in making the tradition of classical rhetoric available to contemporary writing students. Up until the 1960s, the classical tradition was almost entirely nurtured in speech departments, and written rhetoric had lost touch with classical ideas. All that began to change radically in 1963 when Corbett published his first major article on classical applications, "The Usefulness of Classical Rhetoric," in CCC. This article was followed by a number of others, all dealing with the older traditions of rhetoric and their impact on composition issues or with his other area of interest, style in writing. Corbett's best-known articles and essays include "A Method of Analyzing Prose Style" (1965), "A New Look at Old Rhetoric" (1967), "What is Being Revived?" (1967), "The Rhetoric of the Open Hand and the Rhetoric of the Closed Fist" (1969), "The Theory and Practice of Imitation in Classical Rhetoric" (1971), "Rhetoric, the Enabling Discipline" (1972), "Approaches to the Study of Style" (1976), "John Locke's Contributions to Rhetoric" (1981), and "The Cornell School of Rhetoric" (1985). His most important essays have been collected in *Selected Essays of Edward P.J. Corbett*, edited by Robert J. Connors (1989).

Corbett is also the author of a number of well-known books, including his most famous, *Classical Rhetoric for the Modern Student* (1965), *The Little English Handbook* (1973), and *The Little Rhetoric* (1977). He edited *Rhetorical Analyses of Literary Works* (1969) and *The Essay: Subjects and Stances* (1974), and coedited several important collections with Gary Tate, including *Teaching Freshman Composition* (1967), *Teaching High School Composition* (1970), and *The Writing Teacher's Sourcebook* (1981). He also coedited *The Rhetoric of Blair, Campbell, and Whately* with James L. Golden (1968) and *Essays on the Rhetoric of the Western World* with James L. Golden and Goodwin F. Berquist (1990).

One of the primary scholars in the New Rhetoric movement that reshaped college composition teaching during the 1960s and 1970s, Corbett was an important figure in the formation of the discipline of composition studies. His analyses and discussions of traditional rhetorical ideas in composition forums made the classical tradition and the rich intellectual heritage it represented accessible and useful to writing teachers, and his scholarly work broke new ground in understanding the teaching of written discourse. In addition, he remains a man immensely beloved by his students and colleagues, one whose influence was always personal as well as scholarly. A festschrift in his honor, *Classical Rhetoric and Modern Discourse*, edited by three of his students, was published in 1984. He is retired from teaching but remains active in scholarship and in revision of his many book projects.

Robert J. Connors
University of New Hampshire

Bibliography

Connors, Robert J., Lisa Ede, and Andrea Lunsford, eds. *Classical Rhetoric and Modern Discourse*. Carbondale: Southern Illinois UP, 1984.

Corbett, Edward P.J. *Classical Rhetoric for the Modern Student*. 3rd ed. New York: Oxford UP, 1990.

———. *Selected Essays of Edward P.J. Corbett*. Ed. Robert J. Connors. Dallas: Southern Methodist UP, 1989.

———, ed. *Rhetorical Analyses of Literary Works*. New York: Oxford UP, 1969.

Corbett, Edward P.J., James L. Golden, and Goodwin F. Berquist, eds. *Essays on the Rhetoric of the Western World*. Dubuque, IA: Kendall/Hunt, 1990.

Golden, James L., and Edward P.J. Corbett, eds. *The Rhetoric of Blair, Campbell, and Whately*. 2nd ed. New York: Holt, 1980.

Tate, Gary, and Edward P.J. Corbett, eds. *Teaching Freshman Composition*. New York: Oxford UP, 1967.

———, eds. *The Writing Teacher's Sourcebook*. 2nd ed. New York: Oxford UP, 1988.

Correctness

Conformity to a prescribed norm. In rhetoric, *correctness* may signify technical accuracy, stylistic appropriateness, logical validity, or moral propriety; a concern with the need to differentiate the right from the wrong underlies virtually all efforts to conceptualize oratory, informing topics as diverse as error analysis in composition studies and the distinction between success-oriented and consensus-oriented actions in discourse theory. Because of this very general character, it remains largely an implied or latent issue in rhetorical theory. Conflicting assumptions about its definition and application often engage each other in debates on closely related topics, such as criteria or validity, rather than through direct confrontations over the necessity, possibility, and desirability of determining what constitutes the rhetorically correct. In ordinary usage, however, the term usually refers only to conformity to prescribed grammatical and stylistic rules and has as a result been the focus of controversies over grammar and usage.

A preoccupation with correctness dates back to the classical period. Plato in *Gorgias* takes rhetoric to task for creating "a conviction that is persuasive but not instructive about right and wrong" (455a). Aristotle stipulates that "proper and appropriate words and metaphors are alone to be employed in the style of prose" (*Rhetoric* 1404b). In *Rhetorica ad Herennium,* the public speaker should discuss only those matters that "law and custom have fixed for the uses of citizenship" (I.ii.2). And Quintilian goes even further when he suggests in the

Institutio Oratoria that studying the "rules for correctness of speech" should constitute the "first part" of a rhetorical education (I.v.1). Whereas most classical rhetoricians took for granted that it was both necessary and possible to define the correct, they disagreed as to the way it should be defined or the extent to which normative standards should be enforced with prescriptive or proscriptive rigor. And these disagreements in time developed into major differences in attitude toward correctness.

During the Renaissance, for instance, there were prescriptivists as uncompromising as George Puttenham, who, in *The Arte of English Poesie*, declares that "to ridde all lovers o learning from that errour [of mismatching a 'mean' or 'base' style with a 'high' subject]," he will set down "which matter be hie and loftie, which be but meane, and which be low and base, to the intent the stiles may be fashioned to the matters, and keepe their *decorum* and good proportion in every respect" (162). Yet there were also rhetoricians as liberal on the same issue as Erasmus, who states openly in his *On Copia of Words and Ideas* that stylistic improprieties allegedly caused by a striving for *copia* do not "at all concern" him and that he is not "prescribing how one should write and speak" but is "pointing out what to do for training," even though he hastens to add that "it does not seem that we will be acting illogically if we commence the precepts here by forewarning the student of *copia* that, above all, care must be taken that speech be appropriate, be Latin, be elegant, be correct" (14,18).

While Puttenham's attitude foreshadows the hardening of a prescriptive tendency into what Sterling Leonard terms "the doctrine of correctness," embodied in the codification of school grammar and the rise of the current-traditional rhetoric, it is Erasmus's unconcern about adhering to or teaching the rules for "right" speaking that prefigures mainstream thinking about the issue in modern rhetorical studies. When George Campbell suggests in *The Philosophy of Rhetoric* that it is not the business of grammar "to give law to the fashions which regulate our speech," for "[every] tongue whatever is founded in use or custom" (139), or when Richard Whately insists in the introduction to his *Elements of Rhetoric* that rules can be drawn only from the current practice of good composition, they both display an unmistakable affinity with the Erasmian position. In the twentieth century, the general trend has been moving further toward deemphasizing the need to conform to explicitly formulated grammatical or stylistic rules, as is evidenced in the backlash against the current- traditional emphasis on surface correctness, the prevailing of the descriptive over the prescriptive grammar, or the new assumption that "errors" should be viewed as signs of learning, exercises in proficiency, or marks of differences.

Yet this trend belies the increasingly important, even if behind-the-scene, role correctness has been playing in the development of modern rhetorical theory. Just as Erasmus was aware of the "illogicality" of his own stance, so contemporary rhetoricians find themselves in a dilemma when new theoretical insights have enabled them to see clearly that correctness is at once indispensable to and yet not altogether compatible with rhetoric. Subscription to this or that assumption of the right or the normative is a necessary condition for conceptualizing, arguing about, and, in particular, teaching rhetoric. Yet such a subscription would presuppose a more or less *fixed* set of *generalizable* precepts or criteria, which is incompatible with the rhetorical principles of *eikos* and *kairos,* or with the contingency of proofs and the specificity and mutability of situation and audience.

Troubled by a perception of this double bind, theorists such as Richard Rorty suggest that we give up our belief in *criteria* and *argumentation,* and hence our assumption of and expectation for the correct, altogether. Theorists such as Wayne Booth and Jürgen Habermas, on the other hand, call for a reaffirmation of our faith in "reason" or in a solid foundation of the discursively correct and a renewed effort to discover the set of criteria that would enable us to distinguish between right and wrong. Still other rhetoricians try to negotiate a more balanced approach by recognizing both the community-specific, contingent nature of assumed criteria of correctness and the validity and relative stability of these criteria within specific communities. The resultant controversies shed new light on the historical development of the concept and underscore both its importance and its essential recalcitrancy as a theoretical issue.

Yameng Liu
Carnegie Mellon University

Bibliography

Booth, Wayne. *Modern Dogma and the Rhetoric of Assent.* Notre Dame, IN: U of Notre Dame P, 1974.

Campbell, George. *The Philosophy of Rhetoric.* Carbondale: Southern Illinois UP, 1963.

Erasmus, Desiderius. *On Copia of Words and Ideas.* Milwaukee, WI: Marquette UP, 1963.

Finegan, Edward. *Attitude toward English Usage: The History of a War of Words.* New York: Teachers College P, 1980.

Habermas, Jürgen. *The Theory of Communicative Action.* Boston, MA: Beacon, 1984.

Leonard, Sterling A. *The Doctrine of Correctness in English Usage: 1700–1800.* New York: Russell, 1962.

Puttenham, George. *The Arte of English Poesie.* Kent, OH: Kent State UP, 1970.

Rorty, Richard. *Contingency, Irony and Solidarity.* Cambridge: Cambridge UP, 1989.

Shaughnessy, Mina P. *Errors and Expectations: A Guide for the Teacher of Basic Writing.* New York: Oxford UP, 1977.

Whately, Richard. *Elements of Rhetoric.* Carbondale: Southern Illinois UP, 1963.

Cox, Leonard (c. 1500–1599)

A well-known teacher, author, and scholar during his lifetime, but only a very limited number of scholars since the sixteenth century have been acquainted with him and his work. Born near Monmouth, Wales, Cox was educated in England—possibly at Eton. After completing grammar school, he traveled widely in Europe, visiting universities including those at Paris, Wittenberg, Prague, and Cracow. He established contacts with many well-known scholars while traveling, most notably Philip Melanchthon, Desiderius Erasmus, and Juan Luis Vives.

Cox was hired to lecture on classical texts at the Cracow Academy and was highly regarded. For achievements as a lecturer at the school (1519–1527), he received the title of *poeta.* Upon returning to England, Cox earned two Bachelor of Arts degrees (Cambridge University, 1527, and Oxford University, 1529). Upon admission to the Master of Arts degree (1530), he requested dispensation from regency as a schoolmaster at Reading Grammar School (February 19, 1530). He was appointed Reading schoolmaster by Abbot Hugh Farringdon of Reading Abbey.

Following dissolution of the abbey and school and the execution of Abbot Farringdon, Cox left Reading (1539) for Caerleon-on-Usk, Wales. The move appears to have been based on political motives and actions tied to the English Reformation.

Cox received Letters Patent (February 10, 1540/1541) as Master of Reading School with an annual stipend for life. The patent from King Henry VIII read in part:

> for the special care . . . we have . . . for the erudition and education of boys . . . in the arts and sciences of grammar and good letters wishing that such erudition and education . . . may . . . be . . . increased; and for that our subject Leonard Cox, who is sufficiently skilled and learned in the art of grammar, as we have certain knowledge, as yet neither holds nor has received any office or stipend from us for such education . . . we give and grant to the same Leonard Cox the Office of Master or Preceptor of the Grammar School or School of Letters of . . . Reading . . . and constitute him master or preceptor of the aforesaid school by these presents.

Cox returned to Reading soon thereafter and stayed until 1546 or 1547, when the patent was apparently sold. He returned to the Continent to teach Latin and Greek at the Universities of Prague, Paris, and Cracow.

Sometime during the period between 1548 and 1572 Cox returned to Caerleon-on-Usk to teach, but his final years were spent in Coventry, England, as headmaster of the King Henry VIII Grammar School (1572–1599). Cox was described by the school historian as "a very well educated and liberal-minded man and a staunch supporter of the new ideas of religion and education."

Leonard Cox was a prolific writer, polished in both Latin and English. He is known to have composed fourteen works: Four were written entirely in Latin, and the remainder were either in English or translations from Greek or Latin. The best-known work is "The Arte or Crafte of Rhethoryke."

Roselyn L. Freedman-Baum
University of Charleston
and St. John Fisher College

Bibliography

Alston, R.C., comp. *A Bibliography of the English Language from the Invention of Printing to the Year 1800.* Vol. 1. *Grammars Written in English and English Grammars Written in Latin by Native Speakers.* Leeds, England: E.J. Arnold, 1965.

Carpenter, Frederic I. *Leonard Cox's "The Arte or Crafte of Rhethoryke," with an Introduction, Notes, and a Glossarial Index.* Chicago: U of Chicago P, 1899. Rpt. New York: AMS, 1973.

Freedman, Roselyn L. "A Bibliography of Sixteenth-Century English Rhetoric." *Rhetoric Society Quarterly* 11 (1981): 118–36.

———. "Rhetoric in the English Educational System, 1520–1550." Diss. U of Michigan, 1980.

Nelson, William. "The Teaching of English in Tudor Grammar Schools." *Studies in Philology* 49 (1952): 119–43.

Ong, Walter, S.J. "Tudor Writings on Rhetoric." *Studies in the Renaissance* 15 (1968): 39–69.

Pafort, Eloise. "A Group of Early Tudor School-Books." *Library*, 4th series, 26 (1946): 227–61.

Tuck, J.P. "The Beginnings of English Studies in the Sixteenth Century." *Durham Research Review* 7 (1956): 65–73.

Cultural Studies

The interdisciplinary examination of cultural texts and their effects in forming consciousness within economic and political contexts. The beginnings of cultural studies are commonly traced to Marxist influences, particularly as found in the Frankfurt school and, later, in the work of Richard Hoggart, Raymond Williams, E.P. Thompson, and the Centre for Contemporary Cultural Studies at the University of Birmingham. In an alternative genealogy, a number of observers have argued that rhetoric provides the richest historical precedent for this effort. In *Literary Theory: An Introduction*, Terry Eagleton has declared rhetoric as the model for the kind of cultural studies he is recommending: "It [rhetoric] was not worried about whether its objects of enquiry were speaking or writing, poetry or philosophy, fiction or historiography: its horizon was nothing less than the field of discursive practices in society as a whole, and its particular interest lay in grasping such practices as forms of power and perfor-mance." In *The Pursuit of Signs*, Jonathan Culler has likewise used the term *rhetoric* in referring to his proposals for a reformed English studies, although from an admittedly more politically conservative position. James Berlin's "Composition Studies and Cultural Studies: Collapsing Boundaries" has argued that certain schools of rhetoric in North American college English departments have attempted to pursue the projects of cultural studies in the composition classroom since at least the turn of the century.

In "Cultural Studies and Teaching Writing," John Trimbur has described the current conditions that have encouraged the turn to cultural studies in composition, including a resurgence of the participatory political impulse of the sixties, a reaction to the exploitation of composition teachers in English departments, the crisis in the literary canon, and the reaction to poststructuralism. Finally, Patricia Bizzell has argued for rhetorically constituted English studies that include the objectives of cultural studies.

In North American English departments, cultural studies refers to attempts to reshape the discipline by expanding the range of texts considered as well as the methods for reading and writing them. The new objects of investigation include noncanonical literary texts and rhetorical texts as well as movies, television, radio, popular music, and other forms of electronic communication. The productive and interpretive strategies brought to these works call upon structuralist and poststructuralist categories of investigation. Most important, the construction and reception of these varied discourses are examined within the concrete economic and political contexts of their historical moment.

Cultural studies began by contesting the Enlightenment notion of *culture* that has historically been central to English departments. Culture was here regarded as an autonomous category of experience manifested in an exclusive set of canonical texts and in particular ways of reading them. These texts and interpretations were said to be universal in character and thus completely free of temporal economic and political conditions. Against this conception, cultural studies argued for an expansion of the definition of culture. Growing out of Marxist traditions as well as sociological and anthropological formulations, culture came to stand for a complex way of life, that is, the extensive patterns of behavior found in daily activities. Culture is then the entire lived experience of human agents in response to their concrete historical conditions. This definition broke down the distinction between canonical and other cultural texts, arguing that cultural workers, such as English teachers, should consider noncanonical texts and forms of representation typically excluded from concern, such as film, television, popular music, and the like. Furthermore, in a departure from orthodox Marxism, culture was to be treated as a distinct historical force that could never be reduced to a simple reflex of economic and political conditions. At the same time, it could not be altogether separated from these categories.

This notion of culture as lived behavior was eventually challenged by the linguistic turn in cultural studies. Structuralist and poststructuralist thought, as well as American neopragmatism, argued that language constituted rather than reflected experience. Culture was here formulated as a set of representations, with signifying practices—that is, language in its broadest designation—mediating and shaping all experience. This semiotic coding of language was further manifested in the activity of everyday cultural behavior, for example, in the structures of sports and rock and roll as well as in poetry and opera.

The poststructuralist influence led to a number of related developments in the challenge to Enlightenment conceptions of culture. The individual subject was no longer the unified, autonomous, and self-present originator of human experience. Instead, the subject was considered a construction of signifying practices, a multiple and conflicted product of language. While a certain agency is possible in directing human affairs, history —both individual and social—cannot be described as the simple product of individual will. The primacy of signifying practices also challenged totalistic conceptions of history—the grand narratives of Hegel, Adam Smith, or Marx. Thus, the foundational truths on which larger economic and political systems were said to rest were considered transitory historical formations designed to serve the interests of certain ruling groups. Human values, like human subjects, were the products of historically specific signifying practices.

The anthropological notion of culture as lived experience and the poststructuralist notion of culture as signifying practice have been united in recent work in cultural studies. Cultural studies has also been strongly shaped by feminist theory, by African-American studies and by gay and lesbian studies. As a result of these multiple and complex influences, cultural studies has commonly come to be seen as the study of signifying practices in the formation of subjectivities within concrete economic, social, and political conditions. These practices range from the activities of the family, the school, the workplace, and the peer group to the more familiar behavior associated with the cultural sphere, such as the arts and the media and their modes of production and consumption. Cultural studies encourages the examination of the cultural codes of class, race, gender, age, ethnic, and related behavior and their alignments with larger historical events. In short, wherever signifying practices are shaping consciousness in daily life, cultural studies has work to do.

Cultural studies has resisted becoming an academic discipline. Indeed, in its commitment to interdisciplinary methods and its constant self-revisions in response to historical conditions, it is radically antidisciplinary. In North American higher education, it has instead served to critique and revise established disciplinary procedures. In English departments this has taken a distinctive turn. As Robert Scholes has demonstrated, the privileging of canonical literary texts over all other discourses has corresponded to the preference for the disinterested poetic over the interested rhetorical, the private over the public, the contemplative over the active, and the creative over the imitative. Cultural studies argues that the division between the cultivated poetic and the mundane rhetorical or popular is based on class, race, and gender bias and is the result of particular groups forwarding their own interests as universal values. There are thus no disinterested uses of language, since all discourses are involved in ideological endorsements. The social and communal nature of language means the disappearance of the sharp distinction between private and public, with the two domains constantly interacting dialogically. The break between action and contemplation likewise fades as both reading and writing are recognized to be productive acts. Readers as well as writers construct textual significance rather than simply recording preexisting meanings. This means that writing, text production, becomes a serious area of study for English departments, because it serves as the prototype for all textual encounters, receptive as well as productive. Finally, all texts are actively involved in politics and power, in tacitly endorsing platforms of action. Language, as Kenneth Burke has demonstrated, is always a program for performance.

The work of cultural studies within English departments, then, will be the examination of the discursive strategies involved in generating and interpreting textuality broadly conceived. Significantly, the classroom will replace research publications as the center of the discipline. Here teachers and students will develop methods for reading

C

and writing cultural codes, and these codes will cut across the aesthetic, the economic, the political, the philosophical, and the scientific. Furthermore, these responses are never treated as simple accommodations or rejections of textual meaning. Reading and writing are most commonly negotiated critical reactions to experience so that student responses must always serve as points of departure for classroom activities. Students will thus be prepared to engage critically in the variety of reading and writing practices required of them as citizens, workers, and individual sites of desire. English studies will emulate cultural studies in becoming interdisciplinary in methods and materials and in committing itself to a democratic politics of performance within and outside the classroom.

James A. Berlin
Purdue University

Bibliography

Balsamo, Anne. "Feminism and Cultural Studies." *Midwestern Modern Language Association* 24 (1991): 50–73.

Berlin, James A. "Composition Studies and Cultural Studies: Collapsing Boundaries." *Into the Field: Sites of Composition Studies*. Ed. Anne Ruggles Gere. New York: Modern Language Assn., 1993.

Bizzell, Patricia. "On the Possibility of a Unified Theory of Composition and Literature." *Rhetoric Review* 4 (1986): 174–80.

Black Popular Culture: A Project by Michelle Wallace. Ed. Gina Dent. Seattle: Bay, 1992.

Culler, Jonathan. *The Pursuit of Signs: Semiotics, Literature, Deconstruction*. Ithaca, NY: Cornell UP, 1981.

Eagleton, Terry. *Literary Theory: An Introduction*. Minneapolis: U of Minneapolis P, 1983.

Hall, Stuart. "Cultural Studies and the Centre: Some Problematics and Problems." *Culture, Media, Language: Working Papers in Cultural Studies, 1972–1979*. Ed. Stuart Hall, Dorothy Hobson, Andrew Lowe, and Paul Willis. London: Unwin Hyman, 1980.

Johnson, Richard. "What is Cultural Studies Anyway?" *Social Text* 16 (1986–1987): 38–80.

Scholes, Robert. *Textual Power: Literary Theory and the Teaching of English*. New Haven: Yale UP, 1985.

Trimbur, John. "Cultural Studies and Teaching Writing." *Focuses* 1 (1988): 5–18.

Turner, Graeme. *British Cultural Studies: An Introduction*. London: Unwin Hyman, 1990.

Current-Traditional Rhetoric

Term coined by Daniel Fogarty in 1959 to designate the formalist rhetoric commonly used in American writing instruction during most of the twentieth century. Current-traditional rhetoric is characterized by its emphasis on the formal features of the finished product of composing. The current-traditional essay employs a rigorous movement from general to specific. It displays a thesis sentence or paragraph, three or more paragraphs of supporting examples or data, and a paragraph each of introduction and conclusion. The movement from general to specific is repeated within paragraphs, which feature topic sentences—generalized statements that are developed or specified in successive sentences. Highly prescriptive applications of current-traditional theme logic, such as Barrett Wendell's in *English Composition* (1891), prescribe that a general-to-specific relation obtain between subjects and predicates of individual sentences as well.

Current-traditional essays also adhere to the principles of unity and coherence. The first principle mandates that a theme refer to only one subject of discussion. The second mandates that each sentence in a theme demonstrate an obvious, preferably graphic, relation to those that precede and follow it. Current-traditional rhetoric is further characterized by its reliance on the research paper as a major composing assignment; its collapse of invention into a three-step process of selecting, narrowing, and outlining a subject; its division of available genres into four modes of discourse—exposition, description, narration, and argument; and its emphasis on the use of correct grammar, usage, and mechanics.

Current-traditional rhetoric descends from a British rhetorical tradition located in Lockean empiricism but tinctured with a dose of Scottish common-sense realism. Its progenitors were George Campbell's *Philosophy of Rhetoric* (1776) and Hugh Blair's *Lectures on Rhetoric and Belles Lettres* (1783). Several American rhetoric teachers wrote reductivized redactions of these texts during the nineteenth century. The most influential of these was Alexander Bain's *English Composition* (1866), which introduced the notions of the topic sentence and the methods of paragraph development into current-traditional thought. By the turn of the twentieth century, the paradigm essay was firmly in place within mainstream composition textbooks, if not within writing instruction itself. Current-traditional rhetoric dominated textbooks published throughout the first three-quarters of the twentieth century, and its signature can still be seen in the many contemporary composition programs that divide mandatory first-year writing courses between semesters of instruction in exposition and argument or exposition and a research paper.

The hegemony of current-traditional rhetoric is widely thought to have been successfully challenged during the 1980s by process-oriented pedagogy. This pedagogy, however, in which teachers assist students while they are composing, is quite compatible with current-traditional rhetoric, as it accepts the empiricist epistemology that undergirds its older counterpart and as the products of process instruction often look very much like five-paragraph themes. The current-traditional attitude toward subjects as empirical entities that exist entirely apart from people who write about them and its representative theory of language have recently been challenged by composition theorists interested in postmodern theories of authorship and language. This challenge to the preeminence of current-traditional rhetoric, however, has yet to be widely felt in the day-to-day teaching or administration of courses or programs in introductory composition.

Sharon Crowley
Pennsylvania State University

Bibliography

Connors, Robert J. "Mechanical Correctness as a Focus in Composition Instruction." *College Composition and Communication* 36 (1985): 61–72.

———. "The Rise and Fall of the Modes of Discourse." *College Composition and Communication* 32 (1981): 444–55.

Crowley, Sharon. *The Methodical Memory: Invention in Current-Traditional Rhetoric*. Carbondale: Southern Illinois UP, 1990.

Johnson, Nan. *Nineteenth-Century Rhetoric in North America*. Carbondale: Southern Illinois UP, 1991.

Kitzhaber, Albert. *Rhetoric in American Colleges, 1850–1900*. Dallas: Southern Methodist UP, 1990.

Wendell, Barrett. *English Composition: Eight Lectures Given at the Lowell Institute*. New York: Scribner's, 1891.

C

D

D'Angelo, Frank J. (b. 1928)

Professor of English, Arizona State University; B.S. 1960, Loyola University; M.A. 1963, Tulane University; Advanced Certificate 1967, University of Illinois at Champaign (Urbana); Ph.D. 1970, University of Nebraska (Lincoln). Frank J. D'Angelo is in part responsible for the revival of classical rhetoric in the English classroom and has taught and published in a wide range of subjects, including classical rhetoric, rhetoric and literary theory, rhetoric and cultural studies, and composition theory.

D'Angelo's scholarship reveals an extraordinary mastery of classical rhetoric, about which he has advanced numerous theories. Within classical rhetoric arrangement is one of D'Angelo's major fields of study. His article "The Topic Sentence Revisited" (1986) reviews the topic sentence's evolution out of nineteenth-century grammar and emphasizes its establishment of clarity and structure in expository writing. D'Angelo examines criticisms of the topic sentence but also demonstrates how topic sentences can improve reader recall. More important, D'Angelo reveals arrangement's central relationship to the four "master" tropes—metaphor, metonymy, synechdoche, and irony—in nonfiction as well as fiction. His pivotal article "Tropics of Arrangement: A Theory of *Dispositio*" (1990) delineates the use of the master tropes in nonfiction and examines the tropical theories of Aristotle, Giambattisto Vico, Kenneth Burke, Paul de Man, Roman Jakobson, and Hayden White et al. According to D'Angelo, "all texts use tropes [figures of speech]" (103), and all figures of speech are "subsumed" by the four master tropes. These tropes are embedded in both formal and infor-

mal essays; that is, they do not exclusively fall under the purview of formal arrangement. This concept broadens the arena of rhetorical usage to include the informal writing not traditionally associated with rhetoric. Such a stance allows rhetoric to interact as part of the changing canon of literature—and literacy—in modern academia. D'Angelo foreshadows his theories of tropical arrangement in "Prolegomena to a Rhetoric of Tropes" (1987) and extensively develops them in "The Four Master Tropes: Analogues of Development" (1992), relating these tropes to theories of human psychological development.

His academic pursuits have at times taken D'Angelo off the beaten path and into alternative rhetorical forms. In the 1970s his cultural studies culminated in several articles on graffiti. "Sacred Cows Make Great Hamburgers: The Rhetoric of Graffiti" (1974) and "Up against the Wall, Mother! The Rhetoric of Slogans, Catchphrases, and Graffiti" (1976; rpt. 1985) explore graffiti as a source of numerous rhetorical strategies. D'Angelo demonstrates how graffiti's use of puns, alliteration, rhyme, and so forth, generate rhetorical discussion in the classroom.

D'Angelo's study of classical rhetoric extends as well to practical skill development. His many articles on the progymnasmata (preliminary exercises in the art of persuasion), feed into his forthcoming textbook *From Proverb to Argument: Composition in the Classical Tradition*. D'Angelo's practical application of classical rhetoric is also apparent in his now-out-of-print textbook, *Process and Thought in Composition*, which emphasizes student awareness of invention and arrangement. Furthermore, he has explored stylistics both in and out of the classroom. "Style as Structure" applies several stylistic theories to both syntagmatic and paradigmatic structural analyses of a passage from Thomas Wolfe's *You Can't Go Home Again*. D'Angelo's work also ranges contemporary literary theory and literacy in cognition.

Leslie Dupont
University of Arizona

Bibliography

D'Angelo, Frank J. *A Conceptual Theory of Rhetoric*. Cambridge, MA: Winthrop, 1975.

———. "The Four Master Tropes: Analogues of Development." *Rhetoric Review* 11 (1992): 91–107.

———. "Literacy, Cognition, and the Teaching of Writing: A Developmental Perspective." *Literacy for Life*. Ed. Richard Bailey and Robin Fosheim. New York: Modern Language Assn., 1983. 97–114.

———. "Prolegomena to a Rhetoric of Tropes." *Rhetoric Review* 6 (1987): 32–40.

———. "Sacred Cows Make Great Hamburgers: The Rhetoric of Graffiti." *College Composition and Communication* 25 (1974): 173–80.

———. "Style as Structure." *Style* 8 (1974): 322–64.

———. "The Topic Sentence Revisited." *College Composition and Communication* 37 (1986): 431–41.

———. "Tropics of Arrangement: A Theory of *Dispositio*." *Journal of Advanced Composition* 10 (1990): 101–9.

———. "Up against the Wall, Mother! The Rhetoric of Slogans, Catchphrases, and Graffiti." *Rhetoric and Change*. Ed. William E. Tanner and J. Dean Bishop. Arlington: Liberal Arts, 1985. 110–20.

Davidson, Donald (b. 1918)

An innovative and influential analytic philosopher. Donald Davidson indirectly impacts rhetoric because of his antifoundational views, which break with traditional Cartesian dualism and challenge conceptual relativism. His philosophy of language asserts that no conceptual schemes exist to facilitate communication; nothing, not even language or any other systems of categories, mediates between the human mind and the world. For many rhetoricians Davidson's antifoundationalism offers an alternative to the competing foundational theories that locate knowledge in texts, cognitive processes, or discourse communities. Primarily through his considerable influence on the work of Richard Rorty, Davidson's influence has extended to rhetorical theory, especially in the writings of Reed Way Dasenbrock and Thomas Kent.

Educated at Harvard, Davidson was originally an English major; he earned his undergraduate degree in the classics and philosophy. He returned to Harvard for his graduate work in philosophy, studying with Willard Van Orman Quine. Davidson has taught philosophy at Stanford, the University of Chicago, and Princeton. He teaches currently at the University of California at Berkeley.

Davidson calls his view of communicative interaction externalism. Because he believes that no conceptual scheme, such as a system of social conventions, mediates between humans and the objective world, language for Davidson becomes intersubjective and governed neither by internal mental categories nor by discourse communities. His conception of communicative interaction, called radical interpretation, departs from the traditional belief that language is a system of rules and conventions. Instead of conceptual schemes, Davidson bases his language theory on triangulation, the passing theory, the prior theory, and the principle of charity.

Triangulation describes the way thoughts and beliefs develop through the interaction of individual language users, other language users, and objects in the world. As individuals interact with each other and with objects in the world, a baseline of communication and understanding develops. In turn, this interactive and interpretive aspect of communication depends on a passing theory. Because no conceptual schemes exist, humans have no means to guarantee in advance of a communicative situation that communication will succeed. Communication takes place, with varying degrees of success, because both the speaker and interpreter employ passing theories. These largely unconscious adjustments occur continually as people communicate. A speaker continually adjusts to what he or she imagines the interpreter is making of what is being said, and the interpreter makes a reasoned and generally effective guess at what is being said. Prior theories, or the background knowledge possessed by each communicator, also facilitate communication by improving the chances of effective passing theories. While prior theories may make communication easier, they offer no predictive guarantees for success. Basic to all communication is what Davidson calls the principle of charity, a phrase he admits is a misnomer because it does not depend on any conscious charitable acts. He means that people are able to communicate because they share a common world and because each person assumes that, up to a point, other language users are rational beings. The principle of charity states that because people naturally want to communicate they unconsciously make a best effort to understand each other.

Although Davidson's conception of communicative interaction focuses on spoken discourse and not on writing, his philosophy of language nonetheless provides composition specialists with valuable insights about the nature of knowledge, belief, and truth. In particular, social theorists believe that Davidson provides essential arguments against radical skepticism, the doubt that we can know anything with certainty. While maintaining the social dimension of language, Davidson makes the critical connection between the objective world and the way language is acquired and used through interaction with others.

Jane M. Perkins
Iowa State University

Bibliography

Dasenbrock, Reed Way, ed. *Literary Theory after Davidson*. University Park: Penn State UP, 1993.

Davidson, Donald. *Inquiries into Truth and Interpretation*. Oxford: Clarendon, 1986.

Evnine, Simon. *Donald Davidson*. Stanford, CA: Stanford UP, 1991.

Kent, Thomas. "Language Philosophy, Writing, and Reading: A Conversation with Donald Davidson." *Journal of Advanced Composition* 13 (1993): 1–20.

LePore, Ernest, ed. *Truth and Interpretation: Perspectives on the Philosophy of Donald Davidson*. Oxford: Basil, 1986.

Day, Henry Noble (1808–1898)

Congregational clergyman, rhetorical educator, and textbook author who presented a powerful but failed challenge to the development of American composition-rhetoric between 1850 and 1885. Born in New Preston, Connecticut, on August 4, 1808, Day was educated at the Hopkins Grammar School in Hartford, then went on to Yale, where he studied rhetoric under Chauncey Allen Goodrich, graduating with the class of 1828. During his time at Yale, Day lived with his uncle, college president Jeremiah Day, whose Yale Plan was the touchstone of conservative classical college curricula in the nineteenth century.

Between 1828 and 1836, Day taught at a seminary, read law, traveled to Europe and, from 1831 to 1834, held a position as tutor at Yale. In 1836 Day married Jane Marble and was ordained a minister, taking a position at the First Church of Waterbury. In 1840 he was offered the Oviatt Chair of Sacred Rhetoric in the recently established Western Reserve College in Hudson, Ohio. It was during his time there that most of his ideas on rhetoric were developed. The teaching that Day did at Western Reserve was all postgraduate, because the theological department there did not serve undergraduates. It is to that fact that the complex and somewhat forbidding nature of Day's early rhetorical writings may be due.

The theological department of Western Reserve was gradually dismantled during the 1850s for financial reasons, but Day remained in Hudson until 1858, teaching and engaging in business ventures. In 1858 he was asked to accept the presidency of Ohio Female College at College Hill near Cincinnati, which position he held until 1864 when the college failed. Day returned to New Haven, where he lived for the rest of his life, devoting his time to turning out textbooks on a variety of subjects. He died on January 12, 1890.

Day was a classic example of the kind of polymath that nineteenth-century American education sometimes produced. His classical training at Yale was unspecialized, and he chose to read in, master, and then write about many diverse subjects both during and after his teaching career. Between 1844 and 1889, Day wrote textbooks on elocution, rhetoric, composition, grammar, logic, literature, bookkeeping, aesthetics, ethics, psychology, and education. Within this vast compass, however, we can trace a development of Day's thought, which falls generally into two phases: his work on rhetoric, literature, and language, which proceeded from his teaching experience at Yale, Western Reserve, and Ohio Female College, and his more abstract later interests in ethics, aesthetics, and the different forms of "mental science" that we would now classify as philosophy and psychology.

The rhetorical tradition into which Day was born was American Blairian belletrism, and it was Chauncey Goodrich's elocution-tinged version of this strong tradition that he first learned at Yale. Then, in 1828—the year of Day's commencement—the powerful argumentative challenge to Blairian rhetoric presented by Whately in his *Elements of Rhetoric* appeared. Day must have known both of these traditions of rhetoric well, in theory at least, but when he attempted to teach them between 1840 and 1850, he conceived a "disgust" (to use one of his favorite words) for both of them as a result. The result of his dissatisfaction was the creation of Day's own rhetorical theories, many of which are sui generis and were in serious conflict with the received wisdom of his age.

Day's most important statements on rhetoric are all found in his first textbook on the subject, *Elements of the Art of Rhetoric* published in 1850 and in print until 1876. In the preface to that book, Day says that Blairian stylistic rhetoric has the result, "as might naturally be expected where manner is the chief object of regard, that exercises in composition have been exceedingly repulsive and profitless drudgeries" (iii). But Whately's Aristotelian rhetoric, which agreed with this antistylistic view, constrained rhetoric from full use, said Day: "Covering the field of pure discourse as addressed to another mind, [rhetoric] is redeemed from the shackles and embarrassments of that view which confines it to mere argumentative composition, or the art of producing Belief" (v). Day believed that rhetorical instruction must concentrate on invention as opposed to style, and he saw rhetoric as completely multimodal, not merely argumentative.

Day's rhetoric, as exemplified in *Elements, Rhetorical Praxis* (1861), *The Art of Discourse* (1867), *Grammatical Synthesis: The Art of English Composition* (1867), and *The Young Composer: A Guide to English Grammar and Composition* (1870), was both theoretical and practical; his books were meant to be treatises and textbooks at the same time. As an author of textbooks, he had some success; his texts were in print for over forty years. Finally, however, Day's rhetorical ideas represent a dead end, a road that American composition rhetoric did not take. Day favored the ideas of Aristotle, Cicero, and German philosophical writers over those of Blair, Whately, and the early writers on American composition. The moderns, he stated, "have too much regarded rhetoric as a merely critical art. They have directed their attention mainly to pruning, repressing, and guiding; and have almost wholly neglected to apply any stimulus to the faculty of discourse itself" (10–11).

His emphasis on invention and content, his original and complicated taxonomy of discourse types, and especially his claim that rhetoric must be "a developing and invigorating art" rather than a "merely critical art" made Day into a thinker who simply did not fit with the increasingly pragmatic and mechanical needs of American writing instruction, especially after the Civil War. In spite of (or perhaps because of) the immense originality of Day's work, his rhetoric was never as popular as that of his two prewar rivals, George Quackenbos and Richard Green Parker. Never a lively stylist, Day found that his stiff and treatiselike writings on discourse were even less popular after the Civil War, as college education shifted to meet new social needs.

With the development of a sophisticated postwar composition-rhetoric in the works of Alexander Bain, John Hart, Adams S. Hill, and John Genung, Day's rhetoric rapidly dropped in popularity. After he left his teaching positions, he spent most of his later years working on books in nonrhetorical "mental science" disciplines, few of which were successful, and by 1932 the *National Cyclopaedia of American Biography* could say that his books "were of value when published but have long outlived their usefulness." Rhetorical scholars have more recently found much to esteem in Day's emphases on invention and vitality in writing, however, and it is likely that future scholarship will see him as one of the more important theorists to appear in the field of rhetoric in the nineteenth century.

Robert J. Connors
University of New Hampshire

Bibliography

Cramer, C.H. *Case Western Reserve: A History of the University, 1826–1976.* Boston: Little, 1976.

Day, Henry Noble. *Elements of the Art of Rhetoric.* Hudson, Ohio: W. Skinner, 1850.

Genzmer, George Harvey. "Day, Henry Noble." *Dictionary of American Biography.* Vol. V. New York: Scribner's, 1930. 158–59.

"Henry Noble Day." *National Cyclopaedia of American Biography.* Vol 22. New York: James T. White, 1932. 309.

Johnson, Nan. "Three Nineteenth-Century Rhetoricians: The Humanist Alternative to Rhetoric as Skills Management." *The Rhetorical Tradition and Modern Writing.* Ed. James J. Murphy. New York: Modern Language Assn., 1982. 105–17.

See also BLAIR, HUGH; NINETEENTH-CENTURY RHETORIC; WHATELY, RICHARD

Declamation

"Practical exercises" in oratory (Greek *melete;* Roman *declamatio*), originally incorporated into the curricula of Greek and Roman rhetoric schools in order to prepare students for future positions as advocate-politicians; introduced as early as the fourth century B.C.E. and prominent through the Roman and Hellenistic periods.

Declamations typically began with the teacher, or master rhetor, proposing a theme or *cause* (case). This was sometimes a general statement, or *thesis*, such as "It is better for a man to marry," and sometimes a more specific *hypothesis*, like "John was right to marry Christine," in which names and other details were added. Sometimes the teacher added *colores,* details, in order to make a theme more complicated, interesting, or familiar, or simply to add fresh possibilities to a stale theme. The teacher introduced each theme with a *sermo*—a preliminary outline of the situation or case—which included the roles of relevant characters, the principal arguments to be employed (including commonplaces), developments to which it might be susceptible, and potential pitfalls. Frequently, he would perform a "model" declamation for his students to imitate. Students then composed and delivered their speeches to an audience of their classmates,

sometimes in the form of mock trials, after which the teacher would critique their performances. Often, an exercise known as *prosopopoeiae* was included in declamations, requiring that students declaim in the character of the person for whom they were speaking—usually a mythological or historical personage at some critical point in life. Because students were required to attack or defend theses (sometimes both), declamation was often criticized for failing to instruct students in the moral and intellectual responsibilities of the orator. Respected teachers of rhetoric like Quintilian (see, for example, *Institutio* II.x.1–6), Tacitus, and Cicero, however, defended declamation as a potentially valuable exercise, but only to the degree that it cultivated general moral development and remained connected to public oratory.

Although declamation continued to be taught in the East through the Byzantine period, it was particularly influential in Rome, where it acquired prestige and popularity toward the close of the Republic, and remained important until the fall of the empire. Here, however, declamation became a form of "school rhetoric" that became increasingly dissociated from practical oratory. The courts of the Greek *demos* and the Roman Republic had provided environments where free speech thrived, but, under the dictatorship of the Roman Empire, freedom of discussion in the forum and in the schools ceased; consequently, so did the need for orators trained in rhetoric. Indeed, the very real threat of physical abuse, exile, and even assassination effectively deterred those who desired to speak against the emperor on current or controversial issues (such as tyranny, a stock theme in classical declamations), thus forcing rhetoric and oratory to find new contexts and, ultimately, new forms. Under these restrictions, rhetors and their students turned increasingly to fictitious themes, or *scholastica,* wildly improbable, fantastic, and romantic situations involving conflicting laws and shocking crimes such as adultery, rape, incest, murder, and homosexuality. Many of these themes are collected in the elder Seneca's work, *Suasoriae et Controversiae (Deliberative and Forensic Themes)*, which records different treatments of the same themes and the author's own criticism.

Because "safe" worlds about which to declaim literally had to be constructed from scratch out of the imaginations of those dedicated to practicing oratory, invention became a valuable skill during this period. But invention as investigation was largely supplanted by invention as imagination, and rhetoric was increasingly associated with poetic. Moreover, rhetoric and oratory were becoming separate fields of study: The former focused on law and philosophy, the latter on style and delivery. Historians have said that this difference marks the shift from an "old" to a "new" rhetoric. Within this context, declamatory skill was cultivated for amusement, as a social grace, with no necessary connection to historical facts, public law courts, or contemporary realities. And as long as declamations offered occasions to discourse persuasively (and entertainingly) on controversial and complex situations, it seemed irrelevant that they also involved the acceptance of logical impossibilities, perversions of history, and nonexistent laws.

Orators responded in a variety of ways to this new "style" of oratory: Some lapsed into the "theatrical display or insane raving" that Quintilian feared in *Institutio Oratoria* (II.x.8); others continued to promote the intellectual activity for which declamation was originally designed. Still others rented halls and began holding public exhibitions, hoping to attract students with their virtuosity. This trend toward public display further popularized declamation and motivated many teachers of oratory to open their doors to the public several days each year, effectively turning schools into auditoriums. Declamation became an end in itself, unconnected to the law courts and without much substance generally.

Many critics have noted that declamation is proof that style, when cultivated in artificial isolation (that is, without connection to thought), goes bad. They denounce it for its lack of interest in the development of the "whole man," for its perversion of the educational process, and for its general cultivation of mediocrity. But in spite of such negative criticism, declamation continued to be used in the West through much of the medieval period. (St. Augustine, however, ignored it in *De Doctrina Christiana*.) Its emphasis on display found a counterpart in the eighteenth-century elocutionary movement, and its themes survive in composition handbooks from the eighteenth and nineteenth centuries, as well as in handbooks that teach "extemporaneous speaking."

Elizabeth Ervin
University of North Carolina at Wilmington

Bibliography

Baldwin, Charles Sears. *Ancient Rhetoric and Poetic*. New York: Macmillan, 1924.
———. *Medieval Rhetoric and Poetic*. New York: Macmillan, 1928.
Boissier, Gaston. *Tacitus and Other Roman Studies*. Trans. W.G. Hutchison. London: Archibald Constable, 1906.
Bonner, Stanley F. *Education in Ancient Rome*. London: Methuen, 1977.
———. *Roman Declamation in the Late Republic and Early Empire*. Berkeley: U of California P, 1949.
Cicero. *De Oratore*. Trans. G.L. Hendrickson and H.M. Hubbell. Loeb Classical Library. Cambridge, MA: Harvard UP, 1962.
Clark, Donald Lemen. *Rhetoric in Greco-Roman Education*. New York: Columbia UP, 1957.
Gwynn, A. *Roman Education from Cicero to Quintilian*. Oxford: Oxford UP, 1926.
Kennedy, George A. *The Art of Persuasion in Greece*. Princeton: Princeton UP, 1963.
Quintilian. *Declamationes Maiores*. Ed. G. Lehnert. Leipzig: Teubner, 1905.
———. *Declamationes Minores*. Ed. C. Ritter. Leipzig: Teubner, 1884.
———. *Institutio Oratoria*. Trans. H.E. Butler. Loeb Classical Library. 4 vols. Cambridge, MA: Harvard UP, 1921.
Russell, D.A. *Criticism in Antiquity*. Berkeley: U of California P, 1981.
———. *Greek Declamation*. Cambridge: Cambridge UP, 1983.
Seneca. *Controversiae and Suasoriae*. Ed. M. Winterbottom. Loeb Classical Library. Cambridge, MA: Harvard UP, 1974.
Winterbottom, M. *Roman Declamation*. Bristol: Phillimore, 1980.

Deconstruction

Both a critique of the Western metaphysical tradition and a defense of the plurality of meaning. The term *deconstruction* possesses both a philosophical dimension and a rhetorical dimension. The philosophical dimension derives from the writings of the French philosopher Jacques Derrida, and the rhetorical dimension may be associated most directly with American and French discourse theorists who apply Derrida's language philosophy to the study of literary texts. As a philosophical concept, deconstruction constitutes a thoroughgoing critique of essentialism, or what

Derrida calls "the metaphysics of presence"; as a rhetorical concept, deconstruction challenges the notion of unitary meaning and stresses instead the intertextuality that derives from the inherently rhetorical nature—the rhetoricity—of all texts. Although both the philosophical and the rhetorical dimensions of deconstruction share a common and often difficult vocabulary, the differences between these dimensions are important, for the American rhetorical version of deconstruction—represented best by the Yale School—suggests a reading strategy or interpretive methodology that does not align precisely with Derrida's conception of deconstruction.

In his critique of the Western metaphysical tradition, Derrida follows and perhaps ends a line of inquiry represented best by philosophers such as G.F.W. Hegel, Friedrich Nietzsche, Edmund Husserl, and Martin Heidegger. Derrida attacks the presupposition that language—and, consequently, meaning—possesses a metaphysical presence, essence, or center that provides a stable structure or foundation on which we can confidently construct our judgments and beliefs about the world. Reduced to its bare bones, deconstruction constitutes a demonstration that this *metaphysics of presence* contains within itself certain contradictions, or aporias, that lead to its own undoing. Derrida develops this line of thinking in two seminal books, *Of Grammatology* and *Dissemination,* and in two collections of essays, *Writing and Difference* and *Margins of Philosophy*. In these works Derrida employs three key concepts that convey the philosophical project of deconstruction: logocentrism, differance, and the supplement.

For Derrida, the Western philosophical tradition has been dominated by the search for a metaphysical order that possesses at its center an enduring structure of reason, meaning, or essential truth. Derrida employs the term *logocentrism* to refer to the presupposition that a Word, or logos, exists that will stabilize all thought and inquiry. According to Derrida, all the myriad branches of Western philosophy partake of logocentrism, the wistful metaphysical desire for the final Word. As the determination of being as presence, logocentrism always embodies a ground or foundation that privileges certain key concepts while dismissing or negating others. As Derrida points out, philosophers in the Western philosophical tradition have privileged good before evil, the positive

before the negative, the pure before the impure, the simple before the complex, the essential before the accidental, and the imitated before the imitation. These hierarchies, in turn, establish a binary relation based on negation. In the relation permanence/change, for example, permanence represents a positive concept while change represents a negative one, so entities that manifest permanence are naturally privileged over those entities that change. Logocentrism, then, privileges the positive terms in such hierarchical oppositions while treating the inferior second term as the positive term's negation. Consequently, logocentrism may be understood to be the metaphysical presupposition that a stabilizing word, center, or presence exists that enables us to distinguish confidently the differences between things that are positive or good and those things that are negative or bad. In other words, logocentrism corresponds to the desire for an enduring structure or presence that will put an end to difference and that will enable us to locate—within its oppositional hierarchy of positive/negative or good/bad terms—all that can be known.

Derrida attacks the logocentric tradition by turning the logic of logocentrism against itself. Instead of understanding presence as a metaphysical foundation, system, or logos that overcomes difference, Derrida argues that presence and therefore logocentrism actually depends on difference, or what he calls *différance*. In French, the term *différance* sounds the same as *différence*, and the *-ance* ending shows up only in writing. In writing, *différance* takes on the condition of a pun, where the word means both to differ and to defer. According to Derrida, "*Différance* is the systematic play of differences, of traces of differences, of the spacing by which elements relate to one another. This spacing is the production, simultaneously active and passive (the *a* of *différance* indicates this indecision as regards activity and passivity, that which cannot yet be governed and organized by that opposition), of intervals without which the 'full' terms could not signify, could not function" (*Positions*, 38–39). This definition requires a great deal of unpacking, but on its most fundamental level, Derrida's explanation of *différance* makes two important distinctions about language, one temporal and the other spatial. On the one hand, a word or sign stands for something else and, obviously, comes after what it designates; the sign temporally succeeds its referent or

D

differs from it in time. On the other hand, the sign also constitutes a "space" between itself and its referent that *defers* meaning from the referent to the sign. *Différance*, then, refers both to temporal difference and to spatial deferral. Without this *différance*, no signification or meaning would be possible, because the very nature of signification depends on difference and deferral.

In this configuration, however, the term *différance* incorporates a troubling paradox. Because it names nothing that is positive—only that which is deferred—*différance* signifies something that cannot be named; it signifies a quality that is missing within the act of signification. Therefore, *différance* possesses no negative member, in the sense that the term names only a gap or absence that possesses no referent. Of course, a sign without a referent is no sign at all, and we know that, on one level, the word *différance* certainly signifies this gap, absence, or condition of nonreference. On another level, however, *différance* points to an aporia that characterizes the condition of every sign. At once, *différance* signifies both the presence of something—a gap, absence, or condition of nonreference—and its absence, and this condition of nonreference is pure negation without anything to which it can stand as a positive term. Derrida argues that the paradox embodied in *différance*—the presence of absence—denotes the situation of language itself. As a system of relations constituted by difference and deferral, language possesses no foundation, essential structure, or intrinsic presence, so logocentrism's raison d'etre—the presupposition that a presence exists that will stabilize meaning and provide a framework for understanding—evaporates.

A good example that demonstrates how *différance* undermines logocentrism is Derrida's formulation of the supplement. Like the concept of *différance*, the supplement possesses two contradictory meanings. First, a supplement is something inessential that is added on to something else; for example, Rousseau thought that writing was a supplement to speech, something inessential that is added on to speech and that is secondary to speech. However, and here is the second sense of the term, a supplement compensates for a lack in the thing that it completes. In the case of speech and writing, for example, Derrida points out in *Of Grammatology* that

something must be lacking in speech if it requires the supplement of writing. Because the supplement always designates something that is incomplete, speech cannot be complete if it requires writing as its supplement. In fact, because speech exists as only one use of language that supplements other uses, speech itself may be seen as a supplement to writing and to other forms of language within a process of endless supplementarity. As a result of this endless supplementarity, the logocentric desire for a stable presence or foundation for meaning can never be realized because language exists as an endless chain of supplementarity where one aspect of language, such as speech, only supplements all the others. Nothing lies outside our utterances and our texts except other utterances and texts that stand in a supplementary relation to one another. In the realm of meaning, what we encounter is a generalized intertextuality where our utterances and our texts refer only to other utterances and texts.

From a rhetorical perspective, deconstruction extends Derrida's critique of the metaphysics of presence into the realm of textual interpretation. In its rhetorical dimension, deconstruction stresses the indeterminacy of textual meaning through an analysis of the oppositional hierarchies that provide the text with its aura of stability and closure. Although Derrida carefully disassociates himself from any critical or rhetorical methodology, deconstruction in America—especially the version of deconstruction promulgated by Paul de Man and some members of the Yale School—nonetheless embodies a general and codifiable procedure that is frequently employed to reveal a text's plenitude of meaning.

This general procedure embodies two rhetorical moves: First, deconstructionists isolate the hierarchical binary oppositions within a text that give a text its stability or presence, and, second, they destabilize or deconstruct these oppositions by seeking out the aporias that these oppositions suppress. By revealing the aporias that every text suppresses, the deconstructionist produces a new *reading* or interpretation for the text that is supported by the text itself. It is important to note that the deconstructionist does not bring to the interpretive act a predetermined framework of understanding into which the text is inserted. Rather, for the deconstructionist, the text unravels itself and supplies alternative readings within its own language. In other words, the text is self-deconstructive. The interpretive act, then, is interminable, for one reading simply yields another reading that becomes itself the object of deconstructive analysis. To deconstruct a text therefore means to dismantle the oppositions and hierarchies that give a text its aura of stability in order to make known that which the text conceals. Such a move allows the deconstructionist to reinscribe the text within a different order or meaning.

One of the results of this interminable overturning of textual meaning is the awareness of the rhetoricity inherent in all texts. As deconstruction decenters the text to uncover that which the text seeks to conceal, it also reveals the rhetorical operations that give a text its sense of presence and stability and, in so doing, blurs the traditional boundary between the critical act and the creative act. Traditionally, critical analysis has been seen to be parasitic on other texts; that is, a specific instance of critical analysis can occur only if there first exists another text to analyze. Because the critical act has been regarded as parasitic on and secondary to the creation of texts, the creative act of fashioning new meaning has been privileged in our culture over the supposedly less creative analytic act of uncovering meaning. If, however, all texts—including critical texts—are ultimately undecidable and therefore susceptible to plural interpretations, as deconstruction insists, then no clear boundary may be established between the critical text and the creative text. Both kinds of texts engage in the meaning-making process, and both ultimately resist closure and reduction to one stable interpretation. Because the critic and the artist engage in similar activities, the critic does not discover or uncover meaning; the critic, like the artist, creates meaning within the critical text, a text—like the literary text—that harbors the aporias and unstable oppositions that lead to its own inevitable deconstruction.

By revealing the fissures, uncertainties, and gaps latent in every text's structure of meaning and thereby exposing the rhetoricity inherent in every text, deconstruction reveals the futility inherent in the effort to discover an epistemological system that will stop the play of interpretation and stabilize meaning. But, because the Western tradition of rhetoric has been dominated and even defined by the search for just such an epistemological system, we have been historically conditioned to yearn for a methodology or critical technique that will fix meaning and provide an end to interpretation. By disclosing the futility of this logocentric search for a timeless center, deconstruction reveals to us our historical condition and helps us to understand why we yearn for hermeneutical certainty.

Of course, just as we cannot escape our histories, neither can texts escape theirs. Texts cannot escape the structures of meaning imposed upon them by their historical situations, and so every text reiterates its hierarchical historical condition. For this reason, deconstruction does not correspond to a new New Criticism or to a formalist interpretive methodology of close reading, as some critics of deconstruction contend. Derrida, Paul De Man, Geoffrey Hartman, and J. Hillis Miller, among others, have taken great pains to point out that deconstruction does not convert the text into an autonomous artifact that yields up its meaning after it undergoes a close textual analysis; rather, they point out that all texts participate in a process of intertextuality where meaning is always already connected to other texts and to other hierarchies of historical understanding. To say, for example, that every text deconstructs itself does not mean that history, culture, and intersubjectivity are irrelevant to the act of interpretation. In fact, deconstruction acknowledges the truism that every text is embedded in historical, cultural, and intersubjective relations and that no text can escape these complex structures of meaning. By laying bare this rhetoricity—this continual historical, cultural, and intersubjective reshaping of meaning—deconstruction does not sanction a version of formalism but, instead, refutes formalisms of all sorts.

In both its philosophical dimension and its rhetorical dimension, deconstruction challenges and subverts the structures we employ to explain ourselves to ourselves. In this enterprise deconstruction demonstrates the complexity of signification and the inevitability of interpretation, and it continually calls into question the Western compulsion to discover an essential core of human being.

Thomas Kent
Iowa State University

Bibliography

Culler, Jonathan. *On Deconstruction: Theory and Criticism after Structuralism.* 6th ed. Ithaca, NY: Cornell UP, 1989.

de Man, Paul. *Blindness and Insight: Essays in the Rhetoric of Contemporary Criticism.* Minneapolis: U of Minnesota P, 1983.

Derrida, Jacques. *Dissemination.* Trans. Barbara Johnson. Chicago: U of Chicago P, 1981.

———. *Of Grammatology.* Trans. Gayatri Chakravorty Spivak. Baltimore: Johns Hopkins UP, 1976.

———. *The Margins of Philosophy.* Trans. Alan Bass. Chicago: U of Chicago P, 1982.

———. *Positions.* Trans. Alan Bass. Chicago: U of Chicago P, 1981.

———. *Writing and Difference.* Trans. Alan Bass. Chicago: U of Chicago P, 1975.

Gasche, Rodolphe. *The Tain of the Mirror.* Cambridge, MA: Harvard UP, 1986.

Leitch, Vincent. *Deconstructive Criticism.* New York: Columbia UP, 1983.

Norris, Christopher. *Derrida.* Cambridge, MA: Harvard UP, 1987.

See also DERRIDA, JACQUES

Decorum

The standard of what is fitting, becoming, and appropriate in public discourse. *Decorum* is the Latin translation of *to prepon,* one of the requirements of effective rhetorical style discussed by Aristotle (*Rhetoric* III) and later incorporated by Aristotle's student Theophrastus into a systematic doctrine that became commonplace in the classical tradition as the "graces" or "virtues" of style: purity (or correctness), clarity, ornament, and decorum. Although it is well known as a governing concept for the neoclassical literary doctrines that flourished from the sixteenth through the eighteenth centuries (and which are usually traced back to the Roman poet Horace), decorum would appear at first blush to be less significant to the history of rhetoric: a piece of a piece of a vast and comprehensive lore of public discourse that encompasses invention and arrangement as well as style. In actuality, decorum is the most rhetorical of rhetorical concepts, an idea that permeates the whole of classical rhetoric, and an important point of convergence for the social, moral, and aesthetic concerns of the rhetorical tradition.

The success conditions of public discourse, like those of politics broadly considered, are irretrievably situational. It was inevitable, therefore, that despite the profound reservations of Platonists, religionists, and purists of all sorts, the advocates of rhetoric would gravitate (sometimes uneasily, sometimes carelessly) toward a situational ethics, a situational epistemology, *and* a situational doctrine of style and public performance. Clarity, with its orientation to the logical and the true, is of course a preeminent virtue in Aristotle; but already we see in Aristotle a role for *prepon* that is broader than that of the other stylistic virtues and related, significantly, to the ethical doctrine of the golden mean. Ornament, for instance, is a good thing but it can be taken too far, and its effectiveness needs to be measured by the criterion of appropriateness; more broadly, the language of rhetoric in general should be appropriate to its characteristic situations—a mean between the language of poetry and the language of ordinary speech.

Correctness, clarity, and ornament do not always sit easily together; they represent, in fact, rival doctrines of style, rival methods of presenting (and therefore of conceptualizing) the world. Decorum is not merely an additional player but the keeper of the peace, the genial arbiter of conflicting claims, the guardian of moderation and common sense. It is no accident that the characteristic product of rhetorical education—the "gentleman" or statesman—plays a similar role among the vital character types and cultural imperatives (technical, scientific, aesthetic, religious) of the polity. As a form of discourse, rhetoric itself is the keeper of the peace in a successful culture.

One of the paradoxes of culture, however, is that peace and geniality are not always acceptable or even "appropriate." And a paradoxical condition that must be absorbed before the topic of decorum can be fully comprehended is the process by which the consideration of appropriateness, so apparently an antiformalism, devolves rapidly and inexorably into a formalism of its own. In Aristotle, *prepon* is primarily a strategic, rather than an aesthetic or formal concern—it means finding the mode or style of expression that will work best for you under the circumstances. As a purely strategic matter, it is conceivable that appropriateness could encompass a very wide range of styles and forms of self-dramatization, including some that violate canons of politeness and conventional appearance or conduct. In any given historical situation, however, considerations of decorum will inevitably be formal and aesthetic as well as strategic, drawing upon preexisting, conventional symmetries of form and function. In a settled culture, there already exist certain expected ways of doing and saying things, decorum says—a manner as well as a time for all things—and one of the accomplishments of an effective public person is a finely tuned sensitivity to these accepted ways of presenting oneself, that is, to the *decorums* of public life.

In Roman rhetoric the formal and aesthetic dimensions of decorum receive much stronger attention than in Aristotle and come into full flower; a defining feature of Ciceronian humanism, in fact, is its melding of formal, strategic, aesthetic, and indeed moral concerns in the all-embracing concept of decorum. The most prominent embodiment of the doctrine in rhetorical lore is the Ciceronian partition of styles: the plain style for teaching, the middle style for pleasing, and the grand style for moving an audience. The fullest presentation of decorum as a comprehensive aesthetic, moral, and political ideal is contained in Cicero's ethical treatise *De officiis*. Here one finds the fundamental ethical imperative of human existence construed as the doctrine of decorum writ large: In all things, man should behave in ways appropriate to his nature as a rational creature, made for cooperation and society, capable of subordinating impulse to reason, of remembering the past, and of planning for the future. In the moral sphere, interestingly, the counterpart of decorum is the virtue of temperance; and just as decorum performs a governing function among the other three graces of style, so does temperance among the other three cardinal virtues: prudence, courage and justice. "What is proper is morally right," says Cicero, "and what is morally right is proper" (I.93).

So seamless is the fabric of Ciceronian humanism that it is difficult to say whether (as D'Alton claims) decorum is an aesthetic principle applied to life or a moral principle applied to art. In either case decorum is properly associated with harmony, grace, and comeliness as well as timeliness and appropriateness, just as the beauty of nature is associated with its rational design. "And it is no mean manifestation of Nature and Reason that man is the only animal that has a feeling for order, for propriety, for moderation in word and deed. And so no other animal has a sense of beauty, loveliness, harmony in the visible world; and Nature and reason, extending the analogy of this from the world of sense to the world of spirit, find that beauty, consistency, order are far more to be maintained in thought and deed." (*De officiis* I.142). By this logic the good is not only the appropriate but also the attractive and the pleasing. It is of course significant that the word *decorum* and the corresponding verb form *decree* imply *decoration* and pleasing design (even *decor*) as well as appropriateness.

The shortcomings of decorum are the shortcomings of rhetorical culture, and every generation, like that of Plato, should measure these shortcomings against rhetoric's strengths. Decorum is clearly too much at ease in Zion, just as the "gentleman" is too nearly a "mere carrier" (as Richard Weaver put it) of his culture—too prone to equate goodness and effectiveness with politeness and surface harmonies, and perhaps too careless of the fact that conventions of appropriateness can be used to stifle as well as to perfect expression. It should not be forgotten, however, that there are other forms of oppression as well—emanating from the technocrat, the philosopher-king, the prophet, and the myriad low priests of a commercialized, popular culture. To deal with these, a polity could do worse than to call the aging gentleman in the white suit, the genial keeper of the peace, out of retirement.

Walter H. Beale
University of North Carolina, Greensboro

Bibliography

Aristotle. *On Rhetoric: A Theory of Civic Discourse.* Trans. George A. Kennedy. New York: Oxford UP, 1991.

Atkins, J.W.H. *Literary Criticism in Antiquity: A Sketch of Its Development.* Vol. 2. Cambridge: Cambridge UP, 1934.

Bate, Walter Jackson. *From Classic to Romantic: Premises of Taste in Eighteenth Century England.* New York: Harper, 1946.

D

Cicero. *De Officiis.* Trans. Walter Miller. Cambridge, MA: Harvard UP, 1913.
———. *De Oratore.* Cambridge, MA: Harvard UP, 1942.
D'Alton, J.F. *Roman Literary Theory and Criticism: A Study in Tendencies.* London: Longmans, 1931.
Hack, Roy Kenneth. "The Doctrine of Literary Forms." *Harvard Studies in Classical Philology* 28 (1916): 1–63.
Leonard, Sterling. *The Doctrine of Correctness in English Usage, 1700–1800.* Madison: U of Wisconsin P, 1929.
Quintilian. *The Institutio oratoria of Quintilian.* Trans. W.E. Butler. London: W. Heinemann, 1922–1933.
Wimsatt, W.K., and Cleanth Brooks. *Literary Criticism: A Short History.* London: Routledge and Kegan Paul, 1957.

Deduction

The process of reasoning wherein the acceptance of the premises necessitates the acceptance of the conclusion. In logic, conclusions reached through deductive means follow necessarily from the premises. Because rhetoric almost always deals with probabilities or contingent issues, however, the conclusiveness of strict deductive reasoning has little space in the realm of rhetoric. Whereas inductive reasoning puts forward specific cases as evidence for the validity of a general statement, deductive reasoning applies a general statement (All humans are mortal) to a specific case (Aristotle is human) in order to reach a further, indubitable conclusion (Aristotle is mortal).

Deduction in logic takes the form of the syllogism, in rhetoric the enthymeme. While the enthymeme is often expressed in truncated syllogistic form, suppressing the major premise, its form is not what distinguishes the enthymeme from the syllogism. Rather, it is the subject matter: If the premises are demonstrably true, then the argument is a syllogism, but if they are only probable or sometimes true, then the argument is an enthymeme.

Developed about the same time as the *Rhetoric,* Aristotle's *Prior Analytics,* which is a detailed treatment of premises and syllogisms, is the source of his theory of deductive inferences in logic. Deduction in dialectic is the subject of the *Topics.*

Donald E. Bushman
University of North Carolina at Wilmington

Bibliography
Kennedy, George. *The Art of Persuasion in Greece.* Princeton: Princeton UP, 1963.
Thompson, W.N. *Aristotle's Deduction and Induction: Introductory Analysis and Synthesis.* Amsterdam: Rodopi N.V., 1975.

See also ENTHYMEME; INDUCTION; SYLLOGISM

Definition

The act of defining; describing the nature or essential qualities of something, or to state or set forth the meaning of a word or phrase. Understood broadly, definition has been practiced and analyzed since Socrates popularized questions of the form "What is X?" Since then, philosophers and linguists have tried to clarify what definition involves and to improve the analytical tools used in definition.

So-called "real" definitions are efforts to define *things* rather than *words,* to establish facts of essence rather than facts of language usage. When one tries to provide a "real definition" of "death," for example, one is not merely reporting how people use the word *death* but identifying the defining characteristics of what death, itself, "really" is. Strictly speaking, dictionary definitions are *lexical* definitions and not "real" definitions because they report an account of how words have been used in the past. Although most people have lexical definitions in mind when they use the word *definition,* from the standpoint of a "real" definition a lexical definition may be wrong. *Stipulative* definitions are definitional proposals aimed at a specific purpose, as when a mathematician offers a specific meaning for a word as part of a proof. *Ostensive* definitions are merely simple lessons for future word usage based on example, as when a parent points to an object and names the object for a child.

Chaïm Perelman and Lucie Olbrechts-Tyteca made an important breakthrough in *The New Rhetoric* by describing definition as *rhetorical.* Their point in labeling definitions as rhetorical is that even uncontroversial definitions function as claims about how part of the world should be conceptualized, how part of the world *is.* All definitions, whether they are described as "real," "lexical," or whatever, depend on the adherence of language users and hence are conventional. Standard dictionary definitions, for example, represent the temporary agreements of an audience as to how particular words are to be understood. Even the "factual" status of descriptive "real" definitions is maintained only so long as they remain unchallenged. Thus definitions always can be described as rhetorical, whether their rhetorical qualities are, in a given context, a "dormant" or "live" concern of a group of language users.

Definitions are always rhetorical in the sense that each time definition comes up in discourse, language users have the choice of whether to affirm or challenge the current conventional understanding. As Perelman and Olbrechts-Tyteca put it: "A definition is always a matter of choice" (448). Definitions are also rhetorical in the sense that they function as strategies of social influence and control. Definitions tell us when it is "proper" or "correct" to use words in a particular way and, in doing so, they tell us what is in our world.

Edward Schiappa
University of Minnesota

Bibliography

Fetzer, James H., David Shatz, and George Schlesinger, eds. *Definitions and Definability: Philosophical Perspectives.* Dordrecht: Kluwer, 1991.

Perelman, Chaïm, and Lucie Olbrechts-Tyteca. *The New Rhetoric: A Treatise on Argumentation.* Trans. J. Wilkinson and P. Weaver. Notre Dame, IN: Notre Dame UP, 1969.

Robinson, Richard. *Definition.* Oxford: Clarendon, 1950.

Deliberative Oratory

A type of rhetoric concerned with the practical use of discourse in political assemblies. Richard Leo Enos traces the pre-Aristotelian history of deliberative oratory to the emergence of rhetoric as a formal discipline in Syracuse in 467 B.C.E. (*Greek Rhetoric before Aristotle* 52). Because the sophists were primarily concerned with judicial and ceremonial speaking, and because Plato was suspicious of the role of rhetoric in the state, the formal expression of deliberative oratory as a discipline does not begin until Aristotle's description in *The Art of Rhetoric*.

Aristotle divided the art of rhetoric into three classes: forensic, epideictic, and deliberative. While the forensic domain deals with legal activity and the epideictic form focuses on special-occasion speaking, the deliberative type is concerned with counseling the audience about a future course of action in a political forum. In general, deliberative oratory is aimed at expressing arguments about the expediency or harmfulness of a proposed act. More specifically, the deliberative orator addresses ways and means, war and peace, national defense, imports and exports, and legislation. While rhetors reason from either enthymemes or examples, Aristotle claimed that reasoning by example is preferred by deliberative orators.

Following Aristotelian precedence, Cicero discussed deliberative oratory at length. In *De inventione*, Cicero describes deliberative rhetoric as concerned with arguments about the advantageous and the honorable. The advantageous consists of security and power, whether internal or external to the state. He elaborated that the honorable could be subdivided into simple and complex forms. Simple forms of the honorable are those valuable in and of themselves and consist of wisdom, justice, courage, and temperance. Complex forms of the honorable are both meritorious and advantageous, and consist of glory, rank, influence, and friendship.

In the Middle Ages, the classical art of deliberative oratory was subsumed by preaching "once due allowance is made for the differences between terrestrial and celestial city" (Richard McKeon, "Rhetoric in the Middle Ages," in Joseph Schwartz and John Rycenga, eds. *The Province of Rhetoric*, Ronald, 1965, 206). The Renaissance witnessed a return to ancient authorities, particularly Aristotle and Cicero. While deliberative oratory remained central to the study of rhetoric, the "new rhetoric" of 1646 to 1800 moved beyond classical concepts "to become not only the theory of learned and popular oral and written discourses in their didactic and persuasive forms, but also the creative center of speculation about all the types of belles lettres" (Wilbur Samuel Howell, *Eighteenth-Century British Logic and Rhetoric*, Princeton UP, 1971, 442). In the nineteenth century, deliberative oratory continued its classical orientation; little new was contributed to the Aristotelian and Ciceronean concept of deliberative oratory by nineteenth-century rhetoricians. For example, David J. Hill's *Elements of Rhetoric*, published in 1878, explained that "deliberative oratory includes most political and parliamentary discussion. Its themes are war, supplies, finance, and improvement. Its aim is to dissuade from certain measures, and exhort to others. It looks to the expedient" (cited in Nan Johnson, *Nineteenth-Century Rhetoric in North America*, Southern Illinois UP, 1991, 162–63).

D

The twentieth century has noted a continued interest in deliberative rhetoric, but rhetorical theorists have considerably broadened its province. Among the important works that touch upon deliberative discourse are those of Kenneth Burke, Richard M. Weaver, Jürgen Habermas, and Hannah Arendt.

Kenneth Burke's new rhetoric, based on identification rather than persuasion, also treats deliberative rhetoric in a new manner. His seminal essay on the "Rhetoric of Hitler's 'Battle'" indicates that a problem of parliamentary discourse is its babble of voices: "There is the wrangle of men representing interests lying awkwardly on the bias across one another, sometimes opposing, sometimes vaguely divergent" (*The Philosophy of Literary Form*, U of California P, 1971, 200). According to Burke, Hitler was able to unify the divergent expressions by symbolic devices of inborn dignity, projection devices, symbolic rebirth, and commercial use. Burke elaborated literary functions of rhetoric beyond the belletristic tradition of the eighteenth century. In the Burkean system, deliberative oratory does not exist as a separate type; instead, all forms of symbolism have a social function.

Richard M. Weaver believed that the social role of rhetoric extends beyond the immediate political reality to cultural integrity and continuity. For Weaver, rhetoric is an inevitable part of society and is linked to the understanding and promulgation of cultural values. Immediate political reality is no more than argument from circumstance, the bottom tier of his hierarchy of argument. Further up the hierarchy are arguments from analogy, and at the apex of his hierarchy are arguments from genus. In an ideal rhetoric, people will argue from the dialectically secured nature of the issue and will draw upon the poetic qualities of language to invite their audiences to share a part of the rhetor's view of the world and thereby foster ethical action.

Using speech act theory originated by natural language philosophers like J.L. Austin and John Searle, Jürgen Habermas developed a theory of communicative action that operates in the domains of work and power within the society as well as the domain of language. In Habermas's view, the speech act, with its associated validity claims, provides a model of communication that "expresses the ideals of truth, freedom, and justice, thus providing non-arbitrary norms for a contemporary theory of society" (Sonja K. Foss, Karen A. Foss,

and Robert Trapp, *Contemporary Perspectives on Rhetoric*, Waveland, 1985, 237). The social role of rhetoric is clearly linked to the concept of deliberative rhetoric even though Habermas does not make that point explicit in his works.

Hannah Arendt, recognized more as a political theorist than a rhetorician, is nonetheless a moving force in a contemporary account of deliberative oratory. According to Arendt, speech and action are not means but ends in themselves; they reveal the identity of the speaker and agent. Furthermore, political scholars recognize that Arendt believed that "political action is talk about politics" (Kateb 17). Her emphasis of the links among identity, speech, and politics clearly merits her inclusion in the list of contemporary theorists on deliberative oratory.

James Benjamin
University of Toledo

Bibliography

Arendt, Hannah. *The Human Condition.* Chicago: U of Chicago P, 1958.

Aristotle. *Rhetoric.* Trans. George A. Kennedy. New York: Oxford UP, 1991.

Burke, Kenneth. *Language as Symbolic Action.* Los Angeles: U of California P, 1968.

Cicero. *De Inventione.* Trans. H.M. Hubbell. Cambridge, MA: Harvard UP, 1968.

Enos, Richard Leo. *Greek Rhetoric before Aristotle.* Prospect Heights, IL: Waneland, 1993.

Habermas, Jürgen. *The Theory of Communicative Action. Volume I: Reason and Rationalization of Society.* Trans. Thomas McCarthy. Boston: Beacon, 1984.

Kateb, George. *Hannah Arendt: Politics, Conscience, Evil.* Totowa, NJ: Rowman and Allanheld, 1984.

Weaver, Richard M. *The Ethics of Rhetoric.* Chicago: Regnery, 1953.

Delivery

The fifth of the five classical parts, faculties, functions, categories, divisions, or canons of rhetoric; *pronuntiatio* or *actio* in Latin rhetoric; *hypokrisis* in Greek rhetoric; *voice, gesture, expression, orthography, presentation,* or *medium* in modern rhetoric; along with invention, arrangement, style, and memory, one of five essential rhetorical concepts with which rhetors must deal and which they must master, and one of five aspects of rhetorical acts that critics examine and evaluate.

The study of rhetoric is essentially the study of rhetoric's five canons. They are "the sub-disciplines of the main, the lesser arts of the greater" (Connors 64), and they collectively provide a structure for studying the various parts of a complete rhetorical system. In part, the history of rhetoric has been characterized by shifts in the relative importance of the five rhetorical canons, by changing relationships and interrelationships among them. Rhetoric textbooks in both speech communication and composition studies, however, have for years promoted, perhaps unintentionally, a truncated version of the five-canon construct—a version that has focused enormous scholarly and student attention on invention, arrangement, and style issues but has typically ignored, misrepresented, or failed to engage memory and delivery issues. Largely because of this longstanding textbook tradition, the tendency has been, until quite recently, for modern rhetorical theory to neglect, ignore, dismiss, or oversimplify rhetoric's two "problem canons." In speech communication, memory issues have been dropped from textbooks, and delivery issues have usually received incidental treatment. In composition studies the first three rhetorical canons—invention, arrangement, and style—have typically been used to organize the materials presented in textbooks, but the last two—memory and delivery—have typically been ignored or deleted without explanation (Welch passim). The dismissal of memory and delivery, when acknowledged, discussed, and explained, has been attributed most often to the Western world's transition from orality to literacy. For example: "Understandably enough, discussions of delivery, as well as of memory, tended to be even more neglected in rhetoric texts after the invention of printing, when most rhetorical training was directed primarily to written discourse" (Corbett 27–28).

Delivery, however, is the more readily revived of rhetoric's two "problem canons," both theoretically and practically. In composition studies, especially with the advent of word processing and desktop publishing technologies, it has become increasingly popular for both scholars and students to rethink and reemploy delivery issues in rhetorical performance and rhetori-

cal criticism. Current thinking about rhetorical delivery recognizes equivalencies among oral, written, and electronic *pronuntiatio* and *actio*—analogies between voice/gesture and layout/typography, for example. Composition studies focused on technical and computer-assisted writing seem especially to promote a reconsideration of delivery issues in these terms (see Connors, Panetta, and Reynolds for representative treatments).

John Frederick Reynolds
Old Dominion University

Bibliography

Connors, Robert J. "*Actio:* A Rhetoric of Manuscripts." *Rhetoric Review* 2 (1983): 64–73.

Corbett, Edward P.J. *Classical Rhetoric for the Modern Student.* New York: Oxford UP, 1990.

Nadeau, Ray. "Delivery in Ancient Times: Homer to Quintilian." *Quarterly Journal of Speech* 50 (1964): 53–60.

Panetta, Clayann Gilliam. "Teaching Rhetorical Delivery in Freshman Composition." *Thesis.* Old Dominion U, 1992.

Reynolds, John Frederick. "Classical Rhetoric and Computer-Assisted Composition: Extra-Textual Features as 'Delivery.'" *Computer-Assisted Composition Journal* 3 (1989): 101–7.

———, ed. *Rhetorical Memory and Delivery: Classical Concepts for Contemporary Composition and Communication.* Hillsdale, NJ: Erlbaum, 1993.

Welch, Kathleen E. *The Contemporary Reception of Classical Rhetoric: Appropriations of Ancient Discourse.* Hillsdale, NJ: Erlbaum, 1990.

———. "Electrifying Classical Rhetoric: Ancient Media, Modern Technology, and Contemporary Composition." *Journal of Advanced Composition* 10 (1990): 22–38.

See also ACTIO; MEMORY

De Man, Paul (1919–1983)

Proponent of deconstruction. Belgian-born philosopher and critical theorist, Paul de Man was professor of comparative literature at Yale University where (in collaboration with J. Hillis Miller, Geoffrey Hartman, and Jacques Derrida) he became the major proponent of deconstruction in America. De Man practiced, in his own words, a mode of "rhetorical analysis" that sought to "reveal the inadequacy of grammatical models of non-reading" (*Resistance to Theory* 17). He terms traditional interpretations "non-reading" for being overly passive in their acceptance of a text's claims to logical coherence and for failing to acknowledge the radical disjunction between rhetorical and grammatical codes. For de Man, all writing remains at least partially "blind" to this disjunction and the self-contradiction—indeed, the self-deception—it entails. Active, critical reading, however (which he equates with deconstruction), attends to such blindness and to moments of aporia, when reading begins to oscillate between two mutually exclusive meanings—when grammar or logic gives way to rhetoric, and vice versa.

Traditionally, criticism has made rigorous distinctions between philosophical or referential discourse (which repudiates figural language and seeks to "speak the truth" about the world) and literature, which openly acknowledges its fictive, metaphoric nature. De Man refuses these distinctions, arguing that philosophical discourse relies upon metaphor even as it conceals from itself such figural, "fictive" devices. Of course, philosophy privileges logic and grammar over rhetoric in order to protect its truth claims: "Grammar stands in the service of logic which, in turn, allows for the passage to the knowledge of the world. . . . Difficulties occur only when it is no longer possible to ignore the epistemological thrust of the rhetorical nature of discourse, that is, when it is no longer possible to keep it in its place as a mere adjunct, a mere ornament within the semantic function" (*Resistance to Theory* 14). For "rhetoric," once acknowledged in a text, "radically suspends logic and opens up vertiginous possibilities of referential aberration" (*Allegories of Reading* 10). De Man illustrates this conflict between grammatical and rhetorical meanings in the ending of Yeats's "Among School Children," where "two entirely coherent but entirely incompatible readings can be made to hinge on one line, whose grammatical structure is devoid of ambiguity, but whose rhetorical mode turns the mood as well as the mode of the entire poem upside down" (*Allegories of Reading* 12).

Defined as "the study of tropes and of figures," and not as "eloquence" or "persuasion" (*Allegories of Reading* 6), the term *rhetoric*, as de Man uses it, appears reductive. More poignantly, critics are now faced with the anti-Semitic writings (in occupied Belgium during World War II) of his youth, which surfaced after his death. To some, de Man's collaborationist essays "prove" deconstruction's intellectual bankruptcy; to others, the epistemological and linguistic skepticism fueling deconstruction can be "explained" as a symptom of post-Holocaust European culture. Either way, attacks on de Man and deconstruction have become stridently ad hominem, making balanced appraisal difficult.

James S. Baumlin
Southwest Missouri State University

Bibliography

Brooks, Peter, Shoshana Felman, and J. Hillis Miller, eds. *The Lesson of Paul de Man. Yale French Studies* 69. New Haven: Yale UP, 1985.

De Man, Paul. *Allegories of Reading: Figural Language in Rousseau, Nietzsche, Rilke, and Proust.* New Haven: Yale UP, 1979.

———. *Blindness and Insight: Essays in the Rhetoric of Contemporary Criticism.* Ed. Wlad Godzich. Minneapolis: U of Minnesota P, 1983.

———. *The Resistance to Theory.* Ed. Wlad Godzich. Minneapolis: U of Minnesota P, 1986.

Lehman, David. *Signs of the Times: Deconstruction and the Fall of Paul de Man.* New York: Poseidon, 1991.

Norris, Christopher. *Paul de Man: Deconstruction and the Critique of Aesthetic Ideology.* New York: Routledge, 1988.

See also DECONSTRUCTION

Demetrius of Phalerum (c. 350–283 B.C.E.)
Student and friend of Theophrastus, was probably elected *strategos* in Athens several times between 325 and 319. He ruled Athens on behalf of the Macedonian king Cassander from 317 to 307, then fled to Thebes and later to Alexandria where he associated with, and possibly was murdered by, Ptolemy Soter. Diogenes Laertius attributes numerous books to him on history, politics, rhetoric, and the poets, including *On Rhetoric* in two books, and several treatises on Homer. Cicero and Quintilian describe his orations as in the middle style and distinguished by sweetness and frequent use of metaphor.

Modern scholars agree that the work *On Style (peri hermeneias)*, which has been handed down under the authorship of "Demetrius," is unlikely to have been written by Demetrius of Phalerum. The precise date and authorship of *On Style* are unknown. Internal evidence of Attic style has led some scholars (such as Grube) to argue for early Hellenistic composition (c. 270 B.C.E.) and others (such as Roberts and Schenkeveld) to support later (first century C.E.) Atticizing authorship.

While *On Style* shows strong peripatetic influences, and specific echoes of Aristotle's *Rhetoric* and Theophrastus' *On Style* (*peri lexeos*), it differs from Aristotle's *Rhetoric* in its definition of the four types (*charakteres*) of style, inclusion of wit, and some details in its treatment of the period. Its treatment of forcefulness as a separate type of style (*deinos charakter*) is unique among extant authors. It is the only late Greek treatise that does not accord Demosthenes preeminence among orators; Demetrius even goes so far as to consider Demades the equal of Demosthenes in forcefulness. The treatment of letter writing in *On Style* is the earliest extant.

On Style begins with a discussion of sentence structure (Sections 1–36). Just as poetry is divided into lines, so the basic units of prose are clauses (*kola*), which may be combined into periods. Demetrius recommends clauses of moderate length, but allows short phrases (*komma*) for maxims such as "Know thyself." He distinguishes between the periodic style (*hermeneia katestrammene*) of Isocrates, Gorgias, and Alcidamas and the loose style (*hermeneia dieremene*) of Hecataeus and Herodotus, and recommends mixing the two. After distinguishing among narrative (*historike*), rhetorical (*rhetorike*), and conversational (*dialogike*) periods, he discusses stylistic features including antithesis, beginning or ending clauses with similar sounds (respectively, *paromoia* and *homoioteleuton*), clauses of equal length (*isokolon*), and enthymemes.

Sections 36–37 introduce the four styles. Each of the following four sections covers the subject matter, diction, figures, sonic devices, and arrangement appropriate to one style. Means of achieving the virtues of the elevated or grand (*megaloptrepes*) style and avoiding the associated vice of frigidity (*psychron*) are covered in 38–127. The elegant (*glaphyros*) style and the corresponding vice of affectedness (*charakter kakozelos*) occupy Sections 128–89, which also include unusual material on wit. Sections 190–235 cover the plain (*ischnos*) style, its associated vice of aridity (*xeros*), and its application to let-ter writing. The forcible (*deinos*) style and the associated vice of unpleasantness (*acharitos*) occupy the remainder (240–304) of the treatise.

Carol Poster
University of Missouri

Bibliography

Chiron, Pierre. *Demetrios Du Style*. Texte etabli et traduit. Paris: Les Belles Lettres, 1993.

Grube, G.M.A. *A Greek Critic: Demetrius on Style*. Phoenix Suppl. Vol. 4. Toronto: Toronto UP, 1961.

Roberts, W. Rhys. *Demetrius on Style*. The Greek text of Demetrius de Elocutione edited after the Paris Manuscript, with introduction, translation, facsimiles, etc. Cambridge: Cambridge UP, 1902. Rpt. New York: Arno, 1979.

———. *Demetrius on Style*. Introduction, text, and translation. Loeb Classical Library No. 199. Cambridge, MA: Harvard UP, 1927. Rev. 1932. Rpt. 1982.

Schenkeveld, Dirk Marie. *Studies in Demetrius on Style*. Amsterdam: Adold M. Hakkert, 1964. Rpt. Chicago: Argonaut, 1967.

Wall, Bernice Virginia. *A Medieval Latin Version of Demetrius' de Elecutione*, edited for the first time from a fourteenth-century manuscript at the U of Illinois, with introduction and critical notes, thesis. Catholic U of American Studies in Medieval and Renaissance Latin 5, Washington D.C., 1937.

Demosthenes (384–322 B.C.E.)

Greek rhetorician, orator, and statesman. Born in Athens and generally considered the greatest Greek orator, Demosthenes' dates match Aristotle's. Although he achieved fame in his youth for judicial rhetoric, his lasting importance comes through powerful political speeches and, late in his life, a strong self-defense, "On the Crown." Demosthenes reached prominence around 350 B.C.E., when Greek city-states were temporarily autonomous. Sparta and Thebes had weakened, and Philip II of Macedon did not yet control the Attic peninsula. There was considerable unrest, and by the end of Demosthenes' life, the hegemony of the city-states had given way to Alexander's empire. Thus Demosthenes was the final notable Athenian orator.

Biographical details come primarily from his speeches and from Plutarch. He first spoke at age eighteen in a lawsuit against his guardians, who had misappropriated the legacy from his deceased father. His rhetorical skill was already evident, although he finally recovered only part of the inheritance. He became a logographer, a writer of judicial speeches for citizens who, in Athens, had to defend themselves before large juries. Later, he wrote speeches for important public cases. For example, his "Against Androtion" is a speech delivered by Diodorus against a tax collector whose tactics had angered the wealthy. This politically important case demonstrates Demosthenes' conservatism and early allegiance to the wealthy.

At age twenty-nine Demosthenes made his first speech to the Athenian Assembly. Later, in a series of brilliant orations, he warned Athenians against the growth of Philip's power. This series culminated in the "Third Philippic" (341 B.C.E.), a plea for unity among city-states and an appeal to Athenian tradition and character. Thus Demosthenes developed from a defender of the elite into a public spokesman willing to take political risks, a visionary statesman for democracy.

Recognizing Demosthenes' service to the city, Ctesiphon proposed that the Assembly award him a symbolic gold crown. An old rival, Aeschines, objected. The ensuing debate prompted Demosthenes' "On the Crown," widely considered his finest speech. It is a long and vigorous justification of his career and a ringing indictment of Aeschines. In 324, Demosthenes was accused of bribery and escaped into exile. Two years later he committed suicide.

Demosthenes' speeches are important for their literary as well as political qualities. Technically, his rhetorical structure is flexible, seldom mechanical. Despite the possibly apocryphal story of his practicing with pebbles in his mouth at the seashore, his delivery was not distinguished. In contrast with Isocrates and Lysias, his appeal came less through flamboyant rhetoric than through a subtle style, informed by an unparalleled grasp of history and oratorical tradition. He often linked specific cases to a broad vision of Athenian democracy.

Sixty extant speeches are attributed to Demosthenes; about a third of these may have been written at least in part by others. There are also a collection of *proemia* (introductions) and a volume of letters. His speeches are collected in the seven-volume Loeb Classical Library edition by Augustus Taber Murray, James Herbert Vince, et al. (1962).

Ken Autrey
Francis Marion University

Bibliography
Jaeger, Werner. *Demosthenes: The Origin and Growth of His Policy.* Berkeley: U of California P, 1938.
Kennedy, George. "Demosthenes." *The Art of Persuasion in Greece.* Princeton: Princeton UP, 1963. 206–36.
Pearson, Lionel. *The Art of Demosthenes.* Chico, CA: Scholars, 1981.
———. "Demosthenes." *Ancient Writers: Greece and Rome.* Ed. T.J. Luce. New York: Scribner's, 1982. 417–33.

De Quincey, Thomas (1785–1859)

English Romantic essayist who emphasizes uncertainty and intellectual play as elements of rhetoric. De Quincey wrote on a broad range of subjects, including literature, politics, and history. He offers a theory of rhetoric in "Rhetoric" (1828) and "Style" (1840–1881), in which he complains that the writing of his age has become too absorbed with the "determinate questions of everyday life," and wants to return to a premodern rhetoric that he identifies with the meditative and irresolute exploration of abstract issues. This rhetoric is essentially an art of invention in writing: "to hang upon one's own thoughts as an object of conscious interest, to play with them, to watch and pursue them through a maze of inversions, evolutions, and harlequin changes" (De Quincey 97).

De Quincey confronts the popular contemporary definitions of rhetoric advanced by Hugh Blair, George Campbell, and Richard Whately. He criticizes Blair for a mechanical conception of style, Campbell for not distinguishing rhetoric from oratorical eloquence, and Whately for making rhetoric the product of conviction. De Quincey identifies rhetoric with style but does not separate style, or "manner," from content, or "matter." Style materializes the rhetor's exploration of a subject, and since the human imagination is not limited, nor is any subject the rhetor considers. Rhetoric is distinct from oratory because oratory moves audiences toward conviction, while rhetoric involves a writer and his readers as coparticipants in the elaboration of complexity.

De Quincey's most famous works are autobiographical dream-visions, which illustrate both his fascination with the composing imagination and his definition of rhetoric. In his self-proclaimed masterwork, the *Sus-*

piria De Profundis (1845), De Quincey combines autobiography, social criticism, and visionary narrative, and exhibits his typically digressive and excursive style, in order to explicate his contention that the human mind is a "mighty palimpsest." De Quincey's palimpsest is a mental writing surface where the ideas, images, and feelings of one's entire personal history are interconnected with their analogs in the realms of myth, history, and the supernatural. As J. Hillis Miller and others have observed, De Quincey identifies rhetoric, writing, and imagination with the broadly associative intellectual power that the palimpsest represents.

De Quincey's lifelong addiction to opium, announced in *Confessions of an English Opium Eater* (1821) and ratified in *Suspiria de Profundis,* may have affected his conceptions of the composing imagination and the nature of his writing. He repeatedly emphasizes *dreaming* as a central creative activity and maintains that opium has helped him to "dream more splendidly than others." Dream is a term that encompasses all acts of imagination for De Quincey, and his preference for dreaming in solitude corresponds to a theory of rhetoric that appreciates the rhetor-as-dreamer. Before concluding that De Quincey's is a drug-induced, hallucinogenic rhetoric, however, we should note the widespread uncertainty among De Quincey scholars about opium's effects on his writing.

The standard edition of De Quincey's works was edited in 1890 by David Masson, who noted with disapproval that De Quincey's definition of rhetoric was markedly eccentric. René Wellek's 1955 view, that De Quincey's "Rhetoric" has merely "wrenched an acceptable term into a new meaning," can be set against more recent recognitions of De Quincey's contribution to postmodern theories of style and revisionist histories of rhetoric.

William A. Covino
University of Illinois at Chicago

Bibliography

Covino, William A. "Phantastic Palimpsests: Thomas De Quincey and the Magical Composing Imagination." *Composition in Context.* Ed. W. Ross Winterowd. Carbondale: Southern Illinois UP, 1994.
———. "Thomas De Quincey in a Revisionist History of Rhetoric." *PRE/TEXT* 4 (1983): 121–38.
De Quincey, Thomas. *Selected Essays on Rhetoric.* Ed. Frederick Burwick. Carbondale: Southern Illinois UP, 1967.
Lindop, Grevel. *The Opium Eater: A Life of Thomas De Quincey.* New York: Taplinger, 1981.
Miller, J. Hillis. "Thomas De Quincey." *The Disappearance of God: Five Nineteenth Century Writers.* Cambridge, MA: Harvard UP, 1975. 17–80.

Derrida, Jacques (b. 1930)

French critic of the history of philosophy; author of the method of reading known as "deconstruction." Jacques Derrida is currently director of studies at the Ecole des Hautes Etudes en Sciences Sociales in Paris, France, although for many years he was professor of the history of philosophy at the Ecole Normale Superieure. He has lectured and taught at many other European and American universities, including Yale and the University of California at Irvine.

Derrida's work caught the attention of American academics in 1966 when he delivered an essay titled "Structure, Sign and Play in the Discourse of the Human Sciences" at a conference on structuralism held at Johns Hopkins University. This essay, a critique of the intellectual pretensions of structuralism, was representative of Derrida's work throughout the 1960s and 1970s, when he developed the way of reading now called "deconstruction."

The term *deconstruction* refers both to a philosophical attitude about language and to a method of reading. Derrida always reminds his readers that language is an incessant differentiating movement. His deconstructive readings of philosophical texts assume, therefore, that meaning is not stable but fluid. He pays close attention to the temporal and spatial contexts in which texts are composed, arguing that there is no universal or transcendental given (such as truth or human nature) existing outside these contexts that could ground or finalize any interpretation. He assumes further that contexts themselves are never stable but are incessantly being recontextualized. Thus it is impossible to establish

D

a final or completely accurate interpretation of any human utterance, act, or practice. Derrida ordinarily refers to human activity as a "text," in keeping with his insistence that human beings inscribe meaning on the world. He believes that approximate interpretations of texts are possible and useful if interpreters pay close attention to the contexts in which human activity produces effects. Any interpretation of a text immediately becomes part of its context, however, so that texts can never be understood apart from their interpretations. Any meaning assigned to a text deconstructs those previously assigned, and language works at the same time to deconstruct any currently assigned meanings.

Deconstruction depends heavily upon the notion of linguistic differentiation, which Derrida borrowed from the structuralist linguistics of Ferdinand de Saussure. To grasp this notion, it is helpful to think of some set of elements that exists in a series—for example, the letters of the alphabet. Any member of the series—the letter "t" for instance—is significant only insofar as it relates differentially to all other members of the series, such as "i" or "p." In other words, humans are able to recognize the letter "t" only because it differs from other letters. Likewise, the word *to* has meaning for users of English only because it is a member of a sequence or chain of language, all of whose members differ from it even slightly: so and two and on and on. Humans are able to assign meaning to each word only because they see or hear that its letters or sounds differ from those of companion words. Each word has meaning only because it belongs to a system of differentiated relationships. By themselves, letters and words cannot signify; without contexts they are not legible.

Derrida includes both temporal and spatial differentiation in his notion of *différance*. This word is a pun in French, combining the meanings of "differing" (as any set of items lined up in space differ from one another) and "deferring" (as in putting off, delaying in time). Derrida posits that *différance* typifies the movement of human knowledge as well as of language. It is possible to know anything only because knowledge of a thing differs from knowledge of other things. Hence, human knowledge is dynamic, always changing and differing from itself, moving as it does among differentiated items and through differing epochs. Humans make sense of their surroundings by placing boundaries on the movement of *différance,* by including some kinds or forms of knowledge within their ken while marginalizing or excluding others. What a given culture knows at a given time is thoroughly historical, thoroughly written by and within that culture. Knowledge changes over space and time. Its edges become frayed and hence open to new knowledge and ways of knowing. What was marginalized becomes central, relations between parts shift and are redefined, hierarchies are turned on their heads.

In a differential model of knowing, knowledge is necessarily contextualized. That is, no object of perception can be known when it is studied in isolation from the system of rules, laws, or conventions that give it its meaning, or apart from other objects that are related to it and yet differ from it, both in space and time. Indeed, it is impossible to isolate objects from their contexts in order to study them in their pristine essence. For Derrida, meanings lie within contexts rather than within texts or knowers. This is the sense in which his notorious phrase *il n'y pas a de hors-texte* ("there is nothing outside the text") may most usefully be read. Because of his insistence that meaning and knowledge reside in contexts, Derrida has relentlessly critiqued essentialist ideas such as objectivity. The objectivist stance assumes that human beings can have direct access to objects without interference from what Kenneth Burke calls "terministic screens"—the linguistic or ideological networks through which facts are always already read, as Derrida might say.

Because of its reliance on differential and contextualized knowledge, deconstruction offers a radical critique of traditional reliance on transcendental or universal laws as means of authorizing human knowledge and practice. It argues instead that authority derives from human laws and conventions; it follows from this that authority and its attendant privileges are local and timebound. Derrida's preference for metaphors drawn from writing stems from his suspicion of the metaphysics of presence (his nickname for Western philosophy). The metaphysics of presence privileges thought over speech and writing on the ostensible ground that thought is somehow closer to the essence of human being than its expression in language. And within the metaphysics of presence, speech is thought to be closer to the essence of human being than writing because writing occurs in the absence of an other, while reading occurs in the absence of writers. Derrida argues that the crucial feature of written discourse, and the reason for its fallen status within the metaphysics of presence, is precisely an author's absence from a written text. Were writers not absent from readers for temporal or geographical reasons, they would not need to write. Given the necessary absence of its authors, who are not present to authorize a single authoritative reading, writing can generate a plenitude of readings. Thanks to its author's absence, any piece of writing, even the smallest scrap, can make itself available to any readers and other writers, who can and do subject it to a multitude of interpretations.

During the 1970s, Derrida's philosophy of language and his interpretive style were taken up and promulgated by a group of American academics now known as the "Yale Critics": Paul de Man, Geoffrey Hartman, Barbara Johnson, and J. Hillis Miller, among others. These critics produced deconstructive readings of canonical literary texts as well as explications of Derrida's philosophical positions.

The Yale Critics profoundly influenced many members of the English profession during the late 1970s and early 1980s. Several redactions and introductions to Derrida's work were written by well-known critics such as Jonathan Culler, Vincent Leitch, and Christopher Norris. A few literary critics welcomed deconstruction as a badly needed corrective to traditional ways of reading literary texts, and a few teachers of writing explored its potential for altering traditional composition pedagogy. Many more critics and teachers, however, complained that deconstructive readings were relativistic and nihilistic, and they feared as well that deconstruction threatened the institution of academic literary criticism. These fears were well-founded, since traditional criticism depends upon the notion that canonical literary texts are carefully artificed and finished products of a gifted author's specific intentions. Deconstruction immersed all texts, including literary ones, in the infinite differentiating movement and flow of language, thus making it difficult to maintain the traditional positions that some texts are inherently or artistically superior to others and that some authors are naturally or intuitively more capable than others. Deconstruction also threat-

ened traditional composition pedagogy, because it abandoned the traditional notion that composing begins with sovereign authors who are in purposive control of language.

During the late 1980s, academic critics were joined in these complaints by members of the popular press, who lamented deconstruction's supposed relativism and nihilism. The hue and cry intensified with the discovery of Paul de Man's youthful flirtation with Nazism. Critics of deconstruction seized on de Man's personal history as a means of discrediting Derrida and deconstruction altogether. Despite negative reaction to his work, Derrida continued to publish deconstructive readings of philosophical texts during the 1980s and 1990s, and he turned his attention as well to ethical and political issues such as racism and apartheid.

Despite its negative press, deconstruction has radically altered the thinking of many American academics and intellectuals. While it probably bears no direct relation to the development of cultural studies or the canon wars, deconstruction offered a coherent and powerful challenge to traditional attitudes about literary texts, teaching critics to think in theoretical terms and thus paving the way for other challenges to received opinion, such as those mounted by feminism and ethnic criticisms. Its impact has also been felt in fields as disparate as law, film theory, political science, theology, and accounting.

Sharon Crowley
Pennsylvania State University

Bibliography

Crowley, Sharon. *A Teacher's Introduction to Deconstruction*. Urbana: National Council of Teachers of English, 1989.

Culler, Jonathan. *On Deconstruction: Theory and Criticism after Structuralism*. Ithaca, NY: Cornell UP, 1982.

Derrida, Jacques. *A Derrida Reader: Between the Blinds*. Ed. Peggy Kamuf. New York: Columbia UP, 1991.

———. *Of Grammatology*. Trans. Gayatri Spivak. Baltimore: Johns Hopkins UP, 1976.

Neel, Jasper. *Plato, Derrida, Writing*. Carbondale: Southern Illinois UP, 1988.

See also DECONSTRUCTION; DE MAN, PAUL; POSTSTRUCTURALISM

Descartes, René (1596–1650)

Mathematician and founder of modern philosophy, known for his distrust of formal rhetoric. The Cartesian method and effort to achieve philosophic certainty are often cited as a challenge to rhetoric; yet, given Descartes's frequent deployment of rhetorical strategies, it is not surprising that his system makes provision for their provisional use. Furthermore, in spite of Descartes's aspiration toward a philosophy beyond rhetoric, postmodern critics find his system an entirely rhetorical construct.

In Part One of the *Discourse on Method*, Descartes denigrates the utility of formal rhetoric for persuasion, maintaining that clear and distinct ideas suffice. His claim to construct a new philosophic system ignoring previous ones implicitly questions the usefulness of the rhetorical tradition. Proclaiming the unity of all knowledge, he advocated a single method drawing its universal validity not from the specificity of individual disciplines but from the processes of the human mind. Moreover, his adoption of a mathematical model and his aspiration to extend mathematical certainty to all domains caused him to reject the probabilities that had been accepted in rhetoric. His dualism, which assigned highest value to ideas known independently of the senses, led to a distrust of the imagination and passions.

Indeed, the traditional five parts of rhetoric are almost entirely displaced by the four rules of the *Discourse*. If only clear and distinct ideas persuade, convincing arguments are discovered by his method rather than by such technics as the commonplaces. Disposition should sequence ideas from simple to more complex, either in the "analytic" manner by which they were discovered, or in the "synthetic" one that arranges them as a sequence of axioms and definitions that makes clear how each successive proposition follows logically from the preceding one. These clear and distinct ideas should be communicated through a transparent language, with words serving as counters for ideas reduced to their simplest components.

His own practice, however, belies an impersonal speaker addressing a universal audience in a format aping geometry. As Gouhier has shown, Descartes authorizes an instrumental rhetoric necessitated by the residue of childhood prejudices, which retards the complete assurance of certainty that clear and distinct ideas should produce. Fumaroli has described how Descartes aligned himself with Guez de Balzac to reach the emerging audience of *honnêtes gens* by using French instead of Latin, first-person narrative, and a style closer to baroque imagery than to the spare prose of scientific objectivity that is often considered his legacy. Rather than overwhelm his public with the force of his arguments, he modestly proposes to guide them in reenacting his philosophic quest.

Postmodern critics, however, point to the rhetoricity of the entire enterprise. Descartes's physiology, admittedly discredited today, relies not on his method as a heuristic device but on the similes that purport to be only illustrations (Cahné 96). Even his acknowledged contributions to science, like the law of refraction or analytic geometry, cannot validate his method because they were discovered by more piecemeal means (Schuster 213–16). Indeed, revisionist critics suggest that his method is more an instrument of exposition than a tool of invention. Descartes's method, thus, suffers the same fate as the scholastic syllogism, which, according to *Regulae X*, should be transferred from philosophy to rhetoric because it is capable of communicating only arguments that have been discovered by some other means. Moreover, just as the account of his development of his method in the *Discourse on Method* is largely fictional (Schuster 219), the metaphysical foundation of certainty he elaborated for his science in the cogito is paradoxical in that the impersonal subject it requires negates the empirical, autobiographical one that precedes it (Judovitz 108–9). Thus, far from being a mere adjuvant to a method that ultimately precludes it, rhetoric finds itself conterminous with his system's methodological and metaphysical core.

Thomas M. Carr, Jr.
University of Nebraska, Lincoln

Bibliography

Cahné, Pierre-Alain. *Un Autre Descartes.* Paris: Vrin, 1980.

Carr, Thomas M., Jr. *Descartes and the Resilience of Rhetoric.* Carbondale: Southern Illinois UP, 1990.

Flores, Ralph. *The Rhetoric of Doubtful Authority.* Ithaca, NY: Cornell UP, 1984.

Fumaroli, Marc. "Ego scriptor: Rhétorique et philosophie dans le Discours de la méthode." *Problématique et réception du Discours de la méthode et des Essais.* Ed. Henri Méchoulan. Paris: Vrin, 1988. 31–46.

Gouhier, Henri. *La Pensée métaphysique de Descartes.* Paris: Vrin, 1962.

Judovitz, Dalia. *Subjectivity and Representation in Descartes.* New York: Cambridge UP, 1988.

Schuster, John A. "Whatever Should We Do with Cartesian Method?—Reclaiming Descartes for the History of Science." *Essays on the Philosophy and Science of René Descartes*. Ed. Stephen Voss. New York: Oxford UP, 1993. 195–223.

Description

One of the four modes of discourse. In addition to narration, exposition, and argument, description has been used to categorize discourse since the classical period. The modes of discourse have been used to classify types of writing in more composition classrooms than any other form of categorization (Connors 444).

Many current textbooks are replacing the modes, which are ways of breaking down writing according to aim, with the process theory of composing. Within process theory, description and the other modes are considered to be inventive strategies, processes of thought, rather than the current-traditional view that the modes are "forms" of discourse. Mike Rose explains this theory by saying, "[Organizational patterns] should not be conceived of or taught as 'modes' of discourse or as rigid frameworks, but, simultaneously, as strategies by which one explores information and structures by which one organizes it" (116). Also, process theorists see the modes not as distinct categories of writing but as, to use Linda Flower's words, "ways to think systematically about complex topics" (74). Descriptive essays, however, are still commonly used as writing assignments for many levels of composition of instruction.

Descriptive discourse gives an account of physical surroundings. Descriptive words appeal to the senses and can be broken into two subcategories, objective and subjective. Objective description draws a picture using concrete words such as colors and shapes, and that picture can be extended to include smells and sensations. Subjective description also appeals to the senses but in a more abstract way, using words such as *beautiful* or *scary*. Both types of descriptive writing require the use of details to distinguish objects and events from other things. In *Steps to Writing Well*, Jean Wyrick says, "To make any description clear to your reader, you must include a sufficient number of details that are specific rather than fuzzy or vague" (238).

A descriptive essay is a form of writing that evokes a scene, person, object, emotion, or event using distinguishing details. Assignments, such as describing a room in one's house, describing a favorite place, or describing an unpleasant experience, are used to elicit this form of writing from students. Many anthologies used in college composition courses divide writing samples according to the mode of discourse they predominantly use. *The Bedford Reader,* for example, includes E.B. White's essay "Once More to the Lake" and Flannery O'Connor's essay "The King of the Birds" in its description chapter. The editors of that anthology outline the importance of description in their introduction to that section. "You hardly can live a day without describing (or hearing described) some person, place, or thing. Small wonder that, in written discourse, description is almost as indispensable as paper" (87–88).

Julia Kay Ferganchick-Neufang
University of Arizona

Bibliography

Connors, Robert J. "The Rise and Fall of the Modes of Discourse." *College Composition and Communication* 32 (1981): 444–63.

Flower, Linda. *Problem-Solving Strategies for Writers*. New York: Harcourt, 1981.

Kennedy, X.J., and Dorothy M. Kennedy. *The Bedford Reader*. 3rd ed. New York: St. Martin's, 1988.

Rose, Mike. "Remedial Writing Courses: A Critique and a Proposal." *A Sourcebook for Basic Writing Teachers*. Ed. Theresa Enos. New York: Random, 1987.

Wyrick, Jean. *Steps to Writing Well*. 4th ed. Orlando: Holt, 1990.

Dewey, John (1859–1952)

American philosopher, educational theorist, and social critic who helped to establish Pragmatism as a distinctive and influential philosophy. Dewey was a prolific writer who enjoyed a long and productive life: As a boy, he saw his father leave to fight in the Civil War; as a man, he lived through two world wars and worked well into the atomic age. Given the scope of his career, it is helpful to read Dewey's books with an awareness of their place in the seventy-year evolution of his philosophical views. It is also useful to read any part of Dewey's work with an awareness of the broader themes in his philosophy: stability and change, the individual and the community, the instrumental and the consummatory—themes that Dewey sought to balance, without surrendering one to the other.

Dewey saw philosophy as a conversation about values and ways of living rather than a quest for transcendent truth. Thus he believed that philosophy should examine human experience as it is situated in nature and culture, that it should critique and reform social habits, and that it should be concerned with matters of living well. Although no precis of Dewey's views will do justice to their scope and subtlety, notions of "living well"—including such themes as integration, connection, continuity, and growth —run through Dewey's thinking on a range of topics: metaphysics, epistemology, aesthetics, politics, and education.

In Dewey's view, to live well humans must recognize that they are situated in dynamic relation with a natural and social world. Because our ends are emergent and evolutionary, our knowledge and values will be always in process. Hence we should abandon futile quests for certainty, accepting the fallibility of our beliefs and viewing knowledge as a process of inquiry into the problematic rather than a body of fixed and final truths. Even in precarious and problematic circumstances, we can live well if we learn to approach our uncertainties intelligently, using sound procedures modeled on the methods of scientific inquiry—methods of purposeful doubt, protracted investigation, and productive curiosity. And we can live well if we learn to choose well: exercising responsible and wholehearted judgment, sensitizing ourselves to the lives of those who differ from us, and recognizing that we must compose and recompose our ends and values.

This intellectual and ethical activity is always conducted in a social and cultural matrix. Thus, in Dewey's view, humans must create and sustain a political order that fosters a variety of interests, ensures openness of communication, and encourages active participation for all citizens—a society that is radically democratic. Because democracy depends on public discourse, excellence in rhetoric will be necessary for a good life in a good society. Finally, because education must prepare children to live well, Dewey believed that schools stand in special need of reconstruction: Schools should emphasize active, participatory learning, encourage curiosity, teach methods of reflective inquiry, cultivate the imagination and aesthetic perception, and promote citizenship and participation in public life—all of this to enable humans to make their lives works of art.

Dewey's ideas have been influential in the fields of rhetoric, composition, and speech communication, affecting both theory and practice.

To mention but a few examples, Dewey's notions of inquiry and reflective thinking played a key role in the movement to reemphasize invention and problem-solving strategies in the teaching of composition, as well as in the development of the fields of discussion and small-group communication. And his views of education as cooperative, participatory, student-centered learning have figured in such pedagogical emphases as expressive writing and collaborative writing groups. Dewey's prolific and provocative work has been—and remains—a rich resource for scholars and teachers in rhetoric and communication.

Barry M. Kroll
Lehigh University

Bibliography

Alexander, Thomas M. *John Dewey's Theory of Art, Experience, and Nature: The Horizons of Feeling*. Albany, NY: SUNY, 1987.

Boisvert, Raymond D. *Dewey's Metaphysics*. New York: Fordham UP, 1988.

Dewey, John. *Art as Experience*. Vol. 10 (1934). *The Later Works of John Dewey, 1925–1953*. Ed. Jo Ann Boydston. Carbondale: Southern Illinois UP, 1989.

———. *Experience and Nature*. Vol. 1 (1925). *The Later Works of John Dewey, 1925–1953*. Ed. Jo Ann Boydston. Carbondale: Southern Illinois UP, 1988.

———. *How We Think*. Rev. ed. Vol. 8 (1933). *The Later Works of John Dewey, 1925–1953*. Ed. Jo Ann Boydston. Carbondale: Southern Illinois UP, 1986.

———. *The Quest for Certainty*. Vol. 4 (1929). *The Later Works of John Dewey, 1925–1953*. Ed. Jo Ann Boydston. Carbondale: Southern Illinois UP, 1988.

Fishman, Stephen M. "Explicating Our Tacit Tradition: John Dewey and Composition Studies." *College Composition and Communication* 44 (1993): 315–30.

Mackin, James A., Jr. "Rhetoric, Pragmatism, and Practical Wisdom." *Rhetoric and Philosophy*. Ed. Richard A. Cherwitz. Hillsdale, NJ: Erlbaum, 1990. 275–302.

Sleeper, R.W. *The Necessity of Pragmatism: John Dewey's Conception of Philosophy*. New Haven: Yale UP, 1986.

Tiles, J.E. *Dewey*. London: Routledge, 1988.

Westbrook, Robert B. *John Dewey and American Democracy*. Ithaca, NY: Cornell UP, 1991.

Diacope

"Cleft, gash"; the repetition of a word with one or two words in between. "Tomorrow, and tomorrow, and tomorrow" (*Macbeth* 5.5.19). The interposed word can be a qualifying adjective placed between nouns, as in "Company, villainous company, hath been the spoil of me" (*Henry IV, Part One* 3.3.10). It can be an adverb placed between repeated clauses, as in "Put out the light, and then put out the light" (*Othello* 5.2.7). It can also be a noun placed between other nouns, as in "A horse! a horse! my kingdom for a horse!" (*Richard III* 5.4.7). Often, the interposed words render the diacope exclamatory, as in "Light, I say! light" (*Othello* 1.1.145), or "My heart is fixed, O God, my heart is fixed" (Psalm 57).

Arthur Quinn and Lyon Rathbun
University of California, Berkeley

Dialectic(s)

In the classical and scholastic sense, the art and practice of inquiry and argumentation. Although earlier usage often applied *dialectic* to the art and *dialectics* to the practice, today *dialectic* is the preferred term for both the art and the practice. In modern philosophy the term refers to changes in meaning and sequential shifts in socioeconomic conditions, and as such are beyond the scope of this account.

The pre-Socratic philosophers appear to have been the first to develop the art, but Socrates, as portrayed in Plato's dialogues, furnishes the most familiar example of early classical practice. Plato's treatment of dialectic was modified by Aristotle and incorporated as part of the logical methodology described in the *Organon*. His conception of the art was modified by Cicero and Boethius and did not reappear until his philosophical works were recovered in the "Renaissance of the twelfth century." Dialectic reached the peak of its development in the schools and universities of Europe in the thirteenth century. Called the "Peripatetic method" or "scholastic method," it continued to be taught in the universities, where it furnished the basic structure of the examination system for centuries. Following the scientific revolution, the hypothetico-deductive method and experimentation gradually eclipsed dialectic as a method of inquiry. Kant, Hegel, and Marx appropriated the term but not the art of dialectic. Its Aristotelian character was partially revived, only to be merged with rhetoric in the New Rhetoric of Chaïm Perelman in the mid-twentieth century.

Sophistic and Platonic Dialectic

Fragmentary accounts of dialectical practice are first associated with the older sophists, or wise men. One of these, Protagoras, who lived in the latter half of the fifth century B.C.E., is credited with a work variously titled *Truth, Refutatory Arguments,* or *On Being,* in which the technique characteristic of dialectic—contradictory arguments—shapes the content. Protagoras and his followers developed the "eristic art" to a high level, exhibiting their prowess in disputations on many subjects. Noted for their doctrine that "man is the measure of all things," the Protagoreans reputedly advanced relativistic arguments on particular circumstances that "made the weaker cause the stronger." All of the varied approaches to dialectic are, like that of the Protagoreans, embedded in distinct epistemological views.

Dialectic achieves its best known classical form in the "Socratic method" of Plato's *Dialogues*. Socrates regularly questioned his hearers on controversial issues and used the contradictory answers elicited to refine ever more penetrating questions in the expectation of consensus. In Plato's *Phaedrus* Socrates reveals that his purpose in these exchanges is to apply the twin method of definition and division to arrive at essential truths. He explains that definition, collection under one head, and division, partition of the genus into its parts, is the dialectician's method.

Behind the method lies Plato's epistemological view. His dialogues teach that the world we live in contains only images and shadows of eternal forms but that humans have some residue of knowledge of the real from their existence before birth. This knowledge can be recalled when dialectical questioning prompts the respondent to discern the intelligible forms behind the appearances of the world of human experience.

He explains that contradictory opinions exist because the nature of the real has been obscured. Clearing away the irrational elements in the appearances enshrined in opinion (*doxa*) leads to the recognition of truth. Through successive approximations achieved by means of the dialogic process, sense knowledge becomes stabilized and well-based hypotheses can be postulated. Deductions from these hypotheses yield universal truths. Both Plato and Socrates believed that a communal, dialectical inquiry leads to truth. The pursuit of truth, then, is the purpose governing Socratic and Platonic dialectic.

Epistemological Foundations of Aristotelian Dialectic

A realist epistemology underlies Aristotle's teachings on dialectical discourse. He claims that the world is real and knowable through the senses and through innate mental processes that enable us to make sense of it. In the *Organon,* a compendium of his treatises on logic, Aristotle explains the nature of our understanding of reality, the process we use to describe it, and the way we investigate and reason to conclusions about it. He asserts that knowledge is the result of sequential learning that begins with the senses, passes into the memory, is advanced by induction and abstraction, and can issue in the sciences or the practical arts.

As Aristotle explains in the *Categories,* the constituents of being that we perceive in the real world fall into ten categories: substance (essence), quantity, quality, relation, place, time, position, state, activity, passivity. These are not reflections of perfect forms, as in Plato, but are various modes of diverse entities of form and matter. As such, they have specific differences that we recognize. Then, through comparison of our sensory experiences, we conceptualize the nature of things. We note, for instance, the existence of certain kinds of things: Seeing a creature covered with spots with a long neck, we grasp the substance or essence of giraffe. We remark quantity, in that we see more than one such creature, and situation, when we note it stretching its long neck to feed on leaves. The concept "giraffe" follows from our absorption of these sense perceptions about the object on which we are concentrating.

When we move beyond concepts to articulate and reason about these concepts, we employ modes of predication based on the modes of being we observe. We posit a subject and declare something about it. That process and its implications for logical reasoning are described in *On Interpretation of Propositions.* Aristotle terms what we declare or predicate the *predicables.* These exist only in our minds as we think and speak about what we see. The modes of predication are genus, species or definition, property, and accident. Since the predicables refer to what we have observed about the world, they presuppose the categories of being.

Aristotle terms the supreme form of knowledge *scientia,* science. He holds that to have such knowledge in an unqualified way depends on whether we can discover the cause of a thing or the principle that makes it be what it is and no other. Such causes or principles then furnish the middle terms of our reasoning. The middle term enables us to apply a predicate term to a subject term with certainty. The cause furnishes the reason why, for instance, we can say with certainty, "The earth (subject) is a sphere (predicate)." The validity of that reasoning can be tested by means of a categorical syllogism called a "demonstration," which is a deductive argument with a major premise, a minor premise, and a conclusion that is materially and formally valid.

Aristotelian Dialectic

By dialectic Aristotle means a logical method, universally applicable, through which probable answers can be gained to questions or problems for which we have little possibility of gaining certain knowledge; that is, where the causes or principles cannot be discerned. A discussion of the aims and practice of dialectic is found in the *Topics,* another of the books of the *Organon.* Aristotle holds that even though dialectical reasoning can base its premises only in opinion, nevertheless it can arrive at strongly probable truths. While opinion does not enjoy quite the status it had in Plato, it can attain a very high level of probability, depending on whose opinion it is. Aristotle mentions a range: the opinion of the many, the wise, or the best informed of the wise, the experts (*endoxa*). He thinks that such opinion, being based on experience, has truth in it.

Aristotle notes three kinds of problems or propositions as typically treated by dialectic: ethical, logical, and physical. He provides examples of each: for ethics, whether one should obey one's parents or the laws if they are in conflict; logic, whether knowledge of contraries is the same; and physical, whether the universe is eternal or not.

The philosopher further distinguishes between a dialectical problem and a dialectical question, saying that the former is posited as a perplexing problem to be investigated in order to gain knowledge or to take appropriate action, as in the problems just noted in the previous sentence or as a means of solving another problem. The latter takes the form of a challenge to an opponent, such as, "Is it true that the universe is one?" The question in a debate would be posed in the form of a proposition: "The universe is one." The test for logical validity of an argument given in support of or against the proposition would be whether it could be reduced to a valid syllogism. Such a syllogism would be termed "dialectical" because its premises would be based on opinion.

The *Topoi* as Instruments of Discovery and Proof

Dialectic for Aristotle is a purposeful method of winnowing contradictory arguments to arrive at what is most probably true. He further develops the question-and-answer format of Platonic dialectic, employing it as a means of discovery and of proof.

He explains in the *Topics* that in developing an argument based on opinion we can find an abundance of arguments in the predicables. These become tools of discovery, which Aristotle calls *topics* (*topoi*, plural, and *topos*, singular), a term that appears to derive from a physical analogy, implying a place (*topos*) where an argument may be found. Although Aristotle does not further define *topic* in the *Topics*, he notes in the *Rhetoric* that it furnishes the basic element, or the middle term, of the enthymeme, the prime rhetorical argument. Theophrastus, Aristotle's pupil, shed further light on the function of topics. He saw them as laws of inference, saying that they furnished the starting points of arguments.

The *Topics* explains each of the *topoi* in detail, giving many examples of their application in argumentation. Through "genus" one argues from the universal, subsuming category of things that have the same nature but differ in kind, such as animal, which comprises mammals, reptiles, and birds. "Definition" or "species" refers to the universal essence peculiar to the kind. Things of the same species differ only in number. Aristotle remarks that in arguments of definition we try to show the sameness of things and their differences. For example, mammals and birds have the power of locomotion, but we cannot predicate the same kind of locomotion of each. When we show that something is not the same as another, we destroy the definition. But the converse is not true, for to show that one thing is not the same as another does not allow us to maintain a definition.

Argument from "property" employs a universal that does not indicate the essence of something, but rather what always belongs to that species alone and can be predicated convertibly of it: Humans are capable of learning grammar, and whoever is capable of learning grammar is human. "Accident," on the other hand, is what belongs contingently to a species and its individuals, but not necessarily. Hair and eye color vary in the species human being while rationality does not (precluding abnormal cases).

Subsidiary lines of inquiry emerge from the predicables, such as resemblances, dissimilarities, causes, effects, antecedents, consequents, contraries, and contradictories. The possibilities of predication were also multiplied by knowledge of the categories.

While the predications of dialectic are made through logical universals as middle terms, these are still only opinions and so can yield only probable answers. Thus, dialectic as a universal method can be used in any subject; in this it differs from demonstration in a science, where causes are shown to make a particular thing be what it is.

Throughout the discussion of dialectical argument, Aristotle stresses the duty of the dialectician to examine both sides of an issue so as to be able to argue from either side. In this way not only will the arguer be able to anticipate the opponent's arguments, but the most probable solution will also become more obvious. Argument and counterargument constitute the basic form of dialectical argument.

The last part of the *Topics* brings the process of reasoning into the real world of active debate. It treats the debating process itself and offers advice on practical strategies of confirmation and refutation to win over an opponent. The *Sophistical Refutations*, which many scholars think was intended to be the last chapter of the *Topics*, covers fallacies and sophistical refutations that Aristotle says are actually fallacious and not refutations at all.

Benefits of Dialectic

The art of dialectic offers a number of practical benefits, says Aristotle: a means of logical training, an aid in conversation, and a tool for searching out principles of the sciences. Dialectic, then, is a tool for private and communal ends.

Investigation of a dialectical problem leads either to the acceptance or rejection of a choice, say of deciding whether to choose pleasure over duty, or it is a means of discovering truth, as in deciding that the universe is eternal or not. In the latter case, a dialectical investigation may be undertaken as a preliminary step in arriving at a solution in a larger issue. Aristotle notes that dialectic can even be used to consider the basic principles of a science.

The Relationship of Dialectic to Rhetoric

Aristotle speaks of the resemblance between dialectic and rhetoric in the first sentence of his *Art of Rhetoric*, a text that many later scholars classified as part of the *Organon*. Both arts take up any kind of question; both base their premises on opinion, use topics to find middle terms, and employ probable reasoning in their arguments. They differ, however, in their function, aims, and style of argumentation. Dialectic generally is used to debate universal questions in a modified Socratic question-and-answer format with an opponent who is knowledgeable about the subject. The dialectician proposes a position, anticipates objections, refutes them, confirms the proposition, and draws conclusions. Rhetoric is employed to persuade a popular audience to form an opinion or take action on particular issues; its style is more fluid, discursive, and framed in relation to the audience's knowledge of a subject.

Later rhetoricians are quite concerned with these differences in subject matter: Hermagoras, in the second century B.C.E., termed general questions of the type treated by dialectic "theses," and particular questions "hypotheses." Cicero further distinguishes, saying that "questions," being concerned with universal matters, belong to the realm of dialectic or philosophy, while causes, treating of particulars, belong to rhetoric.

Dialectic and rhetoric have similar functions but different aims. Both arrive at the most probable answers to questions through reasoning. Dialectic's aim is to find what is probably true for the sake of truth. Rhetoric also strives to find the most probable answer, but it does so in order to persuade, and for that reason uses more than reason to accomplish its end. Its methods include the authority of the speaker, ethos, and emotional appeals, pathos, in addition to logic, logos. These methods Aristotle calls the artistic proofs because they are invented by the orator. The orator can avail himself also of ready-made proofs, such as documents and witnesses. Antonio Riccobono, writing in the Renaissance, distinguished between the two arts, saying that rhetoric deals with the "persuasible" and dialectic with the "probable."

In the *Rhetoric,* Aristotle refers students to the *Topics* for more intensive treatment of the topics, remarking that he who is skilled in dialectical topics will be the better orator. Aristotle observes, however, that when dialecticians or rhetoricians enter deeply into a science they leave their own realms and enter into the science itself.

Cicero and Boethius on Dialectic

In the Roman period and the early Middle Ages, the complete logic of Aristotle seems to have all but disappeared. What remained of his concept of dialectical argumentation was equated with logic. The topics, which had become the focus of training in dialectic, underwent metamorphoses

with the ascendancy of rhetoric to greater prominence in education than in philosophy.

Although the Romans had little interest in dialectical argument per se, Cicero attempted to explain the dialectical method in his *Topica,* which he thought captured the essence of Aristotle's work on the subject. A bifurcation of dialectic and a blurring of dialectic and rhetoric in the education of the day is evident in Cicero's text. In the introduction to his treatment of the topics, he explains that argumentation (*disserendi*) is divided into two parts: invention and judgment. Judgment is practiced by the Stoics and called dialectic, but the art of the topics is neglected. To practice dialectic, he says, one must resort to the topics, defining a topic as "a region" of an argument. Although he indicates that he plans to carry the work from invention into dialectic, he refers to dialectical argument only once or twice. The realm of dialectical disputation has obviously receded in favor of oratorical argument. The topic then becomes not so much a method of dialectical discovery as one of discovery of arguments in the service of the orator.

Cicero's topic, or locus, takes on the more static character of a set line of argument, a "commonplace," rather than the dynamic *topos* of discovery in Aristotle. The loci are divided into intrinsic and extrinsic. The former inhere in the subject itself while the latter are external, separated from the subject. Cicero lists among the intrinsic topics the familiar ones of Aristotle's predicable, genus and species, adding their derivatives: similarity, difference, contraries, adjuncts, antecedents, consequents, contradictions, cause, effect, comparison according to degree, circumstances, and conjugates. Extrinsic arguments are those dependent on authority and not on "the orator" to invent, he explains. The distinction between artistic and inartistic topics, as noted above, was made by Aristotle in connection with the topics of rhetoric. The illustrations of the topics are almost all placed within the context of legal oratory.

In his *De topicis differentiis,* Boethius attempts to combine the Peripatetic and Ciceronian sense of the topics with that of the fourth-century sophist Themistius, who thought of topics as axioms. The resultant theory is closer to Cicero and Themistius than to Aristotle. Boethius distinguishes between two aspects of the process of dialectical invention, greatly complicating the teaching of it. The dynamic element that drives the predication he thinks of as an axiom, calling it a topical "maxim" (*maxima propositio*), while the individual predicate he terms topical "difference" (*differentia maximae propositionis*), and as such resembles the differences found in the species of a genus. Boethius retains the distinction Cicero made between intrinsic and extrinsic topics, adding a third category, the mixed variety.

What knowledge students had of dialectics in the early Middle Ages came primarily from Boethius, whose topics furnished the standard list. For Boethius, as for Greek scholars, the dialectical structure of question and answer determines the form of argument. An argument produces an answer to a question. But in his scheme the answers are programmatic, further reducing the creative character of the method.

Dialectic in the Schools and Universities

In the early twelfth century, interest in dialectic greatly increased as the *scholares,* or schoolmen, applied dialectic to theology and canon law. In the cathedral schools of Chartres and Laon, dialectic was used to order and reconcile conflicting patristic and canonical texts by defining terms, distinguishing aspects, and reasoning to conclusions. The ordered collections of texts were called *Sententiae* or *Summa sententiarum* (sentences or summaries of sentences). The method, termed the *scholastic method,* was extended beyond doctrines of theology and canon law to those of grammar, logic, and philosophy.

One of the foremost figures of the period, Peter Abelard, sought answers to 158 central problems in theology, collecting the conflicting opinions in the controversial work *Sic et non, Yes and No.* The title accurately reflects the dialectical composition of the subject matter. His use of dialectics in attempting to clarify the Trinity galvanized the opposition of the Cistercians and others against employing the method in matters of theology.

The thirteenth century brought the fullest development of dialectic as the old logic (*logica vetus*) was replaced by the *logica nova,* when missing works of the *Organon* of Aristotle were recovered. The *Prior* and *Posterior Analytics, Topics,* and *Rhetoric* were for the first time fully available in Latin. These works enabled scholars once more to note distinctions among demonstrative, dialectical, and sophistic reasoning that were obscured during the early Middle Ages.

The dialectical method flourished in the newly emerging universities, where it furnished the basic structure of pedagogy and of evaluation. Scholars used dialectics to expose opinions on all sides of central questions (*questiones disputatae*) in their lectures in grammar, philosophy, and theology. The auditors who wished to become bachelors and eventually masters of arts or theology were tested by the dialectical method of disputation. Dialectic so dominated intellectual life in the period that the meaning of the term broadened to include not only the method of investigating truth and probable argument but the art of disputation as well.

Students in the faculty of arts were introduced to the method of disputation in logic classes after brief study of grammar and rhetoric. The *Organon* of Aristotle's Lyceum again furnished the sequence: terms, propositions, types of argument, dialectic, and the fallacies. The higher studies of the traditional liberal arts—arithmetic, geometry, astronomy, and music—received little attention, being overshadowed by the newly recovered works of Aristotle in natural philosophy, moral philosophy, and metaphysics. In these last disciplines, dialectic assumed great importance, as it was brought to bear upon manifold problems where certain knowledge was wanting. Masters generally broached questions and aired opposing and confirming opinions. The same questions became propositions for disputations, which permitted students to learn from advanced colleagues not only the subject matter but also techniques of argumentation. Another type of disputation furnished edifying entertainment, the special free-for-all exhibitions, the *quodlibeta* disputations, held during Advent and Lent, when bachelors or masters offered to answer any question posed.

In the mid thirteenth century, a number of masters of theology undertook to write more extensive and original works, sometimes covering the whole of theology. The best known of these is the *Summa theologiae* of Thomas Aquinas, which has, by synechdoche, become synonymous with the genre. Thomas provides in this work one of the best examples of dialectic in the service of a discipline. Dialectic was applied also by members of the arts faculty who wrote their own, albeit lesser known, commentaries and *summae* on canonical texts in their disciplines. Given the pervasiveness of dialectic, it is not surprising that dialectic influenced the structure of university sermons as well. Definition, division, and other *topoi* were employed to develop proofs of doctrine and Scripture for audiences of scholars.

Decline of Dialectic

The vogue for dialectical complexity reached its greatest heights as semantics and the syntactics of language were given increasing attention in the last half of the thirteenth and the early fourteenth century. The interest in logic itself, with little corresponding concern for the greater philosophical context of epistemology and demonstrative proof, owes much to the writings of Peter of Spain, a contemporary of Thomas Aquinas. Peter's approach has much in common with modern logicians' treatment of quantification in mathematical logic. His logical treatise, the *Summulae logicales* (c. 1246), intended for students in the arts faculty, briefly summarizes the "old logic" and uses Boethius's approach to the topics. It also expands the earlier canon, adding treatises called the *Parva logicalia,* or *Little Logicals,* that take up syncategorematic terms (such as *if, then, all,* and *none*), and goes on to treat suppositions, relative terms, extensions, and exceptives or exponibles (like *only, all but,* and *after*).

The *Summulae* of Peter of Spain, along with commentaries on the work in the fourteenth century, were especially popular in the universities of Northern Europe, where they were often required reading in the arts faculties in tandem with Aristotle's works. It was this tradition of Peter of Spain that most inspired the fulminations of Renaissance humanists against dialectic. The conceptions of logic in the *Summulae,* however, seem to have determined the direction of the reforms undertaken by Agricola and Ramus.

In fourteenth-century England, the teachings of Peter of Spain and his "terminist" followers continued to inspire philosophers. William Ockham and his disciples expanded applications of dialectical *topoi* to investigate the properties of terms and multiply distinctions, producing *insolubilia,* insoluble problems in logic, grammar, and natural philosophy. Topical arguments eventually became known as "consequences," with the term *consequentia* denoting inference.

Renaissance Reforms

Increasing despair in face of the difficulty of conveying the rudiments of logic to young students led to reforms, particularly of dialectic, by scholars of the sixteenth century. They attempted to simplify and reduce redundancy, but in doing so further separated dialectic from its use in philosophical argument. The teaching of logic became formulaic and mechanical. By the next century, many students tended to avoid the subject altogether.

Ruldolf Agricola is the first notable reformer of logic in the Renaissance. His *De dialectica inventione libri tres (Dialectical Invention in Three Books,* 1515) was greatly influential in the Low Countries in the early fifteenth century and at the University of Paris at mid century, becoming popular in Germany, Spain, and England in the later sixteenth century. It seems not to have caught on as well in Italy, where the Aristotelian and Thomistic tradition was stronger.

When Agricola began writing his text at the end of the fifteenth century, Lorenzo Valla was also calling for a new approach to dialectic in his work *Dialecticae disputationes*. He sought to extend the notion of validity in topical argument to bring about a recognition that some arguments are convincing regardless of their form, and he tried to revamp the notion of a hierarchy of argument where demonstrative argument stood at the highest level because of its universality. Instead, he argued, the audience should serve as the criterion for the kind of argument to be employed.

Agricola adopted an approach to reasoning similar to Valla's, going beyond him to conflate dialectic with rhetoric and to accord little weight to demonstrative reasoning. In Agricola's view, the art of logic is dominated by a dialectical logic of topical reasoning. The immediate effect of his work was to move attention away from the preoccupations of terministic dialectic with form and meaning to the arena of practical questions.

Drawing their inspiration from Agricola, other reforms were proposed by such prominent figures as Johannes Sturm, Philipp Melanchthon, and Peter Ramus. Their works and later commentaries on them were to have considerable influence in Northern Europe. The most influential of these was Ramus, who held that the treatment of invention and organization of discourse should be allocated to discourse alone, thus denying to rhetoric those canons; to the latter he accorded responsibility for elegance of expression and effective delivery. Walter J. Ong, in *Ramus, Method and the Decay of Dialogue,* notes that the reforms of Ramus had the effect of eliminating the question-and-answer concept behind dialectic in favor of a spatial model of mental analysis divorced from the external world of things, which, ironically, first gave rise to the art, as the writings of Plato and Aristotle attest. The extent of Ramean influence in England as well as other trends in the teaching of logic and rhetoric are detailed in Wilbur S. Howell, *Logic and Rhetoric in England, 1500–1700.*

While the reforms of Agricola and Ramus might prepare schoolboys more effectively to dispute topics regularly posed in lower-level classrooms, they did not answer the demands of scholars who wished to carry on serious debates in the sciences. Aristotelian approaches to dialectic remained strong in the sixteenth century in Italy, where they flourished concurrently with humanistic approaches. The emergence of Jesuit education in the mid sixteenth century spread Aristotelian logic throughout Europe into Asia and the Americas when its ratio, or method, was adopted in its far-flung colleges. Scholars used disputations to argue points of genuine difference in the sciences. In general they were seriously concerned with real questions, not simply in exhibiting prowess in debate. During the religious turmoil of the Reformation, Protestant and Catholic employed disputation in the hope of resolving religious issues. In the realm of science, dialectic furnished the structure for arguing the relative merits of the Ptolemaic and Copernican theses. Rhetorical appeals entered increasingly into the dialectical exchanges as subjects were aired before the general public.

In seventeenth-century England, dialectical method continued to be the preferred means of dealing with disputed points, even as observation and experiment were increasingly adopted to investigate nature. For instance, John Wilkins, one of the founders and leading figures of the Royal Society, carefully distinguishes between demonstration, dialectic, and rhetoric in works in which he popularized Galileo's discoveries and the Copernican explanation for celestial phenomena.

By the mid eighteenth century, interest in dialectic declined as experiment provided the model for investigation in scholarly circles and discourse attempted to mirror its objective, factual concerns. At the same time, neoclassicism further effaced the stature of demonstration and dialectic. Grounded in the faculty psychology of the day, scholars elevated sense experience in their teachings regarding discourse and argument. Topical invention they held to be needless pettifogging since natural processes supplied the matter.

In the mid twentieth century, a few scholars again turned their attention to dialectic, but for different purposes. Richard Weaver in *The Ethics of Rhetoric* stresses dialectical inquiry as a first step to achieving ethical rhetoric, while Chaïm Perelman and Lucie Olbrechts-Tyteca, in their *La Nouvelle Rhétorique: Traité de l'Argumentation* or *The New Rhetoric* (1958) emphasize the need for a return to a dialectical-rhetorical approach to take full account of the role of opinion in probable reasoning. For Perelman dialectic and rhetoric are essentially the same, because truth is a matter of consensus and all arguments are meant to persuade. Many modern philosophers agree with this view, either abrogating dialectic altogether or making it a subcategory of rhetoric.

Jean Dietz Moss
Catholic University of America

Bibliography

Ashworth, E.J. *Language and Logic in the Post-Medieval Period.* Boston: D. Reidel, 1974.

Boethius. *Boethius's De topicis differentiis.* Trans. and ed., Eleonore Stump. Ithaca, NY: Cornell UP, 1978.

Evans, J.D.G. *Aristotle's Concept of Dialectic.* Cambridge: Cambridge UP, 1977.

Green-Pedersen, Niels J. *The Tradition of the Topics in the Middle Ages: The Commentaries on Aristotle's and Boethius' Topics.* Munich/Vienna: Philosophia Verlag, 1984.

Grimaldi, William M.A. "The Aristotelian Topics." *Aristotle: The Classical Heritage of Rhetoric.* Ed. Keith V. Erickson. Metuchen, NJ: Scarecrow, 1974.

Howell, Wilbur S. *Logic and Rhetoric in England, 1500–1700.* Princeton: Princeton UP, 1956.

Jardine, Lisa. "Humanistic Logic." *The Cambridge History of Renaissance Philosophy.* Ed. Charles B. Schmitt and Quentin Skinner. Cambridge: Cambridge UP, 1988.

McKeon, Richard. "Rhetoric in the Middle Ages." *Speculum. A Journal of Medieval Studies* 17/1 (1942): 1–32. Rpt. *Rhetoric: Essays in Invention and Discovery.* Ed. Mark Backman. Woodbridge, CT: Ox Bow, 1987.

Ong, Walter J. *Ramus, Method, and the Decay of Dialogue: From the Art of Discourse to the Art of Reason.* Cambridge: Harvard UP, 1958.

Peter of Spain. *Summulae Logicales*. Ed. and
trans. J.P. Mullally. Publications in Mediaeval Studies 8. Notre Dame, IN: U of
Notre Dame P, 1945.

Weaver, Richard. *The Ethics of Rhetoric*.
Chicago: Regnery, 1953. Rpt. Davis, CA:
Hermagoras, 1985.

See also ARGUMENT; ARISTOTLE; BOETHIUS;
CICERO; DIALOGICS; PLATO; TOPICS

Dialogics

One of several nouns (others are *dialogism, prosaics*) used to name the critical project of M.M.
Bakhtin and mobilize it as an enterprise in contemporary criticism, theory, and composition
studies. The term is not Bakhtin's, nor is it
securely the property of any of those who have
employed it. Its use sometimes marks differences from uses of "dialogism" (see Holquist) and "prosaics" (see Morson and Emerson) but sometimes does not. The three schools
of thought currently flying the banner of dialogics—focused on the verbal liberal arts, feminist
criticism, and radical critique—have not seriously acknowledged one another or worked
through the likenesses and differences of their
use of the term or of Bakhtin.

Bialostosky (1986), the first to use the term
in a title listed by the *MLA Bibliography*,
advances dialogics as a verbal art correlative to,
but distinct from, the Aristotelian arts of rhetoric and dialectic. He outlines a dialogic critical
practice in which critics deliberately foreground
persons as the bearers of ideas and engage in
discovering their own meanings by differing
with and appropriating the meanings of others.
The practice is open-ended and personal,
whereas rhetoric, in the Aristotelian context, is
decisive and topical. Henderson contrasts Bakhtinian dialogics with Gadamerian dialectic in
order to describe the work of black women
writers. Clark elaborates and modifies the relations of dialogics to rhetoric and dialectic from
a social-constructionist perspective. Bialostosky
(1991) draws the implications of an art of dialogics for the teaching of writing.

Claiming the term for feminist purposes,
Bauer adds "gender considerations . . . to refashion Bakhtin's sociological stylistics into a feminist
dialogics" that she uses to show how the heroines of four novels dialogically construct themselves and misconstrue their situations in a social
world of many voices. Bauer and McKinstry

collect essays that share in a feminist dialogics
"that recognizes power and discourse as indivis-
ible, monologism as a model of ideological dominance, and narrative as inherently multivocal, as
a form of cultural resistance that celebrates the
dialogic voice that speaks with many tongues."

Gardiner features the term in the title of his
assessment of Bakhtin's work for a radical social and cultural theory that practices the critique of ideology. Hitchcock deploys it in the
title of his inquiry into Bakhtin's relevance to
the analysis of subaltern writing. Neither distinguishes *dialogics* from *dialogism*.

Don H. Bialostosky
Pennsylvania State University
Jayme Stayer
University of Toledo

Bibliography

Bauer, Dale M. *Feminist Dialogics: A Theory
of Failed Narrative*. Albany: State U of
New York P, 1988.

Bauer, Dale M., and Susan Jaret McKinstry.
Feminism, Bakhtin, and the Dialogic.
Albany: State U of New York P, 1991.

Bialostosky, Don H. "Dialogics as an Art of
Discourse in Literary Criticism." *PMLA*
101 (1986): 788–97.

———. "Liberal Education, Writing, and the
Dialogic Self." *Contending with Words*.
Ed. Patricia Harkin and John Schilb.
New York: Modern Language Assn.,
1991. 11–22.

Clark, Gregory. *Dialogue, Dialectic, and
Conversation*. Carbondale: Southern
Illinois UP, 1990.

Gardiner, Michael. *The Dialogics of Critique:
M.M. Bakhtin and the Theory of Ideology*. London: Routledge, 1992.

Henderson, Mae Gwendolyn. "Speaking in
Tongues: Dialogics, Dialectics, and the
Black Woman Writer." *Changing Our
Own Words: Essays on Criticism,
Theory, and Writing by Black Women*.
Ed. Cheryl A. Wall. New Brunswick:
Rutgers UP, 1989. 16–37.

Hitchcock, Peter. *Dialogics of the Oppressed*.
Minneapolis: U of Minnesota P, 1993.

Holquist, Michael. *Dialogism: Bakhtin and
His World*. New York: Routledge, 1990.

Morson, Gary Saul, and Caryl Emerson.
Mikhail Bakhtin: Creation of a Prosaics.
Palo Alto, CA: Stanford UP, 1990.

See also BAKHTIN, M(IKHAIL) M(IKHAILOVICH)

Diaphora

"Dislocation, difference, disagreement"; repetition of a common noun to signify both an individual and that individual's associated qualities. Peacham illustrates the figure with the following example: "What man is there living, that would not have pitied that case if he had been a man." He points out that in the repetition, *man* is used to signify humanity, "or compassion proper to man's nature" (*The Garden of Eloquence*). Shakespeare is also using *man* in a diaphora when Alcibiades asks Timon, "Is man so hateful to thee That art thyself a man?" (*Timon of Athens* 4.3.51).

Arthur Quinn and Lyon Rathbun
University of California, Berkeley

Digressio

An anecdote or example inserted into discourse, primarily for illustrating or amplifying existing statements made in the discourse. Although today digression is something that writers and speakers are taught to avoid to excess, the rhetorical technique has roots in classical teachings, where it was termed *egressio, excursus, or excessus,* among others (Lanham 54). *Digressio,* according to Richard Lanham, was seen to have a "technical" and a "general" application. Technically, *digressio* was "a tale or interpolated anecdote which follows the *division,* and illustrates or amplifies some point in it" (54). In general, Lanham defines the term as "any digressive tale or interpolation, especially one prepared on a commonplace subject, and inserted at the appropriate time" (54). Lanham also identifies a specific type of *digressio,* called "paradiegesis, a narrative digression used to introduce one's argument" (107). From these definitions, we see *digressio* as contributing amplification or example to various types of discourse; its applications center on illustrating specific cases or instances in spoken and written forums.

Joseph Colavito
Northwestern State University

Bibliography

Lanham, Richard. *A Handlist of Rhetorical Terms.* 2nd ed. Berkeley: U of California P, 1991.

Diotima of Mantinea (550 B.C.E.–450 B.C.E.)

Prophet, priest, and sophist whose name in Greek connects her with the honoring of Zeus. Uncertainty surrounds the question of whether Diotima wrote, taught, or even existed; no surviving works are attributed to her. Until fairly recently, it was generally accepted that Diotima was a cleverly devised fictional character in Plato's *Symposium.* Scholars argued that Diotima represents Plato's feminization of philosophy, a fictitious creation of Socrates, the erotic stage of the "Socrates" character, or a literary device. At the party depicted in the *Symposium,* Socrates refers to Diotima as his mentor and says that he consulted this sophist on the nature of love, quoting her discourse about Eros. the year 440 B.C.E. is the putative date of the dialogue, which reportedly took place when Socrates met with Diotima in the city of Mantinea. Not until the fifteenth century was the question of Diotima's existence raised.

In works including Lucian's *The Eunuch* and Marsilio Ficino's *Oratio Septima II,* the authors refer to Diotima as a famous woman philosopher. Recent scholarship offers a revision of Diotima as an actual historical figure and not a creation within a cultural context. Archaeological evidence for Diotima's existence includes Paolino Mingazzini's discovery of an overlay for the wooden container that housed the roll of the *Symposium* on which a woman in a long tunic sat engrossed in conversation with a man dressed in simple attire. The male figure on the relief is identical to two fourth-century B.C.E. statues of Socrates.

Recent discussions of Diotima include readings of her speech in the *Symposium,* emphasizing its sophistic and dialectical character. Irigaray argues that Diotima rebuts the claim that love is a great God and argues that love is neither good nor beautiful, but rather something in between, a philosophy or philosopher. Diotima renounces already-established truths and challenges traditional representations of the philosopher. The philosopher is not the well-mannered, educated, all-knowing teacher of already-accepted truths, but rather a barefoot seeker of wisdom and beauty. Irigaray argues that Socrates presents two contradictory positions in the absent Diotima. First, love is intermediary between lovers and neither God nor mortal, but rather demonic. Second, love is a means for procreation and immortality through the birth of children. Diotima laughs at how Socrates seeks truths beyond the everyday reality that he ignores and ridicules his dialectical method that overlooks elementary truths. Diotima views love as an intermediate terrain, a passage between mortality and immortality and asks that her discourse be received as a celebration of Love.

Nye reads Diotima's speech within a historical context, arguing that she is not an anomaly in Platonic discourse but the hidden host of the banquet, speaking for a pre-Socratic world picture against which classical Greek thought is couched. Nye challenges traditional views of Plato as the founder of Western thought and offers him as a rebellious student who transforms the instruction on love and immortality offered by Diotima, an authoritative priest speaking out of a tradition of female power alive in Greek culture.

Edwina Helton
Miami University

Bibliography

Irigaray, Luce. "Sorcerer Love: A Reading of Plato's *Symposium,* Diotima's Speech." Trans. Eleanor H. Kuykendall. *Revaluing French Feminism: Critical Essays on Difference, Agency, and Culture.* Ed. Nancy Fraser and Sandra Lee Bartky. Indianapolis: Indiana UP, 1992. 64–76.

Jahn, Otto. "Socrate et Diotime, Bas-Relief de Bronze." *Annales de l'Institut Archeologique* 13 (1841): 3–4.

Neumann, Harry. "Diotima's Concept of Love." *American Journal of Philology* 86 (1965): 38.

Nye, Andrea. "The Hidden Host: Irigaray and Diotima of Plato's Symposium." *Revaluing French Feminism: Critical Essays on Difference, Agency, and Culture.* Ed. Nancy Fraser and Sandra Lee Bartky. Indianapolis: Indiana UP, 1992. 77–93.

Tejera, V. "Eros and Intellectuality in Socrates' Tale of the Prophetess." *Plato's Dialogues One By One: A Structural Interpretation.* New York: Irvington, 1984. 346–54.

Waithe, Mary Ellen. "Diotima of Mantinea." *A History of Women Philosophers.* Vol. 1. Ed. Mary Ellen Waithe. Boston: Kluwer, 1987. 83–116.

Discourse

Most generally, language in use. An instance of discourse employs a language, as studied by linguistics, and organizes this language into coherent sentences, as studied by semantics. Studying the sentences as discourse, however, focuses on the text's functions in the human world. An instance of discourse may be written or oral.

Discourse has many social functions; that is to say, people use language for a wide variety of purposes. These diverse social functions can be said to give rise to groups of instances of discourse that all share certain conventions of language use, of greater or lesser specificity and binding force, recognized by all users. Thus the term *discourse* may be used to refer to one of these groups, as well as to one instance of language in use.

Theories of discourse typically classify groups of instances of discourse according to broadly defined social functions. For example, Alexander Bain's important premodern theory of discourse classifies discourse types according to what they convey to recipients about their subject matter: "description" sets forth a static scene; "narration" tells a story; "exposition" offers rational explanation; "persuasion" seeks to move to some action concerning the content; and "poetry" arouses pleasurable emotions about the content. James Kinneavy's important modern theory of discourse classifies instances of discourse according to what need of the producer (or "encoder") is primarily addressed: to express feelings ("expressive"); to influence the recipients (or "decoders"; "persuasive"); to convey information about reality ("referential"); or to call attention to the language of the discourse itself ("literary").

The concept of discourse may also be used to refer to more specifically defined groups of instances of discourse, with conventions of language use more narrowly defined within a particular human group. For example, "academic discourse" refers to typical language use within the academic community, shaped by shared conventions of language use among all members of the academic community. Instances of academic discourse might be a student paper, classroom lecture, a scholarly book, or a conversation between two researchers.

Patricia Bizzell
College of the Holy Cross

Bibliography

Bain, Alexander. *English Composition and Rhetoric.* Aberdeen: 1866; excerpted in *The Rhetorical Tradition: Readings from Classical Times to the Present.* Ed. Patricia Bizzell and Bruce Herzberg. Boston: Bedford, 1990.

Crusius, Timothy. *Discourse: A Critique and Synthesis of Major Theories.* New York: Modern Language Assn., 1989.

Kinneavy, James. *A Theory of Discourse: The Aims of Discourse.* Englewood Cliffs, NJ: Prentice, 1971.

Discourse Analysis

The study of texts and readers' interactions with them. Some scholars make a clear distinction between text linguistics and discourse analysis. Given this distinction, those scholars who work in the field of text linguistics are primarily concerned with units of language that extend beyond sentence boundaries, even though a text may consist of a single sentence or even a single word—as in the case of many traffic signs. Those scholars working within the realm of discourse analysis, on the other hand, are interested in how readers/listeners form coherent discourse as they interact with texts. That is, discourse analysts study how readers process texts. While many scholars do make this distinction, others use only the term *discourse analysis* to denote both texts and readers' constructions of meaning from those texts.

In the elementary stages of discourse analysis, scholars looked, for the most part, at the occurrence of syntactic features. In the 1930s, John Firth was one of the first to urge linguists to study language in context, but it was not until 1952 that Zellig Harris, trained in the tradition of structuralist linguistics, published an article titled "Discourse Analysis," in which he addressed the need to describe the formal features of texts. Throughout the 1960s linguists began in earnest to examine texts linguistically, but, because they were primarily trained to examine units at or below the level of the sentence, they tended to look at texts, more or less, as simple strings of sentences. At the same time that interest in larger linguistic units was growing, semantically based approaches to language were emerging as extensions of Noam Chomsky's transformational syntax.

In the early 1970s, scholars began offering a chorus of criticisms of sentence grammars. Alternative views of language came from anthropologists, sociologists, and sociolinguists, who emphasized social interactions within groups of language users. Concurrently, computer scientists were becoming interested in simulating natural language production and comprehension. Psychologists began conducting human memory studies that evolved into an interest in memory for information in texts. Contributions from and interest demonstrated by scholars in all of these fields helped to shape text linguistics and discourse analysis into an integrated field with a broad base of support.

Much of the work in the field throughout the 1970s was concerned with discourse coherence. Some scholars, whose work grew out of the Prague School of linguistics, considered textual coherence as the result of efficient connections between old or given information ("theme") and new information ("rheme"). Other scholars examined discourse coherence within the framework of generative semantics, with coherence as the product of local and global connections within texts. Still others treated coherence as the product of arrangement or organization of texts. The greatest refinement in the study of discourse coherence was that offered in 1976 by M.A.K. Halliday and Ruqaiya Hasan in *Cohesion in English*. Especially in the late 1970s, cognitive psychologists and reading theorists were examining the extent to which readers construct textual coherence in a bottom-up manner (that is, using words as building blocks for larger segments of text) and the extent to which readers construct textual coherence in a top-down manner (using the title of a text as an organizing device for processing the words, phrases, clauses, and paragraphs in that text).

Another major movement in the 1970s was pragmatics, the study of language use and users in context. Perhaps the greatest influence on pragmatics was speech act theory, which examines relations among language forms, intentions, functions, and meanings in context. Related to pragmatics is the ethnography of speaking, whose goal is to describe the linguistic options that are available and situationally appropriate to members of a speech community.

Perhaps the greatest area of interest during the 1980s and into the 1990s has been gender and discourse, which has looked at the intersection of biological sex, culturally constructed gender, and language use. Drawing heavily on feminist theory, sociolinguistics, moral development theory, cognitive psychology, psychoanalytic theory, cultural anthropology, literary theory, and social constructionism, scholars in this area have developed a detailed composite of gendered discourse.

Duane Roen
Arizona State University

Bibliography

Austin, J.L. *How to Do Things with Words.* Ed. F.O. Urmson and Marina Sbisa. 2nd ed. Cambridge, MA: Harvard UP, 1977.

Beaugrande, Robert de. *Text, Discourse, and Process: Toward Multidisciplinary Science of Texts.* Norwood, NJ: Ablex, 1980.

———. *Text Production: Toward a Science of Composition.* Norwood, NJ: Ablex, 1984.

Beaugrande, Robert de, and Wolfgang Dressler. *Introduction to Text Linguistics.* New York: Longman, 1981.

Britton, Bruce K., and John B. Black, eds. *Understanding Expository Text: A Theoretical and Practical Handbook for Analyzing Explanatory Text.* Hillsdale, NJ: Erlbaum, 1985.

Coulthard, Malcolm. *An Introduction to Discourse Analysis.* London: Longman, 1977.

Dillon, George L. *Constructing Texts: Elements of a Theory of Composition and Style.* Bloomington: Indiana UP, 1981.

Halliday, M.A.K., and Ruqaiya Hasan. *Cohesion in English.* New York: Longman, 1976.

Harris, Zellig. "Discourse Analysis." *Language* 28 (1952): 1–30, 474–94.

Meyer, Bonnie J.F. *The Organization of Prose and Its Effects on Memory.* Amsterdam: North-Holland, 1975.

Poynton, Cate. *Language and Gender: Making the Difference.* New York: Oxford UP, 1989.

Saville-Troike, Muriel. *The Ethnography of Communication: An Introduction.* 2nd ed. New York: Basil Blackwell, 1989.

Searle, John R. *Speech Acts: An Essay in the Philosophy of Language.* New York: Cambridge UP, 1969.

Tannen, Deborah. *You Just Don't Understand: Women and Men in Conversation.* New York: William Morrow, 1990.

van Dijk, Teun A. *Some Aspects of Text Grammars.* The Hague: Mouton, 1972.

See also COHERENCE; COHESION; SPEECH ACTS

Discourse Community

A site or social group defined by special kinds of speech and writing, the boundaries and character of which are determined by the communicative practices as well as the social sentiments, shared norms, and cultural values of the members. The concept of the discourse community arises from approaches to rhetoric and composition that emphasize the social qualities of language use. A relatively recent development, the concept emerged during the early 1980s, well after the concept of *speech community* evolved in linguistics (Gumperz; Hymes). It appeared at a time when authors in a variety of fields were applying linguistic analyses to social formations. Thus it corresponds historically and theoretically to the "interpretive communities" of literary critics (Fish), the "communication communities" of sociologists (Habermas), and the new interpretations of "discourse" in philosophy, critical theory, and cultural anthropology (Foucault; Lincoln; Macdonell). Applications of critical theory and ethnomethodology in composition have favored the development of the discourse community concept (Bartholomae; Bizzell; Harris; Killingsworth; Porter). Likewise, in the study of professional and technical communication, the effort to analyze audiences and describe specialized fields and practices of discourse has made the concept attractive (Killingsworth and Gilbertson; Matalene; Porter; Zappen).

Discourse has come to mean more than merely a text longer than a sentence or paragraph. It presupposes social content and cultural as well as cognitive processes. It takes dialogue as the precondition, means, and end of language. Moreover, at least since structuralism, *discourse* encompasses far more than just speech and writing. In addition to nonverbal and electronic communication, it includes other forms of social interchange, notably myth and ritual. Because all communities are to some extent defined by their discourse in this broadened definition and because all discourse is to some extent communal, "discourse community" appears as a critical category that simply draws attention to the discursive qualities of society and the social qualities of discourse.

In one sense, such a construct reaffirms the traditional rhetorical interest in audience and social context. Conjoining audience and forum, it provides authors with a revised view of how and where to direct rhetorical appeals. It adds social, temporal, and spatial dimensions to the notion of audience, and it adds a human dimension to the notion of situation or context. It suggests that instead of directing a speech or written text to an audience type (college-educated American females, for example) or writing for a specific occasion (such as a graduation speech) an author writes with the idea of furthering (or limiting) the goals of a human community. Academic authors, for example, when they promote and extend the favored research agenda of their discipline, tend to use a specialized language that both restricts access to the information and grants privilege to certain viewpoints and behaviors. Their writing thus demonstrates solidarity with some audiences and denies affiliation with or responsibilty toward other audiences.

In a more radical sense, however, the very idea of discourse departs from traditional rhetoric, undermining the integrity of the old author-audience model of communication. The relationship of writer to reader as one mind seeking another yields to a concept of the author and audience as participants in a communication system of interconnected and interrelated individuals, each of whom is already implicated at the time of communication in a complex of social formations. In late structuralism and especially in Foucault's work, individuals can appear only as the sum of the discourses that determine their existence within a field of practice. Reading and writing, interpretation and representation, production and consumption of discourse are seen as interpenetrating processes that instead of being directed by the intentions or purposes of the discourse user actually contribute to the user's own self-understanding and self-definition. The discourse drives the user, rather than vice versa.

The concept of discourse communities appears to be a step back toward the traditional rhetoric, an attempt among compositionists to rescue the individual writer, the subject of rhetoric who, in the most radical notions of discourse, threatens to dissolve into networks of disseminated information. Positioned more firmly in and among discourse communities, the author reappears as the agent or representative of a particular place, social group, or political interest. Though lacking the personal grip on intention that the premodern rhetor commanded, this revised subject of discourse at least has the potential for self-realization among the interests and attitudes of many communities.

The individual may discover affinities either locally or globally. In a local discourse community, such as a biology department at a state university or a regional office of a multinational corporation, individuals come to share habits and norms of discourse through day-to-day contact with one another. They have their favorite topics, their local jargon or shop talk, and their specialized appeals based on relations of political power and personal attraction. By contrast, in global discourse communities, such as the entire discipline of biology or a "school of thought" made up of the adherents of a certain theory or method, members may never meet, but they still share a set of values and behaviors that strongly affect their discourse practices. "Community" for them is a metaphor for their personal commitment to one another's work. If the commitment is strong enough, it may generate conflicts within local discourse communities when members grow dissatisfied and come to identify more strongly with their global interests. A group of research scientists, for instance, may be more interested in furthering the research program of their discipline than in making money for the company that employs them. This preference may show up as a resistance to adopting the discourse practices peculiar to the company.

Whether the rhetorical analyst focuses on local or global communities has been largely a question of method. Empirical study tends to predispose the researcher toward local communities, which can be described with traditional sociological and demographic techniques. Researchers with a predilection for theory usually attend to global discourse communities, which require the more sweeping descriptions of ideological analysis and critical theory.

Considered ideologically, the introduction of the notion of community in composition and rhetoric in the 1980s may have represented a weakening of liberalism among academic researchers and an experiment with communitarianism. Whereas liberalism would prefer a model of rhetoric based upon individual exchange in a free market of information, a communitarian ethos would emphasize the necessity of social constraints upon the individual. But it would nevertheless want to maintain a healthy measure of individualism as a buffer against incorporation by traditionalist interests on the right or socialist interests on the left.

If the concept proves adaptable to shifting historical trends in the field, its proponents still face a number of questions that call for further research: Does community formation and maintenance depend upon a full range of discourse practices, or are certain practices more socially efficacious than others? How do writing and speech contribute to and draw upon other forms of discourse (such as myth and ritual)? How does discourse relate to other methods of community formation, such as inclusion or exclusion by physical force? How do individual discourse users contribute to and draw upon the resources of the discourse community? And, finally, having identified discourse communities, what have we gained? What predictions can we make about how the communities interact with one another and how they ultimately affect the practices and competencies of their members?

While grounding composition and rhetoric in the study of specific sites and social groups, the concept of discourse communities also opens the field toward connections with disciplines and subject matter formerly considered distant from the concerns of the writing and speech teacher and the literary or rhetorical critic. As it raises questions about certain cherished categories, such as author and audience, the new category combines a critical challenge with the promise of revitalizing analytical rhetoric.

M. *Jimmie Killingsworth*
Texas A&M University

Bibliography

Bartholomae, David. "Inventing the University." *When a Writer Can't Write*. Ed. Mike Rose. New York: Guilford, 1985. 134–65.

Bizzell, Patricia. "Cognition, Convention, and Certainty." *PRE/TEXT* 3 (1982): 213–43.

Fish, Stanley. *Is There a Text in This Class? The Authority of Interpretive Communities*. Cambridge, MA: Harvard UP, 1980.

Foucault, Michel. *The Archaeology of Knowledge and the Discourse on Language*. Trans. A.M. Sheridan Smith. New York: Pantheon, 1972.

Gumperz, J. "The Speech Community." *Language and Social Context*. Ed. P.P. Giglioli. Baltimore: Penguin, 1972. 219–31.

Habermas, Jürgen. *The Theory of Communicative Action*. 2 Vols. Trans. Thomas McCarthy. Boston: Beacon, 1984–1987.

Harris, Joseph. "The Idea of Community in the Study of Writing." *College Composition and Communication* 40 (1989): 11–22.

Hymes, Dell. "Models of the Interaction of Language and Social Life." *Directions in Sociolinguistics: The Ethnography of Communication*. Ed. John J. Gumperz and Dell Hymes. New York: Holt, 1972. 35–71.

Killingsworth, M. Jimmie. "Discourse Communities—Local and Global." *Rhetoric Review* 11 (1992): 110–22.

Killingsworth, M. Jimmie, and Michael K. Gilbertson. *Signs, Genres, and Communities in Technical Communication*. Amityville, NY: Baywood, 1992.

Lincoln, Bruce. *Discourse and the Construction of Society*. New York: Oxford UP, 1989.

Macdonell, Diane. *Theories of Discourse: An Introduction*. Oxford: Blackwell, 1986.

Matalene, Carolyn B., ed. *Worlds of Writing: Teaching and Learning in Discourse Communities of Work*. New York: Random, 1989.

Porter, James E. *Audience and Rhetoric*. Englewood Cliffs, NJ: Prentice, 1992.

Zappen, James P. "The Discourse Community in Scientific and Technical Communication: Institutional Norms and Social Views." *Journal of Technical Writing and Communication* 19 (1989): 1–11.

Dissociation

The dissolution of a unitary concept into two aspects in such a way that one aspect is endorsed, while its devalued partner is given new coherence within a particular system of thought. Dissociation is an ingenious rhetorical process differentiating and hierarchically arranging usually two elements of a single concept; the rhetor portrays one element as positive and more highly valued, simultaneously devaluing another element by assigning to it the negative qualities of the formerly unified concept. The purpose of using dissociation is to resolve some troublesome incompatibility, whether theoretical or practical. Resolving this incompatibility may involve either dispelling or creating ambiguity. To disarm a threatening incompatibility, successful dissociation changes the prevailing understanding of a concept by simultaneously transforming and partially preserving its differentiated elements. Thus dissociation does not merely break the links uniting already-independent elements of a concept; instead it profoundly converts and prioritizes the elements in decoupling them.

To illustrate the process of dissociation, consider the case of a jury trial in which the evidence clearly indicates that the accused violated the statute in question but did so in order to achieve what the jurors see as a noble or humanitarian end. Initially, the jurors might struggle with the incompatibility between finding the defendant "guilty" under "the law" and believing that the defendant did the "right" thing. The defense attorney may use dissociation to resolve this incompatibility by dissipating the ambiguity surrounding the nature of the defendant's actions. To do so, the lawyer would differentiate the unitary concept of "the law" into "the letter of the law" and "the spirit of the law." The argument further must subordinate the importance of observing "the letter of the law" to the importance of fulfilling "the spirit of the law," and it finally must show that the defendant's actions satisfied "the spirit of the law," even though they may have breached "the letter of the law." If this dissociation succeeds, the jurors can acknowledge that the defendant "technically" violated a statute, while voting for acquittal because the defendant's actions fulfilled the more significant "essence" of the legal code.

As the illustration implies, dissociation is a strategy that typically opposes "appearance" and "reality." The rhetor identifies the disadvantageous qualities of the dissociated concept as mere "appearance" and the qualities advantageous to the argumentative position as representing "reality." Consequently, dissociation trades on a presumed gap between "appearance" and "reality." Employing dissociation on a theoretical level is especially powerful because, by reconstructing one's conception of "reality," it prevents future reappearance of the same incompatibility.

Dissociation is adaptable enough to transform material as varied as public policy positions, social values, experts' differing philosophical answers to theoretical problems, and knowledge criteria authorizing what counts as acceptable evidence. Dissociation's strategic significance is its versatile ability either to protect or to destroy the viability of concepts or argumentative positions on either a theoretical or a practical plane.

Kathryn M. Olson
University of Wisconsin, Milwaukee

Bibliography

Bass, Jeff D. "The Romance as Rhetorical Dissociation: The Purification of Imperialism in King Solomon's Mines." *Quarterly Journal of Speech* 67 (1981): 259–69.

Olson, Kathryn M. "The Role of Dissociation in Redeeming Knowledge Claims: Nineteenth-Century Shakers' Epistemological Resistance to Decline." *Philosophy and Rhetoric* 28 (1995): 45–68.

Perelman, Ch., and L. Olbrechts-Tyteca. *The New Rhetoric: A Treatise on Argumentation.* Trans. John Wilkinson and Purcell Weaver. Notre Dame, IN: U of Notre Dame P, 1969.

Schiappa, Edward. "Dissociation in the Arguments of Rhetorical Theory." *Journal of the American Forensic Association* 22 (1985): 72–82.

Zarefsky, David. *President Johnson's War on Poverty: Rhetoric and History.* University: U of Alabama P, 1986.

Zarefsky, David, Carol Miller-Tutzauer, and Frank E. Tutzauer. "Reagan's Safety Net for the Truly Needy: The Rhetorical Uses of Definition." *Central States Speech Journal* 35 (1984): 113–19.

D

Dissoi Logoi (Dialexeis)

A sophistic text originally composed c. 400 B.C.E. as a textbook or a compilation of student notes. Influenced by a variety of fifth-century B.C.E. Greek thinkers (predominantly Hippias, Gorgias, Protagoras, and Socrates), the *Dissoi Logoi* explores a diversity of commonplace topics in the rhetoric and philosophy debates of the time, including ethics, epistemology, education, democracy, the art of discourse, and memory. Though probably intended to be a coherent whole, the *Dissoi Logoi* manuscripts were divided by later editors into nine thematic sections.

The first four sections of the *Dissoi Logoi* examine the culture/nature (*nomos/phusis*) controversy in ethical judgments regarding (1) the good and bad, (2) the honorable and shameful, (3) the just and unjust, and (4) the true and false. Each of these first four sections considers contrasting arguments regarding whether ethical judgments (of the good and bad, honorable and shameful, and so forth) are made relative to particular cultural contexts (*nomos*) or according to inherent, natural qualities (*phusis*) in the objects of judgment. For example, in the *nomos* arguments regarding the honorable and shameful, the anonymous sophist writes, "If one were to command all humans to bring together what each considered shameful, and then to remove what each considered honorable, nothing would remain. For we do not all judge things the same way." Thus, judgments of the honorable and shameful (and the good and bad, the just and unjust, and the true and false) are influenced by personal biases and cultural contexts. In the corresponding *phusis* argument, the sophist writes, "I would be surprised if things that were shameful when brought together were to change form and become honorable." Here, ethical judgments are acontextual. The object of judgment holds within its nature the qualities of goodness or badness, honor or shame, and the judgment of the object is favorable if the innate quality of the object is goodness, honor, justice, or truth; the judgment is unfavorable if the innate quality of the object is badness, shamefulness, injustice, or falsity.

The fifth section of the *Dissoi Logoi* explores epistemological relativism from a Protagorean perspective (one object may be both large and small in comparison to other objects) and a Gorgianic perspective (nothing exists in every sense, but everything exists in some sense). Section six presents characteristically Socratic arguments against, and Protagorean arguments for, the teachability of virtue. The seventh section argues for popular elections over selection by lot in democratic governments.

Section eight of the *Dissoi Logoi* examines the art of discourse (*logôn technê*). Practitioners of this rhetorical art must be able to discuss issues in brief style, speak correctly, and understand the rules of the art of discourse; they must also know the truth and be able to teach the nature and origin of all things. This sophistic *logôn technê* incorporates both the pursuit of truth and the art of discourse, which Plato later split into the distinct disciplines of philosophy and rhetoric. Finally, section nine presents several commonplace aids to memory.

Bruce McComiskey
East Carolina University

Bibliography

Robinson, T.M. *Contrasting Arguments: An Edition of the* Dissoi Logoi. Salem, NH: Ayer, 1979.

Doublespeak

A word created in 1971 by the National Council of Teachers of English by blending the words *doublethink* and *newspeak* from the George Orwell (Eric Blair) novel *Nineteen Eighty-Four* (1949). In a famous passage in the novel, Orwell describes doublethink as "to know and not to know, to be conscious of complete truthfulness while telling carefully constructed lies, to hold simultaneously two opinions which cancelled out, knowing them to be contradictory and believing in both of them. . . . Even to understand the word 'doublethink' involved the use of doublethink." Orwell went on to observe that "the subtlest practitioners of *doublethink* are those who invented *doublethink* and know that

it is a vast system of mental cheating. In our society, those who have the best knowledge of what is happening are also those who are furthest from seeing the world as it is." Doublethink is expressed most succinctly in the novel in the three slogans of the Party: War is Peace, Freedom is Slavery, and Ignorance is Strength.

Newspeak is the language invented by the totalitarian government of Oceania to replace standard English, or Oldspeak. In addition to providing the proper language for expressing the ideas of the government of Big Brother, Newspeak was designed to "make all other modes of thought impossible." Newspeak is language "designed not to extend but to *diminish* the range of thought." Once established, Newspeak would make it impossible for an individual even to have an idea in opposition to any government position, insofar as thought is dependent on words. Ultimately, "the intention was to make speech . . . as nearly as possible independent of consciousness" with speech issuing "from the larynx without involving the higher brain centers at all." In Newspeak, for example, any word can be made negative by simply adding the prefix *un*. Thus, *ungood* means *bad*, *uncold* means *warm*, and *unlight* means *dark*. Other words were invented to impose a desirable mental attitude on those using them, words such as *goodthink* (meaning orthodox thinking), *goodsex* (meaning chastity), *crimethink* (meaning any of the concepts of liberty, freedom, and democracy), and *joycamp* (meaning a forced labor or concentration camp). Doublespeak is language that diverts attention away from, or actually conceals, the speaker's true meaning, or what actually is or is not on the speaker's mind.

Doublespeak is language that only pretends to communicate, that makes the bad seem good, the unpleasant appear attractive or at least tolerable. It is language that avoids, shifts, or denies responsibility. Ultimately, doublespeak does not promote or extend thought but prevents or limits it.

Among the uses of language that can function as doublespeak are euphemism, bureaucratese, jargon, and inflated language. In 1984 the U.S. State Department announced that, in its annual reports on the status of human rights in countries around the world, it would no longer use the word *killing* but would use instead the euphemism "unlawful or arbitrary deprivation of life." The U.S. Army no longer refers to "killing the enemy" but instead uses the euphemism "servicing the target." When asked why U.S. military forces lacked intelligence information on Grenada before they invaded the island in 1983, Admiral Wesley L. McDonald responded in bureaucratese that "we were not micromanaging Grenada intelligence-wise until about that time frame." In 1974 Alan Greenspan, then chairman of the President's Council of Economic Advisors, was testifying before a Senate committee and was in the difficult position of trying to explain why President Nixon's economic policies weren't effective in fighting inflation: "It is a tricky problem to find the particular calibration in timing that would be appropriate to stem the acceleration in risk premiums created by falling incomes without prematurely aborting the decline in the inflation-generated risk premiums." In 1988 Greenspan would preface a speech with the observation that "I guess I should warn you, if I turn out to be particularly clear, you've probably misunderstood what I've said." In the doublespeak of jargon, smelling something becomes "organoleptic analysis," glass becomes "fused silicate," a crack in a metal support beam becomes a "discontinuity," medical malpractice becomes "therapeutic misadventure," death caused by medical malpractice is a "diagnostic misadventure of a high magnitude," conservative economic policies become "distributionally conservative notions." In 1977 National Airlines called a crash of one of its airplanes an "involuntary conversion of a 727," thus using a legitimate term of legal jargon as doublespeak to mislead its stock holders. In the doublespeak of inflated language, automobile mechanics may be called "automotive internists," elevator operators "members of the vertical transportation corps," and grocery store checkout clerks "career associate scanning professionals"; television sets are proclaimed to have "nonmulticolor capability." When a company "initiates a career alternative enhancement program" it is really laying off five thousand workers. "Negative patient care outcome" means that the patient died, and "rapid oxidation" means a fire in a nuclear power plant.

Doublespeak is not the product of careless language or sloppy thinking but is carefully designed and constructed to appear to communicate but in fact to mislead. In doublespeak, sexual intercourse becomes "penile insertive behavior"; a tax increase becomes "revenue enhancement" or "tax base broadening." Acid rain becomes "poorly buffered precipitation" or "atmospheric deposition of anthropogenically derived acidic substances"; members of organized crime become "members of a career-offender cartel." A nuclear-armed, intercontinental, ballistic missile becomes a "very large, potentially disruptive re-entry system."

Through global electronic communication, doublespeak spreads quickly both within countries and around the world. The doublespeak uttered in the United States, Canada, England, or another English-speaking country quickly moves into the stream of electronic information communicated to the 750 million English speakers around the world. Doublespeak gains a certain legitimacy when used by public figures, especially leading political figures in the major English-speaking countries, and thus spreads by imitation.

Since 1974, the Committee on Public Doublespeak of the National Council of Teachers of English has each year announced its Doublespeak Award, an ironic tribute given to a public person or organization in the United States who has used public language that is, in the committee's judgment, deceptive, evasive, euphemistic, or self-contradictory. The award is restricted to those uses of public language which have pernicious social, political, or economic consequences. The first winner (1974) of the award was Colonel David Opfer, the United States Air Attache at the U.S. embassy in Cambodia, who, after reporters revealed that American B-52 bombers had accidentally bombed and destroyed a Cambodian village, inflicting a large number of civilian casualties, said to the reporters: "You always write it's bombing, bombing, bombing. It's *not* bombing. It's air support."

Other winners of the award have included the nuclear power industry (1979) for using such terminology as "rapid oxidation" for fire, "energetic disassembly" for explosion, and "abnormal evolution" for accident; the Pentagon (1977) for calling the neutron bomb a "radiation enhancement weapon"; the U.S. Department of State (1984) for creating the phrase "unlawful or arbitrary deprivation of life" to replace the word *killing*; the Exxon Corporation for calling thirty-five miles of oil-polluted beaches in Alaska "environmentally clean" and "environmentally stabilized"; and the U.S. Department of Defense for such doublespeak as "collateral damage" for civilian casualties, "area denial weapons" for antipersonnel bombs, and "servicing the target" for killing the enemy.

William Lutz
Rutgers University, Camden

Bibliography

Gibson, Walker, and William Lutz. *Double-speak: A Brief History, Definition, and Bibliography, With a List of Award Winners, 1974 to 1990*. Urbana, IL: National Council of Teachers of English, 1991.

Lutz, William, ed. *Beyond Nineteen Eighty-Four: Doublespeak in a Post-Orwellian Age*. Urbana, IL: National Council of Teachers of English, 1989.

———. *Doublespeak: From Revenue Enhancement to Terminal Living*. New York: Harper, 1989.

Rank, Hugh, ed. *Language and Public Policy*. Urbana, IL: National Council of Teachers of English, 1974.

Dramatism

A philosophy of symbol-using developed by Kenneth Burke. The tenets of dramatism include the following: (1) Symbol-using is a conventional, arbitrary, and learned form of action socially constructed and uniquely employed by human beings. (2) Symbol-using is an abstraction system that defines and imposes attitudes and meanings upon social activities and phenomena that are not reflected in the physiological nature of sensory experience or reducible to the intrinsic material nature of phenomena. (3) In contrast to the representational function of signal-using abilities characterizing other species, human symbol-using is reflective, feeds back on symbol-users, and this symbolic feedback alters how humans susequently understand and act. (5) Human motivations are uniquely represented in and created by the symbol-using process. (6) Symbol-using is a form of human action independent of but equal to other kinds of human action. (7) Dramatism is not a metaphor for the theatre, but a fixed form that emerges from human physiological processes (for example, the "motion" of brain activity) but ultimately characterizes the independent and literal nature of symbolicity as human action.

Philosophically, Burke has proposed a framework for systematically accounting for human action and knowledge within the context of his concepts, theoretical propositions, and critical methods of analysis. His philosophy of symbol-using stands in opposition to other schemes. Burke has rejected the position of naive realists who hold that symbolic terminologies reflect only the state of nature. He has likewise rejected the posture of rationalists who hold that symbol-using is a symptom or manifestation of reason and experience as the more fundamental criterion for resolving problems. While more controversial, Burke has personally denied that he has employed the postmodern view that symbol-using only reflects and conveys the multiple and contradictory meanings of the diverse cultural systems of symbol-users. Reflecting the broader functions that he would attribute to symbol-using, Burke has maintained that "the notion of *language in general* in shaping the human animal's 'orientation' (notion of 'reality' and behavior accordingly) would encompass a wider field than rhetoric. It would include 'science' even beyond the 'sociology of rhetoric,' or notions of human motivation-in-general (which can be classified with philosophy as in the realm of 'first principles')" (1985:92).

Burke's philosophy of symbol-using emerged and evolved over a seventy-year period. Burke began his career as a critic and philosopher of language in 1920. In 1931, his first published volume of criticism, *Counter-Statement*, examined how works of art, as symbolic forms, can challenge existing and established communication systems. Following *Counter-Statement* and written in the early 1930s, although it was not published for the first time until 1993, Burke maintained in *Auscultation, Creation, and Revision* that all aesthetic works possess pragmatic, social, and rhetorical functions. In *Permanence and Change, An Anatomy of Purpose* (1935) he explored how communication (that is, poetic and critical concepts) defines and affects social and societal problems. In his 1937 volume *Attitudes toward History*, Burke maintained that the entire flow of Western European history can be understood in terms of the rebirthing, purifying, and transformational functions of symbolic action. In *The Philosophy of Literary Form: Studies in Symbolic Action* (1941) he identified specific procedures and techniques for identifying the relationships among situations, attitudes, and strategies. In his sixth critical volume, *A Grammar of Motives* (1945), Burke outlined the basic grammar governing all symbolic or communication systems. He specifically identified a basic class of words—a *pentad* of terms that included *act, scene, agent, agency,* and *purpose*—and the set of operational rules that regulate the grammatical categories of a symbol system. In *A Rhetoric of Motives* (1950) he surveyed the scope and range of symbol-using in practical situations. Using the term *identification* as an organizing and unifying concept—a concept that emphasizes the unifying and diverse functions of all conscious and unconscious appeals in symbol-using—Burke significantly extended the meanings traditionally associated with the word *rhetoric*. In *The Rhetoric of Religion: Studies in Logology,* published in 1961, Burke described the symbolic progression that characterizes the strategies embedded in dominant social discourses, and he proposed a comic alternative to victim-oriented tactics that characterize many symbolic systems. In his ninth and most recent major critical volume to appear thus far, *Language as Symbolic Action: Essays on Life, Literature, and Method* (1966), Burke republished a series of his earlier critical essays, organized to emphasize his developed conception of dramatism.

In 1983 Burke modified his critical scheme, and he proposed "*two* terms for the *one* theory." "Dramatism" should be understood, according to Burke, as an ontological description of "what we humans *are* (the symbol-using animal)," while "logology" was to be understood as an epistemic description of the "*knowledge* that we acquire when our bodies (physiological organisms in the realm of nonsymbolic motion) come to profit by their peculiar aptitude for learning the arbitrary, conventional mediums of communication called 'natural' languages" (1985:89–90).

James W. Chesebro
Indiana State University

Bibliography

Burke, Kenneth. *Attitudes toward History*. New York: New Republic, 1937. 3rd ed. Berkeley: U of California P, 1984.

———. *Auscultation, Creation, and Revision*, circa 1930-1934. *Extensions of the Burkeian System*. Ed. James W. Chesebro. Tuscaloosa: U of Alabama P, 1993. 42–172.

———. *Counter-Statement*. New York: Harcourt, 1931. 2nd ed. Berkeley: U of California P, 1968.

———. "Dramatism and Logology." *Communication Quarterly* 33 (1985): 89–93.

———. *A Grammar of Motives*. New York: Prentice-Hall, 1945. Rpt. Berkeley: U of California P, 1969.

———. *Language as Symbolic Action: Essays on Life, Literature, and Method*. Berkeley: U of California P, 1966.

———. *Permanence and Change, An Anatomy of Purpose*. New York: New Public, 1935. 3rd ed. Berkeley: U of California P, 1984.

———. *The Philosophy of Literary Form: Studies in Symbolic Action*. Baton Rouge: Louisiana SU, 1941. 3rd ed. Berkeley: U California P, 1973.

———. *A Rhetoric of Motives*. New York: Prentice, 1950. Berkeley: U of California P, 1969.

———. *A Rhetoric of Religion: Studies in Logology*. Boston: Beacon, 1961. Rpt. Berkeley: U of California P, 1970.

See also BURKE, KENNETH; SYMBOLIC ACTION

DuBois, W.E.B. (1868–1963)

A major African-American writer, theorist, and political leader. A tireless editor, sociologist, historian, novelist, poet, professor, propagandist, agitator, prophet, enemy of racism, and founder of the National Association for the Advancement of Colored People (NAACP), W.E.B. DuBois both illuminated and helped transform American race relations. As Arnold Rampersad notes, "On the question of race, [DuBois] was the conscience of America."

Born in Massachusetts, DuBois studied in Berlin and earned a Ph.D. at Harvard, where his professors included Barrett Wendell and William James. After first producing scholarly historical and sociological books, in 1903 he wrote *The Souls of Black Folk*—a masterpiece of lyrical argument and prophesy—in which he predicted, "The problem of the twentieth century is the problem of the color-line—the relation of the darker to the lighter races of men in Asia and Africa, in America and the islands of the sea." He claimed that African-Americans were "born with a veil" and possessed a "double-consciousness": "One ever feels his twoness,—an American, a Negro; two souls, two thoughts, two unreconciled strivings; two warring ideals in one dark body, whose dogged strength alone keeps it from being torn asunder." This analysis has been applied and reinterpreted ever since it appeared.

In *The Souls of Black Folk*, DuBois opposed the enormously popular program of racial conservative Booker T. Washington.

D

Acknowledging the success of Washington's institution of vocational training, DuBois attacked Washington's "old attitude of adjustment and submission," which "practically accepts the alleged inferiority of the Negro races." Countering Washington, DuBois insisted that talented blacks deserved university education, not simply technical skills. Further, unlike Washington, DuBois argued loudly for the right to vote, asking, "Is it possible, and probable, that nine millions of men can make effective progress in economic lines if they are deprived of political rights?"

After helping found the NAACP in 1910, DuBois edited its thoughtful journal, *The Crisis*, for the next twenty-four years. During a long, restive life, the independent agitator wrote prolifically, sometimes shifted positions, and often engaged in controversy. Elitist in temperament, he eventually grew more and more radical, joining the Communist Party toward the end of his life and dying an exile in Ghana in 1963.

Arnold Rampersad summarizes DuBois's multifaceted yet coherent achievements:

More than any other individual, [DuBois] was responsible for the conversion of the facts and episodes of Afro-American history into that coherent, though necessarily diffuse, mythology on which collective self-respect and self-love must inevitably be founded. And far more powerfully than any other American intellectual, he explicated the mysteries of race in a nation which . . . has just begun to show remorse for crimes inspired by racism. (293)

Keith D. Miller
Arizona State University

Bibliography
DuBois, W.E.B. *The Autobiography of W.E.B. DuBois.* Ed. Herbert Aptheker. New York: International, 1968.
———. *The Souls of Black Folk.* 1903. New York: New American Library, 1969.
———. *W.E.B. DuBois Speaks: Speeches and Addresses, 1890–1919.* Ed. Philip Foner. New York: Pathfinder, 1970.
Rampersad, Arnold. *The Art and Imagination of W.E.B. DuBois.* New York: Schocken, 1976.

E

Eco, Umberto (b. 1932)

Semiotician known for his conception of semiotics as a philosophy of language and for deploying semiotics in the service of a wide range of cultural criticism. Umberto Eco continues cheerfully to present himself as a semiotician at a time when semiotics as a discipline appears vulnerable. Not only has poststructuralist criticism encroached on the semiotic domain of signification and interpretation but in the process it has also rendered problematic the sign itself as an area of critical investigation. Eco's response to such criticism has been to develop a more flexible theory of semiotics. *A Theory of Semiotics* (1976) and *The Role of the Reader* (1979) were highly influential early texts in promoting the philosophical implications of Eco's semiotic position, the latter in particular being enthusiastically adopted by Anglo-American reader-response critics as theoretical confirmation of the primacy of the reader in textual interpretation. Eco subsequently reinterprets his theoretical stance in *Semiotics and the Philosophy of Language* (1984) while at the same time developing his position as an essayist and a novelist. This development is figured in his best-selling novel *The Name of the Rose* (1983) (later filmed), and in two subsequent commentaries on the novel that outline an interpretive framework for the production and evaluation of literary texts. This fictional turn to the medieval is followed by theoretical texts dealing explicitly with both medieval aesthetics and medieval theories of the sign. Concurrently, Eco conducts a semiotic exploration of various modern cultural sites, ranging from museums to theater, in *Travels in Hyperreality* (1986) and *The Limits of Interpretation* (1990).

The flexibility that Eco brings to semiotics derives from his abandonment of its more scientific, objectivist aspirations and his insistence instead upon the importance of the reader in interpreting "open" texts. This emphasis on individual interpretation has sometimes seemed to move him close to a neopragmatist perspective: Richard Rorty, for example, reads Eco's second novel, *Foucault's Pendulum* (1989), as deconstructing the Western metaphysical idea that texts are really about something other than simply referring to other texts and traditions of interpretation. In *Interpretation and Overinterpretation* (1992), however, Eco maintains that earlier readings of him as champion of a radical openness of texts to interpretation were excessive. He claims rather that the text itself places limits on the process of reading. Although Eco's idea of textuality possesses certain similarities to the radical poststructuralist position that the world is nothing but text, in practice Eco seems more comfortable with the idea of a printed text and a model reader resembling a literary detective who thus deciphers (as opposed to deconstructs) the mystery of the world. Nevertheless, Eco's work, especially the novels, which have been compared with the interrogative historical novels of Kundera and Rushdie, describes a continuity of interpretive problems that is often obscured by the insistence of some postmodernists on a radical break with the past. The vitality of Eco's reader-oriented conception of semiotics as cultural performance has moreover offered an effective answer to criticism of the continuing relevance of the semiotic project.

Mark Mullen
University of California, Irvine

Bibliography

Cannon, JoAnn. *Postmodern Italian Fiction: The Crisis of Reason in Calvino, Eco, Sciascia, Malerba*. Rutherford, NJ: Fairleigh Dickinson UP, 1989.

Coletti, Theresa. *Naming the Rose: Eco, Medieval Signs, and Modern Theory*. Ithaca, NY: Cornell UP, 1988.

Eco, Umberto, et al. *Interpretation and Overinterpretation*. Ed. Stefan Collini. Cambridge: Cambridge UP, 1992.

Ehninger, Douglas W. (1913–1979)

Professor of rhetorical theory and argumentation. Ehninger earned his B.S. and M.A. degrees from the School of Speech at Northwestern University and his Ph.D. in 1949 at Ohio State University. He served on the faculties of Purdue University (1937–1938); Western Reserve University (1938–1943); George Washington University (1946); University of Virginia (1948–1950); University of Florida (1950–1961); and the University of Iowa (1961–1979). Ehninger's doctoral adviser, Harold Harding, was an important influence on his modes of thinking about rhetorical theory. Both men sought to understand rhetorical theory as intellectual practices, as philosophies or systems of public discourse. Especially for Ehninger, definitions of *rhetoric, invention, arrangement, style,* and *delivery* were always grounded in ontological, epistemological, critical, or pragmatic grounds; such definitions may not always be explicit in a rhetorical treatise, but he believed that they could be readily found. Once such definitions were found, the rhetorical scholar's job was to account for the sources and future influences of those definitions.

So Ehninger's work on eighteenth-century British rhetorics unearthed four "dominant trends": a neoclassical rhetoric, grounded in classical ontology and epistemology, with strongly normative features; a belletristic rhetoric, anchored in the nature of language, language use, and genres of discourse, with emphases on creativity (original genius) and critical practice; a psychological-epistemological rhetoric, flowing from the British empiricists and Scottish common-sense epistemologies and featuring speculation on message-mind relationships; and an elocutionary rhetoric, arising from defects in oratorical practices of the time and allied with aural-visual sciences of communication. Each trend, in other words, Ehninger traced to a different source and followed forward to alternative nineteenth-century manifestations.

In his later years, Ehninger devoted more of his work to rhetoric and argument theory. His years as a director of intercollegiate forensics gave him a strong appreciation for argument, and his intellectual style conditioned him to explore the systemic, philosophical aspects of argument. He was an early proponent and explicator of Stephen Toulmin's understanding of argumentation. His essays on the nature of argument were strongly influenced by American analytical philosophy and its understanding of propositional logic and force. Speech-act theory framed his last essays.

A series of essays principally in the *Southern States Communication Journal* from the 1950s contains most of his thinking about eighteenth-century British rhetorical theory. His 1963 edition of Richard Whately's *Elements of Rhetoric* (1846) provides a superb example of his explicative abilities. *Principles and Types of Speech* (with Alan Monroe from the fifth edition, 1962, to the eighth edition, 1978) features his thinking about public communication in general, while *Decision by Debate* (with Wayne Brockriede, 1962/1978) and his *Influence, Belief, and Argument* (1974) show the influence of Toulmin on his thinking. His most enduring essay is "On Systems of Rhetoric" (1968).

Bruce E. Gronbeck
University of Iowa

Bibliography

Brockriede, Wayne, and Douglas Ehninger. *Decision by Debate*. New York: Dodd, 1962.

Ehninger, Douglas. "Argument as Method: Its Nature, Its Limitations, and Its Uses." *Communication Monographs* 37 (1970): 101–10.

———. "Campbell, Blair, and Whately: Old Friends in a New Light." *Western Journal of Speech Communication* 19 (1955): 263–69.

———. "Dominant Trends in English Rhetorical Thought, 1750–1800." *Southern States Communication Journal* 18 (1952): 3–12.

———. *Influence, Belief, and Argument.* Glenview, IL: Scott, 1974.

———. "On Inferences of the 'Fourth Class.'" *Communication Studies* 28 (1977): 157–62.

———. "On Systems of Rhetoric." *Philosophy and Rhetoric* 1 (1968): 131–44.

———. "Validity as Moral Obligation." *Southern States Communication Journal* 33 (1968): 215-22.

———, ed. *Elements of Rhetoric by Richard Whately*. Carbondale: Southern Illinois UP, 1963.

Eighteenth-Century Rhetoric

An important period, dominated by Scottish rhetoric, that was broadly influential, especially in the formation of the North-American composition course as well as in the development of nineteenth- and twentieth-century rhetorical theory and pedagogy.

The most comprehensive overview of eighteenth-century rhetoric is still Wilbur Samuel Howell's *Eighteenth-Century British Logic and Rhetoric*, Alfred Kitzhaber's *Rhetoric in American Colleges*, and the introduction to *The Rhetoric of Blair, Campbell, and Whately*, edited by James L. Golden and Edward P.J. Corbett. There is a helpful bibliographic survey (Barton and Horner) in the new edition of Winifred Bryan Horner's *The Present State of Scholarship in Historical and Contemporary Rhetoric*, which points to further primary and secondary works of the period. Selections from the primary works of John Witherspoon, and the lectures of George Campbell and Hugh Blair in facsimile editions, are available from the Landmarks in Rhetoric and Public Address series, published by Southern Illinois University Press. Edited by outstanding scholars in the field, these editions contain excellent introductions that cover not only the lives and works of these rhetoricians but also comprehensive overviews of the period. Most of the research into this period has centered on important educational figures and texts used in the universities. Much remains to be done in the area of activities outside of these institutions, as well as in the contributions of women and their part in this important period.

Compositionists in North American universities trace their origins to what Edward P.J. Corbett termed the "New Rhetoric" of the eighteenth-century Scottish Enlightenment. In searching out the history of composition, the one course required of almost all American university students in the twentieth century, scholars found its roots in Scottish Enlightenment belletristic rhetoric rather than in the public and civic oral rhetoric of Aristotle, Cicero, and Quintilian. The fact of its widespread influence not only in Europe and England but more importantly in North America has brought a revival of interest in Scottish rhetoric. Hugh Blair and George Campbell dominated eighteenth-century rhetoric, and their published lectures were widely used in the British, American, and Scottish universities well into the nineteenth century.

There were eight colleges in the prerevolutionary American colony, most of them fighting for survival against Indian attacks and natural disasters in the new country. But in spite of the hardships, the colonists, especially the Puritans, considered education a high priority. By the end of the century, twenty-seven new colleges had been founded, although many of them were little more than log cabins.

In the eighteenth century, England had two universities that were in a period of decline because of religious restrictions and general degeneration of educational standards. Scotland, on the other hand, had five well-established institutions that attracted students from all over the world. It was within this enlightened climate of intellectual vigor and liberal humanism that the New Rhetoric thrived during this period. It is out of this cultural zeitgeist that such men as Adam Smith, David Hume, Hugh Blair, and George Campbell came. All of these men held positions of authority in the church and the universities and met often to exchange ideas. All of them considered themselves rhetoricians and taught rhetoric at one time or another. They exerted a powerful influence in Scotland, in England, on the continent, and especially on American education and the founding of the new republic. In addition, hundreds of well-educated Scots immigrated to the American colonies to serve as private tutors or as schoolmasters in local schools, and as instructors in the developing universities. John Witherspoon in particular was instrumental in introducing the Scottish philosophy of education and the New Rhetoric to America. He was a classmate of Hugh Blair's and in 1768 was invited to come to America to be president of New Jersey college, later Princeton University. In that position he introduced many tenets of the Scottish system of higher education to North America.

Philosophy and rhetoric have always been closely related, and the eighteenth century was no exception. René Descartes, Francis Bacon, the empiricists John Locke and David Hume, and the common-sense philosophers, most notably Thomas Reid, influenced the thinking behind eighteenth-century rhetoric in important ways. Descartes had initiated the doctrine of innate ideas, with his famous dictum "I think, therefore I am." Bacon, in turn, questioned the validity of deduction and introduced the scientific method based on induction—with physical phenomena furnishing the basic data. His scientific method permeated thought in a variety of fields and made syllogistic reasoning invalid, an idea that the new rhetoricians readily adopted. Over the next two centuries, every study, including literature, rhetoric, and criticism, became a science. Locke and Hume answered the skepticism of Descartes by assuming that knowledge derived from empirical origins could be organized into principles or theories. The Scottish philosopher Thomas Reid furthered the refutation of Descartes by insisting on an innate knowledge of his own existence and of other things beyond his own physical senses. Such philosophies shaped and enlightened the new rhetoric.

There were a number of other factors that influenced the rhetoric of the Enlightenment—a period of great change and immense intellectual activity. Prior to the eighteenth century, the works and ideals of the classical world had been considered superior to those of the modern world. In the eighteenth century, there was a shift toward the idea that circumstances were in the process of improving and that this improvement was possible in the world of enlightened human endeavors. Instead of the view that civilization was in a steady decline from the classical period and the Golden Age of Athens, the literati of Scotland felt that civilization could be improved through their efforts. And they saw that improvement as their mission.

Before this time the universities were largely devoted to educating men (since the ministry was open only to men) for positions in the church, but this emphasis began to change during the second half of the century with the rise of the merchant class. Finally, the universities began to see their mission as educating merchants and men of business rather than churchmen and aristocrats, and rhetoric responded to this cultural difference. Latin and Greek were no longer appropriate for classroom lectures and were abandoned in favor of instruction in English. The century was one of upward mobility; one of the goals of a rising middle class was a command of "good" English, and "good" English was the London standard. In Scotland, one of the purposes of a university education and rhetoric was to rid the students of their Scottish rusticisms. Consequently, the custom of professors who dictated their lectures in slow and proper English, which their students recorded word for word, prevailed in Scottish and American universities as well. These notebooks of dictated lectures served as course textbooks as well as models of correct English for the students from the provinces.

The eighteenth century saw a tremendous rise in the reading public as books and periodicals appeared in increasing numbers and the society became more and more literate. Rhetoric changed to an emphasis on writing rather than oratory, and as examples from English literature were used as demonstrations of rhetorical principles, interest in the vernacular literature expanded.

Scholars have traced four general trends in eighteenth-century rhetoric (Horner; Howell). There was the neoclassical rhetoric of John Lawson and John Ward based on Aristotle, Quintilian, and the *Rhetorica ad Herennium*. Secondly, the elocutionary movement, most closely associated with Thomas Sheridan, which reduced rhetoric to the fifth canon of *pronuntiatio* or *actio*, held sway in both British and American schools for at least two centuries.

The two important trends with the most long-lasting effects, however, were the empiricist rhetoric of George Campbell and the belletristic rhetoric of Hugh Blair. George Campbell's *Philosophy of Rhetoric*, published in 1776, was widely used in both North American and British universities and still shapes twentieth-century textbooks with its "ends of discourse," directly derived from faculty psychology, which divided the brain into distinct intellectual areas. His famous attack on the syllogism permanantly changed the nature of logic and rhetoric by shifting proofs from the deductive method of Aristotle to the inductive and scientific method of Bacon.

Blair's *Lectures on Rhetoric and Belles Lettres* was adopted at Brown in 1783, at Yale in 1785, at Harvard in 1788, and by the end of the century was the standard text at most American colleges. It was reprinted in a number of languages, including Japanese, and various editions and derivatives were disseminated throughout the world. Blair's concept of taste, an important doctrine of the eighteenth century, was adopted worldwide in the English-speaking countries. Taste was considered an inborn quality that could be improved through cultivation and study. This concept found a ready acceptance, particularly in the provinces of Scotland and North America, where improvement became a basic tenet, and beauty and good were closely connected. The study of English literature spread as rhetoric turned from a generative to an interpretive study. Finally, rhetoric and criticism became synonymous, and both became sciences with English literature as the observable physical data.

The eighteenth century marks a turning point in the history of rhetoric; knowledge of the period is essential for an understanding of the development of North American composition and modern rhetorical theory.

Winifred Bryan Horner
Texas Christian University

Bibliography

Blair, Hugh. *Lectures on Rhetoric and Belles Lettres*. Ed. Harold F. Harding. 2 vols. Edinburgh, 1783. Rpt. Carbondale: Southern Illinois UP, 1963.

Campbell, George. *The Philosophy of Rhetoric*. Edinburgh, 1776. Carbondale: Southern Illiois UP, 1963.

Daiches, David, Peter Jones, and Jean Jones, eds. *A Hotbed of Genius: The Scottish Enlightenment*. Edinburgh: Edinburgh UP, 1986.

Golden, James L., and Edward P.J. Corbett. *The Rhetoric of Blair, Campbell, and Whately with Updated Bibliographies*. Carbondale: Southern Illinois UP, 1990.

Guthrie, Warren. "The Development of Rhetorical Theory in America, 1635–1850: Domination of the English Rhetorics." *Speech Monographs* 15 (1948): 61–71.

Horner, Winifred Bryan, and Kerri Morris Barton. "The Eighteenth Century." *The Present State of Scholarship in Historical and Contemporary Rhetoric*. 2nd ed. Columbia: U of Missouri P, 1990.

Howell, Wilbur Samuel. *Eighteenth-Century British Logic and Rhetoric*. Princeton: Princeton UP, 1971.

Kitzhaber, Alfred. *Rhetoric in American Colleges*. Dallas, TX: Southern Methodist UP, 1990.

McCosh, James. *The Scottish Philosophy*. 1875. Rpt. Hildesheim: Gary Olms Verlagsbuchhandlung, 1966.

Miller, Thomas, ed. *The Selected Writings of John Witherspoon*. Carbondale: Southern Illinois UP, 1990.

Sher, Richard B., and Jeffrey R. Smitten, eds. *Scotland and America in the Age of the Enlightenment*. Princeton: Princeton UP, 19–.

Sloan, Douglas. *The Scottish Enlightenment and the American College Ideal*. Teachers College, Columbia U: Teachers College P, 1971.

Eight-Legged Essay

E

Translation of the Chinese *ba gu wen*. The eight-legged essay was first invented as part of Chinese civil service examinations during the Ming (1368–1644) and Qing (1645–1911) dynasties for the purpose of selecting government officials. It constituted the main form of academic discourse in ancient China, and its influence continues to be felt. The eight-legged essay is characterized by its rigid organizational structure, required topics, and use of ritual language.

An eight-legged essay must have the designated eight parts: *po ti* (leading to the topic), *cheng ti* (taking up the topic), *qi jiang* (the embarking), *qi gu* (the introductory corollary), *xu gu* (the first middle leg), *zhong gu* (the second middle leg), *hou gu* (the final middle leg), and *da jie* (tying the knot). The most important part is the "leading to the topic," usually consisting of two or three sentences, in which the writer introduces the chosen topic and clearly expresses the intended thesis of the essay. In the next six parts, the writer elaborates on the topic for ten to twenty sentences by drawing from the required Chinese classics. Then the writer concludes the essay in two to four sentences. In addition, every part must be carefully balanced through the use of rhymed words, paired phrases, and sentences of matched length. For example, the writer must pair nouns, verbs, and adjectives precisely according to particular features, such as colors, characteristics, and numbers. For instance, if one sentence ends with "white horse," the following sentence must end with "yellow fox" or the like.

In classical times, all topics for eight-legged essays came exclusively from such Chinese classics as the *Four Books* and the *Five Classics*, which convey the thinking and teachings of Confucius, and which set forth the moral and ethical basis of society. Because plainly expressing a personal view might have been offensive to the rulers, the writers usually just paraphrased in the entire essay what the sage said; if they wanted to take some risk, they might briefly express personal views on the topic in the conclusion.

Finally, in order not to offend, the writers also used certain ritual phrases. For example, if writing on a topic such as the virtue and benevolence of the ruler, writers usually compared the ruler to sages in the past ages, saying, "If the wisest man is Confucius, the greatest man is doubtlessly my beloved ruler."

Though the eight-legged essay glorified the beauty of the classical Chinese language, its invention was not for any purely aesthetic or intellectual purpose. Rather, it was used as a tool by the ancient Chinese ruling class to recruit local officials and to ensure its dictatorship. On the one hand, the rigid structure of such essay writing tested the writer's loyalty to and tolerance of the imposition of tyranny. On the other hand, the required topics and use of ritual language tested the writer's willingness to accept the traditional norms set by the sages and rulers to maintain social harmony.

Guanjun Cai
University of Arizona

Bibliography

Cheng, Wangdao. *An Introduction to Rhetorics.* Shanghai, PRC: Writer, 1932.

Geng, Yunzhi. "Reassessment of the May Fourth New Cultural Movement." *Social Sciences in China* 3 (1990): 90–114.

Kuang, Jianxian. "Rhyme-Prose and Eight-Legged Essay." *Literature, History, and Philosophy* 5 (1991): 68–74.

Mao, Zedong, ed. "Oppose Stereotyped Party Writing." *Selected Works of Mao Tsetung.* Beijing, PRC: People's, 1967. 157–69.

Zhang, Jinfan. "A Comprehensive Discussion of China's Ancient Civil Service System." *Social Sciences in China* 2 (1990): 35–58.

Zheng, Zhiyu. *A History of China's Rhetorics.* Taipei, Taiwan: Literature, History, and Philosophy, 1980.

Elbow, Peter (b. 1935)

Teacher and composition theorist, proponent of the writing process movement of the 1970s and 1980s; a central figure in expressive rhetoric. Elbow's focus is pedagogy. His early work includes textbooks for students and articles for teachers addressing classroom practice. His interests are wide ranging. A term as a writing program administrator provided the basis for significant work in portfolio evaluation. More recently, scholarly articles have elaborated the theory underpinning his practice. "Toward a Phenomenology of Freewriting" explores the origin of his practice in existential philosophy, and *What is English?*, an overview of English studies, argues the field's value as a metadiscipline investigating relations between language and knowing in various contexts. For Elbow, theory and practice are correlative and interdependent.

Writing without Teachers (1973) introduced key themes that echo throughout his work. He offers a student-centered pedagogy; the writer as individual, whole person is primary. His "teacherless" class emphasizes freewriting, developed from Macrorie, and peer response groups. In Elbow's scheme, freewriting, spontaneous writing to record immediate impressions and feelings without the mediation of logic or structure, allows writers to generate a "center of gravity" that is subsequently elaborated, then revised and edited as formal writing. His focus is on informal invention, and his aim is to help writers develop confidence. "Growing" and "cooking" are Elbow's metaphors for the writing process. Such organic metaphors demonstrate an allegiance to Romanticism, a common source for expressive rhetoric, for which he serves as a primary theorist.

Elbow does not, however, view the writer as isolated or alienated. He counters this common Romantic tendency with peer response groups, a form of collaborative learning. In the teacherless writing class, students meet regularly to complete structured feedback activities so each writer can "experience her own words *through* seven or more people" (77). Elbow instructs readers to provide "movies of your mind" (85). These immediate affective responses, not reasoned discourse considering formal rhetorical concerns, but freeze-frames, provide a set of data points the writer can use to revise. "Movies of the mind" joins the experiential and empirical aspects of learning, a key theme in *Embracing Contraries: Explorations in Learning and Teaching* (1986).

"The Doubting and Believing Game—An Analysis of the Intellectual Enterprise," an appendix essay in *Writing without Teachers,* provides Elbow's discourse on his own method. He contrasts two forms of inquiry. "Doubting," Cartesian skepticism, challenges the truth value of any assertion. According to Elbow, the domination of doubting has led to a self-limiting anxiety and failure of creativity in young writers. "Believing," an alternative mode of inquiry, accepts assertions as true on face. Through believing, we "have the experience of someone who made the assertion." Thus, we better understand that meaning is not in words, but in people using words (151).

Knowing is an intersubjective act, and meaning is socially contructed. Both doubting and believing are involved in knowing, but, given the domination of doubting, writers, indeed students and thinkers in general, need the systematic introduction to believing provided in *Writing without Teachers.*

Writing with Power, another textbook, develops a key expressivist concept: voice. The locus of "power" in writing is voice: "Voice in writing implies words that capture the individual on the page" (287). Voice emblematizes Elbow's value system. In sympathy with feminists and liberatory teachers, Elbow works to subvert the pedagodical practices and institutional structures that oppress, silence, or appropriate individual voice.

Throughout *Writing with Power,* Elbow stresses process. The context is social and active; the writer is concerned with having an impact on an actual audience, resulting in action. The paradoxical tension between the individual and group allows writers to establish a strong sense of identity in the context of the group or culture. Interdependence is both the source and locus of power. Elbow honors dissensus, tolerance of difference, through which an individual knows herself by recognizing differences between herself and other group members. Voice is the individual identity of the writer working in a community.

Elbow's dominant intellectual method involves working through oppositions. An early book, *Oppositions in Chaucer,* investigates the simultaneous existence of sacred and secular themes in Chaucer. Here and elsewhere, especially in "The Uses of Binary Thinking," paradox is not a logical anomaly; rather, it is a source of productive thinking and creativity. Elbow works through one term to arrive at the other. Practice is not only the ground but the source of theory. Doubting and believing coexist. The text cannot exist apart from an individual writer.

Christopher C. Burnham
New Mexico State University

Bibliography

Burnham, Christopher. "Expressive Rhetoric: A Source Study." *Defining the New Rhetorics.* Ed. Theresa Enos and Stuart Brown. Sage Series in Written Communication. Vol. 7. Newbury Park, CA: Sage, 1993. 154–70.

Elbow, Peter. *Embracing Contraries: Explorations in Learning and Teaching.* New York: Oxford UP, 1986.

———. "Reflections on Academic Discourse: How It Relates to Freshmen and Colleagues." *College English* 53 (1991): 135–55.

———. "Toward a Phenomenology of Freewriting." *Nothing Begins with N: New Investigations of Freewriting.* Ed. Pat Belanoff, Peter Elbow, and Sheryl I. Fontaine. Carbondale: Southern Illinois UP, 1991. 189–213.

———. "The Uses of Binary Thinking." *Journal of Advanced Composition* 13 (1993): 51–78.

———. *Writing without Teachers.* New York: Oxford UP, 1973.

———. *Writing with Power: Techniques for Mastering the Writing Process.* New York: Oxford UP, 1981.

———, and Belanoff, Pat. "State University of New York at Stony Brook Portfolio-based Evaluation Program." *Portfolios: Process and Product.* Ed. Pat Belanoff and Marcia Dickson. Portsmouth, NH: Boynton/Cook, 1991: 3–16.

See also VOICE

Electronic Rhetoric

The study of the influence of electronic media on language and thought; also, the emerging body of principles that suggest how electronic text might best be written, displayed, and read. Media have always been an important focus in rhetorical study, especially the historical shifts from one predominant media to another. The key transitions from orality to literacy, from script to print, from books to television, and from printed pages to computer screens each receives attention from scholars who know that change is concentrated along boundaries and that rhetorical understanding arises from studying the conflicts and tensions of transitional periods.

We are now undergoing a fundamental shift as electronic media assume predominance over print media. Electronic rhetoric is an emerging attempt to describe the changes brought about in language by computers and other electronic media.

McLuhan originally embraced electronic media as a new rhetoric that created welcome extensions of the mind. New forms of communicating and understanding were seen as leading to new forms of cultural organization in a global electronic village. The new media were cool; distances of space and emotion were collapsed in the immediacy of multisensorial communication. The medium was the massage, shaping and constraining meaning.

Other critics have frequently disparaged the products of electronic media, characterizing them as a visual and sonic cacaphony, an MTV flood of visual imagery, fragmentary verbal messages, and musical blasts. Those who adopt this view worry that as a culture we are moving away from the printed word, with its emphasis on rationality, sequencing, extended argumentation, and objectivity. In its place is a rhetoric of ephemera, based on brief, imagistic, nonlogical, and emotional appeals (see especially Postman, *Technopoly*). Ong sees us entering a second period of orality, in some ways similar to that of preliterate cultures. (Secondary orality does depend on literacy as well as on primary orality.) Always, there is a nagging, worrying sense that something essentially literate is being left behind as we move from print to computer screen.

The problem is that we frequently evaluate new media on the basis of the content of the old. What we need to understand about electronic rhetoric are fresh ways of thinking about language and communication. The following is intended to map the key features that together constitute a rhetoric of electronic texts.

What are the key features of electronic text? Electronic texts are *situationally embedded*. The text doesn't stand alone, but is bound up with ongoing activities and events. The text is part of the action. Text is there to be used, to be looked up, to be extracted. Text is increasingly part of a technologically sophisticated hardware environment tied into complex voice, data, and video networks. This is in extreme contrast to books and magazines and has important consequences on design. It makes text more emphatically a technology, and it forces writers to assume the skills of graphic designers, media specialists, or choreographers.

With electronic texts, reading is frequently a more *interactive* process than with printed texts. The text invites readers to be actively engaged—both mentally and physically—rather than passive absorbers of information. The text has a more varied surface structure; there is more *texture* to text on screen. The text has greater functional differentiation. It exists as something to be clicked on, or cut, or blown up, or collapsed. Readers push buttons, launch routines, make changes, adjust features, and generally interact as both readers and writers of their online texts. They *use* text more than *read* text. The heightened interactivity leads to a blurring of boundaries between author and reader.

Electronic text supports reader movement across large pools of information; the text is *spacious* and it is *navigable* in different directions for different readers and purposes. Paper text has always traded off completeness against bulk. Electronic text has no similar constraint, since immense and increasing amounts of text and graphics take little physical space. Large collections of electronic information do, however, pose significant challenges to designers who must help readers confidently navigate within large text/graphic databases. The expectation is that readers will not process text in linear sequence, as they might read a book or article. Jumping around is expected and encouraged (hypertext creates hyperreaders). Neither author nor reader knows what path the reader might follow or where the reader might end up.

These new ways of compiling text for wandering readers push electronic text toward a *modular* structure. Text is composed and presented in self-contained chunks, fragments, blocks; language is *localized,* rather than progressive in its rhetoric. Texts become databases with interchangeable parts used variously by different readers. The text has different levels or layers of embedding; text contains other texts, linked through complex *hierarchical* or loosely associative structures. Modular, hierarchical text leads to wholly new forms of reading, with machine-aided browsing, skimming, zooming, and searching supporting and augmenting traditional reading strategies. This represents a major shift in how texts must create and maintain coherence. The cohesion tends to be local rather than global. Since the writer cannot know from whence the reader arrived, each piece of text must be self-contained, self-referential, understandable out of context with surrounding text.

Electronic text is *graphically rich*: The text exploits and integrates graphic information; it takes advantage of iconic presentation, screen design, font variation, animation, zoom, and other graphic cues to present information and facilitate interaction. In essence, electronic writing is more pictoral and iconic and, perhaps, less alphabetical. The text itself is *fluid*, changing, dynamic; it escapes the impression and binding of print. Electronic text can be customized and owned; the new tools of text make every writer a publisher. Readers become owners and writers; writers become designers and publishers.

In all these ways, computers change literacy: how we write, read, and circulate texts. Many of the changes feel uncomfortable. But the study of the influence of media on language has taught us at least one lesson: that what looks strange and uncomfortable today becomes familiar and natural tomorrow. It is electronic rhetoric that is now mapping the text of tomorrow.

Stephen A. Bernhardt
New Mexico State University

Bibliography

Bolter, Jay David. *Writing Space: The Computer, Hypertext, and the History of Writing.* Hillsdale, NJ: Erlbaum, 1991.

Hawisher, Gail, and Cynthia L. Selfe. *Evolving Perspectives on Computers and Composition Studies: Questions for the 1990s.* Urbana: National Council of Teachers of English, 1991.

Horton, William. *Designing and Writing Online Documentation: Help Files to Hypertext.* New York: Wiley, 1990.

McLuhan, H.M. *Understanding Media: The Extensions of Man.* New York: McGraw, 1964.

Ong, Walter J. *Orality and Literacy: The Technologizing of the Word.* London: Methuen, 1982.

Postman, Neil. *Technopoly: The Surrender of Culture to Technology.* New York: Knopf, 1992.

See also HAVELOCK, ERIC; ONG, WALTER; ORALITY; MCLUHAN, MARSHALL; VISUAL RHETORIC

Ellipsis

The omission of a word or phrase easily understood by the context. Shakespeare used the figure frequently to achieve a sense of compression: "Haply you shall not see me more; or if, a mangled shadow" (*Antony and Cleopatra* 4.2). Ellipsis can also be used to create a telegraphic style, such as "Mother deceased. Burial tomorrow. Sincerely yours" (Camus, *L'Etranger*). Used in interior monologue, ellipses can dramatically suggest a character's anxiety or impatience: "Ambulance . . . Gentlemen . . . good! operate . . . but where? full . . . full . . . full" (G. Bernanos, *Oeuvres romanesques*). Caesar's last words in Shakespeare's play, "Et tu, Brute," or Poe's refrain, "only this, and nothing more," are *absolute ellipses,* which require the reader to supply the omitted material without local textual clues.

Arthur Quinn and Lyon Rathbun
University of California, Berkeley

Elocution

The Elocutionary Movement. Various factors contributed to heightened interest in the study of elocution in both the eighteenth and nineteenth centuries. Numerous scholars recognized that traditional students interested in the ministry or bar were lacking effective speaking skills, and attempts were made to overcome these deficiencies. Beginning in England and continuing in the United States, elocution became the main focus of rhetoric during this time.

Prior to the eighteenth century, the term *elocution* referred to the fifth part of rhetoric, style, which could be detached from other parts of rhetoric and given independent consideration. Aristotle defined delivery, which later became the main focus of elocution, as the correct management of the voice to express emotions; he did not deem it an elevated subject of inquiry. Although Aristotle's definition remained the most common, the most influential of the ancient rhetoricians to the study of elocution are Quintilian and Cicero. Quintilian believed that understanding the material to be read was the most important rule of effective oration. Recognizing that a sincere interpretation of the material was the ultimate goal, he asserted that the speakers had to first understand and experience the material themselves. After achieving this goal, the orators then came to understand the "propriety" surrounding the occasion—that is, those factors that involve effective delivery, including the speaker's expression, gesture, voice, and gait.

From the eighth to the fifteenth century in England, stylistic rhetoric, which emphasized style over all other parts of rhetoric, dominated. The Ciceronian pattern of English rhetoric began with Alcuin (735–?) who wrote *De rhetorica,* the first work by an Englishman on the subject. Primarily interested in invention, Alcuin offered three types of speeches—ceremonial (which emphasize honor), deliberative (which emphasize expediency), and forensic (which emphasize justice). In choosing one's approach, the speakers were encouraged to determine the subject matter of their speeches, then analyze it closely.

What is now known as the Elocutionary Movement began in eighteenth-century England with several factors contributing to its popularity. First, while Latin was being used less frequently, English was rapidly becoming the accepted language, and proponents of its use wanted to elevate its standing. Thomas Sheridan's 1780 dictionary was the most complete guide to pronunciation until John Walker's dictionary appeared eleven years later. The study of phonation led naturally into the study of the delivery of words, and treatises on voice management began to appear, becoming the first elocution manuals. Second, shifting from an oral culture to a literate culture in which provincial accents were no longer accepted, students training for the ministry, bar, or politics were forced to learn a new, more symmetrical mode of oral address. Third, people began to equate the power of public speaking with the power of persuasion, and educators recognized that in order to train and educate future generations a firm understanding of elocution was needed. Fourth, the renewed popularity of the theatre raised interest in the elocutionary movement; two of its major figures, Thomas Sheridan and John Walker, were actors. Fifth, in the universities, linguists such as Thomas Reid became interested in the relationships between language and the mind and language and society. Reid recognized the classical paradox that there could be no social intercourse without language and no language without social intercourse. Whereas eighteenth-century elocutionists viewed elocution as an art, contending that while humanity was governed by natural law the laws of elocution naturally followed the laws of life, nineteenth-century elocutionists viewed elocution as a science. Although the new scholars concentrated almost exclusively on the art of delivery, they still regarded themselves as rhetoricians and claimed that they studied rhetoric.

The change in meaning of several rhetorical terms between 1625 and 1725 reflects the influence of the Elocutionary Movement. Pronunciation, which had once referred to the whole field of delivery, now referred only to the correct phonation of words. Elocution, which had meant the manner of artistic composition, now meant the manner of artistic delivery. And style, which had been a synonym for elocution, now concerned the choice and arrangement of words. In studying elocution, students were primarily concerned with four things: bodily gestures, voice management, pronunciation, and vocal production (the actual formation of the sounds of speech). The principles of analytic elocution included the belief that spoken language related ideas and emotions, that there were two great ends to elocution: (1) to improve and develop the voice to fullest capacity and to adapt it to the correct and natural utterance of thoughts and emotions, and (2) to recognize the five properties of voice—pitch, quality, force, abruptness, and time.

In spite of these common roots, the Elocutionary Movement was divided from the beginning. The Naturalist School believed that the basic principles of delivery came from nature itself. This system of elocution was based on large precepts and the speaker's understanding of the thoughts read or spoken. The Mechanical School also wanted "natural" oration but felt that true naturalness could come only from a study of rules implicit in nature; thus it offered elaborate rules for acquiring naturalness. Although current scholars tend to rapidly categorize elocutionists into one school or the other, it was not uncommon for elocutionists to overlap philosophies. Either way, by 1785 elocution was well established, and the largest number of rhetorical textbooks were on elocution. These texts were normally divided into four sections (voice management, vocal production, bodily action, and pronunciation) and commonly offered selected readings with footnotes as well as occasional background information. These readings could be used for private practice or for social entertainment. Mrs. Fanny Palliser's *Modern Speaker* was one of the more common books used for the latter purpose.

Most major figures of the Elocutionary Movement, whether actually familiar with them or not, claimed to base their rhetorical theories and ideas on either Quintilian or Cicero. Although the most famous and popular elocutionists were English, they had numerous Continental precursors—most notably Louis de Cressolles (1568–1634) and Michel Le Faucheur (late 1500s–1657). Cressolles wrote *Vacationes Autumnales,* a 706-page book that was claimed to be the "largest extant collection of observations by classical authors on the subject of voice and gesture in oratory" (161). The first ninety-nine pages serve as a general introduction; the second "book" suggests oratorical guidelines, and the last 254 pages discuss the management of voice.

Le Faucheur is the more dominant figure, claimed by some to be the founder of the elocutionary movement. In his major work, *Traitte de l'action de l'orateur, ou de la Prononciation et du geste,* he contends that excellence in elocution can make up for deficiencies in invention, arrangement, and style but not vice versa. Envisioning ministers and lawyers as his primary audience, Le Faucheur emphasizes the movement of the hands and eyes. In the seventeen specific rules for the hands, he warns the speaker to avoid gestures such as clapping hands, thumping the pulpit, or beating one's breast. The *Traitte* was translated into English in the early eighteenth century and gained wide popularity and extended influence. The translator liberally inserted the word *elocution,* using it in places Le Faucheur had not, thus extending the scope of this term, which came to dominate all aspects of rhetoric until it became a synonym for rhetoric itself.

The Elocutionary Movement was extremely popular in England, the most famous and influential of the Elocutionists coming from that country. John Ward was one of the first of these men, and in 1759 his *System of Oratory* was published posthumously. Using Quintilian as his theoretical basis while he relied on Cicero for illustration, he divides elocution into two parts: the general characteristics of all verbal expression and the specific rules applied to a certain subject. Contending that the purpose of the art of speaking is to persuade, Ward is the only English elocutionist to rely solely on classical ideas. Unlike John Ward, George Campbell, and Richard Whately, he was not a theologian.

Trying to determine how people come to know things, George Campbell (1719–1796) published *Philosophy of Rhetoric* in 1776; *Lectures on Systematic Theology and Pulpit Eloquence* was published posthumously in 1807. He specifically warns speakers to avoid a theatrical and violent manner, insipid monotony, and a singsong manner, while encouraging them to maintain control of their voice by maintaining the same key, speaking deliberately and slowly, and practicing reading, speaking, and repeating.

Richard Whately (1787–1863) was more interested in how things could be proved; his *Elements of Logic* (1826) and *Elements of Rhetoric* (1828) moved theory in the direction of argument and debate. Ward, Campbell, and Whately discuss three forms of delivery—speaking extemporaneously, speaking from memory, and reading. All prefer the first form and agree that "natural" delivery is the best.

In spite of the popularity of these men, it was Thomas Sheridan (1719–1788) who succeeded Le Faucheur as the English founder of the Elocutionary Movement. In 1756, at the age of thirty-seven, he left his work as an actor and began to write books dealing with education, pronunciation, and elocution. He relied heavily on Cicero but condensed the teachings of the ancient rhetorician to elocution. Initially interested in achieving a standard English pronunciation, Sheridan's 1780 *Dictionary* was the most comprehensive published until Walker's dictionary appeared in 1791. His *Grammar* also appeared in 1780, but his earlier works, including *Discourse being Introductory to a Course of Lectures on Elocution and the English Language* (1759), *Lectures on Elocution* (1762), and *Lectures on the Art of Reading* (1775), were more popular. Contending that ideal delivery included grace, sincerity, and naturalness, he wanted to revive the ancient art of oratory in order to standardize the English language and achieve artistic expression. But in his attempt to achieve these goals, he reduced the ancient art to matters of voice and gesture alone. Sheridan's study of phonation led naturally into the study of the delivery of words, and as he continued to write treatises on voice management, they evolved into elocutionary manuals. Sheridan helped reduce rhetoric to one dimension, and the term gradually evolved until it became equated with empty, meaningless speech.

E

In the United States, the fascination with elocution continued into the nineteenth century. Relying heavily on the English scholars, every important English rhetoric text could be found in one or more major American libraries. Ward's *System of Oratory* was especially popular. In a new country bent on securing a democratic society, elocution flourished in America. The country was expanding, and oratory was needed to proclaim American ideals and debate its problems. Professionally, scholastically, and socially, the United States was ready for the advanced development of elocution.

At first, following the English tradition, elocution was studied systematically, with an emphasis on the speaker's general training and knowledge. Later, there was more interest in the scientific aspects of elocution and more emphasis on the speaker's training in voice and gesture. Although the American elocutionary movement remained similar to that of England, it gradually became less interested in elocution itself and more concerned with intercollegiate debate and argumentation.

John Witherspoon, president of Princeton University, envisioned four goals of speechmaking (information, demonstration, persuasion, and entertainment), while John Quincy Adams emphasized deliberative and judicial oratory. Ebenezer Porter was concerned about the scientific nature of elocution and worried about its lack of feeling. He relied on English elocutionists but adapted their teachings to the unique problems of American students. Dr. James Rush (1786–1869) examined the scientific aspects of vocal production in *Philosophy of the Human Voice* (1827), while James E. Murdoch (1811–1893) was more concerned with performance. In *Analytic Elocution* (1884), he contends that the voice is the most important part of elocution, and in *Philosophy of the Human Voice* he offers a complete system of vocal training. Murdoch was the leader of the Elocutionary Movement in America for over fifty years. A later writer and scholar, Samuel Silas Curry (1847–1921), returned to the more pragmatic philosophy of Porter. A member of the Natural School, he wrote fourteen books, including *Province of Expression* (1891) and *Foundations of Expression* (1907).

The most influential force in late nineteenth- and early twentieth-century America was a French teacher of vocal music and operatic acting—François Delsarte (1811–1871). Although Delsarte wrote nothing himself and there is no single "Delsarte System," the "Delsarte System of Expression" became the most popular method of speech training in America. A supposedly scientific method, this system primarily involved physical training. Based on a philosophy similar to that of the mechanical school, this system reduced the study of rhetoric to the stilted expression of emotion through learned (and practiced) bodily gestures and positions.

Today, elocution no longer exists as a school of thought or mode of study. Communication departments have replaced speech departments, and while they continue to offer students courses in public speaking and oral interpretation, they no longer advocate exaggerated, learned movements or posed stances. Unfortunately, the legacy of the Elocutionary Movement lies not so much in academia as it does in the world beyond, which continues to equate all of rhetoric with empty, meaningless speech.

Brenda Gabioud Brown
University of Science and Arts of Oklahoma

Bibliography

Bahn, Eugene and Margaret L. *A History of Oral Interpretation*. Minneapolis: Burgess, 1970.
Campbell, George. *Lectures on Systematic Theology and Pulpit Eloquence*. London, 1807.
——. *The Philosophy of Rhetoric*. Carbondale: Southern Illinois UP, 1988.
Howell, Wilbur Samuel. *Eighteenth-Century British Logic and Rhetoric*. Princeton: Princeton UP, 1971.
Lawson, John. *Lectures Concerning Oratory*. Ed. E. Neal Claussen and Karl R. Wallace. Landmarks in Rhetoric and Public Address. Carbondale: Southern Illinois UP, 1972.
Murdoch, James E. *Analytic Elocution*. Cincinnati, 1884.
Sheridan, Thomas. *A Course of Lectures on Elocution*. New York: Blom, 1968.
——. *Lectures on the Art of Reading*. London, 1787.
Wallace, Karl R. *History of Speech Education in America*. New York: Appleton, 1954.
Whately, Richard. *Elements of Rhetoric*. 1828. Ed. Douglas Ehninger. Carbondale: Southern Illinois UP, 1963.

See also DELIVERY; EIGHTEENTH-CENTURY RHETORIC; NINETEENTH-CENTURY RHETORIC; SHERIDAN, THOMAS; VOICE; WITHERSPOON, JOHN

Eloquence

A term in the history of Ciceronian-humanist rhetoric. The Latin noun *eloquentia* derives from the verb *eloqui,* "to speak, utter, express." Its basic, popular sense of "effective public address" is present from the beginnings of Latin literature. With the advent of formal rhetorical instruction in Rome in the second century B.C.E., it assumed in addition the more specialized, technical sense of "art of public address" (ρητορικη τεχνη, or simply ρητορικη, from ερειν, "to speak").

In its primary sense of "effective public address," *eloquentia* denoted the practice of the most accomplished Roman orators and, as such, came to represent the primary end of Roman education. Discussing the careers of individual orators in the *Brutus* (46 B.C.E.), Cicero defines *eloquentia* (26) as a "highly finished force and abundance of speaking" (*elaborata dicendi vis atque copia*) while in his *Orator,* composed the same year, *eloquentia* is simply a synonym for "oratory" (3).

In its more specialized sense of "art of public address," *eloquentia* is used as a synonym for ρητορικη, rendered in Latin as *rhetorice* (or *rhetorica*); it was used interchangeably as well for variants on the phrase "art of speaking," such as *ars dicendi* or *ratio dicendi*. In *De Inventione* (90 B.C.E.), a work exercising enormous influence in the Middle Ages, Cicero renders the Greek ρητορικη as *artificiosa eloquentia*, or "public address based on art" (1.6; cf. Quintilian, *Institutio Oratoria* 2.17.2) and treats it as ancillary to statecraft. In his *Institutio Oratoria* (90 C.E.), Quintilian cites *eloquentia* as the Latin term nearest in meaning to ρητορικη but, given the absence of an exact equivalent, prefers the loan word *rhetorice*. Discussing the relationships between ρητορικη and its near equivalents in Latin (2.14.5), Quintilian assigns *eloquentia* a wide sphere of employment encompassing any subject matter requiring rational expression.

Cicero's mature and monumental *De oratore* (54 B.C.E.) provides the *locus classicus* for a third usage: As well as a τεχνη, or rule-bound art, eloquence is there described as a human faculty (cf. the Greek δυναμιζ) and, in fact, as "one of the supreme virtues" (*una quaedem de summis virtutibus*):

All the virtues are equal and on a par, but nevertheless one has more beauty and distinction in outward appearance than another, as is the case with this faculty, which, after compassing a knowledge of facts, gives verbal expression to the thoughts and purposes of the mind in such a manner as to have the power of driving the hearers forward in any direction . . . and the stronger this faculty is, the more necessary it is for it to be combined with integrity and supreme wisdom, and if we bestow fluency of speech (*dicendi copiam*) on persons devoid of these virtues, we shall not have made orators of them but shall have put weapons into the hands of madmen. (*De oratore* 3.14.55)

"This faculty of speaking," Cicero adds, was "designated by the ancient Greeks wisdom (*sapientiam*)" (3.15.56). To the mature Cicero, eloquence is that intellectual virtue that "gives verbal expression" to thought and thus underlies all effective communication, regardless of subject matter and intent. "Fluency of speech" (*dicendi copiam*) is but part of the Ciceronian ideal. In its fullest sense, eloquence becomes the highest aim of the Roman citizen; it is a human faculty capable of training but, more important, its perfection requires that it be united with wisdom and with the ethical virtues as well. Eloquence is a humanistic discipline whose goal, nobly formulated by Cicero's admirer Quintilian, is the creation of the "good man skilled in speaking," the *vir bonus dicendi peritus* (*Inst. Orat.* 12.1.1). For Quintilian, indeed, Cicero was "not the name of a man, but of eloquence itself" (*Inst. Orat.* 10.1.112 *non hominis nomen, sed eloquentiae*). Subsequent uses of the term throughout the history of rhetoric should be examined in the light of this Ciceronian ideal.

Demanding no less than the ethical, intellectual, and artistic perfection of its practitioners, the term invokes one of the central controversies of Western rhetorical tradition: the relation of *eloquentia* to *sapientia*, of language to thought. While Cicero sought always to unite the two, subsequent theorists often encouraged—or lamented—their separation. In Silver Age Latin (14 B.C.E. and afterward), the perceived decline of *eloquentia* proved a common theme in Quintilian's lost *De Causis Eloquentiae Corruptae* ("On the Causes of the Decline in Eloquence") and Tacitus's *Dialogus de Oratoribus* ("A Dialogue on Oratory"). The increasing popularity of *declamatio* was often cited as a cause of this decline (see Caplan 179–80), inasmuch as practitioners of such rhetorical exercises strove above all for striking verbal display. The teachings of Fronto, preeminent Roman orator of the second century C.E., are concerned more with resuscitating literary Latin through an *elocutio novella,* or "new diction," than with reviving Ciceronian eloquence.

Tacitus extends *eloquentia* to cover all forms of literary as well as oral expression, both poetry and prose (*Dialogus* 4.3 and 10.5). This wider, belletristic sense of *eloquentia* is not surprising, given both the rhetorizing tendencies of Roman education and the subjection of primary, oral rhetoric to *letteraturizzazione*—which, as George A. Kennedy defines it, "is the tendency of rhetoric to shift its focus from persuasion to narration, from civic to personal contexts, and from discourse to literature, including poetry. Such slippage can be observed in the Hellenistic period, in the Roman Empire, in medieval France, and in the sixteenth and eighteenth centuries throughout Europe. The primary reason for the *letteraturizzazione* of rhetoric is probably the place given rhetoric in education . . . but the development is of course directly influenced by the opportunities, or lack of opportunities, open to primary rhetoric throughout history" (5). Secondary rhetoric, present whenever techniques "are not being used for their primary oral purpose," emphasizes ornamental effects, often reducing rhetoric to a mode of literary entertainment (Kennedy 5). A problem inherent in the Ciceronian-humanist tradition of eloquence is its tendency toward such reduction.

Espousing the Ciceronian ideal, St. Augustine (354–430 C.E.) claimed for the Christian polemicist a divine wisdom united with forceful expression (*De Doctrina Christiana* 4.2–5). Medieval theorists repeated this sentiment, as evidenced by Robert of Basevorn's *Forma Praedicandi* (1322): "Who will hesitate to say that wisdom and eloquence together move us more than either does by itself? Thus we must insist upon eloquence and yet not depart from wisdom" (347). But while medieval theorists influenced by Augustine sought to unite classical eloquence with Christian wisdom, numerous "formulary" and "stylistic" rhetorics, such as the *Flores Rhetorici,* or "Flowers of Rhetoric" (1087), by Alberic of Monte Cassino and the *Poetria Nova* (1210) of Geoffrey of Vinsauf, emphasized verbal facility and ornament, in effect limiting rhetoric to artful expression separable from invention.

With its great flowering of Ciceronian humanism, the Renaissance may justly be described as an age of eloquence. Desiderius Erasmus's *De Duplici Copia Rerum et Verborum* (1511) presents a "double fluency" (*duplici copia*), a dual concern for thought as well as expression—or rather, for thought united with expression. Of course other rhetoricians, particularly those influenced by the reforms of Peter Ramus (1515–1572), restricted their discussion to lists of figures and verbal ornamentation. Henry Peacham's *Garden of Eloquence, Conteyning the Figures of Grammer and Rhetorick* (1577), typifies the stylistic reductionism of Ramist rhetoric.

In *The Scholemaster* (1570), the English Ciceronian Roger Ascham complained, "Ye know not what hurt ye do to learning, that care not for wordes but for matter" (6). Sir Francis Bacon disagreed totally: To "study words and not matter," he writes in *Advancement of Learning* (1605), is "the first distemper of learning" (24). Such mistrust of verbal artifice—in a word, such anti-Ciceronianism—came to a head in the seventeenth century, when the Royal Society of London (formally chartered in 1662) "renounced the rhetoric of tropes and figures as a guide to scientific writing, and adopted a theory of style that belongs to a new attitude towards rhetoric" (Howell 388). This new attitude, indeed, this new rhetoric, privileged clear and unadorned "exposition" over persuasion and stylistic display. Wilbur S. Howell offers a sociological explanation for the development of this so-called "plain style." By 1688, the year of the Great Rebellion overthrowing the Stuart monarchy in England, "the middle class had established itself as a powerful force; and the new rhetoric had to abandon the unusual pattern of speech that would delight the aristocrat, and to teach the everyday pattern that would convince the commoner" (10).

Howell's point explains the mistrust of eloquence pervasive throughout twentieth-century culture as well. In part a symptom or manifestation of *letteraturizzazione,* "stylistic" rhetoric is typically "a strong trend in centuries of chaos or autocracy" (Kennedy 175)—and a trend, thus, that Bacon and the Royal Society would resoundingly reject. For both seventeenth- and twentieth-century middle-class culture, verbal artifice seems irrelevant or, worse, antithetical to objective scientific discussion and public, democratic political debate. Twentieth-century American prose, both academic and popular, has become thoroughly committed (politically, intellectually, aesthetically) to the "plain style."

The diversity of eighteenth-century theory defies simple outline; nonetheless, the strongly neoclassical aesthetic of the age allowed once again for strands of rhetoric influenced by Ciceronianism. Even belletristic rhetoric, exemplified by Hugh Blair's *Lectures on Rhetoric and Belles Lettres* (1783), offers conventional praise of the Ciceronian ideal:

> To be an eloquent speaker, in the proper sense of the word, is far from being either a common or an easy attainment. Indeed, to compose a florid harangue on some popular topic . . . is a matter not very difficult. . . . [T]he idea which I have endeavored to give of eloquence, is much higher. It is a great exertion of the human powers. It is the art of being persuasive and commanding; the art, not of pleasing the fancy merely, but of speaking both to the understanding and to the heart. (128)

More controversial is George Campbell's *Philosophy of Rhetoric* (1776), which begins: "The word *eloquence* in its greatest latitude denotes, 'That art or talent by which the discourse is adapted to its end'" (145). Thus emphasizing arrangement and style over invention (which it places outside the purview of eloquence), Campbell's "managerial" theory of discourse serves once again to truncate classical, Ciceronian rhetoric.

The term *eloquence* continues to appear in nineteenth-century treatises, such as Richard Whately's *Elements of Rhetoric* (1828). By the mid nineteenth century, however, invention ceased to be taught as an element of rhetoric. Arrangement, as in Alexander Bain's *English Composition and Rhetoric: A Manual* (1866), is reduced to exercises in paragraphing. *Copia* is no longer taught as the foundation of stylistic facility and discussions of figures are greatly abridged. Though largely style-centered, the "current-traditional" rhetoric prominent throughout the late nineteenth and early twentieth centuries has little affinity with classical tradition.

The term *eloquence* fares poorly throughout modern discussions. *The New Rhetoric* (1969) by Chaïm Perelman is typical in this regard. Contemporary audiences are quick to "disqualify" eloquence as "pretence, artifice, a contrived means to an end" (450):

Argument addressed to others and eloquence in all its forms has always been subject to this disqualification and is constantly exposed to it. The attack may be aimed at a particular argument, a particular speech, or even at the whole art of oratory. It is often sufficient to qualify what has been said as "rhetorical" to rob it of its effectiveness.

When treated as oratorical or rhetorical devices, the means of persuasion are pronounced to be artificial, formal, and verbal—terms characteristic of the pairs

artificial	form	verbal
natural	substance	real

This devaluation reaches the point where the spontaneous, unprepared speech, whatever its imperfections, is preferred to the considered, premeditated speech which the hearer considers as a device. (450–51)

Given the disintegration of the Ciceronian ideal uniting *eloquentia* and *sapientia,* modern theory has tended to avoid the term *eloquence* altogether. Although Howell and Kennedy suggest reasons for this avoidance, one is left to consider whether *eloquence*—the term, if not the phenomenon—is dormant or simply dead. In practice, a person may still be said to speak "eloquently," though the term now emphasizes one's passionate conviction more than one's use of verbal artifice. And, even in that regard, attempts "to conquer and inflame are as anachronistic as the amphitheater and the aqueduct. Fiery words of combat have no place on the intimate media of radio and television; fire metaphors and the style they signal have given way to metaphors of electricity and a cooler conversational style" (Jamieson 45). Given our culture's commitment to the "plain style," modern composition and communication theories have been virtually compelled to reject *copia* and the artifice traditionally associated with eighteenth-century belletrism, with Renaissance humanism, and with classical, Ciceronian practice.

James S. Baumlin and Joseph J. Hughes
Southwest Missouri State University

Bibliography
Ascham, Roger. *The Scholemaster. Elizabethan Critical Essays.* Ed. G. Gregory Smith. Oxford: Clarendon, 1904. 1–45.
Bacon, Sir Francis. *The Advancement of Learning.* London: Dent, 1973.

E

Blair, Hugh. *Lectures on Rhetoric and Belles Lettres. The Rhetoric of Blair, Campbell, and Whately.* Ed. James L. Golden and Edward P.J. Corbett. New York: Holt, 1968. 30–137.

Bryant, Donald. *Rhetorical Dimensions in Criticism.* Baton Rouge: Louisiana State UP, 1973.

Campbell, George. *The Philosophy of Rhetoric. The Rhetoric of Blair, Campbell, and Whately.* Ed. James L. Golden and Edward P.J. Corbett. New York: Holt, 1968. 145–271.

Caplan, Harry. "The Decay of Eloquence at Rome in the First Century." *Of Eloquence: Studies in Ancient and Medieval Rhetoric.* Ithaca, NY: Cornell UP, 1970. 160–95.

Cicero. *Brutus.* Trans. G.L. Hendrickson. *Orator.* Trans. H.M. Hubbell. Loeb Classical Library. Cambridge, MA: Harvard UP, 1952.

———. *De Inventione.* Trans. H.M. Hubbell. Loeb Classical Library. Cambridge, MA: Harvard UP, 1949.

———. *De Oratore.* Book III. Trans. H. Rackham. Loeb Classical Library. Cambridge, MA: Harvard UP, 1942.

Golden, James L., and Edward P.J. Corbett, eds. *The Rhetoric of Blair, Campbell, and Whately.* New York: Holt, 1968.

Howell, Wilbur Samuel. *Logic and Rhetoric in England, 1500–1700.* Princeton: Princeton UP, 1956.

Jamieson, Kathleen Hall. *Eloquence in an Electronic Age: The Transformation of Political Speechmaking.* New York: Oxford UP, 1988.

Kennedy, George A. *Classical Rhetoric and Its Christian and Secular Tradition from Ancient to Modern Times.* Chapel Hill: U of North Carolina P, 1980.

Perelman, Chaïm, and L. Olbrechts-Tyteca. *The New Rhetoric: A Treatise on Argumentation.* Notre Dame, IN: U of Notre Dame P, 1969.

Quintilian. *The Institutio Oratoria.* Trans. H.E. Butler. 4 vols. The Loeb Classical Library. Cambridge, MA: Harvard UP, 1920–1922.

Robert of Basevorn. *Forma Praedicandi. Rhetoric in the Middle Ages: A History of Rhetorical Theory from St. Augustine to the Renaissance.* Ed. James J. Murphy. Berkeley: U of California P, 1974. 344–55.

See also COPIA; LETTERATURIZZAZIONE

Emerson, Ralph Waldo (1803–1882)

American essayist, poet, and philosopher. Ralph Waldo Emerson displayed a lifelong concern for the theory and practice of rhetoric. His early journals indicate a close reading of Hugh Blair's *Lectures on Rhetoric and Belles Lettres,* as well as his eventual rejection of its system. On more than one occasion, he regretted that no college had offered him a professorship of rhetoric. Most important, his pronouncements on rhetoric are extensive throughout his published work, most directly in "Nature" (1836) and in his two essays titled "Eloquence," published in 1847 and 1867.

Emerson's rhetoric is grounded in an epistemology in which language is placed at the center of the production of knowledge. As he explains in "Nature," reality is the product of a dialectical interaction of subject and object. The discerning observer brings to experience a set of eternally true ideas that transcend the sensory realm. These, however, are meaningless without concrete manifestation. The material world, on the other hand, offers solid objects, but these are in themselves limited to the incomplete corporeal. It is at this point that language becomes crucial. Ordinary language refers to material objects and so cannot express the eternal. In the language of metaphor, however, the two distinct domains are brought together as the signs for limited material objects, the terms of language, are used to suggest the unlimited realm of ideas. Thus, without the language of the sensory, the ideal cannot be made manifest. Without the ideal, the world of matter is mere dead sense data. The metaphoric language of rhetoric thus enables the realization of the eternal in the finite, the union of the idea and object in mortal experience. Both spirit and matter in dialectical interaction with each other are necessary in discovering knowledge. Rhetoric is thus necessary for the progressive unfolding of eternal truth in the temporal world.

While Emerson's statements in such essays as "The Poet" and "The American Scholar" indicate that this use of rhetoric is the proper sphere of the inspired philosopher or poet, in the two "Eloquence" essays he argues for the democratic possibilities of the process. There he explains that a free democracy is the essential condition for all genuine rhetoric. The writer or speaker must display three features: a love for truth, an ability to engage in dialogue with an audience, and a capacity for analogical thinking. The commitment to truth involves a concern for the good of the community and the rights and capacities of the individuals in it. Emerson was especially wary of the uses of rhetoric for furthering economic self-interest. The dialogic interplay between the interlocutor and audience enables an exchange in which erroneous conceptions and actions are located and corrected. It also encourages the exceptional response to the demands of the situation at hand (the Greek *kairos*), providing the possibility for inspired discourse. The capacity for analogy reemphasizes Emerson's insistence on the metaphoric core of knowledge. Emerson adds that this ability profits from the everyday parlance of the street. This language keeps the interlocutor in touch with the facts of experience, facts necessary to check false ideas and to suggest true ones. It also provides the vividness and energy necessary for communicating truth. Emerson also insists that metaphors must be continually revised in order to resist their appropriation by the enemies of truth, particularly the self-interested commercial classes. Finally, for Emerson, free countries enable all citizens to aspire to the condition of the genuine interlocutor.

Emerson's rhetoric was strongly influential in the democratic rhetorics of schools and colleges early in this century and, more recently, in the thought of Kenneth Burke.

James A. Berlin
Purdue University

Bibliography

Berlin, James A. *Writing Instruction in Nineteenth-Century American Colleges.* Carbondale: Southern Illinois UP, 1984.

Emerson, Ralph Waldo. *The Complete Works of Ralph Waldo Emerson.* 12 vols. Boston: Houghton, 1903.

Ray, Roberta K. "The Role of the Orator in the Philosophy of Ralph Waldo Emerson." *Speech Monographs* 41 (1974): 215–25.

Emig, Janet (b. 1928)

Composition researcher and theorist, former public school teacher, distinguished professor emeriti of English Education at Rutgers University, coordinator of the New Jersey Writing Project, poet and novelist, and past president of the National Council of Teachers of English. Janet Emig remains perhaps the most well known scholar in the field of composition. Her monograph, *The Composing Processes of Twelfth Graders* (1971), has been highly influential in promoting writing as a process and in introducing the case study methodology to composition studies. Early in her career, however, Emig set herself "a goal of trying to suggest all the avenues of research [that composition researchers] could pursue" (personal interview, May 9, 1990). Her scholarly accomplishments over the last three decades indeed reflect the wide diversity and interdisciplinarity of composition scholarship. In the 1980s Emig embraced a philosophy of education that consolidated this diversity and revealed her as one of this field's most important theorists.

Emig's work addresses several overlapping themes. Her basic concern has been the teaching of composition. Her pedagogy, however, has always been firmly entrenched in theoretical considerations. During the 1960s, Emig developed the notion that writing ought to be viewed more as a process than as a product. But her vision of the composing process was complicated by her recognition that thought and language could not be separated during communication. Her earliest conceptions of the composing process were at odds with the simpler view of composing as chronologically set stages. In "The Uses of the Unconscious in Composing" (1964), for example, she demonstrated the preconscious nature and automaticity of writing. In *The Composing Processes of Twelfth Graders* (1971), she described writing as a collection of processes, not simply one monolithic process every writer employs. This recognition of the complexity of written communication remains a significant contribution to her field.

Emig problematized our view of writing processes further with an emphasis on the connections between human cognitive development and rhetorical development. In "The Origins of Rhetoric: A Developmental View" (1969), she suggests that pragmatic and rhetorical abilities develop during infancy and early childhood just like language itself. Complicating matters even further, during the mid-1970s, Emig explored how human physiology, especially that of the brain, affects composing.

In the early 1980s, Emig embraced "constructivism," although a belief in its tenets may well have informed her writing throughout her career. According to Jerome Bruner,

E

constructivism's central idea is that, contrary to common sense, there is no one "real world" preexisting independently of human cognition and language. The "world" is actually a product of human symbolic activity. Emig argues that "as a symbolic, transformative activity of creating text-worlds," writinng participates centrally in human "worldmaking."

Constructivism has significant implications for writing instruction and education generally. If we see learning as the making of more and more sophisticated versions of the world, then we must see communication, including writing, as central to worldmaking. In her most oft-cited essay, "Writing as a Mode of Learning" (1977), Emig argues that writing is a unique and productive way of learning —and thus, of making meaning, of worldmaking. This essay has led the way in the movement to include writing across the curriculum in education. Moreover, if learning is "worldmaking," then students cannot be viewed as empty vessels simply to be filled with a fixed body of knowledge kept in a faculty storeroom; they must be seen as possessing tacit theories of their own, worlds they have already made and that education will inevitably transform. Knowing the power that writing can have, composition teachers must assume a weighty responsibility in directing young writers' worldmaking. Fulfilling that responsibility has required nothing less than a shift in the paradigm that informs composition theory and pedagogy from neglect of writing processes to a view of these processes as being the essence of worldmaking. Emig has been and remains a leader in promoting that shift.

Finally, Emig has been a potent voice against the various forces that threaten English education. From her graduate experiences at Harvard in the 1960s to the present, Emig has confronted the anticomposition bias of those who argue that writing is simply a skill that cannot be improved through thoughtful teacher intervention. Since her earliest graduate experiences at the University of Michigan in the 1950s, Emig also has confronted sexism both personally and professionally. In each case she has argued for maturity, professionalism, and change in the profession of eduation.

Janet Emig problematizes easy classification. While much of her scholarship has examined what goes on inside the writer's head during composing, her theoretical discussions show her to be a far-ranging thinker. Her writings, even the earliest from the 1960s, remain provocative, and, in some cases, the subjects she has bravely broached over three decades we have still yet to fully confront.

Gerald Nelms
Southern Illinois University

Bibliography

Birnbaum, June, and Janet Emig. "Creating Minds, Created Texts: Writing and Reading." *Developing Literacy: Young Children's Use of Language*. Ed. Robert P. Parker and Francis A. Davis. Newark, DE: International Reading Assn., 1983. 87–104.

Bruner, Jerome. *Actual Minds, Possible Worlds*. Cambridge, MA: Harvard UP, 1986.

Emig, Janet. *The Composing Processes of Twelfth Graders*. Research Report No. 13. Urbana, IL: National Council of Teachers of English, 1971.

———. "Journal of a Pessimist: Prospects for Academic Women in the Eighties." *Journal of Education* 162 (1980): 50–56.

———. "On Teaching Composition: Some Hypotheses as Definitions." *Research in the Teaching of English* 1 (1967): 127–35.

———. "The Origins of Rhetoric: A Developmental View." *School Review* 77 (1969): 193–98. Rpt. *The Web of Meaning* 146–56.

———. "The Uses of the Unconscious in Composing." *College Composition and Communication* 15 (1964): 6–11. Rpt. *The Web of Meaning* 3–43.

———. *The Web of Meaning: Essays on Writing, Teaching, Learning, and Thinking*. Upper Montclair, NJ: Boynton/Cook, 1983.

———. "Writing as a Mode of Learning." *College Composition and Communication* 28 (1977): 122–28. Rpt. *The Web of Meaning* 123–32.

Nelms, Ralph Gerald. *A Case History Approach to Composition Studies: Edward P.J. Corbett and Janet Emig*. Diss. Ohio State U, 1990. Ann Arbor: U of Michigan, 1991.

Empedocles (c. 495–430 B.C.E.)

A pre-Socratic philosopher who was born near the dawning of the fifth century B.C.E. in Acragas, Sicily, and lived to about the age of sixty. Some ancient sources claim that Empedocles invented rhetoric, an assertion that has prompted historians of rhetoric to examine his contributions to rhetoric's origin (Enos, *Greek Rhetoric before Aristotle* 67). The few extant fragments of Empedocles' works provide some insight to his views on rhetoric in two respects: his stylistic techniques and his comments on the relationship between knowledge and communication. Empedocles' use of hexameter and elegiac verse is grounded in stylistic techniques of dissociation, metaphor, antithesis, and analogy. Empedocles believed that knowledge was acquired through sense-perception, but man's inherent limitations resulted in observations that were probable, relative, and situational. Empedocles' stylistic techniques of juxtaposing notions and structuring meaning through paradigms and analogies reflect these views on relativism. As the teacher of Gorgias of Leontini, and possibly Tisias of Syracuse, Empedocles provided the conceptual and stylistic framework that grounded the Sicilian sophistic and that is commonly associated with sophistic rhetoric in general.

Richard Leo Enos
Texas Christian University

Bibliography

"Empedokles: 31 [21]." *Die Fragmente der Vorsokratiker.* Ed. Hermann Diels and Walther Kranz. Vol. 1. Dublin/Zurich: Weidmann, 1972.

Enos, Richard Leo. "Aristotle, Empedocles and the Notion of Rhetoric." *In Search of Justice: The Indiana Tradition in Speech Communication.* Ed. Richard J. Jensen and John C. Hammerback. Amsterdam: Rodopi, 1987. 5–21.

———. *Greek Rhetoric Before Aristotle.* Prospect Heights, IL: Waveland, 1993.

Freeman, Kathleen. *Ancilla to the Pre-Socratic Philosophers.* Oxford: Basil Blackwell, 1971.

———. *The Pre-Socratic Philosophers: A Companion to Diels,* Fragmente der Vorsokratiker. 2nd ed. Oxford: Basil Blackwell, 1966.

See also PRE-SOCRATICS

Emphasis

A concept concerning the arrangement of words, sentences, or paragraphs based on their importance in communication as intended by the speaker or writer. Important elements are placed where they can accentuate desired meaning or highlight the importance of an idea.

Emphasis is accomplished through several strategies, one of which is the placement or location of important information in sentences and paragraphs. Important ideas are placed either at the beginning or the end of sentences or paragraphs. Emphasis is also accomplished by the amount of space allocated to those elements being emphasized. Giving fullness of treatment, that is, more space than what is given to less important discourse elements, highlights discourse elements.

Other methods for emphasizing important ideas include use of tags to highlight ideas. Using tags (for example, "most" and "foremost" at the beginning or end of discourse elements such as sentences, paragraphs, or fuller discourse) helps point to information to be highlighted in the discourse.

Repetition is another method of emphasis within discourse. While important ideas are frequently placed in the first sentence of paragraphs and restated or recast in the final sentence of the same paragraph to emphasize their importance, use of repetition for emphasis takes place in other ways. For example, important ideas are repeated within paragraphs. Use of repetition, however, should be done selectively so as to avoid monotony to the reader or to the listener.

Moreover, repetition of words is not the only form of repetition that emphasizes the importance of ideas. When making a point, writers frequently use the same sentence patterns within a paragraph. Such writers or speakers begin their sentences with the same sentence pattern. Lincoln's Gettysburg Address is an excellent illustration of the various types of repetition used to enhance important points or ideas. His repetition of prepositions, "Government of the people, by the people, for the people," along with repeated sentence patterns exemplified by "Now we are engaged . . . We are met on a great . . . We have come to dedicate . . . ," illustrate the use of repetition to highlight the importance of ideas and to accentuate meaning. This use of repetition of parts of sentences, such as prepositional phrases, adverbial phrases, along with introductory clauses, serves to highlight a speaker's or writer's important idea.

Another important stylistic method for "setting apart" or emphasizing significant ideas is placement of the ideas in separate or short paragraphs that contrast with the longer elements within the discourse. While some writers emphasize their points through the use of dashes, hyphens, and other forms of punctuation thought to be "dramatic," these should be used sparingly so that structure does not overshadow meaning.

Further discussions of emphasis are found with discussions of paragraph development and paragraph coherence and unity in many modern writing handbooks.

Louise Rodriguez Connal
University of Arizona

Bibliography

Lazarus, Arnold, and H. Wendell Smith. A *Glossary of Literature and Composition.* Urbana, IL: National Council of Teachers of English, 1983. 104.

Williams, Joseph M. *Style: Ten Lessons in Clarity and Grace.* Glenview, IL: Scott, 1981. 147–50.

Empirical Research

Describes types, uses, and characteristic outcomes of descriptive and hypothesis-testing studies in rhetoric and composition. Surveys of research in written composition in the United States (Braddock; Hillocks; North) reveal growth in both the number and quality of empirical research studies in rhetoric during the last three decades. Braddock and colleagues identified one thousand studies related to composition completed through 1962, five hundred of which they deemed scientific. Only five of these studies, however, were cited as worthy of close analysis. Screening over six thousand studies completed between 1962 and 1982, Hillocks identified over two thousand empirical studies of scientific significance. Finally, North surveyed a variety of "modes of inquiry" in composition, identifying eight methodological communities with the field and a number of significant studies. Despite this evidence of growth, Braddock, Hillocks, and North urge composition researchers to pay closer attention to the complexities of research design and to become more systematic in implementing and reporting their work.

Rhetoricians conduct empirical research in order to answer questions or to solve problems that they confront as scholars and teachers. Two types of empirical studies are quite distinct: *hypothesis-testing studies* and *descriptive studies.* When researchers formulate a hypothesis prior to conducting a study, they seek either a positive or negative answer to a particular question, such as "Is there a relationship between gender and the quality of student writing elicited within a statewide assessment?" or "Do word processors improve or detract from written composition?" Both correlational studies and experimental studies test hypotheses, but the procedures for these two studies are different. In *experimental studies,* researchers manipulate conditions and assign individuals at random to various treatments or groups in order to determine the effects of such conditions or treatments. In *correlational studies* researchers test hypotheses (without manipulating variables) by simply comparing existing phenomena in order to determine particular relationships or patterns.

In contrast to hypothesis-testing studies, *descriptive studies* are designed to describe a situation or event; for example, "What happens in a student-teacher writing conference?" or "How do students conceptualize 'revision'?" Without a specific hypothesis to test, researchers employ various methods that will help them eventually formulate hypotheses or theories about particular domains. Such methods may include *participant observation,* where the researcher becomes a participating member of the group being observed; *protocol analysis,* where the researcher conducts a moment-by-moment observation of individuals as they complete tasks; *in-depth, phenomenological interviewing,* where the researcher interviews individuals over time in order to determine an "insider's perspective"; or *case study analysis,* where the researcher conducts a detailed study of one or more individuals or events.

Although the structure of research reports may vary, most include the following five sections: (1) an abstract of the study; (2) an introduction including a rationale for the study, a review of related literature, and questions addressed in the report; (3) a methods section including information on the participants, research setting, and procedures; (4) a report of results; and (5) a discussion of the author's interpretation of the meaning of the results.

Dana L. Fox
University of Arizona

Bibliography

Borg, Walter R., and Meredith D. Gail. *Educational Research: An Introduction*. White Plains, NY: Longman, 1989.

Braddock, Richard, Richard Lloyd-Jones, and Lowell Schoer. *Research in Written Composition*. Champaign, IL: National Council of Teachers of English, 1963.

Hayes, John R., et al., eds. *Reading Empirical Research Studies: The Rhetoric of Research*. Hillsdale, NJ: Erlbaum, 1992.

Hillocks, George. *Research in Written Composition*. Urbana, IL: National Council of Teachers of English, 1986.

Jaeger, Richard M., ed. *Complementary Methods for Research in Education*. Washington, D.C.: American Educational Research Association, 1988.

Kamil, Michael L., Judith A. Langer, and Timothy Shanahan. *Understanding Research in Reading and Writing*. Newton, MA: Allyn, 1985.

Merriam, Sharan B. *Case Study Research in Education: A Qualitative Approach*. San Francisco: Jossey, 1988.

North, Stephen. *The Making of Knowledge in Composition: Portrait of an Emerging Field*. Upper Montclair, NJ: Boynton/ Cook, 1987.

Seidman, I.E. *Interviewing as Qualitative Research: A Guide for Researchers in Education and the Social Sciences*. New York: Teachers College P, 1991.

See also PROTOCOLS

Enallage

Substitution of one grammatical form for another. Where solecism is the ignorant misuse of cases, genders, or tenses, enallage is their inspired misuse. In declaring "We was robbed," Joe Jacobs created a poetic leap of meaning by using the wrong verb form. Shakespeare did the same in writing "The posture of your blows are yet unknown" (*Julius Caesar* 5.1). In writing "Let us go then, you and I," Eliot showed how enallage can evoke a sense of immediacy ("The Love Song of J. Alfred Prufrock"). Historians regularly resort to enallage when they substitute the present tense for the past to make that past more vivid.

Arthur Quinn and Lyon Rathbun
University of California, Berkeley

E

Enthymeme

A rhetorical syllogism, that is, any statement made in reasoned discourse that is accompanied by substantiation in the form of one or more premises. Although variously used in history, *enthymeme* generally refers to claims in arguments that are supported by probable premises assumed to be shared by the audience.

Enthymeme is of apparently metaphorical origin (*en* = into + *thymos* = soul), known first to appear in reference to rhetoric in Isocrates and Anaximenes. Aristotle in his *Rhetoric* uses the term repeatedly and in a new way, in general to refer to the rhetorical counterpart of the analytic syllogism. Aristotle places the deductive enthymeme alongside the inductive example as one of two modes of logical proof in rhetoric. Yet Aristotle's statements that the enthymeme is the "substance" or "body" (*somos*) of proof and that the rhetor must be skilled in making enthymemes (*enthymematikos*) make it likely that he also considered the enthymeme somehow to govern artistic proofs in general, including ethical and pathetic proofs. This possibility is consistent with his conception of the enthymeme as derived from contingent and practical premises based on beliefs already held by the rhetor's audience. In this sense the enthymeme plays a central role in the process of rhetorical thinking, for Aristotle, insofar as it connects the assumed beliefs of the audience with the conclusions of the rhetor by means of invented arguments. Aristotle contends that, unlike a syllogism, an enthymeme "must consist of a few propositions" and "not carry the reasoning too far back," since to include all the parts of its reasoning would either be too obvious or risk obscurity. This has led some readers of Aristotle to the erroneous conclusion, which has had historical persistence, that he means the enthymeme to be defined as a "truncated syllogism." It seems more consistent with Aristotle's aims to say rather that the Aristotelian enthymeme resembles the logical syllogism but also differs from it significantly in that it is constructed with reference to the assumed beliefs of the audience and is stated according to rhetorical, not formal, needs. Thus Conley has observed that Aristotle's examples of enthymemes also exhibit other rhetorical qualities as "nicely turned sentences or questions raised at climactic points," and that Aristotle also advises that enthymemes be expressed in periodic form, possibly following Isocrates.

There is sufficient ambiguity in Aristotle's text to make *enthymeme* a contested term. It is nevertheless a central term in Aristotle's treatise while it tends to become peripheral in subsequent theories. Having entered the vocabulary of rhetoric, the term is detached from the context of Aristotle's treatise, and used variously by other rhetoricians. Consequently, what enthymeme "really" means must be stated relative to the historical contexts and purposes of the user. The meaning of the term has been in dispute since the first commentaries on Aristotle. Apart from those, it was used to mean different things: a "compressed induction" by Minoukianos or a refutative statement by Rufus in the second century C.E.; any "part" of a syllogism and "a *sententia* drawn from contraries" by Quintilian; an ornamental concluding statement by Hermogenes; a figure of diction in *Rhetorica ad Herennium*; and an "imperfect" (*atelês*) syllogism by numerous Byzantine and Renaissance rhetoricians. Thus the early history of rhetoric includes meanings for *enthymeme* that range from the logical to the stylistic. In more recent times, especially following the influence of Port Royal logic, the term has been dismissed by rhetoricians as unimportant or ignored altogether. Thus Campbell in 1776, given his associationist distrust of deduction, mentions the enthymeme only to link it to a form of argument removed from its source in feeling or to liken it to the figure of antithesis. In the nineteenth century, the term appears infrequently, and when it does it is typically given perfunctory mention as an "irregular form" of argument, as in David J. Hill's *Science of Rhetoric* (1877).

Scholarly interest in the enthymeme revived in the mid twentieth century in part because of the reinterpretation given the Aristotelian enthymeme by Bitzer in 1959. It became a critical term in some kinds of neo-Aristotelian analysis in the study of public address, yet it does not feature in Chicago neo-Aristotelian literary critical theory, even though that theory may finally derive as much from Aristotle's *Rhetoric* as from his *Poetics*. There is, however, something enthymemelike in, for instance, Wayne C. Booth's idea of "co-duction" as presented in his *Company We Keep: An Ethics of Fiction* (1988).

A renewed interest in the enthymeme has also characterized modern composition theory in some quarters, particularly where composition intersects with theories of argument. The first textbook use of enthymeme as a heuristic and structuring device in composition was made by Brandt et al. in *The Craft of Writing* (1969). This idea was subsequently developed by Gage in *The Shape of Reason* (1989). In these pedagogical approaches, the enthymeme provides an alternative to logical formalism. It is presented as a functional basis for generating the overall reasoning of an argument in reference to an audience situation and as a basis in turn for thinking through the requisite rhetorical structure of that argument. This approach links invention with arrangement through the enthymeme and applies the enthymeme also to the teaching of critical reading, on the grounds that any argumentative work will have an underlying enthymematic structure that can be uncovered to reveal the workings of that argument in relation to its implicit audience.

These prescriptive and analytical uses of a "structural enthymeme" in modern composition resemble and overlap with the use of Toulmin's model of argument, with some significant differences. While Toulmin's five-part "layout" (claim, warrant, backing, qualification, refutation) anatomizes basic elements of an argument, it does not put primary emphasis on the relationships among those parts. The four-part structural enthymeme (question-at-issue, assertion, because clause, assumption) focuses attention on the functional relationships among these parts in terms of the interaction of rhetor and audience:

The rhetor's share	The audience's share
assertion	question-at-issue
because clause	assumption

In this schema any explicit statement of assertion and because clause necessarily entails a relationship to an implied question-at-issue and assumption, thereby implying an audience for whom the argument is composed. In this sense the structural enthymeme attempts to define the rational process underlying the invention of an argument by abstracting the most basic elements from which the argument must begin for it to be the kind of argument it is. It is analogous, therefore, to the neo-Aristotelian conception of a "concrete whole," described by R.S. Crane as the rational principle behind works of poetic art, the intuition of which enables "problems" of artistic creation to be conceptualized and solved. Similarly, the structural enthymeme applied to composition is meant to be a conceptualization of the whole argument that enables its needs and possibilities to be understood and its parts to be differentiated. The Toulmin model has no such generative purpose, and hence the components of an argument that it isolates are not conceived of as all necessary to every argument. The enthymeme in this sense overlaps with Toulmin's claim, warrant, and backing only, insofar as any argument must imply these parts whether or not it contains qualifications or refutations. Every argument, however, may be said to be founded on one or more basic question, assertion, line of reasoning, and assumption—with, in other words, an enthymeme or enthymemes as its deep structure.

It is debatable whether this contemporary adaptation of the enthymeme to composition is Aristotelian, and in some senses the question is irrelevant. If Aristotle's enthymeme is "a kind of syllogism," then this contemporary view reverses that relationship by seeming to make the syllogism a kind of enthymeme. Since this view of the structural enthymeme is not dependent on whether any corresponding enthymeme is actually expressed at the sentence level of the argument itself, it is a radical departure from historical usages. But the history of the term seems to have taken radical departures in stride. What the contemporary view does share with Aristotle, arguably, is the sense of connectedness between the reasoning proffered by an argument and the beliefs assumed to be shared with an audience.

John T. Gage
University of Oregon

Bibliography

Bitzer, Lloyd F. "Aristotle's Enthymeme Revisited." *Quarterly Journal of Speech* 45 (1959): 399–408.

Booth, Wayne C. *The Company We Keep: An Ethics of Fiction.* Chicago: U of Chicago P, 1988.

Brandt, William J., et al. *The Craft of Writing.* Englewood Cliffs, NJ: Prentice, 1969.

Conley, Thomas M. "The Enthymeme in Perspective." *Quarterly Journal of Speech* 70 (1984): 168–87.

Crane, R.S. *The Languages of Criticism and the Structure of Poetry.* Toronto: U of Toronto P, 1953.

Gage, John T. *The Shape of Reason.* 2nd ed. New York: Macmillan, 1991.

———. "Towards a General Theory of the Enthymeme for Advanced Composition." *Teaching Advanced Composition: Why and How.* Ed. Katherine H. Adams and John L. Adams. Portsmouth, NH: Heinemann, 1991. 161–78.

Green, Lawrence D. "Enthymemic Invention and Structural Prediction." *College English* 41 (1980): 623–34.

Grimaldi, William M.A., S.J. *Studies in the Philosophy of Aristotle's Rhetoric.* Wiesbaden: Franz Steiner Verlag, 1972.

Hood, Michael. "The Enthymeme: A Brief Bibliography of Modern Sources." *Rhetoric Society Quarterly* 14 (1984): 159–62.

Poster, Carol. "A Historicist Reconceptualization of the Enthymeme." *Rhetoric Society Quarterly* 22 (1992): 1–24.

Toulmin, Stephen. *The Uses of Argument.* Cambridge: Cambridge UP, 1958.

See also DEDUCTION; INDUCTION; PROBABILITY; PROOF

Environmental Rhetoric

A topic or a field of rhetorical practice concentrating on the human relationship to the natural environment and dealing with the forms or systems of discourse arising from ethical and political disputes over environmental protection and developmental planning. Though environmentalism as a social movement has roots in the nineteenth-century Romanticism of writers like Henry David Thoreau and George Perkins Marsh, and though connected with the early conservation movement (both as a form of resistance led by visionaries like John Muir and as a movement of progressive development directed by managers like Gifford Pinchot), environmentalism did not take shape as a widely recognized political perspective until after the publication of Rachel Carson's *Silent Spring* in 1962. Only in the early 1970s, for instance, did the word *environmentalist* begin to be commonly used to denote a person dedicated to the political cause of protecting the natural environment against the encroachments of industrial progress and land development (Killingsworth and Palmer 40–44).

Within a decade of the emergence of environmentalism as a political and social perspective, environmental rhetoric had become a topic of interest among scholars in American universities. Essays and articles devoted specifically to the rhetoric of environmental protection and planning began to appear fairly regularly (Socolow; Oravec; Killingsworth; Miller; Peterson; Killingsworth and Steffens; Throgmorton; Lange; Oravec and Cantrill). By 1992 a full-length study had appeared—Killingsworth and Palmer's *Ecospeak: Rhetoric and Environmental Politics in America*—an agenda-setting book, with forays into the history of the key terms, genres, and topics of environmental discourse and an analysis of the discourse communities and social institutions most prominent in environmental policy-making (political action groups, business and industry, government, the mass media, and the discipline of scientific ecology).

In addition, the interdisciplinary nature of environmental studies has brought forth a number of works in disciplines and fields closely related to, or drawing upon, rhetorical analysis. The literature on "risk communication," for instance, has grown huge very quickly in the last ten years, though it remains beset by difficulties, not the least of which is the problem of defining *risk,* as a number of critics within the field have noted (Krimsky and Plough; Kasperson and Stallen). The study of nature writing has enjoyed a slower and steadier development, but work in this area has not been systematic, and from the perspective of rhetorical analysis it seems highly uneven, ranging from the impressionistic survey by Brooks to the more methodologically sophisticated feminist criticism of Hynes. Work in other disciplines impinges directly upon the study of environmental rhetoric, frequently offering significant if scattered insights into the field. The historical studies of Merchant, the writings of Evernden in environmental studies, and the essays of the biologist Botkin all take a discourse-based approach to interpretation. In social philosophy Luhmann's *Ecological Communication* represents perhaps the bravest attempt thus far to theorize the concept of the environment in relation to discourse. His choice of general systems theory as his main focus, however, leads him quickly away from the problems of communication as defined in the rhetorical tradition.

To date, the study of environmental rhetoric has developed in two directions. The first deals with environmentalism as a topic or an exigency in rhetorical studies. The second represents a more holistic approach, which tends toward the development of a kind of "eco-criticism." This two-branched evolution follows a similar development in gender studies. Feminism created two kinds of critical approaches to speech and writing. First, it generated a set of problems, themes, or issues to be taken up in fairly traditional forms of critical inquiry. Second, it presented researchers with a new form of criticism shaped by the feminist world view. The study of environmental rhetoric may be headed in the same direction.

The great mass of the literature published thus far has followed the first path, applying well-known theoretical approaches to the study and practice of environmental rhetoric. According to this view, environmental consciousness, action, or political interest appears as a special topic involving a rhetor's identification with the land or with a particular region. This identification (an agent-scene ratio, in Burkean terms) either reinforces or interferes with the rhetor's commitment to a particular group, political affiliation, or course of action. Thus, following the famous formula in Aldo Leopold's "Land Ethic," the rhetor raises the land to a new ethical status, which creates special rhetorical problems and opportunities. Dislocations or transformations may appear at the level of the trope, for example, as the land takes on characteristics formerly reserved for descriptions of human beings (the land as victim); or at the level of myth (the land as god or goddess); or at the level of genre (as the land becomes, for example, the subject of historical narrative, rather than merely the scenic background of the mainly human story).

If such dislocations become extensive enough, a dialectical shift may occur, thus creating the conditions for the second development of environmental rhetoric to occur. Whereas in the first approach to environmental rhetoric, the analyst uses knowledge of rhetorical conventions to interpret speech and writing about the environment, in eco-criticism, the analyst or theorist uses ecology to model rhetoric conventions and practice. According to this view, the environment is not just one issue among many, but rather a kind of ur-issue (much as the issue of gender has become the defining category of human relations in feminist studies). In eco-criticism, all rhetoric is to some extent environmental in that all ethical and political decisions have some bearing upon the human relation to nature and, more important, because all writing or speech both creates and participates in a special set of ecological relations. A discourse on war, for example, becomes a text that can make meaning only within a system of relations that are partly historical, partly biological, and partly territorial. The discourse builds upon the cultural resources of language use, working its way among networks of the old myths of dominance and cooperation. Eco-criticism—drawing upon cultural studies and semiotics—maps the paths and systems that such texts depend upon, of which the rhetor may have little awareness. Hence Cooper, for example, can speak of an "ecology of writing," and Luhmann can frame a theory of interaction within systems and resonance between systems under the heading "ecological communication."

These two approaches do not exhaust the possibilities of such a new field; they only indicate the directions that scholars have begun to take. Whether one approach will become dominant or whether both will yield to some yet unimagined development (or, for that matter, be forgotten by history) depends largely upon the power of the exigency of environmental protection and planning. Like environmental polemic itself, studies in environmental rhetoric tend to crystallize around key events in the history of environmentalism—the oil crisis of the early 1970s, for example, or the coincidence of the global warming scare with the twentieth anniversary of Earth Day in 1990. The problems of *growth* and *sustainability*, therefore, appear as key issues not only in environmental planning but also in the developing history of environmental rhetoric.

M. Jimmie Killingsworth
Texas A&M University

Bibliography

Botkin, Daniel B. *Discordant Harmonies: A New Ecology for the Twenty-First Century*. New York: Oxford UP, 1990.
Brooks, Paul. *Speaking for Nature: How Literary Naturalists from Henry Thoreau to Rachel Carson Have Shaped America*. San Francisco: Sierra Club, 1980.
Cooper, Marilyn. "The Ecology of Writing." *College English* 48 (1986): 364–75.
Evernden, Neil. *The Natural Alien: Humankind and Environment*. Toronto: U of Toronto P, 1985.
———. *The Social Creation of Nature*. Baltimore: Johns Hopkins UP, 1992.
Hynes, H. Patricia. *The Recurring Silent Spring*. New York: Pergamon, 1989.
Kasperson, Roger E., and Pieter Jan M. Stallen, eds. *Communicating Risks to the Public: International Perspectives*. Dordrecht: Kluwer, 1991.
Killingsworth, M. Jimmie. "Can an English Teacher Contribute to the Energy Debate?" *College English* 43 (1981): 581–86.
Killingsworth, M. Jimmie, and Jacqueline S. Palmer. *Ecospeak: Rhetoric and Environmental Politics*. Carbondale: Southern Illinois UP, 1992.
Killingsworth, M. Jimmie, and Dean Steffens. "Effectiveness in the Environmental Impact Statement: A Study in Public Rhetoric." *Written Communication* 6 (1989): 155–80.
Krimsky, Sheldon, and Alonzo Plough. *Environmental Hazards: Communicating Risks as a Social Process*. Dover, MA: Auburn House, 1988.
Lange, Jonathan I. "Refusal to Compromise: The Case of Earth First!" *Western Journal of Speech Communication* 54 (1990): 473–94.
Leopold, Aldo. *Sand County Almanac*. New York: Ballantine, 1966.
Luhmann, Niklas. *Ecological Communication*. Chicago: U of Chicago P, 1989.
Merchant, Carolyn. *The Death of Nature: Women, Ecology, and the Scientific Revolution*. San Francisco: Harper, 1980.
———. *Ecological Revolutions: Nature, Gender, and Science in New England*. Chapel Hill: U of North Carolina P, 1989.
Miller, Carolyn R. "Genre as Social Action." *Quarterly Journal of Speech* 70 (1984): 151–67.
Oravec, Christine. "Conservationism vs. Preservationism: The Public Interest in the Hetch-Hetchy Controversy." *Quarterly Journal of Speech* 70 (1984): 444–58.
———. "The Evolutionary Sublime and the Essay of Natural History." *Communication Monographs* 49 (1982): 215–28.
———. "John Muir, Yosemite, and the Sublime Response: A Study in the Rhetoric of Preservationism." *Quarterly Journal of Speech* 67 (1981): 245–58.
Oravec, Christine L., and James G. Cantrill, eds. *The Conference on the Discourse of Environmental Advocacy*. Salt Lake City: University of Utah Humanities Center, 1992.

Peterson, Tarla Rai. "The Rhetorical Construction of Institutional Authority in a Senate Subcommittee Hearing on Wilderness Legislation." *Western Journal of Speech Communication* 52 (1988): 259–76.

———. "The Will to Conservation: A Burkeian Analysis of Dust Bowl Rhetoric and American Farming Motives." *Southern Speech Communication Journal* 52 (1986): 1–21.

Socolow, Robert H. "Failures of Discourse: Obstacles to the Integration of Environmental Values into Natural Resource Policy." *When Values Conflict: Essays on Environmental Analysis, Discourse, and Decision.* Ed. Laurence H. Tribe, Corinne S. Schelling, and John Voss. Cambridge, MA: Ballinger, 1976. 1–33.

Throgmorton, James A. "Passion, Reason, and Power: The Rhetorics of Electric Power Planning in Chicago." *Journal of Architectural Planning and Research* 7 (1990): 330–50.

Epanalepsis

Repetition at the end of a clause or sentence of the word or phrase with which it began. Sidney was using epanalepsis in writing "I might, unhappy word, O me, I might" (*Astrophil and Stella*). As with symploce (q.v.), epanalepsis can be used to evoke a sense of measured balance between clauses: "Blood hath bought blood, and blows have answer'd blows; Strength match'd with strength, and power confronted power" (Shakespeare, *King John* 2.1) Another example: "Rejoice in the Lord always: and again I say, Rejoice" (Philippians 4:4). Because epanalepsis is apparently contrived but can still seem to spring from intense emotion, it is more common in poetry. When epanalepsis is used in prose, it often creates sentences that stand alone as aphorisms: "Nothing can be created out of nothing" (Lucretius). "Men of few words are the best men" (*Henry IV* 3.2).

Arthur Quinn and Lyon Rathbun
University of California, Berkeley

Epanorthosis

The correction of a first thought either to reinforce, to qualify, or to retract it. Jesus was underscoring his point in asserting, "Behold, the hour cometh, yea, is now come, that ye shall be scattered, every man to his own" (John 16:31). Heraclitus qualified his in writing "Religion is a disease, but it is a noble disease." Augustine retracted his in declaring, "Give me chastity, but not yet." Paul illustrated how epanorthosis can be used to create antithesis in writing: "You are a letter from Christ delivered by us, written not with ink but with the Spirit of the living God, not on tablets of stone but on tables of human hearts" (Second Letter to the Corinthians 3.3). When extended throughout a whole work of self-criticism, epanorthosis becomes a palinode, a poem or long passage retracting something said in a previous poem or passage.

Arthur Quinn and Lyon Rathbun
University of California, Berkeley

Epideictic Oratory

A genre of speech that originated during the classical period. Epideictic oratory is also referred to by the following titles: display speech, ceremonial speech, and festival speech. Aristotle designated the genre that grouped together several types of speech prevalent at the time. He was the first to employ the word *epideixeis*, "to show or display," to specify a class of oratory. Prior to Aristotle, the word *epideictic* designated a characteristic or quality that individual speeches might possess, but it was not used to refer to a class of speeches. In later antiquity epideictic expanded to include poetry, history, and even philosophy that bore characteristics consistent with the genre. The genre continues to our own day in the speeches of community and organizational leaders that uphold certain values over others.

Aristotle categorizes oratory into the deliberative, the forensic, and the epideictic in his *On Rhetoric*. He recognizes three elements in the speaking situation: the speaker, the speech, and the audience. It is largely the audience and their role, according to Aristotle, that determines the type of speech that is given. More specifically, his categorization identifies three related concerns: the role of the audience, the time focus, and the ends sought. The audience can play the role of judge or observer. If the audience plays the role of judge, the oratory presented is either forensic or deliberative. It is forensic if the issues in focus arise from the past and deliberative if they involve the future. Finally, Aristotle describes three potential ends or goals that a speech might seek that relate back to the role of the audience and the time focus. In forensic oratory, the audience members determine guilt or innocence relating to events from the past. In deliberative oratory, the audience seeks to determine the best course of action to pursue in the future.

Epideictic, according to Aristotle, contrasts with the other genres on each of the relevant considerations. In epideictic discourse the audience plays the role of spectator or observer rather than judge. Aristotle claimed that "a spectator is concerned with the ability" of the speaker. The time focus of epideictic is the present, and the ends sought in an epideictic speech are to determine "the honorable and the shameful."

Aristotle elaborates further on what he means by epideictic later in *On Rhetoric*, which most scholars consider to be a compilation of his lecture notes. In a section in which he discusses the style appropriate for each of the three genres of oratory, he highlights the different styles necessary for oral and written presentations. In this context he characterizes epideictic as requiring the greatest exactness or attention to style. Epideictic oratory requires the most attention to style because "the epideictic style is most like written, for its objective is to be read." Aristotle's linkage of epideictic to written prose leads some scholars to characterize epideictic oratory as the "display" of a written or memorized text that existed prior to the oral presentation. In contrast, some denigrate epideictic oratory on the basis that it is mere ornamentation or empty style; such a portrayal, however, is inappropriate. Aristotle's purpose is to differentiate three types of speech and the characteristics they possess. As many scholars have noted, all three genres fit into his broader category of rhetoric, and thus each constitutes "available means of persuasion."

Aristotle recognizes that individual speeches may contain elements of each of the categories. For example, he describes how an epideictic speech may include reference to past events and speculations about the future. Aristotle's designation of categories (deliberative, forensic, and epideictic) was an attempt to characterize the oratory of his day. The epideictic category specifically grouped together that oratory that placed the audience in the role of spectator. From his first explanation of it, though, it is clear that he never meant the categories to be seen as a rigid set of boxes into which all possible speeches fit. His original explanation takes the position that a given speech can contain characteristics or elements of more than one of the genres.

Epideictic Speech Prior to Aristotle

Aristotle's classification codified a genre of discourse that did not exist prior to his act of naming it. Although the word *epideictic* was used prior to Aristotle, his use of the term as a specific category of speech was unique. Previous discursive practices were not formalized or thought of in the categories given to them by Aristotle. A fuller understanding of this genre is gained through an examination of the various subgenres that Aristotle drew together to create the epideictic category. Some scholars have concluded that the best way to understand epideictic oratory is as Aristotle's "miscellaneous" category. In this way forensic and deliberative oratory become the primary categories, and epideictic is simply the place to put everything that does not qualify as either of these. Such a perspective on epideictic is unnecessary, as a closer look at what constituted the genre will show. Aristotle's epideictic genre brought together three prominent speech forms existent in the ancient world: the *epitaphios logos, encomium,* and *panegyric.*

The *epitaphios logos* was a eulogy delivered in ancient Athens for those who had died in battle. An annual, public ceremony, it was unique to Athens among Greek states; its purpose was to glorify the state and the values and ideals championed by the state. Only a handful of such funeral orations (*epitaphios logos*) are extant; perhaps the most well known is Pericles' funeral oration as recorded by the historian Thucydides. In introducing this funeral oration by Pericles, Thucydides describes how Athens buried her dead and then had an individual chosen by the state deliver a eulogy. Funeral orations were orations given for particular sociopolitical purposes. On the surface the purpose was to glorify and make heros out of those who had fallen in battle and to praise the state. Behind both of these objectives was the goal of persuading the living that dying in battle for Athens, or having one's husband or son so die, was honorable. It may be that Aristotle, not a native of Athens, had less reverence for the *epitaphios logos* and thus sought to reduce its importance by subsuming it in the larger category of epideictic.

Panegyric, or festival orations, were speeches given at ceremonial occasions and public festivals in Greek cities. The most prominent example of such a festival is the Olympic games. The common elements in the panegyric were praise for the festival itself and the god associated with it, praise for the king or city officials, praise for the city in which it was held, and praise for the contest (such as an athletic event) that would take place during the festival.

Finally, *encomia* were speeches that recounted the deeds and accomplishments of a particular individual. Perhaps the two most prominent examples of this form are encomiums to Helen of Troy by Gorgias and Isocrates. Helen was blamed for inciting the Trojan War by leaving her husband, Menelaus, and eloping to the city of Troy with Paris. Gorgias' encomium details several reasons why Helen cannot be blamed for her actions, because yielding to Paris was unavoidable and inevitable. Isocrates' encomium to Helen praises Helen's actions on the basis that her actions saved the Greeks from becoming slaves. He contends: "Helen is the cause of our not being slaves to the Barbarians." Isocrates' claim is that the Trojan War united the Greeks to a degree that they had not been united before the war.

Thus if we examine classical oratory prior to Aristotle, we see that Aristotle's epideictic genre was a fusion of several preexistent forms. This makes the study of epideictic oratory somewhat muddled, because the determination of what counts in the category is dependent on the definition one gives to the word *epideixeis* prior to Aristotle's *On Rhetoric.* Broader definitions include more speeches and more orators than do more narrow definitions. Because the narrow, technical definition of the word originated with Aristotle, however, it is best to adopt the broader, looser definition in its occurrence in texts prior to *On Rhetoric.* Aristotle's two most prominent contemporaries were Plato and Isocrates. Nearly all of their writings preceded Aristotle yet occurred in the same century. As such, a look at epideictic in their works gives us an excellent look at pre-Aristotelian epideictic. A brief examination of the way they employed the word gives us a snapshot of what *epideictic* referred to before it was named and categorized by Aristotle.

Epideictic oratory has often been vilified on the grounds that it favors "style" over "substance." This response, and the dichotomy that draws it out, originate with Plato who held a similar opinion of epideictic. Plato often uses the word in its most general sense, as "to display or show," in reference to a public presentation of literature or speech. He also uses the word, however, to refer to the speeches of his competitors, in a sarcastic way, in the sense of "mere" display.

Isocrates (b. 436 B.C.E.) is the most prominent example of an epideictic orator. Because he preceded Aristotle by approximately fifty years, he is also a good source for an insight into epideictic speech prior to Aristotle's categorization. Early in his career Isocrates wrote judicial speeches for pay, but he later turned to political and ceremonial speech forms.

In the works of Isocrates, we find uses of the word *epideictic* prior to its designation as a category by Aristotle. He uses *epideixeis* to refer to oratory that evidences style or that is carefully crafted. Often it is a term he employs to criticize the oratory of others as "mere" display or showing off. Isocrates, however, also views epideictic in a more positive fashion. For example, in the *Panegyricus* (c. 380 B.C.E.) Isocrates describes his own oratory: He seeks to employ "the highest kind of oratory" and characterizes "highest" oratory as possessing two qualities. First, the highest oratory "deals with the greatest affairs" of individuals and life. Second, the highest oratory deals with these affairs "while best displaying (*epideiknuousi*) the ability of those who speak." The reason Isocrates seeks to speak in this way is that this type of oratory "brings most profit to those who hear" (4). Later, he differentiates between discourse that evidences "a plainness of style" and that which has been "elaborated with extreme care." He links the former oratory to the courtroom and labels the latter epideictic (11).

Isocrates anticipated Aristotle in that he used epideictic to refer to a characteristic of orations. Broadly speaking, epideictic orations were crafted with great care and exhibited a high degree of style. More specifically, epideictic orations were those that were prepared for a festival or ceremonial event.

Thus, in utilizing epideictic to refer to a class of oratory that included several subtypes, Aristotle chose a word (*epideictic*) that had been used as a more general term for a type of oratory or a characteristic that oratory may have and gave it a technical or specific meaning. Aristotle took a word that had been used to describe specific speeches or a characteristic that speeches could possess and made it into a term that designated a class of oratory.

Epideictic Oratory after Aristotle

It may be helpful to view the history of epideictic as a funnel that first narrows to Aristotle's *On Rhetoric* (where the genre is formed as the confluence of several types) and then broadens again after his day. This broadening includes the inevitable specialization and differentiation that awaits every classification. Finally, the continuation of epideictic oratory stretches to the present day in political, religious, and civic realms.

The broadening of the genre of epideictic oratory can be seen in the writings of Quintilian and Cicero. These authors place both poetry and history within its sphere. Cicero combines epideictic oratory with history and notes how the category differs from discourse that is employed in the law courts and public assemblies (*Orator* 207). Quintilian notes the similarity between epideictic oratory and poetry and then, like Cicero, draws the link to history (*Institutio* X.1.28.31,33). Scholars employing a broad definition of epideictic (for example, as consisting of the elements of praise or blame) locate the genre in the poetry, history, and philosophy of the classical period following Aristotle.

Two Roman authors, Dionysius of Halicarnassus and Menander of Laodicea, discuss epideictic oratory in detail. Dionysius, a first-century author, describes several forms of epideictic oratory in detail in his *Art of Rhetoric*. These include *panegyric* (a festival oration), *gamelion* (a speech given at a marriage), *genethliac* (a speech given at a birthday), *epithalamion* (a speech given on the bride's arrival at her new home), *prosphonetic* (a speech given to a ruler), *epitaphios logos* (a funeral oration), and athletic *protreptic a* (speech given at the athletic games). Dionysius lists the particular content and the arrangement of sections to be included in each form.

Two handbooks on epideictic are attributed to the third-century C.E. author Menander of Laodicea. Like the work of Dionysius, they detail various forms of epideictic and the content appropriate for each. Interestingly, Menander begins by defining epideictic oratory as speeches of praise or blame and then proceeds to discuss only speeches of praise. He traces twenty-three types or forms of praise (including praise of a city, praise of a ruler, and praise of a harbor).

The history of epideictic oratory subsequent to this period includes examples from various realms of society, including the political, religious, and civil. An historical investigation into each of these gives testimony to the importance of epideictic oratory in human affairs from the classical period to the present.

Chaïm Perelman and Lucie Olbrechts-Tyteca in *The New Rhetoric* bring a new perspective on epideictic oratory. They first describe how epideictic oratory became associated more with literature than argumentation. They then set out to bring it back into the latter realm. Specifically, they describe how epideictic oratory elevates adherence to the values already held by an audience. Furthermore, they describe how this heightened adherence to particular values is a key component of persuasion.

This perspective on epideictic is helpful and draws our attention to other contemporary examples of this genre. For example, we can recall Abraham Lincoln's Gettysburg Address, in which he honored those who had fallen in the battle at Gettysburg and elevated the values of belief in God and the equality of individuals. And we can remember President Ronald Reagan's address to the nation on January 28, 1986, following the explosion of the space shuttle *Challenger*. He mourned the loss of the seven astronauts while at the same time he elevated the values of exploration, research, and the U.S. space program. These speeches are contemporary examples of the *epitaphios logos* and fall within Aristotle's categorization of epideictic oratory.

Presidential inaugurations, religious speeches and presentations, and graduation speeches all share characteristics of the ancient category of epideictic oratory. In such speeches rhetors engage in praise or blame and hold up particular values as laudatory and worthy. In such circumstances, the speakers address an audience composed of spectators and not judges. And, in most cases, such speakers seek to present discourse that is well crafted and engaging for the audience. Contemporary epideictic orators would do well to seek Isocrates' conception of the ideal speech: one that deals with the most significant affairs and brings out the best qualities and abilities of the speaker.

David M. Timmerman
Indiana University, Kokomo

Bibliography

Aristotle. *On Rhetoric*. Trans. George A. Kennedy. New York: Oxford UP, 1991.

Burgess, Theodore C. "Epideictic Literature." *University of Chicago Studies in Classical Philology* 3 (1902): 89–254.

Carter, Michael F. "The Ritual Functions of Epideictic Rhetoric: The Case of Socrates' Funeral Oration." *Rhetorica* 9 (1991): 209–32.

Chase, J. Richard. "The Classical Conception of Epideictic." *Quarterly Journal of Speech* 47 (1961): 293–300.

Cole, Thomas. *The Origins of Rhetoric in Ancient Greece*. Baltimore: Johns Hopkins UP, 1991.

Kennedy, George A. *The Art of Persuasion in Greece*. Princeton: Princeton UP, 1963.

———. *Classical Rhetoric and Its Christian and Secular Tradition from Ancient to Modern Times*. Chapel Hill: U of North Carolina P, 1980.

Oravec, Christine. "'Observation' in Aristotle's Theory of Epideictic." *Philosophy and Rhetoric* 9 (1976): 162–74.

Perelman, Chaïm, and L. Olbrechts-Tyteca. *The New Rhetoric: A Treatise on Argumentation*. Trans. John Wilkinson and Purcell Weaver. Notre Dame, IN: U of Notre Dame P, 1969.

Poulakos, Takis. "Towards a Cultural Understanding of Classical Epideictic Oratory." *PRE/TEXT* 9 (1988): 147–65.

Epiphora

The placement of the same word or words at the end of two or more clauses. The Psalmist was using epiphora in writing, "O Israel, trust thou in the Lord: he is their help and their shield. O house of Aaron, trust in the Lord: he is their help and their shield. Ye that fear the Lord, trust in the Lord: he is their help and their shield" (Psalm 115:9). Like its opposite, anaphora (q.v.), epiphora can create an emphatic rhythm that acquires a special emotional charge because the repeated word is used to conclude the sentence or passage. "I'll have my bond! Speak not against my bond! I have sworn an oath that I will have my bond" (*Merchant of Venice* 3.3).

Arthur Quinn and Lyon Rathbun
University of California, Berkeley

Epistemic Rhetoric

A term that came into use with Scott's essay in 1967. It was picked up and used in a number of subsequent essays and books that addressed the question of the relation of rhetoric and "truth," which, in the Western tradition, owes its shape to Plato's questioning of rhetoric. The fundamental effort in the late twentieth century has been to establish rhetorric on a different footing from that of "handmaiden of truth," a phrase common in medieval and Renaissance texts and one that can be read back into the famous opening of Aristotle's *Rhetoric,* that rhetoric is the counterpart of dialectic.

The claim made by the statement "Rhetoric is epistemic," which rather quickly became nearly an aphorism or a battle cry, is that rhetoric itself is a way of knowing, that is, that a test of the merit of ideas and actions is persuasiveness and, moreover, that in acting truth is created.

The notion suggests that the ancient sophists, rather than Plato or even Aristotle, might better guide late twentieth-century rhetoricians in establishing the grounds for an art that would be practical in a world in which diversity is a challenge—that is, the circumstances in which humans are caught and must cope if decent lives are to be possible.

Those who adhere to the claim may well be indebted to the existentialism of the post–World War II era and tend to strike a hermeneutic pose. If so, the word *epistemic* may be noisy in that the idea traditionally closely associated with it, "knowledge," might better be replaced with "understanding," "interpretation," or both. "Knowledge" suggests certainty, and the claim seems to argue that no certainty is possible. Only arguments can be crafted and maintained as the world and human perceptions of it evolve.

In 1978 Leff argued that the claim that rhetoric is epistemic marked the dominant trend in contemporary rhetorical theorizing and posed a number of questions that begged for answers. By that time, some writers attracted by the phrase were deeply concerned by the relativistic suggestions that they found in other adherents of the claim, and wrote to sustain the claim in light of a realistic ontology.

In the 1990s, the energy that had coalesced in a loose debate on the nature and efficacy of the assertion that "rhetoric is epistemic" seems to be playing out. The participants are inclined to shift from an either/or to a both/and stance, modulating what has been the stronger relativistic/realistic claims. If so, it is possible that the controversy has served its purposes or at least shifted focus to the "rhetoric of inquiry" movement, which burgeoned in the 1980s. The early advocates, to be consistent with their claims, will have to agree that if those have any degree of validity, they should be expected to be absorbed as the conversation about the concept of rhetoric evolves.

In 1990 Barry Brummett wrote "A Eulogy for Epistemic Rhetoric," suggesting that those interested in the phrase had erred in failing to take seriously enough the task of turning their abstractions to hard criticism of current discourse. An early landmark in the debate, even though the phrase was not prominent in the essay, is Brummett's 1976 essay in *Philosophy and Rhetoric*. That essay featured the intersubjectivism that has become rather generally accepted by most participants now and tends to mark current rethinking of rhetorical history and efforts to keep the conversation about rhetoric and truth going.

Robert L. Scott
University of Minnesota

Bibliography

Brummett, Barry. "A Eulogy for Epistemic Rhetoric." *Quarterly Journal of Speech* 76 (1990): 69–72.

———. "Some Implications of 'Process' and 'Intersubjectivity': Postmodern Rhetoric." *Philosophy and Rhetoric* 9 (1976): 21–51.

Cherwitz, R.A., and J.W. Hikens. *Communication and Knowledge: An Investigation in Rhetorical Epistemology.* U of South Carolina P, 1986.

Leff, Michael. "In Search of Ariadne's Thread: A Review of Recent Literature on Rhetorical Theory." *Central States Speech Journal* 29 (1978): 73–91.

Scott, Robert L. "On Viewing Rhetoric as Epistemic." *Central States Speech Journal* 18 (1967): 9–17.

———. "On Viewing Rhetoric as Epistemic: Ten Years Later." *Central States Speech Journal* 27 (1976): 258–66.

Epizeuxis

The emphatic repetition of a word with no other words between. "My God, my God, why hast thou forsaken me?" (Psalms 22.1). "O Jerusalem, Jerusalem, thou that killest the prophets, and stonest them which are sent unto thee" (Matthew 23:37). Epizeuxis can be used to express strong emotion or to emphasize a nuance, as Ortega y Gasset did in writing "Curiosity is almost, almost, the definition of frivolity." In writing "O dark, dark, dark, amid the blaze of noon," Milton was emphasizing the contrast between two elements. Epizeuxis can even be used to evoke suggestive sound, as Pope did in writing "To the swinging and the ringing / Of the bells, bells, bells—/ Of the bells, bells, bells, bells, / Bells, bells, bells."

Arthur Quinn and Lyon Rathbun
University of California, Berkeley

Erasmus, Desiderius (1469–1536)

Known especially for his views on style and *copia*. Erasmus was born in Holland, the illegitimate son of a priest. He entered the Augustinian order (the same order to which Martin Luther belonged) in 1488 and was ordained in 1492. As Latin secretary to the Bishop of Cambrai, he traveled to Paris to study theology. From Paris, Erasmus went to England in 1499, where he befriended the humanists John Colet and Thomas More. In 1500 he returned to the Continent to study Greek and work on a new, textually accurate Greek New Testament, which was published in 1516. The book was tremendously influential for the model of humanist scholarship it presented and for encouraging theologians to focus their study more on the early Church Fathers than on scholastic commentaries.

When Henry VIII, of whom the humanists had great hopes of patronage, ascended the throne in 1509, Erasmus returned to England. On that journey he began *The Praise of Folly* (1511) as a gift for More, who would be his host. The work is a satire on scholarly and religious pretensions, including the search for a universal method. Thomas O. Sloane argues that Erasmus, through the persona of Folly, identifies himself with the Greek sophists and their method of exploring arguments through contraries, or *dissoi logoi*, as well as their belief that human knowledge is uncertain and inevitably subject to dispute. Erasmus would, in 1524, attack Martin Luther for claiming that human reason could achieve certainty in religious matters, such as whether or not there was free will.

In England, Erasmus accepted a lectureship in Greek at Cambridge, which he held until 1514. Around 1511 he wrote *Copia: Foundations of the Abundant Style* (usually called *On Copia*) as a Latin textbook for John Colet's new humanist school. This work dominated rhetoric instruction throughout northern Europe for most of the sixteenth century. *On Copia* is divided into two books, the first on "abundance of expression" or "of words" and the second "abundance of subject-matter" or "of ideas." Book I is divided into 206 chapters that catalog a wide variety of figures, tropes, and other methods of amplification. In addition to discussing stylistic devices such as metalepsis, metonymy, and synecdoche, Erasmus lists many ways of expressing syntactic relationships. For example, Chapter 129, "Nothing But," contains the following examples: "You are nothing but a poet, you are nothing else but a poet, you are nothing other than a poet," and so on. Chapter 33 contains the famous example of 150 ways to say "your letter pleased me very much."

The stylistic focus of *On Copia* is typical of many rhetoric texts of the period, Ciceronian and Ramist. Erasmus's relationship to stylistic rhetoric is subtle, however. On the one hand, he opposed the evolution of Italian humanist rhetoric in the direction of courtly conversation. He was distrustful of *sprezzatura,* thought the good style should display learning and wit, and both defended and exemplified the principle that the eloquent man of wisdom should take public stands on important issues of the day. On the other hand, Erasmus valued stylistic ornamentation. Like Cicero, he believed that the most accomplished rhetorician was one who could turn from amplitude to terseness as the situation required. Even during Erasmus's lifetime, however, stylistic elaboration began to cloy some palates. By the turn of the seventeenth century, *copia* was under attack by advocates of the new science and their plainer style.

Bruce Herzberg
Bentley College

Bibliography

Bainton, Roland. *Erasmus of Christendom.* New York: Scribner's, 1969.

Kahn, Victoria. *Rhetoric, Prudence and Scepticism in the Renaissance.* Ithaca, NY: Cornell UP, 1985.

Kaiser, Walter. *Praisers of Folly.* Cambridge, MA: Harvard UP, 1963.

Sloane, Thomas O. *Donne, Milton, and the End of Humanistic Rhetoric.* Berkeley: U of California P, 1985: 72–84.

Thompson, Sister Geraldine. *Under Pretext of Praise.* Toronto: U of Toronto P, 1973.

See also COPIA

Eristic

The branch of rhetoric that deals specifically with controversy or disputation. Benjamin Jowett, the nineteenth-century translator of Plato, succinctly defined it as "the art of fighting with words." The term is derived from the Greek word for strife, *eris*; Homer, for example, says that Athene stirred up *eris* between Agamemnon and Menelaos (*Odyssey* 3.136). For the pre-Socratic philosopher Heraclitus, *eris* seems to denote rivalry as a principle of nature whereby interaction between opposites is the origin of all change.

It is likely that the adjectival form *eristike* was first used to denote a special kind of rhetoric early in the fourth century B.C.E. Schiappa argues that Plato coined the term to mean "seeking victory in argument." The practice so named certainly predates Plato however, and most likely developed among the older sophists of the fifth century B.C.E.

In *Lives of the Great Philosophers*, Diogenes Laertius used the term *eristic* in connection with two of the older sophists, Euclides of Megara and Protagoras of Abdera. Euclides "inspired the Megarians with a frenzied love of controversy," which may explain why some sources refer to eristic as "the Megarian school." Diogenes Laertius credits Protagoras with writing a book titled *The Art of Eristic (Technê Eristikon).* He also says that Protagoras was "the first to institute contests in debating . . . and the first to show how to attack and refute any proposition" (9.52–53; Hicks's translation). An emphasis on either competition or refutation might well have been described as eristic by dialecticians of succeeding generations.

Such methods, though quite appropriate for fifth-century applications in oratorical displays and contests and in legal speeches, were not well adapted to establishing a form of discourse for philosophical speculation. Hence, Plato, Isocrates, and Aristotle were all critical of eristic practices. In *Sophist,* Plato compared a contentious speaker to a prizefighter whose goal is victory rather than knowledge or truth: Eristic lacks legitimacy because it countenances ambiguity. Isocrates offered detailed criticism of other speech teachers in *Against the Sophists* and *Antidosis.* He attacked his contemporaries for their ignorance and defects of character in general, but in particular for their claims to be able to teach standard techniques guaranteeing success.

Aristotle wrote of eristic as both a branch of rhetoric and a type of reasoning. In *Rhetoric* he included eristic among activities that give pleasure—at least to those who have the experience and ability to secure victory (1371a). In a list of ten fallacies, he criticized a specific use of apparent syllogism in eristic (1402a). In *Topics* eristic is identified as one of four types of reasoning, and distinguished from the three others (demonstration, dialectic, and false reasoning): "Reasoning is eristic if it is based on opinions which appear to be generally accepted but are not really so" (100b). In *Sophistical Refutations* eristic is called an unfair kind of fighting (171b).

What these later critics called eristic seems to have emerged in fifth-century Athens as a pragmatic response to political and juridical conditions. It was a loose category of techniques and formulas rather than an organized school of thought. The term, however, has always carried a somewhat pejorative sense. The term *rhetoric* is itself often deployed in much the same way in present-day popular usage.

Janet B. Davis
Northeast Missouri State University

Bibliography

Aristotle. *On Rhetoric.* Trans. George A. Kennedy. New York: Oxford UP, 1991.

———. *Sophistical Refutations.* Trans. E.S. Forster. Cambridge, MA: Harvard UP, 1955.

———. *Topics.* Trans. E.S. Forster. Cambridge, MA: Harvard UP, 1976.

Diogenes Laertius. *Lives of the Great Philosophers.* Trans. R.D. Hicks. 2 vols. Cambridge, MA: Harvard UP, 1959.

Isocrates. *Against the Sophists and Antidosis. Isocrates 2.* Trans. George Norlin. New York: Putnams, 1929. 162–365.

Kerferd, G.B. "Dialectic, Antilogic, and Eristic." *The Sophistic Movement.* Cambridge: Cambridge UP, 1981. 59–67.

Plato. *Plato's Sophist.* Trans. Seth Bernadete. Chicago: U of Chicago P, 1986.

Schiappa, Edward. *Protagoras and Logos: A Study in Greek Philosophy and Rhetoric.* Columbia: U of South Carolina P, 1991.

Ethics

Involves issues and standards concerning degrees of right and wrong, of virtue and vice, and of obligation in human conduct. In Western cultures, for example, such standards as honesty, truthfulness, promise-keeping, justice, fairness, and humaneness typically are used to judge the ethicality of human behavior and practices. Some philosophers draw distinctions between ethics and morals as concepts. Other philosophers use the terms *ethics* and *morals* more or less interchangeably—as will be the case here.

Ethical issues arise in human conduct whenever that behavior could have significant impact on other persons, when it involves conscious choice of means and ends, and when the behavior can be judged by standards of right and wrong. Potential ethical issues thus are inherent in rhetoric because it can be judged on a right-wrong dimension, because it involves potential significant influence on other humans, and because the rhetor (persuader, advocate, arguer) consciously chooses specific ends sought and communicative means to achieve those ends.

Ethical concerns have been central to rhetorical theory and practice at least since Plato condemned rhetoric as sophistry in a negative sense and characterized rhetoric as no more intellectually respectable than mere cookery. In contrast, Aristotle in his *Rhetoric* described rhetoric as an "offshoot" of ethics. Contemporary rhetorical theorists Richard M. Weaver in *The Ethics of Rhetoric* (6, 24) and Kenneth Burke in *The Rhetoric of Religion* (41, 187) argue that all human use of language necessarily involves matters of ethical responsibility.

Ethical Responsibility

Rhetors' ethical responsibilities may stem from a status or position they have earned or been granted, from established ethical principles, from commitments (promises, pledges, agreements) they have made, or from subsequent consequences (effects, impacts) of their rhetoric on others. Responsibility includes the elements of fulfilling duties and obligations, of being accountable to other individuals and groups, of being evaluated by agreed-upon standards, and of being accountable to our own conscience.

The ethics of rhetoric also should encompass both individual and social ethics. What are the ethical virtues of character and the central ethical standards that should guide an individual's choices? What are the ethical standards and responsibilities that should guide the rhetoric of organizations and institutions? For an ethically suspect rhetorical practice, where should individual and collective responsibility be placed? The study of rhetorical ethics should suggest standards both for individual daily and context-bound choices and also for institutional/systemic policies and practices.

Whether persuaders seem intentionally and knowingly to use particular content or techniques is a factor most persons take into account in judging degree of ethicality. If a dubious rhetorical choice seems to stem more from accident, from an unintentional slip of the tongue, or even from ignorance, often people are less harsh in their ethical assessment. In contrast, it can be argued that rhetors have an ethical obligation to verify the soundness of their evidence, reasoning, and terms prior to presentation to others; careless preparation should not be an adequate excuse to lessen the harshness of ethical judgment.

In assessing the ethics of rhetoric, a persistent question is, Does the *end* justify the *means?* Does the necessity for achieving a goal widely acknowledged as worthwhile always justify the use of ethically questionable techniques? To say that the end does not *always* justify the means is not to say that ends *never* justify means. The rhetor's goal simply should be considered as one of a number of potentially relevant ethical criteria from among which the most relevant and appropriate standards are selected. Under some circumstances, such as a threat to physical survival, the goal of personal or national security might *temporarily* take precedence over other relevant ethical criteria such as promise-keeping or truthfulness. A number of scholars have argued that rhetorical *means* employed can have effects on audience thought and decision-making habits *apart from* and in addition to the specific end that the rhetor seeks. No matter the purpose they serve, the arguments, appeals, structure, and language the rhetor chooses do

partly shape the audience's values, thinking habits, language patterns, and level of trust.

Rhetorical Ethics and the Audience

In most public and private rhetoric, a fundamental implied contract or unspoken assumption is that words can be trusted and people will be truthful. Unless there are reasons to be skeptical, audiences expect rhetors to mean what they say. Even if rhetors do not know the absolutely certain "ultimate truth" about something, audiences expect rhetors to say what they believe to be true and not to say what they believe to be false. Various types of rhetorical settings, rhetorical roles, and specific situations also may have unspoken expectations that help define the ethical relationship between persuader and audience. For example, one's expectations concerning honesty, accuracy, and relevance of information probably differ when involved with an American Cancer Society representative persuading one to contribute funds or with the stereotypical used-car dealer. If the Cancer Society representative intentionally uses false statistics, the ethics of that choice could be condemned because the audience does not expect a representative of a reputable humanitarian society to use questionable techniques; in such a situation, the audience would be especially vulnerable.

What are the ethics of audience adaptation? To what degree is it ethical for advocates to alter their ideas and proposals in order to adapt to the needs, capacities, desires, and expectations of an audience? To secure acceptance, some rhetors adapt to their audience to the extreme of so changing their idea that the idea is no longer really theirs. These rhetors merely say what the audience wants them to say regardless of their own convictions. On the other hand, some degree of adaptation in language choice, supporting materials, organization, and presentation to reflect and respect the specific nature of the audience is a crucial part of successful and responsible rhetoric. Rhetors must decide on an appropriate ethical position between their idea in its pure form and that idea modified to achieve maximum impact with an audience.

What are the ethical responsibilities of audience members, of readers and listeners as cocreators of meaning with rhetors? The image held of the rhetorical process may influence the answer to this question. Audience members would seem to bear little responsibility if they are viewed as inert, passive, defenseless receptacles, as mindless blotters uncritically accepting arguments and ideas. In contrast, rhetoric today is typically viewed as a transaction in which both rhetor and audience bear degrees of mutual responsibility to participate actively in the process. This image of audience members as active participants can suggest various responsibilities. Johannesen (135–37) explores two major audience ethical responsibilities: reasoned skepticism and appropriate feedback.

Six "perspectives" for ethical assessment of rhetoric follow. Each perspective represents a major viewpoint or conceptual lens that scholars explicitly, and others often implicitly, use to judge the ethics of rhetoric. These perspectives are not mutually exclusive, nor are they exhaustive of possible stances.

Political Perspectives

A political system (system of government) usually contains within its ideology an implicit and explicit set of values and procedures accepted as crucial to the health and growth of that governmental system. Once these essential political values are identified for a political system, ethical standards for evaluating rhetorical means and ends within that particular system can be derived from those values. The assumption is that rhetoric should foster realization of these values and that communication techniques and tactics that retard, subvert, or circumvent these fundamental political values should be condemned as unethical.

Naturally, each different system of government (such as Italian Fascism, Soviet Communism, or German Nazism) might embody differing values leading to differing ethical judgments. Within the context of American representative democracy, for instance, various analysts pinpoint values and procedures they view as fundamental to optimum functioning of that political system. Rooted in such values and procedures, Haiman espouses a "degree of rationality" ethical standard, and Nilsen develops a "significant choice" rhetorical ethic. Wallace advocates the "four moralities": Habit of Search, Habit of Justice, Habit of Preferring Public to Private Motivations, and Habit of Respect for Dissent.

Human Nature Perspectives

Human nature perspectives, as considered here, focus on the *essence* of human nature. Unique characteristics of human nature that set humans apart from other living things are identified. The assumption is that uniquely human attributes should be enhanced, thereby promot-

ing fulfillment of maximum human potential. Audiences could judge the degree to which a rhetor's appeals and techniques either foster or undermine the development of fundamental human characteristics. They would condemn as unethical a technique that dehumanizes, that makes a person less than human. Both rhetors and audiences could use human nature perspectives to assess the ethics of rhetoric regardless of situation, culture, religion, or governmental form; the assumption would be that a human is essentially human no matter the context.

While they recognize Aristotle's belief that the capacity for rationality is one defining characteristic of humans, Rowland and Womack interpret Aristotle's ethic of rhetoric to be summarized as follows: the sound, relevant, integrated use of both reason and emotion in the service of practical wisdom and the general public good. Wieman and Walter develop an ethic for rhetoric that focuses on the two uniquely human attributes of symbol-using capacity and the need for human beings of other humans. Johnstone roots his rhetorical ethical duties of resoluteness, openness, gentleness, and compassion in the distinctly human capacity to persuade and be persuaded. Scott bases his suggestions for an "epistemic" ethic of rhetoric on the unique human capacity to generate or create knowledge through the rhetorical process itself. And Eubanks advocates an ethic for rhetoric founded on the central human capacity to create and sustain values and to apply them in rendering value judgments.

Dialogical Perspectives

Dialogical perspectives emerge from scholarship on the nature of communication as dialogue rather than monologue. The works of philosopher Martin Buber and humanistic psychologist Carl Rogers have proven seminal in the development of such perspectives. Dialogical perspectives contend that attitudes toward each other among participants in communication are an index of the ethical level of that communication. Dialogical attitudes are held to be more fully human, humane, and facilitative of self-fulfillment than are monological attitudes.

Communication as *dialogue* is characterized by such attitudes as authenticity, inclusion, confirmation, presentness, mutual equality, honesty, concern for the welfare of others, trust, open-mindedness, respect, humility, lack of pretense, nonmanipulative intent, sincerity, encouragement of free expression, and acceptance of others as persons with intrinsic worth regardless of differences over belief or behavior. Communication as *monologue,* in contrast, is marked by deception, superiority, exploitation, dogmatism, insincerity, pretense, personal self-display, self-aggrandizement, judgmentalism that stifles expression, coercion, possessiveness, condescension, self-defensiveness, and the viewing of others as objects to be manipulated. Communication as dialogue flowers most naturally in private, two-person, face-to-face oral communication settings that extend, even intermittently, over lengthy periods of time. Nevertheless, Johannesen (57–77) contends that dialogical perspectives apply in varying degrees to public oral and written discourse, and he explores an ethic for rhetoric rooted in dialogue.

Situational Perspectives
Situational perspectives focus *regularly* and *primarily* on elements of the specific rhetorical situation at hand. Most perspectives discussed here (and others) make some allowances, on occasion, for the modified application of ethical criteria in special circumstances. An extreme situational perspective, however, *routinely* makes ethical judgments *only* in light of each different context. Among the concrete situational factors relevant to making a purely situational ethical evaluation are (1) the role or function of the rhetor for the audience; (2) audience standards for reasonableness and appropriateness; (3) degree of audience awareness and approval of the rhetor's techniques; (4) degree of urgency for implementation of the rhetor's proposal; (5) audience goals and values; and (6) specific audience standards for ethical discourse. From a primarily situational perspective, Rogge argues that unlabeled hyperbole is ethical in a political campaign, that imperiled national security could justify use of otherwise unethical rhetorical techniques, and that in some situations an acknowledged leader has the responsibility to rally support by using emotional appeals that circumvent human rational choice. Also to be explored from situational perspectives could be the nature of ethical standards that should apply to the rhetoric of protest, agitation, and social movements (Johannesen 82–88).

Religious Perspectives
Religious perspectives stem from the moral and spiritual values, guidelines, and rules embodied in the ideology and sacred literature of various religions. Criteria derived from a religion could be used to assess the ethics of rhetoric. For example, the Bible warns against lying, slander, and bearing false witness. Taoist religion stresses empathy and insight rather than reason and logic as roads to truth; citing facts and demonstrating logical conclusions are minimized in favor of feeling and intuition. Griffin (27–41) develops an ethic for Christian evangelism that describes, through the analogy of love, the true lover, nonlover, flirt, seducer, rapist, smother lover, and legalistic lover. Jensen compares the monotheistic Judaic, Christian, and Islamic traditions with the Asiatic religions of Confucianism, Taoism, Hinduism, and Buddhism in a search for potential standards for ethical rhetoric.

Utilitarian Perspectives
Utilitarian perspectives emphasize criteria of usefulness, pleasure, and happiness to assess rhetorical ethics. Some utilitarians expand the concept of happiness to include such intrinsically good consequences as health, friendship, and knowledge. The utilitarian standard for evaluating rhetorical means and ends could be phrased as a question: Does the technique or goal promote the greatest good for the greatest number of people in the long run? Brockriede synthesizes a standard for ethical rhetoric from the influential utilitarian view of English philosopher Jeremy Bentham. Brembeck and Howell (225–47) develop a "social utility" ethic for persuasion that stresses usefulness to the people affected, survival potential for groups involved, and benefits and harms central to a culture's value system.

Some Emerging Perspectivess
Rhetoricians and philosophers continue to explore the constituents of additional ethical positions that profitably may inform the ethics of rhetoric. In *The Abuse of Casuistry*, Albert Jonsen and Stephen Toulmin argue for the rehabilitation and modern adaptation of casuistry (or paradigm case ethics)—a method for ethical reasoning and judgment developed from ancient Greek times through the sixteenth century and a method that could encompass general rules and particular circumstances. Smith explores the use of the casuistic method for the rhetoric of physicians, and Boeyink views casuistry as useful for journalistic ethics. Another issue probed by scholars is the possibility of ethical standards for cross-cultural or intercultural communication. Can there be an overarching, transcendent ethic for rhetoric between people of different cultures? Is the Golden Rule at all adequate for cross-cultural discourse if the person from the other cul-

ture does not wish to be treated as I would like to be treated? Johannesen (216–20) evaluates several sets of suggested ethical standards for cross-cultural rhetoric. In *Ethnic Ethics*, Anthony Cortese attempts to restructure moral theory away from absolute, certain, universal ethical norms to contingent and culture-bound ethics.

An emphasis on duties, obligations, rules, principles, and the resolution of complex ethical dilemmas has dominated the contemporary philosophy of ethics. This dominant emphasis has been true whether as variations on Immanuel Kant's categorical imperative, John Rawls's depersonalized veil of ignorance to determine justice, on statements of intrinsic ultimate good, or on Jeremy Bentham's or John Stuart Mill's utilitarian views. The past several decades, however, have witnessed a growing interest among ethicists in a largely ignored tradition that goes back at least as far as Plato's and Aristotle's philosophies of ethics. This largely bypassed tradition typically is called virtue ethics or character ethics. Most ethicists of virtue or character see that perspective as a crucial complement to the current dominant ethical theories. Ethicists describe virtues variously as deep-rooted dispositions, habits, skills, or traits of character that incline persons to perceive, feel, and act in ethically right and sensitive ways. Also they describe virtues as learned, acquired, cultivated, reinforced, capable of modification, capable of conflicting, and ideally coalesced into a harmonious cluster. Johannesen (1991) explores at length the implications of virtue ethics for the role of "character" in contemporary American political rhetoric. Herrick examines the nature of rhetorical virtues as rooted in rhetoric as a human practice.

Feminist scholars offer critiques of male-dominated ethical traditions with special focus on ways in which traditional ethics have functioned to subordinate or trivialize women's ethical experience; rather, the moral experiences of women and men are worthy of equal respect (Jaggar). Among other things, feminist ethicists question the privileging of rationality over emotion, of universalizability and detachment over particularity and engagement, of the public sphere of discourse over the private sphere, and of individualism over relationships. Feminist scholars argue the case against sexist language, and some argue for the necessity to slant the truth in order to survive in a male-dominated world. Steiner explores the implications of feminist perspectives for an adequate ethics of communication. Gilligan, Noddings, and Manning are three feminist scholars who examine an ethic of care rooted in relationships, interdependence of self and others, compassion and nurturance, and concrete responsibilities as an equal complement to the presently dominant ethic of justice rooted in individual autonomy, impartial rules, rights, and a logic of equality and fairness. In evolution are both a specifically feminist ethic of rhetoric (as part of feminist conceptions of the rhetorical process) and an ethic of rhetoric inclusive of feminist perspectives.

Postmodern theorists and social critics problematize modernist assumptions of truth, reality, and knowledge as certain, immutable, transparent, universal, solely discovered by pure rationality, and uncontaminated by power and historical conditions. Postmodern perspectives see theories as only partial views of their objects and see knowledge, reality, and truth as contingent, constructed in communication, and conditioned by historical circumstances. Most postmodernists question the notion of an autonomous self able to decide apart from the social, economic, institutional, and linguistic context in which that self is immersed and constructed. Postmodern theorists unmask and question the fundamental rules, norms, and procedures imbedded in cultures and institutions that are unquestioned, taken for granted, and simply taken as the way things are. While postmodern theorists differ on a number of concerns, virtually all demonstrate concern for exposing the (often unnoticed) rules, roles, and regulations for discourse and language as major determinants of self, institutions, and cultures. Based on the works of Jean-François Lyotard and of Michel Foucault, Porter sketches a locally and communally based postmodern ethics of composition and rhetoric that centers on how the values of the individual, community, discipline/field, and tradition/culture intersect in the composing process. Cooper builds upon the works of Foucault, Jürgen Habermas, and Nancy Fraser to present a postmodern ethic for political advocacy that focuses on the need to re-create the citizen, on procedures that open up citizen access to means of communication, and on consequences of political discourse that preserve citizens as agents who genuinely can participate in government.

Richard L. Johannesen
Northern Illinios University

Bibliography

Aarons, Victoria, and Willis A. Salomon, eds. *Rhetoric and Ethics: Historical and Theoretical Perspectives*. Lewiston, NY: Mellen, 1991.

Boeyink, David E. "Casuistry: A Case-Bound Method for Journalists." *Journal of Mass Media Ethics* 7 (1992): 107–20.

Brembeck, Winston L., and William S. Howell. *Persuasion: A Means of Social Influence*. 2nd ed. Englewood Cliffs, NJ: Prentice, 1976.

Brockriede, Wayne E. "Bentham's Philosophy of Rhetoric." *Speech Monographs* 23 (1956): 235–46.

Cooper, Martha. "Ethical Dimensions of Political Advocacy from a Postmodern Perspective." *Ethical Dimensions of Political Communication*. Ed. Robert E. Denton, Jr. New York: Praeger, 1991. 23–47.

Eubanks, Ralph T. "Reflections on the Moral Dimensions of Communication." *Southern Speech Communication Journal* 45 (1980): 297–312.

Gilligan, Carol. *In a Different Voice: Psychological Theory and Women's Development*. Cambridge, MA: Harvard UP, 1982.

Greenberg, Karen Joy, ed. *Conversations on Communication Ethics*. Norwood, NJ: Ablex, 1991.

Griffin, Emory. *The Mind Changers: The Art of Christian Persuasion*. Wheaton, IL: Tyndale, 1976.

Haiman, Franklyn S. "Democratic Ethics and the Hidden Persuaders." *Quarterly Journal of Speech* 44 (1958): 385–92.

Herrick, James. "Rhetoric, Ethics, and Virtue." *Communication Studies* 43 (1992): 133–49.

Jaggar, Alison M. "Feminist Ethics." *Encyclopedia of Ethics*. 2 vols. Ed. Lawrence C. Becker and Charlotte B. Becker. New York: Garland, 1992. 361–70.

Jaksa, James A., and Michael S. Pritchard. *Communication Ethics: Methods of Analysis*. Belmont, CA: Wadsworth, 1988.

Jensen, J. Vernon. "Ancient Eastern and Western Religions as Guides for Contemporary Communication Ethics." *Proceedings of the Second National Communication Ethics Conference 1992*. Comp. James A. Jaksa. Annandale, VA: Speech Communication Assn., 1993. 58–67.

Johannesen, Richard L. *Ethics in Human Communication*. 3rd ed. Prospect Heights, IL: Waveland, 1990.

———. "Virtue Ethics, Character, and Political Communication." *Ethical Dimensions of Political Communication*. Ed. Robert E. Denton, Jr. New York: Praeger, 1991. 69–90.

Johnstone, Henry W., Jr. "Toward an Ethics of Rhetoric." *Communication* 6 (1981): 305–14.

Jonsen, Albert, and Stephen Toulmin. *The Abuse of Casuistry*. Berkeley: U of California P, 1988.

Manning, Rita C. *Speaking from the Heart: A Feminist Perspective on Ethics*. Lanham, MD: Rowman, 1992.

Nilsen, Thomas R. *Ethics of Speech Communication*. 2nd ed. Indianapolis, IN: Bobbs, 1974.

Noddings, Nel. *Caring: A Feminine Approach to Ethics and Moral Education*. Berkeley: U of California P, 1984.

Porter, James E. "Developing a Postmodern Ethics of Rhetoric and Composition." *Defining the New Rhetorics*. Ed. Theresa Enos and Stuart C. Brown. Newbury Park, CA: Sage, 1993. 207–26.

Rogge, Edward. "Evaluating the Ethics of a Speaker in a Democracy." *Quarterly Journal of Speech* 45 (1959): 419–25.

Rowland, Robert C., and Deanna Womack. "Aristotle's View of Ethical Rhetoric." *Rhetoric Society Quarterly* 15 (1985): 13–22.

Scott, Robert L. "On Viewing Rhetoric as Epistemic." *Central States Speech Journal* 18 (1967): 9–17.

Smith, David H. "Stories, Values, and Health Care Decisions." *The Ethical Nexus*. Ed. Charles Conrad. Norwood, NJ: Ablex, 1993. 123–48.

Steiner, Linda. "Feminist Theorizing and Communication Ethics." *Communication* 12 (1991): 157–74.

Wallace, Karl R. "An Ethical Basis of Communication." *Speech Teacher* 4 (1955): 1–9.

Wieman, Henry N., and Otis M. Walter. "Toward an Analysis of Ethics for Rhetoric." *Quarterly Journal of Speech* 43 (1957): 266–70.

Ethnography

A branch of anthropology, along with archaeology and linguistics, that tells stories of the experiences of living human beings. Its sites are as profane and sacred as culture, as varied as classrooms and the workplace, prisons and parishes, hospices and homes, ghettos and country clubs. Its subjects are simply people in the act of doing something. Ethnographers observe, describe, inscribe, interpret, and even critique culture, also known as "doing fieldwork." They represent their "data" in ways that include written portraits, storytelling, diaries, case studies, scientific papers full of survey data and demographic tables, and even nonwritten representations such as motion pictures and photographic exhibits. Ethnography today is called an "emergent interdisciplinary phenomenon" (Clifford 13). Its hope is to "enlarge the possibility of intelligible discourse between people quite different from one another" (Geertz, *Works and Lives* 1988: 147).

Culture and Ethnography

The concept of *culture* has evolved over time. How one defines it affects how one represents it. Sir Edward Tylor wrote the "classical" definition of culture, claiming it to be "that complex whole which includes knowledge, belief, arts, morals, law, custom, and any other capabilities and habits acquired by man as a member of society" (1). The classical view of culture stresses organicity, wholes, stability, and objectivity. In a classical view of culture, ethnographers go in search of the essence of a particular culture; in other words, they look for details that represent and describe what the group as a whole is doing and saying. They also produce monologic views of that culture; that is, the ethnographer's voice is pervasive, and all others play a subordinate role as sources or informants who are quoted occasionally. Classical ethnographies are dispassionate, whether written in first or third person. Indeed, any stylistic flourishes or personal voice is considered a weakness, an embellishment of the facts (Clifford 13). These texts proceed as detailed "and then and then and then" descriptions, what Van Maanen calls "realist tales." The ethnographer is the narrator whose authority is never questioned. Ethnographers in the classical vein are considered participant-observers: invisible (therefore not affecting the behavior of the subjects) and objective (detached observers). For well done, classical ethnographies, see Ruth Benedict's *Patterns of Culture*, 1934, or any ethnography by Margaret Mead.

Contemporary representations of culture offer a sharp contrast from the classical definition of culture as "complex whole." Cultures are no longer so neatly circumscribed; indeed, they may be in disarray, have gaps and borders that make us question *how* those gaps came to be. Contemporary cultures are seen as historical and interactive. It follows, then, that ethnographers must now recognize divisions, conflicts, particulars, and subjectivity. *Text* becomes the new metaphor for culture (Geertz 3–30), making culture open to critical theories such as semiotics, deconstruction, and cultural critique.

Briefly, in a semiotic view of culture, human action is considered symbolic, not literal. This leads one to interpret rather than just describe; a semiotic view would capture the gist of a situation, what Geertz calls "thick description" (3–30). Deconstruction's tactics are to follow differences and inconsistences, to unravel a text (culture, in this case) showing how it contradicts its own system of logic. Cultural critique goes further yet, viewing culture as a power, a force full of all sorts of asymmetrical power relationships (observer-participant, ethnographer-informant, teacher-student, outsider-insider, and so forth). The goal in critiquing culture is to expose existing forms of belief in order to challenge the status quo. See Edward Said, *Orientalism,* 1978, for an example of cultural critique.

Contemporary ethnographies are evocative, self-reflexive, and proceed by the force of "because this, then that." Ethnographers are no longer felt to be invisible, the power of observation no longer sacred. The image of ethnographer as lone fieldworker living in the midst of another culture, salvaging it for posterity, has been replaced by the image of "writer," moving around in a moving field, talking with informants who become co-workers, creating a kind of messy, unsystematic text, a dialogue that evolves in conjunction with informants. Indeed, just as "text" is the new metaphor for culture, "dialogue" is the fashionable metaphor for ethnography today, influenced by Mikhail Bakhtin (Marcus and Fischer 681). A dialogic text, then, is one in which textual space is given to the voices of informants. In terms of cultural critique, a dialogic text is one in which the experiences of the culture being studied are used to reflect on one's own culture, in the hope of reshaping some previously held concept of reality (Marcus and Fischer 69).

Besides staging dialogues, a contemporary ethnographer narrates interpersonal confrontations. The process of filtering what the ethnographer sees through the eyes of another has become part of the story. In other words, ethnographers must be aware of both the position from which they write and the position they describe. The struggle now becomes how to represent differences, how to make the process of *doing* ethnography part of the story. Ethnography has become multimethodological; its practice includes observing and collaborating, notetaking, filming, audiotaping, distributing surveys, collecting demographic data, *and* supplementing that with impressionistic and personal accounts of the process of "writing down" and "writing up" the ethnography. Van Maanen calls this style of ethnographic writing "confessional tales." For an example of a dialogic, experimental ethnography, see "Identity at Mashpee" in James Clifford's *The Predicament of Culture* (277–346).

Contemporary Issues in Ethnography

(1) Writing ethnographies. Ethnography has become a literary problem; as such, ethnographic texts are looked *at* as well as *through*. Consequently, the "burden of authorship" is heavier than before (Geertz 138). There are also forces in both the reading and writing of ethnography that are beyond the control of authors and audiences. These "contingencies of writing and reading ethnography—of language, rhetoric, power, and history"—must now be openly confronted in the process of writing (Clifford 25).

(2) Dialogue versus monologue. Characteristics of modernist ethnographic texts (culture as text, curriculum and classrooms as texts) are the "reciprocity of perspectives between insider(s) and outsider(s)" in the ethnographic research situation (Marcus and Fischer 67). Dialogue also encourages the "democratizing of knowledge" (Tedlock 80). It accepts that while the ethnographer is studying informants, the informants have a right to respond to the ethnographer's agenda and a right to have that response incorporated into the text (Rosaldo 206).

Dialogue is problematical for several reasons, however. While dialogue may be the focus and the source for the ethnography, transforming it into an ethnographic text makes it a monologue pretending to be a dialogue. Clifford suggests that we can resist this somewhat by "quoting regularly and at length from informants" (50). Still, quotations are staged by the quoter. Even if an ethnographer claims plural authorship—a joint venture with researcher and subjects—most experiments in plural authorship end up with the ethnographer taking possession of the text as editor-in-chief by the end (Clifford 51). One solution is to write "narrative ethnographies" in which the ethnographer's responses and interpretations are presented along with the informants' responses and interpretations but within a single narrative (Tedlock 69). This goal of producing ethnographic texts that are cooperative ventures (dialogic texts) and that replace monologic presentations of others is called the doctrine of dispersed authority (Clifford 21–54). See Sondra Perl and Nancy Wilson, *Through Teachers' Eyes: Portraits of Writing Teachers at Work*, 1986, for an example of "narrative ethnography."

(3) Personal bias. Another characteristic of contemporary ethnographic texts is their self-consciousness, particularly about epistemological concerns upon which they are constructed (Marcus and Cushman 25). Tedlock points out that in "ordinary 'reflectiveness,' one is conscious of oneself as an other, but in 'reflexivity,' one is conscious of *being self-conscious* of oneself as an Other" (85n). Contemporary ethnographies make problematic the construction of descriptions, interpretations, and writing practices. Pulling this off depends on the skill of the writing, the choice of narrative structures, and the willingness of the reader to tolerate ambiguity and adopt different stances relative to the text. It also accepts that prejudice is the ontological condition of all humans in the world (see Hans-Georg Gadamer, *Philosophical Hermeneutics*, 1976). Modern ethnographers do not bracket, deny, or try to transcend "prejudgments." They lay their cards on the table, so to speak, using their biases as building blocks to new knowledge, making them part of the dialogue as a strategy to engage the audiences' own beliefs and biases.

(4) Verification of ethnographies. James Clifford argues that ethnographic truths are "inherently *partial,*" a point that is resisted by those who "fear the collapse of clear standards of verification" (7). It goes without saying that readers, in evaluating the "truth" of an ethnography, must always recognize the limitations of the story. Clifford suggests that the questions one should always ask of ethnographies are "Who speaks? Who writes? When and where? With or to whom? Under what institutional and historical constraints?" (13).

Ethnographers strive to be believed *and* to be interesting; consequently, they find themselves influenced by more than one epistemology, caught in the middle of the classic debate of hermeneutics: questioning the nature of interpretation (how do I know what I know?) while striving for scientific methods that are systematic and empirical. Empirical evidence may be used, then, to guard against personal bias, to make ethnographies credible and analytical (Van Maanen 29). Other epistemologies influence ethnography as well. Various rhetorical strategies are employed to make ethnography interesting as well as accountable, placing ethnography within a moving continuum between science and art, realism and fantasy, knowledge and ideology, poetics and politics (Clifford 25).

Annie-Marie Hall
University of Arizona

Bibliography

Clifford, J. "Introduction: Partial Truths." *Writing Culture: The Poetics and Politics of Ethnography*. Ed. James Clifford and George E. Marcus. Berkeley: U of California P, 1986. 1–26.

———. *The Predicament of Culture: Twentieth-Century Ethnography, Literature, and Art*. Cambridge, MA: Harvard UP, 1988.

Geertz, Clifford. "Thick Description toward an Interpretative Theory of Culture." *The Interpretation of Cultures*. New York: Basic, 1973. 3–30.

———. *Works and Lives: The Anthropologist as Author*. Stanford: Stanford UP, 1988.

Marcus, George E., and Dick Cushman. "Ethnographies as Texts." *Annual Review of Anthropology* 11 (1982): 25–69.

Marcus, George E., and Michael M.J. Fischer. *Anthropology as Cultural Critique: An Experimental Moment in the Human Sciences*. Chicago: U of Chicago P, 1986.

Rosaldo, Renato. *Culture and Truth: The Remaking of Social Analysis*. Boston: Beacon, 1989.

Tedlock, Barbara. "From Participant-Observer to the Observation of Participation: The Emergence of Narrative Ethnography." *Journal of Anthropological Research* 47 (1991): 69–94.

Tylor, E.B. *Primitive Culture: Researches into the Development of Mythology, Philosophy, Religion, Language, Art, and Custom*. Vol. 1. London: John Murray, 1871.

Van Maanen, J. *Tales of the Field: On Writing Ethnography*. Chicago: U of Chicago P, 1988.

Ethos

Persuasion through the character of the speaker. Throughout the history of rhetorical theory, ethos has been defined in two ways: as a mode of persuasion that draws upon the prerequisite virtue of the speaker; or as a mode of persuasion that relies on the speaker creating a credible character for particular rhetorical occasions. The contrast between these two concepts of ethos can be seen in the difference between Plato's and Aristotle's attitude toward the role of character in persuasion. Plato defined the role of rhetoric as instruction in ideal truth. Observing in *Gorgias* that the object of persuasion should be the cultivation of the moral good, Plato indicted rhetorical practices that strive merely to gratify audiences. Given the noble mission of rhetoric to produce order and proportion, Plato argued that only an orator with intrinsic virtue could hope to instruct others in moral values. Plato's insistence that the speaker must be a philosopher in order to convey a knowledge of the good is linked to his assumption that the goal of rhetoric is to improve the character of the state; strong moral character supports a state governed by reason.

Unlike Plato, who sees virtue in the speaker to be a prerequisite to the kind of rhetoric that contributes to an orderly world, Aristotle's concern with the speaker's character derives from his view of rhetoric as a means of bringing about decisions in matters affecting civil life. Aristotle defined ethos as one of three modes of proof (along with pathos and logos). In the *Rhetoric*, Aristotle equates ethos with conveying credibility. Aristotle refines this definition by explaining that an effective ethos must inspire the audience's confidence in the speaker's good sense, moral character, and good will. Especially important in deliberative and forensic oratory, ethos must be used to offset mistrust and any suspicion that the speaker is not in command of the facts. Not to be confused with a speaker's reputation, ethos must be created in the moment by the speech itself. Aristotle observes that the creation of an effective ethos relies on the speaker's ability to anticipate the kind of good character that different audiences will expect and respond to. In order to project the appropriate ethos in any given situation, the speaker must draw upon an understanding of human nature in order to know how to appear knowledgeable and sincere. The Aristotelian definition of ethos stresses the importance of adaptation to audience, context, and subject; it is not Aristotle's intention to imply that virtue in the speaker can be or should be contrived; his intention is to insist that the construction of ethos, like truth, is relative.

The contrast between Plato's essentialist view of the speaker's character and Aristotle's more pragmatic and relativistic attitude toward ethos as a strategy can also be seen in later definitions of the nature and function of ethos. In *De oratore,* Cicero argues that the goal of rhetoric is to direct the inclinations of the audience in the direction the speaker intends. Cicero makes the point that this cannot be achieved without securing an audience's good will. Cicero's pragmatic approach to ethos is similar to Aristotle's in that Cicero also insists that the presentation of favorable character and moral conduct is the most direct means of securing the audience's good will. Unlike Aristotle, Cicero does not treat ethos under the canon of invention; instead, he treats the presentation of character as an issue that affects stylistic choices and also the speaker's manner of delivery. Cicero's treatment of the principle of ethos is not unusual. Not all rhetoricians specifically use the term *ethos* when discussing the role of the speaker's character, and fewer still treat it as strictly an inventional issue.

What is more typical throughout the history of rhetoric is that the principle of ethos—that the speaker must appear to be knowledgeable, sincere, and of good character—permeate discussions of invention, style, delivery, and the aims of rhetoric as a mandatory consideration; consequently, the obligation of the speaker to present a pleasing character becomes a maxim that rhetoricians acknowledge under various headings. For example, Quintilian's discussion of the speaker's character first appears in *Institutio Oratoria* in a discussion of the importance of moral education for young pupils who aspire to be orators. Quintilian's argument, that pupils should be placed in schools that provide moral instruction, is based on his general assumption that "no one can be an orator who is not a good man." In Quintilian's view, orators must be virtuous or they will not be able to persuade or even speak truly. Like Plato, Quintilian views ethos as the embodiment of a preexisting state of virtue in the speaker. Reminiscent of Plato's and Aristotle's differences of opinion about whether or not moral virtue in the speaker is intrinsic or strategically presented, the contrasting views of Cicero and Quintilian on the nature and function of ethos represent a disagreement between idealistic and pragmatic views of ethos that has persisted throughout the history of the tradition.

Although always asserting itself in treatments of style and delivery, the status of ethos as a central rhetorical principle has fluctuated as rhetoricians in different eras have disagreed as to whether the aim of rhetoric was instruction in the moral good or the facilitation of decisions and action. Predictably, the idealistic definition of ethos as prerequisite virtue flourished in Christian rhetorical theory, which defined the aim of ecclesiastical oratory to be the spreading of religious truth. In Augustine's *De doctrina* (c. 396), the discussion of ethos focuses on the importance of piety in the preacher. Without piety, the preacher cannot interpret the Scriptures; without being able to understand God's word, the preacher cannot explain it to others. Like Plato and Quintilian, Augustine insists that the speaker must already be a virtuous person even before the rhetorical process begins. Because Augustine considers inner piety to be linked to the apprehension of truth, the status of ethos in Augustine's overall theory is quite high. Like Quintilian, Augustine believes that the entire success of oratory depends on a preexisting state of moral character in the speaker. This idealistic view of ethos persisted in the homiletic tradition and in secular rhetorical theories, such as George Campbell's *Philosophy of Rhetoric* (1776) and Hugh Blair's *Lectures on Rhetoric and Belles Lettres* (1783), that treated pulpit eloquence as a form of oratory. Although Christian rhetoric and many secular rhetorics preserved the definition of ethos as prerequisite virtue, this approach to ethos is linked historically to postclassical discussions of preaching and rarely appears in rhetorics designed to provide students and general citizens with instruction in rhetorical skills for professional and civil use. The overall emphasis of rhetoric treatises designed for the academy and for the general public since the Middle Ages has maintained the Aristotelian-Ciceronian approach to ethos, which stressed the importance of adjusting presentation of character to audience and subject.

Campbell's and Blair's approach to ethos actually blends idealistic and pragmatic views: although they both insist that the preacher must have piety in order to influence values and conduct, they also argue that every speaker must be perceived as a wise and good person in order to appeal to the audience's intelligence and emotions. Beginning with the maxim that the speaker must adjust presentation of self to the expectations of those addressed, Campbell and Blair observe that the speaker must convince the audience that he feels the emotions he wants them to feel and that he believes deeply in the truths he argues for. (Historically, rhetoricians have characterized the orator as male.) While Campbell and Blair do not require prerequisite virtue in the lay speaker, they do argue that the speaker cannot persuade if he cannot convey his own commitment to his ideas. Campbell and Blair do not use the term *ethos* but discuss the presentation of the speaker's character in terms of the creation of "sympathy"; the concept of sympathy reveals Campbell's and Blair's epistemological approach to rhetoric. Sharing the assumption that the rhetorician must appeal to the faculties of the mind—the will, the understanding, the emotions, and the imagination—Campbell and Blair argue that the speaker must establish a sympathetic link with the audience in order to engage the emotions that move the will. Nineteenth-century rhetoricians generally treat the principle of ethos as the establishment of sympathy, although they reiterate, as do Campbell and Blair, Aristotelian advice that it is also important to appear to be friendly and sincere. One of the more notable nineteenth-century discussions of the principle of ethos is Matthew Boyd Hope's treatment of the issue as the creation of "presence" in *The Princeton Textbook in Rhetoric* (1859). Predating Chaïm Perelman and Olbrechts-Tyteca's use of the term in *The New Rhetoric* (1969) by a century, Hope argues that the speaker must inspire confidence and appear to be credible (104).

Twentieth-century composition texts and speech manuals have continued the nineteenth-century practice of stressing that the writer and speaker must take presentation of self into consideration when planning an essay or speech. Rarely appearing in modern textbooks under the term *ethos*, the principle of ethos is discussed under a variety of headings, such as "writer's voice," "credibility," and "considering an audience." The idealistic approach to ethos currently finds its expression in homiletic treatments of oratory and also in the theories of rhetorical theorists like Richard Weaver and Wayne Booth, who have both attempted to align rhetorical practice with the pursuit and dissemination of truth and values. Weaver takes the position in "Language is Sermonic" that the rhetorician must draw upon an innate sense of ideal truth in order to show others a better vision of life. In *Modern Dogma and the Rhetoric of Assent* (1974), Booth also discusses the rhetorician as a person of intrinsic goodness whose sense of integrity grounds the rhetorical process of guiding others to identify "good reasons" by which to guide decisions and actions. Despite these neo-Platonic reiterations of the idealistic view of ethos, the modern pedagogical tradition in rhetoric has been governed by the pragmatic and relativistic interpretation of ethos formulated by Aristotle.

Nan Johnson
Ohio State University

Bibliography

Booth, Wayne. *Modern Dogma and the Rhetoric of Assent*. Notre Dame: U of Notre Dame P, 1974.

Cherry, Rodger D. "Ethos vs. Persona: Self Representation in Written Discourse." *Written Communication* 5 (1988): 251–76.

Johnson, Nan. "Ethos and the Aims of Rhetoric." *Essays on Classical Rhetoric and Modern Discourse*. Ed. Robert J. Connors, Lisa S. Ede, and Andrea A. Lunsford. Carbondale: Southern Illinois UP, 1984. 98–114.

Johnstone, Christopher Lyle. "An Aristotle Trilogy: Ethics, Rhetoric, Politics, and the Search for Moral Truth." *Philosophy and Rhetoric* 13 (1980): 1–24.

Yoos, George E. "A Revision of the Concept of Ethical Appeal." *Philosophy and Rhetoric* 12 (1979): 41–58.

Evidence

Criteria for information judged acceptable in support of a claim in rhetorical argumentation; evolved with epistemological and philosophical movements to the point that there is no one model for evidence that crosses all disciplines or situations. The primary criterion is that the audience see the information as relevant to the claim. Evidence in rhetorical argumentation is the information presented to prove or disprove a conclusion or claim. The mere presence of information does not constitute evidence; the informative statements must be accepted as evidence by an audience and believed by it to be relevant to the claim at issue. Evidence can be generally classified as qualitative and quantitative. The former emphasizes explanation and description, appearing continuous rather than discrete, while the latter offers measurement and prediction. Both kinds of information require interpretation, for at no time do the facts speak for themselves.

Classical rhetoricians recognized that because rhetoric, unlike other disciplines, has no subject matter of its own, it is necessary to look elsewhere to find material for arguments.

E

Aristotle identified artistic and inartistic proofs to acquire this material. The inartistic proofs consist of sources such as laws, witnesses, contracts, tortures, and oaths, where the information to support a claim already exists and simply has to be used and interpreted. To the original inartistic sources can be added more modern ones like scientific experiments, written documents, and photographs. The artistic proofs require invention techniques that create the material from which arguments are made. They provide a method of probing a subject to discover material to support a line of reasoning and draw from common topics (definition, comparison, relationship, and circumstance), which apply to any subject, and special topics, which are pertinent to specific kinds of discourse and disciplines. Issues surrounding evidence arise with regard to the criterial questions of verifiability, admissibility, and merit. Personal narratives, biblical texts, trial by ordeal, and so forth, began to have less strength as evidence for claims with the appearance of epistemological movements such as the rationalism of René Descartes (1596–1650) and the empiricism of John Locke (1635–1704) or David Hume (1711–1776). Knowledge of the world, and hence material to support claims, was gained either by reasoning alone or by the five senses. George Campbell (1719–1796) broadened the picture when he argued for both intuitive and deductive evidence. In other words, evidence could be conceived by the mind immediately through intellection (perception), consciousness, or common sense, or conceived by comparisons of related ideas through demonstration or moral evidence, such as experience, analogy, and testimony.

Criteria for judging evidence shifted away from common-sense philosophy in the twentieth century with the growth of the philosophic movement of logical positivism and analytic philosophy. The social sciences and humanities adopted the scientific model of evidence in a search for truth and validity. Evidence was judged according to a verifiability continuum, which put quantitative data above qualitative (that is, statistics and replication of studies) over common sense, analogies, or any other evidence that can admit only degrees of certainty. In the latter part of the century, however, it has been acknowledged that the empirical model of evidence does not allow for historical contexts or human interaction in evaluating the admissibility of evidence.

To account for this weakness, philosophers and logicians such as Stephen Toulmin and Chaïm Perelman have shifted the model of argument from the scientific to ones based more on the law courts and, hence, shifted the criteria for accepting evidence in nonscientific arguments. As a result, evidence is viewed as situation-specific, with different disciplines demanding different forms of evidence. Furthermore, acceptance by an audience rather than some extrinsic criteria determine admissibility of evidence, which puts qualitative material (such as personal narratives or analogies) on a par with quantitative data if it meets three general criteria: (1) the information is pertinent to the critical perspective or discipline; (2) the audience sees it as relevant to the claim; and (3) the information is utilized in a credible and consistent manner. Signs of deficient evidence that cross discipline lines include incomplete, inaccurate, ambiguous, or absent information.

Julie M. Farrar
Saint Louis University

Bibliography

Aristotle. *Rhetoric*. Trans. Rhys Roberts. Ed. Friedrich Solmsen. New York: Modern Library, 1954.

Bitzer, Lloyd F. "A Re-evaluation of Campbell's Doctrine of Evidence." *Quarterly Journal of Speech* 46 (1960): 135–40.

Campbell, George. *Philosophy of Rhetoric*. Carbondale: Southern Illinois UP, 1963.

Fitch, Kristine. "Criteria for Evidence in Qualitative Research." *Western Journal of Communication* 58 (1994): 32–38.

Levine, Michael. "Scientific Method and the Adversary Model: Some Preliminary Thoughts." *American Psychologist* 29 (19): 661–77.

Perelman, Chaïm, and L. Olbrechts-Tyteca. *The New Rhetoric: A Treatise on Argumentation*. Trans. John Wilkinson and Purcell Weaver. Notre Dame, IN: U of Notre Dame P, 1969.

Tompkins, Phillip K. "Principles of Rigor for Assessing Evidence in 'Qualitative' Communication Research." *Western Journal of Communication* 58 (1994): 44–50.

Toulmin, Stephen E. *The Uses of Argument*. Cambridge: Cambridge UP, 1958.

See also PROOF

Example

The form of rhetorical invention that utilizes inductive reasoning. When one uses examples in argumentative discourse, one is arguing from particular instances to a general conclusion, or from known particulars to another unknown one. It is important to remember that rhetorical induction does not actually *prove* anything; it is arguing from the probability that known instances are parallel to and illuminating of those less well known. Whereas full logical induction enumerates all possible instances, the rhetorical argument by example almost always enumerates less than the total. The persuasive impact of such a method of reasoning is increased, of course, as one increases the number of examples.

If one provides examples, for instance, of the voting records of all one hundred U.S. senators to make a general statement about U.S. senators, one is making use of full induction. In a typical rhetorical situation, however, a writer or speaker hasn't the time and a reader or listener hasn't the patience to deal with every possible example. Instead, one chooses representative examples, the persuasive value of which is strengthened by their relevance and by means of their connection to other rhetorical devices.

Aristotle states that "to derive a general law from a number of like instances is in Dialectic induction, in Rhetoric example" (1.2.1356b). Elsewhere in the *Rhetoric,* though, Aristotle notes that use of the example "does not concern the relation of part to whole . . . but of part to part, of like to like. When two things fall under the same genus, but one of them is better known than the other, the better-known is the example" (1.2.1357b). The same idea is expressed in the *Prior Analytics* (2.24.68b). To illustrate this use of the example, Aristotle suggests a situation in which one might contend "that Dionyius, in asking for a body-guard, aims to set up a tyranny." The argument by example would include all other similar cases that the audience would be familiar with—"Theagenes did the like at Megara," and so on (*Rhetoric* 1.2.1357b).

Thus, Aristotle proposed the example as the rhetorical alternative to logical induction and scientific demonstration because of the impracticality of having to lead an audience through a complex series of particulars. Aristotle recognized two main types of examples useful to rhetoric. The first is the historical example, wherein a past event is used to illustrate an unknown instance. The second is the example by invented comparison, in which category falls the fable. Fables and other invented examples can be especially effective, Aristotle suggests, when historical examples are hard to find or when one's audience is indisposed to other, more rigorous forms of reasoning.

The argument by example is one of two possible logical forms in rhetoric, the other being the enthymeme, which is the rhetorical parallel to logic's deductive syllogism. Like an argument from an enthymeme, an argument from example makes use of all the available means of persuasion: not only of the logical appeal of the commonalities apparent between that which is known and that which is under consideration, but also of the emotional and ethical appeals a particular example may denote to a particular audience.

Donald E. Bushman
University of North Carolina, Wilmington

Bibliography

Aristotle. *Rhetoric.* Trans. Lane Cooper. Englewood Cliffs, NJ: Prentice, 1932.

Benoit, William L. "The Most Significant Passage in Aristotle's *Rhetoric.*" *Rhetoric Society Quarterly* 12 (1982): 2–9.

Raymond, James C. "Enthymemes, Examples, and Rhetorical Method." *Essays on Classical Rhetoric and Modern Discourse.* Ed. Robert J. Connors, Lisa S. Ede, and Andrea A. Lunsford. Carbondale: Southern Illinois UP, 1984. 140–51.

Exordium

The first part of a classical oration, designed to introduce and focus the audience's attention on the subject. Contemporary writing textbooks admonish students to use an essay's introduction to "hook" the audience in some way and then follow up by focusing the audience on the purpose or position of the essay via a thesis or forecasting statement. Such suggestions echo the concept of *exordium,* which the *Rhetorica ad Herennium* specifies as "the beginning of the discourse, and by it the hearer's mind is prepared for attention" (1.3.4).

To facilitate this preparation, Richard Lanham notes two types of *exordia* that appeared in classical times: the direct (*pricipium* in Latin, *proomion* in Greek) and the indirect (*insinuatio* in Latin, *ephodos* in Greek) (75). Hugh Blair, in the *Lectures on Rhetoric and Belles-Le ttres* (1783), suggests that audience plays no small role in determining which introductory approach to use. According to Connors and Glenn, Blair saw the *pricipium* as "addressed to well-disposed audience. . . . [It] can proceed with the knowledge that the audience is sympathetic and can go directly to the task of rendering them attentive" (215). The *insinuatio,* in contrast, is

> a less direct, subtler method that prepares a hostile audience for arguments counter to their opinions. . . . [It] generally opens by first admitting the most powerful points made by the opposition by showing how the writer holds the same views as the audience on general philosophical questions or by dealing with ingrained audience prejudices. (Connors and Glenn 215)

In both cases, we see the importance of audience analysis in the construction of successful introductions/*exordia*. Predisposing the audience to accept, or at least acknowledge, a speaker's or writer's viewpoints is paramount in the construction of a piece of discourse; the *exordium,* being the first element of arrangement that the audience encounters, is one of the ways in which rhetors achieve credibility for both topic and presenter.

Joseph Colavito
Northwestern State University

Bibliography

Connors, Robert, and Cheryl Glenn. *The St. Martin's Guide to Teaching Writing.* 2nd ed. New York: St. Martin's, 1992.

Lanham, Richard. *A Handlist of Rhetorical Terms.* 2nd ed. Berkeley: U of California P, 1991.

Rhetorica ad Herennium. Trans. Harry Caplan. Cambridge, MA: Harvard UP, 1954.

Exposition

The setting forth or presentation of subject matter. Expository writing includes nonfictional writing of all sorts, particularly academic essays. Though most experts agree that creative writing is not principally expository, there is less agreement about the defining features of expository text. Some define expository writing by its purpose, that of informing readers about some topic. Others define it by the forms of organization it frequently takes, such as definition, exemplification, causal analysis, comparison, and contrast.

In composition classes, expository writing typically indexes nonfictive discourse where the aim is clear presentation of some topic. Composition textbooks often say that mastery of expository writing involves practicing typical forms or patterns of organization such as deduction, causal analysis, comparison/contrast, and definition.

The term *exposition* is also used outside of composition classes to describe contexts where objects or information will be clearly and effectively presented. Conventioneers attend "technical expositions" where new technologies and products are displayed and information about them is provided by vendors. In fiction, exposition refers to sections of a play or story conveying background information necessary for understanding focal events.

Although most scholars agree that creative writing is not principally expository, there is less agreement about what features other than nonfictional subject matter make expository text expository. Disagreement exists because of the term's definitional breadth, worries about its roots in realist epistemologies, and doubts about the adequacy of traditional expository writing pedagogies. These dissatisfactions have led contemporary scholars to offer reformulated schemes for classifying discourse. In the new schemes, discourse is classified by inferred authorial goals (such as persuading or informing) rather than by subject matter or form. Some scholars have found these reconceptualized discourse classification schemes illuminating; others find them artificial.

In classical Greek and Roman rhetoric, emphasis was placed on persuasive discourse designed principally to gain agreement or action rather than inform or present subject matter. Expository or informative discourse received more attention from eighteenth- and nineteenth-century rhetoricians. George Campbell (1719–1796), for instance, maintained that the human mind worked by universal associative patterns, such as resemblance and causality. These associative patterns were also viewed as the structures composing reality. Campbell believed that rhetoricians first had to establish understanding before they could persuade. Thus, they first had to "expose" their topic clearly by arranging it in one or more of the universally recognized patterns of organization. Subjects exhibited in this manner would be most clearly and fully apprehended by audiences (Golden and Corbett 205–6). Similarly, nineteenth-century rhetoricians such as Henry Day and John Genung believed that expository discourse was most effective when it was organized by the patterns the human mind would most easily recognize. These forms included deduction, generalization, exemplification, and so forth, the "patterns of exposition" still found in composition anthologies today.

The view that students can best be taught to present nonfictional subject matter through practice in expository patterns or modes is still widely shared. In fact, as Berlin (*Rhetoric and Reality*) and Johnson (*Nineteenth-century Rhetoric*) show, expository writing has been the dominant form of text throughout the nineteenth and twentieth centuries. In the last several decades, however, dissatisfactions with traditional conceptions of expository discourse have grown.

There are at least three concerns. First, some scholars find the definitional ambiguity of the phrase *expository writing* problematic. Critics argue that the same phrase has been ambiguously used, referring in some contexts to a particular aim or aims and at other times to patterns of organization or modes.

A second dissatisfaction concerns the realist epistemologies in which the notion of expository writing is rooted. Contemporary scholars maintain that reality is not directly apprehended by the human mind but is instead the result of activities by the perceiver, features of the phenomena perceived, and dimensions of the perceiver's discourse community. This shift toward social constructivist epistemologies encourages theorists to reconsider the old dictum Form follows function. That is, contemporary scholars are increasingly thinking about writing in terms of writers' and readers' purposes rather than the organizational forms necessary for clear exposition. If these forms of exposition are seen as shaped by writers' and readers' social purposes, it makes more sense to understand these purposes and the structures they encourage rather than to study forms of organization by themselves.

A third concern about traditional conceptions of expository writing arises from doubts about the utility of having students identify and practice expository forms as principal means by which they learn to write effective academic and professional prose. When it was believed that the "pure truth" of some topic could best be "exposed" by use of these patterns, focusing instruction on mastery of these forms was warranted. Currently, while appreciation of these forms of organization is seen as important, scholars increasingly maintain that instruction should focus on helping writers to identify their goals and those of their readers and on selecting text forms that best achieve relevant goals in particular contexts.

Three well-known contemporary discourse classification systems are those of James Moffett, James Britton, and James Kinneavy. All three classify discourse principally by functional relations between writers and their readers rather than by form. Moffett classifies discourse according to "speaker-audience" relationships. He says that traditional methods of teaching writing asked students to produce a thesis and then find some pattern of exposition best suited to supporting that thesis. Instead, Moffett maintains that writing should be classified according to speaker-audience relationships or the ways in which writers use language. In his reclassification of discourse types, spoken and written discourse is arrayed according to the degree of speaker-audience "distance" it requires and the degree of speaker–subject matter distance or abstraction it reflects. For instance, at one end of his spectrum, he finds interior dialogue and autobiography; at the other end, where considerable speaker-audience distance is required, he locates science and metaphysics. In Moffett's classificatory scheme, exposition is one of four types of text, classified according to speaker-subject relation. Exposition is text that generalizes about what happens. It requires more distance or abstraction by writers than do recording or reporting, but less than does theorizing (32–36).

Britton and his associates also classify discourse types principally by function. In their reformulation, expository discourse is called "informative writing" and, as they note, their conceptualization of informative writing is an extension of Moffett's. Where Moffett identified four speaker-subject relationships (recording, reporting, generalizing, and theorizing), these authors identify six. These relationships are (in order of least to most abstract): writing to record (running commentary on events occurring at the moment), writing to report (on past events), generalized narrative or description (for example, description of steps taken in performing a scientific experiment), low-level analogic (generalizations are made but not explicitly or in a highly organized fashion), analogic (generalizations made explicit and hierarchically or logically organized), tautologic (highly organized theoretical writing (74–105).

In Kinneavy's taxonomy, as in Britton's, the notion of a set of discourse types that principally present subject matter remains. Like Britton, Kinneavy classifies all discourse by authorial aim. His four types are self-expression, persuasion, reference, and literary. The third type, reference, refers to discourse in which writers chiefly represent some aspect of reality to some audience. For instance, news stories, critical essays, and empirical research would all be classified as referential discourse because in each writers aim principally to "represent" some aspect of reality to some audience. For Kinneavy, expository writing is reference discourse (48–210).

Kinneavy identifies three subtypes of reference or expository discourse: scientific, exploratory, and informative. Scientific or scholarly discourse represents some aspect of reality by proving claims about it. Exploratory discourse (speculative essays) represents an aspect of reality by questioning accepted notions. Informative discourse, found in newspapers, textbooks, popular magazines, and encyclopedias, represents reality by making information accessible to lay audiences.

Notions of expository writing are further reformulated by Rowan ("A Contemporary Theory"), who subdivides Kinneavy's informative discourse into two subtypes: informatory text, designed to create awareness, and explanatory, designed to enhance understanding. A set of stock listings is principally informatory; a newspaper article on why the market is rebounding is principally explanatory. Rowan focuses particularly on explanatory discourse and stresses the importance of function over form. She does not encourage using explanatory techniques such as exemplification and analogy simply because these forms are generally useful in explanation. Instead, she provides a research-based theory of the principal causes of difficulty in understanding complex ideas.

This theory allows writers to detect and anticipate likely confusions readers may face. Specifically, Rowan encourages writers to consider whether an idea will be principally difficult to understand because of a confusing term, a structure or process that is hard to envision, or a notion that is difficult to understand because it is difficult to believe. Arguing that explanatory text should be organized to overcome this principally identified difficulty, she reviews research on text features effective at minimizing each type.

In sum, contemporary classifications of discourse retain notions of expository writing but reclassify expository and all other forms of writing in terms of authorial goals. This reclassification deemphasizes the importance of practicing expository forms for their own sake. Instead, emphasis is placed on analyzing anticipated difficulties, given some set of authorial goals and readers' expectations, and evaluating texts for the extent to which they overcome such difficulties.

Although reformulated discourse classification schemes have been praised by many, they have also been criticized. Some scholars say that all discourse classification systems are overly idealized and artificial: Few actual texts are purely reference discourse or purely persuasive. These theorists note the organic unities one finds among textual purposes and forms. For them, the breadth in traditional notions of exposition is a strength, not a weakness.

Katherine E. Rowan
Purdue University

Bibliography

Berlin, James A. *Rhetoric and Reality: Writing Instruction in American Colleges, 1900–1985.* Carbondale: Southern Illinois UP, 1987.

Britton, James, Tony Burgess, Nancy Martin, Alex McLeod, and Harold Rosen. *The Development of Writing Abilities (11–18).* London: Schools Council Publications, 1975.

Golden, James L., and Edward P.J. Corbett. *The Rhetoric of Blair, Campbell, and Whately.* New York: Holt, 1968.

Johnson, Nan. *Nineteenth-century Rhetoric in North America.* Carbondale: Southern Illinois UP, 1991.

Kinneavy, James L. *A Theory of Discourse.* New York: Norton, 1971.

Moffett, James. *Teaching the Universe of Discourse.* Boston: Houghton, 1968.

Rowan, Katherine E. "A Contemporary

Theory of Explanatory Writing." *Written Communication* 5 (1988): 23–56.

Expressionism

A theory in which "expression" is seen not as a feature of all discourse, but as the highest aim in discourse. Expressionism thus denotes not just a descriptive concept but an argument about value. All discourse is expressive in that if we see an instance of language as discourse, we necessarily infer that someone *expressed* it. In the presence of discourse, we can always consider what we can say about who is doing the discoursing.

In classical rhetorical theory, expressive discourse was not identified as a separate kind of discourse. Classical rhetoricians did hold that a particular persuasive force derived from the listener's sense of the speaker's character. In his *Rhetoric*, Aristotle called this the ethical appeal, and asserted that in situations where the truth was in doubt and persuasion was therefore necessary it was the strongest of the three kinds of appeal a discourse could have. Aristotle also held that evoking emotion was important to the rhetorician and poet, but the emotions in question were those *evoked* by the speaker, not those that the speaker might have *experienced* and then *expressed*.

In the Renaissance and the Reformation, the importance of the experience of the individual was given a boost with the notion that an individual might discover scientific truths about the world by the independent use of the senses, or the truths of the Christian faith by reading the Bible in the printed vernacular. Neither of these developments suggested that "self-expression" had any special importance, however.

The first proponents of what today we would call "expression" as a distinct aim in discourse were the European Romantics of the eighteenth and early nineteenth centuries. The context of "expression" for these thinkers was always a "poetic" one, however.

In the theory of rhetoric and composition since 1960, expression has commonly been taken to be neither a dimension of all discourse nor a feature only of "poetic" discourse, but itself a special kind of discourse. It has been distinguished from discourse, whose primary functions are referential, poetic, phatic, metalingual, or conative (Jakobson, who called it emotive discourse), from discourse whose aims are referential, persuasive, or literary (Kinneavy), and from discourse that has transactional or poetic functions (Britton et al.).

It is not difficult to see how this exaltation of "expression" comported with the rise of individualism, which itself was a crucial aspect of the consolidation of capitalism. In this historical context, freedom came to be defined as freedom to express the self.

Some social reformers in the nineteenth century later noted that while self-expression might be the birthright of the citizens of a democratic society in principle, in actuality self-expression was the province only of those whose power and privilege gave them the leisure and means for such pursuits. Utilitarian critics, in a different critical vein, took self-expression as self-indulgence—the frivolity of the grasshopper who plays the fiddle while the ant toils to accumulate goods against the coming winter.

Not surprisingly, we find contemporary theorists and social critics disagreeing about the value of expressive discourse. In some discussions it is seen as the lowest form of discourse—as when a discourse is characterized as "merely" expressive, or "subjective," or "personal," as opposed to full-fledged "academic" or "critical" discourse. In other discussions, expression is seen as the highest undertaking in discourse—as when literary works (or even works of academic criticism or theory) are seen as works of expression, not merely of communication. In this view, expression may be seen as more importantly a matter of the artifact and its effect on a reader than a matter of the artifact's relation to the author's "self."

In classes and curricula in schools and colleges, distinctions are asserted between expressive writing (often called "creative" or "personal" writing) and writing that is "expository," "technical," or "professional." Sequences of study are commonly built on the assumption that early (private) expression should give way at more advanced levels to (public) communication or persuasion. In educational contexts expressive writing is thus thought to be appropriate only for the immature, developing writer or, at the college level, for the advanced and gifted writer. Here some would distinguish "personal" expression (the "undeveloped" expression of the immature writer) from "creative" expression (which might or might not be personal but which would in any case be artistically accomplished). Expression is thus consigned to "special" circumstances. In most circumstances we are supposed to produce discourse that simply "communicates."

The validity of this "developmental" hierarchy has been challenged by arguing that since the expressive element in discourse is inescapable it must be harnessed, not supposedly "outgrown" or suppressed. The deadening and ultimately counterproductive qualities of much "official" discourse, it is said, suggest that matters of "expression" are not irrelevant to issues of rhetorical or even communicative "effectiveness."

Feminist critics have noted the gendered quality of this hierarchy, which associates subjectivity, emotion, and expressiveness with the feminine, and objectivity, detachment, and professionalism with the masculine.

Political critics have objected to the mystification that results when interests and characters of the persons producing a discourse are hidden. "Objective" (referential, nonexpressive) reporting can be, in this light, a form of bad faith, not an effort to rise above personal bias. The "official" language of the bureaucrat or the professional can be intended to intimidate and exclude, not to embrace and illuminate.

Those who believe that expression should be consigned to an inferior status point to the shallowness and ineffectiveness for any social purpose of much that is justified by its authors as expression and argue that to promote expression at the expense of communication or persuasion is to promote powerlessness. These critics are taking "expression" as meaning "self-expression," of course.

A question that theorists of expression must come to sooner or later, whether they are proponents or detractors, is the nature of the "self" that expresses itself in discourse. This self is not simply given, like the codes in our DNA: That much seems clear. To no small extent, our "selves" are dependent upon and even created by language and culture. Some critics of culture have argued that a culture offers only certain "subject positions" to its members and, furthermore, that access to these positions may be limited by class, race, or gender. To the extent that this is true, self-expression is self-delusion. Other theorists reply that

a "self" arises not by virtue of its taking up a predetermined subject position but by its struggle with what is given in this respect. "Selves" are defined not by their "roles," in other words, but by their choices, some of the most significant of which are choices of language. The "selves" that are thus "expressed" are not necessarily only individual selves: Kinneavy takes the Declaration of Independence as an important example of expression.

In the history of "expression," there is a tension between the idea of movement from the inside out and movement from the outside in. The verb *express* originally carried the connotation of effort, a pressing, or squeezing, or wringing out. We still sometimes speak of "expressing" a mother's milk, though this usage has an archaic ring. On the other hand, *to express* has also meant to form an image by pressure, as in sculpture and painting, a usage that suggests the opposite movement. Today, the most common meaning is "to represent or utter," with the "self" being commonly implicated as that which is represented, a usage that goes back at least as far as Shakespeare and Chaucer.

Authentic expression apparently cannot be just a matter of "getting it out" or "letting go," no matter how therapeutic such an undertaking may be. Acts of expression achieve authenticity (and perhaps achieve their soundest therapeutic benefits as well) only if they are accompanied by acts of reflection. Thus "sincerity" cannot be a sufficient condition for authentic expression: we can be sincere and be quite mad.

Authentic expression would therefore seem to require what the existentialists called "good faith." Good faith entails, among other things, an awareness of the ways in which the self is contingent—on language, on others, and on the world.

Put another way, the discipline of expressive discourse can be said to be a matter of writing, and rewriting, in the largest sense of those terms. In striving for self-expression, it may be best to view ourselves not as instincts but as compositions.

John Warnock
University of Arizona

Bibliography
Britton, James. "The Composing Processes and the Functions of Writing." *Research on Composing: Points of Departure.* Ed. Charles Cooper and Lee Odell. Urbana,

IL: National Council of Teachers of English, 1978.

Britton, James, Tony Burgess, Nancy Martin, Alex McLeod, and Harold Rosen. *The Development of Writing Abilities (11–18)*. London: Macmillan Education, 1975.

Coles, William E., Jr. *The Plural I—and After*. Portsmouth, NH: Boynton/Cook, 1988.

Harris, Jeanette. *Expressive Discourse*. SMU Studies in Composition and Rhetoric. Gen. ed., Gary Tate. Dallas, TX: Southern Methodist UP, 1990.

Jakobson, Roman. "Concluding Statement: Linguistics and Poetics." *Style in Language*. Ed. Thomas A. Sebeok. Cambridge, MA: MIT P, 1960. 350–78.

Kinneavy, James L. *A Theory of Discourse*. Englewood Cliffs, NJ: Prentice, 1971. Rpt. New York: Norton, 1980.

E

F

Fallacy

A topic of fallacies that exists at the intersection of rhetoric with other disciplines, here logic. It might be argued that the notion of fallacy plays a foundational role in logic, or at least in informal logic. Here one notices a disparity, to illustrate which one need only observe that while most rhetoricians would seem to agree that there are *topoi*, yet many logicians and others argue whether there are fallacies, and whether they are always fallacious. In other words, foundational disputes about the very topic of fallacy—how it is to be understood and whether there are any—characterize inquiry to this day.

In common usage, the term *fallacy* has a number of distinct if related meanings. It may refer to a mistaken belief—for example, the gambler's fallacy. Or it may refer to a mistaken inference. Or, finally, it may refer to a mistaken type of argument. Its use in logic and rhetoric is closer to this last sense. The term itself derives from the Latin term *fallax,* which in turn comes from the verb meaning "to be deceived." The rough equivalent in Greek is *sophism.*

In this entry we attempt to give an up-to-date view of research on fallacy. Since the term chiefly inhabits the fields of logic and argumentation theory, that is where we shall find our focus. In distinguishing between logic and rhetoric, we do not pledge allegiance to the ancient antagonism between them. We understand by rhetoric the study of the uniquely human ability to use symbols to communicate with one another, and we take it as well that the paradigm case of rhetoric is the use of the spoken word to persuade an audience. We understand by logic the study of the good and the bad in matters of reasoning. Perhaps the chief contribution of rhetoric to logic and argumentation has been to call attention to the *context* of and the *audience* of argumentation, whereas logicians have tended to be more concerned with matters of structure and form.

The question we propose to raise is: What importance is the study of fallacy for the rhetorician? We will come back to this question at the end. In the next section, we shall give a brief historical overview on the topic of fallacy, after which we move to discuss the issues and problems in current research. We shall first discuss briefly Aristotle's contribution to the subject and then its more recent history.

In logic, as in so many other areas of philosophy, all roads lead back to Aristotle. His work *Prior Analytics* is considered the seminal work of formal logic. Here Aristotle studies the syllogism and does so with a view to discerning valid from invalid forms. The syllogism is meant to be part of Aristotle's theory of scientific reasoning and demonstration. It is customary to trace what is now called informal logic back to the *Topics,* where Aristotle treats of reasoning in which the conclusion follows from the premises *ut in pluribus,* "for the most part." Today we would call this probabilistic reasoning, except that Aristotle understands the term *probable* much less technically than we do. For Aristotle, the term *topos* means "a commonplace of argument"—borrowed, says W.D. Ross (*Aristotle,* 1959) to a large extent from the Academy, and the principal method discussed there is the dialectic. The *topoi* are understood as "the pigeon holes from which dialectical reasoning is to draw its arguments" (Ross 61).

The fallacy tradition, which has become a part of informal logic, goes back to *De Sophisticis Elenchis,* where terms like "begging the question" and "false refutation" are introduced. These are

FIGURE 1.

The Demands of Rationality or Reasonableness (Aristotle's *Organon* revisited)

Thinking/Acting/Talking as Reason Requires

Formal Logic	Natural Science	Ethics	Law & Politics	Informal Logic	Rhetoric
Respecting the demands of basic intelligibility	Respecting the natural grain of the world	Respecting the projects of others (as individuals)	Respecting the projects of others (as collectives)	Respecting the special nature of the present case	Respecting the standpoint of the hearers or readers
Aristotle's *Prior Analytics*	Aristotle's *Posterior Analytics*	Aristotle's *Ethics*	Aristotle's *Politics*	Aristotle's *Special Topics*	Aristotle's *Art of Rhetoric*

Source: Stephen Toulmin. "Logic, Rhetoric, and Reason: Restoring the Balance." Ed. Van Eemeren, et al. *Argumentation Illuminated*, p. 6.

called "sophisms"—the moves that sophists make "to puzzle the plain man by the apparent refutation of his cherished opinions" (Ross 62). Thus, sophisms are false moves within the highly structured kind of discourse practiced in the Lyceum. (Aristotle's *Rhetoric* is not so important a document for our understanding of fallacy.) For an evocative understanding of Aristotle's logical works and their role in his account of reasoning, this diagram due to Toulmin (6) is helpful.

According to Hamblin, whose *Fallacies* (1970) is still treated with great deference, not much happens in the Middle Ages and so we come next to John Locke, who adds the so-called *"ad"* fallacies to the canon, chief among which are the *ad hominem* (attack the person), the *ad verecundiam* (the appeal to authority), and those which may be of special interest to rhetoricians: the *ad misericordiam* (the appeal to pity) and the *ad baculum* (the appeal to force). For the rest, the history of modern logic is largely the history of formal logic. Consequently, scant attention is paid to fallacy. This remains true right through the first seventy years of the twentieth century, which were devoted largely to the development of the logistic systems of modern symbolic (mathematical) logic.

The tide turns in the early 1970s, which witnessed publication of two important books. One was Hamblin's *Fallacy*—a scholarly monograph on the topic of fallacy. The other is Kahane's *Logic and Contemporary Rhetoric*—a college textbook that revolutionized the way in which logic was taught to undergraduates in colleges and universities. Kahane virtually discards formal logic and makes fallacy the critical workhorse. It is ironic that these two develop-

ments, which pull in somewhat different directions, occur virtually at the same moment in history and independently of one another. While Kahane sees fallacy as a new approach to logic and rhetoric, Hamblin is engaged in a critique of fallacy. His castigation of what he calls "The Standard Account" (of fallacy in logic texts) has become famous:

And what we find in most cases, I think it should be admitted, is as debased, worn-out and dogmatic a treatment as could be imagined—incredibly tradition-bound, yet lacking in logic and historical sense alike, and almost without connection to anything else in modern Logic at all. This is the part of his book in which a writer throws away logic and keeps his readers attention, if at all, only by retailing traditional puns, anecdotes, and witless examples of his forbears. (12)

While it is questionable whether the textbook tradition is really as corrupt as Hamblin alleges, his critique struck a responsive chord, and became the platform from which Walton's and Woods's research on the fallacies in the seventies takes off. We turn next to a discussion of the research on fallacy of the last twenty years.

Current research on fallacy tends to have three foci. The first is the question of how to define or understand fallacy, and the related question whether or not there are fallacies. The second issue is the question of whether fallacy theory constitutes a viable theory of criticism. The third focus is the study of individual fallacies. All of these were stimulated by the work of Walton and Wood in the 1970s, which convinced logicians that fallacies could be the sub-ject of serious inquiry.

There is no single conception of fallacy to which all those interested in this topic can pledge allegiance. Until recently, the most fre-quently quoted definition was Hamblin's: "an argument which appears to be valid but is not." The division of labor made formal fallacy the topic of formal logic; informal fallacy became the focus of informal logic.

The last few years have witnessed significant developments in the understanding of fallacy. Eemeren and Grootendorst (1989), founders of the pragma-dialectical school of argumentation, see fallacies as procedural violations of the rules for critical discussion. After repeating the stan-dard charge against fallacies, that fallacies are not always fallacious, Willard suggests, "It is permissible to conceptualize the rules standing behind each fallacy more as *topoi* than as restric-tions" (Willard 235–36). Johnson (1989) criti-cizes the definition given by Hamblin and sug-gests that it be replaced by a more generic and less formalistic account: A fallacy is a violation of the criteria of good argumentation that occurs with sufficient frequency to be worth baptizing. Walton largely agrees with the pragma-dialecti-cal approach and now understands fallacy as "a technique of argumentation that may in principle be reasonable but that has been misused in a given case in such a way that it goes strongly against or hinders the goals of dialogue" (18). Thus it seems that there has been a shift away from defining fallacy either in terms of deceptive intent, or apparent validity, to viewing fallacy as a breakdown in dialogue. Not everyone, how-ever, has followed this trend. Woods views fal-lacies as snares and delusions, which may serve as a launching pad for deeper theoretical inquiry.

The 1980s witnessed a debate about whether there were fallacies and whether fal-lacy theory could be made viable against the standard criticisms.

Karel Lambert and William Ulrich (*The Nature of Argument*, 1980) approach fallacy from the perspective of formal logicians who claim that the very idea of an informal fallacy is incoherent, because a fallacy is a violation of formal criteria (such as the use of an undistrib-uted middle term in syllogistic logic). Finocchi-aro castigates textbook accounts of fallacy and suggests that fallacy typically results from uncharitable reconstruction of the argument; hence it appears that fallacies may exist only in the mind of the critic. Massey, adopting Hamblin's definition of fallacy, argues that there cannot be any theory of fallacy because there cannot be a theory of invalidity.

Govier responds to all three. As against Lambert and Ulrich, Govier argues that their account presupposes a deductivist theory of ar-gument, which, she argues, is much too narrow a view to be satisfactory. As against Massey, she argues that invalidity is neither a necessary nor yet a sufficient condition for fallaciousness: "From the perspective of a pluralistic theory of argument and a nonformalist concept of theo-retical adequacy, Massey's argument against the fallacies is far from evident." As against Finocchiaro, she argues that even granted his point that textbook accounts of fallacy are sloppy and inaccurate and insensitive to context, the sweeping conclusion he appears to draw from this fact is "simply not warranted by the evidence put forward" (196). Johnson (1989) argues that Massey's critique is premised on ac-cepting Hamblin's definition of fallacy, without which the argument is largely disabled.

Tighter and more finely focused book-length studies of fallacy have been more promi-nent in the last decade, and most of them have viewed fallacy in the context of argumentation and have shown the benefits of the rhetorical concern for context and audience. There have also been many more limited studies of the individual fallacies (cf. Brinton). For a useful bibliography of recent work on fallacy and par-ticular fallacies, the reader should consult Han-sen's bibliography.

In spite of challenges and criticisms, the topic of fallacy has remained a significant focus for research. Hamblin's castigation of the study of fallacies, which may have been apt when writ-ten twenty years ago, would not have the same force today.

From the point of view of logicians, the subject of fallacy remains a focal point of both inquiry and controversy. That controversy has been nourished by the concerns of rhetoricians for context and audience, which concerns have gradually been felt in informal logic. Thus arises the question whether a particular move might not be fallacious in one context but perfectly acceptable in another. Recent accounts of fal-lacy have displayed a much greater sensitivity to context, and this appears to be due in no small measure to the influence of rhetorical points of view. Logicians, however, tend to want to retain a normative component in the study of fallacy, which means that the suggestion by

F

some (Ulrich; Willard) that fallacy are *topoi* will face tough opposition.

Ralph H. Johnson
University of Windsor

Bibliography

Note: The current state of research on fallacy remains so disparate that there is no center; there is no one work that all those interested in fallacy theory acknowledge as, if not authoritative, then at least a "must read." The last to so qualify would be Hamblin.

Blair, J. Anthony. "Fallacies in Everyday Argument." *Perspectives on Argumentation: Essays in Honor of Wayne Brockreide*. Ed. Robert Trapp and Janice Schuetz. Prospect Heights, IL: Waveland, 1990. 121–33.

Brinton, Alan. "A Rhetorical View of the *Ad Hominem*." *Australian Journal of Philosophy* 63 (1985): 50–63.

Eemeren, Frans van, and Rob Grootendorst. "A Transition Stage in the Theory of Fallacies." *Journal of Pragmatics* 13 (1989): 99–109.

Finocchiaro, Maurice. "Fallacies and the Evaluation of Reasoning." *American Philosophical Quarterly* 18 (1981): 13–22.

Govier, Trudy. "Four Reasons There Are No Fallacies?" *Problems in Argument Analysis and Evaluation*. Dordrecht, Holland: Foris, 1987. 177–202.

Hamblin, C.L. *Fallacies*. London: Methuen, 1970.

Hansen, Hans V. "An Informal Logic Bibliography." *Informal Logic* 12 (1990): 155–84.

Johnson, Ralph H. "The Blaze of Her Splendors." *Argumentation* 1 (1987): 239–53.

———. "Massey on Fallacy and Informal Logic: A Reply." *Synthese* 80 (1989): 407–26.

Massey, Gerald. "The Fallacy Behind Fallacies." *Midwest Studies in Philosophy* 5 (1980): 489–500.

Ross, W.D. *Aristotle*. Cleveland: World, 1959.

Toulmin, Stephen. "Logic, Rhetoric and Reason: Redressing the Balance." *Argumentation Illuminated*. Ed. Frans H. van Eemeren, Rob Grootendorst, J. Anthony Blair, and Charles A. Willard. Amsterdam: Sicast, 1992. 3–11.

Ulrich, Walter. "In Defense of the Fallacy." *Argument and Social Practice: Proceedings of the Fourth SCA/AFA Conference on Argumentation*. Ed. J. Robert Cox, Malcolm O. Sillars, and Gregg B. Walker. Annandale, VA: Speech Communication Assn., 1985. 110–26.

Walton, Douglas Neil. *The Place of Emotion in Argument*. University Park: Pennsylvania State UP, 1992.

Willard, Charles. *A Theory of Argumentation*. Tuscaloosa: Alabama State UP, 1989.

Woods, John. "Who Cares About the Fallacies?" *Argumentation Illuminated*. Ed. Frans H. van Eemeren, Rob Grootendorst, J. Anthony Blair, and Charles A. Willard. Amsterdam: Sicsat, 1992. 23–48.

Woods, John, and Douglas Walton. *Fallacies: Selected Papers 1972–82*. Dordrecht, Holland: Foris, 1989.

Fantasy Theme Analysis

The line of scholarship that resulted in the development of the symbolic convergence theory, which is an empirically based study of the shared imagination. In addition, fantasy theme analysis is a humanistically based study of rhetorical history and criticism and interpretative approaches to the study of interpersonal, small group, organizational, and media communication.

The social scientific basis for symbolic convergence came from small group laboratories. Studies at Harvard and Minnesota discovered the basic process of group fantasy chains. The chains resulted in the participants' coming to share a group fantasy and the resultant common consciousness with its associated symbolic common ground, emotional evocations, motivations, and group culture. The investigations began with the careful definition of dramatizing messages. Observers then studied the effect of dramatizing on group members. They found that some dramatizations caused a minor symbolic explosion in the form of a chain reaction. As the members shared the fantasy, the tempo of the conversation would pick up. People grew excited, interrupted one another, laughed, showed emotion, forgot their self-consciousness. The people who shared the fantasy did so with the appropriate responses. If the storyteller wanted it to be funny, they laughed; if it was supposed to be serious or solemn, they grew serious and solemn. Further studies revealed that on some occasions group members were apathetic and ignored the dramatizing while on others they rejected the fantasies contained in the dramatizations. Scholars then discovered that the sharing of fantasies also characterized listener responses to a wide range of communication, including conversations, public speeches, and mass media messages.

The symbolic convergence theory has evolved out of fantasy theme analysis over the last several decades as part of a general movement in rhetorical and communication studies to recover and stress the importance of imaginative language (and the imagination) in nonverbal and verbal transactions and upon group consciousness. The efforts at finding some accommodation for imagination, feeling, and envisioning on the one hand and rationality on the other have included investigations into subjects then thought to be more appropriate to aesthetics, art, and literature than to rhetoric. In the 1960s and 1970s, these efforts have often had to face the barrier of rationality. While rhetoricians paid some attention to the imaginative dimension of rhetoric, their attention tended to focus on the logical. Among those who saw themselves as scholars of communication the hegemony of rationality promulgated a view of communication that suggested that myths were false, that stories were fictitious, and that anecdotal evidence was suspect.

Fantasy theme analysis has been controversial, particularly in the early years. Some critics saw it as essentially dealing with the irrational and unrealistic with an undue reliance on Freudian thought. Other critics suggested that while the sharing of fantasies was an important part of small group communication, the move to other contexts was not justified. The proponents of fantasy theme analysis and the symbolic convergence theory have responded by denying the Freudian link and emphasizing the way the sharing of fantasies provides the values and common ground required for logical argument. They have also argued that additional research has demonstrated the sharing process in other communication contexts.

The first fundamental term of fantasy theme analysis is that of *dramatizing message*; the second is of *shared group fantasy*. The point is that people may be exposed to many dramatizing messages without sharing any of them and, if so, *they do not share a group fantasy*: The two technical terms are not interchangeable.

Ordinary usage may focus on one meaning of fantasy, that is, of moonshine, cartoon sorts of things that are opposed to what is real. The technical term, *fantasy*, in fantasy theme analysis denotes the creative and imaginative shared interpretation of events that fulfills a group's psychological or rhetorical need to make sense of its experience and to anticipate its future. Rhetorical fantasies often deal with nonfictitious as well as fictitious dramas. Group fantasies are generally a result of the internal fantasy life of audience members and they are full of images reflecting experience. Often when people dramatize objects of the perceived world, they succeed in getting sharing by shaping and forming them until they are consistent with the fantasies (the existing mental world) of audience members.

Once members of a group have shared a fantasy, they often create another important communication phenomenon in the workings of *symbolic cues* or triggers. The symbolic cue may be a code word, phrase, slogan, or nonverbal sign or gesture. It may refer to geographical or imaginary place or the name of a persona. The symbolic cue is an induction that allows members to symbolize an entire fantasy chain with a brief allusion to it. The inside-joke phenomenon is an example of such a trigger. Only those who have shared the fantasy theme that the inside-joke refers to will respond in an appropriate fashion. But the symbolic cue need not be only an inside-joke. The allusion to a previously shared fantasy may arouse tears or evoke anger, hatred, love, and affection as well as laughter and humor. Inside cues provide the basis for further generalizations. When members of a group have shared several similar fantasy themes, they develop a more abstract recurring form that summarizes the common features of the themes. The more general scenarios constitute a *fantasy type*. Group members can use the fantasy type as a script to explain and evaluate the breaking news or changing experiences and bring these events into line with the values of their group. The Watergate fantasy theme has been generalized to become a type cued by the suffix "gate." Thus new scandals can be typed by using the suffix, as in "Billygate" or "Irangate."

Finally, a community of people may share fantasy themes and types until at some point they fit them into an overarching and coherent view of some aspect of their social reality. The technical term for such a view is *rhetorical vi-*

F

sion. A rhetorical vision is often integrated by a master analogy. The people who share a rhetorical vision form a rhetorical community and participate in a common consciousness.

Fantasy theme analysis forces the scholar to search for the boundaries of rhetorical communities and reveals the complex and complicated symbolic terrain in a given historical period. Such analysis is a strong antidote to interpretations that select out of such complexity a cluster of ideas and suggest that this cluster represents the essence of a historical period in national life. Even selecting out a half-dozen such clusters will often oversimplify the rhetorical diversity in the history of a given time period or geographical region.

Rhetorical criticism involves more than descriptions of discourse and accounts of how it came into being and functioned. Fantasy theme analysts are free to approach their critical work from a variety of perspectives, and they have done so. They always begin, however, by documenting the presence of the sharing phenomenon and the resulting shared consciousness among members of the community. They have been forced, because of the method of criticism, to put the audience back into the rhetorical paradigm. Much rhetorical criticism focuses on the message divorced from an audience that responds or fails to respond to the stimulus. Some criticism focuses on the message and discusses an implied audience or an ideal audience. By contrast, the fantasy theme analyst is encouraged to bring the audience forward into a central position in the study, for until the dramatizing is shared it does not become a fantasy.

Critics who reconstruct the rhetorical visions of communities of people can ask general rhetorical questions in order to analyze the hopes and fears, the emotional tone, and the inner life of the group by examining how the rhetoric deals with basic universal problems. Such insight flows from answers to such questions as these: How well did the communication deal with the problem of creating and celebrating a sense of community? Did it help generate a group and individual self-image that was strong, confident and resilient? How did the rhetoric aid or hinder the community in its adaptation to its physical environment? How did the communication deal with the rhetorical problem of creating a social reality that provides norms for community behavior in terms of the level of violence, exploitation, domi-nance, and injustice? Did the communication create a panoramic vision that served such mythic functions as providing members with an account of the world, the gods, and fate, and that gave meaning to their community and themselves? How well did the vision aid the people who participated in it to live with people who shared different rhetorical visions?

Because fantasy theme analysis incorporates a general social scientific theory of communication (symbolic convergence), it is based on a carefully defined common set of technical terms. Such common terms imbedded in a coherent theoretical structure enable fantasy theme analysts to compare and integrate the findings of a number of separate studies into generalizations about communication. Scholars using the approach often aim to discover knowledge about human communication that transcends communication styles, contexts, and transitory issues. The method allows its practitioners to aim at broad general understandings of human communication in all its varied forms, but particularly as it is used in a rhetorical way.

Ernest G. Bormann
University of Minnesota

Bibliography

Bales, Robert F. *Personality and Interpersonal Relations.* New York: Holt, 1970.

Bormann, Ernest G. "Fantasy and Rhetorical Vision: The Rhetorical Criticism of Social Reality." *Quarterly Journal of Speech* 58 (1972): 396–407.

——. *The Force of Fantasy: Restoring the American Dream.* Carbondale: Southern Illinois UP, 1985.

——. "Rhetoric as a Way of Knowing: Ernest Bormann and Fantasy Theme Analysis." *The Rhetoric of Western Thought.* 3rd ed. Ed. James L. Golden, Goodwin Berquist, and William E. Coleman. Dubuque, IA: Kendall/Hunt, 1983. 431–49.

Brock, Bernard L., Robert L. Scott, and James W. Chesebro, eds. *Methods of Rhetorical Criticism.* 3rd ed. Detroit: Wayne State UP, 1990.

Cragan, John F., and Donald C. Shields. *Applied Communication Research: A Dramatistic Approach.* Prospect Heights, IL: Waveland, 1981.

See also BORMANN, ERNEST G.

Fell, Margaret (1614–1702)

A Renaissance advocate for women's right to speak in public, whose arguments contribute to feminist rhetorical theory. Fell was an early convert to the Society of Friends, the so-called "Quakers," and became an important Quaker leader. She made the estate of her first husband, Thomas Fell, into a sustaining center of Quaker activity in England, spoke extensively in behalf of the new faith, and, with her second husband, George Fox, developed Quaker ideas on egalitarian relations between the sexes.

Margaret married Thomas Fell when she was seventeen, and they had eight children. He was a member of the landed gentry who held influential positions as judge and vice-chancellor of the Duchy of Lancashire. She met George Fox in 1652 and soon converted to his radical religious vision, which founded the Society of Friends. Thomas Fell did not become a Quaker, but he used his position to protect his wife from the persecutions often visited upon Quakers.

At first, Margaret Fell's involvement with the Quaker cause amounted mainly to supporting Fox and other indigent, itinerant preachers of the new faith. After her husband died in 1658, however, Fell became more active. She preached Quaker ideas herself and also solicited legal protection for the new faith, traveling to London in 1674 to convince King Charles II to pardon Fox, imprisoned for his beliefs. In 1684 she delivered petitions that persuaded James II to proclaim tolerance for religious dissent. In 1697 she appeared before William II to plead for continued protection for Quakers.

Fell herself experienced persecution for her religious activities after her husband's death. While jailed in Lancashire Castle from 1664 to 1668, she wrote a tract, first published in 1666, titled *Women's Speaking Justified, Proved, and Allowed by the Scriptures*. "A further Addition" and "Postscript" were added to this text in its second edition, in 1667.

Renaissance rhetorical theory often forbade public speaking by women, on the grounds that they thereby damaged their chastity. Protestant Christianity, however, exerted some counterpressure to this view, for example through female preachers who sometimes addressed very large crowds. Fell wanted the Society of Friends to explicitly permit public religious activity by women and to espouse sexual equality generally. She shaped George Fox's thinking on this subject, especially after they were married in 1669, and the Quaker ideas on relations between the sexes that issued from their collaboration were notably egalitarian. For instance, they denounced the subordination of women to men in marriage.

Fell recognized that women were often persecuted for their religious activities as much because they were women "improperly" appearing in public as because their views were heterodox. Her tract, then, while having as a secondary audience those Quaker men who were not yet convinced of the need for equality of the sexes, was addressed primarily to non-Quakers who held more stringent views against women speaking in public.

In her tract Fell marshals biblical evidence against the inferiority of women, for the wisdom of women and their power as teachers, and for the right of women to publicly proclaim religious truth. Her reinterpretations of these biblical texts resemble revisionist views developed in feminist theology of the twentieth century. Her explanations of what women speakers have to offer sound similar to twentieth-century essentialist feminist explanations of the peculiar merits of the woman's perspective. Fell articulates a public persona for the woman speaker akin to the biblical prophet, entitled to speak in order to denounce public evils and promote public good. Her own ideas on women's rhetoric can be considered as prophetic.

Patricia Bizzell
College of the Holy Cross

Bibliography

Bacon, Margaret Hope. *Mothers of Feminism: The Story of Quaker Women in America*. New York: Harper, 1986.

Fell, Margaret, and Mary Waite. *Women's Speaking Justified / Margaret Fell / Epistle from the womens yearly meeting at York, 1688. A Warning to all Friends / Mary Waite*. 1666, 1667. Rpt. (facsimile) Ed. and Intro. by David J. Latt, Augustan Reprint Society #194, William Andrews Clark Memorial Library, U of California at Berkeley, 1979; and in *The Rhetorical Tradition: Readings from Classical Times to the Present*. Ed. Patricia Bizzell and Bruce Herzberg, Boston: Bedford, 1990.

Ross, Isabel. *Margaret Fell: Mother of Quakerism*. London: Longmans, 1949.

Feminist Rhetoric

Evolved out of women's struggle for the right to speak into a style of discourse, a way of knowing, and a particular form of analysis.

Gerda Lerner's work traces the history of feminist discourse in the European tradition (*Creation of Feminist Consciousness*) and the ideology and practice to which it was a response (*Creation of Patriarchy*). Campbell in *Man Cannot Speak for Her* analyzes the rhetoric of the first wave of feminism in the United States in the nineteenth century; the two-volume reference on early and contemporary women speakers (*Women Public Speakers in the United States*) offers rhetorical biographies of many important figures. Key examples of feminist rhetoric include works by Daly, MacKinnon, and Rich. Janeway's book is a sophisticated analysis of the social mythology against which feminists struggle. Works by Belenky, Bleier, and Okin illustrate feminist rereadings of epistemology, biology, and political theory. Jarratt et al. reexamine rhetorical history from a feminist perspective. Woolf's book is a feminist classic that has influenced deeply the works of others.

Feminist originally meant the same as *feminine*, of the female. Late in the nineteenth century, the meaning shifted to refer to efforts to improve the status of women. Even then, *feminist* had negative connotations because activists were seen as unwomanly—they were selfishly concerned with their own aspirations instead of ministering to others. Moreover, they immodestly asserted their concerns publicly rather than using their influence indirectly at home.

In what follows, feminist rhetoric is treated, first, as the battle to be allowed a voice in public affairs; second, as the effort to appear credible; third, as discourse sometimes based on equality and sometimes on sexual difference; and, finally, as an analysis of patriarchy in which consciousness-raising is a political process, a rhetorical style, and a way of knowing.

Struggling for a Voice

The earliest U.S. feminist agitation was a by-product of women's efforts in support of other reform movements. Women agitating against slavery, alcohol abuse, and prostitution were censured for involving themselves in activities outside the home. Although True Women were believed to be morally superior to men, their efforts to address these issues were severely rebuffed, even by the clergy. Accordingly, what began as moral crusades became efforts to justify woman's right to participate in public deliberation. Feminist rhetoric, then, begins with efforts by women for the right to have a voice in community affairs.

Rhetoric always grows out of prior rhetoric. Thus, early women's rhetoric was shaped by the social mythology that prescribed woman's place and defined her as chaste, spiritual, submissive, modest, and domestic. Until the modern period, when an organized movement emerged, the denial of education to women and the suppression of women's history prevented later generations of women from building on earlier efforts to undermine the social mythology (Lerner 1993). The contradiction between women's allegedly greater purity and piety and their restriction to domesticity ultimately enabled women to justify their right to speak. They responded to the theological, biological, and political/sociological rationales defining woman and denying her any role in public deliberation.

The most troublesome obstacle to woman's right to speak was the theological view that woman's role had been ordained by God, who proscribed a woman's teaching or speaking. Early feminists challenged such interpretations (Lerner 1993). They noted internal contradictions in the Pauline epistles, called attention to female judges, prophets, and leaders in Israel and in the early church, and used the words and actions of Jesus to assert a single moral standard applicable to all, whatever their sex. The issue generated a substantial amount of discourse, including books by such eminent early woman's movement figures as Matilda Joslyn Gage (1826–1898), Elizabeth Cady Stanton (1815–1902), and Frances Willard (1839–1898) (see entries in Campbell 1993).

Early women also were aided by religious ideas. Protestantism's assertion of a "priesthood of believers" was a powerful argument for a woman's spiritual rights. The Society of Friends believed that the "inner light" was in all. Accordingly, Quakers educated girls as well as boys, treated preaching as a form of prophecy open to women, and allowed women to become "public Friends" who addressed outsiders. Quaker women, such as Sarah (1792–1873) and Angelina Grimke (1805–1879), Lucretia Coffin Mott (1793–1880), Susan B. Anthony (1820–1906), and Alice Paul (1885–1977), played major roles in early feminism.

Theology continues to be an important barrier as illustrated by the works of contemporary feminist theologians Mary Daly and Rosemary Radford Ruether. Daly sums up the link between sexism and religion by saying, "If God is male, then the male is God" (1973:19).

In early feminism, beliefs about biology, mostly inaccurate, also were used to justify woman's exclusion from the public realm. If females were educated, it was believed that their ovaries and wombs could not develop properly, as blood needed would be diverted to the brain (Campbell 1989:12). Because women generally are smaller than men, their brains must be smaller, too small for the mental tasks of public deliberation. Their supposedly smaller nerves would be too delicate and fragile to withstand the rigors of the marketplace, the law courts, or the legislature.

In more contemporary times, biology and psychology have been used to argue that woman's traditional roles are "natural." In 1948 Ruth Herschberger published *Adam's Rib,* her pointed and humorous critique of the primate experiments at the Yerkes laboratories that were used to demonstrate that traditional gender roles were part of primate biology. Others have attacked similar conclusions based on primate research, clinical psychology, and sociobiology (Bleier).

A final category of justification is sociological and political, claiming that the family, not the individual, is the fundamental social unit, publicly represented by a male head. Although liberalism is associated with individualism, John Stuart Mill (1806–1873) was the first to argue that the rights of individual women might not be well represented by the family (1979). Laws treating women, particularly wives, differently than men have been the targets of early woman's rights advocates as well as contemporary feminists (Campbell 1989).

Struggling to Be Credible

Once the rhetorical barrier was breached, problems of credibility emerged. Gender is a powerful variable in rhetoric and in personal identity. It is related to rhetoric because qualities admired in rhetoric are those traditionally linked to masculinity: assertiveness, leadership, rational deliberation, refutational and debating skills, and expertise. In addition, public issues are defined as matters best addressed by men: commerce, military matters, legislation, foreign policy, and economic affairs. In other words, those who engage in public discourse are expected to display qualities traditionally associated with masculinity and to discuss issues that are traditionally the concerns of males.

Moreover, because the speaker's character is a matter of great importance in public discourse, gender enters into persuasion. As a rhetor, one's personal ethos depends significantly on community ethos—that is, on the extent to which the individual exemplifies the community's values. To be treated as credible, a woman is expected to exemplify the community conception of femininity. As a rhetor, however, she is expected to embody qualities that traditionally are associated with masculinity. In other words, "any public performance for a woman (except as an actress or a prostitute) is a form of cross-dressing" (Jarratt 2).

Early women's rhetoric offers an array of creative strategies by which women overcame this dilemma. Angelina Grimke, for example, astutely adopted public personae suited to women. Addressing the Massachusetts State Legislature, she compared herself to Queen Esther, who left her private role in order to save her people, and when addressing an abolitionist audience of men and women in Philadelphia, she adopted the role of prophet, for which there were female models in both the Old and New Testaments (Campbell 29–33).

Some strategies were widespread. Many women cited male authorities to establish expertise and to avoid claiming it for themselves. Most addressed audiences as peers or suppliants. Many structured their discourse inductively to draw on personal experience, evidence deemed suitable for women, and to give audiences the illusion that they were drawing conclusions for themselves rather than being led by a woman. Overt refutation usually was avoided, although opposing arguments often were attacked indirectly through debunking illustrations or humorously revealed inconsistencies. As a group, these strategies constitute a *feminine style* (Campbell).

The struggle for the right to speak abated as the nineteenth century ended, but the struggle to be taken seriously continued. Although suffrage advocacy had continued for more than sixty years, only persistent militancy, primarily by the National Woman's Party, led by Alice Paul, moved woman suffrage to the top of the national agenda. Marches, demonstrations, picketing the White House, and burning President Wilson's paeans to a democracy that did not include women, accompanied by a women's press corps to attract media attention, demonstrated women's intense commitment to enfranchisement and kept the issue before the public and Congress, which led to the passage of what became the Nineteenth Amendment.

Equality versus Sexual Difference

The conflict between femininity and feminism also affected the arguments women made. Although activists shared a commitment to improving the status of women, their discourse was not a seamless whole. Some grounded their arguments in equality, others in sexual difference, still others combined them. Natural rights argument claimed legal and political equality for females based on personhood and, in its pure form, made no provision for women's biology. By contrast, appeals based on sexual difference argued that women's unique qualities would benefit the public sphere, and that enlarged rights would enable women better to fulfill their duties as wives and mothers. These often were mixed. Some sought legal and political equality but acknowledged differences that would benefit the public sphere; some called for economic recognition of the social value of maternity and child-rearing. Some argued that equality of opportunity was needed in order to discover what differences were natural. Some argued that women's biology gave them a unique perspective on some issues—for example, that childbirth and child-rearing made women natural pacifists unwilling to risk the lives of sons they had borne and reared.

These differing assumptions continue to be significant because they reflect the relative emphasis given to socialization and biology. Some contemporary feminists blame socialization for the ills of contemporary women. Others blame the patriarchy; still others adopt a "pro-woman line" to argue that women choose traditional paths because these have been the best choices among the options available. Such disagreements have sparked controversy over whether the absence of women in certain categories of employment results from discrimination or from their choice to avoid employment that would interfere with their responsibilities as wives and mothers.

Patriarchy and Consciousness-Raising

The efforts of earlier women laid the foundation for a kind of discourse that in the modern period can rightly be identified as feminist both in content and style. In content, feminist rhetoric drew its premises from a radical analysis of patriarchy, which identified the "man-made world" as one built on the oppression of women (Janeway). Catharine MacKinnon argues that, at least in one sense, women's lot is worse than that of slaves because it was never assumed that slavery was created for the pleasure and enjoyment of the slaves (167–68). Others describe heterosexism as an institution dedicated to the oppression of women (Rich). Feminists call attention to a world in which there is a power struggle between men and women and in which the economic, political, and social systems are designed to maintain female inferiority and dependency (Daly).

Those systems are sustained by policies that exclude women, by attitudes that resist change, and by social norms that define women as personal body servants for their husbands and children, norms enforced through sexual harassment and sexual assault, which are celebrated in and justified by the rhetoric of pornography. In other words, the feminism that emerged in the 1960s was a rude disclosure of the ways in which patriarchy benefited men and disadvantaged women. At its most extreme, feminist rhetoric pointed to the victims of the war between the sexes—to the survivors of rape and incest and the wives and girlfriends battered and murdered by their husbands and "lovers." Feminist scholars also explored the history of patriarchy and identified the emotional and economic grounds for male resistance to change (Lerner 1986).

Feminist rhetoric is a radical and far-reaching analysis of the ideology of patriarchy and the underlying relations between the sexes. In addition, it incorporates a style of communication known as consciousness-raising, which emerged first in the small groups that were typical of the women's liberation movement but that also characterized much of the public discourse through which feminist ideas were articulated. In small groups consciousness-raising was a process through which women shared personal experiences in order to identify what was idiosyncratic and what was systemic. Participants moved from what they had believed were personal, individual problems toward identification of common experiences, a product not of character, personality, or ability, but a function of their status as women. Hence, the familiar slogan "the personal is political."

As a process, consciousness-raising is not entirely personal and experiential. The winnowing that distinguishes the idiosyncratic from the systemic incorporates research and critical analysis. In addition, it requires a relatively homogeneous, leaderless group in which all participate. Thus, as a style of communicating and learning, consciousness-raising is personal, experiential, participatory, and, hence, emotional and egalitarian. It proceeds inductively, moving from personal experiences toward generalizations that reflect the systemically shaped conditions of women generally.

Although usually identified with small groups, consciousness-raising can also be a style of public discourse strategically adapted to women as speakers addressing women as audiences. In such cases, feminists use their own experiences or those of others as a prime source of evidence; they structure arguments inductively to develop conclusions out of a series of instances; they use questions and other devices to prompt the participation of the audience, and they speak as peers sharing experience, not as authorities brandishing academic credentials. The much-praised feminist classic by Virginia Woolf (1882–1941), *A Room of One's Own* (1929/1957), is a prime example of consciousness-raising as a style of writing. Socialization is one reason that women find this style congenial.

Women's traditional tasks are examples of craft learning, a lore developed through trial and error usually supervised by a mentor. Parenting, satisfying the competing demands of spouse and children, and performing most household tasks cannot be learned just by reading books. Through trial and error, one learns the contingencies that affect them. Consciousness-raising style mimics the participatory, experience-based, inductive processes of craft learning, substituting research into and comparison with the experiences of other women for mentoring. Accordingly, although not the exclusive purview of women, this is a style of communicating with which most women as rhetors and audiences feel comfortable.

In some instances the assumption underlying consciousness-raising style—truth emerging out of women's lived experience—has become an integral element in feminist analysis, a feminist epistemology (Belenky et al.). In the thinking of some contemporary feminists, including contemporary French feminists, it is a way of knowing (Jarratt 39-41). Catharine MacKinnon and Andrea Dworkin, for example, call attention to the ways in which pornography silences women, and they speak and write in styles that privilege the voices of women who experience its effects.

Neither the analysis of patriarchy nor consciousness-raising as a small group process, a style of discourse, or a source of human truth is entirely the creation of contemporary feminism. Scattered analyses of patriarchy emerged in the earlier movement. Similarly, consciousness-raising mimics the "testimony" of some religious practices and has been used in revolutionary guerrilla movements. Contemporary feminists, however, have produced far more systematic analyses of patriarchy than their predecessors, and they have used consciousness-raising deliberately and systematically as a way of radicalizing women and of discovering truths about their condition.

Karlyn Kohrs Campbell
University of Minnesota

Bibliography

Belenky, Mary F., Blythe McVicker Clinchy, Nancy Rule Goldberger, and Jill Mattuck Tarule. *Women's Ways of Knowing: The Development of Self, Voice, and Mind.* New York: Basic, 1986.

Bleier, Ruth. *Science and Gender.* New York: Pergamon, 1984.

Campbell, Karlyn Kohrs. *Man Cannot Speak for Her.* 2 vols. Westport, CT.: Greenwood, 1989.

———. *Women Public Speakers in the United States, 1800–1925; 1925–1993: A Bio-Critical Dictionary.* 2 vols. Westport, CT: Greenwood, 1993–1994.

Daly, Mary. *Beyond God the Father: Toward a Philosophy of Women's Liberation.* 1973. Rpt. Boston: Beacon, 1985.

———. *Gyn/Ecology: The Metaethics of Radical Feminism.* 1978. Rpt. Boston: Beacon, 1990.

Janeway, Elizabeth. *Man's World, Woman's Place: A Study in Social Mythology.* New York: Morrow/Dell, 1971.

Jarratt, Susan C., ed. "Feminist Rereadings in the History of Rhetoric." Special issue. *Rhetoric Society Quarterly* 22 (Winter 1992).

Lerner, Gerda. *The Creation of Feminist Consciousness.* New York: Oxford UP, 1993.

———. *The Creation of Patriarchy.* New York: Oxford UP, 1986.

MacKinnon, Catharine A. *Feminism Unmodified: Discourses on Life and Law.* Cambridge, MA: Harvard UP, 1987.

Okin, Susan Moller. *Women in Western Political Thought.* Princeton: Princeton UP, 1979.

Rich, Adrienne. "Compulsory Heterosexuality and Lesbian Existence." *Signs: Journal of Women in Culture and Society* 5 (1980): 631–60.

Woolf, Virginia. *A Room of One's Own.* 1929. Rpt. New York: Harcourt, 1957.

F

Fénelon, François de Salignac de la Mothe (1651–1715)

Archbishop of Cambrai and tutor of the Duke of Burgundy. While Fénelon was best known as the author of Télémaque and of a treatise on the education of girls, his contributions to early modern rhetoric were considerable. Fénelon's *Dialogues on Eloquence* were written in the seventeenth century but not published until 1717. This work put forward Fénelon's theory of speaking in dialogue form to enhance readability and interest. B, an impressionable young preacher, opens the dialogue with an enthusiastic review of an Ash Wednesday sermon he has just heard. When prevailed upon by his interlocutors, A and C, to describe the discourse, B praises its clever use of Scripture, its delicacy of expression, its imagery, and its arrangement.

B's enthusiasm for the affectation, wit, and contrivances of this sermon provides A, who is Fénelon's spokesperson, with the opportunity to react to current speaking practices, of which he disapproves. The preachers of Fénelon's day used topically organized, three-point sermons in which divisions were imposed on the subject and the treatment was loosely connected in a series of insubstantial epigrams, allusions, and narratives. A emphasized instead that organization be coherent and intrinsic to the matter discussed. "When you divide, it is necessary to divide simply, naturally. One must have a division that is found ready-made in the very subject itself; a division that clarifies, that puts material into classes, that is easily remembered, and that helps one to retain everything else" (Howell 1951:61).

Pulpit preaching of the day was frequently epideictic, and its purpose was largely to enthrall and entertain, to call attention to the speaker's skill and artistry. The funeral eulogies of Bossuet and Fléchier, for example, were written in the high style and contained series of rhapsodic periods in praise of the deceased. Fénelon's spokesman, A, objected to these practices, insisting that ostentation be avoided: "Art is clumsy and contemptible whenever it makes itself visible" (Howell 1951:96). Fénelon maintained that virtue and improvement of society should be the aim of all true eloquence: "The good man seeks to please only that he may urge justice and the other virtues by making them attractive" (Howell 1951:62). Disparagement of the florid style does not mean that discourse must be dry and unembellished. Rather, style and delivery should be suited to the thought expressed. Expression should be vivid and engaging, but its vivacity should arise naturally from the subject: "It is necessary not only to acquaint listeners with the facts, but to make the facts visible to them, and to strike their consciousness by means of a perfect representation" (Howell 1951:94).

In his *Letter to the French Academy* (1716), Fénelon again pressed the same themes—eloquence as a way station to moral improvement, proportion, and propriety in style and delivery, and coherence and vivid portraiture in presentation. Fénelon's emphasis on the aesthetics of rhetoric and on the power of portraiture and association presaged the work of Scottish belletrists Adam Smith, Hugh Blair, and George Campbell, who thought highly of his work. In his admiration of Plato, St. Augustine, virtue, and simplicity, Fénelon was neoclassical; in his emphasis on substance, direct expression, and extemporaneous speaking, however, he was modern and a precursor of Enlightenment rhetorical theories.

Barbara Warnick
University of Washington

Bibliography

Goré, Jeanne Lydie. *L'Itinéraire de Fénelon: Humanisme et spiritualité*. Paris: Presses Universitaires, 1957.

Howell, Wilbur Samuel, trans. *Fénelon's Dialogues on Eloquence*. Princeton: Princeton UP, 1951.

———. "Oratory and Poetry in Fénelon's Literary Theory." *Poetics, Rhetoric, and Logic*. Ithaca, NY: Cornell UP, 1975. 123–40.

Litman, Théodore A. *Le Sublime en France: 1660–1714*. Paris: Nizet, 1971.

Warnick, Barbara, trans. *Fénelon's Letter to the French Academy*. Lanham, MD: UP of America, 1984.

Feyerabend, Paul Karl (b. 1924)

Influential philosopher of science. Paul Feyerabend was born in Vienna and educated at the University of Vienna and the University of London. He has taught at the University of London, Berlin Free University, and Yale University. He immigrated to the United States in 1959 and currently teaches at the University of California at Berkeley.

In the philosophy of science, Feyerabend is best known for his formulation of *epistemological anarchism*. By this term he means that no antecedent reason exists that can authorize any one epistemological theory or fixed theory of rationality over another. As a result, no scientific law or rule is final and absolute, nor can be.

It is clear, then, that the idea of a fixed method, or of a fixed theory of rationality, rests on too naive a view of man and his social surroundings. To those who look at the rich material provided by history, and who are not intent on impoverishing it in order to please their lower instincts, their craving for intellectual security in the form of clarity, precision, "objectivity," "truth," it will become clear that there is only *one* principle that can be defended under *all* circumstances and in *all* stages of human development. It is the principle: *anything goes.* (*Against Method* 27–28)

Although this principle of "anything goes" captures succinctly his notion of epistemological anarchism, Feyerabend carefully points out that he does not mean by this term that scientists should proceed without rules and standards. In other words, to claim that no *comprehensive* system of rationality exists does not mean that at particular historical moments, no specific rules or standards exist. Consequently, Feyerabend does not entirely reject rationality; he rejects only the idea that a scientific rule is ever absolute.

If scientific rules are not absolute, then the success of the scientist relies in great part on rhetoric. In place of discovering immutable natural laws through the use of a tried-and-true methodology, scientists actually fashion explanations after the fact. That is, when a scientist begins experimentation, no methodology or rule of rationality exists that will ensure or predict in advance that the results of an experiment will fit the scientist's picture of the world; only in retrospect—by relating a more or less persuasive story—can a scientist account for events in the world. According to Feyerabend, the scientist always *invents* a rational theory to explain the phenomenal world, and these invention strategies, similar to rhetorical strategies, serve to authorize the scientist's claims and, in turn, to persuade others to accept these claims. By critiquing our conventional conceptions of objectivity and rationality, Feyerabend suggests that science constitutes a thoroughly interpretive and, therefore, thoroughly rhetorical endeavor.

Thomas Kent
Iowa State University

Bibliography

Munevar, Gonzalo, ed. *Beyond Reason: Essays on the Philosophy of Paul Feyerabend.* Boston: Kluwer, 1991.
Feyerabend, Paul. *Against Method: Outline of an Anarchistic Theory of Knowledge.* London: Redwood, 1975.
———. *Science in a Free Society.* London: Lowe, 1978.

Figurative Language

Stylistic departure from literal or common usage, according to the tradition of classical rhetoric, aimed at achieving emphasis, enhancing clarity, conveying sentiment, or embellishing language by means of tropes (figures of thought that deviate from the conventional meaning of words) and schemes (figures of speech that diverge from the normal order of words). Thus, in I.A. Richards's felicitous phrase, the classical tradition regards figurative language, even metaphor, as no more than "a happy extra trick with words" that graces speech and enhances its power short of furnishing its constitutive form (90). Contemporary rhetorical theory, however, generally subscribes to the notion that figurative constructions are substantive—thereby eschewing rigid distinctions between form and content, style and argument, emotion and reason, opinion and knowledge, aesthetics and pragmatics, or figuration and literalization. Accordingly, tropes and schemes are thought to prompt arguments and comprise motivating perspectives through an aesthetic impulse that privileges one interest over another in its literalizing presence.

Traditional rhetoric supplies no definitive distinctions between tropes and schemes or any exacting classification of numerous figures of speech and thought. The difference typically maintained between tropes and schemes is confounded by the difficulty of altering the arrangement of words without affecting the meaning conveyed. Even irony, usually identified as one of the master tropes, sometimes appears on lists of schemes as the expression of a given intent by saying its opposite in words that contradict their context. Similarly, litotes (understatement) and periphrasis (circumlocution) sometimes appear as figures of thought, other times as figures of speech, while hyperbole (exaggeration) is commonly considered a trope, although it sometimes is grouped with litotes and irony as a figure of emphasis or understatement to distinguish it from a figure of resemblance or relationship such as metaphor, parallelism, or synecdoche. The latter approach ignores the basic distinction between figures of speech and thought in order to focus on their overlapping functions of comparing, emphasizing, adding, subtracting, substituting, and so forth. Further compounding the confusion, metaphor appears both as a major trope, along with metonymy, synecdoche, simile, personification, and irony, and as the tropological essence of language—thereby reducing metonymy and other tropical coequals to mere varieties of metaphor.

The contemporary focus on metaphor has led to a provocative line of inquiry into the constitutive features and rhetorical force of figurative language. As the rhetorical process that employs the power of fictions to "redescribe reality" (Ricoeur 7), metaphor specifically (and figurative language generally) becomes the source of linguistic ingenium that invents argument and develops perspective. Drawing on the vision of Giambattista Vico, Ernesto Grassi (100) observes that metaphor's ingenium furnishes the middle term of rhetorical deductions. Chaïm Perelman underscores metaphor's conceptual force by treating it as a condensed analogy that influences the "life of notions" (404). Kenneth Burke places metaphor at the organizational base of every perspective, thus featuring its function as a terministic incentive (1984:95). In short, metaphor in its various tropical forms grasps and induces thought, reason, and attitude.

Burke's discussion of the four master tropes (1969:503–17) underscores the constitutive function of figurative language. Metaphor, the trope that presents one thing in terms of another, is extended into its literalized form as a perspective on reality. The line of development from master image, as the point of departure, into a general framework of interpretation requires the assistance of additional figures; each contributing term, however, also contains its own generative principle and thus strains against the organizing principle of the master metaphor. The resulting tension that exists in any relatively coherent line of development produces the potential for a shift of perspective because the metaphors that constitute an established orientation are related to one another through a principle of representation (synecdoche) rather than reduction (metonymy): Just

as the parts can represent the whole, the whole can be restructured from the vantage point of one or more of its parts. Such complexities create the potential for an ironic corrective, or perspective by incongruity, through which the false identities of a perfected metaphor are fractured by oxymoron—thus recasting disharmonies into an essence other than their conventional significance.

Contemporary interest in the constitutive function of rhetorical figures is extended by Hayden White and others into a systematic study of tropes, known as tropology, which explores the cycle of discourse whereby consciousness advances initially from the generative properties of metaphor through subsequent elaborations by metonymy and synecdoche and eventually into the entropic state of irony; its creative energy is regenerated by a return to metaphor, which begins the cycle anew. This investigation of rhetorical figures as ways of thinking precludes the achievement of literality, other than in the sense of equating the literal meaning of a text with its conventional interpretation, for truth and reality are conceived in language that is inherently figurative. The distinction between literal and figurative language, as Friedrich Nietzsche argued, amounts to no more than a distinction between the customary and the novel in discourse. Given that "reality" is a product of frequency, and "fiction" of rarity, figural fictions become literal realities as a matter of common usage. Tropology, then, concerns itself with how the shape of thought reflects the turns of language.

As Steve Whitson and John Poulakos maintain, the aesthetic impulse of figurative language produces only appearances and thus supplants the possibility of objective knowledge, or even of correct perspectives. The artistic act of creating and satisfying appetites orders the chaos of life into hospitable or otherwise appealing forms. Expanding an artistic vision rhetorically into a full framework of interpretation achieves a literalized presence in discourse that momentarily precludes consideration of any alternative views of reality and of the competing interests they serve. Some rhetorical achievements are more hegemonic and lasting than others. None, however, last forever within the vortex of figuration. In the final analysis, figurative language works ironically to deliteralize the significance of one rhetorical turn by inspiring yet another. Accordingly, it is a source of invention and no mere matter of style.

Robert L. Ivie
Indiana University

Bibliography

Burke, Kenneth. *A Grammar of Motives.* New York: Prentice, 1945. Rpt. Berkeley: U of California P, 1969.

———. *Permanence and Change: An Anatomy of Purpose.* New York: New Republic, 1935. Rev. 3d ed. Berkeley: U of California P, 1984.

Cantor, Paul. "Friedrich Nietzsche: The Use and Abuse of Metaphor." *Metaphor: Problems and Perspectives.* Ed. David S. Miall. Atlantic Highlands, NJ: Humanities, 1982. 71–88.

Grassi, Ernesto. *Rhetoric as Philosophy: The Humanist Tradition.* University Park: Pennsylvania State UP, 1980.

Kellner, Hans. *Language and Historical Representation: Getting the Story Crooked.* Madison: U of Wisconsin P, 1989.

Lanham, Richard A. *A Handlist of Rhetorical Terms.* 2nd ed. Berkeley: U of California P, 1991.

Mellard, James M. *Doing Tropology: Analysis of Narrative Discourse.* Urbana: U of Illinois P, 1987.

Perelman, Chaïm, and L. Olbrechts-Tyteca. *The New Rhetoric: A Treatise on Argumentation.* Trans. John Wilkinson and Purcell Weaver. Notre Dame, IN: U of Notre Dame P, 1969.

Richards, I.A. *The Philosophy of Rhetoric.* 1936. Rpt. New York: Oxford UP, 1965.

Ricoeur, Paul. *The Rule of Metaphor.* Trans. Robert Czerny. Toronto: U of Toronto P, 1977.

Vico, Giambattista. *The New Science.* Trans. Thomas G. Bergin and Max H. Fisch. Ithaca, NY: Cornell UP, 1968.

White, Hayden V. *Tropics of Discourse: Essays in Cultural Criticism.* Baltimore: Johns Hopkins UP, 1978.

Whitson, Steve, and John Poulakos. "Nietzsche and the Aesthetics of Rhetoric." *Quarterly Journal of Speech* 79 (1993): 131–45.

See also FIGURES OF SPEECH; IRONY; METONYMY; SYNECDOCHE

Figures of Speech

Any isolatable element of style usually limited to a single word, phrase, or sentence. Such an element usually involves a deviation from ordinary usage. So Quintilian (*Institutio Oratoria* IX.i.11) defines *figura* as "any deviation, either in thought or expression, from the ordinary and simple method of speaking." Nonetheless, the phrase *figure of speech* has since been applied to almost any identifiable turn of phrase, even those quite ordinary and simple.

Over the centuries rhetoricians have distinguished and named literally hundreds of figures of speech. Knowledge of them has been regarded as essential to a rhetorical education. Henry Peacham begins his *Garden of Eloquence* (1593), for instance, by arguing that knowledge of the figures of speech is "so necessary that no man can read profytably, or understand perfectlye eyther Poets, Oratours, or the holy Scriptures, without them: nor any Oratoure able by the waight of his wordes, to perswade his hearers, having no helpe of them."

Often rhetoric handbooks, in particular those that reduce rhetoric to mere style, have been little more than a compilation of these figures, with definitions and examples. Even as recent a work as Brian Vickers's *Defence of Rhetoric* (1988) seems to reduce the whole of modern rhetoric to the study of the figures.

The figures of speech, as collected and classified over the centuries, present two distinct problems for the rhetorician, one theoretical, the other practical. Theoretically, the rhetorician must provide an adequate account of the difference between literal language and figurative language. Such accounts are commonly expected to reveal the nature and potentialities of language itself.

The practical problem presented by the figures of speech derives from their very number and complexity. The rhetorician must provide an accessible classification of the figures, an easily understood and remembered system that consequently will be of use to those wishing to improve their speaking, writing, reading, and listening. The sheer number of figures that need to be defined and classified makes this a daunting task. Moreover, different names have sometimes been given to the same turn of phrase; or the same name has been used to cover quite different stylistic features. The rhetorician needs to sort this all out.

This entry provides such a classification system. (Individual figures of speech are treated in separate entries.) A convenient place to begin to develop this classification system is with the simplest group of figures, those involving spelling. Metaplasm is the general name given for orthographic figures, figures which change the spelling (or sound) of a word without changing its meaning. Such changes are common, for instance, in the permutations to which first names are subjected in ordinary speech. Edward can become Ward or Ed. Ed can become Eddie or Ned or Ted. Ted can become Tad.

In general, there are four ways to change the spelling of a word: addition of letters, their omission, substitution, or rearrangement. So metaplasms themselves can be divided into four types, as can the rest of the figures. Note that both substitution and rearrangement could be considered as combinations of omission and addition. In substitution something is omitted and something else added in the same place; in rearrangement something is omitted and then added somewhere else. Whatever the theoretical significance of this refinement, it is not a useful simplification. Indeed, a fifth mode of figuration should probably be added: repetition. Of course, repetition is simply the addition of something already present. Nonetheless, there are so many figures using this particular kind of repetitive addition that it is useful to treat them as a separate class, however much this might annoy the theoretically fastidious.

The first question to ask of a figure is: How does it change the word or phrase or sentence, by addition, omission, substitution, rearrangement or repetition? Once that is answered, two further questions may be necessary to specify the figure: What? and Where? What exactly has been changed? Where has the change occurred? Surprisingly, these three questions taken together are usually adequate to classify the full range of figures described by the rhetorical tradition. That tradition will then also provide an appropriate name for each, and sometimes more than one name.

Metaplasm provides a simple test for this system. The first group of metaplasms are those made by addition. A prosthesis is the addition of a letter or letters to the beginning of a word. So Shakespeare in his twenty-ninth sonnet writes, "I all alone beweep my outcast state." (Remember that the addition must not change the meaning of the word; so ungrammatical is not a prosthesis for grammatical.) An alternative spelling for the name of this figure is prothesis.

An addition of a letter or letters in the middle of the word is called an epenthesis; visiting,

for example, is rewritten visitating. The addition of a letter or letters at the end is called, alternatively, proparlepsis or paragogue. So Shakespeare's Gelendower claims to be able to call spirits from the "vasty deep" and Matthew Arnold follows by referring to "the vasty hall of death."

The previous metaplasms of addition have been distinguished by where the addition is made. There is also a metaplasm of addition that is distinguished by what is added. Diaeresis is the addition of a syllable. This is done by dividing a single syllable into two. So one might for emphasis pronounce the ao in extraordinary as two syllables. Diaeresis is commonly used in poetry to make the meter regular; so, from observing the metrical patterns, it has been argued that Byron meant the "Juan" in his mock epic Don Juan to be two syllables, and hence a diaeresis.

The metaplasms by omission follow a pattern similar to those by addition. The omission of the beginning letter or letters is aphaeresis. Of the mistreated King Lear, it is said, "The King has cause to plain." Some common poetic aphaereses are indicated by an apostrophe, such as 'neath for beneath.

An omission in the middle is a syncope. Ta'en for taken or saltness for saltiness. Some syncopes become so common they drive the original word to the fringes of the language. It is hard to say if ma'am is still a figure in American English, so much more common is it now than madam.

Apocope is the name for an omission at the end; often becomes oft. In the Merchant of Venice: "When I ope my lips, let no dogs bark." An alternative name for this metaplasm, as rare as it is unpronounceable, is ecthlipse.

There is a special name for the omission of a vowel that entails the contraction of two words into one: synaloepha. The synaloepha is almost always indicated by an apostrophe. Shakespeare was having some fun with this common metaplasm when he used three in one line in Coriolanus: "Take't; 'tis yours. What is't?" A more general name for the omission of a letter that collapses two syllables into one is crasis, as in e'en for even.

A rearrangement of letters is a metathesis: prevert for pervert. So Shakespeare changes fervent in the Merry Wives of Windsor when he writes "With liver burning hot. Frevent." An extreme form of metathesis is the boustrophedon by which the letters come in the reverse order. So James Joyce has a name read in a mirror printed as "mangiD kcirtaP."

A metaplasmic substitution is an antisthecon; *together* becomes *togither*. Note, by the way, that *antisthecon* is occasionally used indiscriminately for metaplasms of both rearrangement and substitution. This seems unwise, since there is already a perfectly good name for rearrangement. Nonetheless, these two figures do belong together for at least one reason. Of all the metaplasms, *metathesis* and *antisthecon* are the ones that risk misunderstanding the most; hence they are quite rare.

Even rarer than these two is the repetition of letters or syllables. This metaplasm of repetition has the wonderfully appropriate name of *echolalia*. So the insistent child may be reported as saying, "Pleeeeease." Most instances of this metaplasm are, to use an *echolalia*, sillilly. Ecostasis, like many metaplasms, involves what might be called purposeful misspelling.

More common are two figures of repetition that can be limited to a single word but do not employ misspelling. The repetition of consonantal sounds is alliteration; this can occur in a single word—*vivacious*—or (more usually) between words—"cool, calm, and collected." The repetition of vowel sounds is assonance. "The tree I will hit to disturb the bird" has two obvious assonances as well as a number of alliterations.

The figures, then, can be classified in terms of five methods of figuration: addition, omission, substitution, rearrangement, and repetition. They can subsequently be subclassified by where the figure occurs (beginning, middle, end) or by what is being figured (in a metaplasm, consonant, vowel, syllable), or on rare occasions by both.

Adequate as such a system is to practical needs, it will still trouble the more theoretically inclined rhetoricians who, following Quintilian, regard a deviation from the ordinary as a defining characteristic of the figure of speech. They will not want alliteration, assonance, or many of the other common figures to be regarded as figures at all. To the more pragmatically inclined, however, this seems a good argument in favor of a looser definition of the figure of speech as simply any isolatable element of style.

Using the figures is, of course, not in itself a guarantee of effectiveness. So among the many terms for particular figures, there are a few additional terms for the ineffective use of the figures. *Brachylogia* is the general term for undue brevity, the overuse of figures of omission. *Battology* is undue repetition. *Synchisis* is a mistake in word order. *Catachresis* is frequently defined simply as a mistaken substitution (a judgment reinforced in the Latin term for this figure, *abusio*). Needless to say, the judgments implied in these terms are often in the eye of the beholder. Or, to risk misusing an old aphorism, one person's *brachylogia* is another's *battology*.

Arthur Quinn and Lyon Rathbun
University of California, Berkeley

Bibliography
Brandt, William. *Rhetoric of Argumentation.* Indianapolis, IN: Bobbs, 1970.
Bullinger, E.W. *Figures of Speech in the Bible.* 1898. Grand Rapids: Barker, 1968.
Cicero. *Rhetorica ad Herennium.* Trans. Harry Caplan. Cambridge, MA: Loeb Classical Library, 1954.
Dupriez, Bernard. *A Dictionary of Literary Devices.* Trans. and adapted by Albert W. Halsall. Toronto: U of Toronto P, 1991.
Fontanier, Pierre. *Les Figures du Discours.* 1821–30. Paris: Flammarion, 1968.
Group MU (J. Dubois, F. Edeline, J.-M. Klinkenberg, P. Minguet, F. Pire, H. Trinon). *Rhetorique Generale.* Paris: Larousse, 1970. Rpt. *A General Rhetoric.* Trans. Paul B. Burrell and Edgar M. Slotkin. Baltimore: Johns Hopkins UP, 1981.
Joseph, Sister Miriam. *Shakespeare's Use of the Arts of Language.* New York: Harcourt, 1947.
Lanham, Richard. *A Handlist of Rhetorical Terms.* 2nd ed. Berkeley: U of California P, 1991.
Lausberg, Heinrich. *Handbuch der literarischen rhetorik.* Stuttgart: Steiner, 1990.
Peacham, Henry. *The Garden of Eloquence.* 1593. Facsimile reproduction. Gainesville, FL: Scholar's Facsimiles and Reprints, 1954.
Queneau, Raymond. *Exercises in Style.* Trans. Barbara Wright. New York: New Directions, 1981.
Quinn, Arthur. *Figures of Speech.* Salt Lake City, UT: Peregrine Smith, 1982. Rpt. Davis, CA: Hermagoras, 1993.
Quintilian. *Institutio Oratoria.* Trans. H.E. Butler. 4 vols. Cambridge, MA: Loeb Classical Library, 1920–1922.
Sonnino, Lee A. *A Handbook to Sixteenth-Century Rhetoric.* London: Routledge and Kegan Paul, 1968.
Vickers, Brian. *In Defence of Rhetoric.* Oxford: Clarendon, 1988.

F

Fisher, Walter R. (b. 1931)

Known for his study of the interdependent roles played by values and reason in human communicative experience. In *Human Communication as Narration: Toward a Philosophy of Reason, Value, and Action*, Fisher argues that humanity may fruitfully be conceived of as *Homo narrans*, that all forms of human communication can best be understood as stories, that individual units of discourse embody "good reasons"—value-laden warrants for believing or acting—and that writers, readers, speakers, and listeners naturally employ a narrative logic that can be used to assess discourse.

Fisher draws on classical and contemporary rhetoric, philosophy, and social theory to articulate a conception of rhetoric contemporary with the best current thinking. He views his work as "strictly experiential" in that his primary test of efficacy is how well a concept enables scholars and lay people to understand how people actually talk and write.

As rhetorical beings, Fisher argues, humans are as much valuing as reasoning animals. But he emphasizes that reason can be found in any elements that provide warrants for adhering to the advice fostered by rhetorical communication, including those that are logical, ethical, and aesthetic. Most theories of rationality obscure this complexity by focusing exclusively on argument. The resulting view is normative, necessary versus prudential whereas narrative rationality is descriptive, offering an understanding of any instance of human choice and action.

The two major features of narrative rationality are coherence and fidelity. Narrative coherence concerns whether a story "hangs together" or is free of contradictions. It encompasses *argumentative* or *structural coherence*, *material coherence*, which is determined by comparing and contrasting the story with related stories, and *characterological coherence*, which concerns the ethos and values of the author. Narrative fidelity concerns the degree to which a story resonates with the critic's experience. One may confirm it against empirical tests, consensus, or reliable and competent witnesses; determine the degree to which the values it embodies characterize one's experience and the experience of others one respects; and assess whether the values fostered by the story are those that would constitute a humane basis for conduct. Humans naturally, typically, regularly, and competently apply these criteria,

Fisher argues, to assess the competing stories they are asked to believe.

One goal of Fisher's recent work is to clarify how his narrative perspective can produce a rhetoric that shares with philosophy a love of *sophia*. He argues that traditional rationality is concerned with "knowledge of that" and "knowledge of how," but not with *knowledge of whether*. Knowledge of "whether" is praxical knowledge, the kind that narrative rationality is aimed to foster and assess. Knowledge of "that" and "how" affirm such values as truthfulness, precision, conformity with past knowledge, and usefulness whereas the bedrock value of praxical consciousness is love, an abiding concern for the welfare and well being of others, which manifests in commitments to justice, happiness, and humanity.

The narrative paradigm has been widely used as a critical tool; Fisher himself has applied it to public moral argument, epic, political communication, philosophical dialogue, historical texts, and scientific discourse.

John Stewart
University of Washington

Bibliography

Fisher, Walter R. "Clarifying the Narrative Paradigm." *Communication Monographs* 56 (1989): 55–58.

———. *Human Communication as Narration: Toward Philosophy of Reason, Value, and Action*. Columbia: U of South Carolina P, 1987.

———. "The Narrative Paradigm and the Interpretation and the Assessment of Historical Texts." *Argumentation and Advocacy* 25 (1988): 50–53.

———. "Narration, Reason, and Community." *Writing the Social Text: Poetics and Politics in Social Science Discourse*. Ed. Richard Harvey Brown. New York: Aldine De Gruyter, 1992. 199–217.

———. "Technical Logic, Rhetorical Logic, and Narrative Rationality." *Argumentation* 1 (1987): 3–21.

Foucault, Michel (1926–1984)

French intellectual with degrees in philosophy, psychology, and psychiatry, who made discursive practice his primary object of study. Foucault's last academic appointment was Chair of History of Systems of Thought at the

College de France. Eschewing attempts by commentators to categorize his work as structuralist, hermeneutic, phenomenological, leftist, or conservative, Foucault described his project as "a pure description of discursive events." His descriptions of discursive events were oriented to the question Who are we now? The answer he provided to this call for a history of the present was that we are thinking beings who make ourselves objects of study, who respond to laws and obligations, and who constitute ourselves as moral agents. His studies of discourse thus investigate the relationship among discursive practice, knowledge, power, and ethics.

The centrality of discourse to his work accounts for interest in Foucault among rhetoricians. His most complete theoretical statements regarding discourse appear in *The Archaeology of Discourse*. There and in other essays and interviews, Foucault explained that discourse was neither a thing, merely representative of thoughts whose source was an author, a work, or a transcendental spirit, nor a process such as reading, writing, or exchange. Instead, he argued that discourse should be treated as an event, intangible and transient yet exhibiting some material substance. He explained the materiality of discourse, the existence of texts, for example, might cause some to treat discourse as static, thereby allowing the creative power of discursive action to occur unnoticed. Foucault argued, however, that the incorporeality of discourse was fundamental to understanding the function of discourse for creating knowledge, power, and ethical systems. Treated as an event, discourse provided sites for investigating the production of knowledge and the formation of human relationships. Moreover, Foucault argued that because of the awesome power of discursive events societies tend to manage discourse by creating taboos, exclusions, categories, and other systems that put parameters around who might talk about what in which circumstances with what effects. Hence, investigation of discursive practices provides a perspective for understanding the history of ideas, institutions, and other human creations across time and culture in the production of systems of knowledge, power, and ethics.

In *Archaeology*, Foucault provides guidelines for examining units of discourse he called "statements." Not to be confused with sentences or propositions that might be explained by linguistics or logic, statements are more akin to speech acts, instances of discursive action that produce objects for our understanding, require assumption of a particular role in order to be uttered, arise within and simultaneously alter contexts in which social relationships and individual identities form, and may be repeated so long as the function of the discourse is the same in subsequent cases. Foucault suggested that a pattern of regularity among statements in terms of knowledge, role, context, and nondiscursive function signals the existence of discursive formations.

Descriptive study of statements and the discursive formations to which they belonged served several ends for Foucault in his major critical and genealogical studies. His early works (such as *Madness and Civilization, The Birth of the Clinic,* and *The Order of Things*) aimed toward explaining how discourse manifests and creates systems of truth and knowledge, frequently calling into question culturally accepted taboos and accepted divisions between reason and folly. Later studies (such as *Discipline and Punish* and *History of Sexuality*: Volume 1) probed the relationship between discourse and power, explaining how discursive practices establish and maintain systems of thought that ground the production of apparatuses that subject human beings to various power structures. Foucault's final project (*The Culture of the Self* and *The Care of the Self*) investigated the relationship between discourse and ethics, defined as the relationship one ought to have with oneself. In these studies Foucault examined discursive practices ranging from Greek pedagogical practices to the Christian confessional in order to explain how discourse constitutes the self and attendant moral obligations differently at different times.

Throughout Foucault's corpus—in his major critical and genealogical works, in his occasional criticisms of single texts (such as *This Is Not a Pipe* and *I, Pierre Riviere, Having Slaughtered My Mother, My Sister, and My Brother*), and in various interviews and essays—his analyses of systems of thought, power, and ethics provide commentary about both repressive powers and forces for liberation within contemporary society. Consequently, various postmodern, feminist, and other contemporary social critics invoke his ideas in their own critique of contemporary culture as it operates within the sphere of discourse.

Martha Cooper
Northern Illinois University

Bibliography

Clark, Michael. *Michel Foucault, An Annotated Bibliography: Tool Kit for a New Age.* New York: Garland, 1983.

DeLeuze, Gilles. *Foucault.* Trans. and ed. Sean Hand. Minneapolis: U of Minnesota P, 1988.

Dreyfus, Hubert L., and Paul Rabinow. *Michel Foucault: Beyond Structuralism and Hermeneutics.* Chicago: U of Chicago P, 1982.

Sheridan, Alan. *Michel Foucault: The Will to Truth.* New York: Tavistock, 1980.

Frege, Gottlob (1848–1925)

German mathematician and philosopher, founder of modern logic. His philosophy influenced key philosophers in the twentieth century (Edmund Husserl, Bertrand Russell, Ludwig Wittgenstein), and his work often is seen as seminal to the analytic philosophy movement. Frege sought to provide logical foundations to mathematics and, for most of his life, attempted to derive the fundamental ideas of mathematics from logical structures.

Given Frege's distrust of ordinary language (including empirical observations) and his commitment to tautological systems, Frege's foundationalism represents a tradition separate from rhetoric. His distinction, however, between *Sinn* ("sense") and *Bedeutung* (often translated as *meaning,* but more easily understood as *reference*) is useful. While Frege recognized the link between thought and language, his interest in their relationship was limited to cognition and the use of language to find truth. To that end he examined aspects of meaning or the meanings inherent in "meaning." He described *Sinn,* the sense of a word, as the thought expressed in a particular presentation. He connected *Bedeutung,* reference, with what a word designates. Thus, the referent of *evening star* and *morning star* is the same planet, but the sense of each is not the same. Frege's distinction among types of meanings precedes discussions of meaning types in the work of rhetoricians such as I.A. Richards, Chaïm Perelman, Lucie Olbrechts-Tyteca, and E.D. Hirsch.

Arabella Lyon
Temple University

Bibliography

Currie, Gregory. *Frege: An Introduction to His Philosophy.* Totowa, NJ: Barnes and Noble, 1982.

Frege, Gottlob. *Translations for the Philosophical Writings of Gottlob Frege.* P. Geach and M. Black. Oxford: Blackwell, 1980.

Toulmin, Stephen. *Human Understanding.* Princeton: Princeton UP, 1972. 52–65.

Freire, Paulo (b. 1921)

Brazilian educator and intellectual whose work has influenced the liberatory or radical pedagogy movement. Freire's work emerges from a largely Marxist theory of culture and from his own varied personal and political experience. Freire grew up poor under the oppressive social conditions established by the Brazilian ruling class. When he had developed his revolutionary pedagogical practice, he was imprisoned and then exiled from Brazil by the military government from 1964 to 1980. He has worked with the adult literacy programs at UNESCO, for the Chilean Institute for Agrarian Reform, and the World Council of Churches. He is currently the secretary of education in São Paulo, Brazil's largest school district. These experiences are important because they help ground Freire's practice and explain his theoretical position, which mixes a modernist commitment to freedom, equality, and social justice with an understanding of ideology and social identity as problematic and shifting.

Freire's early work, most notably *Pedagogy of the Oppressed,* belongs to the tradition of Marxist materialism and social humanism. That is, Freire assumed that reality is constructed through concrete social relations and that these relations are open to critical analysis. As an educator committed to change, Freire also assumed that people are capable of critical self-consciousness, that they can come to comprehend the historical and ideological nature of reality and the social relations within which they live, and, further, that they can change their situation. One of Freire's fundamental assumptions is that the "ontological vocation" of humanity is to develop a conscious recognition of our relations to the social world. Taking a position similar to Antonio Gramsci's theory of hegemony, Freire argued that people are oppressed when they accept historically constructed class relations as necessary and natural.

The pedagogy that Freire developed alongside this theory sees literacy as an essential part of critical self-consciousness and the work of cultural liberation. Freire's practice engages students and teachers together in a dialogue whose starting point is the specific social and material conditions in which the participants find themselves. Because this pedagogy begins with the specific conditions of the students' lives, it often requires that the teacher engage in a kind of ethnographic work both before and during teaching. Sometimes called "problem-posing" education, this practice examines the history and social function of our common-sense understandings in order to problematize the seemingly obvious. The classroom becomes the place where students and teachers together are cultural workers whose reflection on their specific social condition leads to collective action to alter both themselves and their situation—the Marxist notion of praxis. Despite the utopian nature of his theory, Freire recognizes the limitations imposed by existing conditions and calls for a pedagogy of the possible that starts "exactly in the place that we would like to change."

Although Freire has influenced many North American teachers and scholars, transporting his practice directly into classrooms in the United States is difficult at best. At worst it eviscerates his political critique by removing it from the specific political contexts from which it emerged and by ignoring problems of cultural representation in postcolonial relations. A number of recent books written jointly by Freire and North American collaborators—most notably Donaldo Macedo and Ira Shor—attempt to sketch out a Freirean practice for North American classrooms.

Despite the widespread influence of Freire's pedagogical practice, his early work has been criticized for its commitment to an overly reductive conception of social class, for its use of binary oppositions such as that of the oppressor/oppressed, and for the lingering implication that we live under a "false ideology" correctable by Marxist science. In his more recent work, Freire acknowledges that social reality and identity are "ambiguous" and that easy generalizations about homogeneous, unified social structures are unacceptable. Although Freire remains committed to radical change, his theoretical conception of society and the way we live in it has been modified, partially by the way his work is positioned, both by Freire and by other scholars such as Henry Giroux, within the contemporary study of postcolonialism.

Carl G. Herndl
New Mexico State University

Bibliography

Freire, Paulo. *Pedagogy of the Oppressed.* Trans. Myra Bergman Ramos. New York: Continuum, 1989.

———. *The Politics of Education: Culture, Power, and Liberation.* Trans. Donaldo Macedo. South Hadley, MA: Bergin, 1985.

Freire, Paulo, and Antonio Faundez. *Learning to Question: A Pedagogy of Liberation.* New York: Continuum, 1989.

Freire, Paulo, and Donaldo Macedo. *Literacy: Reading the Word and the World.* South Hadley, MA: Bergin, 1987.

Giroux, Henry A. "Paulo Freire and the Politics of Postcolonialism." *Journal of Advanced Composition* 12 (1992): 15–26.

F

G

Gadamer, Hans-Georg (b. 1900)

Contemporary German philosopher and hermeneutical theorist. Throughout his writings, Hans-Georg Gadamer elaborates and critically extends the tradition of philosophical hermeneutics set by Friedrich D.E. Schleiermacher (1768–1834) in biblical studies, Wilhelm Dilthey (1833–1911) in historiography, and Martin Heidegger (1889–1976) in fundamental ontology. Gadamer's hermeneutical theory, with its key concept of historically effected consciousness, involves a careful dialogue with the Western philosophical tradition, starting with Plato and Aristotle and focusing on the perennial question of the conditions of truth and knowledge, by tracing expressions of human understanding from Greek philosophy to Renaissance art (aesthetics) to contemporary critical theory. Gadamer's wide-ranging and uniquely interdisciplinary scholarship is important to scholars in biblical studies, critical theory, legal studies, literature, philosophy, and rhetoric.

In 1960 Gadamer published his major philosophical work, *Wahrheit und Methode* (*Truth and Method*, 1975). Gadamer's study engages the concept of interpretation as it generally relates to continental philosophy and specifically to the Kantian question, What are the conditions of our knowledge? Gadamer's work posits the concept of conditioned knowledge as primary and inescapable. Contrary to the formulations found in the phenomenology of Edmund Husserl (1859–1938), bracketing anything that consciousness does not intend and following Heidegger's break with Husserl's *eidetics* in the "temporal analytics of human existence" (Gadamer 1975:xviii), the concept of *Dasein*, Gadamer argues that the meaning of

language resides in history and tradition prior to residing in the subject. This argument leads Gadamer into a long debate with German philosopher Jürgen Habermas over the status of interpretation, truth, and the roles of language and history in constructing human understanding. *Truth and Method* examines the idea of truth and knowledge as unintended interpretive acts within a mode of being. Initially, Gadamer's book was misunderstood as prescribing an art or technique for understanding that would unseat the established investigative methods in the human sciences (*Geisteswissenschaften*) that begin with German Romanticism in the early nineteenth century and the modern natural sciences (*Naturwissenschaften*). Gadamer argues in the foreword to the second edition that the focus of his study is not on conflicting methods or devising a new method but on the objectives of knowledge. It is the proposition found in the human sciences and the natural sciences claiming the possibility of an unmediated apprehension of truth, grasping the object as it really exists, with which Gadamer finds himself in conflict. Gadamer's concern is in extending the epistemological question raised by Immanuel Kant (1724–1804), How is understanding possible? *Truth and Method* explores this question through an inquiry into the aesthetic consciousness brought on by an experience of an art object, the status of truth and understanding in the human sciences, and a hermeneutics guided by language.

Gadamer describes his own work as not being a dogmatic solution to the question concerning human understanding but a philosophic inquiry into what is common to all modes of understanding. He argues that human understanding is never purely subjective behavior toward a given object but its own history of influence reflected back onto itself. For Gadamer, viewers of art and readers of texts come to an understanding, a hermeneutical consciousness, only under specific historical conditions. Gadamerian hermeneutics offers the questions How does one interpret? and Is objective understanding possible? For Gadamer, one interprets an object through a historical horizon. The interpretation is not a pure grasping so much as it is a dialectical relationship. The historical horizon of the object meets with the historical horizon of the viewer or reader, resulting in an active or productive interpretation. The object under consideration is never completely revealed in the meeting of historical horizons. Gadamer argues for a post-Romantic conception of interpretation that posits the object as in excess of the author's or artist's mind (*mens auctoris*). The meeting of historical horizons is not a recovery of the pure object, or the truth, but a living and dynamic dialogue between past, present, and future, continuing the Western philosophical tradition (*Uberlieferung*) and yielding productive interpretations giving new meanings to human creative acts.

Victor E. Taylor
Syracuse University

Bibliography

Adorno, Theodor, and Max Horkheimer. *The Dialectic of Enlightenment*. Trans. John Cumming. New York: Seabury, 1972.

Gadamer, Hans-Georg. *Philosophical Hermeneutics*. Trans. and ed. David E. Linge. Berkeley: U of California P, 1976.

———. *Reason in the Age of Science*. Trans. and ed. Frederick G. Lawrence. Cambridge: MIT P, 1981.

———. *Truth and Method*. Trans. and ed. Garrett Barden and John Cumming. New York: Continuum, 1975.

Heidegger, Martin. *Being and Time*. Trans. John Macquarrie and Edward Robinson. New York: Harper, 1962.

Palmer, Richard E. *Hermeneutics: Interpretation Theory in Schleiermacher, Dilthy, Heidegger, and Gadamer*. Evanston, IL: Northwestern UP, 1969.

Schmidt, Lawrence K. *The Epistemology of Hans-Georg Gadamer*. New York: Lang, 1985.

Generative Rhetoric

An instructional strategy for generating ideas in sentences and paragraphs developed by Francis Christensen in the early 1960s. To help students develop ideas more fully and add texture to their writing, Christensen used the ancient method of imitation to show students how to generate sequences of syntactical structures that he called *free modifiers* (for example, appositives, participial phrases, subordinate clauses, and other structures that are set off by a pause in speech and by punctuation in writing). First, a model sentence is "outlined" to suggest the interaction of "levels of meaning" and "layers of structure"

1 Jean-Marie has a busy after-school schedule—
   2 tumbling in gymnastics class on Monday,
   2 dancing in ballet class on Tuesday,
   2 and singing in the children's choir on Wednesday.

Next, students imitate the model—filling up the sequence of structures with ideas about a different topic. In the model above, the free modifiers are "coordinate," with parallelism showing that all of the two-level structures modify the one-level structure (an independent clause). Other models have "subordinate" sequences of free modifiers, with nonparallelism showing that each structure modifies another (that is, a two-level modifies a one-level, while a three-level modifies a two-level):

1 Jean-Marie loves her ballet class,
   2 which meets on Tuesday—
      3 the day after her gymnastics class.

In the late 1960s and thereafter, imitation was often complemented by another pedagogical technique, sentence combining, which introduced a new focus on editing text rather than on generating ideas. For example, the sentence about Jean-Marie would be a logical outcome of combining the following simple sentences for conciseness and focus:

Jean-Marie has a busy after-school schedule.
Jean-Marie tumbles in gymnastics class on Monday.

Jean-Marie dances in ballet class on Tuesday.

Jean-Marie sings in the children's choir on Wednesday.

In the other direction—that is, toward expanding rather than condensing—the simple sentences about Jean-Marie could be turned into the topic sentence and main support sentences of a paragraph:

1 Jean-Marie has a busy after-school schedule.

2 First, she tumbles in gymnastics class on Monday.

3 Her favorite event is the high beam, but she also enjoys tumbling and floor exercises.

2 Second, she dances in ballet class on Tuesday.

3 She knows the five basic positions, and she can flow easily from one to the other—so long as her friend Gracie doesn't make her laugh.

2 Third, she sings in the children's choir on Wednesday.

3 Her favorite song is *Johnny One Note*, which she belts out like Ethel Merman.

As this paragraph model suggests, free modifiers serve another purpose: connecting ideas in different sentences and paragraphs (most simply, as in "first . . . second . . . third" above). Thus, the goals of generative rhetoric have broadened to include revision, editing, cohesion, and punctuation—all developing naturally from the original goal of developing ideas by generating free modifiers.

Glenn J. Broadhead
College of the Redlands

Bibliography

Broadhead, Glenn J. "Sentence Patterns: Some of What We Need to Know and Teach." *Sentence Combining: A Rhetorical Perspective*. Ed. Donald Daiker, Andrew Kerek, and Max Morenberg. Carbondale: Southern Illinois UP, 1985. 33–60.

Christensen, Francis, and Bonnijean Christensen. *Notes Toward a New Rhetoric*. 2nd ed. New York: Harper, 1978.

G

Genre

A type of spoken or written discourse, recognized as conventional by members of an intellectual community, that draws together certain substantive and stylistic features in response to a recurrent rhetorical situation. *Genre* in its most general sense is an abstraction, a name given to the human propensity to sort linguistic and artistic artifacts into categories or classifications; thus a genre or genres are instantiations of this classificatory urge. Because the notion of genre deals with types of discourses, it is related to the traditional concept of *arrangement* in rhetorical theory; indeed, one important criterion critics use to claim that a discourse exemplifies a particular genre is the arrangement of its parts. Nearly all theorists of genre, however, maintain that the concept embraces far more than form and arrangement.

Scholars in both literary and rhetorical criticism and theory have explicated the concept of genre. Literary theorists and critics have been most interested in the features of a discourse that allow a reader to recognize it as the instantiation of a particular genre and thus to read it effectively. Literary scholars have also been concerned with how genres emerge and change. Rhetorical theorists and critics have been primarily concerned with the ways genres function as socially active devices, both embodying the current generation of knowledge in discourse communities and constraining the directions it moves in the future.

In common usage, people tend to define genres of both belletristic and "ordinary" discourse by using a kind of genus-species construction. A Shakespearean sonnet is a poem of fourteen lines of iambic pentameter with the rhyme scheme ABAB CDCD EFEF GG. A horror movie is a film featuring monsters that scare human beings. A ballad is a popular, simple narrative song or poem about love. A bad-news business letter is a letter informing the recipient that petitions or proposals have not been accepted. The formula for defining genre is usually *class plus differentia*, with the differentia generally comprising characteristics of either subject matter or form.

Such off-the-cuff definitions enable the sorting of artifacts, but the definitions have at least two other functions as well. Genre definitions that readers have internalized help them to determine what kind of "contract" the writer wants to establish so that readers may comprehend the text at hand successfully. Genre definitions also help writers not only to "write" these contracts themselves but also to make sense of rhetorical situations similar to those they have encountered before. These functions make the concept of genre more than simply the name for a bundle of formal and substantial features. Genre instead is a cognitive construction, a coding template that leads to active, often purposeful, reading and writing.

Literary scholars certainly have not overlooked the simple listing of features that people commonly associate with the notion of genre. Heather Dubrow, for example, points out that genres can be sorted according to subject matter, intended effect, attitude, tone, or some combination of those attributes. Paul Hernadi proposes that genres can be classified according to authors' attitudes, the texts' effects on readers, verbal constructs employed, and the verbal world evoked. Alastair Fowler discusses three highly visible "generic signals": allusions to previous writers or representations of the genre, titles, and text-opening topics. But genre theorists in literary studies have not discussed these features simply as independent entities; instead, they have studied them as features that compose a code that in turn allows a generic contract to form. This contract guides and, ideally, leads to a successful reading of a text.

Fowler offers a useful perspective on this process of contract formation by adapting the Saussurean *langue-parole* distinction, seeing the former as the writer's reservoir of linguistic resources and the latter as the actual linguistic performances, the written artifacts. Fowler proposes that authors of literary works are able to draw upon "a greatly extended *langue*." This extended *langue* not only compensates for a literary work's lack of real situational context by providing "a situation of *literary* context," but it also "reinforces the signal system with additional coding rules" that "confirm the work itself as well as its message, not so much maximizing the efficiency as the integrity and pleasure of its communication." According to Fowler, genre is clearly "the most important . . . of all the codes of our literary *langue*, not least because it incorporates and organizes others." Genre "is an instrument not of classification or prescription, but of meaning. . . . Genre-related features . . . serve not only as information, but as 'instructions' for interpreting other coded information" (22).

While Fowler emphasizes the formative power of superordinate, genre-related text features, other literary theorists describe a more phenomenological power of genre at work in reading and writing processes. Terrence Hawkes, for example, in his comprehensive overview of structuralism, explains that "a theory of genres would have to give an account of those elements of presupposition and expectation" that enable a reader to "recode" a literary work in a manner compatible with the way it has been "encoded" by its author. Hawkes defines "recoding" as "the activity of reducing or 'trimming' all experience to make it fit the categories we have ready for it." He adds, "Genres are the literary aspects of those categories" (103–4). Claudio Guillen approaches genre as principally a writer's meaning-making device. Calling genre "an invitation to form" (109), Guillen explains further:

> Form is the presence in a created, man-made object of a "cause." It is the revelation or the sign of a dynamic relationship between the "finished" artifact and its origins in previous life and history. . . . Form is the visible manifestation of [the] victorious process of formation, making, *poeisis*. The important corollary, as far as genres are concerned, is the fact that a preexistent form can never be simply "taken over" by the writer or transferred to a new work. The task of form-making must be undertaken all over again. The writer must begin once more to match matter to form, and to that end he can only find a very special sort of assistance in the fact that the fitting of matter to form has already taken place. To offer this assistance is the function of genre (111).

Guillen characterizes a genre as "a problem-solving model on the level of form." While such "radicals" and "universals" as narration or lyric verse "fulfill their function at a very early stage," and "details of rhetoric and style play essential but partial and variegated roles, only the generic model is likely to be effective at the crucial moment of configuration, construction, *composition*" (120).

As writers use their notions of genre to construct texts and readers use theirs to recode them in meaningful ways for themselves, a relationship that Dubrow calls "a generic contract" is established:

Through such signals as the title, the meter, and the incorporation of familiar topoi in his opening lines, the poet sets up a contract with us. He in effect agrees that he will follow at least some of the patterns and conventions we associate with the genre or genres in which he is writing, and we in turn agree that we will pay close attention to certain aspects of his work while realizing that others, because of the nature of genres, are likely to be less important. (31)

From the perspective of literary criticism, then, the term *genre* denotes a power, a dynamic, ideally shared contractually by writers and readers, that bundles together features of texts—*topoi,* allusions, themes, syntax, diction, rhyme, and so on—and then "gives presence" to them in varying degrees. The genre dynamic "fronts" those features that cause instantiations of the same genre to resemble one another (for example, the fourteen lines of iambic pentameter and the recognizable rhyme scheme in the Shakespearean sonnet, or the recognition of *hamartia* in a classical tragedy) and "backgrounds," relatively and differentially, those that do not lead to a generic, "family" resemblance.

A few genres, for various cultural or artistic reasons, have stabilized to the point that both their features and the writer-reader contract that allows meaning to emerge are invariable. A haiku, for example, always has three lines, seventeen syllables, and a single, enigmatic proposition. Most genres, however, are not so rigid and, indeed, can change as writers and readers interact in successive instantiations of them. Hans Robert Jauss sees this adaptability as the principal feature of genre:

The relationship between the individual text and the series of texts formative of a genre presents itself as the continual founding and altering of horizons. The next text evokes for the reader (listener) the horizon of expectation and "rules of the game" familiar to him from earlier texts, which as such can then be varied, extended, corrected, but also transformed, crossed out, or simply reproduced. Variation, extension, and correction determine the latitude of a generic structure; a break with the convention on the one hand and mere reproduction on the other determines [*sic*] its boundaries. (88)

Jauss's views that genres have a flexible latitude and that new genres emerge when writers venture beyond their readers' expectations for a genre are echoed elsewhere in literary theory. Tzvetan Todorov, for example, asserts that new genres come "quite simply from other genres. A new genre is always the transformation of an earlier one, or of several: by inversion, by displacement, by combination" (15). Todorov offers an additional perspective on genre, however, a situationally sensitive view that links his definition of the concept to those offered by rhetorical critics and theorists, discussed below. Todorov explains that genres emerge because "a society chooses and codifies the [discursive properties] that correspond most closely to its ideology; that is why the existence of certain genres in one society, their absence in another, are revelatory of that ideology and allow us to establish it more or less completely" (19). To illustrate, he asserts, "It is no coincidence that the epic is possible in one period, the novel in another, with the individual hero of the novel opposed to the collective hero of the epic: each of these choices depends upon the ideological framework within which it operates" (19).

A more sophisticated explanation of how genres change can be found in the work of Mikhail Bahktin, whose essay "The Problem of Speech Genres" also richly informs both the traditional literary view of genre as a contract-inducing code of textual features and the contemporary rhetorical view of genre, discussed below, as a substantive response to social situations. Bakhtin's central idea is that genres, like all utterances, both come in response to previous utterances and invite responses to themselves.

Bakhtin proposes an evocative, but relatively imprecise, definition of his central term, *speech genres,* which can actually be spoken or written discourse:

Language is realized in the form of individual concrete utterances (oral and written) by participants in the various areas of human activity. These utterances reflect the specific conditions and goals of each such area not only through their content (thematic) and linguistic style, that is, the selection of lexical, phraseological, and grammatical resources of the language, but above all through their compositional structure. . . . Each separate utterance is individual, of course, but each sphere in which language is used develops its own *relatively stable types* of these utterances. These we may call *speech genres*. (60)

Proposing that "secondary (complex) speech genres-novels, dramas, all kinds of scientific research, major genres of commentary, and so forth," form as they "absorb and digest various primary (simple) genres" (62), Bakhtin explains that "a more or less fundamental restructuring and renewal of speech genres" occurs when the "literary language . . . (draws) upon various extraliterary strata of the national language" and "(penetrates) into all genres of written language," thereby necessitating "new generic devices for the construction of the speech whole, its finalization, the accommodation of the speech partner, and so forth" (65–66).

Bakhtin proposes three features as constitutive of utterances that stabilize as genres, all of which relate to his central idea of a genre's dialogic nature. The first is the complicated but intriguing characteristic that Bakhtin calls "change of speaking subject":

> Complexly structured and specialized works of various scientific and artistic genres . . . are clearly demarcated by a change of speaking subjects, and these boundaries, while retaining their external clarity, acquire here a special internal aspect because the speaking subject—in this case the author of the work—manifests his own individuality in his style, his world view, and in all aspects of the design of his work. (75)

This "imprint of individuality," Bakhtin maintains, allows the writer to "distinguish this work from other works connected with it in the overall processes of speech communication in that particular cultural sphere: from the works of predecessors on whom the author relies, from other works of the same school, from the works of opposing schools with which the author is contending, and so on." The work, thus, is "like the rejoinder in dialogue" (76).

The second constitutive feature of utterances that stabilize as genres is "the specific *finalization* of the utterance": Bahktin writes that the "finalized wholeness of the utterance"

guarantees "the possibility of a response (or responsive understanding)." Finalization is determined by three factors: the "semantic exhaustiveness of the theme," "the speaker's plan or speech will," and "typical compositional and generic forms of finalization" (76–77). The third constitutive feature is the utterance's *addressivity,* its "quality of being directed to someone": "Each speech genre in each area of speech communication has its own typical conception of the addressee, and this defines it as a genre" (95).

Given the interactive, dialogic nature of his conception of genre, it is not surprising that Bakhtin, like the rhetorical theorists whose works are discussed below, sees genre as emerging from situational contexts: "Genres correspond to typical situations of speech communication, typical themes, and consequently to particular contacts between the meanings of works and actual concrete reality under certain typical circumstances" (87).

Indeed, it is the relations and interactions among typical situations, themes, and interlocutors that lie at the center of theories of genre proposed in recent rhetorical scholarship. While scholars in literary criticism and theory have examined the shared psychology of writers and readers fostered by recognizable patterns of genre-related text features, their counterparts in rhetoric have explained how genres both emerge from, and help make sense of, recurrent rhetorical situations.

The rhetoricians' position is stated most forcefully by Carolyn Miller, who takes it as axiomatic that "a rhetorically sound definition of genre must be centered not on the substance or the form of the discourse but on the action it is used to accomplish" (151). Miller explicitly builds upon a definition of genre developed by Karlyn Kohrs Campbell and Kathleen Jamieson, who view genre as "composed of constellations of recognizable forms"—substantive, stylistic, and situational—"bound together by an internal dynamic" (21). Employing a theory espoused by sociologist Alfred Schutz, Miller argues that speakers or writers come to typify recurrent rhetorical situations. When speakers or writers find themselves in discourse-demanding situations that seem similar or analogous to situations they have experienced before, Miller claims that "what recurs is not a material situation (a real, objective, factual event) but our construal of a type." Viewed as an aspect of this typification of rhetorical situations, the concept of exigence, characterized by Lloyd Bitzer in his famous essay "The Rhetorical Situation" as a kind of personal or private need to accomplish a goal through discourse, becomes for Miller "a form of social knowledge—a mutual construing of objects, events, interests, and purposes that not only links them but also makes them what they are: an objectified social need" (157).

Like literary scholars, Miller holds that genre is more than form; she agrees that genre is a superordinate concept that fuses "lower-level forms and characteristic substance" (163). She differs from her literary counterparts, however, by defining genre as

> a conventional category of discourse based in large-scale typification of rhetorical action; as action, it acquires meaning from situation and from the social context in which that situation arose. . . . A genre is a rhetorical means for mediating private intentions and social exigence; it motivates by connecting the private with the public, the singular with the recurrent. (163)

Charles Bazerman accepts Miller's theory of genre as social action and extends it one step further. Not only do genres emerge from typified construals of recurrent situations; genres themselves provide writers and speakers with a tool to use as they typify situations:

> A genre provides a writer with a way of formulating responses in certain circumstances and a reader a way of recognizing the kinds of message being transmitted. A genre is a social construct that regularizes communication, interactions, and relations. Thus the formal features that are shared by the corpus of texts in a genre and by which we usually recognize a text's inclusion in a genre are the linguistic/symbolic solution to a problem in social interaction. (62)

To recent theorists of rhetoric, then, the concept of genre forms a kind of linchpin in an intellectual community's processes of generating and disseminating knowledge. As she investigates a subject matter appropriate to her field, a scholar typifies and recognizes a recurrent rhetorical situation, and she produces a text that instantiates one of the field's preferred genres, a textual form that requires her to invoke certain *topoi,* create an exigence, effect an appropriate style, and achieve a recognizable purpose. In turn, the genre not only allows the scholar to report her research, but its conventions and constraints also give structure to the actual investigation she is reporting. In a comprehensive summary of this rhetorical perspective on genre, John Swales posits "communicative purpose" as central to genre's formative power. Swales writes:

> A genre comprises a class of communicative events, the members of which share some set of communicative purposes. These purposes are recognized by the expert members of the parent discourse community, and thereby constitute the rationale for the genre. This rationale shapes the schematic structure of the discourse and influences and constrains choice of content and style. Communicative purpose is both a privileged criterion and one that operates to keep the scope of a genre as here conceived narrowly focused on comparable rhetorical action. (58)

In addition to embodying communicative purpose, "exemplars of a genre" also, according to Swales, "exhibit various patterns of similarity in terms of structure, style, content, and intended audience" (58).

The rhetoricians' perspective of genre as both response to and structuring agent for rhetorical situations has been supported by theory from other fields. For example, a group of Australian and British "critical linguists" and educators who view genre as central to the teaching of writing offer a similar perspective. The group's most prominent theorist, Gunther Kress, defines genres as "conventionalized forms of texts" that emerge from "conventionalized forms of the occasions" of a community" (19). According to Kress, "Genres have specific forms and meanings, deriving from and encoding the functions, purposes and meanings of social occasions. Genres therefore provide a precise index and catalogue of the relevant social occasions of a community at a given time (19). Like his counterparts among the rhetorical theorists, Kress sees a genre as comprising an array of forms. He writes that "a genre is not characterized by one or two or a half a dozen linguistic features, but by the totality of the linguistic forms selected in the production of a text" (29).

Perhaps the most eclectic synthesis of theories leading to a definition of genre can be found in the work of Carol Berkenkotter and Thomas N. Huckin. Drawing together structuration theory from sociology, rhetorical theory, interpretive anthropology, Bakhtin's theory of speech genres, and Russian activity theory as it has been manifested in the American field of psychological study called "situated cognition," Berkenkotter and Huckin explain five theoretical principles that support their definition:

1. Dynamism: Genres are dynamic rhetorical forms that develop from responses to recurrent situations and serve to stabilize experience and give it coherence and meaning. Genres change over time in response to their users' sociocognitive needs.
2. Situatedness: Our knowledge of genres is derived from and embedded in our participation in the communicative activities of daily and professional life. As such, genre knowledge is a form of "situated cognition," which continues to develop as we participate in the activities of the culture.
3. Form and content: Genre knowledge embraces form and content, including a sense of what content is appropriate to a particular purpose in a particular situation at a particular point in time.
4. Duality of structure: As we draw on genre rules to engage in professional activities, we *constitute* social structures (in professional, institutional, and organizational contexts) and simultaneously reproduce these structures.
5. Community ownership: Genre conventions signal a discourse community's norms, epistemology, ideology, and social ontology. (478)

Such a thorough fusion of scholarship from a range of the human sciences seems a promising avenue for future explorations of the nature and functions of genre.

David A. Jolliffe
DePaul University

Bibliography

Bakhtin, Mikhail. "The Problem of Speech Genres." *Speech Genres and Other Late Essays.* Trans. Vern W. McGee. Ed. Caryl Emerson and Michael Holquist. Austin: U of Texas P, 1986. 60–102.

Bazerman, Charles. *Shaping Written Knowledge: The Genre and Activity of the Experimental Article in Science.* Madison: U of Wisconsin P, 1988.

Berkenkotter, Carol, and Thomas N. Huckin. "Rethinking Genre from a Sociocultural Perspective." *Written Communication* 10 (1993): 475–509.

Bitzer, Lloyd. "The Rhetorical Situation." *Philosophy and Rhetoric* 1 (1968): 1–14.

Campbell, Karlyn Kohrs, and Kathleen Jamieson. "Form and Genre in Rhetorical Criticism: An Introduction." *Form and Genre: Shaping Rhetorical Action.* Ed. Karlyn Kohrs Campbell and Kathleen Jamieson. Falls Church, VA: Speech Communication Assn., 1978. 9–32.

Dubrow, Heather. *Genre.* London: Methuen, 1982.

Fowler, Alastair. *Kinds of Literature: An Introduction to the Theory of Genres and Modes.* Cambridge, MA: Harvard UP, 1982.

Guillen, Claudio. *Literature as System: Essays toward the Theory of Literary History.* Princeton: Princeton UP, 1971.

Hawkes, Terrence. *Structuralism and Semiotics.* Berkeley: U of California P, 1977.

Hernadi, Paul. *Beyond Genre: New Directions in Literary Classification.* Ithaca, NY: Cornell UP, 1972.

Jauss, Hans Robert. *Toward an Aesthetic of Reception.* Trans. Timothy Bahti. Minneapolis: U of Minnesota P, 1982.

Kress, Gunther. *Linguistic Processes in Sociocultural Practice.* Oxford: Oxford UP, 1989.

Miller, Carolyn R. "Genre as Social Action." *Quarterly Journal of Speech* 70 (1984): 151–62.

Swales, John. *Genre Analysis: English in Academic and Research Settings.* Cambridge: Cambridge UP, 1990.

Todorov, Tzvetan. *Genres in Discourse.* Trans. Catherine Porter. Cambridge: Cambridge UP, 1990.

Genung, John Franklin (1850–1919)

One of the more influential rhetoricians of the late nineteenth and early twentieth centuries. Between 1885 and 1915, John Franklin Genung's rhetoric treatises were the most widely used rhetoric texts in North American colleges and universities. Genung was a professor of rhetoric, oratory, and literature at Amherst College from 1882 to 1918. During that time, Genung produced four successful textbooks: *Practical Elements of Rhetoric* (1886), *Handbook of Rhetorical Analysis* (1888), *Outlines of Rhetoric* (1893), and *The Working Principles of Rhetoric* (1900). Genung's rhetoric texts consistently advanced the definition of rhetoric as "the art of adapting discourse, in harmony with its subject and occasion, to the requirements of a reader or hearer." This definition reveals Genung's debt to the classical tradition as well as to the theoretical orientation of the New Rhetoricians, George Campbell and Hugh Blair, who insisted that the art of rhetoric consists of the ability to apply fundamental principles to various subjects, contexts, and audiences.

Regarding rhetoric as an indispensable art for everyday life, Genung believed that the student of rhetoric should learn to compose for a variety of purposes. His textbooks constructed a course in rhetoric that prepared students to produce the "prevailing literary forms." Conceiving of "prevailing forms" quite broadly, Genung stressed that rhetorical study should take in all possible forms of discourse including the political essay, scientific and descriptive treatises, short stories, editorials, and reporters' columns, as well as the traditional forms of the sermon and the public lecture. Genung's primary pedagogical interest was in offering rhetorical training that would allow students to develop their innate voices as well as prepare them to deal skillfully with all rhetorical occasions.

Genung's theory of rhetoric highlighted the canons of invention and style. Like other influential nineteenth-century rhetoricians, such as Henry N. Day and A.S. Hill, Genung subsumed arrangement under invention as part of the overall process of shaping a coherent composition. Defining invention as the "organization of thought, according to its nature and object, into a coherent and inter-related form of discourse," Genung treated invention as a process that develops an original conception into a completed form that will have a desired effect (*Working Principles* 388). Under invention, Genung discusses the development of a major theme with supporting main ideas and methods of amplification. Genung defined description, narration, exposition, and argumentation as inventional processes that embody different intentions and effects; therefore, the writer must consider the effects of these modes and choose among them appropriately. Genung's discussion of style also focused on strategies that will allow the rhetorician to reconcile subject matter and intention with the intellectual and emotional responses of readers. Defining style as the "manner of choosing and arranging words so as to produce determinate and intended effects in language," Genung focused on the qualities of clearness, force, and beauty and stylistic techniques such as denotation, connotation, sentence structure, and prosaic rhythm. In Genung's view the audience's anticipated responses govern all stylistic choices. Whether treating style, invention, or the importance of rhetoric as a liberal art, Genung promoted the traditional rhetorical principle that the rhetorician's greatest challenge is to communicate effectively.

Nan Johnson
Ohio State University

Bibliography

Berlin, James. *Writing Instruction in Nineteenth-Century American Colleges.* Carbondale: Southern Illinois UP, 1984.

Johnson, Nan. *Nineteenth-Century Rhetoric in North America.* Carbondale: Southern Illinois UP, 1991.

Kitzhaber, Albert R. *Rhetoric in American Colleges: 1850–1900.* Dallas, TX: Southern Methodist UP, 1990.

Varnum, Robin R. "Professor John Franklin Genung, His Life and Works: An Annotated Bibliography." Unpublished manuscript, 1986.

Wichler, George F. "John Franklin Genung." *Dictionary of American Biography.* Vol. 7–8. Ed. Allen Johnson and Dumas Malene. New York: Scribner's, 1946.

Ghostwriting

The practice of presenters of messages pretending they are the authors when others produced the words. When the people involved hide the actual message source, the author's persona takes on a ghostly character.

Ghostwriting has a long history in Western cultures. It was widely practiced in ancient Greece. Some Attic orators, renowned for setting the style for Grecian rhetoric, made their living by writing speeches for others (Lysias was a prolific ghostwriter). Many prominent figures of eighteenth- and nineteenth-century America employed ghostwriters. George Washington gave speeches prepared for him by such men as Alexander Hamilton, James Madison, and John Jay. Andrew Jackson also had ghostwriters.

In nineteenth-century America, people came to prominence in most fields of endeavor through their rhetorical abilities. Many took pride in preparing and delivering their own speeches. Rhetorical skill was the mark of an educated person. Graduating students demonstrated their education publicly at commencement exercises by delivering an oration, defending a thesis, or participating in a debate. Rhetoric was the road to power, influence, and the means by which a good person contributed to society.

Because of the growing importance of eloquence, fewer speakers relied on others to write their messages. Those who used ghostwriters were under pressure to hide that fact, because to admit to doing so was damaging to a person's ethos.

By the early decades of the twentieth century the old emphasis on eloquence had begun to wane, and the practice of ghostwriting became more commonplace. Woodrow Wilson may have been the last American president to prepare his major speeches. He may also have been the last of the eloquent presidents. By the time of Franklin Roosevelt's presidency, the practice of speech writing was widespread in all areas of American society. People could have press agents, public relations specialists, and advertising agencies prepare their messages. Those who could not afford to have a professional rhetorician on staff or on retainer could always hire a ghostwriter from the speech writing agencies that sprang up in all major metropolitan centers. These agencies would write speeches, letters, student papers, theses, dissertations, papers for learned conventions, memoirs, and autobiographies.

Most leaders of business, industry, education, and government (state and local, as well as national) had their important letters, speeches, and reports written for them. Personalities who came to fame or notoriety from their activities, such as actors, or athletes, or because of public relations stunts, unfortunate violence, or victimization had ghostwriters prepare their memoirs and autobiographies. Thus ghostwriting became important by the turn of the twentieth century in the United States. The nineteenth-century tendency to maintain secrecy about who was responsible for rhetorical invention, arrangement, and style tended to carry over into the period of greater use of speech writers. The disparity between appearances and behavior soon resulted in rumor mongers bringing other people's ghostwriters out of the closet. Soon underground rumors spread by inside dopesters were widespread. Gossip about ghostwriting also grew.

Scholars studied the way teams of rhetoricians prepared Franklin Roosevelt's major presidential addresses. They documented the committee-writing techniques under the leadership of chief speech writer Samuel Rosenman. They studied major speeches and other documents to sort out who on the ghostwriting team was responsible for important phrases and slogans. After the Roosevelt administration, the ghostwriters of subsequent presidents became part of the scholarly record. In addition, scholars also began to study the use that state governors and other political figures made of speech writers.

Despite the changes in speech authorship, however, rhetorical critics, political scientists, and political reporters often did not change their criteria for evaluating communication. Critics studied the speeches of presidents such as Kennedy, Nixon, Johnson, Carter, and Reagan and wrote their commentaries and evaluations as though the person who read the script was also responsible for preparing its rhetoric. Media reporters as well as scholarly critics suggested that the rhetoric of various presidents revealed them to have been active or passive, witty or stolid, honorable or given to duplicity, knowledgeable or uninformed, possessed of vision or without inspiration.

By the 1950s the practice of ghostwriting had become controversial. Before this period the practice had been treated, for the most part, humorously or as unimportant. Now some critics charged that ghostwriting relied for its effectiveness on secrecy and deception and thus was inherently unethical. They argued further that such deception denigrated the practice of rhetoric. They suggested that the cynical acceptance of the widespread practice of ghostwriting debased the language of the culture and fostered cynicism.

Defenders of ghostwriting came forward to argue in its behalf. The defenders noted that ghostwriting had been present down through history. The practice was, they claimed, inevitable, and it was therefore useless to decry it or claim that it was unethical. Good ghosts took pains to study the rhetorical style of the client and cast the language in a similar fashion. In the end the ghosts did little more than make sure that they phrased the clients' ideas in the clearest and most elegant style possible. Finally, the defenders argued that if the ghosts were careful to put the clients' ideas into suitable rhetoric and if the clients took responsibility for the ideas, there were no serious ethical problems.

In recent years the clients of speech writers have often acknowledged their presence, and the element of deception disappeared. Often personalities would use a euphemism such as "as told to" and give the actual writer a byline for the autobiography, memoir, or story. By the 1980s the mass media often reported the names of important speech writers, and some speech writers became personalities in their own right. Peggy Noonan wrote eloquent speeches for Presidents Reagan and Bush. After leaving government service, she wrote a book about her experiences and took to the lecture and talk show circuit as a result. Such acknowledgement often resulted in the gossip and rumors dying out. Gradually the term *speech writer* (sometimes spelled *speechwriter*) came to replace *ghostwriter* in instances when the actual authorship was public knowledge.

Ghostwriting is a practice closely related to plagiarism. Plagiarism is taking the rhetoric of another without the author's permission and claiming it as one's own. Plagiarism remains a damaging charge and destructive to the credibility of the person accused or convicted of plagiarism. When allegations were made that Martin Luther King, Jr., plagiarized portions of his dissertation, they caused some consternation for those who admired Dr. King. When Senator Biden's communication team produced a television political spot that appeared to be plagiarized from a British one, he withdrew as a presidential candidate. Ghostwriting also continues

to be troublesome. When charges were made that Margaret Truman was not the author of a series of popular mystery novels to which she had affixed her name, the charges resulted in media coverage.

By the end of the twentieth century, it became apparent that the mid-century debates about ghostwriting were becoming obsolete. Ghostwriting had become but one element in the growing professionalism and software technology that characterizes contemporary communication. Almost every major institution of American society and increasingly of world culture from the United Nations to nation states to local areas has a team of professional rhetoricians. These specialists are narrowly but thoroughly trained in specific communication skills. Some are experts in polling and in-depth interviewing. Others know how to prepare campaign themes and write speeches, letters, and press releases. Others can schedule and buy media time. Still others can prepare commercial messages, radio and film clips, and television programs. Others maneuver to get free media and stage media events. Others brief clients on how to respond to press conference questions and talk show grilling, or questions from the audience. Other specialists have the expertise to create proper lighting and good sound for film and television, write dramatic scripts, and skillfully cut film and construct montages. The team will often include people with professional skills in all the complicated aspects of contemporary mass media communication.

Ghostwriting should now be placed into the context of the professional communication team. The old issues of ethics, deception, and necessity have now become much more complicated. The scholarly critics and media pundits need to develop suitable criteria for evaluating the nature and responsibility involved in creating messages. They need to judge those who read the scripts as well as those who write them, and to understand the ramifications created because they are often not one and the same.

Ernest G. Bormann
University of Minnesota

Bibliography

Bormann, Ernest G. "Ethics of Ghostwritten Speeches." *Quarterly Journal of Speech* 47 (1961): 262–67.

———. "Ghostwriting and the Rhetorical Critic." *Quarterly Journal of Speech* 46 (1960): 284–88.

Brandenburg, Ernest. "The Preparation of Franklin D. Roosevelt's Speeches." *Quarterly Journal of Speech* 35 (1949): 214–21.

Brigance, W. Norwood. "Ghostwriting Before Franklin D. Roosevelt and the Radio." *Today's Speech* 4.3 (1956): 10–12.

Einhorn, Lois J. "The Ghosts Unmasked: A Review of Literature on Speechwriting." *Communication Quarterly* 30 (1981): 41–47.

Enos, Richard L. "The Persuasive and Social Force of Logography in Ancient Greece." *Central States Speech Journal* 25 (1974): 4–10.

Smith, Donald K. "Ghostwritten Speech." *Quarterly Journal of Speech* 47 (1961): 416–20.

Gorgias of Leontini (490?–380? B.C.E.)

An itinerant teacher of rhetoric whom many authorities, both ancient and modern, claim to be the preeminent figure of the Greek sophistic movement. He was a pupil of Empedocles' and a contemporary of Plato's. By most accounts, he lived for more than one hundred years, practicing his profession to the very end. By other accounts, he gave exaggerated estimates of the worth of his pedagogy and amassed great wealth by extracting exorbitant sums of money from his students, two of whom were Pericles and Isocrates. But any effort to provide a balanced and well-developed account of his life and thought is fraught with difficulties. Only two of his compositions have been preserved, the "Encomium on Helen" and the "Defense of Palamedes," and the authorship of those has been disputed. Though two additional works by Gorgias, "On Being" (variously known as "On Nature" or "On Non-Being") and the "Funeral Oration," are available in relatively complete summaries written by others, the most complete accounts of Gorgias and his rhetoric are given by his adversaries. As a result, Gorgias has enjoyed a reputation particularly unpleasant, even for a sophist.

Chief among these adversaries is Plato himself. Gorgias is accordingly portrayed in Plato's dialogues as a pretentious and self-satisfied dolt, incredibly naive despite his years and abundant wealth. Plato's criticism of Gorgias, however, is seldom directed to the man himself, nor even, essentially, to his rhetoric. Nor, least of all, is it the substance of the intellectual challenge that Gorgias brings to bear that is Plato's concern, but more clearly the world view that he so aptly personifies for Plato—one manifest by the whole of early Greek *paideia*, which Plato dedicated his life and philosophy to undo.

In the end, Gorgias emerges in Plato's dialogues as a man remarkably attuned to the workings of the prevailing *doxa* of ancient Greece and ingenious in the ways of exploiting it by means of rhetoric. Indeed, the most crucial constituents of his rhetoric are apparent in their contrast to Plato's world of ideas, and in light of the contrast we see Gorgias espousing a rhetoric that is at once mysterious and eminently practical. It is geared to the world we know through the commonplace experience of the here and now, the singular sanction of any rhetoric's place and purpose. Yet this world is not primary to Gorgias, for he gives precedence to language, to *verba* as opposed to *res*, the conceit of "things that are." In Gorgias' configuration reality is not stable or unchanging, nor is it to be encountered at all except as it resides, as Charles Segal says, "in the human psyche and its malleability and susceptibility to the effects of linguistic coruscation" (110).

Thus, at the heart of Gorgias' rhetorical theory is the belief that language is the great *dynastes,* possessing the potential to make any impression whatsoever on the psyche, for the inspired incantation of words can "drug and bewitch" (*Encomium of Helen*). In this view language is not essentially a set of symbols representing some fundamental reality beyond itself but is autonomous and free. It functions as an independent, external power, whose surest link to reality lies ultimately in its power to evoke reality. It is thereby deceptive, not in a duplicitous or immoral sense, but in terms of *apate,* where deception proceeds as a necessary consequence of the nature of language itself, conveying in Gorgias "the supersession of the world of *logos* over the epic world of things" (Rosenmeyer 232).

In this conception the human psyche is no less ancillary to language than "things that are." Here, we never so much use language as we are used by language. In contrast to Plato's doctrine of the soul, which holds that there is a deep, abiding essence to the self-transcending physical reality, to Gorgias the psyche subsists on a material level, rendering it particularly susceptible to the effects of language, for language engages the psyche with a physical dynamic, having an immediate, almost physical impact on it (Segal 105).

This view of language, the self, and their interactions is decidedly pre-Socratic, evincing a "premetaphysics" to Plato's metaphysics, and thereby making Gorgias' rhetoric akin in many critical respects to the "postmetaphysics" of contemporary thought. Thus, Gorgias has become an important figure in modern rhetorical theory as well, his rhetoric of vital concern to those exploring these connections under the rubric of "postmodern sophistics."

Bernard A. Miller
Eastern Michigan University

Bibliography

Crowley, Sharon. "Of Gorgias and Grammatology." *College Composition and Communication* 30 (1979): 279–84.

Enos, Richard Leo. "The Epistemology of Gorgias' Rhetoric: A Re-examination." *Southern Speech Communication Journal* 42 (1976): 35–51.

Gronbeck, Bruce E. "Gorgias on Rhetoric and Poetic: A Rehabilitation." *Southern Speech Communication Journal* 38 (1972): 27–38.

Jarratt, Susan C. *Rereading the Sophists: Classical Rhetoric Refigured.* Carbondale: Southern Illinois UP, 1991.

Poulakos, John. "Toward a Sophistic Definition of Rhetoric." *Philosophy and Rhetoric* 16 (1983): 35–48.

Romilly, Jacqueline de. *Magic and Rhetoric in Ancient Greece.* Cambridge, MA: Harvard UP, 1975.

Rosenmeyer, Thomas G. "Gorgias, Aeschylus, and Apate." *American Journal of Philology* 76 (1955): 225–60.

Segal, Charles P. "Gorgias and the Psychology of Logos." *Harvard Studies in Classical Philology* 66 (1962): 99–155.

Sprague, Rosmond Kent, ed. *The Older Sophists: A Complete Translation by Many Hands of the Fragments in Die Fragmente Der Vorsokratiker.* Columbia: U of South Carolina P, 1972.

Untersteiner, Mario. *The Sophists.* Trans. Kathleen Freeman. Oxford: Alden, 1964.

See also SOPHISTIC RHETORIC

Gradatio

A series of phrases or clauses each expressing a little more or a little less than what precedes, in accordance with either a mounting or descending progression. "My conscience hath a thousand several tongues, and every tongue brings in a several tale, and every tale condemns me for a villain" (*Richard III* 5.3). As this example indicates, a gradatio can consist of a continued anadiplosis (q.v.) involving three or more members. When a gradatio involves anadiplosis, the figure acquires a distinctive lock-step quality: "And let the kettle to the trumpet speak, The trumpet to the cannoneer without, The cannons to the heavens, the heaven to earth" (*Hamlet* 5.2). Some gradatios arrange thoughts in units of gradually rising importance without using anadiplosis. Tennyson did so in writing "To strive, to seek, to find, and not to yield" ("Ulysses"). Alexander Pope did as well in his line "Renounce my love, my life, myself—and you" ("Eloisa to Abelard").

Arthur Quinn and Lyon Rathbun
University of California, Berkeley

Grammar

The grammar of a language consists of *phonology,* an account of the sounds of that language; *morphology,* the forms of words; *syntax,* sentence structure; *semantics,* meanings of words, phrases, and sentences; and *pragmatics,* the influence of context on language usage.

The term *grammar* has a variety of meanings. The general public, by and large, understand grammar to be a set of normative rules concerning language usage, including such oddities as "Do not end a sentence with a preposition" and "The subjective complement must be in the subjective case," by which regulation "It's me" would never be the "correct" usage. For linguists and other students of language, *grammar* can mean (1) a description of a language, (2) an analysis of the structure of a language, or (3) the set of rules whereby language is generated. These meanings of the term are associated with (1) traditional grammar, (2) structural grammar, and (3) generative grammar. Explanations of each of these kinds of grammar will follow.

Strictly speaking, *grammar* describes language—for example, "The grammar of English allows both single and double negatives" (for example, "Ruby doesn't have any diamonds" and "Ruby doesn't have no diamonds"). *Usage* characterizes appropriateness—for example,

"The double negative is inappropriate in formal language and is often considered evidence of lack of education and culture." Though in popular usage the double negative would typically be called bad grammar, it is more accurately characterized on the basis of its appropriateness and thus could often be called bad or ineffective usage.

This discussion will first turn to what might be called "scholarly grammar" and will then deal with "school" or "pedagogical grammar."

Scholarly Grammar: Traditional, Structural, and Generative Traditional Grammar

Until after World War II, the grammars produced by scholars from Priscian in the sixth century to Otto Jespersen (1860–1943) and George O. Curme (1860–1948) are often called "traditional." Traditional scholarly grammars are typically an amalgamation of notional definitions (definitions based on meanings rather than morphology or structure), structural or syntactic statements, and semantic characterizations. It is easy to see the problems raised by the notionality of traditional grammar. For example, the common definition of *noun* is "the name of a person, place, or thing," but if that is the case, then "blues" and "reds" in the following sentence are either not nouns, or we must greatly expand the definition of "things" to include colors: The *blues* fade more rapidly than the *reds*. In terms of the traditional definition of *noun*, what do we do with "love" and "faith" in "Great *love* creates deep *faith*"?

In order to gain a sense of traditional grammar, some detail is necessary, particularly if one is to appreciate the differences among traditional grammar and the systems that have developed since World War II and that have been influential in rhetorical studies and the teaching of composition.

Curme (*English Grammar,* 1947) defines noun (or substantive) as "the name of a living being or lifeless thing: *Mary, John, horse, cow, dog; hat, house, tree; London, Chicago; virtue*" (11). He subdivides nouns into *common* and *proper.* Here is his explanation of "common noun":

A common noun is a name that can be applied to any one of a class of living beings or lifeless things: *teacher, student, mayor, president, king, man, lion, tiger, cow; house, tree, city, country,* etc.

A common noun may not only be the name of a thing with a definite form, but it may also be the name of a formless mass, a material, as *tea, wheat, sand, water, gold, paper* (but with different meaning in "this morning's *paper*").

A common noun may also be the name of a collection of living beings or lifeless things, here called a collective noun, as *nation, army, crowd,* a *herd* of cattle, a *row* of trees, a *chain* of mountains, etc.

A common noun may also be the name of a quality, action, state, or a general idea, here called an abstract noun: *hardness, kindness . . .* (11)

The structure and coverage of Curme's *English Grammar,* typical of the traditional school, has three major sections: the parts of speech, accidence (inflection or morphology), and syntax. Accidence is a thoroughgoing account of inflections and word changes to show, for example, possession in nouns (Hattie's bonnet, boys' caps), degree in adjectives (good, better, best), and tense in verbs (walk, walked, have walked; see, saw, have seen). Syntax classifies sentences according to intention as exclamatory (That was a horrible blow!), declarative (Chocolate is my favorite flavor), and interrogative (What is your favorite flavor?) and according to clause structure as simple (containing only one independent clause and no dependent clauses), complex (containing one independent clause and one or more dependent clauses), and compound.

The compound sentence consists of different independent propositions or members. These members may be two or more simple sentences, or one member may be a simple sentence and the others complex sentences, or there may be any combination of simple and complex sentences. (74)

Because it was describing written texts, not speech, traditional grammar had no phonological component, and its single focus was what might be called Standard English, for dialects are part of spoken language, not written. Furthermore, traditional grammar pretty much excluded pragmatics, except insofar as grammarians relied on the texts of the "best" writers for their analysis and examples.

This perhaps adequately characterizes traditional grammar, which is important for at least two reasons: the great scholarly grammars—for example, *Modern English Grammar* by Otto Jespersen, and *A Grammar of the En-*

glish *Language* by George Curme and Hans Kurath—are invaluable records of language theory and attitudes; more important, traditional grammar is the basis for most of the pedagogical grammar found in composition textbooks and handbooks.

Structural Grammar

In the twentieth century, and particularly since World War II, various influential grammatical theories and analytical methods have been advanced, one of the more important being structural grammar (often termed "descriptive grammar" or "descriptive linguistics"), "the discipline which studies languages in terms of their internal structures" (Gleason iii). As one of the great structural grammarians, Charles Carpenter Fries, in the introduction to *The Structure of English* (1952), said

> The point of view in this discussion is descriptive, not normative or legislative. The reader will find here, *not* how certain teachers or textbook writers or "authorities" think native speakers of English ought to use the language, but how certain native speakers actually do use it in natural, practical conversations carrying on the various activities of a community. (3)

From the statements by Gleason and Fries, we can derive several axioms of structural grammar. First, it will deal with structure, not meaning (though, of course, any attempt to exclude meaning from grammatical study would be futile, as language *does* mean); second, it will describe what is, not what someone thinks should be (structural grammar will be to the language as anatomy is to the human body); third, it will take speech as primary and written language as secondary (whereas traditional grammar took written language as the all).

Contrasting the structural definition of *noun* with that of the traditionalist (as in Curme, above) vividly illustrates the difference between the two grammars. Fries says,

> A part of speech in English, like a strike in baseball, is a functioning pattern. It cannot be defined by means of a simple statement. There is no single characteristic that all the examples of one part of speech must have in the utterances of English. All the instances of one part of speech are the "same" only in the sense that in structural patterns of English each has the same functional significance. (73)

Fries then defines the first part of speech (which he, significantly, does not call a "noun") as a word that will fit one or more of three frames:

(The) _____	is/was good
	's are/were
The _____	remembered the ___
The _____	went there.

Thus, words such as *coffee, sugar, reports, husband, supervisor, woman, food,* and so on count as members of the first category (that is, as nouns).

Fries divides the lexicon into four parts of speech (corresponding to nouns, verbs, adjectives, and adverbs) and fifteen *function* categories (for example, prepositions, conjunctions, pronouns), and he analyzes the formal characteristics of each class of the parts of speech. For example, words of Class 1 contrast regularly with words of the other three classes:

Class 1	Class 2	Class 1	Class 3
arrival	arrive	bigness	big
departure	depart	activity	active
delivery	deliver	truth	true
acceptance	accept	idealism	ideal

Class 1	Class 4
way	away
day	daily
sea	seaward

Obviously, the traditional names for the classes are (1) nouns, (2) verbs, (3) adjectives, and (4) adverbs. Note, however, that Fries avoids notionality ("a noun is the name of a person, place, or thing"; "an adjective describes a noun") and relies for his "definitions" on structural descriptions.

The influence of structural grammar (and the new linguistics from which it arose) was massive. Textbooks such as Paul Roberts's *English Sentences* (Harcourt 1962) became popular in schools and colleges, and the National Council of Teachers of English furthered the cause of descriptive grammar by publishing such studies as *Language and Learning* (1968), edited by the linguist Albert H. Marckwardt. The whole concept that a grammar of language is a description rather than a normative standard or a set of prescriptive rules set off a number of firefights and minor revolutions.

In *Attitudes toward English Usage* (Teachers College Press, 1980), Edward Finegan gives a lively and instructive account of the storm over *Webster's Third International Dictionary*, published in 1961. For example,

> Editors at *The New York Times* on October 12, 1961, said *Webster's* had "surrendered to the permissive school that has been busily extending its beachhead on English instruction in the schools," a development they found "disastrous because, intentionally or unintentionally, it serves to reinforce the notion that good English is whatever is popular." A fortnight later, *Life's* editors lamented that Webster's had joined "the say-as-you-go school of permissive English" and had "all but abandoned any effort to distinguish between good and bad usage —between King's English, say, and the fishwife's." (121)

A descriptive grammarian would respond that since both the King's English and the fishwife's are part of the language, a grammar should account for both varieties. And it is important to realize that a structural linguist, compiling a grammar, would not claim that the fishwife's language was always appropriate—or that the King's would be appropriate and effective in every situation.

Generative Grammar

The third grammatical system that has impacted composition/rhetoric is called, variously, "generative," "transformational," or "transformational-generative."

In 1964 the author of a little book called *Syntactic Structures* (Mouton) said:

> The fundamental aim in the linguistic analysis of a language L is to separate the *grammatical* sequences which are the sentences of L from the *ungrammatical* sequences which are not sentences of L and to study the structure of the grammatical sequences. The grammar of L will thus be a device that generates all of the grammatical sequences of L and none of the ungrammatical ones. (13)

Noam Chomsky had fired the shot heard round the world. The generative grammar revolution had begun.

For Chomsky (and other linguists), *grammatical* had a special meaning, something like this: Any sentence that a native speaker would be likely to produce is grammatical. Thus, the following are grammatical:

> I don't have any idea where Laura lives.
> I ain't got any idea where Laura lives.
> I ain't got no idea where Laura lives.

But following is ungrammatical:

> I no have no idea where Laura live.

because it would not be produced by a native speaker.

Since the grammar that Chomsky describes would be able to *generate* all of the sentences of a language—which means that the grammar would be a finite set of rules capable of producing an infinite number of sentences—it could not be a series of statements ("a noun is the name of a person, place, or thing") or a set of structural descriptions, any more than a computer program can consist of statements and descriptions. Or, to come at the problem from a different angle: An adequate generative grammar would produce sentences in the same way that the presumed grammar-in-the-human-brain does. Yet another angle: A generative grammar would be a model of grammar-in-the-head. (The computer HAL in *2001: A Space Odyssey* was programmed with an adequate generative grammar.)

The statements or rules in a generative grammar have a form something like the following, in which → means "is rewritten as" "or consists of":

S → NP AUX VP "S[entence] is rewritten as (or consists of) N[oun] P[hrase], Auxiliary, V[erb] P[hrase]."

A series of rules would then define NP, AUX, and VP. Here, for example, is a rule that defines AUX:

AUX→TN (MOD) (HAVE+EN) (BE+ING)

This rule says that tense is essential to the auxiliary. (In other words, a sentence must have tense.) A modal is optional, as are the past participle and the present participle. Thus, the following can be read as

TN   (MOD)   (HAVE+EN)   (BE+ING)
George present   sing
(*George + the present tense of sing = George sings.*)
George present can   have+en   be+ing   sing
(*George + present tense of can + have + past participle of be + present participle of sing = George can have been singing.*)

The point is that the grammar is self-defining and automatic, so that, *if there were an adequate generative grammar* (which, of course, there is not), that grammar could be programmed into a computer, and the computer would generate an infinite string of grammatical English sentences. (In other words, the computer would be able to "talk," as does HAL in *2001.*)

In regard to composition and rhetoric, however, the great influence of generative grammar came with its insight that "kernel" sentences can be combined into multipropositional sentences. Thus, in theory the sentence *Wanting to stay dry, the hikers climbing the trail found a cave that would shelter them from the storm* consists of the following kernel sentences:

The hikers found a cave.
The hikers wanted to stay dry.
The cave would shelter them from the storm.

Very soon after generative grammar emerged, the hopes that it would be "a device that generates all of the grammatical sequences of L and none of the ungrammatical ones" faded. Here is one example of the problems that faced the generative grammarians. Suppose we are programming a computer with a grammar that will generate an infinite string of sentences. From the initial state S, the computer must go to its lexicon to retrieve items that fit the NP and VP slots. Certainly "the carrot" is a noun phrase, and "is singing" is a verb phrase. Certainly "The carrot is singing" is, in one sense, perfectly grammatical; and certainly it is a nonsense sentence. If the grammar is to generate meaningful sentences, it must have a semantic component, and, to make a long story short, words are defined by other words. This being the case, grammar-in-the-computer, like grammar-in-your-head, is unable to escape from the dictionary. An adequate generative grammar is a chimera.

Pedagogical Grammar

Generative Grammar: The influence of generative grammar on composition teaching was massive. (The following discussion of that influence is adapted from W. Ross Winterowd and Barbara Gleason, *A Teacher's Introduction to the Rhetorical Tradition in Composition* [NCTE, forthcoming].) As we have seen, Chomsky's syntactic structures revolutionized grammatical theory by positing that "syntactic investigation of a given language has as its goal the construction of a grammar that can be viewed as a device of some sort for producing the sentences of the language under analysis" (11). In other words, a grammar was to be not merely descriptive, but, rather, *generative.* In 1966 an NCTE monograph, *The Effect of a Study of Transformational Grammar on the Writing of Ninth and Tenth Graders* by Donald Bateman and Frank R. Zidonis, reported on the attempt to apply the theories of "generative grammar" to composition pedagogy.

One insight of the "new" grammar was that sentences can be either "kernels" or agglomerations of kernels. For example, the following are kernels:

The woman ate the meal.
The man prepared the meal.

They can be combined:

The woman ate the meal that the man prepared.

Bateman and Zidonis posited that studying this new kind of grammar would enable students to improve their stylistic virtuosity: "When students can clearly distinguish between kernel and non-kernel sentences, the reconstruction of complex sentences becomes a simple matter" (x). But they were cautious in evaluating their results, concluding nonetheless that "the study of a systematic grammar which is a theoretical model of the process of sentence production is the logical way to modify the process itself" (37).

In a follow-up study, *Transformational Sentence Combining* (NCTE, 1969), John Mellon hypothesized that practice in sentence combining would enhance the syntactic maturity of seventh-grade students, who would learn only enough grammar to understand the instructions or cues for the operation. Here are sample problems (95):

Fact Clause

A. SOMETHING *seemed to suggest* SOMETHING.
Bill finished his lessons in less than an hour. (T:fact)
He had received special help from another student. (T:fact)

B. The fact that Bill finished his lessons in less than an hour seemed to suggest that he had received special help from another student.

WH-Infinitive Phrase:

A. *The instruction manual did not say* SOMETHING.
Someone overhauls the engine sometime. (T:wh+inf)

B. The instruction manual did not say when to overhaul the engine.

Infinitive Phrase:

A. SOMETHING *would be almost unbearable.*
The rocket fails in its final stage. (T:infin)

B. For the rocket to fail in its final stage would be almost unbearable.

Mellon concluded that practice in sentence combining did indeed accelerate growth in the syntax of his subjects, but, obviously, students needed a good deal of grammatical instruction before they could do the combining.

With *Sentence Combining: Improving Student Writing without Formal Grammar* (NCTE, 1973), Frank O'Hare cut sentence combining entirely free of grammar and made it an influential method of instruction, in grade and high school and in colleges and universities. Here, from page 57 of *Sentencecraft* (Ginn 1975), O'Hare's textbook, are examples of how he presents sentence combining:

1. *We tried to explain* SOMETHING.
Our English guest could not understand SOMETHING. (THAT)
SOMETHING had caused so much confusion for some reason. (WHY)
He drove on the left-hand side of the road. ('S + ING)
[We tried to explain that our English guest could not understand why his driving on the left-hand side of the road had caused so much confusion.]

2. SOMETHING *made Anatole wish* SOMETHING.
There was every likelihood of SOMETHING. (THE FACT THAT)

He had to spend the day with his cousin Elmore. ('S + ING)
He had stayed home. (THAT)
[The fact that there was every likelihood of his having to spend the day with his cousin Elmore made Anatole wish that he had stayed home.]

Francis Christensen first published his essay "A Generative Rhetoric of the Sentence" in *College Composition and Communication* for October 1963. In the essay he explained that eight "free modifiers" go to make up what he calls the "cumulative sentence": subordinate clause (SC), relative clause (RC), noun cluster (NC), verb cluster (VC), adjective cluster (AC), adjective series (A+A), absolute (ABS), and prepositional phrase (PP). Examples provide sufficient explanation of the free modifiers and cumulative sentences that they create:

1

1 He dipped his hands in the bichloride solution and shook them,
  2 a quick shake, (NC)
    3 fingers down, (ABS)
      4 like the fingers of a pianist above the keys. (PP)
      (Sinclair Lewis, *Notes* 9)

2

  2 Calico-coated, (AC)
  2 small-bodied, (AC)
    3 with delicate legs and pink faces in which their mismatched eyes rolled wild and subdued, (PP)
1 they huddled,
  2 gaudy motionless and alert, (A+A)
  2 wild as deer, (AC)
  2 deadly as rattlesnakes, (AC)
  2 quiet as doves. (AC) (William Faulkner, *Notes* 9)

Christensen's free modifiers have had less impact on teaching than has sentence combining, which was wildly popular for a decade or so, from about 1970 to 1980, and which has now sifted down into the sections on style in the textbooks.

Traditional Grammar
Instruction in traditional grammar has been and is so much a part of public school English that hopes of dislodging it in the near—or perhaps the far—future are chimerical. Traditional

grammar in the schools loses its descriptive value and becomes almost totally *prescriptive*, setting forth axioms and rules for "polite" or "correct" usage. The following, from the 1963 edition of the Harcourt, Brace classic *English Grammar and Composition* by John E. Warriner, captures the tone and thrust of prescriptive grammar in the schools:

> "Correction" of your English raises the question: Why is one word or one form correct while another is incorrect? What, in other words, is good English? Good English is the kind of English used by educated people. The fact that educated people use a different kind of English from that used by uneducated people can easily be discovered by listening. The educated person will say, for example, "Jim and I weren't able to see anything in the fog." The uneducated person might say, "Jim and me wasn't able to see nothing in the fog." Although the idea expressed is clear in either form, you, as a high school student, would say it the first way, which, since it is the way an educated person would say it, is the "correct" way. (64)

This sounds very much like eighteenth-century pronouncements regarding correctness, and, in fact, the doctrine of correctness originated during the Enlightenment, when "correct" language became as much a requisite for gentility as a fashionable address and modish raiment. (See Sterling Andrus Leonard, *The Doctrine of Correctness in English Usage 1700–1800*, University of Wisconsin Studies in Language and Literature No. 25, 1929.)

The 1963 edition of *English Grammar and Composition* provides a typical example of prescriptivist-traditional pedagogy. The book calls special attention to "Six Special Irregular Verbs" (128–135): lie, lay, sit, set, rise, and raise.

Lie and Lay

The verb *lie* means *to recline, to rest* or *remain in a lying position*. Its principal parts are *lie, lay*, (have) *lain*, (is) *lying*.

The verb *lay* means *to put, to place something*. Its principal parts are *lay, laid*, (have) *laid*, (is) *laying*.

Memorize the principal parts of these verbs:

Present	Past	Past Participle	Present Participle
lie (to recline)	lay	(have) lain	(is) lying
lay (to put)(is)	laid	(have) laid	(is) laying

If you do not habitually use these verbs correctly, you must begin your work on them slowly and thoughtfully. Only by taking time to think through each form you use can you eventually establish the habit of using the verbs correctly. When faced with a lie-lay problem, ask yourself two questions:

1. What is the meaning I intend? Is it *to be in* a *lying position*, or is it *to put something down*?
2. What is the time expressed by the verb and which principal part is required to express this time? (128–29).

In regard to traditional-prescriptive grammar, one question is inevitable: From it, did students learn "educated" usage? In fact, did studying grammar teach them to use grammar? These questions will be addressed in "Learning Grammar," the next section of this discussion.

Structural Grammar

Almost contemporaneous with the 1963 edition of *English Grammar and Composition* was Paul Roberts's *English Sentences* (Harcourt 1962), a text that illustrates the impact of the new linguistics on pedagogy in college, just as *English Grammar and Composition* documents precisely the lack of effect on mainline public school textbooks. To the question "Why study grammar?" Roberts answers that such knowledge can be useful in helping one punctuate and straighten out blunders in writing, but

> Grammar is the heart of language, and language is the foremost of the features that make human beings human. We said earlier that every speaker of English is an English grammar. When you study English grammar, you inquire most intimately into yourself and the way you work. You will surely get most out of the study if you undertake it objectively, with a simple wish to understand what it is like, accepting any practical application as a kind of bonus. (4)

Roberts treats dialect differences (6–11) and, very much like Warriner, points out that the usage of educated people has a prestige that other varieties of English do not have (7–8).

Roberts identifies ten basic sentence patterns—for example:

1. (DETERMINER)	NOMINAL	VERB	(ADVERB)
	Birds	sing.	
The	birds	are singing	merrily.

6. (DET)	NOM	VERB	NOM	NOM
My	uncle	considered	me	a fool.

This structural approach undoubtedly clarifies syntax more effectively than does traditional grammar, but does the structural approach have more pedagogical utility than the traditional?

Learning Grammar

It is obvious that we can *know* grammar in the sense that we are expert users of the language even though we may not *know* grammar in the sense that we can describe the language. The most admired writers and the most eloquent speakers may be unable to give a traditional or a structural description of the language they use and certainly would be unable to propound a generative grammar. Thus, knowing must have at least two senses: being able to use and being able to describe or account for. There must also, then, be at least two senses of *learning*, for if a person can use the language expertly but cannot describe or account for this use, that person has learned in one sense; if that person then studies grammar and becomes able to describe or account for the language, then that person has learned in quite another sense.

Stephen D. Krashen characterizes two kinds of language learning, unconscious acquisition and conscious learning. (See, for example, *Inquiries and Insights* [Alemany Press, 1985].) For convenience, we will use $Learning_1$ (unconscious) and $Learning_2$ (conscious). Children $Learn_1$ language by hearing it, by attempting to communicate, and by receiving meaningful response. Rapidly—and through regular processes and stages—they $Learn_1$ their native language, which is to say that they $Learn_1$ grammar unconsciously and without direct instruction.

Through instruction and conscious effort anyone can $Learn_2$ traditional, structural, generative, or traditional-prescriptive grammar. If a child or an adult has some language deficiency, will $Learning_2$ grammar help to overcome it? We have seen that *English Grammar and Composition* recommends $Learning_2$ the forms and rules

for such verbs as *lie* and *lay* "if you do not habitually use these verbs correctly." It should be obvious, however, that the vast majority of native speakers of English know very little grammar in the sense that they can give adequate descriptions of the morphology and syntax of English words and sentences; that is, these native speakers have $Learned_2$ very little grammar even though they have $Learned_1$ virtually the complete grammatical system of the language. A minutely small number of native speakers of English could do a traditional grammatical analysis of the clauses in a common sentence such as the following: *The idea that the grammar Geoffrey studied in school improved his morals is ridiculous* (The main clause is *The idea . . . is ridiculous*. An embedded noun clause: *that the grammar . . . improved his morals*. An embedded adjective clause: [*that/which*] *Geoffrey studied in school*.) It is difficult to believe that being able to do such an analysis would improve one's use of language. It is obviously possible to $Learn_2$ verb forms (such as *lie, lay, lain* and *lay, laid, laid*), when to capitalize, the use of the comma in series, and other such surface items in traditional-prescriptive grammar, but it is clearly impossible to $Learn_2$ a language, whether native or foreign; for that, $Learning_1$ is necessary. Massive evidence leads one to conclude that systematic grammatical study of any kind does not improve one's writing or speaking ability. (See W.B. Elley et al., "The Role of Grammar in a Secondary School English Curriculum." *Research in the Teaching of English* 10 [1976]: 5–21; Patrick Hartwell, "Grammar, Grammars, and the Teaching of Grammar." *College English* 47 [1985]: 105–127; Richard H. Haswell, "Error and Change in College Student Writing." *Written Communication* 5 [1988]: 479–99; Thomas Newkirk, "Grammar Instruction and Writing: What We Don't Know." *English Journal* 67 (1978): 46–48; William F. Woods, "The Cultural Tradition of Nineteenth-Century Grammar Teaching." *Rhetoric Society Quarterly* 15 [1985]: 1–12; and "The Evolution of Nineteenth-Century Grammar Teaching," *Rhetoric Review* 5 [1986]: 4–21.) Certainly the hours, weeks, and months that children have spent and are spending on grammatical exercises in school are a vandalistic waste of time. Children $Learn_{1,2}$ nothing from underlining nouns, verbs, adjectives, and adverbs in exercise sentences, from diagramming sentences, from reciting paradigms of verb tenses, and other such activities.

W. Ross Winterowd
University of Southern California

Bibliography

Gleason, H.A. *An Introduction to Descriptive Linguistics.* Rev. ed. New York: Holt, 1961.

Klammer, Thomas P., and Muriel R. Schulz. *Analyzing English Grammar.* Boston: Allyn, 1992.

"Linguistics." *Encyclopedia Britannica: Macropedia.* 1992.

Gramsci, Antonio (1891–1937)

Marxist philosopher and political activist. Born in poverty in Sardinia, Gramsci attended university in Turin where he became involved in socialist politics, organized radical workers' unions, and helped found the Italian Communist party. He was imprisoned by Mussolini's courts in 1926 but continued to work in spite of isolation, deprivation, and illness, writing in anelliptical code to confound the prison censors. After his death in a prison clinic, the monumental *Prison Notebooks* were smuggled out of Italy by his sister-in-law.

Gramsci's contribution to rhetoric is the concept of ideological "hegemony." He theorized what Althusser would later call "the crushing reality and manifold mechanisms of all forms of the ruling ideology." According to Gramsci, the "orthodox" Marxists of his time, using a caricature of Marx's historical materialism, dismissed ideology as mere "superstructure" and offered only mechanistic economic analyses of historical events. He attempted to correct what he saw as their oversimplifications and to assert the real power of ideology in history, drawing mainly on Marx's early work, notably *The German Ideology*, which develops the theory that "the class which is the ruling *material* force of society is also its ruling *intellectual* force."

Gramsci recognized that while the state can exercise domination through physical force, civil society can exert controlling influence in a much more diffuse, subtle, and ultimately irresistible way: through ideological "hegemony" promulgated by means of a network of social, religious, and educational beliefs and practices. Therefore, the revolutionary masses must seize the means of not only material production but also ideological production, and so establish the hegemony of their own revolutionary ideology. In fact, in the face of overwhelming physical domination, Gramsci recommended a "war of position" (uniting the workers with revolutionary theory) rather than a "war of maneuver" (direct confrontation with the state).

Gramsci asserted that most intellectuals work, consciously or unconsciously, to support the reigning (bourgeois) hegemony. He, however, defined a different function for revolutionary intellectuals in the proletariat's "war of maneuver": as a force for ideological cohesion among the masses. According to classic Marxist thought, the forces of history provide the necessary revolutionary conditions, but, as Lenin taught, there is nothing inevitable about revolution, and potential revolutionary masses must be radicalized. Professional ideologues (that is, rhetoricians) can contribute to the revolution by helping to free the masses from bourgeois ideological hegemony. Specifically, revolutionary rhetoricians can help workers overcome ideological alienation by working together with them to discover and express the terms of their own alienated (revolutionary) consciousness. Neither an idealist nor an elitist, Gramsci insisted that revolutionary theory must be true to the lived experience of workers and must serve the ends of workers. It must be a "philosophy of praxis."

Gramsci's idea of a diffuse, insidious ideological hegemony has been useful to many theorists of ideology, not least of all Foucault. His attention to the place of language in Marxist theory, particularly its role in the creation of human consciousness, makes his work especially relevant to postmodern rhetorical theory.

Clyde Moneyhun
New Mexico Highlands University

Bibliography

Adamson, Walter L. *Hegemony and Revolution: A Study of Antonio Gramsci's Political and Cultural Theory.* Berkeley: U of California P, 1980.

Althusser, Louis. "Ideology and Ideological State Apparatuses." *Lenin and Philosophy.* Trans. Ben Brewster. New York: Monthly Review, 1971.

Gramsci, Antonio. *Selections from the Prison Notebooks.* Ed. and Trans. Quintin Hoare and Geoffrey Nowell Smith. New York: International, 1971.

Marx, Karl. *The German Ideology: Part I. The Marx-Engels Reader.* Ed. Robert Tucker. New York: Norton, 1972.

Mouffe, Chantal, ed. *Gramsci and Marxist Theory.* London: Routledge, 1979.

G

Grassi, Ernesto (1902–1991)

An Italian/German philosopher devoted to the rediscovery of the philosophical and rhetorical insights of the Italian humanists. Italian by birth, Grassi received his philosophical education in Germany, working for ten years with Martin Heidegger. German idealism was presented as superior to the intellectual efforts of the Italian humanists, which led Grassi to explore the contributions and significance of the philosophical traditions of his homeland. His works include *Rhetoric as Philosophy, The Humanist Tradition, Heidegger and the Question of Renaissance Humanism, Folly and Insanity in Renaissance Literature,* and *Vico and Humanism: Essays on Vico, Heidegger, and Rhetoric.*

Grassi's views of philosophy and rhetoric rely heavily on the work of Giambattista Vico, an eighteenth-century Italian philosopher whom Grassi sees as the best embodiment of humanist thought. According to Vico, the basic concern of philosophy is how humans define and approach the demands of the ever-evolving life situation. Grassi uses Vico's notion of *ingenium* to describe the basic process by which humans manage the world by grasping what is common or similar between things —seeing relationships and making connections between the known and the unknown.

Grassi suggests that *ingenium* manifests itself in three fundamental human processes: imagination, work, and language. Imagination allows humans to offer varied interpretations to the world they observe, while work is the means by which humans act on the basis of imagination to produce what is needed for life. Language is another way of assigning meaning to the world, of grasping the nature of reality by using symbols to label and share experiences.

The Italian philosophers were interested principally in how language embodies *ingenium,* or functions, to allow humans to make sense of the world. The metaphor was valued in particular because it captures the basic process of grasping the similarities between unrelated phenomena. Furthermore, it is the basic process of connecting a symbol to an experience. Finally, metaphoric activity also is at the heart of philosophy because the first principles upon which any philosophic argument are based are nonrational and nondeductive and are understood through an emotional connection with them.

Grassi's exploration of the concept of folly illustrates and embodies the content and method of his approach to rhetoric and philosophy. He analyzes the concept of folly as the humanists did—through searching literature. Folly also functions as a metaphor for the process of *ingenium:* Just as *ingenium* allows humans to see opposite possibilities and to make connections, folly allows humans to project themselves onto new situations, to imagine that things can always be different from what they seem. Folly, then, is not the process of behaving irrationally; it is a basic human process of envisioning alternative possibilities.

Grassi's exploration of humanist texts led him to assert the value of rhetorical speech over rational speech and thus the superiority of rhetoric over philosophy. Rational speech is deductive, universal, and abstract; it is a closed system in which the starting premises for an idea or experience are not questioned or explored. Rhetorical language, in contrast, is concerned with the concrete particulars of life and with the process by which humans "grasp" in a nonrational way—through metaphor, insight, pathos, and wonder—the nature of human experience. Grassi, then, makes rhetoric a primary and original form of knowing that is superior to philosophy with its logical epistemology. Rather than simply a way of expressing the content established by logical deduction—as rhetoric often has been defined—it is the true philosophy, because it grapples with the fundamental questions of human existence upon which rational deduction can only build.

Grassi provides a reinterpretation of the rhetorical tradition of the Italian humanists, who often are seen as groping toward the ideas that were realized in German idealism. He reasserts the value of a tradition that sees rhetoric not simply as a means by which truth is communicated but as a means of generating a truth by which humans choose to cope with the situation in which they find themselves. Ultimately, he privileges the humanities over science as the key to understanding human experience.

Karen A. Foss
Humboldt State University

Bibliography

Foss, Sonja K., Karen A. Foss, and Robert Trapp. "Ernesto Grassi." *Contemporary Perspectives on Rhetoric.* 2nd ed. Prospect Heights, IL: Waveland, 1991. 143–68.

Grassi, Ernesto. *Heidegger and the Question of Renaissance Humanism: Four Studies.* Trans. Ulrich Hemel and John Michael Krois. Binghamton, NY: Medieval & Renaissance Texts & Studies, 1983.

———. *Rhetoric as Philosophy: The Humanist Tradition.* Trans. John Michael Krois and Azizeh Azodi. University Park: Pennsylvania State UP, 1980.

———. *Vico and Humanism: Essays on Vico, Heidegger, and Rhetoric.* New York: Lang, 1990.

Grassi, Ernesto, and Maristella Lorch. *Folly and Insanity in Renaissance Literature.* Binghamton, NY: Medieval & Renaissance Texts & Studies, 1986.

Veit, Walter. "The Potency of Imagery—the Impotence of Rational Language: Ernesto Grassi's Contribution to Modern Epistemology." *Philosophy and Rhetoric* 17 (1984): 221–39.

Greek Rhetoric

The heart and soul of the Greek educational system in the classical period. The word *rhetoric* is used in a variety of senses. Principal among these are a stricter and a looser sense, the latter referring to the phenomenon of persuasive discourse generally considered. In this entry the terms *oratory* and *peithô* (Greek for *persuasion*) will be used to refer to the *use* of persuasive discourse; *rhetoric* will be reserved, in its stricter sense, to refer to the *study* of persuasive discourse. But in whatever sense one uses the term, all must agree that the Greeks figure crucially in its history: They invented the term *rhetoric* itself. They raised the practice of oratory to a position of central importance in their sociopolitical interactions; and they were the first culture in the West to attempt to codify the study of communication as such and to systematize its precepts. And they bequeathed that legacy to the Romans as well. For all these reasons, Greek rhetoric is of fundamental importance to the study of rhetoric (in both senses).

The Archaic Period

In the strictest sense, it is untoward to speak of *rhetoric* in the archaic period of Greek history, as the word itself (*rhêtorikê*) seems not to have existed until the fourth century (Schiappa 1992). (Note: All dates in this entry are B.C.E. unless otherwise noted.) But this does not mean that rhetoric itself did not exist or that its effects were not noted. Even the ancients debated the nature and extent of Homer's attention to the use of oratory in the *Iliad* and *Odyssey* (Kennedy 1957a)—the oldest extant texts of Western literature (composed in the eighth century). Certainly both of those epics are, among other things, profound studies of the successes and failures of human communication. Achilles in the *Iliad* and Odysseus in the *Odyssey,* particularly, are repeatedly the rhetors or audiences of memorable events of persuasive discourse.

But Homeric "rhetoric," such as it is, is presented in narrative (and thus oblique) terms. Hesiod, writing about the same time as Homer, is more straightforwardly analytical in his treatment of the form and function of persuasion. In his *Theogony* and *Works and Days,* he formulates a clear notion of the nature of *peithô* and its place in the universe, the source of oratorical skill, the social function and ethical responsibilities of the rhetor, and the political effects of *peithô* and its specific relation to *dikê,* "justice" (Kirby 1992). For Hesiod rhetorical skill is largely coextensive with poetic, a distinction that is not adumbrated until Plato, and not sketched out fully until Aristotle's *Rhetoric* and *Poetics* (Kirby 1990, 1991). But it is important to see that even at this stratum *peithô* has become the object of conscious study and discussion—an important stage in the history of rhetoric.

The Early Classical Period

Greek rhetoric, properly speaking, flourishes in the high classical period, particularly under Plato and Aristotle. But these philosophers were particularly indebted to their immediate predecessors, those thinkers generally known as the "pre-Socratic" philosophers. The "sophists" may be thought of as a subcategory of the pre-Socratics. Indeed, thinkers typically categorized as pre-Socratics, such as Heraclitus and Parmenides, were deeply interested in issues of language—indeed Empedocles is credited by Aristotle with the invention of rhetoric—while thinkers typically classified as sophists, such as Protagoras and Prodicus, devoted serious study to metaphysical and cosmological issues. Perhaps it would be most useful to characterize the pre-Socratics as thinkers particularly interested in issues of *origin, change,* and *causality,* and to stipulate the sophists as pre-Socratics especially interested in origin, change, and causality *in the realm of language.* For the most part, their work survives only in fragmentary form (collected in Sprague).

The sophists are traditionally credited (or discredited) with the introduction of rhetorical training to Greece. Corax, a Sicilian, is said to have offered in the mid fifth century systematic instruction in the art of oratory, a newly important skill in the nascent democracies of the Greek-speaking world. Already at this early stage, special attention was being paid to the importance of forensic oratory, as the Athenians were a notoriously litigious people (indeed, much of Hesiod's *Works and Days* had focused on the rhetorical significance of a lawsuit). Corax is held to have offered a taxonomy of the parts of a speech—the *prooimion* (Latin *exordium*), the *agôn* or "contest"—which included what was later called the *diêgêsis* (Latin—*narratio*)—and the *epilogos* (Latin *peroratio*). To Corax and his student Tisias are attributed the compilation of the first handbook of rhetorical precepts. Little is known of these two, however, and there is speculation that "Corax" (Greek for *crow*) was merely a nickname for Tisias himself (Cole).

A sophist who has left considerable literary remains (if we may identify him with the orator of the same name—some scholars distinguish between the two) was Antiphon (c. 480–411). Antiphon's teaching style—to judge from the *Tetralogies* he wrote—would have focused on equipping the orator in *antilogikê* (Latin—*argumentum in utramque partem*)—that is, to argue both sides of the case. This early interest in *antilogikê* is also seen in the *Dialexeis* or *Dissoi Logoi* and in the work of the historian Thucydides, who is said to have studied with Antiphon. In fact, it is one of the notable characteristics of sophistic rhetoric overall (Solmsen 1975:11, 16–24, 30–46, 102, 244).

One of the more important sophists, from a rhetorical standpoint, was Gorgias, another Sicilian. Said to have been a student of Empedocles, Gorgias taught in Athens for considerable sums of money. Gorgias is the subject of a dialogue by Plato, and some of his own writings survive as well. His prose style pays much attention (many would say far too much) to rhythm, rhyme, isocolon, and antithesis; he is acutely aware of the inherent power of language, and in his metaphysics and epistemology (see the ancient testimonia to his treatise "On Not-Being") he may be regarded as one of the earliest precursors of deconstruction. Salient doctrines in the instruction of Gorgias were *peithô* as *psukhagôgia*, "leading-the-psyche"—a tribute to the quasi-magical power of persuasive discourse—and the importance of *kairos*, the "opportune moment" for persuasion.

Another well-known sophist, also the subject of a Platonic dialogue, was Protagoras.

Prominent among his teachings was the *"homomensura"* doctrine—that a human is the measure of all things—and that "to every *logos* a *logos* is opposed," another formulation of the notion of *antilogikê*. Hand in hand with the latter may have been his claim to be able to make "the weaker *logos* [the] stronger," though the meaning of this fragmentary citation is disputed (Schiappa 1991:ch. 6). Protagoras was also known for his interest in *orthoepeia,* "correctness of speech," but it is not known whether this referred to grammatical correctness, to the distinction between literal and figurative language, or to the successful determination of the *logos* most rhetorically apt to a situation.

Yet another sophist who is powerfully drawn by Plato (in book 1 of the *Republic*) is Thrasymachus. In the *Republic* he is portrayed, like Callicles in the *Gorgias,* as a proponent of the Might Makes Right school: To such a person, what is important in a rhetorical situation is not truth or justice but winning. This may or may not be historically fair to Thrasymachus; what seems comparatively more certain is that he wrote a rhetorical handbook of some sort (though this may have consisted of a collection of speeches rather than of a set of precepts offered in systematic fashion), and that he was particularly interested in prose-rhythm.

The sophists' pervasive interest in *antilogikê,* together with their often ludic approach to the nature of language, was liable to raise the suspicions of more conservative, antisophistic thinkers, who wanted an uncomplicated, monologic approach to truth and reality. Because of the negative picture many have drawn of them from the dialogues of Plato (but see below), and from some of the reports given of their work by writers of later antiquity, the sophists came to represent trickery, fraud, and the unscrupulous manipulation of language. It is only in the past century and a half that their reputation has begun to be rehabilitated, but the word *sophistry* has yet to be purged of its negative connotations.

The High Classical Period

Certainly one of the pivotal figures in the history of rhetoric is Plato (427–347), the student of Socrates and teacher of Aristotle. Because what we have of his philosophy is couched not in treatise but in dialogue form, it is a matter of exceeding delicacy and difficulty to attempt to formulate a simple "Platonic" doctrine of anything, and rhetoric is no exception. One cannot know, first of all, how much Plato's portraits of

Socrates may be relied upon for historical accuracy, nor how much Plato may have agreed or disagreed with Socrates on any given topic, nor how (or how much) Plato's own opinions may have changed over the years. These factors should induce extreme caution in any scholarly approach to Plato. Common opinion and perhaps the simplest interpretation is that Socrates and Plato represent a conservative reaction to the sophistic movement—a highly moralistic approach to truth and ethics in all walks of life, including the realm of language.

On this account the sophists are the villains of the piece, Socrates the hero. Yet the distinctions are not easy to draw: In the dialogues, Socratic dialectic often seems to involve a sort of logical entrapment. He seems disingenuous about his own (or anyone's) ability to achieve certain knowledge. The process of elenchus in the dialogues often leads merely to *aporia,* a state in which previously unexamined and unsatisfactory positions have been abandoned but are not replaced by positive alternatives. Furthermore, like the sophists, he took students, with whom he was extremely popular, though he seems not to have accepted payment for his teaching; and he pays minute attention to the choice and meaning of words. Finally, he is portrayed in the Platonic dialogues in repeated, and deep, conversation with various sophists. Certainly, if our only evidence were the *Clouds* of Aristophanes, it would be assumed without question that Socrates was a sophist.

The Platonic Socrates, however, does seem to disagree with some of the sophists he converses with on a number of important counts. Perhaps the single most important text in this regard is the *Gorgias,* in which he contends that rhetoric is not in fact a *technê,* an art or discipline with its own discernible rules and methods, because it cannot give an account of its own *arkhai* (first principles). Rather, he argues, it is a "knack" picked up by practice. As a *technê* its goal would be truth; as it is, it is aimed only at flattery. This notion is picked up in the *Phaedrus,* in which (it seems) Socrates allows that there could be such a thing as a philosophical rhetoric, a true *technê.* In the latter dialogue, such a rhetoric is closely aligned with the practice of dialectic. Another Platonic dialogue that offers an acute study of the nature of *peithô* is the *Symposium,* in which a number of people at a drinking party offer formal orations in honor of *erôs* (passionate love, personified as the god Eros). The series of speeches offers a broad disparity of viewpoints on *erôs,* but also a variety of approaches to the nature of discourse. Some of them display features that are recognizably sophistic—for example, an interest in antithesis, fine distinctions in verbal definition, and attention to stylistic matters in the manner of Gorgias. The speech of Socrates, of course, serves as a sort of climax to the series, but in it he claims to have learned everything he knows about *erôs* from a woman of Mantinea, Diotima. Thus his "speech" is actually the account of his dialectical interchange with Diotima.

Many other dialogues focus on rhetorical matters in one way or another. Prominent among these are the *Apology of Socrates,* which dramatizes his defense before the Athenian court that eventually sentenced him to death; the *Cratylus,* which discusses the nature of language; the *Menexenus,* in which Socrates recites a funeral-oration; and the *Protagoras,* in which Socrates explicitly contrasts the use of dialectical question and answer with monologic oratorical delivery.

It must be emphasized again (1) that a careful reading of Plato will keep in mind the fact that Socrates often propounds positions sheerly for the sake of argument and that he will later recant or modify them, so that it is not always easy to tell when he is being ironic; and (2) that, because of his narrative format, it is not entirely clear when Plato is in agreement with his character Socrates, or whether the dialogues may in fact be a critique of the Socratic position. Moreover, one cogent reading of Plato might be that he is deconstructing all positions and all certainties (the "Socratic" as well as the "sophistic").

Aside from Plato and Aristotle, the most important single figure in the history of rhetorical instruction during the high classical period was Isocrates (436–338). Mentioned, perhaps ironically, in Plato's *Phaedrus* as a promising young thinker, Isocrates set up a school in Athens that was the greatest rival to Plato's Academy and Aristotle's Lyceum. Central to its curriculum was rhetorical instruction (Isocrates' term was *philosophia*). Something of his educational philosophy can be learned from his *Against the Sophists, Helen,* and *Antidosis.* Among Isocrates' other remaining works—speeches that were usually revised and published as pamphlets—are the *Areopagiticus, Busiris, Panathenaicus, Panegyricus,* and *Philip.* What has apparently not survived, unfortunately, is Isocrates' rhetorical handbook;

one ancient tradition has it that he destroyed it himself. It is possible that it was an "esoteric" work—that is, intended for use only within the walls of his own school (Kennedy 1963:71–72). Apparently, it included some notion of the genres of oratory, a fairly conventional approach to the parts of the oration, and some discussion of stylistic matters. It is also possible, as in the case of Thrasymachus, that this "handbook" consisted of a collection of Isocrates' speeches.

There is a tradition that Aristotle, on his arrival in Athens, spent some time with Socrates. As this is chronologically impossible, it has been suggested that "Socrates" here is a scribal error for "Isocrates," and that in fact Aristotle studied for a time with Isocrates before going over to Plato (Chroust 1973:1.94–101). This provocative suggestion would, if true, explain Aristotle's early interest in rhetoric; moreover, it would give due recognition to the far-reaching impact Isocrates has had on the rhetorical tradition in the Western world.

If one name were singled out as the most important—for better or worse—in the history of Greek rhetoric, it would have to be that of Aristotle (384–322). His approach to rhetoric, while it owes much to the *Gorgias* and *Phaedrus* of Plato, was unlike anything that preceded it; and it has influenced (if only by way of contrast) virtually every rhetorical system that has followed it in Western culture. In fact, the history of Greek rhetoric might well be written in terms of two strains or systems—the sophistical, which concentrated on teaching the *moria logou*, or parts of the oration, and the Aristotelian (Solmsen 1941), these two traditions finding an eventual synthesis in the rhetorical treatises of Cicero and Quintilian (see the extended treatments of these in Kennedy 1972).

The opening words of the *Rhetoric* are a direct challenge to the contention in the *Gorgias* that rhetoric is antistrophal to cooking: rather, says Aristotle, it is antistrophal to dialectic, Plato's pet practice. By this opening salvo, Aristotle signifies that he is going to situate rhetoric as a genuine *technê,* and to offer a philosophical account of its principles. Rather than take a *moria logou* approach, he breaks rhetoric down according to the species of discourse and according to the parts of rhetoric. The species of discourse are three, each with its own *telos,* or goal, and oriented toward its own time: *sumbouleutikon,* "deliberative" (or "political") oratory, concentrating on the expedient, and aimed toward future action; *dikanikon,* "judicial" (or "forensic") oratory, concentrating on the just, and focusing on the determination of past fact; and *epideiktikon,* "epideictic" (or "ceremonial") oratory, concentrating on praise and blame, and situated primarily in the present. The parts of rhetoric in Aristotle's schema are four, and these account for the overall structure of the treatise: *heuresis* (Latin *inuentio,* the finding of argument), *taxis* (Latin *dispositio,* the arrangement of the parts of the speech), *lexis* (Latin *elocutio,* questions of style) and *hupokrisis* (Latin *actio,* the delivery of the oration). Rather than concentrate on *taxis* and *lexis,* as in the sophistic tradition, Aristotle spends the bulk of his treatise—the first two books—on *heuresis,* which he locates in three—(and only three) modes of proof: ethos, the (perceived) good character of the speaker; pathos, the emotion(s) aroused in the audience by the discourse; and logos, the suasive force of logical argument, as expressed by deduction in the enthymeme or rhetorical syllogism, and by induction in the example. Each of these is proper, or native, to a particular part of the rhetorical situation: ethos to the rhetor; pathos to the audience; and logos to the words of the speech itself. (The latter should be studied in relation to the formal syllogism, which Aristotle was the first, it seems, to discover and to write about, in the *Prior* and *Posterior Analytics;* the *Topics* and *Sophistical Refutations* discuss the use of logic in dialectical situations.)

Issues of *heuresis,* including various topics for enthymeme, various kinds of ethos, and the arousal of various emotions, are treated seriatim in Book 2 of the *Rhetoric.* Book 3 (which may have been written at quite a different time than the rest of the *Rhetoric*) treats the topics of *lexis* and *taxis.* The section on *lexis* includes perceptive discussions of good and bad style; of figured language, such as metaphor and simile; of grammatical correctness; of propriety in style; of prose rhythms; and of periodicity, among other topics. The section on *taxis* (in which Aristotle is on territory especially associated with the sophists) attempts to offer the most philosophical assessment of the topic: The core of a speech is defined as *prothesis* (proposition) and *pistis* (proof); to these may be added proem and epilogue, but the last two parts are not as essential as the first two are.

A treatise that dates from this period (some time before 341) is the *Rhetorica ad Alexandrum* (so called because of a prefatory epistle dedicating the work to Alexander the Great). Formerly attributed to Aristotle, it was probably written by

Anaximenes of Lampsacus. Its particular importance is as a prime example of sophistic rhetoric. It is thought that the *Rhetorica ad Alexandrum* may have been influenced by the *technê* of Isocrates (q.v. above). There are, however, superficial resemblances to the Aristotelian system: Chapters 1–5 correspond in their subject matter approximately to Book 1 of Aristotle's *Rhetoric*; chapters 6–22, to *Rhetoric* 2; and the rest of the treatise to *Rhetoric* 3. (Chapters 23–28 are on style, chapters 29–37 on arrangement, and chapter 38 covers several miscellaneous topics.)

The Postclassical Period

As the tutor of Alexander, son of Philip of Macedon, Aristotle might well be said to have had a direct impact on the shaping of Hellenistic culture. He seems to have fostered Alexander's love of things Greek, and wherever Alexander's empire expanded, the Greek language went too as a *lingua franca*. That of course brought with it the ability to read Greek literature, as well as an *entrée* into Greek rhetorical training. With the rise of Rome, their eventual creation of a republic, and their interest in Greek culture, the avid Roman interest in rhetoric was a natural development.

There was no single Greek theorist after Aristotle who matched his stature in the field of rhetoric, but several Greek thinkers of the postclassical period deserve mention. First among these chronologically would be Aristotle's pupil Theophrastus (c. 370–c. 287), much of whose work is now lost, but whose interesting *Characters* survives, along with some botanical and other scientific treatises and some work on metaphysics. It appears that Theophrastus' rhetorical treatises ran the gamut from invention, arrangement, and style to delivery. He wrote on enthymemes and epicheiremes, on *topoi*, and on the use of humor. Of particular interest is his now-lost *On Style*, which can be reconstructed in a sketchy way from the testimony of Cicero (Kennedy 1957b). While, as has recently been demonstrated, there was already some conscious taxonomy of the *kinds* of style in the fifth century (O'Sullivan), the notion of an array of *virtues* of style had received its earliest clear expression in the *Rhetoric* of Aristotle; it was this hint that Theophrastus picked up in his *On Style*. His categories seem to have been *correctness* (*hellênismos*—that is, the good use of Greek), *clarity* (to *saphes*), *propriety* (to *prepon*), and *ornament* (perhaps *kataskeuê*). It does seem, too, that he offered (but did not entirely originate) a threefold taxonomy of the *kinds* of style—plain, intermediate (or "mixed"), and grand.

It is difficult to date securely the author, known as Demetrius, of a treatise *On Style*. He was formerly identified with Demetrius of Phaleron, an Athenian statesman and orator born c. 350, and a contemporary (and student) of Theophrastus'. It is now thought, however, that this treatise must date from the third, second, or even first century. *On Style* is of particular interest in terms of its contribution to ancient literary criticism. After a discussion of the rhetorical period and its components, the work is arranged around an eightfold taxonomy of literary styles: There are four good kinds, plain (*iskhnos*), elevated (*megaloprepês*), elegant (*glaphuros*), and forceful (*deinos*). Each of these, in turn, has its corresponding vice: arid (*xêros*), frigid (*psukhros*), affected (*kakozêlos*), and unpleasant (*akharis*). For Demetrius, one might say, the vices are virtues *manqués*. In its attention to the virtues of style, the treatise shows some common interest (and possibly filiation) with the work of Theophrastus; on the other hand, it goes beyond what we know of the Theophrastean system in its elaboration of more than one kind of good style. In this respect it prefigures the work of Hermogenes (q.v. below).

One of the "transitional figures" of the postclassical period—a Greek-speaking man living in Rome during the first century and writing for a primarily Roman audience—was Dionysius of Halicarnassus. In addition to his historical work *Roman Antiquities,* he wrote a number of rhetorical works, including *On Mimesis,* which survives only in fragmentary form; *On the Ancient Orators,* which treats of Lysias, Isocrates, Isaeus, and Demosthenes, four of the ten canonical Attic orators; various other essays (some in epistolary form) on Thucydides, Demosthenes, Deinarchus, and Plato; and *On the Arrangement of Words,* which treats of stylistic matters such as composition and euphony.

Dionysius was a proponent of "Atticism" in oratory, as opposed to what he saw as the excesses of "Asianism." Along with Demetrius and Hermogenes, he is one of the great arbiters of rhetorical style in postclassical Greek rhetoric.

Another important treatise from this period, whose author is also uncertain, is *On the Sublime,* formerly attributed (among others) to Dionysius of Halicarnassus and to Cassius Longinus. The latter was a Neo-Platonist philosopher of the third century C.E., and the teacher of Porphyry. *On the Sublime,* however, is now dated (on internal evidence) to the first century C.E. There are significant lacunae in our extant manuscripts of the treatise; what remains to us is perhaps two-thirds of the whole. Unlike the work of Demetrius or Hermogenes, which offers synthetic overviews of various aspects of rhetorical and literary style, *On the Sublime* concentrates on one important virtue of style, *hupsos,* or sublimity. It is traced to five sources, the five having a common ground of *dunamis en tôi legein,* power with language. Two are primarily the product of nature, three of nurture. In the former category are *to peri tas noêseis hadrepêbolon,* sturdiness of ideas (later in the treatise defined as *to megalophues,* inborn greatness), and *to sphodron kai enthousiastikon pathos,* the arousal of vehement emotion. In the latter category are included *he poia tôn skhêmatôn plasis,* the proper construction of figures; *hê gennaia phrasis,* nobility of phrase; and, finally, *hê en axiômati kai diarsei sunthesis,* a general effect of dignity and elevation. The fifth heading is said to encompass the other four.

On the Sublime is an idiosyncratic and very personal work, but deeply perceptive in its literary judgments. Its postclassical status is evident in the elevation of such authors as Homer and Demosthenes to the pinnacle of literary greatness. Quite apart from the critical acumen and sensitivity of the author, we are indebted to this treatise for its preservation of a number of fragments of earlier authors (such as Sappho) that have not otherwise survived the ravages of time.

Perhaps the principal rival to the Aristotelian system, and certainly, during the time before the rediscovery of Aristotle's treatises in the first century, the most influential element of Greek rhetoric, was stasis theory (Latin *status* or *constitutio*). Its first formulation is traditionally ascribed to Hermagoras of Temnos in the second century. His own writings have not survived, but some impression of them can be gained from their apparent impact on the *Rhetorica ad Herennium* and on Cicero's *De inventione.* (Much of what can be known about Hermagoras is reported in Kennedy 1963:303–21.) Hermagoras' system of stasis is said to have been arranged under five headings—probably including those of *stokhasmos* (fact), *horos* (definition), *poiotês* (quality), and *metalêpsis* (transference).

A Greek work on stasis theory that has survived, although from a period later than Cicero, is *On Staseis* of Hermogenes of Tarsus, one of the more important figures of the Second Sophistic. Born around 161 C.E., he was said to be an oratorical child prodigy, so gifted that the emperor Marcus Aurelius came to hear him speak. His system of stasis is much more complex than the Hermagorean system seems to have been (see the treatment in Kennedy 1983:79–86); it depends upon an elaborate process of *diairesis,* or division, in order to determine the question at issue.

Aside from *On Staseis,* Hermogenes' literary remains include *On Invention, On Ideas of Style* (translated in Wooten 1987) and perhaps (though this may be spurious) *Progymnasmata* (translated in Baldwin 1928:23–38). Books 1 and 2 of *On Invention* treat the proem and the narration. Books 3 and 4 concentrate on the proof, with treatments of stasis and of the use of enthymeme and epicheireme; moreover, there is a treatment of style. *On Ideas* offers a sevenfold taxonomy of virtues of style: *saphêneia,* clarity; *megethos,* grandeur; *kallos,* beauty; *gorgotês,* rapidity; ethos, character; *alêtheia,* sincerity; and *deinotês.* Some of these are further subdivided; *deinotês,* literally "awesomeness," is typically translated as "force(fulness)" and (like Pseudo-Longinus's fifth source of sublimity) refers to the effective use of the other six ideas. For Hermogenes the incarnation of *deinotês* (and thus of all the ideas) is the orator Demosthenes, an exact contemporary of Aristotle. A notable difference from the Aristotelian system is the inclusion here of ethos as a matter, not of invention, but of style.

The *Progymnasmata* offers thirteen graduated rhetorical exercises of various types, including the use of *muthos,* fable; *diêgêma,* narrative; *khreia,* anecdote; *gnômê,* proverb; *anaskeuê* and *kataskeuê,* refutation and confirmation; *koinoi topoi,* commonplaces; *egkômion,* encomium; *sugkrisis,* comparison; *êthopoiïa,* character-portrayal; *ekphrasis,* description; *thesis,* logical examination; and *nomou eisphora,* the citation of a law in argumentation. A similar system is found in the *Progymnasmata* of Theon and of Aphthonius; the Hermogenic text was translated into Latin by Priscian in the sixth century C.E. Like the *controuersiae* and *suasoriae* of Latin declamation, the *progymnasmata* were used as rhetorical exercises in the schools.

John T. Kirby
Purdue University

Bibliography

Baldwin, Charles S. *Medieval Rhetoric and Poetic*. New York: Macmillan, 1928.

Chroust, Anton-Hermann. *Aristotle: New Light on His Life and on Some of His Lost Works*. 2 vols. Notre Dame, IN: Notre Dame UP, 1973.

Cole, Thomas. "Who was Corax?" *Illinois Classical Studies* 16 (1991): 65–84.

Kennedy, George A. "The Ancient Dispute over Rhetoric in Homer." *American Journal of Philology* 78 (1957a): 23–35.

———. *The Art of Persuasion in Greece*. Princeton: Princeton UP, 1963.

———. *The Art of Rhetoric in the Roman World*. Princeton: Princeton UP, 1972.

———. *Classical Rhetoric and Its Christian and Secular Tradition from Ancient to Modern Times*. Chapel Hill: U of North Carolina P, 1980.

———. *Greek Rhetoric under Christian Emperors*. Princeton: Princeton UP, 1983.

———. "Theophrastus and Stylistic Distinctions." *Harvard Studies in Classical Philology* 62 (1957b): 93–104.

Kirby, John T. "Aristotle's *Poetics*: The Rhetorical Principle." *Arethusa* 24 (1991): 197–217.

———. "The 'Great Triangle' in Early Greek Rhetoric and Poetics." *Rhetorica* 8 (1990): 213–28.

———. "Rhetoric and Poetics in Hesiod." *Ramus* 21 (1992): 34–60.

Nadeau, Ray. "Hermogenes on Stases: A Translation with an Introduction and Notes." *Speech Monographs* 31 (1964): 361–424.

O'Sullivan, Neil. *Alcidamas, Aristophanes and the Beginnings of Greek Stylistic Theory*. Stuttgart: Franz Steiner Verlag, 1992.

Schiappa, Edward. *Protagoras and Logos: A Study in Greek Philosophy and Rhetoric*. Columbia: U of South Carolina P, 1991.

———. "*Rhêtorikê*: What's in a Name? Toward a Revised History of Early Greek Rhetorical Theory." *Quarterly Journal of Speech* 78 (1992): 1–15.

Solmsen, Friedrich. "The Aristotelian Tradition in Ancient Rhetoric." *American Journal of Philology* 62 (1942): 35–50, 169–90.

———. *Intellectual Experiments of the Greek Enlightenment*. Princeton: Princeton UP, 1975.

Sprague, Rosamund Kent, ed. *The Older Sophists. A Complete Translation by Several Hands of the Fragments* in Die Fragmente der Vorsokratiker. Columbia: U of South Carolina P, 1972.

Wooten, Cecil W., trans. *Hermogenes' On Types of Style*. Chapel Hill: U of North Carolina P, 1987.

Further Reading

General

Cole, Thomas. *The Origins of Rhetoric in Ancient Greece*. Baltimore: Johns Hopkins UP, 1991.

Enos, Richard Leo. *Greek Rhetoric before Aristotle*. Prospect Heights, IL: Waveland, 1992.

Karp, Andrew J. "Homeric Origins of Ancient Rhetoric." *Arethusa* 10 (1977): 237–58.

Murphy, James J. *A Synoptic History of Classical Rhetoric*. New York: Random, 1972.

Vickers, Brian. *In Defence of Rhetoric*. Oxford: Clarendon, 1988.

The Archaic Period

Martin, Richard P. *The Language of Heroes: Speech and Performance in the Iliad*. Ithaca, NY: Cornell UP, 1989.

Solmsen, Friedrich. "The 'Gift' of Speech in Homer and Hesiod." *Transactions of the American Philological Association* 85 (1954): 1–15.

Walsh, G.B. *The Varieties of Enchantment: Early Greek Views of the Nature and Function of Poetry*. Chapel Hill: U of North Carolina P, 1984.

The Early Classical Period

Classen, C.J., ed. *Sophistik*. Darmstadt: Wissenschaftliche Buchgesellschaft, 1976.

Kerferd, G.B. *The Sophistic Movement*. Cambridge: Cambridge UP, 1981.

———. *The Sophists and Their Legacy*. Wiesbaden: Franz Steiner Verlag, 1981.

Lloyd, G.E.R. *Polarity and Analogy: Two Types of Argumentation in Early Greek Thought*. Cambridge: Cambridge UP, 1966.

O'Sullivan, Neil. *Alcidamas, Aristophanes and the Beginnings of Greek Stylistic Theory*. Stuttgart: Franz Steiner Verlag, 1992.

Romilly, Jacqueline de. *The Great Sophists in Periclean Athens*. New York: Oxford UP, 1992.

———. *Magic and Rhetoric in Ancient Greece*. Cambridge, MA: Harvard UP, 1975.

Segal, Charles. "Gorgias and the Psychology of the Logos." *Harvard Studies in Classical Philology* 66 (1962): 99–155.

G

Untersteiner, Mario. *The Sophists*. Oxford: Basil Blackwell, 1954.

The High Classical Period

Allen, R.E., trans. *The Dialogues of Plato. Volume II: The Symposium*. New Haven: Yale UP, 1991.

Cope, E.M. *An Introduction to Aristotle's Rhetoric, with Analysis Notes and Appendices*. London: Macmillan, 1867.

Dodds, E.R. *Plato: Gorgias. A Revised Text with Introduction and Commentary*. Oxford: Clarendon, 1959.

Dover, K.J., ed. *Plato: Symposium*. Cambridge: Cambridge UP, 1980.

Grimaldi, W.M.A. "The Aristotelian Topics." *Traditio* 14 (1958): 1–16.

————. *Studies in the Philosophy of Aristotle's Rhetoric*. Wiesbaden: Franz Steiner Verlag, 1972.

Griswold, Charles L., Jr. *Self-Knowledge in Plato's Phaedrus*. New Haven: Yale UP, 1986.

Kennedy, George A., trans. *Aristotle on Rhetoric: A Theory of Civic Discourse*. Oxford: Oxford UP, 1991.

The Post-Classical Period

Grube, G.M.A. *A Greek Critic: Demetrius on Style*. Toronto: U of Toronto P, 1961.

Kennedy, George A. *New Testament Interpretation through Rhetorical Criticism*. Chapel Hill: U of North Carolina P, 1984.

Russell, D.A., ed. *'Longinus.' On the Sublime*. Oxford: Clarendon, 1964.

Schenkeveld, D.M. *Studies in Demetrius' On Style*. Amsterdam: Hakkert, 1964.

See also ANTIDOSIS; ANTIPHON; ARGUMENT; ARISTOTLE; ATTICISM; CICERO; CORAX; DELIBERATIVE ORATORY; DEMOSTHENES; DIALECTIC(S); DIOTIMA; *DISSOI LOGOI*; EMPEDOCLES; ENTHYMEME; EPIDEICTIC ORATORY; ETHOS; GORGIAS; HERMAGORAS; ISOCRATES; *KAIROS*; LOGOS; LONGINUS; LYSIAS; ORATORY; *PATHOS*; PISTIS; PLATO; *PROGYMNASMATA*; PROTAGORAS; QUINTILIAN; RHETOR; *RHETORICA AD ALEXANDRUM*; *RHETORICA AD HERENNIUM*; *RHÊTORIKÊ*; SECOND SOPHISTIC; SOCRATES; SOPHIST; STASIS THEORY; *TECHNÊ*; *TELOS*; TISIAS

Grice, H. Paul (1913–1988)

Philosopher of language whose notions of nonnatural meaning and cooperation enable the application of language pragmatics to the study of rhetoric. From 1938 until 1967, H. Paul Grice held a position as fellow and tutor of St. John's College, Oxford University. He is probably best remembered as a professor of philosophy at the University of California, Berkeley, where he taught from 1967 until his death.

Grice published several philosophical papers on utterer's meaning and intentions prior to 1967. He is best known, however, for his 1967 William James Lectures at Harvard University, in which he elucidated his ideas about nonnatural meaning and cooperation in conversation. Two of these lectures appeared in volumes of the annual *Syntax and Semantics*, with the promise that full publication of the William James Lectures was imminent. The first paper, "Logic and Conversation," introduced the cooperative principle, along with its related categories and maxims. The second paper, "Further Notes on Logic and Conversation," explained Grice's ideas about how the cooperative principle could explain rhetorical concepts like irony and metaphor. Unfortunately, the promised publication of the lectures did not come until after Grice's death. His complete works were published posthumously as *Studies in the Way of Words*. (All references herein are to this work.)

Grice's notion of nonnatural meaning, which he denoted as meaning$_{NN}$, is important to rhetoric because this notion attempts a precise formulation of meaning as it relates to intentions of speakers. Natural meaning for Grice came in sentences reducible to the form "A means (meant) to do so-and-so by x" (215). In such sentences, meaning is very close to the denotations of the words used in the utterance and to the cultural conventions governing the use of a particular language. In Grice's example "Those spots meant measles" (213), a listener need not stray far from the denotations of the words and the cultural knowledge that spots on the skin are a commonly known diagnostic criterion for measles to understand the meaning.

Nonnatural meaning came in sentences reducible to the form "A uttered x with the intention of inducing a belief by means of the recognition of this intention" (219). In such cases the hearer must recognize the speaker's intention to understand the meaning, especially as the actual utterance may not have a natural meaning that matches the intention. Grice's example of such a case is a speaker uttering "Smith couldn't get on without his trouble and strife" to mean that "Smith found his wife indispensable" (214). In this case the hearer must not only recognize that "trouble and strife" does not refer to what it literally means but in fact refers to a person, but also that the speaker intended the reference to a person.

Nonnatural meaning is the basis of what Grice calls conversational implicature, implicatures based on our understanding of certain conventions of talk exchanges. Grice called these collected conventions the cooperative principle, for which he gives this definition: "Make your conversational contribution such as is required, at the stage at which it occurs, by the accepted purpose or direction of the talk exchange in which you are engaged" (26). Relating to the cooperative principle, Grice distinguishes four categories, quantity, quality, relation, and manner, under which he distinguishes several maxims. The maxims of quantity relate to providing the required amount of information. The maxims of quality relate to providing information that one knows to be true or have reasonable evidence for. The maxims of relation require that each contribution to a talk exchange be somehow relevant to what came before. The maxims of manner require the avoidance of obscurity, ambiguity, and prolixity.

Conversational implicatures occur when conversants observe these maxims but rely on the observance of the maxims to fill in for information that is not present in the talk exchange, as in the following example:

A: I am out of petrol.
B: There is a garage around the corner. (32)

In this example, A must interpret B's response as complying with the maxims of relation and work out the implicature that A could purchase the petrol required at the garage. Speakers, however, sometimes deliberately flout maxims in creating a conversational implicature, as when saying "X is a fine friend" of someone who has just betrayed all of one's business secrets to a competitor (34). In that case the maxims of quality are violated. The utterance is literally not true, but the hearer must assume the speaker is adhering to the maxims of relevance and so understands the irony.

The importance of Grice's work is that it establishes a philosophical basis for understanding the nature of communication exchanges. It has laid the foundation for the merger of linguistics and rhetoric in language pragmatics, one of the subdisciplines of linguistics. Geoffrey Leech, building on Grice, in fact argues that rhetoric is a subdiscipline of linguistics. Dan Sperber and Deirdre Wilson have developed their relevance theory, the most recent perspective on language pragmatics, both as a reaction to and a development of Grice's theories. Practical examples of Grice's impact on rhetoric and linguistics are also available. Rong Chen and Forrest Houlette argue, for instance, that applications of Grice's cooperative principle resolve problems of interpretation surrounding irony, and that most, if not all, figures of speech should be explainable in the same terms. H.P. Grice is, as a result, an important, enabling philosopher to both rhetoricians and linguists.

Forrest Houlette
Ball State University

Bibliography

Chen, Rong, and Forrest Houlette. "Towards a Pragmatic Account of Irony." *Language and Style* 23.1 (1990): 29–37.
Grice, H. Paul. *Studies in the Way of Words.* Cambridge, MA: Harvard UP, 1989.
Leech, Geoffrey. *Principles of Pragmatics.* London: Longman, 1983.
Sperber, Dan, and Deirdre Wilson. *Relevance: Communication and Cognition.* Cambridge, MA: Harvard UP, 1986.

H

Habermas, Jürgen (b. 1929)

German philosopher devoted to the development of a critical theory of society grounded in language and interaction. Associated early in his career with the Frankfurt School of critical theory, Habermas is an eclectic thinker who draws on Marxism, hermeneutics, Freudian psychoanalysis, speech-act theory, and critical theory to suggest a theory of emancipation from domination. His theory has evolved in the course of his writings, which include, among others, *Knowledge and Human Interests, Theory and Practice, Communication and the Evolution of Society, The Theory of Communicative Action* (two volumes), and *On the Logic of the Social Sciences.* His theory can be conceptualized as a four-tiered model that encompasses epistemology, individual language use, communicative action, and critical theory.

The first tier of Habermas's theory of emancipation is his view of human knowledge. Habermas believes that humans have three orientations or interests that structure human activity—work, interaction, and power. *Work* is the basic means by which humans provide for the material aspects of existence. The interest inherent in this domain is technical, which is realized in the empirical/analytic sciences. The domain of *interaction,* by which humans create and maintain social groups, contains a practical interest. The need to interact culminates in the historical/hermeneutic sciences concerned with the interpretation of meaning. *Power,* an inevitable result of the emergence of hierarchies in human societies, is the third aspect of life. Although power is unavoidable, humans have a natural interest in freeing themselves from oppressive forms of power. This desire for greater freedom is the emancipatory interest, which is realized through self-reflection. When formalized, it assumes the form of critical theory. Since work, interaction, and power, with their corresponding interests, are fundamental to human society, Habermas suggests that no domain of humanity is value-free. Each interest shapes a realm of human experience by determining the means for understanding and communicating in that realm.

Universal pragmatics, or the study of general aspects of language use, constitutes the second tier of Habermas's theory. Habermas claims that every competent speaker of a language can use (1) constatives, speech acts that assert a truth claim; (2) regulatives, speech acts that regulate the relationship between speaker and hearer; and (3) avowals, speech acts that deal with the expression of feelings, wishes, and intentions. When using constatives, a speaker is concerned with whether a *truth* claim is valid; with regulatives, a speaker deals with the *appropriateness* of the norms operating in a particular context. Avowals raise the validity claim of the *sincerity* of stated intentions.

The use of these speech acts and the corresponding validity claims are taken for granted in everyday discourse until one of the validity claims is questioned. When this occurs, three options are possible: One or both of the participants can withdraw from the interaction; the problem can be resolved by means of further communication; or the participants can move to what Habermas calls the level of discourse in order to seek resolution. The second option is merely clarification, which may be necessary when sincerity is questioned. The third option—discourse—occurs when either truth or appropriateness claims are discussed.

In discourse, nothing is taken for granted. Participants suspend the usual assumptions about communication and advance data to back their claims. When truth claims are in dispute, participants operate as if the problematic claim is an hypothesis that may or may not be true. When the claim of appropriateness is under scrutiny, participants argue about whether the norms guiding actions are appropriate.

If resolution is not possible through ordinary discourse of this type, participants can move to another level—metatheoretical discourse—where the field or context of an argument is discussed. An additional level of recourse remains if the discussion at the metatheoretical level is unproductive; participants can move to the metaethical level, or critical theory, where the structure of knowledge itself is examined.

The use of discourse presupposes that interaction will be conducted in what Habermas calls an ideal speech situation, in which no constraints are placed on the discussion. This means that all involved have the same opportunity to speak and be heard—the right to freely use constatives, regulatives, and avowals. Full and equal access to all forms of speech acts means that truth (the claim of constatives), justice (the claim of regulatives), and freedom (the claim of avowals) are inherent in language—that there is a rational basis for these dimensions already present in society. The scheme also suggests standards for ethical communication; communication that meets the tests of truth, appropriateness, and sincerity and allows for unrestrained discourse can be considered fair and just.

The third tier of Habermas's theory is communicative action—how the basic building blocks of speech acts play out in society. Habermas suggests that each speech act and validity claim have a corresponding domain of reality that exhibits a particular attitude. The objective world of facts—an extension of truth claims—corresponds with external nature. Speakers communicating in this realm exhibit an attitude of objectivating; the speaker treats the object of discussion as having an independent existence, external to and apart from self. The second domain is the social world of interaction, grounded in the use of regulative speech acts. Here the attitude is conformative, or following norms. Finally, Habermas suggests the existence of a subjective world that deals with those experiences to which the individual has private and personal access. The attitude taken in this domain is expressive—a person makes known a wish, feeling, or other subjective belief.

The final tier of Habermas's model of emancipation is critical theory. In order to assess the possibilities for rationality for a society generally, Habermas distinguishes between the life-world and systems. The life-world is the domain of daily social activity consisting of the general knowledge, traditions, and customs that unconsciously are passed from one generation to the next. Language is the dominant medium in this realm. Systems, on the other hand, are the structural features of life governed by nonlinguistic or speechless media such as money.

As part of his critique of society, Habermas points out that in traditional societies there is a high degree of consensus among participants so that life-world and systems are coherent and unquestioned. In modernity, however, the systemic side of life has dominated the life-world side—institutions, rules, bureaucracies, and economics exert greater influence than language. When this kind of imbalance exists, there is less need to achieve consensus through communication because disputes are solved by recourse to systems. In an emancipated society, however, the life-world is not subjected to the demands of system maintenance; rather, the mechanisms of the system are accommodated to the needs of individuals. For Habermas, then, modernity is a paradox. Its increasing differentiation has forced greater reflection and rationalization but also has allowed the technocratization of the life-world and the devaluing of communication as a means of dealing with human problems.

Karen A. Foss
Humboldt State University

Bibliography

Dews, Peter, ed. *Autonomy and Solidarity: Interviews*. London: Verso, 1986.

Foss, Sonja K., Karen A. Foss, and Robert Trapp. "Jürgen Habermas." *Contemporary Perspectives on Rhetoric*. 2nd ed. Prospect Heights, IL: Waveland, 1991. 241–72.

Geuss, Raymond. *The Idea of a Critical Theory: Habermas and the Frankfurt School*. New York: Cambridge UP, 1981.

Habermas, Jürgen. *The Theory of Commu-
nicative Action, Volume I: Reason and
the Rationalization of Society.* Trans.
Thomas McCarthy. Boston: Beacon,
1984.
———. *The Theory of Communicative Ac-
tion, Volume II: Lifeworld and System:
A Critique of Functionalist Reason.*
Trans. Thomas McCarthy. Boston: Bea-
con, 1987.
McCarthy, Thomas. *The Critical Theory of
Jürgen Habermas.* Cambridge: MIT P,
1978.
Pusey, Michael. *Jürgen Habermas.* London:
Tavistock, 1987. Seidman, Steven, ed.
*Jürgen Habermas on Society and Poli-
tics: A Reader.* Boston: Beacon, 1989.
Thompson, John B., and David Held.
Habermas: Critical Debates. Cambridge:
MIT P, 1982.

Handbooks

In the classical tradition, systematically present
the elements of what would become the five
parts of rhetoric: invention, arrangement, style,
memory, and delivery. This system was firmly
in place by the time of Cicero and may be a
product of the Hellenistic Greek tendency to
categorize, though its seeds can be seen much
earlier.

The handbook tradition reaches back to
the earliest days of the conceptualization of
rhetoric in Sicily during the fifth century B.C.E.
with the fall of tyranny, the institution of democracy, and the teaching of Corax and Tisias.
These men created the first handbooks of rhetoric to enable citizens to speak in the assembly
or to recover property after the tyrants' fall.
Little is known about the contents of handbooks before Aristotle. Corax and Tisias may
have introduced types of argument (probability)
and parts of an oration (introduction, *agön*, and
epilogue). Plato (*Phaedrus*), Isocrates (*Against
the Sophists*), and Aristotle (*Rhetoric*) express
dissatisfaction with the contents of handbooks
because of a lack of a scientific approach to
rhetoric, a tendency toward triviality, and an
emphasis on judicial oratory.

The *Ars rhetorica* of Aristotle (384–322
B.C.E.) is the earliest extant handbook but
presupposes a long tradition of handbooks.
Aristotle seeks to show (against the criticisms of
Plato) that rhetoric can be the subject of a sys-
tematic and useful study and (against other

handbook writers) what the proper contents of
such an inquiry should be. His treatise is broken into three books: Book 1 introduces the
theoretical basis for the study of rhetoric (1–3)
and his three species of oratory: judicial, deliberative, and epideictic (4–15). Book 2 discusses
Aristotle's three types of proof: pathos or emotion (1–11), ethos or character (12–17), and
logos or logical reasoning (18–26). Book 3,
perhaps a later addition, discusses delivery (1),
style (2–12), and arrangement (13–19). Aristotle's treatise is of seminal importance for
its philosophic and logical treatment, for its
rescue of rhetoric from the attacks in Plato's
Gorgias and *Phaedrus,* and for his innovations,
such as the three types of proof and the three
species of oratory.

Also handed down as a work of Aristotle,
but probably the work of a contemporary, is
The Rhetoric to Alexander. Its preface, a letter
presenting the treatise as Aristotle's private lesson to Alexander the Great, is certainly a forg-
ery. The treatise is similar to Aristotle's *Rhetoric* but shows significant differences: It focuses
on seven species of oratory (rather than three),
does not have the logical detail of Aristotle (including the three proofs), and is much weaker
on style. It is most valuable as an example of a
less philosophic handbook from the period.

Since little survives from the Hellenistic
period (neither Theophrastus on the three styles
nor Hermagoras on stasis theory), perhaps the
best example of a traditional handbook comes
from Rome in the first century B.C.E., the *Rhetoric to Herennius.* Long included in the works
of Cicero as the *Rhetorica Secunda,* scholars
now deny Ciceronian authorship and believe
Cornificius to be its author. Its four books again
follow the five parts of rhetoric. Books 1 and 2,
after a preliminary treatment of rhetoric, discuss judicial invention under the organization
of the parts of a speech: introduction, narration,
division, proof, refutation, and peroration. In
Book 1 a major product of post-Aristotelian
conceptualization appears with the treatment of
stasis theory, or the determination of the issue
at hand. Ascribed to Hermagoras of Temnos
(second century B.C.E.), this theory seeks to establish whether the issue at hand is one of fact
(did the defendant commit the crime?), definition (should the act be defined as alleged?),
quality (the act has extenuating circumstances),
or transference (this court is not qualified to
hear the case). This approach is common in
later presentations of invention. Book 2 treats

judicial invention further as it looks to methods of logical argument. Book 3 deals first with deliberative and epideictic oratory, then briefly with arrangement, delivery, and memory. Its treatment of memory is the best of the Graeco-Roman sources. Book 4 is a detailed account of style, the fifth part of rhetoric, and contains an elaborate presentation of figures of thought and speech, another important post-Aristotelian development.

The *Rhetoric to Herennius* enjoyed an immense popularity, partially because it was thought to fill out the ideas on rhetoric of the greatest rhetorician of the Roman Republic, Cicero (106–43 B.C.E.). Cicero's two major contributions to the handbook tradition are *On Invention* and *On the Orator*. The youthful *On Invention* shows Cicero's attempt to bring Hellenistic rhetorical theory into the Roman world. It is thorough and uninspiring, but had a large influence on later handbooks and was known as his *rhetorica prima*. He never completed proposed treatments of the other four parts of rhetoric, and thus the *Rhetoric to Herennius* became a popular supplement. More interesting, and more in the philosophic tradition of Aristotle and Plato, is a work of his maturity. *On the Orator* (54 B.C.E.) presents a discussion between prominent orators of the generation before Cicero: Crassus, Antonius, and Scaevola. Book 1 is given to general discussion and treatment of the question of rhetoric versus philosophy. Scaevola prefers the wisdom of philosophy, but Crassus prefers the orator and argues that he must be a wise man. The second book has Antonius present one of Cicero's main contributions to rhetorical theory, the idea of the three "duties of an orator" (*officia oratoris*): to teach, to please, to move. Here too occurs antiquity's most thorough treatment of humor as a rhetorical tool. In the third book, Crassus treats the issues of style and delivery, which allows him to digress on the importance of knowledge, recalling his remarks in Book 1.

Though other Romans had discussed rhetoric, it was Cicero who established rhetoric at Rome through his numerous discussions of it, both technical and philosophic. The successor to Cicero, and the author of the most thorough treatment of rhetoric from the Graeco-Roman world, is Quintilian (c. 40–95). Under the emperor Vespasian, he was the first to hold an official, state-funded chair of rhetoric. Quintilian's main work, *The Education of the Orator*, consists of twelve books that cover the orator's train-

ing from cradle to grave. Book 1 treats the young boy's prerhetorical education in the Grammatical School. Book 2 begins with the choice of rhetorical schools and teachers, with the bulk being given over to "metarhetoric" issues: definitions, whether rhetoric is an art, rhetoric against philosophy. Book 3 first treats rhetoric's history, origins, and the three species of rhetoric. Then the traditional handbook treatment begins with a discussion of judicial oratory and stasis theory. Book 4 begins the treatment of arrangement of a judicial oration with discussion of the introduction, narration, and digression. Book 5 is devoted to proof and refutation. Book 6 covers the peroration and, connected with it, gives a treatment of emotions. Book 7 treats the theory of arrangement and gives a more in-depth treatment of stasis theory. Books 8 to 11 consider style, with Book 10 offering the famous reading list of which Greek and Latin authors are best to study. This lengthy treatment shows rhetoric's tendency to focus on style in the later classical period and beyond. The second half of Book 11 brings in memory and delivery to complete the five parts of rhetoric. In Book 12 Quintilian presents a postscript on the importance of the orator's being a morally good person (*vir bonus*), perhaps his most significant contribution. He also discusses other topics and methods of studying appropriate for the adult life.

Quintilian is at his best when he gives a thorough and clear presentation of the state of the question on any issue. Most of what he presents is not new, but it is set out in a systematic way for the student. His interest in teaching is apparent, as is his interest in the student as a *vir bonus* and a leading citizen. In this he follows the ideas presented in his great favorite, Cicero. His educational system is thus broad, thorough, and morally sensitive. The prefatory letters to the books, especially to Book 6, in which he talks of the death of his wife and sons, offer a glimpse of a man who was a very successful teacher, if unlucky in his family life. His handbook, once reestablished in its entirety in the fifteenth century, at times eclipsed Cicero's own works as the most influential classical handbook.

Much of the preceding discussion has treated handbooks of oratory. But the Roman Empire also saw rhetoric's increased influence on the literary world, and thus literary rhetoric became a cornerstone of the intellectual world of the empire. As a result, there are several discussions of what might be called "literary rhetoric" during the early empire, as seen, for example, in the work of Pseudo-Longinus, *On Sublimity* (first century). This Greek treatise analyzes what makes literature great. It includes a close discussion of style, thus situating itself in the handbook tradition, but it differs in that its focus is more global and more literary. It is interested in literature, not oratory, and it is interested in what makes a work or passage sublime, not what makes an individual phrase or sentence sublime. Unlike earlier handbook treatments of style that tend to see the trees, *On Sublimity* sees the forest and appreciates it.

A second transformation of the handbook tradition can be seen in the works of Hermogenes, a *wunderkind* of the second century. In the Greek world, handbook treatment came in regularized parts: After beginning with *progymnasmata* (a series of brief exercises for the young student), there came separate treatises on stasis theory, on invention, and on style. Hermogenes is credited with works about all these steps, and his most influential treatise is *On Ideas*, which discusses style. It follows in the tradition of literary rhetoric, analyzing what makes for good oratory, and does this with an elaborate system focusing on seven categories or "ideas" of style: clarity, grandeur, beauty, rapidity, character, sincerity, and force. This system was the basis for later Greek rhetorical and literary analysis, replacing the older concept of the three styles: grand, middle, and plain. Hermogenes' works were vastly influential in the Greek world and inspired numerous commentaries and introductions. Hermogenes and Pseudo-Longinus show the emphasis in the Roman Empire on style as a major focus and on literary analysis as the major medium.

One last transformation of the handbook tradition can be seen in *On Christian Doctrine*, by the rhetor-turned-bishop Augustine (354–430 C.E.). This Latin treatise discusses the ways to find the meaning of the Scriptures (Books 1–3). Book 4 then treats ways of communicating this meaning. The fourth book, therefore, presents an early version of what might be called "Christian rhetoric," leading to the medieval tradition of treatises on the art of preaching. Book 4 is indebted to Ciceronian presentations of the duties of the orator, the three kinds of style, and ethos. It also treats the distinctive characteristics of Christian eloquence.

The classical handbook tradition carried into the medieval period in two ways. First, treatments of rhetoric in the encyclopedic work of Martianus Capella, Cassiodorus, and Isidore of Seville helped to form the ideas of the trivium (grammar, rhetoric, dialectic). This ensured rhetoric's place, if occasionally a subservient place, in the educational system and therefore the handbook tradition. The second medieval manifestation was the concentration on the three arts of verse writing (*ars poetriae*), of letter-writing (*ars dictaminis*), and of preaching (*ars praedicandi*).

The classical tradition of the handbook of rhetoric maintained its life as a member of the trivium, often as nothing more than the treatment of style, into the modern period. The Ciceronian or Aristotelian tradition held sway among students of rhetoric until the twentieth century, when different attempts by Black, Perelman, and others offered new ways to view communication. The classical tradition can still be seen in twentieth-century handbooks of classical rhetoric, such as those by Volkmann (1874, 1901), Lausberg (1960), Martin (1974), and Fuhrman (1984); the histories of Kennedy (1963, 1972, 1980, 1983); composition/communication works, such as those by Horner (1988) and Welch (1990); and the stylistic handbooks, such as that of Lanham (1991).

Terry L. Papillon
Virginia Polytechnic Institute
and State University

Bibliography

The classical handbooks can be found in the Loeb Classical Library (Harvard University Press) with Greek or Latin text and English translation on the facing page. (*Ad Alexandrum* can be found in the volume of Aristotle, *Problems 22–38*. *Ad Herennium* can be found in volume 1 of Cicero's works.)

Black, Edwin. *Rhetorical Criticism: A Study in Method*. 2nd ed. Madison: U of Wisconsin P, 1978.

Cole, T. *The Origins of Rhetoric in Ancient Greece*. Baltimore: Johns Hopkins UP, 1991.

Fuhrmann, M. *Die Antike Rhetorik: Eine Einfuhrung*. Munich: Artemis, 1984.

Horner, Winifred Bryan. *Rhetoric in the Classical Tradition*. New York: St. Martin's, 1988.

Kennedy, George A., trans. *Aristotle, On Rhetoric: A Theory of Civic Discourse*.

Oxford: Oxford UP, 1991.

———. *Art of Persuasion in Greece.* Princeton: Princeton UP, 1963.

———. *Art of Rhetoric in the Roman World.* Princeton: Princeton UP, 1972.

———. *Classical Rhetoric in Its Christian and Secular Tradition from Ancient to Modern Times.* Chapel Hill: U of North Carolina P, 1980.

———. "The Earliest Rhetorical Handbooks." *American Journal of Philology* 80 (1959): 169–78.

———. *Greek Rhetoric under Christian Emperors.* Princeton: Princeton UP, 1983.

Lanham, Richard A. *A Handlist of Rhetorical Terms.* 2nd ed. Berkeley: U of California P, 1991.

Lausberg, H. *Handbuch der literarischen Rhetorik.* Munich, 1960.

Martin, J. *Antike Rhetorik: Technik und Methode. (Handbuch der Altertumswissenschaft, 2nd Abt. 3rd teil.)* Munich: Verlag C.H. Beck, 1974.

Murphy, James J. *Rhetoric in the Middle Ages.* Berkeley: U of California P, 1974.

Perelman, Chaïm, and L. Olbrechts-Tyteca. *The New Rhetoric: A Treatise on Argumentation.* Trans. J. Wilkinson and P. Weaver. Notre Dame, IN: U of Notre Dame P: 1969. French original, 1958.

Volkmann, R. *Die Rhetorik der Griechen und Römer in systematischer Übersicht.* 3rd ed. Leipzig: Teubner, 1901.

Welch, Kathleen. *The Contemporary Reception of Classical Rhetoric: Appropriations of Ancient Discourse.* Hillsdale, NJ: Erlbaum, 1990.

Havelock, Eric (1903–1988)

Classics scholar and author of works on ancient Greek literature, literacy, and culture; major contributor, along with Ong, Goody and Watt, and Olson, to literacy-orality theory. Books include *Preface to Plato* (1963); *Communication Arts in the Western World* (1978); *The Greek Concept of Justice from Its Shadow in Homer to Its Substance in Plato* (1978); *The Literate Revolution in Greece and Its Cultural Consequences* (1982), a collection of his articles; and *The Muse Learns to Write* (1986).

The son of Alfred Henry and Annie Louise (Williams) Havelock, Eric Havelock was born in London. He married first Ellen Parkinson; they had a daughter. His second wife was Christine Mitchell; there are two sons from that marriage. Havelock attended Leys School in Cambridge and Cambridge University, from which he was graduated with highest honors in ancient philosophy.

Havelock taught at Acadia University in Nova Scotia (1926); at Victoria College in Toronto (1928–1947); at Harvard University (1947–1963), where he was chair of the Classics Department; and at Yale University (1963–1971), where he was Sterling Professor of Classics and chair of the Classics Department.

Presenting a forceful argument for the cognitive effects of literacy, Havelock's *Preface to Plato* is one of the germinative works on the so-called "Great Leap" perspective on literacy and orality. According to Havelock, in preliterate, or oral, Greece the bard and audience entered into a "mimetic" spell in which the poetry of Homer was recited and received without question. In this way cultural knowledge—both social values and concrete survival skills—was transmitted. Asserting that literacy was just beginning to be established in Greek society at the time of Plato, Havelock believes that literacy and its ensuing modes of thought break this mimetic spell. For Havelock, literacy based on the Greek alphabet, the only writing system existing in a causal relationship with logic, fosters questioning and releases energy for critical thinking and for the discovery of "selfhood" apart from one's role as a member of the group. This is why Plato banned the poets from the *Republic*: not because their information was necessarily wrong but because their oral performance mitigated against literate modes of thought, held to be abstract, propositional, syllogistic, and prevented systematic analysis, which Plato saw as the means to discovering truth.

According to Halverson, Havelock's work has not been especially well received by his fellow classicists. Havelock's literacy-orality theory, however, has proven compatible with ideas on the growth of rhetoric held by many historians of rhetoric—Kennedy, Murphy, Enos, Horner, Swearingen, and Welch, to name a few. In composition, though, theories based on Havelock's ideas (Ong; Farrell) have been more controversial (Greenberg et al.; Daniell [181–93] in Swearingen; Rose).

Beth Daniell and Karen H. Gentry
Clemson University

Bibliography

Farrell, Thomas J. "IQ and Standard English." *College Composition and Communication* 34 (1983): 470–84.

Goody, Jack, and Ian Watt. "The Consequences of Literacy." *Comparative Studies in Society and History* 5 (1963): 304–45.

Greenberg, Karen, Patrick Hartwell, Margaret Himley, and R.E. Stratton. "Responses to Thomas J. Farrell, 'IQ and Standard English' (with a reply by Thomas J. Farrell)." *College Composition and Communication* 35 (1984): 455–78.

Halverson, John. "Havelock on Greek Orality and Literacy." *Journal of the History of Ideas* 53 (1992): 148–63.

Olson, David R. "From Utterance to Text: The Bias of Language in Speech and Writing." *Harvard Educational Review* 47 (1977): 257–81.

Ong, Walter J., Jr., S.J. "Literacy and Orality in Our Times." *ADE Bulletin* 58 (1978): 1–7.

———. *Orality and Literacy: The Technologizing of the Word.* London: Methuen, 1982.

Rose, Mike. "Narrowing the Mind and Page: Remedial Writers and Cognitive Reductionism." *College Composition and Communication* 39 (1988): 267–302.

Swearingen, C. Jan, ed. *The Literacy/Orality Wars.* Spec. Issue *PRE/TEXT* 7 (1986): 117–208.

Hendiadys

The addition of a conjunction between a word (noun, adjective, verb) and its modifier (adjective, adverb, infinitive), as well as the substitution of this word's grammatical form for that of its modifier. Frequently, the transformed modifier follows the word, leaving it also rearranged. Complicated as it is to describe, examples are straightforward. "Furious sound" becomes "sound and fury." "Nicely warm" becomes nice and warm." Note that a hendiadys that transforms an adjective-noun phrase sometimes also adds articles for emphasis: "The heaviness and the guilt within my bosom / takes off my manhood" (*Cymbeline* 5.2). Note too that the hendiadys that transforms the infinitive-verb phrase cannot involve rearrangement but does require the omission of *to* from the infinitive to become a regular verb.

Thus, "come to see" becomes "come and see." The most common reason for using a hendiadys is emphasis. Grammatically, the modified word is more important than the modifier. A writer or speaker, however, may wish to emphasize what is conveyed by the modifier. Thus, "sound and fury" emphasizes the "fury" of the sound; "nice and warm" makes the fact that it is "nice" at least as important as the fact that it is "warm."

Arthur Quinn and Lyon Rathbun
University of California, Berkeley

Hermagoras (c. 150 B.C.E.)

The most significant contributor to rhetorical theory in the Hellenistic era (322–90 B.C.E.), who wrote in the last half of the second century, a period of transition between the codification of rhetoric and its systematic development in the Roman Republic. According to rhetoric historian James J. Murphy, Hermagoras of Temnos completes the "link" between Greek and Roman rhetorical theory.

Little is known about Hermagoras, and his writings are not extant. His inventional system, however, known as "stasis theory," has been reconstructed from evidence provided by Cicero, Quintilian, and others, who demonstrated that Hermagoras contributed to an understanding of both deliberative and forensic discourse.

Hermagoras modified the Aristotelian structure of rhetoric, stressing its inventional and political dimensions while deemphasizing ethical and emotional proof. He furthered the division of deliberative rhetoric into two interrogative processes that Aristotle had called the "thesis" and the "hypothesis." The thesis was an abstract issue that avoided the particularities of any given case, whereas the hypothesis was a more concrete example of a particular set of circumstances. Consider the following general deliberative question: Is it right or honorable to kill a tyrant? General questions such as this Hermagoras called a thesis. Contrasted with the thesis is the hypothesis: It answers questions on a particular issue, such as, Did the Athenians make the correct choice when they executed Antiphon for treason?

By far the most important contribution that Hermagoras made to rhetorical theory was the topical system for forensic discourse called "stasis theory." The word *stasis* means "strife," "conflict," or "immobility." In rhetorical theory, the stasis of an argument is the basic issue in dispute resulting from an adversarial clash of positions. Stasis is, then, the "stand" between two adversaries resulting from the conflict in allegations between the prosecutor and defendant. Issues are made manifest by an initial claim and counterclaim. The following schematic illustrates an issue and its stasis point:

$$\rightarrow \text{ yes } * \text{ no } \leftarrow$$

The space represented by the asterisk is the immobilized issue. Stasis theory is designed to locate the specific arguments behind an issue and analyzes the points upon which any controversy pivots.

There are four stasis points: conjecture (*coniectura*), definition (*proprietas*), quality (*qualitas*), and procedure (*translativa*). Conjecture involves the question of fact. For example, is gold missing from the state coffers? If the gold is missing, then definition comes into effect. Definition names the kind of act the removal of the gold constitutes. Has the gold been stolen or borrowed? If stolen, quality raises the question of whether the theft was good or bad. Has the stolen gold been selfishly stolen or has it been used to purchase grain for a famine-struck city? Procedure rests on the logistic and legality claims: Has the defendant been treated according to the law or not? Does the court have jurisdiction in this case?

Stasis theory is an inventional system for forensic discourse that became the primary rhetorical system behind the Roman legal apparatus. Stasis theory is the epitome of systematized rhetoric. With Hermagoras, the Aristotelian strand of rhetorical theory had reached its most developed state.

Omar Swartz
Purdue University

Bibliography

Dieter, Otto Alvin Loeb. "Stasis." *Speech Monographs* 17 (1940): 345–69.

Matthes, Dieter. "Hermagoras von Temnos 1904–1955." *Lustrum* 3 (1958): 58–214 [in German].

Nadeau, Ray. "Classical Systems of Stasis: Hermagoras to Hermogenes." *Greek, Roman and Byzantine Studies* 2 (1959): 51–71.

———. "Some Aristotelian and Stoic Influences on the Theory of Stasis." *Speech Monographs* 26 (1959): 248–54.

Hermeneutics

Refers to theories of interpretation, especially in the areas of religious, legal, and literary studies. An extremely influential tradition of German hermeneutics includes the interpretive theories of Schleiermacher, Dilthey, Heidegger, and Gadamer.

The word *hermeneutics* derives from the Greek verb *hermêneuein*, "to interpret," and the noun, *hermêneia*, "interpretation," words associated with Hermes, messenger of the gods and purveyor of language. In the Homeric "Hymn to Hermes," the trickster-god, skillful in cunning words, becomes the herald of the immortals, and in Hesiod's *Works and Days* this guide of souls implants in Pandora a human voice filled with cajoling words of falsehood. In the spirit of such stories, Plato's Socrates explains that "this name 'Hermes' seems to me to have to do with speech; he is an interpreter and a messenger, is wily and deceptive in speech, is oratorical. All this activity is concerned with the power of speech" (*Cratylus* 408a). Interpretation here is tied to a diverse group of linguistic practices, but later Aristotle's treatise *On Interpretation* restricts hermeneutics to studying one sort of language use—the making of propositions, sentences that are true or false—and he separates such an inquiry from rhetoric and poetics, which examine other discursive acts and their effects (17a5). It is the more inclusive sense of hermeneutics, however, as theorizing about the interpretation of all language within speech and writing, that remained most influential, and thus hermeneutics has usually remained intimately linked to rhetorical inquiry throughout their intertwined histories.

Rhetorical theory is to rhetorical practice as hermeneutics is to interpretation. As practices, rhetoric and interpretation denote both productive and receptive activities. That is, interpretation refers to the presentation of a text in speech—as in oral performance—and the understanding or exegesis of a written text; similarly, rhetoric refers to the production of persuasive discourse and the analysis of a text's effects on an audience. In some ways, rhetoric and interpretation are practical forms of the same extended human activity: Rhetoric is based on interpretation; interpretation is communicated through rhetoric. Furthermore, as reflections on practice, hermeneutics and rhetorical theory are mutually defining fields. Hermeneutics is the rhetoric of establishing meaning, and rhetoric is the hermeneutics of problematic situations. When we ask about the meaning of a text, we receive an interpretive argument; when we seek the means of persuasion, we interpret the situation. As theoretical practices, hermeneutics involves placing a text in a meaningful context, and rhetoric requires the contextualization of a text's effects.

Friedrich Schleiermacher (1768–1834) is most often regarded as the founder of modern hermeneutics. He aimed to develop an "art" of understanding, a general hermeneutics, with universal principles of interpretation. Schleiermacher focused on the recovery of authorial meaning and emphasized the primacy of language as a medium of understanding. He claimed that "the unity of hermeneutics and rhetoric results from the fact that every act of understanding is the obverse of an act of discourse, in that one must come to grasp the thought which was at the base of the discourse" ("Outline of the 1819 Lectures"). Beginning a powerful German hermeneutic tradition of reflection on the act of understanding itself, Schleiermacher significantly influenced Wilhelm Dilthey (1833–1911) and his attempt to elaborate a foundational hermeneutics for all the human sciences that would make their claims as objectively valid as those of the natural sciences. He based his general hermeneutics on a methodological distinction between explanation (Erklärung) in the natural sciences and understanding (Verstehen) in the human sciences. For Dilthey, the analysis of culture required not the discovery of natural laws but the understanding of human action, the empathetic interpretation of an agent's motives for historical activity.

The most influential German hermeneuticists of the twentieth century, Martin Heidegger (1889–1976) and Hans-Georg Gadamer (b. 1900) gave up the normative, foundationalist goal of a general, scientific hermeneutics. Though Schleiermacher and Dilthey had recognized the historicity of human activity, their theories methodologically suppressed the interpreter's present situation in attempts to understand the past. In contrast, Heidegger and Gadamer argued for an account of interpretation that gave up the subject-object split assumed by past hermeneutic theories and replaced it with an argument that understanding is the fundamental condition of being-in-the-world. That is, this philosophical hermeneutics viewed understanding not simply as the intermittent reading of texts or actions but more

basically as the ongoing state of being human, with both the subject interpreting and the object interpreted emerging together within the hermeneutic situation. An interpreter's assumptions and beliefs are no longer viewed negatively as prejudices distorting understanding but positively as the enabling ground of that process. In *Truth and Method*, Gadamer argues that "if we want to do justice to man's finite, historical mode of being, it is necessary to fundamentally rehabilitate the concept of prejudice and acknowledge the fact that there are legitimate prejudices." Indeed, prejudices, presuppositions, fore-understandings are the very conditions of historical interpretation.

For Gadamer, these preconditions of understanding are not the private possession of individuals but the shared products of history. Interpreters are always making sense within an historical tradition, and "the element of tradition in our historical-hermeneutical activity . . . is fulfilled in the commonality of fundamental, enabling prejudices." In textual interpretation there is a "fusion of horizons" between interpreter and text within a tradition. In this hermeneutical experience, "there is a tension . . . in the play between the traditionary text's strangeness and familiarity to us, between being a historically intended, distanciated object and belonging to a tradition. *The locus of hermeneutics is this in-between.*"

This reminder of Hermes, the mediator, is amplified in Gadamer's characterization of tradition as thoroughly linguistic in nature. For modern hermeneutics since Schleiermacher, language has been viewed as the "medium of hermeneutic experience," and, for Gadamer especially, "the linguisticality of understanding is *the concretion of historically effected consciousness.*" We might say that Gadamer rhetoricizes the notion of historical tradition by emphasizing the hermeneutic experience as a dialogue or conversation within history. In textual interpretation we question the text, and the text's answers question us. In this fusion of horizons, "the interpreter's own horizon is decisive, yet not as a personal standpoint that he maintains or enforces, but more as an opinion and a possibility that one brings into play and puts at risk, and that helps one truly to make one's own what the text says." For Gadamer's philosophical hermeneutics, "all understanding is interpretation, and all interpretation takes place in the medium of a language that allows the object to come into words and yet is at the same time the interpreter's own language."

The interpretive theories of Heidegger and Gadamer argue for an ontologizing of hermeneutics that views understanding as radically historical and universally linguistic, and it is these two aspects that have provided fruitful ground for some of the more important recent theorizing about the relation between rhetoric and interpretation. In "Rhetoric, Hermeneutics, and the Critique of Ideology," Gadamer analyzes the complex relations among the three theoretical practices of his title. He begins by again emphasizing "the essential linguisticality of all human experience of the world," and in the section on "Rhetoric and Hermeneutics" he explains the interwoven character of their historical development and enabling assumptions. "Where," he asks, "but to rhetoric should the theoretical examination of interpretation turn?" Though he notes that, historically, hermeneutics has focused more on writing while rhetoric has been concerned with "the impact of *speaking* in all its immediacy," he argues that precisely because interpretation of written texts involves the making close of a distant, less immediate object, the interpreter's "grasping of meaning of the text takes on something of the character of an independent productive act, one that resembles more the art of the orator than the process of mere listening." Thus, he claims, "It is easy to understand why the theoretical tools of the art of interpretation (hermeneutics) have been to a large extent borrowed from rhetoric." Gadamer concludes this section affirming that "the rhetorical and hermeneutical aspects of human linguisticality completely interpenetrate each other. There would be no speaker and no art of speaking if understanding and consent were not in question, were not underlying elements; there would be no hermeneutical task if there were no mutual understanding that has been disturbed and that those involved in conversation must search for and find again together."

There have been several attempts to develop the details of a rhetorical hermeneutics in various fields, including philosophy, law, religion, speech communication, composition studies, and critical theory. In speech communication, Michael J. Hyde and Craig R. Smith use Heidegger and Gadamer to explicate the ontological relationship between hermeneutics and rhetoric, claiming that the "primordial function of rhetoric is to 'make-known' meaning both to oneself and to others. Meaning is derived by a human being in and through the interpretive understanding of reality. Rhetoric is the process of making-known that meaning." Within composition studies, Timothy Crusius advocates a "hermeneutical rhetoric" based on Gadamer's philosophy and presented as a pedagogical project that "(a) aims to deepen the process approach to writing instruction (b) by retrieving dialectic as dialogue, as hermeneutic inquiry, (c) within a rhetoric of public discourse emphasis (d) that concentrates on argumentation or the search for 'good reasons.'"

From the perspective of critical theory and legal studies, Stanley Fish has criticized any hermeneutics that tends toward foundationalist theory, that is, "any attempt to ground inquiry and communication in something more firm and stable than mere belief or unexamined practice." For example, Fish attacks E.D. Hirsch for his privileging of "general hermeneutics" over "local hermeneutics." According to Fish, Hirsch means by the former "a procedure whose steps, if they are faithfully and strictly followed," will result in a correct interpretation; while "local hermeneutics" provide only "calculations of probability based on an insider's knowledge of what is likely to be successful in a particular field of practice." A general hermeneutics gives formalizable rules and principles; a local hermeneutics furnishes only rules of thumb, which are unformalizable "because the conditions of [their] application vary with the contextual circumstances of an ongoing practice." For Fish, a general hermeneutics is impossible and thus inconsequential; all we have are variously effective local hermeneutics. We might say that every proposed general hermeneutics is simply a disguised local hermeneutics with foundationalist pretentions. Fish associates antifoundationalist critiques in hermeneutics with the tradition of sophistic rhetoric. "Indeed, another word for antifoundationalism is rhetoric, and one could say without too much exaggeration that modern anti-foundationalism is old sophism writ analytic. The rehabilitation by antifoundationalism of the claims of situation, history, politics, and convention in opposition to the more commonly successful claims of logic, brute fact empiricism, the natural, and the necessary marks one more chapter in the long history of the quarrel between philosophy and rhetoric, between the eternal and the temporal, between God's view and point of view."

A rhetorical hermeneutics is also developing within the field of cultural studies. Following Fish and Richard Rorty, a rhetorical hermeneutics has a negative, therapeutic moment of critiquing foundationalist theories of interpretation. But then, taking a cue from Ludwig Wittgenstein, instead of constructing a hermeneutic ontology in its positive moment, rhetorical hermeneutics examines interpretation as historical events within situated language games. That is, a rhetorical hermeneutics turns theories of interpretation in general into rhetorical histories of specific acts of interpretation. Such a project is a form of cultural rhetoric studies that focuses on specific linguistic acts of interpreting texts, placing those interpretive events in the context of power/knowledge relations of particular historical communities, within the material conditions of diverse institutions and various media, participating in a multivoiced cultural conversation, through which circulate the available tropes, arguments, and narratives of a geographical location and a historical period. This hermeneutics uses rhetorical study to practice interpretive theory by doing reception history.

Steven Mailloux
University of California, Irvine

Bibliography

Bernstein, Richard J. *Beyond Objectivism and Relativism: Science, Hermeneutics, and Praxis.* Philadelphia: U of Pennsylvania P, 1983.

Crusius, Timothy W. *A Teacher's Introduction to Philosophical Hermeneutics.* Urbana, IL: National Council of Teachers of English, 1991.

Fish, Stanley. *Doing What Comes Naturally: Change, Rhetoric, and the Practice of Theory in Literary and Legal Studies.* Durham, NC: Duke UP, 1989.

Gadamer, Hans-Georg. *Philosophical Hermeneutics.* Trans. and ed. David E. Linge. Berkeley: U of California P, 1976.

———. *Truth and Method.* 2nd rev. ed. Trans. Joel Weinsheimer and Donald G. Marshall. New York: Crossroad, 1991.

Hirsch, E.D., Jr. *Validity in Interpretation.* New Haven: Yale UP, 1967.

Hyde, Michael J., and Craig R. Smith. "Hermeneutics and Rhetoric: A Seen but Unobserved Relationship." *Quarterly Journal of Speech* 65 (1979): 347–63.

Mailloux, Steven. "Rhetorical Hermeneutics Revisited." *Text and Performance Quarterly* 2 (1991): 233–48.

Ormiston, Gayle L., and Alan D. Schrift, eds. *The Hermeneutic Tradition: From Ast to Ricoeur.* Albany: State U of New York P, 1990.

Palmer, Richard E. *Hermeneutics: Interpretation Theory in Schleiermacher, Dilthey, Heidegger, and Gadamer.* Evanston, IL: Northwestern UP, 1969.

Ricoeur, Paul. *Interpretation Theory: Discourse and the Surplus of Meaning.* Fort Worth, TX: Texas Christian UP, 1976.

———. *The Rule of Metaphor: Multi-disciplinary Studies of the Creation of Meaning in Language.* Trans. Robert Czerny with Kathleen McLaughlin and John Costello, S.J. Toronto: U of Toronto P, 1977.

See also GADAMER, HANS-GEORG

Heuristics

Strategic thinking for rhetorical inquiry. Heuristics can be viewed as a modern version of the historical concept of *technê* or art. In rhetoric they codify effective tactics used by good rhetors (writers and speakers). Heuristics turn knowledge about discourse (for example, about audience) into procedural plans (such as ways of analyzing and constructing audiences and intertextuality), offering rhetors more help than trial and error efforts, which waste time and effort. Heuristics also work more appropriately in the rhetorical process than rule-governed plans, which exclude intuition and fail to account for complexity. Heuristic thinking in any creative activity is a more flexible way of proceeding than formal reasoning or formulaic steps and a more efficient way than trial and error. Working in tandem with intuition, heuristic thinking prompts conscious activity, which guides a rhetor but never determines the outcome. While learners typically use heuristics deliberately while trying to master them, more experienced users work tacitly, shaping strategies to their own styles. Polya in an early work on heuristics, *How to Solve It*, claims that without a good supply of heuristic method no artist could create, no scientist could discover, no technician could invent. Perkins describes heuristics as tactics that redirect the pattern of thinking itself.

In the 1960s rhetoric and composition theorists, instructors, and textbook authors began to offer students heuristic strategies to guide such inventional acts as question-posing, exploring for insights and supportive material, and constructing arguments. Some widely used inventional procedures include free-writing, the tagmemic perspectives, Burke's pentad and the ratios, and sets of classical topics. Heuristics have also been developed to guide other writing acts, such as audience analysis and revising. Varying in generality, some writing heuristics can be used in a large number of situations and are typically taught in generic writing courses at any level of education. Others are discipline specific and are often learned in writing-across-the-curriculum courses. In either case, heuristic procedures need to be adapted to each writing situation.

Teaching heuristics or rhetorical *technê* has had a long history, starting with the arts of invention, arrangement, and style in Greece. Throughout this history to the present, instruction in heuristic strategies has been controversial. Some have argued that encouraging natural talent, using imitation, and emphasizing practice are preferable pedagogies, while others have maintained that in addition to these three ways of teaching, instruction in heuristics or the arts is important in the development of a rhetor. Some have feared that heuristics will turn into rules or formulas, thereby overdetermining or mechanizing the rhetorical process. This danger was realized at times in rhetorical history when the arts of discourse were taught as inflexible steps for carrying out rhetorical acts rather than as arbitrary but effective guides. Another controversy has stemmed from false expectations about the efficacy of teaching heuristics as a panacea for all rhetorical problems. But they do not supply motivation or subject knowledge but rather depend upon them. Nor do they remedy grammatical problems or provide genre knowledge or syntactic fluency. Advocates of heuristics see them as part of a larger repertoire of rhetorical resources and argue that teaching heuristics shares with students insider knowledge of discourse strategies that can empower them in genuine, compelling, and challenging rhetorical situations.

Janice M. Lauer
Purdue University

Bibliography

Berthoff, Ann. "The Problem of Problem Solving." *College Composition and Communication* 22 (1972): 237–42.

———. "Response to Janice Lauer." *College Composition and Communication* 23 (1972): 414–15.

Lauer, Janice. "Heuristics and Composition." *College Composition and Communication* 21 (1970): 396–404.

———. "Response to Ann E. Berthoff." *College Composition and Communication* 23 (1972): 208–10.

Nickerson, Raymond, David Perkins, and Edward Smith. *The Teaching of Thinking.* Hillsdale, NJ: Erlbaum, 1985.

Perkins, David. *The Mind's Best Work.* Cambridge, MA: Harvard UP, 1981.

Young, Richard E. "Recent Developments in Rhetorical Invention." *Teaching Composition: Twelve Bibliographical Essays.* Ed. Gary Tate. Fort Worth: Texas Christian UP, 1987. 20–34.

Young, Richard E., Alton P. Becker, and Kenneth Pike. "Preparation; Exploring the Problem." *Rhetoric: Discovery and Change.* New York: Harcourt, 1970. 119–36.

See also EPISTEMIC RHETORIC; INVENTION; PENTAD; TAGMEMICS; *TECHNÊ*; TOPICS

Hill, Adams Sherman (1833–1910)

Earned two degrees at Harvard—the B.A. in 1853 and the LL.B. in 1855—then pursued a career as a law reporter before returning to Harvard in 1872 as assistant professor of rhetoric. In 1876 he became the Boylston Professor of Rhetoric and held the chair until 1904. His books on rhetoric include *The Principles of Rhetoric* (1878 and 1895), *Foundations of Rhetoric* (1892), and *Beginning of Rhetoric and Composition* (1903).

Hill insists in *Principles of Rhetoric* that rhetoric is not a science, a means to investigate effectiveness, but an art—a means to achieve effectiveness. Like most other nineteenth-century compositionists, Hill rejects invention, arguing that the content of discourse comes from the subject matter and not from rhetoric itself. Rhetoric conveys the results of thought, but it is not itself a form of thought. It operates through the modes of discourse: narration, description, and argumentation.

Hill attempts to focus rhetoric on its proper subject, excluding all that is peripheral. To this end Hill limits rhetoric to style alone, to the clear and forceful communication of ideas. His textbook thus covers two topics only: grammar and style.

Hill follows George Campbell in defining proper usage as that which is reputable, national, and present. In so doing Hill rejects grammatical and stylistic prescriptions that rely on logic or etymology or "classical" standards of propriety and taste. He does, to be sure, present a conventional prescriptive grammar and usage handbook, but he bases his rules on what he takes to be well-accepted current usage, citing contemporary writers like Disraeli, Macaulay, George Eliot, and Emerson— though he often, paradoxically, cites their "errors" to illustrate rules of usage.

Hill does, however, reject many fallacious arguments about the history and nature of language. He understands the principles of linguistic change—for example, the tendency for slang terms to become part of the reputable vocabulary—and he addresses a practical problem that teachers of rhetoric have by no means solved today—namely, the conflict of descriptive linguistics and the need to teach usage.

The "current-traditional" model of composition teaching that was created in the last years of the nineteenth century combines Alexander Bain's modes of discourse and paragraph unity with Hill's prescriptivism in grammar, usage, and style. This stripped-down rhetoric was a necessity because of the large number of students and the constant turnover of new instructors who needed clear guidelines on how to teach a subject that they generally hoped to leave behind as soon as possible.

Hill says that rhetoric is the use of knowledge not as knowledge but as power. It may seem odd, then, that he treats argument so mechanically, as a patchwork of syllogism, signs, and testimony, and that persuasion gets a perfunctory few pages near the end of the book. But exposition, not argument, is the ideal form in Hill's rhetoric. Composition, under Hill's influence, focuses on correct exposition, and power means the power to earn a living. *The Principles of Rhetoric* spread the gospel of style and usage through the greatly expanded university system that arose after the Civil War.

Bruce Herzberg
Bentley College

Bibliography
Crowley, Sharon. *The Methodical Memory: Invention in Current-Traditional Rhetoric.* Carbondale: Southern Illinois UP, 1990.
Johnson, Nan. *Nineteenth-Century Rhetoric in North America.* Carbondale: Southern Illinois UP, 1991.
Kitzhaber, Albert. *Rhetoric in American Colleges.* Dallas, TX: Southern Methodist UP, 1990.
Reid, Paul. "The First and Fifth Boylston Professors: A View of Two Worlds." *Quarterly Journal of Speech* 74 (1988): 229–40.

Hill, David J. (1850–1932)

Excelled in belles-lettres, oratory, and philosophy, and graduated first in the class of 1874 from Bucknell University. In his senior year at Bucknell, Hill was hired as instructor of ancient languages. In 1877 he became professor of rhetoric, and by 1879 he was president of the college, at age 29 the youngest person ever to hold such a position. He served as president of the University of Rochester from 1888 to 1896, after which he held many diplomatic posts in Europe. He wrote books on rhetoric, socialism, Christianity, psychology, finance, and diplomacy.

Hill is among the first American rhetoricians to focus on writing, not speaking, in response to the development of independent college composition courses. In *The Science of Rhetoric* (1877), he attempts to synthesize the connections between language and psychology that had been developed by George Campbell and Richard Whately and by the compositionists Henry Day and Alexander Bain. Hill begins by excluding several key elements from rhetoric: invention, arrangement, taste, delivery, linguistics, and literature. These elements are all properly treated, he argues, by other disciplines. What is left, he says, is a science of the mental laws that govern the effects of discourse. This is the true province of rhetoric: taking conceptions developed elsewhere and establishing them in the reader's mind.

Thought precedes language, according to Hill, but language conveys thought. There are other ways to convey thought—by drawing and sculpture, for example—but language has special power to convey action and complex ideas. Language addresses reason, imagination, and will (which Hill sorts under "memory"). The means by which the mind is addressed and affected draws on psychology, ethics, and aesthetics, but it is its own special science. Hill follows Bacon's definition of rhetoric, as the application of reason to the imagination to move the will. He uses the modes of discourse in their Baconian form, too—narration, exposition, and argumentation. He borrows Bain's psychology of tropes, dividing them into resemblances, contiguities, and contrasts. His goal is to offer a means of investigating the effects of discourse, and his book is divided into three parts treating the laws of mind, of idea, and of form, which determine rhetorical effects. It is perhaps in this sense that we should understand his desire to see rhetoric as a science. Following publication of his theoretical *Science of Rhetoric*, Hill also published a textbook, *The Elements of Rhetoric and Composition* (1878).

Bruce Herzberg
Bentley College

Bibliography

Ettlich, E.E. "Theories of Invention in Late Nineteenth-Century American Rhetorics." *Western Speech* 30 (1966): 233–41.

Johnson, Nan. *Nineteenth-Century Rhetoric in North America.* Carbondale: Southern Illinois UP, 1991.

Stewart, Donald C. "The Nineteenth Century." *The Present State of Scholarship in Historical and Contemporary Rhetoric.* Ed. Winifred Bryan Horner. Rev. ed. Columbia: U of Missouri P, 1990.

Hirsch, Eric Donald, Jr. (b. 1928)

Educational reformer, literary scholar. E.D. Hirsch, Jr., was born in Memphis in 1928. He completed his B.A. at Cornell in 1950 and his M.A. (1955) and Ph.D. (1957) at Yale. At present he is Kenan Professor of English at the University of Virginia, where he served as department chair from 1968 to 1971 and 1981 to 1983. From 1971 to the present, he has been director of composition. His first books were in Romanticism: *Wordsworth and Schelling, a Typological Study of Romanticism* (1960) and *Innocence and Experience, an Introduction to Blake* (1964). He then turned to hermeneutic theory, publishing the highly influential *Validity in Interpretation* (1967) and *The Aims of Interpretation* (1976).

With *The Philosophy of Composition* (1977), he entered the field of rhetoric directly, since composition is a subdiscipline of rhetoric, just as cardiology is a subdiscipline of medicine. In *The Philosophy of Composition*, Hirsch argued, paradoxically, that composition is not a branch of rhetoric, but is a discipline in its own right, the goal of which is to teach students to write maximally accessible prose. A key term in *The Philosophy of Composition* is "relative readability"—in other words, the text will express the author's intention in the most easily accessible form. Thus, one could not criticize Faulkner's syntax or Joyce's punning, for these features are part of the authors' semantic intentions. In fact, certain syntactic configurations are more easily read than others containing the same propositional content. (For example, when read out of context, active voice sentences are more accessible than their passive counterparts: Mary gave George instructions / Instructions were given by Mary to George.) And as psychologist Walter Kintsch (who greatly influenced Hirsch) demonstrated, paragraphs with limited numbers of semantic tags are more easily read than those with many. (In other words, a paragraph that deals with "tea"—and the family of terms belonging to it: gunpowder, oolong, jasmine, Earl Grey—will be easier to read than a paragraph that deals with tea and coffee and sealing wax and knighthood. The argument of *The Philosophy of Composition* finally boils down to something like this: The goal of composition instruction is to teach students to write accessible sentences and unified paragraphs.

In subsequent work Hirsch discovered that for readers unfamiliar with the content of texts, syntax and the structure of paragraphs made little difference in readability. From this insight came the work for which he is best known: *Cultural Literacy: What Every American Needs to Know* (1987).

Underlying this massively influential book is the principle that readers and writers must share cultural knowledge if they are to communicate, and the belief that more and more children are failing to gain the knowledge that they need in order to enter the literate dialogue. Hirsch cites compelling evidence to support his claim that "cultural literacy" is on the decline among the nation's children in school.

The knowledge that people need to be literate, says Hirsch, is very general, not specific or precise. For example, one does not need to know in great detail about the function of the Supreme Court in order to understand a newspaper article about a Supreme Court decision. Not only is cultural knowledge limited in extent, it is also national, and it is "not the property of any group or class" (*Cultural* 11). The cultural literacy that a Calcuttan speaker of English needs is different from that needed by an American junior high school student. Furthermore,

> Books and newspapers assume a "common reader," that is, a person who knows the things known by other literate persons in the culture. Obviously, such assumptions are never identical from writer to writer, but they show a remarkable consistency. Those who write for a mass public are always making judgments about what the readers can be assumed to know, and the judgments are closely similar. Any reader who doesn't possess the knowledge assumed in a piece he or she reads will in fact be illiterate with respect to that particular piece of writing. (*Cultural* 13)

Hirsch states flatly: "[W]e have accumulated a great deal of evidence that faulty policy in the schools is the chief cause of deficient literacy" (*Cultural* 20). "Although our schools do comparatively well in teaching elementary decoding skills, they do less well than schools of some other countries in teaching the background knowledge that pupils must possess to succeed at mature reading tasks" (*Cultural* 27).

His solution is to provide students in the early grades with the sort of background information that they need in order to read with comprehension. To this end, he and his colleagues Joseph F. Kett and James Trefil have compiled *The Dictionary of Cultural Literacy* (1988), and the Core Knowledge Foundation, of which Hirsch is founder and president, has prepared cultural literacy materials for the public schools.

From *The Dictionary of Cultural Literacy*, here are examples of the sort of knowledge

that Hirsch feels students must acquire during the early years of their schooling:

> *Alexander the Great* A ruler of *Greece* in the fourth century B.C. As a general, he conquered most of the ancient world, extending the civilization of Greece east to *India*. Alexander is said to have wept because there were no worlds left to conquer. In Alexander's youth, the philosopher *Aristotle* was his tutor. (190)

> *cut the Gordian knot* (GAWR-dee-uhn) To solve a notoriously difficult problem in a quick and decisive manner: "The president hopes that his bold new anti-*inflation* plan would cut the Gordian knot." According to Greek legend, an oracle declared that the man who could untie the *Gordian knot* would become the ruler of all *Asia*. *Alexander the Great* impatiently cut it with a single stroke of his sword and proceeded to conquer Asia. (63)

> *inflation* A general increase in prices. (424)

Hirsch's proposals have aroused great controversy, critics charging that he is an elitist. On the other hand, Hirsch's defenders argue that a national cultural literacy will bring together an increasingly fragmented population in the United States.

W. Ross Winterowd
University of Southern California

Bibliography

Hirsch, E.D., Jr. *Cultural Literacy: What Every American Needs to Know*. Boston: Houghton, 1987.
———. "Culture and Literacy." *Journal of Basic Writing* 3 (1980): 27–47.
Kohl, Herbert, and E.D. Hirsch, Jr. "'The Primal Scene of Education': An Exchange." *New York Review*. April 13, 1989: 50–51.
Sledd, Andrew, and James H. Sledd. "Success as Failure and Failure as Success." *Written Communication* 6 (1989): 364–89.
Steiner, George. "Little-Read Schoolhouse." *Rev. of Cultural Literacy. New Yorker*. June 1, 1987: 106–10.

Historiographies of Rhetoric

An accounting for different perspectives on writing history. Historiography, in general, is the study of the different biases of, or attitudes toward, writing history. It is a highly debated and contentious topic. The central question is one of whose interests, in a given history, are being served and whose are being deflected or forgotten. As Kenneth Burke and Paul de Man have said, a way of seeing is a way of not seeing. Though perhaps most historians would give some degree of assent to this bias in language, or in writing-envisioning histories, they would seldom agree that they themselves engage in such biased practices. As Marx would say, they do this without being aware of it. Historiography, therefore, can be conceived of along the lines of whether or not particular historians reflect, and to what degree, on their particular discourse practices, which enable them in the first place to write *the* or *a* or yet *another* history.

So as to inform themselves, historiographers have variously worked out sets of biases over the centuries, especially in contrastive ways during the eighteenth and nineteenth centuries. A contemporary version of signifying practices admits old terms while incorporating new ones. This version is threefold, with the purpose of avoiding structuralist binaries: It includes *current-traditional, revisionary,* and *sub/versive* historiographies.

Current-traditional historiography, which is the most predominant, demonstrates little, if any, awareness of the biases that inform writing histories. Traditionalists write as if archival "facts" speak for themselves in a grand cause/effect narrative. They are guided by positivistic principles of inference or hypothesis-formation, testing, and explanation; by incipient philosophical principles favoring various realisms or Aristotelianisms; or by classical philological, rule-governed principles of textual analysis. Their central virtues are clarity, coherence, and cogency. These historians are seldom, if ever, suspicious of language itself, whereas revisionary historiography is founded on a hermeneutic of suspicion.

Revisionary historians are of two kinds: Either they revise history to achieve disclosure of previously omitted "facts" or alternative interpretations of these "facts," or they revise as a self-conscious critical practice. The first kind attempts to reclaim—given the political interests of the historian—what has been excluded, and usually along the lines of race, class, and sex. Recently, there have been attempts to reclaim the sophists and female rhetors. The purpose, therefore, is primarily to revise the canon by adding what had been excluded and, therefore, forgotten.

The second kind, extending the first, attempts more strenuously to practice a rhetoric of suspicion as established by Freud and Marx. These historians are suspicious of so-called patent meaning in archival "facts" and consequently look for latent meaning. These historians, therefore, attempt to critique traditional, historical discourse to discover how it is coded to prevent members of a field of study from seeing how they are thinking and acting against their own best ethical-political interests. The purpose of a rhetoric of suspicion, then, is not just to revise the canon by adding and correcting, but more so to revise the way that historians, faculty, and students interpret the canon; the purpose, moreover, is ultimately to establish ways to recode the history of rhetoric in terms of a provisional, or strategic, grand narrative of emancipation.

Sub/versive historiography hyperbolically extends the rhetoric of suspicion. While sub/versive historians might favor Freud and Marx, they more so favor Nietzsche and his posthermeneutic of perpetual suspicious, demystification, and decodification. (In other words, they do not believe that the errors of the past or present can simply be recoded, that is, fixed, but must be perpetually decoded, that is, perpetually revised or placed in dispersal.) While revisionists believe in progress or emancipation, sub/versive historians believe in a Nietzschean "cheerful pessimism." While revisionists favor the political over the aesthetic, sub/versives favor the aesthetic over the political. While revisionists assert that history is a function of human beings, sub/versives play at demonstrating how human beings are more so a function of history. While traditionalists favor classical understandings of the *topoi* (commonplaces) and revisionists favor *eutopianisms* (a great, good political place), sub/versives favor *atopianisms* (nomadic drifting). While revisionists engage in negative deconstructions of such binaries as male/female, sub/versives would disengage in affirmative deconstruction by searching for third-subject positions. In other words, sub/versives play and act up so as to show how the sexes, "male/female," are political categories; consequently, sub/versives reach for new understandings of ethos by acting out the proposition that there are as many sexes as individual bodies. While other historians favor strategies with tactics and have clearly stated goals, sub/versives favor tactics without strategies and favor nomadic thinking. Whatever other historians will do for serious purposes, a sub/versive will perform for a (curative) laugh.

Victor J. Vitanza
University of Texas, Arlington

Bibliography

Berlin, James, Susan Jarratt, John Schilb, and Victor J. Vitanza. "Historiography and the Histories of Rhetorics I: Revisionary Histories." *PRE/TEXT* 8 (1987): 9–152; "Historiography and the Histories of Rhetorics II: Revisionary Histories and Ethics." *PRE/TEXT* 11 (1990): 169–287.

Burke, Kenneth. *Attitudes toward History*. 3rd ed. Berkeley: U of California P, 1984.

Connors, Robert. "Writing the History of Our Discipline." *An Introduction to Composition Studies*. Ed. Erika Lindemann and Gary Tate. New York: Oxford UP, 1991. 49–71.

Enos, Theresa, ed. *Learning from the Histories of Rhetoric*. Carbondale: Southern Illinois UP, 1993.

Octolog. "The Politics of Historiography." *Rhetoric Review* 7 (1988): 5–49.

Poulakos, Takis, ed. *Rethinking the Rhetorical Tradition: Historiographies of Rhetoric and Histories of the Classical Rhetorical Tradition*. Denver, CO: Westview, 1993.

Vitanza, Victor J., ed. *Writing Histories of Rhetoric*. Carbondale: Southern Illinois UP, 1994.

Hobbes, Thomas (1588–1679)

Materialist philosopher with deterministic and utilitarian sympathies; universally recognized as one of the first systematic social scientists and often seen as the father of modern analytic philosophy. Born at Westport in Malmesbury, England, and educated at Oxford, Hobbes immigrated to Paris during the English bourgeois revolution. A one-time tutor to Charles II of France and later secretary to Francis Bacon, he also interacted with contemporary luminaries such as Ben Jonson and Galileo Galilei. Hobbes had one of the longest literary careers in recorded history, publishing his first book at age fourteen and his last at the age of ninety-one.

Hobbes believed the traditional approach to philosophy was cluttered with useless abstraction; he systemized Bacon's efforts into the doctrine of mechanized materialism. Hobbes's metaphor for society was that of a machine manipulated by the authority of the mechanic-ruler/king, held together by the prerogative of the king and the loyalty of his subjects. His mechanist tendencies led him to divide philosophy into four "sub-sciences": geometry, physics, ethics, and politics. He believed that all knowledge was empirical; in his doctrine on knowledge, Hobbes attacked the Cartesian theory of innate ideas while admitting that valid general knowledge, conditioned by language, is possible.

Hobbes's primary philosophical concern was the study of bodies and their movements. He believed that in their original state, all men are equal ("nasty and brutish"), and his First Law of Motion states that every organic body has an innate tendency to movement, which leads to his First Natural Right—the right to self-preservation and self-assertion. Hobbes defined the primary condition of life as "collision and conflict," leading to his Second Law of Motion: a voluntary relinquishment by recoiling bodies (humans) of the right to self-assertion for a similar relinquishment on the part of fellow bodies.

Hobbes's political and ethical writings reflected his philosophical basis in determinism and utilitarianism; he made important contributions to the "free will" controversy by asserting that "free" can properly describe only a man's actions, not his will. Hobbes also contributed to the study of linguistics by supplementing the demand for a concreteness of speech with a theory regarding how absurdities are generated by illogical application of different classes of terms.

Hobbes's two most notable works were his *Little Treatise*, published in sections from 1630 to 1637, which was an attack on the Aristotelian theory of sense and which sketched out Hobbes's own new mechanical theory; and *Leviathan: The Matter, Form and Power of a Commonwealth*, published in 1651, which was his most emphatic proclamation that only monarchy, not aristocracy or democracy, could effectively secure peace. A book based in secularism, *Leviathan* estranged Hobbes from French authorities and led to his return to England.

Other publications include *De Cive (Concerning Government)* in 1642, *Politics* in 1650, *De Corpore (On Bodies)* in 1655, *De Homine (On Man)* in 1658, and *Behemoth (Common Laws)* posthumously in 1682. He also did seminal translations of Aristotle, Thucydides, and Homer, and at eighty-six wrote his own autobiography in Latin verse.

Michael E. Doherty, Jr.
Bowling Green State University

Bibliography

Hinnant, Charles H. *Thomas Hobbes: A Reference Guide*. Boston: Hall, 1980.

Reik, Miriam M. *The Golden Lands of Thomas Hobbes*. Detroit, MI: Wayne State UP, 1977.

Sacksteder, William. *Hobbes Studies (1879–1979): A Bibliography*. Bowling Green, OH: Philosophy Documentation Center, Bowling Green State U, 1982.

Sorrell, Tom. *Hobbes*. London: Routledge and Kegan Paul, 1986.

Homiletics

Derived from the Greek *homilia,* "social intercourse." In a Christian context, the word meant a familiar discourse with a group during the Mass, usually about a text suggested by the liturgy of the day or season. The original homily was partly a continuation of the commentary on the Scriptures that was made in the synagogue, but Christian homily from the beginning seemed to add to the explanatory tone of the Hebrew exegesis a persuasive application of the text to the actual life of the Christians.

This persuasive dimension became more crystallized both theoretically and practically in the preaching practices of the ensuing centuries. The distinction between the two tendencies was first crystallized by Origen, who distinguished between the popular exegesis of the homily (Greek *homilia,* Latin *tractatus*) and the more classical oration of the sermon (Greek *logos,* Latin *sermo*). The juxtapositions, oppositions, and combinations of the two genres contribute a major dimension to the history of homiletics.

The Greek and Latin derivations of the terms, however, should not be read as implying that homiletics is a European phenomenon. Indeed, nearly all of the major world religions have involved persons trained to preach. The imam of Islam, the Jewish rabbi, the Confucian sage, the Catholic priest, the Zen master, the Hindu guru, the witch doctor, the Puritan divine—all are preachers in their particular religions. And within each group, there are many subgroups. This is as true of Islam as it is of Christianity and many other religions. The technical training of the groups varies greatly, and the theoretical study of the techniques of preaching also differs widely from religion to religion. Christianity, however, has made many more written attempts to analyze and prescribe methods of preaching than any other religion.

In Christianity the homily dominated until the time of Constantine and the end of the persecutions of the Christians. After that, bishops and priests came heavily from those who had studied in the best rhetorical schools of Athens, Antioch, and Alexandria, Milan, and Rome in the East and the West. Trained in the classical tradition, these preachers adapted into Christianity many of the traditional genres of classical rhetoric, such as the panegyric, the funeral oration, and the thematic oration, particularly as it applied to the liturgical readings of the day.

This was as true of the techniques of invention (as with St. Gregory of Nazianzin) as of the techniques of style (as with St. Basil the Great). Both of those were Greek, but in Latin, St. Ambrose in Milan and St. Augustine in North Africa also applied classical rhetoric to homiletics. St. Augustine, in Book 4 of his *De doctrina christiana,* demonstrated the compatibility of classical rhetorical techniques with Christian preaching, a question that had been hotly debated for three centuries. St. Augustine's preaching ranged from very colloquial homilies to very rhetorical sermons. In the sixth century, the preaching function, that had been largely limited to bishops, was extended to priests. And in the eighth century, the Church emphasized preaching in the vernacular in different countries.

In the Middle Ages, the study of preaching was strongly influenced by Scholasticism in the universities, and by the establishment of two major preaching orders, the Dominicans and the Franciscans, dedicated to itinerate preaching to the populace. Many influential preaching manuals, *Artes Praedicandi,* appeared, often drawing on rhetorical principles. Some populist preaching movements by the Waldenses and the Humiliati, however, were discouraged and eventually prohibited by the Church.

Such populist tendencies were strongly encouraged by the Protestant churches of the Reformation. Lutherans, Calvinists, Presbyterians, and most Protestant theologians had strong and populist views on preaching.

The historical scene from the Reformation on has been covered thoroughly by Harry Caplan and Henry H. King in a series of monographs between 1949 and 1956, with bibliographies on preaching for Italian, Spanish, Scandinavian, Dutch, English, German, and French. All but the last appeared in *Speech Monographs;* the French coverage was in the *Quarterly Journal of Speech.* An update on this material for ten countries was made by Karl Rahner, S.J., in *The Renewal of Preaching: Theory and Practice* (1968); most of his book has to do with Catholic situations.

Probably the most thorough coverage of the history of preaching is the thirteen-volume *Twenty Centuries of Great Preaching,* compiled by Clyde E. Fant and William M. Pinson (1971). A fine one-volume coverage is that of Yngve Brilioth, *A Brief History of Preaching* (1965), which covers up to the middle of this century.

Rhetoric continues to be emphasized in both Protestant and Catholic venues. For example, by far the most influential book in America has been that of John A. Broadus, *The Preparation and Delivery of Sermons,* a book that went through twenty-nine editions between 1870 and 1944. Although the book was intended for Baptist ministers, the audience has already been much larger, possibly because of the deep roots in classical rhetoric. Broadus says, "The author's chief indebtedness for help has been to Aristotle, Cicero, and Quintilian, and to Whately and Vinet." The last two (together with Ripley) had been his textbooks (xiii). These rhetorical, rather than doctrinal, sources are evident in the organization of the text—a quite basic arrangement of argument, style, and delivery—and in the virtues of style—clarity, energy, elegance.

A simple parallel to this in Catholicism is in the *New Catholic Encyclopedia* entry for "Homiletics" (1967). After a brief historical introduction, the article breaks up its material into "Invention," "Arrangement," "Style," and "Memory and Delivery."

Other influences, of course, parallel this tradition. For example, a manifesto for pulpit practice in America for over fifty years has been Harry Emerson Fosdick's famous statement on preaching, "What is the Matter with Preaching?" in 1928. It called for moving away from strict exegesis toward the exploratory and topical treatment of current issues. This has continued to influence such figures as Billy Graham and television evangelists like Jerry Falwell. In this general area is Bruce Rosenberg's *The Art of the American Folk Preacher* (1970).

Possibly the most important theological treatment of preaching in this century remains that of Karl Barth in the first volume of *Church Dogmatics: The Doctrine of the Word of God* (1936–1956). Rudolf Bultman, arguably the single most dominant theologian of the last fifty years, by emphasizing the message of the Gospel, the proclamation function of the minister, and the necessity of presenting the biblical message in modern terms (demythologized from the biblical presentations) heavily influenced Christian preaching theory and practice in both Protestant and Catholic circles.

A countermovement to the Fosdick trend away from exegesis in favor of current issues can be seen in the recent Catholic reassertion of the importance of Scriptural explanations—a return to the early Christian practice. As was pointed out above, both of these movements represent positionings between the relative importance of the homily or the sermon, a recurring concern throughout the history of Christian preaching.

James L. Kinneavy
University of Texas at Austin

Bibliography
Barth, Karl. *Church Dogmatics: The Doctrine of the Word of God.* Rpt. Vol l. Edinburgh: Clark, 1975.
Brilioth, Yngve. *A Brief History of Preaching.* Trans. Karl E. Mattson. Philadelphia: Fortress, 1965.
Broadus, John A. *The Preparation and the Delivery of Sermons.* Rev. ed. Ed. Jesse Burton Weatherspan. New York: Harper, 1944.
Fant, Clyde E., and William M. Pinson. *Twenty Centuries of Great Preaching.* Waco, TX: World, 1971.
Rahner, Karl, S.J., ed. *The Renewal of Preaching: Theory and Practice.* Vol. 33. Concilium, Theology in the Age of Renewal. New York: Paulist, 1968.
Rosenberg, Bruce A. *The Art of the American Folk Preacher.* New York: Oxford, 1970.

See also ARS PRAEDICANDI; HOMILY; PULPIT ORATORY; RELIGIOUS RHETORIC; SERMON

Homily

Derived from Greek ὁμιλία (*homilia*), discourse, converse, intercourse and its attendant verb ὁμιλέμ (*homileo*). Although the word *homily* is now used almost interchangeably with *sermon* in many religious contexts, it has its own history and distinctive meanings. Xenophon (428–354 B.C.E.) in Book 1 of *Memorabilia* uses the word to describe the familiar instruction a philosopher gave to his students. The verb ὁμιλέμ used in the New Testament carries a similar meaning; in Acts 20:11, for example, it denotes Paul's familiar conversation with believers about Christ and his doctrines. It implied an informal, didactic discussion, "question and answer" about the truths shared by believers. It included discussion of the life and sayings of Jesus and of Hebrew sacred literature: exegesis of text.

Long before the advent of Christianity, the Hebrews had developed the practice of carrying on textual exegesis in religious meetings. Passages of sacred text would be read by recognized leaders of the community and expounded on for the instruction and edification of the people. Over the centuries, this practice evolved into complex sermonic forms. A legacy of rabbinical writings was added to the corpus that could be drawn upon for exegesis, and a hallmark of Judaic homilies became, in addition to moral/ethical application, skill in textual interpretation and aesthetics. As in the Christian traditions, the modern meaning of *homilies* and *homiletic literature* in Jewish traditions is now basically synonymous with *sermons*.

In the Christian tradition, the word *homily* for a long time retained its meaning of informal, conversational discourse about spiritual things based on the Hebrew scriptures, the life of Jesus, and the writings of the Christian apostles and evangelists. A distinction was made between the ὁμιλία and more formal, classically structured spiritual/ethical discourse (such as sermons—classified as λόγος—and φιλοσοφία or φιλοσόφημα philosophical discussion). The ὁμιλία, designed to instruct and edify, was intended for the community of already converted believers, whereas sermons and speeches of other kinds were designed to convince the mind (as well as to move the passions and will, depending upon the sort of oration involved). A proselytizing sermon, for example, was qualitatively different from a homily.

These distinctions were still alive up through the medieval period, but they had been fading in varying degrees and in various contexts. The familiar conversations that expounded a text with the faithful became more elaborate and had more distinctions to make, more interpretations to put forward and to correct. The meaning of *homily* also changed because the powerful discourses produced by the Church Fathers and other great preachers through the ages could not be reproduced by every minister in every remote corner of the expanding church—East or West. Both power of words and regularity of doctrine became issues. For this reason the discourses of the prominent preachers came to be collected and read at religious services to compensate for lack of rhetorical power or orthodoxy in other preachers. It also became a tradition to read homilies in connection with the various celebrations of the Church Year. To this day, one of the principal meanings of *homily* is "a written sermon, prepared by some well-known ecclesiastic, and read at religious ceremonies by an officiating person."

The first record we have of a church decree concerning this practice comes from the provincial council of Vaux (probably the third) in 529: Presbyters unable for any reason to adequately prepare their own sermons were enjoined to use the homilies of the Church Fathers. Books of homilies date from the second century and appear in many languages, including Greek, Latin, Coptic, Hebrew, Old English, and Old Icelandic. The first collection into book form of homilies by multiple authors (that we know of) is the *Homilarium,* collected by Paulus Diaconus about 800, first appearing in print in 1482. Other well-known books of homilies include the two collected by the Church of England, published in 1547 and 1571, and containing "sermons or homilies" of contemporary clergy. These homilies, "appointed to be read in churches," stood with the Church of England's *Book of Common Prayer* and the *39 Articles* as repositories of doctrine.

In the modern age, homilies are still delivered during religious services, and books of homilies are still written, collected, and used by clergy. In the Roman Catholic Church, the homily is an official part of the liturgy; according to the *Constitution on the Sacred Liturgy* of Vatican Council II (1963), the homily is "an exposition of the mysteries of faith and the guiding principles of the Christian life expounded from the sacred text read in the liturgy during the liturgical assembly" (52). Some form of "proclamation of the Word" is part of the regular worship in almost all Christian denominations, but if the word *homily* is used to describe that proclamation, it is generally synonymous with *sermon.* Many Christians, however, including Catholics, also use the word *homily* in something like its original sense, distinguishing it from other forms of sacred discourse and referring by it to a minister's or priest's informal, pastoral exposition of scripture for the instruction and improvement of a congregation of believers.

Russel Hirst
University of Tennessee

Bibliography

Bede, the Venerable, Saint, 673–735. *Homilies on the Gospels.* Trans. Lawrence T. Martin and David Hurst. Kalamazoo, MI: Cistercian, 1991.

Bond, Ronald B., ed. *Certain Sermons or Homilies (1547): and, A Homily Against Disobedience and Wilful Rebellion (1570): A Critical Edition.* Toronto: U of Toronto P, 1987.

John Crysostom, Saint. *Homilies on Genesis.* Trans. Robert C. Hill. Washington, D.C.: Catholic U of America P, 1992.

John Paul II, Pope. *The Pope Speaks to the American Church: John Paul II's Homilies, Speeches, and Letters to Catholics in the United States.* San Francisco: HarperSanFrancisco, 1992.

Leontius, Presbyter of Constantinople, 5th/6th cent. *Fourteen Homilies.* Trans. and notes, Pauline Allen and Cornelius Datema. Brisbane: Australian Association for Byzantine Studies, 1991.

Mason, Rex. *Preaching the Tradition: Homily and Hermenutics after the Exile.* New York: Cambridge UP, 1990.

Morris, Richard, trans. *Old English Homilies and Homiletic Treatises of the Twelfth and Thirteenth Centuries.* Rpt. Millwood, NY: Kraus, 1988.

Viladesau, Richard. *The Word In and Out of Season: Homilies for the Sundays of Ordinary Time.* New York: Paulist P, 1991.

See also Ars praedicandi; Homiletics; Sermon

Horace (Quintus Horatius Flaccus) (65–8 B.C.E.)

One of Rome's greatest poets of the Augustan age. Son of a freed slave, Horace belonged to a different social class than did most of the poets and rhetors of his time. Nevertheless, he received an upper-middle-class education, which included training in rhetoric—though he never mentions it—and a period of time studying philosophy in Athens. In 38 B.C.E. he was introduced to the literary circle of Maecenas by Virgil, and he remained under Maecenas' patronage for the rest of his life, turning down a request by the emperor Augustus to become his personal secretary. Horace is known chiefly for his lyric poetry, two books of *Epodes* and four books of *Odes,* inspired by Greek models and exhibiting a perfection of form unparalleled in classical Latin poetry. Other poems include two books of *Satires* (the only Roman literary genre), the *Carmen Saeculare* (a hymn commissioned for the centennial games celebrated by Augustus in 17 B.C.E.), a series of poetic letters, in two books, and the *Ars poetica* (*The Art of Poetry,* also called *Epistle to the Pisos*), which ranks with the lyrics as one of his best-known works. Horace was neither an orator nor a rhetor in the classical sense, but through the *Ars poetica* he influenced rhetorical theory from the first century C.E. through the Enlightenment.

The *Ars poetica* poses as a didactic epistle to fellow poets, the Pisos, on the subject of poetics. The ostensible purpose is to teach the writing of poetry, focusing on epic and drama, by treating first the details of the poem, second the unity of poems, and third the nature of the poet. The *Ars poetica* is difficult to interpret as a whole, even in terms of its own advice; it is far easier to treat as a source of aphorisms, which most critics and imitators have done. Symptomatic of this, a number of our own literary phrases and terms are taken directly from the *Ars poetica*—*purple patch* (15–16), *sub judice* (78), *in medias res* (148), the image of Homer nodding (359), and *ut pictura poesis* (361)—occasionally without regard to their context. Complicating interpretation is the fact that the poem is at once lighthearted and serious; it proffers advice that sometimes agrees with Horace's own practice and other times contradicts it. On the whole, it seems to be in harmony with what we know about the main lines of contemporary poetic and rhetorical theory, though Horace gives indications in his other poems that he may have frowned on the rhetoric of his day.

The *Ars poetica* fuses ancient poetic and rhetorical theories that had been kept relatively distinct since Aristotle, though earlier writers (such as Cicero) admitted that there were similarities. Horace seems to follow the poetic theories of Neoptolemus of Parium, who drew from Aristotle's *Rhetoric* as well as the *Poetics*. Sections of the *Ars poetica* derive directly from Aristotle's *Rhetoric*, such as the ages of man (156–78), the choice and combination of words (45 –72), and the section on characterization (114–24), which would have agreed with any contemporary rhetorical work. It has been thought that Horace appropriated material from Cicero's *Orator* and *De oratore*, but that theory has been disputed (see Brink). It seems safer to say that Horace draws on rhetorical material when it suits his purpose, but that the aims of the *Ars poetica* and Cicero's rhetorical treatises were different.

The *Ars poetica* is also in harmony with the evolution of Roman oratory during the Augustan period. As it moved from the Forum to the salon and teachers emphasized declamation rather than practice in the courts, oratory became a formal, artistic, literary form different from the speeches Cicero delivered. Horace's admonitions to feel the emotions one wants to inspire in the reader (99–111), to choose a model to imitate (119–52), to rewrite and polish (289–94), and to let worthy critics advise one before publishing (385–90) are consonant with the contemporary teaching and practice of declamation. Throughout the poem one finds repeated emphasis on artistic decorum. Likewise, coinciding with developments in rhetorical education, there is an emphasis on the ethics of the poet (309–18). This is reminiscent of Cato's definition of the orator as a *vir bonus dicendi peritus* and foreshadows Quintilian's emphasis on the budding orator's moral development.

The *Ars poetica* became a standard text in the curriculum of the *grammaticus*. The use to which Horace could be put in the schools is shown early by Quintilian (*Institutio Oratoria* 8.3.60), who cites the *Ars poetica* on the subject of decorum. The *Ars poetica* joined the *Ad Herennium* as one of the most popular school texts throughout the Middle Ages and Renaissance, together influencing Geoffrey de Vinsauf and John of Garland. The two works also helped shape the *ars dictaminis* tradition. Because of Horace's stance as a moralist, his poems become important sources for writers of *artes praedicandi* such as Thomas Chabham. Horace's works also appear in the rhetorical treatises of Erasmus and, later, George Campbell.

Robert W. Cape, Jr.
Austin College

Bibliography
Brink, Charles O. *Horace on Poetry*. 3 vols. Cambridge: Cambridge UP, 1963–1982.
Kennedy, George A. *The Art of Rhetoric in the Roman World, 300 B.C.–A.D. 300*. Princeton: Princeton UP, 1972.
Murphy, James J. *Rhetoric in the Middle Ages*. Berkeley: U of California P, 1974.

See also Ars poetica

Howell, Wilbur Samuel (1904–1992)

Ph.D. Cornell University, 1931, long-time professor of rhetoric in the English Department of Princeton University and award-winnning scholar in the history of rhetoric. Howell earned his A.B., A.M., and Ph.D. degrees at Cornell University and taught at Washington University, Harvard, and Dartmouth until he joined the Princeton faculty in 1934. Howell continued and expanded the humanistic research in rhetoric of his mentors Lane Cooper, Harry Caplan, Herbert A. Wichelns, and Everett Lee Hunt, contributing to what became known as the Cornell School of Rhetoric.

A prolific scholar, Howell's most prominent contributions include *The Rhetoric of Alcuin & Charlemagne* (1941), *Logic and Rhetoric in England, 1500–1700* (1956), and *Eighteenth-Century British Logic and Rhetoric* (1971). Howell's final major work, *Poetics, Rhetoric and Logic: Studies in the Basic Disciplines of Criticism* (1975), provides a collection of his most important essays and an introduction that offers an excellent statement of his views on rhetoric. An ardent Aristotelian, Howell provides a strongly argued rationale for distinctions between the nature of poetics and rhetoric, calling the latter a literature of statement whose province is nonmimetic discourse and the former a literature of symbol whose province is mimetic discourse. An outspoken critic of Kenneth Burke's notions of rhetoric, Howell's "Colloquy" with Burke in the February 1976 issue of the *Quarterly Journal of Speech* still provides provocative and convincing arguments on rhetoric.

Howell received many awards for his scholarship on rhetoric. A panel was sponsored by the International Society of Rhetoric in his honor in 1981, and a tribute to his career was published in the spring 1982 issue of the *Rhetoric Society Quarterly*. In 1972 he won the Winans/Wichelns Award of the Speech

Communication Association for distinguished scholarship in rhetoric and in 1985 earned that association's highest honor, the SCA Distinguished Service Award. Wilbur Samuel Howell is commonly considered to be one of the twentieth century's great scholars on the history of rhetoric.

Richard Leo Enos
Texas Christian University

Bibliography

Burke, Kenneth, and Wilbur Samuel Howell. "Colloquy." *Quarterly Journal of Speech* 62 (1976): 62–77.

Enos, Richard Leo. "A Tribute to Wilbur Samuel Howell." Wilbur Samuel Howell. "A Response." *Rhetoric Society Quarterly* 12 (1982): 72–75.

Howell, Wilbur Samuel. *Eighteenth-Century British Logic and Rhetoric*. Princeton: Princeton UP, 1971.

———. *Logic and Rhetoric in England, 1500–1700*. Princeton: Princeton UP, 1956.

———. *Poetics, Rhetoric, and Logic: Studies in the Basic Disciplines of Criticism*. Ithaca, NY: Cornell UP, 1975.

———. *The Rhetoric of Alcuin & Charlemagne*. Princeton: Princeton UP, 1941.

———, ed. *Notes on the Cornell School of Rhetoric*. Riverside, CA: Howes, 1976.

Hudson, Hoyt Hopewell (1893–1944)

Translator, editor, literary critic, rhetorician, academic administrator, educational theorist, poet. Hoyt Hudson, a Renaissance man, slipped easily into any humanistic endeavor with insight and wit. At his death, the Academic Council of Stanford University also cited his nationwide fame as a teacher, "not alone because he was master of his subject and had devoted careful study to the art of teaching, but also because he was to his students guide, counselor, and friend as well as instructor."

Hoyt Hudson was born in Norfolk, Nebraska, on July 6, 1893. He received his B.A. from Huron College in 1912 (where he was a student with Everett Lee Hunt) and his M.A. from the University of Denver the following year. After wandering around doing an assortment of jobs, he accepted Hunt's invitation to do graduate work at Cornell University, arriving just in time to join the famous 1920 seminar in classical rhetoric. He received his Ph.D. in 1923.

During the 1920s Hudson emerged as chief spokesman for the Cornell School of Rhetoric and produced several articles that helped to define the field of rhetoric in American higher education. In "The Field of Rhetoric," he defined rhetoric in the classical sense as the art of persuasion based on probabilities, not scientific certainty or solely limited to public speeches. In "Rhetoric and Poetry," Hudson distinguished between these two allied arts, demonstrating that they are separate endeavors even as they have some overlapping commonalities. These essays gave theoretical bases to the new profession and provided sound arguments for the separation of speech from departments of English. For decades they remained seminal essays in the field.

From Cornell, Hudson went to a series of teaching jobs at the University of Pittsburgh, Swarthmore College, Princeton University, and finally Stanford University, where he was engaged in developing a humanities course of study. During this time he wrote, edited, and translated a number of important works, including his distinguished translation of Erasmus's *Praise of Folly*. He died suddenly on June 13, 1944, leaving behind numerous works including his partially finished *Educating Liberally*, his collection of epigrams titled *The Epigram in the English Renaissance*, and a collection of poems, *Celebration*, which his friends collected, edited, and published posthumously. These works, combined with his previously published books and essays, mark him as one of speech communication's truly Renaissance men.

Theodore Otto Windt, Jr.
University of Pittsburgh

Bibliography

Howes, Raymond F. "Hoyt Hudson, The Renaissance Man." *Notes on the Cornell School of Rhetoric*. Riverside, CA: privately printed, 1976. 11–13.

Hudson, Hoyt H. *Educating Liberally*. Stanford, CA: Stanford UP, 1945.

———. *The Epigram in the English Renaissance*. Princeton: Princeton UP, 1947.

———. "The Field of Rhetoric." *Quarterly Journal of Speech* 9 (1923): 167–80.

———. "Rhetoric and Poetry." *Quarterly Journal of Speech* 10 (1924): 143–54.

———, ed. *Directions for Speech and Style by John Hoskins*. Princeton: Princeton UP, 1935.

———, trans. *The Praise of Folly by Desiderius Erasmus*. Princeton: Princeton UP, 1941.

Hunt, Everett Lee. "Hoyt Hopewell Hudson." *Quarterly Journal of Speech* 31 (1945): 272–74.

Windt, Theodore Otto, Jr. "Hoyt H. Hudson: Spokesman for the Cornell School of Rhetoric." *Quarterly Journal of Speech* 68 (1982): 186–200.

Hume, David (1711–1776)

Empiricist philosopher of the Scottish Enlightenment. Hume applies Newton's "experimental method" in the sciences to moral philosophy, including epistemology and philosophy of mind. The radical empiricism Hume developed reduces all knowledge to immediate sensory experience and what can be deduced from or added to it by the faculties of reason, memory, and imagination. Hume's early philosophical writings were published anonymously and were largely misunderstood and ignored. He first achieved fame as a man of letters, historian of the British monarchy, and diplomatic attaché, rather than, as he is appreciated today, one of the most important English language philosophers.

In his *Treatise* (1739), Hume divides all mental events into impressions and ideas. Impressions are immediate sense contents, passions, or emotions. These are the occurrent experiential data that occupy our sensory fields at any waking moment. They are the colors, shapes, sounds, smells, and external and internal feelings, which, in the empiricist idiom, literally causally impress themselves upon the mind like a stylus on a wax tablet. Ideas are described as faded impressions that may linger behind as an image of an impression after the experience has passed. There are ideas of sensation and of reflection, and the mind supplements the austere raw material of its immediate experiential input by assembling parts of ideas into new combinations, and imaginatively filling in gaps where psychological disposition demands consistency and continuity. Belief and other so-called propositional attitudes such as doubt, hope, and fear are characterized as particular ways in which ideas are conceived. Hume, in one of his more valuable contributions to the analysis of philosophical categories, maintains that causation is experientially unobservable, so that there is no justification for belief in the necessity of causal connection. The concept of causation in Hume's theory is reducible to a particular pattern in the association of ideas that exhibit spatial contiguity, temporal succession, and constant conjunction. Hume attributes the philosophically naive view that causation is a necessary relation between otherwise contingent events to the agency of imagination under the direction of a strictly nonrational psychological compulsion to suppose that causes must produce their effects.

Hume's debt to Ciceronian rhetoric is seen in his posthumous dialogues on religious belief (1779). The exploration of topics in this work is unmistakably modeled on *De Natura Deorum*, and even the names of key interlocutors are borrowed directly from Cicero's criticism of Stoic theocosmology. Hume's admiration and imitation of classical authors is shared by many of his contemporaries, partly as a result of the widespread eighteenth-century educational practice of requiring students to read and write set pieces in the manner of Greek and Latin paradigms. But Hume in his essay "Of Eloquence" (1742), consistently with his declaration that "reason is, and ought only to be, the slave of the passions" (1739:415), praises the pathos and sublimity of rhetorical style among ancient orators and their emotional effect on the audience, by contrast with modern rationalistic preoccupations with argumentative content.

Dale Jacquette
Pennsylvania State University

Bibliography

Flew, Anthony. *David Hume: Philosopher of Moral Science*. Oxford: Blackwell, 1986.

Hall, Roland. *Fifty Years of Hume Scholarship: A Bibliographical Guide*. Edinburgh: Edinburgh UP, 1978 (supplements published annually in *Hume Studies,* beginning Vol. 3).

Hume, David. *Dialogues Concerning Natural Religion*. (1779). Ed. Norman Kemp Smith. Oxford: Clarendon, 1935.

———. *Enquiries Concerning Human Understanding* [1748] and *Concerning the Principles of Morals* [1751]. (1777). P.H. Nidditch, 3rd ed. of L.A. Selby-Bigge (1893) ed. Oxford: Clarendon, 1975.

———. *Essays Moral, Political, and Literary*. (1742). Ed. Eugene F. Miller. Indianapolis, IN: Liberty Classics, 1987.

———. *The History of Great Britain from the Invasion of Julius Caesar to the Revolution of 1688.* 6 vols. (1778). Indianapolis, IN: Liberty Classics, 1985.

———. *A Treatise of Human Nature.* (Books 1 and 2, 1739; Book 3, 1940). P.H. Nidditch, 2nd ed. of L.A. Selby-Bigge (1888) ed. Oxford: Clarendon, 1978.

Norton, David Fate. *David Hume: Common-Sense Moralist, Sceptical Metaphysician.* Princeton: Princeton UP, 1982.

Smith, Norman Kemp. *The Philosophy of David Hume.* New York: Macmillan, 1964.

Hunt, Everett Lee (1890–1984)

Dean of the humanistic school of rhetoric from the founding of the profession until his death in 1984. Everett Lee Hunt based his conception of rhetoric on classical precepts and insisted that rhetoric not become a specialized or scientific study but that it retain its humanistic base and character. He contended that rhetoric dealt with probabilities, with questions that admitted to no certain or conclusive answer.

Hunt was born on October 14, 1890, in Colfax, Iowa. He attended Huron College and upon graduation became a professor of public speaking at the college. He began writing essays for the new *Quarterly Journal of Public Speaking* in response to those, especially Charles Woolbert, who called for scientific studies of public speaking. The early controversies were lively and brought Hunt to the attention of other figures in the field. These eventually led to his appointment at Cornell University in 1917, where he stayed until 1925. In 1920 Hunt offered the famous seminar in classical rhetoric, the first twentieth-century seminar in that subject. It led to a series of articles written from the seminar and culminated in the volume *Studies in Rhetoric and Public Speaking in Honor of James Albert Winans* (1925), which James O'Neill described as "the most significant volume offered to workers in the field of speech in a very, very long time." Hunt's contribution, "Plato and Aristotle on Rhetoric and Rhetoricians," was the seminal work of the volume and remained the standard starting point for studies in classical rhetoric. The volume gave the first scholarly basis for the new profession. In addition, Hunt coedited with Alexander Drummond a collection of controversial essays, *Persistent Questions in Public Discussion,* which was widely used as a textbook.

Hunt moved to Swarthmore College in 1925 and soon devoted his time to being dean of men of the college, a position that eventually left him with little time for scholarly work in speech communication. He wrote several essays on Matthew Arnold, however, and contributed occasional essays on his unique humanistic perspective on rhetoric. In 1949 his essay "Rhetoric and General Education," his response to the Harvard University Report on general education, provoked widespread endorsements and criticism in the *Quarterly Journal of Speech.* After forty-six years of teaching, he retired in 1959. In retirement he held a number of visiting professorships, lectured widely, and wrote a book about his experiences with students, *The Revolt of the College Intellectual* (1963).

Late in his life he summarized his conception of rhetoric: "The case for rhetoric as a humane study may be stated with deceptive simplicity. Rhetoric is the study of men persuading men to make free choices." He continued by saying that choices should be enlightened. "An enlightened choice is a choice based upon a wide knowledge of all the alternatives, but knowledge about the alternatives is not enough. There must be imagination to envisage all the possibilities, and sympathy to make some of the options appeal to the emotions and powers of the will. Such dignity as man may have is achieved by the exercise of free choice through the qualities of learning, imagination, and sympathy; and we should add to these qualities as a fitting accompaniment, what may be called civility." The qualities of knowledge, imagination, sympathy, and civility characterized Hunt's writings, his thought, and his life.

Theodore Otto Windt, Jr.
University of Pittsburgh

Bibliography

Howe, Raymond. *Notes on the Cornell School of Rhetoric.* Riverside, CA: Privately printed, 1976.

Hunt, Everett Lee. "Adding Substance to Form in Public Speaking." *Quarterly Journal of Speech* 8 (1922): 256–65.

———. "Matthew Arnold: The Critic as Rhetorician." *Quarterly Journal of Speech* 20 (1934): 483–507.

———. "Plato and Aristotle on Rhetoric and Rhetoricians." *Studies in Rhetoric and Public Speaking in Honor of James Albert Winans.* New York: Century, 1925. 3–60.

———. *The Revolt of the College Intellectual*. Chicago: Aldine, 1963.

———, and Alexander Drummond, eds. *Persistent Questions in Public Discussion*. New York: Century, 1924.

Windt, Theodore Otto, Jr. *Rhetoric as a Human Adventure: A Short Biography of Everett Lee Hunt*. Annandale, VA: Speech Communication Assn., 1990.

Hypallage

Transposition of the natural relationship between two elements in a proposition. "Melissa shook her doubtful curls" (*Concise Oxford Dictionary*). Like enallage (q.v.), hypallage is an apparent mistake that becomes a figure by expressing an unexpected meaning. Stephano says in Shakespeare's *Tempest*, "Every man shift for all the rest, and let no man take care for himself" (5.1). In *A Midsummer Night's Dream,* Bottom evokes the ineffable wonder of his dream in explaining, "The eye of man hath not heard, the ear of man hath not seen, man's hand is not able to taste, his tongue to conceive, nor his heart to report what my dream was" (4.1). As these examples suggest, hypallage is a figure of arrangement that creates poetic leaps of meaning by deviating from conventional sentence structure.

Arthur Quinn and Lyon Rathbun
University of California, Berkeley

Hyperbaton

Any intended deviation from ordinary word order. Kant used hyperbaton in writing "From such crooked wood as that which man is made of, nothing straight can be fashioned." Euripides was also using this figure in writing "Whom God wishes to destroy, he first makes mad." The deviation from expected word order can add emphasis, as e.e. cummings demonstrated: "pity this busy monster manunkind not." The deviation can also be used to create a rhetorical effect by violating the reader's expectations. Rabelais was playing with his reader's expectations in writing "Few and signally blest are those whom Jupiter has destined to be cabbage planters."

Arthur Quinn and Lyon Rathbun
University of California, Berkeley

Hyperbole

A figurative device using self-conscious exaggeration to emphasize feelings and intensify rhetorical effect; Greek for *overshooting;* also called overstatement, superlatio, overreacher, and loud lyer; contrary to understatement (in Greek, *meiosis*) or litote; one means of amplification.

Hyperbole was first used to mean exaggeration by Isocrates in his *Epistulae* and first identified as a figure of speech by Aristotle, who says: "There is something adolescent about hyperboles, for they express things violently. . . [Their] vehemence. . . . does not suit men of mature years" (*Rhetoric* 1413a). In the apparent first reference to the figure in English, More notes "a maner of speking which is among lerned men called yperbole, for the more vehement expressyng of a mater" (*Dyaloge* IV 110b/I). Sherry argues that hyperbole goes beyond what can be true, such as in "The cry was heard to heaven," and that "[a]nother kind is by increase. . . . It is a miraculous deed to bind a citizen of Rome, heinous to beat him, what shall I say to hang him?" (71). Espy classifies hyperbole as "the boldest figure of rhetoric," one which "enables us to describe what would otherwise be beyond description" (98). In contrast, Cioffi argues that hyperbole "presents a reality that is implausible but not impossible" (524). Marckwardt claims that "the Elizabethan tendency toward hyperbole . . . was, in [America] never submerged by the countermovement toward litotes" that occurred in the English classical revival of the eighteenth century (98–103).

In the American West, hyperbole became the bedrock of frontier braggadocio and tall talk, perhaps most popularized by Davy Crockett's books, in which he asserts that he killed wolves as an infant and was weaned on snake eggs and whisky. More recently, Thompson and Asante note the political use of hyperbole in the exaggeration of America's vulnerability to armed attack during the Cold War and in the arguments against political correctness, resulting in alarmism. While hyperbole has tremendous breadth, it also has important limits. Pericles notes in his "Funeral Oration," delivered in 430 B.C.E., that excess amplification of praise results in jealousy or incredulity.

The amount of exaggeration necessary to have hyperbole can vary from text to text, and the progression of hyperbole is often complexly related to other figures, especially irony and metaphor. The first line of the Parker poem below may be interpreted as straight, metaphoric, or hyperbolic, and is complicated by the poem's developing irony. Finally, hyperbole remains a remarkably diverse rhetorical figure, occurring in political, legal, (in)formal, comic, serious, ironic, condemnatory, and complimentary contexts—among trillions of others: "[T]he world itself could not contain the books" (John 21.25); "They said that/he was a World King, Of men the mildest/and to men kindest, To his people most pleasant" (Beowulf 3180–82); "There lives not three good men unhanged in England, and one of them is fat and grows old" (Falstaff, who is later called "As fat as butter" in Shakespeare's *1 Henry IV*); "a multimonstrous manfrey of heteroclytes and quicquidlibets" (Nathaniel Ward, *The Simple Cobbler of Aggawan*, Laird 353); "My vegetable love should grow vaster than empires and more slow" (Andrew Marvell, "To His Coy Mistress"); "His was the bright star of genius that in early life shot madly forth, and left the lesser satellites that may have dazzled in its blaze to that impenetrable darkness" (Rep. Albert G. Brown on politician John C. Calhoun, to Congress, 1840; Laird 356); "Oh, life is a glorious cycle of song, / A medley of extemporanea; / And love is a thing that can never go wrong; / And I am Marie of Roumania" (Dorothy Parker, "Comment");

"This book weighs a ton" (contemporary colloquial).

Elizabeth Patnoe
Ohio State University

Bibliography

Aristotle. *Rhetoric. Aristotle On Poetry and Style*. Trans. G.M.A. Grube. Indianapolis, IN: Liberal Arts P, 1958.

Asante, Molefi Kete. "The Escape into Hyperbole: Communication and Political Correctness." *Journal of Communication* 42 (1992): 141–47.

Cioffi, Caron Ann. "Criseyde's Oaths of Love: Do They Really Belong to the Tradition of Lying-Songs?" *Journal of English and German Philology* 87 (1988): 522–34.

Espy, Willard R. *The Garden of Eloquence: A Rhetorical Bestiary*. New York: Harper, 1983.

Laird, Charlton. *Language in America*. Englewood Cliffs, NJ: Prentice, 1970.

Marckwardt, Albert H. *American English*. New York: Oxford UP, 1958.

Sherry, Richard. *A Treatise of Schemes and Tropes* (1550). Intro. Herbert W. Hildebrandt. Gainesville, FL: Scholars' Facsimiles and Reprints, 1961.

Thompson, John A. "The Exaggeration of American Vulnerability: The Anatomy of a Tradition." *Diplomatic History* 16 (1992): 24–43.

H

I

Identification

The act of crossing individual boundaries to gain another person's or group's perspective through shared characteristics, experiences, objects, assumptions, beliefs, goals, or languages. A key strand of the lore passed on to initiates in rhetorical studies is the shift from persuasion to identification as the goal of the New Rhetoric. This is, among most rhetoricians, "gospel"—not only in the sense of being treated as a fundamental truth but also in the sense of being understood as "good news": After all, identification is said to be less adversarial, less coercive, less individualistic, more collaborative, more mystical, and more feminist than persuasion.

Traditionally, Kenneth Burke gets the credit for replacing the classical definition of rhetoric as persuasion with the definition of rhetoric as identification, but Burke himself makes clear that one term cannot substitute for the other. Instead, in *A Rhetoric of Motives* he argues that identification between speakers and listeners, writers and readers, is fundamental to persuasion: "You persuade a man only insofar as you can talk his language by speech, gesture, tonality, order, image, attitude, idea, *identifying* your ways with his" (55).

Burke's many uses of "identification" revise rather than replace Aristotle's definition of rhetoric—rhetoric becomes the act of discovering or creating the probable shared grounds or joined interests that make persuasion possible. The appeals to ethos, logos, and pathos become lures to identification. Burke expands the scope of rhetoric beyond the forensic, deliberative, and the epideictic, to apply the term to a limitless variety of acts in which identification is "compensatory to division" (1950:22), ranging from birth and courtship to art, war, and death. He also differentiates the degrees of identification, from pure identification or consubstantiation (1950:20), to formal appeal (1950:65), to a mere sense of recognition because of a shared logo or bumper sticker. For Burke, *animal symbolicum* uses language to bridge the abyss that separates people.

One reason that we hold onto the myth that Burke replaced persuasion with identification and that this substitution holds possibilities for harmony and wholeness is that Burke's rhetoric arises from his faith that people want to participate in the conversation at hand and to unite with others. Although consubstantiation is only one aspect of identification for Burke, the desire for mystical union underwrites his rhetoric.

In general, then, the shift from persuasion to identification promises unity, cooperation, community, dialogue, equality, peace, all components of Burke's "equipment for living" and "strategies for coping." But for Burke and other contemporary critics, identification does not guarantee only harmony in the parlor room where people come and go, putting in their oars and receiving responses. Contemporary critiques of community and conversation make clear, as does Burke himself through images of the Human Barnyard, the Scramble, and the Wrangle of the Marketplace, that conversations are also characterized by "flurries and flare-ups," the "wavering line of pressure and counterpressure, the Logomachy, the onus of ownership, the Wars of Nerves, the War" (1950:23).

Current focus on issues of race, class, gender, and culture introduce further complexities into Burke's parlor room and even into his analyses of the Barnyard, Scramble, and Marketplace. Throughout his writing Burke analyzes situations in terms of order, hierarchy, scapegoating, and victimage, but he does not pinpoint his criticism to issues of race, class, or gender. What is missing from Burke's parlor room anecdote, as well as from his more contentious settings, are the disturbing dynamics and imbalances of power that exclude people from entering the parlor and from participating, once they are inside, because of their positions. Cooperation can disguise competition, unity can deny difference, and collaboration can entail coercion.

Therefore, the shift from persuasion to identification is not unqualified "good news." The shift does not necessarily redefine traditional rhetoric's fundamental goal, which is to change other people's attitudes or actions. Shared interests, common ground, dialogic processes—none of these make a real difference in rhetoric if the rhetor's intent is still to change the other person to maintain or improve one's own position or cause.

Several critics have taken up the challenge to transform the assumed goal of rhetoric. Sally Miller Gearhart argues in "The Womanization of Rhetoric" that any intent to persuade is by nature violent and prevents identification. The "conquest and conversion model" of human interaction should be replaced by a feminine nonpersuasive model of communication, based on the "deliberate creation or co-creation of an atmosphere in which people or things, if and only if they have the internal basis for change, may change themselves; it can be a milieu in which those who are ready to be persuaded may persuade themselves, may choose to hear or choose to learn" (196, 198). Without using the term *identification,* she feminizes its meaning: Rather than being the speaker who persuades, "we are the matrix, we are she-who-is-the-home-of-this-particular-human-interaction, we are a co-creator and co-sustainer of the atmosphere in whose infinity of possible transformations we will all change" (200).

In other words, we must enter into the presence of others with a willingness, an expectation—even a desire—to be changed as well as to effect change. The task of the rhetorician is not to gauge the probable means of persuading another but to create an atmosphere or environment conducive to transformation of all parties. Gearhart directs attention from the grounds for identification, such as a common language,

shared assumptions, and universal calculated appeals, to the attitudes of participants and the flexibility of their roles which allow for possible changes. Ironically, she herself argues to replace or convert the traditional goal of rhetoric in her reader's mind. Also, she seems to assume that there is never a situation in which it may be ethical to seek to change another.

In "Arts of the Contact Zone," Mary Louise Pratt questions a basic assumption in traditional rhetorics, that the person in power changes the other, and she situates *identification* in the changing exigencies of border encounters where people do what they have to do with words in order to cope. In these situations, identities and cultures are changing and heterogenous, not intact, stable, and homogenous. These "contact zones" are where people adapt roles, conventions, and languages to meet specific immediate needs. Her focus is on the specific scenes where cultures meet and where we cannot assume that a "situation is governed by a single set of rules or norms shared by all participants" or that "all participants are engaged in the same game and that the game is the same for all players" (38).

Pratt's critique complicates further the traditional goal of rhetoric, the notion of a single goal, and the conception of identities of people and cultures as intact. Her analysis of contact zones demonstrates that the dominated influence the dominator in what she calls a process of "transculturation." Simple classifications of the colonizer and the colonized, the dominated and the dominator, and the victim and the victimizer cannot account for what happens in specific situations. For Pratt, little is static, and interactions are social reconstructions of all parties. Who's doing what to whom is not as clear as theories often imply because what counts as a "who" is situational and rhetorical rather than constant, intact, and referentially verifiable, and because subjective and objective cases are not fixed categories.

Pratt's term *contact zone,* taken from contact linguistics, connotes competition, combat, and guerrilla warfare. She suggests that the ongoing negotiations about identity and identification, obvious on the borders, are also characteristic of the less-obvious negotiations taking place elsewhere. Her image allows us to see possibilities for change in power relationships and structures when people fight for such changes, using subversive arts. By comparison, Burke's similar image of the "margins of overlap" between people suggests that people share areas of overlap in a somewhat accidental way, despite Burke's own theories of language as action, motivated and consequential. Juxtaposed to these two images, the term *identification* can seem neutral and outdated, perhaps because of its root, *identify*, and the related word, *identity*, which, as Pratt helps us see, too often inaccurately suggests coherence and constancy.

At this point, discussions of "identity politics" can lead us to distinguish between the advantages and disadvantages of "identification" as a key concept in rhetoric, at a time when stable identity has been called into question by social-constructionists and by deconstructionists and when language is understood as context-dependent or contextually motivated. In *Essentially Speaking: Feminism, Nature, and Difference*, Diana Fuss defines "identity politics" as referring "to the tendency to base one's politics on a sense of personal identity—as gay, as Jewish, as Black, as female" (97). She notes, for instance, that identity politics "has been endorsed by both gay men and lesbians as a working theoretical base upon which to build a cohesive and visible political community" (97). While recognizing the expediency of such identifications, Fuss seeks to historicize "identity" in order to illuminate how this political strategy is perpetuated by essentialism.

After acknowledging that the "tension between notions of 'developing' an identity and 'finding' an identity points to a more general confusion over the very definition of 'identity' and over the precise definition of 'lesbian,'" she indicates what she believes is missing from identity politics: "recognition of the precarious status of identity and a full awareness of the complicated processes of identity formation, both psychical and social" (100). Here Fuss recognizes the rhetorical power of an essentialist assertion, but she overlooks the current rhetorical power in her own position and arguments.

Fuss's analysis can help us clarify uses of *identification* by historicizing it as a site where the personal and the public, the socially constructed and the individually constructed, and the essentialist and the rhetorical are recognized as negotiable positions, standpoints, identities, and rhetorics. When recognized as such, people can rewrite them, though not easily, not certainly, and not necessarily with the anticipated results.

Perhaps the most fundamental mode of this ongoing renegotiation of identification, across borders and motives, is the telling of stories. As Walter Fisher proposes in *Human Communication as Narration: Toward a Philosophy of Reason, Value, and Action*, "the world as we know it is a set of stories that must be chosen among in order for us to live life in a process of continual recreation" (65). Wherever we practice identification, we are surrounded by stories that vie for our attention and assent. Though Fisher rightly claims that life requires us to make choices, it is also true that most of us dwell, even as we move through a single day, in several different—sometimes overlapping, often contending—stories at once, and our choices are not clear-cut.

Moreover, in "Argument as Emergence, Rhetoric as Love," Jim Corder elaborates how "each of us is a narrative" and suggests that identification "requires a readiness to testify to an identity that is always emerging, a willingness to dramatize one's narrative in progress before the other" (16, 26). This spinning of our tales, Corder emphasizes, can be a perilous undertaking, especially given the deep-running, long-hidden energy of our diversities. There is no guarantee that others will welcome the stories we are telling, enacting, becoming—or that our lives won't be disrupted, hemmed in, or harmed by the narratives-in-progress that others tell.

Contemporary rhetoric's gospel of identification is a demanding and costly good news. Gloria Anzaldúa in *Borderlands/La Frontera* reveals how, as she tells the story of her "border woman" existence, not only does she awaken to the rage and hatred arrayed against her languages, her cultures, her sexualities, and spiritualities, she also cultivates *la facultad*—a deepening awareness of our motives, our powers, our violations, our mysteries. She speaks of joys, of being not comfortable but present (38).

The more we *practice* identification by dramatizing our narratives-in-progress and by inviting others to do the same, the more we create situations, as Pratt has described it, where no one is excluded and no one is safe (9). But as Audre Lorde reminds us in "The Transformation of Silence into Language and Action," it is time to "learn to work and speak when we are afraid in the same way we have learned to work and speak when we are tired"; she is convinced that "it is not difference which immobilizes us, but silence. And there are so many silences to be broken" (44).

Pat Youngdahl and Tilly Warnock
University of Arizona

Bibliography

Anzaldúa, Gloria. *Borderlands/La Frontera.* San Francisco: Spinsters/aunt lute, 1987.

Burke, Kenneth. *A Rhetoric of Motives.* Berkeley: U of California P, 1969.

Corder, Jim. "Argument as Emergence, Rhetoric as Love." *Rhetoric Review* 4 (1985): 16–32.

Fisher, Walter. *Human Communication as Narration: Toward a Philosophy of Reason, Value, and Action.* Columbia: U of South Carolina P, 1987.

Fuss, Diana. *Essentially Speaking: Feminism, Nature, and Difference.* London: Routledge, 1989.

Gearhart, Sally Miller. "The Womanization of Rhetoric." *Women's Studies International Quarterly* 2 (1979): 195–201.

Lorde, Audre. "The Transformation of Silence into Language and Action." *Sister Outsider: Essays and Speeches.* Trumansburg, NY: Crossing, 1984. 40–44.

Pratt, Mary Louise. "Arts of the Contact Zone." *ADE Bulletin* (1988): 33–40.

Ideological Criticism

An approach to rhetorical analysis that focuses on how conflict, power, and material interests shape and influence social and symbolic interaction. Strongly influenced by the writings of Kenneth Burke, ideological criticism emerged in contemporary rhetoric as a response to a traditional view of criticism that privileges texts over contexts and emphasizes value neutrality and objectivity in the analysis of discourse. Ideological critics argue that criticism is a moral activity that should be used to analyze and challenge hegemonic institutional and social structures. It focuses on the political dimensions of discourse in order to expose the underlying beliefs and assumptions at work in rhetorical theory and practice. Although generally grounded in the oppositional assumptions of Marxist thought, ideological criticism is represented by a number of diverse perspectives and theoretical approaches that transcend the limited conceptualization of ideology as "false consciousness" and "enrich possibilities for analysis of public discourse" (Makus 511).

Ideological critics posit a dynamic relationship between symbolic and material realities by suggesting that the "falsity of an ideology is specifically rhetorical, for the illusion of truth and falsity with regard to normative commitments is the product of persuasion" (McGee 1980:4). Ideological criticism synthesizes a Marxist emphasis on the material foundations of society with a Burkean emphasis on socially constructed realities to explain the articulatory power of ideology, its ability to shape and be shaped by human consciousness, and its decidedly discursive influences. Ideology reflects "a *rhetoric* of control, a system of persuasion presumed to be effective on the whole community." Ideological criticism entails the isolation and analysis of *ideographs,* the "one-term sums of an orientation" that represent the discursive strategies used to defend political and material interests (McGee 1980:6,7). By understanding the analytic and historical dimensions of ideographs, critics are able to decipher relationships between the materialism of "objective" realities and the symbolism of "social" realities.

The deciphering of such relationships undergirds the decidedly moral agenda of ideological critics and their insistence that traditional critical practices mask other interests. Philip Wander articulates this agenda in his explication of an "ideological turn" in contemporary rhetorical criticism. Wander criticizes neoclassical approaches to the analysis of discourse in order to illustrate how traditional criticism's emphasis on technique and the objective analysis of texts obscures the ethical and political issues inherent in the contexts that give rise to discourse. Wander criticizes the works of traditional critics who believe that social and political "struggles can and ought to be transcended" through critical perspectives that emphasize textual analysis (10). Such approaches, like the abstract assumptions of objectivity to which they are wedded, cannot confront the realities of human struggle and conflict attended to by ideological criticism.

Wander offers a definitive vision of ideological criticism: "Criticism takes an ideological turn when it recognizes the existence of powerful vested interests benefiting from and consistently urging policies and technology that threaten life on this planet, when it realizes that we search for alternatives" (18). Wander's essay generated a debate that emphasized the differences between ideological and traditional approaches to rhetorical criticism and focused on the social role and political responsibility of the critic. As a participant in that debate, McGee has observed that ideological critics "understand the moral consequences of believing the fantastic claim that any academic, but especially a rhetorical critic, can and ought in the name of a counterfeit 'objectivity' withdraw from the political economy to participate in a 'timeless dialogue' on this or that ideal abstraction" (50). In further addressing the moral consequences of rhetorical criticism, Wander articulated the idea of a "Third Persona," which represents those marginalized by hegemonic social and discursive structures, "categorized according to race, religion, age, gender, sexual preference, and nationality, and acted upon in ways consistent with their status as nonsubjects" (216). The critic, Wander suggests, can participate in the emancipation of those characterized by the Third Persona by taking the ideological turn or become complicit in their oppression by invoking the analytical abstractions and objective approaches of traditional criticism.

Following Wander, other rhetorical scholars have emphasized the moral and ethical implications of ideological criticism. James F. Klumpp and Thomas Hollihan argue that the ideal of critical objectivity can function as "an ideological ruse for complicity in maintaining the existing social order" (84), and Sharon Crowley contends that traditional criticism implicates its practitioners in epistemological as well as social complicity. Traditional criticism, Crowley argues, is wedded to philosophical essentialism and privileges some critical approaches and perspectives at the expense of others. In addition to limiting the theoretical directions of rhetorical analysis, traditional criticism also undermines rhetoric's practical potential: "To the extent that ordinary citizens are unable to articulate or criticize the discursive conditions that cause and maintain unfair and destructive practices, we academic rhetoricians must bear some responsibility for their silence" (464). Crowley's observations illustrate how the ideological turn in contemporary rhetoric emphasizes the moral and ethical commitments of critics, as well as their social and political roles as participants in the society they analyze and critique.

These two emphases have helped move contemporary rhetorical theory and criticism beyond a limited orthodox Marxist view of ideology and toward a coherent understanding of the relationship between the material and discursive dimensions of social interaction. As Malcolm O. Sillars suggests, ideological critics "acknowledge the material conditions of the power struggles within society, but look for the subtle interactions of these conditions with the ideological symbolizations of all parties" (213). Additionally, ideological criticism has facilitated a self-reflexive sensibility that recognizes and acknowledges its own underlying ideological commitments. Thomas Hollihan and Patricia Riley note that scholars "who study rhetoric and communication are committed to the preservation and conduct of a vital, dynamic, and perhaps even revolutionary public discourse (an ideological position in and of itself)" (273). Ideological criticism has thus had a significant and enduring influence on the discipline of communication, and promises to continue to provide important theoretical directions and practical applications for the field of rhetoric.

Mark Lawrence McPhail
University of Utah

Bibliography

Crowley, Sharon. "Reflections on the Argument that Won't Go Away: Or, a Turn of the Ideological Screw." *Quarterly Journal of Speech* 78 (1992): 450–65.

Hollihan, Thomas, and Patricia Riley. "Rediscovering Ideology." *Western Journal of Communication* 57 [Special Issue on Ideology and Communication] (1993): 272–77.

Klumpp, James, and Thomas Hollihan. "Rhetorical Criticism as Moral Action." *Quarterly Journal of Speech* 75 (1989): 84–97.

McGee, Michael. "Another Philippic: Notes on the Ideological Turn in Criticism." *Central States Speech Journal* 35 (1984): 43–50.

———. "The 'Ideograph': A Link Between Rhetoric and Ideology." *Quarterly Journal of Speech* 66 (1980): 1–16.

Makus, Ann. "Stuart Hall's Theory of Ideology: A Frame for Rhetorical Criticism." *Western Journal of Speech Communication* 54 (1990): 495–514.

Sillars, Malcolm. *Messages, Meanings, and Culture: Approaches to Communication Criticism.* New York: HarperCollins, 1991.

Wander, Philip. "The Ideological Turn in Modern Criticism." *Central States Speech Journal* 34 (1983): 1–18.

———. "The Third Persona: An Ideological Turn in Rhetorical Theory." *Central States Speech Journal* 35 (1984): 197–216.

I

Illustration

Making clear through the use of examples. Derived from the Latin *lustrare,* to make bright, illustration is the speaker's or writer's act of clarifying ideas through the use of examples. Also called exemplification, illustration is one of the more common methods of developing paragraphs and essays.

Classical rhetoricians certainly knew about and discussed illustration, though the closest Latin term to the English *illustration* is probably *exemplum.* Cicero in *De oratore* writes about the importance of amplification (3.104ff). Quintilian in *Institutio Oratoria* discusses exemplum briefly (5.11). He further mentions *enumeration* (5.14) and later defines *enumeration* as "repetition and grouping of the facts" (6.1).

The first cited use of *illustration* in English, in the sense usually associated with rhetoric, is in 1581, when John Marbeck wrote, "It is a figure called Illustration, by the which the forme of things is so set foorth in words, that it seemeth rather to be seene with the eies, than heard with the eares" (*OED*).

The term *illustration* slowly worked its way into the major rhetorics of the eighteenth and nineteenth centuries. In discussing the narrative part of a discourse, Hugh Blair in *Lectures on Rhetoric and Belles Lettres* (1783) emphasizes that the speaker should "illustrate . . . the subject of which one treats." The narration or explication, continues Blair, should "throw light on all that follows" (2:174–75). Richard Whately in *Elements of Rhetoric* (1828) writes of the importance of examples in the chapter on arguments (85–90). Finally, Alexander Bain in *English Composition and Rhetoric* (1866) uses the word *illustration* with reference to "methods of expounding the General Principle, or Proposition" (193). Bain links the use of illustration to the use of figures of similarity—that is, noting resemblances between two objects (196–203).

Many twentieth-century rhetoric texts, modeled after the "modes" approach to writing essays, use illustration as one of the several methods or patterns of organizing expository essays. The terms *exemplification* and *enumeration* are sometimes used synonymously with *illustration,* suggesting that the writer's major method of development is providing many appropriate examples to support the essay's general statements. Since the 1960s, a number of rhetoric texts have begun suggesting that all of the so-called patterns of organization can be used not only for organizing essays but also as systematic ways of exploring various subjects and generating ideas for essays. Using illustration and other organizational methods in this way hearkens back to Aristotle's idea of *topoi,* or topics, which is "a method for probing one's subject to discover possible ways of developing that subject" (Corbett 24). Frank D'Angelo has suggested that illustration and other conventional patterns of organizing paragraphs and essays are systematized ways in which many human minds in the Western tradition process information.

Illustration, then, like all the conventional patterns of organizing paragraphs and essays, is part of both invention and arrangement in the discipline of rhetoric.

David Sabrio
Texas A&M University, Kingsville

Bibliography

Aristotle. *The Art of Rhetoric.* Trans. John Henry Freese. Cambridge, MA: Harvard UP, 1926.

Bain, Alexander. *English Composition and Rhetoric. A Manual.* 1866. New York: Appleton, 1876.

Blair, Hugh. *Lectures on Rhetoric and Belles Lettres.* 1783. Ed. Harold F. Harding. Vol. 2. Carbondale: Southern Illinois UP, 1965.

Cicero. *De oratore.* Trans. E.W. Sutton. Cambridge, MA: Harvard UP, 1942.

Connors, Robert. "The Rise and Fall of the Modes of Discourse." *College Composition and Communication* 32 (1981): 444–63.

Corbett, Edward P.J. *Classical Rhetoric for the Modern Student.* 3rd ed. New York: Oxford UP, 1990.

D'Angelo, Frank. *A Conceptual Theory of Rhetoric.* Cambridge: Winthrop, 1975.

———. "Paradigms as Structural Counterparts of *Topoi.*" *Linguistics, Stylistics, and the Teaching of Composition.* Ed. Donald McQuade. Akron, OH: U of Akron Dept. of English, 1979.

"Illustration." *Oxford English Dictionary.* 1971 compact ed.

Quintilian. *Institutio Oratoria.* Trans. H.E. Butler. Cambridge, MA: Harvard UP, 1920.

Whately, Richard. *Elements of Rhetoric.* 1828. Ed. Douglas Ehninger. Carbondale: Southern Illinois UP, 1963.

See also MODES OF DISCOURSE

Imagery

In literary usage, images produced in the mind by language (effect) or to the imagery-bearing language itself and its signification (cause). The former is mental imagery; the latter is verbal imagery.

A verbal image is often called a "picture" made out of words, but it can appeal to senses other than sight (hearing, smell, taste, and touch), and to internal feelings. The language used to evoke imagery can be figurative or literal or both, as these lines from Elinor Wylie's *Puritan Sonnet* demonstrate:

> I love those skies, thin blue or snowy gray, Those fields sparse-planed, rendering meager sheaves; That spring, briefer than apple-blossom's breath, summer, so much too beautiful to stay, Swift autumn, like a bonfire of leaves, And sleepy winter, like the sleep of death.

Figurative imagery involves metaphor, simile, and other figures of speech (such as metonymy, synecdoche, personification, allegory), by means of which one thing (vehicle) is said while another (tenor) is meant. A figurative image may be said to be abstract or concrete according to whether the vehicle is more abstract or more concrete than the tenor. While concrete images are common, abstract ones are rare. An example of abstract images is from T.S. Eliot's *The Love Song of J. Alfred Prufrock*: "Streets that follow like a tedious argument / Of insidious intent / To lead you to an overwhelming question." In its broad sense, metaphor is not only a figure of speech but also a figure of thought. It is a mode of apprehension and a means of perceiving and expressing something in a radically different way. In such a sense, figurative images are not simply decorative but serve to reveal aspects of experience in a new light.

Images that suggest further meanings and associations in ways that go beyond the vehicle-tenor relationship found in metaphor and other figures of speech are called symbols. The symbolic significance is often achieved through patterning: When images in a literary work are patterned in a special way, they may be invested with symbolic values and become symbolic images. Usually, image patterns are patterns of recurrence: the recurrence of the same image, or different images in a cluster, at intervals throughout the work. The pattern of images, with their symbolic kinship, forms a central image which can reinforce theme, setting, or characterization of the work.

Imagery is one of the more important literary, and especially, poetic devices. It is regarded as the "heart and soul of poetry" (Packard 93): a poet should never explain but imply what he means through imagery. That is what Archibald Macleish means by saying "A poem should not mean / But be" (*Ars poetica*). Even in poetry, however, imagery "must be part of a larger whole and cannot in and of itself constitute a whole. Far from being itself a unifying form, it must be unified along with all the other elements of a poem" (Preminger *et al.* 369).

Ning Yu
University of Arizona

Bibliography

Baldick, Chris. *The Concise Oxford Dictionary of Literary Terms*. Oxford: Oxford UP, 1990.

Cuddon, J.A. *A Dictionary of Literary Terms and Literary Theory*. Oxford: Blackwell, 1977.

Dupriez, Bernard. *A Dictionary of Literary Devices*. Toronto: U of Toronto P, 1991.

Morner, Kathleen, and Ralph Rausch. *NTC's Dictionary of Literary Terms*. Lincolnwood, IL: National Textbook, 1991.

Packard, William. *The Poet's Dictionary*. New York: Harper, 1989.

Preminger, Alex, et al., eds. *Princeton Encyclopedia of Poetry and Poetics*. Princeton: Princeton UP, 1974.

Wales, Katie. *A Dictionary of Stylistics*. London: Longmans, 1989.

See also FIGURES OF SPEECH; METONYMY; SYNECDOCHE

Imitation

Reproducing the style, argument, tone, or purposes of earlier texts. "And it is a universal rule of life," Quintilian writes in *The Institutes of Oratory,* "that we should wish to copy what we approve in others" (10.2.1). Although Quintilian's twelve-volume text treats imitation in the context of schoolroom exercise in rhetorical training, he gives keen importance to imitation's origin within human desire. Describing an institutional role for imitation that influenced rhetorical pedagogy for centuries, Quintilian equates imitation and a "rule of life" because we so often feel two emotions that are central to imitation: admiration and emulation. Rulelike in their processional order, these emotions run through all areas of social life, of which the art of discourse is only one. We admire someone or some quality of conduct; we wish to act like that person, to reproduce that action in our own conduct.

Imitation thus reflects deep-seated tendencies of individuals long before rhetorical pedagogy seized on and developed "doctrine" about rhetorical training based on imitation. "Imitation is natural to man from childhood," Aristotle notes, adding that a human being is "the most imitative creature in the world" (*Poetics* 4.5). Realizing this, we are able to appreciate why imitation has enjoyed such a long and varied history in rhetorical training—and why the history of imitation is beset, as well, by controversy.

As rhetorical practice, imitation has always had to negotiate a path between extremes of influence. On the one hand, excessive admiration for an author invites the attempt to follow the illustrious original too closely. The result is a loss—more precisely, an abdication—of the imitator's individuality. We might say that the prospect of having someone speak with the greatness of a Churchill or a Cicero is not unattractive. But in practice the particular style and inventions of these speakers, if revived with perfect fidelity, would be strange sounding, encrusted with historical idioms, and probably incapable of moving or enlightening an audience. As Erasmus noted in his brilliant attack on the idolatry of Ciceronian imitation, time and circumstance assume fluid shape and are continually reshaped, so that the eloquence appropriate to one season is soon unseasonable, perhaps even laughable.

At the opposite extreme, imitation can be resisted as a contaminating influence, so that the student of language would be unreceptive to the tones, values, and rhetorical devices that could enrich the mind and the expression of that mind. This resistance to imitation would enable the unconscious version of imitation to take over—the rule of admiration/emulation—and so allow nondiscursive models to form the person's character. The irony of avoiding conscious imitation, therefore, is that one remains unconsciously—or semiconsciously—imitative. The act of imitating begins long before a person is interested in formal, conscious effects of language. Aristotle notes that human beings are the most imitative creatures in the world. Most people do not doubt the formative importance of role models in early childhood development and, beyond that, of teenage and adult modulations of selfhood according to peer group modeling of behavior.

The motive for this psychological imitation is a desire for likeness. Carried to ultimate satisfaction, this desire would mean that we think or act exactly like another. We would become that person. Such a hypothetical outcome of imitation is only that, for the resemblance that leads to perfect identity with another is deflected by resemblances to other selves, which also exert their gravitational pull on the self. This movement from "person" as determinate being to person as the collocation of mediated and internalized selves marks the desired end of the academic training in literary and rhetorical imitation.

Imitation highlights a founding assumption of rhetorical art—that language is the crucial agency of community. Our spoken words bridge a physical distance between ourselves and our auditors, but this traversed distance is the allegorical sign of a larger event: Our words seek to effect a convergence of feeling or belief between speaker and auditor. The possibility of this convergence inheres in the basis of rhetorical proof, the enthymeme, which presents as a major premise some statement that everyone finds acceptable. One aim of speech within a Western rhetorical tradition is to produce *pistis* (belief), which will, in turn, produce consensus. A student trained to imitate models, to speak in different ways, could conform language and reasoning to the capacities of different audiences, and thus create that consubstantiality between speaker and audience, the rhetorically created scene of community. In the academic tradition, then, imitative exercises developed the personal potentialities of the individual speaker.

Although imitation is most often perceived in a context of personal influence, by which a model's value, belief, or way of thinking is allowed to color the imitator's, this relation to authorial models represented only one form of imitation. A common practice in composition training was to keep a copybook of phrases, grammatical structures, intriguing figures of speech, philosophical thoughts (*sententiae*)—in other words, a "storehouse" of eloquence built from continual and varied reading. The copybook method avoided the danger of excessive authorial influence in two ways. Often the quoted or paraphrased material was intended to exemplify a rhetorical mode rather than influence any moral value.

With that purpose in mind, Erasmus quotes the famous description of nighttime in Book 4 of Virgil's *Aeneid* as an example of *chronographia* (the device of describing a particular moment): Virgil's description has a larger rhetorical motive—our understanding of Queen Dido after Aeneas' abandonment is made vivid by contrasting nocturnal serenity to Dido's anguished tossing. The particularity of Virgil's description can remain in the literary matrix of his epic, but the procedure of chronographic description as the means to reveal states of human feeling can be used again and again—and in forms far different from that of epic poetry. The student of eloquence can imitate "freely"— finding in the affective values of a description a revealing corollary to psychological "time" or status. In this way the model author becomes a fertile field of imitation, without, however, gaining a predominance in the imitator's mind that would obstruct the entrance of other values and rhetorical modalities.

Imitative pedagogy, however, recognizes the intense affection and emulative desire aroused by individual rhetorical models. In addition to the copybook method, the tradition seeks to parlay attraction to particular authors into formative encounters—either by enjoining the writer to draw into emotional proximity with the model or by forming an adversarial relation to a model, in which the writer, wishing to turn an achievement of the past to resounding new purposes, seeks to "outdo" the original writer.

G.W. Pigman's lucid study of kinds of imitation classifies the first kind as "following," whereby the imitator reproduces the text with only minor adjustments in language, tone, or organization. A greater turn toward independent composition is transformation, which is linked to "following," but involves the literary metamorphosis of the original model's social issue and artistic form into contemporary terms (as in *West Side Story's* following of *Romeo and Juliet*). The third kind of imitation is known as "eristic" (etymologically related to "wrestling"), which involves the effort to surpass the rival author's construction of essential values and actions to which readers had given their allegiance. A classic instance of eristic imitation is Milton's *Paradise Lost*, which diligently observes the conventions of classical epic. These include scenes of ferocious war, compressing identity to a core of will, courage, and stratagem. But Milton's explicit aim is to replace the caparisoned steeds and armor-laden warriors with an ethic of heroic patience—as exemplified in the "greater man," Christ, who delivers us from the inward prison. Milton follows the high road of epic devices, indebted to his models, but he overthrows these in the name of a new purpose, the Christian epic. Imitation's degrees of indebtedness thus range across an index of dependence and identification, beginning with the echoic loyalty of following, and culminating in a rhetorical indebtedness disguised by sharply different purposes and allegiances.

Despite demarcations that allow us to discern graduated stages of learning and skill generated through imitative writing, the processes at work under the heading of "imitation" are in practice less tidy and less conscious than the theoretical descriptions suggest. Speaking of imitation in the Renaissance, Thomas Greene observes that "imitation could mean many things: the adoption of a given author's vocabulary, syntax, and stylistic mannerism, the adoption of his themes, his *sententiae*, his moral style, or the adoption of his characteristic genre with its associated topoi or the specific adaptation of a single work." This does not mean that the tripartite scheme "following, transforming, and overthrowing" is inaccurate as a schematization of imitation's particular processes. It suggests the varying force of our imitative desires. As we have seen, these range from an admiration that seeks union with the model (a desire that accounts for the mysterious continuity of literary traditions) to a receptivity to technical facilities of rhetoric. Learning technical skills from "models" carries along its own continuity. A rhetorical "storehouse" from which we draw different idioms enables us to reach across the sometimes Odysseylike distance that separates individual from individual and group from group.

Daniel Bender
Pace University

Bibliography

Bender, Daniel. "Diversity Revisited: Or, Composition's Alien History." *Rhetoric Review* 12 (1993): 108–24.

Conte, Gian Biagio. *The Rhetoric of Imitation: Genre and Poetic Memory in Virgil and Other Latin Poets*. Trans. and ed. Charles Segal. Ithaca, NY: Cornell UP, 1986.

Greene, Thomas M. *The Light in Troy: Imitation and Discovery in Renaissance Poetry*. New Haven: Yale UP, 1982.

Lunsford, Andrea A., and Lisa S. Ede. "On Distinctions between Classical and Modern Rhetoric." *Essays on Classical Rhetoric and Modern Discourse*. Ed. Robert J. Connors, Lisa S. Ede, Andrea A. Lunsford. Urbana: Southern Illinois UP, 1984. 37–49.

Pigman, G.W. "Versions of Imitation in the Renaissance." *Renaissance Quarterly* 33 (1980): 1–32.

Quintilian. *Institutes of Oratory*. 4 vols. Trans. H.E. Butler. Loeb Classical Library Series. Cambridge, MA: Harvard UP, 1922.

Sullivan, Dale. "Attitudes toward Imitation: Classical Culture and the Modern Temper." *Rhetoric Review* 8 (1989): 5–21.

Inclusio

Using the same word to begin and end a passage, poem, story, or play. J.L. Borges used inclusio in "The Fearful Sphere of Pascal," which begins as follows: "It may be that universal history is the history of a handful of metaphors." The same story ends: "It may be that universal history is the history of the different intonation given a handful of metaphors" (*Labyrinths*). Inclusio is used to create a sense of closure and completeness, as Stephen Crane illustrated: "Do not weep maiden, for war is kind. / Because your love turned wild hands toward the day / And the affrighted steed ran on alone, / Do not weep./ War is kind."

Arthur Quinn and Lyon Rathbun
University of California, Berkeley

Indian Rhetoric (Sanskrit)

In India, the systematic study of language, tracing its history back to the fifth century B.C.E. *Systematic*, in this context, refers to traditional sastraic exposition, involving (1) a study of what constitutes "knowledge" within the context of the specific investigation (*padartha-mimamsa*); (2) a study of the language (*sabda-mimamsa*) involved in the exposition of the knowledge specified in (1); and (3) a study of the validity of critical statements (*pramanya-mimamsa*) made in (1) and (2). The first and third aspects of sastraic exposition fall under the aegis of logic or *nyaya*, the second under grammar (*vyakarana*) and exegetical science (*mimamsa*). Rhetoric might also seem to subsume the activities associated with the second aspect of sastraic exposition.

Sanskrit scholars, however, invariably treat rhetoric as the study of figuration (*alamkara*). In fact, the term *alamkara* is used to denote a school of Sanskrit critics and scholars whose approach to language was essentially formalistic, inasmuch as they believed that formal structure distinguished poetic and rhetorical expression from ordinary utterances. The distinction between primary (*abhidha*) and secondary meaning (*lakshana*) runs throughout Indian thought. What distinguishes the Alamkara School and marks its particular contribution to Indian thought are the principles of "crooked speech" (*vakrokti*, which includes figuration, *alamkara*) and style (*riti*).

At the root of all figures is some element of exaggeration (*artisayokti*), or "crooked" or oblique manner of speech (*vakrokti*). Bhamaha (700–800 C.E.), one of the first writers on rhetoric per se, argued that even the simplest figures require a comparison of dissimilar objects. Bhamaha, however, did not allow that objective description (*svabhavokti*) was essentially figurative. Other writers of the Alamkara school—principally Udbhasta (8–9 C.E.), Dandin (800–900 C.E.), and Rudrata (900 C.E.)—found that even "objective description" was figurative insofar as it required "seeing" objects from a particular perspective. In fact, emotion (*rasa*) itself, which other Indian thinkers wished to view as the ultimate object of "artful writing," was represented by the Alamkara School as something inseparable from the figures required for its expression. The principle dictating the fusion of form and content was called simply "togetherness" (*sahitya*). That "fusion," however, should not be confused with what those of the Alamkara School thought to be the relation of word and sense necessary for intelligible speech. In this context, relating form and content embodies a particular tension (*paraspara-spardha*) between sound and sense—a tension that serves as the ground for one's awareness of the artifice in "crooked speech."

Style is the specific manner by which one is made aware of the artifice in "crooked speech." What is important here is not the specific classification of styles (for example, in terms of clarity [*prasada*] or energy [*Ojas*]), but the implication that style is not to be confused with figuration; style is seen to address some aspect of whatever "beauty" is to be found in language. This distinction is found from the earliest considerations of the subject in India and serves as a starting point for the investigation of Indian rhetorical theories.

David Metzger
Old Dominion University

Bibliography

Bhamaha. *Kavylankara of Bhama*. Ed. with an English translation and notes by P.V. Naganatha Sastri. Delhi: Motilal Banarsidass, 1970.

Chari, V.K. *Sanskrit Criticism*. Honolulu: U of Hawaii P, 1990.

Coward, Harold G., and K. Kunjunni Raja. *Encyclopedia of Indian Philosophies*. Vol. 5. *The Philosophy of The Grammarians*. Delhi: Motilal Banarsidass, 1990.

De, Sushil Kumar. *History of Sanskri Poetics*. 2 vols. 2nd ed. Calcutta: K.L. Mukhopadhyay, 1960.

Deshpande, Madhav H., trans. and ed. *The Meaning of Nouns: The Namarthanirnaya of Kaundabhatta*. Dordrecht: Kluwer Academic, 1992.

Devasthali, G.V. *Mimamsa: The Ancient Indian Science of Sentence Interpretation*. 2nd ed. Delhi: Sri Satguru, 1991.

Sastri, S. Kuppuswami. *A Primer of Indian Logic*. 3rd ed. Madras: Kuppuswami Sastri Research Institute, 1951.

Induction

The process of reasoning wherein individual instances or examples lead to a general conclusion. Inductive reasoning in rhetoric makes use of examples to suggest similarities between that which is known and that which is unknown. In most rhetorical situations, it is impossible (or at least impractical) to lead one's audience through a full induction in which every case is satisfied. Therefore, the inductive argument by example in rhetoric does not result in necessarily true conclusions, since certainty can be gained only through full induction or a complete enumeration of all possible examples. In rhetorical situations, a writer or speaker chooses known examples that are relevant to, and representative of, the unknown case. Generally speaking, as the number of pertinent examples increases, so does the degree of probability attached to the conclusion.

In illustrating some of the differences between reasoning in logic and reasoning in rhetoric, Richard Fulkerson points out that the persuasive impact of inductive reasoning in rhetoric is determined contextually instead of logically. That is, one must consider whether the examples one chooses are sufficient in the context of each rhetorical situation to persuade one's audience to make the necessary inductive leap, not whether they are stringent to logical standards. Fulkerson also cautions against the "ambiguous motion metaphor" contained in definitions of induction that define it as reasoning that "moves from" individual instances to a general conclusion. (The same holds true for similarly worded definitions of deduction.) That is, such definitions suggest that the order in which the parts of the argument are presented is of primary concern, rather than the type of reasoning at work.

Overgeneralization and attributing a cause-effect relationship where none exists are common pitfalls in inductive rhetorical arguments. Since only probable conclusions may be drawn when arguing from examples, one must usually qualify the general conclusions one draws. And when arguing inductively that certain things are the cause of something else, the need exists to be accurate and explicit about the links of the causal chain one develops.

Donald E. Bushman
University of North Carolina, Wilmington

Bibliography

Aristotle. *Rhetoric*. Trans. Lane Cooper. Englewood Cliffs, NJ: Prentice, 1932.

Fulkerson, Richard. "Technical Logic, Comp-Logic, and the Teaching of Writing." *College Composition and Communication* 39 (1988): 436–52.

Thompson, W.N. *Aristotle's Deduction and Induction: Introductory Analysis and Synthesis*. Amsterdam: Rodopi N.V., 1975.

See also DEDUCTION

Informal Logic

The field of intellectual inquiry that concerns the analysis and evaluation of nondemonstrative arguments, arguments in which tentativeness, probability, and contingency characterize the connection between premises and conclusions. In his preface to *The Way of Words* (1976), Ronald Munson tells the story of a friend who asked what he was writing. When Munson said that his book was about informal logic, the friend replied, "There is no such thing." Munson notes that it is disappointing to be told that you are writing a book on a nonexistent topic, but he persisted.

The anecdote can serve as a metaphor for the tension between logic, which for virtually its entire modern history in Western thought has been a formal field, and the relatively new field known as informal logic. Logic has been the study of the argument forms that reflect "valid" reasoning—that is, reasoning in which certain propositions (the premises) if accepted lead necessarily to the acceptance of another proposition, the conclusion. For most of the history of logic, its heart was the Aristotelian syllogism, or the string of syllogisms known as the *sorites*. When these mechanisms were used properly they produced "demonstrative arguments," arguments in which the premises "entailed" the conclusion. When used improperly, they manifested some identifiable error in form, such as the "undistributed middle term" or the "illicit major term."

In the twentieth century, formal logic expanded to include even more complex forms, thereby giving birth to symbolic or predicate logic. Still, two features characterized logic: entailment and formalism. Nonreferential logical variables, *Ps, Qs, Xs,* and so forth, became the key terms in logical expressions. What the variables stood for, or whether they stood for anything in the real world, was unimportant. If P implied Q, and Q was not true, then, necessarily, P could not be true. If P implied Q, and Q also implied R, then necessarily P implied R.

Ever since Aristotle formalized logic in his *Prior* and *Posterior Analytics,* logic dealt with such demonstrative arguments or "entailments." Arguments in which the conclusions followed only probably or contingently from the premises were of no concern. What would a geometry theorem be worth if it said, "Most of the time, the sum of the angles in a triangle is about 180 degrees"?

In one sense, informal logic has a long history: Aristotle laid the groundwork for not only formal logic in his *Prior* and *Posterior Analytics* but also for informal logic in his *Topics, On Sophistical Refutations,* and *Rhetoric.* Yet philosophy and rhetoric had existed in uneasy tension ever since Plato's attacks on the sophists, and philosophy divorced itself from rhetoric almost entirely about the time of the Renaissance. Philosophy claimed logic as its own, granting to rhetoric the leftovers of stylistic embellishment and emotional appeals. Whatever "argument" operated in real-world rhetorical discourse was virtually by definition fallacious and not worthy of logical analysis.

It is impossible to give a date for the modern informal logic movement, but two seminal documents were published in 1958, and a third in 1970. And the First International Symposium on Informal Logic was held in 1978 at the University of Windsor. One paper at the symposium said that in informal logic "there has not been any significant development since Aristotle" (Blair and Johnson 4).

The essential motivation for the seminal works in the field, as well as for the symposium and later the establishment of the journal *Informal Logic,* was "growing disenchantment with the capacity of formal logic to provide standards of good reasoning to illuminate the argumentation of ordinary discourse" (Blair and Johnson 5). (The *Informal Logic Newsletter* was begun by Johnson and Blair at the University of Windsor in 1978. It became the journal *Informal Logic,* published triannually, in 1984. Readers interested in informal logic should also be aware of the quarterly *Argumentation,* which began publication in 1987 in Holland.)

The three seminal modern works on informal logic are Stephen Toulmin's *Uses of Argument* (1958), Chaïm Perelman's and Lucie Olbrechts-Tyteca's *New Rhetoric: A Treatise on Argumentation* (published in French in 1958 and translated into English in 1969), and C.L. Hamblin's *Fallacies* (1970).

The first two books illustrate what might be called the affirmative or direct approach to informal logic, while the third illustrates the negative or indirect. All three share with the informal logic movement as a whole an attempt to answer this question: "In real-world, extended, nondemonstrative arguments, what constitutes a 'good' argument?" Or, to put it another way, "Under what conditions of argument are we justified in assenting to or asserting the truth of a claim?" Blair and Johnson define the field as "the area of logic . . . which attempts to formulate the principles and standards . . . necessary for the evaluation of argumentation" (4).

The affirmative approach to informal logic seeks to describe features of good arguments and to develop methods of teaching students to identify, analyze, and then evaluate extended arguments in real discourse. Toulmin proposed his now well known six-part argument scheme, based on jurisprudence, as a model of what transpires in practical argumentation where solid but rarely necessary conclusions can be reached through rational procedures. Perelman and Olbrechts-Tyteca collected hundreds of instances of argument and created a taxonomy of nondemonstrative argument moves, called "argument loci."

The negative approach to informal argument focuses on identifying the common features of poor arguments, called (material) fallacies. This approach assumes that students who learn to understand and recognize a number of traditional instances of poor argument (fallacies) will be better able to assess arguments in general. The approach also seems to assume that an argument free of significant fallacies is therefore good. (Again, Aristotle is the original source, because he first analyzed a number of fallacies in *On Sophistical Refutations*.) The first full-length modern treatment of fallacies was Hamblin's analysis in 1970, which found that while a great many writers had discussed such fallacies as the *ad hominem* and the *post hoc ergo propter hoc,* the study of fallacy was beset with unsystematic analysis and unclear and overlapping definitions; moreover, it lacked any unifying theoretical approach. A great deal more recent scholarship on fallacies has been produced by Douglas Walton and John Woods.

Currently, the field of informal logic is in its adolescence. It has grown a good deal but does not yet hold the status of a mature field with a reasonably well formed identity. It is making rapid progress but must contend with unresolved internal tensions as well as criticism or rejection by the formal logicians. Its participants agree upon their project, the analysis and evaluation of real-world, usually contingent, arguments expressed in natural language, but they do not yet share a model for their enterprise.

Richard Fulkerson
East Texas State University

Bibliography

Blair, J. Anthony, and Ralph H. Johnson. "The Current State of Informal Logic." *Informal Logic* 9 (1987): 147–51.

———. "The Recent Development of Informal Logic." *Informal Logic: The First International Symposium*. Ed. J. Anthony Blair and Ralph H. Johnson. Inverness, CA: Edgepress, 1980. 3–28.

Golden, James, Goodwin F. Berquist, and William E. Coleman, eds. *The Rhetoric of Western Thought*. 4th ed. Dubuque: Kendall/Hunt, 1989.

Govier, Trudy. "Are There Two Sides to Every Question?" *Selected Issues in Logic and Communication*. Ed. Trudy Govier. Belmont, CA: Wadsworth, 1988. 43–54.

Hamblin, C.L. *Fallacies*. London: Methuen, 1970.

Munson, Ronald. *The Way of Words: An Informal Logic*. Boston: Houghton, 1976.

Perelman, Chaïm, and Lucie Olbrechts-Tyteca. *The New Rhetoric: A Treatise on Argumentation*. Trans. John Wilkinson and Peircell Weaver. Notre Dame, IN: U of Notre Dame P, 1968.

Toulmin, Stephen. "Logic and the Criticism of Arguments." *The Rhetoric of Western Thought*. 4th ed. Ed. James L. Golden, Goodwin F. Berquist, William E. Coleman. Dubuque: Kendall/Hunt, 1989. 374–88.

———. *The Uses of Argument*. Cambridge: Cambridge UP, 1958.

Trapp, Robert, and Janice Schuetz. *Perspectives on Argumentation: Essays in Honor of Wayne Brockriede*. Prospect Heights, IL: Waveland, 1990.

Walton, Douglas. *The Place of Emotion in Argument*. University Park: Pennsylvania State UP, 1992.

Woods, John, ed. *Argumentation: Special Issue on Fallacies*. 1.3 (1987).

I

Invention

In rhetorical studies, usually the process and art of creation, discovery, or problem solving. Like *creation, invention* can refer to original composing; *creation,* however, is a somewhat broader term, since *invention* is usually associated today with the composition of nonfictional discourse, both written and spoken. It can refer to discovery, either deliberate or accidental, of a subject or an idea by intellect or imagination; and it can refer to problem solving, which can be a substantially more complex activity, more akin to creation though more deliberate. *Invention* can also refer to a result of such processes (that is, a concept or judgment, or argument, or solution, or the entire discourse in which such constructs are embedded). It can refer to the writer's or speaker's ability to carry out the process successfully (one can be inventive). It can refer to a theory of the process of original composing and to a formal art (that is, an explicit method) based on the theory, the function of which is to enhance one's ability to engage in the process. And it can refer to a subject of rhetorical pedagogy whose function is to teach the student writer to carry out the process more effectively (the study of invention).

But the definitions of *invention* differ not only in the kind of thing referred to (a process, the outcome of a process, a theory, and so forth). They also have changed over time, often radically. What one finds in the twenty-five-hundred-year history of rhetorical invention is a sequence of reinterpretations in terms of fresh conceptions and different intentions, and these reinterpretations have been met with resistance which itself has often encouraged novel interpretation. Because the meaning of *rhetorical invention* has been so fluid and contested, one is inclined to agree with Friedrich Nietzsche (1844–1900) when he remarks in his *Genealogy of Morals* that terms with histories cannot be defined. At the very least, one can say that *invention* presents special difficulties for anyone seeking to offer a comprehensive definition.

In rhetorical studies, the art of rhetorical invention, which is what *invention* usually refers to, has been traditionally defined as an explicit and organized way of discovering the content of a discourse, especially persuasive discourse. It is usually contrasted with the arts of arrangement, style, memory, and delivery, which, taken together, constitute the classical art of rhetoric. Despite its having become conventional, however, the definition is not wholly satisfactory, for it implies that content and language are sharply separable, a common though questionable assumption. Still other definitions have been offered, each of which implies sometimes very different theoretical assumptions and different methods of composing designed to serve very different purposes. Invention has been defined, for example, as the creative act as it manifests itself in rhetorical composition; as

a conscious procedure for systematically taking an inventory of possible premises and forms of argument; as an investigative research methodology; as a generalized art of inquiry; as an art of devising true or plausible matter that will make a case convincing to a particular audience; as a method for not only finding but also organizing subject matter; as that part of the rhetorical art concerned with the created world of the writer; as an art of questioning in the presence of wonder. None of the definitions wholly capture what happens when the mind engages in its most sophisticated work, though some come closer than others; all end in some form of reduction. Any definition is embedded in history, in the theoretical, psychological, political, ethical, and educational beliefs prevalent at a particular time. That being the case, no definition is likely to satisfy all or for very long.

The definition of rhetorical invention has often included not only the production of discourse but its interpretation as well, readers or listeners being seen as engaging in a kind of secondary composing, re-creating a discourse and its conditions in their own minds. Unlike invention as a method in writing and speaking, however, invention as a method of interpretation is often used with both fictional and nonfictional texts. Different rhetorics can provide explicit methods or, in the absence of explicit methods, orientations for approaching particular texts as well as the theoretical discriminations necessary for a more speculative, philosophic engagement with discourse generally. Different theories of invention offer bases for probing and understanding such critical issues as intention, textual traditions, the place of texts in larger ongoing conversations of the society, and the way beliefs are created and negotiated. Invention, then, has often been regarded as a critical art as well as a productive art, a single set of principles serving for both composing and comprehending. The two arts of composing and comprehending merge in rhetorical criticism, where the critic of a text is at once an audience, whether reader or listener, and a creator of discourse about the text for other audiences. Some critics have argued that rhetorical criticism is one among several methods of practical criticism; others see literary criticism as a special instance of a more inclusive rhetorical criticism. Not surprisingly, rhetorical criticism has taken a number of forms, the result of different rhetorical theories and different understandings among adherents of particular theories.

The Art of Rhetorical Invention

It is possible, of course, to compose and criticize without either theoretical understanding of the processes or formal instruction for carrying them out. But like other complex and fundamentally important abilities, they have from ancient Greece to the present held the attention of many of our best minds and have occupied an important place in academic curricula. Given the complexity of the processes and their significance to our civilization, it is not surprising that they have been the subject of a large body of theory, that numerous attempts have been made to develop arts for improving the ability to engage in the processes, and that extensive efforts have been made to teach the arts in programs of rhetorical instruction.

An art of rhetorical invention is usually thought of as a method or suggestions for proceeding effectively in complex, nonroutine situations, the general purpose being the use of what is known to go beyond it to what is not known. It must not be confused with a theory of invention. An art of invention is not a theoretical system, although it may be embedded in theories of or at least generalizations about expert practice, creativity and inquiry, learning and attitude change, the nature of knowledge, linguistics, and so on. It is to be judged not as we might judge a theory (by its coherence, completeness, and simplicity or by its explanatory power) but by its ability to improve performance.

Formal arts of invention are, basically, heuristic procedures, that is, discovery procedures, *heuristic* being a term in ancient Greek rhetoric for much the same thing referred to by the Latin-derived *invention*. Heuristics are not rigid rules, like algorithms in mathematics, but useful rules of thumb, strategies of proceeding that have proven usefulness. Because any process of discovery moves from the known to the unknown and from the present to the absent, no hard and fast rules can be stated in advance that will ensure the desired results. Heuristics often take the form of suggestions for proceeding or questions to be answered. Their function is to prompt memory, observation, and inference in the conduct of inquiry. A fully articulated art of invention will offer a set or sets of such procedures plus any explanation necessary for their understanding and use.

The art of invention in classical rhetoric can be used to instantiate these generalizations, although it should be kept in mind that other arts may differ from it substantially, not only in the way inventive processes are carried out but in the goals as well. Although there are other possible sources for the arts of rhetoric, Aristotle (384–322 B.C.E.) tells us that his art of rhetoric was based on inductive generalizations about the practice of those who argue effectively. Such generalizations both provide insight into the nature of effective practice and can be used as a foundation for rhetorical arts. What Aristotle and his heirs sought to develop was a discipline for addressing problems and creating arguments in the area of the probable and contingent, where truth is not or cannot be known and proof is impossible. Traditionally, classical rhetoric (if we can for convenience reduce that historical complexity to a single entity) has been concerned with persuasive writing and speaking in the rough and tumble of actual public controversies. It has held out the possibility of intelligent procedure in addressing legal, political, and moral issues that is comparable to but different from the procedures offered for constructing philosophic and scientific arguments, where greater degrees of precision are both possible and necessary for the persuasion of more learned audiences.

The classical art of invention offers procedures for addressing many of the fundamental choices in composing persuasive arguments on public issues; it also offers procedures for criticizing the results of composition, as the art of composing provides the concepts necessary for an art of reading. For example, in a controversy it provides an ordered series of questions that help one consider the main issue to be argued, called the *stasis* or *status*: questions of fact (does it exist? did it actually happen as claimed?), of definition (if it happened, what kind of thing is it that happened?), of quality (is it desirable?), of procedure (in law, does the court have jurisdiction? is the charge proper?). Classical invention also provides heuristics for the various kinds of speeches (deliberative, forensic, and epideictic, which entail, in turn, the ethical considerations of advantage, justice, and honor). And it provides heuristics for developing the various parts of the discourse itself (the exordium, narration, partition, proof, refutation, and conclusion), which entails developing mutually reinforcing appeals to the character of the speaker, to the emotions of the audience, and to logic. For developing the logical dimension of the discourse, it provides heuristics that can be used in shaping any argument (the "common topics" and "proofs") and more specialized heuristics (the "special topics") for the discovery of arguments in particular subject areas. Some have argued that the topics of classical invention are simply an adventitious collection of intellectual moves that have proven to be useful in public argument; others have argued that the topics (or some subset of them) are fundamental acts of cognition that are or should be brought into play any time that one engages in original composing.

The end of an art of invention is not only knowledge (in the form of possible arguments, for example) but also enhanced performance in the creation of effective arguments for particular audiences, a dynamic, highly adaptive, by and large unpredictable process. Artistic performance requires more than knowledge of an art of invention and its underlying principles. It requires substantial training, including repeated practice in imaginative use of method in a variety of rhetorical situations, as the unforeseeable particularities confronted in practice make their own contributions to the development of rhetorical expertise. Artistic performance also requires knowledge of exemplary products of rhetorical processes. Finally, since an art of invention cannot substitute for subject knowledge, skillful performance requires substantial knowledge of the subject at issue, one reason why the tradition of classical rhetoric has been one of the grand intellectual and educational traditions in Western civilization.

Divergent Views

Even among classical rhetoricians, however, where the theory and art of invention have been developed over twenty-five hundred years to a high level of sophistication, there is disagreement over fundamental issues: whether, for example, invention is concerned essentially with a creative process (such as the development of concepts, judgments, and arguments that are both original and functional) or with the retrieval and use in particular situations of already existing concepts, judgments, and arguments—whether it is concerned with inquiry and making or with memory and application. For example, Francis Bacon (1561–1626) in his *Advancement of Learning* compares invention in classical rhetoric and invention in the then emerging natural science and argues that classical rhetoric is concerned primarily with the application of preexisting beliefs widely shared in the community to social problems for the purpose of persuasion. Rhetoric for Bacon is an instrument for addressing social differences, in contrast to science, which is an instrument for producing knowledge of the natural world. For Bacon, rhetorical invention is an aid to the rhetorician in accessing information relevant to the situation at hand: It provides procedures for systematically retrieving information from memory for use in developing a persuasive argument. Others, however, have argued that classical invention is concerned with the creation of new knowledge in situations that call for interpretation and probabilistic argument, as in political argument and rhetorical criticism.

During the eighteenth and nineteenth centuries, a new art of invention emerged that was a radical departure from its classical counterpart. It rests on assumptions that derive not from the observation of expert performance but from eighteenth-century logic and associationist psychology. A component of what is sometimes called "current-traditional rhetoric," it became normative in composition instruction during the early twentieth century and remains the accepted method in many schools throughout the country. Much simpler than classical invention, it offers a three-step procedure that entails selecting and narrowing a subject, composing a thesis statement (usually by making a predication about the subject), and planning the argument (which usually entails constructing a formal outline that will then be elaborated into a fully developed text).

The simple, highly general aspect of this method reflects several broad changes in rhetoric during the last two centuries. One such change has been the gradual extension of the domain of rhetoric to include not only discourse designed for the conduct of public affairs, a characteristic of classical rhetoric, but also learned discourse of all sorts and more personal forms, such as the essay. Among other changes shaping current-traditional invention have been a shift in focus in the discipline of rhetoric away from invention to matters of structure, style, and mechanics, the discipline of logic subsuming many of the concerns of rhetorical invention; the tendency to see the end of rhetoric as the presentation of knowledge acquired by the individual rather than the use of the community's wisdom to address problems of social discord and social policy; and a tendency among educators to regard composing as a formal activity, the goal being the production of texts that meet certain normative requirements (such as unity, coherence, order, completeness), this in contrast with classical rhetoric's goal of psychological change in a particular audience.

Since the 1950s, partly in response to the perceived inadequacies of current-traditional invention, several alternatives have been proposed, among them a method based principally on the work of Gordon Rohman and associated with the term *prewriting*. The method grows out of Rohman's interest in the radically perspectival nature of composing and the psycholinguistic process by which the individual converts events into experiences. Another alternative, still not fully developed and assimilated into modern rhetorical studies, is based on the work of Kenneth Burke. Although his work has been highly influential among rhetorical critics, Burke has not encouraged using his work as the basis of an art of invention designed for the production of discourse. Nevertheless, what has been done to this end is promising enough to invite further effort. Other alternatives to current-traditional invention have been based on the assumptions and methods of tagmemic linguistics, principally in the work of Richard Young, Alton Becker, and Kenneth Pike, and on the work of Linda Flower and John R. Hayes in cognitive psychology.

These last two approaches can be thought of as problem-solving methods, as can to some extent classical invention, largely because of the concept of *status* in Roman rhetoric and the more recently developed concept of rhetorical situation. The heuristics of problem-solving rhetorics are embedded in a process of inquiry that John Dewey (1859–1952) in *How We Think* called "reflective thinking," a process characterized by a felt difficulty (an unanalyzed state of perplexity, hesitation, unease) followed by suggestions for responding to the difficulty and investigations that serve to corroborate or nullify the suggestions. One strength of conceiving of invention as problem-solving is that it addresses the question of motivation in composing in a way that is productive both theoretically and pedagogically, since reflective thought generally and rhetorical situations in particular are seen as having their genesis in felt difficulties. And it expands rhetorical theory and research to include a good deal of the extensive philosophical and psychological literature on the nature of problems and problem-solving and provides a basis for explicit instruction in processes of invention as well. Another strength

is that it can accommodate a very wide range of rhetorical situations and discourse types.

This last claim is not without difficulties, however. It has been argued not only that invention is a natural and necessary part of every discipline and that each discipline develops its own subject-specific arts of inquiry and discourse, but also that the arts are not transferable from one subject area to another and hence that one must learn a new art of rhetoric with every disciplinary community one seeks to enter. As for those generic arts of invention developed for use in more than one discipline, they are either useless or, a less extreme position, less powerful than discipline-specific methods, though they may have some utility in situations where there are no discipline-specific methods or where one has not yet mastered a discipline-specific method. Classical invention's provision of both common topics and special topics seems pertinent to the debate over the relative merits of generic and specialized methods, although in speaking of generic methods, modern rhetoricians are likely to have a much wider range of application in mind than did their classical counterparts when speaking of the common topics.

Early advocates of generic methods tended to overlook the importance of a rich store of knowledge relevant to the problem at hand. They also assumed that heuristics would allow one to access readily what was known and relevant and that transfer across disciplinary contexts and subject matters would happen automatically. Those arguing that cognitive skills are context-bound tended to neglect the potentially useful role of generic heuristics in nonroutine situations and in helping one retrieve and apply domain-specific knowledge and methods. They also tended to overlook the possibility that the absence of necessary conditions for transfer rather than domain specificity might be responsible for a lack of transfer. Though many questions remain unanswered, recent research suggests that under certain conditions people are able to transfer skills, a view that tends to support the utility of arts of invention.

Controversy has also centered on differing assumptions about the relative autonomy of the self and their implications for the inventive act. In what has been throughout much of our history the dominant conception of original composing, the process is thought of as a solitary activity carried out by an autonomous individual who creates new meanings out of his own resources. Recently, largely under the influence of social constructionist theories, invention has been seen as a social act. The social constructionist argues that everyone, including the writer, is a product of a society's distinctive ideology, being constituted by its numerous discourses—in which case the concept of an autonomous essential self takes on something like the status of myth. Thus a text is the product of a social collaboration, either directly through the collaboration of two or more individuals or less directly, but nevertheless significantly through the influence of socially constructed language patterns, actual and imagined audiences, communally shared beliefs, prior texts, social processes, institutions, and so on.

Not all would agree that an art of invention has a place in rhetoric, no matter what form it may take. Many today agree with the Renaissance logician Peter Ramus (1515–1572) that invention is not properly a part of rhetoric, that a concern with the construction of effective arguments belongs in logic, which since the Renaissance has undergone a metamorphosis from the art of learned discourse to the discipline concerned with the nature and conduct of inquiry. Others agree with the eighteenth-century critic Hugh Blair (1718–1800), in his *Lectures on Rhetoric and Belles Lettres*, that a thorough knowledge of the subject thoughtfully considered is more effective in original composing than a formal art of invention. Blair's position can be read, at least in part, as a response to the expansion of the domain of rhetoric during this period to include a much wider range of discourses than those designed for the conduct of public affairs; no single art, he asserted, could help one develop arguments for such a wide range of subjects, audiences, and purposes. Both Ramus's and Blair's positions tend to reduce rhetoric, as a discipline, to matters of organization, style, and presentation; in which case writing and speaking are likely to be conceived of as clothing already developed ideas in effective language. Hence, "mere rhetoric."

Still others, influenced by Romantic literary theorists, have argued that the creative act is highly personal, exceedingly complex, and for the most part unconscious, at least in its essential features, and hence not susceptible either to analysis or generalization. Any explicit art for influencing the creative act is bound to be reductive in conception

and will, when used, distort and impede the creative process. To borrow the popular metaphors, forcing a formal art on an inherently organic process results in mechanical discourse mechanically produced, a view that implies that invention should not be taught, at least explicitly as a formal art. Those holding this position disagree on whether the ability to engage in original composition is a gift that some have and others do not, or an ability characteristic of all human beings. For those arguing that giftedness is a prerequisite to original composition, the study of invention is irrelevant to the discipline of rhetoric, since a gift can be neither taught nor learned. The most that education can do is to cultivate the judgment of the writer, that is, develop a critical ability useful in controlling the exuberance of genius.

Those arguing that creativity is a characteristic human ability are likely to seek ways of nurturing it in the classroom by encouragement and practice, immersion in the subject under consideration, and critical study of original discourse (that is, the products of highly inventive people). The argument of this group probably gave rise to the familiar statement that "writing can be learned but not taught," "writing" here referring to original composing rather than effective use of more conventional features of discourse such as mechanics and usage, which do lend themselves to direct instruction.

Recent research in the psychology of composing, most notably by Carl Bereiter and Marlene Scardamalia, suggests that some of the conflicts among the often very different positions on invention may be the result of at least two fundamentally different strategies people make use of in writing, one that can be characterized as "knowledge telling" and the other as "knowledge transforming." The former is a more naturally occurring ability; the latter, more studied and less common. The two strategies use different methods of proceeding and require different degrees of deliberation and strategic control over parts of the composing process. In original composing the knowledge-telling strategy makes use of cues from the topic, the genre being produced, and the text already produced. The knowledge-transforming strategy incorporates the knowledge-telling strategy; a more complex way of proceeding, it is essentially a problem-solving procedure that entails a reciprocal interaction between developing knowledge and developing text in the process of composing.

Which position on invention one accepts from among the various positions articulated over the twenty-five-hundred-year history of rhetoric has a great deal to do with whether one considers rhetoric itself to be a major discipline concerned with a fundamental and distinctively human activity or whether it has some relatively peripheral place in humanity's intellectual work. Throughout its history, rhetoric's vitality and significance have been closely bound up with the role invention plays in it—that is, with the capacity of rhetoric to deal formally with issues of thought as well as issues of language.

Richard E. Young
Carnegie Mellon University

Bibliography

Bereiter, Carl, and Marlene Scardamalia. *The Psychology of Written Composition.* Hillsdale, NJ: Erlbaum, 1987.

Black, Edwin. *Rhetorical Criticism: A Study in Method.* New York: Macmillan, 1965. Rpt. Madison: U of Wisconsin P, 1978.

Corbett, Edward P.J. "Introduction." *Rhetorical Analyses of Literary Works.* New York: Oxford UP, 1969.

Crowley, Sharon. *The Methodical Memory: Invention in Current-Traditional Rhetoric.* Carbondale: Southern Illinois UP, 1990.

Howell, Wilbur Samuel. *Eighteenth-Century British Logic and Rhetoric.* Princeton: Princeton UP, 1971.

———. *Logic and Rhetoric in England, 1500–1700.* New York: Russell, 1961.

Kennedy, George A. *Classical Rhetoric and Its Christian and Secular Tradition from Ancient to Modern Times.* Chapel Hill: U of North Carolina P, 1980.

Perelman, Chaïm, and L. Olbrechts–Tyteca. *The New Rhetoric: A Treatise on Argumentation.* Trans. John Wilkinson and Purcell Weaver. Notre Dame, IN: U of Notre Dame P, 1969.

Young, Richard. "Invention: A Topographical Survey." *Teaching Composition: 10 Bibliographical Essays.* Ed. Gary Tate. Fort Worth: Texas Christian UP, 1976. 1–43.

———. "Recent Developments in Rhetorical Invention." *Teaching Composition: Twelve Bibliographical Essays.* Ed. Gary Tate. Fort Worth: Texas Christian UP, 1987. 1–38.

Irony

Made its first appearance in Plato's *Republic*. Socrates had one of his interlocutors use the term *eironeia* as a pejorative characterization of his own dialectical method: "a low down way of taking people in." This characterization reveals the Greek suspicion of irony as an abusive and deceptive use of language; anyone who practiced *eironeia* was an *eiron*—a dissembler. In the *Ethics*, Aristotle distinguished irony from its opposite, *alazony,* or boastful exaggeration. Through his other writings, irony shed some of its negative behavioral connotations and became focused into a rhetorical figure. As a figure, the essence of irony for Aristotle was praising by blaming and blaming by praising. Cicero dignified irony by explaining it as the "wholly admirable urbane pretense of Socrates," and he was the first classical scholar to generalize irony according to positive characteristics from a mere figure of speech to an admirable habit of discourse. Quintilian clarified the Ciceronian distinction by developing two categories of irony: "trope" and "schema." Trope refers to a brief figure of speech embedded in a straightforward context. Schema refers to cases of irony. It characterizes an entire speech that is presented in language and a tone that conflicts with the true nature of the situation. Schema also refers to a man's life in which his outward appearance and behavior conflicts with his true, underlying nature.

The Latin word *ironia* was first translated into English as *yronye* in *Thordynary of Crysten men* in 1502. From 1502 to the mid eighteenth century, irony was carried on in the tradition of Cicero and Quintilian, being understood primarily as a rhetorical figure of speech. Typical definitions during that period included "saying the contrary of what one means," "saying one thing but meaning another," and "praising in order to blame and blaming in order to praise." After the concept was adopted into general use in the eighteenth century, scholars began defining and applying irony in significantly new ways, taking irony beyond the realm of "figured" status into philosophical inquiry and speculation. These new conceptions and approaches to irony reflected, as well as influenced, the changing epistemological positions in Europe during the mid 1700s, especially in Germany. Muecke parallels this change with the "heightened philosophical and aesthetic speculation" of the German Romantics. The prominent "ironologists" were Francis Schlegel, August Wilhelm Schlegel, and Karl

Solger. Their major contributions came through their development of the concept "World Irony." Schlegel's conception of irony lay in recognizing that the world was essentially paradoxical. Similarly, Solger argued that genuine irony began from contemplating the fundamental incongruities that existed between the individual and the universe. During the same intellectual expansion, Schlegel developed the concept of Romantic Irony, encompassing the ironies inherent in the very fact of being an artist. To Schlegel, the ironic position of the artist derived from having to occupy polemic positions: (such as subjective/objective, creative/critical).

Thirwall's article "On the Irony of Sophocles" in 1833 represented the next significant contribution to the development of irony. Reflecting the influence of his German predecessors, Thirwall introduced "dialectical irony," a type of irony distinct from verbal, or rhetorical, irony. Thirwall's theory held that irony could be found in life as well as literature. Encompassed in this theory was the idea of "Irony of Fate," that is, irony can exist without an ironist. Expanding Schlegel's notion of irony as paradox, Thirwall argued that irony may reside in the attitude of the ironic observer, or, more specifically, in a feature of a situation that evokes an ironic assessment by the observer.

While irony gained prominence as an intellectual topic during the Romantic Movement, this new conceptualization brought with it a host of issues and problems that scholars continue to address. Booth argued that the Romantic Movement resulted in the "naturalization" of irony. Irony was no longer the creation of an ironist pursuing a rhetorical effect; rather, irony had become a "creature of nature," as it was increasingly viewed as an inherent aspect of the individual's relationship to the universe. The consequences of this naturalization are twofold: It obscured the notion of irony and, furthermore, subordinated the ironist to the ironic effect.

As ironologists have recognized the increasing obscurity and vacuity of irony, they have responded with a plethora of approaches to reestablish the territory of irony. The approaches include taxonomies of and arguments about the definitions of irony, the locus of ironic meaning, and the functions of irony.

Defining irony has been a perennial problem for scholars. The most common definitions have consistently proven inadequate, as they fail to distinguish irony from other major tropes (such as metaphor, allegory, and so forth); furthermore, such definitions fail to address the underlying rhetorical nature of irony.

Muecke's taxonomy of the formal elements of irony and his general two-part classification of irony represent significant inroads to clarifying the distinctive features of irony. Muecke elaborates his definition of irony through a taxonomy of its essential, formal elements, which are distinct from its subjective (irony is not a quality inherent in a remark) and aesthetic (ironic statements exhibit balance and precision) elements. First, irony is a double-layered phenomenon, with the "lower level" containing the situation as it *appears* to the victim of the irony or as it is deceptively presented by the ironist; the "upper level" contains the situation as it *really* is, from the vantage point of the ironist or observer. Secondly, these two levels are always in an oppositional relationship, be it one of incongruity, incompatibility, or contradiction. Finally, ironic phenomena contain a degree of "innocence," which is exhibited either through the victim's confident unawareness of an appearance/reality discrepancy or through the ironist's pretension that no such discrepancy exists.

Muecke's classification of irony into two general types, verbal ("He is being ironic") and situational ("It is ironic that . . ."), echoes the distinction that surfaced during the German Romantic period. The main difference between these two types lies in the role of the ironist. While verbal irony implies an ironist who intentionally creates the irony, situational irony does not; rather, it is a "condition of affairs" that is felt to be ironic. Furthermore, analyzing verbal and situational ironies entails different projects: With verbal ironies, the focus of analysis is on the ironist's techniques, while the observer's ironic sense and attitudes are the focus when analyzing situational ironies.

Muecke's definition and classification have been modified and elaborated by contemporary scholars from literary and rhetorical theory. The seminal contributions of Booth and Kaufer argue that irony is best conceptualized and applied as an essentially rhetorical phenomenon. Both scholars argue that ironic analysis functions as a kind of knowing capable of withstanding skeptical challenges to claims of (and about) knowledge; as such, irony can serve as an exemplar for addressing broader epistemological questions concerning meaning.

Booth's rhetoric of irony represented an attempt to reign in irony and ironic interpretation within the broader context of rhetorical studies. Elevating verbal irony over situational, he argues for the notion of "stable irony" and a four-part heuristic which, taken together, help answer the question "How do we *know* a text is ironic?" Booth defines stable irony as an intentional act of an author, covertly expressed in the text, which is recovered through a stable reconstructive act, resulting in the reader's reconstructing a new local and finite meaning. According to Booth, authorial intention is the necessary element for judging a text to be ironic (or not); the reader's ironic interpretation of a text is limited to the extent that the author intended a specific textual feature to induce an ironic reading.

Kaufer contends that a proper conception of irony requires understanding that its primary rhetorical function is to render evaluative judgments—that is, to negatively evaluate the literal judgment proffered. As such, irony is not discernible in an objective, decontextualized feature of an utterance; rather, ironic opposition resides in the tension between the ironist's subjective attitude and the attitude implied by the expectational context established by the literal meaning of the utterance. Because of irony's more overt content-context interdependencies, Kaufer argues that irony can serve as a prototype for explaining the comparatively covert content-context interdependencies in conventional (nonironic) utterances.

Patricia L. Dunmire and David S. Kaufer
Carnegie Mellon University

Bibliography

Booth, Wayne C. *A Rhetoric of Irony*. Chicago: U of Chicago P, 1974.
Fish, Stanley. "Short People Got No Reason to Live: Reading Irony." *Daedalus* 112 (1983): 175–91.
Frye, Northrop. *Anatomy of Criticism: Four Essays*. Princeton: Princeton UP, 1957.
Kaufer, David S. "Ironic Evaluations." *Communications Monographs* 48 (1981): 25–38.
———. "Irony and Rhetorical Strategy." *Philosophy and Rhetoric* 10 (1977): 90–110.
Kierkegaard, Soren. *The Concept of Irony, with Constant Reference to Socrates*. Trans. Lee M. Capel. London: Collins, 1966.
Knox, Norman. *The Word IRONY and Its Context, 1500–1755*. Durham, NC: Duke UP, 1961.
Muecke, Donald C. *The Compass of Irony*. London: Methuen, 1969.
———. *Irony*. London: Methuen, 1970.
Myers, Greg. "The Rhetoric of Irony in Academic Writing." *Written Communication* 7 (1990): 419–55.
Poetics Today: The Ironic Discourse 4 (1983).
Rorty, Richard. *Contingency, Irony, and Solidarity*. Cambridge: Cambridge UP, 1989.
Welleck, René. *A History of Modern Criticism 1750–1950*. Vol. 2. *The Romantic Age*. New Haven: Yale UP, 1955.
Woolgar, Steve. "Irony in the Social Study of Science." *Science Observed: Perspectives on the Social Study of Science*. Ed. Karin D. Knorr-Cetina and Michael Mulkay. London: Sage, 1983. 239–66.

See also FIGURES OF SPEECH

Isocolon

Repetition of phrases in the same grammatical form but in different words. "In peace, sons bury their fathers; in war, fathers bury their sons" (Herodotus). The parallel elements are usually parallel in length (the same number of words or syllables) as well as in structure. Churchill described the plight of the politician: "He is asked to stand, he wants to sit, and he is expected to lie." While the related figure, polyptoton (q.v.), cannot be extended beyond the sentence without appearing contrived, the isocolon can extend through whole passages, as exemplified in this segment of Paul's Second Letter to the Corinthians: "But in all things approving ourselves as the ministers of God, in much patience, in afflictions, in necessities, in distresses. In stripes, in imprisonments, in tumults, in afflictions, in labors, in watchings, in fastings; By pureness, by knowledge, by long-suffering, by kindness, by the Holy Ghost, by love unfeigned, by the word of truth, by the power of God, by the armor of righteousness on the right hand and on the left. By honor and dishonor, by evil report and good report: as deceivers, and yet true; as unknown, and yet well known; as dying, and, behold, we live; as chastened, and not killed; as sorrowful, yet always rejoicing; as poor, yet making many rich; as having nothing, and yet possessing all things."

Arthur Quinn and Lyon Rathbun
University of California, Berkeley

Isocrates

A rhetor who distinguished himself in the radical cultural changes of fourth century B.C.E. Athens by opening a school of rhetoric and by writing some of the most effective early prose we have. A contemporary and at times a competitor of Plato, Isocrates established in the 390s B.C.E. one of the most important schools in ancient Greece. His extensive course of study provided a model of education for at least twenty-two hundred years and led to Isocrates' designation as one of the founders of the liberal arts. In addition to his pedagogical work, he wrote numerous speeches, twenty-one of which are extant. It is one of the apparent ironies of Isocrates' life that he taught speaking but did not speak in public. While the ancient biographical tradition (and most subsequent commentators) indicate that stage fright and a weak voice led him to present his work in writing rather than in speaking, recent research (for example, Welch 117–24) has offered alternative reasons for this stance. Isocrates was committed to writing as a primary form of communication.

In the public and the private discourse of fourth-century B.C.E. Greece, rhetoric, education, and culture assumed increasing importance. In the years following the Peloponnesian War, the power of language and education acquired new importance. This context of cultural fluctuation produced two important groups that included Isocrates in its number: the Attic orators and the sophists.

The Attic orators have conventionally been numbered as ten. Aside from Isocrates, they include Antiphon, Lysias, Andocides, Isaeus, Demosthenes, Aeschines, Lycurgus, Hyperides, and Dinarchus. Working in the Attic dialect, these accomplished orators and writers composed what George Kennedy has called a literary genre. Part of their writing came about in their roles as logographers, or writers paid to compose court speeches. They flourished in the context of rising judicial importance, the empowerment of many individuals, and a remarkable desire to litigate that was common in the culture. In fact, Greek oratory consisted partly of court speeches written by the sometimes invisible logographers. Isocrates worked as a logographer for ten years until 403 B.C.E. The writing out of discourse that would be spoken (such as the court speeches) and that also would be maintained as writing reveals the unique relationship of writing and speaking in Isocrates' fourth-century context. The canon of the ten Attic orators comes to us in the form

of writing and is either Alexandrian or from the Roman Caecilius of Calacte. The list is probably an arbitrary one.

Isocrates has traditionally enjoyed more prestige in his role as an Attic orator than as one of the sophists. The latter group, who began as largely respectable language teachers, became so sought after that many unscrupulous people joined their profession. A new population needed their training and was seriously attracted to their lectures. The sophists, who were more profit-oriented, contributed substantially to the steadily declining reputation of some members of the group. Isocrates provides an interesting case in the history of sophism because his school made him wealthy, but that wealth did not hurt his reputation. He succeeded at a unique balancing act: He collected large fees at his school and maintained distance from some other sophists, whose equally large fees contributed to their bad reputations. Plato and his Socrates represent a prevalent opinion in their lodging of numerous complaints against the fees charged by the sophists. In spite of this condemnation, and typical of his distinction from other sophists, Isocrates receives praise at the end of Plato's *Phaedrus*. This significant allusion to Isocrates shows the importance his ideas held even among those who disagreed with much of his writing.

One of the reasons that Isocrates was able to avoid absorption into the negative ethos of sophism (a negativism largely constructed and heavily promoted by Plato and Aristotle) lay in his sustained commitment to educational theory. While many sophists presented practical methods of language manipulation, Isocrates stressed rhetoric as an extensive system. His work, therefore, was grounded in theory and so went beyond the familiar sophistic goal of learning how to get what one wants. His system of education depended on approaching the whole person and on the centrality of what later came to be characterized as a liberal education. The intellectual cultivation of whole people with wide-ranging capacities that can be developed defined Isocrates' dominant way of thinking and the course of study at his school. This system was based on rhetoric and included work that we would now call literary studies. Isocrates' definition of his work, in opposition to sophism in general, is presented in the fragmentary *Against the Sophists*. Here he distances his school from other schools, asserting that his emphasis on morality and its relationship to rhetoric makes his school superior to the others. He consistently connected individual education to the health of Greek culture. Deemphasizing the merely factual in education, he maintained that knowledge and understanding should be the center of education and that this emphasis would lead to a healthy culture.

Isocrates and Plato were in agreement with each other on numerous issues, even as they disagreed fundamentally on epistemological, educational, and other central issues. Both thinkers emphasized the educational development of whole human beings and the importance of ethics. Both thinkers also based their educational theory on what each called *philosophia*, although they differed substantially on the definition of that concept. While Plato promoted the idea of the immutable and transcendental Forms, and the relationship of those Forms to the soul and to knowledge, Isocrates did not claim to understand ultimate reality. He was more concerned with *philosophia* as critical wisdom and with palpable issues of practical education. Isocrates was closer to the relativism of Protagoras than to the idealism of Plato, according to W.K.C. Guthrie. Both Isocrates and Plato were much closer in their use of the new technology of writing. Both concentrated their creative and theoretical issues on writing, a form of communication that had developed substantially only in the previous three hundred years. In addition, both thinkers chose to work in written discourse, revealing some awareness of the burgeoning power of the new technology. They both make claims about the centrality of speaking, but each one reveals a commitment to writing in his choice of that medium of communication. Isocrates' work as an orator who shunned public speaking sheds light on the fluctuating relationship between speaking and writing in this important century of rapid and, to many, disturbing change.

Isocrates was born in 436 B.C.E. to Theodorus of Erchia and to Heduto. Aside from her name, we know very little about Heduto. Isocrates had three brothers and one sister. Theodorus was a successful manufacturer of flutes. The Peloponnesian War ended this affluence, a situation that contributed to Isocrates' turning to employment as a logographer. He was educated by some of the best available teachers: Gorgias, Prodicus, and probably (although this is less certain) Socrates. In *Antidosis* he discusses the value of the excellent training he received: He learned how to think, how to apply his mind to problems, and how to use to advantage his native ability.

Gorgias, who arrived in Athens from Leontini when Isocrates was nine years old, appears to have had substantial influence on Isocrates. From Isocrates' extant writing, especially the *Antidosis,* we can see that Gorgias' emphasis on Greek unity and on prose style affected Isocrates significantly. Gorgias, who was greatly popular in Athens, constructed a new genre of discourse. One of his strategies was to apply poetic devices to prose. This new use of language delighted Isocrates and other Athenians, while it angered other people. His unique work provoked both reactions. The dominant critical tradition, from Isocrates' time through the present, tends to reflect these diverse reactions by portraying the Gorgianic influence on Isocrates as an aspect to be admired or tolerated. The influence is difficult to judge now, because Gorgias' whole speeches have not survived. Comparisons must be based on fragments quoted in other people's texts. The critical tradition, which came to be based on Plato's and Aristotle's fervent denunciation of sophism, has been revised at particular historical times, including the present one (Enos; Jarratt; Kerford; J. Poulakos; T. Poulakos; Swearingen; Welch).

Isocrates established these principles in the school he opened in 393 B.C.E. in Chios. The success of his school is partly indicated by the accomplishments of his students, who included the general Timotheus, the Cyprian King Nicocles, and the historian Theopompus, and by the fact that it remained in existence for many decades.

The Peloponnesian War may have deprived him of his inheritance, but it created a necessity for Isocrates to open his school. Working in a general curriculum, the students were trained for a range of occupations because they were taught to develop judgment that could be applied to any situation. In his curriculum, Isocrates recognized the importance of challenging students with difficult material and requiring them to work at a variety of intellectual tasks. The nature of Isocrates' school differs from those of most of the sophists because he did not travel around to teach and to present public speeches. Like Plato, he created a permanent school, requiring students to come to him. Given the serious physical requirements of travel in ancient Greece, a point that Richard Leo Enos has explored, the establishing of one location for his pedagogical experiment enabled Isocrates to devote more time to writing and to teaching, two activities that he found to be mutually reinforcing.

Having chosen not to undergo the rigors of travel over difficult land and water, Isocrates focused his energy on his writing and on his school. He was thereby able to consolidate his power in one location, and the consolidation of his power led to the institutionalizing of his school. The mutually reinforcing strengths of his own influential writing and the success of his school derived partly from a concentration of effort. Part of this concentration can be regarded as a result of the burgeoning power of literacy.

The technology of writing, as Eric A. Havelock, Walter J. Ong, and others have pointed out, leads to a way of living that is more solitary than orally based living is. The requirements of abstraction, among other issues, and the psychological changes in memory brought on by thinking in writing led to different behavior. One change is that the writer requires more time alone. By replacing the work of traveling from place to place with writing in one location, Isocrates was able to produce more prose than many other sophists. The permanence of this prose, as opposed to the ephemeral nature of spoken discourse, led also to Isocrates' writing exerting power for many centuries. While his reputed shyness in public speaking may have caused Isocrates some difficulties, his retreat from the public and from travel to the more convincing circumstances of writing ultimately contributed to his success.

The writing down of speeches resembles generically the fifth- and fourth-century writing of dramatic pieces. The spoken and the written word find a unique merger in both oratorical literature and dramatic literature. It is not a coincidence that these two genres achieved dominance at the same time. The rising power of writing was challenging but not overcoming the hegemony of recitation. Oratorical literature and dramatic literature depended equally on ways of thinking that derive from both speaking and writing. Oratorical literature and dramatic literature arose in and helped to perpetuate a social context that was undergoing radical change because of changes in communication and in political structures. The psychological realities created by the new context of writing and reading gradually empowered these two genres. Oratorical literature and dramatic literature accommodated the demands of traditional oral discourse while partaking of the power of the relatively new written discourse (Welch).

The growing importance of writing contributed to a number of competing theories of education. The centrality of education to Greek culture is revealed in every branch of classical rhetoric, from the sophists, to Plato, to Aristotle, and eventually to Roman rhetorics. The organization of language theory that appears in classical rhetoric always included educational theory. In fact, part of the lasting power of classical rhetoric has been its inclusion of education as a central social and political as well as language issue. This pedagogical concern, which continued with force until the Ramistic cordoning off of the parts of rhetoric in the sixteenth century and with diminished force after that, accounts for much of Isocrates' influence and for his appeal to a broadly based audience through many eras and cultures. Isocratean rhetoric, like Platonic rhetoric and Aristotelian rhetoric, always spoke to a wide audience rather than to a limited audience of specialists. Far from suffering the silence that pedagogy has frequently experienced in the modern period, educational theory was regarded as a matter central to all intellectual concern and to the well-being of the culture. Language training constituted an essential aspect of education. Isocrates' general theory included ideas on what comprised an effective education.

Rhetoric was the central part of that education. Isocrates' *Art of Rhetoric* is lost, but his theory of rhetoric can be determined from his other work. The cornerstones of Isocratean rhetoric are the appeal to many aspects of the listener or reader and an emphasis on values, two ideas that diverged from the guiding principles of many sophists. To bring about multifaceted persuasion, the speaker or writer needed to rely on broad rhetorical training and to rely on a self-presentation that ensured his ability to be believed. To persuade a whole person requires variation in training. The psychological issues that attend the idea of the speaker's or writer's integrity led Isocrates to emphasize ethical conduct. Isocrates' emphasis on ethical conduct became an important basis for Cicero's ideal orator (*vir bonus,* or the good man [*sic*]) and later Quintilian's ideal orator (*vir bonus dicendi peritus,* or the good man [*sic*] speaking well). The emphasis on maintaining high standards of conduct and, as important, the appearance of that good conduct, is one of the reasons that Isocrates' school had a better reputation than those of the sophists who did not emphasize this aspect of rhetoric. Isocrates, then, enacted his own training: He presented his own high standards in a way that contributed significantly to his school's excellent reputation and to his own. In other words, he understood very well the concept of ethos, the general idea of the character presented by a writer or a speaker, and used it to his advantage in his writing and in his curriculum. His understanding of ethos set him apart from other sophists, who did not share his belief in its importance. With this attitude, Isocrates taught one of the first issues in persuasion: credibility. He educated his students in how to engender belief.

The connection of rhetoric, education, and culture appears forcefully in *Antidosis,* a late and autobiographical work. Isocrates, like Plato, extends rhetoric beyond the argumentation of law courts. He privileges instead his idea of *philosophia.* He in fact uses the fiction of a legal defense as a frame for this autobiographical writing. With this writing strategy, he provides an example of how to extend legal oratory. He says, "While those who are thought to be adept at court procedure are tolerated only for the day when they are engaged in the trial, the devotees of philosophy are honored and held in high esteem in every society and at all times" (II.213–14). His *philosophia* consists of work in rhetoric that includes the upholding of moral values.

> It remains to tell you about "wisdom" and "philosophy." It is true that if one were pleading a case on any other issue it would be out of place to discuss these words (for they are foreign to all litigation), but it is appropriate for me, since I am being tried on such an issue, and since I hold that what some people call philosophy is not entitled to that name, to define and explain to you what philosophy, properly conceived, really is. . . . For since it is not in the nature of man to attain a science by the possession of which we can know positively what we should do or what we should say, in the next resort I hold that man to be wise who is able by his powers of conjecture to arrive generally at the best course, and I hold that man to be a philosopher who occupies himself with the studies from which he will most quickly gain that kind of insight. (II.335)

This use of judgment is intended to go beyond speaking in law courts. In other words, legal oratory did not embrace enough of the important issues to define either rhetoric or philosophy, which in the Isocratean worldview applied to every area of human activity. Since responses to situations cannot usually be predicted, the development of a critical faculty through work on rhetoric and *philosophia* enables the individual to meet any circumstance well.

Isocrates established his point about the interrelated issues of rhetoric, *philosophia,* and critical thinking by quoting extensively in *Antidosis* from his earlier works. To some extent the work acts as an anthology of his writing, annotated by himself at the age of eighty-two. The excerpts from his earlier work serve two functions: to explain his life work and to act as an autobiographical argument. Like many autobiographies, the *Antidosis* reads subtextually as a sustained justification of the writer's life and work. The complex series of explanatory prose and of the showing of selected life events leads to an exposition that eventually reads like a justification even though that motive may not be explicitly stated.

The submerged argument of self-justification has for many critics read like a treatise of self-promotion and has contributed significantly to Isocrates' reputation as a person dominated by egocentrism. This traditional view, however, has been revised in the last generation of scholarship, which has reexamined the sophists and has found their work to contain more substantive thinking than often has been attributed to them.

A transcending of the personal occurs with Isocrates' discussion of the relationship of education and language in *Antidosis*:

> We ought, therefore, to think of the art of discourse just as we think of the other arts, and not to form opposite judgments about similar things, nor show ourselves intolerant toward that power which, of all the faculties which belong to the nature of man, is the source of most of our blessings. For in the other powers which we possess, as I have already said on a former occasion, we are in no respect superior to other living creatures; . . . but, because there has been implanted in us the power to persuade each other and to make clear to each other whatever we desire, not only have we escaped the life of wild beasts, but we have come together and founded cities and made laws and invented arts; . . . for the power to speak well is taken as the surest index of a sound understanding. (II.327)

Language for Isocrates permeates every aspect of human existence, and so the development of this ability assumes central importance in the education of the individual.

Isocrates defines the differences between his educational theory and competing theories in the opening of *Helen,* an excellent early example of the encomium. Isocrates asserts that the rival schools ought to "pursue the truth, to instruct their pupils in the practical affairs of our government and train to expertness therein, bearing in mind that likely conjecture about useful things is far preferable to exact knowledge of the useless" (III.63). In this passage and throughout his long writing career, Isocrates wanted to connect education to the useful, including the usefulness of a unified Greek culture. He viewed Athens as the center of this culture. While this idea was held by Gorgias and other thinkers, Isocrates carried the concept further. He promoted a transfer of the fighting among Greek groups to fighting against the Persian empire. In this light he praises Helen, who had been a familiar target for abuse: "It is owing to Helen that we are not the slaves of the barbarians. For we shall find that it was because of her that the Greeks became united in harmonious accord and organized a common expedition against the barbarians, and that it was then for the first time that Europe set up a trophy of victory over Asia" (III.97). Isocrates helped to establish this topic as a typical exercise in rhetorical education. The encomium on Busiris, a mythical king of Egypt, functions in a similar way.

Also centering on the importance of Greek unity is *Panegyricus.* In order to focus Greek energy on cooperation and the power it would bring, Isocrates advocated war against the Persians. He praises Athens extravagantly and forcefully, supplying inspiration to his contemporaries. His persuasion is so impressive and his prose style so attractive that many critics—historically as well as in the modern era—have regarded the *Panegyricus* as his best work. Connecting his unique attitude toward philosophy to the health and potential of Athens, he states:

> Philosophy, moreover, which has helped to discover and establish all these institutions, which has educated us for public affairs and made us gentle towards each other, which has distinguished between the misfortunes that are due to ignorance and those which spring from necessity, and taught us to guard against the former and to bear the latter nobly—philosophy, I say, was given to the world by our city. And

Athens it is that has honored eloquence, which all men crave and envy in its possessors; for she realized that this is the one endowment of our nature which singles us out from all living creatures, and that by using this advantage we have risen above them in all respects as well. (I.147–49)

The health of the state and the health of language education recur as themes in the nine extant letters of Isocrates. All the letters are written to leaders and are characterized by Isocrates' desire for Greek unity through an invasion of Persia. In his letter to the young Alexander (who Van Hook says had probably just begun his training with Aristotle), Isocrates reiterates the centrality of rhetoric: "By means of this study [rhetoric] you will come to know how at the present time to form reasonably sound opinions about the future, how not ineptly to instruct your subject peoples what each should do, how to form correct judgments about the right and the just and their opposites and, besides, to reward and chastise each class as it deserves" (III.429). The other letters—to Philip, to Dionysius, to Antipater, among others—constitute a kind of personal history. His requests, recommendations, and admonitions provide an unusual mixture of the personal and the public and allow us to see historical change in the fourth-century B.C.E. from the unique perspective afforded by the genre of letter writing.

The influence of Isocrates on the classical world was immense. His concept of Greek unity and his system of education based on rhetoric affected ancient Greek history and subsequently Roman culture. Werner Jaeger summarizes his contribution in the following way: "From all his words we can feel the living breath of Hellenism. The new era actually did fall into the forms which Isocrates had thought out before its advent. Without the idea which he here expresses for the first time, the idea that Greek *paideia* was something universally valuable, there would have been no Macedonian Greek world-empire, and the universal culture which we call Hellenistic would never have existed" (80–81). Isocrates was read and quoted extensively partly because his ideas combined cultural and political issues with an agenda for individual education. A major reason for this sustained influence was his readable and evocative prose style. He contributed substantially to the success of Attic prose, extending its limits and creating new structures.

His influence in postclassical cultures was strong as well. Partly through Cicero, Isocrates had an effect on Western lines of thought. With the serious resurgence of classical rhetoric since 1965, interest in Isocrates and the other sophists has grown considerably. Much of the new research offsets the negative attitude toward the sophists that occurs in the work of Plato and Aristotle. Instead of receiving Plato's and Aristotle's views of the sophists, as has been done traditionally, new research examines the work of the sophists according to other perspectives.

Isocrates stands as a central figure in the history of rhetoric and education. He understood the dynamic changes in culture, politics, and language that made the fourth century B.C.E. one of the more important periods of change in the so-called Western tradition. He analyzed a great deal of the fluctuation taking place and sought in his writing and in his school to promote the changes. In other words, he understood the sources of cultural power and embraced the possibilities it offered.

Kathleen E. Welch
University of Oklahoma

Bibliography
Primary Works in English translation.

Isocrates. Three Volumes. Vols. 1 and 2 translated by George Norlin. Vol. 3 translated by La Rue Van Hook. Loeb Classical Library. Cambridge, MA: Harvard UP, Vol. 1, 1928, Vol. 2, 1929, Vol. 3, 1945.

Speeches. Twenty-one extant orations, including six early court speeches. *Against the Sophists* (c. 390 B.C.E.), *Helen* (c. 370 B.C.E.), *Busiris* (between 390 and 385 B.C.E.), *Panegyricus* (c. 380 B.C.E.), *Antidosis* (between 354 and 353 B.C.E.), *To Philip* (346 B.C.E.), *Archidamus* (c. 366 B.C.E.), *To Nicocles* (374 B.C.E.), *Nicocles* (between 390 and 385 B.C.E.), *Evagoras* (between 370 and 365 B.C.E.), *Areopagiticus* (355 B.C.E.), *Panathenaicus* (342 B.C.E.), *On Peace* (c. 355 B.C.E.), *To Demonicus* (between 374 and 372 B.C.E.), *Plataicus* (between 373 and 371 B.C.E.), *Concerning the Team of Horses* (c. 390 B.C.E.), *Trapeziticus* (c. 393 B.C.E.), *Against Callimachus* (402 B.C.E.), *Aegineticus* (c. 394 B.C.E.), *Against Lochites* (c. 404 to 403 B.C.E.), *Against Euthynus* (403 B.C.E.).

Letters. To Dionysius (368 B.C.E.); To Philip I (342 B.C.E.); To Philip II (338 B.C.E.); To Antipater (340 B.C.E.); To Alexander (342 B.C.E.); to the Children of Jason (359 B.C.E.); To Timotheus (345 B.C.E.); To the Rulers of the Mytilenaeans (350 B.C.E.); To Archidamus (356 B.C.E.).

Reference.
Dobson, John Frederic. *The Greek Orators.* London: Methuen, 1919.

Enos, Richard Leo. *Greek Rhetoric before Aristotle.* Prospect Heights, IL: Waveland, 1993.

Guthrie, W.K.C. *The Sophists.* Cambridge: Cambridge UP, 1969.

Jaeger, Werner. *Paideia: The Ideals of Greek Culture.* Vol. 3. Trans. Gilbert Highet. New York: Oxford UP, 1944.

Jarratt, Susan C. *Rereading the Sophists: Classical Rhetoric Refigured.* Carbondale: Southern Illinois UP, 1991.

Jebb, Richard C. *The Attic Orators from Antiphon to Isaeos.* 2 vols. New York: Russell, 1962.

Kennedy, George A. *The Art of Persuasion in Ancient Greece.* Princeton: Princeton UP, 1963.

———. *Classical Rhetoric and Its Christian and Secular Tradition from Ancient to Modern Times.* Chapel Hill: U of North Carolina P, 1980.

Kerford, G.B. *The Sophistic Movement.* Cambridge: Cambridge UP, 1981.

Ong, Walter J. *Orality and Literacy: The Technologizing of the Word.* London: Methuen, 1982.

Poulakos, John. "Rhetoric, the Sophists, and the Possible." *Communication Monographs* 51 (1984): 215–26.

Poulakos, Takis. "Towards a Cultural Understanding of Classical Epideictic Oratory." *PRE/TEXT* 9 (1988): 147–66.

Schiappa, Edward. *Protagoras and Logos: A Study in Greek Philosophy and Rhetoric.* Columbia: U of South Carolina P, 1991.

Swearingen, C. Jan. *Rhetoric and Irony: Western Literacy and Western Lies.* New York: Oxford UP, 1991.

Welch, Kathleen E. *The Contemporary Reception of Classical Rhetoric: Appropriations of Ancient Discourse.* Hillsdale, NJ: Erlbaum, 1990.

Jakobson, Roman (1896–1982)

Structuralist linguist who contributed an influential model of communication and important concepts relating to style. Born in Moscow, Roman Jakobson was a member of the Russian Formalist School and the Prague Linguistic Circle. Jakobson studied at the University of Moscow, serving as research associate from 1918 to 1920, after which he went to Prague. A professor at Masaryk University (1933–1939), the École Libre des Hautes Études in New York (1942–1946), Columbia University (1946–1949), Jakobson wrote extensively on linguistics and literary criticism. In 1949 he became the Samuel Cross Professor of Slavic Languages and Literature, and in 1957 he also joined the Massachusetts Institute of Technology as Institute Professor. By the end of his career, Jakobson had produced over 475 publications, many of interest to rhetoricians.

Roman Jakobson's most important contribution to rhetoric was the model of communication he enunciated in "Linguistics and Poetics," which closed the 1958 Style Conference at Indiana University. In addition, Jakobson redefined Saussure's syntagmatic and paradigmatic dimensions of language as metaphoric and metonymic dimensions. Jakobson based this redefinition on close observation of child language development and aphasic language loss, which he reported in *Fundamentals of Language*. Jakobson's model of communication and redefinition of the dimensions of language enabled him to conduct insightful stylistic analyses, the best known of which is his analysis of Baudelaire's "Les Chats," which he published with Claude Lévi-Strauss.

Jakobson's model of communication saw a communication exchange as undertaken between an addresser and an addressee. The exchange had four additional features: the message, or actual content exchanged; the context, or situation referred to; the contact, or physical or psychological channel of the communication; and the code, or means of encoding a message common to addresser and addressee. Jakobson arranged these six factors according to the following diagram:

Context

Message

Addresser _____ Addressee

Contact

Code

Jakobson believed that the use of language could focus on any one of these six factors. Such a focus he defined as a language function. No single message could fulfill only one function. But the six functions fit into a hierarchical order for any given message, with each message fulfilling a dominant function. Orientation toward the addresser represented the emotive function, toward the addressee represented the conative function, toward the context represented the referential function, toward the message represented the poetic function, toward the contact represented the phatic function, and toward the code represented the metalingual function. Jakobson schematized these functions according to the following diagram, which corresponds to his diagram of factors:

Referential

Emotive _____ Poetic _____ Conative

Phatic

Metalingual

Jakobson's interest in the poetic function of language is of great importance to the study of rhetoric and literature. The bulk of "Linguistics and Poetics," as with most of Jakobson's work on literary topics, is devoted to showing how the two principles of selection (based on the metonymic dimension of language) and combination (based on the metaphoric dimension of language) explain both the structures present in a poem and their function together. Jakobson believed that poetry projected the principle that any item to be selected into the sequence of a poem is essentially equivalent to all possible items onto the principle of combination. Thus items combined in similar sequences become equivalent. This neutralization of sequential elements, making syllable equal to syllable, word equal to word, and line equal to line, enables poetry to create both new meanings and new ambiguities not possible in other functions of language.

Jakobson's views have had significant impact. The Programme in Literary Linguistics at the University of Strathelyde traces its roots to Jakobson. Hosting a retrospective conference on "Linguistics and Poetics," it produced the collection *The Linguistics of Writing,* which summarized Jakobson's pervasive influence on literary criticism and rhetoric.

Forrest Houlette
Ball State University

Bibliography

Fabb, Nigel, Dekek Attridge, Alan Durant, and Colin McCabe, eds. *The Linguistics of Writing.* New York: Methuen, 1987.

Jakobson, Roman. "Linguistics and Poetics." *Style in Language.* Thomas Sebeok, ed. Cambridge, MA: MIT P, 1960. 350–77.

Jakobson, Roman, and Morris Halle. *Fundamentals of Language.* The Hague: Mouton, 1956.

Jakobson, Roman, and Claude Lévi-Strauss. "'Les Chats' de Charles Baudelaire." *L'Homme* 2 (1962): 5–21.

Jamieson, Kathleen M. Hall (b. 1946)

Best known for her contributions to genre theory and political communication. Born in Minnesota in 1946, Kathleen Hall Jamieson was influenced by the work of Edwin Black, who directed her dissertation at the University of Wisconsin, Madison (1972). She extended Black's work on the usefulness of genre in rhetorical criticism and theory in several essays published during the 1970s and early 1980s. More recently, Jamieson is the author or co-author of several books on political communication. She is specifically concerned with the discourse of presidential campaigns and with describing and improving the nature, practice, and effects of such discourse.

Jamieson is currently professor and dean of the Annenberg School for Communication at the University of Pennsylvania. Jamieson has been a member of numerous editorial boards, is a sought-after political analyst and lecturer, and is the recipient of dozens of grants, fellowships, and awards, including several book awards, a Fulbright award, a Ford fellowship, and two MacArthur grants.

Jamieson entered the debate over the "rhetorical situation" in 1973 with her essay "Generic Constraints and the Rhetorical Situation." She brought the perspective of genre to bear on Lloyd Bitzer's (1968) notion that situations are rhetorical and call forth appropriate responses. Genre, Jamieson argued (here and in later essays), serves to structure discourse even more powerfully than does the surrounding situation. She introduced the concept of "antecedent genre," demonstrating that rhetors react to unprecedented situations by calling on their knowledge of existing classes of discourse, whether or not those antecedent genres chosen are appropriate to the situation (1975). Jamieson illustrated the applicability of her insights about the ways in which genres shape and are shaped by institutions with studies of papal rhetoric and presidential discourse.

Several of her recent books investigate the connections between political rhetoric and the mass media, focusing on the (oft-abused) power and (often unfulfilled) promise of broadcasting as a tool for the presentation of political candidates and the education of the electorate. *Packaging the Presidency* represented the first comprehensive study of presidential campaign advertising, which she argues has become "the major means by which candidates for the presidency communicate their messages to voters" (1984:446). *Eloquence in an Electronic Age* traces the "transformation of political speechmaking" across the centuries as a result of social and technological changes. Jamieson examines the ways in which the mass media, in particular, have made a more intimate style of political rhetoric the norm, rendering anecdote and visual innuendo more publicly persuasive than argument, reasoning, and evidence. Similarly, *Presidential Debates* (with David Birdsell) and *Dirty Politics* focus on the decline in the usefulness and ethical standards of various forms of political communication, and conclude with recommendations for ways to improve the political process. Jamieson collaborated with Karlyn Kohrs Campbell on *Deeds Done in Words,* which brought together the two major strands of her research interests in an examination of the generic forms that have created and sustained the United States presidency.

Suzanne M. Daughton and Jennifer L. Rigdon
Southern Illinois University

Bibliography

Campbell, Karlyn Kohrs, and Kathleen Hall Jamieson. *Deeds Done in Words.* Chicago: U of Chicago P, 1990.

Jamieson, Kathleen M. "Antecedent Genre as Rhetorical Constraint." *Quarterly Journal of Speech* 61 (1975): 406–15.

———. *Dirty Politics: Deception, Distraction and Democracy.* New York: Oxford UP, 1992.

———. *Eloquence in an Electronic Age: The Transformation of Political Speechmaking.* New York: Oxford UP, 1988.

———. "Generic Constraints and the Rhetorical Situation." *Philosophy and Rhetoric* 6 (1973): 162–70.

———. *Packaging the Presidency: A History and Criticism of Presidential Campaign Advertising.* New York: Oxford UP, 1984.

Jamieson, Kathleen Hall, and David S. Birdsell. *Presidential Debates: The Challenge of Creating an Informed Electorate.* New York: Oxford UP, 1988.

Jardine, George (1742–1827)

Professor of logic and rhetoric at the University of Glasgow from 1774 until 1824. George Jardine was born in 1742 at Wandal, Scotland, where his ancestors had been tenant farmers for generations. He was educated at the elementary parish school of Wandal and entered the University of Glasgow in October of 1760, where he received recognition for his abilities and enthusiasm. In June of 1774, Jardine was appointed both professor of Greek and assistant professor in logic at the University of Glasgow, and in 1787 he became the sole professor of logic.

Jardine was an outspoken champion of Scotland's democratic philosophy of education and realized that, unlike Oxford and Cambridge, the Scottish universities were designed to train young men for careers in business and science. He radically altered the traditional method of instructing the philosophy and logic class to meet the changing academic, economic, and social needs of his students. During Jardine's tenure at the University of Glasgow, the students were often as young as fourteen and drawn primarily from the working class. Jardine supported discussion and writing as a way of learning in conjunction with lectures for these nontraditional students. His carefully outlined method for teaching philosophy reveals his intense concern about the integrity of language, the separation of writing and speaking from communication, the preparation of students to function in and contribute to society, and methodologies that concentrated simply on correctness rather than on the social nature of writing. Jardine envisioned a comprehensive rhetoric, stressing that the abilities to reason, to investigate, to judge, to write, and to speak are crucial components of a liberal arts education.

Jardine's primary teaching objective was twofold: to cultivate in students the ability to examine their own minds and reactions to outside information as the primary method of acquiring new knowledge, and to encourage them to communicate that knowledge through oral and written language. His practical plan for meeting these goals included sequenced writing assignments, daily free-writing exercises, and peer evaluation—although he does not use those terms. Jardine's approach to education was novel. His colleagues within the Scottish university system were firmly entrenched in the traditional method of systematically lecturing on a prescribed list of topics. Jardine's *Outlines of a Philosophical Education* (1818, 1825) fully discusses his ideas concerning both the curriculum and pedagogical strategies of philosophical education and gives insight into Scottish university education perhaps at its best.

In 1824, Jardine voluntarily retired before he was forced to leave because of old age. Jardine was immensely popular during his own lifetime. The average size of the logic and philosophy class increased from fifty students in 1774 to over two hundred at the time of Jardine's retirement. His successor, Reverend Robert Buchanan, continued Jardine's plan of student-centered instruction in the logic and philosophy class. Unfortunately, Jardine failed to make any lasting mark on educational history. His rhetorical theories were smothered at the end of the nineteenth century by Scotland's philosophical shift from education for the many to education for the select. Jardine died January 27, 1827, following a brief illness.

Lynee Lewis Gaillet
Georgia State University

Bibliography

Gaillet, Lynee Lewis. *A Nineteenth-Century Scottish Rhetorician, George Jardine: Prefiguring Twentieth-Century Composition Theory.* Diss. Texas Christian U, 1991.

Horner, Winifred Bryan. *Nineteenth-Century Scottish Rhetoric: The American Connection.* Carbondale: Southern Illinois UP, 1993.

"Jardine, George." *Chamber's Dictionary of Eminent Scotsmen.* 1868.

"Jardine, George." *Dictionary of National Biography,* 1973.

Jardine, George. *Outlines of Philosophical Education, Illustrated by the Method of Teaching the Logic, or, First Class of Philosophy in the University of Glasgow.* Glasgow: A & J Duncan, 1818. Rpt. Edinburgh: Oliver & Boyd, 1825.

Johnstone, Henry W., Jr. (b. 1920)

Ph.D. Harvard University, 1950, long-time professor of philosophy at Pennsylvania State University, and founding editor of *Philosophy and Rhetoric.* Johnstone's major research contribution is in showing the rhetorical vector inherent in philosophical argument. In revealing how the process of securing validity is inherently rhetorical, Johnstone has made apparent the bonding between philosophy and rhetoric both in theory and in deliberation. Over an extended period of time, Johnstone wrote several articles showing that since philosophical argument seeks and secures validity through its audience, efforts at argument are attempts to secure assent ad hominem—that is, through a particular audience or community.

Johnstone's views are the result of a career-long inquiry; that process is best appreciated through his *Rhetoric and Validity in Philosophical Argument: An Outlook in Transition.* A shorter perspective is found in his essay "From Philosophy to Rhetoric and Back." Johnstone is also credited with introducing the works of other philosophers to American rhetoricians, most notably *The New Rhetoric: A Treatise on Argumentation* by Chaïm Perelman and L. Olbrechts-Tyteca. Johnstone has served as the editor of *Philosophy and Rhetoric* from 1968 to 1976 and from 1987 to the present. At the age of fifty-five, Johnstone began to earn a second doctorate—this time in Classical Studies—and has devoted his most recent efforts to examining the arguments of Greek philosophy as well as continuing his editorial duties for *Philosophy and Rhetoric.*

Richard Leo Enos
Texas Christian University

Bibliography

Johnstone, Henry W., Jr. "From Philosophy to Rhetoric and Back." *Rhetoric, Philosophy, and Literature: An Exploration.* Ed. Don M. Burks. West Lafayette, IN: Purdue UP, 1978.

———. *Validity and Rhetoric in Philosophical Argument: An Outlook in Transition.* University Park, PA: Dialogue, 1978.

Journal Writing

A nonfiction genre related to autobiography but having many forms and serving many purposes. Some typical forms include diaries, learning logs, and field notebooks. As with other genres, journals can stand alone as a complete, fully developed literary product for analysis and rhetorical criticism. They also, however, have a variety of nonliterary uses, such as for personal development, instruction, and therapy. Despite minor differences in form and function, journals usually exhibit highly personalized language and an informal, conversational tone. Because the writer's self is the first and sometimes the only audience, journals are also highly digressive and organized by association. Frequently, journal writing goes no further than the first-draft stage, exhibiting nonstandard language and a lack of concern for grammar and mechanics.

Prototypical journals date back several thousand years to the earliest use of writing, recording daily communal, business, or household transactions, such as the Roman *commentari.* These early forms emphasized recording public, communal life, although some journal forms, such as the pillow book from medieval Japan, expressed both public and private purposes. In the West, journals used as a means of documenting personal and intellectual development and controversy became popular during the Renaissance. Some of these took the shape of commonplace books in which individuals copied quotations from classic writers and added personal commentary. Another type of journal dating from the Renaissance is the travel diary, which served both private and public purposes as an aide-mémoir to the writer and as a guide for others who wished to make the same journey. During the Reformation, journals assumed a personal, spiritual purpose with the goal of documenting a person's progress toward salvation. As with the travel diary, the salvation journal served a public purpose, offering lessons or inspiration for other members of the spiritual community.

The personal journal appeared later than the travel and salvation journals and combines many of their purposes. One of the earliest examples of a personal journal that has also gained literary attention is Samuel Pepys's diary (1660 to 1669). Pepys's diary explored personal values, recorded observations and opinions, and compiled information pertinent to his public life.

Journals have also served as a writer's notebook in which authors discover and shape ideas previous to inclusion in their literary work. Some writers' journals, such as Virginia Woolf's *A Writer's Diary,* also provide important insights into their intellectual and private lives.

Journals have assumed two additional contemporary uses—for writing instruction and for therapy. For example, composition teachers frequently have their students keep journals to develop written fluency as well as for personal and cognitive development. These journals give students formal practice with prewriting, freewriting, problem-solving, or keeping systematic responses to reading or course materials. They have various names, such as "class-room diary," "dialogue journal," "process journal," and "thinkbook."

Since the 1960s and the popularization of psychology, journals have assumed a psychotherapeutic function in recording an individual's psychic growth. Most notable of these programs is Ira Progoff's "Intensive Journal," which has a basis in Jungian psychotherapy and depth psychology. Intensive journals use structured exercises to promote greater self-awareness and growth. Some composition instructors use these structured personal journals, also known as personal development journals, to help students learn the various purposes of journaling and to encourage students to keep a self-conscious record of their personal and intellectual development.

Current trends include incorporating journals into writing-across-discipline programs and computer classroom environments, exploring the social aspects of journal writing, and studying the literary, historical, and pedagogical aspects of gender and journaling.

Christopher C. Burnham and Mary G. French
New Mexico State University

Bibliography

Blythe, Ronald, ed. *The Pleasures of Diaries: Four Centuries of Private Writing.* New York: Pantheon, 1989.

Cozby, Paul C. "Self-Disclosure: A Literature Review." *Psychological Bulletin* 79 (1973): 73–91.

Fulwiler, Toby, ed. *The Journal Book.* Portsmouth, NH: Boynton/Cook, 1987.

Gannett, Cinthia. *Gender and the Journal: Diaries and Academic Discourse.* Albany: State U of New York P, 1992.

Mallon, Thomas. *A Book of One's Own: People and Their Diaries.* New York: Penguin, 1984.

Progoff, Ira. *At a Journal Workshop.* New York: Dialogue, 1975.

J

K

Kairos

Right timing and proper measure—directly related to the rhetorical importance of time, place, speaker, and audience, the proper and knowledgeable analysis of these factors, and the faculty of using the proper means in a particular context to arrive at belief. For the Pythagoreans, *kairos* is one of the laws of the universe referring to the balance between thesis and antithesis.

In order to understand *kairos* better, one must try to understand Greek ways of knowing and thinking. Key elements in Greek thought are thesis and antithesis. Many Greek thinkers explore polarities that lead to a oneness in duality. Only by identifying the polarities and apparent contradictions in the universe can one hope to find a balance that will lead to knowledge. The struggle between polarities such as doubt versus belief, appearance of truth versus reality, and deception versus persuasion is central to classical thought and forms one basis for important debates among rhetoricians. *Kairos* is central to this struggle and the ensuing balance.

The Pythagoreans subscribe to a construct based on opposing concepts. They see the function of *kairos* as allowing these forces to bring harmony to conflicting opposites. For the Pythagoreans, *kairos* represents an "overall sense of rightness—a critical point in time and space . . . the conflict and resolution of form and matter that initiated the creation of the universe and all that is therein" (Carter 102). It is from such a philosophy of balance and harmony embodied in *kairos* that Gorgias and other sophists derive their concept of adapting persuasive discourse to the particular circumstances of each discourse act.

The sophistic search for truth and ethical communication in a relativistic world relies on the choices and balances between competing, conflicting *logoi*. Poulakos suggests two roles for *kairos* in guiding these choices in Gorgianic rhetoric: first, the need for "temporality of the situation" in which the rhetorical act occurs and, second, the "impetus for discourse, the tension in the situation" (Poulakos 39–41). These roles expand on a generative *kairos* that breaks up opposing elements in a rhetorical situation and allows rhetors to persuade themselves and others of the difference between right and wrong (Kinneavy 1979:14). Thus *kairos* exhibits rich ethical implications in addition to its epistemological and rhetorical facets.

Modern uses of *kairos* are linked closely with situational context and have direct applications to a variety of fields. James L. Kinneavy traces the development of classical Greek *kairos* and offers some suggestions for its use in contemporary contexts and in contemporary college curriculum planning. He argues for the inclusion of *kairos* in literary, biblical, legal, and philosophical hermeneutics and insists that *kairos* is implicitly evidenced in speech communication, tagmemics, poststructuralist literary criticism, and in the work of Freud, Kenneth Burke, and E.D. Hirsch (Kinneavy 1986:104). Kinneavy bases his own design for a college composition program around a multifaceted application of *kairos*. He stresses the need to explore the ethical, epistemological, aesthetic, and rhetorical aspects of a complete definition of *kairos,* a concept far richer and more complex than "saying the right thing at the right time."

Sheri L. Helsley
Old Dominion University

Bibliography

Carter, Michael. "Stasis and *Kairos*: Principles of Social Construction in Classical Rhetoric." *Rhetoric Review* 7 (1988): 97–112.

Kinneavy, James L. "*Kairos:* A Neglected Concept in Classical Rhetoric." *Rhetoric and Praxis*. Ed. Jean Dietz Moss. Washington, D.C.: Catholic U of America P, 1986.

———. "The Relation of the Whole to the Part in Interpretation Theory and in the Composing Process." *Linguistics, Stylistics, and the Teaching of Composition*. Ed. Donald McQuade. Akron, OH: Language and Style, 1979.

Poulakos, John. "Toward a Sophistic Definition of Rhetoric." *Philosophy and Rhetoric* 16 (1983): 35–48.

Tillich, Paul. "*Kairos* and *Logos*." *The Interpretation of History*. Trans. N.A. Rasetzki and Elsa Talmey. New York: Scribner's, 1936.

Untersteiner, Mario. *The Sophists*. Trans. Kathleen Freeman. Oxford: Blackwell, 1954.

Kames, Lord Henry Home (1696–1782)

Best known to rhetoricians as a source of the influential theories of Hugh Blair, George Campbell, and Joseph Priestley. Home's *Elements of Criticism* (1762) went through over fifty editions including over thirty in America, where it was a popular college text for a century (see Johnson). *Elements of Criticism* is a prominent example of how introspection was used to establish morality and aesthetics in a science of human nature modeled on the inductive method of Newton and Locke. Home also wrote influential works on education, history, and moral philosophy. His *Essays on the Principles of Morality and Natural Religion* (1751) was the first contribution to Scottish common-sense philosophy, with Home responding to David Hume's skepticism by arguing that introspection demonstrated the existence of an innate common sense that testified to the existence of the world and the reliability of the senses. Home is also important because he apparently persuaded Adam Smith to begin the public lectures on rhetoric and belles-lettres that led to the establishment of Hugh Blair's Regius Professorship of Rhetoric and Belles-Lettres in 1762—perhaps the first university professorship founded to teach English composition, literature, and rhetoric.

Home is a major source for the belletristic and epistemological emphases of eighteenth-century rhetoric (see Bevilacqua). Belletristic rhetoricians such as Blair and Smith and epistemologically oriented rhetoricians such as George Campbell and Joseph Priestley looked to Kames as a source for their shared assumption that the study of discourse should be founded on the laws of human nature. Such assumptions led to the introspective turn of eighteenth-century rhetoric, with discourse no longer judged by classical authorities but by the tastes of the sensitive auditor (see Crowley). Like Shaftesbury, Hutcheson, Hume, and Smith, Kames attempted to apply the inductive method to the study of taste and sensibility. Such efforts tended to conflate aesthetics and ethics in terms of the mental responses of the impartial spectator, a vantage point that proved to be better suited to studying belletristic reactions than the rhetoric of political action.

Home should be more important than he is in research on the intellectual and institutional origins of college English. As discussed by Tytler and later biographers, Home was a mentor to Smith, Blair, and the others who broadened the university curriculum to include modern cultural studies. Home and his colleagues spread the cause of polite refinement outside the classroom in literary societies where Scots gathered to study English and correct their taste and usage. These groups were the original audiences for some of the works that institutionalized the study of English, most notably George Campbell's *Philosophy of Rhetoric*. Home wrote several works that document broader intellectual trends in the Scottish Enlightenment: *The Gentlemen Farmer. Being An Attempt to improve Agriculture, By subjecting it to the Test of Rational Principle* (1776), which advances the cause of social improvement; *Sketches of the History of Man* (1774), which discusses the history of culture and political economy in terms of the progress of such improvement; and *Loose Hints on Education, Chiefly Concerning the Culture of the Heart* (1781), which examines the formation of the polite sensibility. Kames's works sketch out the concern for progress and self-improvement that shaped the cultural and rhetorical theories of Blair, Smith, and the others who first taught English literature, composition, and rhetoric at the university level.

Thomas P. Miller
University of Arizona

Bibliography

Bevilacqua, Vincent M. "Lord Kames's Theory of Rhetoric." *Speech Monographs* 30 (1963): 309–27.

Crowley, Sharon. *The Methodical Memory: Invention in Current-Traditional Rhetoric.* Carbondale: Southern Illinois UP, 1990.

Johnson, Nan. *Nineteenth-Century Rhetoric in North America.* Carbondale: Southern Illinois UP, 1991.

Miller, Thomas P. *The Formation of College English: Rhetoric and Belles-Lettres in the British Cultural Provinces.* Pittsburgh, PA: Pittsburgh UP, 1995.

Ross, Ian Simpson. *Lord Kames and the Scotland of His Day.* Oxford: Clarendon, 1972.

Tytler, Alexander Fraser, Lord Woodhouselee. *Memoirs of the Life and Writings of the Honourable Henry Home of Kames.* 2 vols. 2nd ed. Edinburgh: T. Cadell and W. Davies, 1814.

Kant, Immanuel (1724–1804)

Philosopher who has given modern rhetoric cognitive, moral, and aesthetic implications. Immanuel Kant definitively gave to all fields of philosophical thought the decidedly modern turn, according to which all speculation on the inner ground of things was forever replaced by observation of the special characteristics of the human being. With the *Critique of Pure Reason* (1781), Kant showed the validity of the basic concepts of empirical science to proceed from necessary principles of human understanding, and thereby forever banished metaphysical inquiry into substance. With the *Critique of Practical Reason* (1788), Kant showed that the basic concepts of ethics and law equally derive from the nature of the human will and thereby made otiose any recourse to a divine legislator. With the *Critique of Judgement* (1790), Kant showed that the concept of an end or purpose is indispensable for aesthetic experience, research into organic nature, and moral action, and thereby completely ruled out any hypostatized unity of nature and freedom. In this way he sought to situate human beings with a finite insight into nature, an infinite moral task of freedom, and the permanently problematic destiny of reconciling the two. Kant remains one of the more influential and controversial of modern thinkers.

Kant's explicit comments on rhetoric are few, casual, and derisive. Consequently, he has not been studied closely by rhetoricians. But for those who would reflect on the cognitive, moral, and aesthetic conditions for rhetoric, and would seek ideas for conceiving a new rhetorical art, Kant's work as a whole offers a perspective that can disclose a great wealth of resources.

In his discussion of aesthetics in the Third Critique, Kant says that aesthetic judgments of the beautiful and of the sublime are judgments of "purposiveness without purpose." Such judgments are founded upon a feeling of pleasure in the mere form or formlessness of particular things in nature or of works of art. In this way he distinguishes such judgments from knowledge of objects and from moral perfection and thereby locates aesthetic experience in a uniquely modern and autonomous space. Properly speaking, the pleasure of beauty is the harmonious relation of our mental faculties preparatory to cognition, and the pleasure of sublimity is the sense of our own supreme moral worth in the face of all nature. This harmonious relation, Kant says, is what can properly speaking be called "common sense." And the sense of our moral worth is the true moral feeling, akin to respect. As such, this is what underlies an aesthetic judgment's claim to universal validity, as we can impute to everyone the ability to experience these pleasures. Moreover, they prepare us to embrace our human vocation of using our knowledge of nature in the fulfillment of the moral law. Being relatively autonomous, an aesthetic judgment does not depend upon communication, but it does lay claim to universal communicability. This communicability, says Kant, requires the attainment of a certain measure of culture, the central features of which are a feeling of sympathy for all humanity and the ability to communicate one's inmost self.

Here emerges, then, and in a way that redefines it as independent of but necessary for the attainment of other ends, one of the chief functions of rhetoric: to transform the traditions of the humanities for each new cultural situation. Kant's emphasis on the autonomy of judgments of taste requires that the resources for communication which each culture provides be tested in attempts to express the individual's own experience and, conversely, that each individual learn to discover what it is in that experience that can be expressed with those resources. Kant does not offer rules for such an art of communication (indeed, he insists that true art cannot be learned by rules, but only by emulation of examples), and among existing arts he prefers poetry to oratory because of its comparative freedom from mere utility. Nevertheless, his critique of aesthetic judgment has defined the growth of culture as the real production of intersubjectivity, has indicated that such production is the task not of knowledge or of morality but of art, and has revealed some of the touchstones of the experience to which art should be adequate. This critique helps disclose a uniquely modern function for a rhetoric suited to the rise of individuality and the pluralism connected with it.

Kant goes on in the second part of the *Critique of Judgement* to inquire whether the concept of an end or purpose may have, in addition to its subjective use in aesthetics, an objective use in cognition. The concept of an end is found to have a cognitive use in the understanding of organisms, which can only be known by us as physical ends, but once we have this concept we seek to apply it to nature as a whole. Because of the peculiar constitution of our understanding, which must proceed from a universal to the deduction of particulars as in empirical science, Kant says we conceive an intelligence as underlying nature organized according to a purpose, but this intelligence can nowhere be perceived in nature. Consequently, the idea of this intelligence remains merely regulative for our reflection on nature, and the concept of purpose functions only as a heuristic guide necessary for the organization and description of what are for us the contingent particulars of nature, so that they can be rendered accessible to explanation according to science. The use of this concept issues in a theory of the evolution of nature as a whole. However, the search for an unconditioned end to support this use can only cease in the human being's will to morality, which is an end in itself but requires the development of adequate means. This search therefore implicates the development of the culture and the social relations that facilitate the exercise of this will in nature conceived as a whole with a purpose. Only an intelligence that attains to a system of experience will be impelled to pursue the investigation of nature according to the principle of purpose.

Here again emerges in a wholly new form an especially modern function for rhetoric: to cultivate human beings who are capable of setting ends to themselves and of pursuing these ends in a nature that is thereby revealed to be organized for that end. Kant's claim that the concept of purpose is only a heuristic one makes the exposition of nature's purposiveness a necessary preparation to the organization of nature into genres and species such that it is hospitable to the human being's pursuit of ends. On this view the rhetoric of science concerns not merely the devices and techniques used in scientific writing but also the very discovery of subject matters, the principles of their organization, and the distinctions between fields of study. Similarly, the rhetoric of pedagogy concerns not merely the inculcation of hypothetical maxims but also the very systematization of experience, the investigation of nature's forms, and the capacity of setting ends to oneself. In a highly technological and democratic age, these tasks outline the scope of a modern rhetoric.

Though still not with that name, rhetoric also emerges in Kant's philosophy of history and of the relations of politics and ethics. Kant views history as the struggle between nature and morality in human beings, expressed in the evolution of the state. A polity employs coercion founded on natural inclinations toward pleasure to create a community of legal right in which each citizen is free to pursue the dictates of morality in his or her own way. As such, its commands are absolute, not subject to citizen veto. But a legal command is right only when it enjoins what each citizen would do if that citizen pursued the dictates of morality freely in the creation of a moral polity founded on the performance of duties. The polity is therefore subject to citizen review according to autonomous moral principles. Of course, rhetoric has a function in the state's coercion or persuasion of its citizens. But, in the form of public discussion and criticism, which Kant says is to be allowed complete freedom, rhetoric also mediates between justice and morality. In this role, rhetoric would be responsible for developing the intellectual resources for making history fulfill its mission.

Thus Kant can serve to outline crucial tasks for rhetoric in the modern age, especially as it grows beyond its classically defined limits and emerges in unanticipated places and forms. It will increasingly be the function of an artful, descriptive language not based on scientific concepts to make individual judgments of personal experience generally sharable. This shared fund of experience is, according to Kant, what truly deserves the name of culture. And it is ultimately this culture that underlies the ability of citizens to function as full-fledged members in the historical quest of a moral community. A modern rhetoric will seek to construct and make available such a language.

Clifford Vaida
Ohio State University

Bibliography

Cassirer, Ernst. *Kant's Life and Thought.* Trans. James Haden. New Haven: Yale UP, 1981.

Kant, Immanuel. *Critique of Judgement.* Trans. James Creed Meredith. Oxford: Clarendon, 1952.

———. *Critique of Practical Reason and Other Writings in Moral Philosophy.* Trans. Lewis White Beck. Chicago: U of Chicago P, 1949.

———. *Critique of Pure Reason.* Trans. Norman Kemp Smith. New York: St. Martin's, 1950.

———. *Kants gesammelte Schriften.* 22 vols. Berlin: Preussische Akademie der Wissenschaften, 1900–1942.

———. *Kant's Political Writings.* Ed. Hans Reiss. Trans. H.B. Nisbet. Cambridge: Cambridge UP, 1970.

Kennedy, George A. (b. 1938)

Paddison Professor of Classics at the University of North Carolina at Chapel Hill, author of numerous books and articles on classical rhetoric and oratory, past president of the International Society for the History of Rhetoric. In the foreword to *Greek Rhetoric under Christian Emperors,* George Kennedy himself discusses the genesis of his interest in rhetoric:

> My family took a keen interest in affairs when I was growing up. Among my earliest memories are the voices of Franklin D. Roosevelt and Adolf Hitler, but most of all the great speeches of Winston Churchill over the crackling wireless as events of World War II ebbed and flowed. One of my favorite occupations as a boy was to sit in the gallery of the Connecticut House of Representatives, in which my great-grandfather, grandfather, two great-uncles, an uncle, and a cousin had served. It was not, perhaps, the home of the greatest oratory, but I observed some effective use of ethos and learned that things could be said on both sides of a question. I was also taken to church, where I became an early, if sometimes impatient, critic of the eloquence of the pulpit.

As an undergraduate at Princeton, Kennedy read Plato and Demosthenes in Greek and continued his study of classics as a graduate student at Harvard, where Werner Jaeger encouraged his interest in ancient rhetoric and oratory. It was during graduate school that he conceived the plan to write a history of rhetoric. The first volume, *The Art of Persuasion in Greece,* appeared in 1963; the second, *The Art of Rhetoric in the Roman World,* in 1972. The third volume, mentioned above, came out in 1983. All were published by Princeton University Press. An abridgement of these three volumes into one, *A New History of Classical Rhetoric,* is scheduled to be published by Princeton in 1994. Interspersed with these books, which have become standard reference works in their own time, have been others of interest to those concerned with ancient rhetoric and oratory. His book on Quintilian, published by Twayne, appeared in 1969, and his translation of Aristotle's *Rhetoric,* with introduction, notes, and appendices, was published by Oxford in 1991. He was also the editor of the first volume of the *Cambridge History of Literary Criticism,* published in 1989, for which he wrote the introduction and four chapters.

Kennedy's interests, both geographically and chronologically, have extended beyond the narrow confines of the Greco-Roman world. His book *Classical Rhetoric and Its Christian and Secular Tradition from Ancient to Modern Times* (University of North Carolina Press, 1980) traces the development of classical rhetoric and its influence in Western Europe until the nineteenth century; *New Testament Interpretation through Rhetorical Criticism* applies classical rhetorical theory to the Bible. In recent years his research has looked toward developing a theoretical understanding of rhetoric by comparative study of Western and non-Western culture. An article, "Hoot in the Dark" (*Philosophy and Rhetoric* 25 [1992]: 1–21), extended this to include rhetorical features of animal communication. His books and numerous articles all show extreme clarity of presentation and a meticulous attention to detail. They also exhibit the sort of versatility and ability to take a broad view of the topic that one does not always associate with professional classicists. Because of this, they have had a broad appeal and thus have been instrumental in reviving and revitalizing the study of rhetoric during the twentieth century in the English-speaking world.

In addition to his scholarly activity and his reputation for being a very good teacher, Kennedy has served as the chairman of three departments at the University of North Carolina at Chapel Hill. He has been president of the American Philological Association and is presently the editor of the *American Journal of Philology,* the oldest and probably most prestigious classics journal in America.

Cecil Wooten
University of North Carolina, Chapel Hill

Kinneavy, James L. (b. 1920)

Author of seven books and over thirty articles, best known for *A Theory of Discourse* (Prentice 1971; rpt. Norton 1980). James L. Kinneavy occupies a chair as the Jane and Roland Blumberg Centennial Professor of English at the University of Texas, Austin.

Kinneavy took his B.A. at the College of Santa Fe (1942). His M.A. (1951) and Ph.D. (1956) were both done at Catholic University. His dissertation became his first book, *A Study of Three Contemporary Theories of Lyric Poetry* (Catholic UP, 1956).

After nearly ten years of teaching below the college level, in 1955 Kinneavy became head of the Division of Humanities at the College of Santa Fe. From 1958 to 1963, he taught at the Western State College of Colorado. In 1963 he joined the faculty at the University of Texas. Deeply involved with teaching throughout his career, Kinneavy has worked with the Texas Department of Education in many capacities and as a consultant to public school districts in Texas and elsewhere.

In "James L. Kinneavy: A Bibliographical Essay," Crusius describes Kinneavy's essential project as "the retrieval of the liberal arts tradition within a semiotic framework with practical intent," which means "the yoking together of history, theory, and practice" (352). This description offers a useful framework for summarizing Kinneavy's unique contribution to rhetorical studies.

Fluent in both Greek and Latin, Kinneavy has centered his historical scholarship in classical rhetoric. *Greek Rhetorical Origins of Christian Faith: An Inquiry* argues that the key Christian concept of *pistis* (faith) actually derives from classical rhetoric. At the source of Christian civilization, then, Kinneavy establishes the deep linkage with rhetoric. Moving forward to our own time, he contends that the dissociation of rhetoric from humanistic study explains the latter's loss of relevance and vitality.

Kinneavy's historical thesis about the centrality of rhetoric to our culture in general and to the humanities in particular receives theoretical grounding in semiotics. *A Theory of Discourse* advances the communication triangle to conceptualize the universe of discourse as a set of four basic aims—expressive, persuasive, literary, and referential—each of which foregrounds one of the four elements of the triangle—speaker, audience, language, and reality, respectively. Kinneavy develops a rhetoric for each aim modeled on Aristotle's division of rhetoric into invention, arrangement, and style. The semiotic framework also organizes his comprehensive bibliography, "Contemporary Rhetoric," in Winifred Bryan Horner's *Present State of Scholarship in Historical and Contemporary Rhetoric.*

The classical liberal arts tradition amounted in practice to training students in the various uses of language. Having discriminated the uses (aims) of discourse in *A Theory,* Kinneavy went on to write a practical rhetoric based on those aims, *Writing in the Liberal Arts Tradition* (with William McCleary and Neil Nakadate).

Kinneavy is presently working on a language arts text for secondary education and on the teaching of ethics in college composition. His work continues to evince the integration of history, theory, and practice that has typified his entire career.

Timothy W. Crusius
Southern Methodist University

Bibliography

Crusius, Timothy W. "James L. Kinneavy: A Bibliographical Essay." *A Rhetoric of Doing.* Ed. Stephen P. Witte, et al. Carbondale: Southern Illinois UP, 1992. 351–70.

Kinneavy, James L. "Contemporary Rhetoric." *The Present State of Scholarship in Historical and Contemporary Rhetoric.* Ed. Winifred Bryan Horner. 2nd ed. Columbia: U of Missouri P, 1990. 186–246.

———. "The Exile of Rhetoric from the Liberal Arts." *Journal of Advanced Composition* 8 (1988): 105–12.

———. "Restoring the Humanities: The Return of Rhetoric from Exile." *The Rhetorical Tradition in Modern Writing.* Ed. James J. Murphy. New York: Modern Language Assn., 1982. 19–30.

———. *Greek Rhetorical Origins of Christian Faith: An Inquiry.* New York: Oxford UP, 1987.

———. *A Theory of Discourse.* Englewood Cliffs, NJ: Prentice, 1971. Rpt. New York: Norton, 1980.

Kinneavy, James L., William McCleary, and Neil Nakadate. *Writing in the Liberal Arts Tradition.* 2nd ed. New York: Harper, 1990.

Kitzhaber, Albert R. (b. 1915)

Influential leader in the emergence of composition as an academic discipline in the mid twentieth century. Albert Kitzhaber helped to pioneer the study of nineteenth-century composition and to initiate modern composition's emphasis on knowledge of related fields.

Kitzhaber's 1953 dissertation, *Rhetoric in American Colleges, 1850–1900*, long before it was finally published in 1990, was cited frequently by scholars who followed him in the study of the history of American composition pedagogy. Kitzhaber was a participant in the landmark Dartmouth Conference in 1960, the basis for his 1963 book *Themes, Theories and Therapy: The Teaching of Writing in College* (1963), one of the first books to explore pedagogical approaches to college composition that broke away from the dominant model of nineteenth-century practice. His 1963 address before the Conference on College Composition and Communication, "4C, Freshman English, and the Future," is cited as an initial call for the kinds of changes that characterize the subsequent formation of composition as a discipline in the academy, "taking full advantage," in Kitzhaber's words, "of knowledge available in such fields as language, logic, rhetoric, psychology." Kitzhaber participated in the national debate over composition in the 1960s, especially in relation to his experience as chair of the Conference on College Composition and Communication, president of the National Council of Teachers of English, and as a leader of the earlier federal program called Project English. He began his Ph.D. work in rhetoric in 1948 as a student of Porter Perrin's at the University of Washington, after serving in World War II and teaching English at Iowa State and Washington State colleges. He carried his career through to retirement as Professor Emeritus of English at the University of Oregon in 1980.

John T. Gage
University of Oregon

Bibliography

Kitzhaber, Albert R. *Rhetoric in American Colleges, 1850–1900*. Dallas: Southern Methodist UP, 1990.

———. *Themes, Theories, and Therapy: The Teaching of Writing in College*. New York: McGraw, 1963.

Kristeva, Julia (b. 1941)

Linguist and semiotician born in Bulgaria in 1941 but living in Paris since 1966, contributing important work on relationships between language and gender. Kristeva served as one of the only women on the editorial board of *Tel Quel* and is currently a professor at the Sorbonne and a practicing psychoanalyst. She has worked with Lucian Goldmann, Claude Lévi-Strauss, Jacques Lacan, and Roland Barthes, one of her strongest influences. Her initial and primary theoretical influences are Marxism, Russian Formalism, and Hegel. A combination of socialist and psychoanalytic theories, she believes, is better able to accommodate fundamental differences among all people within an egalitarian structure than can Marxism alone.

Kristeva explains in essays such as "About Chinese Women" that the symbolic realm is the realm of men, of paternity, of linear time, of knowledge and power, of traditional academic discourse; it is a realm from which women are excluded. Women, in contrast, are associated with the unconscious, with *jouissance*, with maternity, with nonlanguage, nonspeech, with the body, with the presymbolic, with the unnameable.

Emphasizing the importance of the disruptive nature of women's marginal discourse, Kristeva sees women's order as outside time, outside traditional notions of truth and falsehood. All discourse bears traces of women's discourse, according to Kristeva; they can be recovered by listening for the unspoken, by emphasizing whatever remains unsatisfied, repressed, new, eccentric, incomprehensible. As she explains in her stylistically innovative essay "Stabat Mater," maternal love is an exit from representation, a shield against death (177).

In "Women's Time" Kristeva discusses the limitations of contemporary feminist movements to solve the problem of the political imbalance between the sexes. The first generation of feminists in struggling for equality aspired to gain a place in linear time as the time of project and history. A difficulty with this approach, however, is that the increase of women in positions of power has not radically changed the nature of that power because women in high positions become guardians of the status quo. A second generation of feminists, according to Kristeva, focus on the specificity of female psychology and its symbolic realizations and seek to give a language to the intrasubjective realizations left mute by culture in the past. The creation of a countersociety by radical feminists, though, results in a kind of inverted sexism. Kristeva calls for a third generation of feminism that includes the two previous generations. This third generation questions the dichotomy man/woman as an opposition between two rival entities and attempts to replace scapegoating with the analysis of the potentialities of victim/executioner that characterize each identity, each subject, each sex.

In "Psychoanalysis and the Polis," Kristeva sees that the interpretation of texts can involve the domination of the text by the interpreter, clearly an undesirable approach. A more desirable approach is to allow the text to speak to the interpreter, thus permitting the constitution of a new theory. Kristeva, however, suggests a third alternative, a posthermeneutic one. This involves a setting off of semantic, logical, phantasmatic, and indeterminable sequences. Such an approach, the method of psychoanalysis, amounts to a return to the archaic mother who is resistant to meaning.

Kristeva's work prepares the way for the development of a poststructuralist or postmodern feminist rhetoric.

Elizabeth A. Flynn and Saralinda Blanning
Michigan Technological University

Bibliography

Bizzell, Patricia, and Bruce Herzberg, eds. "Hélène Cixous and Julia Kristeva." *The Rhetorical Tradition: Readings from Classical Times to the Present*. Boston: Bedford, 1990. 1224–32.

Kristeva, Julia. *About Chinese Women*. Trans. Anita Barrows. London: Boyars, 1977.

———. *Desire in Language: A Semiotic Approach to Literature and Art*. Ed. Leon S. Roudiez, trans. Alice Jardine, Thomas A. Gora, and Leon S. Roudiez. New York: Columbia UP, 1980.

———. *The Kristeva Reader*. Ed. Toril Moi. New York: Columbia UP, 1986.

———. *Powers of Horror*. Trans. Leon S. Roudiez. New York: Columbia UP, 1982.

———. *Strangers to Ourselves*. Trans. Leon S. Roudiez. New York: Columbia UP, 1991.

———. "Women's Time." Trans. Alice Jardine and Harry Blake. *Signs* 7 (1981): 13–35.

Moi, Toril. "Marginality and Subversion: Julia Kristeva." *Sexual/Textual Politics: Feminist Literary Theory*. New York: Methuen, 1985. 150–73.

Worsham, Lynn. "Writing against Writing: The Predicament of *Ecriture Feminine* in Composition Studies." *Contending with Words: Composition and Rhetoric in a Postmodern Age*. Ed. Patricia Harkin and John Schilb. New York: Modern Language Assn., 1991. 82–104.

Kuhn, Thomas S. (b. 1923)

Historian of science who formulated the concept of paradigms. Thomas S. Kuhn is professor of philosophy and history of science at MIT. His writings enormously influenced a variety of disciplines such as sociology, political science, economics, business management, and rhetoric. Kuhn's most widely known book is *The Structure of Scientific Revolutions,* first published in 1962, which examines the making and changing of knowledge in scientific communities. He is usually credited with popularizing the concept of *paradigm*. His work remains of broad interest because of its discussion of how authorized knowledge changes and because of its focus on the communities and the context in which knowledge is created.

As a historian of science, Kuhn examines in detail the cultural setting of a scientist's work. *The Copernican Revolution* (1957) and the *Black Body Theory* (1978) focus on the historical context in which Copernicus and Planck developed their ideas. Kuhn argues in these books that knowledge in science is an integral part of the cultural constraints and assumptions of an era. This claim stands against the commonly held assumption that scientific knowledge is based on an objective reality which exists unaffected by opinions of a particular community of scholars.

The Structure of Scientific Revolutions describes the process of change in science. In a "pre-paradigm" period of an immature science, competing theories coexist. As a science matures, an approach will gain wide acceptance because of its ability to solve problems, a "paradigm" will develop, and normal science will proceed in an orderly fashion. However, when too many anomalies, which cannot be accounted for within a paradigm, are encountered, normal research will be interrupted. A crisis will develop, and a *scientific revolution* will occur. Kuhn argues that this change is not evolutionary but revolutionary. "The transition from a paradigm in crisis to a new one is a reconstruction of the field from new fundamentals, a reconstruction that changes some of the field's most elementary theoretical generalizations as well as many of its paradigm methods and applications" (84–85). Further, the new paradigm will be accepted only through persuasive argument that "converts" the professional community (158).

Kuhn defined *paradigm* in a number of different ways, and in the 1970 edition of *The Structure of Scientific Revolutions* he added an extensive postscript to clarify the term. "Paradigms are something shared by the members of [groups that are] . . . the producers and validators of scientific knowledge" (178). When members of a community share a paradigm, they share commitments, beliefs, values, and a way of looking at the world which allows them to then conduct "puzzle-solving research."

Because Kuhn explores the way knowledge is created and interpreted, his work has been of particular interest to rhetoricians. First, the publication of Kuhn's work coincided with a shift within the field of composition from a focus on the written product (often referred to as the current-traditional approach) to an interest in writing as a process. Rhetoricians found Kuhn's description of changes in what counts as knowledge in science applicable to what is often called the "paradigm shift" in composition, from product to process.

Second, Kuhn's description of how knowledge is generated and gains authority within communities has been adopted and adapted by many disciplines. For scholars interested in rhetoric as epistemic, as a knowledge-making activity, Kuhn's theories provide support because he argues that scientific knowledge is based on the contingent judgment of specific communities rather than on "objective reality." His emphasis on community acceptance as key to validation of scientific knowledge also supports rhetoricians interested in the social construction of knowledge.

While *The Structure of Scientific Revolutions* was initially received with skepticism and even hostility, citation indexes in science, social science, and arts and humanities demonstrate the continuing importance of Kuhn's work.

Lucinda C. Ray
Iowa State University

Bibliography

Barnes, Barry. *T.S. Kuhn and Social Science*. London: Macmillan, 1982.

Bazerman, Charles. *Shaping Written Knowledge*. Madison: U of Wisconsin P, 1988.

Kuhn, Thomas S. *Black-body Theory and the Quantum Discontinuity, 1894–1912*. New York: Oxford UP, 1978.

———. *The Copernican Revolution: Planetary Astronomy in the Development of Western Thought*. Cambridge, MA: Harvard UP, 1957.

———. *The Essential Tension: Selected Studies in Scientific Tradition and Change*. Chicago: U of Chicago P, 1977.

———. *The Structure of Scientific Revolutions*. 2nd ed. Chicago: U of Chicago P, 1970.

Young, Richard. "Paradigms and Problems: Needed Research in Rhetorical Invention." *Research on Composing: Points of Departure*. Ed. Charles R. Cooper and Lee Odell. Urbana, IL: National Council of Teachers of English, 1974. 29–48.

K

L

Lamy, Bernard (1640–1715)

Orator, teacher of philosophy and theology, author of *L'Art de parler*. Fervent disciple of René Descartes and friend of Nicolas Malebranche and Port Royalists Antoine Arnauld and Pierre Nicole, Lamy devoted his life to teaching and writing texts for student use. Lamy taught at the seminary of Grenoble and at Rouen and was exiled twice during his career because of his Cartesian sympathies. Among other works, he published *Entretiens sur les sciences* (1683), *Les Eléments de géométrie* (1685), and *Traité de perspective* (1701), but it is *L'Art de parler* (1675) for which he is best known. Named to mirror the Port Royalists' *L'Art de penser*, Lamy's book went through five editions and nine printings, becoming enlarged as Lamy refined his rhetorical theory during the last twenty years of his life. *The Art of Speaking*, also known as the Port Royal rhetoric, was first published in translation in England in 1676 and reprinted in 1696 and 1708.

A marked departure from neoclassical rhetorics of the late seventeenth century, *L'Art de parler* was intended as a "scientific" (that is, rationalist) account of how discourse works upon the mind. Part I dealt with phonetics and grammar. Following Descartes's injunction to begin with the simplest elements of one's subject and progress by degrees to the more complex, this section described the formation of words, the structure of sentences, and standards for correct language usage.

Part II, on tropes and figures, emphasized the idea that the orator's form of expression should be proportioned to the idea conveyed. For Lamy the tropes and figures were especially significant because they acted as discursive "triggers," exciting desired emotional responses in the listener. Like Descartes, Lamy believed that a listener's passions could be aroused directly by sensible impressions and vivid description. In this section Lamy provided definitions, explanations, and examples for each trope and figure.

Part III discussed the acoustical properties and periodic structure of speech; Part IV considered the relation of style to the situation and genre of expression. In considering historical, philosophical, and poetic styles along with oratory, Lamy anticipated belletrism's concern for taste and good composition across genres. The fifth and last part of *L'Art de parler* treated persuasion explicitly. Lamy disparaged the commonplaces as useless and insisted on demonstrative, syllogistic proofs as the only adequate logical form. He also encouraged use of craft, or *l'adresse*, to gain acceptance for one's views by emphasizing common ground.

Many attributes of Lamy's *L'Art de parler*, taken together, make it unique. It systematically considered the acoustical, phonetic, and periodic properties of speech. It relied extensively on Descartes's psychology in developing an account of how rhetorical appeals acted on the mind. And it expanded consideration of style to the arts of writing in history, philosophy, and literature. In these aspects and others, *L'Art de parler* turned its back on neoclassicism and presaged the major Enlightenment rhetorics.

Barbara Warnick
University of Washington

Bibliography

Carr, Thomas M., Jr. *Descartes and the Resilience of Rhetoric: Varieties of Cartesian Rhetorical Theory*. Carbondale: Southern Illinois UP, 1990.

Lamy, Bernard. *De l'art de parler*. Paris: Pralard, 1676.

LeGuern, Michel. "La Méthode dans *La Rhétorique ou l'art de parler* de Bernard Lamy." *Grammaire et méthode au XVIIe siècle*. Ed. Pierre Swiggers. Leuven: Peeters, 1984. 49–67.

Warnick, Barbara. *Belletristic Rhetorical Theory and Its French Antecedents*. Columbia: U of South Carolina P, 1993.

See also PORT ROYALISTS

Lauer, Janice M. (b. 1931)

Educator whose work focuses on rhetoric as a dynamic discipline operating within institutional communities. Lauer began with an inquiry into rhetorical invention to correct the undervaluing of invention in rhetorical practice in the composition pedagogy of the 1960s and 1970s. Her interests have since extended to include persuasion, the interdisciplinary nature of rhetoric, and the issues of program development and research in rhetoric—particularly with empirical research in collaboration with specialists in psychology, linguistics, and educational measurement. Although this may suggest a diffused focus, in fact it represents a coherent point of view controlled by the following assumptions:

1. A knowledge of the history of rhetoric is a resource for understanding contemporary theoretical problems in rhetoric
2. The value of rhetorical knowledge is in its applications to pedagogical practice based on the resources of empirical, descriptive, and conceptual research
3. Rhetoric is most usefully understood as an inquiry-oriented process
4. Rhetoric runs the risk of being institutionally "ghettoized" if it does not work with other correlated disciplines, especially in the social sciences
5. Assessment scales based on rhetorical/interpretive aspects of writing are more useful than those based on formal/linguistic scales in assessing writing

A substantial part of Lauer's published work is collaborative and interdisciplinary: Much of her published work is collaborative, involving rhetoricians (Richard Enos, Andrea Lunsford, and Janet Emig), linguists (Ulla Connor), psychologists (John Nicholls), and specialists in educational measurement (William Asher). The collaborative process runs deeply and richly through all her work in its situational quality—from her reliance on Richard Young's

tagmemic methods in her writing to her dialectical controversy with Ann Berthoff.

Her work in the history and theory of rhetorical invention has been in the main descriptive and encyclopedic. This historical background, moreover, is frequently drawn on in other works to help to shape the language and models for practice in the development of pedagogical materials and research methods.

Her work in the area of discipline and program cultivation has an axiological flavor: She sees value in disciplines and interdisciplinary teams insofar as they comprise productive communities that are extending the realm of knowledge and practice, and she works to draw on the specialized knowledge and methods of other disciplines, particularly psychology and learning theory, that share issues or problems with rhetoric.

Her work in the area of empirical research demonstrates how empirical, descriptive, historical, and theoretical studies can and should complement and enhance each other. She wrestles with the problems of defining the training requirements for students in a field so broadly defined, and at the same time she models the process of strategically integrating methods and perspectives and collaborating with other disciplines.

Her most important achievement has been to demonstrate the wide applicability of rhetorical knowledge and training. Her publications are a gold mine of applications of rhetorical concepts. The integration of theoretical, empirical, and pedagogical method thus gives her work a decidedly pragmatic cast, which makes the separation of theory and practice appropriately difficult.

Phil M. Keith
St. Cloud State University

Bibliography

Lauer, Janice M. "Composition Studies: Dappled Discipline." *Rhetoric Review* 3 (1984): 20–29.

———. "Issues in Rhetorical Invention." *Essays on Classical Rhetoric and Modern Discourse*. Ed. Robert Connors, Lisa Ede, and Andrea Lunsford. Carbondale: Southern Illinois UP, 1984. 127–40.

Lauer, Janice M., and William Asher. *Composition Research: Empirical Designs*. New York: Oxford UP, 1988.

Lauer, Janice M., and Ulla Connor. "Understanding Persuasive Essay Writing, Linguistic/Rhetorical Approach." *Text* 5 (1985): 309–26.

Lauer, Janice M., and Janet Emig, Andrea Lunsford, and Gene Montague. *Four Worlds of Writing*. 3rd ed. New York: Harper, 1991.

Legal Rhetoric

Any oral or written discourse inscribing or supporting the generation, interpretation, application, amendment, or repeal of laws and contracts in a liberal, representative democracy. Legal rhetoric since Aristotle has been conceived to have two main divisions, forensic and deliberative. It is distinguishable from political rhetoric, whose aim is the praising or blaming of individuals or organizations (for their intelligence, moral character, and past actions) during electoral campaigns.

In its forensic mode, legal rhetoric encompasses the enormous range of discourse conditioned by the settlement of disputes through court litigation and arbitration before neutral third parties. The paradigm forensic situations are considered to involve (1) lawyer-to-judge or (2) judge-to-lawyer rhetoric. Thus there is the lawyer's argument in behalf of a plaintiff or defendant directed to a judge or jury—that is, in trial courts and courts of appeal. Adapting earlier rhetoricians such as Hermagoras, Cicero maintained that all such arguments fall into one of four kinds of stases: arguments of fact (whether or not an act was committed), arguments of definition (how an act, if committed, was to be categorized or described in view of existing laws), arguments of jurisdiction (whether a case was properly tried in a given court at a given time), and arguments of quality (whether an action, even if committed and deemed illegal, might still be deemed just or excusable in view of the equities). At the conclusion of a trial or appellate hearing, modern judge-to-lawyer rhetoric occurs in written judicial opinions that announce and present justification for the court's decision.

Closely connected to this forensic paradigm are many exigencies requiring lawyer-to-lawyer rhetoric, such as when one lawyer attempts to persuade another (opposing lawyer) not to go to trial because the opponent's case lacks foundation in law or fact or when among a team of lawyers there is a debate about the proper arguments to make on a specific legal issue. Other exigencies involve lawyer-to-witness discourse, as when a lawyer uses rhetorical strategies to elicit testimony from a witness before or during trial. Conversely, one also observes legal rhetoric in the efforts of witnesses or clients to shape the perceptions, beliefs, and actions of lawyers concerning the handling of a case. And finally, there is the juror-to-juror rhetoric that occurs during formal jury deliberations at trial.

In its deliberative mode, legal rhetoric encompasses the enormous range of discourse conditioned by the making of laws and binding agreements in assemblies or negotiations. The paradigmatic deliberative situations are thought to involve (1) legislator-to-legislator or (2) legislator-to-citizen rhetoric. There is thus the senator's effort to persuade colleagues to vote for (or against) a particular bill, and the similar effort to drum up or reduce support among the public by members of executive branches of government such as governors, presidents, and prime ministers. Conversely, there are the efforts of citizen, activist, or lobbying groups to persuade legislators to generate or adopt particular bills, or direct citizen-to-citizen rhetoric exercised during initiative and referendum campaigns that sidestep legislative review and enactment to put new laws on popular ballots.

Perhaps the common element in both forensic and deliberative modes of legal rhetoric is the effort by a rhetor to persuade others as to what particular laws or contracts have meant in the past, what they will mean in the future, or what they should mean at present, in view of a particular case or social exigency.

History of Legal Rhetoric

In the indispensable work by Rieke, the historical demarcation of legal rhetoric from rhetoric generally conceived began with the rise of professional schools for lawyers in the late Middle Ages and early Renaissance. These schools tried to shed the legacy of the empty reasoning practiced under the name of rhetoric in the Latin trivium, while at the same time they appeared to lose sight of the philosophical and political necessity for legal rhetorical theory grandly defended in the writings of Cicero and Quintilian. Even the more directly utilitarian, technical methods for discovering legal arguments painstakingly articulated by Cicero in *De inventione,* perhaps the greatest single work on forensic rhetoric and argumentation ever written, seem not to have been assimilated when lawyering and law schools became professionalized during this period. Ever since, rhetorical theory has been forced to maintain an apologetic stance toward law and lawyers, needing to demonstrate its relevance and value in the face of great skepticism.

In Rieke and other scholars, several explanations are offered as to why there has been little later sustained development of classical rhetorical theory for lawyers. One of these explanations, according to Rieke, is that Western democratic legal systems, with their increasingly elaborate rules for evidence and proof, actually absorbed and reflected classical rhetorical theory in an implicit way. That is, to the extent that Aristotle and Cicero addressed themselves in their rhetorical treatises to norms for proper reasoning, Rieke suggests that their work did in fact have influence—but not as rhetorical theory or as legal rhetorical theory per se. A second explanation is that the training of lawyers through apprenticeship and imitation, which began in the late Middle Ages, obviated the need for any comprehensive theorizing; one learned legal rhetoric "by doing it" under the watchful eyes of a mentor. In that sense it might be said that the pre-Aristotelian schools of sophistic rhetoric became the models for lawyers and for legal education in rhetoric.

A third explanation is the Enlightenment view that both making and proving a correct legal decision are matters of scientific logic and deductive demonstration, a view that reached its zenith in Langdell's case method for preparing lawyers at Harvard Law School. That view, perhaps more than any other factor, is what to this day has marginalized the study of legal reading and writing tasks, as well as study of rhetorical theory within professional law schools. As Rieke further details, there were some important experiments in adapting classical rhetorical theory to the preparation of lawyers in American law schools early in their history, particularly at Yale; but those experiments have had little lasting influence, and rhetorical theory is rarely a required course of study in modern American law schools.

Relation of Rhetoric, Legal Argumentation, and Legal Reasoning

Underlying the issue as to whether lawyers draw upon or need rhetorical theory is the deeper question concerning the nature of legal reasoning and legal argumentation. Is legal reasoning different from other forms of reasoning, especially scientific induction and deduction? And if it is different, how should it be described? Much modern inquiry by philosophers, jurisprudential scholars, and rhetorical theorists has addressed itself to this issue. Despite widespread recognition that deductive logic can be used to analyze only certain aspects of legal reasoning and argument, as variously shown in the important works of

Frank, Gottlieb, Stone, Levi, Wasserstrom, Perelman, Llewellyn, Moore, and Parker, a coherent, widely accepted model of the reasoning manifest in legal argumentation has not been realized. As discussed in more recent inquiries, such as those of Stratman, several problems contribute to the difficulty. One is that many theorists confound the theoretically distinct tasks of description with prescription; commonly, how a theorist believes legal arguments and decisions are constructed largely reflects how, from an ethical or epistemological perspective, they believe they should be constructed. This confusion has particularly haunted theorists who, like Wasserstrom, find deductive logic to be the best framework in which to understand legal argumentation.

A second problem is that most theory has uncritically assumed that the rhetorical reasoning of lawyers as advocates and the rhetorical reasoning of judges as decision-makers is fundamentally the same—that is, that there is some single root reasoning process for their activity. For example, until theorists like Perelman, there has been relatively little concern for how audience perception and social cognition generally fit into legal reasoning and argumentation processes.

A third problem, and arguably the most serious, is that theorists have confounded the complex processes of discovering legal arguments and making legal decisions with the texts that are the results—or outputs—of those processes (for example, court briefs or opinions). Thus, for example, Jensen remarks at the opening of his book, "My concern as a student of logic is with the process leading to judicial decisions in so far as they revolve around a question of law, and not with the legal soundness of the decisions themselves. Moreover, only one aspect of the judicial process [will be] considered, namely, the reasoning a judge gives in support of his decisions, and which is also believed to be the reasoning by means of which he arrived at them" (1). Though the problems with this equation are discussed in the literature, most of the major work before 1970 attempts to build theories of legal rhetoric by taking only formal written arguments as relevant data, so that the "processes" of legal rhetoric are reduced to processes that seem inherent in or inferable from these texts.

Research On Legal Rhetoric: Sources

Empirical research on legal rhetoric increasingly examines contexts, social and psychological processes, and genres that extend far beyond lawyers' briefs and judges' court opinions. The effort to widen the scope of inquiry in legal rhetoric can be seen clearly in the educational, sociolinguistic, and anthropological, as well as psychological, communication, and cognitive science research streams. For educational researchers, Wren and Wren provide a careful historical account of how instruction in legal research and written legal genres came to be marginalized in professional law school curricula. For sociolinguists, anthropologists, and students of the history of legal language, the works of Melinkoff, O'Barr, and Danet reflect the ongoing effort to understand the effects of legal rhetoric within larger social and cultural contexts. The effort to understand the relation between cognitive processes involved in the production of legal rhetoric and the cognitive processes involved in its interpretation during attempts at persuasion in appellate courts can best be seen in the work of Stratman and Skinner. Finally, for what is perhaps the most active and intensive empirical research stream—jury instruction, decision and influence processes—the work of Sales, and Hastie, Penrod, and Pennington provide comprehensive overviews.

James F. Stratman
University of Colorado, Denver

Bibliography

Cicero, Marcus Tullius. *De Inventione*. Cambridge, MA: Loeb Classical Library, Harvard UP, 1949.

Danet, Brenda. "Legal Discourse." *Handbook of Discourse Analysis*. Ed. Teun Van Dijk. New York: Academic, 1985. 273–391.

Frank, Jerome. *Law and the Modern Mind*. New York: Brentano's, 1930.

Gaskins, Richard H. *Burdens of Proof in Modern Discourse*. New Haven: Yale UP, 1992.

Goodrich, Peter. *Reading the Law: A Critical Introduction to Legal Method and Techniques*. New York: Blackwell, 1986.

Gottlieb, Gidon. *The Logic of Choice*. New York: Macmillan, 1968.

Hastie, Reid, Steven Penrod, and Nancy Pennington. *Inside the Jury*. Cambridge, MA: Harvard UP, 1983.

Jensen, O. *The Nature of Legal Argument*. Oxford: Blackwell, 1957.

Levi, Edward. *An Introduction to Legal Reasoning*. Chicago: U of Chicago P, 1948.

Llewellyn, Karl. *The Common Law Tradition: Deciding Appeals*. Boston: Little, 1960.

Melinkoff, David. *The Language of the Law*. Boston: Little, 1963.

Moore, Michael. "The Semantics of Judging." *Southern California Law Review* 54 (1981): 151–294.

O'Barr, William. *Linguistic Evidence: Language, Power and Strategy in the Classroom*. New York: Academic, 1982.

Parker, Richard. *Toward a Critical Methodology for Judicial Opinions*. Diss. U of Pittsburgh, 1981.

Perelman, Chaïm. *Justice, Law and Argument*. Dordrecht, Holland: Reidel, 1980.

Rieke, Richard. "Argumentation in the Legal Process." *Advances in Argumentation Theory and Research*. Ed. J. Robert Cox and Charles A. Willard. Carbondale: Southern Illinois UP, 1982. 363–76.

———. "Investigating Legal Argument as a Field." *Dimensions of Argument: Proceedings of the Second Summer Conference on Argumentation*. Ed. G. Ziegelmueller and J. Rhodes. Annandale, VA: Speech Communication Assn. 152–58.

———. *Rhetorical Theory in American Legal Practice*. Diss. Ohio State U, 1964.

Sales, Bruce, ed. *Perspectives in Law and Psychology: The Trial Process*. New York: Plenum, 1981.

Skinner, Anna. *Writing in a Law Firm: Cognitive Processes and Texts Grounded in Social Knowledge*. Diss. U of Texas, Austin, 1988.

Stone, Julius. *Legal System and Lawyers' Reasonings*. Stanford, CA: Stanford UP, 1964.

Stratman, James. "Legal Composition as a Field of Inquiry." *Review of Educational Research* 60 (1990): 153–235.

———. *The Rhetorical Dynamics of Appellate Court Persuasion*. Diss. Carnegie Mellon U, 1988.

Wasserstrom, Richard. *The Judicial Decision: Toward a Theory of Legal Justification*. Stanford, CA: Stanford UP, 1961.

Wellaufer, Gerald. "Rhetoric and Its Denial in Legal Discourse." *Virginia Law Review* 76 (1990): 1545.

Wren, Christopher, and Jill Wren. "The Teaching of Legal Research." *Law Library Journal* 80 (1988): 7–61.

See also CICERO; DELIBERATIVE ORATORY; STASIS THEORY

L

Letteraturizzazione

The tendency of rhetoric, conceptualized in Greece as an art of public address, to become a feature of literary composition and a basis of literary criticism. The Italian term *letteraturizzazione* was perhaps first used in this sense by Florescu (35) and was introduced into English by Kennedy (5) to describe how the teaching of rhetoric has affected written composition and the tendency of writers of prose and poetry to use techniques learned in schools of rhetoric. Although this applies most clearly to the presence in literature of rhetorical tropes, figures, and other features of style, it can also be seen in the use of "topics" and in the adaptation of the structure of a judicial speech (introduction, narration, proof, and conclusion) to other genres, as in the medieval *dictamen*.

Letteraturizzazione is possible because rhetorical energy is a property of all communication. It was facilitated in the classical period by the fact that most literature was publicly performed and by the use of dramatic speeches in epic, drama, and historical works. It was encouraged by the publication of speeches in written form, thus becoming literary models, and by citation by writers on rhetoric, beginning with Aristotle, of examples of rhetorical techniques from literary works, thus suggesting that these works were in some sense rhetorical. The phenomenon is especially evident in those periods when rhetoric retained a central place in formal education while public address was losing ground as a feature of civic life, often accompanied by some loss of freedom of speech: after the fourth century B.C.E. in Greece, under the Roman Empire, and in the Middle Ages or under later autocratic governments. For the Roman period, the classic discussion is Tacitus's *Dialogue on the Orators*. *Letteraturizzazione* is also seen in the assumption of modern literary critics that rhetoric is to be identified with the literary use of metaphor and metonymy.

Evidence of adoption of rhetorical techniques can be found in the highly artificial style characteristic of literature in the periods mentioned, especially the Roman Empire and the Renaissance, in the emphasis on style in rhetorical treatises beginning in the first century B.C.E., and in the use of rhetorical concepts by literary critics (such as Longinus and his Renaissance successors). Christian rhetoric also experienced *letteraturizzazione* as Fathers of the Church from the second to the fourth century drew on the resources of classical rhetoric in their preaching and writing, and again in the Renaissance, when preachers created a Christian epideictic in the grand style.

The concept of *letteraturizzazione* is logocentric insofar as it assumes that the adaptation of rhetoric to literature represents a loss of authenticity. It thus might seem opposed to the concept of "grammatology" as developed by Derrida and his followers, but Derridean grammatology does not deny that writers in the Western tradition since Plato have sought to imitate the living presence of speech; rather, it deconstructs their attempts as a search for fixed meaning that is elusive because of the ambivalent rhetorical quality of all language.

George A. Kennedy
University of North Carolina

Bibliography

Derrida, Jacques. *Of Grammatology*. Trans. G.C. Spivak. Baltimore: Johns Hopkins UP, 1976.

Florescu, Vasile. *La retorica nel suo sviluppo storico*. Bologna: Il Mulino, 1971.

Kennedy, George A. *Classical Rhetoric and Its Christian and Secular Tradition from Ancient to Modern Times*. Chapel Hill: U of North Carolina P. 108–19.

Linguistics

The study of language as a human faculty. Linguistics describes language phenomena of all sorts, from the individual sound through complete discourses. Further, linguistics is a descriptive discipline. Contemporary linguists do not attempt to prescribe how language is used; rather they describe how language is used, primarily by native speakers but also in applied areas such as sociolinguistics and English as a Second Language, as used by nonnative speakers as well. This article will begin with a general discussion of language phenomena, then focus specifically on recent and contemporary applications of linguistics to rhetoric and composition studies. Much of the discussion is based on Raskin and Weiser (1987).

The linguistic disciplines of phonetics and phonology study the phenomenon of sound in language. Phonetics is concerned with the empirical analysis of sound and includes the segmentation of the flow of sounds in speech into discrete units, the inventorying of the sounds of a particular language, the description of each sound, and the description of the elements of pronunciation. Phonology is a theoretical discipline that studies the sound patterns in a language. Working from the descriptions of individual sounds described by phonetics, phonology is concerned with the distinction between similar sounds (for example, the subtle differences between aspirated and unaspirated sounds such as the *p* in *pin* and in *spin*, and the more obvious differences such as that between the initial sounds in the words *pin* and *bin*), the set of "permissible" sound patterns in a particular language (for instance, the absence of the initial combination of "cj" or "ck" in English, though the latter combination is permissible in the middle or end of words, as in *chicken* or *check*), and the range of variation in sound (for example, sounds that are phonetically similar enough to be accepted as the same, accounting for a native speaker's ability to understand a variety of accents and dialects).

Morphology is concerned with the smallest meaningful units of language, those which enable language-users to understand complex individual words. The smallest meaningful parts are called morphemes. Words are composed of one or more morphemes. Words such as *walk, table, desire, frame,* and *elephant* all are single-morpheme words; that is, none can be divided into smaller meaningful units. Words such as *walking, tables, desirable, reframe,* and *elephantine* consist of two morphemes each, while *undesirable* and *reframed* are made up of three morphemes. The division of words into morphemes is thus unrelated to the division of words into syllables because, as the examples of *table, desire,* and *elephant* demonstrate, multisyllabic words may nevertheless consist of only a single morpheme. Similarly, the word *dogs* consists of only one syllable but two morphemes, *dog* plus the plural marker *s*. Thus the distinction between a word and a morpheme is that a word is the minimal meaningful unit that can be used alone within the context of ordinary speech. Such a morpheme is sometimes referred to as a lexical or free morpheme. Other morphemes, called grammatical or bound morphemes, such as most prefixes and suffixes and plural markers, cannot stand alone in this way.

Syntax refers to the system of rules that describe how words are combined into phrases and sentences. Each sentence can be analyzed syntactically by identifying all the phrases that compose it and all the words that constitute each phrase. The analysis of sentences by syntactic rules underlies the concepts of grammaticality and ungrammaticality—that is, whether or not a sentence is considered by native speakers to be a possible sentence of their language. Contempo-

rary syntactic theory has been most heavily influenced by the work of Noam Chomsky. In *Syntactic Structures* (1957), Chomsky proposed a set of rules for describing syntax that formed the basis of generative grammar—a grammar, that is, a system of rules—which can explain or generate the structures of all the grammatical sentences of a language. The key rules of generative grammar, the phrase structure rules, can account for a wide variety of syntactic patterns, but the addition of transformational rules helped account for some more complex structures such as negatives and passives. The main contribution of transformations has been to allow the identification of two levels of syntax: the deep structure, assumed to be the result of the application of the phrase structure rules of generative grammar, and the surface structure, which results from the application of transformations. Thus the deep structure of "The dog chased the cat" and "The cat was chased by the dog" are assumed to be the same, and the difference in their surface structure is attributed to the application of the passive transformation to the sentence generated by the insertion of lexical items into the noun phrase/verb phrase structure of the sentence.

A problem with Chomsky's early theory is that it provided rules for generating not only grammatical sentences but also sentences like his famous "*Colorless green ideas sleep furiously*" (the asterisk is a conventional marker in linguistics for nongrammatical sentences). In his *Aspects of the Theory of Syntax* (1965), Chomsky revised transformational grammar by adding additional rules that accounted for features or properties such as animate, human, singular, and so on for nouns and similar features for other words and combinatorial and selection restriction rules that govern grammatical combinations.

A final point to be made here about syntax and one which has implications for the applications of syntax to rhetoric and composition discussed later is that all languages allow for clauses and sentences to be embedded within one another.

Semantics differs from the linguistic disciplines discussed in the preceding paragraphs. While phonetics, phonology, morphology, and syntax are concerned with linguistic structures, semantics is concerned with the study of meaning in language. Thus semantics encompasses a variety of linguistic structures, from the morpheme, which is the minimal meaningful unit in language, through the text or discourse. Early semantic studies focused primarily on word meaning, with emphasis on the analysis of semantic features. These abstract features, such as human, male, and adult, allowed for words such as *man, woman, boy,* and *girl* to be described according to whether or not they possessed each feature. Thus while each of these four words would be described as "+Human," *man* and *boy* would be described as "+Male," *woman* and *girl* as "-Male," *man* and *woman* as "+Adult," and *boy* and *girl* as "-Adult." Feature analysis is most adequate at describing meaning when it is applied to words with clear, distinct meanings; it is less successful at describing words whose meanings cannot easily be identified in binary features. Words that describe colors are typical examples: It is difficult to determine the features of blue, for example, that would allow one to distinguish it from other colors, both those very different such as yellow and those fairly similar such as violet or blue-green.

A second semantic approach to word meaning focuses on the relations of words to one another. The four commonly studied relationships are synonymy, the relationship among words with identical or very similar meanings; antonomy, the relationship between two words with opposite meanings; homonymy, words with the same spelling and pronunciation but different and unrelated meanings; and polysemy, words with related though different meanings. Unlike synonyms and antonyms, homonyms do not share semantic features: *bear* referring to the animal, *bear* meaning to give birth, and *bear* meaning to tolerate demonstrate this. Homonyms and polysemous words may create ambiguity, as in a sentence like "The bill is large," in which *bill* may refer to the beak of a bird, a part of a cap, or the slip of paper indicating the cost of a purchase. Contextual semantics, discussed later, attempts to address this kind of ambiguity.

Another area of semantic study is sentence meaning. The work of Katz and Fodor (1963) is foundational. Associates of Chomsky's, Katz and Fodor attempted to develop a semantic theory that would do what Chomsky's syntactic theories were designed to do: match the competence of the native speaker. In semantics this meant developing a theory that would account for the ability of native speakers to understand the meaning of sentences, including ambiguity, paraphrase, and semantic anomalies, the latter referring to the deviant property of sentences such as "*Colorless green ideas sleep furiously" that render them meaningless in ordinary, nonmetaphorical use.

The semantic theory of Katz and Fodor and related theories proposed by others focused only on the meaning of the individual sentence in isolation both from surrounding sentences and from the context in which it is used. Such a limitation, however, contradicts the goal of matching the competence of native speakers, as native speakers do indeed interpret sentences in context and in fact are able to disambiguate sentences by interpreting them in the context in which they are used. Contextual semantics and pragmatics offer explanations for this competency.

Contextual semantic theories allow for the expansion of ordinary definitions of words to incorporate semantic information upon which native speakers can draw when they encounter or use a word in a particular context. Raskin uses the term *script* to refer to these more comprehensive semantic constructs. He suggests that the word *doctor* carries with it not only such semantic features as "+Adult," "+Human" but also semantic information that incorporates contextual details such as the activities (study medicine, receive patients, diagnose and treat diseases), places (medical school, hospital, doctor's office), and conditions (physical contact) native speakers associate with the word. Context provides cues for which specific scripts one might apply in a particular situation. Concepts such as scripts thus account for the semantic information that enables people to interpret ambiguous sentences such as "The bill is large" by applying contextual cues to select the appropriate meanings within the context of use.

Pragmatics, sometimes considered a separate linguistic discipline from semantics, typically refers to several specific concepts concerning language users' understanding of how language is used to communicate. The major concepts of pragmatics are presupposition, speech acts, and implicature. Presupposition refers to the assumptions or set of conditions that underlie a particular statement. For example, the sentence "The accident was not my fault" presupposes that an accident occurred and that someone might be at fault. Speech act theory, proposed by Austin (1962) and developed by Searle (1969) is designed to describe the function that sentences perform in discourse. The three basic speech acts, the locutionary act, the illocutionary act, and the perlocutionary act refer respectively to the utterance, the intent of the utterance, and the effect of the utterance. Since there is no correspondence between syntactic structure and speech acts, the same illocutionary act, for instance a request, may be expressed by several locutionary acts. Thus the question "Can you pass me the salt?" and the command "Pass me the salt" and the statement "This soup needs more salt" have the same intention and are understood by both speaker and hearer to produce the effect of the hearer's passing the salt to the speaker. These sentences also illustrate the concept of implicature, developed by Grice (1975), which refers to the use of sentences in nonliteral or unconventional meanings. The sentence "This soup needs more salt" only functions as a request for salt if the appropriate circumstances, such as the presence of a hearer who has access to salt, exist. The same sentence may simply serve as an observation or criticism if it is uttered in a different circumstance, such as to one's dinner companion in a restaurant where neither salt nor server are immediately available. Grice's principles of bona fide communication (Quantity—relate exactly as much information as necessary; Quality—say only what you believe to be true; Relation—speak to the point; and Manner—be succinct) underlie the cooperative principle by which the speaker tells the truth and the hearer recognizes the intention and believes what is said. Implicatures come about when the speaker deliberately violates one or more of the principles, signals the violation to the hearer, and the hearer recognizes the intended meaning of the violation. A fourth pragmatic concept, related to the three discussed thus far, is inference, which might be thought of as the reader's (or hearer's) recognition of what is presupposed.

The previous discussion has focused on principal disciplines of linguistics, but linguistics, like rhetoric, is also an interdisciplinary field. Other areas of linguistics include neurolinguistics, which studies the physiological aspects of language and the brain; historical linguistics; and applied linguistics areas such as psycholinguistics, text linguistics, discourse analysis, sociolinguistics, and second language acquisition (including English as a Second Language). Of these areas, the last four have the most direct connections with work in rhetoric and will be referred to in the following discussion of applications of linguistics to rhetoric and composition studies.

During the 1960s and 1970s, researchers in rhetoric and composition developed applications of the syntactic descriptions from Chomsky's transformational generative grammar. Some researchers believed that because transformational generative grammar so successfully described syntactic relationships, it might prove to be a useful tool for teaching students to avoid errors and to write more effective sentences. In one regard this belief seems naive, as research has consistently demonstrated that formal grammar instruction has neither effect (for summaries of numerous studies, see Braddock 1963 and Mellon 1969). Nevertheless, Chomsky's theories provided the impetus for new research into the relationship between instruction and grammar and the teaching of writing.

One such study, that of Bateman and Zidonis (1964), reported that students instructed in transformational grammar did reduce the number of errors in their writing and, in addition, wrote sentences that contained a larger number of transformations than did students who did not receive such instruction. The apparently positive results of this study stimulated other research designed to identify more accurately the specific causes for the improvement Bateman and Zidonis reported. In particular, Mellon (1969) and O'Hare (1973) questioned the extent to which the growth reported could be attributed to the formal instruction in transformational grammar rather than to the actual practice of applying transformations. Following Chomsky, Hunt (1964) and subsequently Mellon and O'Hare argued that students possess the competence, that is, the inherent linguistic knowledge, that allows them to recognize as grammatical and to use most of the transformations Bateman and Zidonis claimed to have taught. Their research led to the development of pedagogies based on sentence-combining, exercises in which students combine a short series of sentences in order to develop their ability to use a variety of transformations. Though at the height of the interest in sentence-combining claims were made for its efficacy in improving students' writing in a variety of ways, not just syntactically, sentence-combining is currently seen as having a valuable but limited function in helping writers practice a variety of syntactic patterns they might not otherwise attempt to use and in alerting them to numerous options of expressing themselves.

Both transformational grammar and Kenneth Pike's tagmemic grammar have been applied to rhetoric and composition studies as facilitating invention. Francis Christensen's "Generative Rhetoric of the Sentence" (1963) and "Generative Rhetoric of the Paragraph" (1965) loosely borrowed concepts from structuralist and transformational linguistics, which he used to explain how syntactic structures he called cumulative sentences encouraged the "generation" of new ideas. Pike's tagmemics is the origin both of theories of paragraph organization and of a heuristic, developed with Alton Becker and Richard Young, based on Pike's concepts of contrast, variation, and distribution. The work of Pike, Young, and Becker was synthesized in their influential 1970 textbook *Rhetoric: Discovery and Change*. The tagmemic heuristic presented there has been adopted and adapted widely.

With the exception of Christensen's rather metaphoric extension of transformational generative grammar to the generation of ideas in writing and the applications of Pike's tagmemic theory, most efforts to apply linguistic theory to rhetoric prior to the 1980s focused primarily on grammar and syntax. In a sense such an emphasis paralleled the notion of semanticists Katz and Fodor, who, as explained above, argued that semantic theory could account for the meaning of sentences in isolation but not for the meaning of any sentence in context. However, the work referred to earlier in semantics and pragmatics, as well as work in text linguistics, most done in the late 1960s and early 1970s, suggested approaches to understanding both meaning and structure in larger discourses, and such research has been influential in rhetoric and composition.

In particular, linguistic theories have been applied to discourses longer than sentences as means of analyzing and understanding cohesion and coherence. Until the mid 1970s, cohesion and coherence were often used interchangeably, both referring either to a kind of vague sense of wholeness or to a more specific set of relationships definable grammatically and lexically. The work of Halliday and Hasan (1976) influenced scholars and researchers in rhetoric and composition so that, by the early 1980s, the two terms were distinguished. Cohesion is now understood to be a textual quality, attained through the use of grammatical and lexical elements that enable readers to perceive semantic relationships within and between sentences. Coherence refers to the overall consistency of a discourse—its purpose, voice, content, style, form, and so on—and is in part determined by readers' perceptions of texts, dependent not only on linguistic and contextual information in the texts but also on readers' abilities to draw upon other kinds of knowledge, such as cultural and intertextual knowledge.

The most influential work on cohesion has been Halliday and Hasan's *Cohesion in English*.

Halliday and Hasan identify three major types of cohesion—grammatical cohesion, lexical cohesion, and conjunction—and further classify subgroups of each. Grammatical cohesion is attained through the use of cohesive ties such as pronouns, synonyms, comparatives, and definite articles, which link sentences but which do not necessarily add new semantic information. Lexical cohesion depends upon the semantic relationship of one lexical item with another; that is, any word is potentially cohesive but becomes so only when it co-occurs with a semantically similar word. Conjunction connectives, typically referred to as transitions, depend neither upon reference to or replacement of grammatical elements nor upon co-occurrence with another lexical item. For example, in the sentences "The students played soccer. Afterwards it rained" the conjunction *afterwards* makes the two sentences more obviously cohesive by suggesting a specific temporal relationship between them. Each of these types of cohesion can be understood in terms of the concept of presupposition, as the sentence containing the cohesive tie presupposes information that does not appear in that sentence but that is retrievable from the adjacent sentence.

The same kinds of cohesive ties that produce cohesion between two sentences produce cohesion within larger texts. The use of conjunctions, repetition, synonyms, pronouns, and other cohesive devices throughout a paragraph or longer discourse serve to create and indicate cohesion. Analyses of cohesive patterns in longer discourses, derived from the work of text linguists and psycholinguists such as van Dyke, Prince, and Clark and Clark, have been applied in rhetoric by Witte and Faigley (1981) and Witte (1983). In particular, Witte's 1983 "Topical Structure and Revision" provides an excellent summary of theories of topical structure from the Prague School, as well as demonstrating the application of those theories in composition.

Cohesion contributes to the coherence of a text, but because coherence is determined by readers' perceptions of texts, influenced both by the texts themselves and the readers' world or contextual knowledge, contextual semantics and pragmatics also play a part in analyzing and understanding coherence. In particular, script-knowledge, inference, and presupposition contribute to the description of a text as coherent. The presence of incompatible, redundant, or irrelevant scripts in a text is an indication of its incoherence. Texts that are underdetailed, requiring readers to make too many inferences, and texts that are overdetailed, providing readers with information easily inferred, may also be perceived to be incoherent (see Raskin and Weiser 1987:212–16 for examples).

One other application of linguistics that has not been mentioned thus far is directly related to the fact that the goal of modern linguistics is to describe how language is used rather than to prescribe its use. Dialectologists and some sociolinguists study and describe patterns of language use by specific groups of language users. Their work has led to several important recognitions: that the so-called standard dialect (Standard American English) is an idealized dialect that no one really speaks; that all dialects are grammatical, though the grammatical patterns of dialects differ from one another; and that the identification of any dialect as standard, privileged, or preferred is cultural, not linguistic.

The previous discussion of linguistic applications to rhetoric and composition suggests some ways in which linguistic concepts have been borrowed to develop theories, pedagogical applications, and analytical techniques. The contributions of linguistics to rhetoric and composition are thus significant, though not central. And there are limits to linguistic applications to rhetoric and composition, based on both the descriptive nature of linguistics and the broader concerns of rhetoric and composition. Because linguistics is not prescriptive, it does not offer judgments about language quality—that is, it does not provide the basis for judging one of two grammatical sentences as better than the other. And because rhetoric and composition are concerned not only with language but also with the use of language in particular rhetorical situations, there are a number of extralinguistic dimensions of rhetorical effectiveness, such as appropriateness for purpose and audience, the appropriateness of style, conformity to rhetorical conventions for a particular type of discourse, and so on, that linguistics cannot address.

Irwin Weiser
Purdue University

Bibliography

Austin, John L. *How to Do Things with Words*. New York: Oxford UP, 1962.

Bateman, D.R., and F.J. Zidonis. *The Effect of a Knowledge of Generative Grammar upon the Growth of Language Complexity*. Columbus: Ohio State U. U.S. Office of Education Cooperative Research Project 1746, 1964.

Braddock, Richard, et al. *Research in Written Communication*. Urbana, IL: National Council of Teachers of English, 1963.

Chomsky, Noam. *Aspects of the Theory of Syntax*. Cambridge, MA: MIT P, 1965.

———. *Syntactic Structures*. The Hague: Mouton, 1957.

Christensen, Francis. "A Generative Rhetoric of the Paragraph." *College Composition and Communication* 16 (1965): 144–56.

———. "A Generative Rhetoric of the Sentence." *College Composition and Communication* 14 (1963): 155–61.

Grice, H. Paul. "Logic and Conversation." *Syntax and Semantics Vol. 3 Speech Acts*. Ed. Peter Cole and Jerry L. Morgan. New York: Academic, 1975. 41–58.

Halliday, M.A.K., and Ruqaiya Hasan. *Cohesion in English*. London: Longmans, 1976.

Hunt, Kellogg W. *Grammatical Structures Written at Three Grade Levels*. Urbana, IL: National Council of Teachers of English, 1965.

Katz, Jerrold J., and Jerry A. Fodor. "The Structure of a Semantic Theory." *Language* 39 (1963): 170–210.

Mellon, John C. *Transformational Sentence-Combining*. Urbana, IL: National Council of Teachers of English, 1969.

O'Hare, Frank. *Sentence-Combining: Improving Student Writing without Formal Grammar Instruction*. Urbana, IL: National Council of Teachers of English, 1973.

Raskin, Victor, and Irwin Weiser. *Language and Writing: Applications of Linguistics to Rhetoric and Composition*. Norwood, NJ: Ablex, 1987.

Searle, John R. *Speech Acts*. Cambridge: Cambridge UP, 1969.

Witte, Stephen P. "Topical Structure and Revision: An Exploratory Study." *College Composition and Communication* 34 (1983): 313–41.

Witte, Stephen P., and Lester Faigley. "Coherence, Cohesion, and Writing Quality." *College Composition and Communication* 32 (1981): 189–204.

Young, Richard E., Alton Becker, and Kenneth Pike. *Rhetoric: Discovery and Change*. New York: Harcourt, 1970.

See also COHERENCE; COHESION; PRAGMATICS

Literacy

In composition and rhetoric, illuminates the ways that individual acts of writing are connected to larger cultural, historical, social, and political systems. Serving this broadened perspective, interest in literacy has grown as part of a general focus on the social contexts and social ideologies of written language use. Neighboring fields that research literacy, particularly anthropology, psychology, history, and critical education, have helped to enrich writing research, both theoretically and empirically.

By the time the Modern Language Association sponsored the first Right to Literacy Conference at Ohio State University in 1988, *literacy* or *literacy studies* had become an appealing rubric for a wide range of concerns and interests in the field of composition and rhetoric. The term is useful for conceptualizing underlying language abilities that may be common to both reading and writing. It is also useful for identifying pedagogical interests that may be common to teachers of both composition and literature (as well as English teachers in all settings).

Relationships between the oral and the written and their implications for cultural and cognitive development organize many of the key debates among scholars of literacy in anthropology and psychology. In 1968 anthropologist Jack Goody and literary scholar Ian Watt published the influential essay "The Consequences of Literacy." The essay argues that when the Greeks invented a phonetic alphabet, they underwent a transformation from mythical to logical thinking. According to Goody and Watt, thinking in oral societies is concrete, associative, formulaic, synthetic, and conformist, tied always to the present tense. But because the technology of writing allows language and thought to be represented and preserved separately from lived experience, literate thinking can become conceptual, objective, analytical, skeptical, logical, and idiosyncratic, capable of representing both past and future. In Goody's and Watt's view, the epitome of literate thinking is the syllogism, an impersonal mode of thinking not tied to common sense or ordinary experience. Goody and Watt go on to argue that the technology of literacy enabled a host of other social and intellectual innovations, including even democracy.

Walter Ong argues a similar case for the drastic cognitive and social consequences of literacy. Ong's works are concerned with how writing and especially print get interiorized into human psyches, helping to create a modern condition of alienation, detachment, objectivity, and fragmentation, a psychological orientation that is in sharp contrast to a strictly oral one, which he characterizes as holistic, harmonizing, situational, and sounded. These various versions of a "great divide" theory of orality and literacy all attribute intrinsic powers or at least potentials to the technology of writing for transforming consciousness and human societies.

"Great divide" or "great leap" characterizations have been sharply criticized for being ethnocentric, for failing to acknowledge the complexity of oral cultures, for exaggerating the powers of writing, and for trying to disguise literacy as a neutral, technological skill rather than as a cultural practice conditioned by ideology, power, and social context. Scribner and Cole conducted painstaking empirical research among the Vai in Liberia, whose members read and write in three languages, to demonstrate that many of the cognitive consequences attributed to literacy are actually the effects of schooling. Scribner's and Cole's study suggests that whatever consequences literacy brings will be the result of the social practices with which it is associated. In other words, what literacy does to one depends on what one does with it.

Another challenge to "great divide" conceptions of literacy is Shirley Brice Heath's ethnographic comparison of the language habits of working-class and professional communities living in the southeastern United States in the 1960s. Her study demonstrates that literacy is configured in a complex context of class, gender, race, religion, and cultural habits, including problem-solving and storytelling, and that orality and literacy intermingle in complex ways. Revisionist studies argue against a view of literacy as standard or monolithic and offer more cultural, contextual, and political interpretations.

Historical studies of literacy, particularly in North America, provide valuable perspectives for scholars of composition and rhetoric. Historical perspectives are useful especially for understanding the rising standards of literacy in relationship to economic and cultural changes as well as the roots of economic and social injustice that continue to promote illiteracy and limited literacy. Historians tend to examine the motivations that people had at various times for acquiring reading and writing; the institutions that were available to them for literacy education; the material avenues that existed for the dissemination of print; the unequal distribution of literacy by gender, race, class, and region; and the cultural ideologies of literacy that operate during any particular historical period. How to define and measure literacy in any given period has been a thorny methodological question for historians. Studies of the Colonial period generally use the ability to sign one's name as a standard of measure. Other surrogate standards include years of schooling, book ownership or book sales, and, in some cases, personal testimonies. Generally, it is recognized that meaningful standards or measures of literacy must be related to social context. The important question is: What kinds of reading and writing abilities do individuals need to participate in cultural and economic life and to protect and exercise their civil rights?

Another relevant body of research is in the area of "emergent" or "preschool" literacy. A good deal of ethnographic and empirical work has been done on early acquisition of reading and writing. By the time they are two and a half years old, most children in contemporary literate societies have developed some concepts about environmental print—that is, the ubiquitous array of signs, logos, and product labels that they encounter daily. It is generally recognized that long before children master conventional skills of decoding and encoding, they are learning about the functional uses and properties of written language and participating in a number of "literacy events" as part of routine family life. Much informal information about print and reading gets passed from parent to child during storybook reading. Young children also sponsor their own spontaneous efforts to puzzle out the written language system in order to differentiate it from other meaning systems such as drawing or speaking. Traditional methods of reading instruction in school, which emphasize correct decoding and often divorce texts and reading from functional contexts, often fail to provide the rich pragmatic clues that children are able to draw upon in nonschool settings.

Perhaps the most important twentieth-century figure in literacy is the Brazilian educator Paulo Freire, who began working among illiterate peasants in northeastern Brazil in the early 1960s and later took his methods of literacy education to other sites of peasant struggle in South and Central America and Africa. In his highly successful method, learning to read is closely linked to the political realities of the people, their concern for land, food, health care, political empowerment, and self-determination. As written words are decoded, they are also investigated critically for the ideological interests they represent. In Freire's view, "reading the word" cannot be separated from "reading the world." Decoding written language without taking it through one's own critical consciousness is equivalent to illiteracy. He developed a student-centered pedagogy based on nonauthoritarian, dialogic relationships among student and teacher. Curriculum is local and collectively constructed out of "key words" from students' daily lives and concerns. Under the general rubric of *critical literacy* or *critical teaching,* some educators have adapted Freire's methods to North American classroom settings.

Finally, another major area of growing interest is literacy and its intersection with other modern media. Electronic print, computers, and computer networks are transforming written communication, along with what Ong named "secondary orality," the revitalizing of orality through the electronic media of radio, television, and video. These media reinvoke residual orality and the primacy of voice, yet usually do so in decontextualized and distancing ways that more typically characterize literate experience.

Deborah Brandt
University of Wisconsin, Madison

Bibliography

Bolter, Jay David. *Writing Space: The Computer, Hypertext, and the History of Writing.* Hillsdale, NJ: Erlbaum, 1991.

Cornelius, Janet Duitsman. *"When I Can Ready My Title Clear:" Literacy, Slavery, and Religion in the Antebellum South.* Columbia: U of South Carolina P, 1991.

Freire, Paulo. *Pedagogy of the Oppressed.* Trans. Myra Bergman Ramos. New York: Seabury, 1970.

Goody, Jack, and Ian Watt. "The Consequences of Literacy." *Literacy in Traditional Societies.* Ed. Jack Goody. Cambridge: Cambridge UP, 1968. 27–68.

Graff, Harvey. *The Legacies of Literacy: Continuities and Contradictions in Western Culture and Society.* Bloomington: Indiana UP, 1986.

Graubard, Stephen R., ed. *Literacy: An Overview by 14 Experts.* New York: Noonday, 1991.

Harste, Jerome, Virginia A. Woodward, and Carolyn L. Burke. *Language Stories and Literacy Lessons*. Portsmouth, NH: Heinemann, 1984.

Heath, Shirley Brice. *Ways with Words: Language, Life, and Work in Communities and Classrooms*. New York: Cambridge UP, 1984.

Kaestle, Carl. *Literacy in the United States: Readers and Reading since 1880*. New Haven: Yale UP, 1991.

Kintgen, Eugene, Barry M. Kroll, and Mike Rose, eds. *Perspectives on Literacy*. Carbondale: Southern Illinois UP, 1988.

Lunsford, Andrea, Helene Moglen, and James Slevin, eds. *The Right to Literacy*. New York: Modern Language Assn., 1990.

Ong, Walter. *Orality and Literacy: The Technologizing of the Word*. New York: Methuen, 1982.

Scribner, Sylvia, and Michael Cole. *The Psychology of Literacy*. Cambridge, MA: Harvard UP, 1981.

See also ORALITY

Liturgy

In the modern age, denotes a wide range of corporate religious ritual; used in reference to the written formulae for rituals as well as for the enactment of the religious ceremonies themselves; applies to the rituals of the Hopi Indians and Buddhists as well as to those of Christians. For most cultures and religions, liturgy functions in common ways: it commemorates sacred events and personages; it marks sacred time; it thanks, praises, and supplicates deity; it mystically joins humans with God or the Gods or Creation; it binds believers together into communities of understanding, faith, moral conviction, and behavior; and it places humanity within a meaningful cosmic context.

Liturgy refers to the ceremony, song, chanting, reading, preaching, praying, acting, dancing, gesture, use of visual symbols, and every other aspect of communal religious worship. It refers to ceremonies for initiation, healing, marriage, birth, and death, as well as to ceremonies that order the structure of leadership within the religious community. Control of the liturgy has long meant profound influence in the deepest dimensions of human relations—spiritual, psychological, and political.

The word *liturgy* has acquired its broad use only in the past century or so, and it is still not universally used in this way. For example, in Eastern Christendom, the word refers exclusively to the celebration of the Eucharist (commonly called "Mass" in the Roman tradition), the central ritual of all Christian churches. The Eucharist is the ceremony wherein believers eat bread and drink wine or water to commemorate the atoning sacrifice of Jesus Christ in either a symbolic or, as some traditions believe, literal partaking of His flesh and blood. It is the ritual that they believe mystically unites them with the spiritual Body of Christ.

The word *liturgy* is derived from Latin *liturgia*, an adoption of the Greek λειτουργία (ἔργον, "work or act" + λαός, "people, public"—meaning a work for the people. In ancient Greek usage, it referred to works done for the state, usually by wealthy citizens. Early Christians adopted the word to describe the "people's work" of their communal worship of Christ in the Eucharist. The windings of usage of *liturgy* since the early days of Christendom are too lengthy to trace here; modern liturgists use the word in its broad sense both when looking back on religious ritual and when describing modern formulae and practice. This includes reference not only to the Eucharist but also to a broad range of worship services and ceremonies.

A common method of classification is to refer to all the liturgical formulae and practices of a tradition as the "rites" of that tradition—for example, the "Byzantine Rite," "Syrian Rite," "Roman Rite," and so on. Each "rite" contains multiple subgroups, and within each group categories of ritual are recognized—for example, in addition to the Eucharist, there are other ceremonies that may be performed by priests, some that may be performed only by bishops, and some that may be performed by laypersons. The principal liturgical books corresponding to these categories in the Roman Rite have historically been called the "missal," the "pontifical," and the "divine office" (containing prayers, songs, and so forth, to be performed at set hours).

Liturgists generally divide the study of liturgy into three broad categories: biblical and historical, theological, and practical or pastoral (White 1990:2). Some liturgists distinguish the verbal dimension of liturgy from that part which is purely ritualized action, music, or visual symbolism. This is the category of liturgy most directly related to rhetorical studies, yet there is a rhetorical dimension to the entire range of liturgical devices—consider rhetorician Kenneth Burke's definition of human beings as creatures that respond to symbols.

Christian liturgies have undergone vast and varied development over the two millennia since

Christ. Imagine the view from the earliest known codification of Christian ceremony (the *Didache*, c. 100) through the thousands of rule books, lectionaries, prayer books, hymnals, breviaries, missals, and other liturgical books and liturgical rulings and guidelines produced by all the branches of Christianity through the ages. Reflect on developments in church calendars as the number of saints, miracles, and holy days swelled through the years. Review the developments in religious art, architecture, vestments, and the cornucopia of liturgical objects. Consider the writings and sermons of Luther, Calvin, Zwingli, Knox, and all the famous reformers and preachers as they held forth on the spirit and forms of true worship. Consider the combinations and recombinations of liturgical lore as traditions have borrowed from each other, reacted against each other, adapted liturgical doctrines and practices to their cultures, their political and intellectual and spiritual frameworks, their agendas. The history of Christian worship reveals an immense variety of forms.

From the point of view of those who believe that there is only one correct way to worship, this variety can be deeply disturbing. But another point of view rejoices in the diversity of Christian worship, or at least argues to allow it:

> The fact is, that God has established in no church, any particular form, or manner of worship, for promoting the interests of religion. The scriptures are entirely silent on these subjects, under the gospel dispensation, and the church is left to exercise her own discretion in relation to all such matters. . . . The only thing insisted upon under the gospel dispensation, in regard to measures, is that there should be decency and order. . . . But I do not suppose that by "order" we are to understand any particular set mode, in which any church may have been accustomed to perform their service. (Finney 273, 276)

Liturgical evolution within Christianity is integral with the development of Christianity itself, and so has had its periods and places of tight control by church authorities and of freedom. The modern age has seen tremendous freedom in liturgical practice, freedom attained largely through the efforts of "liturgical movements" aimed at adapting traditional rites to the needs of modern communities and cultures. Among the hallmarks of recent liturgical reform has been the *Constitution on the Sacred Liturgy* by Vatican Council II (1963), which brought the work of communal worship closer to the Roman Catholic people by allowing greater lay participation, vernacular language, more emphasis on Liturgy of the Word (preaching/instruction), improved liturgical education, simplification of some rites, and other features designed to make worship more meaningful to laypeople. Many Protestants, for centuries endeavoring to distinguish themselves from Catholic traditions by making preaching the centerpiece of their meetings, have enriched their services by reaching back to draw upon common liturgical sources with Catholics.

At the same time that diversity in religious practice is being more widely celebrated, ecumenical trends are celebrating the common ground shared by Christians. Even so, that common ground does not extend all the way to the Lord's Table in every tradition; many Christians still bar each other from Communion. The center place of Christian liturgy, the Lord's Supper, the place where Jesus invited his disciples to "be one" in him, ironically stands as an age-old barrier to Christian unity.

Russel Hirst
University of Tennessee

Bibliography

Alternative Futures for Worship. 7 vols. Collegeville, MN: Liturgical, 1987.

Baptism, Eucharist, and Ministry. Geneva: World Council of Churches, 1982.

Fink, Peter E., S.J., ed. *The New Dictionary of Sacramental Worship*. Collegeville, MN: Liturgical, 1990.

Finney, Charles G. "Measures to Promote Revivals" (1835).

Jasper, David, and R.C.D. Jasper, eds. *Language and the Worship of the Church*. New York: St. Martin's, 1990.

Jones, Cheslyn, et al., eds. *The Study of the Liturgy*. Rev. ed. New York: Oxford UP, 1992.

Lectures on Revivals of Religion. Ed. William G. McLoughlin. Cambridge, MA: Harvard UP, 1960.

Petry, Ray C. *A History of Christianity: Readings in the History of the Early and Medieval Church*. Englewood Cliffs, NJ: Prentice, 1962.

Thompson, Bard. *A Bibliography of Christian Worship*. Metuchen, NJ: American Theological Library Assn. and Scarecrow, 1989.

White, James F. *A Brief History of Christian Worship*. Nashville, TN: Abingdon, 1993.

———. *Documents of Christian Worship: Descriptive and Interpretive Sources*. Louisville, KY: Westminster/John Knox, 1990.

L

Locke, John (1632–1704)

English philosopher whose theories of language, epistemology, logic, morals, politics, and education profoundly changed rhetorical theory and practice in the eighteenth century and beyond. Particularly relevant to rhetoric are his *Essay Concerning Human Understanding, Some Thoughts Concerning Education,* and *The Conduct of the Understanding,* in which he demonstrates that humans are free and able to use their reason to think and judge reality for themselves. The more theoretical *Essay* shows how human understanding works, emphasizing language and how its "abuse" can defeat the understanding and check the growth of knowledge. The works on education and logic extend similar theories into practice. The popularity of Locke's texts helped bring about the turn from traditional rhetoric toward new theories of knowledge, aesthetics, and psychology in eighteenth-century rhetoric, especially in Scotland.

Locke's family belonged to the smaller landowning gentry of the Puritan trading class. As a reward for his father's battles on the side of Parliament in the Civil War, Locke was able to receive a true gentleman's education and rise in social standing. Early in his career he was an Oxford don and a physician. In 1667 he became physician, secretary, and counselor to Lord Anthony Ashley Cooper (later first Earl of Shaftesbury), liberal politician who influenced Locke's mature, more progressive turn in philosophy. Shaftesbury also introduced Locke to the economic and political activities that would span his career. Locke's early collaboration with the physician Thomas Sydenham strongly influenced him to systematically study medicine. Other important influences were Boyle, Descartes, and Gassendi. Early in his career, Locke spent four years in France. Under suspicion for his association with the radical politics of Shaftesbury, Locke fled to Holland, where he remained in exile from 1683 to 1689, a period of intense philosophical production. He returned to England in 1689, escorting the Princess of Orange, later Queen Mary. In 1691 Locke took up residence at Oates with Sir Francis and Lady Masham. He died at Oates on October 28, 1704.

The *Essay on Human Understanding* was begun shortly after Locke officially became a Royal Society member in 1668. It was not published until 1689, however, after nearly twenty years of constant revision. The next year, *Two Treatises of Government,* written perhaps a decade earlier, was published anonymously. The latter work set forth Locke's critique of Robert Filmer's conservative *Patriarchia,* along with his revolutionary theories of human freedom, labor, and property. *Some Thoughts Concerning Education,* a compilation of advice on child-rearing for a distant relative, first appeared in 1693. His logic, *The Conduct of the Understanding,* was not published until two years after his death in 1704.

In Ayer's terms, Locke's groundbreaking *Essay* sets out a philosophy of "anti-dogmatic realism" coming prior to the subsequent idealism or conceptualism that tends to cloud our own historical vision. The *Essay* takes as its approach the "historical, plain method" of Boyle and Newton, its scope ranging from a first book denying innate ideas through his argument in Book 2 that all knowledge comes from experience, to a discussion in Book 4 of knowledge as a set of mental operations performed upon ideas. Throughout, but concentrated in Book 3, "Of Words," we find Locke's thoughts on language. Locke theorizes that words are signs for ideas, and that all humans can ever know are their own ideas of things, not the real "essences" of the things themselves. Ayers calls Locke's ideational theory "concept-empiricism," in which all our ideas derive from experience, as opposed to "knowledge-empiricism," in which propositional knowledge is ultimately based on sensory knowledge (1:14).

Locke's *Essay* called words "signs of internal conceptions," "marks for the Ideas within [Man's] own Mind, whereby they might be made known to other, and the Thoughts of Men's Minds be conveyed from one to another" (3.i.1.2, 402), a theory linguists have labeled *telementation.* These mentalistic conceptions, or ideas, Locke defines early on in his *Essay* as "whatever is the object of the understanding when a man thinks" (1.i.8.47). This linguistic theory also has been called *semantic idealism,* because statements have no meaning unless they correspond to ideas present in the speaker's mind. The privacy and individuality his language theory entails leads to communicational skepticism because no two individuals will have precisely the same ideas in mind at the same time (although the ideas may have a qualitative sameness). This lack of faith in clear communication poses a problem for scientific discourse and knowledge that Locke attempts to solve in the *Essay* by laying down rules for language use.

Locke's epistemology in the *Essay* revised Aristotelian and late scholastic thinking. Locke describes the process of coming to know as a two-level operation: First the senses perceive, then the mind reflects on these perceptions. Sense-perception itself is involuntary and passive, but reflection is an active process under human control. Along with this perception-reflection duality, Locke offers another pair important to knowledge—that of the primary or secondary qualities of things. Primary or "original" qualities are essential to physical things, while secondary qualities are colors, sounds, smells, and tastes produced in us by the primary qualities. He classifies ideas into the simple or complex—singular ideas or ideas compounded of simples, a traditional framework. Simple ideas cannot be learned from language through a process of definition but must be obtained directly from experience in a passive manner. Complex ideas are voluntary compoundings or combinations of simple ideas. They come more under human control and can generally be transmitted by language, if with difficulty. To understand and communicate clearly, complex ideas must be analytically divided into their component simples and words applied to the simple ideas that make up the complex idea.

The discussion of complex ideas takes up most of Book 3, "On Words," with Locke further breaking down complex ideas into "modes," "substances," and "relations." Modes are further divided into simple and mixed, mixed modes representing our abstract ideas such as "beauty," "gratitude," "glory," and "theft." Locke describes these abstractions as nothing but bundles of ideas tied together by a word used as a "knot" (3.iii.17–19, 417–19). Substances such as "gold," "man," or "horse" (actually mixtures of simple ideas) cannot be adequately known because we can only know the ideas they produce in us. But mixed modes and relations are always adequate to the human-created reality of the mental patterns they represent. Thus through mixed modes in particular, a protoconstructivism enters Locke's *Essay.*

Locke's theory of language, in contrast to earlier Adamic theories, emphasizes the conventional or arbitrary nature of words. He argues against the "double conformity" of signs—their conformity both to the things they represent and, intersubjectively, to others' ideas of things. Not only are signs and signified only arbitrarily linked, words do not reveal essence and knowledge. Instead, they get in the way, like clouded windows, obscuring the possibility of clearly knowing anything.

Despite Locke's frequent emphasis on words, he is not a nominalist because of the priority of mental ideas. However, Locke sees knowledge and words as closely connected, or "scarcely separable," even if they are not the same. Since language is imperfect, the closeness of language to knowledge creates difficulties that he attempts to resolve

by setting rules for language use. In Book 3 (x.490–508), he cites seven imperfections of words and discusses remedies for them. These abuses include first, using words with no clear ideas; using words inconsistently; using jargon or "affected obscurity," taking words for things instead of ideas; making words stand for the real essences of things; using words whose meaning is unclear to others; and finally, using figurative speech, which Locke calls "perfect cheat" in a discourse intended to instruct and where judgment might thereby be influenced by the passions. In expanding on this final abuse, Locke makes his often-cited denunciation of a figural rhetoric, portraying rhetoric as a seductress attempting to deceitfully draw men away from truth (3.x.34, 508).

This Lockean attitude to figurative language was immensely influential in the centuries to come. Nietzsche begins his course in ancient rhetoric by citing Locke's famous passage denigrating rhetoric as proof of the disrepute into which the art of rhetoric had fallen in his day. We should note that in his *Essay* Locke separates "civil" (or rhetorical) and "philosophic" or scientific uses of language, believing that language was adequately communicative for most nontechnical uses. At the same time, his *Essay* attempts to create a new scientific model of discourse as a model for what amounts to all nontrivial communication. Those writing after Locke often accepted his epistemology and accompanying rules for scientific language as extending to all language use. This trend to make scientific discourses the exemplar for all discourses of truth was part of a discursive shift bearing profound implications for future rhetorics.

The *Essay* also included a theory of attraction and repulsion of ideas similar to the Port Royal logic that Locke read while in France. Knowledge, or Truth, to Locke is the perception of the agreement or disagreement of ideas, "as Things signified by them do agree or disagree one with another" (4.v.2.574). Setting up a hierarchy of certainty, Locke writes that knowledge can come directly and immediately through intuition; or, mediately, by reason or demonstration involving chains of inference; or directly by the senses. The bringing of ideas together to compare or judge their agreement or disagreement is a rational, conscious, and controlled mental operation. Involuntary association of ideas is suspect and its connections rejected by Locke as eccentric, even dangerously linked with madness. Likewise, quickness in making connections between ideas is disparaged as "Wit," placed into opposition with the more valued "judgment," as in Hobbes. Theories of associationism shaping eighteenth-century rhetoric are often attributed to Locke; nonetheless, Locke's own theory of association is part of an attempt to control involuntary association and enforce rationality.

Howell represents Locke's views on logic as the pivotal moment in a shift from an old to a new rhetoric. Locke rejects topical invention in both logic and rhetoric and prefers induction and chains of inference to the syllogism. In his chapter on reason in Book 4, Locke vigorously rejects the syllogism along with scholastic logical methods, calling them more aimed at winning disputes than arriving at truth. Locke's *Conduct of the Understanding,* published in 1706 and designed to be an appendix to the *Essay,* contains rules and guides to constitute a new, more effective "method" for gaining knowledge. Howell writes that the work "made twenty appearances in print" by 1805, often being used as a logic text by British universities (278).

Locke, who disparaged the relevance and efficacy of contemporary Latin logic and rhetoric, wrote only scattered comments on rhetoric, and interpretations of his influence on rhetoric vary. The *Essay,* following texts by Ramus, Descartes, and Bacon, implies a rhetoric stressing empiricist values, realism, strict rationality, and the correct use of words coupled with a plain style. These values run consistently through his other texts that allude to rhetoric and writing. *Some Thoughts Concerning Education* began as a series of letters from Holland to a distant relative, Edward Clarke, addressing the problem of educating an average boy who would be a typical member of the English landed gentry. Thus the *Education* writings are about a boy's preparation for "a Gentleman's calling" and view speaking and writing as practical activities and gentlemanly social graces. Locke's advice on writing in this educational treatise emphasizes practice, repetition, and error correction over inventional, aesthetic, or imaginative activities. Perhaps his strongest impact on rhetorical training derived from his advocacy of replacing Latin language education with a "naturalistic" vernacular speaking and writing.

To Locke, the natural way of learning anything, but in particular a language, is by imitation and habit. Thus he objects to teaching children languages by "rules," emphasizing instead repetition and practice to develop good habits (*Education* sec. 167–69, 219–28). An instructor of rhetoric while a don at Oxford, Locke discourages the practice of theme-writing, especially in Latin; he would dispense with written themes in favor of oral questioning of students to train them in English extemporaneous speaking. However, he concedes that if themes must be written, theme-writing should be in English (sec. 171–72, 228–29). His dislike of rules links with his disdain for rhetoric because he equates the "arts" of rhetoric with "rules." Locke's treatise disparages the classically based curriculum in rhetoric and writing and relies on two aspects: the use of models combined with practice and repetition. He offers the Protestant theologian Chillingworth as a model for reasoning and Cicero as a model of "the true *Idea of Eloquence*" (*Education* sec. 188–89, 240).

In "Some Thoughts Concerning Reading and Study for a Gentleman" (published in 1720), Locke offers advice on the art of speaking. He describes two components of the art, "Perspicuity" and "Right Reasoning." The first consists of using the proper words for ideas in the speaker's mind. Locke advises that both perspicuity and right reasoning can most readily be attained through reading models, "since we are more apt to learn by example than by direction" (qtd. in Howell 500). Thus Locke consistently recommends setting aside traditional arts and methods for a "natural" approach based on practice and habit.

Howell, who traces Locke's influence in both logic and rhetoric in his *Eighteenth-Century British Logic and Rhetoric,* has been a primary interpreter of Locke in the field of rhetoric. He portrays Locke as the "hero of an intellectual revolution" at the pivotal point of a major shift in logic. Bevilacqua criticizes Howell's "distinctly Lockean interpretation of eighteenth-century rhetorical theory" (345) and points out the limitations of Howell's Lockean framework in the 1972 *Quarterly Journal of Speech* ("W.S. Howell and the Relatives of Rhetoric" [344–46]). Howell's response in the following issue produces a lively forum (Vol. 59: 215–16). Jerry L. Weedon ("Locke and Rhetoric and Rational Man," *Quarterly Journal of Speech* 56 [1970]: 378–87) and L. Brooks Hill ("Lockean Influences in the Evolution of Rhetorical Theory," *Central States Speech Journal* 26 [1975]: 107–14) have also published on Locke's influence on rhetoric, while John Patton has an article comparing Locke's and Hume's approaches to rhetoric ("Experience and Imagination," *Southern Speech Communication* 41 [1975]: 11–29). Richetti has a chapter on the rhetoric of Locke's own writing in the *Essay* (*Philosophical Writing: Locke, Berkeley, Hume,* 1983). Douglas analyzes class bias in Locke's advice on writing ("Notes toward an

Ideology of Composition," *ADE Bulletin* 43 [1974]: 24–33). In an article first published in 1981, Edward P.J. Corbett inquires into the value of Lockean theory in relation to composition theory, advocating the value of imitation and practice in writing instruction ("John Locke's Contributions to Rhetoric," *College Composition and Communication* 32 [1981]: 423–33). Catherine Hobbs Peaden critiques Locke's language and rhetoric from a feminist perspective ("Understanding Differently: Re-reading Locke's Essay," *Rhetoric Society Quarterly* 22 [1992]: 74–90).

Catherine Hobbs Peaden
University of Oklahoma

Bibliography

Aarsleff, Hans. *From Locke to Saussure: Essays on the Study of Language and Intellectual History*. Minneapolis: U of Minnesota P, 1982.

Attig, John C. *The Works of John Locke: A Comprehensive Bibliography from the Seventeenth Century to the Present*. Westport, CT: Greenwood, 1985.

Ayers, Michael. *Locke, Vol. I: Epistemology; Vol. II: Ontology*. London: Routledge, 1991.

Cranston, Maurice. *John Locke: A Biography*. London: Longmans, 1957.

Hall, Roland, and Roger Woolhouse. *80 Years of Locke Scholarship: A Bibliographic Guide*. Edinburgh: University P, 1983.

Harris, Roy, and Talbot J. Taylor. *Landmarks in Linguistic Thought: The Western Tradition from Socrates to Saussure*. London: Routledge, 1989.

Howell, Wilbur Samuel. *Eighteenth-Century British Logic and Rhetoric*. Princeton: Princeton UP, 1971.

Locke, John. *An Essay Concerning Human Understanding*. Ed. and intro. Peter H. Nidditch. Oxford: Clarendon, 1975.

———. *Locke's Conduct of the Understanding*. Ed. Thomas Fowler. 1881. New York: Franklin, 1971.

———. *Some Thoughts Concerning Education*. Ed. and intro. John W. and Jean S. Yolton. Oxford: Clarendon, 1989.

———. *Two Treatises of Government*. Ed. and intro. Peter Laslett. Cambridge: Cambridge UP, 1965.

Taylor, Talbot J. *Mutual Misunderstanding: Scepticism and the Theorizing of Language and Interpretation*. Durham, NC: Duke UP, 1992.

Yolton, John W. *John Locke and the Way of Ideas*. Oxford: Clarendon, 1956.

Yolton, John W., and Jean S. Yolton. *John Locke: A Reference Guide*. Boston: Hall, 1985.

L

Logic

Associated with rhetoric in one manner or another throughout the twenty-five hundred years of the Western rhetorical tradition. This discussion is confined primarily to those instances where the subject matters of both disciplines have been shared in ways significant to the theory and history of rhetoric. It focuses principally on Western logic, developments elsewhere having relatively little impact on Western rhetoric. Scholars interested in more complete historical treatments of logic and rhetoric should consult works cited in the bibliography.

Overview and Description of Contemporary Logic

Traditionally, logic has been defined broadly. A popular contemporary dictionary of philosophy takes logic to be "the study of the structure and principles of reasoning or of sound argument" (Flew 192). Perhaps the most popular logic text of the twentieth century describes logic as "the study of the methods and principles used to distinguish good (correct) from bad (incorrect) reasoning" (Copi 3). As broad as these definitions are, they begin to narrow the scope of logic from such historically popular definitions as "the science of the laws of thought" or "the science of reasoning," subjects that are more properly the domain of psychological inquiry than of logic (Copi 4–5).

Reflections on the nature and scope of logic, especially since the nineteenth century, until recently resulted in ever more restrictive understandings of the discipline. Although there has been a good deal of interest in recent decades in nondeductive logics such as inductive logic, modal logic, and "practical" or "informal" logic, by the middle of the twentieth century the most concerted efforts in logic centered on one phrase, namely, *deductive inference*—that is, on the logic of deductive reasoning. By mid century, no less a logician than W.V.O. Quine could pronounce that "the chief importance of logic lies in implication. . . .Techniques are wanted for showing, given two statements, that the one implies the other; herein lies logical deduction" (4). Logic has thus become centrally concerned with the study of inferential processes: "Logical inference leads from premises—statements assumed or believed for whatever reason—to *conclusions* which can be shown on purely logical grounds to be true if the premises are true" (Quine 45). However, whether the logician is interested in deduction or some variety of nondeductive logic, "the competence and concern of the logician extend only to the relationship between the truth of the premises and the truth of the conclusion—not to the truth or falsity of the premises themselves" (Blumberg 13). Simply put, the logician's realm of competence and interest includes the "correctness" or "legitimacy" of inferences, where inferences are the move from certain statements (premises) to another statement (conclusion).

Inferences may be judged incorrect or fallacious generally for two reasons. First, conclusions may be *formally* defective if the argumentative structure from which they are drawn departs from the set of argument forms recognized by logicians as valid. The principal criterion of a valid argument form is that from a set of given premises, the propositions of which are arranged properly and which are assumed or known to be true, only a true conclusion follows. A second general category of incorrect inferences includes those that are *informally* deficient. In this case, conclusions are drawn from irrelevant premises or from ambiguous language. It was not until recently that logicians began to pay much attention to informal dimensions of logic. Although the assessment of deductive inference covers both formal and informal reasoning, logicians during much of the twentieth century increasingly turned their attention to formal reasoning and especially to mathematical systems of logic. This occurred because of the widely accepted view among logicians that an expanded scope—one which broaches the broader issues of "proper reasoning" or "the laws of thought"—tends to confuse logic with such disciplines as psychology, sociology, and perhaps rhetoric. The consequence of such a confusion, most logicians contend, is that "the notion of logical form remains impenetrably obscure—indeed it can be explained only in terms of even more mysterious notions, being accounted for as a structure of relations between psychic entities or social behaviour-patterns" (Toulmin 43).

The Relationship of Logic to Rhetoric

The contemporary preoccupation of logic with mathematical systems of deductive inference seems at first glance to have little affinity with rhetoric conceived as the art of persuasion, as an enterprise robustly concerned with human valuing. There is, though, one crucial juncture between logic and rhetoric that has at points in the history

of both disciplines generated topics of common interest: the fact that both deal with *arguments* and hence are inevitably conjoined, however remotely, to *human decision-making*. Despite the clinical precision of deductive systems, especially mathematical systems of logic, and notwithstanding the professed estrangement from prudential issues of those concerned principally with formal validity, logicians frequently pronounce themselves relevant to the same human disputation that has been the focus of rhetoric. Logician Albert Blumberg, for example, avers that "modern logic does offer modern society a precision instrument of great power. It is an essential tool in all the sciences and professions. It is equally needed in the making of social policy and in the life of the individual in society" (vii).

Blumberg's comments suggest a link between logic and rhetoric that is more than fortuitous, for he identifies a connection between the two disciplines that betrays their common heritage. Indeed, it has been argued that logic and rhetoric have a common progenitor, namely, the disputations of the early Greek *sophoi* in the centuries before Aristotle formulated the first systematic logical theory.

The formative, post-Homeric centuries of Greek history, beginning perhaps as early as the eighth century B.C.E., witnessed the emergence of disputation and argument. By the sixth century B.C.E., philosophical speculation spread from Ionia to other parts of the Hellenic world, including Athens. Originally not distinguished by the term *philosophoi*—a term that was not used to describe philosophers in the technical sense until at least the time of Socrates—these early thinkers were the *sophoi*, or sophists. In large measure the characterization of some of these early thinkers as "sophists" and others as "philosophers" has been a matter of their pedagogical emphasis, their basic epistemological position, and the variety of logic they employed in argument. Intellectual historians tend to label thinkers engaged in training and speculation about the physical universe, who take an objectivist position on knowing and being and who employ deductive argument, as *physikoi* or *philosophoi* (physicists or philosophers). Those with wider pedagogical interests, including the teaching of grammar and rhetoric, who aver subjectivist or skeptical epistemologies and who employ an empirico-inductive logic, are called *sophoi*. This general bifurcation of early Greek intellectualism more accurately reveals two competing groups of thinkers whose debates were the spawning ground of both rhetoric and logic as formal disciplines. As philosopher A.N. Prior puts it,

> [R]hetoricians and philosophers were finding themselves compelled to look for ways of refuting the contentions of other rhetoricians and philosophers. This involved analyzing the validity of arguments, and in due course this analysis suggested such stratagems as tentatively accepting the point of view of the adversary and then rebutting it by showing that it implied absurd consequences. (513)

Prior notes the link between this strategy and the basic logical form *modus tollens,* suggesting the inevitable evolution of logic from what, in broad terms, might be called the *rhetorical* milieu of the period. Prior also takes Greek forensic disputation to be the progenitor of an array of arguments, some fallacious, that became topics of discussion for Plato and eventually Aristotle in such works as the latter's *Sophistical Refutations* (513). This relationship warrants further comment and is best illuminated by an examination of the emergence of logic as a formal discipline at the hands of Aristotle.

Aristotle, generally regarded as the "father of logic" as the result of his invention of the syllogism, suggests some initial differences between rhetoric and logic near the end of his *Sophistical Refutations.* There he reminds readers that "on the subject of rhetoric much had been said before, whereas regarding reasoning we had nothing earlier to refer to." Of particular interest in the remainder of the passage is Aristotle's observation that the "paid teachers of arguments" who employ means "rather like Gorgias' method" are to be distinguished by their imparting of "the products of a skill" rather than the skill itself (183b34).

Aristotle implies that logic, by contrast, is a genuine skill because it focuses on the discipline of reasoning, not merely the products of reasoning. Even though logic "did not exist at all" prior to its working out "over a long time by trial and error," the *origins* of the rhetorician's art, like the origins of logic, inhere in the common experience of argument and reasoning. The principal difference between the two arts, so far as argument and reasoning are concerned, is that rhetoricians offer their pupils a ready-made diet of disputation: "Some made their pupils learn rhetorical speeches by heart,

others speeches by questions and answers, it being thought that most of the arguments pro and con were included" (183b34).

Despite Aristotle's complaints about rhetoric's failure to teach a skill or art of reasoning, Aristotelian logic was conditioned by the same considerations of discourse as a practical art that motivated rhetoric. Unlike most contemporary mathematical logics, Aristotle "intends his logic to be of practical service" (Ackrill 87). That this is so is suggested by one explanation for the limitations the Greek philosopher placed on the syllogism. Aristotle recognized only three legitimate general types of "figures" of syllogism, although he gave examples of a fourth possibility. Philosophers have debated why Aristotle would not include this fourth possibility as a fourth figure. One explanation, offered by W.D. Ross, is that although the fourth figure is technically possible, as Aristotle himself recognized, humans simply do not reason in accordance with it (Ackrill 89–90). Likewise, Aristotle does not certify certain figures whose conclusions are weaker than those that might otherwise be drawn. Again, a possible explanation for this omission is that "for practical purposes, in proofs, arguments and conversations, one never wants a weaker conclusion where one could draw a stronger one" (Ackrill 91).

Such considerations of the practical utility of logic, as well as the fact that he saw logic as an *organon* (a tool or instrument) of all the sciences, conjoined with the mutual source of logic and rhetoric in disputation, may have led Aristotle to define rhetoric as the *antistrophos* (counterpart) of dialectic. In any case, by the time Aristotle died, the central role played by logic in dialectic was beginning to erode distinctions between the two terms, and "there is evidence that it [logic] was beginning to be used as the equivalent of dialectic or analytics almost immediately after Aristotle's death" (Kerferd 155).

Despite the erosion of distinctions between logic and dialectic, and notwithstanding Aristotle's insistence in the *Rhetoric* (1355a) that the person who knows most about the syllogism will know most about the central notion in rhetorical proof (the enthymeme), the subsequent history of ideas evidences a varied and oftentimes tumultuous relationship between logic and rhetoric. The two disciplines intersected most closely during the first centuries of the medieval period when rhetoric permeated discussions in all the various disciplines. Richard McKeon has recounted in great detail the story of the development of logic and rhetoric during the medieval period. The relationship of logic and rhetoric, as he notes, was conditioned between the fourth and twelfth centuries by various competing conceptions of the nature and place of *reasoning* in affairs bearing on human conduct. This competition emerged principally among (1) the traditional conception of rhetoric as a practical art concerned with a broad range of civic issues—that is, as an art employing arguments in the treatment of pedestrian affairs; (2) the Christian theological tradition, which, following Augustine, held pagan arts such as rhetoric suspect even while employing its principles to interpret and transmit divine eloquence; and (3) logicians who jealously sought to guard logic as the principal arbiter of reason (McKeon 7–11).

Although the debates among these three emphases were often sulfurous, such discussions served to preserve and extend the rhetorical traditions that were, explicitly or implicitly, at the center of dispute. Drawing on the authority of such classical sources as Hermagoras, Cicero, and the *Rhetorica ad Herennium*—and later Aristotle—medieval logicians were compelled to defend disciplinary distinctions among rhetoric, logic, dialectic, and poetic during the course of disputes on the relationship of art and wisdom, ethics and eloquence, persuasion and demonstration. Depending on the authority in question, the end result of these disputes was chiefly the subordination of rhetoric either to "dialectic" or "logic." For example, Isidore of Seville, who along with Martianus Capella and Cassiodorus was a principal expositor of the rhetoric of the age, held that logic is composed of the two subordinate arts: dialectic and rhetoric. Hugh of St. Victor agreed with that categorization, and an attribution to Rabanus Maurus suggests that logic is a composite of grammar, rhetoric, and dialectic (McKeon 7–11, 15–19).

By the twelfth century, with the discovery and availability of the complete *Organon* of Aristotle, the so-called "New Logic" began to make additional distinctions between such inferential processes as scientific demonstration, on the one hand, and logic and dialectic on the other—the latter arts grouped together on the grounds that they deal with probable proof. Increasingly, logic became separated from rhetoric, the latter employed in the service of the technical aspects of law in the practice of *dictamen,* especially the production of legal letters in the *ars notaria* and in the service of formalized theological exhortation. Ironically, the last vestiges of significant interface between logic and rhetoric were in poetic, which by the thirteenth century was partly subalternate to logic as a genre of argumentation (McKeon 23–25).

Most of the time span between the medieval and modern periods witnessed the subordination of rhetoric as a branch of dialectic or logic. Although it may be argued that the position of rhetoric was clearly tributary to the other arts and sciences during this period, it must be recognized that whatever influence rhetoric enjoyed as a *component* of logic was due to the persistent belief on the part of rhetoricians and many logicians that because rhetoric might be a tool of *rational* persuasion and because logic exercises practical benefits in the evaluation of moral, ethical, and other civic issues, rhetoric must be accommodated. This common belief that logic and rhetoric were more than merely theoretical arts—that they had practical application as well—guaranteed rhetoric an important, if occasionally tenuous, position among the lettered. During the Renaissance this state of affairs was to become rhetoric's undoing at the hands of Peter Ramus.

Although rhetoric had exercised considerable influence among the various arts throughout the medieval period and into the Renaissance, it was continuously playing two tensions off against one another. On the one hand, despite diminished opportunities for the sort of robust rhetorical practice of the classical era, rhetoric could lay claim to praxis, as the instrumental persuasive art of religion, law, and politics. On the other hand, the degree to which this role caused rhetoric to focus on specific questions of day-to-day pedestrian concern diluted its role as a *theoretical* discipline concerned with general conclusions—the sort of conclusions generated by logic and dialectic. But logic and dialectic, developing more and more esoteric methods, faced just the opposite challenge—namely, the potential inability to maintain their traditional ties to day-to-day affairs. Ironically, and in a way not generally recognized by rhetoricians, Peter Ramus's excision of invention and arrangement from rhetoric, and his subsequent application of the two canons to logic, rescued logic for a time from the formalizing tendencies that would eventually lead to the mathematical logics of the nineteenth and twentieth centuries.

The evolution of the relationship between logic and rhetoric from the Ramistic reforms of the early Renaissance to the present day continued with the efforts of Francis Bacon, René Descartes, Gottfried Wilhelm von Leibniz, and John Locke. Whereas Ramus was content to attack Aristotle's logic of terms, replacing it with a logic of invention (discovery) and judgment, these modern thinkers sought to reframe logic within the context of a new age of discovery. Like a number of post-Aristotelian philosophers, in particular the Stoics and Megarians, they endeavored to develop a logic of propositions rather than a logic of terms. For the moderns, the rise of empirical science, replete with new mathematical and inductive methodologies, demanded alternative systems of logic. Yet these explorations rarely made direct contact with the art of rhetoric. Leibniz, in attempting to develop a universal logical language and in working out a logical calculus, ignored rhetoric altogether. Descartes was openly hostile to rhetoric, eventually leading to the "replacement" of rhetoric, at the hands of Port Royal logic, with a doctrine of clear and unadorned transmission of thought. The Port Royalists, in the spirit of Descartes's *Rules for the Direction of the Mind* and his *Discourse on Method,* held that logic was a matter of clear and uncluttered transmission of ideas to the exclusion of all manner of rhetorical artifice. And Bacon, though greatly interested in the perfection of the art of rhetoric, speculated on logic largely independent of rhetorical considerations. Bacon's eventual hostility toward logic in general and deduction in particular led to his belief that human knowledge was a function of circumspect observation, meticulous collection of empirical data, experimental verification, and the most careful assay possible. Similar views were advanced by John Locke, whose opinions, arguably, influenced philosophers of the eighteenth century more than those of any other. Locke's hostility to classical logic, including the syllogism, bordered on derision.

As the importance of traditional logic became questioned, so too the relevance of rhetoric in an age of empiricism. Discovery was now the province of science: Just as logic's ability to tell us anything new about the world was questioned, rhetoric's classical inventional role—the role of discovering substantive arguments on any issue—was also challenged. Here logic and rhetoric fell victim to the same set of historical conditions.

One exception to this hostility to classical logic was the work of Richard Whately. His *Elements of Rhetoric* ran against the current of modern empiricism. In that text, rhetoric is conceived as an "off-shoot from logic" (4). In fact, the book's terms and principles are extracted from logic. Notions of classical validity, contradiction, and the relationship of premises to conclusions, for example, are central to Whately's analysis.

Despite Whately's persistent deference to classical logical principles and despite the influence of his *Elements,* subsequent writers continued to explore alternative principles and systems of logic. The early nineteenth century, for example, witnessed significant advances in mathematical logic, an interest pursued with great vigor into the twentieth century by logicians such as Hilbert, Post, Tarski, Church, Gödel, Lowenheim, Skloem, and others. Whereas logic is generally conceived as a theory of argument and reasoning, mathematics seeks to discover formal methods with which to explain *with great precision* the logical relationships in argument and reasoning. These formal methods, it is argued, may in turn be applicable to such diverse fields as mathematics, computer science, and deontic logics (including questions of law and ethics). Logic and rhetoric intersect here because of the common interest of some mathematical logicians and rhetoricians in issues of law, ethics, and related topics—that is, in *public moral argument*. This obvious interface between logic and rhetoric has been recognized by some rhetoricians, as exemplified by Douglas Ehninger's pursuit of a "logic of ought propositions" (491–99). Rhetoricians have been largely reluctant, however, to exploit this intersection.

Philosophers, too, have failed to capitalize on the aforementioned intersection. Indeed this is ironic given philosophy's recent interest in modal logic. Modal logics investigate concepts such as necessity and possibility. A significant preoccupation of modal logic, then, surrounds issues of what *ought* to be done and the perennial (arguably *rhetorical*) issue of *probability*. Like so many of the developments in logic throughout the history of ideas, inquiries in modal logic highlight one among many untapped but inherent connections between logic and rhetoric.

Another important nineteenth-century development in logic was John Stuart Mill's "canons of induction." Mill's canons displaced classical notions of logic as a means of discovery and exploration with a method for the new sciences. Mill's methodology provided the new sciences with the means by which to exercise intellectual hegemony over an age preoccupied with measuring and counting. The legacy of Mill's canons—and evidence of their influence—is documented by their presence in contemporary discussions in both logic and rhetoric.

The early twentieth century saw a continued interest among logicians in formal logical systems. These systems were perhaps most extensively investigated by Bertrand Russell and Albert North Whitehead in their *Principia Mathematica*. The *Principia* has been regarded by many as the most significant work on logic of the twentieth century and so warrants more than passing comment. Among other important objectives, the *Principia* was intended to demonstrate the broad deductive power of logic beyond the boundaries of logic proper. Although the book has no direct relevance to rhetoric, it contributed significantly to the formalizing tendencies of the first half of the twentieth century and so, in a negative sense, contributed to the widening of the gulf between philosophy—with logic as its central method—and rhetoric. This book, and work subsequent to it, also reinforced mid-twentieth-century tendencies toward positivism.

In its attempt to expand the scope of logic, the *Principia* sought to establish that pure mathematics can be reduced to logic. This reduction, it was argued, may be accomplished by a process of "logical constructionism." Simply put, logical constructionism held that concepts that are inadequately justified or otherwise not well understood can be analyzed in terms of the simpler constituent entities from which they are constructed. By and large, these more simple entities could be verified by empirical observation, reason, and logic. Eventually, Russell applied the method beyond logic to epistemological questions of science and common sense. Another significant contribution of Russell's logical investigations was his "theory of descriptions." This theory was meant to resolve the problem of statements in ordinary language (such as "The present King of France") that seem to aver the existence of nonexistent entities. According to Russell, such statements can be analyzed logically in a way that avoids the apparent assertion of existence.

The logical considerations that prompted the writing of the *Principia,* as well as those that figure in the theory of descriptions, eventually led Russell to the theory of "logical atomism." According to that theory, any and every proposition that is capable of being understood must be constructed out of experiences or out of other propositions themselves constructed out of experiences. Here what began as a logical theory becomes a metaphysical theory—that is, a theory about the basic nature of existence. Included in logical atomism is the view that it is possible to construct an "ideal language" whose structure mirrors reality.

Although Russell frankly admitted that aspects of the theories generated from his logic harbored problems, and while he amended his views frequently, he never abandoned them wholesale. While it is clear that other elements of his philosophy have more direct significance to rhetoric—such as his work in ethics—Russell's logic remains potentially fertile ground for exploring the relationships among logic, language, and the world.

Contemporary Developments in Logic

Clearly, the work of many logicians in the first half of the twentieth century offered few opportunities for discerning the connection between logic and rhetoric. Developments subsequent to World War II, however, provided just such opportunities. Perhaps the most important of these is the interest among philosophers in "informal," or "practical," logic. An illustration is the First International Symposium on Informal Logic held at the University of Windsor in 1978. The symposium was called as a result of the rapid growth of curiosity among logicians in what has been described as "critical reasoning" (informal logic). According to one account, in the first three decades after World War II, fifty-four introductory logic texts devoted at least some space to informal logic; twenty-five of them were published between 1946 and 1970. In the 1970s, at least twenty-nine textbooks devoting some space to the subject of informal logic were published, including at least fifteen devoted exclusively to nonformal treatments of logic. And, by the decade of the nineties, purely formal textbook accounts of logic are a distinct minority. Overall, the evolution of logic from the mid twentieth century to the present has been characterized by a more generalized interest in the related concepts of argumentation and reasoning and by a recognition of the symbiosis between these two concepts (Blair and Johnson 13–14).

Logicians have identified five characteristics associated with informal logic. These characteristics illustrate well the fundamental, if not yet fully realized, convergence of logic and rhetoric. The five include: (1) working with "natural" arguments; (2) the treatment of informal fallacies; (3) consideration of "full" or "extended" arguments; (4) the partial abandonment of the deductive-inductive dichotomy; and (5) the widening scope of informal logic (Blair and Johnson 13–23). These five attributes of practical reasoning demonstrate the marked departure of contemporary logic from logic traditionally conceived as a *formal* inferential process.

One might inquire why there has been such an expansion of the scope of logic in the last decades of the twentieth century. We speculate that the enlarged scope of logic is attributable to the perceived incapacity of traditional logic—as the methodology of philosophy—to provide the discipline with the tools required to assay and ameliorate the egregious problems confronting contemporary society. As some philosophers themselves have observed, traditional logic, caught up in its own technical refinements and discoveries, has failed to step outside itself and inquire as to how such discoveries might apply *in practice* to the world of prudential affairs. Abrogating any responsibility for assessing the soundness of argumentation and persuasion in everyday life, formal logic can be no more than a vacuous, self-contained, hypothetical exercise disconjoined from the human condition.

That this realization is responsible for logic's expansion in recent years may be seen in the work of some of the principle contributors to the literature in practical reasoning. C.L. Hamblin's landmark work *Fallacies* called philosophers' attention to the paucity of treatments of informal fallacies and informal logic, and provided an historical context for further research on the subject. Importantly, the book concerned itself not with hypothetical examples of reasoning from the philosophy seminar but with arguments actually used in the real world of human beings.

Although *Fallacies* is of obvious importance to the field of rhetoric, it has not enjoyed as much prominence among rhetoricians as two other works by contemporary philosophers. Chaïm Perelman and L. Olbrechts-Tyteca's ambitious treatise *The New Rhetoric* sought to navigate between the well-established logics of deduction and induction, demonstrating the significance of a third realm of inference-making, where humans seek the warranted adherence of others on judicial matters. It is noteworthy that treatment of this third realm of inference-making in *The New Rhetoric* is grounded in principles established throughout the history of rhetoric. The effect of this work was to establish and call the attention of logicians to the importance of adherence—the seeking and gaining of the assent of an audience in the process of rational deliberation. One consequence of this approach to informal logic is to render otiose any account of logic or inference-making that ignores context-dependent variables in the argumentation process.

Complementary to *The New Rhetoric* is Stephen Toulmin's *Uses of Argument*. Toulmin makes conspicuous twentieth-century formal logic's evolution on a course that took the discipline to areas increasingly remote from issues and disputations germane to everyday life. Like Perelman and Olbrechts-Tyteca, Toulmin proposes that rational argument be assessed along the lines of jurisprudential models. Viewing arguments as involving a movement from various "supports" or "grounds" *through* "warrants" *to* "claims," Toulmin's work offers both a critique of the practical application of traditional logic and the beginnings of a solution in the guise of a framework for informal logical analysis of everyday practical argument.

As we have mentioned, the work of the aforementioned philosophers, coming as it does from *within* the field of logic itself, yet concerned as it is with practical argumentations or persuasions, establishes common ground for the logician and the rhetorician. Evidence that these common interests of the two disciplines may be explored in a truly interdisciplinary way, although scant, nonetheless exists. One may point to Howard Kahane's *Logic and Contemporary Rhetoric* as an exemplar, despite the fact that Kahane's training as a logician—and a corresponding unfamiliarity with the study of argumentation in the discipline of rhetoric—is evident.

There are trends working against interdisciplinary studies in logic and rhetoric, in addition to the more cooperative tendencies noted above. One can point, for instance, to the proclivity of some recent writers to eschew traditional approaches to logic altogether (Nye; Longino 110–12; Makau 82–94). It is too early to tell whether this strategy can contribute to a better understanding of human reasoning, argumentation, or persuasion. However, the very fact that these contemporary writers have chosen to engage various issues in logic indicates that they are part of its continuing history and traditions. The very compulsion on the part of these scholars to explore logical issues, and the fact that such explorations are of compelling interest to scholars in rhetoric, demonstrates in another, though perhaps ironic way, the inherent interface between logic and rhetoric that has typified the history of Western thought.

Richard A. Cherwitz
University of Texas
James W. Hikins
Ohio State University

Bibliography

Ackrill, John L. *Aristotle the Philosopher.* New York: Oxford UP, 1981.

Aristotle. *Rhetoric and Sophistical Refutations. The Complete Works of Aristotle: The Revised Oxford Translation.* 2 Vols. Jonathan Barnes, ed. Princeton: Princeton UP, 1984.

Blair, J. Anthony, and Ralph H. Johnson, eds. *Informal Logic: The First International Symposium.* Inverness, CA: Edgepress, 1980.

Blumberg, Albert Emanuel. *Logic: A First Course.* New York: Knopf, 1976.

Bochenski, Innocentius. *History of Formal Logic.* Ed. and trans. Ivo Thomas. Notre Dame, IN: U of Notre Dame P, 1961.

Church, Alonzo. *Introduction to Mathematical Logic.* Princeton: Princeton UP, 1956.

Copi, Irving M. *Introduction to Logic.* 8th ed. New York: Macmillan, 1990.

Descartes, René. *Discourse on Method and Meditations.* Trans. Laurence J. Lafleur. Indianapolis, IN: Bobbs, 1960.

———. "Rules for the Direction of the Mind." Trans. Laurence J. Lafleur. *Descartes: Philosophical Essays.* New York: Macmillan, 1961. 145–236.

Ehninger, Douglas. "Science, Philosophy—and Rhetoric: A Look Toward the Future." *The Rhetoric of Western Thought.* 5th ed. Ed. James L. Golden, Goodwin F. Berquist, and William E. Coleman. Dubuque, IA: Kendall/Hunt, 1992. 490–501.

Flew, Antony. *A Dictionary of Philosophy.* New York: St. Martin's, 1979.

Hamblin, C.L. *Fallacies.* London: Methuen, 1970.

Kahane, Howard. *Logic and Contemporary Rhetoric: The Use of Reason in Everyday Life.* 2nd ed. Belmont, CA: Wadsworth, 1976.

Kerferd, G.B. "Aristotle." *The Encyclopedia of Philosophy.* Vol. 1. New York: Macmillan and Free, 1967. 151–62.

Longino, Helen E. "Subjects, Power, and Knowledge: Description and Prescription in Feminist Philosophies of Science." *Feminist Epistemologies.* Ed. Linda Alcoff and Elizabeth Potter. New York: Routledge, 1993. 101–20.

McKeon, Richard. "Rhetoric in the Middle Ages." *Speculum: A Journal of Mediaeval Studies* 17 (1942): 1–32.

Makau, Josina M. *Reasoning in Communication: Thinking Critically about Arguments.* Belmont, CA: Wadsworth, 1990.

Mill, John Stuart. *A System of Logic.* New York: Longman, 1930.

Nye, Andrea. *Feminist Theory and the Philosophies of Man.* New York: Routledge, 1990.

Perelman, Chaïm, and L. Olbrechts-Tyteca. *The New Rhetoric: A Treatise on Argumentation.* Notre Dame, IN: U of Notre Dame P, 1969.

Prior, Arthur N. "Logic, History of." *Encyclopedia of Philosophy.* Vol. 4. New York: Macmillan and Free, 1967. 513–77.

Quine, Willard Van Orman. *Methods of Logic.* 3rd ed. New York: Holt, 1972.

Toulmin, Stephen. *The Uses of Argument.* Cambridge: Cambridge UP, 1958.

Whately, Richard. *Elements of Rhetoric.* Ed. Douglas Ehninger. Carbondale, IL: Southern Illinois UP, 1963.

Whitehead, Albert North, and Bertrand Russell. *Principia Mathematica.* Cambridge: Cambridge UP, 1927.

See also ARGUMENT; INFORMAL LOGIC; PERSUASION

Logical Positivism

An early twentieth-century philosophical movement that opposed the metaphysical tradition and sought foundations for knowledge by (1) developing formal logical analysis to explain the meaning of statements and (2) emphasizing empirical sensory observation as a means of evaluating statements about facts. The movement originated in the ideas of the Vienna circle, a discussion group active from roughly 1922 to 1938, and it linked British and Viennese empiricism (most obviously that of Bertrand Russell and Ernst Mach) with new developments in symbolic logic to realign philosophy with mathematics, logic, and science. Philosophers associated with the movement include A.J. Ayer, Rudolf Carnap, Ernest Nagel, and Moritz Schlick.

In a large generalization, positivism can be seen as concerned with identifying propositions that are potentially true or false and distinguishing them from nonsensical or meaningless propositions. Following a tradition evident in Hume, Leibniz, and Kant, the positivists distinguished two types of true propositions: analytic and synthetic (Kant's terms). Analytic propositions contain the predicate within the subject concept. They are tautological and necessarily true: The propositions of mathematics and logic are prime examples, but some sentences, such as "No unmarried man is married," also qualify. Synthetic propositions require empirical investigation or verification to establish their truth. They are meaningful, that is, verifiable, either by their scientifically testable or observable terms (depending on the theorist, in sensory or physical terms). Propositions that are not analytic or synthetic are characterized as cognitively meaningless or, as later reformulated, as having only emotive meaning.

Logical positivists did not characterize many traditional philosophical fields (metaphysics, ethics, aesthetics) as knowledge. Even ethics becomes characterized as emotive because its conclusions are neither analytic nor synthetic (empirical). Ethical statements are simply expressions of a speaker's position that may evoke a similar response in the listener.

Positivist concerns that people do not accept false beliefs and that they do not accept normative statements as verified are not trivial. The limitation of rational human inquiry to logic, mathematics, and science, however, is clearly too restrictive in its description of most of human discourse as meaningless. Even philosophy itself could not produce meaningful propositions about the world; instead it merely clarified the meaning of existing propositions. Rhetoric's rebirth is, in many ways, a response to the positivists' limited view of rationality and meaning. Clearly, the problems with such a limited view are addressed explicitly by many mid-century rhetoricians (for instance, Kenneth Burke, Susanne Langer, Stephen Toulmin, Chaïm Perelman, Lucie Olbrechts-Tyteca, and Richard Weaver).

Even so, rhetoric's relationship to logical positivism is not simply one of opposition; scholars associated with rhetoric participated in the origination of some of its concepts, and the fields of rhetoric, communication, and composition continue to negotiate the legacy of logical positivism. The positivists' emotive theory of ethics, as developed by A.J. Ayer, provides a good example of the interaction between the fields. It had several earlier incarnations, including C.K. Ogden's and I.A. Richards's *Meaning of Meaning* (1923), which draws a distinction between the symbolic (referential) and emotive functions of language; while Ogden and Richards acknowledged, even emphasized, the interweaving of the two functions, they too were concerned with how truth and meaning exist in and vary between different language functions. In addition to past connections between rhetoric and logical positivism, positivist concerns continue as discussions of verifiability in some of the more social scientific approaches to communication and composition, and these approaches still are read, discussed, and taught within rhetoric.

Arabella Lyon
Temple University

Bibliography

Ayer, A.J., ed. *Logical Positivism*. New York: Free P of Glencoe, 1959. Rpt. London: Greenwood, 1978.

Carnap, Rudolf. *The Logical Syntax of Language*. London: Routledge, 1937.

Kraft, Viktor. *The Vienna Circle, the Origins of Neo-Positivism*. New York: Philosophical Library, 1953.

O'Keefe, Daniel J. "Logical Empiricism and the Study of Human Communication." *Speech Monographs* 42 (1975): 173–83.

Quine, W.V.O. "Two Dogmas of Empiricism." *From a Logical Point of View*. Cambridge, MA: Harvard UP, 1953. 20–46.

Stevenson, Charles L. *Ethics and Language*. New Haven: Yale UP, 1944.

See also AYER, ALFRED J.

Logocentrism

A centering of all meaning. The word *logocentrism* is a neologism, commonly associated with the popularized thought of Jacques Derrida and his critique of metaphysics. (It is easily possible to associate the concept and critique with the *physis* versus *nomos* debate or with such thinkers as Heraclitus, Nietzsche, Freud, Marx, Bataille, and Heidegger.) It is difficult writing about the word *logocentrism*—and especially hazardous to define it—for any attempt can easily force the writer to fall into logocentrisms. It is better "performed" than defined. The writing of performance is often done deconstructively, deconstruction being the discourse tactic and strategy of a critique of logocentrism. When done deconstructively, writing is practiced as a rapid switching of binaries and hierarchies, with a decentering and, therefore, a displacing of a privileged position. However, the whole tradition of the encyclopedia—the tradition of the Enlightenment itself—demands a logocentric bias when considering even logocentrism.

Therefore, one way to think by way of definition about logocentrism is to locate a center in Parmenides', Plato's, Aristotle's, and Kant's similar thinking about logos as reason or logic. These philosophers establish and progressively elaborate on three basic logical principles, or logoscentrisms, which are (a) the law of identity (a statement is either true or false, never both); (b) the law of the excluded middle (a statement is either true or false); and (c) the law of the excluded third (a statement can be only true or false, for there is no third possibility). In the simplest terms, then, all statements are to be centered around these three so-called laws of logic (logos). For example, a human being is either male or female, never both or a possible third. As Michel Foucault, Judith Butler, and Andrea Nye point out, a hermaphrodite must be excluded under these laws, especially that of the excluded third. A similar neologism that functions as a corollary to logocentrism is "phallogocentrism," under which the law of identity is determined by the presence or absence of the penis/phallus. Males have this privileged signifier; females do not; *ergo*, females do not exist, or at best exist as supplements. A negative deconstruction of this state of affairs entails binary "switching," inverting the hierarchy so that the female position is privileged over the male. This strategy has been coined *gynocentric*, and although it offers a pseudocritique of phallocentrism, it nevertheless validates the latter's discrete partner—

logocentrism—by perpetuating the structure of binary thought, a structure that legitimates the unity and totality symbolized by the phallus. Thus, ironically, *gynologocentrism* may be no less grounded on the phallus than is phallogocentrism; there may be no separating the logos from the phallus.

A second way to think about logocentrism can be found in the distinction between the analytic-referential model of thinking (foundationalism) and the hermeneutic-of-suspicion model (antifoundationalism). The former model, following the three basic principles of logic discussed above, posits a possible correspondence between Being (the *physis*/nature of things) and the signified/signifier. In other words, logocentrism posits a possible union between Being and being, so that the "Truth" of things can be known. Hence, there would be a correspondence among logos (reason or cognition), sign (semiotic system), and the world (reality). The latter model, or hermeneutic-of-suspicion, attempts to demystify the notion of this correspondence and the foundation of Truth that such a notion constructs; it sees this or any similar union to establish Truth as the product of particular signifying practices, each always already determined by ideologies, and hence of false consciousness. However, a caveat is necessary, for while Nietzsche, Freud, and Marx are the hermeneuts of suspicion, they vary in the degree of their suspicion and, as has been argued, they themselves at times paradoxically return to logocentric thinking. Derrida himself at times is logocentric. There may be no escape, though many struggle.

The critique of logocentrism manifests itself in contemporary rhetoric in relation to ethos, logos, and pathos. While rhetors in feminist studies, for example, critique and deconstruct the centeredness of patriarchal views of a masculine ethos (a good man speaking), rhetors in gender studies question the male or female binary altogether. While the former engage in negative deconstructions (switching binaries), the latter disengage by way of affirmative deconstructions, no longer inverting binaries but searching for third subject positions such as Monique Wittig's notion of "Lesbian," Gilles Deleuze and Felix Guattari's a "body without organs," or Donna Haraway's "cyborgs." In composition studies a parallel critique of logocentrism figures most prominently in recent work done by the social-epistemic group against the expressivists and the cognitivist groups; this critique is now being further extended by a subversive paragroup that finds the social-epistemic as crypto-foundational. This paragroup employs the tactic of searching for third subject positions. As stated, however, there may be no escape from logocentrism, only a perpetual critique or drifting.

Victor J. Vitanza
University of Texas, Arlington
Diane (Mowery) Davis
Old Dominion University

Bibliography

Baumlin, James, and Tita Baumlin, eds. *Ethos.* Dallas: Southern Methodist UP, 1993.

Berlin, James. "Rhetoric and Ideology in the Writing Class." *College English* 50 (1988): 477–94.

Bizzell, Patricia. "Cognition, Convention, and Certainty: What We Need to Know about Writing." *PRE/TEXT* 3 (1982): 213–43.

Butler, Judith. *Gender Trouble: Feminism and the Subversion of Identity.* New York: Routledge, 1990.

Derrida, Jacques. *Of Grammatology.* Trans. Gayatri Spivak. Baltimore: Johns Hopkins UP, 1976.

———. "Structure, Sign, and Play in the Discourse of the Human Sciences." *The Structuralist Controversy.* Ed. Richard Macksey and Eugenio Donato. Baltimore, MD: Johns Hopkins UP, 1972. 247–64.

Fish, Stanley. "Anti-Foundationalism, Theory, Hope, and the Teaching of Composition." *The Current in Criticism: Essays on the Present and Future of Literary Theory.* Ed. Clayton Koelb and Virgil Lokke. West Lafayette, IN: Purdue UP, 1987. 65–79.

Nye, Andrea. *Words of Power: A Feminist Reading of the History of Logic.* New York: Routledge, 1990.

Vitanza, Victor J. "Three Countertheses: Or, A Critical In(ter)pretation into Composition Theories and Pedagogies." *Contending with Words: Composition and Rhetoric in a Postmodern Age.* Ed. Patricia Harkin and John Schilb. New York: Modern Language Assn., 1991. 139–72.

See also HISTORIOGRAPHIES OF RHETORIC

Logology

L

Kenneth Burke's approach to understanding how language functions as motive. In the latter stages of his career, Burke developed his discussion of logology—initially defined as "words about words." Yet the study of language use goes beyond merely examining language or thinking about language used (words about words) to encompass the whole study of symbolic action. Burke's goal is that we come to understand how we wander through life in a fogbank of symbols. Ultimately, logology becomes the generating principle for studying symbolic action and supplanting dramatism as the god-term of Burke's system.

In *The Rhetoric of Religion* (*RR*) and in *Language as Symbolic Action* (*LSA*), Burke provides both theory and method for this system. An important aspect of logology is Burke's "Definition of Man," in which he labels humans "the symbol-using (symbol-making, symbol-misusing) animal, inventor of the negative (or moralized by the negative), separated from [our] natural condition by instruments of [our] own making, goaded by the spirit of hierarchy (or moved by the sense of order), and rotten with perfection" (*LSA* 16. See also *RR* 40). Burke suggests the importance he places on our ability to represent or symbolize through language: "Can we bring ourselves to realize just . . . how overwhelmingly much of what we mean by 'reality' has been built up for us through nothing but our symbol system?" (*LSA* 5). The study of logology is precisely the study of how this "reality" is created and re-created through constant use of language.

Logology necessarily involves exploring the terms used to name things. The methodology for exploration is the logological formula: "*Pick some particular nomenclature, some one terministic screen . . .* [so] *that you may proceed to track down the kinds of observations implicit in the terminology you have chosen, whether your choice of terms was deliberate or spontaneous* (*LSA* 47, italics in original). Burke notes that there are essentially two types of terminologies, those that stress the principle of continuity and those that stress the principle of discontinuity. Those emphasizing continuity allow us to see two things (for example, events, people, nations) as being substantially the same, while those emphasizing discontinuity allow for no such consubstantiality. Continuity and discontinuity are the generating principles of investigation into terms: They require examination of not only what is consistent or inconsistent with terms. They also require examination of the implications of those terms, the kinds of observations implicit in them.

In considering the kinds of observations implicit in terms, we may consider how those terms are applied. That is, we may consider the efficacy of such terms and whether we ought to revise them. For example, the terms *svelte, skinny, scrawny, sleek, thin,* and *lean* may be used to describe the same person. The one we choose reveals attitudes toward that person. But this example suggests that in selecting such a term to label someone, we clearly do not capture the total reality of that person. Terms can limit our field of vision by focusing us too narrowly. Burke would have us realize the "qualitative difference between the symbol and the symbolized" (*RR* 16) and expand our field of vision so that we would take a broader view than we might otherwise.

Bill Bridges
New Mexico State University

Bibliography

Burke, Kenneth. "Definition of Man." *Language as Symbolic Action*. Berkeley: U of California P, 1966. 3–24.

———. *The Rhetoric of Religion*. Berkeley: U of California P, 1970.

———. "Terministic Screens." *Language as Symbolic Action*. Berkeley: U of California P, 1955. 44–62.

Foss, Sonja K., Karen A. Foss, and Robert Trapp. "Kenneth Burke." *Contemporary Perspectives on Rhetoric*. Prospect Heights, IL: Waveland, 1985. 153–88.

Rueckert, William H. *Kenneth Burke and the Drama of Human Relations*. 2nd ed. Berkeley: U of California P, 1982.

See also: BURKE, KENNETH; DRAMATISM

Logos

Logical appeal ultimately understood as an appeal both to consistency and substantive reasons. As ethical appeal suggests nominally something to do with normative ethics, logical appeal suggests something to do with logical validity. But ethical appeal and logical appeal as rhetorical notions are best directed at understanding not what is good and true but the best means of persuasion. Logic is less important for a rhetoric fashioned for general audiences than for professional and technical disciplines. What is striking about rhetoric studied in speech communication and composition studies is the irrelevance of logical studies to pedagogy. We see this division in the different technical notions of argument found in rhetoric and in logic, a separation that goes back to Aristotle. One needs to analyze the complexity of the topic of logical appeal as a rhetorical concept by viewing it in different contexts of rhetorical, logical, and argumentation theory.

A good starting point to analyze the complexity of the concept is in the interpretations of the Greek term *logos*, which is foundational to classical Greek rhetoric. The fundamental sense of *logos* is *word*. Logical appeal as an appeal to words is an appeal to the consistency in our use and meaning of words. It is ad hominem—that is, our appeals are to what people say *they* believe and not to what *we* necessarily believe. If the meaning of what *they* say is "such and such," then *they* are compelled given *their* meaning to say "such and such." Let's call a logical appeal to words and their meaning *an appeal to semantic consistency*. To say "John is a bachelor, and therefore he is unmarried" is to say what is true of John on the basis of the use of the term *bachelor*. Arguments over semantic consistency are settled by semantic conventions of language usage. Disputes over semantic consistency are resolved by mutually accepted interpretations of the uses of words. Another way of characterizing the same point about an appeal to logos as *word* is that the conclusions of deductive arguments are contained in the premises. What you put into your premises in words is what you get out. Or, expressed succinctly about computers, "garbage in, garbage out."

But if we appeal to logos not *as word*, but *as logic*, the basis of the appeal shifts from semantic to syntactic consistency. In appealing to logos as logic—that is, logical relations that exist between terms—we appeal not to the meaning of sentences and their terms but to the logical form that binds and relates terms. Logical relations exist within sentences between terms, as in term logic, or they exist in the logical connections between sentences, as in sentence logic. Logical relations are generated by the logical grammar within and between sentences—that is, by the logical operators and formation rules that bind and relate phrase structures and constitutive clauses within sentences and that bind constitutive sentences within arguments.

Traditionally, formal logic, which interprets such syntactic foundations of logical appeal, little interests rhetoricians. Nevertheless, logical operations are rhetorical concerns where logical validity is at issue. Therefore, logic is of concern in a rhetoric of the expert disciplines. In contrast, in rhetoric for generalized audiences, there is little need for attention to logical form as such. Native speakers grasp logical form without undue attention to it. Just as native speakers know the grammar of a language without technical formal grammatical knowledge, so native speakers know the logic of their language without technical formal logical knowlege. But speakers do call attention to deductive fallacies by contrasting them with analogous forms of argument where premises are true and conclusions false. Such a refutational strategy appeals to an intuition of form, not to logical rules.

Insofar as rhetorical arguments use gaps, ellipses, and enthymemes, they operate in a context of presumptions. They never depend as do logical arguments on what is explicitly stated. Rather, rhetorical appeals sketch the form of their arguments in a context of linguistic, communicative, and cultural presumptions that audiences intuitively grasp. In contrast, logic demands explicit rigor. Logic demands a full display of logical form. Logic avoids the ambiguity to which rhetorical arguments are prone. Note the ambiguity of the unquantified subject term in "Italians are emotionally expressive." Logic, unlike rhetoric, does not admit of presumption. Logic, to be fully rigorous, unlike rhetoric, demands full and explicit, rigorous annotations of the rules that govern operations. Rarely would one give a rule of inference in rhetorical argument to justify a conclusion. Rhetorical arguments as appeals to presumptive entailments are appeals to syntactic consistency in a context of intuitively grasped communicative presumptions.

To clarify the overlapping and interrelated contrasting concepts of rhetorical argument and logical argument, the term *argument* has four distinct but related uses. First we speak of argument as quarrel, or controversy. This is a sociological interest in argument, a description of social conflict and its companion violence. A paradigm is a domestic quarrel. Second, there is argument as appeal for the acceptance of a claim. This is the use common to forensics and argumentation. It is an appeal for the acceptance of a contention based upon what an audience accepts or is willing to accept. Importantly, rhetorical arguments look to beliefs of an audience to effect changes in them. A paradigm is a lawyer's appeal to a jury. Third, there is argument as deductive argument, traditional to logical studies. Deductive logic is the study of strict entailments—that is, if the premises are true it would be impossible, given the logical form of the argument, to deny the conclusion. A paradigm is a strict mathematical proof. Fourth, there is argument as inductive, as giving evidence to support a probability. Inductive arguments and their validity are the concern of inductive logic and inferential statistics. A paradigm is gathering evidence in scientific experiments to confirm empirical hypotheses. Important to note in relating these four uses of "argument" is that we settle arguments as *controversy* by arguments as *appeals* using *deductive* and/or *inductive* logical arguments.

Appeals to semantic and syntactic consistency are arguments appealing to embodied meaning and logical structures in texts. They focus on the meaning of the wording and the presumptions behind the wording. But such logical appeals are not focal to oratory and public address, argumentation, and forensics. In such disciplines logical appeals are not to logical grounds but to reasons presented as premises, to logos *as reason*. The appeal is to premises, warrants, evidence, facts, data, observations, backing, support, explanations, causes, signs, commonplaces, principles, or maxims. Insofar as the emphasis is on logos as reason, logical appeal is to the substance of premises and/or presumptions and not to meaning or logical form.

The senses of what it is to give a reason are much more numerous than the senses of what it is to argue. Arguments give reasons. Explanations give reasons, but explanations may not be logical appeals. Nor do all explanations provide us with reasons. Rather, explanations in the general use of "explain" respond to interests that an audience might have expressed in the form of questions. Explanations as answers to questions differ widely. We might *explain* what happened, what something is like, how it happened, how something works, when it occurred, in what manner, what caused it, who did it, or for what purpose. Explanations as answers to questions, unless they are theoretical explana-

L

tions, usually involve no logical arguments. Theoretical explanations as premises logically entail the facts to be explained. Facts as entailed conclusions of theoretical explanations are not open to contention. Explanations often exist in communicative contexts where no rhetorical logical appeal is being made. Yet audiences on many occasions demand justification for explanations. They incur a burden of proof. Explanations in such cases are what we argue for.

Narration, description, and exposition as explanations are usually responses, not appeals. Yet often these modes of discourse are used to make appeals indirectly. As such, narration and description function as logical appeals. Note that we question the purpose of explanations. "Why are you telling me that?" "Why are you explaining that to me?" "Why are you pointing that out to me?" Thus, modes often contextually imply claims and contentions. Note that my giving you *my* reasons for *my* believing something may indirectly or contextually imply that *you* ought to believe the same thing for the same reasons. Thus, exposition indirectly appeals by *contextual implication*. For example, literary discourse, historical explanation and narrative, journalistic description, and technological explanations can function contextually as indirect logical appeals. Note that some treatments of enthymemes in logic texts admit as enthymemes explicit premises with implicitly understood conclusions.

Probably the most important epistemological sense of logos as reason is as fact or data, *reason as inductive argument,* that is, as evidential support for the probability of an hypothesis. Inductive argument as appeal gives evidence to support the probability of an hypothesis. With the exception of induction by enumeration, inductive arguments never produce absolute certainty. All hypotheses as conclusions of inductive appeals are potentially open to disconfirmation. Aristotle used enthymemes and examples as the basis for rhetorical arguments. As such, for Aristotle there could be no question of certainty for the conclusions of rhetorical arguments. A problem for Aristotle is how to use probabilistic premises effectively to gain acceptance for contentions that seem only probably true. Using Aristotle's terms, how do we distinguish what is *essential* from what is *accidental* in *species* or *individual substances?*

First, logical appeal in rhetoric for Aristotle in arguing from probabilistic premises is opposed to scientific demonstration, where argument is from certainty to certainty. One interpretation of enthymemes in Aristotle is that they are arguments with probabilistic premises entailing probabilistic conclusions. In contrast for him, the theoretical sciences aim at strict proof with scientific or syllogistic demonstration.

Second, rhetorical induction for Aristotle is argument from example. Examples allow inductive generalization from "some" to "all," *induction by instantiation*. Or, interestingly, an example allows for inductive generalization from "one" typical or representative example or sample to "all." What is missing in Aristotle's account of induction is any numerical quantitative sense of generalized tendencies from aggregations or samples. Missing is any sense of inductive argument by statistical inference. Aristotle's generalizations from common-sense tendencies display a lack of any quantitative concept of probability. Aristotle's deficiency merely reflects the deficiencies of vernacular languages in ascribing with any precision calculations of probabilities. It is the poverty of ordinary language to have few quantitative conceptions to assess probability. For this reason most inductive arguments using natural language are prone to misleading and deceptive assessments of probabilities. As most rhetorical arguments are saturated with inductive arguments by instantiation of instances, examples, cases, or samples, induction in natural languages is prone to hasty generalizations and/or misleading, selective, and deceptive presentations of data.

Modern conceptions of causality too are based upon theories warranted by induction by instantiation of a number of confirming instances, where the correlation of factors in a number of instances in an observation sample is generalized to obtain for a target population. The degree to which we warrant the causal or empirical hypotheses generalized over a target population is relative to the number of instances that correlate in the observational sample.

Inductive warrant for empirical generalizations comes in two flavors: invariant correlations and a probable frequency of a correlation. Importantly, inductive support for statements about invariance are always probable. Equally inductive support for statements about the ranges of probabilities of a correlation are also only probable, a probability of a probability. Apart from induction by enumeration, inductive arguments by instantiation never arrive at logically necessary conclusions about invariance or about probabilistic correlations.

Moreover, besides appeals using warrants by induction from instantiation, we may reinforce the probability of any hypothesis by *induction by systematic coherence*. Any empirical generalization logically entailed by or derived from another hypothesis whose probability has been established has its probability corroborated by that hypothesis. Established theory through its derived tested hypotheses adds to the probability of those hypotheses. Logical coherence thus enhances probabilities.

Insofar as Aristotle presumes examples typical or exemplary, as natural kinds or species, there is a presumption of invariance in Aristotle. What would warrant this invariance? But as indicated in modern conceptions of inductive empirical generalization, hypotheses about invariance are always probable. To establish any presumption of invariance, there must exist a prior inductively and empirically justified argument for the probability of that presumption. If in argumentation from example we grant the presumption of invariance, then one sample or example will do. We assume that all cadavers are anatomically alike, so we assume that any detail in dissection of a cadaver would be like any other cadaver. By granting the presumption of invariance from past experience in anatomical studies, we avoid hasty generalization. Arguments from a single example or case history require such a presumption of invariance to avoid any charge of hasty generalization.

Many traditional logical or rhetorical fallacies are simply confusions about whether appeals are deductive or inductive. Insofar as most rhetorical appeals are inductive, it is rhetorically necessary to be careful about modalities and quantifiers to indicate whether an argument is inductive or deductive. Overstatement and hyperbole tend to confuse these issues. Essentialism and views about natural kinds also tend to blur modal distinctions. That a type is essential or a natural kind is a presumption of invariance that needs to be inductively warranted.

Another distinct kind of reason as distinct from the above accounts of *theoretical reason,* that is, epistemological accounts of reasoning, is *practical reason,* that is, axiological accounts of reasoning. This distinction is strikingly made in speech communication between arguments for propositions of fact and arguments for propositions of value or policy arguments.

Just as we draw distinctions about fact—(1) observations, (2) generalizations about observations, and (3) theoretical explanations of generalizations about observations—so too we can draw distinctions about value—(1) values defined by interests, (2) moral and ethical value, (3) social and political value, and (4) aesthetic value. Importantly, we argue for all these distinctions of fact and value differently, thus multiplying the modes and complexities of logical appeal.

Are ethical and emotive appeals rational? Questions about values are arguably connected to questions of feelings and expert authority. Inductively, we might want to say it is rational to trust one's feelings, or it is sometimes rational to trust the credibility or expertise or authority of another person. In this case, rational means giving inductive reasons to support trust or confidence in the validity of our feelings or our trust in others. Such trust, insofar as it is open to disconfirmation, makes such appeals arguments from probabilities. And again, insofar as such trust may be based upon lived experience, such presumptions about feeling and character are reliably rational. Thus, a taxonomy of appeals as logical, ethical, and emotive as distinct categories breaks down as we assess rationally the persuasive value of ethos and pathos. Using inductive arguments, we may justify the validity of an appeal to our feelings or appeals to authority. Note in particular that an ad hominem abusive need not be a fallacy insofar as it is an inductive argument that discounts an appeal to authority.

It is the character of many commonplaces, proverbs, and maxims of common wisdom to appear trustworthy and highly probable. They are confirmed inductively by common sense. Consequently, common-sense arguments tend to be highly effective rhetorically. Such argument tends to be conservative, as it appeals to traditional or cultural wisdom. Moreover, conventional wisdom is often embodied in language usage. It too reflects conventional and traditional values.

But among traditions of cultural wisdom also are maxims or proverbs about principles of justice, prudence, and personal value such as liberty and property. If you are trying to convince me that I am wrong about my actions, three lines of argument prove rhetorically quite effective against me. First, what I am doing is unfair. Second, what I am doing is not in the long-run good of most people. Third, what I am

L

doing is hurting myself. The first line is about justice. The latter two are about types of prudence: prudence in maximizing public good and prudence in maximizing private good. Insofar as an audience can agree on principles of fairness, public good, and self-interest—and about the priorities of one over the other—arguments about values and policy are rational in the sense that they follow logically from accepted principles. Such arguments form the bread and butter of ethical and political argumentation.

Logical appeal using figures of speech such as metaphor, allusions, or analogies are not based on interpretations of literal terms but on what is contextually implied by such figures. There is in the use of figures, allusions, and analogies in rhetorical contexts and situations a mode of discourse directing attention to a wealth of contextual implications that literal language has no time to take the pains to specify. It is the function of figurative logical appeals to call attention to a ground of presumption in the context of a rhetorical situation. Thus the rhetor has to lay the foundation of a logical appeal in presumption both literally and figuratively by a number of different speech acts, such as reminding or noting, giving testimony or assuring, and citing the testimony of others or reporting the expertise of others. The first pair essentially give focus to what is presumptively available in the audience's experience, the second on the presumptive ethos of the rhetor, and the third on the presumption that the audience is granting credibility and expertise to those cited.

A logical appeal thus ultimately must be understood as an appeal both to consistency and substantive reasons. It is the function of the rhetor to appeal to what is presumptively acceptable by an audience to effect change in an audience's acceptances and commitments. In using all the available means of persuasion, the rhetor uses every means to call attention to a presumptively acceptable ground that will justify to an audience contentions at issue. What seems rhetorically fundamental in logical appeal is using words literally, figuratively, suggestively, and by means of presumption to focus on a ground of audience acceptance, a ground that will reasonably alter what an audience accepts. Unlike the case in logic, this is not a verbally explicit enterprise.

George E. Yoos
St. Cloud State University

Bibliography

Aristotle. *Aristotle. Great Books of the Western World.* Vol. 8. Chicago: Encyclopedia Britannica, 1952.

Beardsley, Monroe C. *Thinking Straight: Principles of Reasoning for Writers and Readers.* 4th ed. Englewood Cliffs, NJ: Prentice, 1975.

Eemeren, Frans H. van, and Rob Grootendorst. *Argumentation, Communication, and Fallacies: A Pragma-Dialectical Perspective.* Hillsdale, NJ: Erlbaum, 1992.

Hamblin, C.L. *Fallacies.* London: Methuen, 1970.

Johnstone, Henry W., Jr. *Philosophy and Argument.* State College: Pennsylvania State UP, 1959.

Kinneavy, James. *A Theory of Discourse.* Englewood Cliffs, NJ: Prentice, 1971.

Perelman, Chaïm, and L. Olbrechts-Tyteca. *The New Rhetoric: A Treatise on Argumentation.* Notre Dame, IN: U of Notre Dame P, 1969.

Sperber, Dan, and Deidre Wilson. *Relevance: Communication and Cognition.* Cambridge, MA: Harvard UP, 1986.

Toulmin, Stephen, Richard Rieke, and Allan Janik. *Introduction to Reasoning.* New York: Macmillan, 1979.

Willard, Charles Arthur. *A Theory of Argumentation.* Tuscaloosa: U of Alabama P, 1989.

Longacre, Robert E. (b. 1922)

An innovative text linguist, associated with the tagmemics school of modern linguistics, who has helped shape discourse theory at the end of the twentieth century.

Robert E. Longacre, born in Akron, Ohio, earned an undergraduate degree at Houghton College in 1943 and a Bachelor's of Divinity at Faith Theological Seminary in 1946 before entering graduate study in linguistics. While taking an M.A. (1954) and Ph.D. (1955) in linguistics from the University of Pennsylvania, Longacre embarked upon a career in "missionary linguistics" with the Summer Institute of Linguistics, the academic arm of the Wycliffe Bible Translators. Longacre has spent much of his career alternating as an indigenous language researcher and Bible translator and as a faculty member in linguistics. In the latter role he served from 1960 to 1967 on the faculty of the

State University of Buffalo and since 1975 has been at the University of Texas, Arlington. He has been the recipient of a National Science Foundation and National Endowment for the Humanities Grant (1974) and numerous other federally sponsored linguistic research grants.

Longacre began a long association with linguist Kenneth Pike and his tagmemic linguistic theory in 1945, attending a Summer Institute of Linguistics seminar led by Pike on tone languages. Since that first exposure, Longacre has become one of the leading expositors and exponents of tagmemic linguistics, which characteristically deals with language data as elements situated within interrelated phonological, grammatical, and referential hierarchies. He is especially associated with the critique of "autonomous linguistics"— for example, the earliest versions of Noam Chomsky's transformational or generative grammar, which ignores social context and language-in-use in its formulation of postulates, rules, and theories of language acquisition. As a linguist and rhetorician, Longacre has thus championed the need for interdisciplinary approaches to situating discourse in its behavioral, sociological, and psychological contexts beyond the individual utterance, whether spoken or written.

Longacre's published research has focused primarily upon the comparative syntax of Mesoamerican languages, the crafting of grammar discovery principles for use in translation work, and theories of discourse above-the-sentence level, particularly the Hebrew narratives of the Bible. His work may be rightly regarded as pioneering in the still-nascent field of text linguistics—in Longacre's estimation simply a species of rhetorical study—a discipline that always has had more practitioners and theorists among continental linguists and rhetoricians than in North American academe. Longacre may also be credited with continuing to shape tagmemic linguistics by his careful criticism of the vocabulary and the tools emerging in the work of Kenneth Pike and other associates of the Summer Institute of Linguistics. His employment of tagmemic insights to an increasing variety of texts and interdisciinary contexts outside of biblical translation has brought tagmemic linguistics to the attention of an ever-greater audience of rhetoricians and linguists.

Bruce L. Edwards
Bowling Green State University

Bibliography
Longacre, Robert E. *An Anatomy of Speech Notions*. Lisse, Belgium: Ridder, 1976.
———. *The Grammar of Discourse*. New York: Plenum, 1983.
———. "Reshaping Linguistics: Context and Content." *New Directions in Linguistics and Semiotics*. Ed. James E. Copeland. Amsterdam: Benjamins, 1984. 79–95.
———. "Why We Need a Vertical Revolution in Linguistics." *The Fifth LACUS Forum, 1978*. Columbia, SC: Hornbeam. 247–70.

See also PIKE, KENNETH L.; TAGMEMICS; YOUNG, RICHARD

Longinus (c. 213–273 C.E.)

Long thought to be the author of *On the Sublime*. This Greek treatise is widely considered to rank with the most original early works on speaking and writing, but there is no mention of it by writers of its time. Modern texts depend on a tenth-century manuscript, a third of which is missing. Until the nineteenth century, *On the Sublime* was thought to be the work of the third-century philologist and statesman Cassius Longinus. It is now generally thought to be the work of an unknown first-century author; the tradition is maintained of using the name *Longinus* to refer to this unknown author. The work became widely known after a Basel edition of 1554. Beginning with a French translation by Boileau (Paris, 1674) and an English translation by William Smith (London, 1739), the work exerted a powerful influence on European literary and philosophical thinking in the late seventeenth and throughout the eighteenth century and has often influenced modern theory through a variety of rereadings.

For Longinus, the achievement of sublimity (sometimes also translated as "elevated" or "great" speaking and writing) is not merely a matter of style, technique, or taste. Rather, sublimity transports the listener out of the self and excites not so much admiration as direct identification with speaker and subject matter. Longinus' rejection of a traditional separation of form and content and his discussion of the problem of the subject anticipate contemporary debates.

Longinus opens his work with a preface and a description of faults (turgidity, puerility, false emotion, frigidity) that may occur in writing that tries but fails to achieve sublimity. He then identifies the signs of sublimity as being in the sense of elevation experienced by the hearer. Longinus then describes the five sources of sublimity: the power of conceiving great thoughts, strong and inspired emotion, figures of thought and speech, nobility of diction, and elevated composition or arrangement of words. These categories are known to traditional rhetoric. Longinus is unusual in his continuing emphasis on the central importance of great thoughts, the measure of sublimity in the transport of the listener, and by his working methods: He is a critic rather than a theorist. Throughout the body of the work, he quotes, comments upon, and evokes through his own style the appropriate response to passages of sublimity in texts he admires: Homer, Sappho, Demosthenes, Cicero, Plato, and the Book of Genesis.

For Longinus, sublimity is not the achievement of mere correctness, consistency, or technique, and it goes beyond poetic beauty or mere persuasion. Sublimity is not in the text or the technique but in the effect, an effect brought about by great moral aspiration, rooted in earthly truth and boldly expressed.

Longinus ends his work with a lament for the decline of eloquence into sterility and flattery, a condition brought about by the collapse of republican government, and producing "an indifference in which, with rare exceptions, all of us live, never laboring or undertaking anything for its own sake, but only for praise or pleasure, never for any benefit worthy of honor or emulation" (58).

Thomas W. Benson
Pennsylvania State University

Bibliography

Fry, Paul H. *The Reach of Criticism: Method and Perception in Literary Theory.* New Haven: Yale UP, 1983.

Guerlac, Suzanne. "Longinus and the Subject of the Sublime." *New Literary History* 16 (1985): 275–89.

Henn, T.R. *Longinus and English Criticism.* Cambridge: Cambridge UP, 1934.

Longinus. *On the Sublime (On Great Writing).* Trans. G.M.A. Grube. New York: Liberal Arts, 1957. Rpt. Indianapolis, IN: Hackett, 1991.

Monk, Samuel H. *The Sublime: A Study of Critical Theories in XVIII-Century England.* Modern Language Assn., 1935. Ann Arbor: U of Michigan P, 1960.

Roberts, Rhys. *Longinus on the Sublime.* Cambridge: Cambridge UP, 1907.

Russell, D.A. *Criticism in Antiquity.* London: Duckworth, 1981.

Russell, D.A., ed. and trans. *"Longinus" On the Sublime.* Oxford: Clarendon, 1964.

Tate, Alan. "Longinus and the 'New Criticism.'" *Collected Essays.* Denver, CO: Swallow, 1959. 507–27.

Lysias (c. 444–380 B.C.E.)

Greek logographer and orator. Born in Athens, Lysias was by descent a Syracusan. Estimates of his dates vary, but he remained a prominent Athenian speechwriter (logographer) from 403 until 380. A friend of Pericles and Socrates, he was a prolific composer of forensic speeches that were models of the plain style.

For a number of years, Lysias and his two brothers lived in Thurii, where Lysias may have studied with Tisias. In 412 they were expelled for political reasons and returned to Athens. In 404, when a revolution brought the oligarchic Thirty into power, he was arrested but escaped into temporary exile. His brother Polemarchus was killed.

Lysias returned in 403 and remained there until his death. According to Cicero, he ran a school of rhetoric for several years before supporting himself solely by selling speeches to litigants. He was prolific, writing at least two hundred speeches, possibly twice that number. Of those, 165 are specifically accounted for; thirty-four exist in complete or nearly complete form.

Only two epideictic speeches attributed to Lysias remain: an Olympic oration and a funeral oration. The *Olympiacus*, probably delivered in 388, advocated union among Greeks and asked Sparta to take the lead. The *Epitaphios*, purportedly spoken during the Corinthian War for Athenian soldiers who supported Corinth, was perhaps only an exercise and is not definitely a work of Lysias'.

Lysias is perhaps best known for a speech he may not actually have written—an argument that a young man should accept the attentions of another who is attracted to him. This speech, referred to in the *Phaedrus,* may actually have been created by Plato after the style of Lysias.

Aside from a deliberative address arguing against subversion of the ancient Athenian constitution, all the other extant speeches are forensic. George Kennedy, along with other critics, believes the greatest of these to be *Against Era-*

tosthenes. The only court speech known to have been delivered by Lysias, it is a strong indictment of Eratosthenes for his role in poisoning his brother Polemarchus. Also, it deals with the character of Eratosthenes and the Thirty in general.

Lysias is known for his pure and graceful prose, a plain style in contrast to the more flamboyant grand style of Gorgias. Lysias eschewed the use of rhetorical figures, except for artistic parallelism or antithesis, which he sometimes used to excess. The naturalness of Lysias extends to his precise diction and straightforward arrangement. His speeches usually include four parts: proem, narrative, proof, and epilogue. He was facile with the first two, uneven in his mastery of proof and epilogue.

Another attribute of Lysias' style is his skill with *ethopoiia*, his ability to tailor a speech to fit the ethos of the person who will give it. Despite early training in the florid Sicilian school, Lysias avoided false brilliance and concentrated on a style that would suit the speaker to whom it was ascribed.

The extant speeches of Lysias are collected in the Loeb Classical Library edition by W.R.M. Lamb (1930).

Ken Autrey
Francis Marion University

L

Bibliography

Dobson, J.F. "Lysias." *The Greek Orators.* Freeport, NY: Books for Libraries, 1919. 74–102.

Jebb, R.C. *The Attic Orators from Antiphon to Isaeus.* Vol. 1. New York: Macmillan, 1893. 140–312.

Kennedy, George. "Lysias." *The Art of Persuasion in Greece.* Princeton: Princeton UP, 1963. 133–40.

M

MacIntyre, Alasdair (b. 1929)

Contemporary moral philosopher, probably best known for his ideas about discourse and ethics, and about rationality and virtue-centered morality. Much of his writing involves critical inquiry into the relationship of classical philosophy to current issues in religion, sociology, and education.

MacIntyre was educated at Queen Mary College of the University of London and at Manchester University. His teaching career has been at various prestigious British and American universities, including Oxford University, the University of Essex, Brandeis University, Boston University, Wellesley College, Vanderbilt University, and Yale University. As of September 1988, he was McMahon-Hank Professor of Philosophy at the University of Notre Dame.

Author of numerous articles and reviews published in various scholarly journals, MacIntyre has also written several important books on humanistic education and moral philosophy, including *Marxism: An Interpretation* (1953), *The Unconscious: A Conceptual Analysis* (1958), *Difficulties in Christian Belief* (1959), *A Short History of Ethics* (1966), *Secularization and Moral Change* (1967), *Marxism and Christianity* (1968), and *Against the Self-Images of the Age: Essays on Ideology and Philosophy* (1971; rpt. 1978). However, MacIntyre is cited most for his more recent books, *After Virtue: A Study in Moral Theory* (1981) and *Whose Justice? Which Rationality?* (1988).

A major portion of *After Virtue* is devoted to tracing the sociological and historical development of modern-day moral practices—a process he identifies as understanding the rise and decline of a morality that is now permeated with the rationality of self-interested individu-alism. The diversity of moral viewpoints within contemporary public discourse disallows any sort of consensus. As a result, the only hope for the reform of human communication and understanding is to adopt a community morality that is based upon an Aristotelian value system—that value system that originally served to bond local communities of "like-minded individuals." *Whose Justice? Which Rationality?*, MacIntyre's later text, is a deeper historical analysis of that moral development and includes an analysis of the nature of the relationship between virtue, justice, and laws.

The focus of MacIntyre's close historical analysis is the breakdown of morality through the rational justification of morals and ethics by what he identifies as "the Enlightenment project." In the twentieth century, this breakdown has become most obvious in such places as academia, where the advent of positivistic, neutral, and objective scholastic inquiry has resulted in such things as an educational curriculum that is fragmented, value neutral, and largely irrelevant. Such curriculum "fails to embody any overall concept of what it is to be educated . . . because it lacks any coherent view of the good or goods to be served by disciplined enquiry" (MacIntyre, "Traditions" 6).

MacIntyre's philosophical insights on discourse, community, and ethical behavior, though not addressing specifically the study of rhetoric, have much relevance to current rhetorical theory. As Thomas S. Frentz suggests, "When tied to a classical conception of rhetoric . . . [MacIntyre's] work provides . . . a paradigmatic form of human communication" (1)—one that is very much rhetorical in nature.

John Paddison
Northern Arizona University

Bibliography

Conrad, Thomas R. "*After Virtue* and Liberal Education." *Liberal Education* 70 (1984): 159–64.

Frentz, Thomas S. "Rhetorical Conversations, Time, and Moral Action." *Quarterly Journal of Speech* 71 (1985): 1–18.

MacIntyre, Alasdair. *After Virtue*. 2nd ed. Notre Dame, IN: U of Notre Dame P, 1984.

———. "Traditions and Conflicts." *Liberal Education* 73 (1987): 6–13.

———. *Whose Justice? Which Rationality?* Notre Dame, IN: U of Notre Dame P, 1988.

Wallace, R. Jay. Rev. of *Whose Justice? Which Rationality?* by Alasdair MacIntyre. *History and Tradition* 28 (1989): 326–48.

Macrorie, Ken (b. 1918)

Writing scholar, teacher, former editor of *College Composition and Communication*. Ken Macrorie has been involved in teaching and studying composition since the late 1940s. His contributions include a number of important scholarly articles and textbooks, his journal editorship, and his discussions of the teaching profession.

In the early 1950s, Macrorie recognized the importance of a writer's commitment to writing and of the writer's development of an authentic "voice," or ethos. As early as 1951 ("Words in the Way"), Macrorie recommended that students read and respond to each other's writing, and he developed the concept of "the helping circle" as a classroom structure for peer-responding. He was also the first to popularize freewriting. In addition, Macrorie has promoted journal writing; teaching revision; viewing research (or "I-search," to use his term) as part of the overall writing process, motivated by the same forces motivating writing generally; and connecting oral language with written language. His *Four In Depth: Readings to Develop the Art of Comparison* (1963) may have been the earliest modern thematic "reader," focusing on only four subjects: work, war, self, and society. And he has been a leader in the movement to minimize the importance of grammar and mechanics and to connect error correction to the overall rhetorical purpose and effect sought by the writer. Pedagogically, Macrorie advocates student-centered education and a vision of the writing classroom as a community of writers.

Like that of Donald Murray, Janet Emig, and James Moffett, his vision of composition instruction encompasses all levels of education, not simply freshman English. His textbooks, such as *Telling Writing*, for example, are not just for college freshmen. They combine the usual composition textbook content (for example, discussions of composing processes and products and writing exercises) with elements of books on creative writing (such as discussions of how to write dialogue) and advice for teachers.

Macrorie has often been labeled a "Romantic" or "Expressivist" (see James Berlin's *Rhetoric and Reality*), but on closer examination, he problematizes easy classification. While he does tend to locate meaning-making in the individual writer, Macrorie finds the origins of that meaning-making in the writer's desire to communicate with others; the writer does not exist for Macrorie without an audience. The social and democratic aspects of Macrorie's theory and pedagogy—his advocacy of peer responding and of the classroom as a community—contradicts Romantic notions of the writer as solitary genius. And he certainly does not limit himself to consideration of writing as self-expression. In addition to discussions of poetry and dialogue, Macrorie includes chapters on report writing and interviewing. He has written a whole book on writing based on research (*Searching Writing*, later titled *The I-Search Paper*). Macrorie's much-neglected textbook *The Perceptive Writer, Reader, and Speaker* (1959), which claims perception as the basis for communication, foreshadows several themes of composition scholarship of the late sixties and early seventies, including a concern of tagmemicists like Richard Young and Alton Becker with multiple perspectives during inquiry and connections between rhetoric and cognition like those made by Janet Emig and James Moffett.

As editor of *College Composition and Communication* from 1962 to 1964, Macrorie oversaw major changes in the journal. He focused it on controversial issues in the field, often devoting a single issue to a particular theme. He published many classic articles by Wayne Booth, Edward P.J. Corbett, Janet Emig, and others.

Several of Ken Macrorie's textbooks remain available, some in fairly recent editions. They stand as testimonies to his long-lasting influence on the study and teaching of written communication.

Gerald Nelms
Southern Illinois University, Carbondale

Bibliography

Graves, Donald H., Jerome C. Harste, Ken Macrorie, and P. David Pearson. *When Bad Things Happen to Good Ideas*. Urbana, IL: National Council of Teachers of English, 1988.

Macrorie, Ken. "Composition as Art." *College Composition and Communication* 15 (1964): back cover.

———. *Four In Depth: Readings to Develop the Art of Comparison*. Boston: Mifflin, 1963.

———. "The Freewriting Relationship." *Nothing Begins With N: New Investigations of Freewriting*. Carbondale, IL: Southern Illinois UP, 173–88.

———. *The I-Search Paper: Revised Edition of Searching Writing*. Portsmouth, NH: Boynton/Cook, 1988.

———. "Mis-Takes." *Iowa English Bulletin* 34 (1986): 35–39.

———. *The Perceptive Writer, Reader, and Speaker*. New York: Harcourt, 1959.

———. *Telling Writing*. 4th ed. Rochelle Park, NJ: Hayden, 1970. Upper Montclair, NJ: Boynton/Cook, 1985.

———. "To Be Read." *English Journal* 57 (1968): 686–92. Rpt. *Rhetoric and Composition: A Sourcebook for Teachers and Writers*. Ed. Richard L. Graves. Upper Montclair, NJ: Boynton/Cook, 1984.

———. *Twenty Teachers*. New York: Oxford UP, 1984.

———. *Uptaught*. New York: Hayden, 1970.

———. *A Vulnerable Teacher*. Rochelle Park, NJ: Hayden, 1974.

———. "Words in the Way." *English Journal* 40 (1951): 382–85.

———. *Writing to Be Read*. Rev. 3rd ed. Portsmouth, NH: Boynton/Cook, 1984.

———. "Writing's Dying." *College Composition and Communication* 11 (1960): 206–10.

Magic

The belief that words have magical power. As early as 415 B.C.E., the sophist Gorgias wrote in his *Encomium of Helen* that speech can "drug and bewitch the soul with a kind of evil persuasion." Magic and rhetoric both traffic in illusion; their common powers worry idealist philosophers from antiquity forward, and become a concern of both Enlightenment scientists and modern social critics. Magic rhetoric is fearful on two counts: (1) The magical imagination is protean, and liable to disrupt prevailing versions of truth; (2) "charismatic" speech can mesmerize listeners into mindless behavior.

Plato calls the sophistic rhetoricians dangerous magicians who—like Proteus—can give truth different shapes. In the fifth century C.E., Augustine warns Christian orators to avoid the "magic arts." In 1500 Gianfrancesco Pico della Mirandola summarizes medieval conceptions of fantasy as a central activity of the composing imagination, and warns against demonic phantasms. In 1667 Thomas Sprat conceives London's Royal Society as the enemy of rhetoric and magic together, allying figurative language and witchery. The Enlightenment castigation of the magical properties of language is met by the Romantic movement's reassertion of an expansive imagination, represented by Coleridge's claim in the *Biographia Literaria*: "I will cause the world of intelligences with the whole system of their representations to rise up before you" (13). Apart from Thomas De Quincey's rather eccentric connection of this generative imagination to a lost art of rhetoric, the Romantic association of magic and language is displaced to poetics, and persists in the neo-Romantic mysticism of William Butler Yeats. New concerns about the magical powers of oratory, advertising, and the "culture industry" in general emerge in the 1940s and 1950s from Frankfurt School philosophers such as Theodor Adorno and Herbert Marcuse, who argue that the language of modern authoritarianism is an automatizing magic. That view is extended by Paulo Freire, who calls "magic consciousness" the opposite of "critical consciousness" in the philosophy of education that he introduces in the 1960s and 1970s, and by radical feminists such as Mary Daly in her 1987 *Wickedary*.

Surveying the history of magic, sociologist Daniel Lawrence O'Keefe has noted that social consensus determines the powers of both rhetoric and magic: Magic, like rhetoric, "works because people agree that it works" (96). O'Keefe's definition of magic as collective social action corresponds with Kenneth Burke's designations of magic throughout his works as symbolic action. For Burke, naming is a magical act because it "decrees" the nature of an object or situation. In *The Philosophy of Literary Form*, he calls "correct" magic the practice of multiplying decrees through the action of broad and irresolute social inquiry. In *A Grammar of Motives* and *A Rhetoric of Motives*, Burke characterizes "false" magic as an arhetorical, dehumanizing act: The use of language to compel motion in objects rather than to engender cooperation in people. With Burke in mind, William Covino contrasts "generative magic rhetoric" and "arresting magic rhetoric": The former is *"constitutive inquiry, or the coercive expansion of the possibilities for action,"* and the latter is *"enforced doctrine, or the coercive reduction of the possibilities for action."*

William A. Covino
University of Illinois, Chicago

Bibliography

Covino, William A. *Rhetoric, Magic, and Literacy*. New York: SUNY P, 1994.

De Romilly, Jacqueline. *Magic and Rhetoric in Ancient Greece*. Cambridge, MA: Harvard UP, 1975.

O'Keefe, Daniel Lawrence. *Stolen Lightning: The Social Theory of Magic*. New York: Continuum, 1982.

Ward, John O. "Magic and Rhetoric from Antiquity to the Renaissance: Some Ruminations." *Rhetorica* 6 (1988): 57–118.

Marxist Rhetoric

Language and the reproduction of society. In everyday usage, *rhetoric* refers to a set of codes or conventions operating when we produce or interpret texts, an analytic practice used to model, define, or critique this production, and a pedagogy derived from such analysis. For Marxism, analysis must come first and would, like all other cultural practices, be subsumed under Marxist theory in general. This follows from the way Marxism locates itself as a theory. In contrast to other rhetorical practices, Marxism does not understand itself as one of many alternative ways of seeing. Indeed, Marxism considers a rhetorical theory much less a formal definition, such as the current one as a material and ideological production circulating in fundamentally oppressive capitalist relations. It would cast the notion of innocent choices between rhetorics as an illusion of individual power that masks relations between economic classes and constructs good political subjects unaware of their conditions. So within classical Marxism, there is no rhetoric. Rather, Marxism offers a theory (its classical practitio-

ners would say a "science") of human social relations that logically precedes all other cultural systems. It offers a narrative of the historical struggle between classes and a set of concepts that inform its analysis of culture. However, because of the importance of communication as part of the material production of culture, theorists interested in rhetoric have adapted the historical narrative of Marxism and many of its concepts.

Perhaps the central questions for a Marxist theory of rhetoric are how language and rhetoric are part of the production of social, especially class relations, and whether rhetoric can help us understand and intervene in the conditions of cultural production. For orthodox Marxism, the answer to the first question is dictated by the architectural metaphor that Marx used to explain social structure. In this theory, the economic base composed of the conditions and relations of production determines all social relations and even the form of our consciousness. Culture, including rhetoric, is part of the superstructure determined by the material conditions under which we live. Language and rhetoric thus help maintain the relations of production that constitute the economic base. This conception of social structure means that the answer to the second question—can we know and intervene in our social condition?—is an emphatic *no*. Since language and rhetoric reside in this superstructure, to imagine that any rhetorical system could transcend the controlling force of materiality is a romantic dream. On such a model, rhetoric becomes part of the production of our "false consciousness," the ideology that submerses us in oppressive class relations.

More recently, however, revisions of this orthodox position by Antonio Gramsci, Louis Althusser, and Raymond Williams have questioned the determining power of the base/superstructure relationship and rejected the orthodox definition of ideology as false consciousness. In doing so, they have vindicated language and rhetoric as critical forces, allowing theorists to reappropriate classical concepts and produce a rhetoric that analyzes the way language reproduces or actively disrupts existing social relations.

Antonio Gramsci is perhaps best known for his concept of "hegemony" and the effect that this concept had on Marxism's thinking about determination and the base/superstructure model. Gramsci separated society into state and civil society, the state composed of official, legal institutions of power, and civil society made up of the whole range of institutions and daily practices that mediate between the state and the economy. Gramsci argued that hegemony was carried out by a range of active and changing strategies within civil society, through which the dominant social class secured the consent of the oppressed. Hegemony worked by diffusing the ideological position of the dominant class throughout the fabric of social practices so that the special interests of the powerful become identified as the interests of society at large, become the "common sense" to which we all automatically subscribe—"what's good for GM is good for America." There are two consequences of Gramsci's insight that created a powerful opening for rhetoric. For Gramsci, hegemony superseded "ideology" and meant that cultural activity was not merely restricted to the economically determined superstructure. Now hegemonic activity helped form economic activity. A second advance created by Gramsci was that hegemonic activity is a process of continual struggle; if there is a powerful dominating hegemony, there are also "counter-hegemonies," competing forms of common sense that disrupt the domination of a particular class interest. This suggests that rhetoric can analyze cultural discourses and identify ways in which they construct a common sense that serves the interests of a limited class and that can identify possibilities for counterdiscourses.

Although his work is very different from Gramsci's, Louis Althusser's revisions of the concept of ideology and his idea of the "Ideological State Apparatuses" and their effect on subjects expanded the opening Gramsci had made for rhetoric. Althusser argued that ideology was the largely unconscious way in which we imagine our relations to the real, and that it is in this realm of representation that power struggles are fought. He also proposed that rather than being controlled by one uniform Ideology, society is composed of a number of ideologies, each constructed in the practices of a number of ideological apparatuses such as schooling, religion, and entertainment. These apparatuses, in turn, interpellate us as subjects. That is, they call us into social being in a position and identity already prepared for us by the dominant apparatuses. Borrowing an idea from Foucault, we can say that every statement creates a position—an identity, authority, social place—for the subject who utters it, and that Althusser's ideological apparatuses regulate the kinds of statements we can make, and thus the subject positions available to us. With this theoretical understanding, rhetoric becomes a tool with which to analyze the way apparatuses use language to represent the real, excluding ideas that are detrimental and privileging those ways of thinking and being that correspond to the interests of the apparatus. Rhetoric also provides a way to explain how an institutional discourse reproduces repressive social relations through the kinds of statements and, thus, the subject positions it makes available.

One problem with Althusser's theory, however, is that it describes subjects as if they were completely determined by the structure of dominant apparatuses and largely ignorant of their condition. Reacting against these two aspects of Althusser's work, theorists such as Anthony Giddens, Chantal Mouffe, and Ernesto Laclau have recently argued that subjects should be understood as cultural "agents" capable of recognizing their place in ideological apparatuses. These apparatuses, in turn, are themselves dynamic rather than static; they exist only in the memory and ongoing practice of social agents. This view of apparatuses as changing and contingent leads to a conception of society as an open and contested space rather than a closed, finite structure. Thus, Chantal Mouffe and Ernesto Laclau argue that social relations are constituted and organized by shifting articulatory practices and that our social character and relations are precarious. For rhetoricians this means that as Mouffe and Laclau argue, the "central problem is to identify the discursive conditions for the emergence of collective action, directed toward struggling against inequalities and challenging relations of subordination" (153). The work of a Marxist rhetoric then becomes the analysis of these discursive conditions and constructing a pedagogical practice as part of this "collective action."

One important site for this collective action is schooling, and Marxism has shaped an influential pedagogical theory. Theorists have argued that schooling has replaced religion as the most powerful apparatus, which can reproduce social relations in at least three important ways. First, schools often offer differential educational opportunities to produce workers trained for jobs associated with different class positions. Less obviously, schooling is also a socialization process, teaching forms of discipline and respect, and through them the discipline and respect for social forms. This "hidden curriculum" teaches students how to behave in hierarchical relations of power. Finally, through a process that Pierre Bourdieu and Jean Claude Passeron call "symbolic violence," schooling legitimizes some forms of knowledge and not others, presenting as fact and common sense knowledges that are historically constructed and tied to material interests. Because the teacher possesses the necessary "cultural capital," education participates in the hegemonic process Gramsci described; it teaches students to consent to essentially oppressive relations. The first task of a Marxist pedagogy is to analyze how the discursive conditions of schooling—particularly the teaching of writing—participate in this social reproduction and to identify ways in which schooling can resist this hegemonic tendency.

Because society is not a closed structure and social agents can come to recognize their conditions, Marxist rhetoric also sees education as a powerful site for ideological resistance and change. This pedagogical tradition, variously called liberatory, radical, or critical pedagogy, attempts to modify both the form and content of education in order to help students and teachers recognize the discursive conditions and thus the social relations in which they work. The most familiar source for this pedagogical theory is the work of Paulo Freire and that of associated theorists such as Henry Giroux and Ira Schor. Freire's fundamental assumption is that education must help us recognize the ways in which language constructs our subjectivity and our relations to the social world. The purpose of education for Freire is to bring students and teachers to a point of cultural self-consciousness, what he calls *conscientizacao*. This pedagogy entails a classroom constructed as a dialogue between students and teachers, and an openness to knowledges and written forms that challenge conventions and offer students and teachers new, less oppressive subject positions from which to speak and act.

Carl G. Herndl
New Mexico State University
Robert L. Brown
University of Minnesota

Bibliography

Althusser, Louis. *Lenin and Philosophy and Other Essays*. New York: Monthly Review, 1971.

Bourdieu, Pierre, and Jean Claude Passeron. *Reproduction in Education, Society and Culture*. Berkeley: Sage, 1977.

Eagleton, Terry. *Ideology: An Introduction*. New York: Verso, 1991.

Freire, Paulo. *Pedagogy of the Oppressed*. New York: Continuum, 1989.

Giddens, Anthony. *Central Problems in Social Theory: Action, Structure and Contradiction in Social Analysis*. Berkeley: U of California P, 1979.

Giroux, Henry. *Theory and Resistance in Education: A Pedagogy for the Opposition*. South Hadley, MA: Bergin, 1983.

Gramsci, Antonio. *Selections from the Prison Notebooks*. Ed. and trans. Q. Hoare and G.N. Smith. New York: International, 1971.

Marx, Karl, and Frederich Engels. *Literature and Art, by Karl Marx and Frederick Engels: Selections from Their Writings*. New York: International, 1947.

Mouffe, Chantal, and Ernesto Laclau. *Hegemony and Socialist Strategy: Towards a Radical Democratic Politics*. New York: Verso, 1985.

Williams, Raymond. *Marxism and Literature*. New York: Oxford UP, 1977.

See also GRAMSCI, ANTONIO; WILLIAMS, RAYMOND

McKeon, Richard P. (1900–1985)

Distinguished American philosopher who studied the theoretic presuppositions behind rhetorical doctrines, traced the changing meanings and applications of rhetorical themes throughout Western intellectual history, and speculated on innovative extensions of rhetoric in philosophy, natural science, practical affairs, and the arts, forming a philosophy of culture in which rhetoric, expanded beyond a simple verbal skill to an intellectual art of invention and inquiry, provides the framework for pluralism and a new organization of learning.

Richard McKeon was born in Union Hill, New Jersey, on April 26, 1900. He studied at Columbia University in preprofessional programs of law and engineering before the First World War interrupted his education. Afterward, his interests shifted to humanistic studies, and he read literature, philosophy, history, and the classics. His Master's thesis in philosophy was on Tolstoi, Croce, and Santayana, and his Ph.D. dissertation, still cited as an important study of seventeenth-century philosophy, was on the philosophy of Spinoza. While at Columbia he studied with Frederick J.E. Woodbridge and John Dewey. In 1922 he went to Paris to study with Leon Brunschvicq, Leon Robin, and Etienne Gilson, leading philosophers and scholars of the day, and received a degree from the University of Paris and l'Ecole des Hautes Etudes. Like Dewey, whose trip to the Far East marked an intellectual turning point, McKeon was stimulated by his experiences in Europe to an interest in communication across cultures and ages that remained a central theme throughout his life. From 1925 to 1935, McKeon taught at Columbia University, where he established medieval philosophy as a serious branch of philosophic studies. In 1935, at the invitation of Robert Maynard Hutchins, he went to the University of Chicago to become dean of the humanities. He was one of the primary architects of the general education program of the "Hutchins College" at Chicago and remained a powerful voice for interdisciplinary studies and the liberal arts in higher education in the United States and abroad.

In the period following the Second World War, McKeon served as an American representative to UNESCO and participated in the Committee on the Theoretical Bases of Human Rights, which helped prepare for the adoption of the Universal Declaration of Human Rights by the United Nations. He was a founding member of the so-called "Chicago School" of literary criticism, reputed to be "neo-Aristotelian" in methodology but, in fact, strongly committed to critical pluralism and an expanded form of rhetorical inquiry that provoked angry responses from the formalist New Critics. Among many other national and international distinctions in a long career in philosophy, he was awarded the highest honor of the American Philosophical Association when he was invited to give the Paul Carus Lectures in New York in 1965.

McKeon was commonly—and mistakenly—described as an "Aristotelian" because of extensive commentaries on Aristotle, important editions of the works of Aristotle, and many essays on ancient Greek philosophy. Although influenced by reading Aristotle's works, McKeon accurately characterized himself as a philosophical pluralist and an American philosopher in the tradition of the pragmatists. His work opened a new direction in American pragmatic philosophy that subtly resonates with C.S. Peirce and John Dewey yet projects the new role of rhetoric in addressing philosophic and practical problems. Some observers argue that McKeon explored the themes of deconstructionism and other late-twentieth-century philosophies decades before their popular emergence but that he avoided relativism and solipsism through the principles of objective inquiry and the possibilities of productive intellectual debate. His active involvement in promoting universal human rights and World Federalism indicates an optimism that stands in sharp contrast to the pessimism over establishing shared understanding that is found in some forms of literary and philosophic deconstructionism. He remained at Chicago until his retirement in 1974 and continued to lecture and publish until his death in 1985.

McKeon was the first major philosopher to recognize the central importance of rhetoric in the philosophic and cultural revolutions that began in the early decades of the twentieth century. He argued that debate in Western culture shifts periodically through a sequence of master topics or commonplaces that he identified as "things," "thoughts," "words," and "actions." The shifting debate progresses from questions of being and metaphysics, to questions of epistemology and forms of thought, to questions of language and the circumstances and consequences of action. In periods of metaphysics and epistemology, the formal discipline of rhetoric often plays a secondary role among the cultural and intellectual arts and is frequently reduced to a mere verbal art, while the devices and themes of rhetoric move informally throughout the arts and sciences. But in a period when debate in all fields and disciplines finds its beginning point in questions of expression, experience, and communication, rhetoric becomes a broadly organizing "architectonic" discipline that provides the issues and instrumentalities for innovation and revolution, leading to new fields of investigation, new disciplines to guide inquiry, and new occupations for men and women in all areas of life.

The rise of rhetoric in the twentieth century began among scientists, artists, and philosophers who revolted against earlier dogma "by seeking meaningful questions in the concrete and real; by cultivating experience and phenomena, existence and nature; by appealing to science and history, common sense and language." However, the presence of rhetorical themes and issues embedded in the new discourse did not ensure the rapid emergence of a new art of rhetoric. Indeed, the progress of twentieth-century revolutions has been frequently blunted and deflected into ideological conflicts and semantic disputes among philosophies by the lack of a new art of rhetoric adequate to the fundamental task undertaken in these revolutions: the formation of a world culture that is both universal in extension and individual and plural in expression. Such an art emerged in the Roman Republic oriented toward practical affairs and law. It emerged in the Renaissance oriented toward beaux arts and belles-lettres. But in the twentieth century, McKeon argued, the new architectonic art of rhetoric would find its orientation, not in the practical or the poetic, but in science and the theoretic. The new rhetoric would be an "art of science" or a "science of art": an intellectual technology that combines theory with practice for new productive purposes.

McKeon's writings—more than 160 articles and eleven books—are a record of his continuing exploration of the dimensions of the new architectonic art of rhetoric directed toward the intellectual and practical problems of the twentieth century. Some of these writings are explicit treatments of rhetoric that shifted the direction of contemporary scholarly inquiry. For example, the seminal "Rhetoric in the Middle Ages" (1942) opened the way for the serious study of medieval and Renaissance rhetoric that forcefully emerged in the second half of the twentieth century. Rhetoric, he argued, is commonly treated as an art with a fixed subject matter, usually a simple verbal discipline. Based on this conception, the resulting histories of rhetoric give only fragmentary accounts and monotonous enumerations of doctrines that fail to explore the influence and development of rhetoric—the spread of its devices and themes—in subject matters far removed from those ordinarily ascribed to it. As a consequence, the history of rhetoric in the Middle Ages appeared brief, equivocal, and unimportant. In contrast, McKeon proposed a history of rhetoric that reflects on the changing conceptions of the subject matter, nature, and purpose of the art, conceptions that rhetoricians employ to distinguish and advance their doctrines in novel applications. When applied to the medieval period, this approach revealed a startling pattern of innovation in the tradition of rhetoricians themselves, in the tradition of philosophers and theologians, and in the tradition of logic, demonstrating not the demise of rhetoric but its renaissance in new forms.

"Rhetoric in the Middle Ages" influenced the course of rhetorical scholarship in the twentieth century, but it also implied the need for a new approach by which to understand the contemporary development of rhetoric beyond the confines of a narrow verbal discipline or a fixed subject matter. In many essays, McKeon explicitly sought to expand the understanding of rhetoric as an intellectual art, showing how the instrumentalities of rhetoric—particularly the common and proper places associated with invention—could be reconstituted to address contemporary problems of culture. Examples include "The Methods of Rhetoric and Philosophy: Invention and Judgment," "Creativity and the Commonplace," "Arts of Invention and Arts of Memory: Creation and Criticism," "Symbols, Myths, and Arguments," and the powerful, provocative essays "Discourse, Demonstration, Verification, and Justification," "Philosophy of Communications and the Arts," and "The Uses of Rhetoric in a Technological Age: Architectonic Productive Arts." In many other essays—the majority of his writings—McKeon implicitly used rhetoric as an intellectual art with which to explore contrasting perspectives on central themes of philosophy and culture, always with a view toward issues in contemporary scholarship, philosophy, science, practical affairs, or the arts. The range of these essays and the scope of treatment of each theme never fail to reveal unexpected connections and intellectual possibilities that remain hidden in narrower or more traditional studies. His goal was a classic expression of rhetoric: to discover new ideas and create new methods that would sustain an ongoing revolution in thought and action to better realize the potential of the human community.

Two rhetorical devices provided the foundation of McKeon's approach to communication: amplification and schematization. Amplification is the device for extending the scope of rhetoric from words to actions, thoughts, and things. He often spoke of the principle of indifference, by which words convert to actions, express thoughts, and refer to things. "Objectivity is the inclusive principle of indifference by which it is recognized that being is grasped only in what we think, and say, and do about it" (McKeon, "Circumstances and Functions" 111). Schematization was the primary device for identifying commonplaces and generating inventions. Schemata are uninterpreted but suggestive relations of terms that might open up possibilities for subsequent interpretation and development in discourse.

Although McKeon traced the many uses of schemata in other philosophies in order to identify topics or commonplaces of inquiry, his own primary schematism was a "semantic matrix," a paradigm for the discovery of meanings in all forms of discourse. He described and illustrated this matrix in "Philosophic Semantics and Philosophic Inquiry" (242–56). The basis of the semantic matrix was a set of four terms which, placed in schematic relationships, formed the commonplaces of discourse: things, thoughts, words, and actions. Variations of these terms (for example, cognates of the verb *to know*: knowledge, knower, known, and knowable) proved to be an ongoing source of discovery for McKeon. He sometimes identified the four issues of the semantic matrix as selection, interpretation, method, and principle, indicating the fundamental issues of all discourse and communication. In essence, the semantic matrix was a highly innovative and unique development of the four scientific questions of Aristotle and the four master topics—the constitutions or questions—of Roman rhetoric.

Using amplification and schematization, McKeon explored four subject matters in a new organization of learning that cuts across traditional disciplinary divisions to reveal interdisciplinary connections. He examined Topics in all areas of thought and action, seeking the sources of creativity and innovation. He investigated Hypotheses in the concrete semantic formulation of inventions that emerge from Topics, seeking the content of doctrines and philosophies. He traced Themes, or the patterns of art that individuals employ to develop their inventions in argument and narration, seeking the lines of thought that open up new connections for investigation and action. He explored Theses, or the fundamental propositions that anchor discourse in what is and what is real, as determined by philosophic systems, the consensus of communities, and the nature of things. Commenting on the new study of discourse that he proposed, McKeon wrote, "Speculation concerning discourse must avoid the fixities of categories, doctrines, methods, and assumptions which discourse assumes in any one form of philosophy or inquiry, if it is to include all the forms which discourse takes in philosophy and in inquiry, action, and production. This is possible because the variety of categories or elements is approached in discourse by way of common topics or 'commonplaces'; the variety of facts or statements of what is the case by way of common hypotheses;

the variety of arts or methods of treating problems by way of common theses; and the variety of assumptions or principles by way of common theses" (McKeon 1950: 45).

The scope and direction of McKeon's work is further revealed in a reshaping of the rhetorical arts. He extended the classic division of the arts of discourse—rhetoric, grammar, logic, and dialectic—into a new rhetorical and philosophic framework:

The new rhetoric may be broadened from persuasion to include all elements of existence and to use commonplaces or topics for discovery of the unknown. The new grammar may be broadened from the composition of statements to include all facts of experience and to use hypotheses of semantics for recovery of the known. The new logic may be broadened from inquiry and proof to include all discursive sequences and all sequential series stated in discourse and to use the themes of the arts for presentation of connections. The new dialectic may be broadened from systems of thought and being to include all ordering principles, elements, and causes and to use the theses of inquiry to unify and transform possible world orders and human orders. The new philosophy can not be a monolithic inclusive shared ideology, but it may oppose the dogmatisms of partial and divisive universalisms to become a philosophy of communications and the arts. (McKeon, "Circumstances and Functions" 119–20).

Richard McKeon was one of the foremost theoreticians of rhetoric in the twentieth century, yet he deliberately resisted systematization of his views on rhetoric or other matters in a body of doctrines or dogma. Instead, he cultivated a new organization of subject matters suited to a dynamic philosophy of culture and a comprehensive set of intellectual arts suited to the exploration of those subject matters. This was so complete a departure from the typical practice of philosophy in the early and middle twentieth century that few contemporaries understood the full significance of his project. For this reason, McKeon remained a problem and an enigma to those individuals who expected a conventional expression of philosophic doctrine and found, in his persistent willingness to consider diverse views on all matters, a tragic waste of a brilliant mind. But many others continue to find in McKeon's work a new path to the organization of learning grounded in rhetoric and suited to the new circumstances of thought and action. As the twentieth century progresses in an ongoing struggle between relativism and anti-intellectual dogmatism—a struggle that McKeon believed to be the unfortunate center of many philosophic and practical problems in this period—the outlines of his philosophy of culture progressively emerge with more striking character and relevance.

Richard Buchanan
Carnegie Mellon University

Bibliography

Callahan, John F. "Richard Peter McKeon: Bibliography of Published Works." *Journal of the History of Ideas* 47 (1986): 654–62.

McKeon, Richard. "Arts of Invention and Arts of Memory: Creation and Criticism." *Critical Inquiry* 1 (1977): 723–39.

———. "The Circumstances and Functions of Philosophy." *Philosophers on Their Own Work*. Ed. Andre Mercier and Maja Svilar. Bern and Frankfurt am Main: Verlag, 1975. 1:95–142.

———. "Fact and Value in the Philosophy of Culture." *Akten des XIV, internationalen Kongresses fur Philosophie, Wien, 2–9 September 1968*. Vienna: Herder, 1969. 4:503–11.

———. *Freedom and History and Other Essays: An Introduction to the Thought of Richard McKeon*. Ed. Zahava K. McKeon. Chicago: U of Chicago P, 1990.

———. "Greek Dialectics: Dialectic and Dialogue, Dialectic and Rhetoric." *Dialectics/Dialectiques*. Ed. Ch. Perelman. The Hague: Martinus Nijhoff, 1975. 1–25.

———. "Introduction to the Philosophy of Cicero." *Brutus, On the Nature of the Gods, On Divination, On Duty*. Trans. Hubert M. Poteat. Chicago: U of Chicago P, 1950. 1–65.

———. "Rhetoric and Poetic in the Philosophy of Aristotle." *Aristotle's "Poetics" and English Literature*. Ed. Elder Olson. Chicago: U of Chicago P, 1965. 201–36.

———. *Rhetoric: Essays in Invention and Discovery*. Ed. Mark Backman. Woodbridge, CT: Ox Bow, 1987.

———. *Thought, Action, and Passion*. Chicago: U of Chicago P, 1954.

Mitchell, Douglas. "Richard McKeon's Conception of Rhetoric and the Philosophy of Culture." *Rhetorica* 6 (1988): 395–414.

McLuhan, Marshall (1911–1980)

Canadian communication theorist and literary scholar. Completed his Ph.D. dissertation on Thomas Nashe in 1942 at Cambridge University. His first teaching position was in English literature at Saint Louis University, 1937–1944; he also introduced a class on rhetoric and interpretation while there, thus extending his New Criticism orientation into the work of F.R. Leavis and I.A. Richards. His scholarship was typical of that of a historian and critic of English literature until the publication of *The Mechanical Bride; Folklore of Industrial Man* (1949), a fanciful, deconstructive study of magazine advertising. It received relatively little attention, however. *The Gutenberg Galaxy: The Making of Typographical Man* (1962), his study of the impact of print upon Western Europe, circulated much more widely and articulated a theory of media determinism: Major shifts in the dominant mass media of societies produce alterations in self-consciousness and social organization. *The Gutenberg Galaxy* was soon followed by the more theoretical and more widely influential *Understanding Media: The Extensions of Man* (1964). This book opened significant topics—hot and cool media, media as extensions of the senses, poets as a society's Early Warning System. It made him internationally famous.

Writing throughout the 1960s, McLuhan offered a causal model of communication and communication systems epitomized in logion "the medium is the message." Like his Toronto colleague Harold Adams Innis, he argued that communication media extend or bias human perception. Media, therefore, are messages in that they determine and embody what is featured in the human sensorium and what is valued in social organizations. Additionally, the evolution of individuals' sensory intake parallels the evolution of cultural structures: oral language dominated tribal cultures; the alphabet, emerging bureaucratic cultures; and electronic communication, retribalized cultures—"the global village."

In the 1970s, as McLuhan settled back into the directorship of the University of Toronto's Centre for Culture and Technology, he focused more systemically on relationships between media and culture, framing a relational-phenomenological theory of communication. In the essays preceding his posthumous *Laws of Media* (1988), he suggested that communication media represent orderings of experiential perceptions of individuals and of relations between humans and (especially) their technological environments. In that they amplify, obsolesce, and re-create or retrieve "something else" when introduced into a social system, communication media structure person–person and person–environment relationships. As well, communication media instantiate figure-ground relationships between stimuli as well as biophysiological relationships between areas of the brain, thereby patterning meaning for individuals. Thus human thought is composed of complex interactions ("resonances") within a web of mediated ideational structures.

Thus, earlier McLuhan offered a theory of influence or diachrony, while the later McLuhan was pursuing a communication theory of resonance of synchrony—a shift from what Carey (1975) identified as a "transmission" theory to a "cultural" theory of communication. The shift was never complete, as McLuhan never completed his "laws of media" project himself, nor did he harden his arguments. He always filtered the practical through the aesthetic; the idea through the metaphor or synecdoche. Yet "the prophet of the electric age" gave impetus and velocity to the critical studies movement in mass media research.

Bruce E. Gronbeck
University of Iowa

Bibliography

Carey, James W. "Communication and Culture." *Communication Research* 2 (1975): 173–91.

"The Living McLuhan." Special Section. *Journal of Communication* 31 (1981): 116–99.

McLuhan, Marshall. *The Gutenberg Galaxy: The Making of Typographic Man.* Toronto: U of Toronto P, 1962.

———. *The Mechanical Bride: Folklore of Industrial Man.* New York: Vanguard, 1951.

———. *Understanding Media: The Extensions of Man.* New York: McGraw, 1965.

McLuhan, Marshall, and Eric McLuhan. *Laws of Media: The New Science.* Toronto: U of Toronto P, 1988.

Molinaro, Matie, Corinne McLuhan, and William Toye, eds. *Letters of Marshall McLuhan.* New York: Oxford UP, 1987.

M

Medieval Rhetoric

A rhetoric, echoing that of the classical period, that emphasized the instruction of speakers or writers (as opposed to the twentieth century's emphasis on hearers or readers) in the creation of some form of communication, but significantly departing from its classical predecessor with a gradual evolution of new shapes corresponding to new functions.

From Antiquity to the Middle Ages

During Greek and Roman antiquity, education prepared citizens for public life, and speech was considered the basis of all social order. Message transmission remained essentially oral, although written documents occasionally served as supplements. Therefore, Greek and Roman schools prepared students to be equally adept at both speaking and writing. In the fifth century B.C.E., the Platonic-Socratic ideal, not unlike the sophistic ideal of Isocrates, promoted rhetoric as a way to unite philosophical wisdom with verbal skill to attain the height of education: a public demonstration of oratory.

After the fall of the Roman Empire in the fifth and sixth centuries, however, large-scale educational decline resulted in a society in which few were capable of reading or writing. Church institutions and a feudal system of government supplanted the classical function of statecraft and legal procedure, rendering public speaking useless on social or political issues. The Areopagus and the Forum were silent spaces. Oratory became the domain of church authorities trained in logic and theology, and writing was left to the few, usually clerics, who were skilled in discourse. Growing complexity in the worlds of both church and state, however, demanded effective communication. Thus, the study of rhetoric fragmented into three new forms: letter-writing (*ars dictaminis*), preaching (*ars praedicandi*), and poetics (*ars poetriae*). Before discussing these forms, it is important to examine briefly the traditions from which they were derived.

Four Classical Traditions

According to James J. Murphy, four distinct classical traditions are represented by the rhetorical texts of antiquity, which were widely copied and circulated throughout the Middle Ages. Murphy designates these as the Aristotelian, Ciceronian, grammatical, and sophistic traditions.

The Aristotelian tradition, a more philosophical, logic-based approach to discourse than the others, was represented by Aristotle's

Rhetorica (c. 350 B.C.E.), the oldest extant text-book on the subject, which reached the West in the thirteenth century via the translations of Arabic commentators. Given the "scholastic" environment and surge of interest in Aristotle during that century, one would assume that his theory of discourse would dominate. Yet Boethius assumed that Cicero's rhetoric should be the standard, and medieval encyclopedists ignored Aristotle's rhetorical theory. His *Poetics* remained virtually unknown until the fifteenth century, and his *Topica* and *De Sophisticis Elenchis* influenced the studies of ethics and political science in the universities of the twelfth through fifteenth centuries far more than they influenced the development of rhetoric. Thus, although *Rhetorica* survives in nearly one hundred medieval manuscripts, its influence on medieval rhetoric has not been definitively determined.

The second tradition, based on precepts originated by Isocrates, was the more practical approach that dominated rhetorical studies during the Middle Ages. Designated by Murphy as the Ciceronian tradition, it includes the seven rhetorical works of Cicero himself (106–43 B.C.E.), the *Rhetorica ad Herennium* (nearly contemporary with Cicero and wrongly attributed to him until 1491), and a mutilated text of Quintilian's *Institutio oratoria* (92 C.E.), the great summary of the classical Latin arts of discourse. This corpus transmitted the Ciceronian scheme of the five parts of rhetoric: *inventio* (finding of material), *dispositio* (arranging of it), *elocutio* (putting words to invented material), *pronuntiatio* (oral delivery), and *memoria* (retention of ideas, words, and their order).

Without doubt, Cicero was the *magister eloquentiae* of the Middle Ages, with the name *Tullius* occurring in nearly every discussion of discourse and among most of the medieval writers, from Thomas Aquinas to Boccaccio. Indeed, his reputation continued through the eighteenth century and beyond. All of the early encyclopedists allude to Cicero as their chief *auctor*. Cicero, along with Seneca, is placed in the first circle (of Limbo) by Dante in his *Divine Comedy*.

Prior to the fifteenth century, Cicero's *De inventione* and the pseudo-Ciceronian *Rhetorica ad Herennium* were the most frequently used rhetorical works. Cicero had constructed his pragmatic scheme of rhetorical elements in close association with Roman law in *De Inventione*, and *Rhetorica ad Herennium* closely parallels it. Therefore, although Cicero composed seven rhetorical treatises over a period of fifty years,

it is his earliest work in *De inventione* that set the pattern for medieval theories of discourse.

Third, a "grammatical tradition" derives from the works of the grammarians Aelius Donatus and Priscian. The two brief grammar treatises of Donatus, *Ars Minor* and *Ars Maior* (350 C.E.), became the most popular elementary texts throughout the Middle Ages. Their author's name, in the form of *Donet*, became a synonym for *primer*, and it is to him that we owe the transmission of such standard concepts as the "eight parts of speech." Abbreviated versions of Donatus's works introduced medieval scholars to Latin, and Priscian's *Institutionum grammaticae* (510 C.E.) became the standard advanced grammar textbook.

Also included in this tradition is Horace's *Ars poetica* (written between 23 and 13 B.C.E.), representing an extension of the basic grammatical process. As Quintilian explains in *Institutio oratoria*, grammar is not only the science of speaking and writing correctly but also the art of interpreting the poets (*enarratio poetarum*). Thus, Horace's *Ars poetica,* consisting of 476 verses of preceptive advice about the composition of poetry, is an important work of the grammatical tradition. Its inclusion as part of the medieval grammar curriculum preserved this significant poetics treatise and transmitted it from antiquity to the Renaissance poets and critics and beyond.

Finally, a fourth tradition arose from the Second Sophistic period (50–400 C.E.), in which two schoolroom exercises flourished—*declamatio* (exercises in fictitious speechmaking) and *progymnasmata* (short exercises in composition). During the Middle Ages, however, the function of the *declamationes* shifted from an emphasis on speechmaking to writing, as the *declamationes* were used as sources for stories or *exempla* (examples). The sophistic tradition, then, emphasized the pedagogy of writing by generating collections of examples and preceptive guides and by its focus on exemplary models, preserving an idea of the connection between the arts of language and ethical behavior. Two representative texts include Priscian's *De praeexercitamentis rhetoricis* (551–560), a translation (or adaptation, some argue) into Latin of part of Hermogenes' *Progymnasmata* and the Elder Seneca's *Declamationes*.

Despite their varying degrees of influence, all four traditions assumed that the arts of discourse could be learned preceptively. Throughout the medieval period, the works of classical tradition and the works of modern theorists existed side by side but never equally. Although the works of antiquity had the advantage of *auctoritas* in a bookish age, modern works had the appeal of the new.

Augustine's *De doctrina christiana*

The first of the "new" emerged in the fifth century and represented a movement toward a modern medieval theory of rhetoric. This was a time of great debate over how much, if any, of Greek and Roman culture should be adopted by the Christian community. In 392 C.E., when the emperor Theodosius formally abolished paganism by decree, many recent converts—among them writers, poets, orators, and artists—reacted violently against their former culture, renouncing paganism completely and never again referring to any pagan poets, rhetoricians, or orators in their works.

Augustine of Hippo (354–430 C.E.), a rhetorician and convert himself, did not regard the culture of the old order with the same revulsion and fear that many of his contemporaries did. Instead, he viewed it more practically as a tool to aid Christian thinkers.

In *De doctrina christiana* (composed between 396 and 426), Augustine used this figure to promote the conscientious use of pagan philosophy:

> Just as the Egyptians had not only idols and grave burdens which the people of Israel detested and avoided, so also they had vases and ornaments of gold and silver and clothing which the Israelites took with them secretly when they fled, as if to put them to better use. (II.x1.60)

Augustine himself took the "Egyptian gold" of Greek and Roman philosophy and logic and skillfully put it to work for the new task of interpreting Christian Scripture, thereby synthesizing old and new.

Augustine was the first theorist of the Middle Ages to establish a clearly preceptive tradition in discourse for the Christian community. *De doctrina christiana* begins with these words: "There are two things necessary to the treatment of Scriptures: a way of discovering those things which are to be understood, and a way of teaching what we have learned" (I.i).

De doctrina is composed of four books. The first three deal with how the words of Scripture may be interpreted by examining language in terms of "signs." Book 3 deals specifically with the problem of ambiguity in both literal and figurative language. Book 4, however, called by some the "first Christian manual of rhetoric," suggests how to teach by pleading for *eloquentia* and advocating the union of pagan rhetorical form (chiefly Ciceronian) and Christian content. *De doctrina christiana* was important not only in establishing a preceptive tradition but also in authorizing Ciceronian rhetorical precepts and advocating *imitatio* as a way to learn eloquence, thereby helping to preserve and transmit the "gold" of classical authors into the Middle Ages.

Transition and Transmission

Classical rhetorical form and pagan content were preserved and transmitted into the Middle Ages via two other means based on the preceptive principle: medieval encyclopedias and educational curricula.

Encyclopedias and Educational Curricula

In the fifth century, Martianus Capella gave this famous description of Lady Rhetoric in his allegorical encyclopedia *De nuptiis philologiae et mercurii* (410–427):

> The garment under her arms was covered by a robe wound about her shoulders in the Latin fashion; this robe was adorned with the light of all kinds of devices and showed the figures of them all . . . indeed it was thought that she could hurl thunderbolts like Jove. For like a queen with power over everything, she could drive any host of people where she wanted and draw them back from where she wanted; she could sway them to tears and whip them to a frenzy, and change the countenance and senses not only of cities, but of armies in battle. (Stahl and Johnson 156)

In addition to this flamboyant portrayal of rhetoric, which cleverly employs the very devices it portrays, *De nuptiis philologiae et mercurii* has been credited with introducing the seven liberal arts—the whole curriculum of the pagan Roman schools and thus rhetoric as well—into the Middle Ages. It should be noted, however, that unlike *De doctrina christiana*, Martianus presents rhetoric and the other disciplines without taking an explicit theological or philosophical stand in the intellectual controversies of his times.

The *De nuptiis* offers seven highly ornamented allegorical portraits of the subjects that made up the Roman educational curriculum in the following order: grammar, dialectic, rhetoric, geometry, arithmetic, astronomy, and music. (By the fifth century, medicine and architecture, which had been included in the curriculum earlier, had been deleted.) Each allegorical portrait is followed by a compendium of the art.

In the next century, Flavius Cassiodorus Senator (480–575), in his *Institutiones divinarum et saecularium litterarum,* and Bishop Isidore of Seville (570–636), in his *Etymologies,* followed the order of the curriculum elements laid out by Martianus in their encyclopedias, thus affirming the elements of the trivium (the first three subjects of the curriculum, which deal with words) and the quadrivium (the last four subjects, which deal with mathematical concepts), the core curriculum throughout the Middle Ages.

Cassiodorus's *Institutiones,* influenced by both Augustine and Martianus, was designed to instruct clerics in their religious and secular studies. Divided into two parts, the first half is devoted to divinity and the second half to the liberal arts; thus its two parts were often copied separately. Rhetoric, in the liberal arts section, is borrowed from second- and third-century works such as the *Artis rhetoricae libri III* of Fortunatianus and Julius Victor's *Ars rhetorica* (the first rhetorical work to include a section on letter-writing).

The last encyclopedist of the age of the Church Fathers, Isidore preserved a large amount of classical lore in his *Etymologia,* but, unlike Cassiodorus or Martianus, he established the seven liberal arts as preliminary to further work in divine studies. *Etymologia* describes a whole educational system in which the first two books, including grammar, rhetoric, and dialectic (the trivium), lay out a general curriculum for all clergy. The remaining seventeen books focus on information particular to various fields and professions.

Thus, during this period of transition, classical rhetorical ideas hardened, via their inclusion in somewhat empty pedagogical formulas such as the seven liberal arts. In theory, the trivium was taught to all students in the grammar schools, while the quadrivium was reserved for only the best students, preparatory to studies for careers in the learned professions of theology, philosophy, law, or medicine. In practice, however, not every school was able to offer a full curriculum; thus grammar was the only universally studied subject (hence, "grammar schools"). Students whose schools offered the entire trivium, however, studied rhetoric, which included in-

struction in the composition of both prose and poetry, with special attention, particularly after the tenth century, given to letter-writing.

By the ninth century, it had become common practice among encyclopedists and educators to assimilate the whole system of classical rhetoric into Christian methodology. However, this began to change when Rabanus Maurus, a pupil of Alcuin's, broke with tradition in his rhetorical treatise *De institutione clericorum* (819 C.E.), by making pragmatic choices and incorporating only those classical concepts that served his purposes.

Instead of adopting only the Ciceronian system as a whole, as Augustine and his followers had done, Rabanus chose his tenets from various sources—sometimes from personal experience or dialectic, as well as from Cicero and Augustine. Although Rabanus clearly borrows most from Augustine, this too is a break with tradition in that he replaces Cicero with a more contemporary rhetoric master.

Authors after Rabanus adopted his method, picking and choosing from classical and other sources according to their needs. The evolution of discourse in the Middle Ages, therefore, shows fragmentation instead of unity: The authors of treatises on letter-writing chose only the parts of works applicable to their art, as did the authors of manuals on preaching and poetics.

The Three Rhetorical Arts
Letter-writing
Because citizens in antiquity were well educated, an orator like Cicero or an emperor like Augustus Caesar was completely capable of composing and transcribing his own thoughts. But because of the educational decline of the fifth and sixth centuries, relatively few were capable of reading or writing in the Middle Ages. The growing complexity in the worlds of both church and state, however, required communication.

The early solution to this problem was the drafting of sets of formulas and exemplary models to be duplicated and adapted to various situations. Medieval formularies, like so many business forms today, usually provided blank spaces for inserting information such as names. Sometimes this was indicated by the letter *N* for *nomen* ("name").

Basically notarial, most medieval formularies dealt with contracts of some type or other, such as this one from Tours:

It is right that those who have promised us unbroken faith should be rewarded by our aid and protection. Now since our faithful subject [name] with the will of God has come to our palace with his arms and has there sworn in our hands to keep his trust and fidelity to us, therefore we decree and command by this present writing henceforth the said (name) is to be numbered among our antrustiones [dependents]. If anyone shall presume to slay him, let him know that he shall have to pay 600 solidi as a wergeld for him. (Murphy, *Rhetoric* 201)

But even several hundred such models could not cover all the intricacies of message transmission and documentation. A new solution was found with the birth of the *ars dictaminis*, or the preceptive art of letter-writing.

The first to link rhetoric with letter-writing (after Julius Victor) was Alberic, a monk of Monte Cassino, who around 1087 wrote formal treatises on the new art: *Dictaminum radii* (or *Flores rhetorici*), which deals with rhetorical ornament, and *Breviarium de dictamine,* which deals with letter-writing specifically. In both, Alberic assumes that rhetorical principles may be employed in writing as well as speaking, in accordance with classical tradition. But he breaks with that tradition when he encourages students to apply Cicero's parts of a speech to the composition of letters.

The next development in *ars dictaminis* shifted attention from Monte Cassino to Bologna, where several significant works on the subject appeared in the early part of the twelfth century. Important theorists included Adalbertus Samaritanus, Hugh of Bologna, and Bernard of Romagna. The first to set forth the standard medieval five parts of a letter, however, was the anonymous author of *Rationes dictandi* (1135 C.E.).

This treatise, written in a pragmatic tone, assumes the reader's acceptance of a basic doctrine of letter-writing by presenting an "approved format" for letters: "There are, in fact, five parts of a letter: the Salutation, the Securing of Good-Will, the Narration, the Petition, and the Conclusion" (Murphy, *Three Arts* 7). The treatise is composed of thirteen sections, the greatest emphasis being on the salutation and the need of the writer to attend carefully to the social level of the letter's recipient. The author presents a range of proper addresses, from greetings to the Pope to "salutations of Delinquent Sons to their Parents." In addition to being an excellent example of a popular letterwriting manual, *Rationes dictandi* also provides an interesting view of the strata of medieval society.

By 1200 many popular manuals were being written, mostly in Italy. The doctrine underlying all of these manuals was the analogy between letter-writing and the Ciceronian parts of a speech. In addition to these letter-writing manuals, several collections of model letters circulated in medieval Europe. After the early thirteenth century, however, few innovations appeared; instead, the masters were copied and used.

Preaching

A second branch of the medieval arts of discourse was the *ars praedicandi,* or the art of preaching. Preaching sermons was an important feature of the Church, and preachers probably followed Augustine's advice to study good preachers instead of good books, or used Cicero's rhetoric as a model. In any case sermons were apparently rather informal, direct, and conversational in tone. Referred to as being in the "homily" style, these sermons did not follow a systematic progression of ideas or a prescribed format.

That situation changed when several Latin sermons patterned in a new way were preached at the University of Paris in the academic year 1230–1231. The new form, called the "university-style," or "thematic" sermon, employed a scriptural quotation as "theme" and then a complex system of division and amplification based on the opening quotation.

Within a few years of the advent of this development, several specialized preaching manuals emerged throughout northern Europe. Nearly three hundred authors of these manuals, written into the sixteenth century, have been identified, with English authors especially prominent.

Robert of Basevorn's *Forma praedicandi,* written at Oxford in 1322, is typical of the art that designates six parts of a sermon, analogous to the Ciceronian parts of oratory. It is distinct, however, from the format described for *ars dictaminis* in that it emphasizes division and amplification. The organizational plan is as follows:

1. Theme: a Scriptural quotation
2. Protheme: introduction for the theme itself, usually followed by a prayer
3. Introduction of a theme (antetheme): explanation of the purpose of the sermon
4. Division of the theme: usually into three (or multiples of three), with *auctoritates* to "prove" each division
5. Subdivision of theme
6. Amplification or dilation of each of the divisions and subdivisions

Even though at first the "thematic" sermon might seem to be rather academic and similar to a spoken gloss, the whole emphasis of the first parts was upon involving the audience, in accordance with Cicero's theory of oration. What distinguishes the *ars praedicandi* from the *ars dictaminis* and other forms of discourse, in fact, was the attention given to the fact of a living audience.

In addition to the preaching manuals that provided the form, medieval preachers made use of other types of aids to supply the matter of their sermons: the Scriptures themselves, collections of *exempla,* concordances and alphabetized lists designed to find material, and collections of sermons.

Poetics
The last of the arts of discourse to be developed in the Middle Ages was the *ars poetriae,* or poetics. Poetics was originally studied as a branch of grammar with three subdivisions of its own. Prose writing, the first of these, was often linked to the *ars dictaminis,* although in France it remained a separate form. *Ars rithmica,* the second form, refers to rhythmical composition for either letters or hymns. The most common form of *rithmus* in letter-writing was the *cursus,* a highly stylized mode of concluding Latin prose clauses with fixed metrical forms.

The third subdivision was the *ars metrica,* or *ars poetria,* and its works were of two types. The first is characterized by many brief, often anonymous treatises describing figures, colors, tropes, and other verbal ornaments. These treatises, appearing all over Europe, usually borrowed examples from Donatus or the *Rhetorica ad Herennium* and were used in elementary schooling as part of the grammar instruction.

The second type of *ars poetriae,* however, consisted of major preceptive works

that took up where Horace left off. Some of the more famous of these include Matthew of Vendome's *Ars versificatoria* (1175), Evardus Allemanus's *Laborintus* (c. 1255), Gervase of Melkley's *Ars versificaria* (1210), and the most famous, the *Poetria nova* (1208–1210) of Geoffrey de Vinsauf, said to have influenced Chaucer.

The *Poetria nova,* composed of more than two thousand Latin hexameters and dedicated to Pope Innocent III, is often singled out as the most representative work of rhetorical influence in medieval poetic theory. It is divided into seven sections—preface, general remarks, disposition, amplification and abbreviation, ornaments of style, memory and delivery, and epilogue—and includes a large variety of rhetorical figures and tropes derived from the *Rhetorica ad Herennium.*

Although its title suggests prosody, the *Poetria nova* actually focuses on precepts of style and structure for poetic narrative. Its recommendations on style do not deviate from what was standard at the time, but its emphasis on an orderly presentation of narrative material was the unique contribution that might have caught Chaucer's attention. Geoffrey de Vinsauf's own highly figured style, too, is worth noting:

> Let that part of the material which is first in the order of nature wait outside the gates of the work. Let the end, as a worthy precursor, be first to enter and take up its place in advance, as a guest of more honourable rank, or even as master. Nature has placed the end last in order, but art respectfully defers to it, leads it from its humble position and accords it the place of honour. (Nims 19)

By the title of this treatise, Geoffrey implicitly hoped to challenge Horace as *magister* of poetic doctrine. By assuming poetics as part of rhetoric and organizing his work on the model of rhetorical manuals, Geoffrey's *Poetria nova* joins with other medieval rhetorical works of letter-writing, preaching, and poetics in their shared notion that the arts of discourse can be learned preceptively.

Aron Morgan
University of California, Irvine

Bibliography

Benson, Robert L., and Giles Constable. *Renaissance and Renewal in the Twelfth Century*. Cambridge, MA: Harvard UP, 1982.

Curtius, Ernst Robert. *European Literature and the Latin Middle Ages*. Trans. Willard R. Trask. Princeton: Princeton UP, 1973.

Faral, Edmond. *Les Arts Poetiques du XIIe et du XIIIe Siecle*. Paris: Librairie Ancienne Honore Champion, 1924.

Miller, Joseph M., Michael H. Prosser, and Thomas W. Benson, eds. *Readings in Medieval Rhetoric*. Bloomington: Indiana UP, 1973.

Murphy, James J. *Medieval Rhetoric: A Select Bibliography*. 2nd ed. Toronto: U of Toronto P, 1989.

————. *Rhetoric in the Middle Ages: A History of Rhetorical Theory from Saint Augustine to the Renaissance*. Berkeley: U of California P, 1974.

————, ed. *Three Medieval Rhetorical Arts*. Berkeley: U of California P, 1971.

Nims, Margaret F., trans. *Poetria Nova of Geoffrey of Vinsauf*. Toronto: Pontifical Institute of Mediaeval Studies, 1967.

Stahl, William H., and Richard Johnson, trans. *Martianus Capella and the Seven Liberal Arts*. Vol. 2. New York: Columbia UP, 1977.

Memory

The storehouse of knowledge, one of five canons of classical rhetoric. Memory in its broadest sense means the mental faculty that holds information about past events, ideas, persons, things, or learned behavior. Within the classical system of rhetoric, rhetoricians defined memory most often as what assisted the orator in retaining a prepared text. Plato considered it a mental art—the revival or recollection of perfect, ideal images; through contemplation and recovery of these ideals, one can reach the divine. Cicero defined memory as part of the virtue of prudence, along with intelligence and providence. Quintilian discussed memory almost exclusively as an art, a prescribed, trainable strategy, though he opened his section on memory with the statement that memory was "the treasure-house of the ideas supplied by Invention."

During the classical period, memory was one of the five canons of rhetoric. This period had little respect for presentations delivered from prepared texts. In the three key Roman texts that described memory in depth, the *Rhetorica Ad Herennium*, Cicero's *De oratore*, and Quintilian's *Institutio oratoria*, each author praised those who displayed unusual feats of memory. These mnemonists combined strong natural memory with specific strategies designed to enhance retention.

In classical texts, memory was said to have two parts, natural and artificial. The classical rhetoricians thought that natural memory was what each individual instinctively exhibited when called on to recall information. Natural memory existed in a set quantity or ability for each individual, could not be altered, and was necessary in abundance for the rhetor. Artificial memory was the trainable function, the teachable side or faculty that could be developed, through training and practice, to enhance recall of information. Classical rhetoricians believed that the student of rhetoric needed to develop the artificial to supplement natural memory. An art of memory came to be seen as a system to improve an individual's recall by using mnemonic strategies.

Within the classical texts, two distinct systems or arts of memory evolved. The loci mnemonic, the oldest existing mnemonic system, was imagistic and synthetic, relying on two image sequences superimposed one onto the other in a prescribed order. According to the loci mnemonic, memories were most easily recalled if ordered mental pictures replaced words in the mind. The individual would develop both background and foreground images. The reusable background images were simply settings, frames such as houses, buildings, or streets that served as storehouses for foreground images. Into each site the rhetor placed an image that served as a key to some idea or word that then revived the matter of the speech. The foreground images were bizarre, vivid, grotesque, or comical. These images were not necessarily tied to the meaning of a speech's particular words but might be related to the words through homonyms, rhymes, or any idiosyncratic personal associations.

Quintilian's alternative system introduced patterning, text analysis, and rehearsal, which were to become the more traditional pedagogical techniques for enhancing recall. Quintilian's system required handcopying texts, reading aloud, concentrating, and taking care in arranging. A cornerstone of Quintilian's textual method was his belief that memory was inextricably linked to arrangement, with a well-organized text easier to remember than an ill-formed one. To enhance organization, a longer text would be sectioned off into more manageable pieces for memorization. These sections could also be marked with representative image symbols.

Discussions of memory before the Romans were either sketchy treatments of the art or general discussions of natural memory, as in Plato and Aristotle. Plato valued only natural memory. He described a loss of memory as a result of an unrealized soul; the body and soul are both needed for perception to occur. Further, Plato viewed memory as a realization of ideal images, which were perfect or true manifestations of the Good or Knowledge. These images were not, however, set by the rhetor but existed apart as a goal in themselves.

Aristotle spoke of the nature of memory itself, describing features that became bases for the later arts of memory. He conceived of any art as a codification of expert performance based upon principles rooted in the nature of the art itself. Aristotle distinguished between memory and recollection. Memory was the apprehension of an image in consciousness, primarily allied with the faculty of sense perception. Memory essentially generated pictures, which were imprinted images of past perceptions conditioned by lapse of time. Recollection was a mode of inference or an act of investigation, which entailed a process of moving from a starting point through a series of ordered movements in which the remembered idea or image resided. These features of natural memory—image, starting points, loci, and ordered movements—became codified later into the art of the loci mnemonic. Aristotle also specified certain broad ordered methods of relating images—similarity, contrariness, and contiguity—that helped to locate starting points in the search for remembered images.

Because classical rhetoricians discussed memory largely as an aspect of delivery, a current misconception is that these rhetoricians used memory solely to facilitate recall of a prepared text; however, they used memory classically to recall material prior

to constructing texts and to recall inventional, topical patterns. In the medieval period, Camillo, Bruno, and others also used memory's arts to aid invention, using the term *Loci*, or places, to describe both the residences for the topics of invention and the seats of memory. The loci mnemonic became widely used as an instrument of religious education wherein ethical principles were transformed into visual images in order to reinforce devotion to virtues and eschewal of vices. In the seventeenth and eighteenth centuries, Bacon related memory to method and invention, Vico attached memory to invention and creativity, and Campbell aligned memory to audience adaptiveness. The nineteenth century highlighted memory in associative and functional psychologies and in style and arrangement rhetorics. Modern discussions of memory are widespread in psychology and reading theory, while modern composition studies have revived interest in the relationship between memory and invention.

Linda T. Calendrillo
Eastern Illinois University

Bibliography
Aristotle. "De Memoria et Reminiscentia." *Aristotle on Memory*. Ed. Richard Sorabji. London: Duckworth, 1972.
Carruthers, Mary J. *The Book of Memory: A Study of Memory in Medieval Culture*. Cambridge: Cambridge UP, 1990.
Cicero. *De Oratore*. Books I–II. Trans. E.W. Sutton and H. Rackham. Loeb Classical Library. Cambridge, MA: Harvard UP, 1924. Revised 1948.
Hutton, Patrick H. "The Art of Memory Reconceived: From Rhetoric to Psychoanalysis." *Journal of the History of Ideas* 48 (1987): 371–92.
Quintilian. *The Institutio Oratoria of Quintilian*. Trans. H.E. Butler. 4 vols. Loeb Classical Library. Cambridge, MA: Harvard UP, 1920–1922.
Rhetorica ad Herennium. Trans. Harry Caplan. The Loeb Classical Library. Cambridge, MA: Harvard UP, 1954.
Yates, Frances A. *The Art of Memory*. Chicago: U of Chicago P, 1966.

See also ACTIO; DELIVERY

Metadiscourse

As a rhetorical term, designates a particular function of language, one that establishes interpersonal bonds and sustains intertextual contact; more specifically, subsumes various kinds of linguistic markers that speakers or writers use to convey their expressive and attitudinal, rather than purely propositional, meanings.

The original assumption underlying metadiscourse goes back to Malinowski (1927), who sees human language capable of not only embodying or reflecting thought but also creating and nurturing bonds of union between interlocutors as well. He dubs this latter function of language "phatic communion." Contemporary studies of metadiscourse, which cover both oral and written discourse, bear a close resemblance to Malinowski's characterization.

Linguists and sociologists study metadiscourse in face-to-face interactions. A number of related terms have surfaced, ranging from *metalanguage,* to *metacommunication,* to *metatalk.* Metalanguage or metalingual function focuses on the underlying code of language, as opposed to other components of any given speech situation, such as the addresser, the addressee, and the message (Jakobson 1960). On the other hand, metacommunication is a much broader term, grouping together such functions as checking or controlling meaning, monitoring the channels of communication, and addressing the relationship between interlocutors. While the distinction between metalanguage and metacommunication is maintained by Bateson ([1972] 1987), Schiffrin (1980) tries to conflate metalanguage with metacommunication into her metatalk, which includes three major indicators: "metalinguistic referents," "operators," and "verbs." She attributes to "metatalk" organizational and evaluative functions.

Researchers in composition and rhetoric generally concentrate on metadiscourse in written discourse. On one level of writing, the writer provides propositional material concerning the subject matter; on the other level, the writer helps her reader react to such material, and to her own authorial presence. It is on this other level of writing that metadiscourse operates, serving both interpersonal and textual purposes. Several taxonomies have been constructed to analyze different kinds of metadiscourse. Vande Kopple (1985), for example, proposes seven, sometimes overlapping, categories; they include "text connectives," "code glosses," "illocution markers," "validity markers," "narrators," "attitude markers," and "commentary." Beauvais (1989), drawing upon speech act theory, characterizes metadiscourse as "expositive" illocutionary acts identified by illocutionary force indicators. He distinguishes primary acts, which use or imply first-person subjects, from secondary acts, which attribute any given act to someone other than the writer. Recent studies have also illuminated, empirically, the link of metadiscourse to ethos, to discourse processes, and to different meaning-shaping rhetorical milieus.

Inevitably, metadiscourse can also signify a more general meaning. Often broadly defined as "discourse about discourse" or "communication about communication," metadiscourse outgrows its concomitant implication of referring to specific linguistic markers; it begins to symbolize the sum total of our discursive means to represent the world to ourselves and to each other. In this sense metadiscourse becomes, indeed, a higher discourse dealing with principles fundamental to human communication; it thus resonates with other postmodern terms like *metahistory* or *metatheory,* and with its own etymological roots.

LuMing R. Mao
Miami University

Bibliography

Bateson, Gregory. "A Theory of Play and Fantasy." *Steps to an Ecology of Mind: Collected Essays in Anthropology, Psychology, Evolution, and Epistemology.* San Francisco: Chandler, 1972. Northvale, NJ: Aronson, 1987. 177–93.

Beauvais, Paul J. "A Speech Act Theory of Metadiscourse." *Written Communication* 1 (1989): 11–30.

Crismore, Avon. "Metadiscourse and Discourse Processes: Interactions and Issues." *Discourse Processes* 13 (1990): 191–205.

———. *Talking with Readers: Metadiscourse as Rhetorical Act.* New York: Lang, 1989.

Crismore, Avon, and Rodney Farnsworth. "Mr. Darwin and His Readers: Exploring Interpersonal Metadiscourse as a Dimension of *Ethos.*" *Rhetoric Review* 8 (1989): 91–111.

Fleischman, Suzanne. "Discourse as Space/

Discourse as Time: Reflections on the Metalanguage of Spoken and Written Discourse." *Journal of Pragmatics* 16 (1991): 291–306.

Halliday, M.A.K. *Language as Social Semiotic: The Social Interpretation of Language and Meaning*. London: Arnold, 1978.

Jakobson, Roman. "Closing Statement: Linguistics and Poetics." *Style in Language*. Ed. Thomas A. Sebeok. Cambridge, MA: MIT, 1960. 350–77.

Malinowski, Bronislaw. "The Problem of Meaning in Primitive Languages." *The Meaning of Meaning*. Ed. C.K. Ogden and I.A. Richards. 2nd ed. New York: Harcourt, 1927. 296–336.

Mao, LuMing R. "I Conclude Not: Toward a Pragmatic Account of Metadiscourse." *Rhetoric Review* 2 (1993): 265–89.

Schiffrin, Deborah. "Meta-Talk: Organizational and Evaluative Brackets in Discourse." *Sociological Inquiry: Language and Social Interaction* 50 (1980): 199–236.

Silverstein, Michael. "The Three Faces of 'Function': Preliminaries to a Psychology of Language." *Social and Functional Approaches to Language and Thought*. Ed. Maya Hickmann. Orlando, FL: Academic, 1987. 17–38.

Vande Kopple, William J. "Some Exploratory Discourse on Metadiscourse." *College Composition and Communication* 36 (1985): 82–93.

Williams, Joseph M. *Style: Ten Lessons in Clarity and Grace*. 3rd ed. Glenview, IL: Scott, 1989.

Metalepsis

A metonymy (q.v.) in which a double substitution seems to have occurred. When Amos states "And I also have given you cleanness of teeth in all your cities" (Amos 4:6), he has associated "cleanness of teeth" with lack of food, connoting famine. The double substitution in a metalepsis is often used to attribute a present effect to a remote cause: "The ship is sinking: damn the wood where the mast grew."

Arthur Quinn and Lyon Rathbun
University of California, Berkeley

Metaphor

By interinanimating two terms, directs our attention to particular aspects of the principal subject, sometimes aspects we would otherwise have overlooked. Metaphors create meaning, move minds, motivate people. They are more than ornaments, intensifiers, or illustrative comparisons. Taken literally, a metaphor is a category error, a semantic/logical contradiction, which asserts or implies "*A* is non-*A*," "men are wolves." We make sense of metaphors by asking ourselves which of the commonplaces associated with the second term (*wolves*) might apply to the principal subject (men). Though with little impact on instruction, the New Rhetoric has, since the 1930s, treated metaphor as a factor in the *logos* of invention and persuasion. To understand why this is a rhetorically radical conception, we need to read it in historical and educational contexts.

The Current Tradition

What do most North American students remember best from what their schooling taught them about metaphor? Burned into their brains is a formal distinction between metaphor and simile. Somewhat bizarrely, our educational system foregrounds this trivial distinction until, more often than not, it blocks out all that is important about metaphor. If the word *metaphor* evokes anything else in students' memories, it is likely the metaphoric distinction between "dead" (cliché) and "fresh" metaphors.

How do textbooks and teachers' professional books present metaphor? Ignoring profound modern and postmodern discussions of metaphor, ongoing since at least I.A. Richards's *Philosophy of Rhetoric* (1936), respected texts continue to replicate the discredited "current-traditional" conception of metaphor we inherit from Renaissance and eighteenth-century rhetoricians. Thus a metaphor is defined as "any comparison that cannot be taken literally" or "an implied comparison between two things of unlike nature that yet have something in common." More typically, texts slight metaphor by saying nothing (or nothing positive) about it. Students are warned against both "dead" and "mixed" metaphors. Strunk and White, whose general advice is to "use figures of speech sparingly," favor similes (in moderation) and say about metaphor only "do not mix it."

Aristotle, in his *Rhetoric*, asserted that prose writers, even more than versifiers, should "pay specially careful attention to metaphor" (Bk. 3, Ch. 2), but the index of *Teaching Com-*

position: 12 Bibliographical Essays, 2nd ed., contains only one reference to metaphor, which refers us to a single sentence in the essay on style: "Those composition teachers who want to peruse the study of tropes will find God's plenty in Warren Shibles, *Metaphor: An Annotated Bibliography and History*" (1971).

In the neoclassical tradition, metaphors (and other figures) are ornaments that can be used to "dress up" discourse or add an overlay of emotion (echoing a "dead" metaphor much favored by Renaissance rhetoricians: "say it with flowers"). Modern composition instruction has for the most part followed this tradition (Seitz), treating metaphors (and other tropes) minimally, and then as techniques for ornamenting or adding emotional impact—both questionable functions in the discursive prose of a scientist society. Like analogy (and simile), metaphor is sometimes also presented as trope of instruction, whereby abstractions can be concretized or the unfamiliar explained by comparison with the familiar.

This view of metaphor is grounded in a neo-Platonic thought/language (*res/verba*) dichotomy. The dichotomy is embodied and epitomized by Peter Ramus, for instance, who moved invention, judgment, and arrangement from rhetoric to logic, thus reducing rhetoric to style, memory, and delivery. With thinking and languaging radically separated, tropes cease to be really figures of *thought*. Metaphor then is no longer understood as a factor in invention and figures in persuasion only in a disreputable sense (that is, as "emotional" appeal).

This reduction matters doubly because metaphor is both a particularly important trope and the representative trope. Hugh Blair calls it "the most fruitful of tropes" and adds, "This figure is more frequent than all the rest put together; and the language, of both prose and verse, owes to it much of its elegance and grace" (Bizzell and Herzberg 817–18). Although *metaphor* names a specific trope, the term is often used more broadly to represent a larger category of tropes or even tropes in general. Thus personification—or simile, or synecdoche, or apostrophe, or *autonomasia,* or *syllepsis,* or even metonymy—may be contrasted with metaphor (narrowly construed) or understood as metaphor (broadly construed). Is it *just* personification (*prosopoeia*) when Joyce Kilmer writes of "A tree whose hungry mouth is prest / Against the earth's sweet-flowing breast" or T.S. Eliot of "the yellow smoke that slides along

the street, / Rubbing its back against the window panes"—or is it also metaphor? In discussions of troping, metaphor may represent all tropes or, as in Roman Jakobson's metaphor/metonymy distinction, an entire mode of troping (and the kind of thinking that goes with it).

Interinanimation

For New Rhetoricians (and for Romantic and symbolist poets, modernists—including New Critics—and postmodernists, structuralists and poststructuralists, semioticians, sociolinguists, and many others), metaphor is much more important and basic than it is in the "current-traditional" rhetoric that dominates our schools and textbooks. This is partly because they tend to treat it really as a figure of thought, but also because they sublate the rough conception of metaphor as a comparison of two things.

Insofar as metaphor involves comparison, it is not of *things,* but of terms. Sounds are not direct signs for things. Rather the sounds we speak (or words we write) are signifiers that evoke signifieds (concepts) in human minds, thus indirectly directing our attention to things (referents) associated with the concepts. A metaphor adds another signifier and thus another set of signifieds to the mediation. Like any signifier, it works not upon empirical similarities between things but upon cultural commonplaces (which may be empirically false); thus it is not empirically factual but socioculturally rhetorical. To make sense of "men are wolves," we think not about wolves but rather of our cultural commonplaces about wolves. Even those of us who know how false these commonplaces are—there is no confirmed case in North America of a wolf ever killing and eating a woman (even if she was not wearing a red cloak) or a man—do not use the true facts about wolves to make sense of the metaphor.

Metaphor, being the interinanimation of two terms, says Richards, we should test for the presence of metaphor by locating and distinguishing the two terms (119), either or both of which may be implicit. Some of the inadequacy of traditional discussions of metaphor arises, he suggests, because we have no names for its parts—worse, *metaphor* names both the whole figure and the second term. Richards suggests we call the term that refers to the principal subject (men) the *tenor,* and the second term (wolves) the *vehicle.* But his terminology has not caught on (and sometimes appears to confuse even Richards himself). It seems clearer to refer to the first term simply as the "subject" (or "principal subject") of the metaphor and, following Chaïm Perelman's suggestion, to call the second term the *phoros*.

For structuralist grammarians, notably Jakobson, metaphor is substitution. The *phoros* substitutes for (stands in place of) the "normal" sign for the principal subject, fills its slot in the sentence. (Jakobson then contrasts two basic modes of thinking, one based on metaphoric substitution, the other on metonymic contiguity.)

This grammatical "substitution" theory is sometimes contrasted with "interinanimation" or "interaction" theories of metaphor. From a broader perspective, however, the two are compatible, for the act of substitution equates the *phoros* with the term for which it substitutes, and we make sense of the substitution by interpreting the implicit apposition.

In Kenneth Burke's phrase, making (or making sense of) metaphor is *term*inistic—that is, it turns perceiving the subject *in terms of* the phoros. "Metaphor is a device for seeing something in terms of something else," he writes, and reminds us that seeing the principal subject "in terms of something else involves the 'carrying-over' of a term from one realm to another, a process that necessarily involves varying degrees of incongruity" (*Grammar* 503–4). The heuristic that Burke calls "perspective by incongruity" generates insight by playfully placing terms in new linguistic contexts, slotting them into sentences where we would not normally use them—thus, by substitution, troping them and generating incongruous perspectives. The purpose of this "verbal atom cracking" is to liberate ourselves from the constraints of the cultural perspectives structured into normal discourse by recontextualizing words to create new, revealing "metaphoric" usages. For Burke, *metaphor* and *perspective* are convertible terms. Where Samuel Johnson deplores "heterogenous images . . . yoked by violence together" (16), Burke sees "hitherto unsuspected connectives . . . which our customary vocabulary has ignored" (*Permanence* 90).

Directing Attention

Metaphors direct our attention, which means of course that they also deflect our attention from whatever insights lie in other directions. Metaphors are not mere devices of style; they are heuristic and persuasive. Creative invention often begins with the discovery of a new metaphor that directs attention to previously deflected observations and insights. In his lectures on rhetoric, Richards speaks of "wretchedly inconvenient metaphors" that underlie misunderstanding, like the neoclassical metaphor that "makes language a dress which thought puts on." He asserts that the "traditional Usage Doctrine" led to ineffective pedagogy because it "treated language on the bad analogy of a mosaic" instead of understanding each word as "a cooperative member of an organism, the utterance" (69). "We shall do better," he asserts, "to think of a meaning as though it were a plant that has grown—not a can that has been filled or a lump of clay that has been moulded" (14). Similarly, will we do better to think of discourse in terms of representation or conversation or symbolic action? Each metaphor orients us differently, motivates different questions, leads to different insights.

Metaphor is also a crucial factor in persuasion. Perelman, who like Jacques Derrida works from a base in philosophy and whose primary concern is to explain how people come to adhere to their beliefs, locates metaphor as "the figure of style corresponding to the argument from analogy" and understands metaphor as "a condensed analogy" (*The New Rhetoric*, cited in Bizzell and Herzberg, 1092–93). But metaphors rarely receive the same critical scrutiny as do analogies.

The New Rhetoricians' point is that our choice of metaphors can be crucial. Perelman asks, Is the mind a *tabula rasa* (clear marble) as Locke would have it, or veined marble as Liebniz retorts? Is science like reconstituting a statue from the broken fragments (Milton) or like developing a living organism (M. Polanyi)? Rationalism is founded on Descartes's rule against skipping a link in "the chain of ideas" lest the chain be broken, but the rule holds only so long as the metaphor is valid: "If we alter the phoros, so that reasoning is . . . likened . . . to a 'cloth' . . . made of interlaced arguments . . . we can no longer affirm that it is . . . no stronger than its weakest link" (Perelman 119–22). The choice of metaphor creates a perspective, directs (and deflects!) our attention, embodies an attitude, leans us toward particular actions—and usually does all this without the critical scrutiny an explicit proposition would receive. With the wrong metaphor, thought is hobbled: Stephen Jay Gould argues, for instance, that eighteenth-century scientists could not discover how heredity works because they lacked player pianos, Jacquard looms, Hollerith's census machines, or any other devices that might have provided a metaphor of programmed instructions. "We must have access to the right metaphor, not only to the requisite information" (150–51). His examples demonstrate the social and material bases of metaphors without which individual genius fails.

This notion that metaphors are heuristic, that they direct our attention, is not new. Classically, of all the figures, "metaphor in particular has been regarded as generative. The sophists made this connection between style and generative thought and have been chastised for it" (Bizzell and Herzberg 6). Aristotle reiterated this, saying that metaphor "adds to our knowledge," "conveys a new idea"; from metaphor "we can best get hold of something fresh" (cited in Derrida 54, 39). Historians of rhetoric should ask when and how and why this insight was lost, forgotten, suppressed, put *and kept* under erasure. (As often, Plato is a good nominee for first villain.)

Root Metaphors

At the root of most, if not all, perspectives are metaphors, which Stephen Pepper in 1948, therefore, dubbed *root metaphors*. Over a decade earlier, in *Attitudes towards History,* Burke made the same point with a different metaphor when he urged philosophers, among others, to make explicit and justify the *master metaphors* that organize their perspectives. Nietzsche had put it even more strongly when he asserted that any apparently literal concept is "merely the *residue of a metaphor*" (cited in Bizzell and Herzberg 892).

A thorough investigation of the master metaphors that constrain our discourse about discourse itself and writing in particular is urgently needed. Two dominant textbook metaphors for writing (process and product) seem to be "writing is construction" (as in building a house) and "writing is a journey." Considering what we know about writing (and reading) processes, constructing a house, with its emphasis on structure, blueprints and advance planning, seems an oddly rigid metaphor to find in composition textbooks. And the journey metaphor implies considerably more linearity than we find in real writers' (or readers') processes. Perhaps these metaphors are more comfortable than the realities they misrepresent.

Feminists have devoted special attention to master metaphors of patriarchal masters. Luce Irigaray calls for "an examination of the 'grammar' of each figure of discourse, . . . its metaphoric networks" (*This Sex* 75). Particularly relevant here is the metaphor of authorship as sexual procreation. Gilbert and Gubar note, among a plethora of similar instances, "thus Anthony Burgess recently declared that Jane Austen's novels fail because her writing 'lacks a strong male thrust,' and William Gass lamented that literary women 'lack that blood-congested genital drive which energizes every great style'" (9). Authorship, it would seem, is fathering, the pen a metaphorical penis. Feminists have resisted this set of master metaphors critically and also creatively. Using the slogan "writing the body," they have created new metaphors for writing, based on women's bodies, sexuality, and reproductive processes.

The investigation—and, when they are "effaced," the reconstruction—of such metaphors is a significant part of what Derrida means by deconstruction (8–9, 19, 60). Master or root metaphors are comparable to the semiotic concept of myth, utterances that constitute common sense, the norm, general opinion (*doxa*). According to Barthes, however, our collective representations today, the signifiers of contemporary myth are typically not narrative, but iconic (broadly, metaphoric).

Language is Metaphoric

Once we adopt this perspective, as Richards emphasizes, we realize that all thinking, insofar as it uses language or concepts derived through language, is metaphoric. Metaphor is not only a figure of thought; for languaging animals all thinking is metaphoric (if not literally, metaphorically). As soon as we name a thing, event, or experience, we juxtapose it with the signified associated with that name, and our attention is directed accordingly. Consider how the revision from "cripple" to "person with a disability" creates a shift of emphasis, redirects our attention (from the disability toward the person). Remember the retired actress who recalled an encounter with Ronald Reagan, when he was already a star and she still a starlet, commenting that today it would be called "date rape"—a powerful term that, together with "'no' means no" brings criminal connotations to experiences that used to be understood much differently (in terms of "asking for it" and "cock teaser"). Consider also how the term "political correctness" may be used to deflect the previous two examples.

M

Thus in the New Rhetoric, metaphor is an extension of this basic characteristic of languaging. Instead of using our usual name for an experience, we juxtapose that name with another, thus doubling the linguistic direction of perception. And the boundary is not distinct. "Date rape" may have begun as a metaphoric extension of our traditional cultural conception of rape, but it was such an effective trope that it is now understood literally, as a subcategory, a type of rape. "Language," Burke asserts, "develops by metaphorical extension" (*Grammar* 506). Etymologically, most of our terms began as metaphors. Rare is the term that does not turn out to be a "dead" metaphor. As Derrida demonstrates, if we take the term *literal* literally and absolutely, it does not exist: all languaging is at least somewhat figurative.

Metaphor is normally part of language, not a deviation but an omnipresent principle of language, especially of abstraction. Burke emphasizes that "implicit in the applying of the same words to different contexts there is a principal of . . . 'metaphorical' extension, . . . the seeing of one situation in terms of another" ("Variations" 181–82); "when we describe in abstract terms we are not sticking to the facts at all, we are substituting something else for them just as much as if we were using an out and out metaphor" (*Permanence* 95).

The scientistic distinction between literal and metaphoric—embodied mundanely in the rule against using *noticeable* metaphors in scientific reports and encapsulated wonderfully by Bram Stoker when the chief scientist in *Dracula* declares, "Metaphor be more disservice to science than wolves be of danger to man"—now breaks down. Nietzsche put it this way:

> The 'thing in itself' (which is precisely what the pure truth, apart from any of its consequences, would be) is . . . quite incomprehensible to the creator of language and something not in the least worth striving for. This creator only . . . lays hold of the boldest metaphors. To begin with, a nerve stimulus is transferred into an image: first metaphor. The image, in turn, is imitated in a sound: second metaphor. . . . We possess nothing but metaphors for things" (Bizzell and Herzberg 890–91).

Burke extends this notion when he asserts that, for wordlings, whatever is named becomes emblematic. Not only do words represent things, but things also represent words, and thus concepts, values, attitudes. Because it is associated with a word, the thing becomes an icon, a signifier that evokes the same concepts as the word. Thus a particular tree, in addition to being its individual self, evokes the idea of "tree" in general (and then perhaps becomes an icon for nature or timber). As soon as people know they are talking with an English teacher, that teacher becomes emblematic of whatever "English teacher" signifies to them (and they usually start to "watch their 'grammar'"). Unnamed, a rose *may* smell as sweet, but it will be less evocative. In Baudelaire's phrase, cited by Burke, we human beings "wander through forests of symbols." It is our nature as wordlings to make iconic all we experience. Strictly, this trope is synecdoche; in Nietzsche's sense it is also metaphor.

For verbal beings, "nonverbal things, in their capacity as 'meanings,' take on also the nature of words" (*Rhetoric* 186) because for us things signify, evoke concepts. As both Burke and Barthes demonstrate, things can become icons and serve the social functions traditionally served by mythic narratives (with the same sorts of ideological implications).

Suppose, to retell a paradoxical Burkean anecdote, an old church with a grand spire ("an image of aspirations 'towards heaven'") stands on a large and very valuable lot in the midst of a burgeoning city. The congregation decides to sell part of the lot not actually occupied by the church and use the proceeds to aid the needy. The purchaser of the land, a multinational corporation, erects its new company headquarters, towering high above the church spire, beside the old church. With paradoxical iconography, "the dialectical realm of ideas" here permeates "the positive realm." An icon of capitalist materialism, emblematic of the profit motive, now overtowers the church spire, emblematic of spiritual aspirations. Though motivated by Christian charity, the congregation has "*really* proclaimed that they live by a 'post-Christian' order of motives[.] . . . If church spires mean anything, they must overtop the buildings that surround them" (*Rhetoric* 186).

Symbolic Action

The New Rhetoricians' insights into metaphor are based in their understanding that language is symbolic action (to use the phrase Burke adopted from Bronislaw Malinowski's appendix to Ogden's and Richards's *Meaning of Meaning*). If metaphors are symbolic action, then we need to ask not just what metaphors mean, but what they do. Once we adopt that perspective, we ask—as we would about any act—what motivates them, what functions they serve, what they *do*. Once we ask what they do, we see that metaphors direct and deflect our attention, create perspectives, shape attitudes, motivate actions.

If some metaphors for writing lead to better pedagogy, if other metaphors for writing deny women equal opportunity to write, then we need some basis for evaluating metaphors. "[A]n idea or notion, like the physicist's ultimate particles and rays, is only known by what it does," claims Richards (5). Some metaphors are "wretchedly inconvenient" because they lead to misunderstandings and bad decisions, because they deflect insights, inventions, and policies that might save us from wars, famines, and ecological disasters. It is no accident that Burke and Richards wrote as they did about metaphor during the Great Depression, a crisis of "overproduction," of economic insanity, when economies floundered and people starved because there was *too much* agricultural and industrial capacity. As Burke put it, "There are certain occasions when the poet . . . give[s] us a correct perspective, a serviceable structure of meanings and attitudes. At other times the integration is inadequate" ("Relation" 170).

It is not enough to ask whether our words are accurate, whether they accurately represent some aspect of reality. Unlike philosophy, which, in the tradition of Plato, has been concerned with Truth absolute, rhetoric has always been concerned with pragmatic decisions made in contexts of probable knowledge. We must ask about metaphors whether they direct/deflect attention in ways that help people achieve their purposes. Thus Burke asks whether they are "representative," whether they have enough complexity to direct attention to all relevant aspects of reality.

Once we understand metaphors in Burke's terms as "equipment for living," as strategies that "size up the situations, name them in a way that contains an attitude toward them" (*Philosophy* 3), rhetoricians must ask with Burke whether the metaphors are "adequate" to our purposes, whether they lead to insights, attitudes, and actions that help us achieve our purposes. Which metaphors for writing encourage the best writing pedagogies? Which economic metaphors lead to material security and well-being? Which, by contrast, lead us into error? Metaphors, not being literal, are neither true nor false; but some are much better than others. And the proof is in the pudding.

Analog

Considered as a mode of thought (for example, in Jakobson's distinction between the metaphoric axis of similarity and the metonymic axis of contiguity), metaphor suggests what modern communication theorists call analog (and, in yet another metaphor, associate with the "right brain"). The analog mode acquired its name because, unlike the arbitrary sounds that constitute human language, its signifiers are analogous to what they represent. Analog communication includes most nonverbal communication: gesture, inflection, rhythm, posture, music, dance, animal communication, dream condensation, Freudian primary process. It is the realm of connotations, of values, of intuition, of art, of the shaman. It lacks quantitative precision, has no tense markers, and cannot represent certain logical structures (if . . . , then . . .; either/or, true negation). In analog one can communicate only in the present about what is present or what can be positively re-presented. For all these lacks, the masculine logic of Western "high" culture has largely relegated the analog to witches, muses, and other feminine or childlike beings (including poets). Because the analog signifier, in the very way it exists, manifests a relationship between signifier and signified, it can express relationships and feelings very fully and subtly. It lacks a definitive either/or (cf. Freud, *The Interpretation of Dreams*, cited in Derrida 46), but it can express infinite gradations of more-or-less and embodies a subtle eye for resemblances (which, according to Aristotle, constitutes a talent for metaphors).

In sum, New Rhetoricians (like some of the oldest rhetoricians) take metaphor seriously as a trope—that is, a substantive figure of *thought*. Discourse—language and thought—is rooted in metaphors. Playing with metaphors is a fruitful heuristic technique. Making sense of an audience's or discourse community's root metaphors is a key to understanding its assumptions and values. Changing an audience's or community's metaphors is a wonderfully effective device for redirecting their attention, persuading them to "see it your way." Especially in a scientistic age, when popular and even educated conceptions of knowledge are typically founded on false assumptions of *literal* objectivity, a critical understanding of metaphor ought to be near the center of general humanistic education.

Richard M. Coe
Simon Fraser University

Bibliography

Aristotle. *The Rhetoric*. Trans. Lane Cooper. Englewood Cliffs, NJ: Prentice, 1932.

Barthes, Roland. *Mythologies*. Trans. Annette Lavers. New York: Hill, 1972.

Beardsley, Monroe C. "The Metaphorical Twist." *Philosophy and Phenomenological Research* 22 (1962): 293–307.

Bizzell, Patricia, and Bruce Herzberg, eds. *The Rhetorical Tradition*. Boston: St. Martin's, 1990.

Burke, Kenneth. *Attitudes towards History*. Rpt. Berkeley: U of California P, 1984.

———. *A Grammar of Motives*. Rpt. Berkeley: U of California P, 1969.

———. *Permanance and Change: An Anatomy of Purpose*. 2nd ed. Indianapolis, IN: Bobbs-Merrill, 1954.

———. *The Philosophy of Literary Form*. Rpt. Rev. abr. ed. New York: Vintage, 1957.

———. "The Relation between Literature and Science." *The Writer in a Changing World*. Ed. Henry Hart. London: Martin Laurance, 1937.

———. *A Rhetoric of Motives*. Rpt. Berkeley: U of California P, 1969.

———. "Variations on Providence." *Notre Dame English Journal* 13 (1981): 155–83.

Derrida, Jacques. "White Mythology: Metaphor in the Text of Philosophy." Trans. F.C.T. Moore. *New Literary History* 6 (1974): 5–74.

Gilbert, Sandra M., and Susan Gubar. *The Madwoman in the Attic*. New Haven: Yale UP, 1979.

Gould, Stephen Jay. "For Want of a Metaphor." *The Flamingo's Smile*. New York: Norton, 1985. 139–51.

Irigaray, Luce. *This Sex which is Not One*. Ithaca, NY: Cornell UP, 1985.

Jakobson, Roman. "The Metaphoric and Metonymic Poles." *Fundamentals of Language*. Ed. Roman Jakobson and Morris Halle. The Hague: *Mouton*, 1956. 54–82.

Johnson, Samuel. *The Works of Samuel Johnson*. Vol. 7. Oxford: Talboys, 1825.

Lakoff, George, and Mark Johnson. *Metaphors We Live By*. Chicago: U of Chicago P, 1980.

Pepper, Stephen C. *World Hypotheses: A Study in Evidence*. 1942. Berkeley: U of California P, 1961.

Perelman, Chaïm. *The Realm of Rhetoric*. Trans. William Kluback. Notre Dame, IN: U of Notre Dame P, 1982.

Richards, I.A. *The Philosophy of Rhetoric*. New York: Oxford, 1936.

Ricoeur, Paul. *The Rule of Metaphor: Multidisciplinary Studies of the Creation of Meaning in Language*. Trans. Robert Czerny. Toronto: U of Toronto P, 1977.

Sacks, Sheldon, ed. *On Metaphor*. Chicago: U of Chicago P, 1979. [Originally *Critical Inquiry* 5 (1978).]

Seitz, James. "Composition's Misunderstanding of Metaphor." *College Composition and Communication* 42 (1991): 288–98.

Tate, Gary, ed. *Teaching Composition: 12 Bibliographic Essays*. Fort Worth: Texas Christian UP, 1987.

See also FIGURATIVE LANGUAGE; FIGURES OF SPEECH

Metonymy

From the Greek "a change of name," a device of symbolic substitution that replaces the subject meant with an attribute or related image. For example, in the expression "from the *cradle* to the *grave*," two concrete images symbolize two abstractions, "birth" (cradle) and "death" (grave). By means of "poetic realism" (Burke), the tangible conveys the intangible.

Giambattista Vico (1744) was the first to identify metonymy, along with *synecdoche, metaphor,* and *irony,* as one of the four figures of thought (*tropes*) to which all others can be reduced. Prior to Vico, philosophers considered tropes—words that "turn" from their literal meaning to a figurative one—merely decorative ways to enrich writing rather than "necessary modes" with which to express reality. Because ancient rhetoricians lacked precise definitions for the tropes, the fine distinction between metonymy and the related figure, synecdoche, has remained unclear for centuries. Despite general agreement that synecdoche functions primarily to substitute the part for the whole—as in "all *hands* [sailors] on deck"—contemporary theorists and dictionaries continue to offer overlapping and contradictory examples of the two figures. The eighteenth-century philosopher Du Marsais held that a synecdoche, because it bears an *internal* relationship with the replaced subject, always forms a whole with it; in contrast, a metonymy, which bears an external relationship, remains "independent" of it. Applying Du Marsais's all-but-forgotten lapidary distinction can serve to disambiguate expressions of these two related but different tropes.

Classical rhetoricians identified several species of metonymic substitutions: *symbol for thing symbolized, cause for effect, effect for cause, controller for controlled, creator for creation, place for activity or industry,* or *administration, container for contained, attribute/ possession for possessor,* and *object used for user* (Quintilian). Many common phrases, newspaper headlines, advertising slogans, song titles, and cartoon captions embody such metonymic concepts: "Bernstein gives up *baton* [conducting]" (symbol for thing symbolized); "Retin-A, the face cream that erases the *years* [wrinkles]" (cause for effect); "These Boots Are Made for Walking"; "He took a swig of *courage* [whiskey]" (effect for cause); "*Bush* [U.S. Air Force] Bombs Iraq" (controller for controlled); "You're never alone with a *poet* [a book of poetry] in your pocket" (creator for creation); "*Detroit* [automobile manufacturers] faces layoffs" (place for industry); "The aircraft returned ten *body bags* [dead soldiers]" (container for contained); "The hired *gun* [killer] confessed" (object used for user). A metonym always expresses some "contiguity" to the subject it represents (Jakobson).

The "compact metonym" (Davis) derives from using a characterizing noun adjectivally; the resulting pithy phrase identifies "one who . . ." or "one that . . ." or "those who . . . ." For example, a "*bag* lady" is one who keeps her possessions in a shopping bag; a "*white-collar* crime" is one that is committed by an office worker; "*convent* girls" are those who are educated in a Catholic school. Compact metonyms form such phrases as *refrigerator* art, *voice* mail, *straphanger, Sunday* painter, *coffee table* book, *bifocal* set, *brown bag* lunch, and *rubbernecking* delays.

Metonymy as a "master" trope (Burke) subsumes all smaller figures of substitution. An *epithet* replaces the person or thing meant with a characterizing phrase: "*man's best friend*" for "dog"; epithets may also be abusive as in "Trickie Dickie" for Richard Nixon. *Euphemism* offers a milder, less blunt way to express an unpleasant subject: "*toss one's cookies*" for "vomit"; "*pass away*" for "die." *Doublespeak* uses deliberately inflated language designed to obfuscate and mislead: "elevator operator" ascends to "*transportation manager*" and "garbage truck" assumes the status of "*resource recovery facilitator.*" In the phrase "*ethnic cleansing,*" euphemism joins doublespeak to both sanitize and disguise "genocide." Another metonymic subtype, *antonomasia,* from the Greek "to name instead," substitutes the name of a famous person or literary character who symbolizes a particular quality: "Your *Romeo* [lover] phoned." Antonomasia informs these headlines: "Bush Is No *Demosthenes* [orator]"; "Leonard Cohen, the *Lord Byron* [Romantic poet] of Rock and Roll"; "Bill Clinton and Food: *Jack Sprat* [who eats no fat] He's Not." Adjectival forms of antonomasia have spawned the dictionary entries *Midas touch, Herculean,* and *quixotic* (from Cervantes' overly romantic character Don Quixote).

Metonymy also comprises extended forms of symbolic representation. The *enactment* aims to show the intended meaning through an action, rather than tell it through a statement, often depicting either a cause or an effect. A country song about aspiring songwriters, "16th Avenue" (Schuyler), enacts their impoverished state: "They've all dialed the phone *collect* to home." A *New York Times* article on gays in the military featured the subhead "Don't Ask, *Don't Drop the Soap,*" an expression warning against a (potential) result by showing a (possible) cause.

A poem, song, story, novel, play, or film whose central image means not only what it says but also something more than it says functions as a *symbolic work:* the lyric to "September Song" (Weill/Anderson), for example, while it describes autumn, simultaneously evokes aging. The white whale of *Moby Dick* and the albatross of *The Rime of the Ancient Mariner* symbolically suggest far more than they literally express. Similarly, a *fable* ("The Fox and the Grapes") and a *parable* ("The Boy Who Cried Wolf") use a literal story to convey a moral lesson by symbolizing how misfortune can result from unethical or immoral behavior. Each of these literary forms, because of its cause-and-effect nature, acts not as an extended metaphor, as so often labeled, but rather as an extended metonymy (Vico). A metaphor, after all, functions as a figure of fanciful comparison, and as such lacks an actual existence: We cannot literally "*jumpstart* the economy."

The common misperception of both the figurative nature of metaphor and the literal basis of metonym and symbol may account for the frequent misapplication of the phrase "*is a metaphor* for. . . . " Often editorial commentary on a contemporary event or situation such as a political scandal, race riot, or public health problem concludes that it "is a metaphor for" something of broader social significance. But Watergate, the L.A. riots, and the AIDS epidemic are literal facts, not figurative fancies. Thus to label a concrete entity "a metaphor for" rather than "a symbol of" is to misperceive the function of both metaphor and symbol.

Given the widespread use of the myriad forms of metonymy, the subject deserves a place in every language arts program, so that future generations will be able to accurately identify and competently use this major means to conceptualize reality.

Sheila Davis
The New School for Social Research, New York

Bibliography

Burke, Kenneth. *A Grammar of Motives.* Berkeley: U of California P, 1945. 503–11.

Davis, Sheila. *The Songwriters Idea Book.* Cincinnati, OH: Writer's Digest, 1992. 110–19.

Du Marsais, Cesar Chesneau. *Des Tropes ou des diferens sens dans lesquels on peut prendre un meme mot dans une meme langue.* Paris: Chez la Veuve de Jean-Batiste Brocas, 1730. 2–3.

Jakobson, Roman. "Two Aspects of Language and Two Types of Aphasic Disturbances." *Fundamentals of Language.* 2nd ed. Ed. Roman Jakobson and Morris Halle. The Hague: Mouton, 1971. 69–96.

———. *Verbal Art, Verbal Sign, Verbal Time.* Minneapolis: U of Minnesota P, 1985.

Lakoff, George, and Mark Johnson. *Metaphors We Live By.* Chicago: U of Chicago P, 1980.

Lakoff, George, and Mark Turner. *More than Cool Reason.* Chicago: U of Chicago P, 1989.

Lodge, David. *The Modes of Modern Writing.* Chicago: U of Chicago P, 1988.

Quintilian. *The Institutio Oratoria of Quintilian.* 4 vols. Trans. H.E. Butler. Loeb Collection. New York: Heinemann, 1922.

Vico, Giambattista. *The New Science of Giambattista Vico.* Trans. Thomas Goddard Bergin and Max Harold Fisch. 4th printing. Ithaca, NY: Cornell UP, 1991. 406–7.

Modes of Discourse

Usually refers to narration, description, exposition, and argumentation, the four forms of discourse that dominated Anglo-American rhetorics of the late nineteenth century. The modes seem to have their roots in faculty psychology and the "new" rhetorics of the late eighteenth century, especially such psychologically based rhetorics as George Campbell's *Philosophy of Rhetoric* (1777). Twentieth-century rhetoricians have condemned modes-based composition pedagogy as formulaic, abstract, and disconnected from social context, but, in their time, the modes may have been a reasonable, albeit not perfect, response to the needs of a changing society.

Divisions of discourse were not a nineteenth-century innovation. The Roman rhetoricians, taking their cue from Aristotle, divided oratory by the nature of the cause, the speaker's intent, and the type of audience. The resulting classification, the *tria genera causarum,* included *genus iudicale,* speeches of accusation and defense, or courtroom oratory; *genus deliberativum,* speeches on future policy, or legislative oratory; and *genus demonstrativum,* speeches of praise and blame, or ceremonial oratory. Medieval rhetoric included the additional divisions of *ars poetriae,* the art of versewriting, *ars dictaminis,* the art of letter-writing, and *ars praedicandi,* the art of preaching.

In the late eighteenth century, however, Scottish rhetoricians developed a view of rhetoric based in faculty psychology and the associative nature of mental activity. George Campbell posited four ends of discourse (to enlighten the understanding, to please the imagination, to move the imagination, and to influence the will) in which each end was associated with a particular faculty of the mind. Nineteenth-century rhetoricians extended these widely held ideas to associate writers' ends with certain kinds of texts and textual features. Samuel Newman's *Practical System of Rhetoric* (1827), Richard Green Parker's *Aids to English Composition* (1844), and Alexander Bain's *English Composition and Rhetoric* (1866) evidence the development of the modes of discourse. By the last decade or so of the nineteenth century, these textual features were ensconced as the standard four (or occasionally five, if "persuasion" were included) modes of discourse noted above. David Jayne Hill, in *The Science of Rhetoric* (1885), gave the rationale for the modes succinctly: "If then we discover the laws of these four elementary forms of discourse, we shall cover the whole ground of the conditions of communication depending on the nature of the idea." The four dominant modes then, were as follows.

Description was that mode in which the parts of a simultaneous whole (such as an object, feeling, or occasion) were exhibited for a particular purpose. Description involved presentation of the whole and enumeration of the parts in such a way as to convey a comprehensive depiction of the subject. Techniques of description were division, classification, and comparison and contrast. The standards by which descriptive writing was judged included cohesion, clarity, and perspicuity.

Narration was that mode in which a successive whole was related, rather than the simultaneous whole that is the subject of description. Narration involved the presentation of a sequence of events or an account of changing circumstances. Techniques of narration included cause-and-effect logic, chronological ordering, and internal summaries. The standards of narrative writing were continuity, unity, emphasis, selectivity, and completeness.

Exposition was the mode in which a general notion was unfolded or explained, and was therefore often allied with scientific discourse. Exposition involved defining the nature of a thing by denoting its general features. Techniques of exposition included analysis (by definition, induction, and deduction) and amplification. The standards of expository writing were clarity, objectivity, and completeness.

Argumentation was that mode by which a proposition was confirmed or proved. Many late-nineteenth-century textbooks were devoted exclusively to argumentation, which included establishing a proposition and proving it through inductive or deductive procedures. These procedures included reasoning by analogy, sign, cause and effect, and example. The standards of good argumentative writing were logical consistency and clarity.

Recently, teachers of composition have criticized the modes of discourse and composition pedagogy based upon them. Whereas earlier schemes were, at their best, allied with instructional techniques that stressed the dynamic interaction among speaker (or writer), subject, and audience, composition pedagogy based on the modes, critics have charged, tended to assume a necessary (but now dubious) connection between certain formal textual features and a corresponding appeal to one of the mental faculties. Critics have urged that, all too often, the result was an over-reliance on convenient, abstract formulae, which in turn led to instruction that was cut off from the vitality of other subjects and of larger social concerns, tended toward the mechanistic, focused on static standards, and ignored the active process of writing.

Like other aspects of rhetoric, however, the modes of discourse developed to meet the needs of the time and place. With the decline of oral culture, the rise of specialized knowledge, and the growth of professional education, modes-based composition pedagogy represents an understandable, if not flawless, system of rhetoric.

Sean Patrick O'Rourke
Vanderbilt University

Bibliography

Baker, Virgil L. "Development of Forms of Discourse in American Rhetorical Theory." *Southern Speech Journal* 18 (1953): 207–15.

Berlin, James A. *Writing Instruction in Nineteenth-Century American Colleges.* Carbondale: Southern Illinois UP, 1984.

Connors, Robert J. "The Rise and Fall of the Modes of Discourse." *College Composition and Communication* 32 (1981): 444–55.

Crowley, Sharon. *The Methodical Memory: Invention in Current-Traditional Rhetoric.* Carbondale: Southern Illinois UP, 1990.

D'Angelo, Frank. "Nineteenth-Century Forms/ Modes of Discourse: A Critical Inquiry." *College Composition and Communication* 35 (1984): 31–42.

Harned, Jon. "The Intellectual Background of Alexander Bain's 'Modes of Discourse.'" *College Composition and Communication* 36 (1985): 42–50.

Johnson, Nan. *Nineteenth-Century Rhetoric in North America.* Carbondale: Southern Illinois UP, 1991.

Kitzhaber, Albert R. *Rhetoric in American Colleges, 1850–1900.* Introd. John T. Gage. SMU Studies in Composition and Rhetoric. Dallas, TX: Southern Methodist UP, 1990.

Miller, Carolyn R., and David A. Jolliffe. "Discourse Classifications in Nineteenth-Century Rhetorical Pedagogy." *Southern Speech Communication Journal* 51 (1986): 371–84.

Stewart, Donald C. "Nothing New under the Sun—or Is There?" *Rhetoric Review* 1 (1982): 64–71.

M

Moffett, James (b. 1929)

A leading discourse theorist, curriculum developer, and educational reformer. James Moffett received his B.A. in English in 1952 and his A.M. in French in 1953, both from Harvard. He taught at Phillips Exeter Academy before becoming a Research Associate in the Harvard Graduate School of Education. Since the mid 1960s, he has also taught at the University of California at Berkeley, San Diego State University, and the Bread Loaf School of English, and worked as a "free-lance curriculum developer—or on some days, reformer."

His first book, *Teaching the Universe of Discourse* (1968, reissued 1983), was one of the founding works of theory for the newly reemerging field of rhetoric and composition. It is built on the proposition that the curriculum in "English" should be determined by the "structure" (a term Moffett defines carefully) of the subject, the subject in this case being "orders" and not just "kinds" of discourse. Moffett says he arrived "intuitively" at this formulation of the universe of discourse and its sequence of development, and that he then involved the work of psycho- and sociolinguists like Piaget, Vygotsky, and Mead to enhance the credibility of his proposals.

In a discussion that is wide-ranging, sophisticated, and richly exemplified, Moffett proposes that at its most fundamental level discourse is a matter of "somebody-talking-to-somebody-else-about-something." A detailed structure and sequence for "teaching" discourse may be ascertained by analyzing each of these elements (the "I," the "you," and the "it") and the relations among them ("I-you" and "I-It") along ladders of increasing "abstraction" (also a term that Moffett defines carefully).

In developing this theory, Moffett said, he was "after a strategic gain in concept," something that could be "utilized" and tested against experience. He warned that the theory should not be applied schematically. Learning to discourse, he has consistently argued, is primarily a matter of "development" in the Piagetian sense (that is, mental growth), not "learning" in the narrow sense. He has urged teachers to recognize that "individualization" should always be the goal in the classroom. Further, he claimed in *Teaching* that "through reading, writing, and discussing whole, authentic discourses—and using no textbooks—students can learn better everything that we consider of value in language and literature than they can by the current substantive and particle approach" (7).

Throughout his career, Moffett has embodied his theory in concrete pedagogical recommendations to an extraordinary extent. In 1968 he published *Student-Centered Language Arts and Reading, K–13* (republished in 1976 with coauthor Betty Jane Wagner and now in its fourth edition), which is "a textbook for teachers . . . in training and a handbook for use . . . on the job." In 1973 he was senior editor for an extensive collection of pedagogical activities, games, recordings, and books for classrooms K–12, called *Interaction*.

In 1981 Moffett published *Active Voice: A Writing Program across the Curriculum*, which is a rewriting of assignments (with advice added about their use) developed while he was teaching at Phillips Exeter in the early 1960s. He later published coauthored anthologies of writing done with these assignments by students in elementary, middle, secondary, and college classes (*Active Voices 1–4*, 1987).

He has also edited (with Kenneth McElheny) *Points of View: An Anthology of Short Stories* (1966) and *Points of Departure: An Anthology of Nonfiction* (1985), both of which organize their selections according to the developmental spectrum structure set out in *Teaching*.

In 1974 Moffett's *Interaction* program was enveloped in "the most tumultuous and significant textbook controversy that North America has ever known"—which is the subject of Moffett's *Storm in the Mountains: A Case Study of Censorship, Conflict, and Consciousness* (1988). In *Harmonic Learning: Keynoting School Reform* (1992), Moffett takes this episode as the point of departure in a book that explores the prospects of integrating the "learning fields" of "family, school, culture and nature."

Essays written by Moffett during and after the 1970s, on various topics, including the social and political contexts of schooling, are collected in *Coming on Center: English Education in Evolution* (1981, 1988).

John Warnock and D.R. Ransdell
University of Arizona

Bibliography

Moffett, James. *Active Voice: A Writing Program across the Curriculum.* 2nd ed. Portsmouth, NH: Boynton/Cook, 1992.

———. *Coming on Center: Essays in English Education.* 2nd ed. Portsmouth, NH: Boynton/Cook, 1988.

———. *Detecting Growth in Language*. Portsmouth, NH: Heinemann, 1992.

———. *Harmonic Learning: Keynoting School Reform*. Portsmouth, NH: Boynton/Cook, 1992.

———. *Storm in the Mountains: A Case Study of Censorship, Conflict and Consciousness*. Carbondale: Southern Illinois UP, 1988.

———. *Student-Centered Language Arts and Reading K–13: A Handbook for Teachers*. Boston, MA: Houghton, 1968. Reissued in 1976 with Betty Jane Wagner and retitled in 4th ed. *Student-Centered Language Arts, K–12: A Handbook for Teachers*. Portsmouth, NH: Boynton/Cook, 1992.

———. *Teaching the Universe of Discourse*. Boston, MA: Houghton, 1983.

———. *The Universal Schoolhouse: Spiritualizing Society*. San Francisco: Jossey-Bass, 1994.

Moffett, James, et al. *Active Voices: A Writer's Reader, I–IV.* (I, grades 4–6, with Marie Carducci Bolchazy and Barbara Friedberg; II, grades 7–9, with Phyllis Tashlik; III, grades 10–12, with Patricia Wixon, Vincent Wixon, Sheridan Blau, and John Phreaner; IV, college, with Miriam Baker and Charles Cooper) Portsmouth, NH: Boynton/Cook, 1987.

Myth

Characters, images, figures, and narratives (specific stories and plots) established by social consensus and usage over time. In a society where "historical" is likely to refer to a favorite soap opera videotaped because of a dental appointment, the fascination with the traditional or *mythic* evident in many other cultures is not immediately self-evident. By contrast, what is regarded as *factual* information is transmitted as scientific data, as instances of legal proceedings (laws), and as part of what one needs to know in order to do well in college entrance competitions. Myths are seldom referred to in such instances, except as examiners test the databases of the competitors (for instance, do they know the characters and stories of Greek and Roman mythology?); nonetheless, mythic language remains somehow *powerful,* effective language. Mythic narrative refers not to external mathematical integers but to materials considered culturally significant. Mythic themes and subject matter; they represent powerful significances because their discourse, like that of poetry and symbolic diction generally, gestures toward suprarational values that cannot easily be reduced to the arithmetic and pragmatic languages of economics and technology.

"It's just a myth that . . . "brings up a second referent beyond that about myths' lacking pragmatic facticity, namely the denunciation of something with which a particular speaker/author disagrees (the myth of the sexually promiscuous African-American, the myth of middle-class support for private schools, and so forth). *Stereotype* or *untruth* is what is meant much of the time: Myth gets tainted with being an "almost truth," or it is considered outdated or primitive in a society that lives by the myth of mythlessness, according to which a contemporary society oriented primarily to science, technology, and economic gain has discarded religion or myth so as to operate "rationally," "scientifically."

Likewise, myth and ideology are treated as synonyms when primary myths are recognized as determining worldviews and ethics. Accordingly, patriarchal domination is blamed for the lack of a sufficient number of heroines to underwrite women's liberation advances today, necessitating searches through previously neglected traditions for new models. Feminist writers have trashed the excessively male heroic monomyth found, for instance, in Joseph Campbell's influential *Hero with a Thousand Faces* (1968), and now replace such a male-dominant monomyth with patterns more appropriate to heroines (see Christ; Donaldson). Nonetheless, elections are influenced still by a candidate's support or rejection of a woman's rights to abortion. And the choice of nonheterosexual individuals to live gay or lesbian lives is still stigmatized by models derived from what are considered to be the normative, prototypical beginnings, those creation myths that also determine patterns of ecology (who dominates what, what sort of "life" counts as important) and social interaction (the expert's chauffeur is not expected to eat at the CEO's table, women get the secretarial jobs).

Already in Bereshith/Genesis 2.19–20, Mudman/*Adamah* gets to *name* everything that has come into existence, as a sign of this creature's power (interpreted, of course, as *His* power, in spite of the explicit multisexual identification in 1.27, "So God created humankind [Hebr. *adamah*] in his image, / in the image of God he created *them*; / male and female he created *them*"). And myths relegate certain aspects of everyday experience to the borders/margins of culture: in one culture dreams count for little, but in another they are so important that they must be enacted immediately, the whole community alert to the possibility that an individual's dream might anticipate changes soon to face them all.

Thus is the importance of the arts, of the artisans whose works probe the yet-incoherent futures of dreams or psychic experiences, and the science fiction explorations of nontraditional gender relationships, and the possibilities that the worlds we inhabit daily are but hints of what is to come. In the arts mythic impulses are heeded as harbingers of new meanings, the advance edges of the new metaphors that will eventually seem the orderly shapes of the everyday. Myths function *conservatively,* passing on revered crystals of human experience (etymologically, *conserve* means "emphatically preserve"; the *servare* root is also the source of *servant* and even *hero*). But they also function *imaginatively,* seeding mythopoetic reassemblings of the metaphors that have become accepted traditions (see the discussions on myth in rhetorical studies in *Communication Studies* 41 [Summer 1990] and 41 [Winter 1990]).

So myths anticipate the future; they guide understandings of the past and the future, the traditional and the anticipated. Each grasping of meaning contributes to meanings-yet-to-come, determines where a society sets its horizons and its limits as to what it considers "truly human." And myths both convey the most important ways to be a "successful" member of society and teach the permitted parameters of behavior that only certain individuals (priests and rulers, artists and musicians, and, today, athletes) may exceed without penalty.

The social ramifications of myths specify boundaries of truth and falsehood, of ours and theirs, meaningful and impossible, conservative and liberal, tory and whig, Republican and Democrat. Hence where touching upon the realms of mythic models, mass communications must tread carefully, lest they inappropriately challenge the status quo. Such political aspects of mythic materials are seldom appreciated even when cherished mythic figures are appealed to in political platforms and national agendas. Another political aspect concerns the control of the literary or rhetorical canon: Whole bodies of mythology may be suppressed or ignored, as has been the case repeatedly with Native American Indian and African-American materials.

The ideological insertion of mythic perspectives into the social order operates at more than one level: Primary beliefs shape what society members consider fundamental, so that deities are considered to be gendered as male or female or beyond gender. Or humans are judged to be dominant over or subservient to the natural order: Females ought to serve males, heterosexual couples get the right of way on the dance floor, gay or lesbian couples are not welcome, and so forth. Secondary reflections of mythic priorities elevate now this, now that oral or literary genre: realistic novels this century, passionate love poetry another; aggressive frontiersmen this time, sensitive new-age guys another. Tracking the secondary refractions of dominating mythic sets is no less difficult than determining how popular culture is to be differentiated from high-brow. Marxian and Culture-Studies perspectives are only beginning to provide critical tools for analyzing how mythico-ideological elements of a society actually operate, although there is a great deal to be learned from (for instance) earlier euhemerism or allegorical interpretation. When Pilgrim (in Bunyan's *Pilgrim's Progress*) carelessly forgets that the Key of Hope is lodged in his bosom, we have a clue to the artificiality of the allegorical frames, the manner in which a particular hermeneutical (interpretive) slogan has overlaid artificially direct relationship to experienced life.

And then there are all those tertiary reflections: names, themes, icons that are seldom "authentic" in terms of originating mythic scenarios, but play well on Broadway, such as the Superman cycles or adventure films that replicate classical mythic scenarios. And finally terms derived from primary mythical stories (narcissism, Oedipus complex, martial heroism) become merely grist for other mills, as when Narcissus becomes a cipher for chastising a congressional candidate, or Mars designates ways a president deals with a situation such as the Bay of Pigs or the Persian Gulf war.

The individualistic psychology of Carl Jung provides consistent semiological or allegorical patterns: The dark side (in Jungian parlance, "the shadow") represents what may yet be developed but has not yet been heeded sufficiently. The androgynous image anticipates an eventual union of the opposites in which everything finally coheres, but a sensation-type personality will have difficulty comprehending why others do not grasp the importance of ecological issues, and so forth. Beyond such (often arbitrary) coding, *the archetypal* usefully names ways in which the repetitively useful, the traditionally significant, make their appearances: Archetypal figures are those whose logarithmic or crystalline structures recur repeatedly in many generations and many different societies. (Frye is useful for understanding archetypal or seasonal, or comic and tragic patterns in literature.)

A particular fairy-tale witch cannot be dismissed out of hand—she is an articulation of the Negative Mother whose manifestations recur across any number of cultural configurations. Or the comic-strip Prince Valiant incarnates the Eternal Youth; and Hemingway's fictional Old Man of the Sea or Faulkner's Bear gain resonances they do not evoke when one is ignorant of the generic, genre-laden qualities that such archetypal figures insert into particular stories. Archetypes represent less essentialist, transcendental instincts or influences from the vague cultural-beyond than repeated constellations of significance shaped historically and politically (ethnocentrically) within specific societies, and experienced variously at different points on the life-cycle or stage of cultural development.

The generic/archetypal/mythical dimension is not produced automatically by some sort of Freudian or physiological libido, nor is its presence evident only from the long-range perspective of hindsight. But its elementary pedagogical, heuristic role in communication cannot be ignored: One hears what one's culture prepares one to hear. A person tells stories that correspond to models long locked into narrative repertoires, models that one dares to revise only if one possesses the stature of Andy Warhol or John F. Kennedy (since Romanticism, the favored model breaks the model, looks new or different). Unfortunately, one's culture has been successful only rarely in finding new myths, in extrapolating (even in science or speculative fiction) imaginative solutions to the same old social problems.

In his critical work on the fictions of J.G. Ballard, Gregory Stephenson usefully suggests:

Myths and symbols may . . . be understood as *tentative organizations of energy and impulse,* as *living shapes,* organic, protean, fluid, and *not as changeless and absolute structures.* If regarded in a rigid, literal sense, if made the basis for some reductive orthodoxy, then the living myth and the fecund symbol become inert, withering into illusion, serving then to stifle and repress the process of change and growth rather than to promote it. (127, emphasis added)

What frequently happens to myths is that they are interpreted literally, the purely local (antiarchetypal, nonuniversal) interpretation restricting the ways mythic patterns provide insights with respect to situations long distant from their origins. In such an instance, such behavioral norms as those of Christianity in the second century become normative proscriptions in contemporary America, and fundamentalist appropriations of mythic beginnings (of Israel, in this instance) become mighty staffs with which to clout any alternative position (see McGee).

Such positions are not restricted to the religiously fervent. Monomythic approaches have dominated politics as well as the technical study of myths, mythography. Accordingly, myths are the accidental residue of cultural rituals; myths represent merely unsuccessful attempts to say in poetic language what the scientist can express in numbers; references to the light and the dark can be translated into astronomical terms (or astrological, or ego-psychological—see the overviews of various approaches in the history of myth study in Doty and Dundes). Myths can be made to mean what the mythteller or mythographer wants them to mean, and their rhetorical power is entirely subject to the prevailing mode of discourse of a particular era or power-elite. Jewett and Lawrence demonstrate a nationalistic appropriation of the apparently universal hero monomyth. It was transformed by Protestantism and frontier values into a secular savior complex that still guides American political behaviors (see Rushing).

What one may express is limited to that with which the audience already has some connections, the *deictic* aspects, elements of experience with which an audience connects cognitively in ritual explications and performances of meanings (see Jacopin). Mythic patterns have provided such cross-referencing intertextual connections for millennia. They do so today—witness George Lucas's acknowledgement of the role of Campbell's *The Hero with a Thousand Faces* in filming *Star Wars.* Hence the patterning of the myths, the resurfacings of certain stories and motifs and figures, may be more important than knowing specific stories from this or that tradition.

A complex, multifaceted approach to myths (advocated repeatedly by Doty and others) rep-

M

resents a realistic, integrative approach to contemporary life and values. Mythic, archetypal, and generic models are not prescriptions but typifying anticipations shaped by the world's mythologies (made helpfully accessible in Smith). A mature mythographic perspective will not be satisfied merely with one local neighborhood's favorites, it will test any attempt at finality by asking whether it contributes to bettering the ways the human race understands itself and interacts with its global environment. Does it last? Can it answer to the repressions of the Nazi or Stalinist repressions? Will its perspectives contribute to expansion of the human enterprise?

"Truth" related by myth reveals communal values and significance rather than factual data; it tells moral consequences rather than abstract logarithms (see Doty). While remaining a component of rational discourse, myth taps as well into the imaginative human propensities evidenced in *the arts* of a culture, in its dance and literature, its music and plastic expression, its photography and architecture. Myths represent historical anticipations of experiences that contemporary persons face daily, even if it may take self-conscious reflection to comprehend cosmological myths in personal terms, the demonic or heroic myth as being relevant today, or myths about the first instances of things as materials that express not only digital information but values as well. Myths are *religious* in the etymological sense of that word: they tie things together in bundles rather than separating them into scientific bits and pieces. And insofar as they are a sort of science of the abstract become concrete, myths may designate meanings within the everyday that are initially discerned in the realms of sacred meanings (Doty 121). Myths suggest that the everyday is not just everyday. They elaborate fundamental elements of basic communicative expressions into their transcendental dimensions by suggesting that even the most trivially mundane aspects of human communication are in some sense divine, culturally important, foundational.

William G. Doty
University of Alabama

Bibliography

Bal, Mieke. "Myth à la lettre: Freud, Mann, Genesis, and Rembrandt, and the Story of the Son." *Discourse in Psychoanalysis and Literature*. Ed. Shlomith Rimmon-Kenan. New York: Methuen, 1987. 57–89.

Campbell, Joseph. *The Hero with a Thousand Faces*. 2nd ed. Princeton: Princeton UP, 1968.

Christ, Carol. *Diving Deep and Surfacing: Women Writers on Spiritual Quest*. Boston: Beacon, 1980.

Daniel, Stephen H. *Myth and Modern Philosophy*. Philadelphia: Temple UP, 1990.

Donaldson, Mara E. "Woman as Hero in Margaret Atwood's *Surfacing* and Maxine Hong Kingston's *The Woman Warrior*." *Heroines of Popular Culture*. Ed. Pat Browne. Bowling Green: Bowling Green State U Popular P, 1987. 101–13.

Doty, William G. "Contextual Fictions that Bridge Our World: 'A Whole New Poetry.'" *Journal of Literature and Theology* 4 (1990): 104–29.

———. "Myth, the Archetype of All Other Fable: A Review of Recent Literature." *Soundings: An Interdisciplinary Journal* 74 (1991): 243–74.

———. *Mythography: The Study of Myths and Rituals*. Tuscaloosa: U of Alabama P, 1986.

Dundes, Alan, ed. *Sacred Narrative: Readings in the Theory of Myth*. Berkeley: U of California P, 1984.

Frye, Northrop. *Anatomy of Criticism: Four Essays*. Princeton: Princeton UP, 1957.

Jacopin, Pierre-Yves. "On the Syntactic Structure of Myth, or the Yakuna Invention of Speech." *Cultural Anthropology* 3 (1988): 131–59.

Jewett, Robert, and John Shelton Lawrence. *The American Monomyth*. 1977. Lanham, MD: UP of America, 1989.

Liska, James Jakob. *The Semiotic of Myth: A Critical Study*. Bloomington: Indiana UP, 1990.

McGee, Michael Calvin. "Secular Humanism: A Radical Reading of 'Culture Industry' Productions." *Critical Studies in Mass Communication* 1 (1984): 1–33.

Rushing, Janice Hocker. "Mythic Evolution of 'The New Frontier' in Mass Mediated Rhetoric." *Critical Studies in Mass Communication* 3 (1986): 265–96.

Smith, Ron. *Mythologies of the World: A Guide to Sources*. Urbana: National Council of Teachers of English, 1981.

Stephenson, Gregory. *Out of the Night and Into the Dream: A Thematic Study of the Fiction of J.G. Ballard*. Westport, CT: Greenwood, 1991.

N

Narratio

The second component of classical argument, which conveys statements of fact furnishing either background information or context for the case being argued. *Narratio*'s translation, definition, and emphasis have changed markedly since the classical age. Originally placed following the *exordium* and preceding the *propositio*, *narratio* chiefly conveys facts. These facts buttress the orator's credibility (a concern of *exordium*) and provide an argumentative scaffold based upon history, precedent, or tradition. This scaffold becomes the basis for a statement of position or thesis conveyed in the *propositio*. Many theorists, classical and contemporary, thus define *narratio*'s function as providing "background information . . . and the circumstances important to the argument" (Woodson 38).

Greek rhetoricians treat *narratio* somewhat passingly; it comes to prominence under the aegis of Cicero and Quintilian. H.M. Hubbell, translator of *De inventione*, translates the term as "narration," thus perhaps leading to some of the confusion over *narratio*'s definition and discourse function. Cicero discusses many of the types of narration/*narratio* in *De inventione*, beginning with the following definition: "an exposition of events that have occurred or are supposed to have occurred" (1.19.27). Cicero also lists three types of narrative. The first type focuses on "the case and . . . the reason for dispute" (1.19.27). A second type contains "a digression . . . for the purpose of attacking somebody, . . . making a comparison, . . . amusing the audience, . . . or for amplification" (1.19.27). The last type of narrative serves a different end—"amusement and training"—and it can concern either events or persons (1.19.27). Cicero identifies three subtypes of narration concerning events: *Fabula*, which uses fictional events; *Historia*, based upon historical precedents; and *Argumentum*, narrative based upon fictional events that could happen (1.19.27).

In addition to cataloguing types of narrative and their respective characteristics, Cicero and, later, Quintilian identify and discuss three crucial traits of effective narrative: brevity, clarity, and plausibility. These characteristics suggest a sense of audience awareness, for they are all cautions to the rhetor against using examples that are too extensive, obscure, or incredible lest the audience become alienated. These characteristics facilitate *narratio*'s appearances in deliberative and ceremonial discourse, as well as forensic discourse.

Today, *narratio* seems secondary to the concepts of narrative or narration, and many theorists have debated the virtues and characteristics of this element of discourse. The concept of narration is particularly significant in the work of Kenneth Burke, whose theories concerning dramatism contribute much to revisions of rhetorical thought. Echoing Cicero in *De oratore*, narration now functions as "the fountainhead from which the whole remainder of speech flows" (2.81.330) and becomes a crucial part of discourse because of its capacity for "applying principles to situations" (O'Banion 66).

Joseph Colavito
Northwestern State University

Bibliography

Cicero. *De Inventione. De Optimo Genere Oratorum. Topica.* Trans. H.M. Hubbell. Loeb Classical Library. Vol. 2. Cambridge, MA: Harvard UP, 1949.

———. *De Oratore.* Books I and III. 2 vols. Trans. E.W. Sutton and H. Rackham. Loeb Classical Library. Vol. 3. Cambridge, MA: Harvard UP, 1954.

Corbett, Edward P.J. *Classical Rhetoric for the Modern Student.* 3rd ed. New York: Oxford UP, 1990.

Fisher, Walter. *Human Communication as Narration: Toward a Philosophy of Reason, Value, and Action.* Columbia: U of South Carolina P, 1987.

O'Banion, John D. *Reorienting Rhetoric: The Dialectic of List and Story.* University Park: Pennsylvania State UP, 1992.

Quintilian. *The Institutio Oratoria of Quintilian.* 4 vols. Trans. H.E. Butler. 1920–1922. Cambridge, MA: Harvard UP, 1976–1980.

Woodson, Linda. *A Handbook of Modern Rhetorical Terms.* Urbana, IL: National Council of Teachers of English, 1979.

Narrative Theory

Began with Aristotle, who in his *Poetics* discussed formal elements not just of tragedy, but also of epic (plot, character, thought, and diction; mimesis and diegesis) that remain concerns of narrative theory today. From the fourth century B.C.E. until the twentieth century, more attention was given to drama and poetry (with poetry often referring to literature) than to narrative as a distinct mode, but after the emergence of the English novel in the eighteenth century, writers such as Henry Fielding, Walter Scott, Nathaniel Hawthorne, Edgar Allan Poe, George Eliot, and others discussed the nature and significance of this new form, its relations to epic, to romance, and to the moral functions of literature.

In the first half of the twentieth century, Henry James and E.M. Forster turned the discussion to matters of novelistic form, with James focusing especially on issues of narration and Forster on the distinction between plot and story and the uneasy tension between character and plot. In the 1960s, narrative theory moved into a new, international phase as the work of the Russian formalists of the 1920s and the contemporary French structuralists was translated and disseminated among Anglo-American theorists, while the work of the Anglo-Americans was translated and disseminated in Europe. Since the 1960s, narrative has received the kind of sustained, sophisticated attention that had previously been reserved for poetry, and narrative theory is now a rich, diverse, and flourishing field.

If we define narrative as a mode of discourse in which at least one narrator recounts to at least one narratee at least two temporally related events, then we can understand the project of narrative theory as the effort to understand the various elements of the mode—narrator, narration, narratee, event, setting, character, plot, and language—the relation of these elements to each other, and narrative's overall nature and significance. Sometimes the term *narratology* is used synonymously with *narrative theory,* but here we shall use it to refer more specifically to the formalist-structuralist account of narrative, and we shall use *narrative theory* to refer to the intersections of narrative studies with critical theory more generally—with, that is, not only formalism and structuralism, but also such movements as Marxism, psychoanalysis, feminism, deconstruction, reader-response criticism, and the various historicisms and cultural studies.

Narratology then, studies "the nature, form, and functioning of narrative" and "examines what all and only narratives have in common . . . as well as what enables them to be different from one another" (Prince). More particularly, the formalist-structuralist model distinguishes among *story* (what happens, in its "natural chronological order"; what the Russian formalists called the *fabula*), *plot* (what happens as it is presented to the audience; what the formalists called *sjuzhet*), and *discourse* (how the event is conveyed; the narration). Narratological work on narrative structure ranges from Vladimir Propp's *Morphology of the Folktale,* which identified an invariable sequence of twenty-nine events occurring in all Russian folktales, to Roland Barthes's "Introduction to the Structural Analysis of Narrative," which distinguished between kernel events (the essential events of a sequence) and satellite events (those that embellish a kernel).

In the Anglo-American tradition, the key early texts followed James's lead and emphasized matters of technique or "treatment," gradually codifying a preference for what was considered an "objective" narration rooted in the center of one consciousness—as practiced by James and theorized by Percy Lubbock. In challenging this dominant view, Wayne C. Booth's *Rhetoric of Fiction* also proposes a general view of narrative as rhetoric and explores the variety of techniques authors may use to persuade their audiences to adopt certain views of characters and events. In addition, Booth's book introduces the widely adopted concepts of *implied author,* the self—distinct from the narrator—whom a writer conveys in constructing a text; *reliable narrator,* who speaks in accord with the norms of the implied author; and *un-*

reliable narrator, who diverges from the implied author's norms.

Gérard Genette advances narratology's investigation into point of view by separating two related but different questions, the question of who sees (a question of vision), and that of who speaks (a question of voice). Genette further unpacks the complexity of narrative discourse by developing a set of categories that addresses its manipulation of time and its relations between a narrator and what is narrated. *Order* refers to the relation between events in the story and events in the text; under this heading Genette includes flashbacks, flashforwards, and other deviations from straight chronology. *Duration* refers to the relation between story time and discourse time; two years of story time may be narrated in a single phrase while five minutes of story time may be narrated for hours upon hours. *Frequency* refers to the relation between repetition in story time and repetition in discourse time; a repeated action may be mentioned only once while a unique event may be returned to again and again in the narration of it. Genette points out that distinguishing between first-person and third-person narration is misleading because all narrators are first-person speakers. He proposes, instead, that we distinguish between *heterodiegetic* and *homodiegetic* narration, between, that is, narration in which the narrator and the characters occupy different narrative levels or spaces (as in, for example, *Tom Jones* or *Beloved*), where the narrators are not characters in the events they portray, and narration in which the narrator and characters are on the same level or in the same narrative world (as, for example, in *Jane Eyre* and *The Invisible Man*).

In *Story and Discourse,* Seymour Chatman synthesizes the work of Genette, Barthes, Booth, and others from the French and Anglo-American traditions, dividing his study into the two parts identified in the title and discussing, under "Story" event, character, and setting and, under "Discourse," varieties of points of view. More generally, Chatman presents what has come to be known as the communication model of narrative analysis. In this linear model, an author creates an implied author who then employs a narrator to address a narratee. As the chain continues, the narratee's understanding is reconfigured by the implied reader (the implied author's hypothetical addressee), and the implied reader's understanding is similarly reconfigured by the real reader.

While researchers in the 1980s and 1990s generally acknowledge the usefulness of the narratological communication model, they have also become increasingly aware of its limitations. Deconstructionist critics such as Paul de Man and J. Hillis Miller would emphasize both the necessity to employ its categories and the inability of the communication to be effected as the model predicts. Arguing that the formalist-structuralist model renders narrative spatial and static rather than temporal and dynamic, Peter Brooks proposes in *Reading for the Plot* that narrative theory attend to the psychic energy of narrative dynamics, the way beginnings generate desires, middles involve a detour on the route to fulfillment, a fulfillment finally delivered (or at least offered) in endings, which can be seen as having determined the whole sequence. But Susan Winnett and others note that Brooks assumes that male sexual desire is the norm for narrative dynamics and, thus, once again implicitly equates *male* with *universal*.

More generally, the narratological model does not have much to say explicitly about ideology, difference, or culture, though it does not preclude its application to these matters. Peter J. Rabinowitz's *Before Reading* extends the model by uncovering the conventions of reading that influence narrative communication in any one work and by showing how the operation of these conventions intersects with the politics of interpretation to influence such larger cultural matters as canon formation. James Phelan proposes a way of thinking about character as a combination of mimetic, thematic, and synthetic components (that is, as person, idea, and plot function), suggests that the relation of these components is determined by progression, and investigates the relation between understanding progressions and resisting them. The translation of M.M. Bakhtin's work in the early 1980s gave theorists a way to link language and ideology and in so doing added yet another layer to the understanding of narrative discourse. Any national language, says Bakhtin, is better thought of as a conglomeration of mini-languages (for example, the language of the marketplace, of the academy, of religion, of politics), each carrying its own ideological values, and the novel is the genre that most dramatically shows these languages and values colliding, contrasting, and challenging each other.

The move of narrative theory toward ideology has been given further emphasis by the work of Marxists and feminists of the last two decades. Fredric Jameson's *Political Unconscious* popularizes the dictum "Always historicize!" and argues that critics need to search for the link between a narrative's form and its often unexpressed or unconscious political agenda. Feminists consistently search for the connections among gender, ideology, and power in narrative and culture. Elaine Showalter, Sandra Gilbert, Susan Gubar, Nancy Miller, Rachel Blau DuPlessis, and others have studied the development of the female narrative tradition as it has developed within a dominant patriarchal culture. Some feminists, such as Judith Fetterley and Patrocinio Schweikart, have focused on the situation of the female reader. Still others have employed the insights of other theorists as part of their investigations of gender and power. To mention just one from a long list, Nancy Armstrong adapts Foucault's ideas of discursive formations to rewrite the origins of the English novel.

Feminist criticism has also made significant contributions to film theory, especially in combination with structuralism and psychoanalysis. Laura Mulvey's landmark 1975 essay "Visual Pleasure and Narrative Cinema" transformed film theory by calling attention to the way Hollywood cinema reinforces patriarchal ideology in the way that it assumes a male spectator and directs his gaze toward an objectified woman. Since Mulvey's essay, film theory has continued to explore the dynamics of the gaze; the phenomenon called *suture*, the process by which the spectator identifies with the film image; the effects of various techniques such as the shot/reverse shot; and in general the relations among form, gender, and ideology.

The two most prominent recent developments in narrative theory are its inflections by the work in new historicism and in multiculturalism. Since the new historicism regards literature as part of a continuous network of cultural texts, it shifts narrative theory's attention to the cultural work performed by narrative. To take just one example, D.A. Miller looks at Victorian fiction through the lenses provided by the new historicism and Foucault's *Discipline and Punish* and argues that the Victorian novel performed a very significant policing function on its readers: In reading *Bleak House,* the Victorian reader internalized culturally sanctioned ways of thinking and behaving.

Work in multiculturalism is now influencing narrative theory in much the same way that it had earlier been influenced by feminism. Henry Louis Gates, Jr., demonstrates how the trope of signifying, so common to African-American oral culture, provides a way to understand the development of the African-American cultural tradition. Gloria Anzaldúa's work on what it means to live and write on the borders of different cultures (figuratively and literally) shows how real readers and writers (as opposed to the abstract, ideal constructs of narratology) have multiple and shifting relations to narrative texts. Theorists of other ethnic literatures and of gay and lesbian literatures also emphasize the difference that difference makes in all elements of narrative, at all points of the communication model—and in the way narrative theory is conducted.

The recent interactions of multicultural and narrative studies have, in a sense, reinforced many of the contributions folklore studies have made to narrative theory. Work ranging from Propp's analysis of Russian folktales (discussed above) to Dundes's structuralist and anthropological approach to folklore has been instrumental in guiding the study of folk narrative as a cross-cultural phenomenon. Barbara Babcock's work on metanarration in folk narrative debunks the myth of "primitive narrative," the idea that oral or folk narrative is "simple, natural, and direct, . . . [u]ncomplicated by . . . self-commentary," a debunking central to the validation of various narratives beyond those of the traditional canon (63). Studies of folk narrative also intersect with literary criticism in the realm of new historicism and ideological criticism. Richard Bauman's work on the performance aspect of verbal art, especially the nature and codes of verbal performance in storytelling, helps us understand not only the representation of performance in written narrative but also the performative dimension of all narrative. In collaborating with Charles Briggs, Bauman also argues that theorists and critics must interpret the performance context but then conduct a reflexive ethnography, which considers the political and ideological influences on both the narrative and the folklorist.

As we hope this narrative shows, narrative theory is indebted to a variety of disciplines and movements, which are, in turn, indebted to it. Perhaps this interaction shows, too, the ubiquity and diversity of narrative, that it exists in numerous, intersecting forms, in everything from the shortest jokes and ballads to the longest films and novels. Because narrative is as common in everyday conversation as it is in formal and informal writing, because theorists are increasingly aware of the importance of the mode, and because it is such a vital component of our lives, we expect narrative theory to continue to flourish as long as people continue to tell and listen to stories—which is to say as long as there are people, language, and social interaction.

Elizabeth Patnoe and James Phelan
Ohio State University

Bibliography

Anzaldúa, Gloria. *Borderlands/La Frontera: The New Mestiza*. San Francisco: Spinsters/Aunt Lute, 1987.

Armstrong, Nancy. *Desire and Domestic Fiction: A Political History of the Novel*. New York: Oxford UP, 1987.

Babcock, Barbara. "The Story in the Story: Metanarration in Folk Narrative." *Verbal Art as Performance*. Richard Bauman. Prospect Heights, IL: Waveland, 1977. First published in *Folk Narrative Research: Studia Fennica* 20 (1976): 177–84.

Bakhtin, Mikhail M. *The Dialogic Imagination*. Ed. Michael Holquist. Trans. Caryl Emerson and Michael Holquist. Austin: U of Texas P, 1981.

Barthes, Roland. "An Introduction to the Structural Analysis of Narrative." *New Literary History* 6 (1975): 237–62.

Bauman, Richard. *Story, Performance, and Event: Contextual Studies of Oral Narrative*. Cambridge: Cambridge UP, 1986.

Blau DuPlessis, Rachel. *Writing beyond the Ending: Narrative Strategies of Twentieth-Century Women Writers*. Bloomington: Indiana UP, 1985.

Booth, Wayne C. *The Rhetoric of Fiction*. 2nd ed. Chicago: U of Chicago P, 1983.

Brooks, Peter. *Reading for the Plot: Design and Intention in Narrative*. New York: Knopf, 1984.

Chatman, Seymour. *Story and Discourse: Narrative Structure in Fiction and Film*. Ithaca, NY: Cornell UP, 1978.

Dundes, Alan. "Folk Ideas as Units of Worldview." *Toward New Perspectives in Folklore*. Ed. Américo Paredes and Richard Bauman. Austin: U of Texas P, 1972: 93–103.

Fetterley, Judith. *The Resisting Reader*. Bloomington: Indiana UP, 1978.

Friedman, Susan Stanford. "Spatialization: A Strategy for Reading Narrative." *Narrative* 1 (1993): 12–23.

Gates, Henry Louis, Jr. *The Signifying Monkey: A Theory of Afro-American Literary Criticism*. New York: Oxford UP, 1988.

Genette, Gérard. *Figures* (1966), *Figures* II (1969), *Figures* III (1972). Paris: Seuil.

———. *Narrative Discourse: An Essay in Method* (1972). Trans. Jane E. Lewin. Ithaca, NY: Cornell UP, 1980.

Gilbert, Sandra M., and Susan Gubar. *The Madwoman in the Attic: The Woman Writer and the Nineteenth-century Literary Imagination*. New Haven: Yale UP, 1979.

Jameson, Fredric. *The Political Unconscious: Narrative as a Socially Symbolic Act*. Ithaca, NY: Cornell UP, 1981.

Miller, D.A. *The Novel and the Police*. Berkeley: U of California P, 1988.

Miller, J. Hillis. *Fiction and Repetition: Seven English Novels*. Cambridge, MA: Harvard UP, 1982.

Miller, Nancy K. "Emphasis Added: Plots and Plausibilities in Women's Fiction." *Publication of the Modern Language Association* 96 (1981): 36–48.

Mulvey, Laura. "Visual Pleasure and Narrative Cinema." *Screen* 16, 3 (1975): 6–18.

Phelan, James. *Reading People, Reading Plots: Character, Progression, and the Interpretation of Narrative*. Chicago: U of Chicago P, 1989.

Prince, Gerald. *A Dictionary of Narratology*. Lincoln: U of Nebraska P, 1987.

Propp, Vladimir. *Morphology of the Folktale*. 2nd ed. Trans. Laurence Scott. Austin: U of Texas P, 1968.

Rabinowitz, Peter J. *Before Reading: Narrative Conventions and the Politics of Interpretation*. Ithaca, NY: Cornell UP, 1987.

Schweikart, Patrocinio P. "Reading Ourselves: Toward a Feminist Theory of Reading." *Gender and Reading: Essays on Readers, Texts, and Contexts*. Ed. Elizabeth A. Flynn and Patrocinio P. Schweickart. Baltimore: Johns Hopkins UP, 1986. 31–63.

Showalter, Elaine. *A Literature of Their Own: British Women Novelists from Brontë to Lessing*. Princeton: Princeton UP, 1977.

Winnett, Susan. "Coming Unstrung: Women, Men, Narrative, and Principles of Pleasure." *Publication of the Modern Language Assn.* 105 (1990): 505–18.

National Council of Teachers of English

Major professional organization for teachers of English at all levels. While NCTE encourages scholarship on the substance of English studies as well as on the teaching of English, it differs from the Modern Language Association (whose members devote themselves primarily to literary scholarship) in focusing on the *teaching*—rhetoric is substantially a *teaching* discipline—of all activities that might be comprehended under "English" (including media studies). It also confines its attention to English (it does not deal, as does MLA, with most other modern or classical languages). Since NCTE once included specialists in speech communication (what was to become the Speech Communication Association was formed in 1914 when members interested in oral language and rhetoric broke off from NCTE to form their own organization) and recognizes the connections between speech and writing, it has an historical concern for oral as well as for written discourse.

NCTE helps to advance the study and practice of rhetoric in several influential ways. First, its conventions offer scholars and teachers wide opportunities to present scholarship on oral and written rhetoric, including the rhetoric of the media. A few sessions on these subjects appear on most programs for the general NCTE convention (held in November), and many more such sessions usually appear on the programs of one of its constituent organizations, the Conference on College Composition and Communication (CCCC). Sometimes a separate program strand, or more than one, at CCCC is devoted to subjects in rhetoric and stylistics. Important theoretical issues in rhetoric and in the teaching of rhetoric are often treated at these sessions. CCCC also sponsors a winter workshop, typically held in early January, focusing on two or three topics of concern to teachers of writing. Topics in rhetorical theory and practice are often among those treated in the workshop.

Some of the professional journals published by the council act as forums for the exchange of research and theory about rhetoric, in particular *College English* and *College Composition and Communication*. (Occasionally one of the council's other journals—for instance, *English Journal,* addressed primarily to teachers in secondary schools—may carry an essay about issues in rhetoric.) Because *College English* carries essays on literature and diverse cultural subjects, as well as on the history of the teaching of English, essays explicitly focused on issues in rhetoric are not numerous, but they are visible. *College Composition and Communication* carries a much larger number of essays about issues in rhetoric, including questions on the relationships of speakers/writers to audi-

ence. (Francis Christensen's essays on the rhetoric of the sentence and of the paragraph first appeared in *CCC,* as did Wayne Booth's well-known piece "The Rhetorical Stance." Edward P.J. Corbett explored the values of classical rhetoric in the pages of *CCC,* and James Kinneavy published in *CCC* an early, compact statement of some of his theories of discourse.) *CCC* has counted among its editors William Irmscher and Edward P.J. Corbett, both well known for their contributions to rhetorical scholarship. *CCC* typically does not carry the kinds of fully documented historical/theoretical essays often carried in the journals of the Speech Communication Association, but it does carry many pieces that deal with written communication in a college setting, and pieces that deal with the teaching of rhetoric and communication.

NCTE also contributes to scholarship on rhetoric through its publications program. NCTE itself publishes, through its own editorial board, some books, monographs, and research reports that treat issues in rhetoric, including topics in linguistics and collaborative composing. More significantly, through its alliance with Southern Illinois University Press in Carbondale, CCCC arranges the publication of the monograph series *Studies in Writing and Rhetoric* (*SWR*) and the annual *CCCC Bibliography on Composition and Rhetoric.* Monographs in *SWR* are typically brief (100 to 150 printed pages) but often deal with important questions in rhetoric, as evidenced by the title of Karen Lefevre's *Invention as a Social Act,* and two historical studies of the teaching of rhetoric by James Berlin. The *Bibliography* lists and classifies, with only the briefest of annotations, all writings, including books and articles, dealing with rhetoric and written communication (and the teaching of them) from all sources published in the year under review. (The council's research-oriented journal, *Research in the Teaching of English,* publishes a semiannual, highly selective, annotated bibliography of research on writing, but the items listed are usually formal research studies—including dissertations.) Apart from the publications programs of the Speech Communication Association and of Southern Illinois University Press, NCTE's publications, as a group, constitute perhaps the most significant single source of scholarly studies about rhetoric now available.

Indeed, NCTE, through publications and through large and small conventions and conferences, stimulates and advances scholarship in rhetoric as much as any single professional group now active.

Richard L. Larson
Herbert H. Lehman College, CUNY

See also CONFERENCE ON COLLEGE COMPOSITION AND COMMUNICATION; SPEECH COMMUNICATION ASSOCIATION

The National Writing Project

The National Writing Project is an expanding network of university-based writing project sites modeled upon the University of California at Berkeley Bay Area Writing Project. Currently, the NWP network numbers 165 sites (152 sites in the United States and Puerto Rico, and 13 sites overseas) which now serve over 100,000 classroom teachers each year.

The National Writing Project has three interrelated goals: improving the teaching and learning of writing in the nation's classrooms, improving university and school continuing education programs for teachers, and empowering successful classroom teachers.

Basic Assumptions

- University and the schools work together as partners, believing that the "top-down" tradition is no longer acceptable as a staff development model.
- Successful practicing teachers are the best teachers of other teachers, having a credibility no outside consultant can match.
- Summer Institutes involve teachers from all levels of instruction, elementary school through university as well as teachers from across the disciplines; writing is as fundamental to learning in science, in mathematics, and in history as it is in English and the language arts.
- Writing needs constant attention and repetition from the early grades on through the university.
- Teachers of writing must also write; the process of writing can be understood best by engaging in that process first-hand.
- Real change in classroom practice happens over time.
- Effective staff development programs are ongoing and systematic, bringing teachers together regularly throughout their careers to test and evaluate the best practices of other teachers and the continuing developments in the field.
- What is known about the teaching of writing comes not only from research but from the practice of those who teach writing.
- The National Writing Project, by promoting no single "right" approach to the teaching of writing, is open to whatever is known about writing from whatever source.

Each NWP site annually identifies up to twenty-five successful teachers of writing, K–university, and brings these teachers together in intensive summer institutes where they (1) demonstrate their own best teaching practices and approaches to writing; (2) examine writing theory and research; (3) experience the process of writing as members of a community of writers; and (4) review each other's written pieces in small editing/response groups.

Following the summer institute, these teachers join other previously trained NWP teacher consultants in planning and conducting year-long staff development workshops in project-sponsored programs in the schools. NWP school-year programs are voluntary and usually offered in a series of ten three-hour workshops spaced throughout the semester or school year. Across the nation, NWP staff development programs will vary somewhat state to state and region to region, but all are consistent with the project's teachers-teaching-teachers model.

Throughout its long history, the NWP has provided initial funding to universities establishing new NWP sites based upon the NWP/Bay Area Writing Project model, program design, and basic assumptions. Federal funding now makes possible continuing support to established NWP sites on these same premises and conditions.

James R. Gray
University of California at Berkeley

Newman, John Henry (1801–1890)

Known in the Victorian literature canon as a religious leader, an educational theorist, an historian, an essayist, a letter writer, a sermon writer, a lecturer, a preacher, a prose stylist, and a poet. Newman was continually engaged during his adult life in some kind of rhetorical activity, either defending his actions or his character or arguing for his stand on some issue. His *Apologia Pro Vita Sua* and *The Idea of a University* are classic examples of the kind of rhetoric that the classical rhetoricians classified as judicial discourse and deliberative discourse, respectively. Newman was also the author of a theoretical work in rhetoric.

Newman's *Essay in Aid of a Grammar of Assent* (1870) is a rhetoric text in the same sense that *Elements of Rhetoric* (1828) by his mentor Richard Whately is a rhetoric text. The central question that Newman seeks to answer in the *Grammar of Assent* is "how it is that a proposition which is not, and cannot be demonstrated, which at the highest can only be proved to be truth-like, not true, such as 'I shall die,' nevertheless claims and receives our unqualified adhesion" (ch. 6). Newman is primarily concerned in this book with how we arrive at the truths that we hold and how we persuade others to respect or to accept what we hold. In short, he wants to explore the psychology of belief or assent.

Newman's theory about the psychology of assent is epitomized in this quotation from Chapter 8 of the *Grammar of Assent*:

> It is plain that formal logical sequence is not in fact the method by which we are enabled to become certain of what is concrete; and it is equally plain from what has been already suggested, what the real and necessary method is. It is the cumulation of probabilities, independent of each other, arising out of the nature and circumstances of the particular case under review; probabilities too fine to avail separately, too subtle and circuitous to be convertible into syllogisms, too numerous and various for conversions, even were they convertible.

There is the quintessence of it—the cumulation of probabilities. The probabilities acquire persuasive weight only in the aggregate, but the cumulation of probabilities is enough to produce immediate, unqualified assent. Involved in the assessment of this cumulation of probabilities is the ratiocinative faculty that Newman calls the "Illative Sense," the faculty that ensures a person that assent to a proposition is justified even though that person is only vaguely conscious of the grounds for the assent.

Newman's exploration of the psychology of assent is carried on throughout most of the book at a very high philosophical level—although with his characteristic lucidity. But when Newman moves out of the abstract, metaphysical level and into the concrete level, he really illuminates his theory. His book is replete with examples, but the presentation of one of his examples will be sufficient to illustrate how he thinks people come to believe certain facts or concepts that they have never been able to confirm themselves.

In Chapter 8 Newman poses the question of how people come to believe that Great Britain is an island, even though they have never circumnavigated that land mass to confirm this fact. He then presents some of the "sufficient reasons" that converge to produce an "overpowering certitude" in the minds of natives and others that Great Britain is indeed an island. Some of the reasons are negative ("Nobody has ever contradicted that claim"), and no one of the reasons by itself (such as "Every map represents Great Britain as an island') would be sufficient to induce a firm belief in anyone's mind that Great Britain is an island. But the aggregate of those reasons is powerful enough to compel belief.

Winning the assent of an audience is the ultimate goal of anyone who composes and delivers a persuasive discourse. In his book, Newman brilliantly explored the mechanism of how we persuade ourselves and others to believe in matters that cannot always be demonstrated conclusively.

Edward P.J. Corbett
Ohio State University

Bibliography

Cronin, John Francis. *Cardinal Newman: His Theory of Knowledge*. Washington, D.C.: Catholic UP, 1935.

D'Arcy, Martin C. *The Nature of Belief*. New York: Sheed & Ward, 1932.

Harrold, Charles Frederick. *John Henry Newman: An Expository and Critical Study of His Mind*. New York: Longman, 1945.

Jost, Walter. *Rhetorical Thought in John Henry Newman*. Columbia: U of South Carolina P, 1989.

Juergens, Sylvester P. *Newman on the Psychology of Faith in the Individual*. New York: Macmillan, 1928.

Newman, John Henry. *An Essay in Aid of a Grammar of Assent*. Ed. Charles Frederick Harrold. New York: Longman, 1947.

New Rhetorics

An umbrella term referring to a variety of reactions against "current-traditional" rhetoric in America. With many strands and substrands, we will limit our consideration to new historicism, modern taxonomies, and cognitive, expressive, and epistemic rhetoric, along with the critiques offered by cultural criticism and feminist rhetoric.

Exigencies require a narrow focus, in this instance on rhetoric and composition studies as practiced in English departments. Scholars in speech communication, however, have made significant contributions to the new rhetorics. They announce their program in *The Prospect of Rhetoric: Report of the National Developmental Project* (1972), sponsored by the Speech Communication Association, with position papers proposing a new agenda, especially for rhetorical criticism, and delimiting speech communication concerns from English studies. Subsequently, Ernest Bormann's work on fantasy dream analysis and Walter Fisher's studies in narrative deserve note. Along with Robert Scott, discussed later, Lloyd Bitzer, Donald Bryant, and Douglas Ehninger have contributed to the conversation concerning epistemic rhetoric. Their work, along with much more, is addressed in *The Rhetoric of Western Thought* (1989 [4th ed.]), a sourcebook drawing extensively on speech communication theory. Currently, speech communication scholars are working in multiculturalism and cross-cultural communication and on the rhetoric of the new media. Their contributions and concerns can only be noted here.

All rhetoric begins as new rhetoric. The Western rhetorical tradition documents a sequence of formulations designed to correct existing debased practice. In the *Gorgias*, Plato condemns rhetoric used to preserve tyranny and the status quo, but in the *Phaedrus* he delimits the correct uses of rhetoric as an aid in discovering truth through the dialogue. The story repeats itself in cycles of various duration: Existing rhetorical practice, withered by conventionalism, is replaced by new theory and practice that revitalizes the tradition. In the twentieth century, modernism and the interest in epistemology fostered by linguistics and poststructuralism have produced several protorhetorics or new approaches to rhetoric. Kenneth Burke in various works contributes dramatism and logology and argues that rhetoric is concerned with the use of language in general, especially that language, as symbolic action, does not merely reflect reality, but, in fact, creates it. I.A. Richards, especially in *The Philosophy of Rhetoric* (1936), attacks the rule-strangled, linguistically misinformed practices of freshman English, arguing for a new approach, that rhetoric "should be a study of misunderstanding and its remedies" (3). He holds that language is metaphoric and that meaning-making is interdependent and context-bound. Other precursors of the new rhetorics, as the term is used here, include Richard Weaver, Chaïm Perelman, Walter Ong, and Steven Toulmin.

Though some controversy exists concerning the specific dating of the new rhetorics movement, all locate it within the period marked by the intensification of the Cold War in the late 1950s and the publication in the early and mid sixties of several critiques of current composition research and practice, including Braddock et al. *Research in Written Composition* (1963), as well as radical textbooks such as Corbett's *Classical Rhetoric for the Modern Student* (1965).

These origins show a symbiosis of rhetoric, composition studies, and the social sciences. Braddock et al. argue that rhetoric and composition studies fall within the social sciences and need to employ social science methodology to design experiments that end with valid and replicable claims. Janet Emig's *Composing Process of Twelfth Graders* (1971) elaborated this argument, offering a method and a model for composition research in the social science tradition.

The social science connection is the origin of cognitive rhetoric, one of the strongest strands of New Rhetoric. Young, Becker, and Pike in *Rhetoric: Discovery and Change* (1970), another radical textbook, introduce tagmemics, adapting metaphors from physics and linguistics to composition, helping writers establish relations between objects and concepts. At base is a view of the mind borrowed from cognitive psychology that describes how humans classify and conceptualize, how we store and recall information, connect it to new information, hypothesize, test, and evaluate new concepts, and especially how the mind manages this problem-recognizing, problem-solving process. Linda Flower elaborates the relation between composing and cognition. From her early "Cognitive Process Theory of Writing," written with John Hayes, she uses protocol analysis, in which subjects verbalize how, as well as what, they are doing while composing. This methodology, though controversial, comes directly from cognitive psychology, again illustrating the strong connection between New Rhetoric and the social sciences. Lately, Flower has recontextualized her work, offering metadisciplinary commentary, placing cognitive rhetoric within epistemic rhetoric, viewing both "not as a tool for communication or persuasion narrowly considered but as a method of inquiry and as a process of social and individual meaning making" (171).

There is little dispute concerning what the new rhetorics reacted against. "Current-traditional" rhetoric, according to Sharon Crowley in *The Methodical Memory*, dominated school rhetoric for more than 150 years. This rhetoric is characterized by a positivistic view of language resulting in an emphasis on grammatical and mechanical correctness; algorithmic form exemplified in the five-paragraph theme and the modes of exposition, a redaction of the classical *topoi*; and a linear view of composing. Handbooks had conventionalized the approach, resulting in unreflective practice by marginalized graduate assistants and adjunct faculty. Crowley examines the sources of current-traditional rhetoric, originally a "new" rhetoric in its own right, in seventeenth-century philosophy's theory of logic and the mind. She argues that in its ultimate form, current-traditional rhetoric is not a rhetoric at all but "instruction in a theory of composition" (148) that cannot be reformed. She suggests a modern application of classical rhetoric, emphasizing invention and ethos, as a remedy.

Crowley's book represents a significant strand within the new rhetorics, new historicism. This movement undertakes a close reading and critique of the Western rhetorical tradition, frequently challenging both the constitution and interpretation of the canon. New historicists argue that history and theory are context-dependent and ideologically driven and thus must be situated and deconstructed. Only by understanding the cultural and epistemological origins of history and theory can we understand their purpose and consequences. New historicists such as Kathleen Welch in *The Contemporary Reception of Classical Rhetoric* question traditional translations of classical texts and demonstrate how the male-dominated Western tradition provides an incomplete and biased view. A concern with the classics, origi-

nating in Corbett and continuing through Frank D'Angelo, Crowley, Welch, and Richard Enos, to name only a few, represents a vital substrand in the new rhetorics. James Berlin, whose work invokes both new historical and epistemic values, and other cultural critics scrutinize more recent history, especially the ideological bases of American school rhetoric. The concern for history culminates in Bizzell and Herzberg's *Rhetorical Tradition* (1990), an anthology designed for use as a textbook; it both constitutes and criticizes the canon.

Complementing the reexamination of rhetorical history is a concern with precise description and analysis of discourse. The taxonomists take such as their project. James Kinneavy's *Theory of Discourse* offers a comprehensive theory based on the aims of rhetoric and using the rhetorical triangle as an analytical framework, and basing his analysis in philosophy, psychology, linguistics, and literary criticism. If a text's primary concern is with communicating information, then it is referential; if with moving an audience to action, then persuasive; if with the writer, then expressive; and if with language and aesthetics, then poetic. James Moffett, James Britton, and Frank D'Angelo offer alternative taxonomies. Kinneavy considers the "critical compatibilities" between all these in "A Pluralistic Synthesis of Four Contemporary Models for Teaching Composition," arguing that considered together they constitute a "metasystem" with Britton providing an empirical approach based in cognitive and developmental psychology, Moffett and D'Angelo providing a psychological approach much under the influence of structuralism, and Kinneavy providing philosophical and critical foundations (52).

While the taxonomists are concerned with text, expressivists are concerned with writers and the experience of writing. This movement is frequently condemned as naive in emphasizing the individual to the exclusion of the social and for being atheoretical, but a close reading such as that completed by Burnham in "Expressive Rhetoric: A Source Study" indicates otherwise. Ken Macrorie, William Coles, Donald Murray, and Peter Elbow are the writers most often associated with expressivism, sometimes labeled neo-Platonic or neo-Romantic rhetoric. Murray's "Writing as Process: How Writing Finds Its Own Meaning" in *Eight Approaches to Teaching Composition* (1980) offers the most comprehensive treatment of composing as viewed by expressivists. He describes a complex, somewhat mysterious recursive process of determining meaning through writing, with the final product coming to be against the original intent of the writer. Elbow's work, considered as a whole, is the most systematic approach to expressivism. In *Writing without Teachers* (1973), a textbook, he offers a writer-centered, experiential approach to writing, using freewriting and structured peer-response groups to create a nurturing, cooperative environment characteristic of his theory of the "believing game," a reaction against Cartesian skepticism, "the doubting game," that has so dominated Western educational practice. Elbow's subsequent work elaborates the theory underpinning his practice. His origins are as disparate as medieval and existential philosophy, depth and transactional psychology, and behaviorism and contemporary learning theory. Paradox emblematizes Elbow and expressivism in general.

Epistemic rhetoric, originally named and defined by Robert Scott and elaborated by Berlin and others, has become itself something of an umbrella term, containing within itself various substrands, including social constructivism, cultural criticism, and liberatory teaching, and the counterrhetoric proposed by feminists. An emphasis on the meaning-mediating function of language, however, characterizes all epistemic rhetoric. According to Berlin in *Rhetoric and Reality* (1987), "In epistemic rhetoric there is never a division between experience and language, whether the experience involves the subject, the subject and other subjects, or the subject and the material world. . . . [J]ust as language structures our response to social and political issues, language structures our response to the material world. Rhetoric then becomes implicated in all human behavior. All truths arise out of dialectic, out of the interaction of individuals within discourse communities. . . . [Truth] emerges only as the three—the material, the social, and the personal—interact, and the agent of mediation is language" (17). And Scott, in "Rhetoric Is Epistemic: What Difference Does That Make?" a retrospective, restates the central value of this movement: "If one argues that whatever may be called truth in the realm of human experience is necessarily contingent by the intersection in experience of human fallibility with whatever is the object of knowledge, then one tends toward the claim that rhetoric is epistemic" (124).

The sense that knowledge is contingent, located in culture, and largely a consequence of social and historical forces is central to social constructivism, perhaps the strongest substrand within epistemic rhetoric. Kenneth Bruffee was an early and influential voice for the social-constructivist view. "Collaborative Learning and the 'Conversation of Mankind'" provides the philosophical and theoretical underpinning for his practice. He uses Kuhn and Rorty, contrasting normal and abnormal discourse, locating the process of learning in the cognitive dissonance implicit in abnormal discourse. Abnormal discourse arises when members of different discourse communities attempt to communicate with one another. Since the conventions that allow for efficient communication within either discourse community—shared values, common vocabulary, and a method for establishing and evaluating claims—are not working in such a situation, discourse participants cannot make assumptions and must negotiate meaning, using language first to establish commonality, then to articulate difference, and finally to arbitrate difference. In Bruffee's application collaborative learning provides members of the outside group, in this case undergraduate students trying to master the disciplinary substance and conventions of their majors, information and procedures that allow them to recognize the values, master the vocabulary, manipulate the methodology, and, ultimately, become initiates. Bruffee provides systematic application of the theory in several articles and a textbook, *A Short Course in Writing* (1985).

Bruffee values negotiation and consensus, a tendency criticized by cultural critics and feminists, other substrands in epistemic rhetoric, for leading to group-think and the uncritical perpetuation of cultural values and practices, especially the social and economic oppression of minorities and women. The cultural critics, working from neo-Marxism and poststructuralism, value diversity and multiculturalism and teach critical self-consciousness of the interdependent and potentially oppressive relation of culture and ideology. John Trimbur, in "Consensus and Difference in Collaborative Learning," offers a thorough critique, arguing that consensus building is the beginning, not the end, the prelude to recognizing dissensus that delineates and accepts, in fact, celebrates, difference. Ira Shor's *Critical Teaching in Everyday*

Life exemplifies the cultural critic's classroom practice, including both Marxist political analysis of American institutions and economics and writing exercises through which students understand and learn to act against the power of popular materialist culture and economics. Shor is a protégé of Pablo Freire, the Latin American radical educator whose *Pedagogy of the Oppressed* (1973) provides the foundation for liberatory teaching. Henry Giroux offers the most systematic liberatory program in several books, especially *Theory and Resistance in Education* (1983).

In rhetoric and composition studies, Carolyn Hill's *Writing From the Margins* (1991) offers a curious but substantive synthesis of expressivism, social-constructivism, cultural criticism, and feminist rhetoric. Caywood and Overing's anthology *Teaching Writing: Pedagogy, Gender, and Equity* (1987) offers a reaction against the social-constructivist project specifically and the male-dominated Western rhetorical tradition in general. These essays offer a counterepistemolgy based on feminist values and the cognitive and developmental psychologies of Carol Gilligan's *In Another Voice* (1982) and Belenky et al. *Women's Ways of Knowing* (1986).

This essay can barely introduce a topic as complex as the new rhetorics. All its various strands and substrands cannot even be named, never mind treated in depth and in relation to one another. Whole volumes, such as *Defining the New Rhetorics* (1993), edited by Theresa Enos and Stuart Brown, tackle complex issues of definition and distinction. Considering the dialectical history of Western rhetoric in which challenges to conventionalized thinking and practice seem always to arise to revitalize the tradition, we best end with Robert Scott's opine, "No doubt, other formal names will better enable us to take fruitful paths in freshening old rhetoric, perhaps to the point at which new becomes fully justified" (183).

Christopher C. Burnham
New Mexico State University

Bibliography

Berlin, James. *Rhetoric and Reality.* Carbondale: Southern Illinois UP, 1987.

Bruffee, Kenneth. "Collaborative Learning and 'The Conversation of Mankind.'" *College English* 46 (1984): 635–52.

Burnham, Christopher. "Expressive Rhetoric: A Source Study." *Defining the New Rheto-rics.* Ed. Theresa Enos and Stuart Brown. Sage Series in Written Communication 7. Newbury Park, CA: Sage, 1993. 154–70.

Crowley, Sharon. *The Methodical Memory: Invention in Current Traditional Rhetoric.* Carbondale: Southern Illinois UP, 1990.

Enos, Theresa, and Stuart Brown, eds. *Defining the New Rhetorics.* Sage Series in Written Communication 7. Newbury Park, CA: Sage, 1993.

Flower, Linda. "Cognitive Rhetoric: Inquiry into the Art of Inquiry." *Defining the New Rhetorics.* Ed. Theresa Enos and Stuart Brown. Sage Series in Written Communication 7. Newbury Park, CA: Sage, 1993. 171–90.

Golden, James, Goodwin Berquist, and William Coleman, eds. *The Rhetoric of Western Thought.* 4th ed. Dubuque, IA: Kendall/Hunt, 1989.

Kinneavy, James. "A Pluralistic Synthesis of Four Contemporary Models for Teaching Composition." *Reinventing the Rhetorical Tradition.* Ed. Aviva Freedman and Ian Pringle. Conway, AR: L and S, 1980. 37–52.

Murray, Donald. "Writing as Process: How Writing Finds Its Own Meaning." *Eight Approaches to Teaching Composition.* Ed. Timothy Donovan and Ben McClelland. Urbana, IL: National Council of Teachers of English, 1980. 3–20.

Scott, Robert. "Rhetoric is Epistemic: What Difference Does That Make?" *Defining the New Rhetorics.* Ed. Theresa Enos and Stuart Brown. Sage Series in Written Communication 7. Newbury Park, CA: Sage, 1993. 120–36.

Trimbur, John. "Consensus and Difference in Collaborative Learning." *College English* 51 (1989): 602–16.

See also BURKE, KENNETH; COGNITIVE RHETORIC; CURRENT-TRADITIONAL RHETORIC; EPISTEMIC RHETORIC; PERELMAN, CHAÏM; POSTSTRUCTURALISM; RICHARDS, I.A.; TOULMIN, STEVEN; WEAVER, RICHARD; YOUNG, RICHARD

Nichols, Marie Hochmuth (1908–1978)

Professor of speech communication at the University of Illinois, rhetorical theorist, and critic. Born Marie Hochmuth in Dunbar, Pennsylvania, July 13, 1908, she earned degrees at the University of Pittsburgh (A.B. 1931, M.A.

1936) and the University of Wisconsin (Ph.D. 1945). She taught at Mt. Mercy College for Women (1935–1939) and at the University of Illinois from 1939 until her retirement in 1976. In 1960 she married Alan G. Nichols and subsequently signed her publications as Marie Hochmuth Nichols. She was editor of the *Quarterly Journal of Speech* (1963 to 1965) and president of the Speech Association of America (which later became the Speech Communication Association) in 1969. She was a visiting professor at the University of Hawaii and the University of Southern California and lectured frequently on other campuses. In 1978, she received the honorary Doctor of Humane Letters degree from Drury College in Springfield, Missouri.

Professor Nichols's early publications included critical studies of William Ellery Channing, Phillips Brooks, and Abraham Lincoln. Her essays in the *Quarterly Journal of Speech* on Kenneth Burke (1952) and I.A. Richards (1958), however, were more significant in their impact. Although later scholars interpreted Burke's work more thoroughly and with greater sophistication, Nichols deserves the credit for giving his ideas their first widespread dissemination in the field of speech communication.

Professor Nichols was recognized as a leading exponent of the approach to rhetorical criticism that came to be called neo-Aristotelian. Her 1954 essay on "Lincoln's First Inaugural," for example, has often been cited as an exemplary case of neo-Aristotelian criticism. She edited volume 3 in the series, *A History and Criticism of American Public Address* (1955), published under the auspices of the Speech Association of America. In the introductory essay, "The Criticism of Rhetoric," she described rhetorical criticism as the humane study of public address wherein the orator is understood as an agent in historical events. The principal tasks in rhetorical criticism are (1) identifying what is to be evaluated (typically public speech), (2) placing the speech in its cultural/historical context, and (3) judging the speech according to standards of rhetoric (typically those derived from Aristotle and other classical writers). The critic must know and account for constituents of the rhetorical act. These include "extraverbal" elements—speaker, purpose, audience, time, and place, and "verbal" elements—arguments, structure, and style. Nichols elaborated her theory of rhetorical criticism in a series of lectures at Louisiana State University in 1959,

subsequently published in a collection titled *Rhetoric and Criticism* (1963). The strong ethical foundations of her approach to criticism are evident in those lectures, especially in the first one, "Rhetoric and Public Address as Humane Study."

In addition to her publications and professional leadership, Professor Nichols influenced the field of speech communication as mentor to scores of graduate students at the University of Illinois. As professor emerita she continued to write, lecture, and advise students until her death.

Joseph W. Wenzel
University of Illinois

Bibliography

Hochmuth [Nichols], Marie. "The Criticism of Rhetoric." *A History and Criticism of American Public Address*. Vol. 3. Ed. Marie Hochmuth. New York: Longman, 1955. 1–23.

———. "Lincoln's First Inaugural." *American Speeches*. Ed. Wayland Maxfield Parrish and Marie Hochmuth. New York: Longman, 1954. 21–71.

Nichols, Marie Hochmuth. *Rhetoric and Criticism*. Baton Rouge: Louisiana State UP, 1963.

Nietzsche, Friedrich (1844–1900)

The most influential philosopher (in both an academic and popular sense) since Plato, Aristotle, and Confucius. His work has made a profound impact on twentieth-century thought, particularly on relatively recent developments in cultural studies, deconstruction, philosophy of language, political science, literary theory, and postmodernism. Many of the crucial figures in twentieth-century intellectual history have written about his work, among them Martin Heidegger, Karl Jaspers, Thomas Mann, Georges Bataille, Antonio Gramsci, Ernst Bloch, Oswald Spengler, Michel Foucault, Jacques Derrida, Stanley Rosen, Martha Nussbaum, Richard Rorty, Luce Irigaray—a manageable list would include twentieth-century intellectuals who have *not* been influenced or infected by Nietzsche. In addition to the effects his work has had on intellectuals, Nietzsche's writings "became an integral part of National Socialist self-definition" (Aschheim 233). However, it is noteworthy that Martin Heidegger's relationship to National Socialism has troubled contemporary academics and intellectuals far more than Nietzsche's role within the realm of Nazi culture and policy. Few seem to give pause to Hans Kern's statement in 1934: "I am convinced that only a conscious National Socialist can fully comprehend Nietzsche" (Aschheim 237), even though it is easy to imagine how Nietzsche's notion of the *Übermensch* (superman) would have appealed to National Socialists.

Except for the work of Geoff Waite, there has not been much attention to the continual, uncritical integration of "Nietzscheanism" within the various manifestations of postmodernism that proceeds without foregrounding Nietzsche's own future-directed plans for "Nietzscheanism," as if Nietzsche did not have a social agenda. Given that Nietzsche holds a central place in rhetoric's history as well as that of the twentieth century, rhetoricians have a particular interest in Nietzsche's case.

Nietzsche grew up in a Protestant family in Saxony. His mother, Franziska, played a prominent part in his life until her death in 1897. His father, a local parson, died early in Friedrich's life. In 1858 Nietzsche attended the famous boarding school of Pforta, which had a distinguished list of former students, including Ranke, Klopstock, Fichte, Novalis, and the Schlegel brothers. At Pforta, Nietzsche concentrated on classics and developed a fascination for ancient Greece, facts that provided direction to his early life.

After Pforta, he went to the university at Bonn to study theology, but during the Franco-German War Nietzsche's studies were interrupted while he served in the military. A riding accident in 1868 cut short his military duties. In 1869 Nietzsche accepted a professorship in classics at the University of Basel, where he wrote *The Birth of Tragedy* (1872), the text that includes his well-known distinction between the Apollonian and Dionysian and his endorsement of the irrational. Nietzsche characterizes Apollo as a god of higher civilization and Dionysus as a god of nature, one associated with "uncivilized," "primitive" behavior (Silk and Stern 63). Scholars cite Nietzsche's contemporary Johann Jakob Bachofen as an influence on Nietzsche's conception of the contrast, as well as the famous composer Richard Wagner, whom Nietzsche knew quite well until the two made a formal break in 1878.

In 1879, partly because of deteriorating health, Nietzsche resigned his post at Basel. The period at Basel and the decade that followed Nietzsche's resignation from academic life mark a period of great productivity, during which he wrote (sometimes dictated) a number of works: "On Truth and Lies in a Nonmoral Sense" (1873); *Human, All Too Human* (1878); *Daybreak* (1881); *The Gay Science* (1882); *Thus Spake Zarathustra* (first three parts published in 1883–84); *Beyond Good and Evil* (1886); *On the Genealogy of Morals* (1887); and *The Case of Wagner* (1888). A number of items appeared after Nietzsche's death through the work of Nietzsche's sister, Elisabeth. The *Nachgelassene Fragmente* were not intended for publication, but the fragments contain an esoteric agenda that needs to be considered along with the published texts. Even in earlier texts, such as *The Birth of Tragedy*, Nietzsche stresses the importance of esotericism by the higher man, the need for secrecy, and for compounding the secrecy, concealing the concealment. Still, many commentaries on Nietzsche read his texts at face value when a Janus face is called for.

This period at Basel is important for rhetoricians because this is the time when Nietzsche gave lectures on rhetoric's history. One of the courses he gave on rhetoric during 1872–1873 attracted but two students, though the weight Nietzsche assigned to rhetoric did not parallel the weight of student interest in the subject. In his "Description of Ancient Rhetoric," Nietzsche says, "The education of the ancient man customarily culminates in rhetoric: it is the highest spiritual activity of the well-educated political man" (Nietzsche 1989:3). Although many view Nietzsche as an "original thinker," it is important to note that these lectures on rhetoric depended heavily on others' work. Nietzsche borrowed material freely from Richard Volkmann's *Die Rhetorik der Griechen und Römer in systematischer Übersicht dargestellt* and from historians of rhetoric such as Gustav Gerber and Friedrich Blass (Nietzsche 1989:xi).

Arguably the most influential essay for the modern history of rhetoric is Nietzsche's "On Truth and Lies in a Nonmoral Sense" (1873), a key text for both deconstruction and postmodernism. As J. Hillis Miller says, this essay is a "decisive moment in the history of rhetoric" (325). Nietzsche's essay is central to both Jacques Derrida's "White Mythology: Metaphor in the Text of Philosophy" (1971), and later to Paul de Man's *Allegories of Reading* (1979). Nietzsche's essay throws suspicion on all of language, for he attempts to show that our usual notions of truth tend to be falsely referential to one degree or another. The problem with this view, according to Nietzsche, is that language points us to itself, to its own system of references that somehow does not lead to enlightenment but to contradiction. The famous passage is:

> What is truth? a mobile army of metaphors, metonyms, anthropomorphisms, in short, a sum of human relations which were poetically and rhetorically heightened, transferred, and adorned, and after long use seem solid, canonical, and binding to a nation. Truths are illusions about which it has been forgotten that they are illusions, worn-out metaphors without sensory impact, coins which have lost their image and now can be used only as metal, and no longer as coins. (1989:250)

Some see this as an emancipatory passage, one that presents a convincing case for textual indeterminacy or heterogeneity. Others, like de Man, view it as a concise statement of the problem with all language, which is that language is defective to the core, a system of illusions that comes about through the misunderstanding and underreading of tropes. For Nietzsche, "language is rhetoric," partly because everything is communicated through tropes. Language can convey opinions or perspectives but not truths, *doxa* rather than *episteme*. We are forever cut off from truth because of its mediation in language. This view provides comfort to rhetoricians who, at least since the days of Plato and the sophists, have felt inferior to scientists and philosophers, who assert that they do not deal in opinion or deceit. Nietzsche's claim is that philosophy and science are as rhetorical as anything else. "Nietzsche developed the notion that truth itself is the product of a certain 'pathos,' that it is an affectively invested figure able to claim no legitimacy beyond the urgency with which it is affirmed. This conceptual move tears the underpinnings from the notion of an arhetorical language of observation: The truth claims of science, in Nietzsche's reading, are themselves merely one rhetoric among others" (Bender and Wellerby 26).

This passage encourages rhetoricians to imagine their discipline in a universal, totalizing way. Since everything is rhetoric, as Nietzsche says, the domain of rhetoricians is everywhere, including, at this late date, the rhetoric of rhetoric.

In 1889 Nietzsche collapsed in Turin and was moved to an asylum. There he was confused about his own identity, "sometimes calling himself the Duke of Cumberland or the Kaiser" (Hayman 339). It was after this collapse that Nietzsche's sister, Elisabeth, began taking on an editorial role in her brother's affairs, creating a Nietzsche archive in her mother's apartment, writing a biography, and having her name changed legally to Elisabeth Förster-Nietzsche. In 1895 Elisabeth gained full control over her brother's works. Nietzsche's books and Elisabeth's biography sold well, and she earned a good deal of money. While her brother's condition deteriorated, she turned him into a showpiece. "She was consciously cultivating a Nietzsche myth. In the summer of 1898, she cut off a lock of his hair and put it in an envelope for the archive. She dressed him in a white pleated robe that made him look like a Brahmin" (Hayman 349). People were paraded in to look at the great man. As one visitor reported, even in his final, sickly days, Nietzsche gave the impression that he could not die. Nietzsche and Nietzscheanism live on.

Bruce Krajewski
Laurentian University

Bibliography

Aschheim, Steven E. *The Nietzsche Legacy in Germany 1890–1990*. Berkeley: U of California P, 1992.

Bender, John, and David E. Wellbery, eds. *The Ends of Rhetoric: History, Theory, Practice*. Stanford, CA: Stanford UP, 1990.

Hayman, Ronald. *Nietzsche: A Critical Life*. New York: Oxford UP, 1980.

Miller, J. Hillis. "Nietzsche in Basel: Writing Reading." *Journal of Advanced Composition* 13 (1993): 311–28.

Nietzsche, Friedrich. *Friedrich Nietzsche on Rhetoric and Language*. Ed. and trans. Sander L. Gilman, Carole Blair, and David J. Parent. New York: Oxford UP, 1989.

———. *Kritische Gesamtausgabe Werke*. Ed. Giorgio Colli and Mazzino Montinari. Berlin: Walter de Gruyter, 1967ff.

Nietzsche-Studien: Internationales Jahrbuch für Nietzsche Forschung. Berlin: Walter de Gruyter, 1979ff.

Silk, M.S., and J.P. Stern. *Nietzsche on Tragedy*. Cambridge: Cambridge UP, 1981.

N

Waite, Geoff. "The Politics of Reading Formations: The Case of Nietzsche in Imperial Germany (1870–1919)." *New German Critique* 29 (1983): 185–209.

———. "The Politics of 'The Question of Style': Nietzsche/Hö[l]derlin." *Identity of the Literary Text.* Ed. Mario J. Valdes and Owen Miller. Toronto: U of Toronto P, 1985.

Nineteenth-Century Rhetoric

A period of transition for the discipline that looks back at the New Rhetoric of the eighteenth century and forward to the "current-traditional" rhetoric of the twentieth. Rhetoric—variously considered to be a science or an art or both—figured more prominently in this century than historians have previously allowed.

Historians once claimed there was little "rhetoric" in the nineteenth century worth studying, but our understanding of nineteenth-century theory and practice has benefited recently from scholarly attention demonstrating that the period actually boasts many different "rhetorics." Combining elements of the New Rhetoric and ancient Greek and Roman rhetoric, nineteenth-century rhetorics are informed by such movements as empiricism, Scottish common-sense philosophy, associational and faculty psychology, Romanticism, scientism, and phrenology. Rhetorics of the period focused variously on the public (civic life), the professional (individual expertise), or the private (individual self-improvement).

It is difficult to determine what precisely falls under the rubric of "nineteenth-century rhetoric." Many of the duties traditionally assigned to rhetoric were being appropriated by other disciplines and arts, as disciplinary boundaries were particularly unstable. A central problem, then, has been formulating a stipulative or working definition of the term *rhetoric*. Historians working out of departments of English have tended to study rhetoric as writing instruction; those working out of departments of speech communication have tended to focus on oratory or elocution. Neither perspective encompasses all that is relevant. In *Nineteenth-Century Rhetoric: An Enumerative Bibliography*, Forrest Houlette points out that although most items catalogued under the term *rhetoric* are composition textbooks, rhetoric was more widely relevant. Searching under related subjects (including the teaching of English and grammar), Houlette identified 3,929 pertinent items written in English published between 1800 and 1920; he predicts that the next bibliography will list between six and seven thousand items bearing upon nineteenth-century rhetoric. This essay will focus on the place of rhetoric in North America and Great Britain, a reflection of the current state of secondary scholarship.

Although the differences among particular rhetorics must be appreciated, generalizations can be made. Stewart, for example, lists five *strands* in British and American rhetoric: classical, elocutionary, psychological-epistemological, belletristic, and practical. Berlin discerns three movements in the United States: classical (based on Greek and Roman theory), psychological-epistemological (based on Scottish common-sense realism and the belletristic movement), and romantic (based in part on the transcendental movement inspired by Emerson). While historians have lamented the decline of rhetoric during this century (Berlin, Guthrie, Kitzhaber), others argue persuasively for rhetoric's continued civil, moral, and cultural importance, as oratory was valued for its facilitation of "the proper workings of the political process, the disposition of justice, and the maintenance of the public welfare and social conscience" (Johnson 166–67; Clark).

During much of the century, Campbell's *Philosophy of Rhetoric* (1776), Blair's *Lectures on Rhetoric and Belles-Lettres* (1783), and Whately's *Elements of Rhetoric* (1828) reigned supreme. "Synthetic rhetorics"—indigenous rhetorical treatises based on the work of Blair, Campbell, and Whately—dominated during the second half of the century (see Johnson and Kitzhaber). Increasingly, rhetorical treatises spoke in terms of the role of language and education in preserving and extending democracy (see Johnson 168–70). Rhetoric emerged in innovative forms as well.

Important texts published during the period include John Witherspoon's "Lectures on Eloquence" (1802) and "Lectures on Moral Philosophy" (1802), John Quincy Adams's *Lectures on Rhetoric and Oratory, Delivered to the Classes of Senior and Junior Sophisters in Harvard University* (1810), and Gilbert Austin's *Chironomia, Or a Treatise on Rhetorical Delivery* (1806). The period's texts reflect radically different understandings of the rhetorical arts—from Austin's exclusive concern with the canon of delivery to the fuller lectures read by Adams.

Well established in American and Scottish schools and universities, though less so in England and Ireland, instruction in rhetoric manifested itself differently according to establishment and time, encompassing some or all of the following: composition (imitation, double translations, themes) and grammar (parsing, editing for correctness), sentence exercises (varying, paraphrasing, and prosing), oratorical activities (disputations, recitations, orations), criticism and reading, elocution, and logic. These terms overlapped as definitions and concepts shifted. Interest in the English vernacular was well established, as the language of the people came to be valued; in all but a few elite institutions, the classical languages no longer dominated language studies. Horner distinguishes between instruction in Scotland's southern universities, which focused on belletristic composition, and instruction in the northern ones, which were more current-traditional. (It is important to note that institutions and regions had different rhetorical orientations.) The rhetorical instruction offered by such Scottish professors as William Edmondstoune Aytoun, Alexander Bain, William Barron, George Jardine, and David Masson prefigures language instruction offered in twentieth-century America.

John Quincy Adams, holder of Harvard's Boylston Professorship of Rhetoric and Oratory, was the century's last great champion of classical rhetoric. (His successor, Joseph McKean, shared the classical bias but left no published record of his work.) Typically, the rhetoric course that prevailed at the beginning of the century entailed a review of the history of rhetorical theory with an emphasis on ancient theory; a brief consideration of the ethics of persuasion; an explanation of the types of oratory (deliberative, forensic, epideictic—or more usually, pulpit) and of the parts of an oration (introduction, narration, argument, refutation, and conclusion); a discussion of the character and education of the rhetor; instruction in invention (the topics), arrangement, and style. The dominance of classical rhetoric was greatly diminished after the opening decades of the century. With Edward T. Channing's *Lectures Read to the Seniors in Harvard College* (1856), for example, its removal seems complete, as the focus shifts from orator to writer and from persuasion to communication generally. Eventually, the ancient precepts are rejected. With Francis Child, the fourth Boylston Chair, rhetoric was abandoned in favor of literary studies. This pattern is not unusual.

During the course of the century, rhetorical theory was altered in consequential ways. Of course, not all rhetorics of the period reflected all of these changes. One crucial change in rhetorical theory was the continuing shift from oral to written discourse, due in part to the increasingly high premium put on the written word in carrying out the political, economic, and legal dealings of society and in part to the impact of the Industrial Revolution on literacy. Written composition no longer served simply as a script for oral performance. The increased affordability and hence availability of printed materials, along with rising literacy rates, necessitated this change. The oratorical culture of early nineteenth-century colleges—characterized by oral performances in literary societies and debate clubs and in classes and before school gatherings attended by the college president himself—had seemed to ensure the prominence of rhetoric. But writing became a more efficient means of exercising and testing the growing numbers of students.

As conceptions of the mission of higher education changed from the preparation of students for a leadership class (for the ministry or government service) to more individually defined careers, instruction in rhetoric was adapted to a more specialized curriculum designed to promote professionalism. By the end of the century, essay topics assigned tended to be more personal, less classical, contributing to what Halloran laments as "the decline of public discourse."

A related change was the increased emphasis on the analysis of discourse, in part the legacy of eighteenth-century Scottish belletristic rhetoric. Belletristic rhetoric emphasized the faculty or power of taste and increasingly focused on aesthetic values, in addition to prevailing moral and societal standards. Its attention to genius diminished the importance of rhetorical invention. Hence, more attention was devoted to style (the canon rhetorical theory rarely omits), with many treatises and textbooks offering detailed analyses of both classical and vernacular (particularly British English) literary works. Many rhetorics of this period, then, continued the eighteenth-century tendency to include literary criticism and appreciation under rhetoric's domain, although literature was understood broadly as including all educated letters. Such rhetorics tended to assume that analysis and production are symbiotic. Writers aimed for an elegant style that had force or energy. Textbooks propagated the belletristic perspective. The most popular was Alexander Jamieson's *Grammar of Rhetoric and Polite Literature* (1820), which saw nearly sixty editions in the nineteenth century (Stewart 162). Resting on Blair's work on taste and style and Campbell's on grammar, it focused on language, especially its aesthetic dimensions. Another important textbook was Samuel P. Newman's *Practical System of Rhetoric* (1827), hailed by Stewart as "the first American text for written composition" (162). (Clark cites Samuel Knox's *Compendious System of Rhetoric* [1809] as the first rhetoric text published by an American.)

By the end of the century, there was a tendency for textbook authors to begin to construe style narrowly, as a matter of perspicuity and grammatical correctness or purity. In general, persuasion became less central to rhetoric, as the modes of discourse—description, narration, exposition, and argumentation—came to dominate textbooks; language was governed by rules for the whole (paragraphs and themes) and for the part (words and sentences).

Another change in the period was the enthronement of written composition. The influential books of Scotsman Alexander Bain, especially popular in America, fueled interest in written composition, so much so that by the century's end the term *rhetoric* came to be synonymous with written composition. A devoted student of psychology, Bain, professor of moral philosophy and logic at Marischal and professor of logic at Aberdeen, grounded his theories of rhetoric and grammar in the principles of the mind revealed by faculty psychology. His prescriptions for the development of paragraphs and for "opening" or topic sentences found many apostles, both among those who taught from his textbooks— especially *English Composition and Rhetoric: A Manual* (1866)—and those who wrote the next generation of textbooks in like manner. His forms or modes of discourse persist in some textbooks today, as does the prescription that paragraphs must have unity, coherence, and emphasis. Although Bain carefully allowed for exceptions that complicated his principles of composition, the pedagogical practices derived from his work were often narrow. Bain is thus considered a founder of "current-traditional rhetoric," a movement whose influence is evidenced by the popularity of textbooks composed by John Franklin Genung, David J. Hill, Adams Sherman Hill, and Barrett Wendell. (This might be called the century of the textbook, a phenomenon made possible by new technologies in printing and paper production and made profitable by the dramatic increase in student matriculation.) These texts have been faulted for an emphasis on "product" and the related neglect of "process," including a diminishment of invention. In general, these texts sadly limit the offices of rhetoric, offering rigid prescriptions for usage and correctness. By the century's end, rhetorical treatises tended to treat only the canons of invention (in truncated form), arrangement, and style, leaving delivery (and occasionally memory) to the elocution manuals.

Other rhetorics emphasized argumentation. An ecclesiastical rhetoric growing out of Whately's desire to defend religious faith in a time of growing doubt, Richard Whately's *Elements of Rhetoric* (1828), for example, treats rhetoric as a theory of argumentation, an important exception to the growing tendency to define rhetoric as the theory of communication broadly conceived. It sought to counter the period's attraction to belletristic rhetoric and elocution and developed an invention of management, for invention proper, in Whately's view, falls under logic's province. Written for the education of boys, it was intended to be a practical textbook, not a philosophical treatise. Its influence was manifested not only by its use as a text in schools and colleges but also by its frequent invocation in subsequent texts. George Pierce Baker's *Principles of Argumentation* (1895) wielded influence in America well into the next century.

The primacy of the reader/hearer, so evident in the New Rhetorics, persisted. Assumptions governing faculty psychology and associational psychology continued to underpin rhetorical principles, as, for instance, "conviction" appealed to the Understanding, while "persuasion" also entailed the Will (see, for example, Samuel P. Newman's *Practical System of Rhetoric* [1834]). David J. Hill's *Science of Rhetoric* (1877) outlines "the three steps" by which "men are moved to action" (44); Henry N. Day's *Elements of Rhetoric* (1866) discusses the ends of "Explanation, Conviction, Excitation, and Persuasion" in terms of the associations of the faculties; Bain's *English Composition and Rhetoric: A Manual* (1866) observes that "the intellectual power named Similarity, or Feeling of Agreement, is the chief inventive power of the mind. By it similitudes are brought up to the view. When we look out upon a scene of nature, we are reminded of other resembling scenes we have formerly known" (3–4). Theorists continued to believe that analyzing effective rhetorical performances revealed the mind's operations.

Some period rhetorics devoted themselves almost exclusively to the canon of delivery. Variously conceived as the art of public speaking, conversation, dramatic performance or oral reading, elocution continued to be popular, and the century saw the publication of such significant books as Gilbert Austin's *Chironomia, or a Treatise on Rhetorical Delivery* (1806) and James Rush's *Philosophy of the Human Voice* (1827). Elocutionary materials were published in America and Britain throughout the century, including such works as *The Art of Elocution as an Essential Part of Rhetoric with Instructions in Gesture and an Appendix of Oratorical, Poetical, and Dramatic Extracts* by George Vandenhoff (Third London Edition, 1862), and *New Science of Elocution: The Elements and Principles of Vocal Expression in Lessons, with Exercises and Selections Systematically Arranged for Acquiring the Art of Reading and Speaking* (1886), written by S.S. Hamill, a professor of rhetoric, English literature, and elocution at several American universities. Its 1889 edition offers four pages of testimonials praising Hamill's teaching of elocution as a theoretical science. William Mathews's *Oratory and Orators* (1878), in its twelfth edition by 1896, takes a more historical approach, offering long, detailed chapters on English, Irish, and American speakers; the eloquent speaker must possess "a strong and masculine understanding with a brilliant imagination, a nimble wit with a solid judgment; a prompt and tenacious memory with a lively and fertile fancy; an eye for the beauties of nature with a knowledge of the realities of life; a brain stored with the hived wisdom of the ages, and a heart swelling with emotion"—in addition to physically rigorous vocal training (63). Manuals often included sketches of human skeletons, explaining human anatomy with detailed accounts of the larynx, epiglottis, the diaphragm, and the posterior arytenoid cartilage. For instance, the Reverend J.J. Halcombe, rector of Balsham, Cambridge, and W.H. Stone, a "late scholar at Oxford," wrote *The Speaker at Home: Chapters on Public Speaking and Reading Aloud* based on a lecture Halcombe had delivered at the Crosby Hall Mechanics' Institute. Addressed to "the younger members of the University," especially those intending to serve in the Church of England ("Preface"), the book went into a third edition in 1874. Running to nearly five hundred pages, King's *College Lectures on Elocution,* published by Kegan Paul in its fifth edition by 1895, recorded the lectures delivered by Charles John Plumptre to the evening classes of this redbrick institution. In addition to formal instruction in schools and universities, elocutionists offered private lessons and public lectures in halls and literary societies. Such lectures were designed for girls and boys, women and men. Disturbed

by the historical neglect of delivery, some elocutionists sought to ground this canon philosophically and empirically; others served to propagate linguistic etiquette, especially for the working and aspiring middle classes and for citizens in the colonial provinces, for whom the London dialect still prevailed as the ideal. Thus treatments ranged considerably in length and in compass from scholarly treatises to the popular how-to manuals. They sometimes offered instruction for the podium, the courtroom, the pulpit, the parlor, or even the stage.

James Berlin has examined countermovements in America in the work of Emerson, Joseph Villiers Denney, Fred Newton Scott, and his student Gertrude Buck, whom Berlin believes views reality "as a linguistic construct arising out of a social act, an interaction among communicator, audience, and language" (80). Scott, who defines rhetoric as "the science and art of communication in language," went on to serve as president of the Modern Language Association and to found the National Council of Teachers of English. Under his tutelage, Buck wrote the initial drafts of *Metaphor—A Study in the Psychology of Rhetoric* (1899), a worthy study of figurative language neglected in its own time that anticipated twentieth-century interest in metaphor.

During the course of the century, rhetoric changed its disciplinary affiliation. In previous centuries the teaching of rhetoric was often associated with classical languages, logic, history, and philosophy. Although the archives of Scottish universities, for example, indicate that writing and rhetoric continued to be taught in connection with history, literature, logic and metaphysics, modern philosophy, moral philosophy, and psychology, rhetoric was indeed gaining a more distinct disciplinary character in the modern university. Departments of English were officially institutionalized in America and Great Britain, though the teaching of the English vernacular had begun much earlier in less official ways. Attention there continued to shift from production to analysis, from the spoken word to the written, from rhetoric to poetic, with the eventual diminishment of composition studies (in prestige as well as in practice) and the enthronement of what became known as "literary studies," the term *literary* eventually encompassing only poetry, fiction, drama, and select essays of the "finer" sort. In his lectures at Glasgow University in 1866–1867, John Veitch, for example, defined rhetoric as "the doctrine or theory of literary composition whether in prose or poetry. . . . Rhetoric enquires into the principle which regulates composition. Literary criticism is therefore viewed in the first instance as the science of analysis—the matter which it analyzes is literary composition" (qtd. in Horner 120–21). Its oral component survived in diminished form in English departments, where it continued to atrophy until the formation of speech departments. Occasionally it flourished in schools of oratory.

Most scholarship on educational practice concerns Scottish and North American rhetorical pedagogy at the secondary level; comparatively little is known about that in England, Ireland, and Wales, where dissenting academies, red-brick universities, and mechanics institutes, for example, had an active interest in language instruction of various kinds. Newman's "Elemental Studies" in *The Idea of a University,* for instance, suggests his desire to incorporate rhetorical studies in Ireland (and might be read alongside his educational treatises). Reconstructing the instruction done in homes, less fashionable primary and secondary schools, and public lectures—records of which are not readily available or perhaps even preserved—makes discerning rhetoric's presence more difficult.

Because rhetorical theory bears relevance beyond the classroom, scholars have begun to explore the fruitful conjuncture of rhetorical (particularly classical and belletristic) and literary theories in British and American Romantic and Victorian writers like Brockden Brown, Byron, Carlyle, Coleridge, Emerson, Fuller, Hazlitt, James, Lewes, Stevenson, Thoreau, Twain, Whitman, and Wordsworth.

Further evidence of rhetoric's belletristic turn is that the canon of style received a great deal of attention outside the classroom. Nineteenth-century theorists offered diverse theories of language, from Herbert Spencer's "Philosophy of Style" (1852), which judges a style's merit based on its readability and economy, to Walter Pater's "Style" (1889), which promotes its aesthetic dimensions. Author of "Rhetoric" (1828), "A Brief Appraisal of the Greek Literature in Its Foremost Pretentions" (1838–1839), "Style" (1840–1841), "Language" (n.d.), and "Conversation" (1847), Thomas De Quincey declared rhetoric to be dead in the modern age. De Quincey's views, including his idiosyncratic reading of ancient rhetoric, broke with the oratorical tradition and embraced the belletristic, especially the informal essay. Rhetoric, which he defined as "the art of aggrandizing and bringing out into strong relief, by means of various

and striking thoughts, some aspect of truth which of itself is supported by no spontaneous feelings, and therefore rests upon artificial aids," is decidedly not the art of public discourse.

Philosophical, political, scientific, and social thought also impinged on rhetoric. The theories of Jeremy Bentham, Thomas Huxley, William James, Charles Sanders Peirce, and John Stuart Mill entailed significant consequences for the function of language in society. In *Lincoln at Gettysburg: The Words that Remade America* (1992), Garry Wills's rereading of the Gettysburg Address in light of its cultural and rhetorical frame demonstrates how interdisciplinary rhetorical studies might enhance social and political history. Clark and Halloran study the transformation of a neoclassical oratorical culture that strove for public moral consensus in early nineteenth-century America to the rhetoric of individualism and professionalism, which understood knowledge as a morally neutral commodity. The periodical press preserves much that is of interest to rhetoric, from advertisements to essays in, for example, Emily Faithful's Victorian Press, founded to publish periodicals promoting socially and politically progressive ideas. Understanding nineteenth-century rhetoric entails not only tracing the influence of the rhetorical tradition so-called but also discerning what implicit theories of rhetoric govern rhetorical practice. The rhetorics governing the discourse of abolitionists and suffragettes like Stanton, the Grimkes, Mary Clarke, Emily Davies, Francis Power Cobbe, and Margaret Fuller have been studied. The Parliament and Congress also offered a forum for lively deliberative oratory, as scores of published collections of speeches indicate (for example, Chauncey Allen Goodrich, *Select British Eloquence* [1852]). The study of rhetorical theory and practice can indeed be a rich index to history. So too pulpit oratory, homiletics, and other aspects of the rhetoric of religion have been little studied, although works such as Newman's *Grammar of Assent* (1870) offer finely argued rhetorical theories.

Although we know a great deal about rhetoric in the nineteenth century, the area begs for attention, both along the lines already attended to and in creative new areas. Additional materials—the proceedings of literary, philosophical, and debating societies, diaries, periodical press pieces, commission reports, and speeches, as well as the more often studied college calendars and catalogs, student and teacher manuscripts, lecture notes, textbooks, prize essays, and so forth—await discovery and study, study that will revise and enrich our understanding of nineteenth-century rhetorical theory, practice, and pedagogy. In summary, although scholarship has treated rhetorical traditions in North America and Great Britain, important work remains. And to be sure, little is known about Continental European and non-Western rhetorics, another area demanding study. Although Spanish and German rhetoric is being examined (see Stewart), comparatively little is known about the rhetorics of other traditions, an absence that is lamentable both for its own sake and for the perspective it might yield on that which is currently studied. In the search for minor figures, scholars may discover new major figures as well.

Linda Ferreira-Buckley
University of Texas, Austin

Bibliography

Berlin, James A. *Writing Instruction in Nineteenth-Century American Colleges.* Carbondale: Southern Illinois UP, 1984.

Clark, Gregory, and S. Michael Halloran, eds. *Oratorical Culture in Nineteenth-Century America: Essays on the Transformation of Rhetoric.* Carbondale: Southern Illinois UP, 1993.

Guthrie, Warren. "The Development of Rhetorical Theory in America, 1635–1850." *Speech Monographs* 13 (1946): 14–22; 14 (1947): 38–54; 15 (1948): 61–71; 16 (1949): 98–113; 18 (1951): 17–30.

Halloran, S. Michael. "From Rhetoric to Composition: The Teaching of Writing in America to 1900." *A Short History of Writing Instruction.* Ed. James J. Murphy. Davis, CA: Hermagoras, 1990. 151–82.

Horner, Winifred Bryan. *Nineteenth-Century Scottish Rhetoric: The American Connection.* Carbondale: Southern Illinois UP, 1993.

Houllette, Forrest. *Nineteenth-Century Rhetoric: An Enumerative Bibliography.* New York: Garland, 1989.

Johnson, Nan. *Nineteenth-Century Rhetoric in North America.* Carbondale: Southern Illinois UP, 1991.

Kitzhaber, Albert R. *Rhetoric in American Colleges: 1850–1900.* Dallas, TX: Southern Methodist UP, 1990.

Secor, Marie J. "The Legacy of Nineteenth Century Style Theory." *Rhetoric Society Quarterly* 12 (1982): 76–94.

Stewart, Donald C. "The Nineteenth Century." *The Present State of Scholarship in Historical and Contemporary Rhetoric.* Rev. ed. Ed. Winifred Bryan Horner. Columbia: U of Missouri P, 1990.

Nomos

A term having two predominant meanings in ancient Greek rhetorical and philosophical texts: first, "custom" (the way things are always done in specific contexts); second, "law" (the way things ought to be done in specific contexts). Though distinguished here for purposes of definition, most classical Greek thinkers recognized the intimate relationship between these two senses of *nomos*. Laws, they argued, cannot be successful unless supported by customs, and customs fade unless reinforced by laws.

In its earliest (pre-Socratic/sophistic) and most common usage, *nomos* is usually translated as "custom," "norm," or "convention." In this sense, *nomos* describes activities done according to tradition or through habitual practice. The sophists viewed *nomos* as one of the keys to rhetorical success. The anonymous author of the sophistic text *Dissoi Logoi* argues, for example, that any practitioner of the art of discourse (*logôn technê*) must know all customs and conventions (*nomoi*), in addition to having skill in the technical aspects of the art (*technê*). The success of any discourse, in other words, is relative to the degree to which that discourse considers the cultural values, customs, and conventions of its audience.

In its second sense (especially in Plato and Aristotle), *nomos* is often translated as "law," "ordinance," or "statute." *Nomos* (and its plural form *nomoi*), in this more prescriptive sense, refers to laws derived through consensus within a cultural setting, as in the laws of Sparta or Athens. Later Greek texts occasionally precede *nomos* with an article, thus attributing laws to a single origin, as in "the laws of nature" or "the law of Moses."

A common debate in fifth and fourth century B.C.E. Greek rhetoric and philosophy considered whether culture (*nomos*) or nature (*phusis*) most profoundly influenced orators' skills in the pragmatic uses of language. The earliest manifestations of this debate, common in pre-Socratic and sophistic fragments, considered whether rituals and laws arise through communal consensus (via *nomos*) or are inscribed in nature (*phusis*) and therein discovered. In later Greek rhetorical texts, the *nomos/phusis* debate considered whether skill in an art is acquired through formal instruction in the rules or "laws" (*nomoi*) of the art, or whether natural ability (*phusis*) is prerequisite and paramount. Most classical Greek philosophers and rhetoricians believed that students of language need both natural talent and good instruction: Education, they argued, is nothing without talent, and talent is wasted without education.

Bruce McComiskey
Purdue University

Bibliography

Guthrie, W.K.C. *The Sophists*. New York: Cambridge UP, 1971. 55–134.
Kerferd, G.B. *The Sophistic Movement*. New York: Cambridge UP, 1981. 111–30.

Nonfiction Prose

Factual writing (biography, essay, and journalism) and creative writing (poetry and fiction). The topic broadly speaks to both genre and textual issues as well as the cultural and ideological presuppositions that shape popular perceptions of literature. In fact, briefly considering how a few of these perceptions have led to the dichotomization of fiction and nonfiction might broaden appreciation for both.

As a preliminary consideration, it is instructive to summarize what, for some, constitutes "literariness." For Northrop Frye and others, imitation, eventually producing an "autonomous verbal structure," informs true literature (Winterowd 1990:5). Conversely, the reportorial nature of nonfiction and the negative connotations associated with the prefix *non* (namely "less than," according to Chris Anderson ix) relegate factual literature to the status of subgenre.

Several historical events mark the current privileging of fiction over nonfiction. The first involves Plato's and Aristotle's respective takes on rhetorical invention. Plato posited that the search for ideas (for him synonymous with truth) was internal and, to an extent, intersubjective, while Aristotle opted for external aids to invention, exploring probability instead of certainty. Thus, as Winterowd suggests, Plato and Aristotle became the progenitors of "creative" and factual literature respectively, Plato relying largely on genius and inspiration, Aristotle on observation and discovery (1993: 12–13). During the late eighteenth and early nineteenth centuries, many other figures contributed to the widening of this chasm, among them Hugh Blair, Ralph Waldo Emerson, and Samuel Taylor Coleridge. More than Campbell and Whately (the two rhetoricians commonly associated with Blair), Blair stressed the written dimension of rhetoric over the spoken. But his focus on "belles-lettres" (fine writing) as well as the aesthetic effects of such writing was used to justify the exaltation of imaginative literature (27, 34). Similarly, Emerson's transcendentalism—somewhat reminiscent of Plato's idealism—uncovered ideas through a type of self exploration (44–47). The poet's inspiration was preferable to the essayist's discovery.

Coleridge's discussion of the primary and secondary imagination significantly projects backward to classical invention (Plato and Aristotle) on the one hand and forward to contemporary literary criticism (Northrop Frye) on the other. By "primary imagination" Coleridge meant the process of copying reality—that is, observation and reporting, whereas "secondary imagination" referred to imitating or re-creating of reality—the first favored the literal, the second the symbolic. Coleridge's own preference for the secondary imagination, as Winterowd notes, "provides the philosophical and spiritual basis for the two great splits in English department humanities," the one between "imaginative" and "nonimaginative" literature and the other between "creative" writing and composition, resulting in "the devaluation of nonfiction literature (the 'literature of fact' and hence composition" (Introduction).

Ironically, the realization of the poetic/nonpoetic division within the university is fairly recent. As late as 1895, for instance, David Mason of the University of Edinburgh included history, biography, expository and oral discourse, poetry, and fiction in his definition of literature. Further, the teaching of what is currently styled "English literature" began at Oxford and Cambridge around 1900; the University of Edinburgh and Harvard appointed their first professors of English literature in 1861 and 1869, respectively. After recounting the above facts, Winifred Bryan Horner concludes: "Thus English literature is a comparatively new member of the academic community" (2–3).

The comparatively recent privileging of "literature" within academia constitutes neither the sole nor major objection that many contemporary scholars raise against the splintering of written discourse. Indeed, many of the objections address either the arbitrariness of the literary/nonliterary distinction or seek to measure certain features of selected nonfiction works by the criteria typically applied to fiction. The introduction to Terry Eagleton's well-known yet provocative study *Literary Theory* suggests that dogmatic views of literature often result from, among other factors, semantic or historical misconceptions. Attempting to objectify a term such as *value* when applied to fiction or poetry is naturally problematic, for "*value* is a transitive term: it means whatever is valued by a certain people in specific situations according to particular criteria and in light of given purposes" (12). Eagleton quickly adds that "value judgments" are not wholly "whimsical," however, but "have their roots in deeper structures of belief which are as unshakable as the Empire State Building" (16). Hence, the concepts of "canon" or "national literature" speak to a particular historical and social "construct," not to universal standards (12).

Moreover, discourse may be "valued" for features that evidently cross the lines of genre. Eagleton accurately affirms that nonfiction works can come to be regarded as "literature," and fiction can be admired for "nonliterary" features—"archeological significance," for example (8). Winterowd and Anderson posit similar notions. Indeed, Winterowd's *Rhetoric of the "Other" Literature* not only questions accepted criteria for literariness but also claims that these criteria are mutually transferable. And Anderson insists: "The traditional hierarchies of literary study are actually porous and fluid," one illustration being the capricious barriers erected between the essay and the story (xix).

Nietzsche's take on rhetoric may also provide a framework for resolving the literature/composition conflict, since, according to Susan Miller, his "treatment defined rhetoric as writing." For Nietzsche, as depicted by Steven Whitson and John Poulakos, there were neither truths nor facts, just "aesthetically generated images";

as a result, "all discourse projects some aesthetic appearance. . . . there is no distinction between the figural and the literal" (138–39). Given the above propositions, arguments over what constitutes literature are meaningless. Nietzsche's position, to this extent, squares with poststructuralist theory—words, be they from a novel or scientific report, can neither access nor represent reality, if reality exists.

If Nietzsche and the poststructuralists have effectively erased the line between fact and fiction, the pedagogical implications are profound and numerous; all texts, fiction, nonfiction, student writing, or professional writing should not be evaluated exclusively by cultural and other ideological constraints. Then, rhetoric will replace reality, and function, form.

David Holmes
Pepperdine University

Bibliography

Anderson, Chris. "Literary Nonfiction and Composition." *Literary Nonfiction: Theory, Criticism, Pedagogy*. Ed. Chris Anderson. Carbondale: Southern Illinois UP, 1989. ix–xix.

Berlin, James. *Writing Instruction in Nineteenth Century American Colleges*. Carbondale: Southern Illinois UP, 1984.

Eagleton, Terry. *Literary Theory: An Introduction*. 12th ed. Minneapolis: U of Minnesota P, 1993.

Horner, Winifred Bryan. "Historical Introduction." *Composition and Literature*. Ed. Winifred Bryan Horner. 2nd ed. Chicago: U of Chicago P, 1987. 1–3.

Miller, Susan. *Rescuing the Subject: A Critical Introduction to Rhetoric and the Writer*. Carbondale: Southern Illinois UP, 1989.

Whitson, Steven, and John Poulakos. "Nietzsche and the Aesthetics of Rhetoric." *Quarterly Journal of Speech* 2 (1993): 136–39.

Winterowd, W. Ross. "A Teacher's Introduction to the Rhetorical Tradition in Composition." Unpublished manuscript, 1993.

———. *The Rhetoric of the "Other" Literature*. Carbondale: Southern Illinois UP, 1990.

N

Ogden, Charles Kay (1889–1957)

Born at Fleetwood, England, on June 1, 1889, entered Cambridge on a Classical scholarship in 1908, making the influence of language upon thought in ancient Greece his field of specialization. Ogden developed and applied this theme in his writing throughout his career.

In 1912 he launched the *Cambridge Magazine,* which originally emphasized philosophy, psychology, aesthetics, religion, and later language. Ogden's best-known book (with I.A. Richards), *The Meaning of Meaning,* appeared first as a series of articles in the *Cambridge Magazine* between 1921 and 1923. Ogden also founded *Psyche,* a journal of general and linguistic psychology, which he edited from 1923 to 1952.

The Meaning of Meaning remains in print today. Its objectives are to create awareness of the misleading power of words, to formalize the study of words as signs of thought, and to provide strategies for avoiding verbal confusion. At the core of the book are a model of meaning as the relationship between symbol (that is, a sign), thought, and what thought is of (referent), as well as six ordered rules, called the canons of symbolism, which reconfigure classical logic. The canons lead to a method for giving definitions of words by a limited set of relations (definition routes) in which a sought referent stands to a known referent.

The writings of Jeremy Bentham (1748–1832) inspired Ogden to develop the notion of definition routes into a method for determining a small number of words that can easily express many others. At the same time, he limited the use of the vast verb system of English to just eighteen functioning as operators (the words operating the others in a sentence) to produce the 850-word system he called Basic English.

Bentham's work not only molded Ogden's views but became the subject of his scholarship: He revised Richard Hildreth's 1864 translation of Bentham's *Traité de législation civile et pénale,* wrote the definitive version of Bentham's notion of linguistic fictions (concrete qualities attributed to a word's referent where none exists), and published many articles dealing with Bentham's ideas about education, extinct languages, grammatical symmetry, translation, metaphor, and so on.

Ogden translated fifteen books from French and German, covering fields as diverse as paroptics and politics, parapsychology and philosophy. These included the first English translation of Wittgenstein's *Tractatus Logico-Philosophicus.* He also edited hundreds of books in the International Library of Philosophy, Psychology, and Scientific Method. He died of cancer at the London Clinic, March 21, 1957.

W. Terrence Gordon
Dalhousie University

Bibliography

Gordon, W. Terrence. *C.K. Ogden: A Bio-bibliographic Study.* Metuchen, NJ: Scarecrow, 1990.

———. "The Semiotics of C.K. Ogden." *The Semiotic Web 1990.* Ed. Thomas A. Sebeok and Jean Umiker-Sebeok. Berlin: Mouton de Gruyter, 1991. 111–77.

See also BASIC ENGLISH

Olbrechts-Tyteca, Lucie (1899–1988)

Belgian researcher and writer whose scholarly collaboration with Chaïm Perelman (1912–1984) resulted in the promulgation of one of the most influential "new rhetorics" of the twentieth century. Madame Olbrechts-Tyteca read economics, sociology, and literature at the University of Brussels and received a licentiate in social sciences (approx. B.Sc.). She never pursued a doctorate and was in her fifties when she began her investigations with Perelman in the late 1940s. Both Perelman and Olbrechts-Tyteca had been greatly influenced by the Belgian sociologist Eugène Dupréel, who held the view that moral standards result from the social evaluation of particular actions and that values form the basis of social groupings.

As a philosopher trained in jurisprudence, Perelman set out to discover an underlying "logic" of value judgments, a means of rendering rational decisions in fields such as philosophy and law where modern formal logic seems virtually ineffectual. To carry out his philosophical mission, Perelman amassed a vast stockpile of actual arguments, culled from a staggering array of disparate sources, ranging from the treatises of philosophers, legal theorists, and historians to the sermons of Bossuet and La Bruyère; the economic and political writings of Bentham, Mill, and Locke; and the works of playwrights, novelists, and poets—ancient and modern. Even the topical satire and parody found in humor magazines became grist for Perelman's philosophical mill. The person who gathered and compiled these materials was Lucie Olbrechts-Tyteca.

The inquiries of Perelman and Olbrechts-Tyteca brought them into contact with the works on rhetoric and dialectic produced by the ancient Greeks and Romans. Aristotle's *Rhetoric* and *Topics* were especially helpful in elucidating the nonformal reasoning procedures whereby agreements or "adherences" are reached on all sorts of questions. In deference to the influence of the classical sources on their thought, the Belgian authors decided to call their theory of argumentation the "new rhetoric."

Although Perelman is usually regarded as the intellectual progenitor of the new rhetoric, Olbrechts-Tyteca coauthored several articles and two books with him. A collection of theoretical probings and partial studies appeared in their book *Rhétorique et philosophie: Pour une théorie de l'argumentation en philosophie* (1952), and the culmination of their joint endeavors bore the title *La nouvelle rhétorique: Traité de l'argumentation* (1958). This latter work was translated into English as *The New Rhetoric: A Treatise on Argumentation* (1969). It contains an exposition of the philosophical assumptions behind the New Rhetoric, as well

as an exhaustive compendium of the techniques used in informal reasoning and persuasion.

Olbrechts-Tyteca's personal account of the "encounter" she and Perelman had with rhetoric can be found in her essay "Rencontre avec la rhétorique" (1963). And several years after their working relationship ended, Olbrechts-Tyteca drew together many of the materials that had not been utilized in *The New Rhetoric* and published *Le comique du discours* (1974). In that book she maintains that all the elements of rhetoric can be perceived as comic objects through distortion or abnormal usage. Her sociological and literary interests are conjoined with philosophical ideas derived from Perelman in order to arrive at a rhetorical theory of humor.

Ray D. Dearin
Iowa State University

Bibliography
Olbrechts-Tyteca, L. *Le comique du discours.* Bruxelles: Éditions de l'Université de Bruxelles, 1974.
———. "Rencontre avec la rhétorique." *Logique et analyse* 6 (1963): 3–18.
Perelman, Ch., and L. Olbrechts-Tyteca. *The New Rhetoric: A Treatise on Argumentation.* Trans. John Wilkinson and Purcell Weaver. Notre Dame, IN: U of Notre Dame P, 1969.
———. *La nouvelle rhétorique: Traité de l'argumentation.* 2 vols. Paris: Presses Universitaires de France, 1958.
———. *Rhétorique et philosophie: Pour une théorie de l'argumentation en philosophie.* Paris: Presses Universitaires de France, 1952.

See also PERELMAN, CHAÏM

Oliver, Robert T. (b. 1909)
Innovative scholar-adventurer whose academic interests span four broad themes: basic communication skills, the history of public speaking in Britain and America, Asian rhetoric, and rhetoric and culture. His investigations have ranged from the power of symbolism to the psychology of persuasion, from conversation to the role communication plays in a healthy personality. He was the first American speech scholar to publish essays on the speech of international relations and on Asian rhetoric.

In the past half-century, Oliver has produced over fifty books and literally hundreds of articles. For over twenty years he headed the department of speech communication at Penn State. For eighteen years he served as counselor, publicist, and speech writer for the Republic of South Korea. He was elected president of both his regional and national professional associations. He is a perceptive rhetorical critic and an experienced journal editor. In short, Robert Oliver is a person of boundless energy, insatiable curiosity, and remarkable perseverance.

Oliver writes in a fresh, lively style. His forte is synthesis and structure: He possesses the ability to absorb large bodies of material and to select from that data the vivid detail that graphically tells a story. His expertise lies in breadth of conception rather than originality, macroscopic overviews rather than microscopic insights. For decades he has been recognized as a scholar willing to tackle challenging assignments no one else would dare undertake.

One key to understanding Oliver is to understand his practical involvement in the speech of international relations. His is not the view of the armchair theorist, isolated from the scene of diplomatic action. Rather, he is one who has himself struggled for years to establish cross-cultural understanding and has closely observed diplomatic negotiation at the UN and elsewhere.

Nations do not always tell the truth to one another, Oliver notes; sometimes they rationalize, presenting socially acceptable reasons to mask the real reasons for their behavior. As early as 1942, in the first college textbook ever published on the psychology of persuasive speech, Oliver argued that there are three avenues of motivation available to the advocate: rational appeal, emotional appeal, and "a process of pseudo-reason . . . termed rationalization." While many of his fellow academics scoffed at the inclusion of rationalization in this trilogy, Oliver himself had no doubt about its efficacy; he remembred all too well Neville Chamberlain's "peace in our time."

A quite different phase of Oliver's rhetorical travels involves his investigation of Asian rhetoric. As one reviewer wrote of his *Communication and Culture in Ancient India and China,* what the book clearly demonstrates is "that rhetoric in one culture is different than rhetoric in other cultures." Oliver's study of Asian rhetorics, the reviewer continued, should "help Western rhetoric shake off its provinciality." No mean achievement that.

A stimulating speaker as well as a prolific publisher, Robert Oliver reminds one of a dauntless traveler ever interested in exploring new ideas and new cultures.

Goodwin Berquist
Dartmouth College

Bibliography

Oliver, Robert T. *Communication and Culture in Ancient India and China.* Syracuse, NY: Syracuse UP, 1971.

———. *Culture and Communication: The Problem of Penetrating National and Cultural Boundaries.* Springfield, IL: Thomas, 1962.

———. *A History of Public Speaking in America.* Boston: Allyn, 1965.

———. *The Influence of Rhetoric in the Shaping of Great Britain: From the Roman Invasion to the Early Nineteenth Century.* Newark: U of Delaware P, 1986.

———. *Leadership in Asia: Persuasive Communication in the Making of Nations, 1850–1950.* Newark: U of Delaware P, 1989.

———. *The Psychology of Persuasive Speech.* Rev. ed. New York: McKay, 1957.

———. *Public Speaking in the Reshaping of Great Britain.* Newark: U of Delaware P, 1987.

———. *Syngman Rhee and American Involvement in Korea, 1942–1960: A Personal Narrative.* Seoul, Korea: Panmun, 1978.

———, et al. *Communicative Speaking and Listening.* 4th ed. New York: Holt, 1968.

———, and D.A. Barbara. *The Healthy Mind in Communion and Communication.* Springfield, IL: Thomas, 1962.

Ong, Walter J. (b. 1912)

Rhetorical theorist and psychocultural critic. Educated at Rockhurst (Kansas) High School and Rockhurst College, he entered the Society of Jesus in 1935 at St. Stanislaus Seminary, and then continued his advanced education: licentiate in philosophy (1940), M.A. in English (1941), and licentiate in theology (1948), all from Saint Louis University. After teaching and research assignments (two Guggenheim fellowships), he received his Ph.D. in English from Harvard in 1954. His tendency to ground his textual studies in social practices was reflected in the work of his Ph.D. adviser, Perry Miller, and his speculative élan rivaled that of his M.A.

adviser, Marshall McLuhan. His simultaneous focus on personal development and the evolution of the universe is reflected in the work of Teilhard de Chardin, with whom he sojourned while on a Guggenheim in France.

Known as a scholar of the Renaissance, president of the Modern Language Association and daring literary critic, regular apologist for American Catholicism, and author of the bestselling scholarly work *Orality and Literacy: The Technologizing of the Word* (1982), Father Ong has had enormous range in his intellectual influences thanks to a six-hundred-item-plus bibliography. In the field of rhetorical studies, Ong is known as a proponent of the New Rhetoric—a student of relationships between and among dominant modes or media of communication, cultural structures, and both individual and collective consciousness. He has been an important reinterpreter of the classical, medieval-Renaissance, modern, and contemporary ages.

His primary weapons are the so-called orality-literacy theorems, which have taken shape thanks to work principally by Ong, Eric Havelock, and Marshall McLuhan. As these scholars studied points of nexus between oral and literate cultures, they discovered that (1) shifts in dominant forms of media are accompanied by shifts in sociopolitical structures and self—and collective awareness; (2) we can define discrete civilizations in the movement from oral to chirographic (written) to print to electronic cultures; (3) the old culture always leaves traces ("residues") in the new culture; and (4) contemporary culture is usefully seen as a period of "secondary orality," a literate culture where characteristics of oral society are reinscribed upon our lives, albeit in the form of electronic rather than face-to-face interactions.

Ong's rhetorical and literacy theories have influenced the teaching of composition. In the late seventies, he counseled that the teaching of writing must be done within an understanding of primary and secondary orality. He claims that a residual primary orality, literacy, and secondary orality interact "vigorously with one another in confusing complex patterns" ("Literacy and Orality in Our Times" 7). Teachers must be sensitive to such interaction while working in a world structured by secondary orality.

Orality and Literacy (1982) offers the most coherent and condensed review of Ong's principal ideas. *Ramus, Method, and the Decay of Dialogue* (1958) contains his foundational ideas, as he examines the impact of print on

intellectual thought and activity. *The Barbarian Within* (1962), *In the Human Grain* (1967), *The Presence of the Word* (1967), and *Interfaces of the Word* (1977) are collections of essays detailing his thought. *Fighting for Life: Contest, Sexuality, and Consciousness* (1981) is a bold historical analysis grounding gendered discourse in biological diversity. *Hopkins, the Self, and God* (1986) is a venture into modernist and postmodernist criticism.

Bruce E. Gronbeck
University of Iowa
Roberta Binkley
University of Arizona

Bibliography

Foley, J.M., ed. "A Festschrift for Walter J. Ong." *Oral Tradition* 2 (1987): 7–382.

Gronbeck, Bruce E., Thomas J. Farrell, and Paul A. Soukup, eds. *Media, Consciousness, and Culture: Explorations in Walter Ong's Thought*. Newbury Park, CA: Sage, 1991.

Lumpp, R.E. "Selected Bibliography of Ong's Writings." *Oral Tradition* 2 (1987): 19–30.

Olson, D.R., ed. *Literacy and Orality*. New York: Cambridge UP, 1991.

Ong, Walter J., S.J. "Literacy and Orality in Our Times." *ADE Bulletin* 58 (1978): 1–7.

———. *Orality and Literacy: The Technologizing of the Word*. London: Methuen, 1982.

Orality

In the "Great Leap" or "Great Divide" models of literacy articulated by Eric Havelock, Jack Goody, Walter Ong, and David Olson, a theoretical construct in binary opposition with *literacy*; as used by Ong, *orality* is often associated with Havelock's *preliteracy* and Olson's *utterance*. Great Leap theories of literacy hold that the alphabetic literacy of Western languages is a causal factor in the development of abstract, logical thinking. Cognition, language use, consciousness, and culture in oral societies are typified as different from, usually opposite, those in literate societies. While the Havelock-Ong depiction of literacy and orality has been exploited by many historians of rhetoric, it has proved more controversial in composition.

Though a concern with literacy and orality runs though the body of Ong's work in rhetoric and literature, the definitive account of orality occurs in his 1982 *Orality and Literacy*. Here, defining *primary oral cultures* as "cultures with no knowledge at all of writing" (1), Ong says that the memory of primary orality requires that valuable information be set in a narrative form with either formulaic or poetic surface features. Like primary orality, *secondary orality*—the orality of the electronic media—is communal, participatory, and formulaic, but unlike primary orality, it is orality based on the written word (136). The informality and spontaneity of secondary orality are self-consciously planned, as are the texts on which it is based (136–37). *Residual orality* is Ong's term to describe pockets of orality that exist "in dominantly high literacy societies, such as urban black subcultures or Chicano subcultures in the United States" (160).

In their strong versions, Great Leap or Great Divide theories assert that simply reading and writing with a Greek-derived alphabet actually causes fundamental advances—great developmental leaps—in human cognition, and that these cognitive leaps then bring about alterations in not only the consciousness of individuals but also in cultures. These models typically present orality and literacy as either a dichotomy or a single continuum contrasting the modes of speech, composition, behavior, and thought of orality—that is, of both oral cultures and oral persons—with those of literacy—that is, of both literate cultures and literate persons. The prototype of an oral culture is held to be Havelock's description of orality in ancient Greece, though in the scholarship, orality is often equated with informal conversation (Elbow). The prototype of literacy is advanced academic literacy in modern industrialized Western countries—that is, the ability to read critically advanced, extended texts and to produce theoretical expository prose, abilities putatively leading to "higher" states of consciousness.

Characteristics of Orality

For Ong, because orality perceives holistically, both its thought and language are said to be additive, aggregative, redundant, conservative, empathetic, participatory, and situational (37–50). Because literacy sees parts and relationships, both its thought and language are described as subordinate, analytic, exploratory, objective, distanced, and abstract (37–50). Oral language therefore relies upon juxtaposition and coordination—that is, parataxis—while literacy employs subordination—that is, hypotaxis (37–38).

According to Ong, oral cultures and oral persons differ from literate cultures and persons in their use of surface language, in attitude and behavior, in elements of the narrative, in views of history, in concepts of self, and in epistemology. In addition to its use of paratactic structures, oral language is distinguished from literate language by surface features that generally serve mnemonic functions—rhythm, alliteration and assonance, repetition, and balanced patterns like parallelism and antithesis (34). Oral cultures also rely on forms that have clearly marked surface structures—proverbs, riddles, and epithets. Oral narrative is also highly redundant (24, 38).

According to Ong, oral cultures see language as "a mode of action," as "power," as "magical" (32). For him, oral cultures are "agonistically programmed" (44), engaged in "triumphalism" (49). This mindset shows up, Ong says, in verbal contests in contemporary cultures that have a high degree of "oral residue"—for example, in the "dozens" in the black communities in the U.S. (44). In Ong's depiction, oral cultures celebrate physical behavior, and their narratives, he says, are marked by the "portrayal of gross physical violence" (44). The characters of oral narratives are "heavy" and stereotyped—Ong uses Nestor and Brer Rabbit to exemplify—not subtle and psychologically complex like those of modern, literate fiction (150).

Oral cultures begin their narratives "in medias res" because, according to Ong, without writing they have "absolutely no way to organize them in strict chronological order" (143). Goody and Watt argue that because narratives in oral cultures serve to justify present social structures, oral societies employ structural amnesia in order to change the story to support present conditions. Ong believes that because oral cultures lack "a sense of difference between past and future" (30), in orality there is no real history.

According to Great Leap models, people in oral cultures cannot separate themselves from the group and therefore do not regard themselves as individuals, but rather define themselves according to the roles and expectations of the society of which they are a part. The oral personality is "more communal and externalized, and less introspective" than the literate personality, Ong writes (69). In oral cultures, according to Ong, "knowing means achieving empathetic, close, communal identification with the known, 'getting with it'" (45–46); participation, not analysis, is the basis of knowledge in oral cultures, Ong says. Oral cultures, he argues, have "a highly traditionalist or conservative set of mind that with good reason inhibits intellectual experimentation" (41).

Some compositionists argue that the oral side of the Great Leap dichotomy or continuum is useful in describing the thought patterns and the language, particularly the written language, of freshman English students and minorities in American colleges and universities (Farrell; Lazerre). According to Ong, "Our deeper understanding of the psychodynamics of orality in relation to the psychodynamics of writing is improving the teaching of writing skills, particularly in cultures today moving rapidly from virtually total orality into literacy as many African cultures are doing, and in residually oral subcultures in dominantly high literacy societies such as urban black subcultures or Chicano subcultures in the United States" (160). But others in composition argue that such claims and the proposals built on them are pedagogically and logically untenable and can be, like Farrell's "IQ and Standard English" article, both psychologically and educationally damaging (Greenberg et al.; Rose; Walters).

The Theory
According to Havelock, in preliterate Greece the knowledge and values necessary for the survival of the culture were transmitted through poetry, particularly Homer's. The content was tradition, the language formulaic. Using oral formulas, the poet, or bard, constructed the poem itself in a public oral performance in which both bard and audience entered into an almost trancelike, or "mimetic," state (Havelock 176). This mimetic relationship prevented the bard from introducing new ideas and the audience from questioning or analyzing. When about the time of Plato literacy became internalized, mental "energy" previously needed for the memorization of the content of the poetry was released for other sorts of cognitive activity. With this new energy, literate persons began to compare texts and note inconsistencies, synthesize conflicting opinions, and question the authority of the oral tradition. As Havelock explains it, Plato's dialectic, a product of these literate modes of thought, was a way of breaking the mimetic spell in which learning had hitherto occurred and thus a method of forcing the audience to question and analyze received information (208–9). Goody and Watt assert

that Aristotle and the next generation of Greek thinkers used these new analytical, logical modes of thought and the concomitant inquiring attitude to develop systematized abstract thinking; they cite as evidence the syllogism, the categories, and the taxonomies in various fields of study.

After the fall of Rome, these literate patterns of thinking were maintained by those possessing what Ong calls "Learned Latin" (112–15). Used almost exclusively by men for academic debate, Learned Latin augmented objective, abstract thought and moved knowledge further into the realm of the theoretical and away from daily life. Next, the invention of the printing press spread both these skills and the consequences of literacy. The technology of print made literacy accessible to more people, releasing more mental energy for abstract thinking in many new fields. Western culture underwent a recapitulation and an extension of the Great Leap. The climax, according to Olson, was the seventeenth-century British essay, which was used by thinkers like John Locke to explore abstract problems and to create new theoretical knowledge (262–69).

Criticisms
The Havelock-Ong Great Leap theory of literacy, along with its orality construct, has been disputed by researchers in a number of fields. Halverson argues, for example, that Havelock's reading of Homer, the basis of the Great Leap depiction of primary oral cultures, is essentially inaccurate. Street refutes Goody's argument by pointing to flaws in both research and logic. Heath's ethnographic work in the Piedmont Carolinas shows that oral language in an African-American community that could be classified as "residually oral" certainly can have far more complex syntax than literate language with the same message, speaker, and audience. Indeed, anthropologists and linguists working in a number of cultural contexts present empirical evidence that calls into question several key assertions of the Great Leap theory, especially those pertaining to orality. Some of this research is briefly summarized in Daniell's *PRE/TEXT* article; papers by Akinnaso, Chafe, Scribner and Cole, Heath, Lakoff, and Tannen, among others, can be found in edited volumes by Frawley; Tannen; and Kintgen, Kroll, and Rose. Most scholars of language use—whether they study other cultures, ethnic subcultures in the U.S., or middle-class, literate Americans—believe that the written and spoken discourse of

actual persons is too complicated, too complex, too rich in meaning and in rhetoric for an oral-literate continuum or dichotomy to have much valid explanatory power.

Other critics charge the Great Leap theory with ethnocentrism. Walters argues that the Great Leap's claim that alphabetic literacy causes its users to think more logically than people in cultures without alphabetic literacy or without any writing system is "an idea that many Westerners find appealing, no doubt because it 'explains' what they perceive to be the superiority of Western culture" (175). Giving substance to this charge is the fact that Ong does not count writing systems such as "cuneiform, Chinese characters, Mayan script, and the Japanese syllabary, and so forth" (3) as real literacy; others assert that such systems are unable to bestow the cognitive benefits of reading and writing (see Farrell's reply in Greenberg et al. 474–76). Ong believes that his term *oral* is "less invidious and more positive" than terms formerly applied to traditional societies, such as *savage, primitive,* and *inferior* (174), despite deconstructionists' assertions that because in a binary opposition one side is always valorized and the other degraded, *literacy* becomes the privileged term and *orality* comes to be associated with the pejoratives.

Other critiques argue that claims of "residual oral culture" are an inadequate explanation for the school failure of inner-city students, since this account omits social, political, and economic conditions (Ogbu; Greenberg et al.). Both compositionists and linguists point out that assertions about the paratactic, oral language of African-Americans ignores linguistic facts (Walters, esp. note 6, 184–85; Hartwell in Greenberg et al.). Marxist critics see changes in education in general and in writing instruction in particular in the nineteenth century not as part of the shift from orality to literacy, as Ong claims, but as a part of the shift from an agricultural economy to industrial capitalism (Berlin; Douglas). Many feminists point to what they see as the essentialism of Ong's association of orality with women: his identification of orality with "mother tongues" (113–15) and breast feeding (*Interfaces* 22–27) and his depiction of orality as focusing on emotion, immediacy, and practicality (but cf. Swearingen).

Some cultural critics point out that many characteristics in Ong's portrayal of orality have been typically listed in academic research as aspects of the language, thought, and behavior

of relatively powerless groups—women, blacks, other ethnic minorities, and the poor (Ehrenreich; Tronto). Others argue that like other developmental theories, the Great Leap model puts its researchers' own values, experiences, and abilities at the top of the hierarchy. Still others criticize the Great Leap theory for its assumption of an isomorphic relationship between thought and language and for its application of historical, cultural, and literary theories to actual individuals and groups.

Beth Daniell
Clemson University

Bibliography

Berlin, James. *Writing Instruction in Nineteenth-Century American Colleges.* Carbondale: Southern Illinois UP, 1984.

Daniell, Beth. "Against the Great Leap Theory of Literacy." *PRE/TEXT* 7 (1986): 181–93.

Douglas, Wallace. "Rhetoric for the Meritocracy." *English in America: A Radical View of the Profession.* Ed. Richard Ohmann. New York: Oxford UP, 1976. 97–132.

Ehrenreich, Barbara. *Fear of Falling: The Inner Life of the Middle Class.* New York: Pantheon, 1989.

Elbow, Peter. "The Shifting Relationships between Speech and Writing." *College Composition and Communication* 36 (1985): 283–303.

Farrell, Thomas J. "IQ and Standard English." *College Composition and Communication* 34 (1983): 470–84.

Frawley, William, ed. *Linguistics and Literacy.* New York: Plenum, 1982.

Goody, Jack, and Ian Watt. "The Consequences of Literacy." *Comparative Studies in Society and History* 5 (1963): 304–45.

Greenberg, Karen, Patrick Hartwell, Margaret Himley, and R.E. Stratton. "Responses to Thomas J. Farrell, 'IQ and Standard English' (with a reply by Thomas J. Farrell)." *College Composition and Communication* 35 (1984): 455–78.

Halverson, John. "Havelock on Greek Orality and Literacy." *Journal of the History of Ideas* 53 (1992): 148–63.

Havelock, Eric. *Preface to Plato.* Cambridge, MA: Harvard UP, 1963.

Heath, Shirley Brice. "Protean Shapes: Ever-Shifting Oral and Literate Traditions." *Spoken and Written Language: Exploring Orality and Literacy*. Ed. Deborah Tannen. Norwood, NJ: Ablex, 1982. 91–117.

Kintgen, Eugene R., Barry Kroll, and Mike Rose, eds. *Perspectives on Literacy*. Carbondale: Southern Illinois UP, 1988.

Lazerre, Donald. "Orality, Literacy, and Standard English." *Journal of Basic Writing* 10 (1991): 87–98.

Ogbu, John U. "Literacy and Schooling in Subordinate Cultures: The Case of Black Americans." *Literacy in Historical Perspectives*. Ed. Daniel Resnick. Washington, D.C.: Library of Congress, 1983. 129–53.

Olson, David R. "From Utterance to Text: The Bias of Language in Speech and Writing." *Harvard Educational Review* 47 (1977): 257–81.

Ong, Walter J., Jr., S.J. *Interfaces of the Word*. Ithaca, NY: Cornell UP, 1977.

———. *Orality and Literacy: The Technologizing of the Word*. London: Methuen, 1982.

Rose, Mike. "Narrowing the Mind and Page: Remedial Writers and Cognitive Reductionism." *College Composition and Communication* 39 (1988): 267–302.

Street, Brian. *Literacy in Theory and Practice*. Cambridge: Cambridge UP, 1984.

Swearingen, C. Jan. "Discourse, Difference, and Gender: Walter J. Ong's Contributions to Feminist Language Studies." *Media, Consciousness, and Culture*. Ed. Bruce E. Gronbeck, Thomas J. Farrell, and Paul A. Soukup. Newbury Park, CA: Sage, 1991. 210–22.

Tannen, Deborah, ed. *Spoken and Written Language: Exploring Orality and Literacy*. Norwood, NJ: Ablex, 1982.

Tronto, Joan C. "Beyond Gender Difference to a Theory of Care." *Signs* 12 (1987): 644–63.

Walters, Keith. "Language, Logic, and Literacy." *The Right to Literacy*. Ed. Andrea A. Lunsford, Helene Moglen, and James Slevin. New York: Modern Language Assn., 1990. 173–88.

See also HAVELOCK, ERIC; LITERACY; ONG, WALTER J.

Oratory

The crafting of persuasive appeals that finds its conditions of possibility in and has the capacity to exceed the context of its production. Sophistic oratory can be read as both a symptom of and a challenge to the socioeconomic, political, and cultural climate of ancient Greece. Emerging out of a society destabilized by the precarious movement from fragmentation and tyrannical rule toward unification and democracy, sophistic oratory was a force of transformation within the polis. Anticipating the Aristotelian division of rhetoric into forensic, deliberative, and epideictic types, sophistic oratory played an active role in the reclamation of property lost in tyrannical rule, the instruction of proper citizenry and just governance, and the inculcation of values through the praise and blame of prominent figures.

The theoretical underpinnings of sophistic oratory, like its practice, responded to and were shaped by the context of their production. Deriving largely from the Gorgian and Protagorean perspectivist critiques of epistemology (critiques initiated at least in part by the need to consolidate and justify the collective identity of particular city-states), sophistic oratory operated from the premise that all claims to knowledge were equally true but not equally valuable. In the Greek judicial system, for instance, the sophists played key roles as orator-hirelings for the propertied elite. The emphasis on value rather than knowledge in sophistic oratory exacerbated the division of subjects into upper and lower classes in ways that enhanced the power of the elite; thus speech in the courts served largely as an instrument of domination. Sophistic oratory operated unabashedly in the service of *doxa* rather than *epistêmê*, belief and opinion rather than knowledge and truth. On this view all claims to knowledge and truth were submitted to the law of value and subject to the play of political economy.

Responding to the decline of the Greek city-state and the predominance of sophistic perspectivalism, Plato devised a theory of governance and a corresponding conception of oratory that sought to ground the polis in the Absolute rather than the transient. Platonic dialectic, facilitated and conveyed by oratory, was designed to reconstitute Greek politics and culture. In an attempt to fulfill the Parmenidean project, Plato sought to disclose the eternal that gives shape to the temporal, the permanent that unifies the multiplicity and flux of lived experience. Often drawing attention to the link between oratory and capital, a link that led him to call the fee-taking sophists prostitutes, Plato advanced his own redeemed theory of oratory in the *Phaedrus*. Here the rift between rhetoric and philosophy is sutured by understanding proper oratory as a means of facilitating the process and, ultimately, transporting the Truth of dialectic.

For Isocrates, Plato's near-contemporary, Panhellenism, or the dream of Greek unification, served as an ideal by which particular values were to be questioned, critiqued, and refashioned. Hence, the function of oratory—be it forensic, deliberative, or epideictic—was to conduct "social surgery" on the body politic, to mend the wounds of a society fraught with internal conflict by extending the influence of Athens. The fragmentation of Greek culture at large was to be repaired, then, by orations whose overwhelming purpose was to promote solidarity by way of the inculcation of Greek values and the construction of an "other" or an enemy against which those values could be measured, indeed valorized. In contrast to sophistic oratory, then, the animating impulse of Isocratean rhetoric is not to advance the needs, desires, or demands of specific communities but, instead, to advocate the interests that bind them together. Taking history and cultural memory as the primary resource for rhetorical invention as well as the warrant for political action, Isocratean oratory seeks to transport the past into the present, thereby articulating a telos that circumscribes action. Hence, Isocratean oratory becomes a mechanism of political change and social control.

What distinguishes the treatment of oratory in Aristotle's *Art of Rhetoric* from that of his predecessors is not merely its comprehensive and systematic character but also its overt refusal to deliberately craft a theory of the art of civic discourse that supports and advances a particular politics. Rather than conceiving oratory as a practice that serves a particular political agenda, Aristotle considers oratory in terms of its pure or generic possibilities. The purpose of the *Rhetoric* appears to have been to lay out a set of general principles of persuasion that would be applicable to any particular situation. But if, on the one hand, the *Rhetoric*'s declared project was to divide oratory into types, temporalities, and *topoi* such that the techniques or strategies might have efficacy in unlimited settings or contexts, on the other hand, the presup-

positions that support and serve as its resource hint at Aristotle's affinity with a form of governance that operates in concert with man's fundamental desire for happiness and the noble life. Indeed, for Aristotle the determining motive of human life and political existence is man's desire for happiness; it is precisely this desire that is the object of persuasive discourse. Hence, whether proofs appeal logically or emotively, syllogistically or enthymematically, at their best they attempt to generate conditions of persuadability that lead to the noble life and, hence, a polis whose governing principle is the common good.

Against the Aristotelian penchant for a generic or universally applicable theory of civic discourse, Ciceronian oratory, in both its theory and its practice, exhibits a renewed commitment to and involvement with the immediate and pressing demands of real-lived political life. Indeed, emerging out of and directing itself to a sociohistorical moment wherein the traditions of republican Rome are virtually in ruins, Cicero's great treatise on rhetoric, *De oratore*, advances a portrait of the active and compelling statesman whose role is to rescue Rome from demagoguery and chaos. Uniting wisdom and eloquence, the arts of thinking and of speaking, the orator integrated theoretical and practical knowledge in an effort to shape the political life of the community.

The movement of the locus of rhetoric from the sociopolitical sphere and into the church gives medieval oratory its distinctive character. Taking as its primary goal the advancement of Christian doctrine, the theorization and practice of oratory issues primarily from the church fathers and preachers rather than from the statesmen and civil servants. To be sure, Augustine's synthesis of Aristotle's theory of words as sensible signs with a Christian notion of the sacrality that provides them with meaning and import in the world, advances a conception of oratory that, in unifying the speculative and dogmatic aspects of rhetoric, functions both as the extrapolation and the transmission of doctrine.

Public sermons that sought to disseminate to a broader public a code of meritorious conduct constituted medieval subjects as individual recipients of the Christian message and as personal agents of virtuous deeds. Although patterned after the informal commentaries on Scripture that typified worship services before Constantine nationalized Christianity, these sermons were now delivered in church sanctuaries rather than in private households. Toward the end of the Middle Ages, a virtual explosion of new preaching manuals, drawing heavily upon the pragmatic and technical approach to persuasion found in Cicero's *De inventione* and in the anonymous *Rhetorica ad Herennium,* instructed preachers in the use of rhetorical devices and forms appropriate to the invention of thematic sermons that encouraged the practice of virtuous conduct.

New forms of preaching in the Reformation emphasized classical principles of intelligibility, clarity, and figuration that constituted the text of the vernacular Bible as the primary locus of authority, thereby encouraging a private encounter with the Scripture as the basis for religious experience, moral decision, and public life for the common man. Because of this shift in theological focus from the practice of virtue to the experience of faith, many preachers of the Reformation relied heavily on rhetorical devices that produced an emotional response on the part of an audience. Reformation sermonizing challenged the ecclesiastical structures of the Roman Catholic Church by privileging, as Lutheran preaching did, the biblical text over the Christian church as the final authority for truth. The authority of the biblical text became the basis for popular preaching that went much further than Luther and other magisterial reformers like Zwingli and Calvin in challenging the status quo. Preachers like Muntzer and Hut, two radical reformers who abandoned the pulpit to preach to embittered peasants and disillusioned commoners, appealed to the authority of textual interpretation over and against the authority of the institutional interpretation of the church. Significantly, the emergence of printing at this time assisted in extending the influence of Reformation oratory beyond the walls of the sanctuary and the confines of local gatherings. Indeed, it is perhaps the reproduction of Reformation oratory in the new mass media of print that enabled the sermon to reach larger and more diverse audiences than had been possible ever before.

The orators of the American and French revolutions used the logic of Enlightenment philosophy to oppose contemporary political arrangements and to cast themselves as historical agents of the common people. Resting their cases for revolution on first principles apparent in natural law, these revolutionary orators constituted public speech as the means to extract liberty and freedom from the bonds of monarchy and aristocracy. For example, Colonial orators such as Samuel Adams, Patrick Henry, and James Otis took on the dramatis personae of soldiers in a battle of ideas with tyrants and oppressors; in courtrooms, public assemblies, and even in churches, these orators opposed personal freedom to British monarchy, an antagonism best exemplified in Patrick Henry's memorable appeal to the Virginia legislature for "liberty or death." In France as in America, the revolution expanded the public sphere, creating audiences for impassioned political oratory in the Republican clubs, the courtrooms, and in the newly formed National Assembly.

Theories of oratory produced in England at this time evidence an Aristotelian revival, albeit with a caveat that is both an effect of and response to the tempestuous character of the age: For George Campbell, Hugh Blair, and Richard Whately, logic and argumentation are taken to be the primary concerns of rhetoric; however, the limits of reason are brought into the calculation. Thus significant attention is paid to the passions that are understood to transport audiences from conviction to a commitment to action. Additionally, George Campbell's *Philosophy of Rhetoric* challenges the presumed universal applicability of the topics and commonplaces laid out in Aristotle's *Rhetoric* by boldly asserting that they simply do not engage modern man.

Between the 1820s and 1860s, the period commonly called the Golden Age of Oratory in America, civic discourse was considered integral to conducting the affairs of the new nation, individual speakers were taken to be folk heroes, and audiences expected to be overcome by the power of eloquence. Shuttling between its two opposing aspects, the playful and the rational, oratory was understood as a craft that on the one hand entertained audiences and, on the other, settled political disputes. Inextricably linked with eloquence and at the same time founded upon the principles of good reason, oratory—whether practiced in congress or on the stump—was perceived to be America's alternative to violence in the struggle over the relationship between the powers and limits of individual states and the federal government. More particularly, in the years immediately preceding the Civil War, multifaceted debates over the rights and responsibilities of individual states were distilled into a bipolar struggle over the emancipation of the slaves.

Abraham Lincoln's "Gettysburg Address" is one celebrated instance of this general trend in American oratorical practice. Similarly, in the post–Civil War period, the dualistic logic that underwrites abolitionist rhetoric is appropriated by the suffragist movement. In both cases oratory shows itself to be a force for social change: the speeches of Frederick Douglass, Sojourner Truth, William Lloyd Garrison, Wendell Phillips, Elizabeth Cady Stanton and others, made visible oratory's capacity to help reshape the sociopolitical landscape of a democratic state in crisis.

By the turn of the century, the American public began again, by and large, to be skeptical of orators and the power of their words to shape the course of history. The general perception—not surprisingly, considering the realignment of social relations effected by the transition to industrial capitalism—was that political decisions were made by business tycoons and party bosses and, hence, that public deliberation, debate, and oratory were practiced only to provide the semblance of democratic decision-making. In short, the once-celebrated statesman was looked upon as the mere pawn of the industrial elite and party machines whose platforms and programs were manufactured with an eye to the accumulation of wealth rather than the preservation and accretion of rights. However, rapid changes in the social, economic, and technical domains during the early decades of the twentieth century fostered powerful upheavals in the practice and theory of oratory. The threat of fascism, the hardships of yet another world war, and the devastating realities of a thoroughly depressed economy transformed the public's earlier cynicism toward the power of rhetoric into a widespread and desperate desire for a new kind of public discourse, one that could nourish the human spirit and inspire collective action by speaking to two sensibilities—realist and romantic—at once. It was FDR's fireside chats that both substantively and stylistically forged an allegiance between the two and thus captured the imagination and earned the trust of Americans.

From the early 1940s to the mid 1960s, rhetorical theories emerged to make sense out of the dynamic changes taking place during the postwar era. New forms of mass culture, consumer society, technology and social unrest (for example, the Civil Rights and Women's Movements) obliged a reinterrogation of received conceptions of the constituent elements of the rhetorical situation. As was the tendency across the human sciences, rhetorical theory was transformed by a hermeneutics of suspicion that demanded a movement beyond the discipline and toward the works of Marx, Nietzsche, and Freud. While Kenneth Burke's "Freudoid" theory of identification and his incorporation of Marx into a reconstructed history of rhetoric in *A Rhetoric of Motives* signified an attempt to uncover the (political) unconscious of the time, Richard Weaver's rehabilitation of Platonic idealism for rhetoric, as well as Chaïm Perelman's theory of the universal audience, signified an attempt to disclose the conscious, albeit sometimes implicit, rationality of modern man to himself.

Transformations in the theory of rhetoric at the time were paralleled by dynamic changes in oratorical practice. Despite similarities between movement goals and media strategies, the discourse of the Women's Movement was substantively and stylistically unlike that of the Civil Rights Movement, its unique character the manifestation of a decidedly different understanding of the role of leadership, constitution of audience, and purpose of public discourse. Unlike the Civil Rights Movement (in which there was some controversy about who should lead but relatively little difference of opinion about whether there should be leadership at all), the Women's Movement was at least conceptually committed to egalitarianism. Hence, since leaders imply followers, a hierarchically organized and orchestrated revolution would violently contradict the overarching goal of the movement: equality among all persons. Additionally, whereas the Civil Rights Movement presumed an already existing black community (in churches, neighborhoods, and schools), the Women's Movement recognized the need to articulate an audience, one whose internal differences (race, class, ethnicity, sexual orientation, geography, religion) could be sublated into a common cause and collective identity. Finally, rather than rely primarily on speeches by great orators in churches and other public spaces in order to move people to act (as was the case for the Civil Rights Movement), the Women's Movement developed a "bottom up" approach to persuasion that anchored itself firmly within "personal" experience.

On the whole, modernist rhetoric and rhetorical theory sought to pose a resolution to the social contradictions and inequities that riddled collective life during the 1940s, 1950s, and early 1960s by looking to an underlying structure or deep logic out of which a coherent liberatory politics might ensue. It was, however, the very persistence of a radical disjunction between the emancipatory promise of Enlightenment rationality and its material instantiation out of which postmodernist rhetorical theories and rhetorics emerged. Lyotard, Habermas, and Derrida, for instance, revisit Auschwitz so as to determine the absolute limit of rational disputation (Lyotard), to make visible the complicity between pure reason and apocalyptic projections (Derrida), and to retrieve rationality from the abuses of *Ursprungsphilosophie* (Habermas). Similarly, the work of the New French Feminists targets Enlightenment rationality as a crucial site of contestation, seeking to supplement a revised conception of reason with a thoroughly libidinalized theory of desire.

No doubt, the critique of Enlightenment rationality was to a great extent spurred on by the radically altered configuration of culture. As if in response to a shift from a generalized sense of alienation to a pervasive feeling of fragmentation, postmodern oratorical practices overwhelmingly exploit fragmentation as the rhetorical means through which decidedly heterogeneous publics can be moved to act in concert, albeit for quite disparate reasons.

The fragmentation that is "the structure of feeling" (Williams) as well as the "cultural dominant" (Jameson) of postmodernity has altered both rhetorical theory and criticism by, amongst other things, decentering the object inquiry. Not only has it become necessary to pay attention to discursive practices that are not verbal but visual (a theoretical-practical shift in the field inaugurated by the Kennedy and Nixon presidential debates); more important, at a time when politics has become the pulpit of industry, the appeal of the fragmentary—understood as a spectacle or simulacra—must be accounted for by refusing to read discursive practices as simply representational or constitutive.

Barbara A. Biesecker and James P. McDaniel
University of Iowa
Susan Biesecker and Gerald Biesecker-Mast
University of Pittsburgh

Bibliography

Barilli, Renato. *Rhetoric*. Trans. Giuliana Menozzi. Minneapolis: U of Minnesota P, 1989.

Baskerville, Barnet. *The People's Voice: The Orator in American Society*. Lexington: U of Kentucky P, 1979.

Campbell, Karlyn Khors. *Man Cannot Speak for Her: A Critical Study of Early Feminist Rhetoric*. New York: Greenwood, 1989.

Jamieson, Kathleen Hall. *Eloquence in an Electronic Age: The Transformation of Political Speech Making*. New York: Oxford UP, 1988.

Kennedy, George. *Classical Rhetoric and Its Christian and Secular Tradition from Ancient to Modern Times*. Chapel Hill: U of North Carolina P, 1980.

McGee, Michael Calvin. "Text, Context, and the Fragmentation of Contemporary Culture." *Western Journal of Speech Communication* 54 (1990): 274–89.

Murphy, James J. *Rhetoric in the Middle Ages: A History of Rhetorical Theory from St. Augustine to the Renaissance*. Berkeley: U of California P, 1971.

Vickers, Brian. *In Defence of Rhetoric*. Oxford: Clarendon, 1988.

The Other

The name recently given to the internal (sexual) differential that is the condition of possibility for rhetorical acts. The question of the relation of self and other is the inaugurating question of Western philosophy and rhetoric. From Parmenides' inquiry into the problematics of the one and the many regarding the unity of Being, through G.W.F. Hegel's formulation of self-consciousness and identity, and to the litany of thinkers working within and against the dialectical tradition, the history of the thinking on the relation of self and other registers the movement from being (ontology) through knowing (epistemology), through doing (ethics) and, finally, to acting (rhetoric).

Traditionally, rhetorical theorists have understood the problematic of self and other as that which merely structures the relationship between speaker and audience. However, Jacques Derrida, arguably the most influential post-Hegelian philosopher, obliges the recognition that alterity resides within rather than simply obtains between those two constituent elements of the rhetorical situation. Taking up the question of acting and rhetoric but working outside the Hegelian morphology, his work invites rhetorical theorists and critics to think the relationship between self and other not in terms of a relationship between interiority and exteriority, but rather as the play of an otherness that inhabits the self.

Of course, from within the framework of the Hegelian morphology, self-consciousness or subjectivity requires a relation to an other. In order for the self to attain self-consciousness, however, the other must be appropriated in a moment of negation, the radical otherness of the other recoded into the idiom of the self. Such recoding is, in Emmanuel Levinas's view, an act of violence. In the moment of sublation (*Aufhebung*), he writes, "the difference [between self and other] is not a difference" (36).

Unlike Hegel and even Levinas, Derrida maintains the integrity of otherness by insisting on its irreducibility to the self, identity, or self-same. Taking as his point of departure Saussure's notion that the identity of any sign is constituted solely through the spatio-temporal relationship between all signs in the system, Derrida goes on to suggest that the sign "is constituted with reference to the trace in it of the other elements of the sequence or system" (26). Similarly, he argues that the subject, like the sign, is operated, indeed is produced by, "the trace of perennial alterity" (xxxix), thus is marked by an internal difference that prevents it from being present in and of itself. Like speech and writing, then, "the subject is constituted only in being divided from itself in becoming space, in temporizing, in deferral" (29). According to Derrida the self is, in short, a subject always already inhabited by the other, always already other to itself.

Derrida's most recent work on the other has radical implications for rhetorical theory and criticism. Most notably, it obliges a rethinking of invention. Typically, rhetorical theorists and critics moving out of Aristotle conceive invention as a process in which an individual speaker generates a message with an eye to an audience and/or an exigence that is exterior to the self. Derrida, however, will find the resources of rhetoric not in the dialectical engagement between a self and an otherness exterior to it but in the play of otherness resident to the self. "The other," Derrida writes, "is what is never inventable and will never have waited for your invention. The call of the other is a call to come, and that happens only in multiple voices" (62).

Derrida's work on otherness and multiplicity has been formative for a host of feminist theorists attempting to displace the dialectical morphology that even Simone de Beauvoir's theorization of woman-as-other was written by. Beginning in the simple observation that throughout history "woman" has served as the name for the other that has made it possible for man to constitute a self, writers such as Hélène Cixous, Luce Irigaray, Julia Kristeva, and Michele LeDoeuff have challenged the more or less implicit suggestion that the relation of self and other can be thought outside the thematic of sexual difference. Indeed, for these thinkers sexual difference is the irreducible differential or excess that disallows the possibility of a dialectical appropriation of other to self in the moment of sublation. Unlike the Hegel of *The Phenomenology of the Spirit* (109) who takes desire as the primordial lack out of which human action as negation ensues (Kojeve 135), these French feminists posit an understanding of feminine desire as a plentitude that persistently refuses any and all gestures of appropriation. Understood as multiplicitous, feminine desire cannot be contained within or controlled by a phallocentric economy that finds it impossible to decipher difference as anything but Other to the Same. Feminine desire or *jouissance* is the general economy of subjectivity as such and, hence, the resource for (symbolic) action.

Recent writings on the other call rhetorical theorists and critics to rethink the Aristotelian formulation of rhetoric as the "counterpart" (*antistrophos*) to dialectic. For if the other is the name to be given to the internal (sexual) differential that guarantees the noncoincidence of the "I" to itself and thus is the condition of possibility for rhetorical acts that are irruptive rather than predictable, then rhetoric cannot be understood as a practice regulated by the law of restricted dialectics; instead, rhetoric must be understood as a practice that always already promises to exceed it.

Barbara A. Biesecker and James P. McDaniel
University of Iowa

Bibliography

Cixous, Hélène, and Catherine Clement. *The Newly Born Woman*. Trans. Betsy Wing. Minneapolis: U of Minnesota P, 1991.

Derrida, Jacques. *Of Grammatology*. Trans. Gayatri Chakravorty Spivak. Baltimore: Johns Hopkins UP, 1976.

———. *Positions*. Trans. Alan Bass. Chicago: U of Chicago P, 1981.

———. "Psyche: Inventions of the Other." *Reading Paul de Man Reading*. Ed. Lindsay Waters and Wlad Godzich. Minneapolis: U of Minnesota P, 1989. 25–65.

Hegel, G.W.F. *Hegel's Phenomenology of the Spirit*. Trans. A.V. Miller. New York: Oxford UP, 1977.

Irigaray, Luce. *The Irigaray Reader*. Ed. Margaret Whitford. Cambridge, MA: Blackwell, 1991.

Kojeve, Alexandre. *Introduction to the Reading of Hegel: Lectures on the Phenomenology of the Spirit*. Trans. James H. Nichols, Jr. Ed. Allan Bloom. Ithaca, NY: Cornell UP, 1980.

Kristeva, Julia. *The Kristeva Reader*. Ed. Toril Moi. New York: Columbia UP, 1986.

LeDoeuff, Michele. *Hipparchia's Choice: An Essay Concerning Women, Philosophy, Etcetera*. Trans. Trista Selous. Cambridge, MA: Blackwell, 1991.

Levinas, Emmanuel. *Totality and Infinity*. Trans. Alphonso Lingis. Pittsburgh, PA: Duquesne UP, 1969.

Spivak, Gayatri Chakravorty. "Translator's Preface." *Of Grammatology*. Trans. Gayatri Chakravorty Spivak. Baltimore: Johns Hopkins UP, 1976.

P

Paradigm Shift

Scholarly coinage that has had enduring popularity. In 1962 in his landmark book *The Structure of Scientific Revolutions*, historian Thomas Kuhn coined the phrase to characterize the Copernican revolution, the change in physical astronomy from a Ptolemaic, earth-centered picture of the universe to a Copernican sun-centered view. Kuhn viewed the Ptolemaic picture of the universe as "incommensurate" with Copernican, so much so that he described the Renaissance astronomers who became Copernicans as converts. In later work, Kuhn was forced to clarify his view on incommensurability. He never meant that Copernican astronomers could not understand the work of their Ptolemaic forebears. He wanted only to emphasize that their intellectual views were so fundamentally different that in some sense they lived in different worlds.

Under the pressure of increasing criticism, Kuhn finally declared himself dissatisfied with the term *paradigm* and suggested the phrase *disciplinary matrix* as a substitute. He felt that *disciplinary matrix* captured two essential meanings of the original term *paradigm:* a set of agreed-upon problems and solutions that constituted scientific training and a set of preferred values and methods that constituted everyday scientific practice, "normal science." A paradigm provided the warrants for and the methods of "normal science," a phrase that characterized what most scientists did most of the time. Occasionally, however, paradigms or disciplinary matrices altered dramatically. These were periods of revolutionary change.

Clearly, Kuhn opined, one could not ground a move from one paradigm to another—for example, from the Ptolemaic astronomy to the Copernican astronomy—on the presuppositions of an *existing* disciplinary matrix. In this sense, and in this sense alone, the justification for change had to be *extra*-scientific: It is for this reason, and this reason only, that Kuhn likened the change to a religious conversion. For him this characterization did not make the move from one paradigm to another irrational or even nonrational. Although converts could not have scientific reasons for moving from one paradigm to another, they could have good reasons.

On this reading of the history of science, its revolutionary practice was open to rhetorical analysis. After Kuhn, it became intellectually respectable to say that paradigm shifts in science—the Darwinian revolution, the Einsteinian revolution—were mediated by rhetorical means. Although this legitimation still holds, it should be emphasized that it does not hold for so-called normal science. Moreover, Kuhn cannot be employed to authorize the rhetorical analysis of science on the premise that he endorses a rhetorical perspective. He does not. His view of science is firmly grounded in the analytical tradition. He is a philosophical realist who believes that one paradigm does not simply replace but also builds on its predecessor. From Kuhn's notion of paradigm shift, therefore, we cannot draw the conclusion that scientific revolutions undermine the idea of scientific progress.

The popularity of the phrase *paradigm shift* has not abated. In the humanities especially, it has been used as an honorific to describe changes of intellectual direction writers regard with special favor. Thus we have had paradigm shifts in composition studies, in rhetorical studies, and in literary studies. It remains an open question whether the analogy holds between these changes and scientific revolutions.

Alan G. Gross
University of Minnesota

Bibliography

Fuller, Steve. "Being There with Thomas Kuhn: A Parable for Modern Times." *History and Theory* 31 (1992): 241–75.

Hoyningen-Huene, Paul. *Reconstructing Scientific Knowledge: Thomas Kuhn's Philosophy of Science.* Trans. Alexander T. Levine. Chicago: U of Chicago P, 1993.

Kuhn, Thomas S. *The Structure of Scientific Revolutions.* 2nd ed. Chicago: U of Chicago P, 1970.

Lakatos, Imre, and Alan Musgrove, eds. *Criticism and the Growth of Knowledge.* Cambridge: Cambridge UP, 1970.

See also KUHN, THOMAS

Parenthesis

Insertion of a word, phrase, or sentence into an otherwise complete sentence. Paul writes, "But wherein any man is bold—I am speaking foolishly—I also am bold. . . . Are they ministers of Christ? I—to speak as a fool—am more" (Second Letter to the Corinthians). Through using parenthesis, an author's or narrator's voice can be inserted into a sentence to express emotion, editorialize, or add information. Horace charged his sentence with emotion when he wrote, "In Rome you long for the country; in the country—oh inconstant!—you raise the distant city to the stars." Carlyle was editorializing in declaring, "Poetry and Religion (and it is really worth knowing) are a product of the smaller intestines." The author of Acts (1:15) was interposing information when he explained, "And in those days Peter stood up in the midst of the disciples and said (the number of names together were about a hundred and twenty), "'Men and brethren, this Scripture must needs have been fulfilled.'" Parentheses are frequently used in interior monologues, where they are often unmarked, and in the digressions-within-digressions that distinguish comic works of fiction, such as Lawrence Sterne's *Tristram Shandy.*

Arthur Quinn and Lyon Rathbun
University of California, Berkeley

Partitio

The section of a classically arranged oration concerned with identifying and enumerating the component parts of the oration. Some writing textbooks suggest that when confronted with a multifaceted issue or focus the writer might do well to construct an introductory section that lists or classifies the component parts of the discussion. This section has its roots in the classical arrangement component known as *partitio*, which is also termed *divisio* or *propositio*. The *Rhetorica ad Herennium* says that the purpose of this section is to "make clear what matters are agreed upon and what contested, and announce what points we intend to take up" (1.3.4). The section thus comes to function similarly to an outline embedded within the discourse, a framework used to focus the audience's collective consciousness on not only the discourse at hand but also elements that helped shape the focus of the discourse.

Richard Lanham offers a closer look at two types of *partitio.* The first, *diaeresis*, sought to "divide a subject into subheadings; amplifying a general fact or idea by giving all of its details; division of a subject into adjuncts, cause into effects, antecedent into consequents" (55). The second type, *anacephalaeosis*, offers a "summary or recapitulation intended to refresh the hearer's memory" (55). In both cases the division assists in cuing the audience's memory or sensibility. *Diaeresis* serves more to inform or enlighten the audience; *anacephalaeosis* seems to rely more upon what the audience may already know about a given situation or topic.

Joseph Colavito
Northwestern State University

Bibliography

Lanham, Richard. *A Handlist of Rhetorical Terms.* 2nd ed. Berkeley: U of California P, 1991.

Rhetorica ad Herennium. Trans. Harry Caplan. Cambridge, MA: Harvard UP, 1954.

See also ARRANGEMENT

Pathos

An argumentative/persuasive appeal to the emotions of the audience. According to Aristotle's *Rhetoric*, there are three types of appeals that the rhetor uses to persuade. Ethos, or ethical appeal, is rooted in the effectiveness of the character of the speaker. Logos, the logical appeal, persuades by means of demonstrating the existence of real or apparent truths. Pathos, or emotional appeal, the third form of appeal, is based upon the rhetor's ability to arouse certain types of emotions in the audience. These emotions can assist in eliciting persuasion because, according to Aristotle in the *Rhetoric,* "when they [the audience] are brought by the speech into a state of emotion . . . [they] give very different decisions under the sway of pain or joy, and liking or hatred" (1.2).

Pathos, as an appeal, tends to have a negative cast attached to it because of its rooting in the focus of its attentions. Audiences may be disinclined to admit that decisions and attitudes may be swayed by manipulation of their emotions, and rhetors, likewise, may not be inclined to reveal that they are appealing to an audience's emotions, as that form of appeal is often associated with underhanded techniques. This negative cast is worthy of acknowledgement, but eschewing emotional appeal as a form of persuasion is to ignore an argumentative technique given much attention by rhetorical theorists throughout the ages. In the *Rhetoric,* Aristotle defines the emotions as "those states which are attended by pain and pleasure, and which, as they change, make a difference in our judgments" (2.1). Aristotle then presents an exhaustive discussion of sixteen "emotions common to public life in the Athenian polis" (Hauser 117). The emotions that Aristotle enumerates and discusses are anger, mildness, love (or friendship), enmity (or hatred), fear, confidence, shame, shamelessness, benevolence (favor or gratitude), pity, indignation, envy, emulation, and contempt (2.2–11). In addition to defining the various emotions and applying them to specific audiences and rhetorical purposes, Aristotle also suggests that the rhetor consider such additional factors as the mental state of the audience induced by each emotion, the focus of the emotion as the audience projects the emotion (for example, "with whom they are wont to be angry"), and what external factors serve to elicit the various emotions (*Rhetoric* 2.1) when appealing via pathos.

In Roman times, the concept of pathos and its accompanying psychological dimensions was no less important. Cicero in *De inventione* takes care to include discussions of placing emotional appeals within sections of orations. In the *exordium,* for example, emotional appeals can function to "bring the mind of the auditor into a proper condition to receive the rest of the speech . . . [and is] accomplished if he [the auditor] becomes well-disposed, attentive, and receptive" (I.xv.20). Cicero discusses the concepts of good will, hatred, and contempt (I.xvi.22) and their effects upon audiences. The emotional appeal, according to Cicero, is of significant influence in the construction of a speech's peroration, which he suggests contains three parts: "the summing-up, the *indignatio,* or exciting of indignation or ill-will against the opponent, and the *conquestio,* or the arousing of pity or sympathy" (I.lii.98). Similarly to Aristotle, Cicero offers extensive discussions of individual strategies designed to elicit these emotions and thus improve an oration. He later expands on these ideas in *De oratore,* noting that "in order to explore the feelings of the tribunal, I engage in a consideration careful, that I scent out with all possible keenness their thoughts, judgments, anticipations and wishes" (II.xliv.186). Once again, the importance of analyzing the audience and its susceptibility to emotional appeals plays a significant role in the theory.

Theories concerning emotional appeals also appear in the thoughts and writings of later theorists. Augustine, in *On Christian Doctrine,* tells us that audiences are "delighted if you speak sweetly . . . , fears what you threaten, hates what you condemn, embraces what you commend" (qtd. in Johnson 157). Eighteenth-century theorists George Campbell and Hugh Blair both offer extensive discussions of pathos and its link to audience analysis. Blair, in *Lectures on Rhetoric and Belles Lettres,* suggests that the orator "paint the object of that passion which we wish to raise, in the most natural and striking manner; to describe it with such circumstances as are likely to awaken it in the minds of others" (qtd. in Johnson 158). On into the twentieth century, emotional appeals become significant contributors to Kenneth Burke's dual concepts of identification and consubstantiality. In order to elicit the sharing of affinities among rhetor, audience, and subject so crucial to achieving identification, the speaker must ally the consciousness of the audience with the subject and the speaker. The speaker must use "identification of interests to establish rapport between himself and his audience," interests that are rooted in subjective responses to issues, people, and presentational styles (Burke 46).

These subjective responses endow emotional appeal with a less than positive cast, particularly since cultures tend to value an objective, rational approach to thinking and conduct over an emotional, subjective posture. This suspicion concerning pathos contributes to a general suspicion toward rhetoric in general, since an uninformed or incomplete view of rhetoric all too often fastens upon the power of words to inflame and in so doing blind an audience. Emotional appeals, admittedly, possess this capability, but as Gerard Hauser suggests, "A responsible rhetoric does not separate our thoughts from our feelings; it unites them by addressing the whole person in terms of that person's experiences and the judgments they support" (119). The place of pathos in the rhetorical tradition is a significant one; emotional appeals constitute a crucial intersection among audience, rhetor, and subject matter, so the connection between audience analysis and rhetorical purpose comes to be an important component of the construction of emotional appeals. As the traditions have suggested, emotional appeals are crucial for providing a vital dimension of rhetorical practice, a dimension full of life and conviction.

Joseph Colavito
Northwestern State University

Bibliography

Aristotle. *The Rhetoric of Aristotle*. Ed. and trans. Lane Cooper. Englewood Cliffs, NJ: Prentice, 1960.

Burke, Kenneth. *A Rhetoric of Motives*. Berkeley: U of California P, 1968.

Cicero. *De Inventione, De Optimo Genere Oratorum,* and *Topica*. Trans. H.M. Hubbell. Loeb Classical Library. Cambridge, MA: Harvard UP, 1942.

Corbett, Edward P.J. *Classical Rhetoric for the Modern Student*. 3rd ed. New York: Oxford, 1990.

Hauser, Gerard A. *Introduction to Rhetorical Theory*. Prospect Heights, IL: Waveland, 1991.

Johnson, Nan. "Reader-Response and the *Pathos* Principle." *Rhetoric Review* 6 (1988): 152–66.

Peacham, Henry (1546–1634)

Ordained in 1574 and subsequently four years as curate of North Mimms; thereafter rector of Leverton in Lincolnshire until his death. Henry Peacham the Elder is best known in the rhetorical tradition for *The Garden of Eloquence* published in 1577 while he was curate at North Mimms. This work is a compendium of figurative language reflecting Peacham's desire to provide a vernacular version of the Latin rhetorical manual and to promote the humanist goal of combining wisdom and eloquence.

When of late I had consydered the needeful assistaunce that the one of these do requyre of the other, that wisedome doe requyre the lighte of Eloquence, and Eloquence the fertillity of Wysedome, and saw many good bookes of Philosophy and preceptes of wysedome, set forth in english, and very few of Eloquence: I was of a sodaine mooued to take this little Garden in hande, and to set therein such Fyguratyue Flowers, both of Grammar and Rhetorick, as doe yeelde the sweete sauour of Eloquence, & present to the eyes the goodly and bewtiful coulors of Eloquution. (sig. A2v–A3r)

Peacham mentions the influence of other authors, notably Cicero, Quintilian, Erasmus, Melancthon, and his countryman Thomas Wilson. He also seems to have been influenced by Johannes Susenbrotus's *Epitome troporum ac schematum,* published in 1540 and widely reprinted in England between 1562 and 1635, and by an earlier English treatise, Richard Sherry's *Treatise of Schemes and Tropes,* 1550.

Peacham divides his treatment of figurative language into tropes and schemes, the difference being that "in the *Trope* there is a chaunge of signifycation, but not in the *Scheme*" (sig. E1v). Tropes are further divided into tropes of words and sentences, and schemes are also divided into grammatical and rhetorical schemes. Grammatical schemes deviate from customs of writing and speaking and are subdivided into orthographical and syntactical schemes. Rhetorical schemes add distinction and "doe take away the wearinesse of our common and dayly speach, and doe fashion a pleasant, sharpe, evident and gallant kinde of speaking, giving unto matters great strength, perspecuitie and grace" (sig. H4v). Rhetorical schemes apply to words, sentences, and amplification.

Although *The Garden of Eloquence* is usually read as a stylistic rhetoric, its treatment of rhetorical schemes blurs the distinction between invention and style, between things and words (*res et verba*). For example, Peacham maintains that "amplifycation is eyther taken of thinges themselves, or else of words" (sig. N3r). Among the amplificatory schemes are *syllogismis* (sig. P2v–P3r), *comparatio* (sig. Q3v–Q4v), *divisio* (sig. R4v–S1r), *paradigma* (sig. U2v–U3r), and *enthimema* (sig. U3v–U4r), all having inventional potential of their own.

In all there are 191 examples of figurative language defined and exemplified from classical literature, contrived examples, and the Bible. Some figures are further subdivided, and there is some overlapping of grammatical and rhetorical schemes. *The Garden of Eloquence*, however, remains a valuable introduction to the Renaissance penchant for the plasticity of language and consequently of thought. The 1593 edition was revised under Ramistic influence and is very different from the first edition. There is an illustrated modern edition of *The Garden of Eloquence* by Willard Espy that incorporates, but also supersedes, Peacham in scope and playfulness.

Grant M. Boswell
Brigham Young University

Bibliography

Espy, Willard R. *The Garden of Eloquence: A Rhetorical Bestiary*. New York: Harper, 1983.

Howell, Wilbur Samuel. *Logic and Rhetoric in England, 1500–1700*. Princeton: Princeton UP, 1956.

Peacham, Henry. *The Garden of Eloquence*. London, 1577. Ed. R.C. Alston. English Linguistics 1500–1800: A Collection of Facsimile Reprints, No. 267. Menston, England: Scholar, 1971.

Sonnino, Lee Ann. *A Handbook to Sixteenth-Century Rhetoric*. London: Routledge, 1968.

Vickers, Brian. "Renaissance Reintegration." *In Defence of Rhetoric*. Oxford: Clarendon, 1988.

See also ELOQUENCE; FIGURATIVE LANGUAGE; FIGURES OF SPEECH; WILSON, THOMAS

Pedagogy

Central to the study of rhetoric, especially at the secondary and postsecondary level; concerned with teaching both the production and analysis of discourse. Tradition has it that rhetoric arose in ancient Greece when the tyrants were overthrown; in the new democracies, citizens needed formal instruction in rhetoric to represent themselves in legal and political assemblies. Many famous rhetoricians were teachers, including Gorgias, Protagoras, Plato, Isocrates, Aristotle, and Quintilian; many famous rhetorical treatises were teaching manuals, including Cicero's *De inventione* and the *Rhetorica ad Herennium*. Both the Middle Ages and the Renaissance retained a curriculum whose most prominent feature was the trivium—grammar, logic, and rhetoric—the study of which led to the Bachelor of Arts; study in rhetoric and grammar would prepare the serious student for later work in dialectic. Throughout this early history, set exercises were common; often rhetorics were prescriptive, laying out rules and providing illustrative examples. Methods included Isocrates' use of models that students imitated and its codification in the popular collections of Aphthonius in antiquity and in the Renaissance; in Plato's socratic method of careful questions and answers; and in the crystallization of Plato's and Aristotle's influence in the scholastic method, a dialectic contrasting arguments for and against a position.

Rhetorical pedagogy was also central to the college curricula of the seventeenth and eighteenth centuries and continued to figure prominently through much of the nineteenth. The influential "New Rhetoric" originated at the University of Edinburgh, where Hugh Blair lectured for twenty-four years; his *Lectures on Rhetoric and Belles Lettres* became one of the most influential textbooks of all times. During the late nineteenth century, however, pedagogy in rhetoric seemed to drift from its rhetorical roots and was reduced at times to formalist, grammatical, and stylistic concerns. Rhetoric was overshadowed by philological and literary studies in newly established departments of English, where "rhetorical" pedagogy was centered primarily in written composition and speech-making.

Although the National Council of Teachers of English (founded in 1911) took seriously the teaching of writing, rhetoric pedagogy fell primarily to the stewardship of newly formed departments of speech communication and their professional organization, the National Association for Academic Teachers of Public Speaking (1914). Instruction in written composition, usually following Scottish rhetorician Alexander Bain's forms (or modes) of discourse—narration, description, exposition, and argumentation—and Barrett Wendell's work on the paragraph, was still entrusted to departments of English, whose instructors remained untrained in the rhetorical tradition. Intermittently, rhetorical concerns of social communication worked themselves into the classroom, especially at the postsecondary level, but rhetoric largely lost its connection with pedagogy in English departments until, in the second half of the twentieth century, scholars like Corbett, Kinneavy, and Weaver reintroduced the rhetorical tradition into composition pedagogy—so much so that today the phrase *rhetoric and composition* is sometimes taken as synonymous with composition. In composition studies, three of the classical canons—invention, arrangement, and style—have received particular attention. But with the maturation of the field, rhetorical pedagogy has become less exclusively centered in classical rhetoric and has benefited from work in such fields as linguistics, psychology, and literary and critical theory. During the last third of the twentieth century, American scholars and teachers concerned with composition have returned to rhetoric, and the body of scholarship has increased exponentially, as the number of books, journals, and articles indicate. Pedagogy in rhetoric and writing has often been centered in the rhetorical situation and has been process-oriented. Outside North America, instruction in rhetorical pedagogy, when offered at all, tends to be offered at the earlier grade levels and to be in oral rather than written composition.

Theorists like Kenneth Burke and Thomas Kuhn have shown how all language and knowledge is shaped, and a growing number of disciplines have become concerned with understanding their rhetorical nature. Sometimes the concern is limited to teaching language conventions, sometimes to the way meaning is shaped by assumptions and language. Most recently, the emergent concern with the social construction of meaning and with cultural studies necessitates that rhetoric play a central role in all pedagogy. In short, rhetoric takes manifold forms in present-day pedagogy under diverse but overlapping rubrics.

Linda Ferreira-Buckley
University of Texas

Bibliography

Bullock, John, and John Trimbur. *The Politics of Writing Instruction*. Vol. 2. Portsmouth, NH: Heinemann, Boynton/Cook, 1990.

Connors, Robert J., Lisa S. Ede, and Andrea A. Lunsford, eds. *Essays on Classical Rhetoric and Modern Discourse*. Carbondale: Southern Illinois UP, 1984.

Corbett, Edward P.J. *Classical Rhetoric for the Modern Student*. 3rd ed. New York: Oxford UP, 1990.

Freedman, Aviva, and Ian Pringle, eds. *Reinventing the Rhetorical Tradition*. Conway, AR: L and S, for the Canadian Council of Teachers of English, 1980. Urbana, IL: National Council of Teachers of English, 1980.

Kennedy, George A. *Classical Rhetoric and Its Christian and Secular Tradition from Ancient to Modern Times*. Chapel Hill: U of North Carolina P, 1980.

Knoblauch, C.H., and Lil Brannon. *Rhetorical Traditions and the Teaching of Writing*. Portsmouth, NH: Heinemann, Boynton/Cook, 1990.

Marrou, H.I. *A History of Education in Antiquity*. Trans. George Lamb. New York: Sheed, 1956.

Murphy, James J., ed. *The Rhetorical Tradition and Modern Writing*. New York: Modern Language Assn., 1984.

———. *A Short History of Writing Instruction from Ancient Greece to Twentieth-Century America*. Davis, CA: Hermagoras, 1990.

Peirce, Charles Sanders (1839–1914)

American philosopher, logician, mathematician; originator of pragmatism, semiotics. Perhaps America's most original thinker, C.S. Peirce has influenced such theorists as Noam Chomsky, Roman Jakobson, Karl Popper, Charles Morris, and John Dewey. He has been called this country's greatest logician and philosopher, yet even today his work remains relatively obscure; it is only recently that his ideas have come into anything near the mainstream of American thought. The paradox of Peirce's importance in philosophy and his outsider status in philosophical thought resulted from a combination of personal idiosyncrasies and the state of American science at the end of the nineteenth century, but the paradox remains crucial to understanding the unique character of his ideas about method, knowledge, and the role of community in the enterprise of scientific inquiry.

Peirce was born in Cambridge, Massachusetts, the second son of Benjamin Peirce and Sarah Mills Peirce. His father was the foremost American mathematician of the time, an inspiring teacher at Harvard who exerted great influence on Charles in his later scientific and philosophical work. The Peirce house was a gathering place for many of the Cambridge intellectual elite, including Louis Agassiz, Margaret Fuller, Asa Gray, Daniel Webster, and Ralph Waldo Emerson. The work of scientists like his father and Agassiz had begun to call into question philosophical assumptions about the nature of belief and the division between faith and science that Darwin's theories were to bring into sharp relief in the next decade. Peirce was deeply affected by the implications of that division, and for the next fifty years his work was dominated by a double inquiry into science and into the role of belief in systems of thought.

Peirce was an erratic student at Harvard, graduating in the bottom half of his class in 1859 but completing a master's degree in chemistry two years later. He often blamed his failures as a student on his left-handedness and on the system of learning by rote. Physical and psychological conditions contributed as well to his difficulties as a student and to later problems in his personal and professional life. Like his father, Peirce was a lifelong sufferer from facial neuralgia, a painful, debilitating ailment that led him to extreme outbursts of temper and that forced him to seek relief in drugs.

His first marriage, to Melusina Fay in 1862, ended when she left him in 1876. In 1883 Peirce divorced her to marry Juliette Pourtalai, and, although this marriage was happy, it offended the Victorian sensibilities of Peirce's academic colleagues and contributed to his problems of finding employment in a university.

Beginning in 1861 and continuing off and on for the next thirty years, Peirce worked for the Geodetic Coast Survey. In *Photometric Researches* (1878), the only book Peirce published during his lifetime, he gave credit to the Survey for supporting his work. His only teaching career was in the Johns Hopkins University, where he was a lecturer in logic from 1879 until he was dismissed in 1884. By 1883 Peirce had acquired an international reputation in astronomy, in geodesy, and in logic, but the academic establishment in the United States did not appreciate the implications of his work until well after the turn of the century and rejected him for his eccentric and unconventional character. From 1890 until his death, Peirce made a meager living writing reviews and articles for such journals as *The Nation* and *Popular Science Monthly*—and by giving occasional lectures in Cambridge, often as a result of the influence of his lifelong friend William James. When he died in 1914 in Milford, Pennsylvania, at his beloved home, Arisbe, he was living almost solely on the proceeds from a fund collected for him by James. He died in deep poverty and neglect, still transforming the doctrines he had begun to explore in his earliest work.

Although Peirce was influenced by many thinkers including Aristotle and Friedrich von Schiller, as well as Duns Scotus and the Scottish common-sense philosophers, his principal influence remained Kant. From the age of seventeen on, Peirce worked to transform Kant's categories, to connect them to emerging conceptions of scientific method. His contributions to scientific and philosophical thought are so varied that it is impossible to discuss them in any detail. His first publication was in chemistry; his second in philology, on the pronunciation of Shakespearean English. His life was devoted to science and philosophy, and to the application of scientific philosophy to mathematics, physics, chemistry, geology, meteorology, and psychology. He was a founder of symbolic logic; he conducted important research in gravity and wrote definitions for the *Century Dictionary* for the terms used in logic, metaphysics, geodetics, meteorology, astronomy, and weights and measures. This breadth of scientific inquiry was not Peirce's attempt to become a nineteenth-century Renaissance man, but to demonstrate what he believed to be true about the nature of knowledge, that underlying all systems is method. "The specialists are doing useful work, taken together," he wrote. "But the higher places in science in the coming years are for those who succeed in adapting the method of one science to the investigation of another" (7.78). The enormous range of scientific inquiry led him to similar conclusions about the way all systems work and the way knowledge progresses. Systems of thought and scientific inquiry he believed connected by principles of logic, which he defined as a method of methods, that allows for an architechtonic growth of ideas.

This devotion to logic—Peirce was the first American to list his profession as logician—and a persistence "like a wasp in a bottle" in investigating a method of methods is evident in his lifelong attention to the discovery of a system of principles that could explain behavior and the growth of knowledge. These principles, which he labeled *first, second,* and *third,* he set forth in a series of Lowell Institute Lectures at Harvard on the logic of science and in the 1867 essay that came from those lectures, "A New List of Categories." Peirce redefined Kantian categories of feeling, knowing and willing to consciousness, consciousness of resistance, and synthetic consciousness. *First* became the quality itself, action unreflected, chance; *second* relation, resistance, continuity; *third* expressed mediation, synthesis, law.

The dynamic of the triadicity of ideas penetrates all of Peirce's thought, as he explores how third principles operate in evolution, psychology, cosmology, logic. Peirce's triadic framework demonstrates how propositions or systems function in life as beliefs and behaviors. The triadicity of ideas allows for the growth of knowledge, in a gradual but inevitable movement from mere action or chance, what he called *tychism,* through tendency toward habit and reaction, *synechism,* toward belief or *agapism.* Peirce believed that any fully formed ideology or system had to be triadic to be realistic but that most systems contented themselves by arguing in terms of second propositions and that their conflicts were therefore self-limiting. The *third,* he argued, encourages progress and knowledge by expressing generalization through a process beginning in doubt, tested by inquiry, and completed by belief.

The new categories illuminate the most important facets of Peirce's work in logic, in sign systems, and in pragmatic philosophy. In logic, Peirce's tripartite logical division into induction, deduction, and abduction or retroduction follow his triadic argument as experiment, hypothesis, testing, and inquiry move toward truth logically and inevitably. Peirce is careful to make room for the imagination within logic; abduction becomes the third or connecting principle that derives in great measure from what he called "the play of musement," or the guess, that sparks both doubt and belief in the inquirer.

Peirce did use the term *rhetoric* to describe part of his system of logic, as logic treated symbols. He included three functions of symbols within logical systems, the third of which he defined as the "formal conditions of the force of symbols . . . and this might be called 'formal rhetoric'" (I.559). He was later to call this third relationship of interpretant to symbol "speculative rhetoric," in part because the symbol's independent relationship to an interpretant constituted an argument.

Peirce is credited, along with Saussure, with the development of semiotic theory, the relationship of signs to meaning. Unlike Saussure's dyadic relationship between sign and meaning, Peirce's semiotic is unsurprisingly triadic, and his theory describes how an object, its represented meaning, and its representation (index, icon, symbol or sign, object, interpretant) function together in perception. The character of semiotics insists that all thought is signs and that humans themselves are signs as they represent thought in action. The sign theory of thought leads to a sign theory of the self and thus into a social theory of logic and of meaning. No experience is unmediated for Peirce. "When we think, then, we ourselves, as we are at that moment, appear as a sign" (5.383). The relationship is irreducibly triadic, rather than dyadic, for a sign gives an instruction to interpret. "In its genuine form thirdness is a triadic relation existing between a sign, its object and the interpreting thought, itself a sign, considered as constituting a mode of being a sign." Peirce's brilliant work in semiotics helps establish the role of consciousness as symbolic, and therefore mediated, active and central to meaning.

As in logic and semiotics, triadic principles underlie Peirce's pragmatic theory, which describes how action and belief function together to create systems of inquiry and of knowledge. Pragmatism enacts Peirce's architechtonic principles, as it allows for systems to rise through adequate analysis of experience and from as many perspectives on experience as possible. Originated in the meetings of the famous Metaphysical Club, which met in Cambridge from 1867 to 1868, pragmatism's doctrines were first developed by Peirce when Chauncey Wright brought to the group Bain's definition of belief as that upon which man is prepared to act. This definition leads to Peirce's definition of pragmatism in his 1871 review of the works of Berkeley: "Consider what effects, which might conceivably have practical bearings, we conceive the object of our conception to have. Then our conception of these effects is the whole of our conception of the object."

The doctrine of pragmatism supplants a priori notions with scientific inquiry, a testing of method and belief toward the aim of understanding the real. It suggests the importance of action and of contingency, and it is these facets of pragmatism that recent neopragmatists like Richard Rorty have highlighted in their own work. But pragmatism is designed to further the development of "concrete reasonableness" and follows triadic principles in identifying its mission with the future and the general as well as with action. Because of its identification with third principles, pragmatism is neither skeptical nor individualistic.

For Peirce, the movement toward knowledge through an awareness of the method of methods depends in great measure on the community. His concepts of logic, semiotics, and of pragmatism are profoundly social theories. Thirdness itself requires a communal spirit, an ability to mediate and locate principles within dialogue. The insistence on the community as part of a scientific system of inquiry led Peirce to see himself not as original or novel but part of a group of inquirers: "Originality is the last of recommendations for fundamental conceptions" (1.360). Peirce's belief in doubt and possibility—his concept of fallibilism—depends on the relationship between individual and community, and the progress toward the real is achieved through a group of inquirers engaged in a devotion to their task. The social exists even within the self—"a sort of public spirit among the nerve cells" (1.354). Given his extreme isolation from colleagues and from students, Peirce grasps the tenets of social theories of knowledge in profound and poignant ways.

Some critics have seen Peirce as a deeply divided thinker who swerved from realism to metaphysical in an attempt to come to terms with his religious faith. Seen dyadically, the two ideologies may be incompatible. But to conceive of the range of his thought in triadic ways illuminates Peirce's breathtaking ability to connect inquiry and belief and thus transform systems of thought. Theorists are only now beginning to realize how thirdness might inform doctrines and bring doubt and truth into dialogue at last.

The first full-length biography of Peirce is *Charles Sanders Peirce: A Life* by Joseph Brent (1993). Peirce's works are available in two major editions in the *Collected Papers of Charles Sanders Peirce*, edited by Charles Hartshorne and Paul Weiss, Volumes 1–6 (1931–1935), and Volumes 7–8, edited by A. Burks (1958). A chronological edition of Peirce's works is in progress as *Writings of Charles S. Peirce: A Chronological Edition*, Peirce Edition Project (1982–), a projected thirty-volume work. A selected group of Peirce's articles and notes are included in *The Essential Peirce*, Volume 1, edited by Nathan Houser and Christian Kloesel (1992). Peirce's correspondence with Lady Welby, in which he explores the concepts of thirdness and semiotic theory, is included in *Semiotic and Significs: The Correspondence between Charles S. Peirce and Victoria Lady Welby*, edited by Charles S. Hardwick (1977).

Hephzibah Roskelly
University of North Carolina, Greensboro

Bibliography

Apel, Karl-Otto. *Charles S. Peirce: From Pragmatism to Pragmaticism.* Amherst: U of Massachusetts P, 1981.

Eisele, Carolyn. *Studies in the Scientific and Mathematical Philosophy of Charles S. Peirce: Essays by Carolyn Eisele.* Ed. Richard Martin. The Hague: Mouton, 1979.

Fisch, Max H. *Peirce, Semeiotic and Pragmatism: Essays by Max H. Fisch.* Ed. Kenneth Ketner and Christian J.W. Kloesel. Bloomington: Indiana UP, 1986.

Freeman, Eugene, ed. *The Relevance of Charles Peirce.* LaSalle, IL: Monist, 1983.

Hookway, Christopher. *Peirce.* London: Routledge, 1985.

James, William. *Pragmatism.* New York: Meridian, 1955.

Sebeok, Thomas. *The Play of Musement.* Bloomington: Indiana UP, 1981.

Pentad

A method developed by Kenneth Burke in *A Grammar of Motives* (*Grammar*) to analyze the inherent drama of human relations or what he labels *dramatism*. Concerned with the motives involved in a given situation, Burke asks, "What is involved, when we say what people are doing and why they are doing it?" (*Grammar* xv).

To answer this question, Burke employs his pentad, a complete method for examining motivation fully: "You must have some word that names the *act* (what took place in thought or deed), and another that names the *scene* (the background of the act, the situation in which it occurred); also, you must indicate what person or kind of person (*agent*) performed the act, what means or instruments he used (*agency*), and the *purpose* (*Grammar* xv).

Any action of a symbolic nature—one that involves language use explicitly or implicitly—is an *act*. Thus a speech, college course, piece of music, painting, physical activity (such as playing a football game or taking a hike) may be viewed as an act. Each of these involves symbolic action that may be examined to discern the actor's motives or purpose in performing the act.

Scene: Burke defines scene as "the background of the act, the situation in which it occurred" (*Grammar* xv). Examining scene involves both time and space. When and where did the act occur? What was the act's context? The examiner may narrow time and space to specific instances (such as "My class in rhetorical invention meets at 10:30 MWF in English 126"), or she may expand the breadth of her investigation as much as she wishes. For example, a class in rhetorical invention (an act) may have as its scene a specific graduate program, a particular university, or a nationwide movement such as the revitalization of rhetoric. The scope of the scene—the various contexts that the examiner elects to examine—determines the range of the examination. To explore scene fully is to examine as many of these contexts as the examiner thinks relevant to the act.

Agent: Who performed or perpetrated the act? Was it an individual or a group of some sort? Considering the agent as an individual requires the investigator to examine the agent's background, to consider such things as where he lives, what brand of politics he practices, his profession, his hobbies, his religious beliefs—all those aspects of the individual that make him who he is and that may have influenced him to act. Burke notes that "personal properties . . . assigned a motivational value, such as 'ideas,' 'the will,' 'fear,' 'malice,' 'intuition,' 'the creative imagination,'" are elements that may be considered in examining the agent. Burke also allows for co- and counteragents in considering the agent, defining these terms as friends and enemies, respectively (*Grammar* xix–xx). The agent may also be a group that may be examined from the perspective of nationality, ethnicity, religion, politics, and geographic locale. Or a particular element of government (such as the Senate, the CIA, or a local Bureau of Land Management office) may stand as an agent.

Agency: The means by which the act was accomplished in the agency. Agency may involve physical or concrete entities (such as the word processor and black ink ballpoint pen used to prepare this piece), or they may be more abstract, including such things as the actor's determination or will to act. Still broader, such entities as war may be viewed as an agency, in that war may be seen as the means to an end.

Purpose: The why behind the act constitutes the purpose. When people act, they do so for a reason or, perhaps, for a number of reasons. In considering purpose, the investigator speculates about these various reasons as she attempts to understand the act as fully as possible.

The pentad becomes a set of probes Burke employs to explore the drama of human relations, and it is at once simple yet complex. As the illustrations above suggest, its terms are "understandable almost at a glance" (*Grammar* xv), but Burke holds that "it should provide us with a kind of simplicity that can be developed into considerable complexity" (*Grammar* xvi) in that it allows him to probe motivation as deeply as he wishes: "By examining [the pentad's terms] quizzically, we can range far because of their possibilities of transformation, their range of permutations and combinations" (*Grammar* xvi). That is, the terms may be used to provide varying perspectives of a particular topic or event under consideration. For example, a body of law may be viewed as an act in that it may be defined as verbal action; but it also may be seen as an agency insofar as that body of law is the means by which a society functions. Further, that same body of law may be viewed as a scene in that it becomes a background or situation that contains or provides a context for the acts of the populace governed by it.

Essential to the use of the pentad are the ratios, which Burke defines as "formal interrelationships . . . among the [pentad's] terms" (*Grammar* xix). Burke lists ten ratios in all. The rationale underlying these interrelationships is that no act occurs in a vacuum; it must necessarily have associated with it a scene, an agent, an agency, and a purpose. The criteria for examining the ratios are "consistency" and "influence"; that is, Burke would have us employ the ratios both to discover whether the two terms of each ratio are consistent with each other and to discover how one term influences the other. For example, in considering a course in rhetorical invention as an act, the investigator would necessarily have to consider how the scene (such as the current movement to revitalize rhetoric) influenced that specific course, how that scene helped motivate the agent (in this case, the teacher) to present the course.

To complete a consideration of motive, the investigator ultimately needs to consider which of the pentad's terms is featured. Each term provides a vantage point or perspective from which a topic may be viewed, and Burke ties each one to a particular philosophical orientation: act corresponds to realism, scene to materialism, agent to idealism, agency to pragmatism, and purpose to mysticism (*Grammar* 128). By considering which term is predominant, the investigator may come to understand more fully the ground of the agent's action, for selecting or proceeding from a dominant term signals the adoption of a perspective, with all other terms and the attendant ratios colored by that selection. Burke offers dramatism, with the pentad as its primary method for analysis, as a counterstatement to various philosophical schools that would attribute motivation to one particular aspect of experience, a view Burke finds too limited. He feels that these schools provide inadequate discussion of motives, that in stressing one factor of motivation over all others, they disregard the complexity inherent in motivation (*Grammar* 318) and, as a result, reduce our actions to the level of stimulus-response. They become, for Burke, "faulty terminologies" (*Grammar* 317). Ultimately, considering which term of the pentad is featured and its corresponding philosophical school may yield rich insights into the motives undergirding a particular act.

Bill Bridges
New Mexico State University

Bibliography

Burke, Kenneth. *A Grammar of Motives.* Berkeley: U of California P, 1969.

Foss, Sonja K. "Pentadic Criticism." *Rhetorical Criticism.* Prospect Heights, IL: Waveland, 1989.

Foss, Sonja K., Karen A. Foss, and Robert Trapp. *Contemporary Perspectives on Rhetoric.* Prospect Heights, IL: Waveland, 1985.

Rueckert, William H. *Kenneth Burke and the Drama of Human Relations.* 2nd ed. Berkeley: U of California P, 1982.

Perelman, Chaïm (1912–1984)

Belgian philosopher whose pursuit of a practical logic applicable to human decision-making led him to elaborate a theory of argumentation in the form of a "new rhetoric." Born in Warsaw, Poland, on May 20, 1912, Chaïm Perelman moved to Belgium in 1925. Perelman received a law degree in 1934 and a doctorate in philosophy in 1938, both from the Free University of Brussels. He became a professor of philosophy and dean of the faculty of philosophy and letters at that institution. He was a leader in the Belgian resistance movement in World War II. After the war he served as director of the Center for the Philosophy of Law and the National Center of Logical Research. In recognition of the renown his work in philosophy had brought to Belgium, Perelman was proclaimed a baron in December of 1983. He died on January 22, 1984.

Perelman's contributions to rhetoric emanated from his philosophic quest to find a nonformal logic capable of playing a role in the behavioral sciences and philosophy analogous to that of formal logic and empiricism in the exact sciences. Although Perelman's early writings reflected the assumptions of logical positivism, which stressed the futility of arguing about values, by the early 1940s an intensive analysis of the concept of *justice*—with its bewildering multiplicity of meanings in various contexts—caused him to broaden his intellectual mission to embrace the problem of *justification* in general. Searching for a "logic of value judgments," Perelman decided to follow the method used by the nineteenth-century logician Gottlob Frege, who had conducted a systematic study of the patterns of reasoning used by mathematicians. Starting in the late 1940s, Perelman undertook, in conjunction with Mme. Lucie Olbrechts-Tyteca, a comprehensive examination of the kinds of arguments actually used by lawyers, moralists, politicians, and others who attempt to "make a rule prevail" in situations where formal logic or empirical evidence cannot settle the matter.

In the course of their investigations, Perelman and Olbrechts-Tyteca "rediscovered" Aristotle's *Rhetoric* and *Topics,* as well as other writings in the classical rhetorical and dialectical traditions. Perelman came to regard rhetoric and dialectic as a unified whole in which dialectic serves as the theoretical underpinning for a theory of argumentation, with rhetoric constituting a practical discipline whereby dialectical techniques are used to convince or to persuade.

The collaboration of Perelman and Olbrechts-Tyteca over a ten-year period resulted in several partial studies, including a collection of essays titled *Rhétorique et philosophie: Pour une théorie de l'argumentation en philosophie* (1952). The culmination of their joint efforts came in 1958 with the publication of *La nouvelle rhétorique: Traité de l'argumentation*. Translated into English as *The New Rhetoric: A Treatise on Argumentation* (1969), the title reflected the authors' decision to associate their theory with rhetoric instead of dialectic. Two reasons were foremost in their minds: (1) the concept of *dialectic,* following the redefinitions of Hegel and Marx, had drifted hopelessly far from its classical moorings; and (2) the idea of *audience* had been recognized as an essential element in all of the ancient theories of rhetoric. For Perelman and Olbrechts-Tyteca, gaining the adherence of an audience seemed to be the objective sought by every arguer. In their new rhetoric, however, the concept of audience is greatly widened beyond the conception of a crowd in the marketplace or courtroom. It embraces an infinite variety of audiences, from the single auditor to the *universal audience* of "all reasonable people" addressed by philosophers. Other noteworthy contributions to rhetorical theory found in *The New Rhetoric* include an emphasis upon the educational function of epideictic discourse, the importance of *presence* in determining the elements that occupy the foreground of a hearer's consciousness, and the role of "quasilogical" arguments in the reasoning process that leads to conviction or persuasion.

Perelman later published a condensed version of the treatise on argumentation under the title *L'Empire rhétorique: Rhétorique et argumentation* (1977), which was translated into English as *The Realm of Rhetoric* (1982). His ideas on rhetoric can also be found scattered throughout more than twenty books and three hundred articles that he wrote on philosophy, logic, sociology, and law. No rhetorical theorist since Richard Whately has been more influential than Chaïm Perelman in expounding a comprehensive theory of rhetoric as argumentative discourse.

Ray D. Dearin
Iowa State University

Bibliography
Arnold, Carroll C. "Perelman's New Rhetoric." *Quarterly Journal of Speech* 56 (1972): 87–92.
Dearin, Ray D. *The New Rhetoric of Chaïm Perelman: Statement and Response.* Lanham, MD: UP of America, 1989.
Loreau, Max. "Rhetoric as the Logic of the Behavioral Sciences." Trans. Lloyd I. Watkins and Paul D. Brandes. *Quarterly Journal of Speech* 51 (1965): 455–63.
Perelman, Ch. *An Historical Introduction to Philosophical Thinking.* Trans. Kenneth A. Brown. New York: Random, 1965.
———. *The Idea of Justice and the Problem of Argument.* Trans. John Petrie. New York: Humanities, 1963.
———. *The New Rhetoric and the Humanities: Essays on Rhetoric and Its Applications.* Trans. William Kluback. Boston: Reidel, 1979.
———. "The New Rhetoric and the Rhetoricians: Remembrances and Comments." Trans. Ray D. Dearin. *Quarterly Journal of Speech* 70 (1984): 188–96.
———. *The Realm of Rhetoric.* Trans. William Kluback. Notre Dame, IN: U of Notre Dame P, 1982.
Perelman, Chaïm, and L. Olbrechts-Tyteca. *The New Rhetoric: A Treatise on Argumentation.* Trans. John Wilkinson and Purcell Weaver. Notre Dame, IN: U of Notre Dame P, 1969.
———. *Rhétorique et philosophie: Pour une théorie de l'argumentation en philosophie.* Paris: Presses Universitaires de France, 1952.

Periodic Style

A style in which the full meaning of a particular thought is suspended until the very end of the portion of speech (or "period") in which that thought is expressed. The term *period* suggests the circuitous movement of such a portion of speech, proceeding from beginning to end, bringing a thought to completion. A period may occur in one sentence or stretch over several.

A periodic style is usually described as "compact" and as being characterized by "suspended syntax." In a periodic sentence, subordinate elements precede the main clause of the sentence; a periodic style is dominated by such constructions. A well-known example of a periodic sentence is the first sentence of the pre-amble to the U.S. Constitution:

> We, the people of the United States, in or-der to form a more perfect union, estab-lish justice, insure domestic tranquility, provide for the common defense, promote the general welfare, and secure the bless-ings of liberty to ourselves and our poster-ity, do ordain and establish this Constitu-tion for the United States of America.

A periodic style is contrasted with a style variously described as "free-running," "cumu-lative," or "loose." The use of a free-running style reflects the combining and intermingling of multiple thoughts, one upon another, and gives the impression that a writer is exploring ideas; the main clause of a loose sentence comes first, and less important details and qualifica-tions follow. A periodic style, on the other hand, is marked by periods and denotes a refinement and a controlled emphasis on the part of the writer.

The control of periodic style is often at-tained through the use of repetition, parallelism, balance, and antithesis, the last of which Aris-totle identifies as a key feature of a periodic style. Such devices are functional in rhetoric because elements of a sentence are understood better when repeated, put side by side with oth-ers, or placed in opposition to other elements. It is important, however, that the full meaning of the sentence, as it is constructed, be sus-pended until its ending.

Donald E. Bushman
University of North Carolina, Wilmington

Bibliography

Aristotle. *Rhetoric*. Trans. Lane Cooper. Englewood Cliffs, NJ: Prentice, 1932.

Kennedy, George. *The Art of Persuasion in Greece*. Princeton: Princeton UP, 1963.

Lanham, Richard A. *Analyzing Prose*. New York: Scribner's, 1983.

Peripatetics

A school of philosophers deriving from Aristotle and his immediate followers. Ancient commentators derive the term either from *Peripatos*, the name of the covered walkway where Aristotle taught, or *peripatein* (to walk), because Aristotle was held to walk with his stu-dents while teaching.

Aristotle's pupil Theophrastus (370–288/5 B.C.E.) of Eresos succeeded him as scholiarch of the Peripatos. His extant works include two treatises on plants, "Characters," "On Metaphysics," and "On Sense Perception." Theophrastus' "Characters" describes the habits, appearance, and psychology of various character types and had significant influence on subsequent ethics, psychology, rhetoric, and new comedy. Ancient sources attribute to Theophrastus a general trea-tise on rhetoric and specific ones on examples, enthymemes, the maxim, nontechnical proofs, praise, statement and narration, style, solecisms, comedy, the ludicrous, and delivery.

Subsequent scholiarchs of the Peripatos included the physicist Strato (scholiarch 286–268 B.C.E.), who wrote many books on logic, and Lyco of Troas (scholiarch 266–225 B.C.E.), a skilled teacher and eloquent speaker with a sweet voice, whose "Characters" appears based on Theophrastus'.

Heraclides of Pontus (fl. 360 B.C.E.), only tenuously associated with the Peripatos, prob-ably studied with Speusippus at the Platonic Academy and was acquainted with Aristotle. His dialogues (none extant), written in the middle style, were admired in antiquity. His books in-clude *Of Public Speaking, or Protagoras* and several works of literary criticism.

Theophrastus' pupil Demetrius of Phalerum (350–283 B.C.E.), probably not the author of the extant treatise "On Style," was skilled in the middle style. He wrote a treatise "On Rhetoric" and several commentaries on Homer.

Later peripatetic rhetoric includes the short undated anonymous *Tractatus Coislinianus*, which summarizes a rhetorical theory of com-edy, distinguishing between funny situations and witty language. Ariston (fl. c. 225 B.C.E.), a peripatetic philosopher known for his elo-quence, may have written "Against the Rheto-ricians." The Greek peripatetic Critolaus (2nd century B.C.E.) demonstrated his eloquence dur-ing an embassy to Rome and amassed argu-ments proving that rhetoric was not an art. His student Ariston of Cos (fl. 2nd century B.C.E.) defined rhetoric as speech designed to persuade the multitude. Aristocles of Pergamum (fl. 2nd century C.E.) studied peripatetic philosophy before converting to rhetoric. Minucian's (fl. 253–268 C.E.) extant peripatetic-influenced "On epicheiremes" covers the three modes of proof and the *topoi*. Cicero mentions both Aristotle's and Theophrastus' rhetorical theories, and peripatetic sources probably influenced his *De inventione, De oratore,* and *Topica.* Quintilian also appears acquainted with the peripatetic tradition.

Peripatetic rhetorical theory is usually held to include the Aristotelian notions of grounding rhetoric in psychology, the *topoi,* the three modes of proof (ethos, logos, pathos), the definition of enthymemes as faulty syllogisms, and the tripartite division of types of rhetoric (deliberative, forensic, epideictic). Later accretions include the five parts of rhetoric (invention, arrangement, style, memory, delivery), the four virtues of style (correct language, lucidity, appropriateness, and ornamentation), the three styles (plain, middle, grand), and the four parts of a speech (exordium, narrative, proofs, and peroration).

Carol Poster
University of Missouri

Bibliography

Erickson, Keith V., ed. *Aristotle: The Classical Heritage of Rhetoric.* Metuchen, NJ: Scarecrow, 1974.

Fortenbaugh, William W., ed. *Peripatetic Rhetoric after Aristotle.* New Brunswick, NJ: Transaction, 1993.

———, ed. *Theophrastus of Eresus.* 2 vols. Leiden: Brill, 1992.

Fortenbaugh, William W., and Peter Steinmetz, eds. *Cicero's Knowledge of the Peripatos.* New Brunswick, NJ: Transaction, 1989.

Gottschalk, H.B. *Heraclides of Pontus.* Oxford: Clarendon, 1980.

Grube, G.M.A. *A Greek Critic: Demetrius on Style.* Phoenix Suppl. Vol. 4. Toronto: Toronto UP, 1961.

Periphrasis

Substitution of more words for less; referring to the "bird of night" to signify an owl. Periphrasis can be used euphemistically to avoid a precise term, as the author of Genesis demonstrated in writing "And thou shalt go to thy fathers in peace; thou shalt be buried in a good old age" (15:15). A writer or speaker can also use periphrasis to describe an elusive experience. A. Malraux did so in writing "There is no word to describe the feeling of marching on the enemy, and yet it is as specific, as strong as sexual desire or anguish" (*Antimémoires*).

Arthur Quinn and Lyon Rathbun
University of California, Berkeley

Peroratio

The segment of a classically arranged discourse charged with summing up the argument and appealing to the audience. Perhaps one of the more straightforward concepts of classical arrangement, *peroratio* is the section of discourse now commonly called the conclusion. The classicists saw this section as combining "impassioned summary . . . [with] a review of previous arguments" (Lanham 114). The Greeks, according to the *Rhetorica ad Herennium,* saw these tasks accomplished via a three-sectioned conclusion concerned with: "summing up (*enumeratio*), amplification (*amplificatio*), and appeal to pity (*commiseratio*)" (Lanham 114). The classical suggestions thus come to reflect some of the suggestions contemporary teachers and writers give and receive when they talk about concluding paragraphs.

Joseph Colavito
Northwestern State University

Bibliography

Lanham, Richard. *A Handlist of Rhetorical Terms.* 2nd ed. Berkeley: U of California P, 1991.

Rhetorica ad Herennium. Trans. Harry Caplan. Cambridge, MA: Harvard UP, 1954.

Persona

Literally a mask. From the Latin word for the mask worn by actors in the classical theater, persona has come to be applied in literary criticism to the "mask" an author puts on in a literary work. It is a useful device for distinguishing between the author and the "character" of the storyteller or poet implied in the story or poem.

The importance of this distinction is most clear in first-person works. For example, in *Gulliver's Travels,* Gulliver is a persona created by Swift for relating his satire. Indeed, the distinction between persona and author is especially useful in criticism of satire because it enables critics to make a link between the implied author and what is being satirized. But it is also helpful in other first-person works. In *Huckleberry Finn,* Huck is a persona that critics are careful to distinguish from Mark Twain. Browning's Duke in "My Last Duchess" and Fielding's Tom Jones in the novel bearing his name are other examples of personae.

However, the concept may be applied in more subtle instances of differentiation between the author and the speaker in the story or poem. In Wordsworth's "Tintern Abbey," for instance, the speaker in the poem seems to be closely associated with the poet himself. Modern criticism, however, questions this identification by using persona to delineate between the author in his or her everyday life and the "character" of the speaker who lives in the lines of the poem, a role that the poet created for the speaker. And the same may be said of third-person narrators of stories and poems, those that do not have a clearly defined speaker. The concept of persona may be used to refer to an implied speaker because all fiction in some sense is told by someone created by the author.

Persona is similar in some ways to the rhetorical concept of ethos. Both allow critics to identify and discuss a "character" created in a discourse, though the former is for literary purposes and the latter for persuasive ones. In fact, it may be argued that the current use of persona in literary criticism provides a way for literary critics to understand the rhetorical nature of literary works through a literary ethos.

Michael Carter
North Carolina State University

Bibliography

Abrams, M.H. *A Glossary of Literary Terms.* 5th ed. New York: Holt, 1988.

Gibson, Walker. *Persona: A Style Study for Readers and Writers.* New York: Random, 1969.

Persuasion

The process by which language or symbolic actions influence the choice-making of others. Though sometimes used interchangeably with the term *rhetoric*, persuasion is most often identified today as the end of a process occurring within rhetorical situations—that is, situations inviting or allowing the exertion of persuasive influence. Persuasion is also typically distinguished from coercion, wherein choice-making is influenced by resort to physical force or extreme punitive actions. Persuasion operates in the realm of practical decision-making, taking for its domain the entire sweep of everyday affairs involving contingent matters in the social sphere, in which people make choices about how to behave, what to believe, and what to value.

In the Western tradition, persuasion was first systematically studied and taught by the sophists, in and around Athens in the fifth and early fourth century B.C.E. Typically, these figures tempered philosophical inquiry with interest in civic affairs. In the two millennia since these beginnings, the study, teaching, and practice of persuasion have undergone several transformations. These transformations were never clean breaks or complete paradigm shifts, however, and especially in modern and contemporary times one can easily find quite different conceptions of persuasion in play at the same time.

These various perspectives toward persuasion are distinguishable by their coordinates along several conceptual dimensions. First, perspectives toward persuasion may differ according to the extent to which they limit their investigations to influence in the public and mass realm or include influence in the private and interpersonal realm as well. Second, perspectives toward persuasion differ according to their inclination to limit persuasion to attempted influence that is explicit, whose persuasive character is conventionally acknowledged, or to include as well the implicitly persuasive potential of forms of discourse not conventionally regarded as persuasive. Third, perspectives toward persuasion differ according to the extent to which they are persuader-centered, regarding persuasion as a function of a communicator's intent to persuade, or audience-centered, regarding persuasion as including—or indeed as limited to—the potential of messages or behaviors to influence others, whether that effect was intentional or not. Fourth, perspectives on persuasion vary according to their approach to the question of ethics in persuasion, some regarding both the means and the ends of persuasion as ethical problems, others focusing on the ethics of persuasive means and regarding the critique of the various ends to which persuasion may be addressed as outside the jurisdiction of the field of persuasion itself.

Within the history of rhetoric, three distinct perspectives toward persuasion are obvious: These may be termed the classical, symbolist, and institutional perspectives. Each of these has its characteristic historical and intellectual traditions as well as its own canon of those social practices that it regards as the proper subject for the study of persuasion.

The classical perspective on persuasion could also, with only little imprecision, be called

P

Aristotelian. It was and remains largely shaped by assumptions tracing back to the *Rhetoric* of Aristotle, in which the various means of persuasion are grouped under the general rubric of rhetoric as the art of selecting among persuasive strategies offered by particular topics and situations, and by the predispositions of particular audiences. While subsequent scholarship within this tradition has emphasized the application of the classical principles to such discursive forms as drama and poetry, epistolary writing, sermons, advertising and public relations, it has most typically retained the original, Aristotelian emphasis on the persuasive power of public address in civic life. This perspective also lays primary emphasis on strategic—hence, intentional—choices among persuasive strategies; even modern social-psychological study of attitude change, on the surface audience-centered, never abandons the assumption that this understanding of audience psychology has strategic implications. Thus the paradigm and rationale of persuasion within the classical perspective is the intentional and explicit attempt by an individual to influence matters of civic concern by directly addressing an audience.

Aristotle identified three primary means of persuasion: the use of evidence and patterns of reasoning within the message (logos), the image and authority of the persuader (ethos), and the predispositions and frame of mind of the audience (pathos). The intellectual and practical traditions represented by the classical perspective have held to these distinctions.

The classical emphasis on use of evidence and argument to appeal to an audience's reason is consistent with the Aristotelian characterization of humans as rational animals. Aristotle identified two resources available to the persuader under this head: examples, and the enthymeme—a deductive argument based on the general and probable, rather than the universal and necessary, that required participation of the audience for its construction. Typically, analysis and evaluation of evidence and argument is accomplished by two general criteria: material validity (the truth of an argument's premises) and formal validity (the correctness of the reasoning from premises to conclusion). Until comparatively recently, these criteria were construed in a manner quite consistent with their origins in formal logic.

The work of contemporary theorists, perhaps most significantly that of Stephen Toulmin, has advanced the general idea that neither reasoning nor reasonableness is limited to the strictures of formal logic. Toulmin's work recognizes that humans construct arguments for the purpose of persuading in those cases where matters are contingent, and thus scientific-style demonstration is not possible. Following Toulmin, scholars have treated the standards of reasoning as more variable by field and social context than was traditionally considered to be the case. In place of the traditional analysis of syllogistic reasoning in terms of major premise, minor premise, and conclusion have come a method of analysis featuring claim, data, and warrant. The claim, the proposition a persuader advances against at least the possibility of disagreement, is supported at minimum by data or grounds, references to examples, testimony, statistical information, authoritative statements, or the like, that an audience might plausibly accept as a foundation for advancing the claim. This movement from grounds to claim in an argument is supported by one or more warrants, principles of legal, religious, ideological, scientific, practical, or other nature that an audience would recognize as justifying the claim in light of the grounds. Other elements of this analysis demonstrate further its departure from traditional syllogistic analysis: the invocation of the warrant may be justified by producing backing, the claim may be qualified based on the strength of the grounds-warrant-claim link, and the possibility of rebuttal conditions may be acknowledged. The Toulmin model is still a formal model, like the traditional syllogism and not strictly either an empirical or prescriptive model, yet it clearly demonstrates a crucial theme in contemporary thinking about reasoning and persuasion: Its standards recognize collaborative, contextual, rhetorical considerations in reasoning, as well as "purely" formal and objective factors.

Aristotelian theory identified three components of the image and the authority of the persuader as a means of persuasion. Demonstrations of the persuader's moral character show that the persuader's values are congruent with those of the audience. Demonstrations of good will toward the audience increase the audience's trust in the persuader, and demonstrations of clear reasoning and command of the subject matter enhance the audience's perception of the persuader's competence. Contemporary research on ethos and credibility, which boomed in the 1960s, added one further dimension, dynamism. This research also concluded that there may be less distinction for audiences between good will and good character than traditionally supposed. Generally, contemporary research has also tended to reduce the issue of a persuader's moral character to the smaller, though important, issue of a persuader's perceived trustworthiness.

Emphasis on the moral qualities perceived to be embodied by a persuader remains crucial, however, in a second area in the contemporary study of persuader image and authority: the phenomenon of charisma. Charismatic individuals wield extraordinary influence, well beyond what might have been duly conferred upon them by formal institutions. Sometimes mistakenly regarded as a matter solely of the personality of the charismatic leader, charisma nevertheless requires a willing audience of followers and a situation ripe for widespread change in the status quo in order for the charismatic leader to emerge. Charismatic persuaders typically articulate a clear vision for change in the status quo and rely on unconventional and highly audience-centered tactics to achieve their ends. Success for charismatic persuaders is frequently ephemeral, since they may lose their following if they can no longer deliver change, and yet if they are successful they often become part of a new status quo within which their once-extraordinary, charismatic persona may appear to become co-opted or irrelevant.

The comparatively rare phenomenon of charisma is based on audiences' longing for heroes, prophets, and messiahs. By comparison, image management—another area of contemporary development on the classical concept of ethos—makes no such demands upon the would-be persuader. Image management, driven by the insatiable demand of a plethora of commercial media for "news," has created a distinctly modern phenomenon: the "celebrity," "personality," or "notable," a figure who is famous not for achievement, power, wealth, virtue, or evil but simply by virtue of being well known. Media images are created strategically, out of simple, vivid, and concrete images, which make sense within the frame of reference of their audience; they rely on the mass media for their dissemination and force. Such celebrity can then be invoked to promote a wide spectrum of persuasive purposes. Image management represents the furthest departure of contemporary developments upon the classical concept of persuader image and character, for

several reasons. First, it represents a weakening of the connection between the managed image of the persuader and the integrity and competence of the persuader's claims. Second, the strategies of image management tend to be more indirect than those of traditional persuader ethos. Image management can attempt to bolster the persuasive power of a source even without that individual's apparent participation; it also creates a reserve of persuasive potential that is comparatively independent of both topic and situation.

The third general means of persuasion identified by the classical perspective is the psychological or emotional state of the audience. Certain states of mind, linked with the experience of pleasure and pain, may predispose audiences to respond in ways consistent with the persuader's purposes. Aristotle identified fourteen different emotions and discussed each in terms of its causes, the experience of pleasure or pain associated with it, the inclinations to act such an emotion may create, and strategies for kindling or extinguishing such emotions in an audience. For example, audiences tend to feel anger when they believe they have received undeserved ill treatment from another. Audiences who feel anger also feel an impulse toward revenge for the slight, and their experience of anger is characterized by pain at the thought of being treated badly and pleasure at imagining revenge or retribution.

Arising from a social scientific context for the study of human behavior, many contemporary studies of audience motivation investigated the effects of rewards and punishments of various types on persuasion. Among the more influential in this line of research were the Yale studies of persuasion conducted during the two decades following World War II and a more recent body of research on fear appeals. This work suggests that rewards are generally more effective than punishments in accomplishing persuasive effects and that moderate fear appeals are more persuasive than extreme ones. Other developments in the study of audience motivations have been in three general areas: equilibrium theories, growth theories, and personality theories. Equilibrium theories include the cognitive balance theory of Fritz Heider and the cognitive dissonance theory of Leon Festinger and associates. Both general perspectives share several key assumptions: First, individuals hold within themselves many different cognitions—thoughts, beliefs, memories, atti-

P

tudes, and values; second, these cognitive elements can come into conflict or tension with one another. According to equilibrium theories, this tension is inherently uncomfortable or unpleasant, and causes the individuals (consciously or unconsciously) to reduce this unpleasant experience by changing their attitudes or behavior to restore equilibrium.

Cognitive balance theory examines the three-part relationship among a perceiver/audience, a second person, and a person or thing toward which the perceiver and other are positively or negatively inclined. In general, balance exists when the various elements and relations are in harmony from the point of view of the perceiver. Where they are not—where, for example, the perceiver is positively disposed both toward the object in question and toward the second person, while the second person is negatively inclined toward the object—the situation is psychologically unstable, and the perceiver experiences an impulse to change his or her attitude toward the other person or toward the object in question. Cognitive balance theory treats this tension reduction as largely automatic and nonreflective.

Cognitive dissonance theory goes beyond cognitive balance theory by attempting to account not only for the valence of the attitude toward other and object but also the intensity of this liking or disliking, as well as the importance to the individual of the attitude in question. Less predictively powerful under controlled conditions than cognitive balance theory, cognitive dissonance theory nevertheless reintroduces a satisfying degree of complexity to description of the attitude change process in persuasive audiences. Cognitive dissonance theory suggests that the pressure to reduce cognitive tension by change in behavior or attitude builds gradually as the number and intensity of dissonant cognitions increases. This theory further assumes that the process of tension-reduction may very well have an external, self-aware social component in it, rather than being a purely psychological reflex.

Compared to equilibrium theories' emphasis on reduction of psychological tension as a motivator of audiences, growth psychology posits that humans are not merely driven by avoidance of pain but also motivated by the desire for growth through the satisfaction of needs. The analysis of human needs as hierarchically ordered, with self-actualization as the apex, is largely the work of humanistic psychology, for which Abraham Maslow was a chief proponent. Growth psychology argues that individuals are motivated not merely by avoidance of pain but by the satisfaction of meeting needs and moving toward self-actualization; it suggests that audiences will be most strongly motivated by persuasive appeals that address their lowest-order unmet need. It differs from equilibrium theories further by its ability to explain how individuals can be motivated to undertake long-term activities, which may do little to reduce stress or tension in the short run but which may over time tend to produce growth.

The classical perspective in its contemporary position retains much of the legacy of its roots in antiquity. It is heavily connected in the distinction between reason and passion. Even today its proponents' insistence that the two are not antithetical terms remains trapped in large measure by the terms of the debate established two and a half millennia ago, when Plato attacked rhetoric, the art of persuasion, as being nothing more than pandering to and gratifying audiences, rather than challenging them with the truth. In the eighteenth century, this tension centered on the so-called conviction-persuasion duality. This division separated persuasion aimed at behavioral change from argument aimed at cognitive change and attempted to separate rational appeals aimed at conviction from emotional appeals aimed at persuasion. This duality has been maintained frequently in the twentieth century, especially as a means of maintaining subdiscipline boundaries. It is also supported by the pervasive modernist cultural belief in "objectivity," the presumption that persuasion, which appeals to "the facts" and to "reason" rather than to the emotions, is both pragmatically more effective and ethically superior. Nevertheless, this distinction has often dissipated within serious theoretical treatments of the subject.

The Platonic attack on the art of persuasion as an art of flattery that disregarded truth set the stage as well for continuing ethical concern about a process of influence that operates in the realm of the contingent rather than from an epistemological position that included an ideal of truth. Because the classical perspective has generally regarded the principles of persuasion as morally neutral, and insisted rather that the ends toward which these techniques are directed are the proper object of ethical critique, persuasion has always been vulnerable to such ethical charges. In response to this, different contemporary approaches to persuasion imply or specify differing levels and perspectives for responsible action on the part of both sources and audience of persuasion.

The symbolist perspective, although generally more modern in temperament than the classical perspective, nevertheless draws upon intellectual roots that are in some cases nearly as old as those of the classical perspective. The symbolist perspective centers on the notion that all persuasion is really to a significant extent self-persuasion, involving the active participation of an audience. Thus symbolist theories explain how audience members decode or interpret a variety of symbolic actions such that influence is accomplished. While the classical perspective emphasizes the intentional and explicit attempt by an individual to influence matters of civic concern by directly addressing an audience, the symbolist perspective departs from—or at least greatly expands—these parameters, taking into account unintentional effects as well as intentional, private or interpersonal interaction as well as public address, implicit forms of persuasion as well as explicit. Because all symbols represent interests and motives, from the symbolic perspective all symbols, and all acts of interpretation, are considered inherently persuasive.

At the heart of the symbolist perspective is the capacity of symbols to represent the interests, motives, and values of those who perceive them. This process of recognizing our own motives represented in the symbolic acts of another has been termed "identification" by Kenneth Burke, whose writings have contributed significantly to the contemporary developments of this perspective. Symbols and symbol-systems are organized as codes, learned conventions shared by cultures and subcultures regarding the interpretation of symbolic message elements. These conventions, again, are generally receiver-centered; while not ignoring the intentional, artistic, and strategic purposes to which persuaders may put symbols, they assume that meaning and interpretation of symbols reside finally within the perceiver of those symbols. Codes shape the influence of symbols and symbolic acts in a variety of media: written and spoken language and dialects, nonverbal behavior as well as architecture and the manipulation of physical objects, film and television production, dance and musical performance, rituals and ceremonies, and so on. They also comprise the conventions of interpretation which define a wide variety of genres and subgenres within each of these media: Within language, they distinguish the creation of meaning in narrative from that in exposition; within narrative, they distinguish comedy, tragedy, and quest—and so on.

The symbolist perspective identifies three broad areas of inquiry and practice on persuasion: language, nonverbal and nondiscursive symbolism, and structure and form. Language is the most obvious and most elaborated code in our experience. In addition to its instrumental function of signification and predication, which was most central to the classical perspective on persuasion, language also serves the constitutive function of creating symbolic reality. Even the most elementary function of language, naming, is itself laden with potentially persuasive consequences, since the act of naming is a cultural expression of the importance of the thing named as well as a demonstration of our power over the thing named.

The traditional analysis of figures of speech and figures of thought also exemplifies this function. Figures of speech include those uses of language for ornament or figuration wherein the words used retain their literal meaning. Rhyming, metrical devices, parallelism, and repetition are examples of figures of speech. Figures of thought, on the other hand, involve the use of language wherein the literal meaning of the words used is no longer able to account for the symbolic meaning of the expression as a whole. Two of the more powerful figures of thought are irony and metaphor. In both cases the figure of thought allows a persuader to evoke powerful identifications that are strongly resistant to translation into literal language.

Nonverbal symbolism is generally built from elements of body movement, visual images, and acoustic images, alone or in some combination. Nonverbal and nondiscursive symbolism enjoyed only small attention within the classical perspective, not infrequently lumped under the bland heading of "delivery." In part this is because of the prevailing Western cultural tendency to view all creation of meaning through the lens of language and linguisticality, as we speak of "body language," "reading a person like a book," and so on. However, nonverbal symbolism tends to be nondiscursive in its form: holistic in its presentation, rather than linear; specific and concrete in its reference, rather than general and abstract; tending toward multiple and sometimes contradictory meanings, rather than univocal and singular. Hence nondiscursive symbolism frequently operates in persuasion in ways that a more language-centered approach will be unable to account for. Nonverbal and nondiscursive symbolism has a content level, at which it reports, conveys, or displays information. It also has a relational level, at which it displays or comments upon the relationship among the parties communicating.

Symbols, discursive or nondiscursive, do not ordinarily exist free floating in a vacuum; they occur linked with other symbols in a structure, which gives shape or pattern to symbolic content or subject matter. These structures themselves are empirical in nature, and a list of general structure types would include rhythm, hierarchy, association, and boundaries. Yet structure alone is insufficient to explain this aspect of the persuasive power of symbols. Symbols influence and motivate us not merely through their referents, content or subject matter. They are also things that we experience, objects of our senses that are (or at least appear to be) located in space and time. This aspect of symbols, their form, is also important to understanding persuasion from the symbolist perspective.

At a psychological level, form refers to the arousal of anticipation followed by the consummation of that anticipation. Once we detect form, we form expectations; a form is completed when it somehow resolves that sense of expectation. This resolution may be temporary or permanent, expected or unexpected. There are several basic forms: Syllogistic progression is any form wherein what comes first somehow requires or demands precisely what comes after. "Syllogistic" does not simply mean "argument;" a well-formed argument is merely one type of syllogistic progression. Qualitative progression can involve variations on a theme, extensions of an idea, or development of some other quality. Repetitive form is the consistent reappearance of a thing—but always in slightly different guise. The "principle" involved in the repetition may be simple and obvious, like rhyming, or subtle and extended, like the repetition of certain kinds of characters or events or imagery. In addition to these more generic forms are the many conventional forms that an audience may understand beforehand from specific cultural experiences. There are many examples of these conventions: church sermons, sonnets, tragic opera, rock concerts, prime-time situation comedies, advertisements, and campaign speeches are just a few instances. Forms can be nested within one another: minor or incidental forms tend to occur in larger or more complex works, or actions, and can be discussed partly independently of the overall work. Forms can be interrelated and may often overlap in a particular work or event. Forms can also conflict with one another, as when one form leads us to expect one thing, while an intermingling form requires some other resolution for itself.

From a purely aesthetic point of view, we judge the artistic merit of a work by how well the outcome resolves the developing form, or how perfectly the form is presented. From a persuasive point of view, we judge the extent to which the formal aspects of a work place the audience in a particular frame of mind, or creates in them a particular motivation.

The structure of persuasive messages is a topic of considerable discussion and inquiry. Both expository and narrative patterns of organization contribute to persuasive effects. While research from the social sciences suggests that didactic organizational patterns emphasizing the clarity of a persuasive argument are effective, there is controversy about the order of presentation of multiple arguments or persuasive appeals. Study of primacy and recency effects argue for the benefits of placing the strongest arguments either first or last in a more complex persuasive message structure. Contemporary developments regarding structure tend to emphasize the persuasive effects of narrative structures like those found in novels or films. Narrative structure appears to be most persuasive when the story presented is both coherent (*narrative probability*) and true to life (*narrative fidelity*). Mythic structures are assumed to be particularly persuasive as their sequence of dramatic action appears often to transcend both time and culture.

The status of ethics is more ambiguous with regard to persuasion from the symbolist perspective than in the case of the classical perspective. Since the emphasis is on audience, rather than persuader, ethical standards for tactics and goals have been discussed less explicitly in this perspective. General consensus seems to exist that persuasion involving symbols or symbolic actions that are themselves inherently degrading or demeaning is unethical, yet even this consensus is not without its unresolved problems. Chief among these is the problem of justifying the censure of a persuader for tactics that an audience finds offensive while simultaneously locating authority for the interpretation of symbols in the audience itself, rather than in the persuader.

Unlike the other two perspectives, the institutional perspective is distinctly contemporary in its scope and theorizing; its intellectual and practical roots extend back scarcely further than the period shortly before World War I. Its context is the modern society, moderated by mass media, which have become both extraordinarily pervasive and interpenetrated with other institutions, all of them large, enduring social collectives empowered by custom or law to perform important social functions. Studies of persuasion from this perspective coincide with the rise of various persuasion industries such as advertising and public relations. The institutional perspective is far less coherent across its entire spectrum than either the classical or symbolist perspective. Its coherence comes from the twentieth-century recognition that once persuasion moves to an institutional context—that is, when institutions serve as audience, source, or context of persuasion—many insights and assumptions of the classical and symbolist perspectives apply only in a qualified form, if at all.

The institutional perspective has as yet no comprehensive theory of persuasion. Rather, four broad areas of practice and inquiry are generally recognized: campaigns, social movements, propaganda, and ideology. Some of these areas, particularly the first three, were at their outset noticeably classical in their orientation, but the ability of the classical perspective to keep from being outpaced by changes in persuasive practices at the institutional level has become uncertain indeed. This can be explained by three contemporary phenomena: Both contemporary theory and practice have significantly blurred the distinction between public and private; the corporate, bureaucratic character of much discourse has rendered problematic the traditional link of persuasion to the moral and ethical choices of a single, identifiable individual; and the increasing hybridization of entertainment in a commercialized mass culture has made the distinction between explicit and implicit persuasion increasingly problematic. Since the classical perspective is defined by fairly sharp distinctions in each of these dimensions, its ability to serve as a basis for theorizing or practice at the institutional level is at least to some extent called into question.

Each of the four broad types of persuasion at the institutional level has its characteristic theoretical and practical concerns. Persuasive campaigns are explicit persuasion for private motives or gain within an institutional context. Campaigns are generally characterized by centralized planning, legitimate leadership, and differing tactical objectives at different stages of the campaign. Product and commercial campaigns tend to exploit both mass and interpersonal communication media, relying on exposure to mass media to create general awareness of a product or idea, and more direct contact with opinion leaders to influence choices regarding the product or idea. Political campaigns typically have structures that are largely shaped as responses to external situations: primaries, ballot deadlines, general elections, and so on. All forms of campaigns typically rely on a highly segmented view of their audience and focus attention on those segments where the greatest support can be garnered with the most efficient use of resources.

Social movements are explicit and implicit persuasion for public gain that attempts to change an institution, its structure, or its practices. By being "outside the system," the range of tactics available to social movements is different from that available to legitimated campaigns. Certain tactics available to "legitimate" or institutionally sanctioned persuasion will not be available to a social movement, while other, perhaps more creative or unconventional tactics become available in their place. Establishing one's legitimate right to leadership can be problematic in a social movement, as can be the need to keep movement members motivated. Social movements typically face the problem of militant and moderate factions within its ranks; such divisions have implications for motivation and discipline of the membership.

Propaganda is explicit, institutionally sponsored persuasion, typically with specific and limited goals, aimed at a mass audience (or "the masses"). Propaganda generally relies on close coordination between media and the institutional source of the persuasion. Its most commonly found strategy is the constant repetition of a fairly simple—and simplified—set of themes or messages. Propaganda is characterized by absolute concern with effects, relies on ideology for its justification, and typically works explicitly or implicitly to repress dissent.

Sociologist Jacques Ellul has noted that propaganda may advance either political or sociological ends, serve either to agitate a mass audience into action or to pacify it into inaction, originate either with the authority of institutional elites or with the pressure to conformity among the masses, and either emphasize or reject the traditional forms of rationality in its messages.

Ideology is implicit persuasion, usually institutionally sponsored, aimed at preserving the institution and its authority. Its building blocks are cultural values, shared myths, and sources and structures of societal power. The goal of ideology is the formation and preservation of a world view and culture, larger in scope and more enduring in scale than anything contemplated by propaganda, social movements, or campaigns. When a clear pattern of values and myths permeates diverse messages and media from diverse, though interrelated, institutions, members of the culture tend to take for granted this pattern and the world view it embodies, not questioning its validity or its relationship to reality outside its own terms. The power of an institutionally backed world view to gain ascendancy within its culture creates or perpetuates a hegemony, whereby the ascendancy of that world view over other possible rivals is preserved. Ideological persuasion is characterized by multiple messages over time and is strongly associated with not only formal institutional channels of communication but also the forms and content of popular culture.

The question of ethics from the institutional perspective is as complex as the problems of theory and practice. Where we consider explicit persuasion that originates "inside" institutions, there are generally formulated ethical codes (as well as legal ones) that may apply. When our concern turns to persuasion that originates from without, as in social movements, or when the persuasion is implicit, like ideology, such judgments become more problematic. This is even more true since in both of the latter cases the source of ethically questionable messages may well be unclear, owing to the bureaucratic nature of institutions and the decentralized nature of movements.

Institution-level persuasion is ethically problematic in yet another way. Both the classical and symbolist perspectives grant a certain reasonable and moral autonomy to their audiences, albeit for different reasons. But most institution-level persuasion depends on reaching a large audience. The scale, and frequently the cost, of such persuasion contributes to a general redefinition of the audience according to the principle of conformity, by which moral autonomy is downplayed in favor of homogeneity and obedience—epitomized in the industrialized West as the consumer.

William L. Nothstine
Portland, Oregon
Martha Cooper
Northern Illinois University

Bibliography

Aristotle. *On Rhetoric: A Theory of Civic Discourse*. Trans. George A. Kennedy. New York: Oxford UP, 1991.

Bailey, F.G. *The Tactical Uses of Passion*. Ithaca, NY: Cornell UP, 1983.

Burke, Kenneth. *Counter-Statement*. Berkeley: U of California P, 1968.

———. *A Rhetoric of Motives*. Berkeley: U of California P, 1969.

Cooper, Martha, and William L. Nothstine. *Power Persuasion: Moving an Ancient Art into the Media Age*. Greenwood, IN: Educational Video Group, 1992.

Ellul, Jacques. *Propaganda: The Formation of Men's Attitudes*. Trans. Konrad Kellen and Jean Lerner. New York: Vantage, 1973.

Keisler, Charles A., Barry E. Collins, and Norman Miller. *Attitude Change: A Critical Analysis of Theoretical Approaches*. New York: Wiley, 1969.

Langer, Suzanne K. *Philosophy in a New Key: A Study in the Symbolism of Reason, Rite, and Art*. 3rd ed. Cambridge, MA: Harvard UP, 1957.

O'Keefe, Daniel J. *Persuasion: Theory and Research*. Newbury Park, CA: Sage, 1990.

Toulmin, Stephen. *The Uses of Argument*. Cambridge: Cambridge UP, 1958.

See also ARGUMENT; AUDIENCE; ETHICS; ETHOS; PROPAGANDA

Phenomenology

A philosophy associated with the human science approach to the study of human conscious experience. Such sciences, including rhetoric and communicology, use an analytic and critical method of description grounded in a logic of discovery. There is both a European and an American tradition in phenomenology beginning in the nineteenth century. The European forerunner of phenomenology was Franz Brentano (1838–1917). He divides the phenomena of conscious experience into (1) representations, (2) judgments, and (3) emotive acts. A philosopher, he had several famous students at the University of Vienna, including the psychoanalyst Sigmund Freud (1856–1939) and the logician Edmund Husserl (1859–1938), who founded phenomenology. In his 1922 London lectures, Husserl defined his methodology as centered on the "manifest multiplicity of conscious subjects communicating with one another."

Within discourse, Husserl specifies the meaning of conscious experience as four domains of rhetorical reference. First, "meaning" signifies (the signifier expression) while "manifestation" refers (the signified perception). Second, "meaning" has "objects." Third, "symbolic meanings" in perception contrast with "intuitive meanings" in expression. Fourth, all "acts of meaning" have a common "ideal meaning." Thus, a phenomenon is the object-referent (*noema*) of the constituting act directed toward it (*noesis*). The whole process is called "intentionality," whereby a person is "conscious of . . . [experience]."

Among the Husserl interpreters are the French philosopher Maurice Merleau-Ponty (1908–1961) and his student Michel Foucault (1926–1984). Merleau-Ponty suggests there are two levels of rhetoric: (1) existential discourse in which a person expresses his speaking in an original and perceptive speech, that is, a "speech speaking"; and (2) empirical discourse that merely expresses what has already been said by others—that is, a "speech spoken." Foucault argues that the empirical level of discourse hides the existential level. This contested process of discourse forms a "rupture" or ongoing discontinuity of levels. He engages his third level, "critical methodology," by using the methods of "archaeology" ("knowledge" as the experience of consciousness) and "genealogy" ("understanding" as the consciousness of experience). That is, the conjunctions of both consciousness and experience in discourse are reversible, reflexive, and reflective in judgment. While Merleau-Ponty examines the place of personal perception in public expression, Foucault critically studies the reverse— that is, the place of public expression in personal perception.

The central personality in American phenomenology is Charles Sanders Peirce (1839–1914), also known for his combination of semiotics and phenomenology. For Peirce, philosophy is a subclass of the science of discovery. Discovery is a logic in which the relation of signs to their objects (that is, consciousness) combines with phenomenology, which for Peirce is the experience of the objective actual world. In this Peircian context, logic is the science of symbols and has three parts: (1) "formal grammar," which concerns the reference of symbols in general; (2) "formal logic," which concerns the truth conditions of symbols; and (3) "formal rhetoric," which studies the force of symbols in appealing to the mind including all general conditions under which a problem presents itself for solution. For Peirce, signs consist of (1) an initial consciousness or "firstness" called a representamen, (2) an "object" in experience or "secondness" and (3) the resulting relationship or "thirdness" constituted between them that is an "interpretant," or the meaning of a phenomenon.

Richard L. Lanigan
Southern Illinois University

Bibliography

Ijsseling, Samuel. *Rhetoric and Philosophy in Conflict: An Historical Survey*. Hague: Nijhoff, 1976.

Kearney, Richard. *Modern Movements in European Philosophy*. Dover, NH: Manchester UP, 1986.

Lanigan, Richard L. *The Human Science of Communicology: A Phenomenology of Discourse in Foucault and Merleau-Ponty*. Pittsburgh, PA: Duquesne UP, 1992.

———. *Phenomenology of Communication*. Pittsburgh, PA: Duquesne UP, 1988.

———. *Semiotic Phenomenology of Rhetoric*. Washington, D.C.: Center for Advanced Research in Phenomenology. UP of America, 1984.

———. *Speaking and Semiology*. 2nd ed. New York: de Gruyter, 1991.

Nöth, Winfried. *Handbook of Semiotics*. Bloomington: Indiana UP, 1990.

Spiegelberg, Herbert. *The Phenomenological Movement: A Historical Introduction*. 3rd enlarged ed. Boston: Nijhoff, 1982.

Philosophical Argument

What philosophers, for the most part, rely on, whether constructive or critical, as a way to truth and the exposure of falsehood. The qualifier "for the most part" is necessary here in order to save for such thinkers as Plotinus and Heidegger, who are not primarily arguers, the status of philosopher.

The statement just made specifies neither necessary nor sufficient conditions for philosophical argument, and so, while objective, is not of much use. But it is possible to go beyond this statement only by abandoning objectivity; for the domain of philosophical arguments is itself a matter of dispute among philosophers. What some thinkers would regard as philosophical arguments others might regard as theological, psychological, sociological, or cosmological arguments, to name a few possibilities, or else as sheer nonsense.

Even if the domain of philosophical argument could be delineated in such a way as to satisfy everyone, the question would remain, "Under what conditions is a philosophical argument *valid?*" Only a rational argument can be valid; this is as true of philosophical arguments as of any others. There is widespread agreement among philosophers that their discipline is rational. (Nonparties to this agreement had perhaps best be treated under some rubric other than that of "philosopher.") But there is no general agreement among philosophers concerning the meaning of "rationality"; this is itself a philosophical question. Philosophers offering different answers to this question—advocates of different ontologies (that is, views of ultimate reality) have regarded different arguments as valid.

Thus the Ontological Argument proceeds from the premise that God is the sum of all perfections to the conclusion that since existence is a perfection, God must exist. This argument is regarded by Descartes as valid, since it is accommodated by his theory of rationality—a theory according to which it is rational to carry out deductions from "clear and distinct ideas" like the idea of God. But Kant, with a narrower view of rationality, rejects the argument as invalid.

Hume's theory of rationality is expressed in the closing page of his *Enquiry concerning Human Understanding* (1748): "When we run over our libraries, . . . [i]f we take in our hand any volume; of divinity or school metaphysics, for instance; let us ask, *Does it contain any*

abstract reasoning concerning quantity or number? No. *Does it contain any experimental reasoning concerning matters of fact and existence?* No. Commit it then to the flames: for it can contain nothing but sophistry and illusion." The metaphysicians he is attacking obviously have a different theory of rationality.

Yet there can be arguments common to a number of different philosophies, committed to different views of rationality, as are the philosophies of Plato and Aristotle. While Plato's view is bound up with his theory of Forms, Aristotle's has no place for Forms but instead endorses the syllogism as the norm of rationality. But the Third Man argument is regarded by both Plato and Aristotle as valid. This argument, used by the character Parmenides in the Platonic dialogue of that name, attacks Plato's own theory of Forms. It proceeds from the premise that if there is a Form of Man, there must also be a Form corresponding to whatever is common between Man and the Form of Man to the conclusion that since the series of Forms and Forms of . . . Man is an infinite regress, a series that goes on forever, there can have been no such thing as the Form of Man in the first place. Plato offers no conclusive response to this argument. But Aristotle adopts it as supporting the central role he assigns to predication, the basis of the syllogism. Predication is not the assignment of a Form to an individual, but the eliciting of a predicate already present in the individual and inseparable from it. There is no need to assign a further predicate to this predicate.

The infinite regress argument is convincing to philosophers worried about infinity but not necessarily to those not bothered by the thought of an unending series. Thus the regress arising from "Every event has a cause" so alarms Aristotle that he attempts to stop it by positing an ultimate Cause of Itself. But most people operating within the framework of contemporary nonquantum science (in quantum theory there can be events without causes) would be entirely comfortable with the idea of the causes . . . of the causes of an event.

The distinction has been made between "vicious" and "nonvicious" infinite regresses (Passmore 28–29), the latter generally to be eschewed, while the former can be innocuous. But this distinction has not been unchallenged (cf. Geach, who thinks that many infinite regresses are no more than simple contradictions).

It is not clear that there are no infinite regress arguments outside the domain of philosophy. It is sometimes claimed that there are examples in mathematics (Waismann; Gardiner). But such claims have been disputed (Passmore).

Another argument acceptable to the partisans of differing positions consists in casting doubt on a thesis by applying it to itself. Such an application has usually been called "self-reference." Of course, some theses can be applied to themselves without harm; for example, "There are truths" is self-exemplifying because it is a truth. But the negation of this thesis—There are no truths—denies its own truth when applied to itself, and so is categorically false.

As further arguments having a distinctively philosophical use, Passmore lists the "Two-Worlds Argument," the "Verifiability Argument," "Excluded Opposites," "Paradigm Cases," and "Allocation to Categories." Fetzer's book includes articles about "Questioning as a Philosophical Method," "The Verifiability Principle," "Ockham's Razor," "The Method of Counterexample," and "The Argument from Ordinary Language," as well as "Infinite Regress Arguments." There is of course some overlapping between these two books.

Henry W. Johnstone, Jr.
Pennsylvania State University

Bibliography

Fetzer, James H., ed. *Principles of Philosophical Reasoning.* Totowa, NJ: Rowman & Alanheld, 1984.

Gallie, W. "Essentially Contested Concepts." *The Importance of Language.* Ed. Max Black. Englewood Cliffs, NJ: Prentice, 1962.

Gardiner, Martin. "The Infinite Regress in Philosophy, Literature, and Mathematical Proof." *Scientific American* 212.3 (1965).

Geach, Peter. *Truth, Love, and Immortality: An Introduction to McTaggart's Philosophy.* Berkeley: U of California P, 1979.

Johnstone, Henry W., Jr. *Philosophy and Argument.* University Park: Pennsylvania State UP, 1959.

Passmore, John. *Philosophical Reasoning.* New York: Scribner's, 1961.

Perelman, Chaïm, and L. Olbrechts-Tyteca. *Rhétorique et Philosophie pour une Théorie de l'Argumentation en Philosophie.* Paris: Presses Universitaires de France, 1952.

Waismann, Friedrich. "How I see Philosophy." *Contemporary British Philosophy: Personal Statements.* Ed. H.D. Lewis. London: Allen and Unwin, 1956.

Philosophy of Rhetoric

Traditionally, the project of grounding rhetorical theory and practice in a philosophical account of persuasion; more recently, the project of tracing the implications of ontological premises regarding the limits of knowledge and the human use of language. The idea of a philosophy of rhetoric begins with the separation of philosophy (as a mode of inquiry) from rhetoric (as the object of this inquiry). In Western thought, the foundation for this separation is established in Plato's *Gorgias* as the difference between true knowledge (*epistêmê*) and opinion (*doxa*). Then, in Plato's *Phaedrus*, Socrates uses this epistemological foundation to ground a philosophical inquiry into the nature of persuasion (*pistis*), which will serve as a true guide (*technê*) for rhetorical practice. This conception of philosophy's relevance to rhetoric provides the model for many later philosophies of rhetoric, including a recent collection of essays on rhetoric and philosophy, which begins with a call for "a philosophical grounding for rhetoric" (Johnstone xv).

But the idea of a philosophy of rhetoric should not be reduced to this one tradition. There is a fundamental complication in the initial separation of philosophy from rhetoric that arises with the recognition that persuasion is a mode of human existence. Early statements of this recognition are found in Isocrates and, later, in Italian humanism (see Grassi). More important, recent work on the relationship between rhetoric and philosophy shows that once persuasion is acknowledged as an ontological fact, it becomes more difficult to circumscribe rhetoric as an object of philosophical inquiry; that is, persuasion interjects itself into all inquiry, including the epistemic purity of philosophical inquiry. The history of the philosophy of rhetoric, then, can be read as attempts to manage the tension between the need for a philosophical grounding of rhetoric and the recognition that persuasion is a basic feature of human existence. In traditional philosophies of rhetoric, this tension is managed by ignoring the ontological status of persuasion; but in more recent inquiries, the ontological premise leads to a rethinking of both philosophical inquiry and rhetoric.

Traditional Philosophies of Rhetoric

Traditional philosophies of rhetoric are characterized by an attempt to provide a psychological account of persuasion. The basic features of such an account were established in Plato's *Phaedrus.* As in the *Gorgias*, Socrates objects to rhetorical practices that produce only opinion in the minds of an audience; but in this dialogue, he acknowledges the possibility of a type of persuasion that produces true knowledge in the audience. Yet this type of persuasion, Socrates warns, also requires a real art of rhetoric—that is, a rhetoric grounded in a rational explanation of how language affects the mind (psuchê). The requirements of this art, he explains, are similar to the Hippocratic art of healing. Just as the doctor must acquire knowledge of the whole body and knowledge of those things that can affect the body, the rhetor should acquire knowledge of the whole mind and those things that can affect the mind. Moreover, just as the doctor's knowledge allows a classification of kinds of bodies and kinds of diseases, the rhetor's knowledge should result in a classification of the kinds of mind and an understanding of how certain rhetorical techniques affect each kind of mind (269e–72c). This model of an art based on the classification of psychological states is more fully developed in Aristotle's *"Art" of Rhetoric,* especially Book 2.

The project of a philosophy of rhetoric is not common in the history of rhetoric following Plato and Aristotle, but its features reappear throughout the history of rhetorical handbooks. In the wake of the Enlightenment, however, with its attempts to ground an understanding of human behavior in principles of scientific inquiry, philosophical accounts of rhetoric reemerge. George Campbell's *Philosophy of Rhetoric* (1776) again establishes rules for rhetorical practice by providing a psychological account of persuasion, describing it as the hierarchical sequence of engaging four mental faculties. Successful rhetoric must (1) provide knowledge to the intellect, (2) present knowledge in such a way that it pleases the imagination, which in turn, (3) affects the passions, and finally (4) influences the will (2). Although traditional, Campbell's philosophy of rhetoric attributes to persuasion a goal that is quintessentially of his time—the attempt to unify the faculties of mind.

New Philosophies of Rhetoric—Linguistic Philosophy and Ontology

The possibilities for a philosophy of rhetoric change significantly when philosophical inquiry is rethought as questions regarding the nature of language. This modern "linguistic turn" has led to a questioning of the traditional privileging of philosophy over rhetoric; and, in some cases, the relationship is reversed such that philosophy is grounded on inquiry defined as "rhetorical" (Nietzsche) or is collapsed such that neither term provides adequate grounding (Derrida). Moreover, this radical shift has led to redefinitions of rhetoric beyond the traditional idea of persuasion. Linguistic philosophy has influenced two new categories of philosophy of rhetoric. The first category is characterized by projects that ground rhetoric in a philosophical account of linguistic meaning. Projects in the second category begin with the assumption that language use is a key aspect of human existence and, in tracing the implications of this ontology, confront the difficulties of the traditional separation of rhetoric from inquiry (see K. Campbell).

In this first category, I.A. Richards's *Philosophy of Rhetoric* (1936) clearly illustrates the influence of the "linguistic turn" in Anglo-American philosophy and an exigency for enlarging the conception of rhetoric beyond persuasion. Richards's project, in fact, takes the basic assumptions of Anglo-American linguistic philosophy and extends their scope to the study of nonphilosophical discourses. The first of these assumptions finds its classic statement in Ludwig Wittgenstein's *Tractatus Logico-Philosophicus* (1922), where the task of philosophy is defined as the clarification of cloudy thought. Richards's debt to this concern for clarification is apparent in his definition of rhetoric as "a study of misunderstanding and its remedies" (3). The second basic assumption is that misunderstanding results from our lack of knowledge about the nature of language. Wittgenstein, for example, claims that most philosophical questions have arisen solely from the failure to understand the logic of language. Similarly, Richards claims that the basic problem of traditional rhetorical theory from Aristotle to Whately is its failure to provide knowledge of "the fundamental laws of the use of language" (7). The final assumption is that language is best examined by analytical methods. Thus, for Richards, knowledge of the laws governing linguistic meaning can be discovered only by examining "the structures of the smallest discussable units of meaning and the ways in which these vary as they are put with other units" (9–10). Although these three assumptions redirect the philosophy of rhetoric away from psychology and toward language, it is important to note that Richards's project remains well within the traditional philosophy of rhetoric in that it still grounds rhetoric in a philosophical account of language use; his account merely replaces the psychological account of persuasion with semantics and thus reproduces the separation of philosophical inquiry from rhetoric that marks the traditional philosophy of rhetoric. A more significant aspect of Richards's project is his break with the traditional definition of rhetoric in terms of persuasion. For Richards, persuasion is merely one "aim" of discourse; yet the study of rhetoric should be concerned with linguistic meaning and, thus, expanded to cover all aims of discourse (23–24).

It is only with the emergence of ontological concerns that the originary separation of philosophical inquiry from rhetoric has come under question. This ontological questioning has developed along two basic lines. The first focuses on human limitations, which imply the impossibility of certain knowledge and the contingency of understanding. This skeptical ontology has led to two conclusions that challenge the traditional project of a philosophy of rhetoric: (1) if certain knowledge is not possible, then philosophical inquiry cannot provide an epistemological grounding for rhetorical theory; and (2) if philosophical inquiry cannot produce certain knowledge, then the traditional opposition between true knowledge (*epistêmê*) and opinion (*doxa*) cannot be maintained and philosophical inquiry cannot be distinguished from rhetoric. This last conclusion has provided the basis for the dominant trend of contemporary rhetorical theory: rhetoric as "epistemic."

The seminal text outlining this new conception of rhetoric is Robert L. Scott's "On Viewing Rhetoric as Epistemic." Scott returns to the ontological skepticism of the Greek sophists to argue that knowledge does not exist prior to action but instead is constructed through action. Most important, this argument for the rhetorical nature of knowledge has raised questions concerning the ethical and political dimensions of action that results in knowledge construction, thus shifting attention from content to conduct. This kind of concern has been developed by theorists and critics associated with the "rhetoric of inquiry" movement, in which the epistemological goal of traditional philosophical inquiry has been replaced by an inquiry that accounts for knowledge in rhetorical terms (for example, argument, audience, narrative, trope) and, often, in sociopolitical terms (for example, gender, institution, professionalism, race). (See *The Rhetoric of the Human Sciences*.)

The second line of ontological speculation is less concerned with the construction of knowledge and, instead, regards the ontological status of language as central to an understanding of human relations and to the possibilities of community. If the first type of ontological rhetoric is "epistemic" in orientation, this second type is "anthropological" (see Blumenberg). This anthropological rhetoric, however, has yet to achieve the academic recognition of epistemic rhetoric, and its conceptions of rhetoric remain scattered in individual texts. Some sense of coherence, though, centers around the philosophical hermeneutics of Hans-Georg Gadamer. Hermeneutics is usually understood to be concerned with interpretation. But in his *Truth and Method*, Gadamer is concerned more specifically with a cultural problem that emerges from the development of the human sciences in the nineteenth century: Culture's sense of its tradition and thus its own identity has been narrowed to "an experimental finding—as if tradition were as alien and, from the human point of view, as unintelligible, as an object of physics" (xxi). The important role of rhetoric in addressing such a problem can be found, according to Gadamer, in the humanist tradition and, more specifically, in Giambattista Vico's *On Method in Contemporary Fields of Study* (1709). Recognizing that a sense of community is maintained through education, Vico argues that instruction must not be limited to the methods of producing scientific knowledge but must include training in the *sensus communis,* the set of beliefs held by a community, in virtue of which the community exists. Instruction in the *sensus communis* is fundamentally rhetorical in that it concerns knowledge of social beliefs (*doxa*). More important for Gadamer, this instruction in social belief establishes the basis for a kind of practical knowledge (*phronêsis*) needed to act wisely in concrete situations, which are always shaped by these social beliefs. It is this concrete, or situated, aspect of human action that the human sciences tend to overlook.

Similarly, Kenneth Burke grounds his "philosophy of rhetoric" in an ontological premise that stresses the role of language in establishing and maintaining community. Looking at research in cultural anthropology, Burke defines rhetoric as rooted in "the use of language as a symbolic means of inducing cooperation in beings that by nature respond to symbols" (*Rhetoric of Motives* 43). Moreover, Burke's ontological approach leads him to, arguably, the most profound reconceptualization of rhetoric since the classical tradition. Attentive to both Freud's and Marx's critiques of a conscious-centered subject, Burke observes that the traditional rhetorical concept of persuasion is inadequate because it entails intentionality. For example, an examination of class relationships will be hampered by "the classical notion of clear persuasive intent" (xiv). Instead, Burke argues, rhetoric should be understood in terms of "identification," allowing examinations of not only an audience's nonconscious identification with certain interests, but also the complexities of the rhetor's identification with the audience, including the sense of audience that the rhetor has internalized through the life-long process of socialization. The philosophy of rhetoric is thus expanded to a project of elucidating "the ingredient of rhetoric in all *socialization,* considered as a *moralizing* process" (39).

James Comas
Syracuse University

Bibliography

Blumenberg, Hans. "An Anthropological Approach to the Contemporary Significance of Rhetoric." *After Philosophy: End or Transformation?* Trans. Robert M. Wallace. Ed. Kenneth Baynes, James Bohman, and Thomas A. McCarthy. Cambridge: MIT P, 1987. 429–58.

Burke, Kenneth. *A Rhetoric of Motives.* 1950. Berkeley: U of California P, 1969.

Campbell, George. *The Philosophy of Rhetoric.* 1776. Ed. Lloyd F. Bitzer. Landmarks in Rhetoric and Public Address. Carbondale: Southern Illinois UP, 1963.

Campbell, Karlyn Kohrs. "The Ontological Foundations of Rhetorical Theory." *Philosophy and Rhetoric* 3 (1970): 97–108.

Derrida, Jacques. "White Mythology: Metaphor in the Text of Philosophy." *Margins of Philosophy.* 1982. Trans. Alan Bass. Chicago: U of Chicago P. 207–71. Trans. of "La mythologie blanche (la métaphore dans le texte philosophique)." First published in *Poétique* 5 (1971): 1–52.

Gadamer, Hans-Georg. *Truth and Method.* Trans. and ed. Garrett Barden and John Cunningham. New York: Continuum-Seabury, 1975. Trans. of *Wahrheit und Methode.* 1960. 2nd ed. Tübingen: J.C.B. Mohr, 1965.

Grassi, Ernesto. *Rhetoric as Philosophy: The Humanist Tradition.* University Park: Pennsylvania State UP, 1980.

Johnstone, Henry W., Jr. Foreword. *Rhetoric and Philosophy.* Ed. Richard A. Cherwitz. Hillsdale, NJ: Erlbaum, 1990.

Nietzsche, Friedrich. "On Truth and Lying in an Extra-moral Sense." *Friedrich Nietzsche on Rhetoric and Language.* Ed. and trans. Sander L. Gilman, Carole Blair, and David J. Parent. New York: Oxford UP, 1989. 246–57. Written in 1873.

The Rhetoric of the Human Sciences: Language and Argument in Scholarship and Public Affairs. Ed. John S. Nelson, Allan Megill, and Donald N. McCloskey. Rhetoric of the Human Sciences. Madison: U of Wisconsin P, 1987.

Richards, I.A. *The Philosophy of Rhetoric.* 1936. New York: Oxford UP, 1965.

Scott, Robert L. "On Viewing Rhetoric as Epistemic." *Central States Speech Journal* 18 (1967): 9–17.

Vico, Giambattista. "On Method in Contemporary Fields of Study." *Vico: Selected Writings.* Ed. and trans. Leon Pompa. Cambridge: Cambridge UP, 1982. 31–45. Trans. of *De nostri temporis studiorum ratione.* 1709.

Phronésis

From *phronéma* for thought or intellect; often used interchangeably with practical wisdom and prudence in the lexicon of Aristotelian ethics and rhetoric. Phronésis was for Aristotle the chief intellectual virtue because its possession enabled one to judge the proper positioning and practice of all other excellences or virtues. So, analogous to the priority of politics in civic life, a master art because it enabled conditions for all the other arts, phronésis may be considered the architectonic virtue of moral life because it allowed and enhanced the prospect for a balanced ethical character. For a philosopher who valued intellect over all else, the importance of phronésis cannot be overestimated.

In the theory of rhetoric, the importance of phronésis depends upon the value attached to prescription or normativity in rhetorical doctrine. To the extent that rhetoric is conceived as an art, capable of practical refinement, phronésis, or practical wisdom, is often considered to be one of the by-products or relational "goods" enhanced and cultivated through rhetorical conduct. For Aristotle, practical wisdom was one of the rhetorical constituents of ethos. But perhaps more important, this overriding intellectual virtue was also cultivated in audiences through the practice of deliberation. In fact, the methods of invention and argument, along with the vast array of commonplaces and *topoi,* may all be conceived as devices for the enhancement of phronésis in speakers and audiences.

The legacy of phronésis for modern rhetorical theory and practice is a controversial one. Some philosophers have claimed that phronésis is a sort of innate, intuitive capacity, further proof that the Enlightenment project of grounding virtue through universalized reason was bound to fail. Still others dismiss the whole language of "virtue" as a kind of wistful nostalgia for what was never fully present in a romanticized civic past. If there is a middle ground in the controversy, it may lie in Aristotle's neglected insight that phronésis is an intellectual quality that we value in ourselves and in others. The question of whether it may be cultivated or taught therefore remains an open one. And as Aristotle long ago introduced his famous treatise on the subject, this question may be viewed as an invitation to further inquiry.

Thomas B. Farrell
Northwestern University

Bibliography

Arnhart, Larry. *Aristotle on Political Reasoning.* DeKalb: Northern Illinois UP, 1986.

Beiner, Ronald. "Do We Need a Philosophical Ethics? Theory, Prudence, and the Primacy of Ethos." *Philosophical Forum* 20 (1989): 230–43.

Farrell, Thomas B. *Norms of Rhetorical Culture.* New Haven: Yale UP, 1993.

Gadamer, Hans-Georg. *Truth and Method.* New York: Seabury, 1975.

MacIntyre, Alasdair. *After Virtue: A Study in Moral Theory.* Notre Dame, IN: U of Notre Dame P, 1981.

Piaget, Jean (1896–1980)

Genetic epistemologist, studied intellectual growth and development of children, noted for a cognitive-developmental theory of learning, sometimes referred to as a stage theory; at sixteen published his observations of mollusks, ultimately leading him to question ways in which humans develop.

Do we learn by modeling the behavior of others or by being rewarded when we "perform" correctly? What role does language play in our learning? How can we account for infants learning to anticipate the reappearance of an object from behind one end of a screen that disappeared behind another end? And why are younger infants unable to anticipate such movement?

These are some of the kinds of questions with which Piaget was concerned. He found answers to them by closely observing children and concluded that cognitive growth was not the result of being reinforced for correct learning. Rather it was affected by physical development, experience with objects in the environment, social interaction, and a system for categorizing new knowledge.

Piaget believed that the child develops schemata as a product of interacting with her surroundings. Schema are structures or categories that allow the child to assign incoming information into understandable concepts. For example, a young child may have acquired a schema for *objects with wings that fly through the air,* which she calls *birdie.* Using this system, she assigns anything she encounters that fits this description into the birdie schema: birds, bugs, airplanes, and so forth. Eventually, however, she develops separate schema for these objects.

Piaget described the process of developing these schemata with two concepts: assimilation and accommodation. A child assimilates new information into an old schema. But when new information cannot be categorized under existing cognitive structures, he must create a new schema to oblige the new information. This is referred to as accommodation. When he is not assimilating or accommodating, the child is in a state of equilibration.

The belief that learning is an interactive process was linked to Piaget's observations of the cognitive stages all children move through; further, this sequence of development is invariant. During the first stage, the sensori-motor, concepts of object permanence (where the child differentiates herself from other objects in the environment) and causality (where the child moves from seeing herself as the cause of all activities to an awareness that other objects can be causes) develop.

Following this period of development is the preoperational stage, in which language development intensifies, thought becomes representational, and behavior becomes more social. The concrete operations stage is recognized by developing logical thought, particularly in the child's ability to understand classification and seriation problems. The last period observed by Piaget was the formal operations. During this stage children develop the ability to understand hypothetical problems while systematically combining all possibilities in solving problems. Transition from one stage to another, which occurs gradually, is initiated by cognitive dissonance, the recognition of an inconsistency of new information with an existing schema.

Another major theme found in Piaget's work and debated in arenas outside of cognitive psychology is the relationship of language to the development of thought. Piaget believed that intelligent thought is present before language, although he also believed that language supports the development of logical thought. He stressed the significance of experiences during the sensori-motor stage as readying the child for language development.

Marlene V. Meisels
University of North Carolina, Chapel Hill

Bibliography

Flavell, Jean. *The Developmental Psychology of Jean Piaget*. Princeton, NJ: Van Nostrand, 1963.

Piaget, Jean. "Autobiography." *History of Psychology in Autobiography*. Ed. E.G. Boring et al. Worcester, MA: Clark UP, 1952. 237–56.

———. *Genetic Epistemology*. New York: Columbia UP, 1970.

———. *Judgement and Reasoning of the Child*. New York: Harcourt, 1928.

———. *The Language and Thought of the Child*. New York: Harcourt, 1926.

———. *The Origins of Intelligence in Children*. New York: International UP, 1952.

———. *The Psychology of Intelligence*. Patterson, NJ: Littlefield, 1963.

Sigel, Irving E., David M. Brodzinsky, and Roberta M. Golinkoff, eds. *New Directions in Piagetian Theory and Practice*. Hillsdale, NJ: Erlbaum, 1981.

Wadsworth, Barry J. *Piaget's Theory of Cognitive Development*. New York: Longman, 1977.

Pike, Kenneth L. (b. 1912)

The originator of tagmemic linguistics and key theorist behind tagmemic rhetoric. Kenneth L. Pike, born in Woodstock, Connecticut, is best known as the originator of tagmemic linguistics, a theory of discourse he began to conceptualize during his experience as a fledgling linguist and Bible translator for the Protestant missionary organization, Wycliffe Bible Translators. After his initial field work among the Mixtec of Mexico in 1935–1936, during which he attempted to codify the phonology, morphology, and syntax of their oral culture, Pike sought formal graduate training at the University of Michigan, studying under the prominent structural linguist Edward Sapir. From 1937 to 1942, Pike combined his continuing investigation of the Mixtec language with his pursuit of the doctorate, in the process becoming especially well known for his insights into the strategies by which linguists may identify the unique phonemes of a dialect from a native perspective.

Earning his Ph.D. in 1942, Pike eventually published his dissertation as *Phonetics* (1943) to much scholarly acclaim. During his academic career, he served as a faculty member in linguistics at the University of Michigan (1942–1979), as president of the Summer Institute of Linguistics, the academic arm of Wycliffe Bible Translators (1942–1979), and as president of the Linguistic Society of America (1961). He has twice been nominated for the Nobel Peace Prize (1984 and 1987) and was elected to the National Academy of Sciences in 1985. Pike is the author of more than twenty books and two hundred articles.

The principles Pike began to develop for his study of Mixtec phonology led him to inquire into ever larger units of discourse beyond the morphological and syntactical levels; this research resulted in his formulation of a new theory of language and language behavior that attempted to account for any and all the relationships embedded both within the discourse itself, and without it—in the complex sociocultural contexts that frame human language use. Pike eventually labeled his theory *tagmemics* after his conceptualization of the *tagmeme*, the key unit-in-context language datum he coined to be parallel in form and scope to the established linguistic terms phoneme and morpheme. Tagmemic linguistic theory is articulated most fully in Pike's 1967 edition of his magnum opus, *Language in Relation to a Unified Theory of the Structure of Human Behavior*. The hallmark of tagmemics is its insistence that the goal of language study cannot be reduced to an "etic" or quasi-objective outsider's account of language phenomena but also must include the attempt to discover an "emic" or native/insider's experience of language and discourse.

Pike's tagmemics eventually came to the attention of rhetoricians and writing instructors in two groundbreaking 1964 articles "Beyond the Sentence" and "A Linguistic Contribution to Composition," published in *College Composition and Communication*. Here Pike presented the basic postulates of what would become a "tagmemic rhetoric." Soon thereafter, Pike allied himself with fellow University of Michigan faculty Richard Young and Alton Becker in their attempts to found a "modern theory of rhetoric." Their alliance resulted in the publication of *Rhetoric: Discovery and Change* in 1970, an innovative textbook well known for its elaboration of the nine-celled heuristic tool that assists students in invention. The tagmemic postulates elucidated in this joint effort and elsewhere in Pike's work since its publication may be seen as congenial to much postmodern thought, emphasizing the construction of knowlege through social encounter and the situatedness of all discourse.

Barbara Toth and Bruce L. Edwards
Bowling Green State University

Bibliography

Edwards, Bruce L. *The Tagmemic Contribution to Composition Teaching*. Occasional Papers in Composition History and Theory. Manhattan: Kansas State U, 1979.

Headland, Thomas N., et al. *Emics and Etics: The Insider/Outsider Debate*. Newbury Park, CA: Sage, 1990.

Pike, Eunice V. *Ken Pike: Scholar and Christian*. Arlington, VA: Summer Institute of Linguistics, 1981.

Pike, Kenneth L. "Beyond the Sentence." *College Composition and Communication* 15 (1964): 129–35.

———. "Building Sympathy." *Practical Anthropology* 7 (1960): 250–52.

———. "Language as Particle, Wave and Field." *Texas Quarterly* 2 (1959): 37–54.

———. *Language in Relation to a Unified Theory of the Structure of Human Behavior*. 2nd rev. ed. The Hague: Mouton, 1967.

———. *Linguistic Concepts*. Lincoln: U of Nebraska P, 1982.

———. "A Linguistic Contribution to Composition: A Hypothesis." *College Composition and Communication* 15 (1964): 82–88.

———. *Tagmemics, Discourse, and Verbal Art*. Ed. Richard Bailey. Ann Arbor: Michigan Studies in the Humanities, 1981.

———. *Talk, Thought, and Thing*. Arlington, VA: Summer Institute of Linguistics, 1993.

Young, Richard, Alton Becker, and Kenneth L. Pike. *Rhetoric: Discovery and Change*. New York: Harcourt, 1970.

See also LONGACRE, ROBERT E.; TAGMEMICS; YOUNG, RICHARD

Pistis

Greek word with two major meanings: (1) "trust in others, faith . . . generally persuasion of a thing, confidence, assurance" and (2) "pledge of good faith, guarantee . . . means of persuasion, argument, proof . . . esp. of proofs of orators" (Liddell and Scott 1408). The first of these meanings is the usual meaning in theology, but the second is the usual meaning in rhetoric. These means of persuasion—*pisteis* is the Greek plural—are usually listed as three. Often they are called the three proofs or the three arguments; sometimes they have been called the three appeals.

These three means of persuasion are based on the elements of the communication process: the writer, the reader, and the subject matter. Aristotle's *Rhetoric* is the first treatise (336 B.C.E.) to use this method of studying persuasion systematically. Writers can persuade by the influence of their own credibility, which is embodied in the writing. This is called the *ethical* appeal (it is not necessarily ethical, in the modern sense of the term, since writers can project entirely false images of themselves). Secondly, writers can persuade by appealing to the interests of the audience: This is usually called the *emotional appeal*. Thirdly, writers can persuade by information or arguments deriving from the subject matter being discussed; this is called *logical appeal*.

The credibility of the authors is usually established by the authors' providing direct or indirect evidence of their own honesty, of their concern for the reader's interests, and of their knowledgeability about the issues involved. Author credibility is often considered the most important of the three appeals—if authors are not believed, everything else they do is wasted effort.

The second major technique of persuasion is the appeal to the audience's interests, biases, prejudices, and emotions. A look at modern advertising for almost any product or listening to political speeches or religious sermons shows the omnipresence of this technique.

The third technique is the appeal by information or arguments relating to the subject matter under discussion. The arguments can be drawn from principles that the writer believes the reader may agree with (deductive arguments) or the arguments may be generalizations from particulars that the author presents (inductive arguments). Frequently, the deductive arguments in persuasion are based on premises and inferences that are only probable. For this reason deductive arguments in persuasion are often called enthymemes. And similarly, inductive arguments often reach only probable conclusions; for this reason, they are often called arguments by "example."

These *pisteis* originated in the study of persuasive discourse, as distinct from scientific or dialectical or literary discourse, though of course there are overlaps of different kinds of discourse. There are nearly always persuasive elements in these other kinds of discourse.

James L. Kinneavy
University of Texas, Austin

Bibliography

Aristotle. *On Rhetoric: A Theory of Civic Discourse*. Trans. George A. Kennedy. New York: Oxford, 1991.

Corbett, Edward P.J. *Classical Rhetoric for the Modern Student*. New York: Oxford, 1990.

Grimaldi, William M.A., S.J. "The Role of the *PISTEIS* in Aristotle's Methodology." *Aristotle, Rhetoric I: A Commentary*. New York: Fordham, 1980. 348–56.

Kinneavy, James L. "Persuasive Discourse." *A Theory of Discourse*. New York: Norton, 1980. 236–75.

Liddell, Henry George, and Robert Scott. *A Greek-English Lexicon*. Oxford: Clarendon, 1968.

See also ARISTOTLE; ENTHYMEME; PROOF

Pizan, Christine de (1364–c. 1430)

First European woman to earn her living by writing; initiator of the *querelle des femmes*. Born in Venice, Christine de Pizan was the daughter of Tommaso da Pizzano, court astrologer and physician to Charles V of France. Having no sons and being a proponent of women's education, her father educated her as he would have a son. Yet in the autobiographical portions of her allegories *Christine's Vision* (c. 1400) and *The Mutation of Fortune* (1405), she claims little Latin and no Greek. At fifteen she was married to a royal notary, Etienne du Castel, who died ten years later, leaving her with three children, her mother, and a niece to support.

Mourning her husband and embroiled in law suits, she took to her pen for consolation and began writing lyric poetry in the courtly love tradition—ballades, rondeaux, and virelays—which came to the attention of the ducal courts. Having secured patronage, she went on to write in several other contemporary genres. She produced a commissioned biography of Charles V and several manuals of practical advice, most notably the *Book of the Three Virtues* (1405), a mirror of honor for women; the *Book of the Body Politic* (1406–1407), a mirror for princes; and the *Book of the Feats of Arms and of Chivalry* (1410), a treatise on warfare. In these latter she anticipated the future, and more famous, handbooks for rulers by Castiglione and Machiavelli, *The Courtier* and *The Prince*. Her best known and most widely read work was her allegory *Book of the City of Ladies* (1404–1405). A response to the misogynistic attacks on women by Matheolus and Jean de Meun, the *City of Ladies* is a celebration of female virtue and wisdom, providing a positive image of womanhood modeled after, but revising, those of Boccaccio and Petrarch.

Christine's direct confrontation of misogyny initiated the *querelle des femmes,* the four-hundred-year-long debate over women's nature and status. It began in 1399 when she composed *Letter to the God of Love,* criticizing Meun's diction and tone, which she felt disparaged women and their virtue. This response, followed by the *City of Ladies,* constitutes perhaps the first Western feminist polemic.

A Christian humanist, Christine presents herself as a moral tutor and argues for women's virtue and women's education. Her work found its way into private libraries throughout Europe as late as the reign of England's Henry VII, who had her *Feats of Arms* translated into English.

No other female voice would be heard for the next hundred years.

Christine's wide erudition was the result of the rigorous program of study she undertook following her husband's death, and it provided the intellectual foundation for her long, publicly active life. The evidence of her scholarship includes her *Feats of Arms,* which is a compendium of military strategies, and the first-known French commentary on Book 1 of Aristotle's *Metaphysics,* which appears in *Christine's Vision.*

Christine died in the convent of Poissy after writing the first tribute to Joan of Arc, *The Tale of Joan of Arc.*

Yvonne Merrill
University of Arizona

Bibliography

Bell, Susan Hoag. "Christine de Pizan (1364–1430): Humanism and the Problem of a Studious Woman." *Feminist Studies* 3 (1976): 173–84.

Kelly, Joan. "Early Feminist Theory and the *Querelle des Femmes*." *Women, History and Theory. The Essays of Joan Kelly.* Chicago: U of Chicago P, 1984. 65–109.

Pisan, Christine de. *The Treasure of the City of Ladies (Book of the Three Virtues).* Trans. Sarah Lawson. New York: Penguin, 1985.

———. *Book of the City of Ladies.* Trans. and Intro. Earl Jeffrey Richards. New York: Persea, 1982.

Quilligan, Maureen. *The Allegory of Female Authority: Christine de Pizan's Cite des Dames.* Ithaca, NY: Cornell UP, 1991.

Willard, Charity Cannon. *Christine de Pizan: Her Life and Works, A Biography.* New York: Persea, 1984.

Plato (427–327 B.C.E.)

Athenian philosopher, first Greek prose writer, originator of dialogue form, inventor of many Greek neologisms, including *rhêtorikê.* Born to Athenian citizen-parents who afforded him the best education available in his day, Plato founded the Academy, a school conducted in the conversational form Plato based on the model of Socrates, and one of the few in Greek antiquity that included women students. Plato's model of dialogue continues to influence classroom discussion practices and tutorial teaching. Although a critic of many of the sophists, and of certain practices of rhetoric, Plato merits credit as the originator of the term *rhetoric,* its first great critic, and its first analyst and reformer. Many of his definitions, and representations, of true rhetoric and philosophy resemble recent social epistemic and rhetoric-of-inquiry approaches to language and knowledge.

Plato's importance to rhetoric is ultimately impossible to gauge. He was at once the first to attempt a full analysis and definition of rhetoric, among its most deft practitioners as a literary and philosophical writer, and its first—perhaps greatest—opponent. Many accounts of Plato's treatment and practice of rhetoric have focused on one of these roles, thereby distorting the complexity not only of Plato's views of rhetoric but also of rhetoric itself during the century when it grew from a practical art of speaking to a widely contended philosophy of language and political psychology.

After Socrates' death in 399 B.C.E., Plato spent twelve years in travel, to Megara among other sites, and taught in Syracuse, where he became increasingly frustrated as counselor to its ruler Dion, a story that is recounted in *Letter VII.* After the founding of the Academy (c. 387), Plato's writing was superseded by teaching activities, though scholars continue to disagree about the chronology, sequence of composition, and revision of the dialogues. Dion asked Plato to return to tutor his son Dionysus (c. 367).

Written between 399 and 387 B.C.E., within one or at most two generations of the sophists they depict, Plato's dialogues span a wide and rapidly changing period in Greek political and intellectual culture: from the great victory at Marathon in 490 B.C.E. to the long, draining Peloponnesian conflict that stretched from 440 to 404 B.C.E. Aristophanes and other dramatists assailed the new culture that accompanied political and economic reforms during the growth of the Athenian empire. Plato's dialogues, borrowing but forever altering the dramatic dialogue genre, presented to the newly literary and philosophical Athenian audience familiar characters for careful scrutiny. Ethos in the rhetorical and dramatic lexicon of the time denoted perceived or perceivable character, the face and literally the "air" (demeanor) of an individual. The literary styles and dramaturgy Plato adopts to characterize the prominent sophists of his day are themselves hallmarks of rhetorical theory and practice.

Among Plato's lasting contributions to rhetorical theory and practice at its inception in Greek language and literature are innovative mergers of genre and the creation of numerous neologisms, among them the use of the term *rhêtorikê* to denote the art, practice, theory, and subject matter that the Athenians had been taught by a number of sophists. The *Phaedrus, Gorgias, Protagoras,* and *Sophist,* along with sections of other dialogues, place rhetoric and the rhetorician under a magnifying lens: Plato's diverse representations of Socratic dialectic illuminate the practices for which Socrates himself was often represented in the literature of the time as a sophist and as a master of rhetorical tricks. Plato has long been credited with instigating a war between the philosophers and poets, as well as with extending the enmity among philosophers, rhetoricians, and sophists. In three areas, then—literary aesthetics, theory and criticism; rhetorical theory and practice; and philosophy—Plato's appraisals and practice of rhetoric continue to be studied. The revision and rebuttal of his treatments of rhetoric by his student Aristotle provide an important record of the debates concerning rhetoric that developed after Plato's initial critiques.

Rhetor and *rhêtorikê* appear primarily in those dialogues that explicitly and extensively address rhetoric: the *Gorgias, Phaedrus,* and *Menexenus.* The *Protagoras, Thrasymachus, Sophist,* and *Symposium* also deal with the character of the sophists and their teachings, as well as with the nature of sophistic knowledge and speeches. The term *rhêtorikê*—"rhetoric" proper —occurs with far less frequency than most English translations indicate. The majority of the passages in which *rhêtorikê* appears occur in the *Gorgias,* with over forty instances. In the *Phaedrus,* a dialogue focusing extensively on rhetoric, the term occurs in only nine passages. The term occurs in only two passages in the *Menexenus* and once in the *Theaetetus, Euthydemos,* and *Cratylus,* respectively. The English *rhetoric* and *speech* provide limited resources for translating the range of words and kinds of language that Plato addresses in the dialogues that deal with rhetoric. Appraisals of Plato's views of rhetoric have begun to take into account the relative infrequency of his use of the term as over and against his very clear and strenuous objections to the art and practice of the sophists.

Plato's appraisals of the sophists' roles in Athens are subtle and varied. A number of Plato's dialogues bear the names of prominent sophists, an important index of the influence on Athenian culture of its teachers before and during Pericles' era. Protagoras and Gorgias were remembered, revered, or rebuked as foreign importers of rhetoric. Plutarch and other biographers record Protagoras' close friendship and advisory role to Pericles over many years; some scholars interpret Plato's and other representations of Aspasia as directed at Protagoras' teachings and specifically at the brand of rhetoric he was remembered as teaching and practicing. Prodicus, Hippias, Thrasymachus, and Anaxagoras were also widely remembered as teachers who had influenced Euripides and Thucydides, among other prominent writers. That Plato, no friend of the sophists' teachings, went to such great lengths to represent and refute their views suggests the respect they continued to hold in many quarters as teachers of language arts, logic, political discourse, and argumentation. In this context the diverse portraits of Socrates in dialogue with a number of sophists take on additional complexities of meaning and import.

The sophists of the first half of the fifth century B.C.E. had been known primarily as cosmologists, mathematicians, and physicists. The role of many sophists in the second half of the century came to be associated with Pericles' political leadership and cultural reforms. As Pericles' popularity waned, the sophists, including Socrates, drew increasingly pointed rebukes in the forms of political censure and dramatic parody. Many sophists and associates of Pericles, including Aspasia, were tried for impiety, on charges that Plato reprises in the *Apology.* The number and nature of the impiety trials attest to the strength of popular objections to Pericles' reforms, many of them attributed to the sophists of his circle and to the rhetorical arts that they taught and practiced. Two female characters appear in Plato's dialogues: Aspasia, Pericles' consort, and Diotima, a priestess from Mantinea, one of the cities ceded by Athens during the Peloponnesian War. Plato gives Aspasia and Diotima the roles of Socrates' teacher; in the *Menexenus,* Aspasia is said to have taught and written speeches for Pericles as well. When Socrates impersonates Diotima's teachings in the *Symposium,* her speech is said to be spoken like a sophist's. Aspasia's speech, delivered by Socrates in the *Menexenus,* is presented as an example of the kind of speech-making and rhetorical teaching that by sample, model, and drill she has, he alleges, given many Athenians, among them Pericles and himself.

What Plato intends by so representing Socrates, and Aspasia, remains a matter of debate. In those dialogues in which Plato places Socrates close to the sophists' teachings, he is represented as capable of their modes of speech-making, roles that are given him in Aristophanes' comedies as well as in classical histories of his own and later centuries. The reliability of these histories is weak by modern standards of accuracy; history in antiquity was regarded as both literary and rhetorical. Nonetheless, the histories record the beliefs and received traditions of their times. Cicero places Plato and Aristotle in a liberal arts tradition in contrast to Socrates' unpopular skepticism and association with the sophists. Some scholars have long held that Plato's depictions of Socrates as a sophist are simply satires. Scholarship reinterpreting the meaning and purpose of such representations will continue to advance differing interpretations of Plato's views of rhetoric as complex, diverse, and difficult to reduce to a single position.

Plato's representations of the sophists and of the charges brought against them—legal, philosophical, ethical, and cultural—remain one of the more comprehensive sources for an understanding of early rhetoric. His portraits of Socrates emphasize several points of resemblance to the sophists: his exchange with Callicles in the *Gorgias*, the contests of speeches in the *Phaedrus* and *Symposium*, his alliance with the poets in the *Symposium* that contrasts so sharply with the banishment of the poets from the *Republic*. In these passages Socrates has traits that the Athenians had come to dislike in the sophists and to attribute to their rhetoric: political opportunism, flashy oratorical and poetic performances, ostentatious impiety, word wrangling, and logic chopping. Understood by the definition he gives it in the *Gorgias*, as the practice and teaching of an art of public speaking, rhetoric is dismissed by Plato on several counts. A well-trained rhetor who knows little or nothing about a subject can, if he has been well trained, be more convincing than a far more knowledgeable specialist. Rhetorical speech is the imitation of an imitation; like writing—a parallel that Plato develops at length in the *Phaedrus*—it gives the surface or pretense of knowledge without any sure measure of credibility or substance. In both the *Gorgias* and the *Phaedrus*, Plato argues that rhetorical training and practice encourage the rhetor and, in turn, the populace, to prefer opinion to truth, probability to proof, and the well-told tale to the more complex details of actual occurrences.

In the *Menexenus,* Aspasia's rendition of a political history of Athens would have been patently false and humorously specious to both its Athenian and modern audiences if it were not also a classic example of encomiastic oratory. Is Aspasia's speech a stand-in for Pericles' famed oration—a speech perhaps that Plato dared not deride? To accept the merits of Aspasia's speech as a model oration is to ignore Plato's implicit critique in representing the speech. To accept it as convicting rhetoric of the crimes Plato elsewhere defines raises the question of why Plato presents Aspasia's skills, like Socrates', as practiced and formidable. If a satire, it is subtle. More obvious villains, such as Thrasymachus and Callicles, bear much heavier measures of Plato's censorious portraiture; their crimes are not limited to rhetorical speech-making. In manner as well as substance, they are presented as advocates as well as practitioners of political and moral philosophies injurious to the individual and to the state.

Recent scholarship on the sophists of Pericles' and Socrates' generation, the mid 450s B.C.E., and particularly on Protagoras, is fostering an improved understanding of the intellectual and political substance of the sophists' teachings and thereby of Plato's objections to them and to rhetoric. Several of the repeated objections to Protagoras are alleged of Socrates as well, though the *Apology* depicts these charges as guilt by mistaken association. Similarly, Aristotle, in his discussion of the arguments from probability in the *Topics* and *Rhetoric* explicitly renounces Protagoras' argument of probability, the *"eikos."* Among the charges Plato levels against Protagoras, and against other sophists as well, were taking fees for teaching, using *antiglogia* and *dissoi logoi*—sharp and somewhat mechanically contrasted arguments for and against an issue—and teaching that virtue or excellence can be taught to all, that the "many" can become "one" by the laws of democracy and through education. Protagoras' man-is-the-measure-of-all-things formula was widely alleged to have led to a false equality of the "one" under the new laws. Virtue (*aretê*)—the ranking of individuals by abilities and talents—was viewed as lost to the goal of commonality advanced under the discussions of nature (*phusis*) versus law (*nomos*). Probability was seen as supplanting truth; the law of averages, it was widely feared, was creating a state in which might makes right. Although it is often conflated with an attack on what today is thought of as relativism, Plato's criticism of Protagoras' man-measure and nature-law formulas is focused on the contention that it is a groundless epistemology and leads to a specious democracy resting on manmade laws and on ever-changing, guilefully manipulated words with no checks to contain those for whom justice is the interest of the stronger.

Though they are enormous subjects in themselves, each of these points of objection surfaces at numerous points in Plato's treatment of rhetoric. It is easy to forget that Athenian democracy was by no means a positive concept in its own time, that "the many" were not highly regarded and that numerous jokes depicted Gorgias, Pericles, and other political leaders as big-headed, many-headed, or swollen-headed miscreants, as chimerical monsters leading gullible "sheep." In a series of puns that provide at least one rhyme analogy with rhetoric, the *rhen* (sheep) are led by the rhetor, whose speech flows like a flooding river (*rhetegmi*). Placed amidst these jokes in the popular culture of the time, Plato's treatment of rhetoric assumes an unexpected respectability of presentation and substance.

Despite his own rhetorical and literary practices, Plato perhaps seeks to distance himself from the widely reviled practices of the sophists and of rhetoric. A singular difference between Socrates and the sophists, and a legacy as well, is emphasized in the setting Plato chooses for the dialogues: the small informal conversation in a home in the evenings. Socrates prefers to meet with people in small groups and to speak informally, at least by the discourse standards of public speeches and teaching to audiences. Plato does not abandon rhetoric entirely as a mode of discourse; he argues for a philosophical and ethical rhetoric that is dialogical and dialectical, that draws upon Socrates' presence in the agora and symposia and his attempts to reintegrate the burgeoning specializations of the sophists—in logic, cosmology, epistemology, mathematics, and language theory—with the life of daily culture in the symposia of educated Athenians.

The paradoxes of Socrates' roles in the dialogues, and implicitly of Plato's views of rhetoric, warrant repeated emphasis in light of the tendency to create a monolithic Plato who simply denounced rhetoric. A paradigm for true rhetoric is sketched in the *Phaedrus* and performed in a number of Plato's dialogues—a dialogical-dialectical method that strongly resembles modern paradigms for a "rhetoric of inquiry." This resemblance and the intriguing juxtaposition of Plato's banishment of the poets alongside his highly literary performances in the dialogues should further warn against easy characterizations of his views as either for or against rhetoric or the poets. Plato's importance as a literary artist instigated the wars between philosophy and poetry, poetry and rhetoric, and rhetoric and philosophy. At the same time, the dialogues are arguably among the first instances of rhetorical uses of literary art and of rhetorical appraisals of literary—then primarily dramatic—art.

The dramatic structure and literary form of Plato's dialogues have received erratic attention, particularly among those who have focused on his war with the poets. In the *Poetics,* Aristotle commends the natural prose style emulating conversational speech in sections of Plato's dialogues and in Euripides' dramas—another reminder of how closely Plato's dialogues approximated literary dramas in their own time. Even today if read aloud as reader's theater or performed in sections, they preserve a sense of how reading aloud and the ability to declaim a speech, as Phaedrus, Socrates, and the participants in the *Symposium* do, were important methods of teaching and learning the art of rhetoric as well as the art of drama. That Plato objects to rote memorization does not exclude his dramatic representations of speeches performed by the sophists and poets of his era. Whether the import of these representations is a singular denunciation of all poetic and rhetorical practice remains debatable, an ambiguity that leaves room for the interpretation of such passages as not only records but also proposals for improving upon the speech-making and dramaturgical workshops of Plato's day.

A number of recent studies of Plato's dialogues have revived attention to his uses of narrative, myth, and lengthy stretches of prose exposition. Conforming to the outline of the rhetorical speech that he mocks in the *Phaedrus,* many of Plato's dialogues begin with an initial statement of the topic or issue at hand, proceed to a narrative—sometimes a myth—delineating the details or nature of the issue, turn to an *agon* or argument among two or more participants debating the issue, sum up the progress of the discussion in one or more recapitulations, and conclude with a narrative or myth prior to the dramatic narrative closing out the evening's symposium. As with the speech by the god that traditionally concluded the Greek dramas, Plato's dialogues often conclude with a traditional myth, invocation, prayer, or allusion to Socrates' ubiquitous daimon.

Dionysus of Halicarnassus and Cicero span the first centuries of classical admiration for Plato's literary exemplarity. Cicero so admired Plato as a stylist, rhetorical theorist and practitioner, and philosopher that he set out to play the same role for Latin culture that he regarded Plato as having played for the Greeks:

to create a prose style by inaugurating a literary language, a philosophical lexicon, and a range of genres for a Latin literature that up to his time had few literate indigenous paradigms. Like Plato, he came to reject the mechanical rhetorical education he had received in the rhetoricians' workshops, and he developed a critique of his teenage *De inventione* in a series of dialogues that he regarded not only as about rhetoric but as models of rhetorical education and practice. Recent work on hermeneutics and dialogics in Plato's and subsequent eras has revived attention to the presence of the dialogue as a vehicle for talking about and practicing both philosophy and rhetoric. Not only Cicero but a succession of dialogue writers in later centuries owe to Plato the sustained integration of literary and philosophical purposes, the retention of metaphor within philosophy and of philosophical substance within literary narrative and poetry that have been recurrently revived in later liberal arts traditions. Inasmuch as the modern expository essay since Montaigne at least is an implicitly dialogical genre, it warrants attention as a successor to the dialogical Plato as much as to the monological traditions of the treatise and school thesis.

In sum, Plato's contributions to rhetoric are perhaps best understood in a narrow and then in larger senses, much as rhetoric as a discipline and practice today has special meanings within disciplines but sustains and builds a larger sense across fields. Defined as a practical political art of public speaking, rhetoric was dismissed by Plato on political, philosophical, and ethical grounds. Understood as a study of interactive discourse and of its goals, rhetoric was given one of its earliest expositions by Plato, who contributed to that paradigm the goal of seeking truth through its collective pursuit. By retaining the rigorous interrogative pattern of Socrates' practice of dialectic, Plato also defined a dialogical rhetorical practice that resembles contemporary rhetorics of inquiry. By inaugurating the literary and dramatic dialogue as a vehicle for conducting and teaching both philosophy and what today would be termed language arts, Plato provided an early written model for classroom and philosophical discourses that was explicitly designed to provide an alternative to the declamation of an outlined or memorized speech that was then current in rhetorical education and political practice.

C. Jan Swearingen
University of Texas, Arlington

Bibliography

Allen, Michael J.B. *Icastes: Marsilio Ficino's Interpretation of Plato's* Sophist. Berkeley: U of California P, 1989.

Arieti, James. *Interpreting Plato: The Dialogues as Drama.* Savage, MD: Rowman, 1991.

Classen, P. Joachim. "Protagoras' *Aletheia.*" *The Criterion of Truth.* Ed. Pamela Huby and Gordon Neal. Liverpool: Liverpool UP, 1989.

———. *Rhetorik.* Wege der Forschung, 187 (Darmstadt 1976).

Coby, Patrick. *Socrates and the Sophistic Enlightenment.* Lewisburg, PA: Bucknell UP, 1987.

Cole, A.T. *The Origins of Rhetoric in Ancient Greece.* Baltimore: Johns Hopkins UP, 1990.

Fornara, Charles W., and Loren J. Samons. *Athens from Cleisthenes to Pericles.* Berkeley: U of California P, 1991.

Friedlander, Paul. *Plato: The Dialogues.* Vol. 2. Trans. Hans Meyerhoff. Princeton, NJ: Bollingen, 1964.

Gadamer, Hans Georg. *Dialogue and Dialectic: Eight Hermeneutical Studies.* Trans. P. Christopher Smith. New Haven: Yale UP, 1980.

———. *Plato's Dialectical Ethics.* Trans. Robert M. Wallace. New Haven: Yale UP, 1991.

Guthrie, W.K.C. *A History of Greek Philosophy.* Vol. 4. *Plato: The Dialogues.* New York: Cambridge UP, 1986.

Jarratt, Susan. *Rereading the Sophists: Classical Rhetoric Refigured.* Carbondale: Southern Illinois UP, 1991.

Kerferd, G.B., ed. *The Sophists and Their Legacy. Hermes* Heft 44. Bad Hamburg: Franz Steiner, 1981.

Kirby, John T. "Aristotle's *Poetics:* The Rhetorical Principle." *Arethusa* 24 (1991): 197–217.

Lewis, D.M., John Boardman, J.K. Davies, and M. Ostwald. *The Cambridge Ancient History.* 2nd ed. Vol. 5. *The Fifth Century.* New York: Cambridge UP, 1992.

Neel, Jasper. *Plato, Derrida, and Writing.* Carbondale: Southern Illinois UP, 1988.

Romilly, Jacqueline de. *The Great Sophists in Periclean Athens.* Trans. Janet Lloyd. Oxford: Clarendon, 1992.

Rosen, Stanley R. *Plato's Sophist, the Drama*

of Original and Image. New Haven: Yale UP, 1983.

Schiappa, Edward. *Protagoras and Logos: A Study in Greek Philosophy and Rhetoric.* Columbia: U of South Carolina P, 1991.

Stokes, Michael C. *Plato's Socratic Conversations: Drama and Dialectic in Three Dialogues.* Baltimore, MD: Johns Hopkins UP, 1986.

Pleonasm

The use of words that can be eliminated without changing meanings. "The inaudible and noiseless foot of time" (*All's Well that Ends Well* 5.3.41). The verbal excess that occurs in a pleonasm can strengthen what is expressed, as when the Psalmist lamented, "By reason of the voice of my groaning my bones cleave to my skin" (Psalm 102:5). Used to excess, pleonasm becomes battology, as William Safire demonstrated: "To be redundant is to be overflowing, unnecessarily wordy, tautologous, overabundant, excessive, or using too many synonyms in a single definition" ("On Language," *New York Times,* Nov. 12, 1983).

Arthur Quinn and Lyon Rathbun
University of California, Berkeley

Ploce

"Plaiting"; repetition of a proper name to designate both an individual and the general qualities that that person is thought to possess. In the sentence "Cicero continued Cicero unto the day of his death," the proper name designates both the man and the patriotism embodied in the man (Peacham). Joyce was using ploce in characterizing some pretenders as "more Irish than the Irish." Paul is also using ploce in Romans when he warns, "They are not all Israel, which are of Israel."

Arthur Quinn and Lyon Rathbun
University of California, Berkeley

Poetics

The study of discourse alternatively called "aesthetic," "literary," "fictional," or "imaginative." In documents and controversies emerging in the West between the fourth century B.C.E. and the end of the nineteenth century, poetics has consisted of theoretical reflections on the mode of being, way of knowing, or art of doing that such discourse evokes or presupposes.

Plato and the Sophists

Plato defines poetics alternatively as mimesis (imitation) and as *enthousiasmos* (inspiration). Plato assigns all artistic objects a lowly epistemological status at a third remove from the highest reality, the forms of truth, ideas accessible only through philosophical inquiry. Having no knowledge of dialectical thinking, the poet has no access to the realm of ideas but can only produce counterfeit copies of external appearances sealed off from truth: imitations of imitations of reality. In *The Republic* Plato banishes poetry from the education of rulers and limits it to state-regulated ceremonial functions.

Plato's definition of *poeisis* as inspired madness appears in later treatises. His explicit statements remain critical, questioning the validity of any knowledge acquired without the mediation of dialectics; yet by relying on myth as a mechanism for representing the moment of dialectical discovery, he harnesses the power of poetics to philosophy.

Twentieth-century historical research on the sophists clarifies the cultural stakes involved in harnessing *poeisis*. Havelock argues that sophistic discourse drew on a tradition of communal participation in rhythmic cadences that appealed to the senses aurally, visually, and kinetically and that conflated the acquisition of knowledge with its expression (1963:146–57). Such discourse was diametrically opposed to the tonality of dialectic, which disengaged speakers from one another and from the object under scrutiny and located the acquisition of knowledge at the end of a temporal chain of question and answer.

Though hostile toward poetics, Plato acknowledges that poetics shapes society and vies with philosophy as a way of knowing. Plato's very attacks on *poeisis* create a space for a theoretically grounded notion of poetic truth.

Aristotle's Poetics

In the *Poetics,* Aristotle treats poetics as a field of knowledge. Assigning poetics the status of a *technê,* or productive art, Aristotle identifies for *poeisis* a structural principle, emplotment; an epistemological production, mimesis; a cognitive incentive, recognition of universal essence in particular form; and a sociocultural rationale, evocation of catharsis; and he systematically interrelates these identifications.

Emplotment crafts an action that pares away the episodic and tangential, revealing a universal truth about the human condition.

Mimesis is not reflective, but productive: It distills complex experience into a characteristically human action. By focusing so strongly on emplotment, Aristotle aligns poetics with the production of form. Central in Aristotle's philosophizing, form is not one dimension of reality among others but the only stay against chaos: Form ensures that attributes cohere into bounded objects and that occurrences over time can reappear as knowable events, not as accidents. Aristotle's emphasis on the unities of time, place, and action is less a mechanism for judgment than an assurance that the insights proffered by mimesis can induce the pleasure of drawing inferences. *Poeisis* affords us the opportunity to learn because it elicits from the flux the structure of reality.

Although Aristotle specifies learning as the goal of mimetic activity, he claims that tragedy has as its goal catharsis, an elicitation of pity and fear in the audience. The term *catharsis* is contested. Is catharsis therapeutic, the purging of excessive emotions? Is catharsis a restoration of moral purity? Or is catharsis an alternative term for intellectual elucidation? The latter definition is consistent with Aristotle's specification of learning as the goal of mimetic activity in the *Poetics* as well as with the stress on intelligibility as the highest philosophical value in the Aristotelian corpus (Preminger and Kerrane 101–3). All these definitions assign to poetics a functional role in the right-working of the polis that contrasts with Plato's vacillation between condemning poetics as a disruption to the state and appropriating poetics in a quest for truth that would bypass human institutions.

Poetics in the Hellenistic Age

The Greek city-states ceased to be the primary centers of reflection on poetics once the locus of political power shifted to the Macedonian empire of Alexander the Great and his successors. The library of Alexandria became a center of textual scholarship. Those who reflected on poetics were interested primarily in collecting, editing, interpreting, and judging discrete texts, not in theorizing.

Several ideas that would provoke debate in later eras emerge in Hellenistic scholarship during the third to first centuries B.C.E.

(1) Literature is defined as a collection of masterpieces from a past age, the excellences of which can never be equaled, let alone surpassed. Lists of such "classics" constitute *canones*, lists of texts appropriate for analysis and edification. Contemporary literature is considered inferior and is kept out of the curriculum (Kennedy 207–8).

(2) The proper focus of analysis is the stylistic excellence of brief passages; no interest is provoked by questions of large-scale formal structure or universal theme.

(3) Genres are distinguished by subject, organization, and style.

(4) A sharp division is maintained between form and content, which provokes debates on the relative importance of delight versus instruction and expressive effects versus subject matter (Preminger and Kerrane 8).

In the Hellenistic age, the scholar-critic emerges as a cultural figure. Years of training authorize scholar-critics to establish textual authenticity through philological procedures, to judge degrees of quality in poetry, and to determine which texts will become part of the curriculum. The Alexandrian scholar-critics limit questions of meaning to those that can be resolved through comparative analysis of parallel passages. Philosophical questions about meaning and cultural significance receive scant attention.

One of these scholar-critics, Callimachus, who was also a practicing poet, formulated stylistic precepts that would be used by Augustan poets to authorize their own poetic choices. Callimachus calls for poetic production calibrated by the needs of his age. Acknowledging the superiority of Homer's epic, he rejects epic in favor of genres displaying "leanness," a narrowing of scope and theme and a focus on precise diction and elegant syntax and meter (Kennedy 202–3).

Each of the philosophical schools of fourth-century Athens that were sustained during the Hellenistic age influences poetics. A representative of the Peripatetic School, Neoptolemus of the third century B.C.E. defends a poetic doctrine reflecting Aristotelian systematicness. Poetics has a three-part structure: (1) *poiema*, the repertoire of stylistic techniques; (2) *poeisis*, the strategies for inventing and arranging subject matter; and (3) *poietes*, the poet, who must put *poiema* and *poeisis* at the service of an audience in need of moral instruction that is both utilitarian and enchanting (Kennedy 204). Stoic philosophy is represented by allegorists, who "find" ethical doctrines in poetry by interpreting figures of speech. Allegory layers the literal and the figurative, demanding imaginative powers from both poet and audience. In the Epicurean school of thought, poetry merges cognition with emotion, subject matter with style, theme with arrangement. Philodemus, an Epicurean of the first century B.C.E., contests reigning assumptions of the Hellenistic age: He rejects didactic aims, ridicules allegorical moralizing, and counters the prevailing division of content from form, insisting instead on organic interrelatedness (Innes 1989).

Poetics in the Augustan Age

Ties between poetics and philosophy remain significant during the Augustan age. But rhetoric's ties with poetics during both the Hellenistic and Augustan periods are even more intimate. The point of differentiation between the two is fluid within as well as across discrete texts. At times the distinction is a formal one between poetry and prose. At other times the distinction references the forum within which a particular composition is expected to appear, with poetics being a collection of genres that entertain or uplift the educated classes. Yet such genres are never outside the realm of rhetorical effectivity, and poetics continues to be framed by an educational system grounded in rhetoric.

In the *Ars poetica,* Horace comes as close as anyone in the Augustan age to acknowledging poetics as a discrete field. Yet most of that document's distinctive doctrines and precepts are shaped by the rhetorical tradition. In fact, the *Ars poetica* is a compilation of legacies, not a new theoretical poetics. Despite its scenario, advice given to an aspiring poet in a personal letter, the *Ars poetica* is closely structured in accordance with Neoptolemus's three-part schema of *poesis,* subject matter; *poema,* compositional technique; and *poeta,* the poet (Innes 259). And like Callimachus, Horace takes the position of the poet-critic seeking options in an age that insists that the excellences of its classical inheritance can be honored but not reproduced.

In Horace we see the Augustan meaning of imitation, a meaning it had acquired in the centuries since the dispersal of Greek culture throughout the Hellenistic empire. Imitation is neither a copying of appearances nor a structuring of a work to elicit form; imitation echoes previous poets, sustaining linkages with the Greek tradition through allusion and adaptation. In addition to advocating imitation of the past over the invention of the new, the *Ars poetica* transmits other tenets to medieval and Renaissance culture. Unity is always an aim but can be achieved through a variety of technical moves. Genres are distinct and must be analyzed as blueprints for poetic production. Decorum is the final arbiter in questions of content inclusion/exclusion and of style. The poet needs knowledge, technical craft, and genius to produce *utile et dulce*, instruction and pleasure.

Latin and Greek Poetics in the Roman Empire

In this period poetics remains imbricated with rhetorical and philosophical traditions that constitute the educational system; "literature" includes any constructed discursive product. The *canones* and the exegetical practices they elicit remain protectorates of rhetoricians and philosophers. The range of positions regarding the nature and worth of poetic production resemble those first codified during the Hellenistic age.

Two movements that arose among Greeks prior to Christianity's ascendancy influenced Western approaches to text reception and production. The Second Sophistic and Neoplatonist movements renew much earlier Greek tradition. Both assume that education in oratory and interpretation provide access to a higher state, secular or sacred, and that classical literature is the source of wisdom. Both movements perpetuate earlier methods of exegesis which, by being practiced in the schools, are inherited by Christendom and passed on to medieval and Renaissance culture.

Latter-day sophists demonstrate the power of oratory in both public and private forums, analyze oratorical effects, invent fictional speeches as part of oratorical training, and attend to theories of figuration. Neoplatonists promote Stoic methods of interpretation: Through symbolization that assigns multiple meanings to all phenomena, they accommodate seemingly irreconcilable philosophies and practices.

[Pseudo-]Longinus's *On the Sublime*

Written sometime in the first or second century C.E. and at one time attributed to Longinus, the Greek treatise *On the Sublime* is a touchstone of classical poetics. A training manual for orators, *On the Sublime* assumes that rhetorical choices anticipate audience response. However, *On the Sublime* is distinctive in its use of the rhetorical tradition. Classical rhetorical distinctions among high, middle, and low styles traditionally served a classificatory purpose: stylistic level coordinated genre, syntax, and diction options for rhetors shaping discourse for the "level" of audience to be affected. But in *On the Sublime*, the evaluative connotations of "high" are drawn out to constitute a qualitative dimension of language that marks a masterpiece, the greatness of which audiences of all times and stations would assent to.

The sublime, *hypsos*, is an eloquence on an entirely different scale than can be produced by mere craft. Pervading an entire work or a brief passage, the sublime uplifts, literally "transports" the audience intellectually, psychologically, and ethically. The experience owes its intensity to the skillful balancing of *poeisis*, the framing of profound thoughts, and pathos, a sustained receptivity to intense emotion. Unless the artist possesses spiritual insight, rhetorical arts of composition, word choice, and figuration cannot effect sublimity.

Like Aristotle's *Poetics* and Horace's *Ars poetica*, *On the Sublime* is a primary text in the history of poetics. If read independently of the rhetorical and philosophical cultures within which they were embedded, these texts present classical poetics as a distinct disciplinary field, and each text becomes a forefather engendering formalist, neoclassical, and Romantic poetics, respectively. This is not to say that later appropriations have no validity, only that those appropriations make programmatic demands upon those texts that effectively rewrite them.

Poetics and Classical Culture Prior to the Middle Ages

Between the third and sixth centuries C.E., issues relevant to poetics are addressed in treatises that teach grammar and demonstrate Neoplatonic allegorizing. Servius's commentary on Virgil, a textbook on Latin grammar that follows the topical procedure of *accessus* initiated by earlier Roman grammarians, will eventually serve as a prototype for the medieval gloss. *Accessus* specifies that a commentary on a poet must first discuss the author's life, then the title of the text under review, then the quality of the poet's verse, then his intent, then the number and order of books within the poem, and finally "explanation," a section explicating figural, metrical, and grammatical usages. Relying on traditional allegorical interpretations of *The Aeneid*, the text moves from line to line to highlight resources for eloquence that a Latin student could appropriate (Kennedy). Medieval commentators would combine the *accessus* with the comparative listing of Greek and Latin canonic *auctores* modeled by Quintilian in Book 10 of the *Institutio Oratoria* to produce treatises called *accessus ad auctores*. Servius's treatise implicitly defines poetics as the line-by-line dissection of standard texts for didactic purposes.

Macrobius's fourth-century commentary on the *Somnium Scipionis* at the conclusion of Cicero's *De republica* illustrates a second curricular location for poetics, moral philosophy. Macrobius follows traditional Neoplatonic explication procedures, announcing the definitional *skopos*, or theme, of the text, linking up *skopos* with textual details, and interpreting each dream event allegorically. Four dimensions of this commentary will be sustained from the early centuries of Christendom through the Middle Ages to the end of the Renaissance: reverence for Virgil's learning and moral stature, reliance on Cicero as a model of prose style and moral thought, use of the dream allegory to teach spiritual truths, and defense of *figmentum* (fictions) as vehicles for integrating delight with instruction in moral philosophy.

Syntheses of Neoplatonic theory remain influential throughout the Middle Ages. For example, Proclus, writing in the fifth century, locates three levels of truth in poetry: the lowest level represents sensory experience; the middle level represents scientific, ethical, and spiritual precepts and reveals a unitary essence underlying being; at the highest level of poetic truth, the rational faculty is bypassed in a direct apprehension of divine truth (Russell 326–27).

In the earliest years of Christendom, scholars disagree regarding the sustainability of the "pagan" arts of rhetoric and poetic within Christian institutions. Augustine's stance toward the relation between discourse and belief is shaped by rhetorical training and Neoplatonic interpretive assumptions. In addition to the explicit allegorizing in the work of St. Paul, Clement of Alexandria at the end of the second century and Origen at the beginning of the third anticipate some of Augustine's arguments in support of poetics.

Augustine's adaptation of the Ciceronian rhetorical tradition to the needs and values of the church ensured rhetoric's imbrication within the educational system and its continuing cultural prestige. Augustine also preserved the hermeneutic traditions transmitted through allegorical procedures of the Stoics and the Neo-platonists. In the first half of *De doctrina christiana*, St. Augustine constructs a theory of interpretation that permits events in the Old Testament to be assigned a Christian meaning. The delight we experience when confronting figurative language is due in part to the sense of reward for the hard work of exegesis and, most important, for the ineffable experience of God that signs can point to but never incorporate.

Poetics in Medieval Europe

Throughout the Middle Ages, poetics has no place of its own: It emerges in each of the disciplines of the trivium at various times. Servius's and Macrobius's association of poetics with grammar and with Neoplatonism dominates the age. In the sixth century, Fulgentius follows these two commentators on *The Aeneid* closely but explicitly links the wisdom of Virgil with the revealed truths of Christianity. He claims that each event in the epic illustrates an issue in moral philosophy and a stage in the journey from birth to death.

Geoffrey de Vinsauf shaped this grammatical and allegorical inheritance into a poetic that contrasts with Horace's rhetoric-centered poetic, the more dominant approach throughout the Middle Ages. Though his *Poetria nova* is a textbook like its rhetorical counterparts, Geoffrey stresses a nonaudience-directed inwardness: Meaning lies within words; ornament is a sign of an inner light, and intention is favored over effect. The mind of the poet, not as it anticipates audience reaction but as it apprehends an invisible truth, shapes the work.

A medieval controversy over the value of poetics emerges in the twelfth-century "standoff" between the humanists, who advocate the traditional grammatical, *auctores*-driven curriculum and the scholastics, who advocate a dialectic-centered curriculum based on what are assumed to be the works of Aristotle. The twelfth-century humanists argue that instruction in how to read the standard list of *auctores* prepares the student for reading scripture and for moral instruction. The scholastics see Aristotle, logic, and dialectic as the appropriate resources for acquiring knowledge and resolving questions of faith. The scholastics reject Neoplatonic interpretive procedures and rhetorical compilations of tropes and schemes for definitional operations based on comparison and contrast.

One hundred years later, the most influential of the medieval Aristotelianists, St. Thomas Aquinas, elaborates definitions for the discourse arts that establish the relative approximation of each to truth. His abstract schema did not displace grammar as curricular preparation for rhetoric. But his scriptural hermeneutic, the fourfold levels of interpretation, is transferred by Dante (1265–1321) to secular and vernacular literature and becomes immensely influential. The fourfold schema begins with the literal level of interpretation and then specifies a movement through three stages of spiritual hermeneutics, from allegorical to moral to anagogical. Dante inherits St. Thomas's attentiveness to the literal level, seen not as a fictive distortion to be overcome but as an initiation into higher truth. Material reality yields figures that elicit our mental powers in an exercise leading to spiritual understanding. In the *Convivio* Dante privileges the realistic texture of narrative and image as a pathway to insight.

De Vulgari Eloquentia breaks new ground in poetics. First, Dante provides no authorizing scholarly predecessors for his assertions that the vernacular is a worthy instrument for poetry and that the many dialects need to be unified into one standard language. He appeals instead to observable social phenomena. Second, though Dante references God's desire for man's spiritual well-being, his focus is on the good that man can derive on earth through intercommunication. Third, grammar and poetics are conjoined mechanisms for unification of Italy's dialects into one language. No longer restricted to the initiation of the young into literacy, grammar and poetics now perpetuate all culture, and the productive poet has a central social function within contemporary society.

Renaissance Poetics

The question of whether to assign poetics to logic, rhetoric, or grammar evolved into a debate that marked the turn in European sensibility and inquiry practices known as the Renaissance. The defense of poetry is part of a larger Renaissance humanist project, the countering of the rationalist categories of scholastic logic with a new cultural and educational program centered on the discursive arts and classical learning. During the Renaissance the defense of poetics becomes a subgenre.

To legitimate poetics, scholars and scholar-poets sought to align poetics with disciplines or arts already validated by the church. In 1315 Mussato first argues for poetics as a worthy servant of theology: Poetry effects a linkage between the earthly and the divine. In correspondence and treatises, Petrarch claims a total congruence between classical poetry and Scripture. Boccaccio's *Genealogiae decorum gentilium,* begun in 1343 and completed in the early 1370s, serves as a compendium of the arguments leveled at poetics by theologians, primarily the Dominicans, who were powerful advocates of scholastic learning based on Aquinas, and of counterarguments earlier constructed by Mussato and Petrarch. In addition, the *Genealogie* is a storehouse of Latin and a few Greek writers of classical myth and pagan legend, whose work had been unavailable to poets and scholars throughout the medieval period.

A series of Italian humanist scholars continue to elaborate ever more powerful and complex defenses of poetics. In the last decades of the fourteenth century, Salutati integrates Petrarch's theory that polytheism is a cover for monotheism with the idea that anthropomorphism helps man conceptualize divinity (Aguzzi-Barbagli 89). Other scholars translate documents from the Greek that reflect the high regard for classical literature of some early Christian writers. In the fifteenth century, Bruni links poetics to oratory and philosophy, fields that had centuries earlier secured an epistemological legitimation despite nonspiritual content; Guarino defends poetics' pedagogical utility and integrates classical literature into his humanistic curriculum.

Thus a place is secured for poetics within the *studia humanitatis,* the cycle of disciplines that centered on the interpretation of Latin and Greek classical texts: grammar, poetry, rhetoric, moral philosophy, and history. Though rhetoric was one of several more or less discrete Renaissance disciplines, rhetoric was also an intellectual and cultural agency that shaped each of its associated disciplines by instituting verbal eloquence as a standard for assessing excellence. By incorporating poetics, both its classical texts and its interpretive procedures, into the cultural program of eloquence, humanist scholars firmly established a social utility for poetics.

From the mid fifteenth century through the sixteenth century, three traditions elaborated theories of poetics: the Horatian, the Aristotelian, and the Platonic or Neoplatonic. Horace's treatise sustained its popularity from the Augustan age through the late classical, medieval, and Renaissance periods. For the Renaissance humanists, the *Ars poetica,* an audience-focused poetics, incorporated the rhetorical ideal of eloquence, the pedagogical rationale for art, and the social value of well-crafted persuasive language. In addition, Horace wrote to encourage Latin poets to emulate Greek predecessors, so the values undergirding a revival of classical texts were evident throughout.

Pazzi's 1536 Latin translation of Aristotle's *Poetics* prompted a series of Latin and then Italian commentaries. All assume that poetry preserves and advocates superior modes of conduct. They share rhetorical presuppositions about the moral and utilitarian ends of poetry, the centrality of conceptions of a readership to poetic production, and the importance of decorum as the principle of artistic selection. Aristotle's *Poetics* was interpreted within this rhetorical frame.

Castelvetro's commentary (1576) was to be of decisive influence in neoclassical poetics. He abandons moralistic and utilitarian rationales in favor of the pleasure rationale and exhibits a distrust of fantastical elements that place undue demands on the imaginative capacities of a general audience. His advocacy of the Aristotelian three unities and the powers of *ingegno,* or wit, becomes doctrine during the next century.

Plato, too, is a resource in the ongoing polemic in defense of poetry. By attempting to align poetic inspiration with that of saints and prophets, Neoplatonic critics try to justify the existence of poetry in an ideal Christian state. They make distinctions among modes of poetry; only divinely inspired poetry can be aligned with truth; most classical literature has no spiritual value. Neoplatonic theorists keep alive the notion of a poetic furor impervious to critical categorization. Patrizi, writing in the 1580s, locates in inspiration and genius the origins of poetic production and initiates renewed attention to the long neglected treatise *On the Sublime* and a new independence from the authoritative controls exerted by cultural reverence for the ancients (Aguzzi-Barbagli 137–39).

One Renaissance theorist stakes out a space that is neither Horation, nor Aristotelian, nor Platonic: Scaliger, an Italian often credited with initiating French classicism, places ethics at the center of poetics: The poet's craft is judgmental rather than inspired or inventive; material with aesthetic potential must be subjected to ethical assessment. Scaliger rejects the imitation of classical models for imitation of physical nature harboring ethical messages.

The distinctions, attitudes, and issues elaborated in the Italian Renaissance are representative of the European and English Renaissance in the last half of the sixteenth century. In France, the *Pleiade* consisted of seven French poets who argued for poetry written in vernacular French. One of the *Pleiade*, Ronsard, wrote in favor of Horatian poetics but extended to the poet the status of seer or prophet. Du Bellay wrote the definitive poetics for the group, *La Defense et illustration de la langue francaise* (1549), arguing for the equal merits of the Greek, Latin, and French languages. In England, Sidney wrote *Defense of Poesie* (1595) with a Platonic framework interlaced with Horatian, Aristotelian, and nationalistic assumptions. Influenced by the Italian critic Minturno's *De poeta* (1559), Sidney synthesizes principles and arguments drawn from as wide a range of positions, but unlike Minturno, Sidney integrates rather than juxtaposes diverse critical stances.

Neoclassical Poetics

The Renaissance defense of poetics succeeded in legitimating poetry. Neoclassical critics, taking poetry's worth for granted, elaborate agendas concerning the proper stance toward the classical past. National literatures and poetics proliferate, and debates on how to appropriate classical tradition are repeatedly staged. Neoclassicism was the dominant poetics throughout the seventeenth century and during the first decades of the eighteenth century.

Neoclassical theorists retain from the Renaissance a belief in audience-centered poetics and a reverence for classical models, especially Roman ones. They cultivate a Neoplatonic concept of "nature." This is not a nature opposed to the human but a universal nature of the human: Greek and Roman poetry is superior because it appeals to a universal human nature. Critics such as Bouhours, Ben Jonson, and Samuel Johnson react against what they deem to be an excess of idiosyncratic imagery and argument in late Renaissance Italian and English poetry. These and others such as Boileau, Swift, Pope, and Corneille seek guidelines for poetic production based on classical models deploying decorum, common sense, lucidity, and universal typologies. Neoclassicists advocate formal symmetry and balance, elegant diction, and strictly defined genre conventions, and they equate inherited ideas with timeless truths.

Neoclassicists call for a poetics of probable correspondences relevant to a universal audience. Aristotle's brief remarks on the value of unity of time, place, and action rigidify into a doctrine congenial to an age dominated by Bacon, Descartes, and Pascal, who sought evidence of rational, orderly systems everywhere. The impossibility of finding models, modern or ancient, that unequivocally exemplify the doctrine led to the elaboration of rationales for the renegade features of beloved works.

In the controversy of the 1680s and 1690s known as the "Battle of the Ancients and Moderns," appeals to the imitation of "nature" mark both sides. Boileau, La Fontaine, and Rhymer, defenders of the ancients, claim that classical adherence to natural rules are often not even approached by contemporary authors; they remain committed to the idea of imitation as imitation of past masters. Perrault and Fontenelle, defenders of the moderns, argue that contemporary authors should bypass classical models and Aristotelian guidelines and turn instead to the direct observation of nature. Dryden and Fenelon zigzag between the two poles: The poet should be educated in the classical tradition so that he could imitate "nature" represented in models, yet he should also attend to nature as manifested in the contemporary world.

Ironically, Boileau, one of the strongest advocates of neoclassicism, introduced a document that complicated the notion of a unified, coherent classical tradition when he translated *On the Sublime* in 1672. His translation initiated the sublime as a *topos* in reflections on poetics by poets, novelists, and philosophers: All use the term to explain powerful encounters with a nature that overwhelms rather than accommodates or represents the human. Initially, the "sublime" serves as a register for intense emotions of fear, passion, awe, horror, or even joy that disrupt the harmonious balance and lucidity valued by defenders of both the ancients and the moderns. Eventually, the "sublime" would justify abandonment of a classical poetics focused on a generalized audience and universal topics in favor of a Romantic poetics that orchestrated intense psychological responses.

Poetics and Eighteenth-Century Philosophy

Poetics became disengaged from its ties to the classical rhetorical tradition as that tradition lost its power to shape Western social and educational systems. Eighteenth-century empiricist theories of mental reception bypass the role of social agency in the production of discourse: Language is a source of ambiguity and fallacy, obstructing access to knowledge.

Despite Locke's attack on figurative language in the *Essay Concerning Human Understanding* (1690), Addison attempts to apply Locke's philosophy to poetics. For Locke, the tabula rasa of the human mind is written on by measurable "primary" experience; secondary qualities such as color and sound are derived from the impact of primary experience on a perceiving subject, and abstract ideas are then derived from simple sense perceptions through mental processes of association. Addison popularized Locke, using his terms *primary* and *secondary* to refer to two different modes of imaginative pleasure, the immediate experience of objects and the secondary experience of their representation. While the faculty of the imagination with which poetics is associated is less valued than the faculty of the understanding, it plays a role in mental functioning. Poetics is retained in eighteenth-century faculty psychology while rhetoric becomes associated with distorted figurative language.

Addison's adaptation of Locke initiates a move away from rhetoric's focus on effective action to a focus on contemplation. Edmund Burke continues this displacement: in *A Philosophical Inquiry into the Origin of Our Ideas of the Sublime and the Beautiful* (1757), he assigns variances in response not to qualities of the object but to the perceiver's "taste." Response to art involves the imagination, an active rearranging of sense data, and judgment, a rational faculty that assesses objects in relation to reason and decorum. Taste is a function of the working together of imagination and reason and can be developed through education and diligent practice. In "Of the Standard of Taste" (1757), Hume disengages taste from judgment, assigning it to the realm of subjective response or sentiment: Taste is regulated by a standard derived from observations of good readers, not from interaction among faculties within a single individual.

Thus British empirical philosophers assume that the human capacity for responding to poetic production should be accounted for within a philosophical theory and demonstrate antipathy to a rhetorical stance. Within Continental philosophy, since language is identified as the preeminent human activity, the status of poetics rises much higher, and poetics retains strong connections with rhetorical theory. Vico defends a rhetorical understanding of language, for which he argues as a resource for understanding historical and contemporary custom, psychology, and cognition. In *The New Science* (1725), Vico develops a tropological theory of human history in which human institutions originate in an originary divine or poetic phase ruled by metaphor. For Condillac as well, figurative language and poetic genres have historical priority, as he argues in *Essays on the Origin of the Human Understanding* (1746).

Condillac influences Rousseau and thereby Romantic poetics. Rousseau agreed that a gestural communication preceded language and that figurative language was historically prior to nonfigurative; but in his *Discourse on the Origin of Inequality among Men* (1755) and in his *Essay on the Origin of Language* (1740–1750), Rousseau also argues that language is not a copying of a gestural order but a product of passionate, perceptual encounter with nature, an encounter that bypasses reason. Lessing continues to cordon off language and poetics from other human acts; opposing Horace's "*ut pictura poesis*," Lessing specifies temporality, the construction of a narrative series of events, as the defining feature of poetics in *Laokoon* (1766). Whereas neoclassicism privileges works of a prior civilization over "barbaric" contemporary works, Romanticist poetics rejects "civilization" as origin and model. The aim of poetics is to present possibilities to the imagination.

The eighteenth-century philosopher whose work would have the most momentous effects on poetics was Immanuel Kant. To all conceptions of poetics, Kant made available for legitimation the notion of an aesthetic realm in *Critique of Judgment* (1790). Kant was not the first to accord importance to the aesthetic, but he granted to the aesthetic an unprecedented role in the structure of a philosophical system: The aesthetic principle, which orchestrates universal yet subjective judgments of taste, unifies and mediates between the theoretical domain of necessary, objective, universal law and the practical domain of free, subjective, contingent moral action. As part of the aesthetic, poetic is linked with apprehensions of pure form possible in encounters with the beautiful or the sublime. Pure form can be observed in poetic products because they exemplify "purposiveness without purpose." In another effacement of rhetoric as a mode of knowledge, Kant reassigns from rhetoric to poetic the mediation between certainty and contingency. Unlike rhetoric, poetics mediates purely, bypassing persuasion and socially exchanged knowledge and thereby securing for the apprehending mind the autonomy that was the highest ideal of Enlightenment morality.

Romantic Poetics

Schiller simplifies Kant by equating art with moral freedom in *The Aesthetic Education of Man* (1793). Schiller also provides an explicit rationale for art's cultural importance: By dialectically overcoming the tension between sensory, temporal experience and formal, atemporal abstraction, by transcending sense and form to allow play, by giving form to an otherwise terrifying nature, art creates freedom within culture. A chief architect of Romanticist poetics, Schiller privileges the poet's relationship with nature. In *On Naive and Sentimental Poetry* (1795), Schiller claims that the naive poet is one with nature and apprehends nature directly through feeling, whereas the sentimental poet is at a second remove from nature. Schelling similarly constructs a dialectic but formulates a spiritual rationale for art: The natural order merges with the psychological order, and the art that results makes incarnate the unity between nature and soul.

Schlegel defines Romanticism as a process of becoming inherent in great poetry of any historical period. Because poetry engages in self-criticism through its alternating, dialectical deployment of wit, or genius, and irony, or skepticism, it perpetuates itself unceasingly.

Like Kant, Hegel assigns aesthetics a role in his philosophical system. Because it concretizes form, art is one means by which consciousness can apprehend the Idea, the infinite totality at the end of history. Within the dialectical unfolding of spirit, Romantic art attains higher level of spiritual embodiment than did symbolic and classical art that historically preceded it, but all art will eventually be superseded by religion.

Nietzsche, too, seeks to establish an objective for aesthetic production. He posits two modes of artistic expression in *The Birth of Tragedy* (1872), Apollonian and Dionysian, coexistent in all of the arts: Apollonian valorizes balance and harmony, Dionysian privileges passion and intensity. Their fusion allows human consciousness to exist despite the impossibility of its desires ever being realized.

In Germany, philosophers elaborate aims and ontologies for Romanticist poetics. In England and North America, practicing poets reflect on Romantic aims, modes, and rationales. Wordsworth launches such reflections in the English-speaking world in his 1802 *Preface to the Lyrical Ballads*. Wordsworth argues that poetry is not a craft but a device for expressing the poet's depth of feeling and intensity of response. Poetics apprehends reality by bringing passion and knowledge, local and universal, into dynamic relation. Subject matter, meter, and diction should be chosen to express the poet's insight, not to instantiate an inherited tradition or to fulfill reader expectations.

Coleridge brings German philosophical concepts into British and American Romanticism. All Romanticist movements reject allegory for the symbol, which unifies the particular and the universal, time and eternity, literal and metaphorical. The high value placed on a harmonious synthesis of "multeity in unity" accounts for the predominance of organic metaphors: Ordering principles are present at the origin as a regulative device. In his *Biographia Literaria* (1817), Coleridge differentiates among the primary imagination, a faculty of perception creative of phenomena, analogous to God's spiritual creation and possessed equally by all, the secondary imagination, possessed most powerfully by the poet, who dissolves phenomena so as to re-create an artistically shaped whole, and the fancy, which conjoins disparate entities but exercises no powers of re-creation.

Shelley constructs a cultural legitimation grounded on spiritual, social, political, and historical claims for Romanticist poetics. Shelley's argument in "A Defence of Poetry" (1821) constitutes an overview of Romanticist attitudes. Linking reason to analysis and differentiation and imagination to synthesis and similitude, Shelley claims that the imagination is an instrument for instituting the moral good. Rather than contribute moral precepts, the poet strengthens the imaginative capacity, which is fundamental to moral action. Shelley credits poetry with sustaining emancipatory projects such as the abolition of slavery and blames economic disparities between rich and poor on the excessive use of reason. Though human nature, beauty, and spiritual truths are universal and transhistorical, social history is progressive: Poets initiate cultural change by apprehending and then helping others apprehend spiritual truths necessary at a particular historical moment. Hence, each age demands new language and new poetic creations.

Emerson's "Poet" (1844) reiterates that poets renew our apprehension of a transcendent reality by rejuvenating language. Symbols mediate between man and nature. The poet transcribes the beauty that originated the universe; his transcription stimulates the imagination to think new possibilities. Poetics is thus fundamental to human freedom and to personal and social renewal.

The Late Nineteenth Century: Disparate Poetics

While pronouncements on poetics and imaginative literature proliferated in the last half of the nineteenth century, for the most part collaborative cultural movements marked by related principles and problematics did not emerge. Poe opposed the didactic "fallacy" ("The Poetic Principle," 1849); Tolstoy upheld it (*What is Art?* 1897). Arnold concerned himself with the social implications of integrating the study of literature into education ("The Function of Criticism at the Present Time," 1864); Pater upheld "art for art's sake" (*Studies in the History of the Renaissance,* 1873). Hippolyte Taine treats literature as documentary evidence in the study of history (*History of English Literature,* 1867); Oscar Wilde assigns to literature formative power over nature and experience ("The Decay of Lying," 1889). One exception to this trend of multiple, idiosyncratic poetic manifestos is the French symbolist movement. A precursor, Baudelaire, devised a notion of the symbol far different from that of the Romantics: Rather than a unifying truth that brings order and significance to the transitory, the Baudelairean symbol remains maximally evocative and indeterminant. Mallarme and Verlaine were at the center of a circle of poets who founded a poetics on the analogy they perceived between music and poetry. Symbolists experimented with phonetic echoes of musical instruments, imagistic interrelations modeled on musical scales, and concrete description resistant to philosophical interpretation.

This study has focused on a standard historical narrative about poetics, one based on theoretical documents and controversies that have circulated within domains from which women, people of color, and the poor have been historically excluded. This does not mean that representatives of these groups have never reflected on poetics. Scholarly efforts both to recover such reflections and to redefine poetics as a more inclusive and variegated domain have emerged only recently. Chapters on historical periods in *Redrawing the Boundaries: The Transformation of English and American Literary Studies* are a good introductory review of scholars attempting to rewrite traditional poetics.

Susan Brown Carlton
Pacific Lutheran University

Bibliography

Adams, Hazard. *Critical Theory since Plato.* Fort Worth, TX: Harcourt, 1992.

Aguzzi-Barbagli, Danilo. "Humanism and Poetics." Vol. 3. *Renaissance Humanism: Foundations, Forms, and Legacy.* Ed. Albert Rabil, Jr. Philadelphia: U of Pennsylvania P, 1988. 85–169.

Greenblatt, Stephen, and Giles Gunn. *Redrawing the Boundaries: The Transformation of English and American Literary Studies.* New York: Modern Language Assn., 1992.

Hardison, O.B. "Medieval Literary Criticism." *Classical and Medieval Literary Criticism: Translations and Interpretations.* Ed. Alex Preminger, O.B. Hardison, Jr., and Kevin Kerrane. New York: Ungar, 1974. 263–490.

Havelock, Eric A. *Preface to Plato.* Cambridge, MA: Harvard UP, 1963.

Innes, Doreen C. "Augustan Critics." *The Cambridge History of Literary Criticism: Vol. I. Classical Criticism.* Ed. George A. Kennedy. Cambridge: Cambridge UP, 1989. 246–73.

———. "Philodemus." *The Cambridge History of Literary Criticism: Vol. I. Classical Criticism.* Ed. George A. Kennedy. Cambridge: Cambridge UP, 1989. 215–19.

Kennedy, George A. "Hellenistic and Philosophical Scholarship." *The Cambridge History of Literary Criticism: Vol. I. Classical Criticism.* Ed. George A. Kennedy. Cambridge: Cambridge UP, 1989. 200–14.

Preminger, Alex, and Kevin Kerrane. "Classical Literary Criticism." *Classical and Medieval Literary Criticism: Translations and Interpretations.* Ed. Alex Preminger, O.B. Hardison, and Kevin Kerrane. New York: Ungar, 1974. 3–259.

Preminger, Alex, and T.V.F. Brogan, eds. *The New Princeton Encyclopedia of Poetry and Poetics.* Princeton: Princeton UP, 1993.

Richter, David H., ed. *The Critical Tradition: Classic Texts and Contemporary Trends.* New York: St. Martin's, 1989.

Russell, Donald A. "Greek Criticism of the Empire." *The Cambridge History of Literary Criticism: Vol. I. Classical Criticism.* Ed. George A. Kennedy. Cambridge: Cambridge UP, 1989. 297–329.

P

Polanyi, Michael (1891–1976)

Born of Jewish parents in Budapest, served as a medical doctor in the Austro-Hungarian army, then undertook an extremely productive career as a research chemist at the Kaiser Wilhelm Institute in Berlin, leaving Germany in 1933 to assume professorial chairs at the University of Manchester and later at Oxford. Through the second half of his life, Polanyi found himself called to philosophy by an essentially rhetorical problem: How can we account for and counter the tremendous persuasive power that political ideologies, especially Nazism and Soviet Marxism, have wielded in the twentieth century?

Polanyi spent his philosophic career articulating an epistemology of personal knowledge that is far more expansive than the objectivist assumptions that had contributed to that crisis. He saw twentieth-century thought and ideological movements rooted in an epistemology of doubt, which has eroded our confidence in our cultural institutions and in ourselves as responsible agents. This orientation has left our moral passions unexamined (and indeed unaccountable) and has led us to seek refuge in the presumably impersonal certainties of science.

But objectivist epistemology is at best an incomplete and hence unfaithful view of the actual workings of science. Its ideological manifestations have threatened scientific activity directly, for instance during the Stalinist purges of the 1930s. It also posits a certainty which has little to do with the progress of science.

Polanyi's epistemology provides us with a complementary picture, one taking its bearings from his understandings of scientific activity but extending to all acts of distinctly human knowing. The scientist works not as an isolated individual but as a member of a mutually accrediting interpretive community, whose work is essential to scientific progress: It accredits new members, embodies shared disciplinary frameworks through which promising problems are perceived and in terms of which they are attacked, and provides forums for the irreducibly persuasive actions necessary in considering a proffered discovery.

Much work of the community is inherently informal and hazardous, in ways that it would not be if findings were merely accumulations of objective, self-evident facts. A true discovery may be dismissed (Polanyi personally experienced this hazard, at the hand of Einstein), or a false one may be embraced. No guarantees can replace responsible judgment.

Polanyi's philosophy takes its bearings most deeply from his understanding of heuristic action, both in the workings of a community of inquirers and in the purposeful efforts of an individual. His epistemology traces the dynamics of an act of discovery, as an objectivist epistemology cannot, and his understanding of discovery encompasses scientific work and human perception. In perceiving a distant object, I attend *from* arrays of clues, as disparate as operations of my eyes and brain and details of the object itself, while I attend *to* making out the comprehensive entity that object is. Likewise scientists attend *from* arrays of clues, embodied in the framework that their discipline offers them, *to* make out what has never been seen before, though the resulting discovery will in some sense irreversibly reshape even the framework that led to it. This integration, by which a person brings *subsidiaries* to bear in making out some *focal* meaning, is the heart of *tacit knowing,* and it informs Polanyi's insistence that "we can know more than we can tell." Tacit knowing undergirds all explicit knowledge and all meaningful affirmations.

Called to philosophy by an essentially rhetorical exigency, Polanyi helps us understand the persuasive powers of this century's ideologies. He places persuasion at the center of communities' work, and its analogue, discovery, at the center of human knowledge. In insisting that all knowledge is personal and in articulating dynamics of the tacit that inform acts of knowing, he uncovers common ground that unites rhetorics which are "expressive" and those which are "social constructivist." Polanyi's aim is to return to us a world in which it is conceivable that human institutions and human beings, although fallible, are responsible agents, a world in which we affirm persons as knowing agents and knowledge as inescapably personal.

Sam Watson
University of North Carolina, Charlotte

Bibliography

Booth, Wayne C. *Modern Dogma and the Rhetoric of Assent*. Chicago: U of Chicago P, 1974.

Emig, Janet. "The Tacit Tradition." *Reinvent-*

ing the Rhetorical Tradition. Ed. Aviva Freedman and Ian Pringle. Urbana, IL: National Council of Teachers of English, 1984. 9–18.

Gelwick, Richard. The Way of Discovery: An Introduction to the Thought of Michael Polanyi. New York: Oxford UP, 1977.

Perelman, Chaïm. "Polanyi's Interpretation of Scientific Inquiry." Intellect and Hope: Essays in the Thought of Michael Polanyi. Ed. Thomas A. Langford and William H. Poteat. Durham, NC: Duke UP, 1968.

Phelps, Louise W. Composition as a Human Science: Contributions to the Self-Understanding of the Discipline. New York: Oxford UP, 1988.

Polanyi, Michael. Knowing and Being. Ed. Marjorie Grene. Chicago: U of Chicago P, 1969.

———. Personal Knowledge: Toward a Post-Critical Philosophy. New York: Harper, 1958.

———. The Tacit Dimension. Garden City, NY: Anchor, 1967. PRE/TEXT: 2 (1981).

Polanyi, Michael, and Harry Prosch. Meaning. Chicago: U of Chicago P, 1975.

Poteat, William H. A Philosophical Daybook: Post-Critical Investigations. Columbia: U of Missouri P, 1990.

———. Polanyian Meditations: In Search of a Post-Critical Logic. Durham, NC: Duke UP, 1985.

Prosch, Harry. Michael Polanyi: A Critical Exposition. Albany: SUNY, 1986.

Scott, Drusilla. Everyman Revisited: The Common Sense of Michael Polanyi. Lewes: Book Guild, 1985.

Wallace, M. Elizabeth, Peter Elbow, Louise W. Phelps, Sam Watson, and Janet Emig. "Polanyian Perspectives on the Teaching of Literature and Composition." Tradition and Discovery 17 (1990–1991): 4–16.

Watson, Sam. "Polanyi and the Contexts of Composing." Reinventing the Rhetorical Tradition. Ed. Aviva Freedman and Ian Pringle. Urbana, IL: National Council of Teachers of English, 1984. 19–25.

———. "Polanyi's Epistemology of Good Reasons." Explorations in Rhetoric: Studies in Honor of Douglas Ehninger. Ed. Ray E. McKerrow. Glenview, IL: Scott, 1982.

Political Rhetoric

The practice of rhetoric traditionally including elements such as persuasion and deliberation, governing and campaigning, issues and images, strategizing and organizing, politicians and voters, mass mediated and nonmediated messages, and public speeches and debates. Exemplars of political rhetoric abound in the annals of American history. For example, while competing against each other for a U.S. Senate seat from Illinois in 1858, Abraham Lincoln and Stephen Douglas met on the same public platform and presented arguments, questioned and refuted each other in front of huge audiences across the state on the most compelling and controversial issues of the day. More than one hundred years later, newly inaugurated president John F. Kennedy called on Americans to "ask not what your country can do for you, but what you can do for your country."

Currently, political rhetoric is characterized by challenges to tradition, challenges fueled by technological advances that have reconfigured the nature of public address in the political life of a community. Did Governor Jerry Brown's use of a toll-free 800 telephone number to establish direct voter contact during the 1992 presidential primaries constitute political rhetoric? Was it political rhetoric when the governor of Arkansas used a computer bulletin board to answer voter questions regarding his stand on specific issues during the 1992 general election campaign (an innovation that went with the governor to the White House when he took office in 1993)? Can the use of computer bulletin boards and toll-free telephone exchanges be classified in the same manner as the Lincoln-Douglas debates and the Kennedy inaugural address?

Because communication technologies and practices are changing so rapidly, the term political rhetoric may best be defined through the identification of a number of relatively stable characteristics that establish its parameters. We argue that political rhetoric can be (1) characterized as strategic symbolic action; (2) produced in response to a perceived exigence; (3) designed to be addressed to particular audiences; (4) oriented within a context of public governance; (5) pragmatic and ritualistic in function within that context; and (6) grounded in an historical tradition of practice.

Some of these characteristics are inherent in all rhetorical activity. For example, like all rhetoric, political rhetoric involves *strategic symbolic action.* Such rhetoric is strategic to the extent that it is the product of a discernible agent, whether it be an individual (such as Senator Robert Dole), a group (such as the National Rifle Association), or an institution (such as the Environmental Protection Agency); is based on some degree of deliberation and inquiry; is consciously planned and structured; and is reflective of the agent's purpose or motive (Bitzer 1981; Black 1978; Burke). Whether employed in political or other contexts, rhetoric encompasses a wide variety of symbolic acts, including oral and written discourse (such as a foreign policy speech); nonverbal symbolic behavior (such as the swastika, a raised fist, or a candidate's shaking hands at the workers' entrance of a factory); and mediated images and sounds (such as a campaign advertisement produced for television). These symbolic acts influence how people interpret their environment and relate to one another within that environment.

Political rhetoric is also *produced in response to a perceived exigence.* The motive for political rhetoric is situational, stemming from the ways in which people define specific contexts that they encounter. People engage in rhetoric when they believe that the nature of a problem they confront requires some level of concerted action beyond the capacity of the individual, and further believe that such cooperative action can be facilitated through the intentional communication of ideas (Campbell; Bitzer 1968; Vatz).

Moreover, political rhetoric *is designed to be addressed to particular audiences.* Like all rhetoric, political rhetoric is reciprocal in that it involves the interaction between senders and receivers. The act of rhetorical transmission can be direct and immediate (such as the mayor addressing a crowd in the city square, answering their questions and responding to their nonverbal feedback), or it can be mediated and delayed (such as a televised broadcast of the mayor's speech and the response of a focus group received by the candidate the next day). Recently, political candidates and their officeholders at all levels have turned to the use of electronic town meetings, structured events in which a speaker takes and answers questions posed by citizens in a setting most frequently designed to disseminate the speaker's ideas to an audience that extends beyond those physically present in the auditorium. This form of political address, while more interactive and dialogic than the traditional speech delivered from the lectern, is nonetheless rhetorical to the extent that it involves the directed, strategic, and purposeful employment of symbolic action to persuade those attending to the message.

One characteristic that distinguishes political rhetoric from other kinds of rhetorical activity is that such rhetoric *is oriented within a context of public governance.* Broadly speaking, public governance involves the creation, enforcement, and legitimation of laws and institutions that regulate the distribution of resources and responsibilities in a community or other social collectivity. Issues (such as abortion) may be subject to public governance when they deal with matters that are defined as having significant effects upon the welfare of a particular community or organization. Acts of public governance occur where the laws, institutions, or customs of a community create forums or spaces (such as the town hall meeting or a session of the state legislature) in which issues of common concern can be debated and decisions made by members of the community or their functional representatives (Bitzer 1978).

Public governance constitutes the substance of political rhetoric. Political rhetoric "deals with matters thought to constitute the public business—that is, all transactions and their consequences which significantly affect the public or its parts" (Bitzer 1981:231). Such rhetoric is orientational in that it strategically positions speaker, message, and audience in relation to particular public issues and deliberative forums. For example, a political advocate may attempt to define an issue such as abortion as constituting the "public's business" and subject to public regulation because such an issue may have significant effects upon the welfare of a particular community or organization (Goodnight 1982).

Political rhetoric also *performs pragmatic and ritualistic functions* in relation to contexts of public governance (Bennett; Gronbeck). Pragmatic functions concern the achievement of practical effects or outcomes of symbolic action. Speakers engage in pragmatic political rhetoric in order to persuade audiences to take specific actions related to the substance and process of public governance. Examples of pragmatic uses of political rhetoric include an electoral campaign speech, a policy debate among legislators, and an address delivered by an antiwar protester (Black 1973; Trent and Friedenberg; Stewart et al.).

Ritualistic functions concern the expression and reinforcement of important principles, values, and community identities. Rather than attempting to accomplish a specific practical outcome, speakers participate with their audiences in traditional and consummatory forms and forums of public address. The mutual engagement of speaker and audience acts to affirm a sense of communal identity. Examples of political rhetoric employed for ritualistic purposes include a speech delivered on a ceremonial occasion, such as an inaugural address (Campbell and Jamieson 1990), and a candidate's speech formally announcing entrance into the political contest (Trent and Friedenberg 1991).

Some forms of political rhetoric attempt to accomplish both pragmatic and ritualistic purposes. For example, the purpose of the acceptance address delivered by the nominee at a major party's presidential convention is to "announce" the issues that will be raised in the campaign and the positions that will be taken as well as to unite the party regulars by reinforcing traditional ideological themes (Farrell 1978).

Finally, political rhetoric *is grounded in a historical tradition of practice*. Politics and rhetoric have always been intertwined. The art of rhetoric in Western civilization has its roots in the political life of ancient Greece. Greek citizens sought an education in public speaking in order to participate in a broad range of civic affairs, and the teachers of the day obliged by designing their rhetorical theories for use by political agents. For example, Aristotle devoted much of the *Rhetoric* to an elaboration of deliberative speech as a major recurring form of address delivered for the purpose of influencing the future course of community policy. The Romans organized elements of rhetorical education into a set of topics or canons that would provide a complete training in the art of public speaking for the purpose of efficient governance (Bitzer 1981). And centuries later, campaign consultant James Carville advised a presidential nominee of the arguments to use in the public comments, debates, and television commercials that by the last decades of the twentieth century had come to characterize American electoral contests. Thus, working from a secure foundation, the theories and practices of political rhetoric have evolved throughout the ages in response to the changing needs of communities for training and expertise in aspects of public deliberation (Kennedy 1980).

While these six characteristics may not provide a definitive answer of what is and is not political rhetoric, they can serve as stable points of reference. As such, they allow us to understand communication innovations in relation to the ongoing traditions in the practice of political rhetoric. The enduring rhetorical concepts of speaker, message, audience, and situation are sufficiently elastic so as to encompass constantly changing means and processes of political talk, from toll-free telephone numbers to computer bulletin boards to the electronic town hall.

Judith S. Trent, Stephen P. Depoe, and
Cady W. Short-Thompson
University of Cincinnati

Bibliography

Bennett, W. Lance. "The Ritualistic and Pragmatic Bases of Political Campaign Discourse." *Quarterly Journal of Speech* 63 (1977): 219–38.

Bitzer, Lloyd. "Political Rhetoric." *Handbook of Political Communication.* Ed. Dan D. Nimmo and Keith R. Sanders. Newbury Park, CA: Sage, 1981. 225–48.

———. "Rhetoric and Public Knowledge." *Rhetoric, Philosophy, and Literature: An Exploration.* Ed. D.M. Burks. West Lafayette, IN: Purdue UP, 1978. 67–93.

———. "The Rhetorical Situation." *Philosophy and Rhetoric* 1 (1968): 1–14.

Black, Edwin. "Electing Time." *Quarterly Journal of Speech* 59 (1973): 125–29.

———. *Rhetorical Criticism: A Study in Method.* 2nd ed. Madison: U of Wisconsin P, 1978.

Burke, Kenneth. *The Philosophy of Literary Form.* 3rd ed. Berkeley: U of California P, 1973.

Campbell, Karlyn Kohrs. *Critiques of Contemporary Rhetoric.* Belmont, CA: Wadsworth, 1972.

Campbell, Karlyn Kohrs, and Kathleen Hall Jamieson. *Deeds Done in Words: Presidential Rhetoric and the Genres of Governance.* Chicago: U of Chicago P, 1990.

Farrell, Thomas B. "Political Conventions as Legitimation Ritual." *Communication Monographs* 45 (1978): 293–305.

Goodnight, G. Thomas. "The Personal, Technical, and Public Spheres of Argument: A Speculative Inquiry into the Art of Public Deliberation." *Journal of the American Forensic Association* 18 (1982): 214–27.

P

Gronbeck, Bruce. "The Functions of Presidential Campaigning." *Communication Monographs* 45 (1978): 268–80.

Kennedy, George A. *Classical Rhetoric and Its Christian and Secular Tradition from Ancient to Modern Times.* Chapel Hill: U of North Carolina P, 1980.

Stewart, Charles J., Craig Allen Smith, and Robert E. Denton, Jr. *Persuasion and Social Movements.* 3rd ed. Prospect Heights, IL: Waveland, 1994.

Trent, Judith S., and Robert V. Friedenberg. *Political Campaign Communication: Principles and Practices.* 2nd ed. New York: Praeger, 1991.

Vatz, Richard. "The Myth of the Rhetorical Situation." *Philosophy and Rhetoric* 6 (1973): 154–61.

Polyptoton

Repetition of words derived from the same root in different cases. "Nothing is enough to the man for whom enough is too little" (Epicurus). The double play of varying sound and contrasting meaning in many aphorisms is achieved through the use of polyptoton. "Few men speak humbly of humility, chastely of chastity, skeptically of skepticism" (Pascal). "Let the people think they govern, and they will be governed" (Penn). "Man would sooner have the void for his purpose than be void of purpose" (Nietzsche). While polyptoton can be used to coin a memorable thought, it is sometimes used purely to make a pleasing play of sound, as in "But day doth daily draw my sorrows longer, / And night doth nightly make grief's strength seem stronger" (Shakespeare, Son. 28).

Arthur Quinn and Lyon Rathbun
University of California, Berkeley

Polysyndeton

"Bound together"; the use of more conjunctions than ordinary usage demands. Stephen Crane employed a polysyndeton in writing "The horizon narrowed and widened, and dipped and rose, and at all times its edge was jagged with waves." A polysyndeton can either emphasize the length of items enumerated or underscore the distinctiveness of each item from the others. The author of Joshua did both in writing "And Joshua, and all Israel with him, took Achan the son of Zerah, and the silver, and the garment, and the wedge of gold, and his sons, and his daughters, and his oxen, and his asses, and his sheep, and his tent, and all that he had" (7:24). While the series can be related spatially or temporally, it can also move from the less important to the more important, or from the general to the specific. Marcus Aurelius moved from the less important to the more important: "Whatever this is that I am, it is a little flesh and breath and the ruling part."

Arthur Quinn and Lyon Rathbun
University of California, Berkeley

Popper, Karl (1902–1994)

Founder of falsificationist philosophy of science and defender of objectivity of linguistic entities. Sir Karl Popper might dislike being included in an *Encyclopedia of Rhetoric,* for he criticized the work of Thomas Kuhn and others for their emphasis on persuasion in scientific discourse. In this, Popper is antirhetorical in the way the mainstream of philosophy has been since Plato, since Locke, and most specifically, since the logical positivism of the Vienna Circle. Born and educated in Austria, Popper moved to New Zealand in 1937 and then to England in 1945; he is known for his work in other fields of philosophy, above all his work in political philosophy culminating in *The Open Society and Its Enemies.* His work in philosophy of science, however, intersects most with the concerns of rhetoricians.

Popper's central contribution to philosophy of science is best known as falsificationism, the idea that science proceeds, not by verifying theories and establishing their truth, but by falsifying them or establishing that they are not true. In this view theories can never be confirmed, but they can be disconfirmed; "knowledge" at any given moment is what has not yet been disproven and is therefore our best current approximation to the truth. This vision of knowledge assigns an important role to language in that the propositions that are disconfirmed are generally linguistic in nature. In Popper's view we have no unmediated access to reality or the truth; our theories and language mediate between us and the world. This does not mean, pace Kuhn, that we have no way to adjudicate between competing theories aside from persuasive rhetoric, but Popper shares common ground with Kuhn in his stress on the linguisticality of science.

Popper insists, however, that attempts to deny the objectivity of scientific knowledge because of its linguisticality are caught up in too simplistic a dichotomy between subject and object, between inner and outer. Popper distinguishes instead among what he calls three worlds, World 1 being external reality, World 2 subjective dispositions, and World 3—his addition to the list—knowledge about Worlds 1 and 2. For Popper, what is mental is not necessarily subjective, and World 3 is the world of what is mental but objective. World 3 cannot simply be identified with language, for certainly some aspects of language would be placed by Popper in the World 2 realm of subjective dispositions, but World 3 is unimaginable without language and our access to it is inescapably linguistic. Yet there is a significant tension in Popper's way of presenting World 3. Does its contents exist before human discovery of those contents? Or is World 3 the totality of what we have discovered to date? In the first case, Popper's model of knowledge seems Platonic in ways that should make rhetoricians uncomfortable; in the second, his model seems Kuhnian in ways that should make Popper uncomfortable, since if World 3 is our construction, it contains many theories destined to be falsified in the future and thus not objectively true. This tension, unresolved in Popper's work, indicates that Popper did not entirely escape a subject-object dichotomy in thinking about knowledge. Nonetheless, his emphasis on the evolutionary development of human knowledge through falsification assigns a powerful role to language and its users and thus can be called rhetorical.

Reed Dasenbrock
New Mexico State University

Bibliography

Lakatos, Imre. "Methodology of Scientific Research Programmes." *Criticism and the Growth of Scientific Knowledge.* Ed. Imre Lakatos and Alan Musgrove. Cambridge: Cambridge UP, 1970. 91–195.

Leech, Geoffrey N. *Principles of Pragmatics.* London: Longman, 1983.

Popper, Sir Karl R. *Conjectures and Refutations.* 6th ed. London: Routledge, 1976.

———. "Normal Science and Its Dangers." *Criticism and the Growth of Scientific Knowledge.* Ed. Imre Lakatos and Alan Musgrove. Cambridge: Cambridge UP, 1970. 51–58.

———. *Objective Knowledge: An Evolutionary Approach.* Rev. ed. Oxford: Clarendon, 1979.

Portfolio

A collection of a student's written work, typically representing a range of purposes, audiences, modes, and styles. The development of student portfolios owes mainly to dissatisfaction with existing methods of assessing students' writing, particularly on a large scale. Test essays written under controlled conditions with little opportunity to revise are not thought to reflect the full range of a writer's abilities. In contrast, portfolios contain several pieces of writing produced under more natural conditions.

In large-scale assessment, portfolios are used to determine whether a writer should enter or exit a specific course or program. In placement assessments, students usually submit a final portfolio from another context (such as a previous course or school) that is then judged against criteria for certification of ability. Similarly, portfolios created in specific courses or programs can be assessed on the basis of exit standards. Because portfolios contain multiple and often diverse writing samples, large-scale portfolio assessment has not met with the same degree of consistency in rankings as more conventional methods of assessment such as the holistic rating of test essays. However, the diversity of samples is also thought to provide a more realistic profile of the full range of a writer's rhetorical and linguistic abilities. In some programs, teachers work collectively in small groups to design their course and agree upon the contents of the portfolio and the criteria for evaluating them, in keeping with broader, programmatic standards for exiting from the course.

From a course-specific, developmental perspective, portfolios are said to provide teachers with more insight into students' needs, processes, improvements, and accomplishments. Papers and other documents become connected in a larger pattern of students' development, instead of representing disconnected texts each created and assessed independently of the others. In some classroom uses, students can continue to work on one or more pieces of writing throughout a course, entering them into the portfolio when they are thought to be ready. Classroom writing portfolios are also said to help students assess their own work and their progress as writers. Students must take on greater responsibility for their own learning and self-assessment, thus replacing a primarily evaluative model of education (characterized by tests of isolated skills, first-draft writing, and little access to students' own intentions or processes) with one that involves greater self-observation and self-critique, and more opportunities for thoughtful achievement.

Related to the student writing portfolio is the teaching portfolio, an innovation for the evaluation and improvement of teaching. Like the student portfolio, the teaching portfolio can be used both for development and assessment. Some documents provide a context for reflection and improvement (such as a commentary on student evaluations, a rationale for a syllabus, or a personal analysis of remarks on students' papers). Other documents, such as a fully worked-out course design, will represent a teacher's best work and might be used for teacher certification, merit review, promotion and tenure, or hiring decisions. The teaching portfolio provides incentive for more thoughtfulness about teaching while its contents also offer richer descriptions of a teacher's abilities and accomplishments.

Chris M. Anson
University of Minnesota

Bibliography

Belanoff, Pat, and Marcia Dickson. *Portfolios: Process and Product*. Portsmouth, NH: Heinemann/Boynton-Cook, 1992.

Daiker, Donald A., Laurel Black, Max Morenberg, and Jeffrey Sommers, eds. *New Directions in Portfolio Assessment*. Portsmouth, NH: Heinemann/Boynton-Cook, 1994.

Edgerton, Russell, Pat Hutchings, and Kathleen Quinlan. *The Teaching Portfolio: Capturing the Scholarship in Teaching*. Washington, D.C.: American Assn. of Higher Education, 1991.

Elbow, Peter, and Pat Belanoff. "Portfolios as a Substitute for Proficiency Examinations." *College Composition and Communication* 37 (1986): 336–39.

Seldin, Peter. *The Teaching Portfolio: A Practical Guide to Improved Performance and Promotion/Tenure Decisions*. Bolton, MA: Anker, 1991.

Tierney, Robert J., Mark A. Carter, and Laura E. Desai. *Portfolio Assessment in the Reading-Writing Classroom*. Norwood, MA: Christopher-Gordon, 1991.

Port-Royalists

Seventeenth-Century French Jansenists, authors of the so-called *Port-Royal Logic and Grammar*. Of the many textbooks written by the Jansenists with ties to the monastery of Port-Royal near Paris, two have significant rhetorical implications: Antoine Arnauld's and Claude Lancelot's *General Grammar* (1660) and, especially, Arnauld's and Pierre Nicole's *Logic or Art of Thinking* (1662). The *Logic* privileges a spare style in which any recourse to the figures must be justified by the subject matter, a distrust of rhetorical methods of invention, and an ideal of transparent language. This approach is born of a convergence of Cartesian epistemology and an Augustinian stress on fallen human nature; its immediate impetus came from the pedagogical experience of the Little Schools run by the Solitaries, the men associated with the monastery, and from the polemics in defense of Jansenist theology, of which the *Provincial Letters* of Pascal (whom the *Logic* praises as having known as much about true rhetoric as anyone has ever known) are the best example.

The Arnauld family was closely linked to the monastery and the Jansenist movement. The convent had been returned to strict observance of its rule by Angélique Arnauld in 1608; most of her sisters and brothers would become nuns in the convent or Solitaries. The most famous was the theologian Antoine Arnauld, who was converted by the Abbé de Saint-Cyran, the monastery's spiritual director, to the intransigent brand of Augustinianism that came to be called Jansenism. Jansenism was a rigorous form of Counter-Reformation Catholicism that refused any compromise with the secular world. Its stress on a penitential ethic and its defense of the doctrine of efficacious grace earned it the enmity of the Jesuits and others who allowed for more accommodation with the world. Its attention to the individual and its condemnation of policies that subordinated the interests of religion and the church to the State incurred the persecution of Richelieu and Louis XIV.

A history of Jansenism's rhetoric would place it at the center of rhetorical trends in seventeenth-century France. In Saint-Cyran one already finds the movement away from the exuberant baroque of the first third of the century. Jansenist preachers like Toussaint Desmares were at the forefront of the call for a simpler, more evangelical style of sermon. Pascal's effort to reach a wide public of *honnêtes gens* in his *Provincial Letters* (1656–1657) led him to create lively, direct prose that was all the more persuasive for forgoing baroque ornamentation, a prose that became the model for the classicism that triumphed later in the century.

The Little Schools (1637–1660) were primary and secondary level classes set up by Saint-Cyran in 1637. In contrast to the regimented curriculum and large classes of the colleges controlled by the Jesuits or linked to the University of Paris, the Little Schools offered a more personalized program that featured close links between masters and pupils; there were at the most some 150 students over the twenty-three years of their existence.

Although the educators of the Little Schools eventually produced textbooks on almost every school subject except rhetoric, rhetoric was far from neglected. Nicole himself taught it at one time, and Arnauld's *Mémoire sur le règlement des lettres humaines* (1690?) probably provides the best account of the spirit of rhetorical instruction at Port-Royal. He rejects what he takes to be the goal of rhetorical studies in the colleges: the composition of elaborate declamations in Latin. Arnauld sets more practical aims: the ability to read with facility the best Latin authors and the sharpening of taste through an appreciation of the masterpieces of antiquity. The ability to express oneself correctly and elegantly in Latin is not ignored but becomes a secondary goal, as it is required in only a limited number of professions. Masters are forbidden to dictate their own lectures on rhetoric; instead, theory and rules are learned by alternating the study of the treatises of antiquity (Aristotle, Cicero, Quintilian) with a modern manual, and here the Jansenist recommends one by the Jesuit Cyprian Suarez. Exercises like amplifications, chria, and compositions take second place to the explication of authors as the foundation of the curriculum.

In the *General Grammar* and the *Logic,* a series of epistemological and linguistic choices, the first two of which show direct Cartesian influence, marginalize but also legitimize rhetoric. The first is the superiority of pure intellection—that is, of ideas perceived without the intervention of the senses or related faculties like the imagination. The second is the independence of thought from language. Were it not for the necessity of communicating our thoughts to others, ideas could be considered in themselves without attaching any exterior linguistic sign to them, although the *Logic* concedes that in prac-

tice the force of habit is so strong that even when alone we think with words. Nonetheless, to the extent that eloquence involves a sensate linguistic medium, it finds itself in a position of inferiority. This inferiority is compounded by the fact that, while eloquence often has recourse to figured speech, the linguistic ideal is a transparent language in which each sign would signify a single clear idea.

Third, Arnauld and Nicole envisage rhetoric in terms of a distinction between the objects of thought and the manner in which these objects are conceived, which derives from their distinction between the two major operations of the mind: Conception is the operation by which the mind sets forth its objects, whether purely intellectual or linked to sensate images; the second operation involves the manner in which the mind considers these objects. Judgment is the chief of these operations by which the mind gives form to its thought, but they also include such inflections of thought as affirmation, wishing, accepting, commands, or entreaties. The *General Grammar* assigns such parts of speech as nouns, articles, prepositions, and adverbs to the first operation, and verbs, interjections, and conjunctions to the second (II.1); rhetoric would seem to have the most affinity with this second operation, which corresponds to the site of a speaker's subjectivity, the personal way in which the idea is conceived.

Indeed, eloquence is most properly identified with just such a manner; rhetorical excellence, according to the *Logic,* requires that the orator conceive the subject matter with force and communicate it vividly, accompanied by movements of the will or emotions: "The chief part of eloquence consists in conceiving things with vigor and in expressing them in such a manner that one communicates to the minds of the listeners a vivid and luminous image that presents not only the things in their bare state, but also the movements with which they are conceived" (III.20.b.1).

While the Port-Royalists protest that it is much worse to be in error about the subject matter than about the manner of its presentation, they concede that failure in the latter respect has more damaging rhetorical consequences. Indeed, the greatest rule of rhetoric is to avoid provoking hatred for the truth by proposing it in a way that shocks the audience (III.20.b.8). Keenly aware of the consequences of original sin on human nature because of their Jansenist orientation, they counsel avoiding as much as possible any manner of presentation that will irritate the audience's self-love (III.20.a.6). The influence of Pascal, who had elaborated an art of pleasing (*art d'agréer*), is particularly evident here.

Finally, the *Logic*'s theory of principal and accessory ideas specifically applies this distinction to the figures employed in eloquence. In addition to a word's primary meaning attached to it by usage, certain secondary connotations adhere to it; sometimes these are a function of general usage, as the suggestion of scorn that accompanies the idea that one is untruthful when accusations of lying are made. At other times, such secondary meanings are added by features of delivery such as tone of voice, inflection, or gesture. In all cases they indicate the manner in which the object, or principal idea, is received. As such they add a personal, subjective quality that can be put to rhetorical use. Figures of speech function in precisely this way by communicating not only a bare idea but also the speaker's emotional reaction to the idea. The rhetorical space for Port-Royal is most properly the accessory conceived in its broadest sense.

However, this marginal position as accessory also legitimizes the rhetorical. While it would be ridiculous, the Port-Royalists maintain, to employ a figured style in speculative topics that can be considered in a calm, impersonal manner, such as some philosophical arguments, a speaker would be equally at fault not to express a reaction when a topic reasonably required it. Such are the truths of salvation, which are proposed not merely to be known but to be loved and revered. Thus the impassioned, figured language of the Church Fathers is entirely appropriate and both more useful and pleasing to their readers than a dry scholastic approach would have been.

Nonetheless, *Logic* belittles rhetorical study. Quoting Augustine's *De doctrina christiana*, it observes that knowledge of rhetorical precepts is not enough to ensure eloquence (III.17). This does not mean that formal rhetorical training is to be ignored. In his 1694 *Reflections on Eloquence*, Arnauld specifically defends such study against Goibaut Du Bois, who had argued that a heart and mind full of one's subject sufficed (Remark 18). Just the same, whether one considers invention, disposition, or style, the *Logic* maintains that rhetoric has little to offer: "As for rhetoric, the aid that it can provide in finding one's thoughts,

one's choice of words or ornaments is not particularly great. The mind furnishes enough ideas, usage provides the wording, and, as for figures of speech and ornaments, there are always too many" (Second Discourse). Arnauld and Nicole assert that their logic manual is more useful in avoiding such faults than most books on rhetoric because the art of thinking helps one focus on the essentials of a subject while paring away stylistic accretions. The most important precepts of rhetoric are negative.

Thus, according to the *Logic,* the topics and commonplaces offer no help in generating arguments and can even impede the mind's natural expansiveness (III.17). The true source of invention is rather the "attentive consideration of the subject." In the tradition of Descartes, who saw attention as the key ingredient in the discovery of truth, logic is above all a set of procedures that allow us to "bring an exact attention to bear on our judgments" (First Discourse).

The *Logic* has little to say on disposition, other than remarking that Cicero's *Pro Milone* can be reduced to the syllogistic form known as an epichirema (III.15). This is not to say that Arnauld would recommend organizing a speech itself in such a rigid progression. In his *Reflections on Eloquence,* he ridicules Du Bois, who had suggested that sermons and orations be arranged in a quasi-geometrical order (Remark 19).

Just as with invention, the *Logic* chiefly offers help in avoiding stylistic excess that too much attention to verbal ornaments can foster (III.20.b.1). Postulating truth as a prerequisite of beauty (III.20.b.2), the *Logic* attacks the highly figured baroque prose that was gradually losing the popularity it had enjoyed earlier in the century, describing it as "an artificial style typical of rhetoric classes, composed of false and hyperbolic thoughts and exaggerated figures" (Second Discourse). The *Logic*'s ideal is "a simple, natural, judicious manner of writing" (Second Discourse) that the best prose of French classicism would exemplify. Nicole's preface to his 1659 collection of Latin epigrams, *Epigrammatum delectus,* supplements the *Logic*'s legitimization of the figures in terms of accessory ideas with a more detailed discussion of how to discern good from bad figures. There, the equivalence between truth and beauty is expanded into a definition of the beautiful as a double congruence with the nature of the thing itself and with that of the audience.

The preface to the *Epigrammatum* is a reminder that while the Port-Royalists subordinate rhetoric to logic, granting the latter jurisdiction over both a discourse's content and its more rhetorical element—its manner of presentation (since any reaction to the content must be reasonable)—the *Logic*'s rather severe strictures concerning rhetoric must be tempered in light of Arnauld's and Nicole's more nuanced treatment of the art in other writings.

Both the *Logic* and *General Grammar* were frequently reprinted through the nineteenth century in France; their views on language, the topics, and the theory of principal and accessory ideas were points of departure for Nicolas Malebranche and Bernard Lamy. Arnauld's *Mémoire* was highly praised by Charles Rollin in his efforts to reform rhetorical education in the Parisian colleges. On a more general level, the sober style the Port-Royalist's championed became the model for French classicism.

Abroad, the *Logic* was made available to a wide European audience through a Latin translation; both it and the *Grammar* were translated into English and were widely cited by British philosophers and rhetoricians. Nicole's *Epigrammatum delectus* was used as a textbook at Eton well into the eighteenth century. In Italy, Vico's attacks against Cartesian method are inspired in great measure by his adverse reaction to the scorn for the topics in the *Logic*.

Thomas M. Carr, Jr.
University of Nebraska, Lincoln

Bibliography

Arnauld, Antoine. *The Art of Thinking*. Trans. James Dickoff and Patricia James. Indianapolis, IN: Bobbs Merrill, 1964.

———. *Réflexions sur l'éloquence des prédicateurs*. Ed. Thomas M. Carr, Jr. Geneva: Droz, 1992.

Arnauld, Antoine, and Pierre Nicole. *La Logique, ou l'art de penser*. Ed. Pierre Clair and François Girbal. Paris: Vrin, 1981.

Carr, Thomas M., Jr. *Descartes and the Resilience of Rhetoric*. Carbondale: Southern Illinois UP, 1990.

Davidson, Hugh M. *Audience, Words and Art*. Columbus: Ohio State UP, 1965.

Delforge, Frédéric. *Les Petites Ecoles de Port-Royal*. Paris: Cerf, 1985.

Dominicy, Marc. *La Naissance de la grammaire moderne. Langage, logique et philosophie à Port-Royal*. Brussels: Pierre Mardaga, 1984.

Howell, W.S. *Logic and Rhetoric in England 1500–1700*. Princeton: Princeton UP, 1956.

Nicole, Pierre. *An Essay on True and Apparent Beauty*. Trans. J.V. Cunningham. Los Angeles: Augustan Reprint Society, no. 24, Clark Memorial Library, 1950.

Sedgwick, Alexander. *Jansenism in Seventeenth-Century France*. Charlottesville: U of Virginia P, 1977.

See also Descartes; Eloquence

Postmodernism

Refers not to a single theory or cultural phenomenon but rather to a cultural conversation between differing but coincident postmodernisms. One of the more influential strands in the conversation is the theorization of a postmodern architecture that emerges in reaction to the Modernist avant-garde aesthetic of purity and functionality. Critics Robert Venturi and Charles Jencks attack the Modernists' portrayal of the city as fallen and their program of urban renewal in which monumental buildings function as foci for the spiritual regeneration of the city. In *Learning from Las Vegas*, Venturi celebrates the schlock and kitsch architecture of the most fallen of U.S. cities; in general, the postmodern architectural critics call for a city with memory, based not upon redemption and unification, but reinterpretation through the ironic, nostalgic and playful quotation of other (frequently incommensurable) architectural styles.

Architectural postmodernism then becomes influential in the construction of a literary postmodernist tradition, providing both a terminological framework and a *raison d'être* in the hostility to Modernism. As a literary style, postmodernism is aggressively eclectic, interested in the play of surfaces, at the same time fascinated by and suspicious of totalizing narratives. Its characteristic modes are those of irony and pastiche enacted through complex references to the past and an elaborate self-consciousness. However, a literary postmodernism is problematic precisely in its assumed opposition to Modernism. Many of the writers who are at first placed in the postmodernist canon, John Barth and Saul Bellow for example, now seem like late-Modernists, and the radical eclecticism so central to postmodernism is shared by many High Modernist texts, such as those of Joyce and Eliot.

Frederic Jameson, in "Postmodernism, or, The Cultural Logic of Late Capitalism," employs a critique of contemporary corporate architecture alongside a consideration of literary and other representational texts in an interrogation of precisely this ambiguous opposition between postmodernism and Modernism. Jameson uses the ambiguity to theorize postmodernism as a new phase of capitalism that develops in the years immediately following the Second World War, in which postmodern spatiality is organized around a shift from imperialist to multinational organization of the flow of global capital. What chiefly distinguishes this postindustrialism from older forms of capitalism is its total commodification of culture, which renders culture not merely a reflection of the economic base but a form of production in its own right, organized around image and information. When applying this to literature, Jameson concentrates therefore not on superficial stylistics but on the texts' engagement with cultural transformation. As a Marxist, Jameson is critical of the postmodern, but in his description of the experience of postmodernity as being simultaneously one of ecstasy and terror, he also reveals a fascination with the endless variety and inventiveness of the postmodern.

The conception of postmodernism as a response to Modernism is also evident in Jean-François Lyotard's response to Jürgen Habermas. Habermas argues that Modernism is an unfinished project, one whose potential is in danger of being overwritten by the neoconservative ideology of postmodernism. Lyotard in *The Postmodern Condition* condemns Habermas's underlying universalist notions as simplistic and argues that the postmodern is instead the period where the two great narratives that have legitimized knowledge in the West (the mythic or traditional-legitimation by reference to primordial origins— and the projective (modern)-legitimation with reference to the future) are disintegrating, giving way to heterogeneous and local histories. Lyotard's notion that postmodernism involves a fundamental epistemological shift in our conception of modernity thus links him with both the poststructuralist critique of the Cartesian subject and the neopragmatist attack on essentialist philosophy.

Individually, and in their relationships to one another, the various strands of the conversation that is postmodernism remain full of contradictions. In addition to postmodernism's uncertain connection with Modernism, there are periodization problems when postmodernism is considered as a new phase of modernity. For example, although Jameson asserts that postmodernism commences after World War II, many of the economic and ideological processes upon which postindustrialism seems to depend appear already to be in full swing in the mid nineteenth century. There is also considerable argument over whether postmodernism represents a critique of enlightenment epistemology or an example of its worst excesses. But the value of postmodernism as a term in these various debates remains its ability to blur the boundaries and to render problematic the distinctions upon which the debates themselves are founded. A concrete definition of postmodernism is, therefore, finally impossible because the various postmodernisms are an attempt to define the one thing that we can never define: ourselves and our relationship to the present moment.

Mark Mullen
University of California, Irvine

Bibliography

Hutcheon, Linda. *The Politics of Postmodernism*. New Accents. London: Routledge, 1989.

Jameson, Frederic. *Postmodernism, Or, the Cultural Logic of Late Capitalism*. Durham, NC: Duke UP, 1991.

Lyotard, Jean-François. *The Postmodern Condition: A Report on Knowledge*. Trans. Geoff Bennington and Brian Massumi. *Theory and History of Literature* 10. Minneapolis: U of Minnesota P, 1984.

Poststructuralism

A term used to describe the analytical strategies of philosophers, linguists, theologians, literary critics, and rhetoricians after the 1960s, when analysis based on structuralist assumptions, particularly in linguistics and literary criticism, had begun to fail. As its morphology shows, *post*structuralism names a field of intellectual discourse that came after structuralism. Four French theorists—Jacques Derrida in philosophy, Jacques Lacan in psychoanalysis, Michel

Foucault in the history of culture, and Julia Kristeva in feminist analysis—first developed the analytical strategies, writing styles, and intellectual habits that one now refers to as "poststructuralist."

Poststructuralist analysis has put many Western assumptions radically in question. Such analysis appears under numerous labels or rubrics, ranging from deconstruction to feminism, from Lacanian psychoanalysis to new historicism, and each of those larger rubrics houses numerous smaller rubrics. New historicism, for example, which grows out of the work of Foucault, can present itself as "cultural critique" or "cultural studies." Under either of these subrubrics, the analyst offers a study of texts of culture from a perspective with no overt political overtones. Any of Stephen Greenblatt's books offers a good example of this sort of historicism. New Historicism can also announce itself as politically motivated—as it does in the work of those British Marxists who operate under the specialized historicist subrubric, "cultural materialism."

The effects of poststructuralism have been felt in rhetoric in the United States in three ways. Each of these three ways results from the economic and political history of the research university English department. In 1900, American university English departments included not only the canonical study of Anglo-American literature, but also both the teaching of speech and the teaching of writing. Because literature professors held these two latter activities in such contempt, in 1914 teachers of speech formed their own professional organization (the Speech Communication Association) and seceded from English departments, taking not only the teaching of public speaking but also the study of the history of rhetoric with them. Then in 1949 teachers of writing did the same thing by forming the Conference on College Composition and Communication. While most writing teachers remain in English departments, the study of rhetoric as a means of persuasion and communication, insofar as anyone in an English department undertakes such activities, is done by faculty who call themselves either specialists in composition studies or specialists in rhetoric/composition. Thus, in discussing the term *poststructuralism* as a term within the field of "rhetoric," one must articulate clearly which strand of rhetorical studies one intends to discuss: the one in speech departments (which now often refer to themselves as communication studies departments), the one informing the teaching of writing, or the one recently resurrected by professors of literature.

In speech (or communication studies) departments, poststructural analysis has operated largely under the phrase "rhetoric as epistemic." Robert Scott introduced this phrase to speech professors in 1967 (the same year that Derrida published *Of Grammatology, Writing and Difference,* and *Speech and Phenomena*) and began a debate that still continues. Some of the most distinguished contemporary scholars in the history of rhetoric have participated in the debate over whether the rhetorical process creates what will then appear as knowledge (the poststructuralist position) or conveys knowledge that exists outside of and prior to the rhetorical process (the antipoststructuralist position). In 1982, Earl Croasmun and Richard Cherwitz published a long overview of the various sides to the dispute, and in 1990 the *Quarterly Journal of Speech* published a "Forum" titled "The Reported Demise of Epistemic Rhetoric," in which Barry Brummett, Richard Cherwitz, James Hikins, and Thomas Farrell reflect on all the arguments about epistemology and persuasion that poststructural analysis introduced to the study of rhetoric.

Among scholars in composition studies or rhetoric/composition (that is to say, among those whose primary task is the teaching of writing, usually in an English department), the effect of poststructuralism is harder to chart. The earliest and most consistent efforts to join rhetoric and composition with poststructural analysis have been made by Patricia Bizzell, Sharon Crowley, Lester Faigley, Susan Miller, and Jasper Neel. These five scholars have worked both from the French theorists mentioned above and from such American poststructuralists as Stanley Fish, Barbara Johnson, Paul de Man, and Hillis Miller.

Poststructuralism has had a variety of effects on theories of writing and the teaching of writing. At one extreme, rhetoric/composition scholars influenced by poststructuralism have tended to oppose empirical research in the teaching of writing because of empiricism's logocentric, positivist assumptions. At the other extreme, rhetoric/composition poststructuralists have struggled with the implications of poststructuralism for the teaching of writing. Poststructuralism does, after all, radically question authorial intent, the self-presence of knowledge, and the validity of interpretation—three presumptions on which the teaching of writing has historically been based. Moreover, the effects of Foucauldian historicism and Kristevian feminism have caused rhetoric/composition poststructuralists to teach with a political agenda, an agenda in which students are required to pay particular attention to race, class, and gender. For the teaching of writing, poststructuralism poses such difficult, occasionally immobilizing questions as, What is an author? What does it mean to write? and To what degree do the privileged, academic discourses of the West write the writer rather than being written by the writer?

The effect of poststructuralism on the term *rhetoric* as it appears in literary studies is both easy and hard to articulate. It is easy because the effect of poststructuralism has been to rehabilitate the term *rhetoric* in literary studies. By 1900 the authors published by the Modern Language Association had so thoroughly degraded the term that few literary critics in the first half of the twentieth century dared use the term. By 1975, however, the term had become so trendy that university press books in the humanities could use *rhetoric* in their titles in hopes of catching a wide reading audience. In brief, the term, when poststructuralist literary critics use it, indicates the author's theoretical biases against Formalist or New Critical principles and toward historicism, psychoanalysis, deconstruction, feminism, or one of the other critical movements that developed after the collapse of structuralism.

Poststructural analysis has led to the rehabilitation of rhetoric because poststructural analysis tends to locate truth and knowledge in the consciousness of a given person or group of people. As a result, rhetoric becomes crucially important because "being persuaded" is the closest one can come to truth. Of course, poststructural analysis also foregrounds its own political and social implications by constantly pointing out the ways in which some consciousnesses are privileged over other consciousnesses.

Jasper Neel
Vanderbilt University

Bibliography

Bizzell, Patricia. *Academic Discourse and Critical Consciousness*. Pittsburgh, PA: Pittsburgh UP, 1993.

Brummett, Barry, et al. "Forum." *Quarterly Journal of Speech* 76 (1990): 69–84.

Croasman, Earl, and Richard A. Cherwitz. "Beyond Rhetorical Relativism." *Quarterly Journal of Speech* 68 (1982): 1–16.

Crowley, Sharon. *A Teacher's Introduction to Deconstruction*. Urbana, IL: National Council of Teachers of English, 1989.

Derrida, Jacques. *Of Grammatology*. Trans. Gayatri C. Spivak. Baltimore, MD: Johns Hopkins UP, 1974.

Faigley, Lester. *Fragments of Rationality*. Pittsburgh, PA: Pittsburgh UP, 1993.

Fish, Stanley. *Doing What Comes Naturally*. Durham, NC: Duke UP, 1989.

Foucault, Michel. *The Order of Things*. New York: Random, 1970.

Kristeva, Julia. *Desire in Language*. Trans. Thomas Gora et al. New York: Columbia UP, 1980.

Lacan, Jacques. *Ecrits*. Trans. Alan Sheridan. New York: Norton, 1977.

Miller, Susan. *Textual Carnivals*. Carbondale: Southern Illinois UP, 1992.

Neel, Jasper. *Plato, Derrida, and Writing*. Carbondale: Southern Illinois UP, 1988.

See also DECONSTRUCTION; DE MAN, PAUL; DERRIDA, JACQUES

Pragmatics

The study of linguistic meaning in a situational context accommodating the interaction of language users. The discipline's foundations are variously attributed to Peircean and structuralist semiotics with philosophical roots in William James, Dewey, and Wittgenstein. Initially confined to ordinary or natural language philosophies such as speech-act and other discursive theories following the work of Austin, Searle, and Grice in the 1960s and 1970s, the field has since expanded to include cognitive, sociological, and affiliated branches of theoretical and applied linguistics treating psychological or cultural phenomena and their instantiation in the linguistic encoding of information structures. More recently, interest in the contextual ramifications of verbal acts has motivated investigations of allied disciplines such as rhetoric and literature, and the establishment of their respective pragmatics. The former examines the suasive effects of both oral and written language; the latter, contextualization in the literary text.

Linguistics informs rhetoric in its assumptions of similar aims in communication—

namely, the intention to convey propositional truth-value in a maximally relevant, understandable, straightforward manner that avoids indeterminacy. The business of both disciplines is the teleology of communication. Both may focus on such elements as deixis, syntax, lexicon, topicality, politeness axioms, modal stance, direct speech acts, and other signification referents. Like linguistics, rhetorical studies are concerned with inferences, implicatures, presuppositions, and other indirect speech acts. However, given its classical denominations—forensic, legislative, and epideictic—rhetoric's historical preoccupation with suasive pressures and their mediation through figurative and stylistic devices entails attention to the affective impact on hearer/reader ethics as well as the epistemology of discursive logic and its illocutionary force. To that end rhetoric must also account for kairotic or situational/occasional import in the attendant circumstances of rhetorical production as event—time, place, person, ethical values and other sociocultural conventions that bear on the subject. The sophistic concept of *kairos* also required that participants in rhetorical acts be aware of a proportionate sense of appropriateness to the situation as well as its timeliness, or historical fulfillment in due course. All these facets of rhetorical context were necessary to judicial resolution, considering the sophists' belief in the metaphysical absence of absolute truth and their alignment with rhetoric's political role in the arbitration of communal affairs.

Pragmatic rhetoric concerns itself, then, with broad contextual or situational phenomena beyond the merely sentential level of coded discourse or referential language, with the practical or empirical consequences of real-world communication. In shifting from a radically linguistic perspective that concentrates on the signified's function in ideational language performance and that posits language as a disinterested medium, rhetorical pragmatics are useful in analyzing semantic and other signifying energies pervading language operations. Thus, when we ask what words *do* to construct the ideological subject, and *how* they engender subjective positions by manipulating audience viewpoint, we inquire into rhetoric's capacity for inducing attitudinal change and the related question of rhetorical purpose.

While rhetorical pragmatics bridge the gap between oral and written communication, in effect spanning all discursive genres, their application to canonical literary studies presents certain obstacles. Here reader-reception theory, the pragmatics of reading process, impinge on the analysis of rhetorical effect. Although linguistic approaches are serviceable with regard to readers' assimilation of the propositional content of sentences, the literary text's ellipses, its hermeneutical constitution, inherent metaphoricity, self-reflexivity, and polyvocality impose inevitable constraints on reader access, which problematize the assumption of unambiguous communication underlying linguistic theories of ordinary public language. The limitations of a linguistic pragmatics in this instance are plain. Dependent on a rationale of salience involving conscious (and conspicuous) indexical communication or saturated coding, idealized norms, and audience familiarity with them, and assuming shared context dependencies like cultural bias, gender, and race, not to mention social situation or other externalities, such a pragmatics cannot justify the underdetermination of meaning in the extralinguistic domain through miscalculation or the failure to communicate, or for illogical, unintentional, or cryptic communication. The fundamentally diachronic nature of literary discourse as opposed to the synchrony of oral articulation also complicates matters. Since rhetorical events are configured differently in each genre, therefore, rhetorical principles must be discretely exercised and adaptable to the generic character. In such a case, the poetics of rhetoricians like Mikhail Bakhtin or Kenneth Burke that eschew more formalist orientations are most successful in addressing the creative mechanisms behind rhetoric's potential tropology (Burke's "symbolic action") and its pertinence to literature. Some literary pragmatists also argue that besides the conditions of interpretation, the contextual environments in which literature is produced warrant further inquiry.

Dianne Armstrong
Santa Barbara City College

Bibliography

Beale, Walter H. *A Pragmatic Theory of Rhetoric*. Carbondale: Southern Illinois UP, 1987.

Clark, Herbert H. *Arenas of Language Use*. Chicago: U of Chicago P, 1992.

Cohen, Philip R., Jerry Morgan, and Martha E. Pollack, eds. *Intentions in Communication*. Cambridge, MA: MIT P, 1990.

Davis, Steven, ed. *Pragmatics: A Reader*. New York: Oxford UP, 1991.

P

Givón, T. *Mind, Code and Context: Essays in Pragmatics*. Hillsdale, NJ: Erlbaum, 1989.

Leech, Geoffrey N. *Principles of Pragmatics*. New York: Longman, 1986.

Lucy, John A., ed. *Reflexive Language: Reported Speech and Metapragmatics*. Cambridge: Cambridge UP, 1993.

Parret, Herman. *The Aesthetics of Communication: Pragmatics and Beyond*. Dordrecht: Kluwer, 1993.

Sell, Roger D., ed. *Literary Pragmatics*. London: Routledge, 1991.

Sheard, Cynthia Miecznikowski. "*Kairos* and Kenneth Burke's Psychology of Political and Social Communication." *College English* 55 (1993): 291–310.

Pragmatism

Refers to a philosophical attitude that looks away from origins and absolutes to consequences and contingencies. As a formal philosophical movement, pragmatism's most widely recognized advocates in the early twentieth century were Charles Sanders Peirce, William James, and John Dewey in the United States and F.C.S. Schiller in England. Peirce described the pragmatic attitude as the consideration of "what effects, that might conceivably have practical bearings, we conceive the object of our conception to have" and then "our conception of these effects is the whole of our conception of the object." James credited Peirce with coining the term *pragmatism* in the 1870s, but it was James, Schiller, and Dewey who developed and popularized the philosophy, especially during the first decade of the twentieth century.

In its most well known exposition, *Pragmatism* (1907), James presented his subject as a method and a theory of truth. As a method, pragmatism asks about the effects of ideas, events, actions: A pragmatist typically "turns away from abstraction and insufficiency, from verbal solutions, from bad a priori reasons, from fixed principles, closed systems, and pretended absolutes and origins" and instead "turns towards concreteness and adequacy, towards facts, towards action, and towards power." As a theory of truth, pragmatism rejects correspondence models, which view truth simply as agreement with reality, and redefines it as the "cash-value" of an idea "in experiential terms." For pragmatism, "true ideas are those that we can assimilate, validate, corrobo-rate and verify. False ideas are those that we cannot. That is the practical difference it makes to us to have true ideas; that, therefore, is the meaning of truth, for it is all that truth is known as."

James's philosophy shares this doctrine of truth with Dewey's instrumentalism and Schiller's humanism, two other forms of pragmatist thought that view truth as "one species of the good." For all these early pragmatists, "the true is the name of whatever proves itself to be good in the way of belief, and good, too, for definite, assignable reasons." The *rhetorical* aspects of pragmatism become evident in such formulations. Not only does pragmatism share with various rhetorical traditions an emphasis on experiential consequences, historical effects, belief, action, and power, the pragmatist notion of truth specifically presents a modern version of the epistemic tradition in rhetoric, especially that of sophistic rhetoric. For example, F.C.S. Schiller argued that pragmatism might best be understood in terms of Protagoras' maxim that humans are the measure of all things, and he noted how all of Protagorean sophistry was grounded in the sophist's rhetorical teachings.

Recently, there has been a dramatic revival of pragmatism in the work of a wide range of humanists and social scientists. Richard Rorty's *Philosophy and the Mirror of Nature* (1979) was especially influential in establishing the current prominence of this neopragmatism. Influenced by poststructuralist thought, Stanley Fish, Giles Gunn, and others have developed a more explicitly rhetorical pragmatism in literary theory and cultural studies.

Steven Mailloux
University of California, Irvine

Bibliography
Fish, Stanley. *Doing What Comes Naturally: Change, Rhetoric, and the Practice of Literary and Legal Studies*. Durham, NC: Duke UP, 1989.

Gunn, Giles. *Thinking across the American Grain: Ideology, Intellect, and the New Pragmatism*. Chicago: U of Chicago P, 1992.

Mailloux, Steven, ed. *Rhetoric, Sophistry, Pragmatism*. Cambridge: Cambridge UP, 1995.

Rorty, Richard. *Philosophy and the Mirror of Nature*. Princeton: Princeton UP, 1979.

West, Cornel. *The American Evasion of Philosophy: A Genealogy of Pragmatism*. Madison: U of Wisconsin P, 1989.

Praxis

A term central to rhetoric, defined as action or practice. In the Aristotelian/Ciceronian strand of rhetorical theory, classical rhetoricians recognized rhetoric as an art that lies on the boundary between ethics and politics and helps people to deliberate in the world of common affairs. While used in a pretechnical sense in Homer, praxis is given a technical meaning by Aristotle. Thereafter, praxis denotes ethical and political action that is done well and manifested through rational choice.

Aristotle presents a tripartite conception of knowledge that includes *theoria* (theory), *praxis* (practice), and *technê* (art). Aristotle's treatise *Peri rhêtorikês* establishes rhetoric as an art that takes thought *(theoria)* and applies it to a given probabilistic situation. Praxis is the part of rhetorical invention that unifies thought with expression to aid humans in reaching their potential within the contingent nature of the polis. Praxis is an activity or action that strives towards *aretê* (excellence) in political affairs. Through praxis the speaker evokes the virtue that characterizes civic life.

An example of the centrality of praxis in later classical rhetorical theory can be found in Cicero's *De oratore*. In Book 1, Crassus argues that the orator is superior to the philosopher on the grounds that the orator has an understanding of praxis. While philosophers are concerned with intellectual matters, they are not able to contribute to the common good, argues Crassus. If one wants to make full "light" of the matter, one is obliged to turn to the orator, who has the power to explain to the populace what the philosopher can only communicate to other technical experts. The philosopher may have knowledge *(theoria)* but not have an understanding of praxis to translate the truth into phronêsis, or practical wisdom, which takes place through the *technê* or art of rhetoric. Cicero emphasizes that praxis lies in the realm of oratory and involves both knowledge of the subject matter, knowledge of the human psyche, and a political awareness.

In modern times praxis was incorporated by Hegel and Marx to designate a consciousness of historical process. Unlike Hegel who considered this process to be idealistic and grounded in *theoria*, Marx regards this consciousness as material. In the material condition, Marx's ideology is actualized as praxis and is the dialectical counterpart of the Hegelian concept of *Geist* (spirit). Ideas achieve their true significance as action in the social realm. For Marx praxis is a revolutionary tool for transforming material conditions and is a central concept in his philosophy. Praxis denotes the correct ideological behaviors of humans struggling to actualize justice within their materially determined conditions.

Omar Swartz
Purdue University

Bibliography

Bernstein, Richard J. *Praxis and Action.* Philadelphia: U of Pennsylvania P, 1971.

Lobkowicz, Nicholas. *Theory and Practice: History of a Concept from Aristotle to Marx.* Notre Dame, IN: U of Notre Dame P, 1967.

Moss, Jean Dietz, ed. *Rhetoric and Praxis: The Contribution of Classical Rhetoric to Practical Reasoning.* Washington, D.C.: Catholic U of America P, 1986.

See also ARISTOTLE; CICERO; MARXIST RHETORIC; TECHNÊ

Pre-Socratics

The pre-Socratics should be read in the context of the massive social and cultural upheaval that characterized Greece during the sixth and fifth centuries B.C.E., when customs were transforming in the face of new economic and political structures and traditional religious views were being questioned. They occupy a place in Western history as the first independent thinkers to reason about the nature of the cosmos and, in so doing, to challenge traditional mythic explanations handed down from Hesiod and Homer. They also developed theories of opposites, posited Being in place of the gods, argued about the relationship between sense perception and reality, experimented with forms of discourse, and speculated on the nature of language. Their preoccupations form a very real background to rhetorical theories put forward by the early sophists, most notably Protagoras and Gorgias. In many cases, early sophistic thought appears to be either directly influenced by or established in opposition to pre-Socratic speculations.

Yet most discussion of the pre-Socratics is firmly embedded in the philosophical tradition. The very term *pre-Socratic* situates the early history of Western speculative thought in relation to a watershed defined by Socrates, thus within a philosophic tradition. This tradition, it should be remembered, was predominantly hostile to rhetoric, likely to minimize sophistic interaction with these early thinkers, and likely to minimize the relation of "philosophic" concepts to their social and political contexts. Released from this philosophic category, these natural philosophers emerge as important predecessors to rhetorical and sophistic thought.

Like the sophists, many of the pre-Socratics engaged in public life. As writers situated between the poetic tradition and new conceptual developments, they sought to transform poetry to argumentative purposes and, in some cases, composed in prose. Even more important from the perspective of rhetoric, their philosophical inquiries constituted an important context for early sophistic rhetorical theory.

In approaching the pre-Socratics, we must remember that relatively little remains of their actual writing. In many instances we know about them primarily from commentators writing much later in antiquity, who view the pre-Socratics from the perspectives of their own philosophical systems. In addition, many of pre-Socratic texts are fragmentary and obscure, lending themselves to multiple interpretations. Thus, it is often difficult to decipher precisely what the pre-Socratics asserted or to say anything definitive about them. Some scholarly consensus does exist, however, providing a basis for this overview of their thought.

The Beginnings of Pre-Socratic Thought

The early pre-Socratics were the first Greek thinkers to apply the reasoning processes of abstract thought to questions about the universe, the natural world, and the role of human beings within it. They searched for principles governing the universe, speculated about its origins and composition, and argued about its nature.

In pursuing such investigations, these early thinkers confronted a rich mytho-poetic tradition originating in dim memories of Mycenean Greece and handed down across the centuries through the works of Homer and Hesiod. Tradition provided polytheistic explanations of the origins of the universe and of natural phenomena, and the anthropomorphic nature of the Greek gods supplied a psychology of human behavior. Yet a revolution in thinking—perhaps associated with the spread of literacy in Greece, and certainly related to the advent of new political and legislative systems—began in the first half of the sixth century, in the city of Miletus, where a small group of Ionians deviated from tradition to assert a new vision of the universe constructed by the reasoning powers of the human mind. They also produced the first prose treatises.

The geographic site of Miletus on the Ionian coast of Asia Minor suggests that the early pre-Socratics probably did not develop their thought in isolation. Knowledge of astronomy, mathematics, medicine, and cosmology may have reached Miletus from Babylonia, Phonecia, and Egypt. From Persian and Hebrew theological accounts, the Milesians may have gained a monotheistic view of religion, a necessary first step toward the unified vision of the universe that underlay their philosophical speculations.

A unified theology suggested an ordered universe, a divine order discoverable by human beings through rational thought. Thus the following became a central question for the pre-Socratics: What is the underlying order of the universe? Eastern theology emphasized the unity of the One, and this mode of thought seems to have led to a second pre-Socratic question: What is the primal substance, the principle source of the universe? These questions, which focus on stasis and unity, contrast with the tendency of sophistic inquiries to focus on change and cultural variation. Though pre-Socratics assuredly acknowledged change (in various ways and to varying degrees), they tended to seek and emphasize the underlying, unifying stability. Though theologically and philosophically radical, the pre-Socratic cosmological focus on unity and stasis probably should be read also as providing analogical arguments against social change and democracy (as Platonic philosophy would later).

The Milesians

Thales (active in 585 B.C.E.) is recognized as the first of the Milesian philosophers. He is thought not to have written any books, and all that is known of him comes from later sources. Like the older sophists, he was knowledgeable in many arts: Herodotus tells us that he was a political advisor and an engineer; he was also known for his expertise in mathematics, geometry, and astronomy, and is said to have predicted an eclipse of the sun, perhaps as a result of access to Babylonian astronomy. In keeping with Thales' place as the founder of Western philosophy, however, most commentary focuses on his cosmological theories. Thales, Aristotle tells us, addressed the problem of why the earth does not fall although suspended in space (*de caelo* B13.2964a28). Thales, who apparently proposed water as the primal substance, suggested that the earth floats on water like a log. While Aristotle dismisses this argument as a form of infinite regress—what, then, does the water rest on?—more recent scholarship (Barnes 10) points to two important aspects of this statement: It is the first attempt to describe the universe not in mythological but in rational terms, and, of greater interest to rhetoricians, the argument rests on an analogy.

Anaximander (said to be sixty-four in 547–546 B.C.E.) was a student of Thales. He was an astronomer and a geographer, famous for making a map of the world. Moreover, he must have been active in public life, for he led a Greek colonizing expedition to Apollonia, a city on the Black Sea. Anaximander proposed that the principle source of the universe was *apeiron*, "without boundary, limit, or definition," indefinite or infinite (Kirk et al. 110). He supported this claim with two arguments that illustrate the rational nature of his thought: (1) since the elements (such as hot fire and cold air) are opposed to one another, if any one were infinite, the others would be destroyed; (2) yet the source must be infinite for generation to persist against its opposite, destruction. Anaximander appears to have been the first writer to conceive of the elements in terms of opposites, a concept that may be important to the later rhetorical theory of opposing arguments. And, perhaps, he implies such a link, for to communicate his idea, he uses a social and political metaphor, describing the processes of exchange between natural opposites in terms of justice/injustice (Kirk et al. 120).

Anaximenes, the youngest of the Milesian philosophers, was a pupil of Anaximander and approximately twenty-four years younger. He is most famous for his theory that air is the primary substance from which all things originate. In his system, air was infinite and divine, and it formed the other elements through processes of rarefaction and condensation: Fire was a rarefied form; water and earth were the result of greater degrees of condensation. Anaximenes does not seem to have forwarded Anaximander's theory of opposites, with the exception of the rare and the dense. But as these opposites (sometimes referred to as the hot and the cold) are responsible for all generation, they hold a central position in his theory. Anaximenes uses an anthropomorphic metaphor to discuss his theory: As breath is the soul of human beings, so air is the breath and soul of the world, and the use of this metaphor suggests a connection to the earlier Homeric age. But in spite of such figurative language, Anaximenes may have been experimenting with a prosaic style, for Diogenes Laertius (II.3) tells us that "he used simple and economical Ionic speech."

The Pythagoreans

Of all pre-Socratic accounts, Pythagorean doctrine is the most difficult to reconstruct. Pythagoras (c. 570–490 B.C.E.) left no writings, and a religious stricture of silence was imposed on many of his teachings. Thus commentators rely entirely on doxographical account, much of which comes from less-than-reliable ancient sources. Pythagoras is said to have been a polymath, revered for his wisdom and perhaps for mystical and psychic abilities. An Ionian by birth, he migrated to southern Italy, where he founded a brotherhood devoted to a religious way of life bordering on the philosophic. He is famous for his doctrine of the transmigration of souls, a doctrine that is of interest primarily for the underlying attempt to describe the soul in personal terms, thus shifting attention from the material concerns of the Milesians and allowing a greater emphasis on the role of human beings in the cosmic order.

In the Pythagorean system, numbers were the primary form of the universe, and cosmic order was modeled on the new mathematical understanding of *harmonia* in music. The study of numbers revealed previously hidden structures of order, and this discovery suggested that the secrets of universal order would yield to a form of mathematical inquiry, a task well matched to the rising confidence in the rational abilities of human beings and consistent with Milesian attempts to discover underlying stasis and unity. In an historical period of social change, when mercantile interests were challenging the hegemony of traditional landed elites and urging relatively egalitarian democratic reforms, such mathematical and cosmological speculations had political implications that historians of philosophy tend to overlook. The Pythagorean Theorem for the hypotenuse of a right triangle ($a^2 + b^2 = c^2$), for instance, was apparently used to demonstrate that "true" equality may exist despite surface appearances of inequality, thus as an analogical argument against egalitarian democratic conceptions of justice (that is, in favor of oligarchy).

P

From a rhetorical perspective, the later Pythagoreans, those of the fifth century, are of primary interest for the doctrine of opposites they proposed. Pythagorean mathematical theory was based on the interaction between unlimited and limited, between even and odd numbers. This attention to opposites and their interrelationships appears to have led to a doctrine of opposites (or contraries). In his *Metaphysics,* Aristotle lists ten primary opposites, which he attributes to Pythagorean sources, and notes that according to this doctrine the substance of matter is created by the interaction of these opposites (A5.986a22). The theory is of interest as a possible precursor to Protagoras' interest in the two *logoi* (contrary theses) in opposition; in fact, Untersteiner has argued that this mixed quality of the universe allows for the possibility that opposing logoi can be proposed for the same phenomenon (24).

Heraclitus

Heraclitus (c. 500 B.C.E.), like many of the pre-Socratics, was deeply interested in the phenomenon of change in the natural world. For Heraclitus, the Pythagorean doctrine with harmony as its center failed to account for the striking feature of shifting appearances in the material world. Thus, Heraclitus posited that strife, not harmony, governed the ceaseless interchange of opposites and accounted for the universal pattern. Yet Heraclitus' vision is not chaotic, for the processes of change are subject to an order, a measure, a Logos that offers stability in the midst of flux by ensuring that no one side of opposing forces will ultimately prevail and reduce generating strife to sterile constancy.

For Heraclitus, the Logos that governs the universe is composed of fire and is present, in a small part, in individuals as the substance of their souls. As a result, processes that govern the universe and the natural world are intimately related to processes that govern human behavior, as all are united by their share in the divine Logos. The place of human beings in this explanation leads to an interesting relationship between physical theory and human behavior and results in an early form of ethics. Thus Heraclitus, somewhat arrogantly, admonishes his audience to dispense with behavior that dampens the soul and with traditional religious practice (except, perhaps, where the ultimate opposites of life and death are involved) and follow the path that leads to an understanding of the universal pattern, the Logos itself.

Heraclitus' insistence on strife as the central force in the universe and the resulting permanence of flux has, as many scholars have noted, profound implications for rhetoric. For Heraclitus the metaphor for the activity of strife is often war, a war between opposing forces that is perpetual and absolutely necessary for continuing existence. Should the war cease, existence would be frozen, subjugated to the dominance of one opposing side. His theory may have influenced the early sophists, who insisted on opposing *logoi* not only as a central feature of discourse but also as a continuing source of generation for language and thought.

The Eleatics

While the Milesians sought an underlying cosmological unity and Heraclitus suggested a universal logos underlying change, the founder of the Eleatic school, Parmenides of Elea (born c. 515 B.C.E.), denied the reality of change. Asserting a sharp distinction between sense perceptions and the true reality, he consequently posited reason as the only means of arriving at truth.

For Parmenides, the central problem is the distinction between "what is" and "what is not." There cannot, he argues, be a negative for existence: "What is not" is impossible. Consequently, since change implies movement between "what is" and "what is not," change itself is therefore a mere trick of the senses, an illusion, which must be dispensed with if true reality is to be perceived. Moreover, "what is" must be eternal, for if it came into being it would once have been "what is not," which is impossible according to Parmenides' system; nor will it perish for the same reason. Finally, existence is one and not many, for diversity suggests a space between existing things, and such a space suggests "what is not." Reality must then be continuous and undivided. And, on the same principle, motion is denied. In sum, this exercise of reason reveals existence as a unified One, freed from time, change, diversity, and motion, and profoundly in conflict with human experience.

In the second part of his single treatise, a long poem, Parmenides does outline the world of sense perception, a world based on mortal belief and opinion. In this system, reality is arbitrarily composed of two opposites, light and night, that interact harmoniously. In positing a world of opposites, Parmenides may be exploring the human sensory experience of appearances, but this explanation asserts the faulty foundations of human opinion. In contrast to true reality, the world of perception is constructed by human beings who have been led astray.

The implications of this philosophical position for rhetoric are many. Protagoras may have written a work attacking the unity of existence, and Gorgias in his treatise *On the Nonexistent* or *On Nature* appears to be directly responding to Eleatic claims, especially about Being. Indeed, sophistic perspectivism can be viewed as a reaction to the constraint of Eleatic monism. Similarly, the important divisions between truth and opinion that inform Platonic criticisms of rhetoric and democracy have their roots in Parmenides' distinction between opinion born of sense perception and truth apprehended through reason. Finally, Parmenides distrusted language itself, for language encouraged a belief in the authenticity of the world of appearance by naming it. The sophists could have found in this philosophical investigation a complex conception of linguistic reference, of language referring to the vagaries of sensory experience, not as directly or simply representing reality.

Zeno (born c. 490 B.C.E.) was a follower of Parmenides and his chief defender. He does not, however, offer arguments in support of Parmenides' system; rather he sets out to demonstrate the absurdity of holding the opposing view. Thus, while Parmenides posits the unity of reality, Zeno examines plurality and shows it to be logically absurd. He is said to be the founder of dialectic and is most famous for a series of paradoxes demonstrating the power of the mind to reason against sense perception. Zeno's famous paradox rests on the concept of unlimited divisibility. If reality is not one but many, then the things that are must be limited. But to distinguish one thing from another, there must be a third thing separating them, and in turn, the third unit must be discrete, and so on ad infinitum. The problem here is that the limited cannot be at the same time unlimited; one cannot stop divisibility at a certain point. Using this principle, Zeno exposes in a series of further paradoxes the logical absurdities of motion, time, and place, and in doing so demonstrates that common perception is at best no more reliable than Eleatic logic.

Apart from his philosophical position, which is in essence Parmenides', Zeno's influence on the sophists is most evident in his form of argumentation. While opposing forces had been common in cosmological speculations, for the first time we see a developed method of argumentation based on opposing *ideas*. The older sophists must have been influenced by Zeno's dazzling display of argumentation, and could have derived their theory of opposing *logoi* from this source.

Against this background, Empedocles (495–435 B.C.E.) emerges as a reconciler, moving away from earlier pre-Socratic positions. While he adheres to some Eleatic doctrine, he seeks to unite sense perception and reality and to integrate Heraclitean strife with Pythagorean harmony. In his system, the four elements replace Eleatic unity. Empedocles proposes strife and love as governing opposing forces and explains change and movement as the principles of attraction (love) and repulsion (strife) between the elements. Thus, in Empedocles' system, the four elements constitute a unity; movement is restored as their interaction and change is explained as their reconfiguration in new forms. In Empedocles, sense perception may be based on a shifting reality, but it yields an acceptable form of knowledge. Probably not coincidentally, he is said to have been a strong supporter of democracy and perhaps responsible for challenging an oligarchic confederation in his native city of Acragas in Sicily.

Empedocles was a polymath of outstanding proportions who demonstrated ability as a poet, orator, mystic, physician, and theologian. A renowned orator, he was, for Aristotle, the founder of rhetoric, yet he does not appear to have written any treatises on the subject. His style is, however, suggestive of his prowess in rhetoric, for his metaphors are frequently drawn from the world of everyday experience, and he summarizes the structure of his discourse, repeating where he has been and outlining where the discourse is going, in what appears to be an effort to communicate clearly (Guthrie, vol. 2, 1965:136). In comparison with the cultivated obscurity of Heraclitus and the awkward style in Parmenides, we can see in Empedocles' texts a new sensitivity to audience.

Empedocles restored the validity of sense perception and constituted a cosmology based on flux, governed by the opposing forces of strife and love. Thus language, referential to sensory experience, again had correspondence with the natural world. This correspondence may have helped sophists concerned with the naming function of language to develop the concept of opposing *logoi* as a condition of existence. Yet Empedocles had created a system that met Parmenides' criteria for existence; thus the problem with negation remained. In Empedocles, as in Parmenides, "what is not" does not exist. Kerferd has argued that this dilemma led to the renunciation of negative statements and produced the doctrine that no false statement could be made (73). Among the older sophists, Protagoras in particular, the categories for distinction changed from true/false to stronger/weaker in order to evaluate the validity of statements.

Empedocles' influence on Gorgias must have been direct, since Gorgias was his pupil. But it is not entirely clear to what extent Gorgias adopted Empedoclean ideas. Gorgias seems to have accepted, and perhaps even extended, Empedocles' defense of sense perception and so to have championed the validity of opinion based on sensory experience. Proclus attributes to Gorgias the claim that "existence is not manifest if it does not involve opinion, and opinion is unreliable if it does not involve existence" (Sprague Frag. 26). In the last section of *On the Nonexistent,* Gorgias may even be arguing for the primacy of logos (here used to signify speech) over sense perception in the realm of communication, thus going beyond his teacher and giving rhetoric an even greater epistemological importance and status.

Conclusion

Until recently, rhetoricians have devoted little attention to the pre-Socratics, focusing instead on the sophists, who developed rhetorical theory and taught rhetorical practice. But the sophists worked in an intellectual context created in large part by the pre-Socratics. Pre-Socratic thinkers challenged traditional religious perspectives with theories of their own making. Though their cosmology may have had conservative political implications, they introduced ways of thinking that celebrated the rational abilities of human beings, thus providing a nontheological basis for speculative and innovative thinking. They experimented with language and developed new forms of argumentation. And they examined the relationship between human language and reality. Pre-Socratic theories of the natural world seem to have provided an intellectual basis for early Greek thinking about language, rhetoric, and society.

Many sophistic concepts likely developed either from or in opposition to pre-Socratic concepts. Pre-Socratic arguments over sense perception, for instance, may have led to sophistic theories on the relationship of sensory experience to language that lie at the heart of early philosophies of rhetoric. Though the pre-Socratics and sophists, insofar as one can generalize about either, may have had different foci and taken divergent positions on various metaphysical, epistemological, political, and social issues, an understanding of the pre-Socratics is important to an understanding of the origins of both sophism and rhetoric.

Anne Hungerford and Richard M. Coe
Simon Fraser University

Bibliography

Barnes, Jonathan. *The Presocratic Philosophers*. 2 vols. London: Routledge & Kegan Paul, 1979.

de Ste. Croix, G.E.M. *The Class Struggle in the Ancient World*. London: Duckworth, 1981.

Enos, Richard Leo. *Greek Rhetoric Before Aristotle*. Prospect Heights, IL: Waveland, 1993.

———. "The Epistemology of Gorgias' Rhetoric: A Re-Examination." *Southern Speech Communication Journal* 42 (1976): 35–51.

Freeman, Kathleen. *Ancilla to the Pre-Socratic Philosophers: A Complete Translation of the Fragments in Diels, Fragmente der Vorsokratiker*. Cambridge, MA: Harvard UP, 1962.

Guthrie, W.K.C. *The Presocratic Tradition from Parmenides to Democritus*. Vol. 2. *A History of Greek Philosophy*. Cambridge: Cambridge UP, 1965. 122–265.

Hussey, Edward. *The Pre-Socratics*. New York: Scribner's, 1972.

Kerferd, G.B. *The Sophistic Movement*. Cambridge: Cambridge UP, 1981.

Kirk, G.S., J.E. Raven, and M. Schofield. *The Presocratic Philosophers: A Critical History and a Selection of Texts*. 2nd ed. Cambridge: Cambridge UP, 1983.

Schiappa, Edward. *Protagoras and Logos: A Study in Greek Philosophy and Rhetoric*. Columbia: U of South Carolina P, 1991.

Sprague, Rosamond Kent. *The Older Sophists*. Columbia: U of South Carolina P, 1972.

Untersteiner, Mario. *The Sophists*. Trans. Kathleen Freeman. Oxford: Blackwell, 1954.

See also SOCRATES; SOPHIST

Preteritio

"To go by; to pass over"; the inclusion of something by pretending to omit it. Preteritio is a subtle way of emphasizing the purportedly omitted information. President Nixon was resorting to preteritio when he declared, "I will not question the motives of those who seek my impeachment." Commonly used expressions such as "I don't need to tell you that . . . ," "I won't remind you how . . . ," "to say nothing of . . ." are preteritios that emphasize a statement only in certain contexts. Preteritio can also be used to summarize information, as when a guest speaker is introduced: "I will not describe the twelve books she has written."

Arthur Quinn and Lyon Rathbun
University of California, Berkeley

Priestley, Joseph (1733–1804)

Rhetorician, born in West Riding, Yorkshire. In 1742, after the death of his mother, he was adopted by his aunt, Sarah Keighley. Priestley entered Daventry Academy in 1751. There he became familiar with David Hartley's *Observations on Man,* a treatise that influenced him extensively (he is reputed to have considered it second only to the Bible as a source of wisdom). In 1761 he was appointed as a tutor of belles-lettres at Warrington Academy and in 1762 was ordained as a minister. In the same year, he married Mary Wilkinson. While at Warrington, Priestley composed *A Course of Lectures on Oratory and Criticism,* which he published in 1777. In 1766 he was elected to the Royal Society for his scientific and philosophical research. During that period he became an intimate of Benjamin Franklin.

In 1767 he left Warrington and became minister at Mill Hill Chapel, Leeds. From 1772 to 1780, he worked as the librarian and literary companion of William Fitzmaurice-Petty, second earl of Shelburne. He continued his scientific work, discovering oxygen in 1774 (the achievement for which he is best known in the twentieth century); ironically, his belief in the phlogistic theory of chemistry prevented him from recognizing the true significance of his discovery. In 1780 he left Shelburne's service and moved to Birmingham. In 1791 a mob believing him to be an organizer of the Constitutional Society's dinner to honor the fall of the Bastille attacked his house, destroying his library and laboratory. In 1794 he immigrated to America, settling in Northumberland, Pennsylvania. He continued to write on various topics until his death in 1804.

Priestley's lectures on rhetoric divide the composing process into four elements: recollection (the task of finding arguments "with which [the] mind is already furnished" (*Lectures* 5)), method (arrangement), style, and elocution. Priestley divides discourse into two realms: narration (which includes both fiction and nonfiction, and writings like geography and botany that may follow an order of place instead of an order of time) and argumentation (which he divides into an inductive mode he refers to as "analysis" and a deductive mode he calls "synthesis"). Priestley's importance as a rhetorician remains open to debate. Bevilacqua and Murphy refer to him as "derivative" and "an index scholar" (Introduction lii), but W.S. Howell in his history of eighteenth-century rhetoric and logic considers many aspects of Priestley's theories worthy of further scholarly examination.

Priestley's theoretical writings on rhetoric represent only a fraction of his intellectual work. A Dissenter, Priestley was often at odds with established religious and political authorities. Besides his numerous scientific writings, he was involved in several philosophical and political disputes. These texts provide scholars of rhetoric with a wealth of material for the examination of eighteenth-century discourse.

Mark Gellis
Purdue University

Bibliography

Fruchtman, Jack, Jr. *The Apocalyptic Politics of Richard Price and Joseph Priestley: A Study in Late Eighteenth-Century English Republican Millennialism. Transactions of the American Philosophical Society.* n.s. 73.4 (1983): 1–125.

———. "Joseph Priestley on Rhetoric and the Power of Political Discourse." *Eighteenth Century Life* 7 (1982): 37–47.

Howell, Wilbur Samuel. *Eighteenth Century British Logic and Rhetoric.* Princeton: Princeton UP, 1971.

P

North, Ross Stafford. *Joseph Priestley on Language, Oratory, and Criticism.* Diss. U of Florida, 1957.

Priestley, Joseph. *A Course of Lectures on Oratory and Criticism.* Ed. Vincent M. Bevilacqua and Richard Murphy. Carbondale: Southern Illinois UP, 1965.

———. *The Theological and Miscellaneous Works of Joseph Priestley.* Ed. John Towill Rutt. 25 vols. in 26. [London] Hackney: George Smallfield, 1817–1832.

See also EIGHTEENTH-CENTURY RHETORIC

Probability

That part of rhetoric involving human contingency rather than absolute certainty. The rhetorical principle of reasoning from what is likely (*eikos*) to be true is known as the argument from probability. Although traditionally credited to Corax of Sicily, the mythical "inventor" of rhetoric, the earliest surviving examples of Greek arguments from probability are found in Antiphon's *Tetralogies*, which are model exercises in forensic speaking. For instance, in the first *Tetralogy*, the prosecutor argues that the defendant was likely to have killed the victim because the victim was likely to do the defendant great financial harm.

The conceptualization of argument from probability is, according to George A. Kennedy, one of the indicators of the awakening of rhetorical consciousness in Greece. Once established as a viable principle for structuring discourse, the argument from probability quickly became a central tenet in sophistic argumentation and was later formalized in Aristotle's rhetorical theory as the enthymeme and the example.

The best historical example of the argument from probability concerns a small man who is accused of attacking a larger one. The accused pleads his innocence, in light of little or no direct evidence, on the basis that it was unlikely he could have perpetrated the assault since the size discrepancy between the two would preclude the weaker man's chance for success. This type of reasoning draws upon a perceived common sentiment and offers a quasi-empirical and experiential method for inducing belief.

The assumption behind the argument from probability is that justice is never clear and knowledge of past and future events is seldom certain. The obvious is not always true. The argument from probability allows for degrees of correctness and tries to account for the contingencies of human affairs.

Aristotle relies heavily on the precept of probability when he declares that rhetoric and dialectic are concerned with general knowledge and do not constitute an exact science. His rhetorical theory is designed to uncover contingent knowledge through artistic proof (*entekhnos pistis*). The enthymeme and example work from the premise that certainty in human affairs is probabilistic and not scientific. A further advantage is that probabilities, unlike oaths and witnesses, do not lie and cannot be subjected to bribes. Furthermore, when direct evidence was absent, Greek juries were dependent upon probable arguments. For example, slaves were tortured before their evidence could be admitted in court because it was believed probable that under such conditions they would be less prone to lie.

Aristotle assumes that people generally act rationally, follow natural social patterns in the pursuit of happiness and the good, and that human nature or the behavior of a particular political body can be predicted. Furthermore, he recognizes that it is seldom the case that an orator has direct evidence to support an argument. Consequently, the orator must build a case from probabilistic knowledge. Usually some evidence exists in a particular case, but the rhetor must go beyond it to construct an effective enthymeme that is grounded more firmly in the expectations and beliefs of the audience.

Omar Swartz
Purdue University

Bibliography

Aristotle. *On Rhetoric: A Theory of Civic Discourse.* Trans. George A. Kennedy. New York: Oxford UP, 1991.

Cole, Thomas. "Who Was Corax?" *Illinois Classical Studies* 16 (1991): 65–84.

Hinks, D.A.G. "Tisias and Corax and the Invention of Rhetoric." *Classical Quarterly* 34 (1940): 59–69.

Smith, Bromley. "Corax and Probability." *Quarterly Journal of Speech Education* 7–8 (1921–1922): 13–42.

See also ARISTOTLE; CORAX; ENTHYMEME; PROOF

Process/Product

A conceptual opposition that was important in the reemergence of rhetoric and composition as an academic discipline. In the New Criticism, the starting point for literary study was the given "text"—that is, the "product." It was considered "fallacious" to consider matters outside the text—such as the writer's "biography" or declared "intention" or the reader's actual "affect"—while doing the work of reading, which was supposed to be aimed at discovering valid interpretations of individual texts.

But English departments also taught (and typically supported their literature classes by teaching) "composition" (and perhaps also "creative writing"). In these domains the "product"—the texts produced by the students—needed to be seen as the outcome, not as the point of departure. Composition teachers, therefore, needed to pay attention to the "process" that produced the "products" in their classes. (Creative writing teachers often took the position, as did their colleagues in literary study, that the process of "creation" was, or needed to be seen as, essentially mysterious: They were not therefore as interested in "process" as were their colleagues in composition.)

Trying to infer the process of composition from its products, said Don Murray, is like trying to infer a pig from a sausage. To make inferences about process, researchers had to look beyond final "products." But the "process" of writing cannot be directly observed; it must be inferred from what we take to be its observable effects. In researching the process, investigators looked beyond final products to notes and drafts and reports of mental activity (Warnock).

The first major empirical study of composing processes—and one of the founding works for the field—was Janet Emig's *The Composing Processes of Twelfth Graders* (1971). Employing the then-unusual method of case study, Emig found that the processes twelfth-grade students used for "school-sponsored" writing were significantly different from the ones they used for "self-sponsored" writing. Students of the writing process also began to pay attention to the self-reports of professional writers. The accounts of Donald Murray, who was also a professional writing teacher, have been found helpful by many teachers.

Other investigators employed careful observation of activities in classrooms (Graves) and of writers writing. A notable line of research employed "thinking aloud protocols,"

records of the spoken accounts of writers at work about what they are thinking as they work. This line of cognitive research has produced the most highly elaborated model of the composing process (Flower).

In composition's struggle to create itself as a field distinct from literary study, "product teaching" has been characterized as the villain of the piece. "Process teaching" has come to occupy a position of honor, in places like the National Writing Project and in a number of writing curricula in the schools and the colleges. In recent years, however, the process approach to teaching composition has not been without its critics.

Some have complained that process teaching neglects issues of the product's meaning, effectiveness, and quality. Process researchers have answered that the aim in studying the process is to improve products, even with respect to such matters as grammatical correctness. To be "effective," however, writers must consider situation and audience. When process teaching does not invite these considerations, invocations of the writing process are otiose. Issues of "meaning" may compel consideration of social, cultural, and literary matters. In achieving "quality," purpose is certainly as important as process (Perkins). To the extent that process teaching takes a writer's purpose as simply given, it makes writing *merely* a process (as opposed to an action).

Sometimes process teaching has been schematized in classrooms and curricula into step-by-step, linear proceedings. Where this has happened, it has happened despite the insistence of many researchers from Emig onward that the process must be seen as recursive and iterative.

John Warnock
University of Arizona

Bibliography

Emig, Janet. *The Composing Processes of Twelfth Graders.* NCTE Research Report No. 13. Urbana, IL: National Council of Teachers of English, 1971.

Faigley, Lester. "Competing Theories of Process: A Critique and a Proposal." *College Composition and Communication* 48 (1986): 527–42.

Flower, Linda, and John R. Hayes. "A Cognitive Process Theory of Writing." *College Composition and Communication* 22 (1981): 365–87.

Graves, Donald H. "An Examination of the Writing Process of Seven-Year-Old Children." *Research in the Teaching of English* 9 (1975): 227–41.

Moffett, James. *Teaching the Universe of Discourse.* Boston: Houghton, 1968. Reissued 1983.

Murray, Donald. *Learning by Teaching: Selected Articles on Writing and Teaching.* Montclair, NJ: Boynton/Cook, 1982.

Perkins, D.N. *The Mind's Best Work.* Cambridge, MA: Harvard UP, 1981.

Warnock, John. "The Writing Process." *Research in Composition and Rhetoric: A Bibliographic Sourcebook.* Ed. Michael G. Moran and Ronald F. Lunsford. Westport, CT: Greenwood, 1984.

See also EMIG, JANET; NATIONAL WRITING PROJECT; PROTOCOLS

Progymnasmata

From the Greek, designating a series of graduated rhetorical exercises common to the schools of Western and Eastern Europe from the Roman republic through the Renaissance. As the term indicates, the exercises were preparatory to the more difficult activities of the *gymnasmata,* known in the Latin schools as the declamations. The *progymnasmata* (Latin, *praeexercitamenta*) were designed to move the student from the relatively easy, elementary exercises in composition to the *suasoriae* and *controversiae,* the more difficult and comprehensive activities of declamation. Each exercise was designed to build on what had come before, thereby reinforcing old lessons while introducing new challenges. The program was also structured so that the student moved from strict imitation to a more artistic melding of the often disparate concerns of speaker, subject, and audience.

The earliest reference to the *progymnasmata* occurs in the *Rhetorica ad Alexandrum* (c. 330 B.C.E.), and the exercises appear to have formed part of the curriculum of the Roman schools from the first century B.C.E. onward. Both Cicero and Quintilian mention them with approval. By the time Quintilian wrote (c. 92–95 C.E.), responsibility for the exercises rested jointly with the teacher of grammar (the *grammaticus*) and the teacher of rhetoric (the *rhetor*). Four hundred years later, when Priscian of Caesarea translated Hermogenes' *Progym-nasmata* into Latin, the *grammaticus* seems to have assumed full responsibility.

The earliest surviving treatises on *progymnasmata* date from the late first and early second century C.E. The texts of Aelius Theon of Alexandria (fl. c. 100 C.E.), Hermogenes of Tarsus (fl. second century), Aphthonius of Antioch (fl. c. 400 C.E.), and Nicolaus of Myra (fl. c. 430–500 C.E.) survive. (Portions of Theon and Nicolaus, as well as the entirety of Hermogenes and Aphthonius, are now available in English translation.) Most later texts were adaptations, combinations, paraphrases, or Latin translations of these early works, or commentaries and glosses on them. These texts, produced well into the seventeenth century, strongly suggest that the *progymnasmata* were an important part not only of the Greek schools of the Byzantine Empire but also of the Latin schools of the West.

With some variation, the *progymnasmata* usually involved the following:

1. *Mythos,* or fable, involved the retelling of folk tales in simple, direct style. Sometimes students were asked to expand or abbreviate the fable, and to identify its moral.

2. *Diêgêma,* or narrative, included providing an account of an action. The action was derived from something that happened or that could have happened.

3. *Chreia,* or anecdote, required students to amplify a famous person's statement or action. The meaning could be developed through praise, paraphrase, statement of the cause, comparison and contrast, and so forth.

4. *Gnômê* (Latin, *sententia*), or proverb, involved the same activity, amplification, as did the *chreia.* It required students to focus on recommending or discrediting an aphorism.

5. *Anaskeuê* (Latin *confutatio*), or refutation, one of the two early assignments in argument, involved disproving a narrative.

6. *Kataskeuê* (Latin *confirmatio*), or confirmation, the other early exercise in argument, involved proving a narrative.

7. *Koinos topos,* or commonplace, required the student to color the subject in shades of good or evil, virtue or vice. Usually the subject of the commonplace was a type rather than a specific person or thing.

8. *Enkômion,* or praise, often went together with the following exercise, *psogos,* and taught the student how to praise a person or thing by expanding upon the virtue of the subject.

9. *Psogos,* or blame, immersed the student in the arts of invective. The assignment was to censure a person or thing for its evil or vicious qualities or actions.

10. *Synkrisis,* or comparison, doubled the subject of the preceding exercises by requiring the student to compare two people or things and to explore shades of virtue and vice.

11. *Prosopopoeia,* or personification, was an exercise in impersonation or characterization, the goal of which was to imitate the ethos of the person portrayed by using language appropriate to the subject and circumstance.

12. *Ekphrasis,* or description, was designed to heighten awareness of language through vivid descriptions of the subject.

13. *Thesis,* or argument, involved logical examination of a general question, that is—one that does not involve specific individuals, such as "Should one marry?"

14. *Nomou eisphora,* or legislation, was the final exercise. In it the student was required to argue for or against a law.

The *progymnasmata* endured in part because they worked and in part because they provided training well adapted to the dominant modes of speaking. Judicial or forensic speaking was served by refutation, confirmation, and commonplace; deliberative speaking by fable, narrative, *chreia,* proverb, thesis, and legislation; and demonstrative or epideictic speaking by praise, blame, personification, comparison, and description. But when, in the late seventeenth century, training in the three classical genera began to lose relevance and the systematic development of Latin themes through imitation and amplification began to lose favor, the *progymnasmata* fell into sharp decline. Nonetheless, the training afforded by the *progymnasmata* has left a strong impression on Western literature and oratory.

Sean Patrick O'Rourke
Vanderbilt University

Bibliography

Baldwin, Charles Sears. "The Elementary Exercises of Hermogenes." *Medieval Rhetoric and Poetic.* New York: Macmillan, 1928. 23–38.

Bonner, Stanley F. *Education in Ancient Rome from the Elder Cato to the Younger Pliny.* Berkeley: U of California P, 1977. 250–76.

Clark, Donald Lemen. *Rhetoric in Greco-Roman Education.* New York: Columbia UP, 1957. 177–261.

———. "The Rise and Fall of *Progymnasmata* in Sixteenth and Seventeenth Century Grammar Schools." *Speech Monographs* 19 (1952): 259–63.

Hagaman, John. "Modern Use of the *Progymnasmata* in Teaching Rhetorical Invention." *Rhetoric Review* 5 (1986): 22–29.

Hock, Ronald F., and Edward N. O'Neil. *The* Chreia *in Ancient Rhetoric: Volume I. The* Progymnasmata. Atlanta: Scholars, 1986.

Johnson, Francis R. "Two Renaissance Textbooks of Rhetoric: Aphthonius' *Progymnasmata* and Rainolde's *A booke called the Foundacion of Rhetorike.*" *Huntington Library Quarterly* 6 (1943): 427–44.

Kennedy, George A. *Greek Rhetoric under Christian Emperors.* Princeton: Princeton UP, 1983. 54–73.

Murphy, James J. "Roman Writing Instruction as Described by Quintilian." *A Short History of Writing Instruction: From Ancient Greece to Twentieth-Century America.* Ed. James J. Murphy. Davis, CA: Hermagoras, 1990. 19–76.

Nadeau, Ray. "The *Progymnasmata* of Aphthonius in Translation." *Speech Monographs* 19 (1952): 265–85.

Prolegomena

In rhetoric, introductions to the history of rhetoric or grammar, including philology, philosophy, and poetics; more generally, readings or intellectual exercises serving as a critical introduction to any subject. Prolegomena to the art of rhetoric were most commonly produced from the third to the thirteenth centuries and fell into four general categories.

First and most typically, they were comprehensive introductory surveys which discussed

P

the definition and principles of rhetoric (or grammar, as in medieval grammar handbooks), its use among gods and literary heroes, and its importance to humans. Hermogenes of Tarsus, for example, wrote a number of important prolegomena summarizing the principles of classical rhetoric and reinterpreting them for his Byzantine audience. The second type of prolegomena was that which introduced a larger work, such as commentaries on Hermogenes. Third, critical introductions from larger works were sometimes compiled into collections, which were also called prolegomena. A fourth kind of prolegomena was a manual of preliminary exercises or principles that served as a pedagogical introduction to rhetoric or grammar. Books 1 and 2 of Quintilian's *Institutio oratoria*, for example, "contain those particulars which are antecedent to the duties of a teacher of rhetoric" (including lectures on poetry, style, and composition), and "consider the first elements of instruction under the hands of the professor of rhetoric and the questions which are asked concerning the subject of rhetoric itself" (including exercises in composition, learning by example, and elementary analysis) (1. Preface 21–22). More recently, and less typically, prolegomena to rhetoric may serve as introductions to a limited topic—a specific rhetorician, rhetorical term, or historical period, for instance, like Frank J. D'Angelo's more recent "Prolegomena to a Rhetoric of Tropes," which suggests rhetoric's connections to epistemology and composition theory.

Hugo Rabe's *Prolegomenon Syllagoge* provides the most complete collection of rhetorical prolegomena, although its reliability is inconsistent. Some examples from the collection represent late reconstructions of rhetorical concepts that use few, if any, source materials (for example, Sopater [Rabe 6A–13]), or that conflict with extant historical documents or primary texts. Others go back to original rhetorical, literary, or historical texts for their information, and are generally considered authoritative (such as Anonymous [Rabe 4], which relies on Sicilian historian Timaeus [4 B.C.E.], who comments on the rhetorical contributions of Corax, as well as his famous lawsuit against Tisias). In any event, early prolegomena provide important information on the roots of rhetoric and suggest rhetoric's reception and influence in subsequent centuries and cultures.

Elizabeth Ervin
University of North Carolina, Wilmington

Bibliography

D'Angelo, Frank J. "Prolegomena to a Rhetoric of Tropes." *Rhetoric Review* 6 (1987): 32–40.

Quintilian, Marcus Fabius. *Institutio oratoria*. Trans. Charles Halm. Leipzig: Teubner, 1868.

Rabe, Hugo, ed. *Prolegomenon Syllagoge*. Leipzig: Teubner, 1931.

Proof

The process of reasoning defined by Aristotle's logical, emotional, and ethical appeals, leading to an emphasis on mathematical demonstration and the syllogism. In the latter part of the twentieth century, it was acknowledged that this argumentative structure did not respond to the uncertainties of natural language and moral issues. New forms of reasoning evolved that emphasize premises and reasons accepted by the audience rather than formal measures of validity.

Proof in argumentation is the process of advancing from specific evidence to a conclusion. Also called the "line of reasoning," it secures belief in one statement by relating it to another one already accepted. Because the proof in mathematical demonstration aims for truth in the conclusion and because the proofs in dialectic and rhetoric aim for only probable conclusions, the models appropriate to these domains of reasoning differ. Mathematical reasoning employs the model of symbolic logic, operating in a closed system and building syllogistic proofs from true premises. Proofs in dialectical and rhetorical reasoning, however, follow a number of different models.

Aristotle classified proofs as inartistic and artistic, with the first deriving from already existing evidence that simply needed to be interpreted and the second for which the rhetorician had to discover the material that would serve as support in the argument. Artistic proofs were divided into appeals to logos, pathos, and ethos. The logical appeal addressed the audience's reason or understanding, the pathetic appeal created emotions to make the audience more receptive to the argument, and the ethical appeal sought to display the character of the rhetorician in a favorable light. Aristotle further broke the logical appeal down into "proof" and "apparent proof," or the enthymeme and the example, respectively. Aristotle's enthymeme was perceived by many over the centuries to be merely a truncated syllogism because one of the two premises was implied rather than laid out.

Cicero defined the enthymeme as a proposition plus a reason. Although this "rhetorical syllogism" addressed only probable conclusions, it often was judged by the same standards of validity as the formal syllogism.

The syllogism served as a dominant model for argumentative proofs. The logical appeal became privileged over the emotional and ethical appeal, especially after Peter Ramus divided dialectic and rhetoric, giving invention and arrangement of proofs to dialectic and style to rhetoric. This division, plus the epistemological movements of rationalism and empiricism during the Enlightenment period, marked a search for a universal structure and criteria for argument, which came more to focus on a search for truth and the validity of formal syllogistic reasoning and less on the audience and the contributions of the emotional and ethical appeals to a rhetorical proof. One significant contribution to this concept during the nineteenth century, however, was Richard Whately's identifying the jurisprudential notion of "burden of proof"—that is, a proof will presume to be good unless sufficient reason is put forth against it; the burden of proof lies on the side of whoever would dispute a claim.

The logical positivism movement in the twentieth century magnified the mathematical and scientific approach to language and argumentation, bringing a resulting rise of scientism in the social sciences and humanities and a focus on deficient proofs, or logical fallacies. Around the middle of the twentieth century, questions arose over the appropriateness of the syllogistic proof as the model to encompass all cases of nonmathematical reasoning. It was perceived of as a complex, closed system that possesses only absolute standards for reasoning that cannot accommodate uncertainties of natural language and the moral issues in daily life. British logician Stephen Toulmin created a new model for argumentative proofs demonstrating a flexibility not known with the syllogism. The foundation of his argumentative structure consists of three parts: (1) the claim, or proposition at issue; (2) the data, or the evidence to support the claim; and (3) the warrant, the inference or bridge, that establishes a connection between the evidence and the claim. To these basic elements, he added backing for the warrant as well as qualifying and rebuttal statements for claims.

Other conceptions of rhetorical proof that question the emphasis on syllogistic reasoning do not offer specific argument structures. They share, however, a concern for the role the audience plays in constructing that proof and return credibility to the emotional and ethical appeals. Logician Chaïm Perelman searched for a "logic of value judgments" and concluded that rhetorical argumentation requires a speaker to gain the adherence of the audience by transferring existing adherence from premises already held to new conclusions based on those premises. Unlike theorists who focus on syllogistic reasoning, however, Perelman shows multiple ways to create a proof from liaisons between premises and conclusions. Arguments are not judged according to validity but to the adherence of an audience to a premise. Rhetorical proofs have also reinvented themselves through the "good reasons" movement, in which reasons replace premises in building an argument. "Good reasons" are statements consistent with each other in support of ought-propositions. Because value statements mean different things in different contexts, the grounds for argument are situation-dependent and judged as "good" by the audience alone. These new rhetorical proofs differ from the self-evident reasoning associated with the syllogism in that they all respond to the situation and involve the audience in their creation and their evaluation.

Julie M. Farrar
Saint Louis University

Bibliography
Aristotle. *Rhetoric*. Trans. Rhys Roberts. Ed. Friedrich Solmsen. New York: Modern Library, 1954.
Brockriede, Wayne, and Douglas Ehninger. "Toulmin on Argument: An Interpretation and Application." *Quarterly Journal of Speech* 46 (1960): 44–53.
Fisher, Walter R. "Toward a Logic of Good Reasons." *Quarterly Journal of Speech* 64 (1978): 376–84.
Perelman, Chaïm, and L. Olbrechts-Tyteca. *The New Rhetoric: A Treatise on Argumentation*. Trans. John Wilkinson and Purcell Weaver. Notre Dame, IN: U of Notre Dame P, 1969.
Toulmin, Stephen E. *The Uses of Argument*. Cambridge: Cambridge UP, 1958.
Wallace, Karl. "The Substance of Rhetoric: Good Reasons." *Quarterly Journal of Speech* 49 (1963): 239–49.
Whately, Richard. *Elements of Rhetoric*. Ed. Douglas Ehninger. Carbondale: Southern Illinois UP, 1963.

See also EVIDENCE

P

Propaganda

A form of rhetorical communication that results when institutions and groups seek to influence a mass audience in the direction of special interests by means of orchestrated or covertly diffused symbols. Propaganda is commonly distinguished from other forms of persuasion on a number of bases: It pertains to organizational rhetoric more than to individual orators; the persons addressed are vast rather than few in number (although propagandists segment their audiences); the aims sought are self-serving rather than geared toward compromise and accommodation in furtherance of a more general good; the form of address is less often a single, direct message and more frequently a massive projection of symbols via the media or a covert infiltration of material into channels of public expression idealized as nonpartisan (such as news, education, entertainment, research reports, and religious preaching).

Unfavorable connotations branding propaganda as hidden, illegitimate persuasion are common in the English-speaking world because of the term's association with the proselytizing efforts of the *Congregatio de propaganda fide* (Society for the Propagation of the Faith) of the Roman Catholic Church. In the United States, the contemporary use of propaganda as a term for hidden mass persuasion began during World War I, when Germany's secret campaign to spur neutralist sentiment was uncovered. Thereafter, *propaganda* became the key rubric for studies of symbolic inducement conducted by American social scientists until the terms *communication* and *persuasion* emerged as replacements in the 1940s. During the 1980s the expression *propaganda* again became common in the United States as a significant theoretical locution for social influence of dubious purpose and tactics.

The term *propaganda* has great utility in helping to mark changes in the style and scope of symbolic inducement since the nineteenth-century era of oratory and pamphleteering. Walter Lippmann noted the increasing inability of twentieth-century urbanites to obtain direct, firsthand experience with key sociopolitical issues and events. Because citizens were now dependent upon secondary accounts in newspapers, Lippmann characterized mass society as increasingly vulnerable to whoever was able to insert biased facts and interpretations into the news. Lippmann's own work with the Wilson administration and with the Army's psychological warfare unit alerted him to certain deep-seated dangers that propaganda posed for democracy. He observed that the political and military administrations of belligerent nations had acted to taint journalism with a self-serving aura. This indictment applied with equal measure to the British, to the Germans, and to the U.S. Committee on Public Information. The Great War brought into bold relief the danger that propaganda might undermine free choice even if the forms of democracy remained unchanged. How might citizens in a republic maintain dominion if their knowledge of events, conditions, and issues were under the sway of the very elites the public was supposed to control?

Lippmann and other intellectuals associated with the Progressive Movement were concerned that the wartime climate of self-serving institutional manipulation would continue in the postwar period. Lippmann's writings, as well as like-minded contributions by John Dewey, Charles Beard, and muckraker Will Irwin, helped establish *propaganda* as a terminological lever in the theoretical arsenal of Progressivism.

The rise of the communication professions (public relations, advertising, and market research) and the emergence of electronic media channels only intensified the worries of Progressives that democratic public opinion was threatened by innovative communicative resources available to institutions and groups. The Great War not only had given all of the communication professions the opportunity to demonstrate their capacity to move the public in behalf of organizations and causes, but the war had also highlighted how trends of promotion and publicity, emerging since the Age of Jackson, called into question the assumption of orthodox democratic theory that an independent public could form and articulate its will. Certain antecedents of the propaganda nexus were emerging as early as the 1830s, when large-circulation penny newspapers, supported by advertising, began to replace smaller subscription organs that had been directly subsidized by commercial or political elites. Now that news was popularized for purposes of gathering a large readership, politicians began to recognize that news coverage offered more opportunity for self-promotion than did oratory. At the same time, circus and theater promoters, the precursors of public-relations counselors, began to ply their trade in behalf of railroads and, later, politicians. In the latter nineteenth century, advertising became a popular communication art when rival agencies began to prepare and place copy for clients that targeted not merely retailers and wholesalers but also the general public.

The term *propaganda* frequently has been associated with governmental manipulation and with the competition of alliances and large ideological blocs. In the Nazi literature, propaganda represented the art of playing upon the emotional vulnerabilities of the public for purposes of control. National-Socialist propaganda aimed at maintaining the regime by means of whatever tactics would undermine enemies of the state and would solidify support for the leader. In the Soviet-Marxist literature, propaganda is described as a scientific system for penetrating public consciousness with correct Marxist-Leninist principles. As an offshoot of Marxist ideology, Soviet-style propaganda has endeavored to inculcate a world view that makes clear in a particular case the proper duties of the working class and the responsibilities of the Communist Party.

Not only has the connection of propaganda to governmental-ideological machinations been characteristic of European approaches (that of Jacques Ellul excepted), but this was the predominant use of the term during the 1940s and 1950s in the United States when American opinion leaders were preoccupied with the struggles of liberal democracy against fascism and communism. As studied in the U.S., however, the term *propaganda* more often has been used to designate efforts by domestic institutions and groups to co-opt important and ostensibly apolitical channels and forums of social expression. Both between the world wars and after the Vietnam War, significant literatures emerged that critiqued communications from civil-service-protected governmental agencies as well as from research bureaus, news organizations, educational establishments, religious bodies, and entertainment media. Currently, a large number of works are available that uncover propagandistic tendencies in federal programs, private foundation grants, television news practices, textbook content, televangelism, and in the plots and characters of popular films.

Most writers on propaganda in the U.S. have taken up the post–World War I view of Progressives that institutional orchestration and covert manipulation are subversive to democracy. However, other students of the subject demur either as to whether propaganda is antithetical to democratic public opinion or as to whether the public is competent at all to form opinions on the basis of communication. Three other significant schools of thought on propaganda emerge in the works of communication practitioners, communication scientists, and proponents of critical thinking.

Practitioners of advertising, public relations, and market research (polling), as well as programmers in the mass media, recognize from experience that persuasion is not always easily attained. They fault propaganda critics for overstating the influence of modern promotional culture on citizens. From the practitioners' point of view, propaganda represents an elaboration of traditional American boosterism. Advertisers, on their part, credit their craft for making possible an unprecedented degree of consumer choice in both the commercial and political spheres. Public-relations spokespersons argue that propaganda enlightens society by enabling and encouraging institutions to adjust their policies and products to what they understand is the public will. Pollsters frequently tout their own work as uniquely valuable in ascertaining democratic opinion.

Scientists who conduct quantitative studies of communication tend to accept the view of practitioners that the competition of propagandists (enhanced by communication professionals) renders twentieth-century persuasive practices socially benign. Political scientist Harold Lasswell became a major spokesperson for this school of thought, arguing that propaganda is an alternative to force and that symbolic cultivation of the masses is necessary both because of the scale of mass society and given humanity's psychological frailties. On these bases, communication scientists justified their assistance to large governmental and mercantile persuaders.

The critical-thinking approach to propaganda dates from the 1920s, when a number of social critics and social scientists, appropriating concepts from crowd psychology and from Freudian psychoanalysis, argued that the failure of public opinion during the war years owed more to the cognitive incompetence of the public than to institutional manipulation of opinion. Proponents of critical thinking contended that sociocognitive phenomena, such as the extreme anti-German manias of 1917–1918, could not be controlled unless citizens were taught scientific principles (hypothesis, experiment, and conclusion) and logical forms (inference, proof, and validity).

Propaganda is a verbalism used not only by Progressives, ideologists, practitioners, scientists, and critical thinkers but also by polemicists, whose writings on symbolic machinations have produced a considerable literature that greatly enhances academic and professional understandings of the term. In the United States, the polemical literature on propaganda divides itself into two bodies. First are works that result from a political appropriation of the term *propaganda* as a club to anathematize enemies; second are works by intellectuals associated with political movements whose exegeses explicate symbolic manipulations by opposing partisans.

Illustrative of propaganda analysis as a direct political weapon was the work of the House Committee on Un-American Activities (1934, 1938–1975). Captured in 1938 by an anti–New Deal faction led by Congressman Martin Dies of Texas, HUAC diluted its mandated duty to expose communist and Nazi propaganda directed from overseas by also pursuing various evocative but questionable forays into such agencies of the New Deal as the Federal Theatre Project. HUAC endeavored to paint the FTP as procommunist on the basis that the agency produced plays critical of bankers and industrial leaders. However, these hearings were far overshadowed by the committee's later work to blacklist certain writers on the basis that these playwrights (despite the strictures of the studio film-production system) had injected procommunist propaganda into American movies. HUAC occasionally produced work of a public-service character; however, the committee gained a reputation for harassing nonconformist liberals and dissident socialists with charges often based more on innuendo and guilt by association than on reasonable analysis.

The excesses of HUAC notwithstanding, polemical propaganda analysis is not necessarily less credible than propaganda studies that aim for dispassionate academic inquiry. One may turn to a considerable body of interesting and generally well-reasoned propaganda critique contributed by intellectuals who have been closely associated with the political Left and Right. Critical investigations of journalism by George Seldes (*Lords of the Press,* 1938) and I.F. Stone (his self-published weekly newsletter) constituted useful propaganda critiques, and Noam Chomsky and Edward S. Herman (*Manufacturing Consent,* 1988), along with

Herbert I. Schiller (*Culture Inc.,* 1989), have continued this left-of-center tradition. Politically committed intellectuals on the Right who have contributed propaganda critiques include William F. Buckley, Jr. (*God and Man at Yale,* 1951) and Dinesh D'Souza (*Illiberal Education,* 1991).

Educators tend to share the dominant view (dating from the Progressive Movement) that propaganda represents a social problem because it taints public opinion. The Institute for Propaganda Analysis (1937–1942) undertook the most comprehensive effort to construct curricula that would defuse the propaganda problem. The institute's monthly bulletin and educational materials directed the attention of teachers and students to propaganda in various media channels (newspapers, radio, film), in various professions (such as public relations), and also provided case studies of propaganda by political and commercial organizations. However, the institute was (and is) best known for developing the seven propaganda devices: name-calling, glittering generalities, transfer of authority or respect, celebrity testimonials, the plain-folks appeal, overemphasis by means of card stacking, and the bandwagon ("everybody is doing it") appeal. Despite the wide circulation and influence of the institute's materials, the concept of educational propaganda analysis fell out of favor when opinion leaders began to express concern that this kind of universal critique of symbolism might prevent Americans from rallying to the antifascist crusade of World War II. During the 1940s critical-thinking pedagogies replaced propaganda analysis in the public schools. The post-Vietnam revival of antipropaganda curricula is best exemplified by the Public Doublespeak program of the National Council of Teachers of English, which, although heavily oriented to semantics and logic, also has attended to major propagandists and propaganda tactics.

If demagoguery is the chief threat to democracy in an oratorical epoch, then propaganda is the specter of a mass-mediated promotional culture. The questions of whether propaganda is necessary for mass society and whether, and to what extent, propaganda imperils democratic public opinion raise issues that weigh heavily on modern and postmodern societies.

J. Michael Sproule
San Jose State University

Bibliography

Bernays, Edward L. *Propaganda*. New York: Liveright, 1928.

Doob, Leonard W. *Propaganda: Its Psychology and Technique*. New York: Henry Holt, 1935.

Ellul, Jacques. *Propaganda: The Formation of Men's Attitudes*. New York: Knopf, 1965.

Jowett, Garth S. "Propaganda and Communication: The Re-Emergence of a Research Tradition." *Journal of Communication* 37 (1987): 97–114.

Jowett, Garth S., and Victoria O'Donnell. *Propaganda and Persuasion*. 2nd ed. Newbury Park, CA: Sage, 1992.

Lasswell, Harold D. *Propaganda Technique in the World War*. London: Kegan Paul, 1927. Rpt. Cambridge, MA: MIT UP, 1971.

Lee, Alfred McC. *How to Understand Propaganda*. New York: Rinehart, 1952.

Lee, Alfred McC., and Elizabeth B. Lee. *The Fine Art of Propaganda*. New York: Harcourt, 1939. Rpt. San Francisco: International Society for General Semantics, 1979.

Lippmann, Walter. *Public Opinion*. New York: Macmillan, 1922.

Smith, Ted, III. *Propaganda: A Pluralistic Perspective*. New York: Praeger, 1989.

Sproule, J. Michael. "Propaganda Studies in American Social Science: The Rise and Fall of the Critical Paradigm." *Quarterly Journal of Speech* 73 (1987): 60–78.

See also CHOMSKY, NOAM; DOUBLESPEAK; PERSUASION; POLITICAL RHETORIC

Protagoras (b. c. 490 B.C.E.)

Of Abdera, the earliest of the so-called older sophists. Often described as one of ancient Greece's first great humanists, Protagoras is one of the first Greek thinkers to give an account of language and reality that functioned ideologically as a defense of democracy and open debate. Though he taught before the formalization of the discipline of rhetoric, his notions of *dissoi logoi,* twofold discourses, and the correct use of discourse, *orthos logos,* are important forerunners to later theories of rhetoric.

Protagoras' most famous aphorism is "of all things the measure is Human: Of that which is, that it is the case; of that which is not, that it is not the case." The scholarly consensus is that Protagoras made this statement in response to Parmenides and his followers. For Parmenides, contradiction signaled error and misunderstanding. If one person feels the wind is cold and another feels it is not cold, one or both have to be wrong, for the wind cannot both *be* cold and not-cold. Protagoras resolved this contradiction with a nascent notion of relativism. The wind may be cold to *one person* and not-cold *to another.* For Protagoras, it makes no sense to say that one or both people are mistaken; both accounts can be true. It is human beings, not the gods or "divine" philosophers, who decide what is or is not the case.

Protagoras is often called the father of debate, in part because he is credited with declaring that "there are two contrary accounts (*logoi*) concerning everything." Of these two *logoi,* one is stronger at any given point in time. Just as the wind may be cold and not-cold, a law may be just to one polis yet considered unjust by another. According to Aristotle, Protagoras promised to teach how "to make the weaker argument stronger," by which Protagoras apparently meant how to turn a losing cause into a winning cause, such as changing a city's perceptions about a law.

Protagoras is also credited with beginning a treatise with the following: "Concerning the gods I am unable to know, whether they exist or whether they do not exist, or what they are like in form; for there are many hindrances to knowledge—the obscurity of the subject and the brevity of life." Though undoubtedly an expression of agnosticism, it is possible also that Protagoras wrote these words as the beginning of a treatise that represents what we would now call an anthropological approach to religion.

Protagoras is credited with giving lectures, engaging in "Socratic questioning," and conducting two-sided debates. Protagoras' teaching and conceptualization of discourse was undifferentiated and precategorical—that is, it was independent of context and did not distinguish between types of discourse on the basis of distinctive principles or degrees of certainty. Plato's description of Protagoras' educational activities in the dialogue *Protagoras* did not limit him to the oratorical training of rhetors in the sense the term was used in the fifth and fourth centuries.

Edward Schiappa
University of Minnesota

Bibliography

Kerferd, G.B. *The Sophistic Movement.* Cambridge: Cambridge UP, 1981.

Schiappa, Edward. *Protagoras and Logos: A Study in Greek Philosophy and Rhetoric.* Columbia: U of South Carolina P, 1991.

Sprague, Rosamond. *The Older Sophists.* Columbia: U of South Carolina P, 1972.

See also SOPHIST

Protest Rhetoric

Broadly speaking, any and all discourse or symbolic action directed toward removing alleged injustices. Usually, however, we think of protestors as persons or groups operating outside official channels of influence, or in marginal roles with respect to them. Thus, mainstream political candidates may register all manner of objection to government policies, and their support may be enlisted by protest groups; but they are not generally considered protestors in their own right.

Although individuals may protest on their own, the focus here is on protest by or in the name of an organized protest group or protest movement. These vary from informal, grassroots undertakings to highly professionalized movement organizations such as Amnesty International and the Sierra Club. Those who affiliate with protest groups may be among the direct beneficiaries of successful protest, or they may be persons acting out of conscience for the benefit of others, or they may be pressing universalistic claims for which they and others could benefit.

Protest rhetorics vary with goals, audiences, and situations. Protest may be directed at state authority or, as has commonly been the case in recent years, it may seek to politicize nongovernmental institutions. The contemporary women's movement, for example, has practiced a "cultural politics" that has included activities designed to redefine the meaning of womanhood through changes in language structure. It also has sought alteration of images of women in advertising and pornography and has attempted to combat stereotypes of women as only mothers and wives.

One goal of protest may be to enhance the status of the protesting group. Beyond that, the aims of protest may consist of throwing the rascals out, altering policies or practices, transforming public beliefs and values, or, as is commonly the case, preventing alleged wrongs from being perpetrated. The more ambitious the goal, the more likely it is to be resisted. A key strategic question for protestors is whether to influence targets of protest directly or to build a sufficient base of support that targets will feel constrained to comply.

All protest movements must mobilize material and personnel resources, exert external influence, and resist counterinfluences. These needs give rise to more specific functions. Mobilization, for example, involves recruiting new recruits and energizing existing supporters. Recruitment is seldom a matter of enlisting isolated individuals to the cause. Rather, volunteers tend to be recruited from within established networks of interaction, such as churches, trade unions, universities, and friendship circles.

Fireman and Gamson speak of four stock arguments for participation in protest activities: necessity, opportunity, solidarity, and responsibility. Potential activists must be convinced that just outcomes are unlikely without their participation (necessity), that these outcomes are likely or at least possible with their participation (opportunity), that their personal interests are linked with the group's interests (solidarity), and that the need for action is urgent and requires their principled commitment (responsibility). Absent significant material benefits for participation in sustained protest activities, protestors need especially to be provided with nonmaterial incentives such as solidarity appeals. Protest leaders may also need to provide definition of that which is ambiguous in the social situation, give structure to anxiety and a tangible target for hostility, and articulate wish-fulfillment beliefs about the protest group's power to succeed.

To energize supporters and to sustain their commitments in the face of counterpressures, protest leaders generally must provide rationales for movement goals and tactics; offer "correct" interpretations of the past, present, and future; delegitimize competing ideologies; offer defenses against counterarguments; and provide immunizing rationales for potentially embarrassing situations. Symbolic acts of defiance and protest also serve as points around which the movement may coalesce.

Protest rhetorics are moral rhetorics: They seek to legitimize the group's own interests and to delegitimize the opposition. Moral rhetorics by protest groups are addressed not only to supporters but also to third parties, such as the news media. In seeking to legitimize their own cause, protestors may appeal to logic, to rights, to fairness or goodness, to feelings or sentiment, or to kinship. Enlisting support is generally a matter of fitting a protest group's ideological frame to that of a culturally sanctioned frame. For example, recent "identity politics" have involved efforts to win benefits and protections for some groups (for example, gays and lesbians) that had earlier been established as civil rights for others. "Rights" claims have often been based on the assertion of a formal similarity in kinds of identity, from racial and ethnic to class, gender, and sexual identity. Snow and his colleagues speak in this connection of "frame alignment processes" as an ongoing and interactional accomplishment that may involve frame bridging, frame amplification, frame extension, or frame transformation.

The verbal rhetoric of protest groups may be arrayed on a moderate-to-militant continuum. In general, the militant tend to express greater degrees of dissatisfaction. Whereas the moderates tend to ask "how" questions, the militants ask "whether" questions. If the moderate sees inefficiencies on a given issue, the militant is likely to see inequities. The moderate tends to regard authority figures as misguided though legitimate, while the militant tends to regard them as willfully self-serving and illegitimate. Both the moderate and the militant are apt to pay homage to law, but the latter is more apt to derogate existing laws in the name of higher law. Finally, the moderate tends to restrict the scope of opposition, whereas the militant is apt to cast the net widely, extending it even to ordinary citizens. For example, Queer Nation and Operation Rescue have argued that "the people" are engaging in genocide condoned by a passive state.

Verbal appeals are often combined with collective actions, such as demonstrations, picketing, boycotts, sit-ins, and the like, ranging all the way to rioting and guerrilla warfare. These too can be arrayed on a moderate-to-militant dimension. Whether social disturbances are viewed as legitimate protests—or as deviant or rebellious acts, for example—apparently depends on a variety of factors, among them whether the activists are seen to be part of an aggrieved group; whether they are viewed as helpless to achieve their ends by lesser means; whether they show signs of moral virtue, such as being habitually law-abiding; and whether

they combine attention-getting threats with sympathy-inducing appeals. The media play an important role in attending to or ignoring movement actions and in conferring or denying legitimacy to them.

A recurring dilemma for protest movements is the need to combine sympathy-inducing appeals and attention-getting threats. Getting attention from targets and from the news media may require illegal, violent, or otherwise militant forms of collective action, yet these power strategies may undermine the movement's moral appeal. Thus, protest movements may alternate between persuasion and power or synchronize the activities of their moderate and militant factions. Protest groups may also engage in collective actions intermediate between those of the moderate and militant. A favorite tactic has been to confront opponents in ways designed to force them to embarrass themselves publicly by their manner of response—or else acquiesce to the protestors' demands. Here, as with other protest activities, favorable media response as well as support from other third parties tend to be crucial. Benefits are most likely to be won when protest groups are able to exploit divisions among elites and/or antagonisms toward particular targets by mass publics.

Finally, protest movements must deal with a variety of counterinfluences. Insofar as protest movements challenge accepted ways of doing things, they are likely to engender resistance from government or other established institutions, each of which deploys its own rhetorics of justification and social control. Protest movements may also generate countermovements or other backlash effects as powerful as the initiating movements themselves. Then too there tend to be internecine struggles within movements over goals, strategies, or personal allegiances. Even among organizations with broadly similar goals, the relationship is rarely one of pure cooperation. Thus, for example, African-Americans, feminists, and Marxists have found common cause in their indictments of discrimination based on race, gender, and class, while at the same time competing for the attentions and resources of potential supporters. Given the cross-pressures protest movement leaders predictably confront, it seems a truism that whatever rhetorical strategies they devise to mobilize supporters, exert external influence, and combat counterinfluences will inevitably create new problems requiring new rhetorical adjustments.

Herbert W. Simons, Philip Bakelaar, and Cynthia Patton Temple University

Bibliography

Fireman, B., and W. Gamson. "Utilitarian Logic in the Resource Mobilization Perspective." *The Dynamics of Social Movements: Resource Mobilization, Tactics and Social Control.* Ed. J. McCarthy and M. Zald. Cambridge, MA: Winthrop, 1979.

Fuentes, M., and A. Frank. "Ten Theses on Social Movements." *World Development* 17 (1989): 179–91.

Gamson, W. *The Strategy of Social Protest.* 2nd ed. Belmont, CA: Wadsworth, 1990.

Offe, C. "New Social Movements: Challenging the Boundaries of Institutional Politics." *Social Research* 52 (1985): 817–68.

Simons, H., E. Mechling, and H. Schreier. "The Functions of Human Communication in Mobilizing for Action from the Bottom Up: The Rhetoric of Social Movements." *Handbook of Rhetorical and Communication Theory.* Ed. C. Arnold and J. Bowers. Boston: Allyn, 1984. 792–867.

Snow, D., et al. "Frame Alignment Processes, Micromobilization, and Movement Participation." *American Sociological Review* 51 (1986): 464–81.

Stewart, C., C. Smith, and R. Denton. *Persuasion and Social Movements.* Prospect Heights, IL: Waveland, 1989.

Protocols

A conceptual framework and vocabulary for talking about composing and establishing an agenda for further research that has examined the ways in which acts of cognition mediate different rhetorical contexts for writing. Studies in composition have shifted during the last twenty years, from analyzing written texts to understanding how texts are constructed. Renewed interest in rhetorical invention, planning, and revision has brought with it an important research method, protocol analysis. Researchers have used think-aloud protocols to capture a glimpse of writers' moment-to-moment thinking as they compose a text through analyzing writers' tape-recorded reports of their writing process. Think-aloud protocols, first used in studies of problem-solving strategies in cognitive psychology, have enabled writing researchers to explore what is involved in the act of writing, specifically how writers orchestrate the underlying cognitive processes of composing.

Perhaps most notably, the work of Flower and Hayes in the late 1970s and 1980s, based on protocol analysis, drew upon rhetoric and cognitive psychology to ask how we might model or describe the basic, underlying, goal-directed processes that go on in composing. While think-aloud protocols have been quite useful in helping researchers understand more about the *what* of writing, researchers have begun to pose a different set of questions, not so much about *what* writers do, but *why*. These *why* questions arise from our increasing concern with rhetorical situations and our growing sensitivity to the diverse assumptions and goals that influence writers as they move in and across these different contexts. One of the more striking examples of this shift is in the study of novice writers. In the 1980s, researchers such as Flower and Hayes and Bereiter and Scardamalia were using protocols to describe whether and how novice performance differed from that of experts. Expert/novice comparisons also laid the groundwork for a new approach to teaching by showing that effective writers had a distinctive repertoire of problem-solving strategies. Education could indeed intervene where it mattered by teaching the process of writing, not just showing how to analyze a written product. At the same time, process instruction has raised important questions about whether it is possible to teach a natural process of activities and ignore goals and strategies and how we can scaffold the transition to new, often more difficult strategies.

Researchers in the 1990s are building on this work by asking why such differences exist, why writers recognize and attend to some strategies but not others, and whether the idiosyncratic behaviors we observe in different groups of writers possess a "logic" of their own. Researchers who ask such questions argue that differences in performance and strategies are not always best described in terms of deficits and failures. Using think-aloud protocols, we have learned that other factors—for example, writers' past experiences with writing, the evaluative climate of the classroom, or their assumptions about the task—can influence their writing decisions and performance. The purpose of this growing body of research is to clarify and understand some of these situational and cognitive influences.

Think-aloud protocols, used alone or in conjunction with other methods, such as text analysis and retrospective interviews, have enabled researchers to build a rich understanding of the relationship among texts, situational factors, and writers' constructive processes. Most important, think-aloud protocols have provided a window into writers' thinking, opening up more grounded and sensitive ways to understand the strategies writers bring to the act of composing, the logic they invoke, and the ways teaching could foster the process of learning.

Stuart Greene
University of Wisconsin, Madison

Bibliography

Bereiter, Carl, and Marlene Scardamalia. *The Psychology of Written Composition.* Hillsdale, NJ: Erlbaum, 1987.

Emig, Janet. *The Composing Process of Twelfth Graders.* Urbana, IL: National Council of Teachers of English, 1971.

Ericsson, K. Anders, and Herbert A. Simon. "Verbal Reports as Data." *Psychological Review* 87 (1984): 215–51.

Flower, Linda, and John R. Hayes. "A Cognitive Process Theory of Writing." *College Composition and Communication* 32 (1981): 365–87.

Smagorinsky, Peter, ed. *Verbal Reports in the Study of Writing: Problems and Potentials.* Newbury Park, CA: Sage, 1994.

Swarts, Heidi, Linda Flower, and J.R. Hayes. "Designing Protocol Studies of the Writing Process: An Introduction." *New Directions in Composition Research.* Ed. Richard Beach and Lillian Bridwell. New York: Guilford, 1984. 53–71.

Pulpit Oratory

A rhetorical perspective on Christian preaching. Rhetoricians characteristically are drawn to the intersections of theory and practice, and pulpit oratory is an art that exemplifies the creative dynamics between the two. Contemporary historians of rhetoric, though, tend to focus on certain events in the development of preaching theory, especially events that are seen as central to the unfolding of the classical tradition. Most accounts thus emphasize Augustine's endorsement of Greek and Roman rhetoric for Christian purposes; the importance of preaching (along with letter-writing and verse-writing) as one of the three rhetorical genres of medieval Europe; the proliferation of manuals on the thematic sermon in the thirteenth century; and the influence of Blair, Campbell, and Whately, the British triumvirate of minister-rhetoricians who reinterpreted classical traditions for modern times. Attention to broader theoretical and practical developments, however, offers a more encompassing perspective.

The practice and theory of preaching, so often associated with Euro-American Christianity, are rooted in the rhetoric of ancient Palestinian Judaism, especially as embodied in the first-century synagogue. Both Jesus of Nazareth and the Apostle Paul, whose discourse practices shaped the communities of faith that produced the New Testament, were immersed in this richly developed Hebrew interpretive and oratorical tradition. At the same time, from the earliest days of the church, Christian preachers have been informed by the legacy of classical Greek and Roman rhetors—especially Isocrates, Aristotle, and Cicero. Currently, the twentieth-century renaissance in rhetoric has encouraged an unprecedented illumination of the power claims encoded in biblical texts, hermeneutical precepts, and ecclesiastical practices. Such investigation is proving to be particularly generative for the work of feminist preachers.

The proclamation of the Christian message (*kerygma*) emerged as a few of the disciples began to announce their conviction that Jesus, the crucified messiah, had been raised from the dead. This is the core of the church's gospel (*euangelion*), and according to the New Testament, the believers proclaimed it first to other followers of Jesus, often evoking disbelief, and later to Jews and Gentiles beyond their nascent community of faith.

Since nearly all of the earliest disciples were Jewish, they interpreted the crucifixion and resurrection events by drawing not only on their memories of the words and actions of Jesus but also on the elaborate store of imagery, narrative, ritual, and conviction provided by their thousand-year-old religious heritage. As the new faith spread, oral traditions were superseded by written forms (letters, collections of sayings, accounts of the passion and resurrection, and finally, gospels). Eventually, Christian worship came to include the pattern of preaching established in the synagogue: a reading from the sacred texts was followed by an explication of its meaning, which sometimes included an application or exhortation to members of the congregation.

Christian oratory also received a formative imprint from the traditions of classical rhetoric. To begin with, as James Kinneavy has shown, the concept of faith inscribed in the New Testament reflects the influence of Greek theories of persuasion. Kinneavy argues that the New Testament writers and their audiences understood *pistis* (usually translated "faith") to refer not only to human trust in God (the concept of faith emphasized in the Hebrew scriptures) but also to the human process of giving free assent, despite some uncertainty, to a new perspective (the notion of persuasion exemplified in the writings of Isocrates and Aristotle). The early church assumed, as Kinneavy's analysis reveals, that persuasion to the faith was not a once-and-for-all event, essential only for potential converts, but an ongoing process, a day-by-day assent that would likely increase in depth and power as doubt was explored and commitment was tested.

During the early chapters in the church's life, Christian orators designed a variety of approaches to this task of ongoing persuasion. At first, worship took place in the homes of believers, and the preacher offered what Origen would later call a homily (*homilia*, "conversation"), colloquial in style, which typically followed the scriptural text verse by verse. After Nicea (325), when imperial persecution had ended and worshipers gathered in large churches, some preachers began to employ a more artful expression. In the Eastern church, preachers tended to draw upon the classical rhetor's devices more freely than did their Western counterparts. At the extreme was John Chrysostom, bishop of Constantinople, who endeavored (without success) to keep his congregation from interrupting his eloquence with applause.

In the West, by contrast, church leaders were more reluctant to use secular strategies for Christian persuasion. Partly as a response to this dilemma, Augustine, bishop of Hippo, developed a Christian theory of rhetoric. Far more than simply giving permission for pulpit orators to cultivate Greek and Roman modes of expression, Augustine reinvented classical theory by articulating a Christian perspective on the nature of signs, the art of interpretation, and the relations between speaker and hearer. Augustine's *On Christian Doctrine* (*De doctrina christiana*, 427) is the treatise most explicitly oriented to the preacher's work. Books 1–3 advise the Christian rhetor on how to discern the truth in scriptural texts, while Book 4 focuses on how to convey that truth so as to persuade one's hearers. Though most of Book 4 is devoted to an application of Ciceronian theory to the preacher's style, Augustine insists that wisdom is more important than eloquence, and his bias toward the preacher as teacher is clear.

Augustine's more innovative rhetorical proposals, however, are expressed in *Concerning the Teacher* (*De magistro*, 389) and *On Catechizing the Uninstructed* (*De catechizandis rudibus*, 399) as well as in Books 1–3 of *On Christian Doctrine*. Of particular interest here is Augustine's exploration of words as "prompts"; his emphasis on the creative participation of the reader or hearer in making meaning and effecting persuasion; his awareness of the mutual transformation involved in every rhetorical interaction; and his insistence on the "rule of love" as a guide for interpretation, teaching, and preaching. These ventures prefigure several tenets fundamental to the "new rhetorics" of our own day.

During the medieval era, preachers continued to adapt their methods according to the exigencies of audience, context, and purpose. Even Robert of Basevorn, whose *Form of Preaching* (1322) offers advice on how to compose and deliver the intricately structured "thematic" or "university style" sermon, acknowledges that there have always been nearly as many ways of preaching as there are skillful preachers. Robert's manual typifies the hundreds of treatises on the art of preaching (*ars praedicandi*) that circulated in this period, promoting the use of the thematic sermon form.

The early preaching of Luther, for instance, reflects the influence of thematic structures; as the Reformation took root, however, and as his passion for educating the whole community of faith increased, Luther's sermon form became less complex and more direct. This commitment to instruction, along with the reformers' renewed emphasis on the preaching of the Word, has left a lasting impression on the ministry and mission of the church.

A balance between tradition and innovation has characterized pulpit oratory in the United States. Teresa Toulouse has analyzed major homiletical influences and shifts through the sermons of Cotton, Colman, Channing, Emerson, and Coleridge. Ernest Bormann has traced the development of a "rhetoric of romantic pragmatism" beginning with Jonathan Edwards and culminating in the speeches of Abraham Lincoln. Henry Mitchell has chronicled the emergence and influence of a distinctive African-American homiletic. David Buttrick has offered a contemporary manual, including an extensive bibliography, which brings the resources of rhetorical theory to the preaching task.

A significant issue often neglected in the scholarship on preaching has been the exclusion of women from interpreting and proclaiming the Word. Women of faith have long responded to this prohibition with rhetorical insight and ingenuity. Even when the ordination of female preachers was still unthinkable among church officials, a few women managed to transgress the boundary set down between them and the pulpit. One of these was Hildegard of Bingen, the twelfth-century abbess whose portrayal of her visionary prophetic call so impressed the bishops and the Pope that she succeeded in making several preaching tours among the cities of the Rhineland, calling for spiritual renewal and church reform.

Margaret Fell's prison epistle, *Women's Speaking Justified, Proved, and Allowed by the Scriptures* (1666), offers a deft and elaborate argument in support of women preachers, anticipating some of the hermeneutical moves practiced by feminist interpreters today. To refute those who appeal to Pauline proscriptions of women's speaking, Fell demonstrates how to read the Bible not as dogma but as drama—as a sacred story centered in Christ, who not only welcomed the ministry of women but also commissioned them, according to Matthew and John, to proclaim the Easter gospel. Her treatise and leadership encouraged an abiding commitment to sexual equality in the Society of Friends.

This century has witnessed the ordination of women preachers in nearly every major Protestant denomination. Yet Christian feminists continue to struggle with the Bible, acknowledging its primal role in their faith communities and in their own spiritual formation, while also recognizing the dangers of its pervasive androcentric bias. Over the past twenty years, feminist scholars have conducted a many-faceted examination of the rhetorical aims and power claims inscribed in scriptural texts, hermeneutical methods, and patterns of church life. One key revelation has been the construction of the canon as a reassertion of patriarchal hegemony against what Elisabeth Schüssler Fiorenza has called "the discipleship of equals," which originally gathered around Jesus and to which the New Testament provides only fragmentary witness. In her 1987 presidential address to the Society of Biblical Literature, Schüssler Fiorenza called for a reorientation of biblical studies in rhetorical terms. Her locus of authority is not the texts of the Bible but the community of believers, specifically those who struggle for liberation from the interlocking oppressions of patriarchy.

Feminist investigation thus undermines the mystique of canonical status by insisting that the divine Word (whether present in Christ, in the Bible, or in a sermon), is always mediated by communities of believing, wondering, arguing, transforming people like ourselves. Such a conviction reconstitutes the traditional authority relations among community, text, and preacher, as Christine Smith has shown. The implications of a feminist hearing and preaching of the Word are becoming evident in Christian liturgy, theology, and ethics—indeed, in the very religious imagination of the faithful.

Several important aspects of preaching remain unexplored here. Concentrating on developments in Europe and the United States, we have not attended to Christian proclamation in South Africa, Central America, or Asia, for instance. And given our focus on Christianity, we have not considered the traditions of Jewish or Islamic preachers. As religion so often turns out to be a catalyst for violent conflict, continuing study and conversation are essential, and it is all the more urgent to investigate the interplay between rhetoric and faith.

Pat Youngdahl
University of Arizona

Bibliography
Bormann, Ernest G. *The Force of Fantasy: Restoring the American Dream.* Carbondale: Southern Illinois UP, 1985.

Buttrick, David. *Homiletic.* Philadelphia: Fortress, 1987.

Kennedy, George A. *Classical Rhetoric and Its Christian and Secular Tradition from Ancient to Modern Times.* Chapel Hill: U of North Carolina P, 1980.

Kinneavy, James L. *Greek Rhetorical Origins of Christian Faith*. New York: Oxford UP, 1987.

Mitchell, Henry H. *Black Preaching*. Nashville, TN: Abingdon, 1990.

Murphy, James J. *Rhetoric in the Middle Ages: A History of Rhetorical Theory from Saint Augustine to the Renaissance*. Berkeley: U of California P, 1974.

Schüssler Fiorenza, Elisabeth. *But SHE Said: Feminist Practices of Biblical Interpretation*. Boston: Beacon, 1992.

Smith, Christine. *Weaving the Sermon: Preaching in a Feminist Perspective*. Louisville: Westminster, 1989.

Toulouse, Teresa. *The Art of Prophesying: New England Sermons and the Shaping of Belief*. Athens: U of Georgia P, 1987.

Volz, Carl A. *Pastoral Life and Practice in the Early Church*. Minneapolis, MN: Augsburg, 1990.

See also Ars praedicandi; Homiletics; Homily; Sermon

Purpose

Some or all of the factors of the rhetorical situation—the historical and cultural contexts, the particular exigence that called the discourse forth, the conventions of genre, and the needs and expectations of readers, as well as judgments of authorial intention and attention to lexical clues. To inquire about something's purpose is to ask why it exists and what particular character it has. Determining the purpose of speech or written text is notoriously difficult. Purpose would seem to be related to authorial intention, but the two are not identical, for the realized intentions of a text, as judged by its impact or the consensus of its readers, may be different from what an author intended. Similarly, while discourse sometimes offers reliable clues to its purpose, this is far from always the case. Since rhetorical discourse is by definition situational, discovering the purpose of rhetorical discourse requires going beyond the author and the text.

Purpose is generally thought of as a comprehensive term, determinative of genre. As a result, discussions of purpose historically have tended to occur in the context of attempts to create taxonomies of discourse.

Classical Period

Aristotle, who distinguishes rhetorical discourse from scientific and poetic, derives the purposes (*teloi*) of rhetorical discourse from the institutional roles audiences play in the public forums where rhetoric is practiced. In the Athens of his day, these forums were principally the legislative assemblies, the law courts, and part of public ceremonies such as occasions of state. In the assembly, the audience is cast as a judge of whether a recommended action is advantageous or not. In the courtroom the jury similarly judges, but of whether an action is just or unjust. In the public ceremonies, the audience plays the role of a spectator (since it takes no effecting action), accepting or rejecting the rhetor's praise or attack on the subject. By locating purpose in the social action the audience takes, Aristotle's approach to purpose provides him with a basis not only for classifying rhetoric into his famous three types—deliberative, forensic, and epideictic—but also for deriving characteristic lines of argument appropriate to the persuasion of an audience in a given institutional context.

While Cicero's discussion of the types of rhetoric follows Aristotle's taxonomy, he also introduces a new set of terms that become most influential in subsequent discussions of purpose. In *De optimo genere oratorum* and in *Orator,* Cicero insists that the ideal orator should instruct, delight, and move. Generally, Cicero presents these three ends of discourse as appropriate at different points within a single oration: to please the hearers in the exordium, to instruct them in the narration and confirmation, and to move them in the peroration. But in paralleling these ends with the three styles (plain, middle, and grand) and maintaining that particular subjects and types of discourse have an appropriate style, Cicero allows the inference that the three ends apply to different types of discourse.

Enlightenment

In the *Philosophy of Rhetoric,* George Campbell cites Cicero's three ends of rhetoric as the basis for his four types: "All the ends of speaking are reducible to four: every speech being intended to enlighten the understanding, to please the imagination, to move the passions, or to influence the will" (1). Campbell makes no reference to the public purposes that rhetoric plays and, while he locates purpose with reference to the audience as Aristotle and Cicero had also done, he does not define the audience in terms of an institutional role. Because Campbell's goal is to contribute to the Enlightenment's project of articulating the universal laws of each discipline, he derives the purposes of discourse from what he assumes are universal faculties of the mind. He also assumes that discourse manifests which of these faculties (singly or in combination) the rhetor targets.

Modern Period

James Kinneavy and Walter Beale have contributed influential modern treatments of purpose within this taxonomic tradition. Kinneavy evolves the purposes of discourse from the communication triangle, with its three legs of reader, reality, and writer and its enclosed area representing language. The dominant component of the triangle as revealed in the rhetorical choices manifest in the text is the text's purpose. If the revealed basis for choice is reader accommodation, the discourse's purpose is persuasive; if achieving an accurate representation of reality, it is referential; if self-revelation, it is expressive; if beauty of expression, it is literary. The implication of Walter Beale's theory is that purpose is a combination of two factors of discourse: the degree to which it aspires to describe reality or not—is referential or tropological—and the degree to which it aspires to effect action—is contemplative or active. This framework yields four general purposes for discourse: instrumental discourse, the aim of which is to govern, guide, and control or execute human activities (active, referential); scientific, which aims to discover, construct, and organize knowledge (referential, contemplative); poetic, which aims to present an object of aesthetic enjoyment (tropological, contemplative); and rhetorical, which aims to influence the understanding and conduct of human affairs (active, nonreferential).

Composition

Within composition theory, the approach to purpose taken by the taxonomic tradition has been criticized as being unhelpful to those trying to create essays and speeches, even misleading. One focus of attack has been Alexander Bain, who wrote an influential textbook, *English Composition and Rhetoric* (1866). Following Campbell, Bain validates the three Ciceronian purposes (to inform, persuade, and please) on psychological grounds: they correspond to the Understanding, the Will, and the Feelings. Bain associates modes of discourse with these purposes, listing, for example, the presence of description, narration, and exposition as indicative of the informative purpose. This approach is faulted for seeming to suggest that including a particular method of development, such as narration, is a way to achieve a particular purpose, thus separating purpose from the dynamic elements of a rhetorical situation.

Arthur E. Walzer
University of Minnesota

Bibliography

Beale, Walter H. *A Pragmatic Theory of Rhetoric.* Carbondale: Southern Illinois UP, 1987.

Connors, Robert J. "The Rise and Fall of the Modes of Discourse." *College Composition and Communication* 32 (1981): 444–55.

Crowley, Sharon. "Response to Robert J. Connors, 'The Rise and Fall of the Modes of Discourse.'" *College Composition and Communication* 35 (1984): 88–91.

Flower, Linda. "The Construction of Purpose in Writing and Reading." *College English* 50 (1988): 528–50.

Kinneavy, James L. *A Theory of Discourse.* 1971. New York: Norton, 1980.

Knoblauch, C.H. "Intentionality in the Writing Process: A Case Study." *College Composition and Communication* 31 (1980): 153–59.

Walzer, Arthur. "The Meanings of 'Purpose.'" *Rhetoric Review* 10 (1991): 118–29.

Q

Quackenbos, George Payn (1826–1881)
Educator and author of educational works, including several influential textbooks dealing with composition, rhetoric, and grammar. G.P. Quackenbos responded to a need at midcentury for more practical applications of the highly theoretical yet widely expounded ideas of the New Rhetoric—evident in works such as George Campbell's *Philosophy of Rhetoric* (1776), Richard Whately's *Elements of Rhetoric* (1828), and Hugh Blair's *Lectures on Rhetoric and Belles Lettres* (1783). While many of his contemporaries strove to fashion American versions of these highly influential imports from Britain, Quackenbos synthesized the most prominent features of the New Rhetoric, simultaneously pitching their delivery in decidedly practical terms. The result—the *Advanced Course of Composition and Rhetoric* (originally published in 1854)—was a rhetoric that approached the composition process based on the faculty psychology of Campbell and in so doing treated the invention process as chiefly composed of selection and "careful, deliberate, concentrated thought."

Quackenbos was among the first composition textbook authors to attenuate the selection process by providing lists of subjects (topics) for composition. Quackenbos's notion of "thought" most clearly demonstrates the epistemology of the New Rhetoric by the way it seems to be merely a filter for phenomenon: "This is an analysis of the subject, or a drawing out of the various heads which suggest themselves to the mind as appropriate to the theme of discourse." Quackenbos signaled the practical nature of his book by including an exhaustive section on grammar, a subject typically ignored in the more abstract treatises on rhetoric. At the same time, he nodded in the direction of Hugh Blair and the belletristic tradition by including long discussions of taste, the sublime, and prosody.

Some scholars have suggested that Quackenbos was the originator of the modes of discourse (description, narration, exposition, argumentation), while others maintain that such a distinction belongs to Alexander Bain, Henry Day, or Samuel Newman. Regardless of who justly deserves credit (or blame) for the development of so influential a pedagogical approach, it seems fair to propose that Quackenbos was certainly among the first to make the modes an integral part of composition pedagogy.

In 1896 John Duncan Quackenbos (son of George Payn) published *Practical Rhetoric*, a textbook that reflects much of his father's synthesis of the New Rhetoric but that eliminates the lists of subjects and recommends an expanded use of the imagination in the process of invention.

Creighton Lindsay
University of Oregon

Bibliography
Crowley, Sharon. *The Methodical Memory: Invention in Current-Traditional Rhetoric.* Carbondale: Southern Illinois UP, 1990.
Johnson, Nan. *Nineteenth-Century Rhetoric in North America.* Carbondale: Southern Illinois UP, 1991.
Kitzhaber, Albert R. *Rhetoric in American Colleges, 1850–1900.* Dallas: Southern Methodist UP, 1990.

Quadrivium
The segment of medieval and Renaissance education concerned with arithmetic, geometry, astronomy, and music. In the wake of the declines of the Greek and Roman civilizations, the scope

and face of education underwent a variety of changes. As the Middle Ages developed, the Roman Catholic Church rose to the forefront of educational services, and this institution fostered an amalgamation of the three formerly dominant cultures (Greek, Roman, and Hebrew). This amalgamation is particularly apparent in the case of educational curricula, of which the Quadrivium is generally acknowledged as being similar to a contemporary Master's Degree (Corbett 603).

Taken in conjunction with the disciplines composing the Trivium (grammar, rhetoric, and dialectic), the four segments of the Quadrivium (geometry, astronomy, music, and arithmetic) came to represent the seven liberal arts. Each strand was cross-disciplinary: a student might, for example, study the "rudiments of geography [in] . . . geometry . . . [or find that] . . . astronomy included physics" (Cordasco 25). In arithmetic, according to Ellwood P. Cubberley, an historian of educational practice, the student would consider "the uses of arithmetic in determining church days, calculating the date of Easter, and interpreting passages in the Scriptures involving measurements" (159). Cubberley suggests that music appeared to be the most advanced and thoroughgoing of the Quadrivium's strands, owing mainly to the importance of music and the organ to the church (162).

Cubberley also notes that the Quadrivium came to be less emphasized than the Trivium, which itself was often reduced to focused studies of grammar, "the foundation and source of all the Liberal Arts" (155). In those schools not offering instruction in the Quadrivium, the student might find elements of the four areas of study in the textbooks used to study the Trivium (Cubberley 158). Perhaps a forerunner of our contemporary concerns for language, writing across disciplines, and cultural studies, the Quadrivium provided the rounding of the medieval and Renaissance mind.

Joseph Colavito
Northwestern State University

Bibliography

Conley, Thomas. *Rhetoric in the European Tradition*. New York: Longman, 1990.

Corbett, Edward P.J. *Classical Rhetoric for the Modern Student*. 3rd ed. New York: Oxford UP, 1990.

Cordasco, Francesco. *A Brief History of Education*. Paterson, NJ: Littlefield, Adams, 1963.

Cubberley, Ellwood P. *The History of Education: Educational Practice and Progess Considered as a Phase of the Development and Spread of Western Civilization*. 1920. Cambridge, MA: Riverside, 1948.

See also TRIVIUM

Quine, Willard Van Orman (b. 1908)

One of the foremost contemporary American philosophers of logic, language, and epistemology. Quine has made important contributions to the logical foundations of set theory and the semantics of logic and natural language. He is widely known for original work in the development of formal criteria for the existence commitments of competing scientific theories; behaviorist speech act semantics; translation and language learning theory; and the interrelation between truth, concept acquisition, and theory construction.

Quine is an extensionalist semanticist, attempting to explain language in terms of public objects and events rather than private mental contents. In his landmark treatise (1960), Quine interprets the holistic structure of sentence usages in a language community as a causally interconnected network multifariously linked to nonverbal behavioral stimuli. Language use is verbal behavior, and in Quine's early treatment is understood like other animal behaviors in an operant conditioning model, in which dispositions to respond to situations by the utterance of a particular speech act exhausts a sentence's semantic content in what Quine calls its stimulus-meaning. The sentence "This is red" just *means* those occurrences, typically encounters with objects that appear red, in which English speakers are disposed to utter the expression.

Semantic holism combined with the empirical-behaviorist semantics in Quine's extensionalist philosophy of language entails his thesis of the indeterminacy of radical translation. When interpreting alien speech structures, even the ideal field linguist must impose familiar logical and conceptual categories on the observed linguistic behavior of language users in the presence of common public stimuli. Quine maintains that except for the determinate universal application of basic propositional connectives such as negation *not,* conjunction *and,* and disjunction *or,* all other terms in a language are subject to multiple conceptual categorization, so that translation from one ideologically remote language into another is never epistemically determinate. Field linguists are unjustified in trusting absolutely the accuracy or exact conformity of term and sentence equivalences proposed hypothetically as translations. If the linguist discovers speakers uttering "Gavagai" in the presence of what English users refer to as a "rabbit," to cite a favorite example of Quine's, the empirical evidence of stimulus-meanings in a holistic semantic context is indeterminate with respect to whether the speakers really mean "rabbit," "undetached rabbit parts," "connected succession of rabbit-stages," or the like. From this it is not far to conclude that distinct language groups can communicate only with probable agreement in understanding, as measured by pragmatic standards of successful cooperation in shared actions mediated by discourse.

Consistently with his epistemic and semantic holism, Quine has repeatedly insisted that his philosophy must be considered as a whole and with respect to each interrelated thesis in order to be fully understood and properly evaluated. This brief account of some central Quinean views about logic, language, and knowledge must be put in perspective in a more complete and comprehensive exposition of his work to avoid distortion and to appreciate the implications of his thought for the theory and practice of rhetoric.

Dale Jacquette
Pennsylvania State University

Bibliography

Davidson, Donald, and Jaakko Hintikka, eds. *Words and Objections: Essays on the Work of W.V. Quine.* Dordrecht: Reidel, 1969.

Gochet, Paul. *Ascent to Truth: A Critical Examination of Quine's Philosophy.* Munich: Philosophia Verlag, 1986.

Hahn, L.E., and P.A. Schilpp, eds. *The Philosophy of W.V. Quine.* LaSalle, IL: Open Court, 1986.

Quine, Willard Van Orman. *From a Logical Point of View.* Cambridge, MA: Harvard UP, 1961.

———. *Methods of Logic.* 3rd ed. New York: Holt, 1972.

———. *The Roots of Reference.* LaSalle, IL: Open Court, 1974.

———. *Word and Object.* Rev. ed. Cambridge, MA: MIT, 1961.

Quintilian

One of the most influential writers in the Western rhetorical tradition, second only to Cicero; a lawyer-turned-teacher who retired after twenty years in the classroom to compose a book that not only presented a complete survey of rhetorical theory but also described in full detail the Roman school system that was to dominate European education for the next eighteen hundred years.

Marcus Fabius Quintilian was born in the Roman city of Calagurris (modern Calahorra), Spain, between 30 and 40 C.E. His father took him to Rome for further education in 50, but in 59 Quintilian returned to Spain as a lawyer and teacher. When the governor of Spain, Galba, went to Rome in 59 as emperor, Quintilian went with him. He lived in Rome for the rest of his life.

Quintilian was Rome's most famous teacher, gaining both honors and official government subsidies for his school: The Emperor Vespasian's grant to him in 72 established what was to become an official policy of state support for schools over the next four centuries. His illustrious pupils included Tacitus, Suetonius, Juvenal, and Pliny the Younger. The Emperor Domitian granted him consular rank in his retirement—an unusual privilege. It is thought that Quintilian died shortly after the end of Domitian's reign in 96.

His major work has survived: *Institutio oratoria (Education of the Orator).* In the *Institutio* (6.Pref.3), however, he mentions another work titled *De causis corruptae Eloquentiae (On the Causes of the Decay of Eloquence).* It is interesting to note that because of the similarity of title and presumed subject matter, many Renaissance editors falsely assumed that Quintilian was the author of the *Dialogus de oratoribus (Dialogue on the Orators),* actually written by Tacitus. Nor was Quintilian the author of two sets of school debate exercises (*declamationes*) often printed as his.

The Institutio Oratoria

Completed in 95 C.E., the *Institutio oratoria* is a distillation of both Roman rhetoric and the educational system in which rhetoric was the core. The book has four main parts, as Quintilian makes clear at the onset.

My first book will be concerned with the education preliminary to the duties of the teacher of rhetoric. My second will deal with the rudiments of the schools of rhetoric and with problems connected with the essence of rhetoric itself. The next five will be concerned with Invention (in which I include Arrangement). The four following will be assigned to Elocution, under which head I include Memory and Delivery. Finally there will be one book in which our complete orator will be delineated; as far as my feeble powers permit, I shall discuss his character, the rules which should guide him in undertaking, studying and pleading cases, the style of his eloquence, the time at which he should cease to plead cases and the studies to which he should devote himself after such cessation. (1.Pref.21–22)

What makes the *Institutio* especially valuable is Quintilian's sensible and humane approach to the issues he treats. Earlier treatises, like Cicero's *De inventione* and the Pseudo-Ciceronian *Rhetorica ad Herennium*, lay out their rhetorical doctrines in matter-of-fact, almost schematic fashion; both are essentially expanded outlines. Quintilian, on the other hand, typically discusses varying viewpoints even while he makes his own position clear. In Book One, for example, he stresses the value of public (that is, group) education at the same time he considers—and rejects—several arguments for private or tutorial education. In Books Eight and Nine, he considers a large number of tropes and figures, not just defining them but also analyzing their particular use in oratory. As a result the *Institutio oratoria* is an admirable introduction to Roman education and rhetoric, presenting not only Quintilian's views but a survey of many others' as well.

The Educational Process

Quintilian describes an educational system in which boys were trained daily in language use from the age of six to about seventeen or eighteen, when they became adults under the law. Through a complex set of increasingly difficult exercises, their masters strove to instill in them what Quintilian calls *facilitas*—facility in devising appropriate language to fit any speaking or writing situation. All of the pedogogical methods were inherited from the Greeks, but the

Roman advance was to shape them into a system.

The first stage was at home—"in the cradle" Quintilian says. Aware that language acquisition begins with the earliest words heard by the child, Quintilian urges parents to make sure that only the best Latin is spoken in the presence of babies and children. Parents, he says, should have the highest hopes for their children. Even the child's companion, the *paedagogus* who travels with him to school, should be an educated person so that the child will always have good linguistic examples around him.

Two levels of masters teach the child in this system. The first is the *grammaticus,* who leads the child through the simplest kinds of imitations (*imitatio*) and introduces him to the simplest types of speaking and writing exercises (*progymnasmata*). The rhetor handles more advanced levels in these two areas, and then moves the student into the final phase of declamation (*declamatio*), or fictitious speeches on assigned subjects.

This was not a time-based system. Quintilian says that the child should advance to studies with the rhetor only when he is ready. Moreover, the same types of classroom exercises continue throughout the boy's career in school, whether with the *grammaticus* or the rhetor, the only changes being in their advancing complexity.

Rhetoric was not taught as a separate subject. Rather its elements were introduced throughout the program as needed; for instance, the *grammaticus* might well ask his charges to identify some differences in style between, say, Virgil and Thucydides, but it would be the rhetor much later who could ask the same questions in terms of technical rhetorical terms like propriety or types of amplification. The fourteen year old should know the principles of partition (under arrangement) to prepare successful declamations, while an eight year old could reasonably be expected only to paraphrase a speech without knowing that there are technical names for its parts. It is important to note that the rhetorical theory Quintilian treats is not an invention of his but is exactly the same as that outlined almost two centuries earlier by Cicero and the Pseudo-Cicero—it is the standard "Roman" rhetoric of five "Parts" or "Canons." The same thing could be said for the rest of the teaching program for the young laid out in Books One and Two.

In Book Ten, after seven books discussing the rhetorical causes of invention, arrangement, and style, Quintilian returns to the educational process—but this time for the self-educating adult. He urges the adult orator to continue the processes of imitation and declamation he had learned in school, stressing the importance of keeping in mind the important relations between reading, writing, speaking, and listening that informed his childhood education. (Quintilian's treatment of self-editing and rewriting, together with his sensitive analyses of numerous writers and orators, makes Book Ten one of the more important critical documents of antiquity.)

The ancient teaching process of imitation (*imitatio*) is much misunderstood today. Most modern uses of the term *imitation* make it mean "false" or "fake." For almost two thousand years, though, the term described a systematic learning activity designed to equip the learner with a wide range of language abilities. In essence, imitation proposes that emulating the writing/speaking attributes of good models in this way will enable the imitator to attain the ability to employ any of those attributes in his own future discourse. A person who "imitated" twenty-five other writers, for example, would have twenty-five possible ways to form his own writing or speech in the future—he would thus enlarge his arsenal of possibilities when it came time to decide what to say.

This is not, however, a haphazard activity. It has sequential steps. Each step depends on the one before. Perhaps the best way to describe the whole process is to list its elements as found in Quintilian's descriptions:

a. Reading aloud (*lectio*)
b. Master's detailed analysis of a text (*praelectio*)
c. Memorization of models
d. Paraphrase of models
e. Transliteration (prose/verse and/or Latin/Greek)
f. Recitation of paraphrase or transliteration
g. Correction of paraphrase or transliteration

Also much misunderstood today is the ancient process of *progymnasmata*. This is a set of composition exercises arranged in order of increasing difficulty, with each new exercise depending on all the ones before it. Twelve such were common by Cicero's time:

1. Retelling a fable
2. Retelling an episode from a poet or a historian
3. *Chreia*, or amplification of a moral theme
4. Amplification of an aphorism (*sententia*) or proverb
5. Refutation or confirmation of an allegation
6. Commonplace, or confirmation of a thing admitted
7. Encomium, or eulogy (or dispraise) of person or thing
8. comparison of things or persons
9. Impersonation (*ethologia, ethopoeia, prosopopeia*), or speaking or writing in the character of a given person
10. Description, or vivid presentation of details
11. Thesis, or argument for/against an answer to a general question (*quaestio infinita*) not involving individuals
12. Laws, or arguments for or against a law

Roman boys were drilled for ten or eleven years in the tasks of imitation and *progymnasmata* to sharpen their inventive and stylistic abilities. Then they were set to work making declamations (*declamationes*), or practice speeches, on assigned subjects. This was the culmination of all their training, preparing them for the real world of courtroom and assembly. There were two types: The political (*suasoria*) dealing with deliberative matters, and the forensic (*controversia*) dealing with legal cases. The students debated each other in front of their peers. Understandably, the assigned issues are as difficult as the masters can make them; this is an important point, because surviving examples of declamation topics—cases of pirates, poisons, inheritances, rapes, and the like—have led some modern observers to ridicule declamation as a trivial and fanciful activity. Rather, the surviving examples demonstrate the capacity of Roman schoolmasters to devise intricate problems to test the rhetorical mettle of their charges. Cicero says that he valued declamation so much that he practiced it every day of his life.

One final note should be made about the Roman teaching process Quintilian describes. That is, it constantly stresses the interrelation between reading, writing, speaking, and listening. Book Ten of the *Institutio*, in particular, lays out the principles behind this correlation.

All in all, Quintilian portrays a teaching system in which purposeful language activities are systematically used over a dozen years to bring the young man to a state of *facilitas*—endowed with the ability to improvise effective language in any situation. Rhetoric is at the heart of the enterprise, but it is imbued in the student by constant practice in its principles rather than by lecture or memorization of its theories.

Quintilian's Rhetoric

Books Two through Nine and Book Eleven treat in detail the standard five parts of Roman rhetoric familiar since the time of Cicero: invention, arrangement, style, memory, and delivery. His survey of rhetorical theory is especially valuable because he often discusses alternative views before stating his own conclusions on a point. On the question of "what is rhetoric?" (2.xv), for example, he analyzes the views of Isocrates, Ennius, Plato, Cicero, Theodorus, and Cornelius Celsus before declaring his judgment that rhetoric is "the science of speaking well." Quintilian's discussion of the "questions" proper to rhetoric (3.v.4–16) includes an equally careful survey of numerous other writers.

This habit of reflective discussion makes Books Eight and Nine especially valuable for the modern reader. Quintilian stresses the importance of relating words to matter and criticizes his contemporaries who struggle more over a single word than they do about seeking out proofs for their case. It is his subtle observations on the tropes and figures, however, that set out for the first time in Roman rhetoric a clear rationale for their use. Both Cicero and the Pseudo-Cicero had taken them for granted. Quintilian defines a trope as "the transference of expressions from their natural and principal signification to another." He says a figure is "a form of expression to which a new aspect is given by art." He notes "a considerable difference of opinion among authors" on the matter, so his treatment is carefully broad, surveying various opinons before delivering his own on each trope and figure. The result is an encyclopedic coverage of ancient theories.

In sum, while Quintilian's treatment of rhetoric does not present us with major new theoretical advances, his urbane and reflective analyses do provide another dimension for understanding Roman views on the subject.

The True Orator as a "Good Man Skilled in Speaking"

Quintilian's stated aim in the whole *Institutio oratoria* is "to form, then, the perfect orator, who cannot exist unless he is above all a good man" (Pref. 9). Although Book Twelve contains the most direct descriptions of the ideal orator, Quintilian uses the phrase *good men* (*vir bonus*) twenty-three times throughout the work. His argument is that moral goodness cannot be separated from rhetorical efficiency because the active citizen-orator who helps shape the community is responsible for its welfare—not just his own. Therefore, he must be wise, strong, and filled with a sense of duty.

This is a direct break with prior views—including those of Aristotle and Cicero—that made persuasion alone the goal of oratory and rhetoric. For Quintilian, rhetoric is the "science" (as he says in 2.xv), while oratory is the practical application of that science in human affairs—an essentially moral arena. Hence he says that "the orator must above all things devote his attention to the formation of moral character" (12.ii.1). Mere eloquence does not make a true orator: There will always be some, he quips, who would rather be eloquent than good. An evil man who speaks well is therefore not fulfilling the true aim of oratory. Quintilian also stresses his belief that criteria for the perfect orator should always be kept in mind even if such a paragon has not yet been found.

Quintilian's Influence

The history of Quintilian's influence is not yet written. There have been three main peaks of interest in his work. His honors, and the fame of his pupils, indicate his immediate influence in first-century Rome. During the so-called "Renaissance of the Twelfth Century" in France, his *Institutio* played a role in revitalizing education and spurring new interest in classical authors. Nevertheless, medieval readers had only a partial text of the book, and when Poggio Bracciolini discovered a complete copy at a monastery in St. Gall, Switzerland, in 1416, he was so excited by his find that he personally set down and copied out the entire text over a period of thirty-six days. Humanists were enthralled, of course, but so were later figures like Desiderius Erasmus and Martin Luther. An even one hundred editions of the *Institutio* were published in the first eighty-five years of printing. The reformer Peter Ramus thought him such an important pillar of the educational establishment that in 1549 he published a book attacking every idea in the *Institutio*, including the "good man" concept. "It will be clear from all this, " says F.H. Colson, "that the influence of Quintilian, especially with writers and thinkers on education, was throughout this period immense."

By the middle of the nineteenth century, his influence began to wane, along with that of other classical authors. In recent years, however, there has been a revival of interest in his concepts of reading, speaking, writing, and listening; meanwhile, numerous individual precepts or exercises continue to appear in textbooks written by authors unaware of their antecedents.

James J. Murphy
University of California, Davis

Bibliography

Bonner, Stanley F. *Roman Declamation in the Late Republic and Early Empire*. Berkeley: U of California P, 1949.

Clark, Donald L. *Rhetoric in Greco-Roman Education*. New York: Columbia UP, 1957.

Colson, F.H. *M. Fabii Quintiliani Institutionis oratoriae Liber 1*. Cambridge: Cambridge UP, 1924.

Erickson, Keith V. "Quintilian's *Institutio oratoria and Pseudo-Declamationes*. A Bibliography." *Rhetoric Society Quarterly* 11 (1981): 45–62.

Kennedy, George A. *The Art of Rhetoric in the Roman World*. Princeton: Princeton UP, 1972.

———. *Quintilian*. New York: Twayne, 1969.

Little, Charles E. *Quintilian the Schoolmaster*. 2 vols. Nashville: George Peabody College for Teachers, 1951.

Marrou, Henri-Irenée. *A History of Education in Antiquity*. Trans. George Lamb. New York: New American Library, 1964.

Quintilian on the Teaching of Speaking and Writing: Trans. from Books One, Two, and Ten of the *Institutio Oratoria*. Ed. James J. Murphy. Carbondale: Southern Illinois UP, 1987.

Quintilian. *The Institutio Oratoria of Quintilian*. Trans. H.E. Butler. 4 vols. Cambridge, MA: Harvard UP; London: Heinemann, 1922.

Quintilian's Institutes of Oratory: or, Education of an Orator. Trans. John Selby Watson. 2 vols. London: George Bell, 1892.

Ramus, Peter. *Arguments in Rhetoric against Quintilian: Translation and Text of Peter Ramus's* Rhetoricae Distinctiones *in Quintilian*. Trans. Carole Newlands; Intro. James J. Murphy. De Kalb: Northern Illinois UP, 1986.

Winterbottom, Michael, ed. *Institutionis Oratoriae Libri Duodecim*. Oxford: Clarendon, 1970.

Q

R

Ramus, Peter (1515–1572)

Writer and teacher who succeeded in separating rhetoric and philosophy, leaving to the province of rhetoric only style and delivery. Peter Ramus was the Latinized academic name of Pierre de la Ramee, who was born to impoverished parents in Picardy. The family was able to prepare him to study Latin and send him to Paris at age eight. He entered the University of Paris at age twelve. Like many other poor scholars, Ramus worked his way through school as a servant to wealthier students. He took his master of arts degree in 1536 at the age of twenty-one.

Ramus taught dialectic and rhetoric in various colleges of the university. In 1543 he published two extremely controversial books: *Aristotelicae animadversiones,* attacking Aristotelian dialectic in its classical and scholastic avatars, and *Dialectical partiones,* advocating a new intellectual method.

In these books Ramus condemned the argumentative methods in use at Paris since at least the twelfth century and offered a new method. This was such an affront that all three graduate faculties of the university successfully petitioned the French king Charles I to forbid Ramus to teach from the two books. Far from being chastened by this censure, Ramus mounted a campaign to gain acceptance for his ideas. Between 1545 and 1549, seven books appeared by either Ramus or Omer Talon (Latinized as Talaeus), Ramus's collaborator. Ramus also defended himself in public disputations with other professors.

The books most pertinent to Ramus's views on rhetoric are his attacks on Cicero, *Brutinae questiones* (1547), and on Quintilian, *Rhetoricae distinctiones in Quintilianum* (1549), and two books by Talaeus outlining a new program for rhetoric, *Audomari Talaei Institutiones oratoriae* (1545) and *Audomari Talaei Rhetorica* (1548). Scholars believe that Ramus published some of his own work under the name of Talaeus to avoid the royal ban on his ideas. Both rhetoric texts may be his.

The ban on Ramus's works was lifted in 1547 when Henry II became king and Charles of Lorraine, a former college classmate of Ramus's, interceded on his behalf. Thereafter, Ramus's career prospered. In 1551 he was appointed a Regius Professor of the university. He continued to publish revised editions of his early controversial works, French translations of them, grammars for Latin, Greek, and French, studies of Cicero's oratory, and more. He continued to fight with other professors. In 1565 he was named dean of the Regius Professors, a group that later became the College de France.

Meanwhile, in 1561 Ramus had become a Protestant. Religious violence was increasing in France in this period, but for some time Ramus's highly placed friends were able to protect him and to get him out of Paris when danger threatened. This protection evaporated when the Roman Catholic Catharine de'Medici became regent. She ordered the Saint Bartholomew's Day massacre of Protestants in 1572, and Ramus was one of its victims.

Between 1550 and 1650, some 750 editions of works by Ramus and Talaeus appeared in Europe. Ramus's explosive influence may be attributed in part to his image as a doughty warrior opposing all stultifying traditions. He attacked scholasticism in Paris, its greatest bastion. And since scholasticism, and the Paris faculty, were still strongly associated in people's minds with the Roman Catholic Church, Ramus's academic arguments took on overtones of religious reform, an aura intensified by the manner of his death. He was seen as a martyr.

Moreover, in attacking scholasticism, Ramus departed from the usual humanist strategy of castigating the schoolmen for burying precious classical thinkers under trivialities. Ramus attacked the classical thinkers as well. He even downplayed the importance of education in the classical languages and elevated the vernacular. Those looking for reform in the study of science could claim that Ramus was making a space for them.

Ramus's program calls for the union of philosophy and eloquence, to be effected by strictly separating philosophy—meaning dialectic—from rhetoric. Like Agricola, Ramus arrogates to dialectic three traditional canons of rhetoric: invention, arrangement, and memory. Invention uses ten topics (causes, effects, subjects, adjuncts, opposites, comparisons, names, divisions, definitions, and witnesses) culled from the classical commonplaces.

Arrangement, for Ramus, should follow the structure of the syllogism, starting with the general principles of the subject under discussion and working down through levels of generality to the particulars. This process typically proceeds by creating dichotomies at each level. Any subject can be analyzed in this way. Moreover, such arrangement renders other arts of memory unnecessary: Because this arrangement, Ramus asserts, embodies the natural structure of both the world and the human mind, anything organized in this way is retained easily and thoroughly. For Ramus, these versions of invention and arrangement constitute the universally applicable method of inquiry that so many intellectuals of his day were seeking. Evidently, many of them agreed with him.

Ramus frequently advertises the usefulness of his dialectical method. Ramus does not have a specific use, such as statecraft, in mind. He claims that his method is useful for any worldly activity a person might undertake. The decontextualization of knowledge that Ramist dialectic sought to accomplish had dire consequences for rhetoric. For Ramus, the province of rhetoric was style and delivery only. Moreover, delivery was really of very minor importance to Ramus. Style was simplified—Ramus reduced all tropes to metonymy, irony, metaphor, and synecdoche—and reduced to rule.

After Ramus, rhetoric seemed to be concerned with nothing but ornamentation—at best a frivolous and at worst a meretricious, manipulative concern. The elevation of a supposedly unornamented style for serious business was developed further in religion by the Puritans and in academia by the Royal Society. Thus eloquence as the Italian humanists had conceived it was marginalized, if not absolutely exterminated.

Bruce Herzberg
Bentley College

Bibliography

Duhamel, Pierre Albert. "The Logic and Rhetoric of Ramus." *Modern Philology* 46 (1949): 163–71.

Grafton, Anthony, and Lisa Jardine. *From Humanism to the Humanities*. Cambridge, MA: Harvard UP, 1986.

Ong, Walter, S.J. *Ramus and Talon Inventory.* Cambridge, MA: Harvard UP, 1958.

———. *Ramus, Method, and the Decay of Dialogue*. Cambridge, MA: Harvard UP, 1958.

Sharratt, Peter. "Peter Ramus and the Reform of the University." *French Renaissance Studies 1540–70*. Ed. Peter Sharratt. Edinburgh: Edinburgh UP, 1976.

———. "Recent Work on Peter Ramus (1970–1986)." *Rhetorica* 5 (1987): 7–58.

See also DIALECTIC; TALON, OMER

Readability

"Accessibility or ease of understanding," traditionally defined as effective (simple, straightforward, quick, and accurate) conveyance of the author's semantic intention (usually specific, predetermined ideas or feelings) to the mind(s) of a given or intended audience. Readability, however, is beginning to be defined as the total "success" of interactions between the characteristics of particular texts and those of particular readers, in terms of efficacy, understanding, and interest.

Today's "readable" writing, theorists believe, should compromise stylistic and semantic concerns to fulfill writers' *and* readers' purposes, finding a balance between surface-level difficulty and overall comprehension. Never oversimplistic, it should generally provide discourse cohesion, textual clues to organization, timely semantic closure, psycholinguistic redundancy, and reasonable inference load. In addition to real and implied readers' purposes, it should also consider their expectations—expectations based on culture, prior knowledge, and interest; on linguistic, grammatical, and generic conventions.

Practice, however, largely contradicts current readability theory, appearing to emphasize "transparent" linguistic coding. To some, our society has increasingly conflated "easily processed" with "better." Theorists ask: Can we categorize texts by type and amount of optimum readability? How do different audience-conceptions—real, fictive, passive, information-seeking, social-constructionist—influence texts? How are texts made more "accessible" to specific or general audiences? Does society really *want* to award status and power on the basis of stylistic complexity? Which purported causes of reading "problems" can readability ameliorate?

Theorists now consider reading comprehension more relative, more contingent upon particular comprehension tasks. "Constructive" and "discursive" reading models show active readers building textual reality-constructs. Readers use content schemas, text structure schemas, global predictions, and personal reading goals as they decode, parse, and assign "local meanings" before creating summative "meaning" from interactions of all factors.

Many scholars remain unconvinced of the most-used readability formulas' applicability to this updated model of reading, despite the availability of more than one hundred different formulas and political, legal, and commercial pressures for their use. Many consider these most-used formulas, developed decades ago for young children, invalid and unreliable—based on the formulas' statistical models, sampling and scaling procedures, "circular" correlations, emphasis on surface-level style, and elision of social and cultural differences. Formula supporters disagree on how and for whom formulas measure text "difficulty," while consensus maintains that writing to formulas often creates mechanistic, less comprehensible texts.

Formulas' much-criticized simplicity, however, has led to computer adaptations and ever greater use. More cost-effective than human assessments, formulas are quantitative and—since purportedly "objective"—usable as legal and contractual criteria.

Many assert that our only choices are between using existing formulas and developing improved, pragmatic alternatives. Newer formulas—using broader criteria like content and audience factors—seem more reliable and valid, and a society that wants to "define" readable texts (positivistically and ideologically, some believe), may force the use of some formula. Readability researchers now call for further study of reader demographics, audience constructs, and reader comprehension. They hope to find higher-level text features more correlated with or causative of text difficulty, along with better ways to use "real," human audiences for assessments.

John M. Clark
Bowling Green State University

Bibliography

Chall, Jeanne S. *Readability: An Appraisal of Research and Application.* Columbus: Bureau of Educational Research, Ohio State U, 1958.

Davison, Alice, and Georgia M. Green, eds. *Linguistic Complexity and Text Comprehension: Readability Issues Reconsidered.* Hillsdale, NJ: Erlbaum, 1988.

Harrison, Colin. *Readability in the Classroom.* Cambridge: Cambridge UP, 1980.

Klare, George R. *The Measurement of Readability.* Ames: Iowa State UP, 1963.

———. "Readability." *Handbook of Reading Research.* Ed. P. David Pearson. New York: Longman, 1984.

Zakaluk, Beverley L., and S.J. Samuels, eds. *Readability: Its Past, Present, and Future.* Newark, DE: International Reading Assn., 1988.

Reader-Response Criticism

A term used to describe a set of loosely related critical approaches to literary study with a common interest in focusing attention on readers more so than on texts or authors. Reader-oriented criticism has had a long history, going as far back as Aristotle's theories regarding the cathartic response of audiences at tragic performances and continuing through the early twentieth century with the work of Louise Rosenblatt and I.A. Richards. But the term *reader-response criticism* has generally been understood to apply to a set of critical theories that began to appear in the late 1960s and early 1970s and is most often associated with the work of such figures as Wolfgang Iser, Stanley Fish, Norman Holland, and Jonathan Culler.

It would be misleading to characterize reader-response criticism as a *school* or *movement;* such terms imply a degree of unity of theory and practice that is not found in the distinct, sometimes contradictory, critical modes of the most widely recognized reader-response critics. As Susan Suleiman writes in her introduction to *The Reader in the Text,* "Audience-oriented criticism is not one field but many, not a single widely trodden path but a multiplicity of criss-crossing, often divergent tracks that cover a vast area of the critical landscape in a pattern whose complexity dismays the brave and confounds the faint of heart" (6). Common ground in reader-response criticism tends to be located not in the answers arrived at but the questions asked: To what extent (if any) does the written text "determine" the act of reading? What happens to the reader during this act? How do the structures of extratextual knowledge and understanding within the reader's mind inform the art-event? How is meaning made in the reading process, and to what end? These and related questions have formed the center of gravity in reader-response criticism.

Some Varieties of Reader-Response Criticism
Wolfgang Iser, in his two major works of the 1970s, *The Act of Reading* and *The Implied Reader*, portrays the reading act as being substantially determined by the text but leaving the reader the essential task of "gap-filling." That is to say, for Iser, the text may be conceived as a set of instructions that is to some degree incomplete, so it is the job of the reader to act as co-creator of the work through filling in the areas of textual incompletion in a process of "concretization." While this role is indispensable, Iser's reader is nevertheless subordinate to the text, as the act of reading is no more than the realization of that which is implicitly laid out in the work of the author.

The early work of Stanley Fish, his so-called "Affective Stylistics," can be contrasted with Iser's approach in that while Iser tends to scan the overall picture of the reader's evolving attitudes toward a given text, Fish's practice began by focusing on the phrase-by-phrase, sometimes word-by-word, process of negotiating through a written text. In his important work, "Interpreting the Variorum," Fish asserted that whatever happens in the process of reading—even "misreadings" of the text—constitute the text's meaning. Later, Fish abandoned his earlier objectivist theoretical claims and developed the idea of the "interpretive community" as a means of reconciling the infinitude of possible readings of a given text with the fact that of course with many exceptions, texts do tend to successfully function as means of communication. The collection of essays *Is There a Text in This Class?* chronicles this evolution of Fish's theories of reader-response.

Norman Holland and David Bleich are the names most often associated with psychoanalytic theories of response. Holland's central thesis is that "interpretation is a function of identity"; that is to say, unity in a text and identity in a human being are to be seen as analogous. Thus, readers are held to respond to works of literature and to life experience in parallel ways. One of Holland's key terms in his development of this theory in *5 Readers Reading* is the "identity theme." According to Holland, each person develops a more or less consistent pattern of carrying on transactions with his/her life experiences; this style of dealing with life is like a musical theme subject to nearly infinite variations. When encountering a text, a reader's identity theme interacts with that of the author, and so the text is re-created through the process of this transaction. David Bleich's psychology of response differs from Holland's in that Bleich challenges the notion of the stability of meaning in a text and of readers' "identity themes." Instead, Bleich identifies language as the means of objectifying experience, including the experience of reading a text. Bleich's brand of reader-response theory is emphatically individual oriented and is to be distinguished from Iser's approach in that Bleich argues that literary texts do not at all determine or constrain the act of reading and that there is no "objective" meaning to a text at all. Nevertheless, while for Bleich an individual reader may respond to a work of literature in a way that is wholly subjective, this experience is "objectified" as it is expressed in language and validated (or not) by the "community of interpreters" to which the reader belongs.

Jonathan Culler's *Structuralist Poetics* develops a theory of reader-response from the perspective of French structuralism. As Jane Tompkins writes in her introduction to *Reader-Response Criticism,* "Culler's basic assumption is that the shape a text assumes for its readers is determined not by the text itself but by the complex of sign systems readers conventionally apply to literature" (xvii). Thus, Culler identifies "literary competence" as a *grammar* of literature, internalized in the same way as is a person's competence to speak and understand his/her language. Just as Stanley Fish emphasizes the fact that the reception of any given text always occurs in a situation that determines the nature of the reader-response, Culler argues that every work of art and every reader is ineluctably bound up in historical, social, and cultural systems of signification.

The preceding overview of the theories of Iser, Fish, Holland, Bleich, and Culler is intended to provide a brief, and necessarily limited, overview of some of the more widely recognized theories in this field. There are many other contributions that have been highly influential in the field; among them are George Poulet's phenomenological approach to reader-response, Hans Robert Jauss's reception aesthetics (focusing on response as an historical phenomenon), Michael Riffaterre's semiotic theory, and Steven Mailloux's rhetorical theory. (A fuller view of reader-response work through 1980 may be obtained by referring to the extensive, annotated bibliographies in the Suleiman and Crosman and the Tompkins anthologies.)

The State of the Art
The most innovative and active period in the development of reader-response theory was the 1970s and early 1980s, and today many of its main practitioners have distanced themselves from their earlier positions. Elizabeth Freund asserts in her retrospective critique, *The Return of the Reader*, that reader-response has a past but not a future, and Wolfgang Iser, one of the figures who helped to launch the reader-response "movement," now speaks of reader-response in the past tense. Nevertheless, a sizable body of criticism focusing on the reader in literature continues to be produced, although the emphases tend to have changed. One of the more recent books to be published on the subject, Richard Beach's *Teacher's Introduction to Reader-Response Theories,* is an example of one of the current trends in response criticism—pedagogical applications of the theory. Articles published in the last several years show a rising curve of interest in the specific application of response theory and criticism in the English classroom. Another marked trend in contemporary reader-response criticism falls under the category of cultural criticism, with especial attention being paid to problems of racial and gender bias in the construction of "the reader." Feminist critics, in particular, have been very productive in helping to construct a body of theory on the politics of reading. While the pedagogical and cultural-critique approaches play a prominent role in the current literature, reader-oriented criticism and theory continues to be produced in a rich variety of forms.

Although what Freund calls "the return of the reader" is no longer the force in contemporary theory that it was a decade ago, this may be a result of its successes more than its failures. That is to say, whereas at one time a serious discussion of matters of literary reception was often dismissed as an example of the "affective fallacy," now the relevance of reader-responses to literary works tends to be accepted axiomatically; the roles of reader and author, text and context, are generally seen as interdependent, indispensable components in literary theory and criticism.

Clifford Johnson
University of California, Irvine

Bibliography
Beach, Richard. *A Teacher's Introduction to Reader-Response Theories*. Urbana, IL: National Council of Teachers of English, 1993.
Fish, Stanley. *Is There a Text in This Class? The Authority of Interpretive Communities*. Cambridge, MA: Harvard UP, 1980.
Freund, Elizabeth. *The Return of the Reader: Reader-Response Criticism*. London: Methuen, 1987.
Mailloux, Steven. "The Turns of Reader-Response Criticism." *Conversations: Contemporary Critical Theory and the Teaching of Literature*. Ed. Charles Moran and Elizabeth F. Penfield. Urbana, IL: National Council of Teachers of English, 1990. 38–54.
Suleiman, Susan R., and Inge Crosman, eds. *The Reader in the Text: Essays on Audience and Interpretation*. Princeton: Princeton UP, 1980.
Tompkins, Jane P., ed. *Reader-Response Criticism: From Formalism to Post-Structuralism*. Baltimore, MD: Johns Hopkins UP, 1980.

Reception Study
Refers to historical investigations of how texts have been interpreted, evaluated, and used by individual readers and reading communities. Though studies of literary reception have a long history within various scholarly traditions, the German theorist Hans Robert Jauss initiated the most influential recent version with his landmark essay "Literary History as a Challenge to Literary Theory" (1970). Jauss's reception aesthetics emphasizes how "the literary work is not

an object that stands by itself and that offers the same view to each reader in each period." Rather than treating the work as a "monument that monologically reveals its timeless essence," Jauss focuses on the "dialogical character" of the literary work, which is "more like an orchestration that strikes ever new resonances among its readers." Thus, "the history of literature is a process of aesthetic reception and production that takes place in the realization of literary texts on the part of the receptive reader, the reflective critic, and the author in his continuing productivity." Jauss discusses reception in terms of historical readers' shared horizons of expectations: preunderstandings of past genre conventions, present relations among surrounding texts in different literary genres, and the opposition between literary and nonliterary discourses.

Reception history and theory are often distinguished from other reader-oriented approaches. Reception study analyzes the historical effects of reading texts while reader-response criticism examines the reading process itself; reception study describes how historical readers interpreted and used texts while reader-response criticism looks at actual or hypothetical readers during the activity of reading. In the preface to *The Act of Reading* (1978), Wolfgang Iser, Jauss's colleague at the University of Constance, draws a parallel distinction between the theories underlying their two approaches to readers reading: A theory of response deals with how a literary work and its "hitherto unformulated situation can be processed and, indeed, understood" while a theory of reception "always deals with existing readers, whose reactions testify to certain historically conditioned experiences of literature. A theory of response has its roots in the text; a theory of reception arises from a history of readers' judgments." Though reception study and reader-response criticism can be contrasted in these ways, both approaches are theoretically and practically interrelated as can be seen in the introduction and essays collected in James Machor's *Reader in History* (1993).

There are at least two ways that reception analysis directly relates to rhetoric. First, and most obvious, reception study examines the effects of texts on specific historical audiences. Second, and less obvious, is the fact that inquiry into reception history necessarily emphasizes the reader's rhetoric in responding to texts. That is, in examining historical acts of interpretation, reception study engages in rhetorical analysis of how particular readers argue their interpretations and evaluations within the cultural conversations of their specific historical communities. Thus, reception study can make significant contributions to what might be called the study of cultural rhetoric—the tropes, arguments, and narratives circulating in a culture at particular historical moments.

Steven Mailloux
University of California, Irvine

Bibliography

Holub, Robert C. *Reception Theory: A Critical Introduction*. London: Methuen, 1984.

Jauss, Hans Robert. *Toward an Aesthetic of Reception*. Trans. Timothy Bahti. Minneapolis: U of Minnesota P, 1982.

Johnson, Barbara A. *Reading* Piers Plowman *and* The Pilgrim's Progress: *Reception and the Protestant Reader*. Carbondale: Southern Illinois UP, 1992.

Machor, James L. *Readers in History: Nineteenth-Century American Literature and the Contexts of Response*. Baltimore: Johns Hopkins UP, 1993.

Mailloux, Steven. *Rhetorical Power*. Ithaca, NY: Cornell UP, 1989.

Refutatio

Or, refutation, the part of a speech wherein the rhetor uses arguments to weaken, disprove, or impair the adversary's confirmation or proof, as defined by Cicero in *De inventione*. In fifth-century B.C.E. Greece, handbooks on rhetoric included refutation as part of the structure of judicial oratory, along with introduction, narration, proof, and conclusion (Kennedy 20). The Romans retained this division.

Aristotle devotes the concluding chapters of Book 2 of the *Rhetoric* to a discussion of refutation, stating that arguments may be refuted by either raising a countersyllogism or an objection. The same topics may be used for countersyllogisms, or refutative syllogisms, as for demonstrative, since both are based upon probabilities. However, refutative syllogisms are more favored by audiences because things that stand in juxtaposition are always clearer to audiences.

Aristotle says that objections may be raised by means of refutation in four ways: they may be derived from the opponent's enthymeme, from what is similar, from what is opposite, or from former decisions of well-known men. Most objections, however, only manage to demonstrate that the argument is not *necessarily* true—not that it is improbable. The most potent refutative objections are those that manage to establish both that the opposing argument is unlikely to be true and that it need not be true.

Signs, discussed in Book 1, may be refuted if they cannot form the basis of a logical syllogism. Such signs are called probable signs and are related as the universal to the particular. But signs that can serve as the basis of a logical syllogism, or necessary signs, cannot be refuted.

Enthymemes may be refuted in the same ways that one might refute any other argument based upon probability. A single fact that contravenes an opponent's example will suffice to refute it, by showing it as not necessarily true. However, if the opponent has numerically more or more frequent examples, then the refutation must show that the present example is dissimilar to the other examples given by the opponent, that the event did not happen in the same way, or simply point to some other kind of difference that makes the examples inapplicable. But if the examples are preponderant, and the situation is clearly a true example, then it becomes irrefutable because it becomes a logical demonstration.

Cicero discusses refutation in *De inventione*. One may refute an argument by not granting one or more of its assumptions; by granting assumptions but denying that a conclusion follows from them; by showing an argument to be fallacious; or by meeting a strong argument with an argument equally strong or stronger.

Quintilian, in the *Institutes of Oratory*, differed from most preceding rhetorical theorists by opposing the practice of anticipating arguments in order to preemptively refute them. He contended that they both had to be made to appear weak, and the adversary could argue that the speaker would never have raised them, had the speaker not recognized their power.

Mary Foertsch
Bentley College

Bibliography

Aristotle. *Rhetoric*. Trans. John Henry Freese. Cambridge, MA: Harvard UP, 1975.

Cicero. *De Inventione, De Optimo Genere Oratorum, Topica*. Trans. H.M. Hubbell. Cambridge, MA: Harvard UP, 1949.

Kennedy, George. *Classical Rhetoric and Its Christian and Secular Tradition from Ancient to Modern Times*. Chapel Hill: U of North Carolina P, 1980.

Quintilian. *Institutio Oratoria*. 4 vols. Trans. H.E. Butler. Cambridge, MA: Harvard UP, 1958.

Religious Rhetoric

Hearing, speaking, reading, writing, and knowing as acts of faith. For most North Americans in the late twentieth century, the notion of "religious rhetoric" will likely call to mind not only discourses that unfold in officially designated sacred spaces such as temples, kivas, churches, and mosques but also occasions when the language of faith invades the conduct of everyday life. As the kicker attempts the extra point, someone in the stands behind the goalposts, positioned in view of the television audience, raises a placard scrawled with "John 3:16"; a scan among other channels during the commercial break reveals an evangelist in mid exhortation. At the close of an Alcoholics Anonymous meeting, attenders stand and recite the serenity prayer. Letters to the editor in mainstream newspapers quote Leviticus as grounds for societal censure of lesbian and gay citizens. The president concludes a State of the Union address with a benediction. Fundamentalists representing a bewildering variety of faiths assert their claims through public actions such as bombings, kidnappings, assassinations, rapes, and wars.

Such "intrusions" of religious visions and values into secular contexts are nothing new. In fact, allusions to the numinous are so much a part of ostensibly nonreligious discourse that they are not always recognized. One potentially clarifying response would be to limit the scope of what we call *religious rhetoric* to situations in which people explicitly refer to a divine presence as they seek to implicate hearers or readers in a unifying myth and mission. Seen this way, religious rhetoric would become a specialized genre of persuasive discourse—a genre whose purposes and strategies for creating identification were peculiarly its own. The insights of contemporary rhetorical theory, however, suggest that it may be more fruitful—not to mention more accurate—to view religious rhetoric as a more extensive domain. Indeed, perhaps we would do well to understand all rhetoric as religious; in other words, to concede that one cannot hear, speak, read, write, or know without making a leap of faith.

Not surprisingly, this proposal has been found to prompt spirited resistance, especially among people who grant to scientific inquiry a privileged epistemological status. Still, scholarship in rhetoric has called such privilege into question by its analysis of the relationship between language and knowledge, including the persuasive processes by which knowers come to agree on what is known. Several researchers have suggested, in their own ways, that all knowing begins with faith, for scientists as well as theologians. As Michael Overington has shown, the "allegedly self-evident character of scientific knowledge" masks the drama of negotiation, consensus-building, and belief-shaping by which its facts and theories are generated (161).

Similarly, in Karl Popper's estimation, "scientific discovery is impossible without faith in ideas which are of a purely speculative kind . . . a faith which is completely unwarranted from the point of view of science, and which, to that extent, is 'metaphysical'" (38). Michael Polanyi likewise characterizes the move from one epistemological paradigm to another as a "conversion to new premises not accessible by any strict argument from those previously held"; such moves are made "in the hope of achieving thereby closer contact with reality. We take a plunge only in order to gain a firmer foothold" (105, 106). Everybody, it seems, must walk by faith.

Accordingly, in the perspective of Ernesto Grassi, all human speech is grounded in experiences of wonder and revelation and shared belief—experiences which are, in a basic sense, religious. Grassi argues that all rational speech is preceded by rhetorical speech, which is the more primal. Such "original speech" is uttered by "the wise man [or woman], the *sophos,* who is not only *epistetai,* but who with insight leads, guides, and attracts" (32). Further, Grassi asserts the primacy of metaphor in all human speaking and knowing. Even as we "make 'sensory' observations," he contends, "we are forced to 'reach back' for a transposition, for a metaphor" (33). Thus, rhetorical speech, which is the matrix for rational speech, has an essentially "'evangelic' and 'prophetic' character" (21).

An appreciation of rhetoric as religious in this sense can serve to foster reflection about the shaping of truth and action through the metaphors we reach for, the questions we ask, the politics we enact, the stories we tell and hear and inhabit. It is perhaps not accidental that concurrent with the affirmation of the essentially religious character of rhetoric there has emerged a renewed awareness of the thoroughly rhetorical nature of religion. The transformative possibilities of this latter insight have not been lost on feminist scholars. One illumination of their work is *Weaving the Visions: New Patterns in Feminist Spirituality,* a compilation by Judith Plaskow and Carol P. Christ, which demonstrates how women of many different religions, races, and cultures are increasing their rhetorical power and freedom within and beyond their communities of faith.

Pat Youngdahl
University of Arizona

Bibliography
Grassi, Ernesto. *Rhetoric as Philosophy: The Humanist Tradition.* University Park: Pennsylvania State UP, 1980.
Overington, Michael A. "The Scientific Community as Audience: Toward a Rhetorical Analysis of Science." *Philosophy and Rhetoric* 10 (1977): 143–64.
Plaskow, Judith, and Carol P. Christ. *Weaving the Visions: New Patterns in Feminist Spirituality.* San Francisco: HarperCollins, 1989.
Polanyi, Michael. *Personal Knowledge: Towards a Post-Critical Philosophy.* 1958. Chicago: U of Chicago P, 1962.
Popper, Karl R. *The Logic of Scientific Discovery.* New York: Basic, 1959.

See also ARS PRAEDICANDI; HOMILETICS; HOMILY; PULPIT ORATORY; SERMON

Renaissance Rhetoric
A complex subject of great geographical scope and temporal longevity in which hundreds of rhetoricians endeavored to recover ancient learning and adapt it to the needs of the early modern age. Rhetoric was an essential element in the intellectual enterprise called the Renaissance. Writers, schoolmasters, theologians, lawyers, and poets contributed to the development of rhetorical theory and practice in the Renaissance. Hundreds of books were written about

rhetoric, and hundreds more were influenced by its doctrines. Because rhetoric so pervades Renaissance culture, the subject of this entry resists ready reduction. At best, only a broad outline of the career of rhetoric in the fifteenth, sixteenth, and early seventeenth centuries can be sketched. It may be reasonable to say that the history of Renaissance rhetoric is characterized by recovery and reform. That is, the Renaissance sought to recover rhetoric's true past and, using this knowledge, to reform rhetoric so that it might serve the changing shape of the European world in the early modern era.

The recovery of rhetoric's past was initiated by Italian humanists in the fourteenth and fifteenth century. These humanists believed that medieval conceptions of rhetoric were distorted because medieval rhetoricians did not have access to the entire literature of classical rhetoric. Renaissance "bookhunters" systematically searched for those treatises that had disappeared or survived only in part following the collapse of the Roman empire. Beginning in the late fourteenth century, a series of discoveries gradually revealed the true nature of ancient rhetoric. In 1416 Poggio Bracciolini rediscovered the complete text of Quintilian at St. Gall, and in 1422 Bishop Andriani rediscovered the text of Cicero's *De oratore*. With the recovery of these two texts, in particular, the understanding of classical rhetoric expanded considerably. The authority of Cicero, already considerable in the Middle Ages, increased dramatically as the Roman orator became the arbiter of both theory and practice. Cicero's conviction that rhetoric was the force that created and sustained the possibility of humans living together in a political community was enthusiastically embraced by Renaissance humanists. The Ciceronian conception of rhetoric as a great art composed of five parts—invention, disposition, style, memory, and delivery—became a model for emulation or received wisdom requiring refutation before rhetoric might advance. Either way, the persona of Cicero as preeminent philosopher and master practitioner is manifest in every Renaissance consideration of rhetoric.

The recovery of Roman rhetoric was accompanied by a similar restoration of the Greek tradition of rhetoric originating in the Byzantine world. The division of the Roman Empire into eastern and western portions and the ascendancy of Latin in the West meant that Greek treatises were largely unknown to medieval rhetoricians. The most important of those introducing Greek thought into Western rhetoric was George Trebizond (1395–1472), in particular for introducing Hermogenes into Western rhetoric. In *Rhetoricorum Libri V* (1433 or 1434), he presented a compendium that integrated the Greek and Roman traditions in rhetoric. Trebizond influenced future rhetoricians, and his work presaged later Renaissance treatises in which Roman theory would be augmented by contributions from ancient Greece. Thus by the end of the fifteenth century, the humanists had established a sophisticated view of rhetoric that may have shared more with their ancient sources than it did with their medieval predecessors.

This fuller understanding of the classical conception of rhetoric provided the incentive to render rhetoric more faithful to the past and more useful to the present. The earliest, and perhaps the most influential of such reformers was Rudolphus Agricola (1443–1485). Agricola initiated a reform, some would say a revolution, in the relationship between rhetoric and dialectic. The Humanists were disgusted by medieval scholasticism and Boethian logic, which subordinated rhetoric to logic. The effort of Agricola and those who followed was to rearrange that relationship. In his *De inventione dialectica* (1515), Agricola develops a view of logic that is distinctly rhetorical. Central to Agricola's reform of dialectic was the elevation of the *topoi,* or topics, over the predicaments, or categories. Whereas traditionally the topics had been treated by both rhetoric and dialectic, after Agricola the *topoi* would be increasingly restricted to the latter art.

Juan Luis Vives (1493–1540) was one of the first to propose the rehabilitation of rhetoric consistent with the Agricolan reform of dialectic. In his encyclopedic *De disciplinis* (1531), Vives indicts scholasticism for its sterility and its corrupting influence on all disciplines. Despite his admiration of Cicero, Vives rejects the classical conception of rhetoric for its redundancy and irrelevancy. Vives believes that only *elocutio* is unique to rhetoric. The other parts of the Ciceronian system are useful in a variety of arts and hence not the exclusive property of rhetoric. Invention is therefore an element in many arts, but it is best studied in dialectic. In *De ratione dicendi* (1533), Vives develops a theory of rhetoric consistent with his indictment in *De disciplinis*. Vives's alternative to the five-part Ciceronian system is a detailed and systematic investigation of style.

Of all the sixteenth-century reformers, the best known is probably Peter Ramus (1515–1572). Like Vives, Ramus was an opponent of scholastic logic and classical conceptions of rhetoric. He wrote a series of books in which he attacked Aristotle (*Aristotelicae animadversiones,* 1543), Cicero (*Brutinae quaestiones,* 1547), and Quintilian (*Rhetoricae distinctiones in Quintilianum,* 1549). Ramus's argument is much the same in all three works: the ancient authorities have confused dialectic and rhetoric. Ramus's mission, to clarify this ancient misunderstanding, is undertaken in a series of books including *Dialecticae institutiones* (1543) and two books published under the name of his collaborator, Omer Talon: *Institutiones oratoriae* (1543) and *Rhetorica* (1548). Although Talon is identified as the author of the two latter works, Ramus was certainly involved in their preparation and may have been the actual author of the *Rhetorica.* These works were reissued in numerous editions in Latin and French.

Ramus's proposed solution to the classical muddle proved to be appealingly simple. Invention and disposition had traditionally been elements in both dialectic and rhetoric, thus creating confusion and redundancy. Ramus therefore assigns *inventio* and *dispositio* to dialectic while reserving *elocutio* and *pronuntiatio* for rhetoric. He omits *memoria* altogether. Thus the two arts of discourse, dialectic and rhetoric, are each neatly separated from one another and, in keeping with Ramus's fondness for dichotomy, are each subdivided into two principal components. This dichotomizing continues: elocution is divided into figures and tropes; pronunciation, into voice and gesture. Ramus's approach, however, is not quite as balanced as it might seem. *Pronuntiatio* was never developed as fully as *elocutio* by Ramus or his followers and was often ignored. The obvious consequence of such a realignment was that style would become the predominant, or exclusive, concern of Ramistic rhetoricians.

The reforms of Ramus were remarkably well received and readily disseminated throughout Europe. Probably the first work to show Ramistic influence outside France was the *Organum dialecticum et rhetoricum* (1579) by the Spaniard Francisco Sánchez de las Brosas (1523–1601). Ultimately, however, Ramism proved particularly appealing to Protestant countries. Ramus was killed in the St. Bartholomew's Day Massacre of French

Huegonauts, and his martyrdom may explain the association of Ramism and Protestantism. In England several important works with Ramist rhetoric were published. These include Dudley Fenner, *The Artes of Logike and Rhetorike* (1584); Abraham Fraunce, *The Arcadian Rhetorike* (1588); Charles Butler, *Rhetoricae libri duo* (1598); and his *Oratoriae libri duo* (1629). The widespread influence of Ramism demonstrates the appeal to Renaissance thinkers of systems that were both precise and practical.

Precision and practicality were important to Renaissance reformers who, for the most part, were not much interested in speculation without application. Vives, Ramus, and others were educational reformers intent to improve education in general and the teaching of rhetoric in particular. By the early sixteenth century, rhetoric had again assumed a dominant place in the classroom; therefore, any question of educational reform almost inevitably involved rhetoric.

The importance of rhetoric to Renaissance education is clearly evident in the work of Desiderius Erasmus (1465–1536), another of the great reformers of rhetoric. His *De ratione studii,* published in 1512, but circulating earlier, was one of the inspirations for a sixteenth-century innovation—the English grammar school. St. Paul's, the first of these schools, was established by John Colet to realize the educational ideals of Erasmus and other humanists. The education Erasmus has in mind in *De ratione studii* is a rhetorical one: to bring students to "a credible degree of eloquence." The first step in attaining credible eloquence was to master Latin grammar, broadly conceived. For Erasmus, Latin was a living language that should become as familiar as one's native tongue. Thus the curriculum consisted of translating from the vernacular into Latin and back again, paraphrases, and original compositions. There were four principal composition exercises in the grammar school: letter-writing, verse-making, the theme, and the oration. While the oration was deemed to be the most difficult and hence the final exercise, all exercises involved oral and written aspects. The distinctions between writing and speaking, well established in the twentieth century, would have been meaningless in the sixteenth.

Erasmus not only provided the grammar schools with much of their pedagogical inspiration, he also gave them their first textbook, *De copia* (1511). He wrote the book as a text for St. Paul's, but its frequent reprintings throughout the sixteenth century attest to its use in a variety of schools. *Copia* is often translated as copiousness or abundance. Neither term, however, entirely captures what Erasmus had in mind. *De copia* expresses a stylistic ideal, a conception of language that values richness, variety, and facility as the essence of eloquence. Variety, in particular, is essential to the formulation of good style. "There is absolutely nothing, however powerful," says Erasmus, "which is not dimmed if not commended by variety." Much of *De copia,* then, is devoted to explaining how the capacity for variety might best be achieved. This discussion of variety culminates in the best-known portion of the work. Erasmus displays his own ability at variety by producing 195 varieties on the sentence "Your letter pleased me mightily." This virtuoso performance by Erasmus is designed to demonstrate the infinite variability of expression. Students were expected to emulate such performances in the process of becoming eloquent themselves. The English grammar schools devoted enormous effort to ensure that their students might meet Cicero's expectation that the orator be able to speak, or write, "with fullness and variety on any subject whatsoever." There is considerable evidence that they were often successful in that endeavor. The list of English writers who studied at such schools is perhaps testament enough: Milton, Shakespeare, Spencer, Marlowe, Jonson, Sidney, and others. Of course, education cannot take full credit for genius. But there is little question that the art of these writers was shaped by the lessons learned in the grammar schools.

The success of these writers also illuminates another central feature of Renaissance rhetoric: its identification with literature of all kinds. Indeed, rhetoric and literature are inseparable in the Renaissance. Rhetoric offered the only fully developed theory of literature and was therefore applied to all literary forms. Poetry and prose, plays and propaganda, were all seen as essentially and inescapably rhetorical. Not surprisingly, in such a view of literature, the oration maintained its place as the preeminent literary form. The classical oration exerted a formal control over a wide variety of genres. The six-part division of the classical oration (*exordium, narratio, propositio, confirmatio, confutatio,* and *peroratio*) were viewed as an appropriate pattern for virtually any discourse. Thus Sidney's *Defense of Poesie* is in the form of an oration and Milton's "Paradise Lost" is "An Oration to Justify the Ways of God to Men."

The union of the literary and the rhetorical underscores the preoccupation of Renaissance rhetoricians with *elocutio* or style. Erasmus, Vives, Ramus, and others argued in various ways for the priority of style in rhetoric. If the goal is to create an eloquent human being, then it is inevitable that *elocutio* would occupy a favored position among the five parts of classical rhetoric. Thus Renaissance rhetoricians expended great energy identifying and naming the resources of language available to writers and speakers. In this endeavor they were consistent with the technique and terminology found in their classical sources. In particular, Renaissance rhetoricians elected to treat style by means of the figures of speech. The figures had been regarded from antiquity as artful deviations from ordinary language which could be identified and categorized. Compilations of the figures were to be found in Quintilian's *Institutio oratoria* and in the *ad Herennium.* Renaissance writers followed the lead of these ancient authorities in presenting rather detailed catalogs of these linguistic devices. Important works that feature the figures include Johannes Susenbrotus, *Epitome troporum ac schematum* (1540); Richard Sherry, *A Treatise of Schemes and Tropes* (1550); Henry Peacham, *The Garden of Eloquence* (1577); Angel Day, *English Secretorie* (1586); and George Puttenham, *The Arte of English Poesie* (1589).

The authors of these treatises typically present long lists of figures. These lists are then further subdivided. Although the terminology varies among writers, the figures are most often divided into schemes and tropes. Peacham, in the 1593 edition of the *Garden of Eloquence,* defines tropes as "an artificial alteration of a word, or a sentence from the proper and natural signification to another not proper, but yet nigh and likely." Day defines the figure as "no change in signification . . . certain mean whereby from a simple and ordinary kinds of speaking, we grow into a more cunning and excellent deliverie." Tropes, then, involve deviations in the meaning of words, whereas schemes involve deviations in the patterns and arrangements of words. In *A Treatise of Schemes and Tropes,* Sherry presents about 180 figures, which he names, defines, and usually illustrates with examples "gathered out of the best Grammarians and Oratours." The termi-

R

nology that Sherry chose to use, despite writing in English, is the Greek and Latin names for the figures. The names of the figures never successfully translated into the various vernaculars and, of course, the ancient labels have persisted.

The fondness for the figures found in Sherry, Peacham, and a great many other writers is not entirely the product of an acute aesthetic sensibility or a compulsion for categorization. Rather, Renaissance rhetoricians emphasized the figures because they believed in the utility of the schemes and tropes. This belief is clearly expressed by Peacham: It is through the use of the figures that "the oratour may leade his hearers which way he list, and draw them to what affections he will: he may make them to be angry, to be pleased, to laugh, to weepe, and lament: to loue, to abhore, and to loath: to hope, to fear, to couet, to be satisffyed, to enuye, to have pittye and compassion: to meruaile, to beleeue, to repent: and briefely to be moued with any affection that shall serue best for his purpose." In short, it is the figures by which the emotions are engaged, and persuasion is essentially an emotional process. Without figurative language, the efficacy of rhetoric would be seriously impaired, if not rendered impotent. Little wonder, then, that Renaissance rhetoricians devoted so much energy to a mastery of the figures.

As the work of Sherry, Peacham, and others indicates, the figurative approach to language was applied with equal enthusiasm to Latin and to the vernacular languages. While the Renaissance began with an intimate connection with the Latin language, the concerns with communication readily transcended that language and became at home in the development of the national idioms. Translations of rhetorical texts into the vernaculars had begun in the late Middle Ages and continued into the Renaissance. As early as 1260–1266, Bruno Latini produced a French version of *De inventione* in Book 3 of his *Tresor*. At about the same time, Guidotto Bologna wrote an Italian compendium of *De inventione* and the *ad Herennium*. John Gower includes an English resume of rhetoric in his *Confessio Amantis* (1393?), which was derived from Latini's *Tresor*. In 1427 Enrique de Villena produced a Castilian version of the *ad Herennium*.

Early Renaissance vernacular treatises progressed beyond direct translation but remained derivative of Greek and Latin sources. These translations, paraphrases, and epitomes met the important need of providing accessibility to the rhetorical tradition to those unlearned in Latin. Thus Miguel de Salinas justifies his *Rhetórica en lengua Castellana* (1541) on the grounds that everyone uses Spanish while few know Latin. Rendering rhetoric into the vernacular was sufficient service; originality was not required as well. Leonard Cox in *The Arte or Crafte of Rhethorike* (1530), the first English work devoted explicitly and exclusively to rhetoric, is relatively modest about his own contribution: "I have partly traunslatyd out of a werk of rhetoryke wrytten in the lattyn tongue, and partly compyled of myne owne, and so made a lytle treatise in maner of an introduccyon into this aforesaid scyence and that in the englysshe tongue." While Cox suggests his source is Cicero, his book is derived principally from Philip Melancthon's *De rhetorica, libri tres* (1519) and *Institutiones rhetoricae* (1521). Cox's work is restricted, in the manner of Cicero's *De inventione*, to a discussion of invention. Thus while *The Arte or Crafte of Rhethoryke* is of limited scope and originality, it nevertheless marks an important step in the development of rhetoric in the English language. Cox's work was followed by Sherry's *Treatise of Schemes and Tropes*, a work restricted, of course, to a consideration of *elocutio*.

It is not until the publication in 1553 of *The Arte of Rhetorique* that a complete, comprehensive Ciceronian rhetoric appears in English. The author of this work, Thomas Wilson (1525–1581), is heavily influenced by classical and Continental authorities, yet he shows a remarkable degree of independence from those sources. Early in the *Arte of Rhetorique*, Wilson says that an orator "must fasten his mynde first of all, vppon these fiue especiall pointes that followe, and learne them euery one." These special points are, not surprisingly, the five parts of Ciceronian rhetoric, and they provide Wilson with the fundamental organization of his work. *The Arte of Rhetorique* is divided into three books, one devoted to invention, one to disposition, and one to elocution, with some attention to memory and delivery. In skillfully anglicizing Ciceronian rhetoric, Wilson helped ensure that the ancient rhetorical tradition would continue to influence the development of English language.

Just as rhetoric was closely related to the rise of national languages in Europe, so too was it a part of another great fragmentation—the religious controversies and reforms that ruptured Christian Europe. Much like the monarchs and princes of Europe, rhetoricians were usually associated with the Protestant or Catholic causes. Ramus and the German educator Philip Melancthon (1497–1560) were influential in Protestant countries, while the Dominican Luis de Granada (1504–1588) and the Jesuit Cypriano Soarez (1524–1593) exercised greatest influence in Catholic countries. While Catholic and Protestant writers alike attempted to render rhetoric consistent with the appropriate theological views, religious rhetorics share certain important features. Both Protestant and Catholic rhetoricians were intent to adapt classical rhetoric to the needs of the preacher. The Reformation made it clear that there was a greater need than ever for effective preaching. While Augustine and other early church figures had accommodated Christianity to rhetoric, Renaissance writers believed that accommodation was not yet complete. The preaching manuals of the medieval *ars praedicandi* were far from complete Ciceronian rhetorics. Thus, as with Renaissance rhetoric in general, much of the effort of religious rhetorics was to ensure that Ciceronianism and Christianity were finally and fully integrated.

This interweaving of the Christian and Ciceronian traditions is particularly pronounced in the work of Granada. His *Ecclesiasticae rhetoricae* (1576?) was in part a response to the Council of Trent's initiative to reinvigorate Catholic preaching in response to the rise of Protestantism. Granada believes that the Protestant challenge can best be met by realizing the Ciceronian ideal of the union of wisdom and eloquence in the person of the preacher. Granada claims that while preachers were adequately taught theology and philosophy, their training in rhetoric was neglected. To address this neglect, he presents a theory of rhetoric that is Ciceronian in spirit and structure.

Like other Renaissance rhetoricians, however, Granada is not reluctant to refashion the Ciceronian system to meet his, and the church's, needs. Granada alters the three genres of classical oratory. He dismisses judicial oratory as irrelevant to preaching, and while he retains the two remaining genres, deliberative and epideictic, he alters their functions. Granada assigns to deliberative the function of correcting the faults of sinners, and he assigns to epideictic the duty of praising the saints. Similarly, he accepts four of the five traditional parts of rhetoric, dismissing only memory because it is a part of nature rather than of rhetoric. At the same time, Granada virtually elevates *amplificatio* to a constituent part of rhetoric, nearly equal to *inventio* and *elocutio*, with which it shares some functions. Amplification is important to Granada and many other Renaissance writers because amplification, by exploiting the figures, exploits the emotions. The *Ecclesiasticae rhetoricae* is not a conversion manual; Granada assumes that the preacher's audience is at least nominal Christians. The task, therefore, is to get them to behave according to their beliefs. Doing so is an emotional rather than a rational process, and so the preacher must master *amplificatio*. The *Ecclesiasticae rhetoricae* is a Ciceronian rhetoric, but it is a thoroughly Christianized one. In it Granada transforms Cicero's ideal orator into the image of the preacher, defending the faith and exhorting the faithful.

As an intellectual movement, the Renaissance was inspired in large measure by the recovery of ancient rhetorical texts. From its very inception, then, rhetoric had a central place in the Renaissance that it never relinquished. Although reliant on classical models, Renaissance rhetoricians were not enamored of ancient authorities because of ardent antiquarianism. Rather, classical rhetoric was appealing because it appeared relevant, or could be made so, to the needs of the early modern age. Even the critics of the Ciceronian system were willing to concede that Cicero was a master practitioner who deserved emulation. And following Cicero, rhetoric was viewed as a civilizing force and thus the centerpiece of a humane education. To be educated was to be eloquent, and Renaissance schoolmasters relentlessly pursued the goal of eloquence. Their success can best be seen in the rhetorical nature of the literary artifacts of the age. *Elocutio* was cultivated by Renaissance rhetoricians because style speaks to the human emotions, the very passions that propel human beings to action.

Rhetoric maintained continuity with its ancient origins while also cognizant of the great political, religious, intellectual, and linguistic changes of the Renaissance. Indeed, rhetoric, as the art of eloquence and the art of persuasion, was often an instrumentality of those transformations. Rhetoric was at the very center of the Renaissance experience. It is difficult to fully understand the meaning of the Renaissance without understanding the meaning of Renaissance rhetoric.

Don Paul Abbott
University of California, Davis

Bibliography

Abbott, Don Paul. "The Renaissance." *The Present State of Scholarship in Historical and Contemporary Rhetoric*. Ed. Winifred B. Horner. Rev. ed. Columbia: U of Missouri P, 1990. 84–113.

———. "Rhetoric and Writing in Renaissance Europe and England." *A Short History of Writing Instruction from Ancient Greece to Twentieth-Century America*. Ed. James J. Murphy. Davis, CA: Hermagoras, 1990. 95–120.

Howell, Wilbur S. *Logic and Rhetoric in England, 1500–1700*. Princeton: Princeton UP, 1956.

Monfasani, John. "Humanism and Rhetoric." *Renaissance Humanism: Foundations, Forms, and Legacy*. Vol. 3. *Humanism and the Disciplines*. Ed. Albert Rabil, Jr. Philadelphia: U of Pennsylvania P, 1988.

Murphy, James J. *Renaissance Eloquence: Studies in the Theory and Practice of Renaissance Rhetoric*. Berkeley: U of California P, 1983.

———. *Renaissance Rhetoric; A Short Title Catalogue of Works on Rhetorical Theory from the Beginning of Printing to A.D. 1700*. New York: Garland, 1981.

Ong, Walter, S.J. *Ramus, Method, and the Decay of Dialogue: From the Art of Discourse to the Art of Reason*. Cambridge, MA: Harvard UP, 1958.

Shuger, Debora K. *Sacred Rhetoric: The Christian Grand Style in the English Renaissance*. Princeton: Princeton UP, 1988.

Vickers, Brian. "Renaissance Reintegration." *In Defence of Rhetoric*. Oxford: Clarendon, 1988.

See also CICERO; COPIA; ERASMUS, DESIDERIUS; FIGURES; PEACHAM, HENRY; RAMUS, PETER; STYLE; TREBIZOND, GEORGE; TROPES; WILSON, THOMAS

Repetitio

Repetition of the same word, phrase, or clause. "Vanity of vanities, saith the preacher, vanity of vanities; all is vanity" (Ecclesiastes 1:1). While repetition without purpose denotes carelessness, repetitio can be used to add emphasis as Catullus demonstrates in "I hate and I love. Why I do so, perhaps you ask. I know not, but I feel it and I am in torment." In the following passage, Paul uses repetitio to emphasize the warmth of his vehemence: "Here come more voices.—Your voices! For your voices I have fought; Watch'd for your voices; for your voices bear of wounds two dozen odd; battles thrice six I have seen and heard of; for your voices have done many things, some less, some more. Your Voices!" (Corinthians 2.3.120).

Arthur Quinn and Lyon Rathbun
University of California, Berkeley

Reynolds, Sir Joshua (1723–1792)

First president of the Royal Academy of Arts, 1768 to 1790. Although he is primarily known as an artist—he was arguably the most famous portraitist of his day, and was prolific—Reynolds also left an important legacy in art theory, chiefly in the form of the annual lectures he delivered at the Academy. These lectures, and other of his writings, achieved wide and lasting influence. They are important not only in the history of art criticism and literary studies but in the history of rhetoric because classical rhetorical theory figures significantly in Reynolds's formulation of aesthetic theory.

Reynolds's fifteen lectures, known as the *Discourses,* were printed in pamphlet form immediately after each lecture; they were also collected and published in numerous editions. Receiving high praise, they established Reynolds's reputation as a writer and critic. Reynolds sought recognition as a man of letters deliberately; the literati of the day were constant guests at his table. He was a prominent figure in the "Literary Club" and wrote essays for Samuel Johnson's *Idler* series. Boswell's *Life of Johnson* is dedicated to Reynolds. During the years of Reynolds's presidency, there were accusations that Johnson or Edmund Burke, or both of them, had written parts or all of the *Discourses*. Reynolds's biographers take pains to demonstrate that although he had recourse to the critical judgment of his famous literary friends and although the *Discourses* contain a few phrases penned by these editors, Reynolds is certainly the author. The *Dictionary of Literary Biography* notes that although Reynolds's output of "creative literature" was not great, he was, "in fact, one of the most significant figures in the literature of his time" (253). Hilles, author of *The Literary Career of Sir Joshua Reynolds,* quotes the following lines from an effusive poem by one of Reynolds's friends: "[Reynolds] Has of *two* arts attain'd the lawrel'd heights; / Paints with a Pen, and with a Pencil Writes!" (90).

From the point of view of rhetorical studies, the most significant thing about Sir

Joshua's writings is the way he fuses classical rhetorical theory with his views about the education of the artist and the production and appreciation of art. Bevilacqua argues that "Reynolds took painting not merely to be *like* rhetoric but indeed equivalent to rhetoric in conception, treatment, and effect, and thus presumed a corresponding dictum [to Horace's *ut pictura poesis*]—*ut rhetorica pictura*": as rhetoric, painting (64). Reynolds conceived of all art, whether painting, sculpture, music, poetry, or oratory, as having the object of producing particular effects in those who viewed or heard the artistic productions. Grounding himself in the idioms of neoclassical rhetorical and aesthetic theory, he used analogous reasoning to discuss the processes of the painter's invention, arrangement, style, and "delivery" that would produce the desired effects. The most important effect, accomplished through the "grand style" of painting (an analogy to Cicero's grand style in oratory), was the education, uplift, and ennoblement of an audience by communicating sublime thoughts and feelings. Reynolds is generally credited with theoretical promotion of the grand style and with successful application of it, but some critics have opined that he himself did not fare well in his own attempts at the grandest style in historical painting, but excelled in a less grand style that nevertheless glorified the subjects of his contemporary portraits, portraits that made him a wealthy man.

Aesthetic theory that draws analogies between the arts is of course not peculiar to Reynolds; it is at least as old as Horace, and it was common in Renaissance art theory. After Bacon's discussion of the "one universal science" in *The Advancement of Learning*, the search for common ground between the arts became even more common (Alexander 158). Reynolds was strongly influenced by treatises that take this approach and that employ terminology and psychological assumptions from classical rhetoric, such as Franciscus Junius's *Painting of the Ancients* (1638), Gerard Vossius's *De graphice* (1660), and Jonathan Richardson's *Essay on the Theory of Painting* (1715), to name just a few of the titles that Reynolds himself acknowledges or that his biographers cite (Bevilacqua).

Reynolds's *Discourses* and other writings describe the education of the artist, the nature of artistic imagination, and the rules that govern the production of great art. Reynolds championed the classical doctrine that great art is not the product of "inspiration" or inherent genius alone but is the result of the highly disciplined, lifelong application of learnable rules. Those rules, as articulated by Reynolds, have been the subject of scholarship for centuries and are applicable to fields as seemingly diverse as poetry, painting, technical communication, and rhetoric.

Russel Hirst
University of Tennessee

Bibliography

Alexander, John M. "Eighteenth-Century Justifications for Analogical Comparisons among the Arts." *Enlightenment Essays* 11 (1971): 158–66.

Bevilacqua, Vincent M. "*Ut Rhetorica Pictura*: Sir Joshua Reynolds' Rhetorical Conception of Art." *Huntington Library Quarterly* 34 (1970–1971): 59–78.

Hilles, Frederick Whiley. "A Bibliography of Sir Joshua's Writings." *The Literary Career of Sir Joshua Reynolds*. Hamden, CT: Archon, 1967. 277–300.

———. *The Literary Career of Sir Joshua Reynolds*. Hamden, CT: Archon, 1967.

Leslie, Robert Charles, and Tom Taylor. *Life and Times of Sir Joshua Reynolds*. 2 vols. London: Murray, 1865.

Novak, Matthew Stephen. *Sir Joshua Reynolds and Composition Theory: The Value of the 'Discourses' for the Modern Professional Writer*. Diss. Case Western Reserve U, 1989.

Reynolds, Sir Joshua. *Discourses on Art*. Ed. Robert R. Wark. San Marino, CA: Huntington Library, 1959.

———. *Letters of Sir Joshua Reynolds*. Ed. Frederick Whiley Hilles. Cambridge: Cambridge UP, 1929.

Rogers, Pat. "Sir Joshua Reynolds." *Dictionary of Literary Biography: Vol. 104. British Prose Writers, 1660–1800*, 2nd series. Ed. Donald T. Siebert. Detroit, MI: Layman, 1991. 251–60.

Rhetor

Orator belonging to the period when rhetoric, in its earliest form, was a systematic study of oratory and applied to the training of orators for debate and other forms of public speaking in classical Greece and Rome. During this time, persuasion was administered almost entirely by the spoken word. Effective public persuasion through speech was known only in the free states, as the arts of oratory were comparatively unknown prior to this time. Earlier empires, like the Assyrian and Egyptian civilizations, practiced a kind of leadership that had yet to include public persuasion. The people then were driven rather than persuaded because none of the refinements of public speaking existed.

In Greece the principles of training speakers arose with the development of democracy in Syracuse in the 460s B.C.E. The egalitarian government allowed the people a chance to voice their opinions and argue their claims before a group of fellow citizens. So important was the ability to speak well that rhetors were sought after by dispossessed landowners. Similarly, in the early ages of Rome, rhetoricians taught upper-class men to be effective rhetors on affairs of the state.

Rhetoric, coming from a rhetor, means the art of speaking with propriety and elegance. A rhetor focuses on the use of words in an effective manner to persuade the audience rather than to inform or to entertain. His goal is to attempt to change the view of his audience and in turn their behaviors or attitudes. The rhetor's discourse is argumentative. As a pleader, his duty is to influence and win over his audience, the judges of a controversy. Devices in rhetoric, evidence, lines of reasoning, and logic are some of the elements incorporated in the argumentative persuasion. Hence, the primary purpose of a rhetor is to persuade the audience through the effective use of a detailed formulaic pattern. The principles of the art were expressed in discourses by rhetoricians such as Aristotle, Cicero, and Quintilian. Among the many prominent practitioners were Demosthenes and Cicero.

Three types of oratory were performed by rhetors in ancient Greece and Rome: legal, political, and ceremonial. The most characteristic type of oratory in ancient Athens was legal (forensic) oratory, often used in defense of individual rights and freedom. The Romans, however, saw little of legal oratory during the existence of the monarchy because legal proceedings were uncommon and public speeches were mainly for entertainment purposes.

The golden age of Grecian eloquence extended from the time of Solon (about 600 B.C.E.) to that of Alexander (336 B.C.E.). Within this span of time, the most renowned rhetors flourished. Rhetors eventually developed theories for successful speechmaking, or rhetoric. Thus, a group of men, called rhetoricians, emerged, and were especially plentiful during the Peloponnesian War.

Siew C. Burroughs
Bowling Green State University

Bibliography

Bizzell, Patricia, and Bruce Herzberg, eds. *The Rhetorical Tradition: Readings from Classical Times to the Present.* Boston: St. Martin's, 1990.

Bowersock, G.W. *Greek Sophists in the Roman Empire.* Oxford: Clarendon, 1969.

Connors, Robert J. "Greek Rhetoric and the Transition from Orality." *Philosophy and Rhetoric* 19 (1986): 38–65.

Corbett, Edward P.J. *Clasical Rhetoric for the Modern Student.* 3rd ed. New York: Oxford UP, 1990.

Dobson, John F. *The Greek Orators.* Freeport, NY: Books for Libraries P, 1971.

Enos, Richard Leo, and Ann M. Blakeslee. "The Classical Period." *The Present State of Scholarship in Historical and Contemporary Rhetoric.* Ed. Winifred Bryan Horner. Rev. ed. Columbia: U of Missouri P, 1990. 9–44.

Hunt, Everett Lee. "Plato and Aristotle on Rhetoric and Rhetoricians." *Historical Studies of Rhetoric and Rhetoricians.* Ed. Raymond F. Howes. Ithaca, NY: Cornell UP, 1961. 19–70.

Kennedy, George A. *The Art of Persuasion in Greece.* Princeton: Princeton UP, 1963.

———. *Classical Rhetoric and Its Christian and Secular Tradition from Ancient to Modern Times.* Chapel Hill: The U of North Carolina P, 1980.

Se also RHETORICIAN

Rhetorica ad Alexandrum (Rhetoric to Alexander)

Among the works collected under the name of Aristotle. The prefatory letter claims that the work is by Aristotle, tutor of Alexander the Great, and is written to the pupil as a personal treatise. Its style and content prove, however, that it is not by Aristotle; rather it is thought to be by a contemporary of Aristotle's, Anaximenes of Lampsacus, because of Quintilian's description of the latter's work (3.4.9).

The treatise's contents are similar to what is known about technical treatises of the fourth century and may be broken into four major sections: introductory comments on the seven species of rhetoric (encouragement and dissuasion, praise and blame, accusation and defense, and examination); discussion of types of proofs (direct and supplementary); treatment of style;

and treatment of arrangement. There is also a very brief appendix with miscellaneous and spurious material. A more detailed outline of these sections follows:

I. Introductory Comments on the Species (§§1–6):
    Deliberative Oratory (§§1–2)
    Epideictic Oratory (§3)
    Judicial Oratory (§4)
    Investigation (§5)
    Concluding comments on the species (§6)
II. Invention (§§7–21):
    Logical Proofs (§§7–17)
        Direct (§§7–14)
            probabilities, examples, tokens, considerations, maxims, signs, refutations
        Supplementary (§§14–17)
            opinion of speaker, voluntary evidence, evidence under torture, evidence under oath
    Audience-related Proofs (§§18–19)
        Anticipation, Postulates
    Recapitulation (§§20–21)
        Irony
III. Style (§§22–28):
    Elegance, Length, Diction, Attractiveness, Clarity, Antithesis and Parallelism
IV. Arrangement (§§29–37):
    General Comments (§§29–33)
        introduction (§§29)
            attention, goodwill
        narration (§§30–31)
            clear, brief, attentive, well-ordered
        proof (§§32–33)
            confirmation, anticipation
        recapitulation (§33)
    Deliberative (§34)
        with comment on pathos
    Epideictic (§35)
    Judicial (§36)
        prosecution and defense
        with fuller comments on peroration
    Examination (§37)
V. Miscellaneous and Spurious Material (§38)

The treatise is similar to Aristotle's *Rhetoric* in some superficial ways and may be dependent upon it (it recognizes Aristotle's three species of rhetoric). Some correspondences may show only that both treatises depend on a common source or are involved in the broader tra-

dition of technical handbooks (the supplementary proofs of *The Rhetoric to Alexander* are akin to the inartistic proofs of Aristotle's *Rhetoric*). More importantly, *The Rhetoric to Alexander* differs in significant ways from Aristotle's *Rhetoric*: It posits seven species (over Aristotle's judicial, deliberative, epideictic); it has little interest in the three proofs (logos, ethos, and pathos) or the logical detail of Aristotle (such as the enthymeme); its discussion of style is much less clearly organized and lacks discussion of metaphor; it also lacks any interest in philosophic discussions about the definition and nature of rhetoric or the ethical issues of abuse that are common in Aristotle. Thus it cannot be said to possess the scope or originality of Aristotle's *Rhetoric*. Still, its greatest value is as an example of a less philosophic handbook from the fourth century B.C.E. to compare with Aristotle.

Terry L. Papillon
Virginia Tech

Bibliography

The Greek text with an English translation may be found in the *Loeb Classical Library* Series. It appears in the volume titled *Aristotle: Problems II, Rhetorica Ad Alexandrum*, edited by H. Rackham. Cambridge: Harvard UP, 1933, revised 1957.

Kennedy, G.A. *The Art of Persuasion in Greece.* Princeton: Princeton UP, 1963.
Wendland, P. *Anaximenes von Lampsacus.* Berlin, 1905.

Rhetorica ad Herennium (c. 89–86 B.C.E.)

The earliest, most complete manual of Roman rhetoric. An extensive amount of scholarship has been done to determine the date and authorship of the *Rhetorica ad Herennium*. For much of the history of rhetoric, scholars believed that Cicero was the author; in fact, it is reasonable to conclude that the *Rhetorica ad Herennium* survived because it was included among Cicero's *Rhetorica*. Cornificius and Marcus Antonius have been proposed as possible authors, but the best scholarship on the subject has been done by Harry Caplan, who concluded in his edition of the text for the Loeb Classical Library of Harvard University Press that the author is still unknown.

The *Rhetorica ad Herennium* is the oldest known manual of rhetoric in Latin and was probably written between 86 and 82 B.C.E. It is the first text in rhetoric to explicitly discuss the five canons of rhetoric: invention, arrangement, style, memory, and delivery. The first of the four books of the *Rhetorica ad Herennium* provides detailed treatment of *constitutio,* the Latin equivalent of *stasis,* particularly as it relates to forensic rhetoric. Extensive treatment of arrangement and invention are offered, along with memory and the epicheireme, a five-part rhetorical syllogism. The discussion of style, to which much of the treatise is devoted, is categorized into three levels (*gravis, mediocris,* and *attenuata*), and the treatment of tropes and figures provides a comprehensive presentation of terms and precepts. As mentioned above, the Loeb Classical Library edition by Harry Caplan (Harvard University Press, 1954) offers an excellent English translation facing the Latin text as well as a lucid introduction. Caplan's introduction is reprinted in *Of Eloquence: Studies in Ancient and Medieval Rhetoric by Harry Caplan,* edited by Anne King and Helen North (1970). Augustus S. Wilkins provides a clear (but dated) analysis of the *Rhetorica ad Herennium* in his introduction to Cicero's *De oratore.* Ray Nadeau's translation and commentary of Book 1 of the *Rhetorica ad Herennium* (*Speech Monographs,* 1949) is the only other substantial scholarship on the topic.

Richard Leo Enos
Texas Christian University

Bibliography

Caplan, Harry. "Introduction to the *Rhetorica ad Herennium*" and "A Medieval Commentary on the *Rhetorica ad Herennium.*" *Of Eloquence: Studies in Ancient and Medieval Rhetoric by Harry Caplan.* Ed. Anne King and Helen North. Ithaca, NY: Cornell UP, 1970. 1–25, 247–70.

[Cicero] *Ad C. Herennium De Ratione Dicendi* (*Rhetorica ad Herennium*). Trans. and Intro. Harry Caplan. Cambridge, MA: Harvard UP (Loeb Classical Library), 1954.

Nadeau, Ray. "*Rhetorica ad Herennium,* Commentary and Translation of Book I." *Speech Monographs* (now *Communication Monographs*) 16 (1949): 57–68.

Wilkins, Augustus S. "Introduction: 5. Analysis of the Treatise *Ad Herennium De Arte Rhetorica.*" *M. Tulli Ciceronis De Oratore Libri Tres.* Hildesheim: Georg Olms Verlangsbuchhandlung, 1965. 56–64.

See also ROMAN RHETORIC

Rhetorical Criticism

The interpretation and evaluation of rhetorical texts and performances; more broadly, any mode of criticism that takes into account the relationships that exist between and among the speaker or writer, the performance or the text, and the audience or reader. The goals of rhetorical criticism are to understand how rhetoric works, to influence thought and action, and to contribute to rhetorical theory.

What Terry Eagleton says about literary criticism in *Literary Theory: An Introduction* may also be true of rhetorical criticism. Rhetorical criticism has neither a distinctive method nor a distinctive object. Until recently, rhetorical critics would not have seriously doubted that the basic task of rhetorical criticism is to analyze, interpret, and evaluate a wide range of texts deemed rhetorical, including speech, oratory, public address, and any other kind of text that has designs on an audience. But rhetorical criticism may be dissolving into literary criticism, literary criticism may be dissolving into rhetorical criticism, and both may be dissolving into some form of cultural studies.

The Critical Object

In antiquity, the object of rhetorical criticism was the whole field of discursive practices in society, including oratory, poetry, drama, epic, history, and philosophy. Protagoras, for example, made discourse itself an object of study by critically analyzing the epic poets. In Plato's dialogue *Phaedrus,* Socrates criticizes Lysias' speech because it is repetitive and because it lacks structure. In the introduction to the *Rhetoric,* Aristotle critiques Plato's view of rhetoric as well as rhetoric as it was currently practiced. Throughout the *Rhetoric,* Aristotle uses quotations from prose and poetry to make rhetorical points. Like Aristotle, Cicero drew on both prose and poetry to make critical remarks about rhetoric. And Quintilian drew on poetry, history, philosophy, and all the arts to illustrate his observations about rhetoric. Quintilian is one of a long line of rhetoricians who considered the *Iliad* a rhetorical text. He praised Homer's speeches for their eloquence.

In the twentieth century, the critical object has been a subject of considerable interest and debate in speech communication. Hoyt H. Hudson suggested that critics should study speeches or some kind of persuasive discourse. In an attempt to separate rhetorical criticism from literary criticism, Herbert H. Wichelns took speech as the object of criticism, especially the study of great speakers of the past. In contrasting rhetorical criticism with literary criticism, Wichelns argued that rhetorical criticism "is not concerned with permanence, nor yet with beauty. It is concerned with effect. It regards a speech as a communication to a specific audience, and holds its business to be the analysis and appreciation of the orator's method of imparting his ideas to his hearers" (209). S. Judson Crandell wanted rhetorical critics to study the rhetoric of social movements as well as speeches. Ernest J. Wrage advocated studying issues and ideas in public address. A number of critics wanted to expand the object of criticism beyond the limits of speech and public address, and proposed novels, plays, editorials, and journalistic writing as subject matter for rhetorical criticism. More recently, critics have proposed studying a wider range of discursive practices and objects including television, radio programs, film, graphic arts, music, and advertising, thereby moving rhetorical criticism into cultural studies. But perhaps the most controversial approach to the critical object in speech communication is that proposed by Michael McGee in a special issue on rhetorical criticism in the *Western Journal of Speech Communication* 54 (1990). Virtually all of the critics represented in that issue agreed that the range of rhetorical acts and artifacts extends well beyond speech, oratory, and public address. But McGee claims that in this postmodern era, in which American culture is in a state of fragmentation, we no longer have a unified text but discursive fragments of issues, texts, arguments, and context. In his view, the role of the rhetorical critic is to invent a text "suitable for criticism."

In English departments the situation is more complicated. There is no metaphorical "school" of rhetorical criticism as there is of New Criticism, Russian Formalism, or Deconstructionism. However, over the years there have been scholars of Milton, Shakespeare, Donne, or Pope who have applied rhetoric to the analysis of imaginative literature, but who would not necessarily think of themselves as rhetorical critics. One of the earliest rhetorical critics in English departments is Wayne Booth, whose *Rhetoric of Fiction* is often cited as spreading interest in rhetorical criticism beyond the field of speech. Edward P.J. Corbett's *Rhetorical Analyses*

of Literary Works also contributed to a renewed interest in rhetorical criticism in English departments. Whereas Booth's book dealt with the rhetoric of fiction, Corbett's anthology presented a variety of critical objects, including poems, plays, fiction, apologies, history, and satire. Other critics who might loosely be called rhetorical, such as reader-response critics, structuralists, and deconstructionists, focused their analyses on a wide range of critical objects, including philosophical, literary, and critical texts composed in French, German, and English. But the rhetorical criticism of these scholars is neither a unified philosophy nor a coherent set of practices. It might best be summed up by Paul de Man's term *rhetoricity,* which he sees as a feature of all texts.

The Critical Method

Just as there is no single object of rhetorical criticism, there is no single or correct method that can be applied to all texts. Some critics believe that the critical object should determine the method. Others believe that it should come from an existing critical method or theory. Mark Klyn in "Toward a Pluralistic Rhetorical Criticism" argues that rhetorical criticism only means "intelligent writing about works of rhetoric . . . in whatever way the critic can manage it" (147).

In the period between 1925 and 1945, the dominant method in speech communication was Neo-Aristotelian Criticism. However, rhetorical critics drew not only on Aristotle but also on Cicero and Quintilian to analyze speeches and public address. But Edwin Black's *Rhetorical Criticism* and Donald C. Bryant's *Rhetorical Dimensions in Criticism* attacked Neo-Aristotelian Criticism for slavishly following the Aristotelian categories of invention, arrangement, style, memory, and delivery; the three modes of proof; and the three kinds of speeches. As a result of these and other criticisms, critics argued for a plurality of critical methods. Kenneth Burke's theory of dramatism was shown to be applicable to a variety of rhetorical texts. The first edition of Robert L. Scott's and Bernard L. Brock's *Methods of Rhetorical Criticism* listed the Neo-Aristotelian approach, the eclectic approach, the sociocultural-psychological approach, the grammatical-semantic approach, and the dramatistic approach. More recently, Roderick P. Hart's *Modern Rhetorical Criticism* and Sonja K. Foss's *Rhetorical Criticism* exemplify a variety of critical approaches, including narrative, generic, fantasy theme, Feminist, Marxist, deconstruction, and cultural, thus moving rhetorical criticism into literary theory and cultural studies.

In English departments, early on, the dominant method has been classical rhetoric. But Edward P.J. Corbett in *Rhetorical Analyses of Literary Works* argued that the rhetorical techniques and terms derived from Greek rhetoric could not be made to cover all kinds of literary texts, and he urged the use of new rhetorical methods and a new vocabulary.

Traditionally, scholars in English departments have distinguished rhetorical criticism from literary criticism. Yet Roman Jakobson, Jacques Lacan, Hayden White, J. Hillis Miller, Paul de Man, and Jacques Derrida have sometimes described the kind of critical analyses that they do as rhetorical. Although not all of these scholars were in English departments, their theories have been appropriated by scholars in English departments to analyze texts.

In "The Function of Rhetorical Study at the Present Time," J. Hillis Miller argues that the key to the integration of reading and writing in English departments is "rhetorical study." He labels deconstruction "a form of literary study that concentrates on the rhetoric of literary texts, taking rhetoric in the sense of the investigation of the role of figurative language in literature." In "Rethinking the Graduate Curriculum," Jonathan Culler calls for a revival of rhetoric and the use of rhetorical categories, particularly tropes, to describe how meaning is produced in discourse.

Roman Jakobson finds the distinction between metaphoric and metonymic processes in language useful to describe patterns of discourse. In a work of literature, for example, a discourse may move from topic to topic metaphorically or metonymically. These two poles of language are connected to the paradigmatic and syntagmatic relations of the sign and are modes of thinking common to everyone. Rhetorical analysis can get at these relationships. Lacan, following Jakobson, claims that Freud's dream processes show up in a dream as metaphor and metonymy. In elaborating unconscious dreams, the unconscious uses a veritable

"rhetoric." At the end of a Freudian interpretation, a dream is revealed as a configuration of densely packed figures. The task of the psychoanalyst is to get at those figures. Therefore, psychoanalysis is textual exegesis.

Rhetoric enters the historical text in any number of ways, according to Hayden White: in the mode of emplotment, in the mode of argument buried in the narrative, in the historian's ethical stance, and in the use of tropes. Since tropes are analogs of *topoi*, tropes are inventive strategies that historians use to prefigure the data of a historical field and constitute it as an object of thought.

The word *rhetoric* appears often in de Man's critical vocabulary. Following Nietzsche, de Man contends that the basic structure of language is figural (that is, rhetorical) rather than literal. In arguing with the French structuralists, who evidently saw no problem in assimilating rhetoric to grammar, de Man sees a radical discontinuity between the two. Rhetorical analysis, for de Man, consists of reading the literal as if it were figurative and the figurative as if it were literal.

Finally, Derrida maintains that it is impossible for philosophy to free itself from rhetoric or from literary devices. The use of tropes in philosophy is part of its strategy for producing changes in belief. These can't always be accomplished by straightforward rational argument. Tropes are rhetorical strategies that all writers use to change attitudes and gain adherence.

There is a growing belief in English departments that all criticism is rhetorical criticism and that the study of rhetoric is central to what they do. Jonathan Culler, for example, in *Framing the Sign,* comments that "a surprising number of thinkers have called for criticism to become a generalized rhetoric, studying the production, structure, and reception of texts of all sort." Stanley Fish, in *Is There a Text in This Class?*, argues that "no one can claim privilege for the point of view he [or she] holds and therefore everyone is obliged to practice the art of persuasion." In *Literary Theory,* Eagleton urges scholars in English departments to return to "the oldest form of literary criticism in the world"—rhetoric. If all criticism is rhetorical, then literary criticism is dissolving into rhetorical criticism, just as rhetorical criticism is dissolving into literary criticism.

Rhetoric of Inquiry

Increasingly, scholars in a variety of disciplines are talking about what they do in rhetorical terms. They are beginning to examine the kinds of writing they do as forms of persuasion. In the view of many of these scholars, all scholarly writing is rhetorical. Anthropology, whatever else it may be, is a kind of writing. Yet few anthropologists teach their students how to write or how to persuade audiences. Economics is a kind of persuasion. Yet few students know how economists argue. The writing of history is rhetorical. Yet few historians think of themselves as rhetoricians. Like their counterparts in anthropology or economics, they simply "write up" the results of their research. Law is more than a system of rules. It is an art of persuasion, and like rhetoric it is concerned with justice and injustice. Science uses argument, and its texts are designed to persuade.

This kind of talk about the rhetoric of scholarship has been labeled the *rhetoric of inquiry*. It was given impetus by scholars from the humanities, the social sciences, and the natural sciences who met at the University of Iowa from March 28 to March 31, 1984, to talk about the "rhetorical turn" in academic discourse. They were not the first, of course, to make academic discourse an object of rhetorical analysis. Hayden White has commented on the rhetorical nature of history writing. Derrida argues that philosophical writing is rhetorical through and through. What is new is that scholars, regardless of discipline, are asking how scholars actually argue, whether they use common topics, how they appeal to audiences, and so forth.

However, critics who attended the Iowa conference point out that in looking at how rhetoric is used in the various disciplines, it might be more proper to talk about *rhetorics* of inquiry, rather than the rhetoric of inquiry, because rhetoric has many different functions. John Lyne in "Rhetorics of Inquiry" lists five functions—rhetoric as argument, rhetoric as socializing discourse, rhetoric as configuration, rhetoric as critical practice, and rhetoric as a means of empowerment. As argument, rhetoric is the art of persuasion as practiced in each discipline. As socializing discourse, rhetoric constructs discourse communities. As configuration, rhetoric uses narrative plots and tropes to argue. As critical practice, rhetoric criticizes not only texts but also social institutions and practices, looking for instances of ideology and hegemony. And as a means of empowerment, rhetoric gives people power over situations.

Rhetoric and Cultural Studies

Although rhetorical criticism was not a critical method espoused by early proponents of cultural studies to "read" the lived experiences and texts of working-class culture, cultural studies is rhetorical through and through. The cultural studies movement began in Great Britain in the 1950s. It took *culture* as a contested term. To the earlier cultural critics, such as Raymond Williams, Richard Hoggart, and E.P. Thompson, culture is not something inscribed in high cultural texts. Nor is it to be identified with the aesthetic or with "the best that has been thought and said." Culture is the lived experience of working-class people—what they do for a living, what they read, what movies they see, what television shows they watch, and so forth.

The later cultural critics, such as Stuart Hall and Richard Johnson, at the Centre of Contemporary Cultural Studies in Birmingham, England, did not conceive of cultural studies as an academic discipline but as a field of study to which scholars in the different disciplines could contribute. Nevertheless, social scientists attacked cultural studies for overstepping its proper limits. Literary scholars regarded culture as embedded in the texts they were studying.

In contrast to literary studies, cultural studies takes neglected, everyday texts as its object of study. It analyzes, interprets, and evaluates texts taken from popular culture and the mass media such as film, television programs, radio broadcasts, newspapers, advertisements, popular romances, soap operas, and song lyrics. Or it might juxtapose the study of literary texts with the study of everyday texts, subjecting them to critical analysis, focusing on issues of class, education, gender, sex, race, and ethnicity.

Cultural studies uses, among other methods, the methods of literary criticism. In the 1950s the dominant methods used were historical materialism and ethnography. But more recently, scholars interested in the cultural studies approach are bringing a wide range of methodologies, including rhetoric, to bear on popular culture and cultural texts. What makes cultural criticism a kind of rhetorical criticism is the emphasis it places on the *effect* that discursive practices have on the lives of everyday people. To the extent that cultural studies submits issues of class, education, gender, sex, race, and ethnicity to theoretical critique, it is engaging in rhetorical criticism. To the extent that cultural studies points to instances of ideology and hegemony in everyday texts and shows how they operate to change attitudes and beliefs, it is engaging in rhetorical criticism. Rhetorical criticism, then, no longer has a unitary method or a fixed object. It is becoming instead a generalized rhetoric, using a variety of critical methods and focusing on a variety of texts.

Frank J. D'Angelo
Arizona State University

Bibliography

Black, Edwin B. *Rhetorical Criticism: A Study in Method.* New York: Macmillan, 1978.

Booth, Wayne C. *The Rhetoric of Fiction.* Chicago: U of Chicago P, 1961.

Brantlinger, Patrick. *Crusoe's Footprints: Cultural Studies in Britain and America.* London: Routledge, 1990.

Bryant, Donald C., ed. *Rhetorical Dimensions in Criticism.* Baton Rouge: Louisiana State UP, 1973.

Corbett, Edward P.J., ed. *Rhetorical Analyses of Literary Works.* New York: Oxford UP, 1969.

Culler, Jonathan. "Rethinking the Graduate Curriculum." *ADE Bulletin* 62 (September–November 1979): 19–26.

Eagleton, Terry. *Literary Theory: An Introduction.* Minneapolis: U of Minnesota P, 1983.

Easthope, Anthony. *Literary into Cultural Studies.* London: Routledge, 1991.

Fish, Stanley. *Is There a Text in This Class?* Cambridge, MA: Harvard UP, 1980.

Foss, Sonja K. *Rhetorical Criticism.* Prospect Heights, IL: Waveland, 1989.

Gaonkar, Dilip Parameshwar. "Object and Method in Rhetorical Criticism: From Wichelns to Leff and McGee." *Western Journal of Speech Communication* 54 (1990): 290–316.

Hall, Stuart. "Cultural Studies and the Centre: Some Problematics and Problems." *Culture, Media, Language.* Ed. Stuart Hall et al. London: Hutchinson, 1983. 15–47.

Hart, Roderick P. *Modern Rhetorical Criticism.* Glenview, IL: Scott, Brown Higher Education, 1990.

Johnson, Richard. "What Is Cultural Studies Anyway?" *Social Text* 6 (1987): 38–80.

Klyn, Mark S. "Toward a Pluralistic Rhetorical Criticism." *Essays on Rhetorical Criticism.* Ed. Thomas R. Nilsen. New York: Random, 1968. 146–57.

Lyne, John. "Rhetoric of Inquiry." *Quarterly Journal of Speech* 71 (1985): 65–73.

Miller, J. Hillis. "The Function of Rhetorical Study at the Present Time." *ADE Bulletin* 62 (September–November 1979): 10–18.

Nelson, John S., Allan Megill, and Donald N. McCloskey, eds. *The Rhetoric of the Human Sciences.* Madison: U of Wisconsin P, 1987.

Nilsen, Thomas R., ed. *Essays on Rhetorical Criticism:* New York: Random, 1968.

Scott, Robert L., and Bernard L. Brock, eds. *Methods of Rhetorical Criticism.* New York: Harper, 1972.

Simons, Herbert W., ed. *Rhetoric in the Human Sciences.* Newbury Park, CA: Sage, 1989.

Stewart, Charles J. "Historical Survey: Rhetorical Criticism in Twentieth Century America." *Explorations in Rhetorical Criticism.* Ed. G.P. Mohrmann, Charles J. Stewart, and Donovan J. Ochs. University Park: Pennsylvania State UP, 1973. 1–31.

Wichelns, Herbert A. "The Literary Criticism of Oratory." *Studies in Rhetoric and Public Speaking in Honor of James Albert Winans.* New York: Russell, 1962. 181–216.

Rhetorical Question

A stylistic approach to evoke emotion by posing a question that is not meant to be answered, where the answer itself is implied in the question. Used as an approach to gain attention, the timing and positioning of the words in a rhetorical question are carefully selected to surprise the respondent, invoke emotion, or appeal to one's sense of morals. Rhetorical questions are not used for information gathering but for effect.

As a form of irony, the position of the words in the question would make it impossible to answer the question without incriminating oneself. An example would be, "Do you still use drugs?" Another approach to the rhetorical question is to ask a series of questions, which again, are not meant to be answered but are used to elicit an emotional response. Politicians use this approach in their speeches: "Are we going to let them get away with this? Are we going to let the government take away everything we work for? Are we going to stand here and not fight back?" Along these same lines, to emphasize a point, one may quickly ask a series of questions, one following the other immediately: "You're leaving? When did you decide this? Why are you going? How are we going to get in touch with you?" Rhetorical questions can be used as an avenue to set up an ironic or sarcastic scene by asking a question that implies the opposite already took place, or by asking a question at an inappropriate moment: Handing back a failed paper to a student, the teacher remarks, "Study all night?"

This device is commonly found in classic texts, such as those by Plato, Isaeus, and especially in Demosthenes.

Diane L. Hendrix
New Mexico State University

Bibliography

Corbett, Edward P.J. *Classical Rhetoric for the Modern Student*. New York: Oxford UP, 1971.

Cuddon, J.A. *A Dictionary of Literary Terms and Literary Theory*. 3rd ed. Worcester, MA: Andre Deutsch, 1977.

Fogelin, Robert J. *Figuratively Speaking*. New Haven: Yale UP, 1988.

Holman, C. Hugh, and William Harmon. *A Handbook to Literature*. 5th ed. New York: Macmillan, 1986.

Preminger, Alex, ed. *The Princeton Handbook of Poetic Terms*. Princeton: Princeton UP, 1986.

Rhetoric and Fiction

Denotes the techniques writers use to influence the emotions, knowledge, beliefs, opinions, values, and judgments of their audiences. Although fictional rhetoric has been an object of critical concern since Plato's banning of poetry from the ideal state because it appeals to the passions rather than reason, the intensive study of rhetoric in fiction is a twentieth-century phenomenon that begins with Henry James and is significantly advanced through the work of Wayne C. Booth, Gérard Genette, and Mikhail Bakhtin—and of course through the larger critical discussions surrounding these figures. In the prefaces to the New York edition of his novels (1907–1909), James, in richly metaphoric language, discusses the evolution of his techniques, especially his preference for narrating through the central consciousness of a character and, more generally, for scenic presentation of information and character rather than for narrative summary. James's preferences gradually became codified into Rules for Writers based on the assumption that dramatic presentation is more objective, less rhetorical and, therefore, more artistic than summary or commentary from an omniscient narrator. The primary rules were show don't tell, prefer scene to summary, use first-person or third-person center of consciousness narration rather than omniscient narration.

Booth's *Rhetoric of Fiction* argues against the codification of these rules by exposing the problems of the underlying assumption. All techniques, Booth shows, have rhetorical dimensions; the writer's choice is not between rhetoric and objectivity but among different kinds of rhetoric. Booth argues further that judgments about a writer's choices ought not to be made by applying abstract rules; instead, such judgments should be made according to how a particular rhetorical means contributes to a larger artistic end. Booth also develops a set of influential concepts for analyzing author-narrator-reader relationships. A writer creates an *implied author*—that is, a "second self" who is the consciousness behind all the choices made in writing the fiction. The implied author, in turn, creates a narrator—that is, the voice and perspective from which the action is recounted. The narrator may be *reliable,* in which case he will speak in accordance with the norms of the implied author, or *unreliable,* in which case he will deviate from those norms. The reader of an unreliable narrator will be aware of considerable *distance* between that narrator and the implied author; the reader of a reliable narrator will sense minimal distance between the two.

Gérard Genette, in his three-volume *Figures*, portions of which have been translated as *Narrative Discourse: An Essay in Method* (1980) and *Figures of Literary Discourse* (1982), develops an additional set of concepts for analyzing narrative discourse. First, he divides point of view into the distinct categories of *vision*—who sees—and *voice*—who speaks. Sometimes narrative discourse will offer both the vision and voice of a single consciousness (narrator's or character's) as, for example, in the first sentence of *Middlemarch*: "Miss Brooke had that kind of beauty which seems to be thrown into relief by poor dress." At others it will split vision from voice, as, for example, when the mature narrator's voice in Joyce's

"Araby" describes the young boy's vision of his feelings about Mangan's sister: "my body was like a harp and her words and gestures were like fingers running upon the wires."

Genette also points out that classifying points of view according to differences in grammatical person is misleading, since any narration implies a speaker and, hence, the grammatical first person. Genette proposes instead the term *homodiegetic* to refer to a narrator who is capable of interacting with characters and, thus, exists at the same fictional (or diegetic) level as they do, and the term *heterodiegetic* to refer to a narrator who observes the world of the characters but is not herself an actor in that world. Thus, for example, Huck Finn is homodiegetic, Eliot's narrator in *Middlemarch* is heterodiegetic, and the Showman of *Vanity Fair* shifts between the two. Genette also develops the concepts of *order, duration,* and *frequency* in order to refine the analysis of narrative representations of time. Order refers to the relation between chronological sequence and discourse sequence: In his analysis of Proust, Genette shows how easily narrative discourse lends itself to analepsis (flashback) and prolepsis (flashforward) and how these manipulations of order can intersect with variations in duration and frequency. Duration refers to the comparative lengths of story time and discourse time; a period of several years may be narrated in one sentence or a period of a few moments may be narrated for pages or even chapters. Frequency refers to the relation between repetition in story time and repetition in discourse time: An event that occurs only once in story time may be returned to again and again in the discourse, whereas frequently repeated events in the story may be summarized in a single sentence in the discourse.

Bakhtin's work, conducted in Russia in the 1920s and 1930s, became well known in the United States and Western Europe only in the 1980s. His books, *The Dialogic Imagination, Problems of Dostoyevsky's Poetics,* and *Rabelais and His World,* propose a view of narrative discourse as shot through with ideological values and of narrative itself, especially the novel, as the genre that uses discourse to put social values into dialogic relations with each other. Bakhtin's view of narrative discourse derives from his more general conception that a given national language is not a unified system but rather a collection of mini-languages— for example, the language of the aristocracy, the language of the working class, the language of the academy, each of which reflects the social values of its group. In representing diverse characters, the novel naturally represents these different mini-languages or, to use Bakhtin's term, tends toward *heteroglossia.* Different novelists will establish different dialogic relations among these mini-languages: Some will clearly privilege one over others or use one to expose the values of others, and, in so doing, may either reinforce the existing hierarchy of dialogic relations in society or critique it; other novelists, such as Dostoyevsky, for whom Bakhtin reserves his highest praise, may make several languages and their attendant ideological values equally attractive and in this way may resolve their plots without resolving their dialogues.

Many other critics and theorists have sought to continue the work of Booth, Genette, and Bakhtin (see Chatman and Rimmon-Kenan), and some of the more promising current work focuses on complicating the rhetorical formalism of Booth and Genette with the concern for the relation between technique and ideology reflected in Bakhtin's work (see Rabinowitz and Lanser). Furthermore, the work of Booth, Genette, and Bakhtin intersects in complex ways with work in reader-response criticism. But rather than continuing what is inevitably a superficial survey, I would like to round off this entry by illustrating how the concepts I have discussed can be usefully applied. Consider this short passage from Charlotte Brontë's *Jane Eyre,* part of Jane's account of her flight from Thornfield:

I would have got past Mr. Rochester's chamber without a pause; but my heart momentarily stopping its beat at that threshold, my foot was forced to stop also. No sleep was there: the inmate was walking restlessly from wall to wall; and again and again he sighed while I listened. There was a heaven—a temporary heaven—in this room for me, if I chose: I had but to go in and to say—

"Mr. Rochester, I will love you and live with you through life till death," and a fount of rapture would spring to my lips. I thought of this.

That kind master, who could not sleep now, was waiting with impatience for the day. He would send for me in the morning; I should be gone. He would have me sought for: vainly. He would feel himself forsaken; his love rejected: he would suffer; perhaps grow desperate. I thought of this too. My hand moved toward the lock. I caught it back and glided on. Drearily I wound my way downstairs.

In James's terms, this passage is a scene rather than a summary; Brontë is showing rather than telling. Consequently, the rhetoric of the passage invites its reader to reach most of her conclusions through inference. We are required to be active readers here, in part because the homodiegetic narrator is giving us her vision and voice at the time of the action (though the use of the subjunctive subtly reminds the reader of the retrospection). The technique—and our active inferencing—add to the dramatic power of the scene, a desirable effect here because of the centrality of Jane's relationship to Rochester to the whole narrative. This event comes in the chronological order that Jane's account, for the most part, follows, and this is the first and last time that the event will be narrated. It is the climax of the series of events, again unfolded in the discourse according to the chronology of story, that began with Jane's initial meeting of Rochester, developed into their courtship and engagement, and suddenly got reversed by the revelation of Rochester's marriage to Bertha Mason. Although it is difficult to determine how long in story time Jane stood in front of Rochester's door, Brontë certainly extends the moment in the discourse by stopping to reveal what Jane heard, what she thought, what she imagined saying. Furthermore, she breaks the description of Jane's hand movement over two sentences ("My hand moved toward the lock. I caught it back and glided on"), a device which seems to suggest that the movement was slow and that she hesitated before either seizing the handle or pulling back. The dramatic quality of the scene, its singularity in Jane's account, and the extended duration combine to stress its importance in both Jane's life and her narrative.

In looking at the norms in play here, we see that the scene emphasizes the conflict between Jane's sense of rectitude and the desires of her heart. Jane knows that she cannot accept Rochester's offer to live with him while he is married to Bertha, knows that she must leave Thornfield. But Brontë knows that in order to

show the depth of Jane's feeling, this leave-taking cannot be easy. By the end of the passage, we certainly feel that Jane has acted in accord with the norms of the implied author. But Brontë also introduces some slight distance into the scene, also asks us to see more than Jane realizes that she is telling us. The first distance comes in Jane's explanation of why she stops before Rochester's door: because her heart stops, her foot is also "forced" to stop. The distance occurs with Jane's choice of *forced*, a word that Bakhtin would call "double-voiced" because it simultaneously participates in the discourses of two different languages. In Jane's overt discourse, the word is part of a physiological discourse, implying some connection between the arrest of her heart and that of her foot. But the word also participates in the discourse of romantic love—Jane's heart stops because it is overflowing with feeling, and this overflow of feeling "forces" her to stop at Rochester's door. *Forced* is both an apt and a misleading term: Jane must stop, she cannot simply walk past Rochester's room, but she also stops voluntarily, following the dictates of her heart.

Before following out what her sense of rectitude tells her she is also "forced" to do, she gives her imagination some play, as she thinks about the alternative to leaving. Brontë introduces a dialogue between the language of incarceration—Rochester is an "inmate"—and the language of romantic love—his room is a potential "heaven"; her promise would be to love and live "through life till death"; "a fount of rapture" is waiting for her. By giving in to the dictates of her heart, she could turn Rochester's room from a prison cell into a bower of bliss.

Jane's imagination goes further and projects itself into his state of mind and proleptically into the probable future. She thinks through the stages of a narrative whose culmination would surely be Rochester's suffering and even perhaps his suicide. It's almost as if she is painting the picture bleakly enough and dwelling on each stage just long enough to justify changing her mind: How could I do this to him? It wouldn't be fair. This prolepsis not only reveals the power of Jane's temptation and the depth of her investment in the ideology of romantic love but it also invites questions about the motives behind her imagined narrative. In attributing so much to Rochester's feelings, she is also telling us volumes about her own. The apparently altruistic appeal of her narrative—

how can I make him suffer so?—gives way to our recognition of what she does not fully admit, the power of her own desire—how can I make myself suffer so?

Brontë takes Jane right to the edge, moving her hand toward the lock, until suddenly Jane's sense of rectitude reasserts itself. The language of romantic love drops out and Brontë returns to unadorned narration—"I caught it back and glided on." Having seen the power of Jane's temptation so vividly, we are left to infer the superior strength of her will and her sense of rectitude. It would be extremely difficult for Brontë to show this strength without overt moralizing, without in fact destroying the mimetic power of the scene. She lets the cost to Jane be conveyed in the now heavily loaded adverb of the last sentence: "Drearily I wound my way downstairs." Brontë asks her reader both to admire Jane's strength and to understand and sympathize with heart's desire. Powerful as they already are, this scene and these norms are given even more importance later, when the implied author endorses Jane's rejection of St. John's appeal to her sense of rectitude in favor of the dictates of her heart, dictates that take the form of Rochester's voice calling to her across the miles.

James Phelan
Ohio State University

Bibliography

Bakhtin, Mikhail. *The Dialogic Imagination: Four Essays*. Ed. Michael Holquist. Trans. Caryl Emerson and Michael Holquist. Austin: U of Texas P, 1981. Original Russian ed., *Voprosy Literary I: Estetiki*, 1975.

———. *Problems of Doestoyevsky's Poetics*. Trans. Caryl Emerson. Minneapolis: U of Minnesota P, 1984. Russian ed., 1965.

———. *Rabelais and His World*. Trans. Helene Iswolsky. Cambridge, MA: MIT P, 1968. Russian ed., 1965.

Booth, Wayne C. *The Rhetoric of Fiction*. 2nd ed. Chicago: U of Chicago P, 1983.

Chatman, Seymour. *Coming to Terms*. Ithaca, NY: Cornell UP, 1991.

———. *Story and Discourse: Narrative Structure in Fiction and Film*. Ithaca, NY: Cornell UP, 1978.

Genette, Gérard. *Figures*. Paris: Seuil, 1966.

———. *Figures II*. Paris: Seuil, 1969.

———. *Figures III*. Paris: Seuil, 1972.

Lanser, Susan Sniader. *Fictions of Authority: Women Writers and Narrative Voice*. Ithaca, NY: Cornell UP, 1992.

Rabinowitz, Peter J. *Before Reading: Narrative Conventions and the Politics of Interpretation*. Ithaca, NY: Cornell UP, 1987.

Rimmon-Kenan, Shlomith. *Narrative Discourse: Contemporary Poetics*. London: Methuen, 1983.

Veeder, William, and Susan Griffin. *The Art of Criticism: Henry James on the Theory and Practice of Fiction*. Chicago: U of Chicago P, 1986.

Rhetoric and Poetry

Relationship between rhetoric and poetry. If separation of the two arts, rhetoric and poetry, is a desideratum, we have Aristotle to thank for our first and most enduring example of how the separation is to be conducted. Western literary tradition, *mutatis mutandis* and with very few serious challenges, has accepted his example as embodied in the *Rhetoric* and the *Poetics*. But some of the acceptances might have astonished, if not appalled, Aristotle. Here is T.S. Eliot, echoing John Stuart Mill, on true poetry: "If the author never spoke to himself, the result would not be poetry, though it might be magnificent rhetoric." The poet under this dispensation must be "speaking to himself—or nobody," relegating the rest of us to the role of eavesdroppers. This version of the separation concedes rather too much to rhetoric. For Aristotle, after all, the highest type of poetry, tragedy, is also the most rhetorical. And he would hardly be prepared to accommodate Homer and Hesiod, neither of whom is much given to speaking to himself, as subspecies of rhetoric.

Aristotle, of course, was not on the side of a "pure" poetry, composed and heard in splendid isolation. Though he seems to view the two arts as having fundamentally different ends—for rhetoric, practical persuasion; for poetry, aesthetic pleasure—he sees places for their convergence. For example, when in the *Poetics* he discusses thought or reasoning (*dianoia*), he refers to the section in the *Rhetoric* that treats of the same subject. Further, critics have often noted how heavily the latter work relies on poetry for its examples, a fact that suggests that he saw nothing wrong with the dependence, at times, of one art on the other.

But perhaps the most significant area of convergence appears in the species of rhetoric Aristotle terms epideictic or ceremonial. In this species is found oratory that, through praise or blame, affirms and sometimes reforms, the values of a community, often foregrounding some individual as example. But the category has proved somewhat troubling for critics, and for the obvious reason that, unlike the other two species—forensic (juridical) and deliberative (political) debate—it does not accomplish its ends by argument for or against some judgment or action. The asymmetry here has sometimes prompted a dismissal of epideictic as relatively unserious, more a mode of self-display, removed from practical concerns, from—in Cicero's phrase—"the battles of life," and thus free to indulge in verbal pyrotechnics. While it can provide material for the other two, it cannot in itself claim equal status with them, being—Cicero again—"fitter for the parade than for the battle . . . spurned and rejected in the forum," and mainly of use as a schoolboy's drill for serious things to come.

Such interpretations—and they did not end with Cicero—recognize a real inconsistency in the *Rhetoric,* and this inconsistency can be read another way. This way understands epideictic as the oldest of the three species and, as some critics (Elroy Bundy, for example, and Jeffrey Walker) have argued, it finds its roots in the Greek poetic tradition. In Hesiod's *Theogony* (c. 700 B.C.E.), the Muse Kalliope "grants her ready attendance to honorable kings," whose inspired speech explains laws, dispenses justice, and settles serious disputes. This surely suggests an understanding of rhetoric, though one founded in powers that preside over *poiesis,* the making of poetry.

One kind of such making was the ceremonial poem celebrating victory at the Games (*epinikion* or *enkomion*), those of Pindar being the most famous. In these, the victor's home, family, background, and character are drawn upon to compose poetry that is surely epideictic, its relation to ceremonial prose hardly at issue—certainly not to the post-Aristotelian rhetoricians who admitted all kinds of poetry, not just that of praise or blame, into the epideictic category.

Thus if we cannot propose a simple and exhaustive definition of the kinship (or differences) between rhetoric and poetry, we can at least recognize that they converge at important points. We can perhaps go further and assert that poetics must be a part of any rhetoric with pretenses to being complete, just as rhetoric must be a part of any poetics that claims to be inclusive. The poetics of rhetoric is found most obviously in the concern for stylistic means—the use of trope, say, or syntactic patterning—and, more subtly, in the concern for projecting credible ethical presence. The rhetoric of poetry is pervasive, entering wherever there is concern for effects on audience expectation.

It would appear, then, that in the matter of the separateness of the two arts, much depends on *how* separate separate is.

Aristotle (in Kennedy's translation) defines the art of rhetoric as "an ability, in each [particular] case, to see the available means of persuasion." If epideictic is part of rhetoric and also exploits poetic means for its somewhat special ends, Aristotle's definition can be made to apply to certain kinds of poetry: those which, like certain kinds of rhetoric, deploy means to compose a discourse that, in professor Kennedy's words, "praises, corrects, modifies, or strengthens an audience's belief about civic virtue or the reputation of an individual." The convergence of the two arts here is so obvious that any account that ignores the strong presence of either is incomplete.

It is, however, possible to conflate the rhetoric and poetics, or subordinate one to the other, in ways that distort them or play down their real differences. There is, in fact, a sort of tradition of antiseparatism, wherein one of the arts dominates the other: poetics in Gorgias and "Longinus"; rhetoric in Horace (of "*Ars poetica*") and, in the Renaissance, Robortello. Edmund Burke in the mid eighteenth century offers a suggestive alternative to radical separation in an argument against Aristotle's poetics of mimesis (representation, imitation). Burke observes that both arts "do not exceed in exact description so well as painting does: their business is to effect rather by sympathy than imitation; to display the effect of things on the mind of the speaker, or of others, than to present a clear idea of the things themselves." If in this passage "the mind of the speaker" suggests an expressive rather than a persuasive purpose—anticipating Romantic aesthetics—still Burke recognizes a critical truth frequently overlooked: that imitation is but one means, not the defining characteristic, of poetry, and the analysis of (rhetorical) effect is a better way of understanding the workings of poetry than exploring its proximity to some model.

Antiseparatists, of course, owe much to Socrates, Plato, and Aristotle; but perhaps even more to Isocrates, whose ideal was a practical rhetoric grounded in a principled, philosophic one, embodied in the best epideictic and poetic models. This was Cicero's ideal, for all his contempt for display, and also the ideal of Quintilian and Aristides.

In our own day, Wayne Booth has brought the two arts together without subverting the integrity of either. Reminding us of the dangers of a formalist version of Aristotle and the ideal of a "pure" art, he insists that we must accept the presence of a rhetorical element in the very inception of a literary work: "At the instant when [Henry] James exclaims to himself, 'Here is my subject!' a rhetorical aspect is contained within the conception: the subject is thought of as *something that can be made public,* something that can be made into a communicated work. Insofar as it turns out to be a true subject, its means of communication will spring from the essence and seem, when perfected, in harmony with it."

And thus we come back to "available means." But critics wary of any conflation of the arts argue that ends, not means, are the distinguishing criteria in this matter, and rhetorical ends have to do with practical reality, not some imagined representation of it offered for aesthetic pleasure. And this is perhaps why, as did Cicero, they find it expedient to demote epideictic rhetoric to a form of personal display. But at least on the level of theory, even if we grant a profound difference in ends between practical and ceremonial rhetoric, we cannot dismiss their sharing of means, and it would seem wise here to follow the sensible judgment of Quintilian when he notes that "all three kinds rely on mutual assistance of the other."

This is not to deny differences in the two arts, but these might be better understood, not as categorical but as matters of degree and emphasis spread along a continuum whose one extreme would be the most commonplace court case, whose other would be Mallarmé's purest poem. Between lies a vast range of choices, each a member of one whole, a family in Wittgenstein's sense, where "a" and "z" are distant kin but still kin.

This unschematic scheme would still allow for important differences that operate where one art (a name now, not for a thing, but for a sector of choice) leaves off and another begins. Difference would now, as in practice it does, leave room for overlap and convergence. For example, one difference of poetry is that it often transcends its occasion—we still read Homer, Sappho, Pindar. But then we still read the "Gettysburg Address." Again, poets have the power to represent many voices, but so have orators when occasions require. And again, poems are usually constituted of especially intense patterns of syntax, figure, and idea. But so too is the prose of Gorgias, John Lilly, and Sir Thomas Browne. And finally, poems are usually composed in meter, except of course for prose-poems and free verse. And Aristotle himself—perhaps unfairly—withheld the term *poem* from versified philosophy because it was not mimetic.

In fact, what a study of rhetoric and poetry seems to suggest is that rigorous, all-or-none schemes of definition and difference do not much reflect actual practice in these arts, and that we had better be ready to accept considerable ambiguity in their relationship. For if they are not one, neither are they quite two. And further, we must learn to accept the unromantic pragmatism that dictates actual compositional practice of even the purest authors. In a famous poem, Rilke, contemplating a beautiful, though headless, statue of Apollo, turns in the last line to his audience and in a flagrantly rhetorical gesture, declares: "You must change your life." Thus, a poem that might have been expected to offer only aesthetic pleasure suddenly demands that we act, that we see the statue, maimed though it is, as a sort of proof that something is wrong with our lives, and an aesthetic end becomes also an argumentative one.

The lesson Rilke's example offers us is that the individual artist—rhetorician or poet—will use any means available, whatever its name or class, to consummate a desired end. Our theories ought then, to reflect this reality if they are to be taken as serious accounts of the way rhetoric and poetry actually work.

Leonard Nathan
University of California

Bibliography

Aristotle. *On Rhetoric: A Theory of Civil Discourse.* Trans. George A. Kennedy. New York: Oxford UP, 1991.

———. *Poetics.* Trans. Richard Janko. Indianapolis, IN: Hackett, 1985.

Booth, Wayne C. *The Rhetoric of Fiction.* Chicago: U of Chicago P, 1961.

Crane, R.S., ed. *Critics and Criticism: Ancient and Modern.* Chicago: U of Chicago P, 1952.

Russell, D.A. *Criticism in Antiquity.* Berkeley: U of California P, 1981.

Walker, Jeffrey. "Aristotle's Lyric: Re-Imagining the Rhetoric of Epideictic Song." *College English* 51 (1989): 5–28.

Wimsatt, W.K., and Cleanth Brooks. *Literary Criticism: A Short History.* New York: Knopf, 1957.

Rhetoric and Psychiatry

Rhetorical perspective as applied to the theory and practice of psychiatry. Until recently, the field of rhetoric has largely overlooked one of the most effective rhetorical systems in existence: the rhetoric of the theory and practice of psychiatry. It is difficult to account for this, except to speculate that in much of the extant work on health communication that has a psychiatric component psychiatric orthodoxies often provide accepted and unexamined foundations and premises for theory and practice. Regardless, major communications journals have published virtually no significant rhetorical analysis or rhetorical criticism of the concepts and practices of psychiatry. Yet for over a generation, the disciplines of psychiatry and clinical psychology, along with the practice of psychotherapy, have been the subject of critical analysis by scholars outside of rhetoric, some of whom utilize rhetorical perspectives in their critiques.

Psychiatrist Thomas Szasz is by consensus the most important critic of psychiatry and psychoanalysis, and his criticism has been largely framed from a rhetorical perspective. Szasz's theories of what psychiatry, psychology, and the other fields of mental health deal with and how these professions sell themselves have considerable implications for rhetorical study.

Since his 1960 publication of *The Myth of Mental Illness*, a depiction of "mental illness" not as disease but as semiotic behavior, he has been prolific in arguing that the behavior we call "mental illness" rarely is the result of brain disease, and represent instead unusual or unacceptable communication.

Thus, Szasz argues that to understand both the behavior called "mental illness" and the practice called "psychotherapy" one must understand not medicine but rhetoric and metaphor: "Psychiatry, using the methods of communication analysis, has much in common with the sciences concerned with the study of languages and communicative behavior. In spite of this connection between psychiatry and such disciplines as symbolic logic, semiotics, and sociology, problems of mental health continue to be cast in the traditional framework of medicine" (1974:3). Psychiatry is, therefore, ultimately a linguistic enterprise closely related in the tradition of Aristotle to ethics and politics (Szasz 1961:212) and having as its end moral suasion rather than medical cures. Only if psychiatry is understood as rhetoric and persuasion, rather than medical science, can one begin to understand, for example, why psychiatrists are seen as medical practitioners even though they don't practice medicine; people are seen as patients despite the fact that they have no demonstrable illness; and psychiatrists' nonscientific and nonmedical opinions are seen as scientifically and medically based.

Szasz and others who attack the medical model of mental health claim that these communications and behaviors are labeled as "illness" for the purpose of strategic persuasion and for the purpose of effecting social control. Moreover, Szasz maintains, the mental health industry enjoys much immunity from scrutiny and criticism due to its medical ethos.

Szasz argues that what we call psychiatric "treatments" or "therapies," from the "talking cures" of psychotherapies to provocative sexual therapies, to the sometimes torturous "behavioral therapies," are pseudomedicine, though he does not maintain that such interventions do not help some people improve the quality of their lives.

In what is essentially rhetorical criticism, Szasz argues that the metaphors and paradigms of illness and science that underlie psychiatric research and therapeutic methods are either incomplete or, worse, misleading and deceptive. Recent attacks on the mental health field in general and psychoanalysis in particular have been particularly virulent. For example, the trial of John Hinckley tended to demystify psychiatry and psychiatrists for much of the public. Hinckley was found not guilty by reason of insanity in the attempted assassination of President Reagan, unleashing public outrage and causing general public skepticism regarding the "diagnostic" integrity of psychiatrists and psychologists, particularly in the forensic setting. To many, Hinckley seemed simply dangerous and self-indulgent, not bizarre or legally "insane." Under pressure in the wake of the Hinckley acquittal, the American Psychiatric Association and the American Bar Association, among other medical and psychological associations, created ad hoc committees on the insanity plea that examined the plea by focusing on its language and rhetoric.

Much of the onslaught against the scientism of psychiatry has focused on Freudian psychoanalysis (perhaps because of the cost), the perceived elitism and arrogance of its practitioners, and its hierarchical position as the granddaddy of psychotherapy. Freudian theory is now experiencing the greatest avalanche of criticism, much of it rhetorically based, since Karl Popper's landmark attack almost a generation ago, in which he saw psychoanalysis as "pseudo-science" and compared the psychoanalytic theories of Freud, Adler, and Jung to "astrological lore."

Attacks on Freudian theory and therapy have expanded to include imputation of sexism as well as the charge by Jeffrey Masson (detailed in his 1984 work, *The Assault on Truth*), who was director of the Sigmund Freud Archives, that Freud suppressed evidence in molding his seduction theory. But the most enduring and penetrating attack has been the rhetorical assault on the foundation of the scientific metaphor in psychoanalytic theory: its claim of a "scientific" basis for its theories and practices. Such attacks on the central metaphor of the helping professions imply as well the invalidity of much psychiatric and clinical psychological theory and practice.

It was Sigmund Freud's goal, he wrote, "to furnish a psychology which shall be a natural science." Those who consider Freud's theories "scientific" sometimes appear to mean that whatever "scientists" do is, ipso facto, science. And since the vast majority of psychoanalysts hold M.D. degrees, they are by this view practicing "science." Critics who argue that Freudian theories and practices are not scientific often argue that, to be scientific, an enterprise must rely on the application of a specifiable method—that is, the scientific method. Freudian theory, they maintain, does not.

Most conspicuous in reaction to the identity crisis in mental health is the coming of the "new biologism" or "molecular psychiatry." New technology, such as positron-emission transverse tomography (PETT), permits the tracing of biochemical changes in the brain. This and other advances have created a new flourishing field of biological psychiatry, a field whose public relations have created another mystifying myth about the nature of present-day psychiatry, for biological psychiatry is populated by less than a small minority of psychiatrists and a much, much smaller population of the mental health field in general.

The rhetorical implications of the heralded neuropsychiatric frontier are significant for both the direction and selling of psychiatry. We are in the throes of an acclaimed revolution in psychiatry of which it is said, for example, in a recent Pulitzer Prize–winning series of newspaper articles, that "psychiatry today stands on the threshold of becoming an exact science" (Franklin). The rhetorical perspective on psychiatry and psychoanalysis represents the major critique of this view, a view that is widely shared by both professionals and the public.

Richard E. Vatz
Towson State University
Lee S. Weinberg
University of Pittsburgh

Bibliography

Conrad, Peter, and Joseph W. Schneider, eds. *Deviance and Medicalization: From Badness to Sickness.* St. Louis: Mosby, 1980.

Franklin, Jon. "The Mind Fixers." *Baltimore Evening Sun.* July 23–31, 1984.

Szasz, Thomas. *The Myth of Mental Illness: Foundations of a Theory of Personal Conduct.* 2nd ed. New York: Harper, 1974.

———. *The Myth of Psychotherapy: Mental Healing as Religion, Rhetoric, and Repression.* Garden City, NY: Anchor, 1978.

Vatz, Richard E., and Lee S. Weinberg. "The Rhetorical Paradigm in Psychiatric History: Thomas Szasz and the Myth of Mental Illness." *Discovering the History of Psychiatry.* Ed. Mark Micale and Roy Porter. New York: Oxford UP, 1993.

Vatz, Richard E., and Lee S. Weinberg, eds. *Thomas Szasz: Primary Values and Major Contentions.* Buffalo: Prometheus, 1983.

Rhetoric and Technology

A topic or a field of rhetorical practice concentrating on the ethical and political relationships between technical instrumentalities, systems of discourse used to interpret these instrumentalities, and the meaning of "technology" itself.

The rhetorical study of technology has developed in two primary directions. The first treats technology as a topic or an exigence in contemporary rhetoric. Bytwerk's set of recommendations for implementing new technologies provides an early example of this approach. Hyde develops the critical potential of this perspective, arguing that rhetoricians should scrutinize technology with a philosophical rigor wherein examination elucidates understanding, understanding promotes open communication, and communication encourages further questioning. Farrell and Goodnight exemplify this approach in a critique focusing on technological language's inability to explain the breakdown at the Three Mile Island nuclear power generation plant. Postman's incisive critique of technology in *Technopoly: The Surrender of Culture to Technology* spans the distance between the first type of analysis, which is grounded in neo-Aristotelian criticism, and the second, which takes a more radical approach. The book's broad appeal indicates the developing public interest in technological critique. In it he speaks eloquently of the need to offer resistance against technological assumptions that shape attitudes and direct behavior in contemporary life. The second research trend is grounded in Heidegger's claim that the ethos of technological society resides in instrumental consciousness, which is both logically and historically prior to any given technology. It relies on Ellul's concept of "la technique," or the reduction of everything in the world, including humans, to a derivative status as means to something else. Ellul's work emphasizes that criticism of the cultural transformations caused by technology must entail careful examination of the particularly influential effects of communication technologies. Miller offers one of the first rhetorical analyses of technological consciousness, explaining how it influences debates over both specific technologies and broad social issues. Medhurst, Gonzalez, and Peterson argue that the roots of the technological ethos are found in general cultural presuppositions about discourse itself.

Perhaps no structure of relevance has had a more pronounced effect on contemporary Western culture than that embodied in the term *technology*. The technological society is manifested not only in the form of technically sophisticated instruments but also in the patterns of thinking and valuing that motivate and warrant the behavioral habits of its citizens. The term *technology* comes from two Greek words— *technê* and *logos*—that were central terms for classical rhetorical theory. Classical rhetoric can be read as an ongoing debate between these two concepts. From one perspective rhetoric was considered to be a craft *(technê)*, while from the other it was conceived of as a creative art that primarily relied on invention, reason, and judgment *(logos)*.

Despite the theoretical distinctions that can be made between science and technology, the history of modern technology is also a history of science. In other words, the growth of technology is largely the result of technology's appropriation of scientific values ranging from measurement to rationality. One can, however, draw a fundamental distinction between technology and science by examining the purpose of each. While the traditional goal of science is the discovery of universal truths, technology aims to accomplish something that becomes possible because of the truths understood to science. This leads to the general conclusion that technology serves an instrumental function. Rather than seeking to discover, it utilizes discovery to achieve a predetermined end.

Given technology's instrumental nature, studies of specific technologies tend to rely on the criterion of effectiveness to evaluate the interpretation and use of technical information in policy deliberations. They suggest message strategies and language choices that can be used to construct images emphasizing the benefits of novel and large-scale technical systems. For example, Bytwerk suggests that proponents of a new technology should (1) keep the debate low key, (2) minimize any negative or harmful effects of the technology, and (3) demonstrate practical benefits of the technology.

Contemporary rhetorical analysts who treat technology as a topic of study use knowledge of rhetorical conventions to interpret the relationship between technology and society. Most of the literature following this path applies well-known theoretical approaches to the study of society's relationship with technology in general, or with specific technologies. This relationship is shown either to reinforce or interfere with attempts to improve the human condition. A large body of work examines difficulties associated with transmitting and translating messages containing complex information. Although not explicitly acknowledged, much of the burgeoning field of "risk communication" relies on concepts developed in traditional rhetoric. This work analyzes both means whereby technology can be made palatable to the general public, and social problems associated with its development.

Analyses of problems associated with new technologies examine the impact of these technologies on traditional institutions and the impact of an increasing preference for technical reasoning and instrumental values in new contexts. For example, the use of computers in the public schools fundamentally alters the educational system, and the use of instrumental reasoning to decide whether to have children does the same for the family context. In each case behavior and ideas that are not conducive to a given technique's instrumentality are reduced or eliminated by the technique.

The failure of an unreflective reliance upon technology to manage adequately social and political situations has been further noted. Postman offers a biting critique of technological society in which he points out that because of the close relationship between technology and science, the two become melded into the rhetorical persona of the expert. Technical discourse, then, derives authority by intimidating the public with its complexity. He examines both the strategies and social consequences of marginalizing nonexperts when deliberating solutions to social problems. The increasing acceptance of technical jargon in which to discuss public issues leads to intimidation and limited participation by those whose lives are directly affected by policy decisions. Within this scenario discussions of topics such as nuclear energy, genetic engineering, and space-based defense systems evolve into lectures wherein experts command docility rather than participation from their audience.

Farrell and Goodnight's critique highlights the failure of technical knowledge to resolve social, ethical, or political dilemmas. They argue that in public, deliberative discourse, technical reasoning becomes the dominant force constraining decision-making. The cultural preeminence of technical reasoning severely restricts the range of responses available to rhetors who need to respond to exigencies created by technological failures, such as the partial meltdown at the Three Mile Island nuclear power generation plant. Critiques such as these point out that the primacy of technology has scrambled traditional patterns of familial, organizational, and political communication without offering alternative designs. Accordingly, the most dangerous aspect of technology, and its accompanying instrumental reasoning, is not that it alters or replaces social values and norms, but that it trivializes the very concept of normative structures.

One potential weakness of the approach described above is that it invites either the glorification or vilification of technology. Hyde argues that this dichotomous perspective toward technology is dysfunctional. He writes that criticism of technology must move beyond the limitations of either/or to a dialectical pro-gression of questioning that elucidates understanding. Without this more holistic approach, society either trusts technology completely or distrusts and wants to abandon it. In both situations a thorough critique becomes unfeasible. In the first, society allows a lazy contentment to prevent it from questioning technology; in the second, it allows the discomfort that accompanies lack of understanding to block questions to technology.

The most significant advantage of the dialectical approach toward the analysis of technology is that reflection serves as the critical impulse. This basis in critical reflection provides investigations of technology with an external means of validation that is missing from nondialectical work. Without this means of validation, technology becomes a vehicle whereby advocates and critics advance their personal interests rather than the object of study. Thus, the understanding of technology becomes distorted, for these analyses present a technology clothed in the presuppositions of an individual interest. Hyde argues that "any assertion about technology, when communicated on the basis of such understanding, is more an expression of self than it is of technology." Critical reflection, alternatively, brackets the presuppositions of both selves and their accompanying interests. This allows technology to assume a central role in the attempt to acquire understanding of the human condition. This perspective suggests that since technology has become the universal medium between individuals and their interaction with both other human beings and the natural world, it is essential that it be understood in an accurate way.

Rhetorical critiques that consciously promote the development of a dialectical mode of inquiry offer one means for achieving an accurate assessment of technology's effects on the human condition. This work asks what effects the intensification of technology has upon the structure and dynamics of society and it elucidates manipulative features of technology that both restrict and facilitate social interaction. It explores the invariant features of the technological transformation of human communication, including the transformation of face-to-face dialogical situations by technology. Because people take this mediating factor for granted, they fail to comprehend the effects that technology imposes on the communicative dimension of the human condition. The technological dialectic between people and their tools, for example, has been shown to limit the creative development of humanity. Other work explores how technological processes directed toward the materialization and the commercialization of political ideals alter the "American way of life." Essentially, this approach examines the modern dilemma of learning to coexist with technology without becoming technologized.

A more radical approach to the analysis of technology uses it as a metaphor for discourse, thus representing a broad range of rhetorical conventions and practices as technologies. According to this view, technology is a dimension that cuts across and influences all symbolic action, rather than an issue (Medhurst, Gonzalez, and Peterson). Because one cannot avoid becoming technologized, criticism is represented as "technological criticism." In technological criticism all discourse is seen as technological because it is the fundamental tool used to create and participate in social relations. Symbol use, then, becomes the most indispensable technology for human agents who, by their natures, construct and manage images of a desirable and sustainable collective life.

This intrinsically dialectical approach, which explores and critiques the technological metaphor, argues that instrumental consciousness projects a world that is nothing more or less than a composite of material resources, waiting to be used for human purposes. All things, human and nonhuman, can be reduced to a set of known facts and categorized according to measurably useful instrumental actions. Ellul argues that in this technological world, everything has been defined in terms of how it serves as means for maintaining economic, political, and social forms of the all-inclusive technological system.

In contrast to Hyde's claim that rhetorical critique should be centered on technology rather than on human interests, this approach claims that it is not technology that constitutes the problem. Instead, the ways humans have conceptualized, communicated, and created various cultures with this technology is problematic. Human nature rather than technology is in need of reexamination, for it is out of human desire that technological miracles come into being. Further, it is human culture that supports values, attitudes, and incipient belief systems; that privileges some people and disenfranchises others; that revolutionizes concepts of selfhood and understandings of who we are; that takes on a life of its own, apart from conscious, individual decision-making.

Technology, however, is not irrelevant to the project of technological criticism. Miller points out that human cultures become increasingly complex as a function of the tools they make. As a culture becomes more reliant on its tools, the tools make increasingly legitimate demands for production, maintenance, improvement, and coordination. Technology, then, becomes self-justifying. The resulting technological consciousness leads to undoing previous patterns of rationality in all contexts. Miller argues that the consciousness that develops in technological cultures shares certain features, including (1) the acceptance of means as ends, and the proliferation of the ends entailed in that acceptance; (2) substitution of closed system logic for open-system reasoning and an attendant acceptance of logical form over rhetorical substance; (3) self-justifying objectivity evidenced by the explanation of problems and potential solutions in terms of available technology rather than external realities; and (4) conceptual confusion between the universal features of technology (such as tool use) and historical features of a particular technological system. Technological consciousness has become so significant to human society that it defines, inevitably, what we believe to be ethical.

Technological criticism is grounded in an exploration of technological discourse, or language used to structure human action according to rules of closed systems (Medhurst, Gonzalez, and Peterson). The rhetorical critic who engages in technological criticism examines how technological discourse damages both institutions and individuals who make up those institutions by its idealization and precise definition of social hierarchies. Within the resulting mindset, experience that cannot be managed, or manipulated, is discarded as worthless. It becomes unspeakable, therefore nonexistent. In technological communication, either the dialogical means for any conversation are determined by preexisting ends, with each step predetermining the next, or acceptance of prevailing interaction patterns is so complete that questions regarding appropriateness never arise. Technological discourse thus masks its own temporality, while provoking participants to forget alternatives. As this awareness is suppressed, technological discourse is progressively judged by rules reflecting technical values and assumptions, and generated by a concern for "la technique." Thus, technological discourse shapes both consciousness and culture.

R

This approach to technology views cultural evolution as a social construct that is engineered by members of a technologized world rather than a biological process. Technological critics emphasize that while communication is a tool, the act of communicating is more than the use of a tool: It is the primary means of constituting the world and the self. Working from the assumption that technology is never politically neutral, they critique the processes whereby it privileges some interests over others. Related to this critique is the examination of how the censure of forms of reasoning other than those based on Aristotelian and Enlightenment models has further marginalized already disadvantaged groups within society. Technological criticism analyzes the modern faith in technology that enables the ideology of expertise to legitimize the continuation of existing forms of domination and to extinguish alternative visions of social structure.

In one sense, the development of technological criticism reaffirms the classical rhetorical focus on prudential judgment. Such judgment can never be absolute, its conclusions never final, nor closed to debate. However, rather than viewing technology and the rhetoric surrounding it as a response to a rhetorical situation, technological criticism assumes that technology induces discourse that in turn induces culture. Accordingly, the rhetorical critique of technology has become less about "it," and more about us. Thus it leads to the assumption that one cannot claim to understand technological facts fully unless one also understands the ethos of a community in which such facts are treated as believable and significant, for technology, like rhetoric, never operates in a vacuum, divorced from the contingencies of time and place. Rather than a topic of study, technology becomes a metaphor for language and culture.

At this point in our understanding of technology, rhetorical scholars are just beginning to look carefully at what technology tells a culture about its own potential as a viable human community. Terms such as *progress, quality of life, future security, economic advancement,* and *control* require further investigation. Technological criticism suggests that the problem of rhetoric and technology is primarily a matter of substituting creative thought and interaction for mindless, automatic systems. Its potential stems largely from the productive tension between Ellul's pessimistic view of the human condition and the optimistic view of rhetoric as an art with the power to call ideas into being, to create the world through human speech, thereby endowing it with purpose and meaning.

Tarla Rai Peterson
Texas A&M University

Bibliography

Bytwerk, Ronald. "The SST Controversy: A Case Study in the Rhetoric of Technology." *Central States Speech Journal* 30 (1979): 187–98.

Ellul, Jacques. *The Technological Society.* Trans. John Wilkinson. New York: Knopf, 1964.

———. *The Technological System.* New York: Continuum, 1980.

Farrell, Thomas, and G. Thomas Goodnight. "Accidental Rhetoric: The Root Metaphors of Three Mile Island." *Communication Monographs* 48 (1981): 271–300.

Heidegger, Martin. "The Question Concerning Technology." *Martin Heidegger: Basic Writings from Being and Time (1927) to the Task of Thinking (1964).* Ed. David F. Krell. New York: Harper, 1977. 287–317.

Hyde, Michael J., ed. *Communication Philosophy and the Technological Age.* University: U of Alabama P, 1982.

Medhurst, Martin, Alberto Gonzalez, and Tarla Rai Peterson, eds. *Communication and the Culture of Technology.* Pullman: Washington State UP, 1990.

Miller, Carolyn. "Technology as a Form of Consciousness: A Study of Contemporary Ethos." *Central States Speech Journal* 29 (1978): 228–36.

Postman, Neil. *Technopoly: The Surrender of Culture to Technology.* New York: Knopf, 1992.

Rhetoric of Film

A mode of rhetorical criticism investigating the interpretation of motion pictures. At its most focused, the application of rhetorical frames to film theory and criticism has interpreted the persuasive dimensions of films designed to advance an argument, whether they are documentary or fiction films. Such approaches sometimes confine themselves to the vocabulary of classical rhetoric for tools of analysis. A much broader approach encompasses rhetoric as the study of symbolic inducement, reaching beyond films that are didactic or propagandistic, and employing the whole range of tools common to humanistic inquiry into cultural forms and investigating issues of text, genre, myth, gender, ideology, production, authorship, the human subject, meaning, the construction of cinematic ways of knowing, response, and reception.

In practice, most rhetoric of film work has been in criticism rather than in theoretical discourse as such, though typically a variety of theoretical interrogations is part of the criticism. A core practice of such criticism is the close examination of films as inducements to audience response. Close readings of films from a rhetorical perspective challenge both received rhetorical doctrine and some popular modes of film criticism.

Some film theorists and critics have conceptualized the place of rhetoric within film studies in reference strictly to films intended as persuasion, or to the importation into filmic texts of traditional rhetorical figures, such as metaphor, metonymy, synecdoche, and irony. Such restrictive definitions of rhetoric sometimes are used as a way of denying that rhetoric should be part of the mainstream of film studies.

Institutionally, most of the scholarship identifying itself as rhetoric of film has been written by scholars in communication studies and literature. Such critics argue that rhetoric is central to film study and is the set of organizing theoretical principles for any inquiry into human symbolic action, subsuming more specialized theoretical approaches such as semiotic, structuralist, poststructuralist, feminist, psychoanalytic, and Marxist analysis, and transcending particular media and genres, such as speech, literature, film, and so on. Most critics practicing rhetoric of film criticism also work with other genres as well. In defining rhetoric of film as broadly as most of them do, these critics from speech communication and English departments affiliate their work not only with their own disciplines but also with the work of those film critics who are engaged in close reading of film texts, film criticism as part of critical and cultural studies, or film as an issue of reader-response or historical poetics—even though the gesture of affiliation is often not reciprocated.

Rhetorical criticism of film within the institutional tradition of speech communication raised doubts about persuasion as the core element of response to symbolic form, questioned the habitual distinction of form and content (wherein a decision to persuade an audience to a predetermined end led to a set of formal choices about how to achieve assent), and created doubts about the boundary between public and private, about the place of intention and language in communication, and about the domain of rhetoric as a discipline. These critics have been especially interested in the persistence of significant form (including generic and ideological forms) and the interpretive activity of the spectator. At its best, such criticism has hoped not only to contribute to a fuller exploitation of the rhetorical tradition in inquiring into human symbolic action but also, by introducing new methods and questions, to refresh the study of what has always been inarguably a core subject of rhetoric: public, argumentative discourse. Rhetorical criticism of film in the tradition of literature departments has employed the full range of contemporary approaches to literature to film texts and has at the same time been part of a broader challenge to the canon of high-cultural literary texts. Hence, rhetorical critics of film are a reminder of the unsettled and often contentious place of rhetorical studies (both institutionally and theoretically) in academic inquiry since classical times.

Thomas W. Benson
Pennsylvania State University

Bibliography

Benson, Thomas W. "Respecting the Reader." *Quarterly Journal of Speech* 72 (1986): 197–204.

Benson, Thomas W., and Carolyn Anderson. *Reality Fictions: The Films of Frederick Wiseman.* Carbondale: Southern Illinois UP, 1989.

———. "The Ultimate Technology: Frederick Wiseman's Missile." *Communication and the Culture of Technology.* Ed. Martin J. Medhurst, Alberto Gonzalez, and Tarla Rai Peterson. Pullman: Washington State UP, 1990.

Bordwell, David. *Making Meaning: Inference and Rhetoric in the Interpretation of Cinema.* Cambridge, MA: Harvard UP, 1989.

Browne, Nick. *The Rhetoric of Filmic Narration.* Ann Arbor, MI: UMI Research, 1982.

Chatman, Seymour. *Coming to Terms: The Rhetoric of Narrative in Fiction and Film.* Ithaca, NY: Cornell UP, 1990.

Medhurst, Martin J., and Thomas W. Benson, eds. *Rhetorical Dimensions in Media: A Critical Casebook.* 2nd ed. Dubuque, IA: Kendall/Hunt, 1991.

Rhetoric of Science

The rhetoric of science is a new discipline built on an old foundation: Aristotle's *Rhetoric*. But Aristotle would have rejected without question the central concern of rhetoric of science: the rhetorical nature of knowledge. Classical rhetoric concerns opinion only—matters we cannot know with any certainty. It concerns the past as it is reconstructed in courts of law, the future as it is determined in the laws and policies of deliberative bodies. But in its view, genuine knowledge is timeless; natural science tells us about what always was and always will be. In speaking about Darwinian evolution and Einsteinian relativity, then, we pay tribute to the departed discoverers of ever-present laws.

The notion that these laws are, in any sense, inventions, especially rhetorical inventions, was bound to be controversial and certain to be resisted. On this issue, contemporary rhetoricians are divided. Some maintain their essential conservatism by dealing only with the rhetoric of science policy, others by dealing with science as communication; only a few insist on radicalism, on dealing with scientific knowledge itself.

Rhetorical studies of science policy may be divided into two categories: those that ignore and those that address the science and technology involved in decisions. Science policy certainly involves deliberative issues, issues that fall readily within the traditional concerns of those trained in the rhetorical analysis of public address. Nevertheless, so strong was the traditional focus of the emerging discipline of speech communication on political oratory that the first rhetorical study of science policy was not made until 1953, by Richard Weaver. Weaver is concerned with an early climax of a continuing conflict in American public education, the place of Darwin's theory of evolution in the curriculum. The focus of his study is the Scopes trial. In that trial, Weaver concludes that the prosecution and the defense argued at cross purposes. The issue at hand was not the law against teaching evolution but the legality of Scopes's conduct under the law. Given this stasis, the scientific testimony in favor of evolution was irrelevant. Indeed, even in the legislature the question was not the truth of evolution but the right of the state to exclude from the curriculum what was, for the people of Tennessee, academic knowledge perhaps, but religious heresy certainly.

More recent studies of policy issues relating to science—John Lyne on sociobiology, and Alan Gross and Arthur Walzer on the *Challenger* disaster—also subsist entirely within the traditional bounds of Aristotelian theory. In this sense these studies do not constitute a theoretical advance over Weaver.

This is not to say that they do not deepen and extend our understanding of science policy. Lyne claims that sociobiology is a paradigm example of the need for a rhetoric of public policy. According to sociobiologists, biology is, to some large but still largely undetermined extent, the cause of social behaviors, of friendship and fraud. But even if this were true, even if there were, for instance, genes for friendship or for fraud, the real question, the deliberative question, would be: what ought we to do about this fact? In Lyne's view only rhetoric can address this question.

Alan Gross and Arthur Walzer claim that the cause of the *Challenger* disaster was not, as the presidential commission suggested and many communication scholars confirmed, faulty O-rings compounded by faulty communications. It was, rather, a cognitive and ethical failure, a failure of the deliberative process that should have led to the postponement of the launch.

In the study of science policy, then, deliberative issues continue to be addressed. Nevertheless, no rhetorician of science has addressed substantive issues, has taken the science seriously. That this can be an error, philosopher of science Helen Longino has shown in her study of the public policy implications of low-level radiation. Science, she says, offers us three models for the effects of such radiation, models that vary widely in the lethality they attribute to the rays. But, currently, there is no *scientific* way of deciding among *scientific* models. This absence opens up a deliberative space and justifies current rhetorical study. Longino's study implies that rhetoricians of science policy cannot routinely ignore the scientific status of the knowledge that motivates public debates. It may make a difference whether evolutionary theory is ideology or fact, whether sociobiology is knowledge or nonsense, whether the *Challenger* engineering was sound or faulty. Notice that Longino's work also implies that this space may eventually close. Indeed, if it were eventually discovered that low-level radiation was no more worrisome than summer sunlight, there would be for Longino nothing left to deliberate.

The focus of rhetoricians on science itself— science that scientists would call science—represents a definite break with tradition. In this sense at least, all rhetoric of science is radical. Nevertheless, it is possible to analyze even the primary texts of science—Galileo's *Two World Systems,* Newton's *Opticks,* Darwin's *Origin*—without opening the science in these works to rhetorical scrutiny: One can treat these texts as communications designed to persuade relevant members of scientific communities concerning scientific claims that are *already* true, true as the result of a scientific, rather than a rhetorical process. On the other hand, more radically, one can treat these same texts as if the science they contain is also an object of rhetorical scrutiny.

More Conservative Views

The most important critics of scientific texts as vehicles of communication are Charles Bazerman, John Angus Campbell, and Greg Myers. Of the three, Campbell, whose discipline is speech communication, has been publishing for the longest time. His work on Charles Darwin, begun a quarter-century ago, continues and matures to this day. Originally focused on the *Origin,* Campbell's work has since moved forward and backward in time, forward to Darwin on orchids, backward to Darwin's *Notebooks.* In all of his work, Campbell's central message is the same: Darwin is the master rhetorician, willing even to distort and disguise his religious and scientific views if he believes that distortion and disguise will attain conviction on some issue central to evolutionary theory. Darwin is a master-rhetorician even in his *Notebooks,* whose audience is only Darwin himself. These notebooks are a testing-ground for Darwin's theories, theories tested against the imaginary audience of such important potential objectors as his geological mentor and friend, Charles Lyell.

Charles Bazerman ranges more widely than Campbell: from Newton to Compton, from the style manual of the American Psychological Association to the reading habits of physicists. Unlike Campbell, Bazerman's training is as a literary critic. The difference shows in his close, careful readings of the text, exegeses typical of literary criticism. These readings illustrate both the successes and the failures of communication. In his chapter on Newton, for example, Bazerman shows in great detail why the great scientist's first optical paper failed. He also demonstrates how Newton learned from that failure to present essentially the same material in his later *Opticks* in more convincing

form. In his chapter on the APA style manual, we are the witnesses to the paradox of success. All scholarly papers in psychology are bound by the behaviorist strictures of the manual, despite the fact that the field as a whole has left behaviorism far behind. Bazerman's analyses are always searching. But as the title of his book indicates, he sees the rhetoric of science as shaping, not as creating knowledge.

Because Greg Myers routinely expands the notion of text to include drafts as well as final versions, his work resembles sociology and ethnography as much as rhetoric. Indeed, he sees rhetoric as an adjunct to and a deepening of sociological analysis. In a typical chapter, he follows two papers in biology through the process that leads to their final placement in a scientific journal. Initially, the claims in these papers exhibit the considerable breadth required of the prestigious general journals to which they are sent for review; but as rejection follows rejection, these broad claims are negotiated downward. Eventually, these papers are published in specialist journals with claims no wider than their specialist audiences will comfortably accept. This negotiating process is tied inextricably to persuasion and to rhetoric; clearly, it is knowledge that is being negotiated, or negotiated away. But Myers shrinks from saying knowledge is rhetorical; presumably, he rests his rhetorical conservatism on the bedrock that it is the *breadth,* not the *nature* of the claims that is the object of contention.

Campbell, Myers, and Bazerman are not the only relatively conservative rhetoricians of science. Jean Dietz Moss, Lawrence Prelli, Carolyn Miller, and Jeanne Fahnestock have also made significant contributions. Moss and Prelli would, perhaps, be the most comfortable with a conservative label; Miller and Fahnestock would, perhaps, be the least. Moss has spent half a scholarly lifetime on Galileo's rhetoric, on placing that rhetoric firmly within his times and his intellectual milieu. In a typical paper, "Reinterpreting Galileo," Moss claims that there was, between the *Letter to Christina* and the *Two World Systems,* a shift in Galileo's rhetorical strategy: In the former he is sure that he will soon find proofs of Copernicanism; in the latter, lacking such proofs, he seemingly leaves the issue open. But Moss shows that Galileo's actual audience was not deceived concerning his real motive in the *Two World Systems:* to propagandize in favor of heliocentricity. Still, for Galileo, rhetoric was rhetoric; science, science: Moss's central point is that Galileo is everywhere a man—and a scientist—of his time.

Prelli's conservativism rests squarely on his project to create a topical rhetoric of science, an inventional system on classical lines that can generate the arguments scientists use. In his analysis of the controversy over whether the great apes can use language, for example, Prelli is concerned exclusively with the type of arguments used by proponents and opponents. In his discussion, Prelli shows that the opponents of research into ape language rely on the scientific norm of universalism as an argumentative strategy: They accuse the researchers of systematically avoiding the judgment of peers and interfering subjectively with the outcomes of experiments. Because of this breach, the researchers are not really scientists. The proponents of such research, on the other hand, argue in favor of a counternorm, a kind of particularism: Their research must use such methods because it is crucial in such experiments to gain the trust of the subjects involved. Theirs is the only way to do simian linguistics. Prelli is not concerned with the substantive issue: Is science universal or particularist? He is concerned only with the rhetorical use of these values to persuade others.

Jeanne Fahnestock and Carolyn Miller are conservatives with a difference. On epistemological issues they may be agnostic, but they have strong views concerning the social and ethical implications of scientific practices. In a typical paper on the rhetoric of decision science, Miller faults it for its purported misrepresentation of the way people actually make decisions. She has, she believes, two strong arguments in favor of her view. Decision science is intellectually flawed; moreover, despite its scholarly reputation, decision science is little used in actual practice. She suggests an alternative for managerial deliberation, the ancient art of rhetoric. It is this ancient art and not its modern alternative that in her view best represents the way people actually decide about important issues.

Jeanne Fahnestock is also concerned with the social and ethical implications of her analyses. In an examination of the rhetorical differences between science and its popularizations, Fahnestock makes the rhetorical point that science is written in the forensic genre, its popularizations in the epideictic. As a result, scientific claims in the popular media distort science, making its claims seem more certain than they actually are. In many cases this is ethically indifferent. But not always. Fahnestock takes as her example a scientific paper that claims that boys may be better at mathematics than girls— genetically better. The original scientific claims are hedged and were soon disputed on various grounds. In the popular press, however, the claim was not at all hedged; moreover, there were no follow-up stories concerning its controversial nature.

More Radical Views

Radical rhetoric of science comes in two varieties, feminist and epistemological. The feminist variety has many proponents, but none within rhetoric; the epistemological variety has only one proponent in the rhetorical camp. The lack of interest in the first variety is significant for the opportunity it offers; the lack of interest in the second variety is significant in itself.

According to the feminist story, the progress of the natural sciences has been purchased at too high a cost. As presently constituted, the natural sciences depend on a self-blindering narrowness of vision; moreover, this narrowness is shared by the human sciences, humanistic scholarship, and society as a whole, insofar as these depend for guidance, as they surely do, on the methods and results of the natural sciences.

For its own purposes, then, feminist criticism of science broaches the question of whether historians, philosophers, and social scientists have been asking the wrong questions. Typically, traditional scholars of history, philosophy, and social science tell their stories as if the natural sciences were *already* special; they do not ask how they got to be special, and why. In addressing these latter questions, feminist studies of the natural sciences purport to give, not another, but a better picture of the natural sciences as one set of human enterprises among many. Insofar as feminist criticisms of science are political, rather than purely cognitive, they are emancipatory in intent, their purpose being to free the natural sciences from their confining self-images, and to free society from the natural sciences so confined.

Feminist analysis of science has a short but distinguished history: Evelyn Fox Keller's *Reflection on Gender and Science,* Helen Longino's *Science as Social Knowledge,* Donna

Harraway's *Primate Visions*, Sandra Harding's *Whose Science? Whose Knowledge?* These are only four well-known and well-respected books in a growing field. But there seems to be no book or article in which a feminist scholar trained in rhetoric focuses on the work of science.

The possibilities inherent in such a focus are evident from an article by anthropologist Emily Martin, published in the feminist journal *Signs*. By a careful analysis of textual evidence, Professor Martin establishes the claim that textbook and research depictions of the egg and the sperm suffer in large part from masculine biases that give the first a passive, the second an active role. Current research indicates, however, that these depictions are grossly inaccurate, that in fact conception is characterized by the mutuality of two active agents. Professor Martin's excursion into biology moves the cause of feminist criticism of science a step closer to the inner sanctum of the "hard" sciences, and it does so largely through rhetorical analysis.

In the past fifteen years, at least three books have appeared that have as their subject the generalization of radical critique, characteristic of feminism, to the essence of scientific knowledge: *Laboratory Life* by Bruno Latour and Steve Woolgar, *Science in Action* by Bruno Latour, and *The Rhetoric of Science* by Alan Gross. Each has a different character, a different method: The first is a sociological reconstruction; the second, a cultural critique; the third, a rhetorical analysis. The first traces the establishment of scientific facts entirely to everyday interactions in the laboratory; the second traces this establishment entirely to the consolidation of social and political power in centers of influence; the third traces this establishment entirely to successful rhetorical encounters between scientists and their chosen audiences. So described, each of these books may seem reductive, a search for one simple explanation for the fact and success of the natural sciences. In fact, from each the natural sciences emerge as enterprises of great complexity and interest, enterprises that can survive explanations that do not presuppose their special character.

The radical cultural critique of the natural sciences shows that their methods came into being and that their results achieved their special, almost sacral character by means of interactions that are, initially, indistinguishable from the interactions of everyday social life. Darwin's *Notebooks* are a good example of the process. They enact the genesis of evolutionary theory; as such, we see them as testimony to his scientific genius. But individually, the entries do not constitute this genius; indeed, they are barely coherent. Only as a whole, and only as seen through the spectacles of subsequent science and subsequent history do Darwin's *Notebooks* exhibit the methods and results of a new, revolutionary biology. And Darwin's *Notebooks* are only an example, a synecdoche for all of science, none of which is, on this reading, mysteriously exempt from radical analysis.

The nature of radical rhetorical explanation can best be gauged by comparing Bazerman and Gross on Newton's *Opticks,* and Campbell and Gross on Darwin's *Notebooks*. To Bazerman, the movement from Newton's unsuccessful early paper to his successful later book is an exercise in audience accommodation; to Gross, this same movement is evidence of the radical instability of physical optics as a science, the rhetorical plasticity of the facts and theories it presents to the world. To Campbell, Darwin's *Notebooks* trace his early progress toward a theory of evolution; to Gross the *Notebooks* enact not an orderly progress toward eventual stability but an untidy and continuing emotional and intellectual struggle. On this reading, the *Origin* is not so much one long argument as the adventitious imposition of form on ideas whose epistemological status was, and remained, fluid through Darwin's lifetime.

It is too early to tell whether these books will actually radicalize the rhetoric of science, or whether such radicalization, if undertaken, would benefit rhetoric as a discipline. But it is not too early to notice the growing resistance to the threat of radicalization. The resistance to these deflationary views by philosophers, historians, and the more traditional among the social scientists is understandable, given their deep professional investments in traditional views of science as a social enterprise. Acceptance of this deflationary view would deflate the worth of their own work as they see it, work that lives in large part in the reflected light of the sciences themselves.

The resistance of rhetorical critics and theorists is less easily understandable. The central concern of conservative critics is the leap from rhetorical analysis, broadly conceived, to philosophical conclusions about what there is and how we know it. Conservative opposition crystallizes around the validity of the Platonic division between knowledge and opinion; the radical attack takes its impetus from an interpretation of the sophists that finds the distinction between rhetoric and philosophy intellectually uninteresting. The conservative critic excludes epistemology from rhetoric; for the radical critic, rhetoric and epistemology are two descriptions of essentially the same enterprise.

Radical rhetoric of science does not require radical rhetorical theory. Indeed, despite their differing views of the relationship between rhetoric and science, Bazerman, Campbell, Myers, and Gross make do with a theory of persuasion that differs little in its essentials from that of Aristotle. These rhetorical critics are innovative, not in rhetoric theory, but in applying classical principles to texts for which they were not meant; Gross is radical, not as a theorist, but only in drawing from rhetorical analyses general inferences that Aristotle would think illegitimate. But that the rhetoric of science should rely so heavily on so primitive and antiquated a theory of persuasion, one so wedded to an outmoded folk psychology, is a view that must be open to question in any discipline properly self-conscious about its foundations.

To make the case for a radical theoretical view, one that involves the virtual abandonment of classical rhetoric, we must demonstrate the fundamental inadequacy of this rhetoric in its encounter with the texts of the natural sciences; we must read rhetoric of science as a history of theoretical failure. We must say that any text can be redescribed in terms of appeals and intended audience. Nevertheless, this universality is a consequence not of the explanatory power of classical rhetoric but of its theoretical vacuity. Like an oversized coat, classical rhetoric, because it covers everything, fits nothing. To say that in his first optical paper, Newton uses the common topic of cause and effect or that its single diagram gives his experiment presence is only to redescribe the obvious in rhetorical terms; it is to say nothing much and nothing interesting.

To make the case for this radical view, we must also find that the lack of theoretical bite of traditional analyses comes as no surprise, given the origins of classical rhetoric. Aristotle, Cicero, and Quintilian were not trying to explain but to teach. They were creating a system designed to produce speakers with strong memories, a ready wit, and a shrewd understanding of the means for swaying large audiences of ordinary citizens. Aristotle, Cicero, and Quintilian were writing handbooks—superior handbooks, to be sure—not treatises. They knew the difference; contemporary rhetoricians of science, apparently, do not.

There is a second, equally disabling problem that confronts those who wish to rely on the principles of classical rhetoric to analyze the texts of science. Classical rhetoric was designed for a society of speaking opportunities fixed in time and place, of well-defined audiences, and of clear potential outcomes. In contemporary societies, these conditions apply only to special cases: juries, for example. They most assuredly do not apply to the intricacies of so involved a social system as science.

Finally, the radical theorist must attack the epistemological presuppositions of a classical rhetoric of science. In a vanished world, texts had stable meanings, authors stable identities and recognizable intents, audiences and authors purposes in common. In that world, reason and its strategies were the primary tools of persuasion. These assumptions are also the assumptions of classical rhetoric. Even Aristotle's analysis of emotional appeals in the *Rhetoric* provides evidence in favor of this logocentric claim. His analysis is relentlessly rational; moreover, it is made in the unquestioned service of the strategic control: Speakers manipulate the emotions of their audiences in the interest of their persuasive purposes.

The radical critique of a classical rhetoric of science is not itself ideological. Its endorsement requires only a sensitivity to the shaping forces of an intellectual world and a cultural climate that is our common experience. One does not have to be a Marxist to abandon the notion that human beings are in full control of their history; one does not have to be a Freudian to abandon the notion that they are in full control of their thoughts and actions; one does not have to be a feminist to see that our most important cultural productions bear the unmistakable marks of masculine bias; one does not have to be a deconstructionist to see the futility of trying to recover the *real* meaning of a text, the *actual* intent of its author, the *true* disposition of its audience.

The endorsement of this radical critique does not mean the end of rhetoric of science. But it does mean that rhetoric of science must rethink its theoretical foundations. To endorse this radical critique is to call for a renewal of rhetorical theory, a renewal that takes both

modernism and postmodernism into consid–
eration.

As with all new disciplines, the rhetoric of
science must find an institutional and intellectual place in an academy all of whose niches are
already filled. The means for so doing are social
and political: the establishment of new niches
within existing structures, the creation of doctoral programs, the founding of journals and
learned societies. Philosophy of science is a
model new discipline in this sense. Although
only three generations old, it is now a recognized specialty within departments of philosophy, one that generates its share of doctorates.
Moreover, philosophy of science has a learned
society, the Philosophy of Science Association,
and a journal, *Philosophy of Science*. In a manner analogous to philosophy of science, rhetoric of science has so far established new niches
in departments of speech communication and
English. It has also established doctorates in
rhetoric of science in at least a half-dozen institutions. Its contributions are readily accepted in
a variety of disciplinary and interdisciplinary
journals. But it still does not have a learned
society or a journal of its own. And it lacks status in the English and speech communication
departments within which it is practiced. It
lacks the prestige of Shakespeare, let us say, or
of mass communication.

This lack of institutional status makes it
difficult for rhetoric of science to establish itself
intellectually. Older disciplines, such as history
or philosophy of science, simply ignore rhetoricians and will not publish their papers in their
journals. Newer, less secure disciplines, such as
the sociology of scientific knowledge, attack its
alleged pretensions. At the same time, both
newer and older science studies disciplines appropriate to a rhetorical sensibility without the
benefit of formal rhetorical instruction or of
formalized rhetorical knowledge: Historian
Martin Rudwick and sociologist Steve Woolgar
have produced sensitive rhetorical analyses of
science, apparently without benefit of rhetorical training or terminology. If this is possible,
the argument runs, can rhetoric of science be
necessary?

As a result of these factors, rhetoricians of
science suffer from a poor intellectual balance
of trade: While they readily cite other disciplines, other disciplines rarely cite them. So long
as this is so, these neighboring disciplines will
see little need for a separate academic presence
for rhetoricians of science.

Rhetoric of science is an emerging discipline that takes classical rhetorical theory as its
intellectual tool and the texts of science and
science policy as its target of analysis. It is too
early to predict its institutional or intellectual
fate. Institutionally, it is just beginning to establish itself; intellectually, it must overcome considerable challenges if it is to gain the continuing respect of established disciplines.

Alan G. Gross
University of Minnesota

Bibliography

Bazerman, Charles. *Shaping Written
    Knowlege: Genre and Activity of the Ex-
    perimental Article in Science*. Madison:
    U of Wisconsin P, 1988.
Gross, Alan G. *The Rhetoric of Science*.
    Cambridge, MA: Harvard UP, 1990.
Harding, Sandra. *The Science Question in
    Feminism*. Ithaca, NY: Cornell UP, 1986.
Keller, Evelyn Fox. *Reflections on Gender in
    Science*. New Haven: Yale UP, 1985.
Myers, Greg. *Writing Biology: Texts in the
    Social Construction of Scientific Knowl-
    edge*. Madison: U of Wisconsin P, 1990.
Prelli, Lawrence J. *A Rhetoric of Science: In-
    venting Scientific Discourse*. Columbia:
    U of South Carolina P, 1989.
Simons, Herbert W., ed. *Rhetoric in the Hu-
    man Sciences*. London: Sage, 1989.
———. *The Rhetorical Turn: Invention and
    Persuasion in the Conduct of Inquiry*.
    Chicago: U of Chicago P, 1990.
Weaver, Richard M. *The Ethics of Rhetoric*.
    Chicago: Henry Regnery, 1953.
Woolgar, Steve, ed. *Knowledge and Reflexiv-
    ity: New Frontiers in the Sociology of
    Knowledge*. London: Sage, 1988.

Rhetoric of Silence

The influence on public attributions of meanings exerted by intentional failure to communicate. Most rhetoric takes the form of words or
gestures with meaning. But *silence* can also be
rhetorical. Not all silence is rhetorical. Silence
functions rhetorically when it is used *strategically* (rather than happens randomly) in *political* (rather than interpersonal) contexts. Rhetorical silence has four characteristics: It violates
expectations, it is intentional, it generates predictable meanings, and it influences the meanings of its context more than context influences
its meanings.

The rhetoric of silence occurs when a failure to communicate *violates expectations*. Silence in a place of worship, or at a funeral, does not call attention to itself as a strategy because it is expected. A leader who should speak to the public about a crisis but does not, or who cancels a well-advertised speech without good reason, is being silent against expectations. Rhetorical silence is therefore an inexplicable or at least unexplained silence. If it *can* be, or is, explained or rationalized, then the expectations are reordered and the silence no longer violates expectations.

Silence is rhetorical when it seems to be *intentional*. The failure to communicate must be perceived to be a deliberate act rather than simply a lapse, laziness, or the result of pressing business elsewhere. Public reactions may not be what the silent person planned, but the choice to be silent against expectations must be seen to be deliberate.

Rhetorical silence generates *predictable meanings*. The meanings of silence in interpersonal settings will vary from one situation to another. Silence between spouses, for instance, may mean friendly intimacy, hostility, or something else, depending on the people involved and the specific context. But rhetorical silence is public. Because it is public, it has political import. Specifically, rhetorical silence replaces *talk* in politics. Talk performs specific, invariable functions in politics, and strategic silence has certain meanings precisely because it is *not* talk, which was expected. In other words, because talk has definite and predictable functions in politics, the silence that replaces it has predictable meanings. Talk is a way of defining *relationships* in politics; rhetorical silence therefore means *mystery* and *uncertainty* among people, in place of relationship. Talk is a form of *action* in politics; rhetorical silence therefore means *passivity* and *relinquishment* of initiative in politics. Suppose the president sends the U.S. Marines to intervene in a South American military conflict. They immediately suffer heavy casualties in a crushing defeat. Suppose the president says nothing at all, neither in speech nor press conference, about the disaster. Certainly, suspicions that he is no longer "in charge" would surface in the press. Speculation about why he is silent, and what it portends, would abound. Suspicions of presidential passivity, questions about mysterious motivations or policies behind the silence, are very

likely to be among the predictable meanings that the silence would draw.

Messages draw much of their meaning from their contexts. But because rhetorical silence generates predictable meanings insofar as it replaces political talk, rhetorical silence reverses the flow of meaning: It *influences its context's meanings*. Rhetorical silence encourages the public to see its context as one of mystery and uncertainty in relationships, as one of passivity and relinquishment of action. Suppose that a foreign crisis threatens war, yet the president refuses to address the public about it. The context of war and the president's policies will not influence what the silence means so much as the silence will encourage the public to attribute meanings of mystery, uncertainty, passivity, and relinquishment to the president, his actions, his relationships to foe and to the public, and so forth. The crisis, the president, and what he does will be perceived in certain ways because of the silence, more than the silence is perceived in certain ways because of the context.

Rhetorical silence is theoretically interesting because it is centered on the audience rather than the rhetor. Although silence may certainly be used as a strategy, the rhetor only initiates it. What it means, and how those meanings influence perceptions of the particular context within which silence occurs, is determined by a process of attribution and meaning construction carried on by the audience itself. By contrast, rhetors take more of a role in urging specific meanings upon an audience in other forms of rhetoric. The rhetoric of silence is therefore distinct from much rhetorical theory that describes the process of message construction and strategizing from the perspective of rhetors.

Barry Brummett
University of Wisconsin, Milwaukee

Bibliography

Brummett, Barry. "Towards a Theory of Silence as a Political Strategy." *Quarterly Journal of Speech* 66 (1980): 289–303.
Bruneau, Thomas J. "Communicative Silences: Forms and Functions." *Journal of Communication* 23 (1973): 17–46.
Jensen, J. Vernon. "Communicative Functions of Silence." *ETC., A Review of General Semantics* 30 (1973): 249–57.
Johannesen, Richard L. "The Functions of Silence: A Plea for Communication Research." *Western Speech* 38 (1974): 25–35.

Scott, Robert L. "Rhetoric and Silence."
 Western Speech 36 (1972): 146–58.

Rhetoric Society of America

An interdisciplinary professional organization concerned with all aspects of rhetoric. The Rhetoric Society of America (RSA) is an interdisciplinary professional organization dedicated to the promotion and distribution of knowledge in all areas of rhetoric. To these ends, RSA sponsors a biennial conference and a quarterly journal, *Rhetoric Society Quarterly*. Founded on and sustained by a view of rhetoric as a powerful, multifarious activity that is at once central to all disciplines and itself the hub of all disciplines, RSA has forged important links between scholars from such diverse fields as English, speech communication, philosophy, linguistics, classics, computer science, anthropology, sociology, and psychology.

RSA emerged from an invitational workshop on rhetoric organized by J. Carter Roland for the 1968 Conference on College Composition and Communication. Participants from several disciplines who shared a common interest in rhetoric gathered and defined the tripartite purpose of RSA: (1) to foster communication among those interested in rhetoric, (2) to distribute knowledge of rhetoric to the uninitiated, and (3) to encourage research, scholarship, and pedagogy in rhetoric.

In December of 1968, the first RSA newsletter was compiled by then-Executive Secretary Nelson J. Smith, III. The fledgling society struggled initially; the newsletter appeared sporadically between 1968 and 1972. The struggle can be attributed in part to the members' desire for a vigorous scholarly forum that avoided simply reproducing other professional organizations. While intense commitment from the members helped to sustain RSA (see correspondence among members in Winterowd 3–6), the society was finally galvanized by the creation of a constitution drafted by Richard Larson and ratified by members in 1971 and by the appointment of an editor. Instructed by the newly formed board of directors to nominate someone from outside of English studies to edit the *Rhetoric Society Newsletter*, Larson enlisted George Yoos, a philosopher.

Under the skillful editorship of George Yoos (1972–1992), *RSN* was transformed from a practical tool for exchanging news items, descriptions of works-in-progress, and program descriptions to a sophisticated scholarly journal. The transformation was marked in 1976 when the journal was upgraded and renamed *Rhetoric Society Quarterly*. In addition to insightful articles, *RSQ* provides invaluable bibliographies on various topics concerning rhetoric. These rich bibliographies have been gathered in a metabibliography (Seefeldt 99–105).

Given the shaky economy of the early 1970s, which limited departmental funding for conferences at many institutions, RSA members chose at first not to hold a conference but to convene associated meetings at various national and regional professional conferences, a practice that continues today. In 1984, however, Charles Kneupper organized the first RSA biennial conference at the University of Texas at Arlington. With a nod to George Orwell's *1984*, the theme of the conference was "Old Speak/New Speak: Rhetorical Transformations." This conference was important for establishing strong collegial ties (Feehan 242). Since then, RSA has held a conference every other year, attracting speakers and participants from all over the world.

Through both its journal and its conferences, RSA has traversed disciplinary and geographical boundaries to make vital contributions to the study and development of rhetorical theory, history, practice, and pedagogy. In the pages of *RSQ* and on the floors of RSA conferences, authors have tackled such reciprocal topics as the theory of rhetoric and the rhetoric of theory, the history of rhetoric and the rhetoric of history, the philosophy of rhetoric and the rhetoric of philosophy, the criticism of rhetoric and the rhetoric of criticism, the pedagogy of rhetoric and the rhetoric of pedagogy. These dynamic pairings attest to RSA's commitment to explore the multiple dimensions and power of rhetoric.

Maureen Daly Goggin
Carnegie Mellon University

Bibliography

"Constitution of the Rhetoric Society of America." *Newsletter of the Rhetoric Society of America*. Sept. 1971: 7–10.

Corbett, Edward P.J. "A Note from the Chairman." *Rhetoric Society Newsletter* 3 (1973): 1–2.

———. "Statement from the Chairman." *Rhetoric Society Newsletter* 2 (1972): 2.

Feehan, Mike. "Ruminations Round Remaginations of a Society-in-Process." *PRE/TEXT* 5 (1984): 241–43, 251–53.

Rhetoric Society Newsletter 1 (1968): 1–2.

Seefeldt, Charles W. "Fifteen Years of the Rhetoric Society Quarterly: A Bibliography of Bibliographies." *Rhetoric Society Quarterly* 16 (1986): 99–105.

Vitanza, Victor J. "For Charles." *Rhetoric Society Quarterly* 22 (1992): 1–5.

Winterowd, W. Ross, ed. "RSA: Genesis and Direction." *Newsletter of the Rhetoric Society of America.* Sept. 1971: 3–6.

Yoos, George E. "Ich Gelobe Meine Treue Dem Banner." *Rhetoric Society Quarterly* 20 (1990): 5–12.

Young, Richard. "Working on the Margin: Rhetorical Studies and the New Self-Consciousness." *Rhetoric Society Quarterly* 20 (1990): 325–32.

Rhetorician

Strategist responsible for finding the means of persuasion as well as showing the persuasive product. The history of the term *rhetorician* goes back to the earliest system of higher education in ancient Greece (c. 470–399 B.C.E.). During this period, changes in the population and the development of city states shifted the Athenian government toward democracy. The Greeks also achieved significant sophistication and specialization in life styles to give them the money and leisure to seek intellectual disciplines.

Early rhetoricians originated from a group of professional teachers called the sophists. They became prominent when the principles of "training" speakers arose with the development of democracy in Syracuse in the 460s B.C.E. In Sicily, Corax taught effective speech structure, a schematized rhetoric, to fellow citizens of the Greek colony of Syracuse. Under the egalitarian government, the people had a chance to argue their claims before a group of fellow citizens, and rhetoricians like Corax were able to make use of their study of the power of language.

These professional teachers also brought the means to successful political life on mainland Greece. In Athens, rhetoricians taught the arts of persuasion to the aristocratic class, who could afford to attend lectures as they sought practical training in their political and legal careers. As a result, public speaking on local and foreign affairs became a common engagement for the Greeks in their quest toward political action.

While early rhetoricians saw rhetoric as the art of persuasion, Aristotle expanded this view to include the absolute truth, only achievable through pure science. Rhetoric is then seen as a useful art whereby systematic investigation is required. Hence, the rhetorician becomes the identifier of rhetorical language or expression. In the narrow Aristotelian sense, the pure rhetorician is the strategist of persuasion who spends time analyzing the means of persuasive speech and writing, but leaves the application of the art to others.

In the early ages of Rome, rhetoricians served as teachers to upper-class men on affairs of the state, usually between the patricians and the plebeians. The political situation in Rome ensured forensic speeches to become common practices for the defense of the Roman law. Roman rhetoricians from around the time of Quintilian to the fall of Rome in 410 C.E., however, were participants of the Second Sophistic movement. They shared the interests of the early Greek sophists in language. However, the latter rhetoricians catered their use of language more toward literary purposes rather than social and political goals.

In the discussion of the rhetorician, it is difficult to separate theory from practice. The rhetorician and the orator (rhetor) were often the same person because rhetoric in ancient times meant the whole art of persuasion. While the rhetorician was a professor of the art of rhetoric, especially in ancient Greece and Rome, he was also a professional orator. He can also be seen as an eloquent writer, one who used rhetorical language or expression.

Siew C. Burroughs
Bowling Green State University

Bibliography

Bizzell, Patricia, and Bruce Herzberg, eds. *The Rhetorical Tradition: Readings from Classical Times to the Present.* Boston: St. Martin's, 1990.

Connors, Robert J. "Greek Rhetoric and the Transition from Orality." *Philosophy and Rhetoric* 19 (1986): 38–65.

Corbett, Edward P.J. *Classical Rhetoric for the Modern Student.* 3rd ed. New York: Oxford UP, 1990.

Enos, Richard Leo, and Ann M. Blakeslee. "The Classical Period." *The Present State of Scholarship in Historical and Contemporary Rhetoric.* Ed. Winifred Bryan Horner. Rev. ed. Columbia: U of Missouri P, 1990. 9–44.

Horner, Winifred Bryan. *Rhetoric in the Classical Tradition.* New York: St. Martin's, 1988.

Hunt, Everett Lee. "Plato and Aristotle on Rhetoric and Rhetoricians." *Historical Studies of Rhetoric and Rhetoricians.* Ed. Raymond F. Howes. Ithaca, NY: Cornell UP, 1961. 19–70.

Kennedy, George A. *The Art of Rhetoric in the Roman World: 300 B.C.–A.D. 300.* Princeton: Princeton UP, 1972.

———. *Classical Rhetoric and Its Christian and Secular Tradition from Ancient to Modern Times.* Chapel Hill: U of North Carolina P, 1980.

Kerferd, G.B. *The Sophistic Movement.* London, Cambridge: Cambridge UP, 1981.

See also RHETOR

Rhêtorikê

The ancient Greek word ῥητορική translated as "rhetoric" in English. *Rhêma* is a word that can be traced back to Homeric days and refers to a "saying" or "that which is said." In the *Iliad*, Achilles is referred to as a *mythôn te rhêtêr* (9.443), a phrase that is usually translated as "a speaker of words" but in context is better understood as a "teller of tales." The word *rhêtêr* appears only once in all of the surviving texts prior to the middle of the fifth century B.C.E. During the fifth century, the masculine form *rhêtôr* emerged as a quasi-technical legal term used to refer to those who spoke often in the assembly or in the law courts. Though *rhêtôr* literally means "speaker," the word conveyed a sense similar to the modern-day word *politician,* as all political discourse of the time was presented orally.

The *-ikê* ending in Greek connotes skill or art. Thus, *rhêtorikê* literally means "art or skill of the *rhêtôr.*" *Rhêtorikê* can be used as an adjective such that one can call someone or something "rhetorly" or "rhetorical," or it can be used as a substantive, as in the word *rhetoric.* The Greek word *rhêtorikê* cannot be found in any text that can be dated confidently prior to Plato's dialogue *Gorgias,* usually dated 385 B.C.E. Though it is certainly possible that the word was in use prior to this date, several scholars have conjectured that Plato may have coined the word in order to describe the teachings of his competitors and to distinguish it from his own teachings. Such a conjecture has been supported by the absence of the word *rhêtorikê* in many texts of the same era (including the surviving texts of Isocrates), and by Plato's documented habit of coining many new words with *-ikê* endings to describe various arts. In particular, a series of verbal arts were first described by Plato with such terms as *dialectic, eristic,* and *antilogic,* making it a respectable possibility that *rhetoric* is also a Platonic coinage.

Edward Schiappa
University of Minnesota

Bibliography
Cole, Thomas. *The Origins of Greek Rhetoric.* Baltimore: Johns Hopkins UP, 1991.

Schiappa, Edward. "*Rhêtorikê*: What's in a Name? Toward a Revised History of Early Greek Rhetorical Theory." *Quarterly Journal of Speech* 78 (1992): 1–15.

Richards, I.A. (1893–1979)

English-born rhetorical and literary theorist, educator, critic, and poet. Focusing on "how words work" and "the study of misunderstanding and its remedies," Ivor Armstrong Richards proposed a new role for rhetoric in his 1936 *Philosophy of Rhetoric.* Following in the intellectual footsteps of George Campbell's 1776 *Philosophy of Rhetoric,* Richards suggests that rhetoric be seen as "the art by which discourse is adapted to an end" (*Interpretation* 12). He argues that language is the key to understanding thought, a "discipline aiming at a mastery of the fundamental laws of the use of language" (*Philosophy* 7) and as the means to draw on and to extend the disciplines of linguistics, psychology, philosophy, anthropology, education, and literary studies.

After receiving a degree from Magdalene College, Cambridge, in moral sciences in 1922, Richards taught in Cambridge's first literature studies program and began collaborating with C.K. Ogden on *The Meaning of Meaning.* Teaching at Cambridge led to *Practical Criticism* and *Principles of Literary Criticism,* texts that became foundations for the New Criticism developing in America. After visits to China, where he worked to establish Basic English, a simplified form of English developed with

Ogden, Richards joined Harvard's College of Education. Convinced that theory without application is useless, Richards argued for revising concepts of language teaching in *How to Read a Page* and *Speculative Instruments,* in his studies of cartooning and other media aids, and in his extensive language teaching series co-produced with Christine Gibson.

Rhetoric, for Richards, is not the Aristotelian counterpart of dialectic. As an advocate for a new or reformulated rhetoric, Richards centralizes the idea that "language is an instrument for controlling our becoming" (*Speculative* 9) and "the instrument of all our distinctively human development" (*Philosophy* 131). In Richards's scheme language reflects both human character and human development. Over history, as humans developed language abilities, language in turn developed its users. Language "has become a repository, a record, a reflection, as it were, of human nature" (*Practical* 208). Convinced of the pervasiveness of language in thought processes, he argues, its use is both personal and social, both forming and formative. Richards thus establishes a new direction for rhetoric, bypassing the fixation on persuasion. Deeply embedded in this reformulation is the need for a "systematic study of *the inherent and necessary opportunities for misunderstanding* which language offers" (*Speculative* 74). In other words, a study of *meanings,* that "notoriously uncontrollable word" (99).

Richards moves rhetoric into the twentieth century by making its subject matter more inclusive, by attempting to reconcile the roles of reader, writer, and text. For Richards, a principal question was "whether our views of the mind can really influence our mind's development" (*Mencius* 45). This focus is necessarily subject to a "persistent, systematic, detailed inquiry into how words work" (*Philosophy* 23). The methodology for this, he argues, must apply "not only, as with the old Rhetoric, on a macroscopic scale, discussing the effects of different disposals of large parts of a discourse—but also on a microscopic scale by using theorems about the structure of the fundamental conjectural units of meaning and the conditions through which they, and their interconnections arise" (*Philosophy* 23–24).

Richards's scheme emphasizes the conjectures made, the conditions or contexts of language use, the "interinanimations" among words that occur and affect the outcome, and the meanings derived from the encounter. He argues the need to develop instruments to examine these features in their contexts as opposed to promoting an analysis of their isolated, and decontextualized, components.

Central to this conception is the inherent metaphorical nature of language. Understanding metaphor, the processes of thinking or feeling about one thing in terms of another, enables a deeper awareness of the relations of language to thought. Language is integrally linked with thought, and thought with language. Closer attention to metaphor provides access to both improved understanding and improved use of language. He introduces the now commonplace terms *tenor* and *vehicle* as means to analyze these processes.

Richards's New Rhetoric focuses attention on the study of meanings—what they are and how they come about—as more inclusive than the Aristotelian assumption that it is the study of persuasion. Rather, rhetoric is the study of all discourse. Richards's further extension is that language is not the fixed record of an experience to be recaptured, but rather "an instrument for the pursuit and control of meanings" (*So Much Nearer* 128). To understand how meaning occurs is to investigate how multiple meanings, or "misunderstandings," result.

The New Critics, beginning with John Crowe Ransom, draw on his early theorizing about the nature of reading and criticism in *Principles of Literary Criticism* and his work with student protocols as outlined in *Practical Criticism* as integral to textual study. Reader-response theorists also point to his early work as pivotal in the development of that critical movement. Richards, however, said he was less after a theory of literary criticism than an instrument for comparing meanings, for understanding meaning as dialectic.

Encountering a text sets up a realm of choices that activate the entire spectrum of language, including that not actually present in the utterance. Meaning is constructed with interpretative choices, choices guided by purposes and selected from previous choices by the reader. Interpretation, or perceived meaning, is the process of categorizing and sorting previous and immediate responses to these choices, often with little recognition or consciousness of doing so. Comparison becomes the principal activity of comprehending. But comparison is initiated by the text and its features. Richards's attention is fixed on the means of meanings. A reader's purpose is to derive approximate meanings, to interpret *from* that record. Richards, following his studies of the classical Chinese philosopher Mencius, came to prefer the term *translate*. Translation involves not just the exchange of one symbol system or language for another but the transformation of a text on historical, cultural, and psychological, as well as lexical, grounds.

The effect of text results in a reconciliation of tension generated by all of the differing entities involved. Readers assume authorial intent behind a text, either explicitly or implicitly. Those intentions, represented by the text, conflict or concur with the reader's own experiences and particular reading of that text. The author, constrained by the specific context of that text during its creation as well as the continual struggle with the limits of the language being used, conveys the author's own tensions. The text, an approximate rendering of that struggle and its context, reflects this to the reader. Perception of the text becomes an interpretation as the reader selects certain features to recognize or respond to and ignores others.

Examining this almost automatic, unconscious process led to C.K. Ogden's and Richards's now famous echo of Aristotle's triangle (as they reinvent C.S. Peirce's version) in *The Meaning of Meaning*. The triangle represents the basic processes of communication, a dialectical process between speaker and listener that invokes social and psychological factors as well as purposes, effects, and attitudes. Text is where presentation (by the author) and representation (by the reader) meet.

Richards distinguished emotive language from referential language. Referential language (science) refers to reality. Emotive language expresses speaker attitude to listener or reader (feeling), speaker attitude toward the subject (tone), and speaker purpose underlying the text (intent). Pure expository or referential language hardly exists "outside the routine of train services and the tamer, more settled parts of the sciences" (*Philosophy* 41). He later proposes a more inclusive set of terms: scientific, rhetorical, and poetic. These exist on a continuum where pure referential discourse is science, pure emotive discourse is poetry, and the points in between are rhetoric (55).

Richards's conception of *dialectic* is critical to examining the processes of understanding and as a point to reexamine author-text-reader relationships. He takes the term from Plato, arguing that Plato meant dialectic as a means for truth as opposed to *eristic*, or word-fighting, as a means to victory. Dialectic is the art of "making clear in any discussion what the participants are really saying and thinking" (*Plato* 9). Richards's understanding of Plato is that "dialogue and dialectic for him go together, the participating minds redressing one another's mistakings, as our two eyes see better than either can alone" (*Plato* 10).

Richards, aligning his own rhetoric with an understanding of psychological principles and the concept that language is representative of experience, can then argue that the character of the speaker meets the character of the listener through the mediation of the utterance. Encountering text, the reader engages in a dialogue, moving back and forth between what the reader meets in the text and what the reader brings to the encounter. Rhetoric is the study of this process.

In attempting to unify what he perceived as a split between the views of Plato and Aristotle, Richards proposes a "virtuous" approach to language, a means of discovering the self through the discovery of meaning. He argues that "we are so busy with WHAT we may have to say that we underconsider both how we shape what we say and how we shape our understanding of what we take as being said" (*So Much* 16).

Perceiving words as resourceful rather than as the more problematic "ambiguous" is key to Richards's scheme or theory of meanings. He argues instead for a "contextual theorem of meaning" to counter "the proper meaning superstition," or the argument that words have inherent meaning. The meaning of a discourse continually shifts as contexts change. As readers or writers attempt meaning, they uncover and make use of the meanings within a given context, on both global and local levels. Richards was, however, wary of surrendering meaning totally to the reader: "The *original* difficulty of all reading, the problem of *making out the meaning*" (and not succumbing to the tendency to *make* the meaning) is to allow different aspects of meaning to be distinguished (*Practical* 174).

Rather than allow "a hundred verdicts from a hundred readers" (*Practical* 173), he identifies four "lenses" as aids to interpreting a text. *Sense* is the recognition that speakers speak to say something and listeners listen for something to be said. *Feeling,* and other "connative-affective" aspects, notes the attitudinal and expressive nature of language. *Tone* is the recognition that the speaker has an attitude toward the audience. As audiences vary, so does the speaker's *"recognition of his relation to them"* (175). The fourth feature is the conscious or unconscious effect the speaker or writer is "endeavouring to promote" (176). All of these attributes are identifiable, to one degree or another, in most discourse.

Investigating the occurrence of these functions and their effect is the role of the reader. "As a rule," he says, "meaning does contain a concept—so wrapped up with other functions as to be unintelligible and untranslatable apart from them" (*Mencius* 88). The more familiar the meaning, the more difficult "to distinguish what we are thinking of from what we are feeling about it or what we want to do with it" (88). Recognizing and accounting for responses to a text thus becomes as important a responsibility as comprehension, an awareness that enables greater flexibility in the decisions made about a text.

Close attention to textual understanding leads to "'knowledge how' not 'knowledge of.'" Drawing on his understanding of both Mencius and Coleridge, Richards suggests that this understanding provides self-realization in the sense of coming into being of the full self, thus encouraging "the development of the possibilities in human nature" (*Mencius* 39–40). A reader's encounters with a text are encounters with potentiality. The author's role, via the text, is to select and present those opportunities. An audience's responsibility is to attend more closely to the activity that occurs, to the choices presented and the decisions made in resolving those choices. A reader necessarily must be an active participant in the exchange that occurs when encountering a text.

"Words are not a medium in which to copy life. Their true work is to restore life itself to order," Richards proposes (*Philosophy* 134). Language study therefore should be directed toward developing tools, or "speculative instruments," to aid thinking. Echoing Augustine, Richards argues that the aim of rhetoric is instruction in these processes. He applies the modern perception that a quest for ideal truth, for certain meaning, is inadequate. Rather than Aristotle's argument that "neither rhetoric nor dialectic is the scientific study of any one separate subject: both are faculties for providing arguments" (1356a, 26), Richards indicates that both are faculties for speculating about meanings.

Language use is purposive and complex and pervasive, the only means to understanding self and others. In Richards's new rhetoric, meanings are both composed and derived from the complex chain of past and present, personal and social events. Rhetoric provides the means to pursue an understanding of language and how it is used. He argues, "It is no preliminary or preparation for other profounder studies" (*Coleridge* 231).

Stuart C. Brown
New Mexico State University

Bibliography

Berthoff, Ann E., ed. *Richards on Rhetoric: I.A. Richards, Selected Essays, 1929–1974.* New York: Oxford UP, 1991.

Foss, Sonja K., Karen A. Foss, and Robert Trapp. "I.A. Richards." *Contemporary Perspectives on Rhetoric.* 2nd ed. Prospect Heights, NJ: Waveland, 1991. 27–54.

Ogden, C.K., and I.A. Richards. *The Meaning of Meaning: A Study of the Influence of Language upon Thought and of the Science of Symbolism.* 1923. San Diego: Harcourt, 1989.

Richards, I.A. *Coleridge on Imagination.* 1934. Bloomington: Indiana UP, 1960.

———. *How to Read a Page: A Course in Effective Reading, with an Introduction to a Hundred Great Words.* New York: Norton, 1942.

———. *Mencius on the Mind: Experiments in Multiple Definition.* 1930. Westport, CT: Hyperion, 1983.

———. *The Philosophy of Rhetoric.* New York: Oxford, 1936.

———. *Practical Criticism.* London: Kegan Paul, 1929.

———. *Principles of Literary Criticism.* London: Kegan Paul, 1924.

———. *So Much Nearer: Essays toward a World English.* New York: Harcourt, 1968.

———. *Speculative Instruments.* New York: Harcourt, 1955.

———, ed. and trans. *Plato's Republic.* Cambridge: Cambridge UP, 1966.

Russo, John Paul. *I.A. Richards: His Life and Work.* Baltimore: Johns Hopkins UP, 1989.

Ricoeur, Paul (b. 1913)

French educator and philosopher who linked issues of human will, evil, and psychoanalysis to theories of linguistic interpretation. Ricoeur taught at a number of schools, including the Sorbonne and the University of Chicago. His career in philosophy began as a phenomenologist, using a method that attempts to reach a pure description of experience. But his philosophical thinking took a "linguistic turn" as he recognized that many philosophical issues have their roots in language and particularly the interpretation of language, or hermeneutics.

Ricoeur's major early work was the *Philosophy of Will* (1950–1960), which consisted of three books. The first was *Freedom and Nature: The Voluntary and the Involuntary*, a phenomenological study of the issue of freedom and necessity in human action, showing how each depends on the other. The second, *Fallible Man*, concerns the existence of human fault and questions of evil. In the third, *The Symbolism of Evil*, Ricoeur makes a significant shift in methodology toward a hermeneutical understanding of indirect representations of evil as found in symbols and myths.

Ricoeur's interest in the linguistic properties of evil led him to explore psychotherapy in *Freud and Philosophy* (1965), an attempt to search out the ties between philosophical reflection and hermeneutics. It is in this book that he makes his famous distinction between two kinds of hermeneutics. The first is the hermeneutics of faith, characterized by an openness to meaning, a trust that the facade of a structure will reveal a truthful interpretation of that structure. The other, the hermeneutics of suspicion, begins with doubt. The masters of the hermeneutics of suspicion—Marx, Nietzsche, and Freud—see interpretation not as revelation but as a tearing off of the masks of false consciousness. After a detailed interpretation of Freud's writings, Ricoeur cannot find a resolution to this conflict of interpretations but hints at the possibility for a dialectical relationship.

Ricoeur's career then turns directly to issues of language. *The Conflict of Interpretations: Essays on Hermeneutics* (1974) represents his struggle with structuralism. He rejects the latter's focus on the abstract structure of language (*langue*) at the expense of language as used (*parole*). For Ricoeur, both the meaning and the event of language may be crystallized in the word. In *The Rule of Metaphor* (1975), Ricouer investigates two opposing views of metaphor and offers a third that combines the best of the two. The interpretation of metaphor consists of two movements, a semantic clash that marks a collapse of meaning and a semantic construction of new meaning on the ruins of the old. *Interpretation Theory* is a useful distillation of Ricoeur's work in hermeneutics. In this series of lectures, he looks at theories of written discourse, metaphor, and symbols. Finally, in the ambitious, three-volume *Time and Narrative* (1983–1985), Ricoeur explores the inherent linguistic and symbolic nature of human existence through an extensive study of mimesis or imitation.

Michael Carter
North Carolina State University

Bibliography

DiCenso, James. *Hermeneutics and the Disclosure of Truth: A Study in the Work of Heidegger, Gadamer, and Ricoeur.* Charlottesville: U of Virginia P, 1990.

Klemm, David E. *The Hermeneutical Theory of Paul Ricoeur: A Constructive Analysis.* Lewisberg, PA: Bucknell UP, 1983.

Reagan, Charles E., ed. *Studies in the Philosophy of Paul Ricoeur.* Athens: U of Ohio P, 1979.

Ricoeur, Paul. *Hermeneutics and the Human Sciences.* Ed. John B. Thompson. Cambridge: Cambridge UP, 1981.

Rogerian Rhetoric

Refers to theories and practices derived from psychologist Carl R. Rogers's ideas about communication and teaching. The introduction of Rogers to the field of rhetoric and composition is attributed to Young, Becker, and Pike (1970) and Hairston (1976). Early debates centered on the applicability of Rogerian strategies for teaching argument. Later Hairston (1982) broadened the discussion to adapting Rogers's educational ideas in writing classrooms. Moreover, Rogers's social and political engagement, first described as a political rhetoric by Zappen (1980), has influenced strategies for negotiation, mediation, and problem-solving for consensus.

Initial questions about the usefulness of adapting Rogers's ideas to rhetorical theory and teaching writing asked whether Rogerian principles constituted a rhetoric distinct from Aristotelian argumentation and whether they could be transferred to writing from the face-to-face, oral communication of individual and group counseling or negotiation. Rogers objected to the formulaic use of his principles as techniques or steps abstracted from specific therapeutic situations. Trying not to be reductive, however, some teachers extended Rogers's "person-centered" principles into invention and oral discourse for "active listening," peer response groups, and collaborative writing.

Pedagogically, Rogerian principles apply to all aspects of the composing process, from individual or group activities before drafting to writing the final product. For argumentation and problem-solving, where they have been taught most often, Rogerian strategies differ from the approaches of forensic and adversarial argument. Rogers stressed the interconnections of thought and emotion, not only in specific acts of communication but also in explanations of the transactions.

In an influential 1951 paper, Rogers stated, "Real communication occurs when we listen with understanding . . . to see the expressed idea and attitude from the other person's point of view, to sense how it feels to him . . . , to understand his thoughts and feelings so well that you could summarize them" (331–32). "Active listening" was the name Rogers and colleagues gave to this strategy of empathy and restatement.

Rogerian empathy is bound up in ethos and ethics. Although Rogers recognized that empathy could be used for hostile as well as growth-enhancing ends, he objected to the use of his principles manipulatively for the adversarial purpose of winning an argument. He proposed that if you achieve empathic understanding of another's views, "if you are willing to enter [another's] private world and see the way life appears to him, without any attempt to make evaluative judgments, you run the risk of being changed yourself" (333). To take the risk of changing rationally and emotionally on an issue is, for Rogers, to make an effort to cooperate and negotiate for mutually satisfactory solutions to problems.

Rogers's rationalistic assumptions for conflict resolution reflect the influences of John Dewey and William H. Kilpatrick's ideas of education, pragmatism, and social responsibility. From the understandings achieved through mutual communication, Rogers held that differences could be resolved rationally and harmonious relationships established. He extended his principles from the therapist-client situation to that of larger groups: teacher-students, labor-management,

even hostile factions in international political disputes.

However, critics and proponents alike recognize that Rogerian rhetoric is not applicable in all discourse situations. Feminist and social critics, in particular, object to Rogers's psychologizing rhetoric and humanistic psychotherapy. Yet Rogers's contributions to the theory and practice of mutual communication and student-centered, experiential learning form a rhetoric that facilitates individual and social development.

Nathaniel Teich
University of Oregon

Bibliography

Brent, Doug. "Young, Becker and Pike's 'Rogerian' Rhetoric: A Twenty-year Reassessment." *College English* 53 (1991): 452–66.

Hairston, Maxine. "Carl Rogers' Alternative to Traditional Rhetoric." *College Composition and Communication* 27 (1976): 373–77.

———. "Using Carl Rogers' Communication Theories in the Composition Classroom." *Rhetoric Review* 1 (1982): 50–55.

Kirschenbaum, Howard, and Valerie Land Henderson, eds. *The Carl Rogers Reader.* Boston: Houghton, 1989.

Rogers, Carl R. "Communication: Its Blocking and Its Facilitation." *On Becoming a Person.* Boston: Houghton, 1961. 329–37.

Teich, Nathaniel, ed. *Rogerian Perspectives: Collaborative Rhetoric for Oral and Written Communication.* Norwood, NJ: Ablex, 1992.

Young, Richard E., Alton L. Becker, and Kenneth L. Pike. *Rhetoric: Discovery and Change.* New York: Harcourt, 1970.

Zappen, James P. "Carl R. Rogers and Political Rhetoric." *PRE/TEXT* 1 (1980): 95–113.

Roman Rhetoric

An elaborate program of study and training, designed to produce an individual who could, as the occasion demanded, respond with appropriate and effective language. The system itself endured almost two thousand years. From the second century B.C.E. well into the eighteenth century, Roman rhetoric was taught, learned, and practiced. The concept of Roman rhetoric is something of a misnomer. Actually, the Greeks had developed rhetorical theory and rhetorical pedagogy to a remarkable state prior to the takeover of Greece by Rome in the second century. Nonetheless, the Romans in the first and second century did much to modify existing Greek rhetorical theory so that it would be better suited and better adapted to their own civic and political purposes.

For the Romans, prior to the second century B.C.E., the tutorial method of instruction was the predominant educational practice. A Roman young man would apprentice himself to an older, more established individual and would learn from this older person what was required in a given profession. For example, if one wished to become a legal advocate, one would apprentice oneself—or one's family would apprentice him—to an already successful individual. Much like contemporary guild systems wherein one progresses through a lengthy apprenticeship to master a craft or trade, the early Roman tutorial format had both advantages and weaknesses. The relatively small number of aristocratic, patrician families made professional apprenticeship possible. Without doubt one could learn politics or military science or legal pleading from the precepts and daily practice of an experienced mentor. As an educational arrangement, however, tradition is privileged over innovation, custom over creativity. As the Republic began to expand and as Rome's middle class also expanded, the situation became susceptible to change. The Greek method of rhetorical schooling met the cultural need.

When Greece was conquered by the Romans, many of the teachers of rhetoric were taken to Rome as slaves. Their knowledge and experience in teaching the art of persuasion, an art with pragmatic and utilitarian consequences, was perceived as valuable for a young Roman destined for a civic career. As some of these educated slaves gained their freedom, they established schools. Teaching rhetoric to the young Romans caused them to be expelled in 161 B.C.E., in part because their teachings seemed not practical and ill-suited to the Roman belief in the customs of their ancestors and the old ways of learning. Nonetheless, the inherent practicality of rhetoric, particularly in the law courts and assemblies, soon proved to be an indispensable skill, and once recognized as such, rhetoric became an accepted requirement for Roman aristocrats.

We know, for example, that L. Plotius Gallus was teaching in Latin a system of rhetoric when he was censored in the first century. By this first century, however, the way rhetoric was taught had become codified into five interrelated arts. Two extant treatises, Cicero's *De inventione* (89 B.C.E.) and the *Rhetorica ad Herennium* (86 B.C.E.), clearly attest to the concretization and codification of Roman rhetoric as early as the first century B.C.E. This program of study and training was broken down into a three-part system. Precepts, rhetorical rules, were taught and had as their goal theoretical understanding which would undergird performance and practical application. Second, practice of various forms and modes of discourse formed a significant part of the Roman rhetorical schema; finally, imitation was used to reinforce and expand what was learned in the precept and practice configurations. One can easily see the impact of Isocrates and his teaching of nature, art, and practice in the fourth and third centuries B.C.E. in this three-part methodology. Each of these three will be considered in turn.

The Precepts of Roman Rhetoric

Our sources for the codified rules of Roman rhetoric are the *Rhetorica ad Herennium,* Cicero's *De inventione, Partitione oratoria, Topica, Brutus, Orator,* and Quintilian's *Institutio oratoria.* From these primary sources, one learns that the theoretical material of Roman rhetoric was divided and subdivided, and classified and subclassified. The three genres— judicial, deliberative, and demonstrative— formed a structural pattern under which the precepts could be addressed. Knowing that the Romans were litigious and that one could attain fame in the Roman culture by distinguishing oneself in the law courts, it is not surprising to discover that most of the attention of the rhetoricians was focused on the judicial or forensic genre.

Invention

The first of the five great arts of Roman rhetoric, invention, involved finding true or probable material that would make a case believable. The interaction and intersection of various philosophical schools can be read into the rhetoricians' development of invention. How might one find true and probable material? An elaborate array of topics and the stasis system were employed. A student was required to first deter-

R

mine the genre in which he would be speaking and then use the inventional aids.

If a speaker were going to give an epideictic speech, for example, the rhetoricians taught a set of topics (*De inventione* 1.xxiv.34). One would consider the name, nature, manner of life, fortune, habit, interest, and so forth, of the individual being praised and then, in addition, explore what were considered the goods of an individual's mind or body or chance (*De inventione* II.lix.177). Goods of the mind would be such things as an individual's wisdom, intelligence, or virtue, and goods of the body would include such things as a person's health and physical attractiveness. Money, friends, and power, for example, were considered goods of chance, which, if an individual were fortunate enough to have them, could also be points around which discourse could be developed to praise a given person. These topics (*loci*) functioned as a checklist, facets of the subject that needed to be considered for the sake of completeness.

If an individual, on the other hand, were going to learn about deliberative speaking in an assembly, such a student would need to learn that the goal of any discourse in a deliberative setting is to secure advantage and honor and avoid disadvantage and baseness. Certain things were to be sought. Virtue, knowledge, and truth were things to be sought because they were considered components of honor and as such were valuable in and of themselves. Glory, rank, and influence were goods that were considered external to a speaker but valuable nonetheless. Glory, for example, "consists in a person's having a widespread reputation accompanied by praise" (*De inventione* 2.liv.166). Knowing this precept would allow one to address the concept of glory in a speech and develop the concept as well. Long lists of topics such as these needed to be learned and integrated into the student's habitual way of locating material in a deliberative case.

In forensic oratory, the major emphasis of Roman rhetoric, the stasis system, came into its own (*De inventione* 2.iv.14ff). A student learned to begin his analysis with the conjectural issue: whether or not a thing happened. A prosecutor needed to thoroughly explore the motive of the accused person; the deed committed needed to be scrutinized under the headings of acts caused by impulse and premeditation. When speaking for the defense, one needed to master a set of rules that helped one deny and minimize the alleged action. Additional lines of investigation were available to speakers in this

context: lines of investigation from an individual's character, a person's name or fortune, various emotions, and so forth. Lines of investigation were available from the act itself in terms of where and when the act took place, the occasion, and the facilities.

When preparing a case that revolved around the stasis of definition, what something should be properly called, if one were prosecuting, for example, one learned a procedure wherein one could define the action and relate the act to the offered definition. Again, if one were on the defense, a student learned how to offer countering definitions to engage the dispute (*De inventione* 2.xvii.52–56).

The qualitative stasis, that arena in which extenuating circumstances could be addressed, received considerable attention by the Roman rhetoricians (*De inventione* 2.xxi.62–115). When the question at hand concerned the impact, nature, and kind of an action committed, students immediately would determine whether they could profitably pursue legal inquiries into the types and sources of laws or equitable considerations involving issues of right and wrong. Commonplaces were taught in which a student could magnify the baseness of a deed, produce a vivid verbal picture of a deed, or counter with a shifting of the blame or argue degree of guilt.

Often, the translative stasis came into play and, accordingly, was taught as a set of precepts (*De inventione* 2.xix.57–61). This would be used when an inappropriate procedure was involved. That is, if a case were being tried in a wrong court or at the wrong time or under a wrong statute, the Roman rhetoricians taught students ways of expressing this inappropriateness. Civil law prescribed certain courts for certain offenses. A case of bribery had to be heard in a prescribed court; otherwise, an advocate could argue that the case was being tried in the wrong arena. Although this argument to shift from one court to another was not often used in a forensic speech because of the elaborate preliminary work done before hearing a case, nonetheless an advocate needed this knowledge and it was taught as a required component of Roman rhetoric.

Arrangement
Nowhere else in the extant Roman rhetorics is the tendency to codify as apparent as it is in the rhetoricians' discussions of the ways in which a speech needed to be structured.

The *exordium,* the introduction to a persuasive address, required a student to select materials that would either enhance or make repugnant the case at hand (*ad Herennium* 1.4; *De inventione* 1.xiv.19ff; *De oratoria* 1.143). Topics could be found by analyzing the ethos of the speaker, the character of the opponent, the audience, and the facts of the case. Again, working much like a checklist, the catalogs of topics provided a highly systematized and apparently thorough way of exploring every conceivable dimension from which material could be located for the purposes of producing a powerful and impact-filled introduction. The function of the *exordium* was to render the listeners attentive and well disposed, as well as set the tone for the remainder of the oration. However, if a speaker found himself in a weak position, methods of using an indirect approach were taught to undermine and sabotage an opponent's case—in the introduction—by use of humor, apparent agreement, and insinuation.

The second part of the classical oration, the narrative (*narratio*), was divided into types with attendant rules for each. A narration could be either a straightforward offering of facts or a story in which facts were interwoven within the entire speech or a presentation that was essentially unconnected with the case. The emphasis always was on traits of character, regardless of which type was selected. The rules for the narrative tended to be unequivocal. The narrative, according to the Roman rhetoricians, should contain only the essentials, should be clear, should be sequenced and plausible. Even when the facts of the case contained in the narrative were true, one should still make them plausible because, according to the rhetoricians, the narrative serves as an anticipatory reputation. When an orator builds the story so that what happens fits with what is considered usual or expected or natural, the motives of the persons involved in the case can be made quite apparent to an audience.

In a typical classical forensic oration, a division (*divisio*) occurred next (*ad Herennium* 1.x.17). This was a section of the speech in which agreements and disagreements were covered and an overview of the entire case presented to the auditors.

Gaining belief from one's audience was paramount. The fourth main section of the classical oration, proof (*confirmatio*), was designed specifically to work on existing beliefs (*ad Herennium* 2.xviii.28). By using the stasis formula, one could determine the crux of a case and argue either from conjecture or definition or quality or transference. Much as in the narrative, rhetoricians placed great stress on motives and probabilities as central concerns of the speaker. Here, rules were provided for: speaking for and against witnesses, testimony, rumors, documents, conflicting laws, and so forth. Lists of topical headings for each of these were committed to memory in the schools of the rhetoricians. In addition, various commonplaces were considered proper in the proof section of a speech. These commonplaces were designed for recommending pity or attacking the prosecutor. Roman rhetoricians more or less agreed on the structure that a proof should take. Most seemed to favor the *epicheireme,* a five-part form into which propositions and proofs could be put. In an *epicheireme* one began with a proposition and offered a reason for the proposition and then followed this with a further proof of the reason. Then, an orator was expected to provide embellishment and a resume, thereby completing the five-part formula. Not surprisingly, extensive rules for each of the five parts were supplied.

The refutation (*refutatio*) formed the fifth part of the oration and had as its purpose the recognition of faults and flaws in the proofs offered by one's opponent. Then, an orator was expected to add the final part, the peroration, which would sum up the key features of the case, amplify the salient points via commonplaces, and add any final appeals.

Style

The Roman rhetoricians taught that there were three levels of style—the grand or high, the middle, and the low or plain. Each of these levels, however, were thought to require four virtues: clarity, correctness, appropriateness, and ornateness or distinctness. The quality of ornateness received the most emphasis in the rhetorical treatises and the rhetoricians had a proclivity to produce long lists with many nuanced distinctions between and among ways in which words could be used and configured. For example, the rhetoricians divided language into figures of diction and figures of thought (*ad Herennium* 4.xii.17). Figures of diction concerned the ornate use of words, for example, an interrogation. Figures of thought involved distinctions that came from the idea and not the word itself. Understatement, for example, would be a figure of thought.

Delivery

All the Roman rhetoricians agreed that delivery contributed greatly to the impact of a speech (*ad Herennium* 3.xi.19; *Institutio oratoria* 11.iii.2). The rules and precepts for delivery were influenced, without doubt, from the prescriptions and training given to professional actors. Delivery included both vocal quality and physical movement. The rhetoricians prescribed exercises and ways to develop this skill that were derived not only from the regimen of acting but also from the disciplines of music, nutrition, and medicine. Delivery, for a Roman orator, required physical strength and control, as the speeches typically were presented in the out-of-doors and frequently crowded areas. Rules were taught for using various pitches, rates, and volumes, as well as for moving the feet and hands and assuming various facial gesticulations. As a nonverbal element of persuasion, delivery was accorded high status in the rhetorics of Rome.

Memory

The fifth and final art of an orator, memory, derives from a kind of mental association and may have been based on a kind of learned or reinforced iconic memory (*ad Herennium* 3.xvi.28). The rhetoricians recognized two types of memory: natural and artistic. Natural memory was inherent and a gift that an individual might possess, but even natural memory, according to the rhetoricians, needed extensive training. Artistic memory, on the other hand, used a system of backgrounding and foregrounding of images onto which an orator would mentally place parts of a speech if not actually the individual words of each section of a speech. This associative type of mnemonic device served the Roman orators well, and the various phases of the school exercises interlocked with this canon of oratory much as it did with the other four. An educated Roman, it must be noted, was expected to master all five of these arts of oratory.

The School Exercises

Better known as the *progymnasmata,* the school exercises involved both writing and oral performance to produce rhetoricians, persons able to use language fittingly as a situation or subject demanded. Our most complete treatment of the school exercises can be found in Quintilian's *Institutes.* Here, Quintilian notes that a student would need to master grammar before proceeding into the schools of rhetoric wherein the school exercises were taught. In matter of fact,

however, grammarians often did teach some of the exercises, and some of the rhetoricians, no doubt, found it necessary to return initially to some grammatical exercises before moving into the stages of the *progymnasmata.*

The *Progymnasmata*

Taken as a whole, this system of school assignments has an underlying architectural model as its foundation. The exercises themselves are patterns to follow, and they are graded from the simple and easy to the more complex and difficult. Each of the exercises adds to what was learned in the exercise before, and each contains key component skills for later use in public and civic discourse. Each of the exercises was perceived as important in itself, as well as for its later practical use. The school exercises, the *progymnasmata,* began with the fable. This was a fictitious narrative giving the semblance of truth, with the moral at either the beginning or end of the story. A rhetorician would provide models of fables upon which the students could then either pattern their own compositions or, in some cases, they could create stories of their own. The fable, as a pedagogical device, introduced students to a simple narrative form, a form that would be used not only in later exercises but also in actual court cases and in deliberative settings. The fable legitimizes for students the use of literary forms and encourages production of discourse that directly addresses moral behavior. Moreover, the fable introduces concepts of statement (the moral) and development. As such, a primitive structure into which one could then assemble arguments in subsequent situations was introduced at the outset of the course of training. Finally, the narrative form invites an imaginative response to a situation and, as such, would encourage creativity in a student at the very outset of his learning process.

After the fable, students were assigned the tale. This was an exposition of a thing done or imagined as done. The exercise introduced a form related to but distinct from the fable. It too involved the moral dimension of human activity, and it concerned itself with six distinct elements: the agent, the act, time, place, manner, and cause. By learning to manipulate multiple components, a student could begin developing the cognitive skills of keeping a number of important points alive for an audience in his fictive discourse.

Next a student was assigned the *chreia.* This exercise involved a brief bit of advice bearing appropriately on some person. It could be constructed in various ways, to be sure, either as a panegyric or as an exhortation from a cause or testimony from the ancients. The *chreia* was a simple, manageable prototype of deliberative discourse. As such it begins to show a student the connection between the deliberative genre and the epideictic genre introduced in the first two exercises. Moreover, the *chreia* introduced a student to the possibility of using a variety of developmental forms in assembling and producing discourse.

Next, students were taught the proverb. This exercise was a concise expression in the form of a statement promoting something or opposing it. As a pedagogical tool, it moves from a single individual in the *chreia* to a more universal application in this exercise. The hortatory, an advisory dimension, is present in that it involves moral conduct. And the proverb could be developed and amplified in the same forms as the *chreia*. Doing so would reinforce what was already learned as well as anticipating what was to come.

The Romans placed a high premium on skill in forensic oratory and it is no surprise, then, to discover that the next exercise in the *progymnasmata* was one called refutation. This exercise involved an overthrowing of anything set forth. This exercise and the one following are often considered to contain all of the power of rhetoric. The procedure for producing a refutation involved a set of steps: state the false assertion, explain the problem, and then develop discourse showing the false assertion to be obscure or unconvincing or impossible or inconsistent or improper or irrational.

One might wonder why refutation is prior to proof. The exercise trains one in analysis, and a student would then be better equipped to locate weaknesses in a case before attempting to construct one. The exercise is obviously preparation for forensic oratory, but it is also directly linked to deliberation. Obviously, in the Senate or Roman Assembly, one would need to know the methods of refutation, as attacking a position is always easier than establishing one. This exercise, the refutation, moves a student from the moral area of discourse into the logical dimension. In addition, students would recognize that it is an actual part of the classical oration.

Next, the student was expected to exercise his rhetorical learning in the confirmation. This project involved a showing of proof for anything set forth. Since the student had already learned the procedure for refutation, one needed only reverse the procedure to prove a point. That is, one could and was expected to develop one's confirmation

by deriving material from the refutation of the proponent and then showing how the position is obvious or convincing or possible or consistent or proper or rational. Here, too, a main part of the classical oration is introduced as part of the school training exercises, but it is introduced and learned after the preceding preparatory exercises have given a student ways of manipulating material as well as ways of structuring it.

Then the student learned the commonplace. This exercise was an amplification of the evil things connected with anyone. The project was called common because these passages or pieces of discourse would apply at a general level to all individual evil doers within a given category, such as liars, traitors, patricides, and so forth. An extensive and expected sequence for creating a commonplace formed part of the training. A student was expected to show how incompatible with moral precepts a given behavior was and then compare or contrast it to magnify the evil, attack the motive, or digress to enhance the reproach. Finally, most commonplaces had a section involving the rejection of any mercy, given the magnitude of the evil that had been perpetrated. Pedagogically, commonplaces would be used throughout an oration and particularly in forensic speeches, as they frequently involve moral issues. These moral issues, it should be noted, were already introduced in several of the earlier exercises and their applicability would be reinforced by learning and producing commonplaces.

Next, students were given the assignment to produce an *encomium*. This assignment was a speech bringing out the good points of someone. In other words, students were taught to praise an individual. In some ways this exercise is the opposite of the commonplace, but it contains the cultural values prized by a society and teaches students a performative way to use these values. The objects of praise range from plants to persons, virtues to seasons to locales, but regardless of the focus of the praise, students were required to use an exact formula for developing this type of discourse. For example, students were expected to use the topics of genus, education, achievements (physical, spiritual, and those from fortune), and then use comparisons to magnify the value of their object of praise. Here, too, one notes a return to the earlier exercises that stressed moral action. However, this exercise extends to one's civic community, whereas the earlier ones do not do so necessarily. Highly practical and relevant for funeral eulogies, forensic addresses, and other discourse forms, the encomium gave a student a formula for discovering and using the available means of cultural praise.

Since students could anticipate a career in which they would need to blame as well as praise, one ought not be surprised to learn that the next exercise in the *progymnasmata* was vituperation. This exercise was a speech bringing out the bad points in someone. It is the opposite of an *encomium* to be sure, but it involves heavy accusation. The training here is ideally suited for later use in forensic settings, and it uses the same pattern as the *encomium,* only in a reverse formula. That is, exploring the topics of genus, education, achievements, and so forth, one could discover moral faults that could be used as the basis for blame.

Students were then given the project of comparison. This exercise involved the study and production of a speech that juxtaposes one thing with another to demonstrate greatness. No doubt an early and primitive form of logical reasoning, this exercise trained one to perceive differences and similarities and to express these differences and similarities easily and purposefully.

Characterization was the next in the sequence of exercises. Here, a student was given the task of imitating the character of a proposed person. Closely related to drama, this project emphasized ethos. By learning how to characterize, a student was learning a form that could be used simultaneously to enhance an argumentative point and mask a speaker and the speaker's intention.

The very nature of speech involves the use of mediating agencies—voice and gesture—to present something real to an audience. The students in the *progymnasmata* of the Roman rhetoricians were taught description as a discrete exercise. This assignment was an expository speech distinctly presenting to view a thing being set forth. Learning how to describe an object or an event or a set of happenings enabled one to use language that depicts and portrays and paints. In other words, description as a rhetorical device works primarily in the visual realm, which would strengthen and reinforce ordinary, expositional language. Two types of theses were next taught. As a reasoned examination of anything under consideration, a student could produce a political thesis concerned with the city or a speculative thesis that involved issues of the mind. This exercise required a stu-

dent to develop analytical skills, offer opposing views, and refute these opposing views. The thesis was a primitive type of dialectic inquiry that encouraged a blending of speculative generalization with practical application. As a derivative from the procedures used in the schools of philosophy, this exercise broadened a student's culture and outlook. For example, developing a thesis such as "The wise man alone is rich" would require conceptual thought put into pragmatic discourse.

Next the student was given the exercise in proposing a law. This task involved an advocacy of and an opposition to an established law. In addition to sharpening one's ability to anticipate consequences, enjoin moral codes, and consider distinctions between and among the just, the useful, and the possible, this school assignment prepared one directly for a lifetime of activity in the assembly and senate. Upon completion of this exercise, students would then continue their training in the schools of declamation. Sometimes these were taught by the rhetoricians as an extension of the *progymnasmata,* and sometimes they were simply taught separately. Of importance, however, to understanding the power of the school exercises, one must remember that orators practiced and rehearsed and trained with these exercises, particularly the next two, throughout their entire adult careers.

The *suasoria* and *controversia* were the two exercises most closely associated with the schools of declamation. The *suasoria* was an exercise in persuading or dissuading a person or an assembly to or from a given course of action. Quite directly, the exercise was training for deliberative assemblies and at best encouraged creativity and practice in coping with dilemmas. At its worst this exercise could lead to excess in creating unusual and bizarre situations. The *controversia* was an exercise in which one argued for or against a fictive person caught between a law and an unusual set of circumstances. An exercise that was excellent training for the law courts could easily be turned into a performance for one's peers or one's students and, indeed, this was a common practice in the first and second centuries C.E. Nonetheless, when taught under the careful guidance of a rhetorician, the *suasoria* and *controversia* were the capstone achievements of the school exercises, and between the two of them, they incorporated much of what had been taught in the preceding projects.

Imitation

The genius of Roman rhetoric resides in the use of imitation throughout the school course to create sensitivity to language and versatility in its use. Isocrates, the Greek rhetorician, used imitation extensively in his school of rhetoric, but whether the Roman adaptation is a carbon copy of his procedure remains uncertain. We do know that in the Roman schools of rhetoric, imitation was a system by which students learned to model their language usage upon that of other language users to enhance their originality. Imitation, for the Romans, was not copying and not simply using the language structures of others. On the contrary, imitation involved a series of steps, which, taken together, yielded the desired results.

At the outset, a written text was read aloud by a teacher of rhetoric, and this text was invariably carefully chosen. It could be an essay or a speech, a section from a history or a poem. The teacher would use both strong and weak pieces for instructional purposes, but the student would immediately hear both the form of the text and the ideas expressed.

Next, a phase of analysis was used. The teacher would take the text apart in minute detail. The structure, word choice, grammar, rhetorical strategy, phrasing, elegance, and so forth, would be explained, described, and illustrated for the students. Both what the passage contained and what the passage concealed were displayed. As a consequence, a student would learn what judgments others had made in their language choices and what results would accrue from these choices.

Next, students were required to memorize good models. This task would provide an abundance of phrases and figurations for subsequent use, and the exercise in and of itself would strengthen a student's memory, one of the five arts of oratory.

Students were then expected to paraphrase models. By retelling a text in their own words, the exercise could be as simple as retelling a fable or as complex as retelling the plot of a tragedy. This phase of imitation reinforced students' abilities to perceive and actually reproduce the structural elements of a selection.

Then, students recast the ideas in the text under consideration. Many forms were possible—for example, a student might translate from one language to another (Roman aristocrats were bilingual); they could move from a verse to a prose form; they could shift from one level of style to another. This recasting involved both writing as well as speaking, and it should be noted that all of the exercises and phases of imitation involved both composition as well as oral expression. Recasting places a premium on prose and verse forms, intricate knowledge of grammar, and vocabulary.

As part of imitation, students would then read aloud a paraphrase or a recasting of one's own text for the teacher and for his classmates before moving to the final phase, which involved correction by the teacher. Because correction was done in public, one can imagine a great deal of peer pressure to excel. Thus, the judgments of both the teachers and one's peers were learned and implemented. Adults as well as school children followed the steps of imitation throughout their lifetime.

Roman rhetoric, then, involved the mastery of an intricate set of rules and precepts, the successful working through of the exercises in the *progymnasmata*, and an internalization and continued practice of the steps and phases involved in imitation. Little wonder that Roman rhetoric endured for over two thousand years as the premier method of language development, linguistic understanding, and language performance.

Donovan J. Ochs
University of Iowa

Bibliography

Baldwin, Charles Sears. *Ancient Rhetoric and Poetic*. New York: Macmillan, 1924.

Bonner, Stanley. *Education in Ancient Rome*. Berkeley: U of California P, 1977.

———. *Roman Declamation*. Liverpool: Liverpool UP, 1949.

Clarke, Martin L. *Rhetoric at Rome: A Historical Survey*. London: Cohen, 1953.

Kennedy, George. *The Art of Rhetoric in the Roman World: 300 B.C.–A.D. 300*. Princeton: Princeton UP, 1972.

Yates, Frances. *The Art of Memory*. Chicago: U of Chicago P, 1966.

See also Arrangement; Cicero; Imitation, Invention; *Progymnasmata*; Quintilian; Stasis Theory

Rosenblatt, Louise M. (b. 1904)

Reader response theorist and practitioner. As Margaret Mead notes in her autobiography, when she and Louise Rosenblatt were undergraduate roommates at Barnard College in the early 1920s, they and their closest friends (Leonie Adams, Eleanor Pelham Kortheuer, Deborah Kaplan, Viola Corrigan, and Hannah Kahn) formed a group that came to be called the Ash Can Cats, a name given to them by Minor W. Latham, one of their favorite professors. She earned her B.A. in English from Barnard in 1925, her doctorate in comparative literature from the Sorbonne in 1931. She was professor of English education at New York University from 1948 to 1972. In 1991 she was awarded an honorary doctorate from the University of Arizona.

When Rosenblatt first published *Literature as Exploration* in 1938, she encouraged teachers to help adolescents "experience" literature by responding to it, rather than simply criticizing it. In 1978 Rosenblatt offered the notion of "efferent" and "aesthetic" psychological stances that readers assume when reading a text. She derives the term *efferent* from the Latin *effere*, meaning "to carry away," and explains that this is what happens when one reads a text primarily to extract information from it. "Aesthetic" reading, on the other hand, is concerned with literature as art, with the "lived through" experience of the text, with what happens "during the actual reading event." It is possible that different aesthetic transactions can occur with the same text and different readers—depending on the "nature, state of mind, or past experience of the reader." The main distinction, then, between aesthetic and nonaesthetic readings of texts has to do with what the reader does or does not do (1978:24–28).

To Rosenblatt, reading is an activity that occupies a continuum between aesthetic and efferent stances, with an aesthetic stance being necessary for literary reading. The psychological stance of the reader, though, is often contingent on the "socio-physical" setting (1978:78). In other words, the reader's attitude and the context for reading, rather than the text itself, are the determining factors in whether the reader has an "aesthetic" or "efferent" experience. In the classroom context, what Rosenblatt calls the "nonverbal setting" (the aims and objectives of the lesson and the teacher) is also important in fostering an aesthetic reading because it clues the student as to which stance to take (1978:78). In fact, it is the English teacher's responsibility to "keep alive this view of the literary work as personal evocation,

the product of creative activity carried on by the reader under the guidance of the text" (1983:280). Drawing on the works of Charles Sanders Peirce, William James, and John Dewey, Rosenblatt argues that reading literature is a two-way process, a transaction between the reader and the text. In this view, meaning resides in the experience that a reader brings to a text, tempered by accountability to the limits of the text itself.

Anne-Marie Hall
University of Arizona
Duane H. Roen
Arizona State University

Bibliography

Karolides, Nicholas J., ed. *Reader Response in the Classroom: Evoking and Interpreting Meaning in Literature*. New York: Longman, 1992.

Mead, Margaret. *Blackberry Winter: My Early Years*. New York: Morrow, 1972.

Rosenblatt, Louise. *L'Idee de l'Art pour Art*. New York: AMS P, 1977.

———. *Literature as Exploration*. 4th ed. New York: Modern Language Assn., 1983.

———. *The Reader, the Text, the Poem: The Transactional Theory of the Literary Work*. Carbondale: Southern Illinois UP, 1978.

See also READER-RESPONSE THEORY

Rousseau, Jean-Jacques (1712–1778)

French philosopher whose ideas have broadly influenced Western thought, particularly through Romanticism, of which he is considered a father. Rousseau figures in the rhetorical tradition as a critic of language and education. His emphasis upon individualism and the self influenced the epistemological reorientations that rhetorical theory and practice underwent in the eighteenth century.

Born in Geneva, Rousseau spent many years of his youth in Turin and Chambéry under the care of Mme. de Warens, a woman twelve years his senior who later became his lover. In 1742 Rousseau arrived in Paris and failed to achieve notoriety with the numerical system of musical notation he had invented, but he did become familiar with Diderot and other *philosophes*. In 1745 Rousseau began a lifelong liaison with Thérèse Lavasseur, an uneducated servant girl. They had five children, all of whom he sent to an orphanage. Rousseau's fame began in 1750 upon winning the Dijon Academy's prize for the best essay on the question "Whether the reestablishment of sciences and the arts has contributed to purify morals." His "Discourse on Sciences and the Arts" denounced the ill effects wrought upon people as they are taken from a state of natural goodness into the artifices and inequalities of society. This established Rousseau's public identity as a critic of society and the corrupting influences of its institutions. In 1761 Rousseau's popular novel *La Nouvelle Héloise* appeared, followed in 1762 by his famous *Du Contrat Social* and *Émile,* Rousseau's revolutionary educational "treatise." After *Émile* was condemned for challenging Christian dogma, Rousseau visited England as David Hume's guest but returned to France after his recurring paranoia caused his rupture with Hume. In his later years he wrote autobiographically, especially his *Confessions* (1782).

Rousseau influenced rhetoric by advancing the concept of a universal human nature, making the faculty psychology of George Campbell and others possible. Rousseau also gave impetus to the subjective epistemologies of his century, favoring private, expressive, and intuitive models of discourse over formal, social, or artificial ones (the "vitalists" of twentieth-century composition still bear this influence). Rousseau may fairly be called antirhetorical because he rejects formal language and literary instruction and attributes a society's ills to its eloquence. The education he advocates in *Émile* omits linguistic and moral inculcation. Instead, students rely upon their own authority and experience, learning from the book of nature rather than anything printed, and exercising their bodies as much as their minds. Rousseau explicitly rejects rhetoric in *Émile,* claiming that practice in the art of persuasion is too often empty verbiage.

In his "Essay on the Origin of Languages," Rousseau acknowledges a close relationship between language and the passions, thus aligning himself with eighteenth-century rhetorical thought. Rousseau posits the fundamentally figured nature of language, as well as a reciprocality between the mores of a society and its eloquence. Hugh Blair draws obliquely on this essay in his own on the same subject; Derrida has given more painstaking attention to its contents, uncovering Rousseau's consciousness of the complexity of language and rhetoric.

Gideon Burton
University of Southern California

Bibliography

Annales de la société Jean-Jacques Rousseau. Geneva: A. Julien. 1903– .

Babbitt, Irving. *Rousseau and Romanticism.* New York: Houghton, 1919.

Blair, Hugh. "Origin and Nature of Figurative Language." *Lectures on Rhetoric and Belles Lettres.* 2 vols. London, 1783. Rpt. in facsimile. Harold F. Harding, ed. 2 vols. Southern Illinois UP Series, Landmarks in Rhetoric and Public Address, edited by David Potter. Carbondale: Southern Illinois UP, 1965.

Cassirer, Ernst. *The Question of Jean-Jacques Rousseau.* Trans. and ed. Peter Gay. New York: Columbia UP, 1954.

Derrida, Jacques. *Of Grammatology.* Trans. Gayatri Chakravorty Spivak. Baltimore: Johns Hopkins UP, 1974.

Guehenno, Jean. *Jean-Jacques Rousseau.* Trans. John and Doreen Weightman. New York: Columbia UP, 1966.

Oliver, Robert T. *The Influence of Rhetoric in the Shaping of Great Britain.* Newark: U of Delaware P, 1986.

Schinz, Albert. *État présent des travaux sur J.-J. Rousseau. Études Français.* New York: Modern Language Assn., 1941.

Wright, Ernest Hunter. *The Meaning of Rousseau.* London: Oxford UP, 1929.

R

Royal Society of London

The first and foremost society of natural philosophers, later scientists, in Great Britain; publishers of the *Philosophical Transactions of the Royal Society.* Chartered in 1662, it has provided a forum and institutional basis for the development of modern science, influencing scientific communication by its overt programs of language reforms; the media, institutions, and practices of communication that it fostered; and the overall social practice of scientific knowledge-making that it helped develop, which both provided a context for scientific communication and made that communication instrumental in the growth of knowledge. Despite an overt philosophy that at times has eschewed rhetoric, the Royal Society has helped set the social and disciplinary terms within which the modern rhetoric of science operates.

The Royal Society, chartered by King Charles II of England in 1662, brought together a group of natural philosophers who had been meeting in London, largely at Gresham College, with the "invisible college" centered on Samuel Hartlib and a third group meeting at Oxford since 1648, overlapping with the first two. The society has since met regularly, at Gresham College of the University of London, until 1710, when it moved to Crane Court; in 1780 the society moved to its present location at Somerset House. Over the years its membership has changed from a mixed group of aristocrats, gentlemen, and tradesmen into a select group of preeminent scientists.

From the earliest years, the society has been dedicated to empiricism and the free circulation of knowledge. Early meetings were devoted to the presentations of demonstrations of empirical phenomena for the communal witnessing and validation of events and the sharing of philosophic communications from throughout the world. In 1665 the society's secretary, Henry Oldenburg, founded as a private venture the first English-language scientific journal, *The Philosophic Transactions of the Royal Society,* following by only three months the founding of the French *Journal des Scavans,* which was the first scientific journal. Ownership of the journal was taken over by the Royal Society, which has published it continuously since then. By means of the *Philosophic Transactions,* the demonstrations and communications of the society were made available more widely. Appropriate genres for the reporting, arguing for, synthesizing, and criticizing of findings and claims developed, establishing the modern forms for the communication of science. At first a wide range of topics were considered proper for the natural-philosophic concerns of the society, including reports of non-European learning and culture, archaeological findings, and educational experiments. Throughout the eighteenth and nineteenth centuries, however, subjects of interest narrowed and became specialized into modern disciplinary divisions of the natural and physical sciences. Other societies and journals were founded in the wake of the Royal Society of London, at first to serve different regions but then to serve different classes of people, as the Royal Society came to serve a specialized group of increasingly elite scientists, and different branches of knowledge and technology, as differentiated professions developed in the nineteenth century.

Historians of rhetoric and style have most frequently attended to the society's overt program of cleansing language of the figures of rhetoric in order to create a universal philosophic language that places words in direct relation to true objects. This program derives from Francis Bacon's concern to establish a philosophic language based on a proper naming of things freed from the four "idols": the Tribe (from human nature), the Cave (from individual idiosyncrasy), the Marketplace (from human interchange, including language), and the Theater (from dogma and philosophy). Such programs and the consequent discussion of them, however, have usually not taken into account Bacon's full concern for the role of both concepts and experiment in formulating knowledge, for the conventional nature of language, and for the nature of rhetoric. Nonetheless, under the banner of Bacon, Thomas Sprat in his *History of the Royal Society,* published in 1667, denounced tropes, figures, metaphors, and other "ornaments of Speaking" and described the language policy of the Royal Society as:

> a constant Resolution to reject all the amplification, digressions and swellings of style; to return back to the primitive purity and shortness, when men delivered so many things almost in an equal number of words. They have exacted from all their members a close, naked, natural way of speaking; positive expressions; clear senses; a native easiness; bringing all things as near the Mathematical plainness as they can.

John Wilkins in *An Essay Towards a Real Character and a Philosophical Language* proposed in 1668 an ideographic lexicon that embodied and ordered all concepts and objects, while expelling words that did not refer to true things. Although such projects of language purification have regularly been criticized (in the Hobbes-Locke-Hume-Berkeley tradition) and even ridiculed (as in Swift's *Gulliver's Travels*) as misguidedly optimistic about possible relations between world and word, they have continually served as heuristic goals for much scientific discourse since then, although scientific language necessarily labors under the same constraints and dynamics as all languages and other symbolic formations. Programs of language purification also stand behind projects of lexical ordering of language, expressed through taxonomies, nomenclature debates, and dictionaries, which have been a regular concern since then of not only science but of all branches of knowledge. The spare style proposed by the early Royal Society has also served as heuristic for much English style since then, although proving statistical correlation has proved elusive.

Whatever the impact of the overt proposals of language purification on written style in limited scientific and more general discursive domains, the Royal Society has concretely influenced rhetorical history by creating new forums and institutions within which new kinds of communication took place. The early meetings, which organized discussion around common witnessing of demonstrations, not only provided new criteria for credibility of claims but also put constraints on argument about ideas removed from shared concrete experience. Data, facts, and reports of specialized occurrences removed from the common experience of life became increasingly important warrants for claims within natural philosophic discussion and the more general public sphere. Further, the society created a sequestered forum for discussion of ideas about the nature of the world removed from the contentiousness of public political debate. Such a move to diffuse public contention over fundamentally divisive issues has been seen by modern commentators as both major motive and major consequence of the formation of the society. There is a direct line between this Restoration political solution to the enthusiasm of the Puritan Revolution and the removal of many public issues today to the worlds of specialized expertise, which are considered objective and scientific.

The extension of the society's discussion (along with the attendant system of letter-writing) into the first English-language scientific journal created a new kind of print forum, which has blossomed into the wide range of scientific and professional journals that today are primary vehicles for proposing, arguing for, and archiving knowledge and that provide the intertext upon which new investigations and claims are asserted. The reports of demonstrations in the *Philosophic Transactions* began the development of the narrative modes, in which events to be taken as evidence of natural phenomena are presented for the virtual witnessing of the readership and of the form of the modern experimental report. Other genres of scientific communication also developed within the pages of this and consequent scientific journals.

As the *Philosophic Transactions* developed over the eighteenth and nineteenth centuries, it gave rise to many of the social and institutional features of modern science, including the crucial role of journals in arguing for scientific claims, sponsorship of journals by professional societies, expert readership, expectation of focused criticism according to anticipatable professional and methodological criteria, the system of the prior review of articles by experts in the field to ensure appropriate quality, and specialization.

A further underlying rhetorical consequence of the formation of the society, the specialization of its discourse, the increasingly focused strictures placed on the character and quality of the spoken and print discourse, the credentialing of membership, the formation of strong professional networks among members, and the public dominance over certain questions gained by the membership of the society and its professional extensions has been to create a new source of ethos that breeds trust internally among members of scientific communities and that warrants individual scientists speaking to the wider public with the ethical probity of the entire communal endeavor of science. Currently, in the United Kingdom, being Fellow of the Royal Society grants one not only honor and respect but great credibility within science and to the wider public. Similar honors and statuses in the United States and elsewhere carry similar public force.

Charles Bazerman
Georgia Institute of Technology

Bibliography

Bazerman, Charles. *Shaping Written Knowledge: The Genre and Activity of the Experimental Article in Science.* Madison: U of Wisconsin P, 1988.

Dear, Peter. "*Totius in Verba*: Rhetoric and Authority in the Early Royal Society." *Isis* 76 (1985): 145–61.

Hall, Marie Boas. *All Scientists Now: The Royal Society in the Nineteenth Century.* Cambridge: Cambridge UP, 1984.

Hunter, Michael. *Science and Society in Restoration England.* Cambridge: Cambridge UP, 1981.

Jacob, Margaret. *The Newtonians and the English Revolution, 1689–1720.* Ithaca, NY: Cornell UP, 1976.

Jones, Richard Foster. "Science and English Prose Style." *Publications of the Modern Language Association* 45 (1930): 977–1009.

Shapin, Steven. *A Social History of Truth: Gentility, Credibility, and Scientific Knowledge in Seventeenth-Century England.* Chicago: U of Chicago P, 1994.

Shapin, Steven, and Simon Schaffer. *Leviathan and the Air Pump: Hobbes, Boyle, and the Experimental Life.* Princeton: Princeton UP, 1985.

Slaughter, M.M. *Universal Languages and Scientific Taxonomy in the Seventeenth Century.* Cambridge: Cambridge UP, 1982.

Stimson, Dorothy. *Scientists and Amateurs: A History of the Royal Society.* New York: Henry Schuman, 1948.

Russell, Bertrand Arthur William (1872–1970)

British philosopher, mathematician, educator, social theorist, and liberal activist whose principal work was in developing symbolic logic and applying it to philosophy and mathematics. He attended and became a fellow of Trinity College, Cambridge University. Russell endorsed the application of logic to all aspects of thought and language. In 1944, as the third Earl Russell, he became an active member of the British House of Lords, was elected a fellow of the Royal Society, and in 1950 received the Nobel Prize for literature. Russell is recognized as one of the most influential thinkers of the twentieth century and his most important work, *Principia Mathematica* (1910–1913), written with Alfred North Whitehead, is acknowledged as the most important twentieth-century treatise on logic.

Russell's early work focused on an analysis of propositions. He held that a linguistic expression can only be understood if it either refers to something experienced or is defined by such expressions. Much of his writing was directed toward providing a minimum vocabulary for nonmathematical knowledge.

Principia Mathematica demonstrated that the theorems of pure mathematics follow the principles of logic and that all mathematical concepts may be defined in terms of the vocabulary of logic. Only three "undefined" terms are needed, terms described as constituting a "minimum vocabulary" for mathematics and logic. Russell posits an ideal language that would have a structure identical to the structure of reality.

Our Knowledge of the External World (1914) explains this logical atomism and holds that all propositions that are statements about experienced reality can be broken down into logically irreducible subpropositions. Russell also provides a method for translating statements about physical objects into statements referring solely to their appearances. Reference to an object can then be regarded as a logical construction with no need to treat it as an inferred metaphysical entity lying beyond sense data.

He contends that inferences to unknown entities should be replaced by logical constructions out of known ones: a program of translation. Statements are used that are capable of serving the same theoretical purposes but that make reference only to things of whose nature and existence we are more sure. Russell did not make a final identification of these "more sure" entities.

In proposing a theory of descriptions, Russell demonstrates that grammatically correct sentences may be devoid of meaning for logical reasons. He maintains that the logical form may be obscured by the grammatical form and that analysis may display a description coupled with a false assertion of existence. Russell introduced "contextual definitions." They provide a method of substituting for the statements themselves other statements of a different structure not containing descriptive phrases.

Russell believed that the possibility of such definitions indicates that the grammatical form of the defined statement furnishes no clue as to its real meaning. In tackling the problem of assertions about things that do not exist (the golden mountain does not exist!), Russell's theory of descriptions offers a systematic technique for eliminating such phrases.

Ken Guyer
New Mexico State University

Bibliography

Eames, Elizabeth R. *Bertrand Russell's Theory of Knowledge.* New York: Braziller, 1969.

Klemke, Ed, ed. *Essays on Bertrand Russell.* Urbana: U of Illinois P, 1970.

Ludlow, Peter, and Stephen Neale. "Indefinite Descriptions: In Defense of Russell." *Linguistics and Philosophy: An International Journal* 14 (1991): 171–202.

Russell, Bertrand. *The Autobiography of Bertrand Russell.* 1951. Boston: Little, 1967.

———. *Basic Writings of Bertrand Russell.* New York: Simon, 1961.

———. *An Inquiry into Meaning and Truth.* New York: Norton, 1940.

———. *Our Knowledge of the External World.* London: Open Court, 1914.

———. *Why I Am Not a Christian.* New York: Simon, 1957.

Russell, Bertrand, and Alfred North Whitehead. *Principia Mathematica.* 3 vols. London: Cambridge UP, 1910–1913.

Smiley, T.J. "The Theory of Descriptions." *Proceedings of the British Academy* 67 (1981): 321–37.

R

S

Salisbury, John of (c. 1115–1180)

Medieval author of works on political and pedagogical theory, renowned letter-writer, defender of the Trivium, and writer of the *Policraticus* and the *Metalogicon.*

John of Salisbury was born in southern England, journeying thence to Paris and Chartres in 1136 in order to study with, among other great teachers of his day, Abelard and (later) the rhetorician Thierry of Chartres. After ordination to the priesthood, he returned to England in 1154, having been appointed secretary to the then–Archbishop of Canterbury, Theobald. During the following years he composed his *Policraticus,* a treatise on political theory, as well as his *Metalogicon,* a defense of the study of the liberal arts and one of the central texts in the history of medieval pedagogy. (Two collections of the letters of John of Salisbury also survive, and as a Latin letter-writer in the twelfth century, as a practitioner of the *ars dictaminis,* John is unparalleled.) Both of John's major works were upon completion sent in 1159 to Thomas Becket, then chancellor to Henry II; when Becket became archbishop himself in 1161, John continued to serve as his secretary, becoming his close friend. He was exiled along with Becket by Henry II, and saw the murder of his friend in 1170. John himself died on October 25, 1180.

Though not a rhetorical treatise per se, the *Metalogicon* is John's most important work from the perspective of the history of rhetoric, for its subject is "logic" in the broadest of senses: the arts relevant to both reasoning and, more generally, verbal expression. In other words, "logic" in the *Metalogicon* is more or less synonymous with the Trivium itself. Written to refute an increasingly popular position, attributed to one "Cornificius," which insisted that skill in eloquence and reasoning was attributable more to natural talent than formal study—which amounted to an attack on the very relevance of the study of grammar, rhetoric, and logic—the *Metalogicon* defines rhetoric as one of the two areas (along with dialectic) of probable logic. Probable logic, as distinct from demonstrative and sophistical logic, included (among other topics) argumentation. Like many medieval theorists, moreover, John grants grammar much of the inventive and interpretive power classically accorded to rhetoric. Works having the greatest influence on John's ideas on rhetoric, grammar, and pedagogical theory include Cicero's *De oratore* and *De inventione,* the *Rhetorica ad Herennium,* and Quintilian's *Institutia oratoria;* the most frequently mentioned authors in the *Metalogicon,* however, are St. Augustine and especially Aristotle, who figures prominently in the *Policraticus* as well. Aristotle, in fact, was a special passion for John, and his knowledge of the *Topics, Categories,* and *Posterior* and *Prior Analytics* was as thorough as anyone's of his time. John's works survive as impressive testaments to twelfth-century scholarship and humanism.

Daniel J. Pinti
New Mexico State University

Bibliography

Liebeschütz, Hans. *Mediaeval Humanism in the Life and Writings of John of Salisbury.* London: Warburg, 1950.

McGarry, Daniel D., trans. and introd. *The Metalogicon on John of Salisbury.* Berkeley: U of California P, 1955.

Nederman, Cary J., and Catherine Campbell. "Priests, Kings, and Tyrants: Spiritual and Temporal Power in John of Salisbury's Policraticus." *Speculum* 66 (1991): 572–90.

Webb, C.C.J., ed. *Metalogicon*. Oxford: Oxford UP, 1929.

Wilks, Michael, ed. *The World of John of Salisbury*. Oxford: Blackwell, 1984.

Salutatio

Technically, the part of a Latin letter salutation that conveys the sender's greetings to the addressee; here, the complete tripartite salutation: *intitulatio* (the sender's name, with any attributes), *inscriptio* (the addressee's name, with any attributes), and *salutatio*, a noun or phrase of greeting (typically *salutem*, meaning both "greeting" and "good health"; compare English "farewell"), with a third-person-singular verb of wishing or sending understood—in its simple classical form, *"Caelius Ciceroni salutem"* (Caelius to Cicero [sends] greeting). Greek letter salutations were equally formulaic.

The earliest examples of Latin letter salutations appear in plays of Plautus, early second century B.C.E. For such prolific letter-writers of the classical period as Cicero and Pliny the Younger, the epistolary framework was of no stylistic interest. Many letter collections lack salutations because later copyists replaced them with rubrics that merely identified sender and addressee. We can nonetheless trace a pattern of increasing elaboration in each part of the salutation from late classical times through the twelfth century.

Honorific titles of social rank appear in the *inscriptio* from the first century C.E. From the early fourth century, the *inscriptio* began regularly to be placed first as a mark of respect, freighted with flattering epithets designed to win the addressee's good will (for example, from Augustine to Jerome, *"Domino dilectissimo et cultu sinceriissimo caritatis observando atque amplectando fratri et conpresbytero Hieronymo Augustinus,"* in which all but the last word belong to the *inscriptio*). At about the same time, the Christian ideal of humility suggested for the *intitulatio* such epithets as *humilis, peccator,* and (standard for the pope after Gregory I) *servus servorum Deo;* it always remained acceptable, however, for the writer to give himself *no* attributes—and so dramatize his own humility.

For the *salutatio*, early Christian writers added to the already twofold meaning of *salutem* a third, religious sense of "salvation," and wrote, for example, *"praesentem et futuram salutem";* after the Carolingian era, less formulaic, even message-bearing, phrases such as *"in adversis fortitudinem, in prosperis humilitatem"* often replaced the *salutem* phrase. By the twelfth century, we find such elaborate programmatic salutations as (from the bishop of Chartres to the king of France), *"Domino suo Philippo magnifico Francorum regi, Ivo humilis Carnotensium episcopus, sic militare in regno terreno ut non privetur aeterno."*

Rhetorical theory regarded the beginning of a speech (exordium) as especially important for capturing the attention and good will (*benivolentia*) of the audience. In letters, the salutation took the place of the *captatio benivolentiae,* and letter-writers and epistolary theory alike devoted a disproportionate amount of attention to it—especially to the *inscriptio* and the *salutatio* proper. The *artes dictaminis*, handbooks of epistolary theory and practice that proliferated from the early twelfth century on, prescribed detailed rules for correspondence between members of various social groups. Although these handbooks discussed all parts of a letter, they always emphasized the three-part salutation, and often included sample salutations as well as model letters.

Carol Dana Lanham
University of California at Los Angeles

Bibliography

Constable, Giles. *Letters and Letter-Collections.* Typologie des sources du moyen âge occidental 17. Turnhout: Brepols, 1976.

———. "The Structure of Medieval Society According to the *Dictatores* of the Twelfth Century." *Law, Church, and Society: Essays in Honor of Stephan Kuttner.* Ed. Kenneth Pennington and Robert Somerville. Philadelphia: U of Pennsylvania P, 1977. 253–67.

Erasmus, Desiderius. *De conscribendis epistolis [On the Writing of Letters].* Trans. Charles Fantazzi. *Collected Works of Erasmus* 25–26. Ed. J.K. Sowards. Toronto: U of Toronto P, 1985.

Lanham, Carol Dana. "Salutatio" *Formulas in Latin Letters to 1200: Syntax, Style, and Theory.* Diss. UCLA, 1973. Münchener Beiträge zur Mediävistik und Renaissance-Forschung 22. Munich: Arbeo-Gesellschaft, 1975.

Sappho (fl. 610–580 B.C.E.)

Archaic Greek poet. A lyric poet from Lesbos, Sappho remains an enigmatic figure for biographers. Scholars such as Joan deJean and Jane M. Snyder have demonstrated the ways in which writers from the death of Sappho to the present have created fictions of the Greek poet. Both critics show the ways in which constructions of Sappho represent specific cultural moments in historical and literary study. In spite of the numerous legends that surround Sappho's life, biographers do know that she was a member of an aristocratic family.

Sappho was the daughter of Skamandronymous and Kleis and had three brothers: Erigyios, Charaxos, and Larichos. She also had a husband, Kerkylas, and may have been a mother. Some authors have even suggested that Sappho ran a school for girls, though no concrete evidence substantiates this position. Still, in much of her poetry, Sappho referenced female audiences and vividly described young women who might have attended such a school. While a scarcity of evidence about Sappho's life has encouraged fictionalized accounts of the poet, the eroticized language of the verse itself has elicited numerous critical responses. For instance, Jack Winkler argues for Sappho's awareness of gender, suggesting that in each of her poems she uses two cultural scripts: the language of a predominantly masculine cultural world and the language of a woman's world to negotiate her presence as a poet and express her desire as a woman. Page duBois claims that when Sappho ascribes agency to Helen she redefines the terms of narrative structure, and Eva Stehle Stigers explores the ways in which Sappho constructs a romantic discourse in her poetry.

While Sappho's vocation as a teacher still remains in question, her position as a poet is well documented by her contemporaries. Although only one complete poem, "The Hymn to Aphrodite," exists, scholars have attributed approximately two hundred fragments to Sappho. These poems exist in many forms, including wedding songs, prayers, and amatory verse. While the archaic lyric in which she wrote was used primarily for public audiences, many of Sappho's poems are intensely personal, exploring issues of desire, passion, and power. The ways in which she treated these themes blurred the distinctions between private and public discourse.

Not only did Sappho's verse provide a model for future poets, both male and female, but it also offered a model of feminist rhetoric, one that predated the emergence of sophistic rhetoric a century later. Sophists upheld the concept of *nomoi* logos, or something believed to be right by a particular audience. This position subverted the idea of Truth or the possibility of a transcendent perspective. Sappho anticipated this rhetorical strategy in her poetry when she refused to privilege one subject-position or perspective. For example, as she explored and illuminated relationships between lovers, Sappho oscillated between the roles of subject and object, lover and beloved. She thereby deflected the speaker's authority in the poems, offering a challenge to a hierarchical system already in place in ancient Greek thought. Sappho's contribution to the history of rhetoric lies in this poetry, in which she developed an alternative to the masculine rhetorical strategies that developed the following century.

Teresa A. Lyle
Miami University

Bibliography

DeJean, Joan. *Fictions of Sappho: 1546–1937*. Chicago: U of Chicago P, 1989.

DuBois, Page. "Sappho and Helen." *Women in the Ancient World: The Arethusa Papers*. Ed. John Peradotto and J.P. Sullivan. Albany: SUNY, 1984. 95–105.

Snyder, Jane McIntosh. *The Woman and the Lyre: Women Writers in Classical Greece and Rome*. Carbondale: Southern Illinois UP, 1989.

Stigers, Eva Stehle. "Sappho's Private World." *Reflections of Women in Antiquity*. Ed. Helene P. Foley. New York: Gordon, 1981. 45–61.

Winkler, Jack. "Gardens of Nymphs: Public and Private in Sappho's Lyrics." *Reflections of Women in Antiquity*. Ed. Helene P. Foley. New York: Garden, 1981. 63–89.

Saussure, Ferdinand de (1857–1913)

Swiss scholar whose discoveries concerning the organization of language depend on an analysis we call *structural*, and whose theories have influenced modern linguistics, and structuralist and poststructuralist thought generally. Son of a prominent naturalist and member of a family with a noteworthy background in the natural sciences, the young Saussure was introduced to linguistic studies at an early age. By fifteen he had learned a number of modern languages in addition to the compulsory Greek and Latin. It was at this time that he began his lifelong reflection on a "general system of language" (qtd. in Culler 21).

In 1875 he entered the University of Geneva and, in the tradition of his family, enrolled as a student of physics and chemistry, all the while continuing courses in the ancient languages. After a year he convinced his parents to send him abroad to Leipzig to study Indo-European languages. After four years at the university, he made acquaintances with some of the most famous linguists of his day and published the well-received *Memoir on the Primitive System of Vowels in Indo-European Languages*. He left for Paris and began to teach Sanskrit and eventually Indo-European philology. In 1891 he was offered a professorship at the University of Geneva and returned to Switzerland, where he married, fathered two children, and wrote less and less. He gave lectures in general linguistics until his death in February of 1913. He was fifty-six years old.

In his famous *Course in General Linguistics*, a posthumous compilation of his lecture notes from the University of Geneva, Saussure puts forth the concepts of language's structure. These are best summarized as a series of dichotomies: *synchrony* and *diachrony, language (langue)* and *speech* or *speaking (parole), paradigmatic* and *syntagmatic, signifier* and *signified,* and by notions of the linguistic *sign* (Lepschy 43). The *Course* arose from Saussure's dissatisfaction with the existing theories of linguistics. Rather than regarding human speech-acts as merely "physical events," he argued that they were events with "meaning," "a system of social conventions" (Culler 63).

Of the three dichotomies—*langue-parole,* paradigmatic-syntagmatic, synchronic-diachronic —the first two have correlatives that must be studied together. In the case of the third, says Saussure, inverting key concepts of historical linguistics, the terms can be studied independently.

In other words, elements of a system can change, he believes, in isolation, in a "non-systematic" manner and eventually produce new systems.

A language can be analyzed synchronically —that is, by looking at a particular point in time, not fixed temporally, either in the present *or* the past. Or it can be analyzed diachronically —that is, by accounting for shifts in language from one point in time to another. The sign, being arbitrary, is totally subject to history, and the combination at a particular moment of a given signifier and signified is a contingent result of the historical process. Paradoxically, it is also ahistorical, defined solely as a relational entity, in its relations to other signs at a particular moment. "In asserting the priority of the synchronic description," Saussure stresses the "irrelevance of historical or diachronic facts in the analysis of *la langue*" (qtd. in Culler 47).

Langue and *parole* roughly correspond to language and speech respectively. In Saussure's lexicon, however, the two separate terms—the social and abstract (*langue*) and the individual and concrete (*parole*)—are conflated into one. The social part of language, outside of the individual speaker, beyond his control, and the individual, physiological, psychological reality of particular speech-acts are indistinct. Briefly, "*langue* and *parole* [are] logical and necessary consequence[s] of the arbitrary nature of the sign and the problem of identity in linguistics. . . . [I]f the sign is arbitrary then . . . it is a purely relational entity, and if we wish to define and identify signs we must look to the system of relations and distinctions which create them" (qtd. in Culler 45). Pronouns are obvious illustrations of differences between *langue* and *parole.* The statement "I am happy," for example, acquires different meanings depending on the context. The "I" does not refer to anyone in particular but can be appropriated by any speaker at any time. Saussure implies that there are two kinds of meaning: one that is relational based on a linguistic system (*langue*), and one that emanates from actual situations of utterance (*parole*). In separating the two, Saussure writes, "We are separating what is social from what is ancillary or accidental" (qtd. in Culler 41).

For Saussure, the sign is not a vehicle for representing something else, but a "relationship" between two entities—the signifier and the signified. The sign, according to him, has two primary features: "It is arbitrary . . . , and its [signifier] is linear"

(Lepschy 48). When one refers to the sign's arbitrary nature, one must separate "extralinguistic" from "intralinguistic" relationships: "The extralinguistic . . . is the relationship between language units and things meant, the intralinguistic is the relationship between two planes of expression and content" (Lepschy 49).

Saussure's second principle of the signifier's linearity is not fully explained in the *Course* but is arguably very important for modern linguistic theory. Clearly for Saussure, relationships between signs are essential to their definition. Such relationships are of two kinds: syntagmatic and paradigmatic. Signs have a syntagmatic relationship with other signs in a sentence—that is, a relationship "between elements . . . which are all present in the message" (Lepschy 50). Signs have another relationship with those signs not present in a particular message. This is called a paradigmatic relationship and its basis is one of association, because all signs, regardless of the particular message, belong to the language: "Paradigmatics and syntagmatics" may also be interpreted in terms of *langue* and *parole* respectively.

Saussure's reflections on the sign and on sign-systems were fundamental to later developments in linguistic theory. In terms of interdisciplinary study, he has had a profound impact on psychoanalytic criticism as developed by Jacques Lacan and later by Julia Kristeva, and his notion of linguistics as the model for understanding all sign systems has been of utmost utility for semioticians like Roland Barthes and Umberto Eco.

Catherine Lappas
Saint Louis University

Bibliography

Culler, Jonathan. *Ferdinand de Saussure.* Rev. ed. Ithaca, NY: Cornell UP, 1986.

Holdcroft, David. *Saussure: Signs, System, and Arbitrariness.* Cambridge: Cambridge UP, 1991.

Lepschy, G.C. *A Survey of Structural Linguistics.* Rev. ed. London: Andre Deutsch, 1982.

Saussure, Ferdinand de. *Course in General Linguistics.* Ed. Charles Bally and Albert Sechehaye. New York: McGraw, 1966.

Scesis Onomaton

The omission of the main verb from a sentence. Henry Peacham both defined and exemplified scesis onomaton: "When a sentence or saying doth consiste altogether of nouns, yet when to every substantive an adjective is joined, thus: A man faithful in friendship, prudent in counsels, virtuous in conversation, gentle in communication, learned in all learned sciences, eloquent in utterance, comely in gesture, pitiful to the poor, an enemy to naughtiness, a lover of all virtue and goodliness" (*The Garden of Eloquence*). As Peacham's example demonstrates, scesis onomaton can string together phrases to form an accumulatio (q.v.). Scesis onomaton can also be used to evoke a sense of immediacy in describing particulars: "Hog butcher of the world / Tool maker, stacker of wheat, / Player with railroads and the nation's freight handler; / Stormy, husky, brawling, / City of the big shoulders" (Carl Sandburg, "Chicago").

Arthur Quinn and Lyon Rathbun
University of California, Berkeley

Scholasticism

Activities of Medieval and Renaissance writers who sought "to join faith to reason," and who did so in cloistered settings, first in monasteries or ecclesiastical schools, and later in universities. Each of the key terms in this formulation—*faith, reason, join,* and *school*—has correlates in the history of rhetoric, but where rhetoricians sought action or commitment in the face of uncertain knowledge, the schoolmen sought a science of increasingly certain knowledge in a world where immediate action was not foremost. While rhetoricians sometimes drew upon scholastic studies, and while some schoolmen worked in rhetoric, more often the two orientations diverged, and the attitudes of the various participants ranged from mutual indifference to antipathy. The word *scholasticism* first appears in the sixteenth century as a term of dismissal or abuse; it survives today as a broad and imprecise term, since the individuals and doctrines commonly embraced by it often have little in common.

Scholasticism as a school activity describes a rational approach to investigations in theology, philosophy, and the liberal arts. It was based largely upon the logic of Aristotle and his improvers, and was used both to conduct research and to teach. It was thought that authorities from antiquity had made substantial contributions and that contemporary advances on those authorities would be incremental and cumulative, but only if those authorities were well understood. The two principal features of scholastic procedure—*exposition* and *disputation*—each developed as a response to the fragmentary recovery of materials from late antiquity. Exposition was needed at first to understand obscure or difficult texts, which were often studied in isolation from recognizable contexts. From marginal notes, scholia, and glosses, exposition developed into lectures and lengthy commentaries, and in time the mastery of texts entailed the mastery of massive amounts of earlier exposition. Disputation was used at first to confront the conflicting patristic interpretations of Scripture, and in time was adapted to problems in areas beyond biblical hermeneutics.

With the recovery of more materials from antiquity, the greater numbers of practitioners, and the institutionalization of inquiry, the sheer amount of exposition and newer doctrine became overwhelming. Researchers and students alike needed guides to this body of information, and schoolmen responded with introductions, synopses, and compendia. By the fifteenth century, these aids to exposition had themselves become part of the material to be mastered, and less ambitious students were apt to substitute mechanical guides for attention to the original subjects. And as the body of information became more settled, or as some issues settled into unresolvable impasses, the procedures of disputation became routine and self-referential.

The effort to join faith to reason, to unite revealed Christianity with classical philosophy and science, began with two competing strains of thought. One, attributed to Boethius, asserted the adequacy of God's gift of reason for comprehending revelation. The other, drawn from Pseudo-Dionysius the Areopagite, asserted the inadequacy of the human mind to apprehend divinity. Shifting notions during the medieval period, on the constituents of faith, the operations of reason, and the nature of conjunction, led to divergent positions on questions such as the rational proof of God's existence, divine providence and human freedom, the relationship between will and intellect, and the adequacy of human language for comprehending human experience. Thus Anselm's effort (eleventh century) to rely exclusively upon reason to demonstrate the tenets of faith was countered by Bonaventure's charges (Franciscan, thirteenth century) that Aristotelianism had paganized Christianity, only to have Thomas Aquinas (Dominican, thirteenth century) attempt a reconciliation by reserving reason and faith for separate spheres, while still insisting on their mutual dependence.

The terminology and logical tools used to discuss these complex issues became increasingly precise and sophisticated, but schoolmen never developed a symbolic logic adequate to their needs. They instead appropriated ordinary language to do the work of a specialized philosophical discourse, thus creating a hybrid discourse that was difficult for practitioners and incomprehensible to laymen. After notable advances in theocentric philosophy during the eleventh through fourteenth centuries, scholastic inquiry reached limits of what it could do with its tools. Practitioners had arrived at insurmountable impasses, while nonpractitioners had a sense of meager results purchased at the price of linguistic unintelligibility. The Renaissance movements for the recovery of classical Latin and toward simplified modes of reasoning were in part responses to late scholasticism, but scholastic inquiry survived these challenges and continued to make advances in political and ethical thinking through the eighteenth century.

Lawrence D. Green
University of Southern California

Bibliography

Brehier, Emile. *The History of Philosophy: The Middle Ages and the Renaissance*. Paris: F. Alcan, 1926–1932. Rpt. Trans. Wade Baskin. Chicago: U of Chicago P, 1965.

Copenhaver, Brian P., and Charles B. Schmitt. *Renaissance Philosophy*. Oxford: Oxford UP, 1992. 358–431.

Gilson, Etienne. *History of Christian Philosophy in the Middle Ages*. New York: Random, 1955.

Grabmann, Martin. *Die Geschichte der scholastischen Methode*. 2 vols. Freiburg: Herder, 1909–1911. Rpt. Berlin: Akademie, 1988.

Hackett, Jeremiah, ed. *Medieval Philosophers*. Detroit: Gale, 1992.

Kretzman, Norman, Anthony Kenny, and Jan Pinborg, eds. *The Cambridge History of Later Medieval Philosophy*. Cambridge: Cambridge UP, 1982. 893–977.

Maurer, Armand A. *Medieval Philosophy: St. Augustine to Ockham*. 2nd ed. Toronto: Pontifical Institute of Mediaeval Studies, 1982.

Pieper, Josef. *Scholasticism: Personalities and Problems of Medieval Philosophy*. Trans. Richard Winston and Clara Winston. New York: Pantheon, 1960.

Schmitt, Charles B., Quentin Skinner, and Eckhard Kessler, eds. *The Cambridge History of Renaissance Philosophy*. Cambridge: Cambridge UP, 1988. 842–930.

Seidel, Helmut. *Scholastik, Mystik und Renaissancephilosophie*. Berlin: Dietz, 1990.

Wulf, Maurice de. *History of Medieval Philosophy*. 3 vols. London: Nelson, 1951. (From 6th ed., rev. Louvain: Institut Supérieur de Philosophie, 1934–1947.)

Scott, Fred Newton (1860–1931)

American professor of rhetoric, first president of the National Council of Teachers of English. Fred Newton Scott was one of the most original American rhetoricians. He headed the Michigan Department of Rhetoric from 1903 until retiring in 1926. He became the twenty-fourth president of the MLA (1907) and the first president of the NCTE (1911–1913). His approach to rhetoric was well ahead of its time. His influence faded after his death in 1931, but thanks to the work of Donald C. Stewart, he is now more widely known.

Scott was born August 20, 1860, in Terre Haute, Indiana. He earned three degrees from the University of Michigan and remained there throughout his career. In 1903, largely because of his efforts, the university created a department of rhetoric. His students included Gertrude Buck, Sterling Leonard, Charles Fries, and numerous other distinguished scholars.

Scott was astonishingly active as a professional leader. Besides heading the MLA and NCTE (for two terms), he subsequently served as president of the North Central Association of Colleges and Schools (1913–1914) and president of the American Association of Teachers of Journalism (1917). Until his retirement he was in heavy demand as a speaker.

Scott's ideas about rhetoric and pedagogy, developed in over a hundred articles and speeches, place him at odds with the current-traditional theory of his time. He was open to other disciplines such as psychology and linguistics and believed that English teachers on all levels should know rhetorical history. He contrasted sophistic and Aristotelian rhetoric with the Platonic perspective that he favored. "Rhetoric Rediviva," a 1909 speech edited by Stewart and published long after Scott's death, argues that for Aristotle rhetoric was merely the art of persuasion, while Plato "broadened the scope of rhetoric enormously, and took toward it the attitude . . . of the speculative philosopher intent solely upon the truth" (415).

Scott's views on natural language acquisition were also remarkably modern. He believed that "schoolmaster's English" squelches the child's enthusiasm, devaluing personal language experience. In "English Composition as a Mode of Behavior," Scott links poor writing to societal problems and argues against mere mechanical correction of themes. Scott responded sharply to reports in the 1890s by a Harvard committee that exposed poor writing on entrance exams. Scott argued that the grading of such exams overemphasized superficial errors and encouraged a "feudal" attitude and arbitrary entrance requirements. In contrast, he suggested an "organic" approach to college admission that would recognize varied factors and foster more continuity of purpose between schools and colleges.

Scott coauthored some fifteen textbooks; the most successful was *Paragraph Writing*, written with Joseph V. Denney. It presents the paragraph as a flexible unit of composition, a sort of miniessay. His textbooks are dated and relatively tradition-bound; however, they emphasize composing as a holistic, multifaceted endeavor, not merely a set of mechanical skills. Similarly, his grammar book, written with Gertrude Buck, recognizes social context as a factor in language use and presents a descriptive rather than a prescriptive view of usage.

Ken Autrey
Francis Marion University

Bibliography

Berlin, James A. "An Alternate Voice: Fred Newton Scott." *Writing Instruction in Nineteenth-Century American Colleges*. Carbondale: Southern Illinois UP, 1984. 77–84.

Scott, Fred Newton. "English Composition as a Mode of Behavior." *English Journal* 11 (1922): 463–73.

———. "Rhetoric *Rediviva*." *College Composition and Communication* 31 (1980): 413–19.

Scott, Fred Newton, and J.V. Denney. *Paragraph Writing*. Boston: Allyn, 1893.

Stewart, Donald C. "Fred Newton Scott." *Traditions of Inquiry*. Ed. John C. Brereton. New York: Oxford UP, 1985. 26–49.

———. "Rediscovering Fred Newton Scott." *College English* 40 (1979): 539–47.

Scott, Robert L. (b. 1928)

Author of the phrase "rhetoric is epistemic." Robert L. Scott reinvigorated the debate over the relationship between rhetoric and truth, arguing for an intersubjectivist stance. He employed this perspective in his critical analysis of the rhetoric of Black Power.

Robert L. Scott was born on April 19, 1928, in Fairbury, Nebraska. His Ph.D., gained at the University of Illinois in 1955, led to a professorship at the University of Minnesota. He edited the *Quarterly Journal of Speech* from 1972 to 1974.

With his article "On Viewing Rhetoric as Epistemic" (1967), Scott reignited the centuries-old debate about the relationship of rhetoric to truth. Drawing on existentialist insights, Scott rearticulated the sophistic perspective that rhetoric is the means by which human beings come to understand themselves and their world.

This perspective conceived "truth" as probabilistic and historically grounded understanding rather than as certain and timeless universals. Scott explained that this position was intersubjectivist rather than relativist. Consequently, human worldviews could be understood as grounded in tradition, but not held captive to those traditions. He developed the claim that the intersubjectivist position encouraged moral goodness because it required humans to accept responsibility for the values they constituted in communicating. In applying this epistemological perspective to the categorization of the history of rhetorical theory, Scott emphasized the tendency of objectivist formulations toward elitism in contrast to the more egalitarian orientations of intersubjectivist stances. These efforts anticipated the later focus on audience-centered rhetorical theory.

Scott's second major contribution, his studies of the rhetoric of Black Power, extended this epistemological stance to the practice of rhetorical criticism. Scott worked with Wayne Brockriede (1969) to examine press coverage of Stokely Carmichael and the response of white leaders to the Black Power slogan. They revealed the ways in which white opinion leaders cast Black Power as a racist threat to white America rather than elaborating the constructive side of Black Power as they might have done. Scott also explored the structure of Black Power rhetoric from an empathic perspective that sought to understand how it functioned as a worldview for black people rather than from a dismissive perspective that denied it status as objective truth. Despairing that a "police state for us all" was the sole alternative, in 1968 he concluded, "A relatively peaceful working out of Black Power may often seem a dim hope, but it is the only sensible hope for which Americans can work." Scott then turned his critical studies back toward middle-level theory building, offering a theoretical account of the rhetoric of confrontation that described its symbolic functions, its powerful resources, and its limits.

For these works Scott received the first Charles H. Woolbert Award in 1981, along with the James A. Winans Award in 1970, and the Douglas Ehninger Distinguished Rhetorical Scholar Award in 1989. In 1992 he received the award "For a Distinguished Career in the Study of Human Communication" at the Speech Communication Association Convention in 1992.

Celeste Michelle Condit
University of Georgia

Bibliography

Scott, Robert L. "On *Not* Defining 'Rhetoric.'" *Philosophy and Rhetoric* 6 (1973): 81–96.

———. "On Viewing Rhetoric as Epistemic." *Central States Speech Journal* 18 (1967): 9–17.

———. "Rhetoric as Epistemic: Ten Years Later." *Central States Speech Journal* 27 (1976): 258–66.

———. "A Synoptic View of Systems of Western Rhetoric." *Quarterly Journal of Speech* 61 (1975): 439–47.

Scott, Robert L., and Wayne Brockriede. *The Rhetoric of Black Power*. Glenview, IL: Scott, 1969.

Scott, Robert L., and Donald K. Smith. "The Rhetoric of Confrontation." *Quarterly Journal of Speech* 55 (1969): 1–8.

Scottish Enlightenment

An intellectual movement to develop a "science of man"—a systematic account of human thought, society, morality, and institutions. The Scottish Enlightenment occurred in the latter half of the eighteenth century (c. 1750 to the 1780s), and its sites were Edinburgh, Aberdeen, and Glasgow. The Scots' accomplishments during this period were prodigious. David Hume's *Treatise of Human Nature* (1739, 1740) considered how knowledge was acquired, explored sources of distortion in perception and reasoning, and articulated a skeptical philosophy grounded in empiricism. Henry Home, Lord Kames's *Elements of Criticism* (1762) considered the nature and origins of taste and discussed qualities of excellence in literature and composition. And Adam Smith's *Inquiry into the Nature and Causes of the Wealth of Nations* (1776) provided a coherent account of the economic life of society based on detailed empirical evidence. In these works and others, the Scots literati identified and delineated the general principles of human activity in morals, literature, aesthetics, economics, and other arenas. They thus laid the groundwork for intellectual approaches that later became disciplines in their own right (Chitnis 6). The pioneering of social science and major advances in science and medicine were among their accomplishments.

The rhetorics of the Scottish Enlightenment differed markedly from the neoclassical rhetorics that preceded them. Traditional rhetorics had been concerned with production—how a good speech was constructed argumentatively and stylistically. The belletristic rhetorics of the Scottish Enlightenment were concerned as much (if not more) with reception. In the service of studying human nature and its institutions, these Scottish rhetorics examined the workings of language, taste, and style to discover how discourse worked upon the mind. They distinguished the varieties of aesthetic experience and explained how each variety caused certain responses in the hearer or reader. Their works were influenced by Francis Hutcheson, who had held that there was a "sixth sense"—an internal reflex sense that responded to certain qualities. For example, one quality might be novelty, and the orator who introduced something strange and unfamiliar could surprise the hearer and excite curiosity. Or the orator might describe a grand object or magnanimous action, thus evoking the sublime response in which the soul expanded and experienced grandeur.

Because it had long studied genres and qualities of discourse, rhetoric provided a fertile field for examining human response. One of the Scots' aims was to investigate the principles of mind by which hearers were led to understand and believe what they heard. In regard to style, Scottish rhetorics emphasized clarity, vivacity, and propriety. Clarity facilitated comprehension of what the speaker said. Vivacity made experience immediate and proximate, thus simulating sensation. And propriety called for speakers to order events according to their natural connections and to portray characters and situations so as to conform to cultural experience. Discourse that had these qualities appealed to its listeners and readers because it aligned with their experience.

Two of the three major works of this period were pedagogical. One publication was based on Adam Smith's lectures at Glasgow in 1762. Smith had begun his lectures on rhetoric and belles-lettres in Edinburgh in 1748, and when he accepted the chair of logic at Glasgow in 1751 he continued these lectures in his new location. Smith's lectures were never published, but a student copyist's "Notes of Dr. Smith's Rhetorick Lectures" were discovered by John M. Lothian in 1961 and first published in 1963 as *Lectures on Rhetoric and Belles Lettres*. Although the first lecture is missing and the recorded lectures are only an approximate version of what Smith said, the notes do provide an indication of the lectures' content. The second pedagogical rhetoric is Hugh Blair's *Lectures on Rhetoric and Belles Lettres* (1783). Blair had attended Smith's early lectures and continued the tradition by lecturing at Edinburgh for over twenty years.

Both Smith and Blair lectured to audiences of young men who were interested in becoming proficient in the arts of discourse. Their students particularly wished to develop skill in composition as well as good taste in judging others' works. Smith and Blair thus discussed the standards of good language use, linguistic purity, the avoidance of Scotticisms, and development of a good English prose style. Taste was an important topic in their lectures. Reading, attending plays and performances, and discussing the literary merit of various works provided a primary form of leisure entertainment in Scottish society, and so taste was a means of improving one's quality of life. Smith and Blair themselves served as model critics for their audiences, discussing the works of authors such as Shaftesbury, Addison, and Swift and exemplifying proper critical response.

Rhetorical study during the Scottish Enlightenment was considerably broadened to include genres of writing and speaking other than oratory. Smith and Blair discussed various genres—poetry, drama, history, and description—as well as deliberative, epideictic, and judicial speaking. As a Presbyterian clergyman, Blair also discussed pulpit speaking. A recurrent pattern in their works was to identify a genre, describe its elements, and then criticize well-known examples. There was great interest in work of this sort. Blair's lectures were translated into French, Italian, Russian, and Spanish, and they were subsequently issued in twenty-six editions in Great Britain and thirty-seven in the United States.

It is unfortunate that Smith ordered his lecture notes destroyed prior to his death. His was an excellent and penetrating intellect, and his lectures must have offered innovative views on the origin and structure of language and the virtues of style. Blair's lectures, on the other hand, have been generally condemned as pedantic and unoriginal (Howell 655). Blair's was not intended as a theoretical treatise, however. His purpose was merely to initiate readers into his subject, to cultivate their taste and form their style. His *Lectures on Rhetoric and Belles Lettres* were a melange of conventional wisdom, neoclassical and romantic doctrines, and contemporary and classical literary examples. As a compendium of secondary source material and digestible theory, Blair's lectures popularized rhetoric and made it accessible to a very large readership, and therein lies the nature of his contribution.

The third major rhetoric of the Scottish Enlightenment was George Campbell's *Philosophy of Rhetoric* (1776). This work, which was technical and meant for a learned audience, was intended to be a philosophical examination of rhetoric. That is, Campbell aimed to explain, not only *how* certain messages influence certain audiences, but *why*. Furthermore, Campbell aspired to attain increased knowledge of human nature by studying the workings of rhetoric. He defined rhetoric very broadly as "that art or talent by which discourse is adapted to its end" (Campbell 1). In this art he included discourse intended to enlighten understanding, please the imagination, move the passions, or influence the will. Thus, Campbell was interested in the rhetori-

cal (or "influencing") dimension of many kinds of discourse, informative as well as persuasive.

The British empiricist tradition of Francis Bacon, John Locke, and David Hume had a strong influence on Campbell's theory of rhetoric. Like Hume, Campbell believed that the mind was moved by sense impressions and by memory. Thus discourse that made the ideas it evoked resemble sensation and memories would be influential. Campbell emphasized comparison and portraiture as means of simulating sensation. He emphasized the concrete, the specific, the use of the sensible to represent the intelligible. Campbell held that the orator could succeed by making general ideas concrete, lively, and vivid, by bringing near what seems remote, and by generally increasing the presence of the ideas discussed. Ironically, Campbell also folded into his theory of rhetoric the common-sense principles of Thomas Reid, a major opponent of Hume. These ideas or principles include the following: that things that come into our consciousness have a cause, that our memories are reliable, and that the future will resemble the past. Such beliefs contradicted Humean skepticism, yet Campbell believed that they were necessary to a coherent theory of rhetoric.

The projects undertaken in the rhetorics of the Scottish Enlightenment (developing a taxonomy of aesthetic elements, spelling out the dimensions of discursive propriety, and considering the bases of receptive competence) have not been fully developed elsewhere in the rhetorical tradition. The Scottish belletrists cast aside the common topics and other stock persuasive strategies and instead generated psychological and physiological explanations of discursive influence. Their entire enterprise, however, was grounded in the assumption that a theorist's personal predilections could ground general truths about aesthetic experience. Belletristic aesthetics was "empirical" only in the sense that it was based on *the critic's* response to discursive elements as approved and accepted by his readers. Scottish Enlightenment rhetorics were nonetheless very well suited to a society concerned with taste, correct expression, and the development of style. They also provided useful analyses of second-order reference and of the reasons why certain speeches and narratives resonate with the lives and experiences of their hearers and readers.

Barbara Warnick
University of Washington

Bibliography

Blair, Hugh. *Lectures on Rhetoric and Belles Lettres*. Ed. Harold F. Harding. Carbondale: Southern Illinois UP, 1965.

Campbell, George. *The Philosophy of Rhetoric*. Ed. Lloyd F. Bitzer. Carbondale: Southern Illinois UP, 1988.

Chitnis, Anand C. *The Scottish Enlightenment: A Social History*. London: Croom Helm, 1976.

Daiches, David, Peter Jones, and Jean Jones, eds. *A Hotbed of Genius: The Scottish Enlightenment, 1730–1790*. Edinburgh: University P, 1986.

Howell, Wilbur Samuel. *Eighteenth-Century British Logic and Rhetoric*. Princeton: Princeton UP, 1971.

Sher, Richard B. *Church and University in the Scottish Enlightenment*. Edinburgh: University P, 1985.

Smith, Adam. *Lectures on Rhetoric and Belles Lettres*. Ed. J.C. Bryce. Oxford: Clarendon, 1983.

Warnick, Barbara. *The Sixth Canon: Belletristic Rhetorical Theory and its French Antecedents*. Columbia: U of South Carolina P, 1993.

See also BELLES-LETTRES; BLAIR, HUGH; CAMPBELL, GEORGE; SMITH, ADAM

The Second Sophistic

Where, as in the first, the "ancient quarrel" between rhetoric and philosophy is brought once again to the fore, and the intimate connections between those two disciplines are thereby highlighted. The First Sophistic (though it is not usually called that) included an efflorescence of self-conscious interest in the nature and function of discourse—including formal tuition, for pay, in rhetoric—in Athens of the fifth century B.C.E. The impact of this phenomenon on the history of rhetorical theory (and indeed of philosophy) cannot be overstressed. Philostratus, in his *Lives of the Sophists*, calls this the "Ancient Sophistic" (*arkhaia sophistikê*), pointing to the work of Gorgias of Leontini for its origin. He sets this Ancient Sophistic in contradistinction to a "Second Sophistic" (*deutera sophistikê*), which he dates from the exile of the Attic orator Aeschines to Caria and Rhodes in the late fourth century B.C.E. But the Second Sophistic is not new, he says; it too is ancient.

It would seem that these categories of Philostratus are based on logical rather than on chronological distinctions: While the first was concerned with issues such as courage and justice, as well as the origin and nature of the universe, the second focuses on types of human character and on specific topics (*hupotheseis*) "to which history leads." What he seems to be saying here in very compressed terms is that the First Sophistic focused on more abstract and metaphysical issues, the second on more pragmatic and social or political ones. On such an account it is possible to imagine both sophistics existing side by side, even in the same culture.

The First Sophistic, says Philostratus, was a "philosophical rhetoric" (*rhêtorikê philosophousa*), while in the second, some thinkers most properly categorized as philosophers were often thought of as sophists; accordingly, he is willing to include them in his work. This confusion of categories is an instructive and useful guideline for our own assessment here. Wilamowitz, one of the greatest classical scholars of modern times, denied that there had ever even been a Second Sophistic. While his position has since lost favor, it nonetheless reminds us that such categories are themselves human constructs designed to make sense out of history. In this entry, then, in addition to those that the ancients labeled *sophists* in the strictest sense, some mention will be made of other figures writing in Greek during this period whose work was influential and remains important for students of rhetoric. (A complete literary history of the era would include the New Testament documents and the early Church Fathers; the Greek novelists [Achilles Tatius, Chariton, Heliodorus, Longus, Xenophon Ephesius]; philosophers such as Plotinus; and such Latin writers as Apuleius, Calpurnius Flaccus, Aulus Gellius, Macrobius, Seneca the Elder, Petronius, Tacitus, Valerius Maximus, and of course the author of the *Rhetorica ad Herennium*, Cicero, Quintilian, and the pseudo-Quintilianic *Declamations*.)

After Aeschines, no other figure of the high classical period is named; Philostratus begins the Second Sophistic with him, perhaps, in order to anchor his notion of the movement securely in the antiquity of classical Athens, and to bolster his assertion that the Second Sophistic, like the first, is "ancient." The continuum from Aeschines (in the fourth century B.C.E.) to Nicetes (in the age of Nero) is eased by the inclusion of such philosophers as Carneades (c. 213–129 B.C.E.), the Skeptic philosopher who headed the ("New") Academy in the mid second century B.C.E.

The genuine sophists of Philostratus' own era were best known as orators or teachers of rhetoric. Some may have been more restrained, others more Asianic or (as Philostratus says) "dithyrambic" in their style. But generally this was an era of great interest in standards of Atticism, in terms both of diction (choice of individual words) and of composition (syntax and phrasing).

Much of the rhetorical training offered in the schools of the time centered around declamation (known in Greek as *meletê*, "practice"). This aspect of the curriculum had been emphasized in Greek schools since the third and second centuries B.C.E., and in Rome since the age of Cicero. One might be asked to treat a general theme in abstract terms (Gk. *thesis,* Lat. *quaestio*) or a more particular one, grounded in specific persons or situations (Gk. *hupothesis,* Lat. *causa*). In the Roman schools, declamation was divided under the headings of *suasoria* and *controuersia.* A *suasoria* addressed the course of action, in a particular situation, of an individual (whether mythical or historical): For example, "Should Sulla resign his dictatorship?" A *controuersia* dealt with the arguments on both sides (*in utramque partem*) of an imaginary legal case. Greek declamation was often on historical themes, concentrating on Athens of the high classical (pre-Hellenistic) period. Before going on to study declamation with a sophist, students of rhetoric would typically first work through the elementary exercises of a rhetorical handbook—the so-called *progymnasmata,* which included the use of fable, narrative, *khreia* or anecdote, encomium, comparison, and so forth.

Besides the historical works of Philostratus and Eunapius, other ancient sources useful for the study of the Second Sophistic include the histories of Diodorus Siculus and Suetonius, the *On Style* of Demetrius, the *Lives and Opinions of Eminent Philosophers* of Diogenes Laertius, the works of Synesius of Cyrene, the *Attic Nights* of Aulus Gellius, the *Deipnosophistae* of Athenaeus, the lexicon of Harpokration, the *Bibliothêkê* of Photius, and the tenth-century literary encyclopaedia known as the *Suda.* Following is a list of sophists and other major figures of the period:

- Aelian (Claudius Aelianus) of Praeneste (c. 170–235 C.E.): a writer of history rather than a declaimer; author of a *Varia Historia* in fourteen books and *On the Characteristics of Animals* in seventeen; some of his letters survive as well. He was attracted to the doctrines of Stoicism.
- Antipater, Aelius of Hierapolis (2nd to 3rd century C.E.): governor of Bithynia and consul under the emperor Severus. Teacher of Philostratus and of the emperor Caracalla. A talented extemporaneous declaimer, he was known also for his letters and his history of Severus.
- Appian (Gk. *Appianos*) of Alexandria (fl. 160 C.E.): wrote, in Greek, a lengthy history of Rome (some of which survives) spanning from the earliest period to the accession of the emperor Vespasian.
- Apsines (Valerius Apsines) of Gadara (fl. 235 C.E.): a friend of Philostratus, he taught in Athens. He wrote an *Art of Rhetoric* and *On Figured Problems.* A great admirer of the oratory of Demosthenes.
- Aristeides (Publius Aelius Aristeides Theodorus) of Hadrianutherae (117–189 C.E.): educated at Athens and Pergamum. His skill was not in extemporaneous declamation. Fifty-five of his orations survive, among which are a *Panathenaicus,* an *Encomium of Rome,* and two rejoinders (*On Behalf of Rhetoric* and *On Behalf of the Four*) to Plato's *Gorgias.* The Neo-platonist philosopher Porphyry attempted in turn to write a response to Aristeides.
- Dio (Gk. *Diôn*) Cocceianus of Prusa (c. 40–after 111 C.E.): Greek orator/philosopher, later known as *Chrysostom,* "golden-mouthed"; not to be confused with the historian Dio Cassius (c. 150–235 C.E.). Studied Stoicism at Rome. Banished by the emperor Domitian; restored by Nerva. About eighty extant orations have been attributed to him; some are political, some display pieces; among these are his *Euboeic Discourse, Trojan Discourse, Olympic Oration,* and four speeches *On Kingship,* as well as an *Encomium of Hair.* Among those lost are a *Eulogy of the Gnat* and *Eulogy of the Parrot.*
- Dionysius of Halicarnassus (1st century B.C.E.): rhetor/historian who taught in

Rome. A great proponent of Atticism. Author of *Roman Antiquities* and of works discussing the Attic orators and Thucydides, as well as a treatise *On the Arrangement of Words.*

- Eunapius of Sardis (346–414 C.E.): studied rhetoric at Athens before returning to Sardis to teach. Author of a detailed *Universal History,* which survives only in fragments, and of *Lives of the Philosophers and Sophists*, an important source for fourth-century sophistic.

- Favorinus (2nd century C.E.): orator/philosopher, a hermaphrodite, born at Arelatê (modern Arles) in Gaul; learned Greek in Massilia (modern Marseille). A pupil of Dio's, teacher of Herodes Atticus, and friend of Plutarch and Fronto. Fluent in improvised declamation. Prominent in Rome under the emperor Hadrian, but banished by him c. 130. Recalled by Antoninus Pius. One or two speeches attributed to Dio (nos. 37 and perhaps 64) are probably by Favorinus.

- Fronto, Marcus Cornelius (c. 100–c. 176 C.E.): eminent Roman orator, born in Africa. Consul in 143 (with Herodes Atticus). Tutored the future emperor Marcus Aurelius. Favored a classicizing style. His writings are extant in both Greek and Latin.

- Galen (Gk. *Galênos*) of Pergamum (129–190 C.E.): physician to the emperor Marcus Aurelius and a prolific writer on medicine and other topics including philosophy. Widely read and translated in the Middle Ages.

- Hermogenes of Tarsus (b. 161 C.E.): an oratorical child prodigy; the emperor Marcus Aurelius came to hear him declaim. A great admirer of the style of Demosthenes. Author of *On Ideas of Style, On Staseis,* and *On Invention;* the *Progymnasmata* attributed to him may be spurious. His work on stasis theory apparently offered a system alternative to that of his contemporary Minucian.

- Herodes Atticus (Lucius Vibullius Hipparchus Tiberius Claudius Atticus Herodes) (101–177 C.E.): celebrated Roman sophist and philanthropist, born at Marathon to a family of vast wealth. Consul in 143 (with Fronto). Friend of Aulus Gellius. The extensive literary output of Herodes described by Philostratus has perished, with the exception of *On the Constitution* (if that is genuine).

- Himerius (Gk. *Himerios*) of Bithynia (c. 310–c. 390 C.E.): a contemporary of Eunapius; taught rhetoric at Athens to pupils including St. Gregory of Nazianzus and St. Basil. Declaimed before the emperor Julian. Twenty-four of his speeches survive, including an *epithalamion.*

- Libanius (Gk. *Libanios*) of Coele Syria (314–c. 393 C.E.): born to a noble family of Syrian Antioch; went to Athens to study in 336. An admired declaimer and teacher of rhetoric in Constantinople, Nicomedia, and Antioch. Taught St. John Chrysostom and possibly St. Gregory of Nazianzus. A voluminous written output survives, which is an important source for the culture and literature of the fourth century.

- Lollian (Publius Hordeonius Lollianus) of Ephesus (2nd century C.E.): teacher of Theodotus; served under the emperor Antoninus Pius as archon at Athens, where he also held a municipal chair of rhetoric. Famed for his rhetorical invention and style. His written work survives in fragmentary form.

- "Longinus" (Gk. *Logginos*) is the name generally given to the anonymous author of the brilliant essay *On Sublimity.* Formerly attributed to Cassius Longinus of Palmyra (3rd century C.E.), it apparently dates from the principate of Augustus or of Tiberius. In it, sublimity (*hupsos*) is traced to five sources: loftiness of thought, powerful emotion, figures of diction and of thought, nobility of diction, and distinguished rhetorical style.

- Lucian (Gk. *Loukianos*) of Samosata (c. 120–after 180 C.E.): satiric philosopher, originally trained in sophistic rhetoric. Much interested in issues of religion. Best known for his *Dialogues of the Dead, Dialogues of the Gods, Dialogues of Courtesans,* and for his so-called *True History.*

- Maximus of Tyre (c. 125–185 C.E.): sophist/philosopher, author of 41 *Dialexeis.* Lectured in Athens and in Rome under the emperor Commodus. His lectures—diatribes in the Platonist and Cynic vein—exhort the audience to moral virtue.

S

- Menander (Gk. *Menandros*) of Laodicea (3rd century C.E.): not to be confused with the playwright (342–c. 292 B.C.E.) of Attic New Comedy, author of the *Dyscolus*. To Menander Rhetor are attributed two treatises on epideictic speeches, which discuss the composition of such items as hymns, prayers, *epithalamia* (marriage-songs), *genethliaka* (birthday speeches), the *lalia* or "talk," *paramuthêtika* (consolations), *epitaphioi* (funeral speeches), and panegyrics of various kinds.
- Minucian (Minucianus) of Athens (2nd century C.E.): orator in the time of the emperor Antoninus Pius; author of speeches, a commentary on Demosthenes, an art of rhetoric, and of works on stasis theory and *progymnasmata*.
- Philostratus, Flavius of (?) Lemnos (b. c. 170 C.E.): studied rhetoric at Athens and Ephesus; a courtier of the Syrian empress Julia Domna (wife of Septimius Severus). Author of *Lives of the Sophists* and coiner of the term *Second Sophistic*.
- Polemo (Gk. *Polemôn*) of Laodicea (2nd century C.E.): not to be confused with Polemôn, the head of the Platonic Academy (313–270 B.C.E.). Sophist and most prominent citizen of the city of Smyrna, of which he was a great benefactor. A friend of the emperors Trajan, Hadrian, and Antoninus Pius; studied under Dio. Famous for the fluency of his extemporaneous declamation, for the passion and intensity of his delivery, and for his egregious arrogance.
- Porphyry (Gk. *Porphurios*) (233–c. 301 C.E.): Neo-Platonist philosopher, brought up at Tyre; studied with Cassius Longinus and Plotinus; eventually headed the Neo-Platonist school at Rome. Famed for his eloquence. Wrote *Against Aristeides*, in seven books, and other works on a vast variety of subjects, including language and literature.
- Ptolemy (Gk. *Ptolemaios*) of Naukratis (2nd century C.E.): studied under Herodes Atticus and Polemo. Famed for his extemporaneous declamation.
- Rufus of Perinthus (2nd century C.E.): sophist born into a wealthy and influential family; studied under Herodes Atticus. Famed for his extemporaneous declamation.
- Sopater (Gk. *Sopatros*) (5th century C.E.?): not to be confused with the comic playwright of the same name (4th century C.E.). Taught rhetoric at Athens; wrote *Diaireseis Zêtêmatôn* ("Divisions of Questions"), a *catalogue raisonné* of eighty-one topics for declamation. A commentary on Hermogenes' *On Staseis* is also attributed to him.
- Synesius (Gk. *Sunêsios*) of Cyrene (c. 370–413 C.E.): orator/poet, member of the Neo-Platonist school of Alexandria, pupil of the mathematician Hypatia. Author of letters, hymns, a treatise *On Dreams,* and discourses including the *Diôn* and an *Encomium of Baldness* (indebted to Dio's *Encomium of Hair*). Became bishop of Ptolemais (in Libya) in 410.
- Themistius (Gk. *Themistios*) of Paphlagonia (c. 317–388 C.E.): sophist/philosopher, teacher of rhetoric in Constantinople. Tutor to the future emperor Arcadius. Contemporary of (but not mentioned by) Eunapius. Thirty-four of his orations are extant.
- Theodotus (Gk. *Theodotos*), Iulius (2nd century C.E.): king-archon at Athens; pupil of Lollian; contemporary (and secret political opponent) of Herodes Atticus. Chosen for a chair of rhetoric by Marcus Aurelius.
- Theon (Gk. *Theôn*), Aelius of Alexandria (1st or 2nd century C.E.): author of notes on Demosthenes, Isocrates, and Xenophon, as well as a *Rhetoric* and a handbook of *Progymnasmata*.

John T. Kirby
Purdue University

Bibliography

Anderson, Graham. *Philostratus: Biography and Belles-Lettres in the Third Century* A.D. London: Croom Helm, 1986.

———. *The Second Sophistic: A Cultural Phenomenon in the Roman Empire.* London: Routledge, 1993.

———. 1990. "The Second Sophistic: Some Problems of Perspective." *Antonine Literature*. Ed. D.A. Russell. Oxford: Oxford UP, 1990. 91–110.

Bowersock, Glen. *Greek Sophists in the Roman Empire.* Oxford: Oxford UP, 1969.

———, ed. *Approaches to the Second Sophistic.* Papers Presented at the 105th Annual

Meeting of the American Philological Assn. Ephrata, PA: Science, 1974.

Bowie, E.L. "Greeks and Their Past in the Second Sophistic." *Past and Present* 46 (1970): 1–41.

Jones, C.P. "The Reliability of Philostratus." *Approaches to the Second Sophistic*. Ed. Glen Bowersock. Papers Presented at the 105th Annual Meeting of the American Philological Assn. Ephrata, PA: Science, 1974. 11–16.

Kennedy, George A. *The Art of Rhetoric in the Roman World*. Princeton: Princeton UP, 1972. 553–641.

———. *Classical Rhetoric and Its Christian and Secular Tradition from Ancient to Modern Times*. Chapel Hill: U of North Carolina P, 1980.

———. *Greek Rhetoric under Christian Emperors*. Princeton: Princeton UP, 1983.

———. "The Sophists as Declaimers." *Approaches to the Second Sophistic*. Ed. Glen Bowersock. Papers Presented at the 105th Annual Meeting of the American Philological Assn. Ephrata, PA: Science, 1974. 17–22.

Lesky, Albin. *Geschichte der griechischen Literatur*. 2nd ed. Bern: Francke Verlag, 1963. Trans. James Willis and Cornelis de Heer. *A History of Greek Literature*. London: Methuen, 1966. 829–45.

Norden, Eduard. *Die Antike Kunstprosa*. 2 vols. Leipzig: Teubner, 1898.

Penella, R. *Greek Philosophers and Sophists in the Fourth Century* A.D.: *Studies in Eunapius of Sardis*. Leeds: Cairns, 1990.

Russell, D.A., ed. *Greek Declamation*. Cambridge: Cambridge UP, 1983.

———. *Dio Chrysostom: Orations VII, XII, XXXVI*. Cambridge: Cambridge UP, 1992.

———, ed. *"Longinus" On the Sublime*. Oxford: Oxford UP, 1964.

Russell, D.A., and N.G. Wilson, eds. *Menander Rhetor*. Oxford: Oxford UP, 1981.

Rutledge, Harry. "Herodes the Great, Citizen of the World." *Classical Journal* 56 (1960–1961): 97–109.

Wooten, Cecil W. *Hermogenes' On Types of Style*. Chapel Hill: U of North Carolina P, 1987.

See also DECLAMATION; GORGIAS; GREEK RHETORIC; SOPHISTIC RHETORIC

Semantics

Related to a family of Greek words: *semanticos*, "significant," *semainein*, "to signify," and *sema*, "a sign" or "a mark" (*sema* also an inscribed headstone). One can trace the development of semantics at least as far back as the sophist Prodicus, who was said to have collected lists of words and to have been very concerned with the exact meanings of words. The first semantic theorist may have been the sophist Gorgias, as suggested by *On Nature or On Non-Being*. But certainly semantics had developed to a theoretical level by the time Plato wrote *Cratylus*. *Parmenides* and the *Sophist* are also concerned with semantic theories.

The primary questions of philosophical semantics concern the possible relations between words and things. Is it nature or convention that attaches certain words to specific things? Are these attachments systematic or idiosyncratic? Given that words refer to things beyond themselves, do they refer to ideas (referential idealism) or objects (referential realism) or both (referential behaviorism)? Is it possible that words do not refer to anything at all, but rather are meaningful because of the relative place they hold in a closed system of words? As a branch of linguistics, semantics is concerned with determining the linguistic conditions that make words or sentences unambiguously meaningful in and of themselves. Unlike pragmatics, which considers meaning as a function of human action, semantics brackets human actions and historical factors to concentrate exclusively on words and sentences as elements of a closed system, much as Saussure bracketed *parole* in order to concentrate on *langue*.

In a related exclusion, semantics does not examine exclamations or questions. It analyzes propositions only. One approach to analyzing the meaning of a proposition, known as truth conditionality, is to determine if the proposition in question is verifiable or could be verified in a possible world. In other words, to know the meaning of a proposition is to know the conditions under which it could be proven true. The intension of a word is the set of properties that enables us to pick out all the objects (real or hypothetical, that is possible) to which that word refers, or could refer. The intension of *cat* is the set of feline properties. The extension of a word is the set of all beings (real or imaginary) to which the word refers or could refer. So, we use the intension to establish the extension. At the level of propositions, the intension allows us to determine what the contents of the extension is or could be. The proposition "The present king of France is bald" is currently meaningless in that the intension, "the present king of France," refers to a null set, but it is meaningful in the sense that if there were a king of France, it could be proven that he was or was not bald.

In addition to determining truth conditionals, semantics is concerned with such linguistic phenomena as synonymy, homonymy, polysemy, semantic fields, computer languages, encryption, and decoding. In general, semantics is the branch of linguistics concerned with determining what makes meaning possible.

George L. Pullman
Georgia State University

Bibliography

Gordon, Terrence W. *Semantics: A Bibliography, 1986–1991.* Metuchen, NJ: Scarecrow, 1992.

Korzybski, Alfred. *Science and Sanity: An Introduction to Non-Aristotelian Systems and General Semantics.* Lakeville, CT: International Non-Aristotelian Library, 1958.

Morris, Charles. *Signs, Language, and Behavior.* New York: Prentice, 1946.

Odgen, C.K., and I.A. Richards. *The Meaning of Meaning: A Study of the Influence of Thought upon Language and of the Science of Symbolism.* New York: Harcourt, 1946.

Semiotics

Theory and science of sign systems in language, derived from Greek *simeion* (sign) and *semeiotikos* (one who interprets or divines the meaning of signs). The first known awareness of signs as signs can be seen in early Greek physicians, who diagnosed illnesses by interpreting the body's physical signs. Passages in *Cratylus, On Interpretation,* and *Rhetoric* indicate that Plato and Aristotle realized that the interpretation of signs depends on the influence of *physis* (Nature) and *technê* (Culture) because signs do not have the same meanings. Later, St. Augustine called for a unified *doctrina signorum,* or doctrine of signs, in *On Christian Doctrine.* Likewise, in his defense of empiricism in *Essays on Human Understanding* (1690), which defined experience as the foundation for all knowledge and ideas, John Locke divided human inquiry into three areas, the last being *semeiotike,* or the doctrine of signs. Lamenting the ambiguity of language, Locke attempted to clarify the communication of knowledge, offering directions from the perspective of signification.

By concluding his essay with a proposal for a semiotic historiography, Locke showed an appreciation for the complicated nature of signs.

In his *Course in General Linguistics* (1915), Swiss structural linguist Ferdinand de Saussure (1857–1913) introduced the study of the life of signs within society, which he calls "semiology." Saussure focused on *langue* (systems of linguistic conventions, rules, and their internal relations), regarding *parole* (discourse and usage) as the domain of psychology. Saussure's primary concern was identifying an objective structure of signs and their governing laws. Signs involve two dichotomous albeit inseparable components—the signifier (set speech sounds or marks on a page) and the signified (the concept, idea, and meaning). The relationship between signifier and signified is arbitrary and unnaturally connected, usually historically and culturally negotiated. Because of this completely arbitrary relationship, Saussure proposed that language is a system of signs, defined by their differences from other signs within that same linguistic system. Focusing on the differences, he reoriented linguistics, emphasizing a synchronic investigation of signs, interested in what binds coexisting terms. However, Saussure's logocentric model discounted any element beyond the domain of signification, including epistemological concerns.

Unlike Saussure, American pragmatist Charles Sanders Peirce (1839–1914) built on Locke's theories, demonstrating that signs can never approach or contain any definite meanings. The founder of "semiotics," Peirce distinguished three fundamental kinds of signs: the icon (which resembles its conceptual object—for example, a portrait or photograph resembles a person); the index (which depends on an associative relationship—for example, the direction in which a weathervane points allows the interpreter to conceptually identify the direction the wind is blowing); and the symbol (which depends on social and cultural convention or established usage—for example, a red traffic light means "Stop!"). Every sign has three irreducible parts—the sign or representamen (stands for something to a person), the object (the thing it stands for), and the interpretant (the thought or concept generated in relation to the sign and the object). Peirce's interpretant regresses infinitely, not unlike Umberto Eco's notion of unlimited semiotics: the interpretant can and often does become a sign that requires a new interpretant. Thus, the process of interpretation is not limited to the mere substitution of certain signs for others. Peirce's understanding of interpretation threatens Saussure's concept of arbitrariness because it underscores the necessity and mediated character of interpretation; understanding comes not merely from the decoding of signs but from cognitive processes.

By transforming the medieval Trivium (grammar, logic, and rhetoric) into a semiotic trivium, Peirce offered Speculative Grammar (classifying the various possible sign functions), Critical Logic (codifying the circumstances surrounding truth, reality, and knowledge), and Speculative Rhetoric (analyzing patterns of communication and the relationships among signs). Because Peirce defined rhetoric as the "secret of rendering signs effective," the study of Speculative Rhetoric focused on language as the mediating factor among subject, reality, and community (Peirce 1978:149). It involves the discursive norms that are publicly objectified, the ways signification embodies habits, and the relationship between the interpreter and interpretant when signs enter human thought and behavior. For Peirce, words are not only tools for communication but also a system of relationships indicated in language use. Peirce's concept of mediation involves both patterns of communication and other codes of inquiry that lead to growth. However, a community's significatory habits can also approach a regulatory domain.

Influenced by Peirce's trichotomies, C.K. Ogden (1889–1957) and I.A. Richards (1893–1979) saw sign interpretation as the context for discussing meaning. Later, Richards used the term *interinanimation of words* to suggest that meanings are derived from context and past experiences of the way words are used. Synthesizing Saussure's and Peirce's theories, Russian formalist Roman Jakobson (1896–1982) applied semiotics to poetics, rejecting the possibility of separating sound from meaning in language. Emphasizing the importance of context, Jakobson offered an understanding of poetics through the rhetorical tropes metaphor (where similar signs are substituted for each other) and metonymy (where spatially, temporally, or intellectually contiguous signs are combined). Improving on Saussure's theories, Roland Barthes (1915–1980) theorized that signification cannot and must not be divorced from the operations of myth and ideology; it always implies a larger cultural arena. Stressing the concept of connotation, Barthes investigated how emerging signifying systems build on already existing systems, usually influenced by class interests and values.

Barthes highlights the role of myth and ideology in his analyses of popular culture, including fashion and wrestling. Other popular applications of semiotics include narratology (A.J. Greimas), cultural anthropology (Claude Lévi-Strauss), cognitive and behavioral development (Jean Piaget and Charles Morris), psychoanalysis (Jacques Lacan and Julia Kristeva), film (Christian Metz), literary analysis (Michael Riffaterre and Barbara Herrnstein Smith), and philosophy (Ernst Cassirer and Susanne Langer). In the 1980s and 1990s, the study of signs extends to semiotic analyses of cultural phenomena (cultural studies).

Sue Hum
University of Massachusetts, Dartmouth

Bibliography

Barthes, Roland. *Elements of Semiotics.* Trans. Anetto Lavers and Colin Smith. New York: Hill and Wang, 1968.

Benveniste, Emile. *Problems in General Linguistics.* Trans. Mary Elizabeth Meek. Coral Gables, FL: U of Miami P, 1971.

Bordwell, David. *Making Meaning: Inference in Rhetoric in the Interpretation of Cinema.* Cambridge, MA: Harvard UP, 1989.

Bouchard, Guy. "Semiotics and the Logic of Argumentation." *Canadian Semiotic Association* 6 (1986): 264–85.

Eco, Umberto. *A Theory of Semiotics.* Bloomington: Indiana UP, 1976.

Jakobson, Roman. *Verbal Art, Verbal Sign, Verbal Time.* Ed. Krystyna Pomorska and Stephen Rudy. Minneapolis: U of Minnesota P, 1985.

Lacan, Jacques. *The Language of the Self: The Function of Language in Psychoanalysis.* Trans. Anthony Wilden. New York: Dell, 1968.

Lyne, John R. "Rhetoric and Semiotic in C.S. Peirce." *Quarterly Journal of Speech* 66 (1980): 155–68.

Ogden, C.K., and I.A. Richards. *The Meaning of Meaning: A Study of the Influence of Language upon Thought and of the Science of Symbolism.* 1923. San Diego, Harcourt, 1989.

Peirce, Charles Sanders. *Complete Published Works Including Selected Secondary Material.* Ed. Kenneth L. Ketner et al. Greenwich, CT: Johnson, 1977.

———. "Ideas, Stray or Stolen, about Scientific Writing, No. 1." *Philosophy and Rhetoric* 11 (1978): 147–55.

Saussure, Ferdinand de. *Course in General Linguistics*. Ed. Charles Bally and Albert Reidlinger. Trans. Wade Baskin. New York: Philosophical Library, 1959.

Sebeok, Thomas A. *Semiotics in the United States*. Bloomington: Indiana UP, 1991.

See also PEIRCE, CHARLES SANDERS; SAUSSURE, FERDINAND DE; SIGNIFIED/ SIGNIFIER/SIGNIFYING

Sermon

Derived from Latin *sermo*, meaning talk, discourse, speech and a few related concepts (see *sermo*, *Oxford Latin Dictionary*); used synonymously with *homily* in various contexts and *homiletics*, which designates the art of composing and delivering both homilies and sermons. Although form critics are often ambiguous in their use of the terms *homily* and *sermon* (Black 2), there are profound differences in the kinds of address that are called "homilies" and "sermons." Most important, "homily" has often been used to designate informal discourse about spiritual things or a celebration or exegesis of Scriptures or beliefs *with a gathering of believers*. "Sermon," on the other hand, refers primarily to the rhetorical genre "sacred orations," which can be divided into multiple categories based on audience, occasion, form, content, method of delivery, purpose—even "faculty of mind primarily addressed." Some rhetorical theorists have regarded the sermon as a type of epideictic address, while others have placed it in a unique category because of its special purposes, materials for invention, and connection with divine inspiration (see J.Q. Adams, *Lectures on Rhetoric and Oratory*, 1810). Its primary purpose is *persuasion*. A sermon may celebrate, but its main work is argument.

The Christian sermon, to which this entry confines itself, is rooted in Judaic rhetoric of the Hellenistic period and has carried on a relationship with classical rhetorical theory almost from its beginning. Some scholars affirm the relationship right from the start of the Gospels, seeing even in the written accounts of Jesus' *Sermon on the Mount* and *Sermon on the Plain* significant features of classical rhetoric. Scholars debate the nature and degree of the influence of classical rhetoric on Christian sermons and other forms of address up through the first century, but consensus improves dramatically from the mid second century onward. No one maintains that Christian preaching was entirely a product of classical rhe-

torical arts, but the impact of classical rhetoric on Christian sermons is increasingly evident, as we look into the second century and see the pervasive influence of the Second Sophistic and other rhetorical trends. So profound were these influences that prolonged struggles ensued between those Christians who welcomed and those who feared the classical arts. Tertullian, in about 200, summarized the conflict with the words "What hath Athens to do with Jerusalem?"

Perhaps the most influential answer to this question came from Augustine, whose *De doctrina christiana* (finished in 427) synthesized Ciceronian rhetoric with Christian doctrines and purposes. His treatise provided preachers with useful theoretical foundations and with powerful arguments for bringing the "plundered gold" of classical learning into the service of God. The early homiletic manuals, the medieval *ars praedicandi* (art of preaching), and the hundreds of treatises on preaching that have guided sermonic composition and delivery up to the present, bear witness to the many productive syntheses of secular and sacred rhetorical theory.

In American homiletic theory, the nineteenth century provides a particularly clear view of the way "literary and conservative" homileticians fused the art of preaching with traditional oratory and the care they took to distinguish the sermon from any other kind of address. Here, for example, is part of a definition of "sermon" written by Austin Phelps, professor of Sacred Oratory at Andover Theological Seminary from 1848 to 1879:

> A religious exhortation, for instance, is not a sermon. A part of a sermon it may be; but exhortation standing alone is not preaching. Informal remarks in a meeting for religious conference are not a sermon. Woven into a sermon they may be, but isolated they are not preaching. A sermon is a structure: it is something put together with care. It has unity, coherence, proportion, a beginning, a middle, and an end. As a literary production, it has a philosophical construction as truly as a tragedy or an epic poem. (14)

Although Phelps uses the term *literary production* to emphasize the "philosophical construction" of a sermon, he goes on to insist that a sermon is not a "poetic" production; it is distinctly a rhetorical act because persuasion is central. A sermon is "an oral address to the popular mind on religious subjects as contained in the Bible and elaborately treated *with a view to per-*

suasion" (14, italics added). Phelps, typical of the traditional homileticians of his day, goes on to discuss the forms of oratorical address in classical systems (such as Quintilian's "Introduction, Narration, Proof, Refutation, Conclusion") and to show that sermonic form is similar. His treatise on the art of preaching, like dozens of others of his day, is based on the classical canons of invention, arrangement, style, and delivery. None of this is to say that Phelps or any of his colleagues believed human persuasion alone could bring people to believe in Christ and live godly lives, only that God's emissaries should, as Augustine said, "obtain [rhetorical skill] for the uses of good in the service of truth" (4.ii.3).

The waning of secular "oratorical culture" has been paralleled to a large degree in sacred oratory, and at many seminaries, the traditional art of making sermons is no longer the central pillar it once was. However, modern preachers in some denominations and settings still rely significantly on traditional bodies of rhetorical lore to produce "elaborate" religious addresses designed to persuade hearers to faith and righteousness—that is, sermons.

Russel Hirst
University of Tennessee

Bibliography

Black, C. Clifton, II. "The Rhetorical Form of the Hellenistic Jewish and Early Christian Sermon: A Response to Lawrence Wills." *Harvard Theological Review* 81 (1988): 1–18.

Fasol, Al. *Essentials for Biblical Preaching: An Introduction to Basic Sermon Preparation.* Baker Book House, 1989. 157–62.

Gorman, G.E., and Lyn Gorman. *Theological and Religious Reference Materials: Practical Theology.* Bibliographies and Indexes in Religious Studies, No. 7. "Homiletics: Bibliographies, Dictionaries, Handbooks." New York: Greenwood, 1986. 170–86.

Kennedy, George. *Classical Rhetoric and Its Christian and Secular Tradition from Ancient to Modern Times.* Chapel Hill: U of North Carolina P, 1980.

———. *New Testament Interpretation through Rhetorical Criticism.* Chapel Hill: U of North Carolina P, 1984.

Phelps, Austin. *The Theory of Preaching.* New York: Scribner's, 1887.

Webber, F.R. *A History of Preaching in Britain and America.* 3 vols. Milwaukee, WI: Northwestern, 1952–1957.

See also Ars praedicandi; Homiletics; Homily; Pulpit Oratory

S

Shaughnessy, Mina (1924–1978)

Founder of the basic writing movement and supporter of open admissions. Shaughnessy was also director of the CUNY Basic Writing Program and founding editor of the *Journal of Basic Writing*. Because of her early death, Shaughnessy wrote only one book and published fewer than a dozen essays, but her work continues to be a seminal source for current research in basic writing. Above all, Shaughnessy was a great, compassionate, and humane teacher. In the early 1970s, City University of New York implemented an open admissions policy, which guaranteed all high school graduates an opportunity for a college education. Teachers were confronted with severely underprepared students, and many considered these students uneducable. These students' educational and cultural backgrounds had not prepared them for "college level" work. Shaughnessy, however, taught the discipline how to read these student writers' texts. Where others had understandably seen ignorance and error, Shaughnessy found intelligence, logic, and order.

In her influential volume *Errors and Expectations: A Guide for the Teacher of Basic Writing* (1977), Shaughnessy reconceptualized attitudes toward basic writers. It was her humane understanding of error that established *Errors and Expectations* as a classic in the field of composition. She rigorously examined each student writer's errors, demonstrating that errors are rarely random and illogical. By entering into her students' minds and imaginatively re-creating the thought processes beneath writing errors, Shaughnessy discovered patterns in errors. Thus a text that contained fifteen errors could be understood to have only four patterns, or four types, of errors.

Shaughnessy's method of reading basic writing texts continues to inform methodologies of current research in basic writing. But it is as important to recognize the moral and ethical quality of Shaughnessy's scholarship. Never before had students' writing been treated as texts to be studied. In the past, such texts were conveniently hidden away, allowing academe and society to ignore these students who, after attending school for twelve years, could not write an acceptable paragraph. To focus on basic writing texts would expose problems in our academic and social systems. And no one wanted to claim responsibility for these students. Shaughnessy, however, created no scapegoats in her description of what had gone wrong in education. She instead brought dignity to the basic writing student and teacher. For a generation of writing teachers who were not sure of the worth and validity of their accomplishments, Shaughnessy legitimized their work. For the basic writing student whose writings had been viewed as failure, Shaughnessy discovered meaning in their writing.

Of late, Marxist and poststructuralist critics have described Shaughnessy's work as innocent, as formalistic, and as denying students a right to their own language. Shaughnessy's stance on students' right to their own language is somewhat ambivalent. Though she did not encourage her students blindly to obey the formalities of academic discourse, she at times urged them to write for the university; however, in other instances, she encouraged her students to write against the formal conventions of academic discourse. And while Shaughnessy's methodology is perhaps formalistic, her interaction with students moved teacher and student beyond constraints of a formalist methodology. Colleagues of Shaughnessy's tell of her dancing with students in the cafeteria when she tired of classifying their errors.

Several awards have been created in memory of Shaughnessy. The Mina P. Shaughnessy Writing Award is given to the best article published in *Journal of Basic Writing*. The Mina Shaughnessy Scholars Program is designed to support practitioners to improve teaching and learning at the postsecondary level.

Amy Patterson
Texas Christian University

Bibliography

Bartholomae, David. "Released into Language: Errors, Expectations, and the Legacy of Mina Shaughnessy." *The Territory of Language: Linguistics, Stylistics, and the Teaching of Composition.* Ed. Donald A. McQuade. Carbondale: Southern Illinois UP, 1986. 65–88.

D'Eloia, Sarah G., ed. "Toward a Literate Democracy." *Journal of Basic Writing* 3.1 (1980): 1–119 (entire issue).

DeMott, Benjamin. "Mina Shaughnessy: Meeting Challenges." *Nation.* December 9, 1976: 645–48.

Lu, Min-Zhan. "Redefining the Legacy of Mina Shaughnessy: A Critique of the Politics of Linguistic Innocence." *Journal of Basic Writing* 10.1 (1991): 26–40.

Shaughnessy, Mina. "Diving in: An Introduction to Basic Writing." *College Composition and Communication* 27 (1976): 234–39.

———. *Errors and Expectations: A Guide for the Teacher of Basic Writing.* New York: Oxford UP, 1977.

See also BASIC WRITING

Shelley, Percy Bysshe (1792–1822)

A Romantic poet who most clearly articulates his rhetorical theory in his unfinished essay *A Defense of Poetry* (1821). In *The Rhetoric of Romanticism*, Paul De Man argues that Shelley's rhetorical theory of language is provocatively entangled in his poetry. Deborah Esch's critique, "A Defense of Rhetoric/The Triumph of Reading: De Man, Shelley, and *The Rhetoric of Romanticism*," launches De Man's discussion further by questioning the rhetorical theory Shelley's poetry and *Defense* espouse. In "Prose Preface and Romantic Poets: Insinuation and Ethos," John F. Schell connects Shelley and his work to rhetorical history by explaining how he employs the *insinuatio* for the sake of ethos. The use of this ploy begins to bridge the classic and Romantic traditions. In "The Exoteric Species: The Popular Idiom in Shelley's Poetry," Stephen C. Behrendt argues that poetry written around 1811 maintains the classical connection because of its pathos-steeped narrative form.

While Shelley's esoteric verse is marked by a deliberately simplified style, some of his esoteric works, such as *The Mask of Anarchy* and *Queen Mab,* reveal his struggle to reduce sublime concepts. Shelley even declares, "I have the vanity to write only for poetical minds, and must be satisfied with few readers" (qtd. in Behrendt 474). Such a statement suggests Shelley's contention that poetry should be preserved only for those who have the mental capacity to appreciate its introspection. Thus, such a statement not only separates and evaluates other writing in relation to poetry, it also defines and separates respective reading audiences. Finally, in *Shelley's Style*, William Keach clarifies the division Shelley establishes by explaining that the keystone to understanding

Shelley's style is his frequent use of "mentalistic images (that is, 'imagery drawn from the operations of the human mind.' [Preface to *Prometheus Unbound*])" (Quinn 97).

Shelley's definitions of *reason* and *imagination* in *Defense* not only mark his rhetorical perspective, they also resonate with Coleridge's splitting of the imagination into the Primary and the Secondary in *Biographia Literaria*. While for Shelley the former term refers to "the enumeration of quantities already known," the latter "is the perception of the value of those quantities" (204). These definitions underscore Shelley's preference for the imagination. Furthermore, reason is considered to be amoral, while imagination is considered to be moral. For Shelley, poetry is the imagination expressed. Poetry comes from genius (or those who are able to tap most uniquely into the imagination), not from craft. Therefore, poetry, imagination, and morality are necessarily inherent in each other.

Furthermore, although linguistic skepticism pervades much of Shelley's work, he does define language as "that imperial faculty whose throne is curtained within the invisible nature of man" (208). Because, for Shelley, poetry is expressed through language that comes from within, and what is deep inside is revered over what is learned, poetry is esteemed over other genres. Shelley's evaluation maintains the larger Romantic, rhetorical tradition in which he writes—one that values inward looking as a means to writing.

Dawn M. Formo
University of Southern California

Bibliography

Behrendt, Stephen C. "The Exoteric Species: The Popular Idiom in Shelley's Poetry." *Genre* 14 (1981): 473–92.

De Man, Paul. *The Rhetoric of Romanticism.* New York: Columbia UP, 1984.

Engelberg, Karsten Klejs. *The Making of the Shelley Myth.* London: Mansell, 1988.

Esch, Deborah. "A Defense of Rhetoric/The Triumph of Reading: De Man, Shelley and the Rhetoric of Romanticism." *University of Toronto Quarterly* 57 (1988): 484–500.

Keach, William. *Shelley's Style.* New York: Methuen, 1984.

Quinn, Mary A. "Book Review: Shelley's Style." *Modern Philology* 85 (1987): 96–99.

Schell, John F. "Prose Preface and Romantic Poets: Insinuation and Ethos." *Journal of Narrative Technique* 13 (1983): 86–97.

Shelley, Percy Bysshe. "A Defense of Poetry." *Percy Bysshe Shelley: Selected Poetry and Prose.* Ed. Alasdair D.F. Macrae. London: Routledge, 1991.

S

Sheridan, Thomas (1718–1788)

Thomas Sheridan received a classical education from his father, Dr. Thomas Sheridan, and the M.A. from Trinity College, Dublin. His son, Richard Brinsley Sheridan, became the famous playwright. Sheridan was the godson of Jonathan Swift, to whose influence he attributed his passion for the English language and his Augustan love of the ancients. Swift and Sheridan endorsed the idea of "ascertaining" or correcting the language by fixing rules for usage.

His interest in correcting English led Sheridan to forgo an acting career to become a proselytizer for elocution. From 1756 to 1762 he gave his successful lecture course, published in *Lectures on Elocution* in 1762. He later published *A Plan of Education* (1769), *Lectures on the Art of Reading* (1775), and *A General Dictionary of the English Language* (1780), all of which reiterated in some form the argument that Sheridan had first made in 1756 in a work called *British Education: Or, The Source of the Disorders of Great Britain. Being an Essay towards proving, that the Immorality, Ignorance, and false Taste, which so generally prevail, are the natural and necessary Consequences of the present defective System of Education. With an attempt to shew, that a revival of the Art of Speaking, and the Study of Our Own Language, might contribute, in a great measure, to the Cure of those Evils.* Reviving oratory and elevating it to the status it held in ancient Athens and Rome would, Sheridan insisted, lead to improvement in religion, morality, and the fine arts. Sheridan's connection between "Ignorance, Immorality, and false Taste" is typically Augustan: The knowledge and proper appreciation of classical culture will inevitably raise one's moral values. Sheridan adds that because of their superior religion and form of government, the British can rise even higher than the ancients.

Sheridan thus found an ideal forum for his own talents and interests, abetted by the contemporary desire for linguistic self-improvement and educational reform. Sheridan argues that just as language is the medium of reason (as Locke had shown), voice and gesture are "the natural language of the passions." Sheridan appeals to science, reverence for the ancients, linguistic anxiety, religion, and morality, bringing to bear every possible argument for the importance of elocution. His overvaluation of elocution led to criticism and undervaluation of Sheridan's project, but his arguments are not without substance and his principles for public speaking are quite reasonable. His practical instruction consists of advice to be natural, to practice correct grammar and usage, and to speak, for reasons of social expediency, the refined dialect of the educated English gentleman. He urges attention to the meaning of sentences in order to determine the placement of emphasis and pauses. Gestures should be natural. But, he notes, the meaning of gestures is conventional, an action attached to an idea: "Natural" therefore means "not mechanical" rather than "springing from human nature."

Though Sheridan's own fame diminished, he had many imitators, and the substance of his lectures was abstracted into many textbooks, notably Blair's lectures, and appeared in elocution courses offered by colleges in Britain and the United States from his time to ours.

Bruce Herzberg
Bentley College

Bibliography

Bacon, Wallace. "The Elocutionary Career of Thomas Sheridan (1719–1788)." *Speech Monographs* 31 (1964): 1–53.

Benzie, W. *The Dublin Orator: Thomas Sheridan's Influence on Eighteenth-Century Rhetoric and Belles Lettres*. Leeds: U of Leeds School of English, 1972.

Howell, W.S. *Eighteenth-Century British Logic and Rhetoric*. Princeton: Princeton UP, 1971.

See also ELOCUTION

Sidney, Sir Philip (1554–1586)

Cosmopolitan literary and cultural figure of the English Renaissance, known for his poetry, prose romances, and literary criticism, as well as for embodying the virtues of an ideal courtier. Sir Philip Sidney is recognized as a sophisticated writer of the sonnet sequence (*Astrophil and Stella*), the prose romance (*The Countess of Pembroke's Arcadia*), and literary criticism (*A Defence of Poesy*). Sidney's *Defence* argues that literature "delights" and "instructs" its readers, serving as a force for moral and social improvement. This affective critical theory, borrowing

much from Horace, emphasizes the rhetorical nature of literary work in persuading people to lead virtuous lives. The influence of humanist rhetoric can be seen throughout Sidney's writing, but it also shows through in his life. He fashioned himself as a figure who combined Ciceronian and chivalric ideals into a courtier hero widely admired by his contemporaries, while his early death also encouraged a mythologizing that continues even in today's Sidney scholarship.

Sidney's approach to rhetoric and literature was by no means remarkable for his time. *A Defence of Poesy* offers cogent arguments for the value of literature, particularly an English vernacular literature, but these positions merely amplify critical commonplaces about the rhetorical function and moral purpose of literary work. Kenneth Myrick has shown, however, that Sidney's *Defence* is itself an elegant realization of the rhetorical art, shaped as a traditional Ciceronian oration. Though not a theoretical innovator, Sidney still proved an experimental writer, adapting the traditional love sonnet to reflect greater subtlety, irony, and complexity of emotion. Even more experimental was his ambitious attempt to shape the prose romance into a form that could encompass the complications and paradoxes of Elizabethan England. Though neither version of his *Arcadia* achieves this goal, both demonstrate Sidney's considerable invention, imagination, and rhetorical skill. The *Arcadia* also foregrounds oratory in action through the central characters, Musidorus and Pyrocles, both of whom display an oratorical dexterity rooted in the Ciceronian tradition. At least in the second version (the *"New" Arcadia*), they also represent the courtier ideals embraced by Sidney.

Sidney's overall importance to Renaissance rhetoric derives from the rhetorical practice evident in his literary work, where he advocates and embodies the ideals of humanist rhetoricians and where he reveals his own mastery of the rhetorical arts. Sidney's personal reputation, though a product of obvious "self-fashioning" and of subsequent appropriation by others, still reveals Sidney's attempt to fulfill the ideals set forth by Renaissance humanists. Elyot, Ascham, and others concerned with the education of political leaders had argued for the value of both rhetorical skills and the ideals of the orator hero found in Cicero's *De oratore*. Cicero had presented the orator as the ideal blending of warrior courage with intellectual depth and verbal skill. Renaissance humanists adopted this ideal while

Castiglione combined it with the courtly elements of the chivalric tradition (see *Il Cortegiano*). Sidney acknowledged and espoused these ideals as the template for both personal action and fictional representation, achieving the fullest realization of the courtier hero.

Vincent Casaregola
Saint Louis University

Bibliography

Casaregola, Vincent. "Inventions for Voice: Humanist Rhetoric and the Experiments of Elizabethan Prose Fiction." Diss. U of Iowa, 1989.

Connell, Dorothy. *Sir Philip Sidney: The Maker's Mind.* Oxford: Oxford UP, 1977.

Duncan-Jones, Katherine. *Sir Philip Sidney: Courtier Poet.* New Haven: Yale UP, 1991.

Greenblatt, Stephen. *Renaissance Self-Fashioning: From More to Shakespeare.* Chicago: U of Chicago P, 1980.

Kinney, Arthur. *Humanist Poetics: Thought, Rhetoric, and Fiction in Sixteenth-Century England.* Amherst: U of Massachusetts P, 1986.

Kinney, Arthur, ed. *Essential Articles for the Study of Sir Philip Sidney.* Hamden, CT: Archon, 1986.

Myrick, Kenneth. *Sir Philip Sidney as a Literary Craftsman.* 1935. Lincoln: U of Nebraska P, 1965.

Ong, Walter J., S.J. *Rhetoric, Romance, and Technology: Studies in the Interaction of Expression and Culture.* Ithaca, NY: Cornell UP, 1971.

Stump, Donald V., Jerome S. Dees, and C. Stuart Hunter. *Sir Philip Sidney: An Annotated Bibliography of Texts and Criticism (1554–1984).* New York: Hall, 1994.

Signified/Signifier/Signifying

Products of linguistic convention that produce signs and that in turn enable communication of meaning within a system. A relationship between *signifier* (sound image or its graphic counterpart) and *signified* (the concept referred to) constitutes the *sign,* in Saussurian terminology; but this relationship is fundamentally arbitrary, sustained only by context. The structural relationship for example between the signifier "rose" and the signified rose constitutes a linguistic sign—the basic component of language. No necessary "fitness" exists in the connection between the *rose* or its signified, and the rose growing in nature. The word *rose,* in short, lacks any "roselike" essence, and there is no access to a "reality" beyond the structure of language. The word *rose* means the physical thorny object with petals growing in nature because the *structure of language* validates it when it does so (Hawkes 1977:25).

Language is self-defining, self-generating, and so enclosed and complete. It is capable of "transformation"—that is, of creating new meanings in response to new experience. These capacities language renders possible precisely because it allows no appeals to a "reality" beyond itself. In the end it constitutes its own reality. According to Saussure: "Language is a system of inter-dependent terms in which the value of each term results solely from the simultaneous presence of the others" (Hawkes 1977:26).

If language is based on relations, Roland Barthes explains how the "associative total" of the sign, through the example of a bouquet of roses, signifies passion. The bouquet of roses is the signifier, the passion the signified. The relation between the two (the "associative total") produces another term, the bouquet of roses as a sign. And *as a sign,* the bouquet of roses is entirely different from the bouquet as a signifier, that is, as a thorny, petally, physical entity. As a signifier, the bouquet of roses is "empty," as a sign it is "full." What fills it (makes it signify) is a complex of the lover's "intent" and the "nature of society's conventional modes and channels" that present a "range of vehicles" for the expression of love (Hawkes 1977:131). This range, it is important to remember, may be "conventionalized" and "finite," but only until it invents new ways of signifying (that is, articulating *like* a language). By then language's grounding in *différence* (or distinctions) also implies a commitment to *différance* (or deferring). As Saussure puts it, "In language there are only differences."

In the aesthetic use of language, signs do not signify in the "normal" way because they signify themselves. Ordinarily a signifier refers to a signified beyond itself with the least possible ambiguity; the "fit" between signifier and signified is exact. However, in literary discourse signifiers manifest a high degree of sanctioned ambiguity, a concept very similar to Jakobson's view that poetry represents "organized violence committed on ordinary speech" (Erlich 1973:219).

Catherine Lappas
Saint Louis University

Bibliography

Barthes, Roland. *Mythologies*. Trans. Annette Lavers. London: Paladin, 1973.

Culler, Jonathan. *The Pursuit of Signs: Semiotics, Literature, Deconstruction*. Ithaca, NY: Cornell UP, 1981.

Erlich, Victor. "Roman Jakobson: Grammar of Poetry and Poetry of Grammar." *Approaches to Poetics*. Ed. Seymour Chatman. New York: Columbia UP, 1973.

Hawkes, Terence. *Structuralism and Semiotics*. Berkeley: U of California P, 1977.

Saussure, Ferdinand de. *Course in General Linguistics*. Ed. Charles Bally and Albert Sechehaye. Trans. W. Baskin. 1959. New York: McGraw, 1966.

Smith, Adam (1723–1790)

Early proponent of the new rhetoric. Lecturing on rhetoric from 1748 to 1763, first to public audiences in Edinburgh and later at Glasgow University, Adam Smith was among the first to articulate the new rhetoric that emerged in Britain during the second half of the eighteenth century. His lectures fall into two broad divisions: The first breaks with rhetoric's traditional focus on persuasion, adopting *communication* as a more inclusive concern, and the second analyzes various *forms of composition,* encompassing poetry, history, and scientific writing as well as traditional rhetorical genres.

The first section of Smith's lectures focuses on perspicuity, the "origin and design of language," and the principles of prose style. In these lectures Smith employs approaches to language characteristic of the new rhetoric: (1) comparing languages to identify relative strengths and "defects"; (2) emphasizing the vernacular while illustrating arguments with examples from both classical and contemporary writers' works; (3) linking grammatical and stylistic standards to national custom interpreted according to models of progress and social hierarchy (for example, distinctions between "primitive" and advanced languages and between the usage of "the lower sort of People" and that of "men of rank and breeding").

In his treatment of style, Smith takes pains to distance himself from rhetorical tradition. He establishes a single governing principle of arrangement—"whatever is most interesting in the sentence, on which the rest depends, should be placed first; and so on thro' the whole" (19)—arguing that other traditional rules "do not deserve attention" (24). Similarly, he refuses to offer a detailed taxonomy of tropes and figures, calling ancient and modern treatises emphasizing such taxonomies "a very silly set of Books" and arguing that it is not figures themselves but their relations to the sentiments, characters, and circumstances of speakers that make such expressions agreeable and effective (26).

The second section of Smith's course concerns various "Species of Composition" (62). These lectures formulate principles governing the ends, means, arrangement, and manner of expression appropriate to each form of composition. Smith also analyzes the work of writers who "have succeeded most happily in all these branches" (63), accounting for differences among them in terms of their characters and "the different condition of the countries in which they lived," thus linking rhetorical theory and practice to cultural contexts (160).

Smith's taxonomy of composition begins with a division between discourses whose purpose is "barely to relate some fact" and those that aim additionally "to prove some proposition" (62). The first kind he calls narrative, which he eventually divides further into descriptive and historical writing, the former a general method of relating facts, the latter a distinct form of composition. The second kind he divides into didactic and rhetorical composition, distinguished by ends and means. Didactic or scientific writing aims primarily at instruction and only secondarily at persuasion; therefore, it "proposes to put before us the arguments on both sides of the question in their true light" (62). Rhetorical writing aims primarily at persuasion and only secondarily at instruction; therefore, it "magnifies all the arguments on the one side and diminishes or conceals" arguments that favor the opposing side (62). Thus, since Smith also considers poetry and drama in his lectures, his broad treatment of communication and composition encompasses discursive territory that once belonged to the realms of rhetoric, dialectic, and poetics (Howell 1971:575). Arguably the first to articulate the new rhetoric of the eighteenth century, Smith undoubtedly helped to shape a pivotal movement in the history of rhetoric.

H. Lewis Ulman
Ohio State University

Bibliography

Bevilacqua, Vincent M. "Adam Smith and Some Philosophical Origins of Eighteenth-Century Rhetorical Theory." *Modern Language Review* 43 (1968): 559–68.

Hogan, J. Michael. "Historiography and Ethics in Adam Smith's Lectures on Rhetoric, 1762–63." *Rhetorica* 2 (1984): 75–91.

Howell, Wilbur S. *Eighteenth-Century British Logic and Rhetoric*. Princeton: Princeton UP, 1971. 536–76.

Lightwood, Martha Bolar. *A Selected Bibliography of Significant Works about Adam Smith*. Philadelphia: U of Pennsylvania P, 1984.

Smith, Adam. *Lectures on Rhetoric and Belles Lettres*. Ed. and Intro. J.C. Bryce. New York: Oxford UP, 1983. Vol. 4 of *The Glasgow Edition of the Works and Correspondence of Adam Smith*. 6 vols. 1976–1983.

Spencer, Patricia. "Sympathy and Propriety in Adam Smith's Rhetoric." *Quarterly Journal of Speech* 60 (1974): 92–99.

Social Construction

The view that language practices construct the social realities that enable individuals and groups to enact their purposes in the world. *Social construction* is a cover term that refers to a number of related intellectual currents, ranging from poststructuralism and neopragmatism to Marxism and feminism, that have sought to redescribe the relations among mind, language, and reality in ways that resist earlier empiricist and idealist accounts.

The central proposition of social construction holds that individuals do not encounter the world directly and then use language to describe these encounters, as empiricists generally maintain. Instead, social constructionists believe that individuals and groups draw upon the linguistic resources available within particular cultures and specialized social milieux in order to constitute reality and to position themselves as speakers, writers, and actors in relation to these locally constituted realities, to each other, and to social institutions. By the same token, unlike idealists in Cartesian and Kantian traditions, social constructionists do not think of the mind as consisting of inherent mental properties that can be known a priori as the foundation of philosophical method, but rather they think of the knowing subject as the result and instrument of social and discursive practices. For these reasons, in social constructionist theory, statements that are accorded the status of truth are matters neither of matching language to the world in accurate representations nor of applying philosophical method successfully but instead are matters of what the philosopher Richard Rorty in *Philosophy and the Mirror of Nature* calls "socially justified beliefs." That is, the available means of validating statements reside not in the correspondence of ideas to objects and events or in the internal workings of the mind but instead in the persuasiveness of statements within particular communities.

According to Rorty, philosophers such as Dewey, Heidegger, and the late Wittgenstein compose an "edifying" tradition that seeks to demystify all forms of transcendental support as the foundation of philosophy by calling attention to the figurative properties of philosophical discourse. In this regard the cluster of ideas associated with social construction represents a significant break with earlier traditions of rhetoric. For social constructionists, language use is persuasive in part because it is epistemic—because it produces versions of reality capable of eliciting consent and participation among groups of people who share particular discursive practices. This view of the intersubjectivity of knowledge production and authorization signals an important departure in rhetorical theory from traditional Aristotelian assumptions that scientific knowledge and ethical principles are impervious to rhetorical practice and that rhetoric should therefore be limited to the arena of public discourse, where absolute certainty is impossible and opinions are divided. Social constructionists, on the other hand, define rhetoric by function, not content, thereby blurring the distinctions between rhetoric and poetic, rhetoric and science, and rhetoric and ethics. Social constructionists describe all discourse—including literature, science, and philosophy—as rhetorical in nature, involved not only in representing and interpreting the world but also in establishing and legitimizing the social practices that reproduce and maintain social relations within discourse communities. In this sense the activities we call science, literature, and philosophy need to be analyzed, from a social constructionist perspective, as communal events that produce and sustain social institutions through a broad range of discursive and textual practices.

The notion of social construction has always been implied in Marxist theory, following Marx's famous dictum that "people make history but in conditions not of their making." The term itself, however, appears initially with Berger's and Luckmann's (1966) *Social Construction of Reality*, a sociological account of how ordinary people construct a practical knowledge of their worlds. Subsequently, the studies of particular intellectual communities by theorists such as Thomas Kuhn (1962) in *The Structure of Scientific Revolutions*, Bruno Latour and Steve Woolgar (1979) in *Laboratory Life*, Stanley Fish (1980) in *Is There a Text in This Class?*, and James Clifford and George Marcus (1986) in their edited collection *Writing Culture* have been labeled *social constructionist* for their challenges to the positivistic view of knowledge as an incremental and progressive accumulation of facts and concepts. The label *social construction* has come to refer to the view that academic and professional fields rely on locally determined paradigms and disciplinary matrices as the conditions of possibility that enable and constrain intellectual and practical work. Social constructionists, therefore, tend to focus on the persuasive and normalizing functions of discourse in constituting objects of inquiry, leading questions and research programs, and terms of validation and criticism that bind discourse communities together as coherent social and linguistic systems. In this sense, social construction offers an important reinterpretation of the nature and authority of knowledge by figuring knowledge not in terms of demonstrable certainties but instead in terms of contingent rhetorical negotiations.

Social construction has generated a body of scholarly research into the context-specific rhetorical practices of academics and professionals. Charles Bazerman (1988) in *Shaping Written Knowledge* and Greg Myers (1990) *Writing Biology* have studied the social construction of scientific knowledge. Collections such as Odell's and Goswami's (1985) *Writing in Non-Academic Settings* and Bazerman's and Paradis's (1991) *Textual Dynamics* look at writing in a variety of professional settings, and the rhetoric of inquiry in collections such as Nelson's, Megill's, and McCloskey's (1987) *Rhetoric of the Human Sciences* and Simons's (1989) *Rhetoric in the Human Sciences* has investigated the social construction of

knowledge in particular academic and professional contexts.

Just as social construction has challenged traditional assumptions about the nature and authority of knowledge, so has it challenged traditional assumptions about the relationship between language and thought. For social constructionists, what individuals experience as private or personal acts of cognition are in fact social in character, the result, as Vygotsky describes it, of internalized conversations with others. What philosophers and rhetoricians have conventionally thought of as the mind or the knowing subject is, according to the tenets of social construction, not a naturally given faculty but an artifact created by the extension of social experience inward, a "polyphony" of others' voices, as Bakhtin put it, contending for a person's attention and social allegiance. In this view, the rhetor cannot be the autonomous creator of utterances but rather is as much the product of the discourses a person participates in as the producer of these discourses.

Feminist, African-American, and postcolonial theorists, moreover, have argued that such apparently common-sense categories as gender, race, and nationality are themselves social constructions, based not on biological or geographical realities but rather on politically interested discourses that organize differences between male and female, white and black, metropolis and colony in relations of domination and subordination. From this nonessentialist perspective, individual and group identities are not naturally given but are produced, socially and discursively, as available subject positions. As Stuart Hall puts it, identities and interests are not so much determined by social position as they result from the ways individuals and groups articulate subjectivities to the social formation.

Because of its resolutely antifoundationalist disposition toward issues of truth, knowledge, meaning, and value, social construction has been embroiled in a number of debates. For some critics, the social constructionist view that there is no measure to judge knowledge claims beyond the local practices of particular discourse communities amounts to a kind of moral and epistemological relativism incapable of distinguishing between truth and force. By way of reply, social constructionists argue that the desire to establish a secure method for determining the good and the true results from a misguided evasion of the rhetorical character of human experience and amounts to an attempt to ground thought and action on first principles instead of on rhetorical negotiation. To disclose the conventionalism of belief and practice, social constructionists argue, is not to lapse into a debilitating relativism but rather is to hold individuals morally responsible for conventions and their social consequences.

For others, such as the philosopher Donald Davidson, social constructionists have gone too far in their efforts to codify the conventionalized practices of discourse communities. According to Davidson, there are no "conceptual schemes" or background conditions an individual can have prior to a communicative interaction that will guarantee intelligibility. Instead, communicative situations will always be enacted in indeterminate and incomplete ways through intersubjective and interpersonal relations that cannot be predicted in advance. In other words, while social constructionists tend to emphasize the shared language practices that make communication possible within particular institutions and discourse communities, Davidson wants to emphasize the unpredictable and uncodifiable hermeneutical interactions by which individuals work their way into and make sense of discursive situations.

Finally, leftwing critics of social construction have charged that its conventionalism neglects how discourse communities establish and maintain asymmetrical relations of power and differential access to the means of producing and distributing knowledge. From a leftwing perspective, social constructionists have failed to pay adequate attention to the way discourse communities enfranchise or marginalize participants on the basis of status, credentials, race, class, gender, age, and so on. According to leftwing critics, the notion of consensus that social constructionists use to explain the dominant concerns of discourse communities obscures the fact that specialized, consensually based academic and professional fields constitute social formations of insiders and outsiders: monopolies of experts, on one hand, and client populations dependent on professional authorities, on the other. In other words, while social constructionists have provided useful accounts of the production of knowledge, they have largely evaded the question of how the means of producing knowledge are articulated to wider systems of distribution and exchange.

Social construction is by no means a finished or codified intellectual tradition, and the issues surrounding it remain volatile and open ended. While social constructionists hold to the view that entities such as ideas, concepts, and facts are linguistic constructs that have proved useful to particular discourse communities, the issue of how language organizes and makes sense of reality at the level of lived experience remains largely underdeveloped within social constructionist thought. Similarly, while it is axiomatic in social construction that discourse communities are based upon particular social and linguistic practices, the matters of how individuals appropriate and internalize these practices, inhabit multiple and overlapping discourse communities simultaneously, and resist or evade acculturation to communal practices and beliefs are only recently topics of exploration. Finally, social constructionists are just beginning to address the problem of intercultural communication, where incommensurable discourses meet, by elaborating notions of boundary conversation, or what Mary Louise Pratt calls the "arts of the contact zone," to explain the hybrid, sometimes subversive, and often parodic forms of expression that result from unequal cultural encounters.

John Trimbur
Worcester Polytechnic Institute

Bibliography

Bruffee, Kenneth A. "Social Construction, Language, and the Authority of Knowledge: A Bibliographic Essay." *College English* 48 (1986): 773–90.

Kuhn, Thomas. *The Structure of Scientific Revolutions.* 2nd ed. Chicago: U of Chicago P, 1970.

Latour, Bruno, and Steve Woolgar. *Laboratory Life: The Social Construction of Scientific Facts.* Beverly Hills, CA: Sage, 1979.

Rorty, Richard. *Philosophy and the Mirror of Nature.* Princeton: Princeton UP, 1979.

Sociolinguistics

The study of all aspects of the relationship between language and society. Emphasis in sociolinguistic research is on the range of variation exhibited in language related to any number of social or cultural factors, including age, sex, education, occupation, ethnicity, or socioeconomic class. A wide range of issues are investigated, such as social attitudes to language, standard and nonstandard forms of language, patterns and needs of national language use, regional and social varieties, or the social basis of bi- and multilingualism. In addition to linguists, among those interested in investigating these issues are anthropologists, social psychologists, sociologists, philosophers, educators, and political scientists.

Sociolinguistics became established as a field in the late 1960s and early 1970s, a development consistent with the various social and cultural movements of that period. Researchers from a range of disciplines recognized that differences in the way people use language often have social consequences. Among the issues given scholarly attention were the disadvantages associated with the use of nonstandard varieties of English, most notably black English; educational failure and nonstandard language use; sexism and language; policy and planning issues in linguistically diverse countries; and the language rights of minorities. The following describes a few areas in which sociolinguistic research is conducted and illustrates the breadth of the field and ways in which research findings can be applied.

Dialectology

Over a century before sociolinguistics became recognized as a field, linguists in Europe were researching language variation in dialectology studies. Work in this area continues to the present. The focus of this research is regional differences in language form, particularly variations in pronunciation and vocabulary, and in determining the geographic location of the pronunciations observed. Data is generally collected through dialect surveys that interview speakers on a range of items. For example, the Indiana Dialect Survey has found that 44 percent of those surveyed refer to nonalcoholic carbonated beverages as "pop," while 34 percent prefer to call all soft drinks "Coke," and another 10 percent say "soda." The remainder used "sody," "sody water," or "Pepsi." Seventy-one percent pronounce "greasy" as "gree-see," and 29 percent prefer "gree-zee." One goal of this research is the identification and documentation of the various varieties of a language. While dialectology was originally concerned with the dialects of rural speakers, contemporary studies have also investigated urban dialects as well as class and ethnic dialects. Attention has also been given to differences in grammar as well as vocabulary and pronunciation.

Language and Gender

Of interest to sociolinguists in recent years is the relationship of language and gender. One approach is to examine differences in the use of language to refer to women and men and the connection between this use and the connotations and values associated with the two sexes. For example, it has been observed that terms referring to women more frequently describe food items (*cupcake, cheesecake,* or *peach*) or animals (*vixen, chick, kitten, pet*). Terms of reference for men more often connote strength or sexual prowess (*he-man, stud, hunk,* or *jock*). Differences have also been noted in the development of the meanings of such word pairs as *master-mistress, bachelor-spinster,* or *governor-governess.* Another approach to sex differences is to examine female-male differences in the use of language and the social factors that influence these differences. Variation has been documented in the use of color words; it has been claimed that women use color words that men do not, such as *chartreuse, lavender, magenta,* or *mauve.* Adjectives such as *adorable, charming, divine,* or *lovely* are also more likely to be used by women than men. Other differences documented are in men's and women's styles of speaking in mixed-group conversation. For example, women generally ask more questions, encourage others to speak, use *you* and *we* more often, and protest less than men when interrupted. Men however interrupt more, challenge, dispute, and ignore more, and try to control the topic more. These differences can lead to misunderstandings, much like the miscommunication observed between members of different cultures. One such instance is women's use of *mhhmmmm,* which more often is intended to mean "I'm listening," while men are more likely to interpret it as "I'm agreeing."

Educational Failure and Language Use

Research into language variation has provided insight into the relationship between the use of language and failure in school. One line of research has sought explanations for the failure of children from poorer working-class families to do well at school. One explanation is that the school variety (the so-called standard variety) is different from that learned by children growing up in such families; these children use a so-called nonstandard variety. These differences (for example, the school variety is more grammatical and varied in syntax and vocabulary) interfere with the ability of poorer working-class children to participate and succeed in the educational process and affect teachers' responses to and expectations of these children. Another line of research has pursued the effects of the use of black English on educational failure and remedies for lack of success. One aim of studies has been to demonstrate that black English is a legitimate variety of English that by no means limits its speakers' expressive and communicative abilities and that its speakers use this variety to mark group membership. This insight into language as a symbol has helped explain why black English–speaking children may be resistant to the school's efforts to get them to stop using black English and to switch completely to use of the standard.

English in the World Context
A developing area of interest is the investigation of the different Englishes (Indian English, Nigerian English, European English) used and learned around the world. Scholarship in this area investigates the forms and uses of these varieties of English, both native and nonnative, in diverse cultural and sociolinguistic contexts. This research is particularly relevant to the concerns of language planners and policy-makers, writers and literary critics, linguists, and English language teachers and teacher educators. Addressed are public attitudes toward the learning and use of English in countries and regions where this language is spreading (such as Europe) or is being retained (such as former colonies in Asia and Africa); creative expression through the use of English in nonnative, or colonial, literatures; the multiple cultural identities and traditions associated with English in non-Western contexts; the impact of English on other major languages of the world and the resultant language change; and norms and standards for newly developed or developing varieties.

Discourse Analysis
Sociolinguists have also given attention to written texts. This focus on written units of language larger than a sentence is referred to as discourse analysis. An important perspective connected with discourse analysis is that language cannot be studied in isolation from the communicative intentions of the users and the social and cultural context in which they use a language; a text, or a discourse, is socially situated. The structure of a text and the purpose it is intended to serve can be understood and determined by reference to the norms and expectations of the writer and the reader. These norms and expectations will differ in significant ways within and across cultures and social groups. Those engaging in discourse analysis seek to discover the nature of these differences. Of particular interest are the devices that provide a structural framework to texts and the cohesion necessary for a text to be considered an organized whole. One line of research is the identification of cohesive ties, which are devices that refer to preceding or subsequent elements in a text, such as pronouns presupposing an earlier or later occurrence of a noun. Decoding the pronoun depends upon knowing or being able to find that noun. Other research investigates the overall structure of discourse in different genres (such as instruction manuals, research reports, or direct-mail solicitation letters) and disciplines (for example, law, technology, or journalism) to determine the norms guiding the creation and evaluation of written texts in various discourse communities. Particularly productive have been studies of discourse in a variety of cultural and linguistic contexts, which illustrate the diversity of means of organizing written information. An expository text written by a Hindi speaker, for example, contains passages that an American English reader unfamiliar with Hindi text structure would consider distracting digressions.

From the study of single sounds and pronunciations of individual speakers to the use of a world language as a lingua franca, sociolinguistics makes significant contributions to a wide range of disciplines and social concerns. Collectively, the insights gained from the study of language and society contribute to an understanding of the way language functions as a means of human interaction and communication and ultimately to an understanding of humanity.

Margie Berns
Purdue University

Bibliography
Bernstein, Basil. "Social Class, Language and Socialization." *Language and Social Context*. Ed. Pier Paolo Giglioli. Harmondsworth, England: Penguin, 1972. 157–78.

Davis, L.M. *English Dialectology: An Introduction*. University: U of Alabama P, 1983.

Hudson, R.A. *Sociolinguistics*. Cambridge: Cambridge UP, 1980.

Kachru, Braj B. *The Other Tongue: English across Cultures.* 2nd ed. Champaign: U of Illinois P, 1982.

Labov, William. *Language in the Inner City: Studies in the Black English Vernacular.* Philadelphia: U of Pennsylvania P, 1972.

Lakoff, Robin. *Language and Women's Place.* New York: Harper, 1975.

———. *Talking Power.* New York: Basic, 1990.

Stubbs, Michael. *Discourse Analysis: The Sociolinguistic Analysis of Natural Language.* Chicago: U of Chicago P, 1983.

Thorne, Barrie, and Nancy Henley, eds. *Language and Sex: Difference and Dominance.* Rowley, MA: Newbury, 1975.

Wardhaugh, Ronald. *An Introduction to Sociolinguistics.* 2nd ed. New York: Blackwell, 1992.

Socrates (469–399 B.C.E.)

Athenian citizen and philosopher who took a great interest in the role of persuasion. Inasmuch as Socrates wrote nothing, his ideas are difficult to ascertain. Various sources provide details of his life, though these sources often conflict. Socrates influenced the significant shift in philosophic inquiry from consideration of natural science to ethical (and later epistemological) concerns.

In Plato's *Apology,* Socrates states what may be his life's central idea, that the unexamined life is not worth living. In his pursuit of virtue through knowledge, he differed from both the natural science of earlier philosophy and the interest in success attributed to the contemporary sophists. His complete devotion to this idea and its implications brought serious results both for him and for those around him: He neglected his own surroundings, and he ended his life in poverty, having come to realize the unimportance of material things. His desire to foster such ideas in others (describing his behavior with the metaphors of a gadfly stinging a horse to action or a midwife helping others to brings ideas to birth) created devotion in many followers as well as hostility among his interlocutors.

His method of inquiry, known now as the "Socratic method," was to use questions and answers to get at essential definitions and divisions of a topic, usually revealing inconsistent beliefs in his interlocutor before developing positive knowledge. Plato's *Euthyphro* or the *Protagoras* are good examples of this method; his words in Plato's *Apology* describe the often

antagonizing effects that may have led eventually to the attack brought against him. In 399 B.C.E., Socrates was tried on charges of corrupting youth and introducing new gods. He spoke in his own defense, but was convicted; he offered a sizable fine as a counterproposal to the death penalty, but was condemned to death by poisoning (hemlock). He did not take advantage of an opportunity to escape from prison presented to him later (as described in the *Crito*), and he died in the presence of his sorrowful friends (*Phaedo*).

Even though the picture of Socrates handed down comes predominantly from the *Apology* and Plato's other dialogues, these other dialogues are less sure sources for information. The "Socratic Question" of who the "historical" Socrates was depends, therefore, on a wider scrutiny of the sources, most important among which are Aristophanes, Plato, and Xenophon.

Socrates is presented by his contemporary Aristophanes in the comedy *The Clouds.* The plays of Aristophanes that mention Socrates are the only sources from his lifetime and therefore offer an important source of information about popular opinion. *The Clouds* attacks the role of the sophists in the cultural atmosphere of the day. This play offers the view that Socrates was a part of the sophistic movement and was no different from other sophists; he is money-seeking, immoral, and an impractical searcher after irrelevant knowledge. Because Socrates offered a new kind of education and (often) paradoxical thought, he could be equated with the newness of the sophists. But his approach (as shown in the Platonic works and in Aristotle's references to him) differed from that of the sophists, especially in his interest in dialectic over set speech and in knowledge over opinion.

Socrates' death in 399 B.C.E. inspired a great deal of emotion and creativity. Further attacks were made, which led to the writing of several versions of what Socrates had said in his own defense when on trial. From the works of his influential follower Plato (429–347 B.C.E.) comes the fullest picture of Socrates and his ideas on rhetoric. Socrates' own practice of oratory and his ideas about the efficacy of rhetorical principles may be detected in Plato's *Apology.* Socrates asserts there that he differs from the sophists, addressing the claims made by Aristophanes and others about his relation to that new school of thought. Plato's Socrates is a man who is concerned about the definition and aims of persuasion (*Gorgias*), who is aware of the technical traditions existing at the time (*Phaedrus* and *Menexenus*), and who perhaps sees some hope for the field if it is carefully subordinated to philosophical truth (*Phaedrus*). Other dialogues that show Socrates' interest in the topics of rhetoric include the *Symposium, The Protagoras, The Theaetetus,* and *The Republic.*

Whether the views presented in these works by Plato are those of Socrates, however, is a question open to discussion, given contradictions in sources other than Plato and even within Plato's dialogues. Many scholars think that Plato's earlier works may better present the ideas of the "historical" Socrates. Plato's later works would then increasingly use Socrates only as a mouthpiece for the development of Plato's own ideas. If this is so, then the fact that many early dialogues are not dogmatic, but aporetic (left with no answer to the question posed), may indicate something of Socrates' approach to philosophic method and his subsequent attitude toward persuasion. These show Socrates very much in control of the art of persuasion (*Apology*), but also very hostile toward its moral ambiguity and its claims to be an art (*Gorgias* and *Protagoras*). They do not, however, offer conclusions.

Xenophon (428–354 B.C.E.), the historian and philosopher who claimed to be a follower of Socrates', also presents characterizations of Socrates in several of his works: his own version of *The Apology of Socrates* and a *Symposium,* and his account of Socrates' thought in *The Memorabilia* and *The Oeconomicus.* Xenophon's presentation lacks the sophistication of Plato's and as a result has suffered much negative criticism. Still, the presentation by Xenophon may balance the lofty image in Plato's dialogues. They, along with references from Aristotle, may indicate which portions of Plato's presentation are attributable to the "historical" Socrates.

Terry L. Papillon
Virginia Tech

Bibliography

The works of Plato are most easily found, in Greek, in the five volumes of the *Oxford Classical Text* series (edited by John Burnet) and in English in *The Collected Dialogues of Plato* (edited by Hamilton and Cairns [Princeton UP, 1961]). The other primary sources are collected in Ferguson.

Brickhouse, T.C., and N.D. Smith. *Socrates on Trial.* Princeton: Princeton UP, 1989. Corrected ed. 1990.

Ferguson, John. *Socrates: A Sourcebook.* London: Macmillan, 1970.

Kennedy, George A. *Art of Persuasion in Greece.* Princeton: Princeton UP, 1963.

Kidd, I.G. "Socrates." *Encyclopedia of Philosophy.* Ed. P. Edwards. New York: Macmillan, 1967. Vol. 7. 480–86.

Vlastos, Gregory. *Socrates: Ironist and Moral Philosopher.* Ithaca, NY: Cornell UP, 1991.

See also GREEK RHETORIC; PLATO

Sophist

A professional teacher of political excellence in ancient Greece noted for giving traveling lectures on rhetoric for a fee. The ancient Greek term *sophist* was used in both a general and a specific way, both of which carried positive and negative connotations that its user might highlight. In its general use, *sophist* can be found in references dating from the sixth century B.C.E. that draw upon its literal translation as "wisdom-bearer." Such sophists were respected teachers or professors who sought to impart wisdom to others; the "educational" role of poets and philosophers in Greek society marked them as "sophists" in this sense. A suspicion of sophists who were "too clever for their own good" (or for the good of society) added negative connotations to this term, much as the disparaging use of "intellectual" does today.

By early in the fifth century B.C.E., the term became associated with the rising professional class of traveling teachers who professed to teach *aretê,* or political excellence, for a fee, especially through lectures and courses in rhetoric. These sophists were educational innovators responsive to social and political changes that made the ability to speak effectively a valuable commodity. In Athens particularly, the democratic reforms begun by Solon, continued by Cleisthenes, and completed by Pericles and Ephialtes by the middle of the fifth century B.C.E. ensured broad participation in public life: in the Assembly, where all citizens might speak, in the courts where litigants were heard by huge lay juries who decided civil and criminal cases on matters of law as well as matters of fact, and on ceremonial occasions such as public festivals.

The useful training offered by the sophists gained them attention and respect, though it also brought jealousy, anger, suspicion, and fear from those who saw the most promising young men drawn away from friends and families who would have been their mentors in political life, and drawn toward these foreigners who charged money on the promise that they could impart practical wisdom to their students. In *Against the Sophists,* Isocrates (436–338 B.C.E.) complains that some of these competitors with his school of rhetoric promised more than they could possibly deliver. In *Gorgias,* Plato (427–347 B.C.E.) suggests that they make the worse case seem the better by teaching this "form of flattery" that persuades without educating. Plato's concern over the sophists' teachings did not merely reflect his bias against rhetoric, but rather a deeper philosophical difference summed up in the statement of Protagoras of Abdera (490?–420? B.C.E.), one of the earliest and best known sophists, that "man is the measure and the measurer of all things." Unlike Plato, the sophists doubted whether absolute truth existed or could be known by humans. They believed that laws and customs were not handed down from the gods or rooted in a natural order but were the products of human creation. And although they differed on the allegiance they believed was owed to human-made laws and customs, they did believe that citizens could take an active role in the rhetorical processes that created them, confident that persuasive arguments could be made on either side of a given controversy. Such philosophical relativism could not but offend Plato and threaten defenders of the status quo.

Among the prominent early sophists were Protagoras of Abdera, probably the first to charge fees for his teaching; Gorgias of Leontini (480?–380? B.C.E.), known for the jingling poetic style evident in his *Encomium on Helen*; Prodicus of Ceos (470?–370? B.C.E.), who insisted on the precise use of language; Hippias of Elis (465?–395? B.C.E.), a teacher with broad knowledge who taught a wide range of courses and developed a mnemonic system for speakers; and Thrasymachus of Chalcedon (465?–410? B.C.E.), who made original contributions to a theory of rhetorical style, emotional appeals, and delivery.

History has been less kind to the sophists, perhaps, than their contributions warrant. Little of the sophists' writings have survived, while Plato's criticisms of them are readily available. Yet, as practical educators, the sophists wrote for their own age more than for posterity.

J. Clarke Rountree, III
University of Alabama, Huntsville

Bibliography

Barrett, Harold. *The Sophists.* Novato, CA: Chandler, 1987.

Guthrie, W.K.C. *The Sophists.* Cambridge: Cambridge UP, 1971.

Sprague, Rosamond Kent. *The Older Sophists.* Columbus: U of South Carolina P, 1972.

Sophistic Rhetoric

A modern phrase used to refer to a collection of rhetorical practices and doctrines attributed to the "older sophists" of fifth-century B.C.E. Greece. The term *sophist* (*sophistês*) means a person of *sophia* (skill or wisdom). In ancient as well as modern times, the label *sophist* is assigned rather inconsistently according to the perspective of the writer. In ancient times, people as diverse as Prometheus, Homer, Hesiod, Damon, Solon, Thales, Pythagoras, Anaxagoras, Empedocles, Zeno, Plato, Socrates, and Isocrates were called sophists. Aeschines, Eudoxus, and Protagoras are included in Philostratus's *Lives of the Sophists* as well as in Diogenes Laertius' *Lives of Eminent Philosophers.*

In modern times, the group most often meant by the phrase "the sophists" includes Gorgias, Protagoras, Hippias, Prodicus, Thrasymachus, Critias, and Antiphon. However, some scholars add some or all of the following to the list: Polus, Euthydemus, Dionysodorus, Callicles, Socrates, Antisthenes, Alcidamas, Lycophron, as well as the authors of *Dissoi Logoi,* the *Anonymus Iamblichi,* and the *Hippocratic Corpus.*

The idea of a distinct "sophistic rhetoric" is a relatively recent notion. In classical Greece "sophistic" and "rhetoric" were considered distinct, though sometimes overlapping, arts or *technai* (cf. Plato's *Gorgias*). In no surviving Greek text—not even Plato's or Aristotle's—will one find the exact phrase "sophistic rhetoric." While in contemporary scholarship a distinct "sophistic rhetoric" is sometimes contrasted to "philosophical rhetoric," classical authors did not draw such a distinction. In *Lives of the Sophists,* for example, Philostratus even claims that "we must regard the ancient sophistic art as philosophic rhetoric" (1.480).

One of the earliest efforts to describe a distinct "sophistical" rhetoric was made in 1855 by Edward M. Cope. Since that time, many scholars have taken the category "sophistic rhetoric" for granted. Nonetheless, it is important to recognize that the categories with which ancient writers classified doctrines and practices are not always consistent with contemporary categories. Because of the diversity of the projects that have been labeled *sophistic,* it is more useful and accurate to speak of multiple "sophistic rhetorics" than to posit a singular and monolithic sophistic rhetoric.

When contemporary scholars refer to sophistic rhetorics, typically they refer to one (or more) of three concepts: specific rhetorical practices, implicit or explicit theories of rhetoric, and particular pedagogical practices attributed to the sophists. The two sophists most often cited by contemporary scholars of rhetoric are Protagoras and Gorgias, so it is from them that most of the examples below are drawn.

Of the sophists' various rhetorical practices, the most often discussed are their general composition styles, their use of specific figures and tropes, and their cultivation of two-sided argumentation (*dissoi logoi*). The sophists wrote during a time when written prose was still a novelty. Archaic Greek culture relied almost exclusively on oral modes of composition and communication. The earliest "literature" of Greek culture was epic poetry that rhapsodes memorized and passed on from generation to generation. Some of the first written compositions (other than lists or basic property markings) were records of these orally composed mythical poems. Composition in oral Greek society originally evolved to serve the needs of memory, as it was through repetition and memorization that one generation passed on to the next what it had learned. For example, the vocabulary of an oral dialect is usually limited to a few thousand words, while modern English has a recorded vocabulary of one and a half million. The need to remember also affects syntax and composition, making verse, song, and story the best vehicles in which to "store" the records of Greek oral culture.

Some of the earliest theoretical or "philosophical" writings were created during a time when the habits of an oral culture dominated composition. Parmenides, often considered the parent of Western philosophy, wrote in the sixth century B.C.E. and used the same hexameter verse as did Homer. Parmenides tells his philosophy in the form of a mythic journey of discovery in which he encounters a goddess. Heraclitus wrote in easily memorized aphorisms. By the middle of the fifth century B.C.E., the time of the older sophists, writers were experimenting with different forms of composition that were both indebted to, and broke from, previous poetic forms of composition. In Plato's dialogue *Protagoras,* the title character gives a speech that begins with a mythical account (mythos) of the origins of human political arts, but then moves to a well-reasoned account (or logos). Gorgias' speeches known as *Helen* and *Palamedes* follow the traditional habit of treating time-honored mythical themes, but do so in the process of developing sophisticated (for the time) forms of reasoning. It is difficult to make generalizations about the prose compositions of the sophists because they are not as poetic or mythic as earlier writings, yet they also are not as spare and analytical as later writings. As contemporary theorists explore different modes of composition and discuss "secondary orality" as encouraged by electronic media, the "mixed" composition style of the older sophists has provided an interesting set of texts to consider.

A good example of a "sophistic rhetoric" described by contemporary scholars is "Gorgianic rhetoric," which makes use of various figures of speech. Gorgias' texts were carefully crafted compositions that drew heavily from earlier poetic modes of writing. The following is from Gorgias' *Epitaphios:*

> What did these men lack that men should
> have?
> And what did they have that men should
> lack?
> May what I say be what I sought to say,
> and what I sought to say what I ought to
> say—
> free from the wrath of gods,
> far from the envy of humanity

In Gorgias' surviving prose compositions, one finds the use of alliteration, asyndeton, antithesis, isocolon, *parison, homoioteleuton,* assorted types of assonance, *epanalepsis, paronomasia,* rhetorical questions, and the use of compound words, metaphors, and "poetic" terms. Often when contemporary writers use "sophistic rhetoric" to describe a particular style of composition that is highly experimental or figurative, it is Gorgianic discourse that they have in mind. At the same time, it is worth noting that Gorgias' prose in many respects is clearly rational and logical. For example, he argues using the apagogic method by which an advocate enumerates a series of possibilities and addresses each in turn. Also, Gorgias uses certain Greek particles as logical connectives in his texts in a way that distinguishes his style and reasoning from that of traditional poetry.

We do not have complete speeches by Protagoras that are confidently regarded as authentic. Instead we have two speech re-creations found in Plato's *Protagoras* and *Theaetetus* and a series of short aphorisms. One such aphorism declares that there are two contradictory accounts (*logoi*) possible about everything. A text titled *Dissoi Logoi* or *Dialexeis* from around 400 B.C.E. demonstrates the idea by presenting arguments on both sides of a series of topics. Thus, another important practice often referenced as "sophistic rhetoric" is the idea of acknowledging and enacting a two-sided form of reasoning sometimes called "antilogy" or *antilogia*. Some contemporary theorists suggest that the practice of *dissoi logoi* is based on an explicit sophistic or Protagorean theory about discourse and the world. Such a theory is influenced by Heraclitus' declaration that reality itself is made up of conflicting opposites. Just as what is real at any given time is the result of a battle of opposites, what is understood as true at any given time by humans is the result of a battle of contradictory discourses.

There are a number of theoretical doctrines attributed to the sophists that are sometimes lumped together under the rubric of "sophistic rhetorical theory." However, the Greek word for rhetoric, *rhêtorikê*, was not coined until the early fourth century B.C.E. (possibly by Plato) and is not found in any extant text or fragment of the fifth-century sophists. Strictly speaking, it is more historically accurate to call these sophistic theories of discourse or persuasion than of rhetoric. Another option is to consider such doctrines *implicit* or *incipient* theories of rhetoric, in order to distinguish them from later doctrines that are more direct and explicit efforts to describe and theorize "rhetoric" as a specific subject.

Rhetorical theorists draw upon the sophists' texts for a variety of insights that are relevant to contemporary theories of discourse and composition. For example, many writers have shown great interest in the epistemological doctrines of the sophists. Protagoras, for example, declared that "humanity is the measure of all things" rather than the gods, and thus he has been characterized as an early humanist. While certain Greek thinkers viewed contradiction and disagreement as a sign of human error,

Protagoras saw them as evidence of a contradictory reality. If to one person the wind feels cold and to another it feels not-cold, then is the wind "really" cold or not-cold? Protagoras would say both, while many Greek thinkers, including Plato and Aristotle, would say that such contradiction is impossible—the people disagreeing do not really know what they are talking about. Protagoras has been characterized as a relativist because he would say that the truth of statements about the wind are relative to the person experiencing the wind.

Contemporary theorists who stress that "truth" is not an absolute concept and argue that different discourse communities understand the world differently find precedent for their theories in the doctrines attributed to Protagoras. It is worth noting, however, that throughout twentieth-century philosophy, Protagoras has been appropriated by a variety of sometimes conflicting philosophical positions, including positivism, pragmatism, skepticism, phenomenalism, empiricism, utilitarianism, and social-constructionism. It is not surprising, therefore, that very different projects have shared the label of *sophistic rhetorical theory*.

Gorgias is another sophist whose texts have been found to contain numerous explicit or implicit theoretical doctrines. In *Helen*, Gorgias describes the workings of logos, or speech. Gorgias begins the relevant section by declaring that "*Logos* is a powerful lord that with the smallest and most invisible body accomplishes most god-like works. It can banish fear and remove grief and instill pleasure and enhance pity. I shall show how this is so." In the process of describing the workings of logos, Gorgias develops an analogy that proved to be very influential: "The power of speech has the same effect on the condition of the psyche as the power of drugs to the nature of the body; for just as different drugs dispel different secretions from the body, and some bring an end to disease and others to life, so also in the case of logos—some bring pain, others pleasure, some bring fear, others instill courage in the hearers, and some drug and bewitch the psyche with a kind of evil persuasion." Based on these and other passages, theorists have identified Gorgianic theories of discourse that have been likened to contemporary aesthetic, psychological, and speech-act theories of language.

Another influential Gorgianic text is known as *On Nature* or *On Not-Being*.

Though the original text is lost, Gorgias' arguments have been retold by later writers such as Sextus Empiricus. According to Sextus, "Gorgias says nothing 'exists'; if it exists, it is unknowable; and if it is knowable, it cannot be made evident to others." Though the precise meaning of the Greek word translated here as "exists," or *esti*, is open to argument, Gorgias' text is a provocative assault or parody of metaphysical writers in general and monists such as Parmenides and Melissus in particular. Gorgias' arguments, though not always formally valid, challenge the reader to rethink in what ways humans come to know and communicate about the world around us. As before, a variety of contemporary interpretations have been offered that position Gorgias as everything from a profound thinker to a radical nihilist, a skeptic to a trivial jokester. Regardless of how Gorgias is interpreted now, it is clear from references in Isocrates and Sextus that Gorgias' arguments about existence and knowledge were widely discussed in classical Greece.

Contemporary theorists have postulated all sorts of implicit or explicit theories in Gorgias' various texts, including "theories" of art, style, catharsis, and knowledge. Such claims are potentially misleading, inasmuch as they overestimate the maturity of theory development and imply more coherence and completeness than can be supported with the available evidence. Nonetheless, as in the case of Protagoras, Gorgias' texts serve as inspiration for a variety of contemporary thinkers interested in "sophistic rhetoric."

The sophists also are utilized as inspiration for contemporary approaches to pedagogy. Based on evidence that some of the sophists, Protagoras in particular, were supporters of Athenian democracy, some contemporary writers describe "sophistic pedagogy" as empowering students to participate effectively as citizens of the modern polis. Some writers have described "sophistic rhetoric" as pedagogy that is emancipatory, subversive, empowering, or aimed at cultural critique, while others simply contend that the most useful aspect of sophistic teaching was that it aided participation in the democracy. It should be noted that, once again, it is difficult to make generalizations about the sophists' political doctrines as a group. While the evidence is clear that Protagoras was an explicit ally of Periclean democracy, such evidence is not available about all sophists, and some sophists even opposed democracy as a form of government and worked against the democracy in ancient Athens.

In sum, it may be helpful to refer to a multitude of "sophistic rhetorics" rather than to posit a singular notion of sophistic rhetoric. Although there has evolved a standardized list of the "older sophists" of the fifth century B.C.E., the term *sophistic* has been used to describe a variety of people who have little in common other than being Greek. Even among the sophists on the standardized list, the different practices and doctrines resist easy generalization. The phrase "sophistic rhetoric" has been used to describe a collection of very different rhetorical practices, from a heavy reliance on poetic figures of speech to the development of two-sided debate. It has been used to denote a variety of explicit theories and doctrines about discourse in general and rhetoric in particular. And, finally, it has been used to describe certain forms of pedagogy that are consonant with participatory democracy.

It may be useful to draw a distinction between two types of scholarly projects that engage the texts of the sophists. "Historical reconstruction" is work that attempts to understand the contributions of past theorists and practitioners in their original historical context. A scholar interested in the historical reconstruction of different sophistic rhetorics might try to answer questions such as these: Who were considered "sophists" in fifth-century B.C.E. Greece? In what ways does Plato distinguish between fifth- and fourth-century B.C.E. sophists in his dialogues? How did Protagoras theorize about logos? What were the political implications of the discourse of Hippias? What were the cultural ramifications of Gorgias' version of the traditional Athenian funeral oration? How do fifth-century B.C.E. texts that theorize about logos differ from fourth-century B.C.E. texts that theorize about *rhêtorikê*?

A somewhat different sort of scholarly engagement can be labeled a *contemporary appropriation* of sophistic texts that is aimed at producing new or *neosophistic* rhetorical theory, criticism, or pedagogy. Rather than describe past theories and practices as they evolved through the contingencies of the past, scholars who attempt the contemporary appropriation of classical texts do so to shed light on rhetorical concerns manifest in the present. A scholar interested in contemporary appropriation for the purposes of describing neosophistic theory, criticism, or pedagogy might try to answer questions such as these: Who are today's "sophists"? Can we devise a postmodern neosophistic theory of rhetoric? Which aspects of Gorgias' composition style can inform contemporary composition studies? Can Protagoras' vision of education serve as a useful model today? Such questions direct and develop the concerns of ancient authors in ways probably not anticipated by those authors. Instead, contemporary needs and interests guide the process of selectively appropriating aspects of past authors' texts.

As mentioned previously, Gorgias' texts were simultaneously poetic and logical for the time in which they were written. Typically, however, contemporary theorists who champion a "Gorgianic" style tend to highlight the poetic and figurative side and downplay Gorgias' use of systematic reasoning. Such selective appropriation is desirable because a primary goal of neosophistic rhetorical studies is to chart possible futures of rhetorical theory and practice. Whereas historians may feel obligated to describe aspects of sophistic doctrines that they may find problematic or even obnoxious, neosophistic scholars are free to value those aspects of sophistic rhetorics that they find useful and explore their potential for future directions in theory, criticism, and pedagogy.

Of course, historical reconstruction and contemporary appropriation of sophistic rhetorics are related endeavors. Historians tend to be drawn to the study of the sophists for contemporary reasons that inform their interpretations (such as an interest in style), and contemporary theorists often depend on the work of historians to guide their understanding of sophistic texts. Sometimes the line between these two types of scholarship is hard to draw. Nonetheless, the methods, goals, and values associated with historical reconstruction and contemporary appropriation can be delineated with sufficient clarity that scholars may find it useful to distinguish between historical studies of the various sophistic rhetorics and the advancement of neosophistic rhetorical theory, criticism, and pedagogy.

Edward Schiappa
University of Minnesota

Bibliography

Barrett, Harold. *The Sophists*. Novato, CA: Chandler, 1987.

Cope, Edward M. "On the Sophistical Rhetoric." *Journal of Classical and Sacred Philology* 2 (1855): 129–69; 3 (1856): 34–80, 252–88.

Guthrie, W.K.C. *The Sophists*. Cambridge: Cambridge UP, 1971.

Jarratt, Susan C. *Rereading the Sophists: Classical Rhetoric Refigured*. Carbondale: Southern Illinois UP, 1991.

Kerferd, G.B. "The First Greek Sophists." *Classical Review* 64 (1950): 8–10.

———. *The Sophistic Movement*. Cambridge: Cambridge UP, 1981.

Poulakos, John. "Towards a Sophistic Definition of Rhetoric." *Philosophy and Rhetoric* 16 (1983): 35–48.

Schiappa, Edward. *Protagoras and Logos: A Study in Greek Philosophy and Rhetoric*. Columbia: U of South Carolina P, 1991.

———. "Sophistic Rhetoric: Oasis or Mirage?" *Rhetoric Review* 10 (1991): 5–18.

Sprague, Rosamond Kent. *The Older Sophists*. Columbia: U of South Carolina P, 1972.

See also GORGIAS; GREEK RHETORIC

Speaking and Writing

An explication of the relationship between speaking and writing by noting that there are really three relationships involved: (a) between speech and writing in themselves, (b) between how speech and writing are used, and (c) between the mentalities or cultures that may go along with speech and writing.

Comparing Speech and Writing in Themselves

Speech consists of nothing but sound waves that come to the ear and thus exist in the medium of time. Writing is visible and comes to the eye and exists in the medium of space. Thus speech is ephemeral and goes out of existence at the moment it comes to be; writing persists, so we can "step out of time" with writing and go back and revisit the words or skim through the text quickly or read sections in any order.

(Note, however, the following complicating factors. Texts also exist in time, not just in space. That is, we cannot take in a text all at once as we can a picture; we can only read a text bit by bit in time. Also, speech is more like writing when we speak onto tape recorders and answering machines: These devices make speech more lasting so we can listen again or skip around. Furthermore, sophisticated computers now permit a hybrid medium: They take speech as input and produce writing as output.)

In any culture, babies start learning to speak from an early stage without any instruction at all, as long as there is another person around who speaks and listens. It is almost as though the human baby is "wired" to talk—and indeed, that is Chomsky's influential hypothesis. It is not that infants do not struggle and practice as they learn to speak, but they do so without urging or instruction. Indeed only peculiarly forceful conditions can *stop* a child from learning speech.

After we learn to speak (by means of a learning process we are seldom conscious of—at least in retrospect), we almost never experience ourselves having consciously to form our words: Usually the intention to say something is enough to result in the words' issuing from our mouth. (Note, however, that some people learn to be virtually as fluent in writing as in speaking by means of frequent practice, for example, with freewriting.)

Children usually speak before they can write. Infants can manage the physical act of speaking before the movements needed for writing. (However, children can learn sign language *before* they can manage the more delicate physical coordinations required for speech.) Thus most people's primary relationship to language is to speech rather than writing: Most people mentally *hear* what they read and write; in most cultures writing is a representation of speech sounds.

Speech has two dimensions of audibility: the *quality of sound* people make, based as it were on their physical "instrument" (and how they use it to produce sound), and the kinds of rhythms, tunes, and styles they use in "playing on their instrument." It is hard to change or control either dimension of speaking, but the quality of sound is particularly hard to change—being at least partly dependent on the body.

In comparison to writing then, speaking is harder to control and usually less self-conscious than writing—closer to automatic behavior. Thus speaking usually gives a more naked or candid picture of how we are feeling, and indeed often even of what we are like. It is usually harder to hide how we feel in our writing than in our speaking. People can often detect our mood after hearing nothing but our "hello" on the phone. Thus people can often detect a difference between what we *say* and how we feel (for example when we say something cheerful but betray ourselves to be sad or angry), whereas it is usually harder to detect a difference between what we *write* and how we feel.

Thus even though our speech may sometimes hide our mood, and some people are bril-

liant actors, speech is usually more intimately tied to the speaker than writing to the writer. Few written sentences have markers that link them with one particular writer, but a spoken sentence could have been produced only by one speaker. "Voice prints" are as reliable as fingerprints as markers of individual identity. Speech is also more likely to reveal the geographical and class origins of the speaker than writing. We see an etymological link between voice and the speaker's identity in the word *person*: It means both self and body, and *persona* was the word for the mask that Greek actors wore to amplify their voices (*per + sona*). (However, *handwriting* is also unique to each person; like speech, it consists of near-automatic behavior.)

Speech has more semiotic channels than writing—more channels for carrying meaning. Consider the subtle or not so subtle pauses we make as we speak, the little intensities or lengthenings of a syllable—and all the other ways we complicate the messages we speak. To list more systematically the semiotic dimension of speech: There is volume (loud and soft), pitch (high and low), speed (fast and slow), intensity (relaxed and tense), accented or not. And note that these are not just binary items, for between each pair there lies an extensively usable range of differences of degree. In addition, in each case there are patterned sequences: For example, tune is a *pattern* of pitches; rhythm is a pattern of slow and fast and accent. Furthermore, there is a wide spectrum of timbres (breathy, shrill, nasal, and so forth); there are glides and jumps; there are pauses of varying lengths. Combinations of all of these factors make the possibilities dizzying, and they all carry meaning. Writing lacks many or most of these markers.

Comparing How Speech and Writing Are Used
In most cultures, infants are invited to learn speech without formal instruction, while writing is usually *taught* in formal and structured ways—usually in schools. But this powerful and pervasive difference is not inevitable. Just as any child can learn sign language without instruction (earlier, in fact, than learning to speak), children can and sometimes do learn to write without instruction just as they learn to speak: simply by finding themselves in the midst of people who write and who invite them to imitate and to engage in conversational written discourse.

We tend to experience writing as more *difficult* than speaking, but this bears further investigation. That is, we tend to assume that writing requires the *additional* skills of forming letters and spelling words and punctuating sentences. Yet if someone learned to write before speaking, we would say that pronouncing words and conforming to the subtle conventions of speech were daunting "additional skills." Indeed, it may be that the conventions of speech are more complex than the conventions of writing because scholars seem to understand them less well. If a child had as much practice with writing as with speech (naturally motivated practice, not coerced practice), would that child not be as fluent in writing as in speaking?

We most often speak in the presence of others and speak in "turns," such that the speaker alternates with other speakers. We most often write alone in the form of "monologues." That is, we usually write out completed discourses in text without getting any answer or response from a reader—for a long while, if ever. Thus speech is often used in a more social way than writing. A significant function of much speech is to establish and foster connection between persons; speech tends to have more "phatic" content than writing (words and locutions whose function is simply to establish and keep up the connection).

As a result, speech usually contains more *awareness* of audience and context—but by the same token, less *explicit articulation* of audience and context. Writing, in contrast, often suffers from lack of awareness of audience and context: We often write something without even knowing exactly who will read it and what context these readers will be in. Here then is an additional difficulty of writing: not only to form letters and spell words but also to "decontextualize" the discourse—that is, to spell out messages about audience and context so that the message will be clear to readers distant in time and place—readers who are not there to reply, to ask questions, or to show when they do not understand.

Because writing is in fact indelible, it tends to connote permanence and thus seems to call for more planning, care, and organization. Because speech is in fact fleeting, it tends to connote the temporary and thus to invite less planning and deliberation, more vacillation and change. People characteristically write more carefully or deliberately than they speak—planning and pondering before writing or else crossing out, ripping up, rewriting. Thus, speech is characteristically used in such a way as to record the mind *in action* or in process as it thinks, feels, moves and changes. Writing is characteristically used in such a way as to record mind having *already* thought and felt, moved, changed, and reached a conclusion. People thus often get more sense of drama in their speech than in their writing.

Notice that most of the differences just described are not characteristics of how speech and writing *must be used*, but only of how they are *most often used*—and, perhaps more important, of the sites where they are most often researched. That is, everything just said really describes speech as it occurs in informal conversation and writing as it is used more formally. But people do not speak only in informal conversation; they sometimes "give speeches"—formally or ad hoc. That is, they often speak whole and uninterrupted discourses with no turn-taking, sometimes getting little or no response as they go along. And speech is often extremely careful and planned in certain speech situations (such as in job interviews or when people are speaking "up" to listeners with a great deal of authority over them). In such situations speech may be far from fluent, and the speaker may rehearse each word in mind before speaking it. And when people use voice-mail and phone machines, they often speak when they are alone and distant from the hearer—often even in a somewhat decontextualized way.

Similarly, people often write in an *informal, social* setting in the presence of others—for example, in workshops, classrooms, committee meetings, brainstorming sessions, and when passing notes. With computer networking and E-mail (and teletypewriters or telecommunication devices for the deaf), it is now common for people to "converse" in writing—that is, to write actual dialogue, with turn-taking in real time exactly like conversation. In these communication settings, and even in the writing of conventional letters, writing functions in the contextualized way speech does: It assumes audience and context and thus refrains from spelling out many cues about them.

Furthermore, when we compare the actual uses of speech and writing, speech usually *functions* more "indelibly" than writing. That is, we seldom talk except in the presence of listeners, and once we have said something we can never take it back. When we have written something, on the other hand, we can usually change it or throw it away before anyone else sees it. Thus writing is an ideal medium for temporary, tentative, exploratory discourse—an ideal medium for exploiting the mind's capacity for chaos, play, experimentation. In writing we can more easily be incoherent, chaotic, unconventional, or explore what is taboo than we can when we speak in the presence of others.

Comparing the Mentalities or Cultures that May Go Along with Speech and Writing

Many people have come to talk about a *mentality* or *culture* of orality as opposed to literacy because of the following facts:

- Speaking comes before writing for individuals and in the development of cultures.
- Most oral cultures make more use of narrative and poetry, while most literate cultures put more emphasis on the logical, conceptual, expository uses of language.
- Historically speaking, the development of logic and careful, detached thinking seems to have gone along with the development and dissemination of writing.
- Writing permits more distance and detachment from our discourse; therefore, if we want to examine and question and correct our thinking, writing is better than speaking. Even with the technological advantage of tape recorders, speech is still at a disadvantage, because writing helps us see more of our discourse at once. And we tend to be more caught up in our speech than our writing.
- Writing and conceptual thought have often come to seem more "mature" or advanced—and orality more juvenile and something to be moved past, gotten away from. Schools tend to teach narrative to younger children or to students at the start of a writing course—and then move on to the more "advanced" forms of exposition and argument.

Despite those facts, speech and narrative can be every bit as sophisticated, cognitively complex, and mature as writing. There is research on the Vai culture—where some people learn writing in a nonschool setting—that seems to indicate that the commonly asserted link between writing and more conceptual detachment and attention to logic may be ascribed as much to the process of *schooling* as to the medium of writing itself.

Weak student writing is often blamed on students' not having moved past the oral mentality. On the basis of this diagnosis, some teachers and theorists say that students should *distance* their writing further from speech—try to feel writing as different from speaking. But sometimes these students do better at writing when they are invited to bring *more* "orality" into the process rather than less. When they practice "speaking onto paper," as in freewriting, they may retain some of the carelessness of speech, but they often attain the two things that are most difficult about writing: a fluent naturalness of syntax and an awareness and connection with audience.

A Note on "Voice in Writing"

This is a slippery and much disputed concept but one that is surprisingly prevalent among writers, critics, teachers of writing, and many theorists. The notion of voice in a text is much more useful if care is taken to note three different senses: writing with pronounced speechlike or audible features; writing with a strong implied author or persona; writing that reflects the actual voice qualities or character of the real author.

Peter Elbow
University of Massachusetts, Amherst

Bibliography

Bolinger, Dwight. *Intonation and its Parts: Melody in Spoken English*. Stanford, CA: Stanford UP, 1986.

Derrida, Jacques. *Of Grammatology*. Trans. Gayatri Chakravorty Spivak. Baltimore: Johns Hopkins UP, 1974.

Elbow, Peter. "The Persistence of Voices in our Discourse." *Voices on Voice: A (Written) Discussion*. Ed. Kathleen Yancey. Urbana, IL: National Council of Teachers of English, 1994.

———. "The Shifting Relationships between Speech and Writing." *Conference on College Composition and Communication* 36 (1985): 283–303.

Havelock, Eric. *The Muse Learns to Write: Reflections on Orality and Literacy from Antiquity to the Present*. New Haven: Yale UP, 1986.

———. *Preface to Plato*. Cambridge, MA: Harvard UP, 1963.

Kintgen, Eugene R., Barry M. Kroll, and Mike Rose, eds. *Perspectives on Literacy*. Carbondale: Southern Illinois UP, 1988.

Kroll, Barry M., and Robert J. Van, eds. *Exploring Speaking-Writing Relationships*. Urbana, IL: National Council of Teachers of English, 1981.

Ong, Walter. *Orality and Literacy: The Technologizing of the Word*. New York: Methuen, 1982.

———. *The Presence of the Word*. New Haven: Yale UP, 1967.

Oschner, Robert S. *Physical Eloquence and the Biology of Writing*. Albany, NY: SUNY P, 1990.

Scribner, Sylvia, and Michael Cole. *The Psychology of Literacy*. Cambridge: Cambridge UP, 1982.

Tannen, Deborah. "Oral and Literate Strategies in Spoken and Written Discourse." *Literacy for Life: The Demand for Reading and Writing*. Ed. Richard Bailey and Robin Fosheim. New York: Modern Language Assn., 1983. 79–96.

———. *Talking Voices: Repetition, Dialogue, Imagery*. Cambridge: Cambridge UP, 1989.

Vygotsky, Lev. *Mind in Society: The Development of Higher Psychological Processes*. Ed. M. Cole, V. John-Steiner, S. Scribner, and E. Souberman. Cambridge, MA: Harvard UP, 1978.

———. *Thought and Language*. Trans. Eugenia Hanfman and Gertude Vakar. Cambridge, MA: MIT P, 1962.

Speech Acts

The set of abstract acts people do in spoken or written utterances. Since 1962 the concept of speech acts has been central in roundly debated philosophical and linguistic studies of meaning and communication, the results and methods of which have been applied to theoretical and pedagogical problems in rhetoric.

Studies of speech acts are based on a provisional dichotomy between utterances that describe states of affairs (constatives), which are true or false, and utterances that perform actions (performatives), which are felicitous or infelicitous. An assertion, for example, is true or false, whereas a promise is made more or less happily. Performatives illustrate how language is related to contextual conditions such as social conventions or "rules"; intentions, beliefs, and feelings of utterers; and the interpretation of such internal states by audiences, which is part of an audience's "uptake" or recognition of a speech act. When an utterer makes a promise, for example, an audience recognizes the utterer's intention to commit to some future conduct. The concept of speech acts is thus consistent with the position that meaning and communication are at least partly dependent on an audience's recognizing that an utterer intends for the audience to recognize an intention.

The dichotomy between constatives and performatives collapses when certain abstract acts are taken to be performed simultaneously in all utterances. According to Austin, these abstract acts are of three kinds (94–108). First, a locutionary act is performed when a sentence is uttered with sense and reference—"meaning" narrowly construed. Second, an illocutionary act is performed when an utterance is made and understood to be made with a certain "force," which consists of the utterance's conventional social status as an assertion, promise, bet, demand, and so on. Third, a perlocutionary act is performed when an utterance has certain effects on an audience (such as belief, confidence, fear), these effects not necessarily having any conventional status but being related to the particular situation of utterance and uptake. One of the more contentious issues concerning these three acts is the degree to which the force of an utterer's illocutionary act is reducible in one way or another to the meaning of the locutionary act. Various acts besides these three have also been proposed.

The term *speech acts* commonly refers to only illocutionary acts, the forces of which have been classified according to a number of criteria, including the "point" or purpose of the acts in their situational contexts. In one scheme illocutionary acts are of five kinds: (1) assertives, such as claiming, arguing, and accusing, which represent that something is the case; (2) commissives, such as promising, offering, and betting, which commit the utterer to doing something; (3) directives, such as asking, commanding, and recommending, which attempt to get the audience to do something; (4) declaratives, such as resigning, endorsing, and christening, which make something the case; and (5) expressives such as apologizing, thanking, and greeting, which express the utterer's attitude toward something (Searle and Vanderveken 179–216). There is no one-to-one relationship between illocutionary acts and English verbs.

J.L. Campbell
Henderson State University

Bibliography

Austin, J.L. *How to Do Things with Words.* 2nd ed. Ed. J.O. Urmson and Marina Sbisa. Cambridge, MA: Harvard UP, 1975.

Searle, John R. *Speech Acts: An Essay in the Philosophy of Language.* Cambridge: Cambridge UP, 1969.

Searle, John R., and Daniel Vanderveken. *Foundations of Illocutionary Logic.* Cambridge: Cambridge UP, 1985.

Winterowd, W. Ross. *Composition/Rhetoric: A Synthesis.* Carbondale: Southern Illinois UP, 1986.

See also AUSTIN, J.L.

Speech Communication

A discipline that formally came into being in 1914, although its ancestry can be traced back to the rhetoricians of Greece and Rome. In the nineteenth and early twentieth centuries, oral discourse was taught in American schools and colleges from two perspectives. One of the approaches has come to be known as the Elocutionary Movement. Its proponents based their teaching on the work of writers such as Thomas Sheridan, Gilbert Austin, John Lawson, François Delsarte, and Charles Darwin. The result was a field that focused exclusively on physical presentation. Little or no interest was shown for the content, language, and form of discourse. Elocution concerned itself with physiology and the adaptation of gesture and vocal tone to the emotion of the discourse.

The second perspective was rooted in the rich rhetorical tradition of the eighteenth and early nineteenth centuries. At the same time that elocution was flourishing, rhetoric was preserved in the early departments of English in the United States. The typical rhetoric and composition text of that period was derived from the belletristic rhetorics of the previous century. They did not draw a clear difference between written and oral communication. Material dealing with invention, taste, structure, conviction, and persuasion was equally applicable to both modes of communication. Indeed, most of the texts contained fairly specific material on oratory. By the early years of the twentieth century, many departments of English contained divisions of oral English. When the National Council of Teachers of English was established, it included an Oral English section. A few colleges and universities had even instituted separate departments of public speaking. As oral English developed, elocution, in the scientific environment of the developing American universities, came to be considered as irrelevant or even spurious.

The establishment of the ancestor of speech communication occurred at the 1914 meeting of the NCTE in Chicago. Seventeen of the more than one hundred members of the Oral English section voted to form a separate organization of teachers of public speaking. The departure was hardly a revolution, as for a number of years the new National Association of Academic Teachers of Public Speaking continued to meet at the same time and place as the NCTE; they even adjourned their meetings when the Oral English section of the council met.

Although "Public Speaking" was prominent in the name of the new association, it quickly embraced almost all of the oral arts. The early issues of the association's journal included articles dealing with such matters as theater, debate, voice and diction, and speech correction as well as public speaking. Not much later it would embrace other divisions, such as group discussion and radio broadcasting.

The strongest motivation for the establishment of the new profession was political rather than intellectual. Many of the members admitted that they wanted to escape the domination of English departments. Since public speaking was almost entirely a performance-oriented field, in its early days it sought to determine how it could conduct research. The search brought about a dispute that has not been settled to the present day as to whether the new field should be a humanistic or scientific field. The chief exponents were Everett Hunt for the humanities and Charles Woolbert for science.

Within the first years of its founding, the association began to publish rhetorical criticisms and articles on Greek and Roman rhetorical theory. Almost all of the criticism was informed by a strong classical, even Aristotelian, orientation. Most of the early articles, however, were concerned with pedagogy and sharing of information.

After the 1950s, speech communication underwent significant changes. The "Social Science Revolution" of that period affected speech communication as it did other disciplines. Under the influence of the social sciences, the discipline extended its interest to a new diverse group of subfields, including interpersonal, small group, and organizational communication. While speech communication was expanding, it was also contracting. Formerly subordinate fields such as theater, speech correction, and broadcasting left the protection of the parent body to form organizations of their own.

The study and teaching of rhetoric also was modified. Much of the classical orientation disappeared, to be replaced by rhetorical theory and criticism derived from literary figures such as Burke, Weaver, McKeon, and Booth, as well as social thinkers including Foucalt, Adorno, Habermas, and Toulmin. Rhetoric, in speech communication, ceased to be restricted to the spoken word; it declared its domain to include most forms of verbal and nonverbal discourse, including film, architecture, and costume.

In its present state, speech communication is a discipline that partakes of and contributes to learning both in the humanities and the social sciences.

Herman Cohen
Pennsylvania State University

Bibliography

Benson, Thomas W., ed. *Speech Communication in the 20th Century.* Carbondale: Southern Illinois UP, 1985.

Wallace, Karl R., ed. *History of Speech Education in America: Background Studies.* New York: Appleton, 1954.

Winans, J.A. "The Need for Research." *Quarterly Journal of Public Speaking* 1 (1915): 17–23.

Woolbert, Charles H. "The Organization of Departments of Speech Science in Universities." *Quarterly Journal of Public Speaking* 2 (1916): 64–77.

Speech Communication Association

A major national professional association of communication scholars, teachers, and practitioners. The Speech Communication Association (SCA) includes approximately seven thousand individual members and three hundred organizational members from every state in the United States and from many other countries as well.

The mission of SCA is to promote study, criticism, research, teaching, and application of the artistic, humanistic, and scientific principles of communication.

SCA was founded in 1914 as the National Association of Academic Teachers of Public Speaking, an organization formed by seventeen disaffected members of the National Council of Teachers of English who were convinced that the fundamental differences between English and speech were not recognized by that body. There have been a series of name changes over the years: National Association of Teachers of Speech (1923), Speech Association of America (1946), and the current name, adopted in 1970. These changes reflect a progressive broadening of the scope of members' interests and concerns.

From the beginning, SCA has been strongly focused on rhetoric and the humanities. Early members were predominantly teachers of public speaking and debate. As scholarship in the field matured, theorists and historians of rhetoric and public address played a prominent role in the association. Since World War II, they have been joined by scholars in the social and policy sciences and by communication practitioners, but there has been a continuing commitment to the humanistic study of communication.

SCA publishes six journals. Three of them—*Quarterly Journal of Speech, Critical Studies in Mass Communication,* and *Text and Performance Quarterly*—are predominantly oriented toward the humanities and publish scholarship of interest to theorists, historians, and critics of rhetoric. Essays in the other three journals—*Communication Monographs, Communication Education,* and *Journal of Applied Communication Research*—also frequently are of interest. Each journal is published quarterly. Membership benefits include the choice of one journal subscription; additional journals are available for a fee.

Each year SCA holds an annual meeting attended by nearly half the members. The annual meeting typically includes eight hundred or more business meetings and programs. Convention programs address issues and concerns in the philosophy, theory, practice, history, and criticism of rhetoric. The convention also includes seminars, short courses, and other special programs, and affords opportunities for scholarly and professional interaction.

SCA members may affiliate with three units (known as divisions, sections, or commissions, based on their size and function); additional affiliations require payment of a fee. Divisions focused largely on rhetoric include Rhetorical and Communication Theory, Public Address, Argumentation and Forensics, and Political Communication. Other divisions such as Instructional Development, Performance

Studies, Mass Communication, Organizational Communication, and Theater also may sponsor programs and meetings of interest to students of rhetoric.

An active list of nonserial publications complements the association's journals. Foremost among these is the *Index to Journals in Communication Studies,* published every five years, which is the most comprehensive index to the journal literature in the field. SCA publications also include series in education and instructional development and in applied communication. The association also is the publisher of record for a variety of conference proceedings, including those of the biennial Summer Conference on Argumentation sponsored jointly by SCA and the American Forensic Association.

Other SCA activities include sponsorship of summer conferences and research seminars, faculty development projects, government relations activities, affirmative action, sponsorship of an international debate exchange, a placement service, and an extensive program of awards and recognition for distinguished teaching, research, and service. Among the most prestigious awards in rhetoric are the James A. Winans/Herbert A. Wichelns Memorial Award for Distinguished Scholarship in Rhetoric and Public Address, the Douglas Ehninger Distinguished Rhetorical Scholar Award, the Franklyn S. Haiman Award in Freedom of Expression, and, for young scholars, the Karl R. Wallace Award.

The SCA National Office is at 5105 Backlick Road, #E, Annandale, Virginia 22003; telephone (703) 750-0533. The national office staff includes an executive director, two associate directors, a controller/operations manager, and a publications manager, with appropriate support personnel.

David Zarefsky
Northwestern University

Bibliography

Wallace, Karl R., ed. *A History of Speech Education in America.* New York: Appleton, 1954.

Work, William, and Robert C. Jeffrey, ed. *The Past is Prologue: A 75th Anniversary Publication of the Speech Communication Association.* Annandale, VA: SCA, 1989.

Stasis Theory

A system taught in the rhetorical schools of antiquity to aid in identifying the point at issue in any verbal conflict. Both the Greek term *stasis* and its Latin counterparts *status* or *constitutio* signify the standing point, or stopping point, at which argument commences. There is evidence that Greek rhetoricians as early as the fifth century B.C.E. understood the utility of clearly identifying the point at issue, especially for speeches in the law courts, and Aristotle lists four kinds of stasis in his *Rhetoric* (1417b21). However, stasis theory as a formal codifying system was a development in post-Aristotelian Hellenistic rhetorical theory that is attributed to Hermagoras of Temnos, who lived in the second century B.C.E. (For what is known about Hermagoras' lost text, see Matthes 1958.) Both Cicero and the author of *Rhetorica ad Herennium* learned stasis theory as part of their education in rhetoric, and both cover it in their own manuals (*De inventione* 1.10–19, 2.12ff; *ad Herennium* 1.11–17). However, the most complete exposition of a fully developed stasis theory was written in about 176 C.E. by Hermogenes of Tarsus in his technical treatise *On Stases.* Hermogenes' definitive text survived as a mainstay of rhetorical education for well over a thousand years, throughout the later Roman and Byzantine empires, and appeared in printed versions in the West starting in 1508. Available English translations are by Nadeau (1964) and Heath (forthcoming).

Stasis theory falls under the rhetorical canon of invention, or discovery of material. In the realm of particular problems (*hypotheses,* as opposed to general problems, which Hermagoras called *theses*), an accusation, or a proposal, is met by a denial. Out of this opposition arises the question (*zetema*), or the matter that is to be resolved; this matter can be classified as a stasis. The rhetor proceeds through a prescribed series of dichotomizing questions to locate and identify the unresolved matter. Locating a stasis within the system presents the rhetor with not only a name for a category of argument but also a recommended strategy for pursuing it.

In the basic four-part system attributed to Hermagoras, the first stasis is that of fact (also called conjecture: *stochasmos* in Greek, *status coniecturalis* in Latin). It responds to this question: Is there a cause for dispute? If of two parties one denies that there is cause for dispute, that issue in itself becomes the first difference to be resolved. Example: A man is found burying a corpse in an isolated place and is accused of murder. He claims the death was from natural causes. Argument will center on the factual question of whether the death was a natural one or not.

If the parties agree that there is a cause meriting action, the point to be settled may be at the second stasis, that of definition (Greek *horos*, Latin *status definitivus*). It responds to the question What are the essential characteristics that define the fact? Example: A theft has occurred in a temple. The prosecution defines the act as sacrilege; the defendant responds that it was simple theft if the goods involved were not possessions of the temple but private property. Argument will center on the definition of the act, and in particular the name that should be given to it.

Many times, people who acknowledge a dispute may give it the same name yet still disagree about certain circumstantial (or nonessential) features. Their descriptions diverge at the third stasis, that of quality (Greek *poiotes*, Latin *status generalis*). They must argue the question What circumstances have bearing on the settlement of our dispute? Example: In 1832 Samuel Houston was charged with an assault on William Stanbery, a U.S. representative from Ohio. Houston defended himself on grounds that he made the assault without premeditation, over a published libel (not words spoken in the House), and that Stanbery furthermore had shot at him with a pistol. There were mitigating circumstances, and Houston took the stasis of quality as the site of argument.

The fourth stasis, called *metalepsis* by Hermagoras (*status translativus* in Latin), denotes objection of a procedural nature. It responds to the question Is our dispute being argued in the proper manner, or in the right place? In the ancient world, an objection might be that the action was being brought before the wrong court—that a plaintiff who had lost his civil rights was bringing suit in the citizens' court, for instance. Present-day rhetors use the stasis of objection when they protest that a technical matter is being argued "before the court of public opinion."

In addition to the stases just enumerated, Hermagoras' system also accommodated four legal questions and four asystatic cases. The legal questions identified issues of a specifically forensic nature (letter versus spirit of the law; contradictory laws; ambiguous laws; and infer-

ence from written to unwritten law). The asystatic cases included exceptional situations in which argument is not expected to reach resolution: the overwhelmingly one-sided, the totally equal, the convertible (when each party appropriates the opponent's ground), and the insoluble, such as disputes involving dreams or predictions.

Some three hundred years after Hermagoras, toward the end of the second century C.E., the rhetorical prodigy Hermogenes reorganized stasis theory into a system so comprehensive that it has never been superseded. His treatise *On Stases* still survives in its entirety, as one part of a five-part text known as "Hermogenes' Art of Rhetoric." Since Hermogenes' treatise is complete, whereas that of Hermagoras is fragmentary, comparison between the two versions of stasis theory must be speculative. It is clear, however, that Hermogenes' system is the more complex because it includes thirteen stases, increases the number of asystatic cases to eight, and adds three near-asystatic cases. Yet the move to greater complexity was not uniquely Hermogenean; we know from later commentators that a contemporary rival of Hermogenes named Minucianus also taught a thirteen-stasis system, although (like Hermagoras') Minucianus' text is now in fragments.

Other differences between Hermogenes' system and its simpler four-part predecessor are, first, that Hermagoras applied the theory to all three genres of rhetoric, including epideictic, whereas Hermogenes addressed only the deliberative and the judicial. Second, Hermagoras' seems to have been a coordinate system in which the four stases were equal, whereas Hermogenes' was a subordinating system in which twelve succeeding stases developed out of the stasis of conjecture.

Still, Hermagoras' well-established terminology was not so much changed as augmented by its heirs. The thirteen stases presented by Hermogenes were as follows:

1. Conjecture. Is it clear or unclear that an act was (or should be) committed? If unclear, this is the matter that must be argued. If clear, proceed to 2.
2. Definition. Is a term available to give a description of the act that is essentially complete? If available description is incomplete, then argue here. If complete, proceed to 3.

3. Quality. Of a future act (for deliberative speeches): Is it practical? Hermogenes directs that "the practical issue" be considered under the headings of legality, justice, advantage, capability, honor, and outcome. Of a past act (a juridical issue): Was it just or unjust, legal or illegal? The stases immediately following are concerned with what is just. If one party denies the act was wrong, proceed to 4.

4. Justification. Argue that the act is not forbidden, nor generally held to be actionable. If it cannot be so justified, proceed to 5.

5. Counterplea. Argue that an error was made, but a corresponding benefit was achieved thereby. If no such benefit can be claimed, proceed to 6.

6. Counteraccusation. Using this stasis, a rhetor who is unable to justify the act or claim it was beneficial argues that the victim deserved it. If the victim is unassailable, proceed to 7.

7. Transfer of blame. Argue that responsibility for the act lies elsewhere, perhaps with some third party. If blame cannot be transferred, proceed to 8.

8. Plea for leniency. At this stasis, the argument is based on what we might call "human nature": Hermogenes here mentions sleep, or feelings of pity, as mitigations. Say, however, that we are proceeding from stasis 3 on grounds not of justice but of legality. The next four stases offer ways of arguing an act was not illegal. Readers will recognize Hermagoras' four legal questions, now fully incorporated as stases within the system.

9. Letter versus spirit of the law. For example, foreigners are denied access to a city's walls, but a foreigner fighting on the walls helps to save the city. Is his transgression punishable?

10. Conflict of laws. When a case involves two or more laws, a choice may have to be made about which law gives a rhetor the greater advantage.

11. Ambiguity of laws. The technological constraints of ancient writing (without punctuation or spaces between words) undoubtedly encouraged use of this stasis, but modern examples are not unknown.

12. Inference from written to unwritten law. Hermogenes' example concerns theatrical performances of comedy. If there is a law against ridiculing anyone by name in the theater, but a production featured characters with identifiable masks, was the law broken?

13. Objection. As in the four-part system, this stasis denotes objection of a procedural or technical nature. Hermogenes apparently refined it by distinguishing documentary from nondocumentary grounds for objection.

These were the thirteen stases. To the four asystatic cases of Hermagoras were added four more: the impossible, the incredible, the contemptible, and the case without motivating circumstances. The possibly new category of near-asystatic cases included those in which evidence was ill-balanced—that is, cases in which the evidence, though not overwhelming, was much heavier on one side than on the other; flawed, such as those assuming circumstances contrary to historical evidence; or prejudiced.

Hermogenes' system probably owes its longevity to the comprehensiveness that made it such useful material for educational purposes. Clearly, it focused on judicial rhetoric and may have had some utility for training legal practitioners, but the idiosyncrasy and antiquity of some of the examples used suggest that it was intended primarily for schooling the young in rhetoric, not in law. Learning to apply stasis theory in speaking exercises and declamation would encourage taking a systematic approach to the discovery of material, at the same time fostering a certain flexibility and resourcefulness of mind. When the students reached adulthood, it is easy to imagine them as educated amateurs applauding an especially inventive use of counterplea, say, or nondocumentary objection, in a rhetorician's performance. Above all, however, stasis theory was meant to be practical, geared to "rational dispute on a particular matter, based on the established laws and customs of any given people" (Hermogenes 2, Heath's translation).

Janet B. Davis
Northeast Missouri State University

Bibliography

Cicero. *De Inventione.* Trans. H.M. Hubbell. Cambridge, MA: Harvard UP, 1949: 3–345.

[Cicero]. *Ad C. Herennium (Rhetorica ad Herennium).* Trans. H. Caplan. Cambridge, MA: Harvard UP, 1954.

Heath, Malcolm. *Hermogenes' On Issues: Strategies of Argument in Later Greek Rhetoric.* Oxford: Oxford UP, 1995.

Hermogenes. "Peri Staseon." *Opera.* Ed. H. Rabe. Stuttgart: Teubner, 1911. Reissued 1985.

Kennedy, George A. *The Art of Persuasion in Greece.* Princeton: Princeton UP, 1963. 303–14.

Matthes, Dieter. "Hermagoras von Temnos, 1904–1955." *Lustrum* 3 (1958): 58–214.

Nadeau, Ray. "Classical Systems of Stases in Greek: Hermagoras to Hermogenes." *Greek, Roman and Byzantine Studies* 2 (1959): 53–71.

———. "Hermogenes' *On Stases*: A Translation with an Introduction and Notes." *Speech Monographs* 31 (1964): 361–424.

Russell, D.A. *Greek Declamation.* Cambridge: Cambridge UP, 1983. 40–73.

Stewart, Donald C. (1930–1992)

An historian of nineteenth and twentieth-century rhetoric and writing pedagogy who championed the development of individualistic, "authentic voices" in apprentice writers. Donald C. Stewart, born in Kansas City, Missouri, earned his undergraduate (1952) and master's degrees (1955) at the University of Kansas and the doctorate in English from the University of Wisconsin (1962). Stewart had a distinguished teaching, editing, and publishing career, which began at the University of Illinois (1962–1968) and continued until his death at Kansas State University (1968–1992). Stewart held numerous posts in the National Council of Teachers of English (NCTE) and the Conference on College Composition and Communication (CCCC), including program chair and chair of CCCC, respectively, in 1982 and 1983; he also edited *Kansas English* from 1971 to 1980. Stewart's textbooks, *The Authentic Voice* (1972) and *The Versatile Writer* (1986), well represent his interest in teaching apprentice writers to develop an "authentic" voice—that is, one that exemplifies their unique, personal vantage point on the world and their commitment to a particular set of values, devoid of affectation or false collaboration contrived from the experience of schooling. Stewart was also an avid outdoorsman who spent many summers in Yellowstone National Park as a ranger, writing a memoir of his experiences, *My Yellowstone Years* (1989).

In his research Stewart focused his attention on the roots of modern rhetorical theory and practice in nineteenth-century American university settings, noting deleterious influences as well as offering rehabilitations of prescient thinkers whose contribution to rhetoric he wanted contemporary teachers and researchers to consider. One of Stewart's major contributions to twentieth-century rhetoric is his articulation of what he called the "Harvardization" of American English, an institution whose early twentieth-century legacy, he believed, reduced writing instruction to concern for superficial correctness, disassociated writing instruction from meaningful social context, and helped drive a wedge between composition and literature instruction in the profession. Stewart must also be credited with the "rediscovery" of Fred Newton Scott, a turn-of-the-century professor of rhetoric at the University of Michigan, whose conceptualizations of rhetoric and whose writing program Stewart often presented as a positive counterexample to Harvard's and as a harbinger of later innovative twentieth-century classroom writing pedagogy.

In the later years of his career, Stewart found himself a somewhat reluctant crusader against what he viewed as a prevailing tide of collaborative and social-constructionist views of the role of invention in the writing process. Such views seemed to him to dismiss too quickly the individual personality of the writer and its role in framing subject matter and style and, worse, inadvertently reestablished impersonal, institutionalized prose as a goal of writing instruction. In such critiques Stewart consistently argued against what he termed a renewed positivism in composition studies that parodied his concern for authenticity as radical autonomy in invention, an anachronistic remnant of a Romantic individualism. While conceding the impact of groups on individual identity and consciousness, Stewart maintained that each writer possesses a single, unique voice that the practice of writing could assist in manifesting and could serve the individual in negotiating meaning and communicating the self in the external world.

Bruce L. Edwards
Bowling Green State University

Bibliography

Stewart, Donald C. *The Authentic Voice*. Iowa City: Brown, 1972.

———. "Cognitive Psychologists, Social Constructionists, and Three Nineteenth-Century Advocates of Authentic Voice." *Journal of Advanced Composition* 12 (1992): 279–90.

———. "Collaborative Learning and Composition: Boon or Bane?" *Rhetoric Review* 7 (1988): 58–83.

———. "Harvard's Influence on English Studies: Perceptions from Three Universities in the Early Twentieth Century." *College Composition and Communication* 43 (1992): 455–71.

———. "Nineteenth-Century Rhetoric." *Historical Rhetoric: An Annotated Bibliography*. Ed. Winifred Bryan Horner. Boston: Hall, 1980.

———. "Rediscovering Fred Newton Scott." *College English* 40 (1979): 539–47.

———. "Rhetorical Malnutrition in Prelim Questions and Literary Criticism." *College English* 39:2 (1977): 160–69.

———. *The Versatile Writer*. Lexington, MA: Heath, 1986.

Stoics

Characterized by an ascetic moral heroism. Zeno of Citium founded the Stoic school of philosophy near the end of the fourth century B.C.E. Stoicism held that logic provided a person the method to attain true knowledge. For the Stoics, physics contained the principles by which the universe was organized, and the discipline of ethics built on these principles for precepts upon which one must live one's life. The Stoics believed that the highest good in life was virtue, a concept in which human behavior was in accord with the laws of nature, the human will with the divine will. In other words, a practicing Stoic was expected to live life according to their view of nature. Only the wise person, they believed, could attain this state of virtue. The sage, the wise one, recognized that whatever was external to oneself was indifferent. Wealth or poverty, health or illness, pain or pleasure were all matters of indifference. A life in accord with nature was paramount.

As a moral code, stoicism found favor with many Romans both for its intellectual base and for its proximity to their own cultural value of *severitas*. Enduring hardship and disaster with a spirit of equanimity was deeply ingrained in the Romans. Sternness in the face of difficulty, along with the unquestioned belief in a strict moral code of civic responsibility, made stoicism attractive and easily understood. Indeed, the ethical dimensions of stoicism are apparent in the extant Latin works of Seneca (4 B.C.E.–65 C.E.). Anger, wisdom, the happy life, consolation, and leisure are but a few of the subjects he addressed.

The Stoics recognized emotions as kinds of excessive impulses that are contrary to nature. Oratory as practiced by the Romans did make appeals to desire, fear, pain, and pleasure; not surprisingly, the Stoics rejected rhetoric and its practice. Instead, they valorized language characterized by brevity, restraint, and the absence of passion and ornament. Any use of language not crafted to instruct the intellect (that is, the language of dialectic) was considered deceitful, unnatural, and a vice. Language, for the Stoics, ought be used only to communicate truth.

Far too many of the tenets of stoicism were at odds with Roman rhetoric to have much, if any, impact. Cicero, for example, ever the statesman and ever the pragmatist, believed that oratory, by definition, entailed both wisdom and virtue. While agreeing that rhetorical language would instruct, Cicero also believed that an orator must charm and persuade an audience. Truth, for him, remains inaccessible unless and until it is given life and energy via rhetoric and its use of aesthetically pleasing style. The Stoics were wrong, Cicero believed, in their rejection of ornate language.

Stoicism did not mix well with rhetoric. In the political and ethical arenas, stoicism did form an important base for the Romans in the conduct of their civic and personal lives.

Donovan J. Ochs
University of Iowa

Bibliography

Annas, Julia. *Hellenistic Philosophy of Mind*. Berkeley: U of California P, 1992.

Colish, Marcia L. *The Stoic Tradition from Antiquity to the Early Middle Ages*. New York: Brill, 1990.

Erskine, Andrew. *The Hellenistic Stoa: Political Thought and Action*. London: Duckworth, 1990.

Style

The third canon of rhetoric. Style is the canon that is concerned with the arrangement and depiction of words in discourse. It has been used as a self-conscious, strategic, rhetorical device at least since the time of Gorgias of Leontini (c. 480–380 B.C.E.). Gorgias' method of rhetorical composition included what became known as figures—*homoeoteleuton, isocolon, antithesis,* and *parison.* These figures addressed forms of repetitive endings, syllabic balance, opposition, and parallelism. The effect of the devices was a jangling, rhythmic language that created aural responses on the part of an audience that facilitated persuasion. Although antithesis could be argued to provide semantic variation, the Gorgianic figures were devices that attended more to the aural dimensions of language and were grounded in a culture that was sensitive to such concerns. Rhetorical style and the figures continued to be an important part of subsequent rhetorics. Isocrates is said to have followed in the Gorgianic tradition, while Aristotle offered less attention to the aural dimension of style and placed his stylistic focus on more semantic devices such as metaphor, simile, and antithesis. Theophrastus, Aristotle's successor at the Lyceum, developed additional doctrine on style, stressing the qualities of purity, clarity, appropriateness, and the ornamentation of language.

By the first century B.C.E., style had burgeoned into an extensive doctrine. The author of *Rhetorica ad Herennium* identified three levels of style—grand, middle, and plain—that are achieved through the use of some sixty-four figures. The grand style featured the use of ornate and impressive words for stirring the emotions and moving an audience to action. The plain style featured the basic idioms of standard speech. The middle style was something of a cross between the two, utilizing more colloquial language and the Gorgianic figures. The figures were divided into two types, forty-five figures of words and nineteen figures of thought.

The first thirty-five figures of words were devices with which a rhetor arranged, warped, and manipulated language for persuasive effect. In particular, they were means of achieving repetition, opposition, strategic advantage, structure, and rhythm. The repetitive devices (*epanaphora, antistrophe,* interlacement, transplacement, reduplication, synonymy) involve the reiteration of words for emphasis. The devices of opposition (antithesis, reasoning by contraries, reciprocal change) allow for the comparison, contrast, and interaction of words. The strategic devices (interrogation, ratiocination, *hypophora,* elimination, correction, *aposiopesis, paralipsis,* surrender, and indecision) feature the use of expression aimed at shaping thought to the rhetor's advantage. They range from questioning patterns to ploys and forms of innuendo. Several are overtly argumentative, orienting the audience toward the orator's position. Structural devices (definition, transition, and climax) allow the rhetor to arrange ideas. They focus more on general organizational features such as transitions and summaries. Finally, a significant number of devices (clause, phrase, period, *isocolon, homoeoptoton, homoeoteleuton,* disjunction, conjunction, adjunction, asyndeton, and *paronomasia*) deal with the manipulation of clauses, sentences, phrases, cases, and word endings for rhythmical and metrical effect.

The last ten of the figures of words are what are now known as tropes. Each involves a variation in the act of naming or identifying phenomena. Conventional meanings of words are vacated and replaced with tangential phenomena connected to the original meaning by means of substitution (metaphor, *antonomasia,* allegory), exaggeration (hyperbole), part-to-whole and whole-to-part relationships (synecdoche), representation (metonymy), circumlocution (periphrasis), change in word order (*hyperbaton*), and creation of words (catachresis, onomatopoeia). The tropes allow for the creativity of the rhetor; they reassign, exploit, and create meaning.

The nineteen figures of thought are devices that facilitate organization, expression, comparison, and description. The organizational figures (distribution, vivid description, accumulation, dwelling on the point, division, antithesis, and comparison) deal with the way thought is arranged to emphasize and demonstrate a point. Various devices arrange thought to consider the consequences of an action, assign functions or roles to people or things, use a variety of analogical relationships, and use certain organizational patterns for emphasis. The expressive figures (frankness of speech, understatement, refining, personification, emphasis, and brevity) involve a variety of ruses used to facilitate persuasion. The comparative figures (simile and exemplification) employ models and examples to support a particular point. Finally, descriptive figures use a variety of means to describe: physical traits, character traits, patterns of speech used by particular people, and vivid description to depict an event. Taken together, the rhetorical figures provide the rhetor with the strategies that make language persuasive and rhetorical rather than didactic.

Cicero, in *De oratore* (55 B.C.E.) and, more particularly, in *Orator* (46 B.C.E.), linked the three levels of style with three "duties of the orator": to teach, to delight, and to move. The plain style was used to facilitate instruction, the middle style to delight, and the grand style to move. This system emphasizes the use of language as the primary means of persuasion and mitigates the influence of argument. In the fourth and fifth centuries, St. Augustine utilized Ciceronian rhetoric for the transmission of Christian instruction. His application of the duties of the orator and the levels of style was wholesale, but with a greater emphasis on instruction as the most important duty. Style was used as a means of persuasion, but only when associated with transmission of truth or knowledge, in this case Christian doctrine.

Accounts of rhetorical style are less in evidence in the encyclopedic rhetorics of the early Middle Ages; indeed, most of the more substantive accounts of the figures are found in the grammatical tradition, a tradition with a different emphasis from the rhetorical. The rhetorical tradition of style was a preceptive one that used the figures as heuristic devices for the facilitation of persuasive discourse. The grammatical tradition, on the other hand, used the figures as a means of criticizing and interpreting discourse, particularly literature. The grammatical figures were subsequently absorbed into the rhetorical tradition. The most influential grammar of the period, perhaps in history, Aelius Donatus's *Ars grammatica,* explained language from its foundations, identifying such basic components as sounds, letters, syllables, and words and then adding to those components the parts of speech (noun, verb, and so forth) and the distinctions between those parts (such as gender, number, and case). Variations in the correct forms of these grammatical distinctions were referred to as faults in language: barbarisms and solecisms. Barbarisms are faults derived from misspellings, mispronunciation, and the like. Solecisms are faults derived from im-proper grammatical usage. A barbarism used in poetry is called a metaplasm, and a solecism in poetry is called a scheme. Barbarisms and solecisms, then, become allowable faults when used in poetry.

The schemes are what had previously been called figures. Donatus noted the traditional distinction between figures of thought and figures of words but declared that only the figures of words apply to grammarians, as figures of thought were the province of the orator. Donatus also discarded the figures of words that consisted of a strategy or ploy. The tropes are the only part of Donatus' grammatical system that do not follow as variations of his basic grammatical foundation. They were additions to the grammatical system necessitated by their existence in Latin literature. Donatus' failure to account for the tropes in his interrelated grammatical system is no doubt due to the open, amorphous nature of tropes. Nonetheless, he adhered to his grammatical focus by considering the tropes as a means of analyzing texts, particularly the classics of Latin literature.

The figures excluded by Donatus and other grammarians often circulated separately in the Middle Ages as rhetorical "colors" but were reunited with the remaining figures in the preceptive grammars of the twelfth and thirteenth centuries. A new discourse genre, *ars poetriae* (arts of poetry and prose), also evolved during that time, featuring an innovative combination of both rhetorical and grammatical figures. The role of figures in *ars poetriae* is neither as descriptive (as in the grammatical tradition) nor as generative (as in the rhetorical). Rather, the figures were used as a means of reworking traditional themes and achieving particular rhymes or meters. The tropes were used as a means of converting words to different and varied forms. Geoffrey de Vinsauf, Gervasius of Melkley, and John of Garland incorporated the figures into their innovative doctrines of conversion, determination, and *transsumptio*—systems used literally to convert, determine, and transform discourse. Along with some categories of grammar, then, the figures perform the function of the topics in classical rhetorical systems. They are the devices first applied to the rhetorical situation.

An equally important component of rhetorical style is discussed in a variety of treatises

S

from late antiquity through the Middle Ages: *cursus* and *rhythmus*. These are prescribed systems of rhythmic emphasis used in various types of discourse. They are featured prominently in each of the three medieval rhetorical genres, *ars poetriae, ars praedicandi* (art of preaching), and *ars dictaminis* (art of letter-writing). Much work remains to be done to understand this important area of rhetorical style, a style that all but disappeared in the rhetorical shift from an oral to literal emphasis.

A complete survey of Renaissance rhetorical theory has yet to be written. In general, however, Renaissance rhetorical theory is marked by two particular movements that influence style: humanism and Ramism. Both emphasized style at the expense of the other rhetorical canons. The Humanists hoped to regain what they regarded as the cultivated learning of classical Greece and Rome. Accordingly, they sought the recovery of classical texts that had been generally unavailable in the Middle Ages. Of particular interest were Cicero's *De oratore* and *Orator* and Quintilian's *Institutio oratoria*. The Renaissance appropriation of style moved more to one of ornamentation, rather than one of depiction and persuasion. The evolving shift from an oral rhetoric to a literal one also had an effect as the emphasis on rhetorical figures moved from aural ornamentation to literal ornamentation. The emphasis on stylistic adornment produced whole treatises on style, notably Henry Peacham's *Garden of Eloquence,* planted with 191 grammatical and rhetorical figures.

Peter Ramus reorganized the arts of the Trivium in the sixteenth century, arguing that there was too much overlap and duplication among grammar, dialectic, and rhetoric. In the process of his reorganization, however, the province of rhetoric was reduced to two of its five canons, style and delivery. He reduced the number of tropes to four—metaphor, metonymy, synecdoche, and irony—though a number of other tropes were included as subcategories, a structure that was later adopted by Giambattista Vico and Kenneth Burke as the Master Tropes. The effect of Ramus's system, ultimately, was the almost exclusive association of rhetoric with style.

Eventually, these ways of thinking were overturned by the new intellectual perspectives advanced in the seventeenth century. Francis Bacon, René Descartes, and others rejected the prevailing, scholastic view of logic. Scholastic logics concerned themselves with justifying previously reached conclusions; their material was the received wisdom of classical sources, and their method was the arcane division, labeling, and arrangement of arguments. The critics of scholasticism posited logic as an art of inquiry, proceeding inductively from rigorous observations to testable conclusions. For the scholastics, rhetoric had concerned the invention of argument. For their philosophic critics, the role of rhetoric was confined to the accurate transmission of scientific knowledge. In this scheme, logic and sophistic had particular roles in the transmission of thought, but rhetoric was the vehicle of the imagination. This is known as the "managerial" function of rhetoric.

The second development affecting eighteenth-century rhetoric was the emerging study of psychology. The concept of "faculty psychology" ascribed specific faculties (such as reason, imagination, and will—or perception and preference) to the mind. In general, rhetoricians recognized the fact that individuals might be convinced of the truth of a position, without being persuaded to act upon the truth. Effective persuasion could occur only when each independent faculty had been addressed, so in Bacon's famous dictum, "the duty and office of rhetoric is to apply *Reason to Imagination* for the better moving of the will."

As reason was only one of the faculties of the mind, rational argument could be only one of the tools of the rhetor. Appeals to other faculties of the mind involved, of necessity, arousing the passions and inflaming the imagination with vivid, lively images. Those images were portrayed by means of the figures. Rhetoricians were at pains to point out that such appeals were, in George Campbell's words, "not the supplanters of reason, or even rivals in her sway; they are her handmaid." This scheme is slightly reminiscent of the duties of the orator, though style is used as the means of achieving only one of the components. Nonetheless, rhetorical style is central to the communication of ideas. The Baconian combination of logic and rhetorical style and the consideration of psychological concerns were defining characteristics of modern rhetorical theory.

The intrinsic pragmatism of rhetoricians mediated the influence of these theories. The province of rhetoric had always been action—that is, the rhetor worked to produce a change in the world. For pragmatic reasons, some rhetoricians rejected these new insights. In doing so they argued that the classical canons had always worked in the past and would do so in the future. These "nonphilosophical" rhetorics are exemplified by Vico's *Institutio oratoriae* (1711) and John Ward's *System of Oratory* (1759). Such works tended to be thoroughly Ciceronian in approach, stressing a multitude of figures, places, and rules.

The majority of eighteenth-century rhetorics proceeded differently. Authors such as John Holmes, George Campbell, Joseph Priestley, and Hugh Blair accepted all five classical canons, recognized the attenuation of invention, and stressed the elements of style. They tried to reconcile the divergent offices of rhetoric by stressing both perspicuity and passion.

Nineteenth-century rhetorical studies have been dismissed by twentieth-century scholars. In Europe and North America, the period was marked by wrenching economic and social change. Encouraged in part by the spectacles of the American and French revolutions, most European nations rose in revolt by mid century. Monarchies were replaced with various forms of democracy. The population shifted from overwhelmingly rural to predominantly urban. Employment shifted from artisanship to mass industry, with the result that life became both anonymous and regimented. The *Communist Manifesto* (1845) vied with *On the Origin of Species* (1859) for space on bookshop shelves.

Nonetheless, nineteenth-century teaching on rhetorical style sailed on, unconcerned. Rhetoric, taught at private colleges to an elite audience, retained a conservative attachment to its classical and Enlightenment forebears. Richard Whately's widely reprinted *Elements of Rhetoric* (1828) reiterated the eighteenth-century wisdom: The best style was perspicuous, energetic (or vivid), and elegant (or beautiful). With minor repackaging, Campbell's and Blair's dicta on taste and style were incorporated in most university courses. Similarly, most rhetoricians (through the 1870s) accepted the belletristic assumption that all forms of communication were joined: Rhetoric textbooks focused simultaneously on writers and speakers, readers and hearers, oratory and poetry. Finally, these rhetoricians accepted the earlier notions of decorum, or elevated speech, as the hallmark of all good communication. In addition to Whately, works in this tradition include Samuel Newman, *Practical System of Rhetoric* (1827);

Alexander Jamieson, *Grammar of Rhetoric and Polite Literature* (1844); Henry Day, *Elements of the Art of Rhetoric* (1850); and A.S. Hill, *Principles of Rhetoric* (1878).

The style of rhetoric taught in the academy was increasingly at odds with rhetorical practice. Politicians, appealing to an indifferently educated lower- or middle-class audience, adopted a much more colloquial style of discourse. This style substituted homely examples for classical allusions and was often less sublime than bombastic. The preferred speaking style of "gentlemen" became associated with pomposity and aristocratic pretension.

Two defenses for the continued teaching of an elevated style can be adduced. First, some historians argue that this style served to shape a progressive ruling elite. By stressing the importance of concepts such as sublimity, taste, and imagination, rhetoricians subtly inculcated values essential to the success of society's upper class. The teaching of style, then, served much the same propagandizing function as the epideictic oratory of centuries past. Second, the old style of the upper class became mimicked in the lower class. Many common citizens, disoriented and discomfited by accelerating social and economic changes, sought to reaffirm their self-worth and identity by adopting the refined style of the elite. A plethora of authors catered to the interests of the socially insecure through articles in popular journals, manuals of etiquette, household encyclopedias, and other works.

Belletristic rhetoricians had proceeded from the assumption that poetry, oratory, and historical essays were controlled by the same rules of style. Under the probing of philologists (later, linguists) and teachers of composition, the belief that all forms of discourse were governed by the same natural rules began to unravel late in the nineteenth century. This change was due in part to the changing nature of a university education. Where college degrees were once the domain of the upper class, the needs of an industrial society and the rise of the state universities brought far greater numbers of students who were pursuing a college degree as a vocational matter. This change had two effects: First, it created a student body that studied rhetoric for its practical application to their careers. Impatient with literary or belletristic frills of traditional rhetoric courses, students pursued training in clear writing. Second, it created a student body more poorly prepared for college than their predecessors.

Articles in the 1880s, for example, complained of the illiteracy of young people and the need for instruction in composition. These factors helped propel the split between spoken and written rhetoric. Rhetoric texts, such as John F. Genung's *Practical Principles of Rhetoric* (1886), began to specialize in written composition by the 1880s. The first "freshman writing" course was introduced at Harvard in 1885 and was a common element of university curricula by 1900.

In this new realm, rhetoric was shorn of all pretension and reduced to its most utilitarian core. The goal was to produce workers capable of writing clear, technically correct prose. The mechanism for such teaching was frequent, small writing assignments. The time once devoted to literary models was turned over to the writing of daily themes. The preferred style for such rhetoric was classically plain. The best exemplar of this school is William Strunk, *The Elements of Style* (1918). E.B. White, in the introduction to his famous revision of Strunk's work, reduced Strunk's lesson to "Rule Thirteen. Omit needless words. Omit needless words. Omit needless words." While such courses continued to be offered under the title "Rhetoric," they were divorced from the traditional civic and moral functions of rhetorical training.

Nineteenth-century practice influenced the twentieth century. Speakers of the late nineteenth century strove for power through simplicity of style. Albert Beveridge, a renowned Senate orator at the turn of the century, warned speakers: "Refrain from what is called rhetoric. Shun the ornate. Never try to be eloquent." Like the Church Fathers of an earlier era, Beveridge felt that eloquence would flow naturally from the power of the speaker's ideas. It could not, he argued, "be manufactured like a hat or a shovel." The approved style was clear, direct, objective, impersonal, and forceful.

A second factor influencing rhetorical style was the technological ability to reproduce the human voice through electronic amplification and, later, broadcast. Before the advent of amplification, speakers needed to fill vast halls with the power of their voices. To would-be orators with insufficient lung capacity, John Quincy Adams recommended "some occupation more compatible with their tenderness of constitution." This fact of delivery interacts with style in two ways. First, it eliminated certain rhetorical styles from public discourse, since not all styles are equally compatible with being shouted into a great hall. Second, along with other prejudices, the emphasis on powerful voices systematically excluded women from the ranks of public speakers. Amplification weakened these constraints; broadcast eliminated them. As discourse became a matter of a single speaker addressing a dispersed broadcast audience, addresses were styled as conversations with listeners rather than assaults upon them. The tendency of television to further decrease the psychic distance between speaker and listener mandated a new style. Kathleen Jamieson argued that "the intimate medium of television requires that those who speak comfortably through it project a sense of private self, unself-consciously self-disclose, and engage the audience in completing messages that exist as mere dots and lines on television's screen. The traditional male style is, in McLuhan's terms, too hot for the cool medium of television."

It is not surprising that style has been reduced to the single dictum Be clear. Where the nineteenth century associated eloquence with pomposity, the twentieth century linked it with insidious manipulation. At best, the eloquent speaker was trying to sell something; at worst, to mask tyranny behind high-flown language. This aversion is reflected in Franklin Roosevelt's decision to match Goebbel's Ministry of Propaganda with a simple Office of Facts and Figures.

With even the canon of style now attenuated, the teaching of rhetoric is largely confined to matters of presentation. The rhetorical tradition has not, of course, been abandoned. It flourishes instead as a tool for the criticism of discourse. Scholars such as Kenneth Burke (whose "Four Master Tropes" derive from Ramus and Vico) or Henry Louis Gates (who proposes "Signification" as the master trope in Afrocentric rhetoric) continue to explore the mind of the speaker revealed through the speaker's rhetoric. Ironically, Burke's essay on the Master Tropes appears in his *Grammar of Motives*, placing criticism and tropes back into the realm of grammar outlined by Donatus. The question of whether this tradition survives the practice of having rhetors merely parrot the words of pollsters and speech writers remains to be resolved.

William M. Purcell
University of Washington
David Snowball
Augustana College

Bibliography

Bevilacqua, Vincent. "Philosophical Influences in the Development of English Rhetorical Theory: 1748 to 1783." *Proceedings of the Leeds Philosophical and Literary Society* 12 (1968): 191–215.

Cmiel, Kenneth. *Democratic Eloquence: The Fight over Popular Speech in Nineteenth-Century America.* New York: Morrow, 1990.

Conley, Thomas M. *Rhetoric in the European Tradition.* New York: Longmans, 1990.

Howell, Wilbur Samuel. *Eighteenth Century British Logic and Rhetoric.* Princeton: Princeton UP, 1971.

———. *Logic and Rhetoric in England, 1500–1700.* Princeton: Princeton UP, 1956.

Jamieson, Kathleen Hall. *Eloquence in an Electronic Age: The Transformation of Political Speechmaking.* New York: Oxford UP, 1988.

Johnson, Nan. *Nineteenth-Century Rhetoric in North America.* Carbondale: Southern Illinois UP, 1991.

Kennedy, George. *The Art of Persuasion in Greece.* Princeton: Princeton UP, 1963.

———. *The Art of Rhetoric in the Roman World, 300 B.C.–A.D. 300.* Princeton: Princeton UP, 1972.

Murphy, James J. *Rhetoric in the Middle Ages: A History of Rhetorical Theory from St. Augustine to the Renaissance.* Berkeley: U of California P, 1974.

See also FIGURATIVE LANGUAGE; FIGURES OF SPEECH; STYLISTICS; TROPES

Stylistics

The study of style, which is the manner of setting forth linguistic expression that distinguishes one person or group from another. "Style" is used to refer to any kind of manner or way of doing something (cooking, painting, designing buildings or clothes), especially something in which an aesthetic component resides, thus specifically a manner of writing.

As a discipline stylistics is not ancient: The word itself is German in origin, and its earliest known uses in English date from c. 1800 and refer only to the attempt on the part of a writer to develop a competent method of self-expression (a good or "correct" rather than an individual style). Until the end of the eighteenth century, individuality of style, though acknowledged and often commented on, was not considered an asset to a writer. Deviation from the standard was called "singularity" and considered either bad manners or akin to madness. During the nineteenth century, however, individuality of all kinds became valued, while at the same time the scientific study of language began. As a result of the confluence of these trends, the moment was appropriate for the study of individual linguistic expression, or style. This interest sometimes took bizarre forms: Vossler tried to link various European languages with what he thought was the national character of their speakers; others attempted to solve the Shakespeare authorship question by counting the number of nouns in his (and Marlowe's and the Earl of Oxford's works) and developing profile or fingerprint curves (Mendenhall), and some examined metaphors to determine the previous work experience of playwrights (Spurgeon).

Methods of studying style are basically of two kinds: impressionistic and quantitative. The impressionistic method (used almost exclusively from the beginning of stylistics well into the present century and probably still by some) proceeds as the observer notes certain characteristics of the text and decides that they have a specific importance, significance, meaning, or the like. For example, critics who described Henry James's prose as convoluted concluded that he had reservations about the phenomena he was narrating. Those commenting on Hemingway's fiction emphasized the shortness of his sentences and his repeated adjectives and related these features to his manly outlook: strong men do not care about style. Similarly, Gibbon's style was considered effete and feeble perhaps because his portraits showed a short and portly gentleman holding a snuffbox. Although these examples may be extreme, they are also typical of impressionistic stylistics. Some impressionistic critics (Leo Spitzer and Michael Riffaterre) have been close observers and their findings have been accepted, but not so much as the result of their methods as of their extensive erudition and their own analytic gifts.

The difficulty residing in impressionistic stylistics is that it frequently involves a prior decision that a subject style is good or bad, interesting or long-winded, casual or scholarly, and leads to searches for evidence in the prose to support the decision, thus turning the scientific method on its head. Standard scientific procedure begins with phenomena, leads to a hypothesis that is tested by experiment and confirmed, modified or abandoned.

In the 1930s Rickert and others began to apply the methods of science to stylistics, and quantitative methods became popular, especially because statisticians found that the distribution of words provided an interesting field to which to apply their new hypotheses (Williams; Yule; Herdan). In an important sense, however, all stylistics is quantitative because any statement about the occurrence of linguistic phenomena, no matter how free of quantification it may appear, is only a disguised statement about frequency. The remark that Hemingway uses short sentences is merely a version of the statement that he uses more short sentences than the norm, or than other writers, or than might be expected, all of which are quantities. So impressionistic critics of style are in the position of making casual quantitative statements without being aware of it and tacitly denying the necessity of precision about quantities. Thus, impressionistic statements about short or long sentences, frequent adjectives and the like are untenable and harbor a claim about the independent value of nonquantitative statements about style.

The quantitative efforts of the statisticians and linguists of the 1930s (based on extensive hand counting) gave way after the end of World War II to computers, which vastly multiplied the possibilities of explicit quantitative stylistics. The linguists who adopted this tool (Booth; Locke) saw its possibilities for machine translation and with the support of federal grants worked actively for several decades in what ultimately became a lost cause. Their work inspired others, however, especially biblical and classical scholars, who applied their new methods in a search for evidence of the authenticity of certain books of the Bible and the sequence and chronology of the works of Plato (Morton).

Literary scholars, traditionally cautious about science and mathematics and devoted to outmoded and comfortable methods—long suspicious about the use of typewriters—eventually joined the many who were discovering the power of computers to perform repetitive tasks at vertiginous speeds, whether these were inventories of hardware parts or instances of function words in poems or plays.

In the late 1960s a series of reference works (called "concordances" and consisting of an alphabetical list of the major vocabulary items together with context and location in the works of an author) for such British literary figures as Matthew Arnold, Blake, Byron, Johnson, and Swift, and such others as Emily Dickinson, Yeats, and *Beowulf,* began to be issued by Cornell University Press under the direction of S.M. Parrish. Earlier concordances to the poetry of Wordsworth, the plays of Shakespeare, and the Bible had required substantial portions of the lifetimes of their compilers. The new computerized concordances required only minutes of computer time after the text had been keyboarded and verified. These new tools were not as carefully devised as the handmade ones—distinctions between homographic parts of speech are usually ignored—but with all their defects they are at least available when scholars need them.

From concordances and bibliographies, it was a short step to the analysis of the texts themselves. Once a text had been keyboarded, it resided on a medium (cards, tape, disk, mainframe memory) and could be processed endlessly without requiring the labor of keyboarding a second time. The archival existence of these texts afforded stylisticians easy access for analysis of poetry and prose of any era. In addition, scanners were developed that could convert printed text to binary codes directly, without keyboarding, a development that seemed ready to further reduce the drudgery of the preliminary work. Although these promised to be extensively labor-saving, they did not actually prove very satisfactory. The scanning devices required that the texts to be read be printed in familiar fonts, crisply and without smudges. Indeed, some scanners could accurately read only texts printed by typewriters using special elements. Also the intervention of a person was often necessary to determine whether errors had taken place when the scanner detected what appeared to be a letter but might simply be a mark of some kind, or when it could not distinguish between similar characters.

After a text has been prepared for processing, the actual study of style proceeds in one of three ways: (1) "manocular," a term that refers to the hand and eye procedure of the scholar; (2) computerized programs; and (3) corpus-based. The actual details of the stylistic procedure depend on the purpose of the analysis, which may be one of the following: (1) description of an individual or group style; (2) determination of authorship (attribution); (3) literary criticism or interpretation; and (4) linguistic or rhetorical inventory. The first or basic purpose of stylistics is the *description* of the style of an individual (sometimes a group). A second purpose is the determination of authorship or *attribution*. A more general use of stylistics is to aid in the *interpretation* of a literary work or of its parts. Finally, stylistics plays a role in compiling an *inventory* of the resources (linguistic or rhetorical) of a language, an author, a work, or a group.

In *describing* the style of an individual author, the stylistician identifies stylistic features by examining either selected works or random samples of them and comparing them with a norm. It is never practical to attempt to make a stylistic study of the entire body of work of an author (or "canon") and uneconomical as well; hence, random samples representing only a fraction of the total are drawn with the help of a random number table to ensure that the bias of the researcher does not enter in. (In a random sample, every unit of the text has an equal chance of being selected.) An alternative method uses "stratified" samples, in which a set number of words, lines, sentences is taken from every page, every tenth page or the like, in order to compile a representative selection from the work or the canon. Tests have shown that stratified samples are slightly more representative than random samples.

The comparison with a norm is a critical aspect of this kind of analysis. Any experienced reader or scholar can detect the peculiarities of a writer's prose simply by noting what appears different from the usual. In a sense, the reader/scholar has an internalized norm. Every writer applies this process to determine whether he or she recalls having written an unfamiliar piece of writing. We recognize our own prose because its features are part of our internal norm. We examine a sentence, for example, extract the content, and match a grammatical representation of that content with the form in which we would state it ourselves. If the match is close, we conclude that it is ours. That is how one realizes that a story by Hemingway is not a translation from a foreign language, or a symphony by Beethoven is not something composed by a Chinese musician. Implicit norms play an important part in our daily use of language.

Norms can also be explicit: Makers of dictionaries and others interested in the quantitative features of language provide us with rank-ordered lists of word frequency (such as the million-word Brown Corpus) against which we can compare the work of any writer. In describing a prose style, the researcher determines what features are of literary or linguistic interest and finds a way of estimating their frequency, which is then compiled into a census of features constituting a profile. If the features are commonplace (sentence-length, word-length, frequency of function words, word-size), they can be compared with existing norms. Otherwise, the stylistician is obligated to devise a norm ad hoc. This would be the case if the features to be examined were semantic, rhetorical, or cognitive in nature, for which there are no or almost no existing norms.

Features of style are, in theory, numberless. But they can be arranged in several categories: *Lexical* features are vocabulary items, words or phrases that occur in a certain often regular frequency in the writings of an author; *Grammatical* features refer to preferences among syntactic alternatives, for example, whether modifiers are adjectival, attributive, phrasal, or clausal; *Rhetorical* features involve the use of figures of speech, such as metaphors or word-order alteration (for example, inversion) and other ways of creating emphasis, sometimes by placement of lexical items. It should be recalled that reference to features of style is always quantitative. And it can be quantitative in more than one way. The function word *the* is the most frequent in any sample of prose in English: therefore it has rank-order one. Its actual frequency may, however, be five or six or seven percent of the total number of words. Rank-order statistics tend to blur quantitative differences. And of course the significance of these quantities can be determined only contextually, usually by means of a norm. Another aspect of lexical frequency has to do with the position of a word in the sentence: *however*, like many sentence adverbials, can occur in a variety of places in a sentence from word-initial to word-final and at the boundary of constructions in between. An inventory of such positional preferences provides more information about individual style than the bare rank or frequency.

If the stylistic purpose of the analysis is the *attribution* of an unknown text or the authentication of a text of doubtful authorship, the process is essentially similar to description. The main difference concerns the features of interest. A stylistician describing a text is interested in the features that characterize the individual author and that may be interpreted in terms of personality or literary significance, whereas another interested in attribution will concentrate on those features that are most likely to differentiate one author from another. These are not necessarily different, but they may be affected by genre or context.

For example, the description of the style of an author must take into account what is present in all the writings of that author, the irreducible minimum of style. Thus, Jonathan Swift is known to use some function words (for example, connectives) in initial position in nearly all his writings, so this feature could be used both to characterize him and to help detect his hand in unknown texts. Initial connectives, however, tend to occur more often in argumentative or persuasive genres than in expository or expressive or others, and this feature might not therefore be conclusive in attribution determination for all writers. Such features as sentence-length and word-length are extremely genre-sensitive and are not always considered reliable for attribution. Because some writers are partial to certain letters or combinations of letters, a knowledge of these peculiarities could be of great usefulness in attribution but would have only a very limited function in characterization.

Early in the twentieth century, stylistics was perceived as an instrument for the *interpretation* of literature. That is, by studying the linguistic patterns of Henry James or Flaubert, one might be able better to understand either the intentions of the authors or the meanings of the text. Much of this kind of stylistics was based on impressionism rather than on rigorous quantification: The stylistician read the text, made some observations about the regularities to be found in it, and then interpreted these according to his own intuition. Spitzer, the foremost name in this kind of analysis, specifically discounted attempts at analysis that did not proceed from this starting point, rejecting any that employed what he called "ready-made categories." He believed, for example, that Diderot's interrupted sentences revealed the author's sexual preoccupations, and that the play with words in the writings of Rabelais, displaying great linguistic instability, reflected his political attitudes, which were irreverent and subversive. The subjectivity of such a procedure is self-evident. Nonetheless, it can play a valid role in certain kinds of investigation. A careful analysis of the speeches of each character in a play can reveal that the author attempted to provide "signature" stylistic features to each in an effort to give the character recognizable language. In addition, such an investigation provides valuable insight into the playwright's notions of language and the relation between language and personality.

For the attribution of an unidentified work to its author, reliable identification and descriptions of potential authors are necessary. It is seldom the case that an unidentified work is without a possible author, except in the case of ancient and medieval works, none of whose possible authors are known because the literary context of the period is full of gaps (for example, *Beowulf,* the riddles, mystery plays). In works of the Renaissance or later, a possible author can always be hypothesized, except of course that anything written in the second half of the sixteenth century will first of all be ascribed to Shakespeare!

Of the well-known attribution cases, those of the Junius Letters and the Federalist Papers may serve as illustrative. The letters of Junius attacked the government of the king and the king himself (George III) during the period 1769 to 1771. Although many could have written them, they contained information known mainly to members of Parliament, which reduced the number of possible authors to several hundred; a few well-known political figures who disagreed with the ministry were most often considered likely. Ellegard examined the text of the letters and chose to do a lexical analysis, identifying the words and phrases that "Junius" repeated often. He then compiled a large norm of political writings of the period and developed a list of Junius's "plus terms" and "minus terms" and compared them with the norm, thus achieving a distinctiveness ratio, positive or negative, for each word or phrase. He then selected a dozen or so possible competing authors and did the same for them. The one who matched the letters the best was Sir Philip Francis, and Ellegard therefore identified him as the probable author. Attribution by statistical means cannot of course be used to prove that a particular person was the *actual* author, but it can effectively indicate that one or more are *unlikely* to have been. Paternity by means of blood typing is a parallel case.

The Federalist Papers were, it is known, written by Hamilton and Madison, but the question that long troubled scholars concerned which disputed papers were written by which man, most having been identified by external evidence. The solution proposed by two statisticians eager to test the usefulness of the Bayes theorem in such problems involved testing the frequency of certain function words, in part because they occur frequently and in part because they offer the opportunity for personal preference, there being numerous alternative choices, evidenced in such pairs as *on* and *upon, for* and *because, though* and *although.* On the basis of this complex study, Mosteller and Wallace concluded that Madison had written all the disputed papers. Unfortunately, their lack of acquaintance with the literature of the period led them to ignore the possibility that Madison probably edited the disputed papers (which might have been written by Hamilton) and changed the target words according to his own preference.

Attribution problems in such authors as Chaucer illustrate the difficulty of identification before books were printed, when scribes and copyists had considerable latitude in their reproduction of the works that they were responsible for copying. Thus the "final" form of a work could not be safely considered to be what the author had originally written, and even the most definitely authenticated works left room for uncertainty. The nearer we approach our own time, the more likely it is that an attribution problem can be solved. But now that records are kept of every transaction and books must be copyrighted by a government office, it is extremely unlikely that any significant attribution problems will surface or will require the assistance of stylistic analysis.

In considering the contribution of stylistics to the *interpretation* of a literary work, it is necessary to settle first what "interpretation" means and what it is. In the simplest sense, the term implies that a work means something other than it appears to be. Thus Hemingway's *Old Man and the Sea,* which narrates the pursuit, capture, and eventual loss of a large fish in the Caribbean, is interpreted as meaning something other than this simple transaction, something like the necessity of showing courage in defeat, for example. Although this conclusion can be reached without the intervention of stylistics, it is made more probable by a study of the vocabulary, in which such words as *unintelligent, kindness, virtue, respected, happy,* and *good* appear often, more often perhaps than in an account of an ordinary fishing expedition.

Similarly, Gibbon's manner has excited much comment of various kinds as a result of the feelings of the commentators about his criticism of religion and his ironic approach to that criticism. So his style has often been called "ponderous," or "formal," terms that have no specificity in describing style. If a syntactic inventory of Gibbon's prose is taken, one will find extensive nominalization (the preference for nouns over verbs), which is associated with formal documents and statements made on formal occasions, and a considerable use of certain figures of speech, such as periodic sentences and zeugma. Such a census, which would yield a quantitative formulary of these preferences, can lead to a better appreciation both of the text and of the effect of its features on the reader.

For any of these conclusions to be valid, a kind of linguistic or rhetorical *inventory* must have taken place. Obviously, the state of the art is not adequate for a complete inventory of any part of the literary language. Even the lexical aspect, which has attracted the most attention, is only partially understood. For example, although there are million-word corpora (the Brown Corpus, the Lancaster-Oslo-Bergen Corpus), and other larger ones on the horizon, it is not known how large a text mass would be necessary to contain any specific proportion of the lemmas (stems of words) in the language, without even taking into account the steady and constant increase in the vocabulary of the living language. It is clear that a million-word corpus, containing some fifty thousand types (fewer lemmas, of course), would not even include all the words in a collegiate dictionary, to say nothing of an unabridged dictionary (approximately 500,000).

An inventory of the syntactical possibilities of English has been done only sporadically, as a special problem may have interested a particular researcher—for example, "On the cleft and pseudo-cleft construction in English," in a journal devoted to corpus linguistics. Corpora are now becoming the major resource for the study of the details of the language, as they provide text masses whose contents have been examined closely and evaluated and which can serve as data bases for any further investigation and the provision of norms for stylistics. Nonetheless, it should not be supposed that there is an inevitable link between stylistics and literary criticism, though the former was at one time considered a topic under the latter.

The interpretation of literature is a field that has been treated to a variety of theoretical fashions. At one time, it was considered appropriate to see genres as organisms with a life of their own, subject to Darwinian evolution. At another time, context was considered irrelevant and only the text itself was the source of information about the author's meaning or intention (New Criticism). To make investigation more complex, the author's intention was declared unknowable and therefore dropped from the vocabulary of literary criticism. And more recently the existence of the author has been brought into doubt by the practitioners of deconstruction. Society, according to Derridean theory, is the agent, the speaker, of any literary work, which is therefore not the work of any author. The language, it is said by those theorists, "speaks the author." It is therefore useless to attempt to find individuality of authorship in any text. If that is so, society not literature, and especially not literary works, ought to be the field of study for literary critics and stylisticians.

This intriguing theory, which requires students of literature to become social critics and undermines the essential linguistic nature of literary work, has been found seductive by a good many whose interest in historical, rhetorical, and philological matters was inadequate or inactive. Ideology about gender, sexuality, and oppression has affected a great deal of what some considered to be included under stylistics, but which is primarily social theory. Narratology, the study of the trajectory of plot in fiction, narrative poetry, and film, and reader-response theory in which the impact of the elements of the text on the reader, who reorganizes it during each reading, have become active fields for speculation. Nonetheless, these developments, though they are theoretically of interest, do not really fit into any definition of stylistics that is based on the individual use of language. Theories of literature that ignore the individual writer may be plausible and intellectually stimulating, but they are primarily speculative exercises, just like the Berkeleyan view that all sense data are subject to interpretation and must be distrusted. They are more attractive than plausible and plainly contradicted by the experience of mankind. We know that there are authors and we can recognize their work, when it is mature and original. Without doubt authors are influenced by society but in as many different ways as there are human beings. Society, if it speaks through authors, has many different colors and views. Hence Derrida's theory must be considered a mere episode in a continuing struggle to understand the remarkable phenom-

enon we call literature. Despite the arguments of those who wonder whether style exists and those who therefore have no room in their view of scholarship for stylistics, it has a clearly defined role and existence. It is a little like the bumblebee, which, according to some aerodynamic engineers, lacks sufficient wing surface to fly but seems unaware of this failing.

Stylistics is the field of study, based on quantitative linguistics, that can specify the particular resources of the language peculiar to a particular author or group of authors, which give their literary works their characteristic nature, and can help to decode the linguistic, semantic, rhetorical meaning of those works. Despite the flux of argument, this interest has not flagged in the centuries since Aristotle. With the new tools at the stylisticians' command, it can be expected that progress in this field will yield valuable results for the understanding of the practical use of language.

Louis T. Milic
Cleveland State University

Bibliography

Butler, Christopher S., ed. *Computers and Written Texts*. Cambridge: Blackwell, 1992.

Ellegard, Alvar. *A Statistical Method for Determining Authorship: The Junius Letters, 1769–1772*. Goteborg: Acta Universitatis Gothoburgensis, 1962.

Herdan, Gustav. *Language as Choice and Chance*. Groningen: Noordhoff, 1956.

Johannson, Stig, and Anna-Brita Stenstrom, eds. *English Computer Corpora: Selected Papers and Research Guide*. Berlin: Mouton de Gruyter, 1991.

Kucera, Henry, and W. Nelson Francis. *Computational Analysis of Present-Day American English*. Providence, RI: Brown U, 1967.

Ledger, G.R. *Re-Counting Plato*. Oxford: Clarendon, 1989.

Leed, Jacob, ed. *The Computer and Literary Style*. Kent, OH: Kent State UP, 1966.

Leitner, Gerhard, ed. *New Directions in English Language Corpora: Methodology, Results, Software Developments*. Berlin: Mouton de Gruyter, 1992.

Locke, William N., and A.D. Booth. *Machine Translation of Languages*. Cambridge, MA: MIT P, 1957.

Mendenhall, T.C. "The Characteristic Curves of Composition." *Science* 9 (1887): 237–49.

Milic, Louis T. *Style and Stylistics: An Analytical Bibliography.* New York: Free, 1967.

Mosteller, Frederick, and David L. Wallace. *Inference and Disputed Authorship: "The Federalist."* Reading, PA: Addison, 1964.

Rickert, Edith. *New Methods for the Study of Literature.* Chicago: U of Chicago P, 1927.

Riffaterre, Michael. *Essais de stylistique structurale.* Paris: Flammarion, 1971.

Spitzer, Leo. *Linguistics and Literary History.* Princeton: Princeton UP, 1948.

Spurgeon, Caroline. *Shakespeare's Imagery.* Cambridge: Cambridge UP, 1935.

Vossler, Karl. *The Spirit of Language in Civilization.* Trans. Oscar Oeser. London: Kegan Paul, 1951.

Williams, C.B. *Style and Vocabulary.* London: Griffin, 1970.

Yule, G. Udny. *The Statistical Study of Literary Vocabulary.* Cambridge: Cambridge UP, 1944.

Suetonius (Gaius Suetonius Tranquillus) (c. 69–c. 140 C.E.)

Roman antiquarian, biographer, and historian of grammar and rhetoric. Suetonius is most famous for his accounts of prominent Romans, including *The Lives of Illustrious Men* and *The Lives of the Caesars.* Suetonius was educated in the Roman schools of declamation and became a teacher of rhetoric. Emperors Trajan and Hadrian provided Suetonius with secretarial appointments that provided the opportunity to research the history of Roman rhetoric. Among his archival efforts, Suetonius wrote *De grammaticis et rhetoribus,* an account of early schools of declamation in Rome. Of particular importance in this work is Suetonius' meticulous chronicling of the two occasions when the teaching of rhetoric was outlawed in Rome. This fragmented work was known through the second century C.E. but lost until its rediscovery in the mid fifteenth century.

Richard Leo Enos
Texas Christian University

Bibliography

Enos, Richard Leo. "When Rhetoric Was Outlawed in Rome: A Translation and Commentary of Suetonius's Treatise on Early Roman Rhetoricians." *Speech Monographs* [now *Communication Monographs*] 39 (1972): 37–45.

Suetonius. Trans. J.C. Rolfe. 2 vols. Loeb Classical Library. Cambridge, MA: Harvard UP, 1970.

Syllepsis

Use of a single word in both its literal and figurative senses. The syllepsis is often formed out of a zeugma (q.v.): Sallust's phrase "Waging war and peace," like Puttenham's "My Ladie laughs for joy, and I for wo," are at once zeugmas and syllepses. La Rochfoucauld's insight that "Neither the sun nor death can be regarded steadily" is another syllepsis that is also a zeugma. Although most syllepses are zeugmas and while the most striking zeugmas are syllepses, rhetoricians continue to distinguish these figures. While not necessarily a zeugma, the syllepsis always plays on the different connotations of a word understood differently in relation to the words that it modifies or governs. The advertising slogan "Toshiba: We mean business" is a syllepsis that is not a zeugma, as is the sylleptic simile "Bad prose, like cholera, is a communicable disease."

Arthur Quinn and Lyon Rathbun
University of California, Berkeley

Syllogism

A form of deductive argument; also the intellective strategy of legal analogy. Aristotle offered the first technical definition of syllogism in his *Prior Analytics*: "an argument in which certain things having been assumed, something different from the assumptions follows by necessity on account of these things being as they are." For Aristotle, the assumptions in a syllogism are premises, each comprising subject and predicate terms. Accordingly, within Aristotle's paradigm of the syllogism, two premises share one term, such that their conjunction leads to the conclusion, which draws its subject term from one premise and its predicate term from the other. For example, if all A are B, and all B are C, then all A are C (*Prior Analytics* 1.4, 7, 25). Aristotle divided syllogisms into the demonstrative (philosopheme), dialectical (epichireme), and rhetorical (enthymeme), insisting that all were governed by the same general principles (*Prior Analytics* 2.23). Conceiving enthymemes as persuasive, Aristotle devoted much of his *Rhetorical Art* to explication of their contents, signs, and probabilities, as well as their forms, special and general topics.

During Hellenistic times, syllogism remained the focus of rhetorical argument theory, although rhetoricians of the period apparently found the enthymeme less attractive than the epichireme (Cicero, *De inventione* 1.34; *Rhetorica ad Herennium* 2.18). Also in this period, Hermagoras added a new sense of syllogism to rhetorical theory—namely, the legal question or disputable issue concerning application of a law to circumstances uncontemplated in the law.

Within the imperial period, enthymeme and epichireme were frequently distinguished as shorter and longer versions of the syllogism; this crystallization of argument forms encouraged theoretical treatment of multiple forms in individual rhetorics (Quintilian, *Institutio oratoria* 5.14; Fortunatianus, *Artis rhetoricae* 2.28–29). Concurrent development of syllogism as legal question included a sharpening of its definition to emphasize the relation between written and unwritten law (Hermogenes, *De statibus* 2.14; Fortunatianus, *Artis rhetoricae* 1.25).

Interest in syllogism as argument and legal question persisted subsequent to the classical era. Both senses of syllogism are significant in Byzantine commentaries and early medieval rhetorical theories (Stephenus, *In artem rhetoricam Aristotelis* 1.9; Maximus Planudes, *Scholia ad Hermogenis status* 2.14; Aurelius Augustine, *De rhetorica* 11; Martianus Capella, *De nuptiis Philologiae et Mercurii* 5.16). So too, in late medieval rhetoric, argumentative forms of syllogism appear in preaching theory as modes of elaborating sermon themes ([Pseudo]-Bonaventure, *Ars concionandi* 3.37; Robert of Basevorn, *Forma praedicandi* 31). During the Renaissance, rhetoricians in the humanist tradition revitalized the forms of syllogism for argumentative purposes, frequently with recourse to the principles of logic (Trapezuntius, *Rhetoricorum libri* V 3; Cox, *Art or crafte of Rhetoryke* fol. B1r). The relation between logic and rhetoric was adjudicated somewhat differently in revisionist theories of discourse; these insisted upon syllogism as an instrument of argument but separated invention of arguments from rhetoric (Ramus, *Dialecticae libri duo* 1.1, 2.3; Bacon, *Advancement of Learning* 2). In modern times, syllogistic argument was criticized as useless by rhetorical theorists influenced by empiricism and faculty psychology (Locke, *Human Understanding* 4.17.6; Campbell, *Philosophy of Rhetoric* 1.6). Still, syllogism maintained importance in certain modern theories (Lawson, *Lectures concerning Oratory* 8; Whately, *Elements of Rhetoric* 1.2.1). Twentieth-century rhetoric has been informed by attacks on the syllogism as ambiguous and overly restrictive (Toulmin, *Uses of Argument* 3; Perelman, *Nouvelle Rhétorique* Introduction).

Robert N. Gaines
University of Maryland

Bibliography

Howell, Wilbur S. *Eighteenth Century British Logic and Rhetoric.* Princeton: Princeton UP, 1971.

———. *Logic and Rhetoric in England, 1500–1700.* Princeton: Princeton UP, 1956.

Marciszewski, Witold. *Logic from a Rhetorical Point of View.* Berlin: Walter de Gruyter, 1994.

Murphy, James J. *Rhetoric in the Middle Ages.* Berkeley: U of California P, 1974.

Volkmann, Richard. *Die Rhetorik der Griecher und Römer in systematischer Übersicht.* 2nd ed. Stuttgart: B.G. Teubner, 1885.

Symbolic Action

A concept that pervades the humanities and the social and behavioral sciences; refers to the multiple levels of meaning involved in human activity. Kenneth Burke sees essence of humanness in the creation, use, and abuse of symbols through which human sensory perceptions and knowledge are stabilized. Symbols, then, are the means through which human interaction, identification, and shared meaning are attempted, and, at whatever level is possible, achieved.

Rhetorical behavior is grounded in the fundamental conceptualization that humans are symbol-makers, symbol users, and symbol abusers. Symbols are structured through an abstractive process involving selection, choice, and purpose. The act of creating and using symbols is motivated by the fact that individual human beings are unique—each is divided from every other—and the concomitant fact that humans perceive the need to identify with and to influence each other. Symbol systems (languages) are created to interpret human actions, both physical and mental. The symbolic system engages the motives or purposes that distinguish human action from simple animal motion. Language used to influence or persuade others exerts influence also on the user—the self.

The concept of *action* includes the aspects of conflict, purpose, reflection, and choice. It is intrinsically dramatic, as well as rhetorical. As symbols describe, induce, or explain action, they shape the perceptions of the actor, and those who witness the act, as it is performed, or through symbolic re-creation of past events or precreation of a future. Symbols manifest aspects of the agent, the agency or means, and the scene or situation, as well as the act itself and its purpose.

Ambiguity, deceit, and negation are inherent and essential qualities of any symbolic or linguistic system—thus, of symbolic or linguistic action. These qualities are sometimes, though not by any means always, minimized, avoided, or devalued. At other important times, they provide opportunities for learning or making new associations, abstractions, classifications, or hierarchic orderings. These mental symbolic actions, in turn, can give rise to physical or linguistic symbolic actions that also induce or influence perceptions.

Symbolic action is a concept adapted and adopted in social and behavioral sciences, as well as by literary and rhetorical scholars. In particular, political scientists, sociologists, cultural psychologists, and philosophers employ the analytic perspectives and the language of dramatism in order to perceive, process, and express their understandings of the complexities of human behavior.

Symbolic action extends beyond the idea that symbols are simply denotative and connotative. Humans depend on symbols, rituals, and myths to formulate their experiences, and to frame events or situations. Symbols create or construct meanings. Meanings, in turn, generate the action chosen as a strategic response. As situations recur, and individuals come to share meanings and the symbols of those meanings, societies or cultures develop by means of those collective symbols.

Symbolic action provides the ground for critical analysis and interpretation of the literature, the myths, the rhetoric, and the institutions and interactions of human societies and cultures.

H.L. Ewbank
University of Arizona

Bibliography

Boesch, Ernest E. *Symbolic Action Theory and Cultural Psychology*. Berlin: Springer-Verlag, 1991.

Burke, Kenneth. *A Grammar of Motives*. New York: Prentice, 1945.

———. *Language as Symbolic Action: Essays on Life, Literature and Method*. Berkeley: U of California P, 1966.

———. *A Rhetoric of Motives*. New York: Prentice, 1950.

Duncan, Hugh Dalziel. *Symbols in Society*. New York: Oxford UP, 1968.

Edelman, Murray. *Politics as Symbolic Action: Mass Arousal and Quiescence*. Chicago: Markham, 1971.

———*The Symbolic Uses of Politics*. Urbana: U of Illinois P, 1964.

Gregg, Richard B. *Symbolic Inducement and Knowing: A Study in the Foundations of Rhetoric*. Columbia: U of South Carolina P, 1984.

Gusfield, Joseph R., ed. *Kenneth Burke on Symbols and Society*. Chicago: U of Chicago P, 1989.

Langer, Susanne. *Philosophy in a New Key*. New York: New American Library, 1958.

Mead, George Herbert. *The Philosophy of the Act*. Chicago: U of Chicago P, 1938.

See also Burke, Kenneth; Dramatism

Symploce

"Intertwining"; the repetition of one word or phrase from the beginning of successive clauses, sentences, or passages at their end. Paul was using symploce in writing "Are they Hebrews? So am I. Are they Israelites? So am I. Are they of the seed of Abraham? So am I" (Second Letter to the Corinthians 11:22). Symploce can add a sense of measured balance to the rhetorical effects achieved through either anaphora (q.v.) or epiphora (q.v.). Paul demonstrates this in "Are they Hebrews? So am I. Are they Israelites? So am I. Are they of the seed of Abraham? So am I." Symploce can also string together clauses to create either a catalogue (q.v.) or gradatio (q.v.): "For want of a nail, the shoe was lost / For want of a shoe, the horse was lost / For want of a horse, the rider was lost / For want of a rider, the battle was lost / For want of a battle, the kingdom was lost."

Arthur Quinn and Lyon Rathbun
University of California, Berkeley

Synecdoche

From the Greek "act of taking together," a figure of substitution taking two inverse forms: substituting the part for the whole or the whole for the part. For example, in the phrase "we don't own *wheels*," a significant part (wheels) represents the whole (a car). In the headline "*America's* Collapsing and Buckling," the whole (America) substitutes for its troubled parts, collapsing bridges and buckling highways.

The eighteenth-century philosopher and rhetorician Giambattista Vico was the first to identify synecdoche, metaphor, metonymy, and irony as four fundamental "modes of expression" (409). Ancient rhetoricians, who had considered these figures merely "ingenious inventions of writers," failed to clarify the distinction between synecdoche and the related figure of substitution, metonymy. Consequently, theorists have long held conflicting views on these two major *tropes:* Kenneth Burke considered synecdoche the basic figure of speech and metonymy merely "a special application of synecdoche" (1969:509); Roman Jakobson argued that metonymy subsumed synecdoche (Lodge 75); contemporary theorists Lakoff and Johnson, following Jakobson, classify synecdoche as "a special case of metonymy" (36).

Without regard to the hierarchy of the two tropes, the classical rhetorician Du Marsais (87) drew a clear distinction between them: In a synecdoche, the substituted part always forms a whole with the subject it represents, as in "many *hands* [people] make light work." In a metonymy, however, the substituted image remains independent of the subject it represents, as in "the *pen* [literature] is mightier than the *sword* [warfare]." Applying Du Marsais's criterion helps to tease apart the two tropes in two proverbs. In "The *hand* that rocks the *cradle* rules the world," a synecdoche represents the whole person by the substitution of an integral part (hand) and a metonymy represents *baby* by the substitution of a symbol (cradle). In "His *bark* is worse than his *bite*," bark and bite function as metonymic metaphors for a human's loud words (bark) and cruel actions (bite). These proverbs also serve to illustrate Burke's observation that metonymy "ovelaps" both synecdoche and metaphor (1969:507).

The following types of synecdochic substitutions fulfill Du Marsais's criterion of forming an internal relationship with the replaced subject: particular for general, species for genus, product for producer, trade name for general product, raw material for finished product, general for particular, genus for species, and place for one-time event. The substitutions of cause for effect and container for contained, however, though cited by some contemporary theorists as synecdoches, do not form a whole with the replaced part, and thus are more properly considered metonymies.

Because synecdoche functions mainly to compress, newscasters and headline writers readily employ the figure: "New *Blood* [people] in Congress Inspires Hope" (part for whole); "*Argentina* and *Banks* [administrators of] Sign Pact" (whole for part); "When *Trucks* and *Trains* [management of their companies] Unite" (product for producer); "The Twenty-Fifth Anniversary of *Woodstock* [concert that took place there]" (place for one-time event). Advertisers find synecdoche effective in the substitution of raw material for finished product: "Where the *rubber* [tire] meets the road." Medical practitioners draw on synecdoche's part for the whole in such phrases as "There's a *compound fracture* in the emergency room and a *heart attack* in Room 4." Synecdoche helps songwriters create memorable lines by substituting species for genus, as in "diamond bracelets *Woolworth* [a dime store] doesn't sell, baby" (Fields).

Applying Vico's dictum that a major trope subsumes all lesser related figures (409), the following qualify as synecdochic subtypes: *abbreviatio* (L. "shortening"), any common form of abbreviation such as *NY* for *New York* and *M.D.* for *medical doctor; curtatio* (L. "shortened"), a shortening of words such as *celeb*(rity) or *sten*(ography); *aphaeresis* (Gr. "taking away"), the elimination of the initial letter or syllable of a word, *'em* for *them* and *phone* for *telephone; syncope* (Gr. "cutting"), an elision within a word, *o'er* for *over* and *s'pose* for *suppose; apocope* (Gr. "cutting off"), a clipping of the final sound in a word, as *ope'* for *open* and *runnin'* for *running; synaloepha* (Gr. "melting together"), a contracting of two words into one: *we're* for *we are* and *wannabes* for those who *want to be; prosonomasia* (Gr. "naming"), a readily identifiable nickname, such as "I like *Ike* (Dwight Eisenhower)"; *acronym* (Gr. "outer end" plus "word"), a pronounceable form made by linking initial letters in a verbal string, such as *AIDS* for *acquired immune deficiency syndrome; partitio* (L. "dividing"), a replacing of the subject meant with a list of its parts—for example, a health club ad eschewed the word *exercise* in favor of the invitation to "swim, stretch, lift, run, row, step, cycle, sit-up, push-up, pump, jump, serve."

Empirical evidence from split-brain language studies with aphasic patients lends support to the hypothesis that synecdoche and metaphor function as two opposing modes of thought (Davis). Synecdoche, in reducing the whole to an integral part, contracts meaning; metaphor, in comparing two disparate realms and thus creating a new semantic concept, expands meaning. The right (figurative) hemisphere processes information in a holistic manner and is dominant for the interpretation of metaphor; the left (literal) hemisphere excels in internal details and breaking the whole into parts (Burns et al.), constituents of synecdochic thought. Similarly, metonymy and irony function as opposing processes: metonymy, in replacing an abstraction with a congruent image, solidifies meaning; irony, in juxtaposing incongruities within a context, dissolves meaning. We may thus visualize the "four master tropes" (Burke 1969:503) as a cross of two pairs of polar-opposite conceptual systems mediated by the split brain—the horizontal axis composed of synecdoche in the left hemisphere and metaphor in the right, and a vertical pole with irony at the top of the cerebral cortex and metonymy at the bottom, "overlapping" synecdoche and metaphor. Brain-research findings bearing on this model indicate that the transfer of visual images, essential to metonymy's symbolizing process, occurs in the occipital (rear) region of the cerebral cortex (Springer), and abstract thinking, a component of irony, takes place in the frontal lobes (Gershon). This plausible hypothesis of a fundamental synecdoche-metaphor, irony-metonymy polarity invites further interdisciplinary investigation. As linguist Linda Waugh has noted regarding the blurred distinction among the tropes, "[M]uch more work needs to be done for a thorough structural reanalysis of those figures" (163).

Sheila Davis
New School for Social Research, New York

Bibliography

Burke, Kenneth. *A Grammar of Motives.* Berkeley: U of California P, 1969. 503–17.

———. *The Philosophy of Literary Form.* Chicago: U of Chicago P, 1973.

Burns, Martha S., Anita S. Halper, Shelley I. Mogil. *Clinical Management of Right Hemisphere Dysfunction.* Rockland, MD: Aspen, 1985. 1–38.

Davis, Sheila. *The Neurology of Psychological Type and Language Style.* New York: Solar Systems, 1993. 7–38.

———. *The Songwriters Idea Book*. Cincinnati, OH: Writer's Digest, 1992.

Du Marsais, Cesar Chesneau. *Des Tropes ou des diferens sens dans lesquels on peut prendre un meme mot dans une meme langue.* Paris: Chez la Veuve de Jean-Batiste Brocas, 1830 ed. 87.

Gershon, Elliot S., and Ronald O. Rieder. "Major Disorders of Mind and Brain." *Scientific American.* September 1992: 129.

Group u: J. Dubois, F. Edeline, J.-M. Klinkenberg, F.P. Minguet, H. Trinon. *A General Rhetoric.* Trans. P. Burrell and E. Slotkin. Baltimore: Johns Hopkins UP, 1981.

Lakoff, George, and Mark Johnson. *Metaphors We Live By.* Chicago: U of Chicago P, 1980. 36.

Levin, Samuel R. *Metaphoric Worlds.* New Haven: Yale UP, 1988.

Lodge, David. *The Modes of Modern Writing.* Chicago: U of Chicago P, 1988. 73–81.

Springer, Sally P., and Georg Deutsch. *Left Brain, Right Brain.* New York: Freeman, 1989. 53.

Vico, Giambattista. *The New Science of Giambattista Vico.* Trans. Thomas Goddard Bergin and Max Harold Fisch. Ithaca, NY: Cornell UP, 1991. 406–9.

Waugh, Linda. "The Poetic Function and the Nature of Language." *Roman Jakobson: Verbal Art, Verbal Sign, Verbal Time.* Ed. Krystyna Pomorska and Stephen Rudy. Minneapolis: U of Minnesota P, 1985. 143–68.

See also FIGURATIVE LANGUAGE; FIGURES OF SPEECH; METAPHOR; TROPES

Tagmemics

A modern theory of linguistics and, derivatively, of rhetoric, originated by Kenneth L. Pike, that has influenced language study through its advocacy of multiperspectival approaches to language inquiry. The term *tagmemics* denotes a set of theoretical and practical insights into textuality and human language behavior derived primarily from the research of linguist Kenneth L. Pike. Pike began his career as a virtually self-taught translator among the Mixtec of Mexico and was eventually more formally educated as a linguist under the tutelage of Edward Sapir at the University of Michigan. His earliest publications, c. 1937–1942, focused on phonetics, as Pike attempted to assist linguists and translators facing the bewildering task of understanding and describing languages in primary oral cultures that lacked an alphabet or codified grammar. He concluded that this endeavor was not well assisted by existing structuralist and behaviorist models of language, given their limiting conceptual vocabulary, notation system, and field methods. Consequently, Pike and other early tagmemicists such as Robert E. Longacre addressed these concerns with an aggressive and innovative inquiry into the social foundations of the phonology, morphology, syntactics, and ethno-epistemology of the peoples among whom his translator teams were living.

How, Pike asked, might language researchers discern and articulate dimensions of human language use that are deeply embedded in culture and not apparent in the surface language behavior of indigenous language users? How do concepts of "sameness" and "difference" operate, not only in the sound and syntactic systems of languages under study but also in larger units of discourse and beyond, into the very fabric of human relationships and behavior between and among various individuals, groups, and tribes?

Pike's incisive responses to these questions comprise his major contribution to twentieth-century linguistics and rhetorical theory and are epitomized in his conceptualization of the tagmeme, a neologism for "unit in context," and the foundation for Pike's own linguistic theory, which he labeled *tagmemics* in reference to this term. The *tagmeme* denotes any unit or "chunk" of language or language behavior that can be identified, classified, differentiated, and employed, in itself, in a system, or as a system within a particular universe of discourse or cultural context. That is to say, a tagmeme might be a sound, a word, a sentence, a chapter in a book, a speaker, a writer, a reader, a tradition—any recognizable unit or feature of a unit that has distinguishable functions and effects in a particular language situation. The linguist's—and the rhetorician's—task is inevitably to locate an appropriate "tagmeme" with which to enter a language field and to begin fruitful inquiry into solving a language issue or problem.

A rhetoric founded upon tagmemic premises is thus preeminently a "social rhetoric," for at the heart of Pike's tagmemic rhetoric is an anthropology that refuses to treat language apart from the human beings as persons who use it, hence the title of Pike's magnum opus, *Language in Relation to a Unified Theory of the Structure of Human Behavior* (1967). Pike believed that traditional linguistics had always been too preoccupied either with micro-level etymological issues (for example, philology), or, after Noam Chomksy, sentence-level operations—thereby excluding necessary context-based analysis. In contrast, Pike's tagmemics insists upon understanding human language use as a defining feature of human rationality, apart from which neither language nor humanity can be understood. Within tagmemics, reality is conceived as a multifaceted entity that, while it exists independently of the observer, is nevertheless in some sense constructed by an individual observer through discourse—both public and private. Because people's vision is always partial and finite, tagmemic rhetoric posits, the use of language is always approximate, never fully apprehensive of the reality it seeks to name. Therefore, from the viewpoint of tagmemic rhetoric, meaning is not an independent given whose import and intent is self-evident in an utterance or text but something that each individual, already embedded in a particular social context, must play a part in negotiating within this community or universe of discourse.

For the tagmemic rhetorician, translation is not a unique or specialized activity only for "missionary linguists" but is the prototype of all human communication. All people who attempt to communicate do so by articulating their private worlds in a public language that is constrained by the shared experiences and lexicon of the hearers. Tagmemics also asserts that its axioms hold for all human behavior and not just for language use; there are "tagmemes" of behavior just as there are of text structure. For Pike and other tagmemicists, this means that rhetorical models of communication must refrain from abstracting both discourse and language users themselves from the textual, cultural, and social context in which they are situated. Therefore, no purely mechanical or "autonomous" model of language as a "system" can ever successfully account for meaning or purpose in the human use of language.

Innumerable theoretical insights and practical discovery tools for the field of rhetoric have thus been derived from Pike's original and evolving inquiry. Among them is the tagmemic axiom that language users view the world in repeatable units, experiencing the world as particles (discrete bits), waves (merging of units and overlapping borders that change over time), or fields (as points in a set of relationships). From Pike's point of view, each of these perspectives may, and in fact must, come into play in understanding the nature of phenomena; they are indigenous to rationality and are not to be understood as mutually exclusive vantage points.

Tagmemically, human communication problems may be classified partly according to the tendency of language users to view the world through monolithic perspectives. An exclusively particle view of the world may yield nothing but discreteness—that is, unconnected, decontextualized, randomized bits of experience; an exclusively wave view may yield nothing but unstable, ever-shifting strings and combinations of experience that elude articulation. An exclusively field perspective may yield nothing but a universe of relations that comprise no substantive, tangible entities that bear discernible features of their own. Inquirers, observers, or writers, assisted by tagmemic theory, are asked to employ such multiperspectival viewpoints to solve misunderstandings, bridge gaps in knowledge, or untangle unnecessary ambiguities in discourse so that an exchange of information can occur and meaningful change may be voluntarily considered or achieved.

Tagmemicists often use a game, and quite often the sport of baseball, to illustrate such principles and postulates. In attending a baseball game, for instance, a spectator can adopt a particle, wave, or field view of the events and participants. A particle view, for instance, might focus on the individual acts within the horizon of the stadium: a throw to first base, the pitcher picking up the rosin bag, an outfielder putting on his sunglasses, a vendor tossing a bag of peanuts—oblivious to any continuous action or the larger frame that these individual deeds might play in the game as a whole. A wave view might focus on the flight of a baseball driven over the fence for a home run, the subsequent scramble to retrieve the ball by fans, and the eventual pride of a father and son who return home to show off the ball to neighbor friends—a focus on continuous action and change—again oblivious in some sense to individual components or larger frameworks beyond the changes that occurred as a result of the flight of that particular ball. The field view might focus on the relationships that prevail on a team of nine players, each of whom has his own special prowess, defensive strength, or offensive role; one notes how in the late innings the weak-hitting shortstop uses his turn at bat to sacrifice a runner over to second so the line-drive hitting right-fielder has a better chance to get an RBI so the home team can get an insurance run.

In each case, the perspective employed does not so much exclude or falsify another as subsume it and make the observer temporarily oblivious to other kinds of information that might be received and processed. But the game of baseball is not merely the sum of its parts, and its "meaning" is dependent not only upon what actually occurs on the field but also upon that which the observer has brought to the game. Here tagmemics enlists the help of Pike's concepts "etic" and "emic" (derived from "phonetic" and "phonemic") to distinguish what he calls the "outsider's view" from the "insider's view." To the novice baseball fan—that is, the etic observer—much of what occurs on the field goes unnoticed. This observer identifies peak events, such as when runs are scored, and who wins the game, but the subtleties and little dramas and battles of the game escape the novice's vision. If accompanied to the game by an experienced fan (an emic observer), the novice can be directed to watch and absorb other kinds of detail and thereby be assisted in putting a greater number of factors into perspective, thus increasing an understanding of the game.

One could say that the "etic" observer, the outsider, is confronted with a kind of dizzying pluralism when attending the baseball game. In a sense, this observer has too much information, and the most instinctive response to the game is governed by a particle view, for the novice knows too little about what is supposed to be "seen" to effectively employ an alternative or interlocking wave or field view. Therefore, the etic observer picks up on the minutiae, even though unable to place them in proper perspective except in the most limited way. For the emic observer, the potential pluralism of experience is greatly diminished by a greater familiarity and initiation to the game; the insider knows when and how to move in and out of the various perspectives that yield true insight into the game.

Tagmemic theory thus argues that human beings must, and in fact do, bring multiple perspectives to their communication efforts. But they do so selectively and often unconsciously, and tagmemic rhetoric attempts to systematize this multiperspectival inquiry. In the baseball example, the emic/insider's knowledge of the game is not exhaustive, but it is richer, more realized, and more sophisticated than that of an etic/outsider friend. The emic observer's task is to "translate" for the companion—that is, to use particle, wave, and field perspectives to move the friend from an etic knowledge toward an increasingly emic one, in other words a

bridge to new knowledge and unfolding vision. Pike's tagmemics ultimately grounds speech, textuality, and communication in a rhetoric of participation wherein communities of writers and readers are seen as sharing the responsibility for meaning-making within specific, nonarbitrary historical contexts and in a publicly available discourse, thus rejecting the more dubious, positivistic notion that a static, self-evident, extractable core of meaning inheres in an utterance or text itself.

Tagmemics first came to the attention of rhetoricians and writing instructors more directly through Pike's 1964 *College Composition and Communication* articles, "Beyond the Sentence" and "A Linguistic Contribution to Composition Teaching: A Hypothesis," and the work of Richard Young and Alton Becker, colleagues of Pike's at the University of Michigan. Young and Becker sought to exploit Pike's heuristic insights into language for a "modern theory of rhetoric" that would overcome what seemed to them a moribund current-traditional model that emphasized arrangement and style to the neglect of the problem-solving, discovery process they believed rhetoric must become to serve modern students. Their collaboration with Pike resulted in an influential 1970 textbook, *Rhetoric: Discovery and Change,* that drew attention to the peculiar insights of tagmemics into how language unitizes experience into repeatable units and how writers and readers recover, store, discover and create knowledge that serves their mutual purposes.

Since the publication of *Rhetoric: Discovery and Change,* tagmemics has come to be associated in the field of rhetoric and composition primarily with certain "discovery tools," or heuristics, found in it that attempt to restore invention and problem-solving to the center of the writing and critical thinking process. Of special note is Young, Becker, and Pike's nine-celled discovery matrix, which invites users to employ particle, wave, and field perspectives to explore topics within a compact grid that yields insights into the topic's contrastive or identificational features, its place within a dynamic flow or larger system, and its nature as a system itself with component parts.

In the 1970s and 1980s, researchers and theorists such as Janice Lauer and Lee Odell continued inquiry into the effectiveness of Young, Becker, and Pike's original tagmemic work, verifying experimentally the utility and theoretical soundness of many of the tagmemic postulates. Ironically, ongoing advances in tagmemic rhetoric have tended to be overshadowed over time by the attention paid to tagmemic heuristics, obscuring the anticipations and alternatives that tagmemic theory may present to both linguists and rhetoricians at the end of the twentieth century.

Bruce L. Edwards
Bowling Green State University

Bibliography

Brend, Ruth M. *Kenneth L. Pike: Selected Writings*. The Hague: Mouton, 1972.

Edwards, Bruce L. *The Tagmemic Contribution to Composition Teaching.* Occasional Papers in Composition Theory and History. Manhattan: Kansas State U, 1979.

Headland, Thomas N., et al. *Emics and Etics: The Insider/Outsider Debate*. Newbury Park, CA: Sage, 1990.

Jones, Linda Kay. *Syntax and Semantics*. Vol. 13. Ed. Edith A. Morovcsik. New York: Academic, 1980.

Pike, Kenneth L. "Beyond the Sentence." *College Composition and Communication* 15 (1964): 129–35.

———. "Language as Particle, Wave and Field." *Texas Quarterly* 2 (1959): 37–54.

———. *Language in Relation to a Unified Theory of the Structure of Human Behavior*. 2nd rev. ed. The Hague: Mouton, 1967.

———. *Linguistic Concepts*. Lincoln: U of Nebraska P, 1982.

———. "A Linguistic Contribution to Composition: A Hypothesis." *College Composition and Communication* 15 (1964): 82–88.

———. *Tagmemics, Discourse, and Verbal Art.* Ed. Richard Bailey. Ann Arbor: Michigan Studies in the Humanities, 1981.

———. *Talk, Thought, and Thing*. Arlington, TX: Summer Institute of Linguistics, 1993.

Young, Richard, Alton Becker, and Kenneth L. Pike. *Rhetoric: Discovery and Change*. New York: Harcourt, 1970.

See also LONGACRE, ROBERT E.; PIKE, KENNETH L.; YOUNG, RICHARD

Talon, Omer (1515?–1562)

Classical scholar, writing commentaries on Cicero's *Topics*, Porphyry's logic, and Aristotle's *Ethics* as well as a shorter discussion of Plato. Omer Talon (Audomarus Talaeus) was born around 1515 in either Amiens or Beauvais, son of an Irish colonel settled in France. Except for a brief period teaching at the College of Beauvais in Paris, his whole career was associated with Peter Ramus. As Walter Ong observes, "Talon was Ramus's man" (1983:271).

Talon's close connection to Ramus—and Ramus's own habits of publication—make it difficult to identify the exact nature of Talon's own works. As Peter Sharratt has pointed out, it is never certain how much is the personal contribution of Ramus and how much is the work of his collaborators. Ramus used Talon's name in 1546 to smuggle into print his own revision of his 1543 *Institutio dialecticae;* he was unable to use his own name at the time because he was under a royal prohibition against teaching or writing on philosophy. Ramus's lifelong companion and biographer, Nicolaus Nancel, reports that in at least one other case, a book replying to an attack by Adrien Turnèbe, Ramus wrote the book (in only three days) then published it under Talon's name.

This use of names is a significant factor in assessing the most famous book published under Talon's name—the *Rhetorica* of 1548. It was wildly popular, going through 103 editions in a dozen countries within the next century. Strictly Ramistic, it defines rhetoric as "the theory of expressing oneself well" and declares that it consists only of style and delivery. Style, the adornment of speech, consists of tropes and figures; the four kinds of tropes—"no more are possible"—are metonymy, irony, metaphor, and synecdoche. There are twenty-nine kinds of figures, including *numerus* or prose rhythm. Delivery, apt expression of language, consists of utterance and gesture. These are Ramus's own ideas, clearly expressed elsewhere in such works as his attacks on Cicero (*Brutinae quaestiones*, 1547) and on Quintilian (*Rhetoricae distinctiones in Quintilianum*, 1549).

Interestingly, Talon had published only three years earlier a much more generalized *Training in Oratory* (*Institutio oratoriae*, 1545). (A summary is available in Ong's *Method*, 272–74.) Although Father Ong sees this work of Talon's as an early stage in the Ramus-Talon thinking about rhetoric, the fact is that Ramus had already enunciated these same ideas two years earlier in his attack on Aristotle. Moreover the *Institutio* is so traditional (and so unspecific compared with the 1548 *Rhetorica*) that it seems more likely that Talon's 1545 book is after all original only with him—and that the 1548 *Rhetorica* is not at all original with its supposed author, Omer Talon. Rather, it seems likely that Peter Ramus is the actual author of the "Talon" *Rhetorica* of 1548. Talon never wrote anything so precise and economical. Moreover, after Talon died, Ramus declared that it was his own work and proceeded to make various alterations in the text (as he did all his life with his other works).

Omer Talon, then, can be seen as a disciple of Ramus, a part of the team of researchers, editors, and writers Ramus gathered about him to help him produce the fifty books he published during his lifetime.

James J. Murphy
University of California, Davis

Bibliography

Nadeau, Ray. "Talaeus versus Farnaby on Style." *Speech Monographs* 21 (1954): 59–63.

Ong, Walter J., S.J. *Ramus and Talon Inventory: A Short-Title Inventory of the Published Works of Peter Ramus (1515–1572) and of Omer Talon (c. 1510–1562).* Cambridge, MA: Harvard UP, 1958.

———. *Ramus, Method, and the Decay of Dialogue.* Cambridge, MA: Harvard UP, 1958. Rpt. New York: Octagon, Farrar, 1974. Rpt. Cambridge, MA: Harvard UP, 1983.

Sharratt, Peter. "Recent Work on Peter Ramus (1970–1986)." *Rhetorica* 5 (1987): 7–58.

See also FIGURES OF SPEECH; RAMUS, PETER; TROPES

Technê

Transliteration of the Greek word for art. In many histories of rhetoric, the terms *technê* and *technai* (plural) refer to the extensive handbook tradition of rhetoric that reportedly goes back to Corax and Tisias in the fifth century B.C.E. Used this way, *technê* denotes a collection of rhetorical precepts that might include schemes of discourse classification, treatments of the parts and arrangement of a speech, principles of style and possibly stock phrases, and some discussion of the offices of rhetoric.

Technê also appears in Greek literary traditions that go back to Homer and Hesiod, where it is identified with art, skill, cunning, and even subterfuge. *Technê* is thematized in the Prometheus narratives of Hesiod, where it is associated with fire that enables craft production and the potential for invention that shifts the balance of power between humanity and the gods. *Technê* is consistently contrasted with necessity, force, and chance. For example, in Aeschylus's version of the Prometheus myth, Prometheus's *technê* contrasts with Kratos (force) and Bia (compulsion), the agents of Zeus. In fifth-century medical treatises, *technê* appears as a well-defined model of knowledge. In the treatise *On Art,* attributed to Hippocrates, the *technê* of medicine is characterized as intervening in processes that without art might appear to be governed by chance or subject to the necessary laws of nature. Thucydides refers to the *technê* of seafaring and warfare as a means of mitigating chance and indeterminacy in nature and war.

In the Aristotle corpus, *technê* is identified with the "making" (*poesis*) associated with productive knowledge. This category of knowledge is carefully distinguished from the other two domains of Aristotle's epistemological taxonomy, theoretical knowledge and practical knowledge. Examples of *technai* in the Aristotelian corpus include medicine, architecture, poetics, and rhetoric. In the *Nicomachean Ethics,* Aristotle describes art as concerned with the contingent and the possible, "with contriving and considering how something may come into being which is capable of either being or not being" (1141.a.10). Aristotle explains in the *Metaphysics* that "art arises when from many notions gained by experience one universal judgment about similar objects is produced" (981a); and *technê* continues to contrast with chance: "experience made art . . . but inexperience luck" (981a). In these contexts, *technê* is more than rules or instrumental technique; rather, it is a complex model of knowledge.

Janet M. Atwill
University of Tennessee

Bibliography

Barnes, Jonathan, ed. *The Complete Works of Aristotle.* Rev. ed. 2 vols. Bollingen Series 71. Princeton: Princeton UP, 1984.

Cope, Edward M. *An Introduction to Aristotle's* Rhetoric. London: Macmillan, 1867.

Technical Communication

Communication of scientific and technical information, as well as discourse concerning science and technology; also, the concept of language as a machine or system. Technical communication refers most commonly to the use of documents, speech, and various mixed media for the recording, storage, retrieval, transmission, and reception of information on scientific or technical subjects. In industry, technical communication concerns the information needed to design, install, and operate sophisticated equipment; it also refers to the processes, systems, and software integral to using such equipment. Much technical communication involves interactions among two or more specific technical disciplines pursuing a joint project (for example, mechanical, structural, and chemical engineers designing a petroleum refinery). More broadly, technical communication also refers to the explanation or justification of various technologies for a nontechnical audience, as in the sales literature and user manuals directed at consumers or in the advocacy literature on technology and public policy directed at voters. Finally, theories that regard language as essentially systematic and mechanistic provide a cultural foundation for technical communication, sometimes allowing it to become a paradigm for all communication.

Historical Bases

Technical communication seems a relatively recent rhetorical category. I.A. Richards's 1908 *Guide to Technical Writing* is one of the first books specifically addressing the subject (Souther in Fearing and Sparrow 4). However, the roots of technical communication lie further back. Walter Ong has argued that the "technologizing of the word" through printing led to the scientific revolution in seventeenth-century Europe. In the mechanistic process of printing, Ong finds the first instance of mass production technology. Likewise, he argues that printing greatly amplified the objectification of knowledge (first made possible by writing) and, therefore, that modern science and technology grew first from the printing press.

Regardless of the cause, technical writing is definitely rooted in the Enlightenment's search for a scientific communication style, one free of rhetorical interference. Viewing language as a "lens" through which could shine the "light" of reason, scientific writers increasingly strove for clarity and logic. During the subsequent two centuries, scientific discourse continued to evolve as Europe and America developed into industrial powers. Enlightenment philosophical assumptions, made into cultural commonplaces by the socioeconomic realities of the industrial revolution, provide the historical bases for technical communication.

Theoretical Context

The theoretical foundation for technical communication lies in the often-unquestioned belief that language is essentially a highly complex information system. In this view, all "natural" human language operates on the same principles of symbolic logic that govern the relatively closed, highly rule-governed code systems called "computer languages." Conceived of in this way, language becomes another means of data processing (that is, recording, storing, retrieving, and so forth). Accompanying this view is an objectification of knowledge as that which can be observed, recorded, stored, and retrieved. As "knowledge" is reduced to manageable "information," language becomes a conduit for the flow of information from points of sensory recording and transmission to points of reception and storage. In practice, of course, the less language used, the better, because technical communication often involves such intricate detail that only the sparest of styles seems effective.

Though rooted in the Enlightenment, scientific views of language achieve full theorization in modern structural linguistics, which offered systematic models of language (cf. C.S. Peirce, I.A. Richards, Ferdinand de Saussure, and Roman Jakobson). In particular, Jakobson's discourse model presents an addresser (encoder) sending a message to an addressee (decoder), the message involving a code, context, and contact. Communications theorists often focus on the encoding and decoding factors, emphasizing not only a systematic but also a mechanistic view of language (one based in telecommunications and computers). By presenting a scientific (some say "scientized") theory of language, structuralism also provided a theoretical basis for the already common but untheorized assumptions of technical communication. Many practitioners, however, remain unaware of their theoretical foundation because structuralism's influence is so pervasive in all fields of communication.

Despite the growth of technical communication, recent rhetorical and literary theories have questioned its fundamental assumptions. Various poststructuralists have consistently attacked the discourse of Enlightenment philosophy and science, especially as realized in structuralist theories of language and culture. Others have critiqued scientific and technical discourse as a cultural phenomenon (cf. Kuhn, Rorty). However, scientific and structuralist views of language still exert considerable influence. Thus the increasing significance of technical communication masks its problematic theoretical foundation.

Practice and Pedagogy

Technical communication focuses most intensely on practice and pedagogy, addressing the communication needs of complex, technical disciplines and institutions, along with those of a technology-intensive marketplace. Apparently a subcategory of organizational communication, technical discourse provides the underlying "systems paradigm" on which organizational structure is based. In both settings, communication is viewed as a mechanistic activity, not unlike data transfer. Because organizational structure derives from machine and systems models, technical communication actually creates the dominant paradigm of all forms of organizational communication.

Technical communication pedagogy, in both academic and industrial sites, trains practitioners in organizational schema, stylistic clarity, and sophisticated media design while also touching on analytical and logical skills often developed through collateral study of mathematics. The pedagogy stresses careful editing to achieve clear organization and verbal economy while still employing accurate terminology. The emphasis on clarity has helped communication generalists like Rudolph Flesch and Robert Gunning to gain a wide acceptance for their simple readability formulas, and these are frequently cited in the vast handbook literature on technical communication.

Both pedagogy and practice give significant attention to document and media design, especially the blending of writing, graphics, sound, video, and computers into multimedia presentations. Media complexity has led to specialized academic programs in technical communication (for example, that of Rensselaer Polytechnic), and also to separate "technical communication departments" in the workplace. Both academic and industrial training programs also work to improve the communication skills of students and working professionals in specific technical fields. Finally, cognitive composition theorists (such as Linda Flower) have tried to develop a general discourse pedagogy derived from the problem-solving process so ingrained in scientific and technical communities.

Vincent Casaregola
Saint Louis University

Bibliography

Anderson, Paul V., R. John Brockmann, and Carolyn Miller, eds. *New Essays in Technical and Scientific Communication: Research, Theory, Practice.* Farmingdale, NY: Baywood, 1983.

Fearing, Bertie E., and W. Keats Sparrow, eds. *Technical Writing: Theory and Practice.* New York: Modern Language Assn., 1989.

Flower, Linda. *Problem-Solving Strategies for Writing.* New York: Harcourt, 1981.

Kenner, Hugh. "Machinespeak." *The State of the Language.* Ed. Leonard Michaels and Christopher Ricks. Berkeley: U of California P, 1980. 467–77.

Kuhn, Thomas. *The Structure of Scientific Revolutions.* 2nd ed. Chicago: U of Chicago P, 1970.

Nelson, John S., Allan Megill, and Donald N. McClosky, eds. *The Rhetoric of the Human Sciences: Language and Argument in Scholarship and Public Affairs.* Madison: U of Wisconsin P, 1987.

Ong, Walter J., S.J. *Orality and Literacy: The Technologizing of the Word.* London: Methuen, 1982.

Rorty, Richard. *Philosophy and the Mirror of Nature.* Princeton: Princeton UP, 1979.

Sides, Charles, ed. *Technical Communication Frontiers: Explorations of an Emerging Discipline.* Minneapolis, MN: Association of Teachers of Technical Writing, 1993.

Telos

A Greek term meaning end or completion or purpose, much used by Aristotle, translated into Latin as *finis,* thus the sources of our notions of teleology and final causality, respectively.

Under the general meaning of end, Aristotle introduces nuances in different contexts and also associates *telos* with other Greek terms that further specify the meaning intended. Thus a *telos* or end may be viewed under several formalities: (1) as terminating or ending a given function or activity, allied to *eschaton,* meaning last or ultimate end; (2) as bringing a particular function or work (*ergon*) or nature (*phusis*) to completion or actualization, allied to *energeia* and *entelecheia,* meaning actuality and full actuality respectively; (3) as what is aimed at or intended, allied to *skopos,* meaning aim; (4) as causal or as exercising a determining influence on actions being placed, allied to *to hou heneka,* "that for the sake of which"—that is, the final cause; and (5) as the perfect form or the good intended, allied to *eidos, agathos,* and *aristos,* meaning form, good, and best, respectively.

A few examples may serve to illustrate and clarify these nuances. As terminal (1), the *telos* is merely the point at which a process ends—say, the end of a trip; intermediate stopping points may then be viewed as means to the ultimate end. As completion or actualization (2), end has different meanings, depending on whether the work is one of art or of nature. In the case of an art such as rhetoric, which itself is a faculty (*dunamis*), it is the actualization or functioning of that faculty, putting it to work (*en-energeia*), say, at finding the means of persuasion. In the case of nature, in the generation of a plant or an animal, it is the full actualization of the generative process tending toward a state of completion (*en-telecheia*)—that is, the production of a new individual of the species. As intentional (3), the end at which rhetoricians aim is to persuade; this is their *telos,* and it remains their aim even though they are not successful in finding the proper means of persuasion. As causal (4), the determining influence on rhetoricians is again to persuade, just as that on doctors is to restore health. Surgeons who perform operations intend to restore their patients to health; it is this goal that dictates every action they and their assistants perform. Should the patient die on the operating table, that is the end of the operation in the terminal sense; it clearly is not "that for the sake of which" the surgeon performed the operation. As perfective (5), the end is that which brings the agent to a completed or fulfilled state, without "defect," the way in which Aristotle saw happiness as the aim of all human living, individual and in common (1360b.4–5).

The final cause is regarded as the "cause of causes"—that is, of the other three causes (matter, form, and agent), and is particularly helpful as a *topos* for crafting enthymemes in the fields of ethical and political enquiry.

William A. Wallace
University of Maryland, College Park

Bibliography

Bonitz, Hermann. *Index Aristotelicus.* 2nd ed. Graz: Akademische Druckund Verlagsanstalt, 1955.

Moss, Jean D. "Aristotle's Four Causes: Forgotten Topos of Renaissance Rhetoric." *Rhetoric Society Quarterly* 17 (1987): 71–88.

Peters, F.E. *Greek Philosophical Terms: A Historical Lexicon.* New York: New York UP, 1967.

Wallace, William A. "Aitia: Causal Reasoning in Composition and Rhetoric." *Rhetoric and Praxis.* Ed. Jean D. Moss. Washington, D.C.: Catholic U of America P, 1986. 107–33.

Terministic Screens

A concept central to logology; Kenneth Burke's term for the systematic study of language as symbolic action. Essentially, terministic screens are verbal "filters" through which we perceive reality. Burke speaks of them as terminologies that cause us to focus on certain elements of situations we encounter rather than on others, a process he labels as the directing of the attention ("Terministic Screens," *Language as Symbolic Action* 45).

As a verbal construct, a particular screen contains all those terms we associate with a particular event or person, and we use them to categorize elements of the situations we encounter and so to bring order to those situations. In essence, our use of screens enables us to interpret the situations we encounter.

These screens, while giving us an "accurate" picture of these situations (accurate in the sense that they allow us to interpret situations, or reality, as we must see them), are potentially harmful, for, as Burke notes, "Even if any given terminology is a *reflection* of reality, by its very nature as a terminology it must be a *selection* of reality; and to this extent it must function also as a *deflection* of reality" (*LSA* 45). For example, an ardent football fan may view students of his university's archrival as near-cretins whose knuckles are callused from dragging on the ground as they walk. That view serves as a reflection and selection of reality; yet it also deflects—and may do so dangerously—the more human aspects of those students, their qualities as intelligent beings who are studying medicine, English, or biology and who also make positive contributions to the people they encounter and to their communities by being effective friends, parents, and civic workers.

Terministic screens, by deflecting reality, by directing attention, are indeed powerful. They may motivate us to engage in acts we may otherwise see as abhorrent, in that they may spur us to discriminate on the basis of age, gender, race, or ethnicity. Ultimately, they allow us to justify whatever cause or causes we engage in as right. With his concern for our nature as the symbol-making, -using, and -misusing animal ("Definition of Man," *LSA* 3–24), Burke directs our attention to such screens, to understand better how they manipulate us. In doing so we may reinforce those screens that allow us to treat others with respect or repair those screens that allow us to engage in actions potentially harmful to others.

Bill Bridges
New Mexico State University

Bibliography

Burke, Kenneth. "Definition of Man." *Language as Symbolic Action.* Berkeley: U of California P, 1966. 3–24.

———. "Terministic Screens." *Language as Symbolic Action.* Berkeley: U of California P, 1966. 44–62.

Rueckert, William H. *Kenneth Burke and the Drama of Human Relations.* 2nd ed. Berkeley: U of California P, 1982.

Tisias (c. 487–c. 420 B.C.E.)

Rhetorician from fifth-century B.C.E. Syracuse, Sicily; considered to be one of the "founders" of rhetoric as a discipline. Corax (q.v.) and Tisias are credited with establishing rhetoric as a discipline in 467–466 B.C.E. and in nurturing the development of sophistic rhetoric. Arguments about the accuracy of Corax's contributions, and even his very existence, persist (Cole). Yet, scholars of rhetoric have much more precise evidence about Tisias and his influence in rhetoric (Enos). Some ancient sources credit Tisias with founding rhetoric (Cicero, *De inventione* 2.2.6) but most sources present Tisias as the student of Corax. It is known that Tisias wrote a *technê*, or manual of rhetoric, and taught such famous rhetoricians as Gorgias, Lysias, Thrasymachus, and possibly even Isocrates. Both Tisias and Gorgias went to Athens, spreading the study of rhetoric and the Sicilian sophistic in general. Ancient sources credit Tisias with promoting theories of probable argument and the importance of structure and arrangement of discourse. The most current scholarship focuses on the political forces that shaped rhetoric; as we come to better understand the appeal of rhetoric as a source of power in democracies, we can (albeit indirectly) better understand the impact of Tisias and his followers.

Richard Leo Enos
Texas Christian University

Bibliography

Cole, Thomas. *The Origins of Rhetoric in Ancient Greece.* Baltimore: Johns Hopkins UP, 1991.

Enos, Richard Leo. *Greek Rhetoric before Aristotle.* Prospect Heights, IL: Waveland, 1993.

Schiappa, Edward. *Protagoras and Logos. A Study of Greek Philosophy and Rhetoric.* Columbia: U of South Carolina P, 1991.

Tmesis

Rearrangement of compound words through separating the parts, usually with another word inserted between them. "Whatsoever things," for example, becomes "what things soever." Most often, tmesis is applied to compounds of "ever." "Which way soever man refer to it" (Milton); "that man—how dearly ever parted" (*Troilus and Cressida* 3.3.96); "how heinous e'er it be, / To win thy after-love I pardon thee"

(*Richard II* 5.3.34). However, the syllable of any word can be separated: "Oh so lovely sitting abso-blooming-lutely still" (A. Lerner and F. Lowe, *My Fair Lady*). Or "See his wind—lilycocks—laced" (G.M. Hopkins, "Harry Ploughman"). Tmesis is also commonly used in terms of British slang, such as "hoo-bloody-ray."

Arthur Quinn and Lyon Rathbun
University of California, Berkeley

Topics

Guides for rhetorical invention. One of rhetoric's earliest features as an art was a set of topics, or *topoi*. Aristotle argued that an art could be taught and allowed the user to engage more effectively in an activity, understanding the reasons for the results. He defined the art, or *technê*, of rhetoric as knowledge of strategies or principles, gleaned from the practice of successful *rhetors*, to guide the activity of discoursing. Among these strategies were sets of topics—resources, seats, places, or haunts of effective arguments including lines of reasoning, types of evidence, and appeals to audiences. Although the sophists and Plato deployed numerous topics deftly and Isocrates used the term *topoi*, Aristotle was probably the first to offer an explicit theory and extensive list of these strategies. Because his conception has shadowed subsequent topical treatments, it will be examined here first.

Aristotle distinguished between two types of topics: common and special. His common topics were defined as lines of reasoning useful across three rhetorical situations: deliberative, forensic, and epideictic. He listed twenty-eight common types of arguments, including opposites, correlatives, consequences, definition, parts, and cause and effect. He also described two kinds of special topics. The first, according to Grimaldi (*Studies*), were categories governing specific material appropriate as evidence in each of the types of discourse. For example, his deliberative topics included ways and means, peace and war, national defense, and food supply; forensic topics included motives, states of mind, kinds of wronged persons, and just and unjust actions. Epideictic topics pointed to virtues such as justice, courage, temperance, and wisdom. These special topics did not supply information but rather prompted the rhetor to find it. Aristotle noted that such topics approached the fields of ethics and politics, in which the content

could be found. Another type of special topics were the appeals for ethos and pathos. For ethos, Aristotle proposed showing good sense, good moral character, and good will. For pathos, he offered a list of possible emotions, identifying them, discussing their causes, and indicating how they might be excited.

Aristotle's conception of the purpose of the topics has been a matter of debate among historians of rhetoric. Scholars such as Conley, Hill, and Cope hold that the topics were aids to memory, a checklist or inventory of forms of argument or available premises for enthymemes to help a rhetor convince an audience of a judgment already held. The topics were warrants linking premises to already held conclusions, finding rather than creating judgments. Other scholars argue that Aristotle's topics had an epistemic function, guiding the rhetor to new knowledge or new probable judgments, and thus giving an epistemological cast to the entire rhetoric. Grimaldi, for example, refers to the topics as forms of inference within a rhetoric that apprehends reality and determines probable truth. McKeon sees Aristotle's topical analyses as aiming to discover new propositions. Enos and Lauer view some of his topics as heuristics—socially shared instruments for creating probable knowledge.

In the Roman rhetorical treatises the distinction between common and special topics disappeared, as did their inferential function. The author of *Rhetorica ad Herennium* multiplied topics, positioning them under the three types of discourse (judicial, deliberative, and epideictic), under the issues (conjectural, legal, and juridical), and under the parts of the text (introduction, narration, proof, and conclusion), thereby stressing their function as methods of textual development. In *De inventione,* Cicero identified two superordinate topics, person and act, viewing topics as methods of discovering material for arguments. In *De oratore,* he ignored his earlier topics of person and act, constructing instead a method of invention common to dialectic and rhetoric. Quintilian positioned his topics under the three types of discourse, drawing on sets of strategies from prior rhetoricians. Under judicial discourse he used Cicero's early two-part set (persons and things/actions) and also listed some of Aristotle's topics, such as definition, division, similarities, consequences, and causes. Under demonstrative discourse he grouped topics of praise or blame under subject categories such as gods (their majesty of nature, special powers, and so forth) and men (their life period: character, advantages, and so forth; before their birth: parents, ancestors, and so forth; after death: monuments; children, arts, and so forth). For deliberative discourse he catalogued a variety of civic virtues such as honor, expedience, and justice. These sets of topics were similar to Aristotle's special topics, guiding the rhetor to subject matter as evidence for different rhetorical situations. Stressing the education of the rhetor, Quintilian advocated deliberate practice with a roster of topics to expand the argumentative repertoire of learners so that later, as mature rhetors, they could intuitively select arguments prompted by the specific rhetorical situation. These Roman topical treatments underwent further transformations in subsequent periods.

In the early medieval period, Augustine treated the topics primarily as hermeneutical guides for interpreting the Scriptures to obtain matter for sermons, a function that continued through the development of the *ars praedicandi* (the art of preaching). McKeon explains that in the early medieval phase the topics drifted from rhetoric into logic, with invention going underground to influence the development of the scholastic and the scientific methods, while the late medieval period saw a resurgence of the rhetorical topics. Leff argues that Boethius considered the rhetorical topics (grouped in categories of intrinsic, extrinsic, and intermediate) as subordinate, concrete instances of the purer forms of inference in dialectic and that the late technical treatises reified the topics, setting them up in coherent structures with little practical application. Throughout this long medieval period, rhetorical invention, both in theory and education, was subordinate to theological and philosophical ways of knowing.

In the Renaissance the classical topics reappeared briefly but ultimately gave way to logical topics and schemes and tropes. Wilson's *Arte of Rhetorique* reiterated the topics of several previous rhetoricians. For demonstrative discourse he used Cicero's topics of persons and deeds, listing under persons Quintilian's topics for periods of a man's life. Under deeds he enumerated qualities and circumstances, but also sent the rhetor to the "places of logike." For deliberative discourse he provided a catalogue of virtues. For judicial discourse he followed *Rhetorica ad Herennium,* enumerating a selection of "common" topics under the types of issues: conjectural, legal, and judicial. In contrast, Ramus set out to simplify topical systems by referring the rhetor to the topics of logic, a move that ultimately eliminated a rhetorical way of knowing from both theory and practice. In the late Renaissance, Bacon denied rhetorical topics the status of invention because he claimed that they merely recovered what was already known. This unargued characterization stuck to the rhetorical topics through subsequent periods. In the eighteenth century, Blair described the function of rhetoric (without topics and invention) as that of polishing the valuable substance of a composition that had been generated through knowledge and science.

The inventional topics remained outside rhetoric for several centuries. In the early twentieth century, many composition instructors in the United States, for example, directed students to logic, readings, subject matter fields, or methods of development for their ideas, their reasoning, and their content. Rhetoric as a whole, even discourse, had become a tool for elaborating and communicating knowledge that had been constructed through introspective processes or the scientific method. Since the mid twentieth century, however, scholars have been reinstating rhetoric's inventional function, including the topics. Perelman has identified lines of informal reasoning being used in modern rhetorical situations. Proponents of rhetoric as epistemic have argued for rhetoric's knowledge-making functions in contexts ranging from the social to all situations. Rhetoric and composition specialists have made connections between the topics and heuristic procedures (nonrigorous inquiry strategies that guide discovery) and have constructed new sets of topics, including the tagmemic perspectives, adaptations of Burke's Pentad and ratios, and new clusters of classical topics.

This brief historical sketch suggests that although specific sets of topics have changed in different eras and cultures and have had varied purposes, rhetoricians persist in identifying and teaching topics as guides for invention.

Janice M. Lauer
Purdue University

Bibliography

Conley, Thomas. "Logical Hylomorphism and Aristotle's Koinoi Topoi." *Central States Speech Journal* 29 (1978): 92–97.

Cope, Edward. *An Introduction to Aristotle's "Rhetoric" with Analysis Notes and Appendices.* London: Macmillan, 1867.

Crowley, Sharon. *The Methodical Memory: Invention in Current-Traditional Rhetoric.* Carbondale: Southern Illinois UP, 1990.

Enos, Richard, and Janice Lauer. "The Meaning of 'Heuristic' in Aristotle's *Rhetoric* and Its Implications for Contemporary Rhetorical Theory." *A Rhetoric of Doing.* Ed. Stephen Witte, Roger Cherry, and Neil Nakodate. Carbondale: Southern Illinois UP, 1992. 79–87.

Grimaldi, William. *Aristotle, "Rhetoric": A Commentary.* 2 vols. New York: Fordham UP, 1980–1988.

———. *Studies in the Philosophy of Aristotle's Rhetoric.* Wiesbaden: Franz Steiner Verlag GMBH, 1972.

Hill, Forbes I. "The *Rhetoric* of Aristotle." *A Synoptic History of Classical Rhetoric.* Ed. James Murphy. Berkeley: U of California P, 1972. 19–76.

Kennedy, George. *Aristotle on Rhetoric: A Theory of Civil Discourse.* Trans. and ed. George Kennedy. New York: Oxford UP, 1991.

Leff, Michael. "The Topics of Argumentative Invention in Latin Rhetorical Theory from Cicero to Boethius." *Rhetorica* 1 (1983): 23–43.

McKeon, Richard. "Aristotle's Conception of Language and the Arts of Language." *Critics and Criticism: Ancient and Modern.* Ed. R.S. Crane. Chicago: U of Chicago P, 1952.

———. "Rhetoric in the Middle Ages." *Speculum* 17 (1942): 1–32.

Ochs, Donovan. "Aristotle's Concept of Formal Topics." *Speech Monographs* 36 (1969): 419–25.

———. "Cicero's *Topica*: A Process View of Invention." *Explorations in Rhetoric: Studies in Honor of Douglas Ehninger.* Ed. Ray McKerrow. Glenview, IL: Scott, 1983.

Perelman, Chaïm. *The Realm of Rhetoric.* Trans. William Kluback. Notre Dame, IN: U of Notre Dame P, 1982.

Young, Richard E. "Recent Developments in Rhetorical Invention." *Teaching Composition: 12 Bibliographic Essays.* Ed. Gary Tate. Fort Worth: Texas Christian UP, 1987. 1–38.

See also ARGUMENT; ENTHYMEME; EPISTEMIC RHETORIC; ETHOS; INVENTION; PATHOS; TECHNÊ

Toulmin, Stephen (b. 1922)

British philosopher whose "radical re-ordering of logical theory" has had a significant impact on modern rhetoric and informal logic. Toulmin graduated from Kings College, Cambridge, in 1942, with a degree in mathematics and physics. After serving as a junior scientific officer during World War II, he earned a doctorate in philosophy at Cambridge in 1948 with a dissertation on "Reason in Ethics." Toulmin held a succession of academic posts at Oxford, Melbourne, and Leeds before moving to the United States in 1959. Here he has taught at numerous universities, including Stanford, Columbia, the University of Chicago, Brandeis, Michigan State, and Northwestern, where he is currently the Avalon Foundation Professor of the Humanities.

Toulmin's most influential work for rhetoric is *The Uses of Argument* (1958). In it he criticizes the traditional approach of logicians to logic and argumentation. To philosophers, *logic* (and thus argument) has been a formal study of the canons of deductive validity. A good argument is one in which the premises lead inevitably to the conclusion on the model of Euclidean geometry. Such arguments are called analytic, in contrast to arguments in which the premises make the conclusion likely but fail to guarantee it, arguments that Toulmin refers to as "substantive."

Toulmin criticized the standard treatment of logic on the basis that (1) it is "doubtful whether any genuine, practical argument could *ever* be properly analytic"; (2) the traditional distinction between deductive (analytic) and inductive arguments was a "crude muddle," and (3) that contrary to the viewpoint of traditional treatments of logic, argumentation is essentially a field-dependent phenomenon, in which different fields of rational inquiry must supply the standards of what makes a "good" argument. To provide a comprehensive system for analyzing arguments across fields, Toulmin proposed his own six-part argument schema, the Toulmin model.

The book offended professional philosophers because of its rejection of formal/analytic logic, and after several negative reviews, Toulmin says he assumed it would die a quick death. But the argument scheme he presented was introduced to American speech rhetoricians in early 1960 by Wayne

Brockriede and Douglas Ehninger, and it became popular in the U.S., first in the field of speech, which had long been concerned with substantive arguments, then as part of the informal logic movement; eventually it made its way into a number of English textbooks.

Toulmin holds that most actual fields of argumentation cannot accommodate the claims to "timeless" and absolute knowledge that are required by formal logic, modeled on mathematical deductions. This insight makes his argument theories directly relevant to the rhetorical issue of what provides satisfactory "proof" on topics that are by their nature contingent. For an answer, Toulmin turned to legal reasoning, rather than geometry, as an appropriate model of rational thought. "Logic (we may say) is generalised jurisprudence."

According to the Toulmin model, all arguments, no matter what the field of discussion, have six parts (although they may not all be made explicit by the arguer). Thus the general structure of argument is field-independent, while the canons of evaluation are field-dependent. The core of argument involves a set of data or grounds (the information or knowledge base one has to work with) plus a claim based on those grounds. Connecting the grounds to the claim, and authorizing the movement from one to the other is some sort of warranting principle, a procedural "rule of thumb" or "inference license." Often the warrant is an unstated operating principle of the field of argumentation, but it can be exposed for argument analysis, by treating the argument as an enthymeme.

In a law court, the facts of the case as testified to are the grounds, the assertion of guilt or innocence is the claim, and the relevant legal principles provide the warrant for interpreting the grounds.

In addition, the Toulmin model contains three other features. Since the model is meant to apply to arguments over contingent issues, it contains a modal qualifier, often a single adverb within the claim, a word like *surely, probably,* or *possibly,* indicating the relative degree of confidence one can have in the conclusion, based on the grounds and warrant. Moreover, since there may be known exceptions to the warrant, a fifth part of the model is an explicit set of "rebuttal conditions"—conditions that if true would keep the warrant from applying to

the grounds in this case. The rebuttal conditions can usually be expressed easily in a clause attached to the claim and beginning with an exceptive transition such as "unless." (Illustration: "The defendant is surely guilty of murder in the shooting death of her husband, unless it is decided that the years of abuse she suffered make this a case of self-defense.")

Perhaps the most problematic element of the Toulmin model is "backing." Backing is proof that the warranting principle itself is acceptable, should it be challenged. In the legal model, the backing would include previous court interpretations of the language of a statute, as well as such peripheral information as legislative debate about it. But "in each field, great differences begin to appear: the kind of backing we must point to if we are to establish [the warrant's] authority will change greatly as we move from one field of argument to another." Since an anthropologist does not reason in the same way as a lawyer, or a physicist, or an economist, the appropriate substantive argument principles will differ from field to field. "Arguments within any field can be judged by standards appropriate within that field, and some will fall short; but it must be expected that the standards will be field-dependent, and that the merits to be demanded of an argument in one field will be found to be absent (in the nature of things) from entirely meritorious arguments in another." In practice, then, only experts in the relevant field can hope to be able to assess the adequacy of an argument.

Richard Fulkerson
East Texas State University

Bibliography

Brockriede, Wayne, and Douglas Ehninger. "Toulmin on Argument: An Interpretation and Application." *Quarterly Journal of Speech* 46 (1960): 44–53.

Toulmin, Stephen. *Cosmopolis: The Hidden Agenda of Modernity.* Chicago: U of Chicago P, 1990.

———. "Logic and the Criticism of Arguments." *The Rhetoric of Western Thought.* 4th ed. Ed. James L. Golden, Goodwin F. Berquist, and William E. Coleman. Dubuque, IA: Kendall/Hunt, 1989. 374–88.

———. *The Uses of Argument.* Cambridge: Cambridge UP, 1958.

See also INFORMAL LOGIC; WARRANT

Translation

A term representing either the process of producing in a target language the closest natural equivalent of the source-language text or the text resulting from this process. A failure to make this distinction has been the subtle source of much misunderstanding in the past. Therefore, it is important to speak about *translating* when the focus is on the process and *translation* when the referent is the resultant text.

Translating is essentially an act of communication and can be judged properly only in terms of the extent to which the intended audience adequately comprehends and appreciates the resultant text. But no translation can perfectly represent all the features of content and form of a source text any more than any discourse within a single language is perfectly understood by the intended audience. In all communication there is always some loss and distortion because no two speakers of any one language have exactly the same language experience or respond to an utterance in precisely the same manner.

Furthermore, no text treats a subject in a completely exhaustive manner. Because the participants in any original communication already possess certain shared information, a text does not need to be exhaustive. In fact, an important maxim of communication specifies that one need not and should not communicate more than is required because of the purpose of the text or the needs of the target audience. This means that all texts leave a good deal of information implicit. As a result, translators rendering a text for an audience having a very different culture must often make explicit, either in the text or in marginal notes, information that is crucial to the proper understanding of the message.

Translating inevitably involves varying degrees of paraphrase because no two languages express the same concepts in the same manner. Languages do not differ substantially in the concepts they can represent, but in the ways in which they do so. Unfortunately, the term *translating* has too often been understood as referring to word-for-word transfers from source to target language, while *paraphrase* has been used to characterize those transfers that are regarded as being unnecessarily altered in the number and meaning of words or in the divergency of grammatical constructions. Accordingly, *translating* has been regarded as proper and *paraphrase* as inferior or wrong. Translating and paraphrase are not, however, antithetical but represent complementary and overlapping processes.

The extent of legitimate paraphrase depends largely upon the linguistic and cultural differences between the source and target languages. In general, differences of culture lead to more radical paraphrases than do differences of language structure. For example, it is easier to translate from German to Hungarian, which belong to two different language families but share essentially the same culture, than from German to Hindi, which belong to the same language family but differ appreciably in culture.

The problems encountered by translators are of two major types: linguistic and cultural. The linguistic problems range from subtle plays on the multiple meanings of words because of similarities in sounds (that is, puns) to the difficulties in adequately representing intricately structured poetic patterns (for example, sonnets). Linguistic problems arise because of the diversities of language structures, while the cultural problems result primarily from the diverse ways in which people use and value verbal communication, an area of study normally referred to as sociolinguistics. For example, a translation of the parallel lines in Hebrew biblical poetry is sometimes vigorously rejected by the speakers of some languages because they regard the repetition of the same ideas, although in different words, as being an insult to the intelligence of the audience. On the other hand, in some other languages, poetic parallelism is such a crucial factor that single lines in a source-language poem must be expanded into two lines if the poem is to be acceptable to target-language speakers.

The linguistic and cultural differences between source and target languages have led some persons to deny the possibility of adequacy in translating, despite the fact that more and more effective translating is constantly taking place. Translating is possible for three principal reasons: (1) the underlying structures and the functions of all languages are amazingly similar; (2) the basic functions and values of all cultures are much more alike than diverse; and (3) all people have imagination, and even though they may regard the ideas and behavior of other language-cultures as being strange and even reprehensible, they can comprehend why other people believe and act differently as the result of distinct presuppositions. Those language-culture features that unite people are far more numerous and important than those that separate them.

Ideally, a translation should be of such a quality as to permit a target-language audience to respond intellectually and emotively in essentially the same way as the original audience did, but such a hypothetical and maximal ideal is never realized in view of the linguistic and cultural differences between the respective speech communities. At the same time, there should be a minimal level of adequacy for translations: A target-language audience ought to be able to understand and appreciate a translation in such a way as to comprehend how the source-language audience must have understood and appreciated it.

The most common problems faced by translators result from the structural differences between languages, while the most serious problems arise because of crucial distinctions in the practices and values of the respective cultures. The most overlooked and misleading difficulties, however, are sociolinguistic, the area of interpenetration between language and culture.

Although punning is universal, the precise correspondences can only rarely be duplicated in translating. But the extent to which languages may employ punning for particular types of discourses differs widely. For example, such plays on the meanings of words are almost a hallmark of the Hebrew prophets, while in English punning tends to trivialize preaching but enhance advertising.

No two words in any two languages ever coincide completely in designative and associative meanings, and the specificity of designation may differ greatly. For example, Mandarin Chinese has eight words for *cousin,* while English has only one. These nonconformities can usually be readily sorted out. What is far more difficult is the existence of disconformity in certain crucial distinctive features that are easily overlooked. One missionary in Africa obtained from informants a word for *virgin,* which was immediately incorporated into a translation of the New Testament. The term did refer to virgins, but it also indicated their initiation into a fertility cult involving ritual sexual intercourse. The rapid increase in the membership of this cult was strongly defended by local people on the basis that the mother of Jesus had evidently been a member of this cult. Words have meanings only in terms of the cultures of which they are a part.

Differences in the usual order of syntactic elements can generally be handled with little or no difficulty. The sentence order of subject-verb-object can be almost automatically changed to verb-subject-object if the latter is the normal pattern in the target language. Similarly, the prenoun order of attributives in a source language can be readily shifted to a postnoun order in a target language. What is far more complicated is the nonconformity in subtle tense-aspect particles or affixes. Hebrew prophetic utterances normally employ a completive aspect to emphasize the certainty of a prophetic utterance, but it is not always clear whether the completive aspect refers to a future or past event. Translators from English into many other languages have great difficulty with the ambiguities of English auxiliaries, because *can* and *could* may refer to either ability or permission, and *may* and *might* may involve either possibility or permission. Furthermore, the past tense forms *might* and *could* often add a modal element of uncertainty.

Disconformities in discourse patterns and usage are particularly difficult to sort out. Some languages require that language order and historical order be parallel, and as a result the typical flashbacks in English narratives must be reorganized in translating. In many languages the levels of language (ritual, formal, informal, casual, and intimate) must be carefully tuned to the status of the interlocutors and to the subject matter. If parables are not clearly marked, they may be interpreted as factive, and myths are likely to be regarded as history.

Most people assume that only those who speak languages with a long literary tradition can comprehend and appreciate the wide range of diverse literary genres—for example, narratives, history, biography, laws, prophecies, commands, ultimatums, epic poetry, genealogies, dreams, prayers, visions, riddles, and proverbs. The oral literature of all cultures either already has all these various discourse types, or they can be readily assimilated into the local "literary inventory." Functional equivalence on the level of discourse is far greater than many persons presume.

Theories of translation have been of three major types: philological, linguistic, and communicative. Philological theories have generally been based on the practice of translating literary texts, and the principal concerns have centered around the issue of literalness and freedom of expression. Is the reader to be brought back to the forms of the original or is the original to be adjusted to the comprehension of the reader? Present-day philological theories of translation have incorporated a number of insights from semiotics.

Linguistic theories of translation arose primarily after World War II, when comparative and descriptive linguistics were making particularly important contributions to an understanding of the differences and similarities between languages belonging to entirely different language families. At the same time, these linguistic approaches to translating have contributed significantly to the semantics of words, grammar, and discourse, because translators must give priority to semantic correspondence on all levels of structure.

The communicative theories of translation have been based on communication theory, with its focus on source, message, medium, target, noise, feedback, and setting, as well as on the paralinguistic and extralinguistic features involved in any interlingual communication. Unfortunately, too many persons have regarded translating as merely a matter of decoding the source text and encoding a target text without realizing that communication always involves a bundle of related codes and that the meaning of the words may be completely altered by such features as the tone of voice, the setting of the communication, or the format of the text. One translator of the Psalms into English decided not to have the text printed as poetry because, as he said, he wanted people to believe that "the text was true and not just poetry."

There is no generally accepted theory of translating, even as there are no similar theories of language, anthropology, psychology, communication, and culture, on which translating largely depends and with which it is intimately linked. There is, however, increasing agreement as to certain broad principles of interlingual communication, and there exist many helpful handbooks and commentaries that spell out for translators the major problems and useful solutions.

Eugene A. Nida
American Bible Society

Bibliography

De Waard, Jan, and Eugene A. Nida. *From One Language to Another*. Nashville, TN: Nelson, 1986.

Snell-Hornby, Mary. *Translation Studies: An Integrated Approach*. Amsterdam, PA: Benjamins, 1988.

Steiner, George. *After Babel: Aspects of Language and Translation*. London: Oxford UP, 1975.

Trebizond, George of (1395–1472 or 1473)

Rhetorician, translator, and teacher who assimilated Byzantine and Latin rhetoric and translated Greek writings into Latin. Although he taught privately, most of his career was sponsored by patricians and popes. George of Trebizond is a misnomer; his great-great grandfather emigrated from Trebizond to Crete before Trebizond's birth.

As a young Greek scholar, Trebizond was hired by Venetian patrician Francesco Barbaro. After moving to Italy, Trebizond mastered Latin and started teaching it. His handbook on Latin grammar, *De partibus orationis ex Prisciano compendium*, went through five editions. During the same period, Trebizond made Hermogenes of Tarsus's work available through a synopsis of Peri idion and a treatise on style, *De suavitate dicendi*.

Dissatisfied with teaching younger pupils, Trebizond accepted the Chair of Greek at Florence, which gave him time to write. His opus magnum, *Rhetoricorum libri V*, summarized rhetoric from antiquity to Trebizond's time but concentrated on the teachings of Byzantine scholars Dionysius of Harlicarnassus, Maximum the Philosopher, and Hermogenes. *De laudibus Ciceronis* and *De artificio Ciceroniane orationis Pro Q. Ligario* interpreted Cicero through a Byzantine outlook. *Isagoge dialectica* became a popular textbook for logic.

As a translator, Trebizond's major project was Aristotle's *libri naturales*. With the exception of *Rhetorica ad Theodecten*, however, few of his translations made the transition from manuscript to print. Trebizond's translations were well received by fellow scholars, but his commentaries on his translations of *Almagest* and *Hundred Sayings*, Ptolemy's texts on mathematics and astrology, caused severe criticism. Modern scholars have found his translations somewhat careless, but his efforts made many Greek works available.

Controversy marked Trebizond's life. His harsh assessments of other scholars, including mentor Guarino Veronese, cost him friends and positions, yet Trebizond responded to examinations of his own work in an angry, aggressive manner. He argued at length with humanist Lorenzo Valla and was jailed after coming to blows with Poggio Bracciolini. Trebizond wrote Protectio to criticize his contemporaries. In *Comparatio philosophorum Aristotelis et Platonis,* he used his disenchantment with Plato to proclaim Aristotle a better scholar and Christian but also to imply that his Neo-Platonist rivals, including Greek Cardinal Bessarion, were morally corrupt.

Trebizond wrote many treatises on religion, including warnings about the infidels (Moslems). Although he was employed by the Curia for many years, few popes were interested in his apocryphal visions. After Constantinople fell in 1453, Trebizond feared that Mehmed II would soon rule the world, so he wrote treatises urging the ruler to become Christian and to join Islam with Christianity. Trebizond traveled to Constantinople to meet Mehmed II but was not granted an audience. Instead his adventure cost him four months in an Italian prison; he was freed on the basis of earlier writings and the good will of Pope Paul II, a former pupil.

Trebizond and his Cretan wife, Galitia, had five daughters and two sons, Andreas and Iacopo, who followed their father's footsteps in the service of the Curia.

D.R. Ransdell
University of Arizona

Bibliography

Monfasani, John. *George of Trebizond: A Biography and a Study of His Rhetoric and Logic.* Leiden: Brill, 1976.
———, ed. *Collectanea Trapezuntiana: Texts, Documents, and Bibliographies of George of Trebizond.* Binghamton, NY: Medieval and Renaissance Texts and Studies, 1984.

Trivium

The traditional medieval curriculum, composed of grammar, dialectic (or logic), and rhetoric. The Trivium, "an intersection of three roads," was a four-year program of study equivalent to the Bachelor of Arts degree; in educational histories it is typically paired with the Quadrivium (arithmetic, geometry, astronomy, and music), the equivalent of the Master of Arts degree, to form the seven liberal arts. Isocrates is usually credited with developing the educational system that was eventually codified in the Trivium, the *enkyklios paideia*. A comprehensive curriculum for young male aristocrats with rhetorical instruction at its center, Isocrates' liberal arts system was used in Greece, Rome, and parts of Europe, permeating higher education for approximately a thousand years.

In the medieval period, however, the elements of the Trivium were reshuffled to represent what some scholars have described as the delayed educational triumph of Plato over Isocrates: the main emphasis of the college and university shifted radically from rhetoric to dialectic—specifically, the defense of ideas in a debate with one's classmates or teachers. While during the classical period academic success depended on a student's ability to declaim, in the Middle Ages academic progress was measured by the ability to engage in dialectical debate; indeed, the scholastic debate became practically synonymous with education and dominated higher education until the nineteenth century.

In 429 C.E. Martianus Capella, a contemporary of Augustine's, finished a long allegorical poem, *The Marriage of Philology and Mercury,* which reflected the new emphasis on logic and provides a definitive listing of the seven liberal arts and their medieval reception. In it, dialectic occupies the superior position in the Trivium, replacing rhetoric as the favored means of philosophical dispute. Grammar, based largely on the writings of Priscian, holds the second position, and includes as its main concern the reading and analysis of literary texts as well as the study of language. Rhetoric holds the third position in the Trivium and is depicted by Martianus as a beautiful but fierce woman, ornamented with figures and tropes and armed for battle. This portrayal suggests that during this period the teaching of rhetoric within the Trivium was characterized by the use of classical figures of speech, hence primarily concerned with style; this interpretation of rhetoric strongly influenced the three rhetorical arts of the medieval period—preaching (including saints' lives and devotional treatises), letter-writing, and poetry (particularly vernacular poetry)—and remained virtually unchanged until the Renaissance. Even so, Martianus apparently understood the importance of rhetoric during the classical period, for he refers readers to Cicero for a more authoritative discussion. About one hundred years later, probably because of the custom of the classical schools and the growing popularity of classical texts, Cassiodorus moved rhetoric back to the second position in the Trivium. Although this essentially reduced rhetoric to a link between grammar and dialectic, renewed interest in rhetoric suggests that it may resume its original position as the capstone of a basic liberal arts education.

Elizabeth Ervin
University of North Carolina, Wilmington

Bibliography

Cordasco, Francesco. *A Brief History of Education: A Handbook of Information on Greek, Roman, Medieval, Renaissance, and Modern Educational Practice*. Paterson, NJ: Littlefield, 1963.

Kennedy, George. *The Art of Rhetoric in the Roman World*. Princeton: Princeton UP, 1972.

Murphy, James J. *Rhetoric in the Middle Ages: A History of Rhetorical Theory from Saint Augustine to the Renaissance*. Berkeley: U of California P, 1974.

Paetow, Louis John. *The Arts Course at Medieval Universities with Special Reference to Grammar and Rhetoric*. Champaign: U of Illinois P, 1910.

Parker, H. "The Seven Liberal Arts." *English Historical Review* 5 (1890): 417–61.

See also QUADRIVIUM

Truth, Sojourner (1790–1883)

The soldier of women's suffrage, temperance laws, and the abolitionist movement. Sojourner Truth was born Isabella Baumfree in 1790, the slave of a Dutch master in upstate New York. This proud and relentless woman was freed in 1827 as a result of a state law that gradually emancipated all New York slaves. Truth worked as a nurse in Washington, D.C., during the Civil War, but is best known for her efforts to ensure the rights of freed slaves, secure women's suffrage, and pass temperance laws.

In spite of never learning to read and write, Truth gave courageous speeches and worked tirelessly to better the human condition. As an illiterate former slave, she addressed many audiences with the religious fervor of her great African-American male peers, including Frederick Douglass. An impromptu speaker guided by inner strength and spiritual faith, Truth was successful in compelling audiences to listen to her—to acknowledge her will to survive and her demand for humane conditions not just for African-Americans and women, but for all people.

This brave orator decided to take the name *Sojourner Truth* while walking down a street in Brooklyn and receiving inspiration from God. She exclaimed, "Why, thank you, God. . . . Thou art my last master, and thy name is Truth; and Truth shall be my abiding name till I die!"

In 1852 Truth participated in a Women's Rights Convention in Akron, Ohio. In her candid reply to a man who argued that women endure a harsher life because of the sin of Eve, Truth said, "If de fust woman God ever made was strong enough to turn the world upside down, all alone—dese tegedder ought to be able to turn it back and get it rightside up again." Another male speaker claimed that because of their fragile natures, women should be assisted into carriages and over mud puddles. After explaining that she had never received such aid, Truth asked, "And arn't I a woman?"

At an abolitionist rally in Indiana, Truth became infamous for baring her breasts to a crowd when several listeners accused her of being a man. She announced to the rude audience, "I will show my breasts to the entire congregation. It is not my shame but yours that I should do this." Heaping further embarrassment on the crowd, she boldly asked, "Do you wish also to suck?"

Sojourner Truth was buried in Battle Creek, Michigan, after receiving effusive tributes from comrades in the antislavery movement. The great African-American heroine was then prepared to preach in a new land in which her most attentive listener would be her faithful God.

Chris McCloud
Arizona State University

Bibliography

David, Jay. *Black Defiance*. New York: Morrow, 1972.

Fauset, Arthur. *Sojourner Truth: God's Faithful Pilgrim*. New York: Russell, 1971.

Twentieth-Century Rhetoric

Characterized by a concern for rhetorical theory and practice returning once more to the center of intellectual life, somewhat displacing both scientific and aesthetic models of language with a more socially constructed understanding of communication that applies to all forms of discourse. The twentieth century opened with the rhetorical arts at their cultural nadir, their place in education and intellectual life largely co-opted either by extreme, "scientized" views of communication or equally extreme aesthetic approaches to language. Rhetorical arts had largely deteriorated to limited and superficial exercises in elocution and performance, almost completely separate from any concerns for invention and for discourse as a "knowledge-making" activity. Since the late sixteenth century, invention had increasingly become the province of dialectic, while concerns for the aesthetics of style had become the province of literary criticism. Rhetoric was restricted to the social niceties or political necessities of everyday discourse among the polite or the powerful. J.S. Mill had said that "Eloquence is heard, poetry is overheard," and by the end of the nineteenth century, "eloquence" or rhetoric was heard as the mere social surface of discourse, having little importance for either epistemology or art.

However, just as changes in media technology and patterns of cultural representation during the Renaissance had presaged a rebirth of interest in rhetoric, so too in the twentieth century, new communications media, particularly broadcast media, began to change the ways in which culture viewed language and linguistic performance. Likewise, the development of a high-technology, industrialized society led to a growth in advanced education, resulting in the founding or expansion of numerous universities. University education in rhetoric had persisted in the traditional curriculum for centuries, albeit on an increasingly marginalized basis, and the expansion gave rise to a new interest in rhetoric, especially for its practical usefulness in business and commerce.

At the same time, philosophers of language increasingly questioned the fundamental assumptions of Enlightenment thought and its attendant scientific views of discourse. As the century progressed, and especially during its latter half, the prevailing intellectual climate shifted from one in which language was viewed as a vehicle for meaning to one that viewed all meaning as rooted in acts of discourse, subject to the limits of language and society.

Rhetorical Theory and Philosophy
During the twentieth century, concern for the relationship between language and epistemology led to a reconsideration of the importance of rhetoric for all forms of inquiry, including the foundational discourse of philosophy itself. The rationalism of Enlightenment philosophy, along with the earlier Ramistic educational tradition, had eroded the central role of rhetoric in traditional intellectual life. Throughout the eighteenth and nineteenth centuries, this erosion continued, as scientific discourse became increasingly influential and as industrialization

helped to support more mechanistic models of human communication. Mechanistic models were further encouraged by communication technology that reduced language to rule-governed codes or electronic signals that could be transmitted through wire.

Early in the century, many philosophers began to view language as a relatively closed system, similar to those constructed from the principles of symbolic logic, assuming that the structure of language should be studied separately from the particulars of experience. Language philosophers and linguists (including C.S. Peirce, Ferdinand de Saussure, Ludwig Wittgenstein, Bertrand Russell, I.A. Richards, and others) attempted to formulate the principles of such a language system and articulate its operations. In doing so, however, they began to confront the limitations of philosophical language, leading some to abandon the effort. Others persisted, and Saussure's semiological approach became particularly foundational to structuralist theories of language, literature, and culture, while Richards's blend of structuralist principles and literary formalism helped serve as a basis for New Criticism. Both Saussure and Richards had significant effects on language theory and literary criticism through the mid century. Rhetoric, in either its traditional or more contemporary incarnations, was not a central element in semiotic, structuralist, or new critical theories, but each of these theories drew attention to problems and questions about language and meaning that would lead to greater influence for rhetorical theory.

While some language philosophers sought a rarefied approach to constructing philosophical discourse and others designed grand theories of linguistic structure, J.L. Austin, John Searle, and other "speech-act" theorists valued "ordinary language" as interpreted and understood in practice, emphasizing the contextual, customary, and communal aspects of discourse. Likewise, Kenneth Burke examined how all forms of discourse (literary, philosophical, practical, and so forth) still reflected human motives and values, calling individual interpreters to understand themselves and their discourse in the context of a social environment. He designed the "dramatistic pentad" to represent the rhetoric of discourse in various social contexts (including act, scene, agent, agency, and purpose). Both speech-act theory and Burke's rhetorical criticism helped to reestablish the role of rhetoric in the creation of meaning while also emphasizing the socially constructed nature of discourse and the interpenetration of literature and other forms of writing. Both schools of thought became influential in the study of speech communication from the 1960s to the present.

In his *Rhetoric of Fiction,* Wayne Booth brought a Burkean approach into some level of popularity in literary criticism, competing somewhat with new critical and structuralist approaches. Of course, Booth's rhetorical literary criticism also echoed more traditional views, never quite overcoming the influence of these early twentieth-century theories. Rhetoric's return to literary theory would come, oddly enough, from within the structuralist tradition itself, as some of its second-generation adherents grew dissatisfied with the grand schemes and hegemonic claims of structuralism. In the 1960s and 1970s, Jacques Derrida (among others) began an ongoing critique of structuralist theory and Enlightenment thought. This "*post*structuralism" pushed Saussure's theory of signification to its logical extreme and, emphasizing the arbitrariness of signs, poststructuralists began to deconstruct the binary distinctions upon which structuralism, and the Enlightenment project itself, had been founded. Derrida's *Of Grammatology* was the first of a number of influential works to be translated into English and to shape not only continental but also Anglo-American assumptions about language and meaning. Derrida and other poststructuralists brought a new kind of rhetorical theory into the context of literary interpretation while opening up ground to be explored even by more traditional rhetorical theories.

Like the structuralists before them, poststructuralists also questioned the relationship between language and reality, but they went further, questioning as well the systematic model of language based on the signifier/signified dichotomy. Arguing that all signifieds were themselves signifiers, poststructuralists placed the ongoing act of interpretation in the foreground of discourse where meaning is never present but always deferred, followed through traces of potentially endless chains of signifiers, which reveal how the discourse deconstructs itself before the reader. For poststructuralists, the universal propositions central to Western philosophy, and essential to language philosophers who wished for philosophy to transcend the limits of language, had suffered erasure. The construction of meaning was placed once more in the immediate, probabilistic, and indeterminate arena of linguistic performance, a place well known to even the ancient practitioners of traditional rhetoric.

The influence of Derrida and other poststructuralists extended beyond the fields of language, literature, and communication, bringing fundamental questions to bear on the methodologies of all disciplines and highlighting the rhetorical nature of all forms of inquiry. At the same time, historian-of-science Thomas Kuhn and philosopher Richard Rorty cast doubt on apparently unassailable epistemology of scientific investigation. This interrogation of intellectual inquiry has become commonplace in the academic literature since the 1970s, and specific research groups, such as the Project on the Rhetoric of Inquiry at the University of Iowa, have engaged in a persistent examination of the use of rhetoric in all fields, in the process generating works such as *The Rhetoric of the Human Sciences*.

Still, not all philosophers and rhetoricians support the poststructuralist project and its derivative interrogations in other disciplines, but all those concerned with the process of intellectual inquiry and philosophical discourse must now account for the rhetorical features of the experiences, conceptions, and representations from which they construct models of reality. The ancient on-again/off-again war between philosophy and rhetoric has entered a new phase, one in which neither the universalizing tendency of philosophy nor the local and performative concerns of rhetoric have achieved hegemony. For all those who find philosophy to have suffered erasure, there are equal numbers who are advancing the claims of new or previously marginalized forms of philosophical discourse (for example, feminists, Marxian theorists, theorists of *différence,* and others). Still others, such as Ernesto Grassi, have developed a neohumanistic approach to rhetoric wherein it becomes coequal with philosophy, acknowledging that all philosophy begins in rhetorical assumptions and ends in rhetorical practice. Yet whether the focus be on the theoretical or pragmatic, the universal or the local, the twentieth century ends with a common acknowledgement, among rhetoricians and philosophers alike, that insofar as philosophy is embedded in language it is inevitably interwoven with rhetoric.

Rhetorical Theory and Ideology
The modern understanding of rhetoric and ideology has focused largely on how rhetoric serves

specific beliefs, values, and communities, and this has often led to a negative view of both terms. Even simplistic political arguments label their opposition as *mere rhetoric*. More sophisticated critiques may describe a particular political discourse as using a deceptive rhetoric to conceal its ideological significance or of being naively unaware of its own rhetorical nature and ideological site. Throughout the century, politicians and intellectuals alike have often ignored, avoided, or disclaimed connections with either "rhetoric" or "ideology," since these terms imply a limit on the truth claims of any political discourse.

Earlier in the century, two independent intellectuals from distinctive historical sites began reexploring the connection between theories of meaning and the politics of discourse. In the United States, Kenneth Burke argued that literature, along with all other forms of discourse, is inevitably rhetorical. In 1931 Burke's *Counter-Statement* contested the trend toward a scientized textual criticism, but this work had only limited influence. Somewhat earlier than Burke (c. 1920), the young Soviet intellectual Mikhail Bakhtin began writing the first of his many works that explored theories of language and society in relation to individual acts of discourse. Though his own ideological site is much disputed, recent scholarship demonstrates that he most likely did not write the specifically Marxist works issued under the names of Medvedev and Voloshinov (works traditionally attributed to him). Bakhtin resisted the systematizing efforts of any particular ideology (including Marxism) while still arguing for the deeply social implications and moral consequences of all discourse. His early work (for example, *Toward the Philosophy of the Act*) examined the problem of individual moral responsibility in a socially constructed environment of language. He argued, there and elsewhere, for a dialogic basis of meaning that demands that we take responsibility for acts of discourse even though we cannot completely control the circumstances of language and meaning. We are still responsible for our actions, each of which exists in a unique, "unfinalized" historical site, leaving us "no alibi for being."

Despite the later significance of both Burke and Bakhtin, neither exerted a major influence until after World War II. Burke's major work appeared during the first two postwar decades, and as it gained a greater audience, he was joined by critics such as Wayne Booth and Richard Weaver in reemphasizing the persuasive agenda of all discourse. Bakhtin, suffering political repression in the Soviet Union, would not have his reputation "rehabilitated" until the 1960s. His work has influenced Anglo-American thought only slowly, but since the 1970s, Bakhtin has become a major voice in literary, cultural, and rhetorical studies.

With an intellectual environment already prepared by earlier theories, it remained for Michel Foucault to provide the most influential discussion of how discursive practices intricately interweave with cultural exchanges of power. Foucault recognized that all knowledge-making practices are both political and rhetorical at once. In *The Order of Things, The Archeology of Knowledge,* and subsequent works, Foucault brought his broad experience in psychology, philosophy, and history to the study of fundamental cultural conditions in which we establish meaning and value. He demonstrated that both our intellectual traditions and social institutions exist as patterns of discourse designed to manipulate power. Ironically, his attempt to dislodge hegemonic and totalizing institutional discourses and practices has in some cases led to the academic institutionalization of both cultural studies and discourse theory. Still, these fields have done much to explore the rhetorical practices and ideological sites of supposedly neutral knowledge-making methods of other intellectual disciplines and cultural institutions.

Foucault's work helped to initiate a general interrogation of all cultural practices that allegedly establish transcendent truth unmediated by rhetoric and untouched by ideology. Together with the critical practices of Derridian deconstruction, Foucauldian cultural criticism has opened opportunities for scholars from a number of fields to explore the rhetoric and ideology of all discursive practices while encouraging resistance to the more hegemonic of these practices. Among the most prominent of these scholars are those representing a variety of "theories of difference," including feminism (such as Hélène Cixous and Julia Kristeva), Marxian theory (Fredric Jameson), postcolonial studies (Gayatri Spivak and Edward Said), and black studies or Africana studies (Henry Louis Gates, Jr.). Though not rhetorical theorists per se, they have advanced the status of rhetoric by reminding us that all cultural institutions and methods of inquiry exist in particular historical and cultural sites, with the attendant rhetorical practices and ideological assumptions of those sites. These scholars and their followers have also contested the unacknowledged rhetoric of hegemonic ideologies, offering resistance on the basis of gender, race, ethnicity, class, and numerous other social positions. Their work has both directly and indirectly influenced the fields of rhetorical theory and composition studies, especially benefiting social-constructionist theory and revisionist histories of traditional rhetoric. Thus the connection between rhetoric and ideology in the twentieth century evolves from an ongoing intellectual project that explores the rhetorical and ideological implications of all cultural practices. This project has intensified overall interest in rhetorical studies and has provided new insights for both the history and theory of rhetoric.

Rhetorical Theory and Argumentation

A renewed interest in the relationship between rhetoric and argumentation began slowly in the mid twentieth century. Previously, their relationship still had been affected by Ramus's split of rhetoric and dialectic and by the influence of the analytic methods championed by so many philosophers, from Descartes and Hume to Bertrand Russell, all of whom looked to syllogistic logic as the model for argument. This tradition viewed rhetoric as an ornament that lent an emotional tone to argument and saw dialectic as the use of reason to establish truth or falsehood.

Early twentieth-century discussions of argumentation were located either in philosophy (which focused on formal logic as a model for argument) or in speech communication (which directed its attention to formal rules of debate and other public-speaking performances). University English departments showed little interest in argumentation, concentrating primarily on belles-lettres and reflective writing. An argumentation revival began in the late 1950s and early 1960s, however, as theorists and practitioners in the diverse fields of philosophy, speech communication, and English began to acknowledge and study the limits of traditional logic as a model for argumentation.

The shift in the theoretical perspective of argumentation grew from a realization that the rules of formal logic, based on validity and self-evident propositions, were appropriate neither for reasoning in most arenas of everyday life (politics, morals, law, the social sciences, and so forth) nor for use with natural, nonmathematical language. Basic questions arose: What is an ar-

gument? Where is argument situated? What does it mean to be reasonable? Are the standards for good arguments the same across the disciplines, or does it vary from one to another? The greatest influences on argumentation theory came from Stephen Toulmin and Chaïm Perelman, both of whom, though working independently, published their most influential works in 1958. Toulmin's *Uses of Argument* and Perelman's *New Rhetoric: A Treatise on Argumentation* (written with Lucie Olbrechts-Tyteca; translated into English in 1969) brought new perspectives to argumentation without making a complete break with the classical tradition to which they were responding.

Toulmin began his work as a traditional philosopher and logician, but he questioned whether criteria for determining the soundness of an argument are the same for argumentation in everyday life as for formal logic. Turning to the judicial system for examples, he developed an analytic model of argument different from the traditional syllogism. It consisted of six parts: the claim or proposition, data (facts on which the claim is based), the warrant (a general principle on which the claim is based), a rebuttal, a qualifier, and backing statements. In addition, he analyzed arguments for both field-invariant and field-dependent features, concluding that there were no universal norms of argument and so putting himself at odds with many colleagues in philosophy. While Toulmin did not acknowledge any debt to or awareness of rhetorical theory in developing his new model of argument, he moved farther away from traditional logic and closer to rhetoric.

Perelman was also a philosopher and logician who looked to the law courts for models of argumentation. With his colleague Lucie Olbrechts-Tyteca, he explored whether apparently arbitrary values were necessarily irrational. This study eventually took him from logic back to rhetoric and Aristotle, resulting in his theory of a "new rhetoric," which viewed all argumentation as rhetorical and socially constructed. His treatise discussed the object, the starting point, and the techniques of argumentation, proposing that argument must develop in terms of an audience, and so audience adherence must be both the object and the starting point of argumentation. Rejecting formal logic and the syllogism as models for all nonmathematical argument, he directed his attention to the reasonable rather than the rational in argument, as did theorists such as Henry

Johnstone, Jr., Wayne Booth, and Richard Weaver, who saw a connection between ethics and rhetoric. They claimed that speakers do not operate in a vacuum because argument requires social interaction between reasonable human beings with some shared values. They emphasized the need to present reasons in a way acceptable to an audience, showing that audiences would interpret evidence in their own terms.

Concern with audience was also central for what might be termed the "good reasons" movement of rhetoric and argumentation. Karl Wallace, Walter Fisher, Joseph Wenzel, and others worked to identify a logic of good reasons. Their movement examined the use of value judgments in discourse and how proof could be seen as rational. Validity was not the measure of an argument's success; reasons replaced premises in building an argument. "Good reasons," as defined by Wallace, were statements consistent with each other in support of ought-propositions. Fisher examined how to choose between compelling good reasons to generate a sense of what is good as well as what is reasonable. Wenzel argued that value statements mean different things in different contexts, so the grounds for argument are situation-dependent. As a result, it is necessary to determine the context and criteria for each field in order to recognize good reasons.

Other argumentation work focused on propositions and still relied heavily on symbolic logic rather than rhetoric for its models. The reconciliation between rhetoric and argumentation (or dialectic), however, marked a concern for the practical application of ordinary language in reasoning. In the process it created a value- and audience-centered approach that, while not offering a model for argument as basic as the syllogism, did define argument more accurately as a social act. This trend in argumentation theory paralleled a more general movement (noted in the previous sections) toward a situationally and socially constructed sense of meaning where truth claims were interpreted in rhetorical terms.

Rhetoric and the Academy

At the turn of the century, the rhetorical arts did not hold a very prominent place in the university. Rhetoric was associated with elocution and public speaking, with an emphasis more on arranging and presenting the discourse than creating it. Industrial growth, however, combined with the development of new media technology, brought greater interest in practical language skills, especially as university enrollments began to increase.

When teachers of speech communication established their own departments separate from English departments, they also took with them the study of rhetoric and dialectic, although they continued to emphasize the management of knowledge rather than its creation. Most English teachers were not trained in the art of rhetoric; however, it usually fell to them to instruct the rising number of college students in the skills of critical thinking and writing. Because professors were better trained in and more dedicated to their research in literary history and criticism, they viewed the writing courses as a "service" curriculum concerned with the teaching of grammar, punctuation, and paragraph development. In English departments, composition courses therefore remained the responsibility of untrained, overworked, and underpaid graduate students, part-time instructors, and junior faculty.

For the first half of the twentieth century, discourse pedagogy continued as it had in the nineteenth. Following the so-called "current-traditional" approach, composition courses primarily taught the modes of paragraph and essay development derived from Alexander Bain. However, the 1950s and 1960s saw a slow stirring of interest in rhetorical history and theory, especially in the neo-Aristotelian movement at the University of Chicago, which viewed rhetoric as public discourse and mutual inquiry. At the same time, theorists of media and culture such as Marshall McLuhan and Walter Ong began to explore the impact of media technology on the practice of discourse, and a new generation of rhetorical theorists and historians began to reexamine rhetoric from its earliest beginnings to its contemporary applications. The theories of Richards, Burke, Toulmin, and Perelman were analyzed as possible foundations for both scholarly and pedagogical practice. Textbooks such as Edward Corbett's *Classical Rhetoric for the Modern Student* and theoretical analyses like James Kinneavy's *Theory of Discourse* brought the rhetorical tradition back to the composition classroom while Wayne Brockreide and Douglas Ehninger applied Toulmin's model to speech communication pedagogy.

Literary critics incorporated both rhetoric and language philosophy into the teaching of literature and writing, drawing on the work of a wide range of different theoretical communities (such as Marxist, feminist, structuralist, poststructuralist). Graduate programs in rhetoric, situated primarily in English and communication departments, appeared from the 1960s to the 1980s, increasing the amount and quality of research pursued in this field. Early work by Richard Lloyd-Jones, Richard Braddock, Janet Emig, and Janice Lauer (along with that of many others) helped to shape a disciplinary research agenda for the emerging specialists in "composition studies," a field that draws on linguistics, rhetorical theory, cognitive psychology, literary theory, and cultural studies while focusing on the issues specific to writing pedagogy. Finally, during the 1980s and 1990s, James Berlin and a number of other theorists of composition studies have focused the discipline particularly on the socially constructed nature of discourse and on the ideological concerns of writing pedagogy.

Rhetoric did not remain an isolated field, because researchers in both speech and composition stepped outside of the humanities and into empirical studies. They adapted the cognitive psychology theories of Jerome Bruner and Jean Piaget, turning attention to the cognitive processes of discourse and reintroducing the act of invention, which had been abandoned by the scientized view of communication. This application was seen most readily in the work of James Britton and Janet Emig, as well as in the problem-solving models of Linda Flower and John Hayes. In addition, rhetoric offered a means for interrogating all forms of discourse, so the scholarly works in many disciplines began to apply theories of rhetoric to their own fields. At the same time, growing concerns for basic literacy and communication skills led universities to pay closer attention to introductory writing and communication curricula. Education, linguistics, and psychology programs directed their studies toward language acquisition and cognitive development at all levels. Rhetoricians moved into both business and engineering programs, to study and to teach organizational and technical communication. Working in tandem with computer specialists, they also investigated applications of computer-assisted instruction to writing pedagogy. As universities began to recognize writing as a fundamental tool for learning, they developed writing-across-the-curriculum programs that encouraged all departments to explore the relationship between rhetoric and knowledge acquisition in their own discursive practices.

Despite the growing interest in rhetorical issues at both the scholarly and pedagogical levels, universities still have done little to change the usually low status of those who teach basic writing and speech courses. Ironically, the revival of rhetoric as a scholarly discipline may have encouraged an even greater internal division between rhetorical theorists and composition researchers, on the one hand, and those academics who devote most of their efforts to teaching the actual writing and speech courses. As the century closes, a failure to address this continuing inequity might damage the whole academic discipline of rhetorical studies, negating the progress made from the 1950s through the 1980s.

As the century reaches its close, we find that its intellectual life has been shaped, at least in part, by an increasing interest in and exploration of the rhetorical nature of all forms of discourse and inquiry. After nearly three hundred years during which rhetorical arts suffered limitation and decline, we once again find ourselves in a culture where an understanding of rhetoric is fundamental to full participation in the most advanced intellectual movements of our time. The universalizing discourse of science, amplifying the basically arhetorical or antirhetorical principles of Enlightenment philosophy, has been actively challenged both by a revitalized appreciation for the rhetorical tradition and by a range of new rhetorical theories.

Although the current intellectual environment is one of great flux and even confusion at times and although many of the new and revived approaches to rhetoric question and conflict with each other, we have reached a common acceptance that all philosophical discourse and all explorations of epistemology must take into account the local, the social, and the rhetorical, as they attempt to establish the propositions from which the conversation of philosophy will derive. Likewise, new theories of argumentation, and new concerns for the social and ideological values, which form the need and basis for argumentation, have refocused interest on the social function and ideological weight of discourse. In addition, academic institutions, playing an ever more expansive role in intellectual life and exerting ever greater influence on everyday living, have reshaped both rhetorical theory and practice, not only through the work of departments of English or communications but also through the broad-based concern for literacy and communications skills. Finally, explorations of early childhood language development and of the relationship of language to cognition have brought departments of psychology and education into a discussion traditionally rooted in the humanities.

Regardless of the sites in which rhetoric is practiced or investigated, both as an intellectual discipline and as a pragmatic field of action, twentieth-century rhetoric has proved to be versatile, dynamic, and increasingly influential. From the most arcane discussions of philosophical discourse and literary theory to the most pragmatic concerns with the practice of communication in everyday life, rhetoric is as important in the twentieth century as it has been in any age. As we move into the next century, we are likely to continue to witness the growing influence of rhetoric in all aspects of culture. Given the widespread growth of interactive communication technologies, multimedia representations, and hypertext and cyberspace environments, we may very well be entering into the most important period ever known in the history of rhetoric.

Vincent Casaregola and Julie Farrar
Saint Louis University

Bibliography

Bakhtin, Mikhail. *Toward a Philosophy of the Act*. Trans. Vadim Liapunov. Austin: U of Texas P, 1993.

Berlin, James. *Rhetoric and Reality: Writing Instruction in American Colleges, 1900–1985*. Carbondale: Southern Illinois UP, 1987.

Bizzell, Patricia, and Bruce Herzberg, eds. *The Rhetorical Tradition*. New York: Bedford, 1990.

Booth, Wayne. *Modern Dogma and the Rhetoric of Assent*. Notre Dame, IN: U of Notre Dame P, 1974.

———. *The Rhetoric of Fiction*. Chicago: U of Chicago P, 1961.

Burke, Kenneth. *Counter-Statement*. 2nd ed. Chicago: U of Chicago P, 1957.

———. *A Grammar of Motives*. Rpt. Berkeley: U of California P, 1969.

———. *A Rhetoric of Motives*. Rpt. Berkeley: U of California P, 1969.

Corbett, Edward P.J. *Classical Rhetoric for the Modern Student*. 3rd ed. New York: Oxford UP, 1990.

Derrida, Jacques. *Of Grammatology*. Trans. Gayatri Spivak. Baltimore: Johns Hopkins UP, 1976.

———. *Writing and Différence*. Trans. Alan Bass. London: Routledge, 1978.

Faigley, Lester. *Fragments of Rationality: Postmodernity and the Subject of Composition*. Pittsburgh: U of Pittsburgh P, 1992.

Fisher, Walter R. "Toward a Logic of Good Reasons." *Quarterly Journal of Speech* 64 (1978): 376–84.

Flower, Linda. *Problem-Solving Strategies for Writing*. New York: Harcourt, 1981.

Foucault, Michel. *The Archeology of Knowledge*. Trans. A.M. Sheridan Smith. New York: Harper, 1972.

———. *The Order of Things*. New York: Vintage, 1973.

Golden, James L., Goodwin F. Berquist, and William E. Coleman, eds. *The Rhetoric of Western Thought*. 4th ed. Dubuque, IA: Kendall/Hunt, 1989.

Grassi, Ernesto. *Rhetoric as Philosophy: The Humanist Tradition*. University Park: Pennsylvania State UP, 1980.

Jarratt, Susan. *Rereading the Sophists: Classical Rhetoric Refigured*. Carbondale: Southern Illinois UP, 1991.

Kinneavy, James. *A Theory of Discourse*. New York: Norton, 1971.

Kuhn, Thomas. *The Structure of Scientific Revolutions*. 2nd ed. Chicago: U of Chicago P, 1970.

Morson, Gary Saul, and Caryl Emerson. *Mikhail Bakhtin: Creation of a Prosaics*. Stanford, CA: Stanford UP, 1990.

Nelson, John S., Allan Megill, and Donald N. McClosky, eds. *The Rhetoric of the Human Sciences: Language and Argument in Scholarship and Public Affairs*. Madison: U of Wisconsin P, 1987.

Ong, Walter J., S.J. *Orality and Literacy: The Technologizing of the Word*. London: Methuen, 1982.

Perelman, Chaïm, and L. Olbrechts-Tyteca. *The New Rhetoric: A Treatise on Argumentation*. Trans. John Wilkinson and Purcell Weaver. Notre Dame, IN: U of Notre Dame P, 1969.

Richards, I.A. *The Philosophy of Rhetoric*. Rpt. New York: Oxford UP, 1964.

———. *Principles of Literary Criticism*. New York: Harcourt, 1924.

Rorty, Richard. *Philosophy and the Mirror of Nature*. Princeton: Princeton UP, 1979.

Toulmin, Stephen E. *The Uses of Argument*. Cambridge: Cambridge UP, 1958.

Wallace, Karl. "The Substance of Rhetoric: Good Reasons." *Quarterly Journal of Speech* 49 (1963): 239–49.

Weaver, Richard. *The Ethics of Rhetoric*. Chicago: Regnery, 1953.

———. *Language is Sermonic*. Ed. Richard L. Johannesen et al. Baton Rouge: Louisiana State UP, 1970.

See also COMPOSITION STUDIES

U

Ultimate Terms

As used by twentieth-century rhetoricians Kenneth Burke and Richard M. Weaver, a phrase that represents the ideas or values that hold primary motivational potency or preeminent ranking in the public discourse of an era, culture, or community. In *A Grammar of Motives* (74), Burke notes that "God-terms" are the "names for the ultimates of motivation" and that such terms characteristically embody the principles of necessity and freedom. In *A Rhetoric of Motives* (183–97), Burke presents a lengthy analysis of positive, dialectical, and ultimate terms. Positive terms have an empirical referent, whereas dialectical terms imply an opposite term and are value-laden. An ultimate term would be the "guiding idea" or the "unitary principle" behind a diversity of related or competing terms. There would be gradations of terms "with reference to their relative distance from a single norm." The ultimate term would place competing terms "in a *hierarchy*, or *sequence*, or *evaluative series*, so that, in some way, we went by a fixed and reasoned progression from one of these to another, the members of the entire group being arranged *developmentally* with relation to one another." Later in *A Rhetoric of Motives* (298–301), Burke catalogues the rhetorical names for God, or the "extension of 'God' into the area of 'god-terms' generally." His long list of possibilities includes such god terms as *freedom, necessity, history, science, justice, duty,* and *money*.

In *The Ethics of Rhetoric* (211–32), Richard M. Weaver directly, but without acknowledgement, employs many of Burke's insights on ultimate terms and also adapts and extends these ideas for his own purposes (Johannesen). In the chapter on "Ultimate Terms in Contemporary Rhetoric," Weaver describes a "god term" as a "rhetorical absolute," an expression below which "all other terms are ranked as subordinate." The god term's force "imparts to the others their lesser degree of force, and fixes the scale by which degrees of comparison are understood." In an extension of Burke's idea, Weaver explains: "This capacity to demand sacrifice is probably the surest indicator of the 'god term,' for when a term is so sacrosanct that the material goods of this life are rendered up to it, then we feel justified in saying that it is in some sense ultimate." The god terms that Weaver identifies for the early 1950s reflect necessity or certainty: progress, science, fact, modern, efficient, and American. In an original contribution, Weaver discusses "charismatic terms" such as freedom and democracy and "devil terms," the ultimate terms of repulsion, such as *un-American, communist,* and *prejudice*.

Weaver's view of ultimate terms warrants comparison to his analysis of "uncontested terms," those values, premises, and conclusions assumed already "fixed by universal enlightened consensus" for an era or culture (166–74). In addition, Weaver's discussion of ultimate terms, god terms, devil terms, charismatic terms, and uncontested terms must be understood in the context of his premise that the conscious life of humans revolves "around some concept of value." "So true is this that when the concept is withdrawn or forced into competition with another concept, the human being suffers an almost intolerable sense of being lost." For Weaver, persons must know where they are in the "ideological cosmos" in order to coordinate their activities, and "probably the greatest cruelty which can be inflicted" on the human mind "is this deprivation of a sense of tendency" (213).

Richard L. Johannesen
Northern Illinois University

Bibliography

Burke, Kenneth. *A Grammar of Motives.* New York: Prentice, 1945.

———. *A Rhetoric of Motives.* New York: Prentice, 1950.

Johannesen, Richard L. "Richard M. Weaver's Uses of Kenneth Burke." *Southern Speech Communication Journal* 52 (1987): 312–30.

Weaver, Richard M. *The Ethics of Rhetoric.* Chicago: Regnery, 1953.

Unity

May be methodological, metaphysical, textual, or epistemological. The unified authorial subject is a product of the Enlightenment, and our modern legacy. But as the academy addresses itself to issues of gender, diversity, and postmodernity, it becomes difficult to assume the value and meaning of unity, either as an aesthetic for writing or an ethic for cooperatively living. Perhaps for rhetoricians, the achievement of unity has never been taken for granted. Kenneth Burke explains that words and their histories motivate people to act in ways that both distinguish themselves from one another and seek commonality. Bakhtin expresses an analogous tension in his concepts of the centrifugal, or univocal, and centripetal, or polyvocal, tendencies of texts. And the sophistic tradition has always reconciled truth with circumstance or *kairos,* suggesting a contingent unity.

Philosophically, the origins of unity can be traced to Pythagoras (number one as constituent of all things), Plato (one as interpenetration of beauty, truth, and good), Aristotle (correlation of unity and being), Plotinus (God as One), Aquinas ("transcendental unity"), and Kant ("transcendental unity of apperception"). Non-Western traditions (such as Native American and Hindu) appear to express similar notions of cosmological unity. But in a modernist context, unity has served utilitarian sociopolitical purposes, particularly as it has been manifested in written communication. To function as a unified, productive body of consumers, the eighteenth-century emergent middle class needed to read and write. The shift from a simple market to an industrialized economy increased the demand for information, and the printing press accelerated its dissemination. Likewise, the masses required and demanded education. As a result, writing was routinized and standardized, which in turn made proper taste in speech and writing an object of consumption. Proper literature, for example, was Aristotelian, exemplifying a unified plot, the tragedy being the highest expression of this unity, replete with rising action, climax, and denouement or resolution. The letter and, in turn, the essay, also produced and modeled unity, Hugh Blair's (1718–1800) Man of Letters the enviable, unified, learned authorial subject. A learned man (gender significant) was a rational, observant man, a Spectator, to apply the title of one of the popular coffeehouse newspapers of the time, a single, unified voice. Perhaps the strongest academic influences on unity were two mid-nineteenth-century rhetoricians: Alexander Bain, who, deriving from faculty psychology, prescribed a paragraph unified in purpose and shape, and Henry Noble Day, for whom discourse was a rational procedure that should be singular in its aim and its subject in order to best represent a natural combination of the two. The two-plus-centuries-old five-paragraph theme and current-traditional rhetoric's emphasis on method reflect further the expedience and utility of unity.

Although the Romantics celebrated a personal genius transcending didacticism, they nevertheless subscribed to the ideal of unity. The text lives and spontaneously arises whole from nature; as Coleridge claimed (borrowing from Bacon), it expresses a natural and perhaps divine quality through the harmony of its parts and can be constructed through an equally divine, unified method. Turning away from expressionistic aesthetics, New Criticism emphasized the structural, linguistic coherence of the text, but still confronted the problem of a unity that excludes, in this case the reader.

In an increasingly complex world, the question remains as to how unity can function ethically without collapsing difference and aesthetically without misrepresenting the subject.

Andy Crockett
University of Arizona

Bibliography

Adams, Hazard, ed. *Critical Theory since Plato.* 2nd ed. Orlando: Harcourt, 1992.

Bizzell, Patricia, and Bruce Herzberg, eds. *The Rhetorical Tradition.* Boston: St. Martin's, 1990.

Crowley, Sharon. *The Methodical Memory.* Carbondale: Southern Illinois UP, 1990.

Faigley, Lester. *Fragments of Rationality.* Pittsburgh: U of Pittsburgh P, 1990.

Rosenblatt, Louise M. *The Reader the Text the Poem.* Carbondale: Southern Illinois UP, 1978.

V

Vico, Giambattista (1668–1744)

Professor of Latin eloquence at the University of Naples and author of the *New Science*. Vico was born in Naples and left only once, to tutor the children of the Rocca family for nine years (1686 to 1695) at their castle at Vatolla in the Cilento, south of Naples. He considered himself an autodidact, having acquired his adult education by reading in the library of the convent of Santa Maria della Pietà at Vatolla. He won appointment to the university at the age of thirty-one (1699). The position was poorly paid, which caused him to accept commissioned works, such as the life of the military figure Antonio Carafa, and to offer private lessons to young students preparing for the law. In 1723 he lost his bid for a better chair. This experience became the turning point in his career. In 1735 Vico was appointed royal historiographer, and in 1741 he was succeeded in his professorship by his son Gennaro.

His family had little means. His father came to Naples from the country and acquired a small bookshop; the family slept in a small room above. In a city and age when institutions were dominated by class, social position, and wealth, it is remarkable that Vico could rise to a university position. His success is due to his enormous erudition, coupled perhaps with something of the enterprising spirit demonstrated by his father. In his *Autobiography* he describes his temperament as melancholy, after he fell and fractured his skull at age seven. Vico lived at the same time as the historian Giannone and composer Scarlatti, but Naples was a cultural and political backwater, ruled then by Spanish and Austrian viceroys and, in the last decade of Vico's life, by Charles of Bourbon. Vico slowly attained some prominence, especially among leading scholars in Padua and Venice, but received no recognition (which he sought) from scholars of Northern Europe, except for favorable reviews by Jean LeClerc of the first two volumes of his work on universal law (*Il diritto universale*). Vico's major work, the *New Science* (lst ed. 1725; 2nd ed. 1730; 3rd ed. 1744), to which he felt free to devote himself after being refused the better position, received very limited recognition. He states in his *Autobiography* that some thought him a fool or more kindly said he had "odd ideas." He sent a copy of the *New Science* to Newton, which may have reached Newton in the year Newton died.

The great rediscoverer of Vico's work in the nineteenth century was Michelet, who translated the *New Science* into French. In the twentieth century, Croce revived Vico both as a source of his own philosophy and in an attempt to make him the Italian Hegel, holding that Vico's views of history and knowledge are similar but also prior to Hegel's. In literature Coleridge and Yeats made reference to Vico, but it was James Joyce who introduced Vico to many readers in this century; he used Vico's conception of cycles in the *New Science* as a "trellis" for *Finnegans Wake* and may have also been influenced by Vico's conceptions of language and myth.

Since the 1970s there has been a renaissance in Vico studies in the English-speaking world and there now exists a body of scholarship on Vico in almost all fields of humanities and humanistically oriented social science.

In rhetoric, among those who have interpreted and employed Vico's views are Ernesto Grassi (in relation to Renaissance humanists such as Salutati, Landino, Vives, and others), Michael Mooney (the humanist tradition generally), Donald Verene (philosophy and the nature of the imagination), and Andrea Battistini (the history of rhetoric and contemporary rhetoric generally). Vico is important to rhetoric in three ways: (1) as a teacher; (2) as a practicing rhetorician; (3) as a philosopher engaged in redefining the nature of philosophy on rhetorical principles.

(1): Vico's primary duties were to prepare university students for the law, which was understood as based in training to speak successfully in the courts and before the public. He was fully knowledgeable in the classics of Latin literature, especially Cicero, Quintilian, Horace, and Tacitus. Vico's readers encounter at every turn his profound and detailed knowledge of the full range of Latin texts. He claims in his autobiography that he could write Latin as well as his own language. The manual he wrote and taught survives as *Institutiones oratoriae*. In his last public address, a short oration to the Academy of Oziosi, "The Academies and the Relation between Philosophy and Eloquence," he says: "I hold the opinion that if eloquence does not regain the luster of the Latins and Greeks in our time, when our sciences have made progress equal to and perhaps even greater than theirs, it will be because the sciences are taught completely stripped of every badge of eloquence."

(2): Vico was required to deliver an oration in Latin to inaugurate the academic year. The first six of these were not published during his life. The seventh, given in 1708, was expanded and published (1709) as a book, *On the Study Methods of Our Time.* In addition to these and the oration to the Academy of Oziosi, he gave another, "On the Heroic Mind," and he quotes from yet another (the full text is now lost) in his autobiography. These orations are built upon rhetorical principles and deal with themes in human education, its nature and importance for the individual and society. He not only taught rhetoric, he practiced it professionally. In addition to academic exercises in rhetorical speech and thought, Vico wrote commissioned and occasional pieces as a practicing rhetorician and poet—funeral and marriage orations, an oration for the arrival of Philip V in Naples, a history of the Spanish succession in Naples, and much else. Vico's commissioned and occasional rhetorical writings and poetry have no special literary status apart from their importance as part of his career and thought.

(3): Vico's most interesting ideas for the contemporary rhetorician are in his conception of human education expressed in his orations, especially the *On the Study Methods of Our Time*, and in the *New Science*. In the *Study Methods*, Vico argues against the Cartesian, Port-Royal conception of basing the education of the young on the study of logic, to the exclusion of the arts of topics, imagination, and memory. Vico argues that the very study of logic, the abstract concepts of metaphysics, and analytic geometry ruins young minds because, although they may become proficient at an early age at evaluating the validity of arguments, they are cut off from developing those powers of mind necessary for the creation of arguments and the general thinking of new and original thoughts. Vico holds that young minds naturally excel in poetry, grasp of metaphor, and exercise of memory, all of which are necessary, later in life, for the practice of jurisprudence and civil wisdom. Further—for a mind able to find new beginning points and principles (*archai*) for thought in the sciences—logic, metaphysics, and analytic geometry (as opposed to Euclidian geometry, which employs figures and images and is quite suitable for the young) should be undertaken later in the mature students' education, once the groundwork in metaphor, memory, and imagination has been laid.

In the *New Science*, Vico carries over this view of the rhetorical and poetic focus of speech and thought as the foundation of his conception of human history. He regards all nations as living out a life cycle beginning in a stage of "poetic wisdom," in which the world is formed through "imaginative universals." Vico, like modern anthropologists and mythologists such as Lèvi-Strauss, understands the myths of any culture to be a first form of thought, through which the world is originally ordered. Reflective thought, which Vico understands as based in "intelligible universals," appears later in the course of a nation. Vico's "intelligible universals" are those of Aristotelian class logic, what are commonly understood in the process of definition by genus and species.

Vico speaks of a "sensible topic" (*topica sensibile*), a kind of *topos* or commonplace that is formed, not in the intellect, as Aristotle would hold, but as a kind of bodily locus that is felt by the first humans in their intense power of sensation. From these physical loci, the first humans of any nation's history are able to organize a common life that is framed in their myths as the mental life of imagination that overlays their ritual and social order. As part of this poetic wisdom, which dominates the first ages of a nation, Vico distinguishes four tropes, based on the rhetoric of Johannes Voss: metaphor (which, Vico says, is a fable in brief), metonymy, synecdochy, and irony. Vico claims that irony is as such not part of poetic wisdom; it occurs only when philosophic and reflective thought develop.

Vico insists that human speech—based in the powers of metaphor and imagination—precedes, in culture and in the order of human thought itself, the principles of logical and rationalistic thought and gives the subject matter studied by rhetoric priority over the traditional intellectual instruments of scientific and philosophical thought. The subject matter of rhetoric, being the nature and manner of human speech itself, becomes foundational for any scheme of human knowledge and for an understanding of human culture.

At the end of his autobiography, Vico states that in his teaching he always strove to embody the ancient Latin and humanist ideal of "wisdom speaking" (*sapienza che parla*). He based his thought in an attempt to revive and preserve, in the face of the ongoing development of rationalist and empiricist philosophy, the humanist ideal of the interconnection of *sapientia, eloquentia,* and *prudentia*—wisdom, eloquence, and prudence—in other words, to think well, to speak well, and to act well. For Vico, each of these was of a single order, the expression of which can be found in Cicero and in the rhetorical tradition of Italian humanism. Vico attempts to set these rhetorical ideals against the rise of modern philosophy in the hands of Descartes and Locke, who, along with Kant, made their famous distinction between rhetoric (as merely the attempt to sway opinion) and true knowledge (which was to be based in the logical proposition and the fact). Against this view of the founders of modern philosophy, Vico identifies rhetoric with the power of human speech itself, which is the essential element at the basis of the process of human knowledge, not simply a means of influencing opinion.

Donald Phillip Verene
Emory University

Bibliography

Battistini, Andrea. *La degnità della retorica. Studi su G.B. Vico.* Pisa: Pacini, 1975.

Grassi, Ernesto. *Rhetoric as Philosophy: The Humanist Tradition.* University Park: Pennsylvania State UP, 1988.

———. *Vico and Humanism: Essays on Vico, Heidegger, and Rhetoric.* Ed. Donald Phillip Verene. New York: Lang, 1990.

Mooney, Michael. *Vico in the Tradition of Rhetoric.* Princeton: Princeton UP, 1985.

New Vico Studies 1 (1983)– . [Contains articles, translations, and reviews as well as annual cumulative bibliography of work on Vico.]

Verene, Donald Phillip. *The New Art of Autobiography. An Essay on the 'Life of Giambattista Vico Written by Himself.'* Oxford: Clarendon, 1991.

———. *Vico's Science of Imagination.* Ithaca, NY: Cornell UP, 1981.

Vico, Giambattista. *The Autobiography of Giambattista Vico.* Trans. Max H. Fisch and Thomas G. Bergin. Ithaca, NY: Cornell UP, 1944. Rpt. 1990.

———. *The New Science of Giambattista Vico.* Trans. Thomas G. Bergin and Max H. Fisch. Unabridged, including Vico's "Practice of the New Science." Ithaca, NY: Cornell UP, 1948. Rpt. 1984.

———. *On Humanistic Education. Six Inaugural Orations 1699–1707.* Trans. Giorgio A. Pinton and Arthur W. Shippee. Ithaca, NY: Cornell UP, 1993.

———. "On the Heroic Mind." Trans. Elizabeth Sewell and Anthony C. Sirignano. *Vico and Contemporary Thought.* Ed. Giorgio Tagliacozzo, Michael Mooney, and Donald Phillip Verene. Atlantic Highlands, NJ: Humanities, 1979.

———. *On the Most Ancient Wisdom of the Italians, Unearthed from the Origins of the Latin Language.* Including the Disputations with the *Giornale de' Letterati d'Italia.* Trans. L.M. Palmer. Ithaca, NY: Cornell UP, 1988.

———. *On the Study Methods of Our Time.* Trans. Elio Gianturco; includes "The Academies and the Relation between Philosophy and Eloquence." Trans. Donald Phillip Verene. Ithaca: Cornell UP, 1963. Rpt. 1990.

Vinsauf, Geoffrey de (fl. c. 1210)

Author of the *Ars poetria* and *Documentatum de arte versificandi*. Little is known of the life of Geoffrey of Vinsauf, the single most important figure in the development of the *ars poetriae* in the Middle Ages. He indicates that he left England for Rome (*Poetria nova* 1.31), and he likely served in Rome during the Pontificate of Innocent III (1198–1216), for his best-known work is dedicated to "Papa Nocenti." Internal references in his works indicate that he was probably active between 1199 and 1215. References in Hunterian Museum Manuscript 511 (*Causa Magistri Gaufredi Vinesauf*) add two details: He was educated in Paris and employed as a teacher in Hampton in England.

Geoffrey's central work is the *Poetria nova*, dated variously between 1200 and 1214. It seems to have been completed in a preliminary version by 1200 to 1204 and revised by Geoffrey or others until approximately 1210 to 1215. A Latin verse treatise of 2,116 lines, the work outlines approaches for both the practice and theory of poetry. Geoffrey is also generally accepted as the author of a Latin prose treatise on the same subject: the *Documentum de arte versificandi*, likely completed around 1210. The two treatises incorporate generally the same subject matter. Of the two, the *Poetria nova* is far better known and appears to have been more influential.

Primary influences on the work appear to be the *Rhetorica ad Herennium* (believed in the Middle Ages to have been written by Cicero) and the *Ars poetria* of Horace. At least one critic (Gallo) has also taken note of interesting parallels with Quintilian's *Institutio oratoria*. Since the *Poetria nova* is aimed at both practitioner and theorist, its influence in the Middle Ages is significant. Among scholars and rhetorical theorists, Geoffrey is mentioned specifically by Gervase of Melkley in the *Ars versificatoria* (before 1216), Eberhard in the *Laborintus* (before 1280), and Nicholas Trivet in *Annales* (before 1328). Works by both Eberhard and John of Garland show Geoffrey's direct influence.

Among literary figures, Chaucer has been suggested as Geoffrey's most famous student. John Matthews Manly argued that Chaucer specifically acknowledged and employed Geoffrey's precepts in *The Canterbury Tales*. James J. Murphy subsequently argued that Manly's arguments lacked certainty. Cases for Geoffrey's direct influence on other writers remain uncertain; however, he serves as a touchstone for students attempting to bridge medieval literary theory and practice. His codification of ancient literary theory into a brief, comprehensible treatise ensured his influence on both literary theorists and poets.

Robert L. Kindrick
University of Montana

Bibliography

Faral, Edmond, ed. "Documentum de mode et arte dictandi." *Les arts poetiques du XIIᵉ et du XIIIᵉ siècle.* Paris: Edouard Champion, 1923. 263–327.

——— "Poetria nova." *Les arts poetiques du XIIᵉ et du XIIIᵉ siècle.* Paris: Edouard Champion, 1923. 194–262.

Gallo, Ernest, ed. and trans. *The* Poetria nova *and Its Sources in Early Rhetorical Doctrine.* The Hague: E.J. Brill, 1971.

Manly, John M. "Chaucer and the Rhetoricians." *Proceedings of the British Academy* 12 (1926): 95–113.

Murphy, James J. "A New Look at Chaucer and the Rhetoricians." *Review of English Studies* 15 (1964): 1–20.

Nims, Margaret F., trans. Poetria nova *of Geoffrey of Vinsauf.* Toronto: Pontifical Institute of Mediaeval Studies, 1967.

Parr, Roger P., trans. *Documentum de modo et arte dictandi.* Milwaukee, WI: Marquette UP, 1968.

Visual Rhetoric

Narrowly, the study of the design of text on pages; more generally, the study of all visual signs, including the semiotics of the graphic arts, television, and other media. Traditionally, rhetorical study has defined within *delivery*, one of rhetoric's five canons, the visual dynamics of speech. The recognition that a speech is, in part, a visual event and should be accompanied by appropriate gestures has been recognized since classical times. During the late eighteenth century, an emphasis on delivery led to elaborate elocutionary manuals showing, among other things, all possible hand movements, postures, and facial expressions that might accompany and embellish an apt delivery. The modern inheritors of this tradition treat the visual rhetoric of face-to-face verbal interaction under such headings as *kinesics* (or body language) and *proxemics* (or the study of how speaker/interlocutor distance, posture, and touch affect interpersonal communication). The lesson of such study is that much of the meaning in an interpersonal exchange is tied up not in the words exchanged but in the physical posturings, in observable behaviors that are seen and can be interpreted as meaningful aspects of the encounter.

The emerging field of visual rhetoric, however, is concerned more with written text than spoken. A written text must be visually apprehended, and the spread of ink on paper carries meaning. At the level of the whole text, the visual gestalt communicates to a potential reader whether the text is inviting or forbidding. Written texts are visually examined for meanings: for cues to genre, organization, emphasis, or beginnings and endings. Writing forces writers to indicate divisions and hierarchies, to show what goes with what, to create chunks of text that together constitute a whole. In contrast to the flow of speech, the graphic quality of writing heightens boundaries and discontinuities.

The visual design of the text filters the information on the page. Because writing indicates hierarchy, the reader is cued as to what is necessary to read, what is important to read, and what can be skimmed or skipped. A visual format, such as that which informs a research article, allows a reader to find general information quickly in the abstract, introduction, or conclusion sections. Readers use the visual design to find their place, locate specific information, or skip whole sections that they do not feel the need to read. A newspaper is another good example of a visually informative text, one that provides multiple cues to readers about the status of various sorts of information. Headlines, column rules, captions, font size variation, and conventions of body versus advertising copy all work together to provide a highly informative visual design. Because of the design, the reader can use highly efficient processing strategies, scanning large blocks of text and using highly evolved strategies to process large amounts of information in very little time.

Printed text offers an impressive array of visual features that have no exact counterparts in speech: punctuation, symbols such as asterisks or bullets, numerals, indentation, margins, white space. Type itself, with rich variation recently made available to writers through desktop publishing tools, becomes a powerful element in the rhetoric of the text, with meaningful variation expressed in type fonts (bookish Times Roman versus trendy Avant Garde or anachronistic Courier), type sizes (the larger the point size the more important the information), and type styles (with italics, small caps, shad-owed, double underlined, and other variations all carrying their own meanings, whether playful or emphatic).

When text becomes visually informative by exploiting its graphic potential, the rhetorical meanings of that text are then shared between the logical/semantic/interpersonal meanings that are expressed verbally and those supporting or complementary meanings that are expressed visually. The visual features of the text work together with verbal features to structure meaning. Writers can indicate and readers can infer what sort of text it is in a holistic way simply from the text's appearance. The visual features guide reading, suggesting what is most important and what is less so; what should be read first, last, or not at all; what sections are subordinate to other sections; and so on.

The visual rhetoric of texts also subsumes those elements collectively referred to as "the visuals": pictures and illustrations, line drawings and photos, charts and graphs. Each of these visual elements makes meaning by being interwoven with the written text itself, with words referring to the visuals and providing reference and naming, elaboration, direction of attention, or emphasis. The visuals themselves have their own rhetoric of display, and well-developed principles apply to designing visuals that are efficient, informative, emphatic, honest, relevant, and sufficient. Studies of perception, for example, show that people are good at comparing the height of columns across two bar charts but not so good at comparing the relative sizes of two shaded areas across two pie charts. Knowing such principles allows writers to choose among line graphs, bar charts, or pie charts for certain sorts of data display. The rhetoric of visuals also provides principles that lead to honest representation: using scales appropriate to the data, being careful not to combine one- or two-dimensional data with three-dimensional (as in faulty comparisons of height to volume), using zero baselines or clearly indicating otherwise, and presenting data in context. These are only a few examples of rhetorical generalizations that derive from the study of visuals.

Visual rhetoric is hugely influenced by desktop publishing. A personal computer, a laser printer, and some software give a writer full control of the appearance of the text. In addition to granting control over typography, desktop publishing makes text into manipulable objects, moveable pieces of language that can be

V

combined with graphic objects. Text as object can be stretched, fit to curves, flowed around objects or within boundaries, overwritten, screened (printed at less than 100 percent density), given color, or otherwise manipulated and composed. A whole terminology has sprung up around desktop publishing, with terms and concepts borrowed from graphic design: leading, kerning, alignment, rule, body type, style, descender, gutter, grid, and separation. All indicate control: control granted to the writer (rather than the printer) of the shape of the text.

It is difficult to overestimate the importance of desktop publishing to visual rhetoric. The technology redefines the role of writer into writer/designer. The world is now inundated with publications that attempt to combine words and images into strong and interesting designs. The technology reinvigorates the word *composition,* making writing less a matter of words and sentences and more a matter of effectively integrating verbal and visual elements into a pleasing and effective whole. Writers who wish to become text designers must develop aesthetic insight and an affinity for the art of an informed practice with its basis in graphic design. In some ways, desktop publishing suggests a return to the earlier scribal tradition of illuminating manuscripts. The scribe is both writer and artist.

Another key influence on visual rhetoric is the transition of media from print to screen. Screens as a medium of composition differ dramatically from paper. They afford easy visual/verbal integration and the luxury of open space. They provide easy access to color and to special textual effects: inverse lettering, animation, and all the manipulation of text that is characteristic of desktop publishing, only in a more dynamic medium.

Principles of visual rhetoric for screen design are only beginning to emerge. We know readers have little tolerance for extended reading on screen, that they frequently become lost in large textbases, and that they need to develop new strategies for navigation. Books—whether computer manuals or popular magazines—cannot simply be put into electronic files and be useful. Information must be designed for the screen to be effective. Readers of on-screen text need to know how to open the text and adjust its display. They need to be constantly reminded of where they are and where they have been. They need to know how to make the text work, how to find what they need and remember it. They need to know how to customize the text

and what to do if they make unintentional changes. New roles and responsibilities are emerging for writers and readers.

In its more abstract manifestations, the boundaries of visual rhetoric tend to blur with those of media criticism, aesthetic theory, advertising, physiology of vision, and semiotics. Suffice it to say that like many areas of rhetoric, it is extremely difficult to draw tight boundaries on what constitutes visual rhetoric versus other related areas of inquiry. Rhetoric is fundamentally cross-disciplinary, and visual rhetoric is a prime case in point. To ask how language functions as a visual experience is to open wide the doors to many other disciplines.

Stephen A. Bernhardt
New Mexico State University

Bibliography

Barton, Ben F., and Martha Lee Barton. "Trends in Visual Representation." *Technical and Business Communication.* Ed. Charles H. Sides. Urbana, IL: National Council of Teachers of English, 1989. 95–136.

Bernhardt, Stephen A. "The Shape of Text to Come: The Texture of Print on Screens." *College Composition and Communication* 44 (1993): 151–75.

Bolter, Jay David. *Writing Space: The Computer, Hypertext, and the History of Writing.* Hillsdale, NJ: Erlbaum, 1991.

Tufte, Edward. *Envisioning Information.* Cheshire, CT: Graphics, 1990.

———. *The Visual Display of Quantitative Information.* Cheshire, CT: Graphics, 1983.

White, Jan. V. *Graphic Design for the Electronic Age.* New York: Watson, 1988.

Voice

A term used in composition and rhetoric to refer to the representation of the writer in discourse. As a designation of the writer, voice is similar to the concepts of ethos and persona. Traditionally, however, these classical concepts refer to a writer's character or to a role a writer assumes in discourse, designating more limited attributes of the writer than suggested by voice. Other rhetorical terms related to voice that pertain to the representation of the writer include *tone* and *stance,* which refer to a writer's attitudes toward audience and topic. In addition, the aural qualities of written discourse suggested by tone and the position a writer takes on a topic suggested by stance also connect to ideas often associated with the concept of voice. But voice is a more inclusive concept than either tone or stance, and a more elusive one. None of these similar or related concepts adequately accounts for what is meant by voice, because voice more extensively encompasses notions about human subjectivity. In composition and rhetoric, contested assumptions about subjectivity are foregrounded in issues of voice concerning presence, agency, control, and text-ownership.

The degree to which a writer achieves *presence* in discourse is a contested issue of voice that concerns the authenticity of voice. Authenticity pertains to origins, and an authentic voice is one that is thought to originate from within the writer's inner self. Considering the self the site of origin of voice underscores a connection between voice and speech that for many composition scholars is as actual as it is metaphorical. According to some compositionists who believe that an authentic voice gives a writer presence, speech represents an ideal model for writing. Proponents of one common approach to voice, for example, advocate that writers listen to the voice that resides within them and allow it to become liberated by tuning out external constraints that tend to stifle its natural expression. This expressionistic account of voice suggests that writing needs more closely to approximate speech in order for voice to be authentic. Speech is considered closer to the self, its source of origin, than writing, and therefore less constrained and more honest, natural, and spontaneous. Similarly, some compositionists claim that writers discover what they want to say when they allow writing to flow as naturally as when they speak. According to this vitalistic view, voice enables a kind of self-discovery, for honest expression reveals who a writer really is.

Certain conceptions of style also assume a correspondence between voice and self based on the connection between voice and speech. In accordance with one long-standing stylistic approach, voice is the culmination of the stylistic choices a writer makes with regard to the rhetorical situation, disclosing who the writer is in relation to other components of discourse. Although versions of this approach to voice often provide classifications of prose styles according to registers of voice, many scholars nevertheless believe that the element of choice ensures each individual voice to be unique to the writer. Phonological aspects of speech such as pitch, rhythm, intonation, and so on inhere in writing, and these sounds are thought to convey the personality of the writer. Voice thus gives the writer presence according to the extent to which readers are able to hear the writer speak from the page.

Authorial presence is one of the more contested issues of voice. In fact, some scholars in composition and rhetoric so strongly object to the notion of presence that they take issue with the very concept of voice. They contend that there is no way to conceive of voice as representing the writer in discourse without basing that view on an assumed relationship between speech and self, an assumption they reject. Regarding the components of a discourse situation, including the writer, as socially constructed, these compositionists subscribe to poststructuralist notions about language. In particular, many social constructionists employ the well-known deconstructive maneuvers of opposition and reversal to assign priority to writing over speech and to problematize the concept of self-hood. Accordingly, any instance of language is a "written" instance, an inscription made possible by previous inscriptions. What inheres in any utterance, then, spoken or written, are inscriptions from previous contexts, detached from any recoverable source except language itself. The result of this deconstruction is a dismantling of the idea of an originary self and a refiguring of the concept of presence with the concept of absence. Without its connection to the self, speech loses its authenticity, and so too, then, does voice.

Some composition scholars have become critical of what they consider to be a reductionary view of voice and subjectivity that results from the emphasis poststructuralism places on language and textuality. When the model of speech is replaced by a textual model, linguistic codes are thought to govern all discursive productions, including the construction of the writer. Softening the textual model, many scholars have aligned themselves with postmodernism, which, like poststructuralism, problematizes the notion on an originary self, but not to the extent that the possibility of voice is dismissed. According to these compositionists, voice concerns the positions a writer takes in discourse. These "subject positions" are thought to be constructed by social forces such as race, class, gender, ethnicity, institution, and so on to which writers can both submit and resist. A subject position is thus considered a site where meaning and identity are negotiated, and voice refers to a writer's active role in those negotiations.

Agency, the controlling force or forces of discourse production, is an issue of voice that arises from debates about discursive practices. Discursive practices entail the ways in which writers interact with cultural, social, and rhetorical constraints during the production of discourse. Voice pertains to the relations of power such interactions involve, for at stake in how power relations are constituted is a writer's ability to be an agent in discursive productions of meaning and subjectivity.

Some composition scholars have sought to understand discursive practices better by investigating the cognitive processes of writers. Although they do not dispute that discourse production is regulated in part by social forces, these researchers focus primarily on human agency. According to some cognitive-process theorists, writers perform as agents as they interact in responsive ways with contextual constraints to construct goals and purposes and implement plans for achieving them.

Other compositionists believe that research on agency needs to focus more on the social forces that regulate discourse production. For some who advocate this emphasis, social forces govern virtually all categories of existence, including subjectivity. According to this conception of subjectivity, the ability of a writer to perform as an agent is already limited. Social forces are also thought to constitute the discursive practices that differentiate discourse communities. Certain sets of practices for communicating—how questions are raised, what methods of investigation are accepted, what kinds of issues get treated, how authority is constructed, what textual forms are used, and so on—are textual conventions that are thought to define discourse communities and further constrain a writer's voice.

Discourse community theorists believe that questions concerning agency need to center on how writers gain access to discursive practices in order to become "insiders" in discourse communities. This approach is contested, however, by compositionists, who argue that having to adopt the discursive practices of a given discourse community represents a gatekeeping tactic that prevents those who do not have access to certain discursive practices from having a voice. In fact, some composition scholars claim that achieving an insider's status merely produces a "Pygmalion" effect, whereby the absorption of voice by the conventions of a community constitutes the loss of identity. Scholars who share these critical views of discursive practices believe that having a voice requires writers to perform as agents of not only discourse but also the practices that regulate discourse. Voice thus involves taking a self-aware stance to challenge authoritarian constructs of language, knowledge, and subjectivity, which often entails developing or rediscovering language practices that better reflect one's identity.

Although there have been attempts to move beyond accounts of agency that tend to dichotomize the individual and the social, debates about who or what has more control and in what ways that control is exerted continue. *Control* is an issue of voice that reconfigures the individual/social opposition as a dichotomy between situation and art, opposed by depictions of subjectivity as fragmented and conflicted on the one hand or sovereign and transcendent on the other.

Compositionists who regard voice as the assertion of human agency believe writers have recourse to strategies they can use to help guide them in their writing efforts, including their efforts to disclose themselves in certain ways. These composition scholars focus on writing as an art, as an act of producing by means that are relatively discernible and able to be described in general ways. Necessarily inexact—an art cannot supply formulas—the descriptions of what writers do when they write have offered some compositionists the bases upon which they have designed composing strategies (various heuristic procedures such as tagmemics, guides for analyzing audience, idea trees for clustering, and so on). They contend that use of such strategies can help to foster or develop the capacity of writers to respond effectively to their situatedness in discourse.

Composition scholars who promote composing strategies have been criticized for allegedly holding a conception of the writer as a free agent who is able to transcend the situation of discourse and exert control over it. Some strategies have been offered for writers to use to deliberate about voice directly. Even though such strategies usually involve writers in investigating their relationships with audience, topic, and so on, some critics still claim that the methods presuppose that a writer has ultimate authority in composing activities, making voice central to the production of discourse.

Those who regard voice as far more situationally determined than a focus on writing as an art supposes think that generalized accounts of human activity are suspect. They question how valid generalizations about even a particular individual can be when subjectivity is itself fragmentary and indeterminate, constituted by multilayered and complex subject positions that often conflict with one another. These scholars also contend that strategies for composing are themselves discursive formations, so even though strategies might seem to offer a writer control over a discourse situation, the social forces operating in such strategies exert just as much control over the writer. Focusing their criticisms on the views of human subjectivity some strategies seem to imply, rather than dismissing a writer's recourse to compositional arts per se, some scholars advocate methods for composing that engage writers in critique, with the composing methods included in what is brought under critical scrutiny. Failure to adopt such a critical posture, it has been argued, makes writers unknowingly complicitous with the dominant forces regulating discourse, "voice" serving to reinforce the relations of power already in place within discursive practices.

As the representation of the writer in discourse, voice is a concept frequently associated with the idea of authorship. But rather than being a synonym for voice, authorship is more closely aligned with an issue of voice, namely *text-ownership*. Like the idea of authorship, text-ownership concerns the extent to which discourse that results from a writer's discursive actions can be considered as belonging to the writer. Arising from debates about intervention and composition pedagogy, the issue of text-ownership is contested according to how a writer's deliberations are thought to affect voice.

The notion that writers have recourse to strategies they can use for composing suggests that they are able to intervene in the production of discursive formations, voice serving as part of what constitutes the social forces and power relations that comprise discourse. At the same time, voice is itself part of what becomes constructed, pointing to the idea that writers can intervene in the formation of their own subjectivities.

It is not necessarily the case that compositionists who believe that voice in writing accords the writer a great deal of text-ownership promote the notion of intervention. Some hold that interventional methods place distance between a writer and voice, focusing on a writer's deliberations of external constraints that inhibit the spontaneous expression of the writer's own voice. Although these scholars do endorse such composing strategies as freewriting, a method intended to enhance introspection, they are opposed to methods that they think encourage too much deliberation. They recognize that the distance required for deliberating creates a space for others, besides the writer, to intervene, allowing the voices of others into the composing process and thereby making considerations of external factors truly deliberating.

For other compositionists, creating a space for intervention is the only way voice can be asserted, albeit a voice that is not solely the writer's own. Even if a strategy like freewriting does liberate a writer's inner voice, that voice, some maintain, is already filled with public language. They also contend that intervention makes the teaching of writing possible, which in itself suggests that others have some stake in discourse. Among these scholars, some believe that having a stake in discourse obliges them to teach strategies that help writers to be critical of the ways in which discourse is both regulated by and serves to reinscribe dominant social forces, value hierarchies, and power relations. In accordance with their views of voice as critical intervention, these compositionists promote hermeneutic procedures as composing strategies. Such methods acknowledge writing to be, in part, an interpretive enterprise, which precludes the idea that a text can be filled with the subjectivity of one individual writer.

Others who share the view that intervention is part of that which shows the unavoidable collaborative aspect of writing and social nature of voice nevertheless remain reluctant to endorse pedagogical practices that they consider too over-determining. Although they concur that intervention requires a distanced and critical perspective, some scholars believe certain interpretive strategies seem to demand that writers produce critiques and sometimes even to lead to particular positions. These scholars suspect that such requirements can greatly reduce even the partial ownership of discursive productions voice grants writers.

Debra L. Jacobs
University of South Florida

Bibliography

Aronowitz, Stanley, and Henry A. Giroux. *Postmodern Education: Politics, Culture, and Social Criticism.* Minneapolis: U of Minnesota P, 1991.

Berlin, James A. "Composition Studies and Cultural Studies: Collapsing Boundaries." *Into the Field: Composition Studies.* Ed. Anne Ruggles Gere. New York: Modern Language Assn., 1993. 99–116.

Brooke, Robert. "Control in Writing: Flower, Derrida, and Images of the Writer." *College English* 51 (1989): 405–17.

Elbow, Peter. *Writing with Power: Techniques for Mastering the Writing Process.* New York: Oxford UP, 1981.

Flower, Linda. "Cognition, Context, and Theory Building." *College Composition and Communication* 40 (1989): 282–311.

Hickey, Dona J. *Developing a Written Voice.* Mountain View, CA: Mayfield, 1993.

Porter, James. *Audience and Rhetoric: An Archaeological Composition of the Discourse Community.* Englewood Cliffs, NJ: Prentice, 1993.

See also ELBOW, PETER; ETHOS; PERSONA; SPEAKING AND WRITING

Vygotsky, Lev Semenovich (1896–1934)

One of the foremost Soviet psychologists of the twentieth century. From 1924 until his untimely death from tuberculosis in 1934, Vygotsky held a series of prestigious positions in various Soviet psychological institutes. While a large part of Vygotsky's writings remain unpublished, his theoretical insights and research have enjoyed a growing popularity in the past few decades. His translated works include *The Psychology of Art, Thought and Language* and *Mind in Society: The Development of Higher Psychological Processes.*

Thought and Language, the most influential of Vygotsky's works published outside of the Soviet Union, examines the child's inner life and how it shapes, and is subsequently shaped by, socialization. Jean Piaget, the leading developmental psychologist in the 1930s, claimed that cognitive development in children begins when the personal, autistic mental states characteristic of inner speech are gradually socialized into egocentric speech, and finally mature in the form of social speech. Vygotsky, working from an assumption opposite to Piaget's and that of the school of psychology that assumed ontogenetic development to be based in individualistic principles, argued for the social foundations of higher mental functions.

In his examination of the ontogenetic development of children, Vygotsky begins with the assumption that "the primary function of speech, in both children and adults, is communication, social contact" (*Thought and Language* 34). At a certain age, social speech transforms into egocentric and communicative speech. The former, which eventually becomes inner speech, emerges when "the child transfers social, collaborative forms of behavior to the sphere of inner-personal psychic functions" (35). In this model, Vygotsky posits the direction of development as "not from the individual to the social, but from the social to the individual" (36).

Vygotsky was also concerned with the ontogenetic and cultural effects of the interiorization of writing. To this end he distinguished between everyday, spontaneous concepts (natural spoken language) that children acquire unconsciously, and scientific, nonspontaneous concepts that children learn consciously in formal academic settings. Spontaneous concepts are learned primarily in direct face-to-face contact with others, an example of how external, social relations are interiorized by the individual. In reference to context, "the child is not conscious of concepts because his attention is always centered on the [nonlinguistic] object to which the concept refers, never on the act of thought itself" (171). Everyday concepts are saturated with experience and are based on the sense of words rather than their meaning.

Scientific concepts, according to Vygotsky, constitute different types of signs because they stand in a different relation to the object. These concepts are formalized and relatively static because they are based on "relations of generality" (190). In the scientific concept, the meaning of the word predominates over the sense. Formal school instruction guides children away from "primitive wordless perception to perception of objects guided by and expressed in words—perception in terms of meaning" (170).

Vygotsky singled out the role of writing as representative of the sign systems that make possible higher mental functions. The scientific concept, encoded in written discourse and introduced through formal instruction, is mediated through another linguistic concept. Written language, he concluded, "is a separate linguistic function, differing from oral speech in both structure and mode of functioning" (180). Writing, as an artificial instrument that is consciously interiorized, represents a "second degree of symbolization" governed by "a high level of abstraction" and the absence of an interlocutor (181).

By focusing on the social foundations of higher mental functions and the interiorization of language and other sign systems ("psychological tools"), Vygotsky's thought has contributed to both theory and practice in recent composition, rhetoric, and literacy research. His theory of inner speech calls into question the paradigmatic conceptualization of thought as atomistic and uniquely individual. Karen Burke LeFevre, for example, uses Vygotsky's ideas about the cultural origins of inner speech to support a model of rhetorical invention based on collaboration and social interaction. Vygotsky's research has also influenced the debates about literacy over the last fifteen years. Current criticisms of standardized literacy tests focus on the narrow definitions of such tests. These textual definitions of literacy may accurately reflect the forms of written, academic discourse in institutionalized education, but they quickly lose their descriptive power in the multiple contexts across which communication occurs. As Vygotsky hypothesized and his student Alexander Luria demonstrated, syllogistic and abstract thought is tied to specific forms of institutional instruction. Both Shirley Brice Heath's research in the southeastern United States and Sylvia Scribner's and Michael Cole's research with the Vai in west Africa have confirmed and extended Vygotsky's ideas about multiple literacy.

Wade Williams
Ohio State University

Bibliography

Heath, Shirley Brice. *Ways with Words: Language, Life, and Work in Communities and Classrooms.* Cambridge: Cambridge UP, 1983.

LeFevre, Karen Burke. *Invention as a Social Act.* Carbondale: Southern Illinois UP, 1987.

Luria, Alexander R. *Cognitive Development: Its Cultural and Social Foundations.* Cambridge, MA: Harvard UP, 1976.

Scribner, Sylvia, and Michael Cole. *The Psychology of Literacy.* Cambridge, MA: Harvard UP, 1981.

Vygotsky, L.S. *Mind in Society: The Development of Higher Psychological Processes.* Cambridge, MA: Harvard UP, 1978.

———. *The Psychology of Art.* Cambridge, MA: MIT P, 1971.

———. *Thought and Language.* Cambridge, MA: MIT P, 1983.

Wallace, Karl R. (1903–1973)

Rhetorical theorist known for his original contributions to rhetorical theory and his interest in Renaissance rhetorical theory, primarily that of Francis Bacon. As a theorist, Wallace conceives of rhetoric as "something more than a methodological art. Its principles reflect men's behavior in their conversing, discussing, and speech-making, when they are in practical settings rather than in specialized or professional ones." He focuses on the nature of the rhetorical act and on the substance of rhetorical discourse. To see a person in his or her rhetorical character is to see this person behaving humanistically, reflecting both "the cognitive and affective materials of experience" and revealing one's "entire being" as he or she relies ultimately upon our "ordinary language" to make a "meaningful response to a meaningful situation."

Wallace conceives of the rhetorical situation as occurring in the area of the contingent, where choice-making is possible, bringing "practical reason into play" and actively exhibiting three modes: deliberation, justification, and explanation. Since the "stuff" of rhetorical discourse springs from the essential character of the speaking/writing act, it is ethically grounded. His focus on the primacy of substance and ideas and on rhetoric as advisory leads him to center on the substance of rhetoric as "good reasons." A *good reason* "is a statement offered in support of an *ought* proposition or of a value-judgment." The rhetor, then, should focus on one or more of three essential value categories: the desirable, the obligatory, and the praiseworthy. Both rhetor and listeners/readers are necessarily concerned with choices, ought-statements and their justifications as they are "indicated or implied in statement form as reasons, warrants, premises, laws, principles and beliefs."

Asserting that invention is at the very heart of rhetorical activity, Wallace treats of the *topoi* and their systematic development at length. Fully aware of the reciprocal nature of rhetorical action, both rhetor and audience must participate in inventing activity as "an orderly way of searching for meaningful utterances." Since rhetoric is governed by intentions and justified by values, Wallace outlines four basic "moralities of communication": the duty of search and inquiry; the allegiance to accuracy, fairness, and justice in the selection and treatment of ideas and arguments; the willingness to submit private motivations to public scrutiny; and the toleration of dissent.

In addition to his emphases on the primacy of substance and ideas, a concern for the ethical grounding of discourse, and a vision of the rhetorical person as the *whole* person, a fourth, clearly, was Wallace's "bias" as "that of a teacher," arguing that the teacher of rhetoric must "stand for truth and justice in communication because the health and welfare of a free society depends upon the integrity of the communicator."

In addition to his own body of theory, Wallace concentrates on discovering and explicating the work of Francis Bacon. Placing Bacon's communication theory within the fuller body of Bacon's "comprehensive interests," Wallace stresses the "amplitude" of Bacon's mind, the source of movement and energy that is to be found in the unity of his thought and purpose. Within his conception of rhetoric as a "unifying study," Wallace probes, for example, the relationships Bacon drew between and among Understanding, Reason, and Rhetoric.

Jane Blankenship
University of Massachusetts

Bibliography
Wallace, Karl R. "Bacon on Understanding, Reason, and Rhetoric." *Speech Monographs* 38 (1970): 79–91.

———. *Francis Bacon on Communication and Rhetoric, or The Art of Applying Reason to Imagination for the Better Moving of the Will.* Chapel Hill: U of North Carolina P, 1943.

———. *Francis Bacon on the Nature of Man: The Faculties of Man's Soul.* Urbana: U of Illinois P, 1967.

———. "The Fundamentals of Rhetoric." *The Prospects of Rhetoric.* Ed. Edwin Black and Lloyd Bitzer. Englewood Cliffs, NJ: Prentice, 1971. 3–20.

———. "The Substance of Rhetoric: Good Reasons." *Quarterly Journal of Speech* 49 (1963): 239–49.

———. "*Topoi* and the Problem of Invention." *Quarterly Journal of Speech* 57 (1972): 387–95.

———. *Understanding Discourse: The Speech Act and Rhetorical Action.* Baton Rouge: Louisiana State UP, 1970.

Warrant

One of six elements in the Toulmin model of argument. The (1) warrant is a general principle, a rule of thumb, which justifies the move from the (2) data (or grounds) to the (3) claim. The other three elements are (4) backing for the warrant, (5) possible exceptions to the argument called "rebuttal conditions," and (6) a qualifier (such as "certainly" or "probably"). Just as a search warrant authorizes a law officer to perform certain acts, an argument warrant authorizes the inference from evidence to conclusion.

In enthymemes, warrants are often unstated but recoverable. In "alcoholic beverages should be outlawed in the U.S. because they cause death and disease each year," the first clause is the conclusion, and the second the data. The unstated warrant is fairly phrased as "In the U.S. we agree that products causing death and disease should be made illegal." Sometimes leaving the warrant unstated makes a weak argument seem stronger; recovering the warrant to examine its other implications is helpful in argument criticism. The warrant above would also justify outlawing tobacco, firearms, and automobiles.

Toulmin based his model on legal argumentation. The facts of the case constitute the data/grounds, and the conclusion is the guilt or innocence of the defendant. The warrant is the law itself, whether statute or precedent.

In certain senses a warrant is similar to the major premise in a traditional syllogism. In the chestnut about the mortality of Socrates, the major premise/warrant is that "all men are mortal." However, Toulmin's warrant cannot be simply equated to a major premise. First, in some valid syllogisms neither premise is a warranting principle. Consider this syllogism:

Some Americans believe in gun control.

All Americans believe in first amendment rights.

[Therefore] Some supporters of the first amendment believe in gun control.

It is valid reasoning, but the first premise (the major) is not a rule of thumb that "applies" to the second one.

Second, in proposing his model, Toulmin rejected the traditional notion of logic as a formal deductive system represented by the syllogism. His model applies equally to traditional deduction and induction.

Third, still other modes of reasoning fit the Toulmin model well. Consider "John was the only student with a key to the copying room. The stolen test was locked in the copying room and later found in John's desk; moreover, though he claims to be innocent, he failed a lie detector test. It seems likely that he stole the test." Such an argument (from fallible sign) is difficult to analyze as a syllogism or as an inductive generalization, but it is easily examined from the Toulmin perspective. It rests on a warrant such as "Someone who has access to a stolen item later found in his possession and who fails a lie detector test probably stole the item." In a similar manner, arguments by analogy and authority can be explicated using Toulmin's idea of a warrant as a procedural rule that relates evidence to conclusion.

Richard Fulkerson
East Texas State University

Bibliography

Toulmin, Stephen. "Logic and the Criticism of Arguments." *The Rhetoric of Western Thought*. 4th ed. Ed. James Golden, Goodwin F. Berquist, and William E. Coleman. Dubuque, IA: Kendall/Hunt, 1989. 374–88.

———. *The Uses of Argument*. Paperback ed. Cambridge: Cambridge UP, 1963.

Toulmin, Stephen, Richard Rieke, and Allan Janik. *An Introduction to Reasoning*. 2nd ed. New York: Macmillan, 1984.

See also INFORMAL LOGIC; TOULMIN, STEPHEN

Weaver, Richard M. (1910–1953)

American rhetorical theorist and educator. Richard Weaver, rhetorical theorist, social philosopher, and literary critic, personified the ideals of liberal learning to which, he observed, the Southern gentleman of the last century had been committed. Born in Asheville, North Carolina, he earned his B.A. at the University of Kentucky, where he was briefly a member of the Socialist party; his M.A. at Vanderbilt University under the tutelage of the Southern Agrarians, whose influence led him to a lifelong interest in conservatism; and his Ph.D. at Louisiana State University, where he wrote his dissertation, "The Confederate South, 1865–1910: A Study in the Survival of a Mind and a Culture."

Despite his partisanship for the conservative South, he spent most of his professional life expatriated from his native environment as a professor of English in the undergraduate college of the University of Chicago. There he distinguished himself as a teacher and an influential writer on the themes of conservatism, composition, and a brand of rhetorical theory that was wound together tightly with the strands of his conservative philosophy. His largest audience, particularly during the 1950s and early 1960s, when he was most active, were like-minded conservatives; but his rhetorical writings, although influenced by his political philosophy, belong to the canon of modern rhetorical theory.

Weaver's controversial first book, *Ideas Have Consequences* (1948), established him as one of the leading voices among postwar conservatives, who, like Weaver, felt outnumbered by liberals and alienated from a society they believed had been set adrift upon a sea of social policy, government bureaucracy, and a burgeoning commitment to the authority of science and social science at the expense of philosophy and religion. Weaver's *Ethics of Rhetoric* (1953) was his most important statement on the ethical and cultural role of rhetoric. In 1955 he published a composition text, and his last book, *Visions of Order*, appeared in 1963, the year in which he died of a heart attack at the age of fifty-three. Weaver also published numerous articles, many of which have been anthologized in posthumously published books. One of these, *Language Is Sermonic* (1970), is a useful collection of his essays on rhetorical themes.

Similarities between Weaver's and Plato's visions of the rights and responsibilities of people in society have led many to call Weaver a neo-Platonist. In his partisan political writing, in his treatment of the decline of Western civilization, in his argument for the historical and philosophical bases for these stances, and in his arguments for noble rhetoric, Weaver evinces a decidedly Platonic attitude. He believes that relativism is corrupting society and its underlying culture; that a philosophical realism provides the metaphysical defense for a better society; and that a noble rhetoric, using dialectic and inspiration, is the only defensible use of language.

Weaver develops his triad of "neuter rhetoric," "base rhetoric," and "noble rhetoric" from his reading of the *Phaedrus*. The first rubric includes scientific and technical communication, much business and bureaucratic communication, and increasingly the discourse of the humanities and social sciences. Its ostensible purpose is expository, and its hallmarks are attempts at objectivity and clarity. The second rubric includes advertising, propaganda, and much political discourse. Its purpose is persuasion, and its hallmarks are emotional appeals, a lack of interest in logical support, and a flexible, self-serving ethic. The third rubric includes very little of modern society's discourse, although its goal—to lead interlocutors toward the truth—he believes ought to include all discourse. Its hallmarks are a logical base for argument as well as effective rhetorical display.

Noble rhetoric is conscious of the appropriate topics for argument. Weaver differentiates among arguments from definition, similitude, consequence and circumstance, and testimony and authority, and he claims that the noblest rhetoric uses definition and the least noble uses circumstance. (Testimony and authority are differently judged.) This hierarchy has drawn criticism from Weaver scholars, who claim that it lacks both clarity and consistent application.

Noble rhetoric also is aware of a society's ultimate terms—both its "god terms" and its "devil terms"—and is aware of the charismatic charge some terms carry. Charisma is the nonlogical force a term has in a society's discourse, and Weaver correctly notes how such terms can be used by unscrupulous rhetors in the place of a noble, logos-based argument. Besides ultimate terms, Weaver also discusses positive and dialectical terms, the former having material referents and the latter dependent upon cultural and group values. Although he claims that these terms are implicit in Plato's *Phaedrus,* his discussion mirrors one in Burke's *Rhetoric of Motives,* a book that Weaver read in manuscript form before he wrote *The Ethics of Rhetoric,* the book in which these terms occur.

Perhaps the most important similarity between Weaver's and Plato's concepts of rhetoric is in the nature of dialectic and its relationship to rhetoric. Using his analysis of the *Phaedrus* as his point of departure, Weaver places dialectic early in a rhetorical process that identifies questions at issue, investigates possible resolutions and determines the best one, and presents this choice eloquently to an audience; the placement at times threatens to give to dialectic at least the canon of invention and limit rhetoric to style and perhaps arrangement. Also Platonic is Weaver's perception of dialectic as the means for providing the subject matter for rhetoric; thus, one does not invent arguments simply on the basis of what an audience will believe but rather selects only those arguments that originate in dialectical truth.

Style is presented as the means of giving shape to the truths arrived at dialectically; as Weaver says, it renders the logical analogical. Thus, Plato's "winged charioteer" in the *Phaedrus* is a figure said to resemble the soul, an imaginative representation in human language, adapted to a particular audience. In Weaver's rhetorical criticism, style also provides an index to the character of the rhetor, the audience, and culture. For example, Weaver admires the "spaciousness" of nineteenth-century rhetoric, its "widths of sound and meaning," which he sees as an accommodation to the settled beliefs of the age. Nineteenth-century oratory was spacious because it celebrated unchallenged tenets of democracy and religion. Such celebrations, in the pattern of epideictic rhetoric, did not require the mustering of empirical evidence but compelled the orator to find language by which to reexpress the presumptive truths that lent coherence to the society. The grandiloquence of nineteenth-century rhetoric, its breadth, glittering generalizations, and abundance of rhetorical figuration and amplification, was a function of the orator's inclination to view the world as a cultural creation in which metaphysical ideas about the human charter took precedence over mere fact. In this homogeneous society, the great orator assumed the role of public philosopher who occupied a position of ethical authority rarely granted speakers today. Modern scientifically dominated culture, which assumes that facts can be understood independently of the filter of cultural truths, has little need of the old orator whose role was precisely to remind audiences of how things should be seen. The function of reminding audiences of what they already know is one that Plato in the *Phaedrus* ascribes to written discourse.

The existence of Platonic truths is at the core of Weaver's metaphysical position. He articulates a philosophy of realism—a belief in the existence of eternal, unchanging, and absolute truths that give a rationale and shape to our ethical systems and thereby determine the quality of our acts and ideas. Weaver admits that our limitations as human beings make us unable to know these truths directly, so, despite his distaste for modern relativism, in his rhetorical theorizing he accepts a position more in keeping with Protagoras than Plato, and similar to Burke's perspectivism.

Despite his implicit acceptance of a relativistic stance, Weaver is explicit about the major cause for the decline of Western civilization: the fourteenth-century defeat of realism by the nominalism of William of Occam. Weaver's cultural criticism is highly critical of the consequences of nominalism's victory, specifically the rise of science and the subsequent enshrinement of technological progress, and the separation of fact from value and the subsequent establishment of a modernist relativism in matters not scientific. Results of realism's defeat include the loss of liberal education to vocationalism, of art to entertainment, of the pursuit of truth to the acceptance of opinion. Weaver posits the antebellum South, due to its roots in feudalism, its chivalric code, its gentleman class, and its religiousness, as a culture to be emulated.

This preference for a lost reactionary society provides the basis for Weaver's more partisan writings. He is very much the political conservative in many speeches and written pieces for *National Review* and *Modern Age;* he also takes reactionary positions in his examination of the South and of Western history. He is opposed to vocational education and the weakening of core requirements in the liberal arts, opposed to women's entrance into the workplace, and opposed to modernist influences in art; he is wary of egalitarian sentiments in general and comes close to approving of the institution of slavery. However, his conservatism also opposes technological developments and the growth of big business, putting him squarely at odds with the conservatism preached by politicians and corporate leaders.

Weaver variously expresses his distrust of modern scientific and technological culture. He challenges the presumptive authority of science by rearguing a case long ago closed in the court of history, Tennessee's right to ban evolutionary teaching, which sparked national public interest in the celebrated Scopes trial. He argues that the state's dialectic should take precedence over the allegedly more rhetorical pleadings of the defense, which claimed for science an authority superior to that of religious teachings. According to Weaver, scientific fact and theory must be evaluated in reference to metaphysical propositions, which include, he claims, the cultural autonomy of the state. Therefore, if the state believed that evolutionary doctrine threatened the welfare of its inhabitants, it could legislate its exclusion from the public school curriculum. The scientific validity of evolutionary doctrine or its importance to the scientific enterprise was immaterial.

Scientific and technological culture undermined ethical philosophy by making the locus of contemplation the material, rather than the ideational, world. While scientific culture created the specialist and expert, traditional culture glorified the orator who, with an intimate knowledge of culturally derived rhetorical commonplaces, gave perspective to a wide range of topics. Weaver's ideal orator acted to preserve culture constituted by sentiment, memory, and prejudgment.

Drawing upon the insights of Burke and conservative economist Friedrich von Hayek, Weaver expresses grave concern over the increasing role of the social scientist and stingingly criticizes social scientific rhetoric. His primary targets, however, were sociologists, for they were most conspicuous in assisting the architects of the New Deal to reconstruct the social order. The first sin of the social scientist was to claim scientific status. Weaver believed that sociologists were in fact deliberative orators whose research was a prelude to government intervention in the social world. Social scientists treated dialectical terms such as *poverty* and *underprivileged* as though they were positive terms, as though they had material referents. Unrealistically optimistic about the possibility of resolving social problems, their diction tended toward Latinate language that euphemized the problems they described. Yet the social scientists distrusted metaphor when metaphor could be exploited as an effective means of discovery and expression. They also exhibited a "caste spirit," an absorption in the norms and language of their disciplines, which led to a formulaic, unnecessarily tentative, and turgid exposition of ideas.

Weaver's criticisms of scientism extend to General Semantics. He believes that the urging of General Semanticists to adopt a more purely referential form of speech is symptomatic of a scientific culture distrustful of evocative and more traditionally rhetorical uses of language. General Semanticists attempt to "plane the tropes off of language." By focusing upon objective referents, they deny the reality of ideas and the cultural importance of sentiment. According to Weaver, the role of language is not the faithful representation of the material world but the movement of audience toward the right thought and action. However, language is inescapably tendentious, and its use is necessarily "sermonic."

Although Weaver has relatively little literary theory and criticism, one can hear Platonic overtones in his comments about divine inspiration and the importance of realizing the power literary works have to form and sustain individual and societal attitudes. His much richer body of work on rhetorical and composition theory suggests that although he is of the "current traditional" school of composition theory he does reintroduce into the discipline elements from rhetorical theory that are of great benefit to the teaching of communication.

Bernard K. Duffy
California Polytechnic State University
Martin J. Jacobi
Clemson University

Bibliography

Beale, Walter H. "Richard M. Weaver: Philosophical Rhetoric, Cultural Criticism, and the First Rhetorical Awakening." *College English* 52 (1990): 626–40.

Bliese, John R.E. "Richard M. Weaver and the Rhetoric of the Lost Cause." *Rhetoric Society Quarterly* 19 (1989): 313–25.

Duffy, Bernard K., and Martin Jacobi. *The Politics of Rhetoric: Richard M. Weaver and the Conservative Tradition.* Westport, CT: Greenwood, 1993.

Goodnight, Gerald Thomas. "Rhetoric and Culture: A Critical Edition of Richard M. Weaver's Unpublished Works." Diss. U of Kansas, 1978.

Johannesen, Richard L. "Richard M. Weaver's Uses of Kenneth Burke." *Southern Speech Communication Journal* 52 (1987): 312–30.

Johannesen, Richard L., Rennard Strickland, and Ralph T. Eubanks. Intro. *Language Is Sermonic.* Ed. Richard Johannesen, Rennard Strickland, and Ralph T. Eubanks. Baton Rouge: Louisiana State UP, 1970.

Sproule, J. Michael. "Using Public Rhetoric to Assess Private Philosophy: Richard M. Weaver and Beyond." *Southern Speech Communication Journal* 44 (1979): 289–308.

See also ULTIMATE TERMS

Wendell, Barrett (1855–1921)

One of the most successful popularizers of the term *composition*. Barrett Wendell was the author of *English Composition* (1891), one of the more influential late-nineteenth-century treatises that defined the study of composition as the study of style, or, in Wendell's terms, "the study of expression." Originally hired in 1880 to assist Adams Sherman Hill in teaching composition to Harvard undergraduates, Wendell taught both composition and literature at Harvard until 1917. Wendell was an advocate for the belletristic perspective that the study of composition should be accompanied by the study of great literature; his own professional interests combined his commitment to composition instruction and his passion for literature. During his career, Wendell published not only the well-known *English Composition* but also several literary studies, including a biography of Cotton Mather, *Cotton Mather, the Puritan Priest* (1891), and a widely used history of American literature, *A Literary History of America* (1900). Wendell initiated the Harvard course in American literature in 1898.

A popular speaker on education and the study of literature and composition in particular, Wendell promoted the Harvard approach to composition instruction as an ideal. Wendell insisted that no one who hoped to develop clear powers of thought could do so without training in written expression. He explained in a commencement address at the College of Charleston in 1909 that the end of the college years should be "a strengthened power of composition. . . . [Y]our best philosophers, too, your wisest men, are those who compose at once most vigorously and most truly—with the least eccentricity and the most courage" (155). Following Adams Sherman Hill's habit of equating composition primarily with the mastery of style, Wendell defined composition as the expression of thought and feeling in words. For Wendell, "expression" is a key concept. Like Hill he focused on how thoughts were to be conveyed, not on how thoughts were to be invented. In *English Composition*, Wendell reiterated several nineteenth-century principles of style, including the definition of the qualities of style as clearness, force, and elegance; the definition of unity, emphasis, and coherence as principles of composition affecting sentence structure and paragraph organization; and the general rule that stylistic choices should be governed by a consideration of how the text will affect the reader.

In assessing Wendell's equation between composition and the study of style it must be kept in mind that, to Wendell, style encompassed more than the mastery of correct diction or sentence structure. Given to highly belletristic sentiments regarding the somewhat mysterious alchemy between thought, emotion, and words, Wendell stressed that composition was a process in which each writer applied basic principles to the expression of individual truth. Wendell also argued that the art of composition demands that each writer strive to present valuable and challenging ideas that will "inform, influence, guide, and inspire" (192).

Nan Johnson
Ohio State University

Bibliography

Douglas, Wallace. "Barrett Wendell." *Traditions of Inquiry*. Ed. John Brerton. New York: Oxford UP, 1985. 3–25.

Howe, M.A. De Wolge. *Barrett Wendell and His Letters*. Boston: Atlantic, 1924.

Self, Robert T. *Barrett Wendell*. Boston: Twayne, 1975.

Wendell, Barrett. *The Mystery of Education and Other Academic Performances*. New York: Scribner's, 1909. 137–94.

Whately, Richard (1787–1863)

Logician, rhetorical theorist, essayist, preacher, lecturer, public controversialist. Whately was born in London on February 1, 1787. As a shy, frail child, he received early instruction at home. During this period he became recognized as a mathematical prodigy of the type then known as "ready reckoner"; but by the time he entered Mr. Phillips' school near Bristol, this aptitude had left him. When he entered Oriel College, Oxford, in 1805, he had become tall, robust, and fond of fishing and hiking. He took his B.A. degree in 1808, was elected fellow of Oriel in 1811, took his M.A. in 1812, and in 1814 was ordained an Anglican clergyman. In 1819, during his residence at Oxford, he wrote and published anonymously *Historic Doubts Relative to Napoleon Bonaparte*, a witty satire showing how Hume's excessive skepticism concerning testimony for miracles could be applied to prove that Napoleon never existed.

In 1821, soon after his marriage, Whately accepted a pastorate at Halesworth, Suffolk, but returned to Oxford in 1825 as principal of St. Alban Hall, with John Henry Newman as first vice-principal. During this period, until 1831, when he was appointed archbishop of Dublin, he wrote *Elements of Logic* (1826), *Elements of Rhetoric* (1828), and many of the other works that ensured him a prominent place in nineteenth-century intellectual history. In 1837 he wrote his celebrated treatise *Christian Evidences*, translated during his lifetime into more than a dozen languages. At a later period he contributed to popular education with his *Easy Lessons on Reasoning*, on *Morals*, on *Money Matters*, on *Mind*, and on the *British Constitution*. After an extended illness, he died in Dublin on October 1, 1863.

From a rhetorical perspective, at least three aspects of Whately's achievement continue to challenge scholars. First, recent researchers have discovered an unusually close relationship between Whately's logical system and rhetorical theory and also between these and his actual rhetorical practices. Whately's decision in the *Elements of Rhetoric* to treat "Argumentative Composition, *generally* and *exclusively*" rested upon, and was intended as "an off-shoot" from, his prior treatment in the *Elements of Logic* of deductive inference generally and exclusively. Therefore, a team of scholars would render a prime professional service by producing a single-volume critical edition of both works with all textual variants and cross-references from edition to edition collated and indexed.

Again, despite the fact that (as more than one researcher has noted) there have been nearly three times as many scholarly articles published on Whately as on any other nineteenth-century rhetorical figure, little agreement exists on the meaning and value for us of such basic Whatelian notions as presumption, burden of proof, the drift of propositions, and "natural" delivery.

Finally, though Whately was one of the more prolific writers in the history of rhetoric, having published nearly one hundred separate works during his lifetime, fewer than 20 percent of these have so far been examined and evaluated critically. To what extent any of these works *persuaded* persons not already agreeing with their central ideas remains to be determined. Yet it seems clear from the *Elements* books and the *Easy Lessons* series alone that Whately excelled in what has recently been termed "the rhetoric of explanation."

Ralph S. Pomeroy
University of California, Davis

Bibliography

Akenson, Donald H. *A Protestant in Purgatory: Richard Whately, Archbishop of Dublin*. Hamden, CT: Shoe String, 1981.

Anderson, Floyd D., and Merwyn Hayes. "Presumption and Burden of Proof in Whately's Speech on the Jewish Civil Disabilities Repeal Bill." *Speech Monographs* 34 (1967): 133–36.

Bentham, George. *Outline of a New System of Logic: With a Critical Examination of Dr. Whately's "Elements of Logic."* London: Hunt and Clarke, 1827.

Berlin, James. "Richard Whately and Current-Traditional Rhetoric." *College English* 42 (1980): 10–17.

Bowen, Desmond. *The Protestant Crusade in*

Ireland: 1800–1870. Montreal: McGill-Queen's UP, 1978.

Connors, Robert. "The Rhetoric of Explanation: Explanatory Rhetoric from Aristotle to 1850." *Written Communication* 1 (1984): 189–210.

———. "The Rhetoric of Explanation: Explanatory Rhetoric from 1850 to the Present." *Written Communication* 1 (1985): 49–72.

Edney, Clarence W. "Richard Whately on Dispositio." *Speech Monographs* 21 (1954): 227–34.

Ehninger, Douglas. "Campbell, Blair, and Whately: Old Friends in a New Light." *Western Speech* 19 (1955): 263–69.

———. "Campbell, Blair, and Whately Revisited." *Southern Speech Journal* 28 (1963): 169–82.

———. "Dominant Trends in English Rhetorical Thought, 1750–1800." *Southern Speech Journal* 18 (1952): 3–12.

———. "Whately on Dispositio." *Quarterly Journal of Speech* 40 (1954): 439–41.

Einhorn, Lois J. "Consistency in Richard Whately: The Scope of His Rhetoric." *Philosophy and Rhetoric* 14 (1981). 88–99.

———. "Richard Whately's Public Persuasion: The Relationship between His Rhetorical Theory and His Rhetorical Practice." *Rhetorica* 4 (1986): 51–65.

Fitzpatrick, William J. *Memoirs of Richard Whately, Archbishop of Dublin.* 2 vols. London: Richard Bentley, 1864.

Freeman, William. "Whately and Stanislavski: Complementary Paradigms of Naturalness." *Quarterly Journal of Speech* 56 (1970): 61–66.

Golden, James L., Goodwin F. Berquist, and William E. Coleman. "The Rhetorics of Campbell and Whately." *The Rhetoric of Western Thought.* 4th ed. New York: Holt, 1989.

Gronbeck, Bruce E. "Archbishop Richard Whately's Doctrine of 'Presumption' and 'Burden of Proof': An Historial-Critical Analysis." Thesis. U of Iowa, 1966.

Jongsma, Calvin. "Richard Whately and the Revival of Syllogistic Logic in Great Britain in the Early Nineteenth Century." Diss. U of Toronto, 1982.

Leathers, Dale G. "Whately's Logically Derived Rhetoric: A Stranger in Its Time." *Western Speech* 33 (1969): 48–58.

Lee, Ronald, and Karen King Lee. "Reconsid-ering Whately's Folly: An Emotive Treatment of Presumption." *Central States Speech Journal* 36 (1985): 164–77.

McKerrow, Ray E. "Campbell and Whately on the Utility of Syllogistic Logic." *Western Speech Communication* 11 (1976): 3–13.

———. "The Ethical Implications of a Whatelian Rhetoric." *Rhetoric Society Quarterly* 17 (1987): 321–27.

———. "'Method of Composition': Whately's Earliest 'Rhetoric.'" *Philosophy and Rhetoric* 40 (1978): 43–58.

———. "Probable Argument and Proof in Whately's Theory of Rhetoric." *Central States Speech Journal* 26 (1975): 259–66.

———. "Richard Whately and the Revival of Logic in Nineteenth-Century England." *Rhetorica* 5 (1987): 163–85.

———. "Richard Whately: Religious Controversialist of the Nineteenth Century." *Prose Studies: 1800–1900* 2 (1979): 160–87.

———. "Whately's Philosophy of Language." *Southern Speech Communication Journal* 63 (1988): 211–26.

———. "Whately's Theory of Rhetoric." Diss. U of Iowa, 1974.

———. "Whately's Theory of Rhetoric." *Explorations in Rhetoric: Studies in Honor of Douglas Ehninger.* Glenview, IL: Scott, 1982. 137–56.

Parrish, Wayland M. "Richard Whately's *Elements of Rhetoric.*" Diss. Cornell U, 1929.

———. "Whately and His Rhetoric." *Quarterly Journal of Speech* 15 (1929): 58–79.

———. "Whately on Elocution." *The Rhetorical Idiom: Essays in Rhetoric, Oratory, Language, and Drama.* Ithaca, NY: Cornell UP, 1958. 43–52.

Pence, Orville L. "The Concept and Function of Logical Proof in the Rhetorical System of Richard Whately." *Speech Monographs* 20 (1953): 23–28.

Pomeroy, Ralph S. "Whately's Historic Doubts: Origin and Argument." *Quarterly Journal of Speech* 49 (1963): 62–74.

Prior, Arthur N. *Logic and the Basis of Ethics.* Oxford: Clarendon, 1949.

Prior, Mary. "Richard Whately." *Encyclopedia of Philosophy.* Vol. 8. New York: Macmillan, 1967. 287–88.

Rashid, Salim. "Richard Whately and Christian Political Economy at Oxford and

Dublin." *Journal of the History of Ideas* 38 (1977): 147–55.

———. "Richard Whately and the Struggle for Rational Christianity in the Mid-Nineteenth Century." *Historical Magazine of the Protestant Episcopal Church* 47 (1978): 293–322.

Rigg, James Harrison. "Richard Whately." *The Dictionary of National Biography.* Vol. 20. London: Oxford UP, 1882. 1334–40.

Sproule, J. Michael. "The Psychological Burden of Proof: On the Development of Richard Whately's Theory of Presumption." *Communication Monographs* 43 (1976): 115–29.

Van Evra, James. "Richard Whately and the Rise of Modern Logic." *History and Philosophy of Logic 5* (1984): 1–18.

Whately, Elizabeth J. *Life and Correspondence of Richard Whately, D.D.* 2 vols. London: Longman, 1866.

———. *Miscellaneous Remains from the Commonplace Book of Richard Whately, D.D., Late Archbishop of Dublin.* Rev. ed. London: Longman, 1864.

Whately, Richard. *Elements of Logic* [1827]. Ed. Ray E. McKerrow. New York: Scholars' Facsimiles and Reprints, 1975.

———. *Elements of Rhetoric* [1846]. Ed. Douglas Ehninger. Carbondale: Southern Illinois UP, 1963.

———. *The Errors of Romanism, Traced to Their Origin in Human Nature* [Essays: Third Series]. London: Fellowes, 1830.

———. *Historic Doubts Relative to Napoleon Bonaparte* [1862]. Ed. Ralph S. Pomeroy. Berkeley: Scholar, 1985.

———. *Introductory Lectures on Political Economy.* Oxford: John Parker, 1832.

———. *Miscellaneous Lectures and Reviews.* London: Longman, 1861.

———. *On Some Peculiarities of the Christian Religion.* [Essays: First Series]. London: Longmans, 1825.

———. *Some of the Difficulties in the Writings of the Apostle Paul* [Essays: Second Series]. London: Fellowes, 1826.

———. *The Use and Abuse of Party Feeling in Matters of Religion* [The Bampton Lectures]. Oxford: John Parker, 1822.

Winans, James A. "Whately on Elocution." *Quarterly Journal of Speech* 31 (1945): 1–8.

Wichelns, Herbert August (1894–1973)

Widely known for two major essays, "The Literary Criticism of Oratory" and "Ralph Waldo Emerson." The first of these essays established a basis for advanced study of rhetoric, and it continues to be republished as a landmark in the resurgence of study in rhetoric and rhetorical criticism. Recent republications of this essay appear in Martin J. Medhurst, *Landmark Essays in American Public Address* (Hermagoras, 1993) and in Thomas W. Benson, *Landmark Essays in Rhetorical Criticism* (Hermagoras, 1993). It may fairly be said that this essay was the pioneer proposal for scholarly study of strictly rhetorical discourse, especially oral. The above essays and his rigorous training of young scholars constitute Wichelns's major contributions to modern studies of the history and methods of practical rhetoric.

Wichelns was born in New York City, attended high school there, and then entered Cornell University, graduating with a B.A. degree in humanities and a doctorate in comparative literature. He served in the United States Army during World War I but was not stationed overseas. He taught briefly at the University of Pittsburgh but returned to Cornell University where, with occasional temporary assignments at other universities, he spent the rest of his active career in Cornell's Department of Speech and Drama. He chaired that department for several years. He retired in 1964 but continued to teach occasionally at Cornell. Ultimately he returned to the New York City area, where he died.

Wichelns was an active member of what became the Speech Communication Association, taught a variety of courses in speech and rhetoric, and directed numerous graduate studies.

Carroll C. Arnold
Pennsylvania State University

Bibliography

Wichelns, Herbert A. "The Literary Criticism of Oratory." *Studies in Rhetoric and Public Speaking in Honor of James Albert Winans.* Ed. A.M. Drummond. New York: Century, 1925.

———. "Ralph Waldo Emerson." *A History and Criticism of American Public Address.* Vol. 2. Ed. William Norwood Brigance. New York: McGraw, 1941.

Wilkins, John (1614–1672)

A founder of the Royal Society and an advocate of establishing a universal language upon the nature of things. In the 1650s John Wilkins served as warden of Wadham College, Oxford, where Robert Boyle and others gathered to discuss scientific inquiry. Upon the Restoration, many of the Oxford group moved to the capital, and the Royal Society was established there in 1662. Wilkins's half-dozen works on science are more speculative than experimental, most notably *The Discovery of a New World; or a Discourse tending to prove, that it is probable there may be another habitable World in the Moon* (1638) and *Discourse Concerning the Possibility of a Passage to the World in the Moon* (1638). Wilkins was one of the first in England to write a book-length treatise proposing a universal language. Before becoming bishop of Chester in 1668, he also wrote a treatise on preaching that was one of the first works to use the term *elocution* for the art of delivery.

While drawing widely on classical theories, Wilkins's *Ecclesiastes, or, A Discourse concerning the Gift of Preaching* (1646, with at least seven editions by 1700) is a pivotal text in the transition away from Ciceronianism. As with Robert Boyle, Joseph Glanvill, and others associated with the Royal Society, Wilkins advocated the plain style as more consistent with the unadorned truths of the Bible and with Baconian doctrines of nature's own language. Wilkins argued for an "experimental acquaintance" with religious truths on the assumption that the inductive method of the new science would instill a rational understanding of the religious experience. Wilkins was perhaps the first to depart from classical sources to use *elocution* for delivery rather than style or *elocutio*, but he maintained a classical conception of the arts of rhetoric, devoting but a single page to the art that elocutionists would make almost synonymous with rhetoric (see Howell 451–64). Like his work on preaching, Wilkins's *Discourse Concerning the Gift of Prayer* (1651) drew on the moderns' interest in method to investigate mental faculties and argue for the plain style as the language of nature.

Wilkins's *Essay towards a Real Character, and a Philosophical Language* (1668) is "generally regarded as the most comprehensive and elaborate attempt at a universal language" (Asbach-Schnitker xxvi). Wilkins's *Essay* includes "An Alphabetical Dictionary" that defined all words according to the essential characteristics and logical relations of natural objects. The work was published under the auspices of the Royal Society and, like others in the group, Wilkins believed that a universal language was essential to promoting international "commerce," "improving natural knowledge," and eliminating religious differences that arose from the vagaries of mere words (*Works* 170). Wilkins's *Mercury or the Secret and Swift Messenger* (1641) also argued for a universal language as the most efficient means to advance knowledge, for "that great part of our time which is now required to the learning of words, might then be employed in the study of things" (*Works* 54).

Wilkins's works thus document some of the trends involved in seventeenth-century debates between the ancients and moderns, and he is also historically important as one of the founders of the institution commonly identified with the origins of the new science.

Thomas P. Miller
University of Arizona

Bibliography

Asbach-Schnitker, Brigitte. Introductory Essay. *Mercury: Or the Secret and Swift Messenger. . . Together with an Abstract of Dr. Wilkins's Essay Towards a Real Character and a Philosophical Language.* John Wilkins. *Foundations of Semiotics* 6. Amsterdam: Benjamins, 1984.

Howell, Wilbur Samuel. *Eighteenth-Century British Logic and Rhetoric.* Princeton: Princeton UP, 1971.

Wilkins, John. *The Mathematical and Philosophical Works of the Right Rev. John Wilkins.* 1708. London: Cass, 1970.

Williams, Raymond (1921–1988)

One of the leading left intellectuals in twentieth-century Britain. Raymond Williams wrote or edited over thirty books as part of his engagement with socialist theory, which led him to develop what he called "cultural materialism: a theory of the specificities of material culture and literary production within historical materialism" (*Marxism and Literature* 5). Williams's work is remarkable not only because of its breadth—he wrote novels, plays, and scholarship on literature, history, popular culture, and Marxism—but also because of his style and his relation to established disciplines. Williams's style is unusual in the way he makes intricate theoretical arguments in widely accessible language. His work is also unusual in the way it borrows the methods and concepts of literary studies, Marxist theory, and history, adapting them to his own project while providing a powerful critique of their uses. Because of the subject and style of his work, he is one of the more influential modern writers on culture and language and a founding figure of contemporary cultural studies.

Williams's work belongs to the movement of British socialist scholars such as Edward P. Thompson and Richard Hoggart. Williams combines a socialist concern for history with his working-class Welsh background and a sensitivity to textual form and nuances. Because of these multiple affiliations, Williams's work always has a critical relation to what were at the time accepted disciplinary traditions. To borrow one of his own, now famous, terms for describing social processes, his work represented an "emergent" cultural practice. For Williams, an emergent, as opposed to "residual" or "dominant," practice is one that is not merely novel but "alternative and oppositional" (*Marxism and Literature* 124). The concept of the "structure of feeling," which is central to Williams's work, and his early books *Culture and Society* and *The Long Revolution* characterize both his intellectual position and his dedication to intervening in contemporary culture.

The paradoxical term *structure of feeling* first appeared in the *Preface to Film* (1954) and appeared in revised form throughout Williams's work. Initially developed to analyze the relation of a text to material social processes, the structure of feeling was generalized as "a structure in the sense that you could perceive it operating in one work after another which weren't otherwise connected—people weren't learning it from each other; yet it was one of feeling much more than thought—a pattern of impulses, restraints, tones" (*Politics* 159). In this formulation, Williams acknowledges the reality of lived experience as the basis of cultural "feeling" and rejects the structural and Marxist notion that experience is secondary and determined by economic structures. Nevertheless, this definition also recognizes the historical and material basis of experience, avoiding the purely formal analysis of Leavisite criticism. Williams repeats this strategy in his famous critique of the Marxist concept of the "base/superstructure" opposition (*Marxism and Literature* 75–82) and his analyses of material and social production of literature and popular culture.

In *Culture and Society*, Williams explores how the idea of "culture" develops through history. By examining a number of texts written between 1780 and 1950, he corrects what he saw as the selective redefinition of "culture" at the hands of critics like T.S. Eliot and F.R. Leavis, who set culture against democracy, socialism, and the working-class experience. Williams later argues that culture is ordinary, that it is everyday common experience rather than a specialized aesthetic. Similarly, in *The Long Revolution*, he offers an historical analysis that argues that the three revolutions in British history—the industrial, democratic, and cultural revolutions—are all one integrated process of social change and advance rather than decline.

Carl G. Herndl
New Mexico State University

Bibliography

Eagleton, Terry. *Raymond Williams: Critical Perspectives*. Boston: Northeastern UP, 1989.

Williams, Raymond. *Communications*. 2nd ed. Baltimore: Penguin, 1968.

———. *The Country and the City*. New York: Oxford UP, 1973.

———. *Culture and Society, 1780–1950*. New York: Columbia UP, 1958.

———. *Keywords: A Vocabulary of Culture and Society*. New York: Oxford UP, 1976.

———. *The Long Revolution*. London: Chatto & Windus, 1961. 2nd ed. New York: Harper, 1961.

———. *Marxism and Literature*. New York: Oxford UP, 1977.

———. *Politics and Letters: Interviews with the New Left Review*. London: New Left, 1979.

———. *Problems in Materialism and Culture: Selected Essays*. London: Verso, 1980.

———. *Writing in Society*. London: Verso, 1983.

Wilson, Thomas (1523 or 1524–1581)

Tudor scholar, author, and statesman. Thomas Wilson rose from a wealthy yeoman's family to become a member of Elizabeth I's privy council and Master of St. Katherine's Hospital. He entered King's College, Cambridge, in 1542 and secured his Master of Arts degree in 1549. When the Catholic Queen Mary came to the English throne four years later, Wilson, a committed Protestant, followed his English co-religionists into exile in Italy. There he continued his studies, demonstrated his legal skill as an advocate at the papal court, and secured his Doctor of Civil Laws from the University of Ferrara in 1559. Upon his return to England in 1560, he began to establish contacts with members of Elizabeth's government. Attracting the eye of William Cecil, Elizabeth's most powerful counselor, Wilson embarked on his career as a crown servant, acting as ambassador to Portugal and the Low Countries. His service in this capacity so impressed Elizabeth and Cecil that after his second mission to the Low Countries, Elizabeth appointed him privy councilor and principal secretary, an office he shared with Francis Walsingham.

Wilson continued his scholarly activity for most of his career. At Cambridge he edited several volumes, wrote the first English-language logic text, *The Rule of Reason* (1551), and produced *The Arte of Rhetorique* (1553). During his public life, he translated the *Orations of Demosthenes* (1570) and published *A Discourse upon Usury* (1572). Thomas Wilson's present fame derives primarily from *The Arte of Rhetorique,* in which he adapted classical Roman rhetorics for the needs of the Tudor period. The audience intended for his rhetoric (as well as his logic) was the socially mobile professional class, including lawyers and merchants, of which he was a prominent member. Appropriating the ancient categories of forensic, deliberative, and epideictic discourse, Wilson reinterpreted them to suit the practical needs of Renaissance speakers and writers. Moreover, *The Rule of Reason* treated logic simply and systematically so that men of little education could have access to the processes of formal reasoning. These texts represented a movement toward the democratization of the arts of discourse, making it available to a wider group of people. Both books, in fact, underwent numerous editions and reprints throughout the sixteenth century, a tribute to their popularity and their usefulness to many members of the rising classes in Tudor England.

John C. Weaver
Purdue University

Bibliography

Derrick, Thomas J. Introduction. *Arte of Rhetorique*. Thomas Wilson. New York: Garland, 1982. vii–cxl.

Howell, Wilbur Samuel. *Logic and Rhetoric in England 1500–1700*. Princeton: Princeton UP, 1956.

Medine, Peter E. *Thomas Wilson*. Twayne's English Authors Series 431. Boston: Twayne, 1986.

Winans, James Albert (1872–1956)

A major figure in the revival of rhetorical studies, especially oral, in the United States. Winans was born in rural New York state and died in Ithaca, New York. He attended Hamilton College, where he received the B.A.; he thereafter assumed a teaching post at Cornell University. There he taught speech, with few breaks, until 1920. For much of this period, he headed what emerged as the Department of Speech and Drama. In 1920 Winans moved to Dartmouth College where he served as professor until his retirement. After retiring from Dartmouth he taught during World War II at the University of Missouri, then settled for the rest of his life in Ithaca. In the early years of his service at Cornell, Winans also took a degree in law. He did not practice law, but during his tenure at Dartmouth he created and taught a widely known course in legal argument.

Winans was dissatisfied with the thrust of college courses in elocution, and, in 1915, some sixteen years after coming to Cornell, he privately published his textbook *Public Speaking.* The book was soon taken over by Century Press. After the book had gone through several editions, he replaced it with *Speech-Making,* first published in 1938. Both textbooks were widely used in American colleges and universities. Both were strongly rooted in contemporary psychology as well as in standard rhetorical theory, and both emphasized a theory of oral composition stressing a "keen sense of communication" and "full realization of the content of your words as you utter them." In the year of his death, he published *Daniel Webster and the Salem Murder,* a critical study on which he and his late colleague, Howard A. Bradley, had worked for years. The founding of the Eastern Public Speaking Conference, now the Eastern Communication Association (and part of the Speech Communication Association), gave Winans many additional opportunities for professional commentary and intellectual exchange, both of which he highly valued. His contributions to rhetorical theory are in most circumstances still applicable, and they are found chiefly in his two textbooks.

Carroll C. Arnold
Pennsylvania State University

Bibliography

Bradley, Howard A., and James A. Winans. *Daniel Webster and the Salem Murder*. Columbia, MO: Artcraft, 1956.

Winans, James A. *Public Speaking*. New York: Century, 1917.

———. *Speech-Making*. New York: Appleton, 1938.

Winterowd, W. Ross (b. 1930)

American theorist of rhetoric and composition whose wide-ranging studies have contributed to our understanding of rhetoric as a global art. In 1972, at the forefront of renewed interest in the theory and history of rhetoric and its relation to other fields, Winterowd founded the doctoral program in rhetoric, linguistics, and literature at the University of Southern California. He directed this program from 1972 to 1984, and again beginning in 1987. The RLL program, as it has become known, embodies Winterowd's conception of rhetoric as an interdisciplinary study that entails a broad and substantial body of research and methodology from the social sciences and the humanities. This global view of rhetoric delivers it from an exclusive academic identification with the teaching of composition, at the same time as it emphasizes composition as a rich intellectual and practical enterprise. Winterowd's RLL program was recognized as a model for doctoral training in rhetoric, and its influence is apparent today at a number of universities.

Winterowd's 1986 book *Composition/Rhetoric: A Synthesis* collects essays of his that have become classics in the field, and that, taken together, indicate the range of his scholarship: for example, "Brain, Rhetoric, and Style" discusses the relationship of cerebral hemisphericity to "propositional" and "appositional" modes of thinking and writing; "The Rhetoric of Beneficence, Authority, Ethical Commitment, and the Negative," is an investigation of speech act theory and case grammar as interactive models for the creation of sentences. "Creativity and the Comp Class" is a comprehensive digest of creativity theory as it affects rhetorical invention.

As Winterowd himself has noted, this 1986 book echoes the title of his 1968 *Rhetoric: A Synthesis*, which was one of the first efforts to survey the emergence of current-traditional rhetoric in the eighteenth century and to assess its influence on prevailing conceptions of style, as well as an introductory treatment of the rhetorical theory of Kenneth Burke. Winterowd's love of Burke has influenced all of his work, and Winterowd's "Kenneth Burke: An Annotated Glossary of His Terministic Screen and a 'Statistical' Survey of His Major Concepts," remains a unique guide to Burke's theoretical perspectives.

Winterowd has been a major innovator of composition pedagogy, and English education generally. Working with the Huntington Beach High School District in Southern California from 1976 till 1982, he planned and developed "Project Literacy," a curriculum that represented the successful application of theory to practice and became a model for schools nationwide. In much of his work on literacy and English education, Winterowd observes a tendency in the humanities to aggrandize "imaginative" literature (fiction and poetry) and devalue what Winterowd calls "the literature of fact": autobiography, biography, history, the essay. This distinction between the imaginative and the factual has led, Winterowd believes, to the denigration of composition in the academy.

William A. Covino
University of Illinois at Chicago

Bibliography

Winterowd, W. Ross. *Composition/Rhetoric: A Synthesis*. Carbondale: Southern Illinois UP, 1986.

———. *The Culture and Politics of Literacy*. New York: Oxford UP, 1989.

———. "Kenneth Burke: An Annotated Glossary of His Terministic Screen and a 'Statistical' Survey of His Major Concepts." *Rhetoric Society Quarterly* 15.3–4 (1985): 145–77.

———. "Literacy, Linguistics, and Rhetoric." *Teaching Composition: Twelve Bibliographcal Essays*. Ed. Gary Tate. Fort Worth: Texas Christian UP, 1987. 227–64.

———. *Rhetoric: A Synthesis*. New York: Holt, 1968.

Witherspoon, John (1723–1794)

Noted as the author of the first work on rhetoric produced in America, but more widely known as a signatory of the Declaration of Independence, a founder of the American Presbyterian Church, and a teacher of James Madison. While Witherspoon and Hugh Blair were classmates in the first classes on English literature, rhetoric, and composition offered at Edinburgh University, Witherspoon became a leading opponent of the Moderate party of clergymen that Blair helped establish. Witherspoon's popular satire of the moderate sensibility, *Ecclesiastical Characteristics* (1753), attracted the attention of the evangelists who were trying to prevent the established clergy from gaining control of the college that they had founded at Princeton, and in 1768 Witherspoon was persuaded to immigrate and become president of the college. His courses on rhetoric and moral philosophy introduced such students as Madison to the civic ideals and natural rights doctrines that shaped American revolutionary rhetoric. Witherspoon maintained the classical ties between rhetoric and moral philosophy that were central to the civic humanist tradition, but his approach had far less impact on the emerging field of college English studies than the belletristic orientation of his former classmate.

Witherspoon's *Lectures on Moral Philosophy, and Eloquence* were published in 1810, although they had appeared earlier in his *Works* (Philadelphia 1802; Edinburgh 1804). Witherspoon never revised his lectures for publication, and their rough form helps to explain why they did not become as popular as Blair's textbook. Like Blair, Witherspoon is less important as an original theorist than as an index to popular assumptions. Blair's belletristic perspective appealed to provincials' cultural insecurities, while Witherspoon's civic approach to rhetoric and moral philosophy suited the political needs of revolutionary America. Witherspoon did not share Blair's view that the composition of public discourse had become less important than belletristic criticism. Witherspoon reiterated rhetoric's classical focus on popular political discourse and confined his discussions of taste to a final concluding lecture. He provided a practical survey of the classical precepts of rhetoric, but like other "new" rhetoricians, he rejected topical aids to invention and the elaborate style and form favored by classicists (see Howell 671–91). Witherspoon treated rhetoric as a political art closely related to moral philosophy, and his *Lectures on Moral Philosophy* drew on civic humanists like Aristotle and Cicero as well as the most important Scottish theorist of the time, Francis Hutcheson, Adam Smith's predecessor and teacher as professor of moral philosophy at Glasgow.

Witherspoon was less interested in theorizing about rhetoric than in speaking to the public controversies of the time. He helped bridge the rift between evangelicals and the established clergy and became the first moderator of the reunified Presbyterian Church. Witherspoon's sermon *The Dominion of Providence over the Passions of Men* (1776) is widely viewed as the most influential statement of support for independence to be delivered from an American pulpit. Witherspoon had achieved notoriety as head of the radical delegation to the New Jersey Assembly that was instrumental in removing the royalist governor, William Franklin, and Witherspoon went on to become a delegate to the Continental Congress. Conservatives used the late arrival of the New Jersey delegation to argue that the time was not yet ripe for independence, and Witherspoon responded by delivering a famous speech in which he said that the colonies were "not only ripe for the measure but in danger of becoming rotten for the want of it" (*Selected Writings* 31). Witherspoon was thus far more influential as a practicing rhetorician than as a rhetorical theorist.

Thomas P. Miller
University of Arizona

Bibliography

Collins, Varnum Lansing. *President Witherspoon*. 2 vols. Princeton: Princeton UP, 1925.

Halloran, S. Michael. "Rhetoric in the American College Curriculum: The Decline of Public Discourse." *PRE/TEXT* 3 (1982): 245–69.

Howell, Wilbur Samuel. *Eighteenth-Century British Logic and Rhetoric*. Princeton: Princeton UP, 1971.

Miller, Thomas P. "Blair, Witherspoon and the Rhetoric of Civic Humanism." *Scotland and America in the Age of Enlightenment*. Ed. Richard Sher and Jeffrey Smitten. Edinburgh: Edinburgh UP; Princeton: Princeton UP, 1990. 100–14.

———. "John Witherspoon and Scottish Rhetoric and Moral Philosophy in America." *Rhetorica* 8 (1992): 381–403.

Sloan, Douglas. *The Scottish Enlightenment and the American College Ideal*. New York: Teachers College P, 1971.

Witherspoon, John. *Selected Writings*. Ed. Thomas P. Miller. Carbondale: Southern Illinois UP, 1992.

Wittgenstein, Ludwig (1889–1951)

Twentieth-century philosopher of language. Wittgenstein was born in Vienna, where he was educated at home until he was fourteen. He attended school at Linz for three years and then studied mechanical engineering for two years in Berlin. In 1908 he traveled to England and enrolled at the University of Manchester to study engineering. While in England his interests shifted from engineering to problems in pure mathematics, and in 1912 he enrolled at Cambridge to study with Bertrand Russell. At the outbreak of World War I he volunteered to serve with the Austrian army, and during his army service he continued to work on the book he began under Russell's tutelage. In 1918 he completed the manuscript, and in 1921 the book appeared in German. One year later, the English version was published with the title *Tractatus Logico-philosophicus*.

After the war Wittgenstein earned a teaching certificate, and in 1920 he began teaching children in a village school located in Lower Austria. In 1926 he resigned his teaching position and occupied himself for the next two years helping to build an elaborate house for his sister. During this time Wittgenstein attended a few meetings of the Vienna Circle, and through his discussions with Moritz Schlick, one of the founders of the Circle, Wittgenstein became an important influence on logical positivism. In 1929 Wittgenstein enrolled once again at Cambridge where he submitted the *Tractatus* as his dissertation. He began teaching at Cambridge in 1930 and assumed the chair in philosophy in 1937. During World War II, he relinquished his teaching duties and worked in a London hospital. He resumed his teaching position at Cambridge in 1944 and began work in earnest on the *Philosophical Investigations*. In 1947 Wittgenstein gave up his chair at Cambridge and led a solitary life in Ireland and England until his death in 1951.

Wittgenstein's most influential writings are the *Tractatus* and the *Philosophical Investigations*. In general, the *Tractatus* attempts to reveal the relation between language and reality. Perhaps the central concept in Wittgenstein's analysis of this relation is his formulation of the picture theory of language. By picture theory Wittgenstein means that constructing thoughts about the world consists in our ability to form meaningful sentences, and a sentence is a picture of reality in the sense that a sentence corresponds directly to what it represents. Consequently, anything that cannot be stated or pictured in a sentence cannot be thought. The primary function of philosophy, then, consists in relating what can and cannot be said.

In the *Philosophical Investigations*, Wittgenstein disavows almost completely the philosophy of language he promulgated in the *Tractatus*. In particular, he drops the picture theory of language in favor of something he calls "language games." In the *Tractatus*, Wittgenstein presupposed that language is basically uniform; it possesses an essence—the ability to picture reality—that all individual utterances share. In the *Philosophical Investigations*, however, Wittgenstein eschews essentialism and regards meaning as a product of the uses of language within different kinds of language games. These games might bear a superficial resemblance to one another, but no two language games ever will be precisely the same. Wittgenstein's anti-essentialist stance regarding language means that a sentence may be understood only within the context of a language game. Since concepts or words do not possess an essence or absolute meaning outside of a specific language game, no rules exist or could exist that describe how language operates to produce meaning. In fact, Wittgenstein argues that linguistic rules derive from the language games we play; therefore, the linguistic rules that we follow are shaped by social practice and not the other way around.

Building on his concept of a language game, Wittgenstein attacks the ubiquitous idea of a private language. Reacting against the idealist formulation that words stand solely for ideas in the mind of a language user, Wittgenstein argues that the context or circumstances of language use determines meaning. When we employ language to communicate, we must follow certain shared rules or agreements. In order to be shared, these agreements must be public and accessible to other language users; obviously, they cannot be private. Consequently, the very idea of a private language is self-contradictory. Wittgenstein's argument against the possibility of a private language constitutes yet another attack on essentialism and on his own picture theory of language, and it calls into question any theory of language that attempts to explain meaning exclusively in terms of mental categories or universal grammatical structures.

Wittgenstein's conception of language represents a singular achievement in the history of philosophy, and it continues to influence a wide range of philosophers, rhetoricians, and literary theorists interested in the relation between language and meaning.

Thomas Kent
Iowa State University

Bibliography

Griffiths, A. Phillips, ed. *Wittgenstein Centenary Essays*. New York: Cambridge UP, 1991.

Malcolm, Norman. *Ludwig Wittgenstein: A Memoir*. New York: Oxford UP, 1984.

Wittgenstein, Ludwig. *The Blue and Brown Books: Preliminary Studies for the* Philosophical Investigations. London: Blackwell, 1958.

———. *Philosophical Investigations*. Trans. G.E.M. Anscombe. New York: Macmillan, 1953.

———. *Tractatus Logico-philosophicus*. New York: Harcourt, 1922.

Women Rhetoricians

Women who have studied persuasive uses of language. Women have contributed to the traditional Western rhetorical canon, which has been directed primarily at male speakers using persuasive language for public purposes such as political debate or preaching. Women have written about more private forms of persuasive language, deemed more suitable for women in patriarchal societies. Some women's work with persuasive language treats areas not traditionally defined as rhetoric.

This diversity of definitions suggests the scholarly problem of dealing with the almost total exclusion of women from the traditional canon, arising from its focus on the use of persuasive language in public, where women's participation was banned. But no one should assume that because of this ban no women contributed to rhetoric; as in revisionist research in literature, a wealth of texts by women are being uncovered where there had been thought to be "nothing" before. More work is also being done on rhetorics by women outside the West, and on entirely oral rhetorics.

Looking only at the Western tradition preserved in written texts—and at oppositional spaces carved out within or alongside this tradition—reveals resources on women rhetoricians. In ancient Greece the (male) sophists questioned the social exclusions visited on Greek women, and this may have helped to create spaces for women in education. Plato may have admitted some women to his school, and there were also schools for women only, with curricula similar to those of the men's schools. Sappho headed such a school. Inscriptions suggest that by the second century B.C.E., enough girls were attending such schools that cities funded competitions for them in oratory. Classical texts by male authors present women learned in rhetoric as important characters—for example, Diotima and Aspasia.

Nevertheless, only a tiny minority of Greek women, among the economically privileged, were studying rhetoric, and practicing it only in highly controlled conditions such as the sanctioned competition. Educated women such as Aspasia could serve as teachers of rhetoric, not only to young girls but also to adult men. But these activities did not include participation in public uses of rhetoric such as political debate.

The picture in ancient Rome is very similar. Only a tiny minority of women, mostly the socially privileged, could get any education at all. They might study at home with tutors or, especially later in the imperial period, in schools for girls, or sometimes even in coeducational schools that also included a tiny number of indigent students with imperial scholarships. Nevertheless, women's education was not to be used in public. Women might influence their male relatives; Cicero comments upon the importance of a well-educated mother to her son's success as a political leader. Women may also have participated in private competitions in declamation, to which men, too, were increasingly restricted by late imperial censorship.

The Christian clergy controlled formal education in Europe after Rome fell, especially from about 500 to 1200 C.E. The rise of Christianity broadened educational opportunities for women slightly, in that the available opportunities were to be equally due to any true Christian and not the exclusive province of the upper social classes. Educational opportunities for all, however, declined during the medieval period, and Christian education downplayed the importance of rhetoric. Moreover, the women who did manage to get some education—for example, in women's religious establishments, where students from poor families were accepted—were still largely banned from speaking in public. Religious women, such as Hildegard of Bingen, could have influence through their writings. Women could write poetry influenced by rhetorical stylistic devices. But only aristocratic women, such as the daughters of Charlemagne, who were educated in the same court school with their male relatives, could hope for any public scope for the exercise of rhetoric.

The familiar pattern of scanty private education plus even scantier public opportunity continued in Renaissance rhetorical education for women. Rhetoric, however, enjoyed an upsurge of attention in the schools founded by Renaissance humanists, and these schools often included all the children, male and female, of the sponsoring aristocrat, as well as some indigent children supported by the patron. The few women who did receive an education in the Renaissance learned more about rhetoric than any women had since classical times. Moreover, slightly more opportunities existed for the public exercise of rhetorical talents, such as by the child prodigy, such as Cassandra Fedele, or the female monarch, such as Elizabeth of England. At the same time, however, and perhaps in response to women's increased ability to practice rhetoric, arguments against women's use of rhetoric in public became even more strident.

Attention to women's use of persuasive speech in nonpublic situations was sanctioned, however, and highly developed by well-educated women humanists such as Christine de Pizan and Laura Cereta. Moreover, women's literacy increased in the Renaissance period, influenced by such factors as the Protestant Christian emphasis on individual Bible study and the spread of printing. Texts by Renaissance women that can be considered as rhetoric include Christine's *Treasure of the City of Ladies* (1405), which gives advice on the private use of persuasive speech, and Margaret Fell's *Women's Speaking Justified, Proved, and Allowed by the Scriptures* (1666), which boldly argues for a public role for women in moral exhortation.

Although access to literacy varied with social class, race, and region, about 50 percent of women in Europe and America were literate by the end of the eighteenth century, and more women were educated above the grammar school level. Texts by women that could be construed as rhetorical proliferated, such as on how women should use persuasive speech in private forms, such as letters and conversation.

See, for example, Catharine Macauley's *Letters on Education* (1790) and Hannah More's *Strictures on the Modern System of Female Education* (1799). More texts also began to appear in which women argued for increased public roles, primarily as moral agents. For example, Sarah Grimke's defense of women speaking in public (1838) was intended to justify her and her sister Angelina's activism in behalf of abolition.

The nineteenth century offers a rich field of texts by women that can be construed as rhetorical. These texts may deal with education, social activism, or religion, but are being reread as accounts of how women defined, claimed, and justified active public voices for themselves. By the late nineteenth century, many women in Europe and America were becoming powerful political actors—including women of color such as Sojourner Truth and Frances E.W. Harper—and were receiving university educations on a par with men's. Rhetoric scholars are recovering these women's reflections on their persuasive practices—for example, in the memoirs of Elizabeth Cady Stanton, a powerful speaker for abolition and women's suffrage. Women also began to write rhetoric textbooks for any student, such as Gertrude Buck's *Argumentative Writing* (1899).

This outpouring of work has continued into the twentieth century. The same sites identified above as productive of much work by women on rhetoric are also being developed in the twentieth century, augmented by the observations of the increasing number of women who have held political office and other leadership positions in this period.

This century has also seen the first development of a large body of academically trained women scholars whose focus is rhetoric. Women scholars in such fields as philosophy, speech communication, composition studies, and the history of rhetoric make up the largest body of women rhetoricians, perhaps, who have ever lived. Their work not only studies rhetoric but may also itself be studied to elucidate its rhetorical strategies.

Twentieth-century work on women and rhetoric has considered whether women use language in distinctive ways. Traditional rhetoric may have said that women use language in ways inferior to men's ways. Contemporary linguist Robin Lakoff has argued that these inferior ways, with such features as hypercorrectness and tag questions, are forced on women to make them appear chaste, indecisive, and unintelligent—that is, as fulfilling acceptable patriarchal images of women.

In contrast, the work of Carol Gilligan on women's concepts of morality and of Mary Field Belenky and her colleagues on women's approaches to academic work suggests that while women may indeed use language as Lakoff suggests, these language-using habits should not be viewed negatively, as signs of oppression, but rather positively, as signs of a more caring, noncompetitive world view peculiar to women, a world view that could be seen as morally superior to the more aggressive attitudes conveyed in "male" styles of language use.

Some contemporary feminists have thus developed an intellectual discourse that transgresses traditional academic conventions in order to valorize ways of using language previously denigrated as feminine. For example, many feminist scholars routinely use the first person in their scholarly writing, discuss the influence of their personal experiences on their work, and otherwise violate academic objectivity. A powerful example of this style, as well as a compelling theoretical justification for it, may be found in the work of bell hooks (see, for example, *Talking Back: Thinking Feminist, Thinking Black* 1989).

Others, such as French feminist Hélène Cixous, go further and fashion a discourse that is emotionally expressive, poetic, allusive, and nonlinear—all "faults" in traditional academic discourse. Cixous links this decentered discourse to female sexuality with its multiple erogenous zones, and thus claims to be "writing the body," allowing the banned female form a public voice.

Cixous also uses more traditional academic discourse, what she calls the "discourse of mastery," to assert authority over her students. Cixous terms this a "rhetorical discourse" because it aims to master or control the audience, a persuasive power Cixous seeks for women. At the same time, Cixous suggests that even in adapting traditional academic discourse to feminist purposes, a new, less imperious kind of rhetorical power must be developed. Some contemporary feminists have suggested that one way to make this power less imperious is to bring out the presence in any discourse—and any individual— of multiple voices, a conviction that works

out in pedagogy through allowing more student participation and collaboration in the classroom.

These strands of work on women and language use are weaving into new views of rhetoric that are uniquely women's. Scholarship to articulate the traits of women's rhetorics may look at almost any writings or recorded speeches by women to see what persuasive features they exhibit, even if the women did not record explicit reflections on language use. Thus a woman whose writings are judged to be rhetorical, or to be employing persuasive devices, may be nominated ex post facto as a woman rhetorician. The possibilities for research here seem broad indeed.

Patricia Bizzell
College of the Holy Cross

Bibliography

Belenky, Mary Field, Blythe McVicker Clinchy, Nancy Rule Goldberger, and Jill Mattuck Tarule. *Women's Ways of Knowing: The Development of Self, Voice, and Mind.* New York: Basic, 1986.

Bizzell, Patricia, and Bruce Herzberg, eds. *The Rhetorical Tradition: Readings from Classical Times to the Present.* Boston: Bedford, 1990.

Campbell, Karlyn Kohrs. *Man Cannot Speak for Her.* 2 vols. New York: Praeger/Greenwood, 1989.

Cixous, Hélène, and Catherine Clement. *The Newly Born Woman.* Trans. Betsy Wing. 1975. Rpt. Minneapolis: U of Minnesota P, 1986.

Gilligan, Carol. *In a Different Voice: Psychological Development and Women's Development.* Cambridge, MA: Harvard UP, 1982.

Jarratt, Susan C., guest editor. "Special Issue: Feminist Rereadings in the History of Rhetoric." *Rhetoric Society Quarterly* 22 (1992).

Lakoff, Robin. *Language and Women's Place.* New York: Harper, 1975.

Lunsford, Andrea A., et al., eds. *Reclaiming Rhetorica.* Pittsburgh: U of Pittsburgh P (in press).

Phelps, Louise Wetherbee, and Janet Emig, eds. *Feminine Principles and Women's Experience in American Composition and Rhetoric.* Pittsburgh: U of Pittsburgh P (in press).

Writing across the Curriculum

A movement aimed at incorporating writing into all educational contexts, especially courses with specific disciplinary content. Often identified by the acronym WAC, the movement includes scholarly theorizing on the nature of writing in different settings; empirical research focusing on contexts, writers, teachers, disciplinary genres and epistemologies, the acquisition of discipline-specific writing abilities, and the nature of writing as a medium for general intellectual development in all subject matters; historical accounts of writing in different fields; studies and practical information on implementation and program assessment; and an extensive pedagogical literature focusing on specific classroom and programwide strategies for using writing in different school settings (see Anson, "Multidimensional"; Anson, Schwiebert, and Williamson).

Although both the theory and practice of writing across the curriculum has deep historical roots, most scholars and practitioners credit its beginnings to a movement in Britain in the 1960s and 1970s that advocated the increased use of language activities in the public schools. This curricular emphasis gained momentum with the publication in 1975 of Britton, Burgess, Martin, McLeod, and Rosen's *Development of Writing Abilities (11–18),* which reported large-scale research on the functions of writing in British public schools, demonstrating its increasing impoverishment as a tool for intellectual development throughout the later years of schooling. In the United States, the WAC movement has several nineteenth-century historical antecedents documented by Russell in his comprehensive history, but the earliest attempts by literacy educators to help integrate writing instruction into courses across the curriculum seem to have begun about thirty years ago, corresponding with the national attention to language instruction in the U.K. In some ways the movement is a natural response to increasing compartmentalizing and marginalizing of writing into centralized programs that are unable to reflect the great diversity of genres, conventions, and uses of writing in all school and professional settings.

As the WAC movement spread in the United States, it began to divide in the mid 1980s into two parallel emphases. The first of the two emphases, reflected in the more popular name "writing across (or in) the disciplines," focuses on the use and development of writing as a medium for communication in specialized subject matters, profes-

sions, or areas of scholarship. Acknowledging the varieties of discourse and "ways of knowing" of these diverse fields, this strand of WAC aims to help novice writers to acquire the discipline-specific skills necessary to produce writing acceptable to members of a specific discursive community such as the field of history, economics, or mechanical engineering. Students learn to write texts *in* a specific field, following the norms established by its members. Recognizing the continuum of specialized writing from school-based disciplines to nonacademic settings, WAC scholars began to look more closely at the forms and processes of written communication in professional fields (see Odell and Goswami; Bazerman and Paradis). Some of this information, in turn, has informed the teaching of discipline-specific writing in public and higher education.

WAC advocates working with teachers in other disciplines on ways to incorporate writing into their courses, however, reported various sources of resistance to the idea of specialized disciplinary writing: The teachers did not think themselves qualified to teach writing; they did not see it as their responsibility; they felt it would "add" new material to their already full curriculums instead of enhancing students' learning; and they argued that it took time away from their other responsibilities as teachers. A parallel movement, known as "Writing to Learn," began to develop in response to these and other rejections of WAC. That emphasis, perhaps better suited to early schooling and to general education curriculums in colleges and universities, does not have the explicit goal of improving students' writing abilities. Rather, it sees writing as an excellent and often neglected medium for enhancing the learning process. Informal writing—especially in journals, "freewrites," and short reaction papers—is assigned to help students to articulate and examine new ideas, integrating them into what they already know. The mastery of discipline-specific genres of writing—a goal more common in advanced or specialized course—is secondary to the use of writing as a tool for general intellectual development and the learning of new subject matter. Because writing is incorporated into existing subject matter, it is less likely to be seen as an "add-on" to the curriculum or as something to be explicitly taught apart from existing course material. Because teachers use writing in the service of learning rather than as a way to evaluate accumulated knowledge, they are less likely to see it as a burden or as something in which they have little pedagogical expertise. Theorists of this strand of WAC point out that the mere practice of writing as a tool for learning may lead to improved writing ability, though this is not the most primary goal of writing to learn.

The attempt to revitalize writing in all educational settings has also led to new conflicts and debates about the role of literacy development in schooling. Many unresolved questions remain: Whose job is it to monitor and teach writing? What should become of centralized writing programs? Who should be empowered to carry out faculty development in the area of writing instruction? How can insights in the field of written literacy be conveyed to teachers who have other scholarly interests within their own disciplines? How can we assess the effectiveness of WAC programs? To what extent should all forms of discourse be respected on the basis of the communities in which they are produced? Should WAC encourage increasing specialization of writing, especially in light of the consequent exclusion of nonspecialists from the making and sharing of knowledge in different fields? These and other questions continue to fuel a movement that began modestly at a few schools and now has developed into a subfield of rhetoric and composition in its own right.

Chris M. Anson
University of Minnesota

Bibliography

Anson, Chris M. "Toward a Multidimensional Model of Writing in the Academic Disciplines." *Writing in Academic Disciplines.* Ed. David A. Jolliffe. Norwood, NJ: Ablex, 1988. 1–34.

Anson, Chris M., John E. Schwiebert, and Michael M. Williamson. *Writing across the Curriculum: An Annotated Bibliography.* Westport, CT: Greenwood, 1993.

Bazerman, Charles, and James Paradis, eds. *Textual Dynamics of the Professions.* Madison: U of Wisconsin P, 1991.

Britton, James, Tony Burgess, Nancy Martin, Andrew McLeod, and Harold Rosen. *The Development of Writing Abilities (11-18).* London: Macmillan, 1974.

Odell, Lee, and Dixie Goswami, eds. *Writing in Nonacademic Settings.* New York: Guilford, 1985.

Russell, David R. *Writing in the Academic Disciplines 1870–1990: A Curricular History.* Carbondale: Southern Illinois UP, 1991.

Y

Young, Richard E. (b. 1932)

A modern rhetorical theorist, educator, and professional leader. Richard E. Young received his B.A. (with honors) and Ph.D. in English from the University of Michigan, and his M.A. in English from the University of Connecticut. He has been chair of the Department of Humanities in the College of Engineering at the University of Michigan and head of the Department of English in the College of Humanities and Social Sciences at Carnegie Mellon University, where he is currently the Thomas S. Baker Professor of Rhetoric and English Literature. Among his awards are the Elliot Dunlop Award for teaching and contributions to education given in 1993 at Carnegie Mellon and an honorary doctorate of humane letters from St. Edward's University in Austin, Texas.

Among his many contributions to rhetorical studies, primary has been his pioneering work in helping to develop a field of rhetorical inquiry on written discourse. His scholarship, graduate program development, and extensive professional activities have significantly influenced the introduction of rhetoric as a field of study within departments of English.

In 1970, with Alton Becker and Kenneth Pike, he published *Rhetoric: Discovery and Change*, a modern rhetorical theory called tagmemic rhetoric, which stimulated interest in rhetorical invention, sensitivity to cultural difference, and writing as a process of inquiry guided by heuristical procedures. An epistemic rhetoric, this theory entailed a conception of writing as a process, thinking as multiperspectival, audience as participatory, and the text as embedded in larger contexts. This work became one of the models for theory-building in composition research.

As one of the organizers of the Rhetoric Society of America in the 1960s, Young stressed the importance of multidisciplinary research on writing to study the complexities of writing and teaching. His own studies with linguists Becker and Pike and with psychologists Koen and Hayes further testify to his dedication to multimodality in rhetorical scholarship.

In many seminal essays and in over one hundred conference papers for different forums (for example, CCC, NCTE, MLA, NIE, ADE, and NEH), he has argued for writing as an intellectual activity of discovery and change, as a strategic art. His recent publications and presentations examine theoretical issues in Writing across the Curriculum and propose strategies for critically reading empirical studies on writing. His lectures at numerous seminars and workshops in colleges, universities, and organizations around the country and abroad have disseminated an understanding of modern rhetorical studies and stimulated others to pursue such research.

Another major contribution has been Young's development of graduate programs and courses in rhetoric within departments of English. During the seventies, he provided courses in rhetoric for interested doctoral students in English and education at the University of Michigan. In the 1980s, in the English Department at Carnegie Mellon, he helped to establish three graduate programs and one undergraduate program: a master's in English with a concentration in rhetoric; a Ph.D. in rhetoric; a master's in professional writing; and an undergraduate major in rhetoric. These programs, among the first opportunities for rhetorical study in departments of English, have prepared outstanding younger scholars. He has also offered four NEH summer seminars on "Rhetoric: Modern Developments in the Art of Invention" and one year-long fellowship in residence: "Rhetorical Invention and the Composition Process," thereby introducing many others, including a number of prominent current scholars, to emerging research in rhetoric and composition.

Throughout his career, Richard Young has helped establish a rigorous multidisciplinary field of rhetorical inquiry and to motivate and empower others to participate in a community dedicated to the study and teaching of writing.

Janice M. Lauer
Purdue University

Bibliography

Young, Richard E. "Arts, Crafts, Gifts, and Knacks: Some Disharmonies in the New Rhetoric." *Reinventing the Rhetorical Tradition.* Ed. Aviva Freedman and Ian Pringle. U of Central Arkansas: L and S, 1980. 53–60.

———. "Problems and the Composing Process." *Writing: Process, Development and Communication.* Ed. C.H. Fredericksen and J.F. Dominic. Hillsdale, NJ: Erlbaum, 1981.

Young, Richard E., and Alton Becker. "Toward a Modern Theory of Rhetoric: A Tagmemic Contribution." *Harvard Educational Review* 35 (1965): 450–68.

Young, Richard E., Alton Becker, and Kenneth Pike. *Rhetoric: Discovery and Change.* New York: Harcourt, 1970.

Young, Richard E., John R. Hayes, et al. *Reading Empirical Research Studies: The Rhetoric of Research.* Hillsdale, NJ: Erlbaum, 1992.

See also HEURISTICS; INVENTION; ROGERIAN RHETORIC; TAGMEMICS

Z

Zeugma

"To yoke"; the use of a single verb for several clauses: "Waging war and peace" (Sallust). Bacon demonstrated the capacity of a zeugma to condense contrasting ideas in "Histories make men wise; poets, witty; the mathematics, subtile; natural philosophy, deep; moral, grave; logic and rhetoric, able to contend." The contrast can be highlighted by yoking abstract with concrete terms, as Dickens did in writing "with this permission and the front-door key, Sam Weller issued forth" (*Pickwick Papers* Ch. 38). In *The Arte of English Poesie* (1589), George Puttenham distinguishes between the prozeugma, mesozeugma, and hypozeugma. In the prozeugma, the verb is expressed in the first clause: "Her beauty pierced mine eye, her speech mine woeful heart, / Her presence all the powers of my discourse." In the mesozeugma, the verb is expressed in the middle clause: "Fair maids' beauty (alack) with years it wears away, / And with weather and sickness, and sorrow as they say." The hypozeugma is the contrary of a zeugma, a sentence in which every clause has its own verb. Zeugma is sometimes confused with syllepsis (q.v.).

Arthur Quinn and Lyon Rathbun
University of California, Berkeley

Zoellner, Robert (b. 1926)

Developed the "talk-write" model for teaching the composing process, a model adapted from behavioral psychology. Zoellner attacks the "think-write" metaphor, the idea that the written word is thought on paper. He objects to methods for teaching writing that assume that writing problems stem largely from deficiencies in students' thinking. He views writing as a behavioral process, a pattern of responses that produce the finished essay. He is one of the first theorists to give serious attention to the composing process.

Zoellner envisions a classroom devoid of desks and chairs, where students stand at easels and write on large pads of paper with felt-tip markers. (Zoellner actually practiced this method in a large classroom equipped with large blackboards stretching from floor to ceiling.) The talk-write part of the pedagogy comes in the interaction between teacher and student and between student and fellow student. The teacher attempts to bridge the gap between vocal performance and scribal performance by having students talk out what they meant to communicate in an unclear passage. If the utterance helps the teacher understand the passage, then the teacher has the student revise the passage by transcribing that utterance on the pad of paper. The teacher makes further inquiries about the written piece, encouraging the student to explain further what he or she meant to communicate. As students try to clarify their writing through speech, they become models of the writing process for other students.

The talk-write model has seven basic principles. First, the teacher focuses on the verbal and scribal behavior of the individual student—the writing act—rather than on the product of scribal behavior, the finished essay. Second, the teacher builds on the "naive behavioral repertory" of the student, the vocal and scribal skills the student already possesses. Third, the teacher works with "freely emitted behavior": The teacher does not expect the student to write or speak in a predetermined way but rather builds upon those verbal behaviors the student freely exhibits. Fourth, the talk-write environment allows the student to respond a number of times, providing immediate reinforcement of positive behaviors. A student can react immediately to a piece of writing or a teacher's inquiry, making revisions in what he or she has written. Fifth, the emphasis on free utterance and spoken language allows a low duration of response. Students can respond quickly and are in a position to respond again immediately. Sixth, the teacher reinforces approximate behavior immediately through both verbal and nonverbal cues. Seventh, the teacher reinforces not only "correct" behavior but also each bit of behavior that approximates the behavior the teacher desires the student ultimately to exhibit, any behavior that moves in the direction of good writing.

Although Zoellner's model received harsh criticism, his ideas have influenced subsequent models of the relationship between speech and writing in the composing process.

Gary Layne Hatch
Brigham Young University

Bibliography

Hatch, Gary. "Reviving the Rodential Model for Composition: Robert Zoellner's Alternative to Flower and Hayes." *Rhetoric Review* 10 (1992): 244–51.

Hatch, Gary, and Margaret Walters. "Robert Zoellner's Talk-Write Pedagogy." *Writing Ourselves into the Story*. Ed. Sheryl Fontaine and Susan Hunter. Carbondale: Southern Illinois UP, 1992.

Heilker, Paul. "Public Products/Public Processes: Zoellner's Praxis and the Contemporary Composition Classroom." *Rhetoric Review* 10 (1992): 232–38.

Walters, Margaret. "Robert Zoellner's 'Talk-Write Pedagogy': Instrumental Concept for Composition Today." *Rhetoric Review* 10 (1992): 239–43.

Zoellner, Robert. "Talk-Write: A Behavioral Pedagogy for Composition." *College English* 30 (1969): 267–320.

Index

Cognitive balance theory, 508
Cognitive development, 219, 752
Cognitive-developmental theory, 519
Cognitive dissonance, 520
Cognitive dissonance theory, 508
Cognitive linguistics, 550
Cognitive process, 385
Cognitive psychology, 572, 738
Cognitive rhetoric, 108–109
Coherence, 110, 111, 147, 156, 193, 222, 390
Cohesion, 10, 110–111, 193, 390, 447
Cohesive ties, 110–111
Cole, Thomas, 723
Coleridge, Samuel Taylor, 73, 111–112, 474, 536, 634
Coles, William E., 113
Collaboration, 114–115, 636
Collaborative learning, 208
Collaborative writing, 55
College Composition and Communication, 138, 420
College composition textbooks, 39
College English, 372, 768
College English, 458
Committee on Public Information, 566
Commonplace, 562, 641
Commonplace books, 369
Commonplaces, 80, 116–117, 427
Common sense, 93
Common-sense philosophy, 204, 372
Common topics, 724–725
Communication, 635, 674, 730
    ecological, 226, 227
    gendered, 262–265
    models of, 365
    technical, 720–721
Communication Education, 692
Communication media, 428–429
Communication model of narrative, 455
Communication Monography, 692
Communication theory, 117–121
Communication triangle, 121–122, 376, 577
Communitarianism, 195
Community, 48, 195, 499
    discourse, 194–196, 750
Compact metonym, 445
Company We Keep, The (Booth), 82
Comparatio, 495
Comparison, 122–123, 145–146, 447, 563
Compendium, 6, 96
Completeness, 447
Complicity, 341
Composing process, 219, 778
Composing Processes of Twelfth Graders, The (Emig), 219
Compositio, 35
Composition, 53, 63, 321–322, 322–323, 760
    emergence of, as discipline, 377
    1950s, 420
    1960s, 420
Composition exercises, 583
Compositionism, 750

Composition studies, 123–133, 738
Composition theory, 577
Computer applications in rhetoric, 134–136
Computer-mediated communication, 49
Computers, 721
Conative, 365
Concept, 118
Conclusio, 36, 96
Conclusion, 504
Concordances, 704
Concrete operations stage, 520
Condillac, Etienne Bonnot, Abbé de, 136–137, 535
Conditionality, 145
Cone, Carl B., 89
Conference on College Composition and Communication (CCCC), 123, 124, 137–138, 377, 458
Confirmatio, 33, 138–139, 562, 639
Confirmation, 87, 562
Confrontation, 658
Confucianism, 100–101
Confucius, 139–140, 207
Confutatio, 138, 562
Congregatio de propaganda fide, 566
Conjecture, stasis of, 693–694
Conjunction, 111
Connotation, 667
Consciousness
    human, 512
    shared, 260
Consciousness-raising, 264–265
Consensus, 636
Conservatism, 757
Consolation of Philosophy (Boethius), 80
Constatives, 690
Constitutio, 604
Constraints, 76
Constructivism, 219–220
Consubstantiality, 140
Consumer, 44
Contact, 365
Contact zones, 338
Content, form and, 143
Context, 109, 365, 371, 453, 550
Contexts, 141, 178
Contextual definitions, 648
Contextuality, 141–143
Contextual semantics, 388
Contingency, 144–145
Continuing education, 459
Continuity, 447
Contrast, 122, 145–146, 447
Contrastive rhetoric, 146–148
Controursia, 662
Controversia, 562, 583, 642
Controversy, 17
Conversational implacature, 307
Conversation analysis, 18
Conviction-persuasion dualism, 22
Cooper, Lane, 330
Cooperative principle, 307
Cope, Edward Meredith, 29

Freud, Sigmund, 513, 635
Freudianism, 259
Fries, Charles, 657
Frigidity, 415
Fronto, Marcus Cornelius, 216, 663
Frye, Northrop, 474
Functional equivalence, 729
Functionalism, 119
Funeral oration(s), 229–230, 231
    Pericles', 41
Fussell, Paul, 89

G

Gadamer, Hans-Georg, 190, 277–278, 317–318, 517
Gage, John, 123
Galen, 663
Galilei, Galileo, 325
Gallus, L. Plotius, 637
Gardiner, Alan H., 122
Gates, Henry Louis, 702
Gates, Henry Louis, Jr., 5, 735
Gaze, 456
Gellius, Aulus, 661, 662
Gender, 456, 621
    language and, 678
Gendered communication, 262–265
Genealogy, 513
General reader, 44
General Semantics, 759
Generative grammar, 292–293, 387, 415
Generative rhetoric, 278–279
Genesis, 416
Genette, Gérard, 609–610
Genre, 35, 77, 279–284, 621, 708
Genre theory, 366
Genung, John Franklin, 285, 702
Genus deliberativum, 446
Genus demonstrativum, 446
Genus iudicale, 446
Geoffrey of Vinsauf, *see* Vinsauf, Geoffrey de
Gerard, Alexander, 71
German idealism, 298
German Romanticism, 94
Gesture, 172
Ghostwriting, 285–287
Giftedness, 354
Gilligan, Carol, 464, 772
Giroux, Henry, 464
Gleason, Barbara, 128
Gnômê, 562
God terms, 741, 758
Golden Age of Oratory, 486
Good faith, 252
Good men, 584
Good reasons, 755
Good reasons movement, 565
Good will, 243
Goody, Jack, 314, 392
Gorgias (Plato), 524, 682
Gorgias of Leontini, 150, 221, 288–289, 300, 421,
    553, 558, 665, 682, 683–685, 698, 723
Governance, 539–540

Governments, 102
Gradatio, 289
Grading, 56–57
Graffiti, 159
Grammar, 289–296, 402, 427, 667, 730, 731
    descriptive and prescriptive, 152
Grammar handbooks, 564
Grammatical correctness, 561
Grammaticus, 562, 582
Gramsci, Antonio, 297, 422–423
Granada, Luis de, 599
Grand style, 32, 51, 698
Graphic(s), 747
Grassi, Ernesto, 298, 594
Graves, Donald, 561
Great divide characterizations, 392
Great Leap theory, 314, 480–483
Greece, ancient, education in, 770
Greek handbooks, 602–603
Greek rhetoric, 299–304, 569, 680–681
Greek Sophists, 630
Gregory the Great, St., 70
Greimas, A.J., 667
Gresham College, 646
Grice, H. Paul, 306–307
Grimaldi, William M.A., 29
Grimke, Sarah, 771
Grootendorst, Rob, 19
Group communication, 119
Guarino of Verona, 533
Guido Faba, 37
Gunn, Giles, 552
Gunning, Robert, 721
Gymnasmata, 562
Gynocentric, term, 408

H

Habermas, Jürgen, 172, 277, 309–310
Hadrian, 70, 709
Haiman, Franklyn S., Award in Freedom of Expression, 693
Haldane, J.B.S., 68
Halliday, M.A.K., 193
*Handbook of Rhetorical and Communication
    Theory* (Arnold), 30
Handbooks, 311–313, 719
    Greek, 602–603
Harding, Harold, 204
Harmony, 371
Harper, Frances E.W., 771
Harpokration, 662
Harris, Zellig, 102, 193
Hartley, David, 559
Hartlib, Samuel, 646
Harun Al-Rashid, 14–15
Harvard University, 59, 657, 696
Hasan, Ruqaiya, 193
Havelock, Eric, 314, 528
Hayes, John R., 353, 461
Heath, Shirley Brice, 392
Hebraic tradition, 75
Hegel, Georg Wilhelm, 488, 536, 553

Knox, John, 395
Koina, 29
Koinos topos, 562
Krashen, Stephen D., 296
Kristeva, Julia, 377–378, 667, 735
Kuhn, Thomas S., 48, 378–379, 491, 542, 676, 734

L

Lacan, Jacques, 667
Lakoff, Robin, 771–772
Lamy, Bernard, 381, 547
Lancelot, Claude, 544
Landow, George P., 94
Langer, Susan K., 73
Langer, Susanne, 667
Language, 200–201, 509, 621, 666, 673, 728, 765
    of dramatism, 711
    and gender, 678
    as heuristic, 73
    law and, 72
    and reality, 769
    and society, 677–679
    universal, 72
Language and Learning (Britton), 84
Language games, 23, 769
Language in Relation to a Unified Theory of the Structure of Human Behavior (Pike), 520
Language origins, 136
Language Research, Inc., 68
Language study, 634
Langue, 654, 665
Lasswell, Harold, 567
"La technique," 617, 619
Latour, Bruno, 625, 676
Lauer, Janice M., 129, 382, 717, 738
"Laugh of the Medusa, The" (Cixous), 105
Law(s), 164, 473, 642
    language and, 72
    of thought, 400
Lawrence of Aquilegia, 37
Layers of structure, 278
Learning logs, 368
Leavis, F.R., 31, 428
Le Comique du discours (Olbrechts-Tyteca), 478
Lectionary, 328
LeDoeuff, Michele, 489
LeFevre, Karen Burke, 753
Legal argumentation, 384
Legal question, 710
Legal reasoning, 384
Legal rhetoric, 383–385
Legislation, 563
Leibniz, Gottfried Wilhelm von, 403
Lemmas, 707
Leonard, Sterling Andrus, 295, 657
Leontini, 221
Lerner, Gerda, 5
Lessing, Gotthold Ephraim, 535
Letteraturizzazione, 216, 386
Letters, 36–37, 99
Letter to the French Academy (Fénelon), 266
Letter-writing, 429, 432–433

Letter writing models, 95
Levels of meaning, 278
Lévi-Strauss, Claude, 667
Lexical, 102
Lexical cohesion, 111
Lexicon, 102
Libanius, 663
Liberal arts, 6, 95, 425, 580, 731
Liberal arts tradition, 376
Liberalism, 195
Liberatory pedagogy, 275, 424
Life-world, 310
Lincoln, Abraham, 487, 539
Linear communication model, 44
Linguist, 102
Linguistic fictions, 72, 477
Linguistic markers, 437
Linguistic reform, 72
Linguistics, 10, 102, 119, 192, 325, 386–391, 666, 728
    cognitive, 550
    tagmemic, 415, 520–521
    text, 193, 415, 715
"Linguistics and Poetics" (Jakobson), 365, 366
Lippmann, Walter, 566
Lispector, Clarice, 105
Listener, 43
Literacy, 210, 314, 323, 392–393, 554
    women and, 770–771
Literacy-orality theorems, 480
Literary Club, 600
Literary criticism, 505, 606
"Literary Criticism of Oratory, The" (Wichelns), 763
Literary history, 592
Literary pragmatics, 550
Literary self, 113
Literary study, 561
Literary style, 386
Literature, 474, 621
    of fact, 767
Literature and Dogma (Arnold), 31
Litigation, 383
Litote, 334
Liturgy, 328, 394–395
Liu Xie, 101
Lloyd-Jones, Richard, 738
Loci mnemonic, 435
Locke, John, 71, 136, 396–399, 403, 535, 666
Locutionary act, 54, 690
Logic, 20, 22, 58, 136, 184, 255, 274, 348–349, 352, 399–406, 407, 410, 497, 580, 651, 667, 731, 766
    classical, 477
    of discovery, 512
    relationship of, to rhetoric, 400–404
    rhetoric and poetic and, 86
Logical appeal, 521
Logical atomism, 404, 648
Logical commonplaces, 149
Logical constructionism, 404
Logical fallacies, 565
Logical positivism, 58, 246, 406–407, 542, 769
Logocentricism, 408–409

Logocentrism, 165–166, 408–409, 549
Logographers, 358
Logoi, 556
    opposing, 556
Logology, 201, 409–410, 722
Logos, 29, 408, 410–414, 504, 506, 556, 564
Logos, 65, 300, 617
Lollian, 663
Longacre, Robert E., 414–415, 715
Longinus, 303, 415–416, 663
Longus, 661
Lorde, Audre, 5
Loud lyer, 334
Love, 191
Lucian, 663
Lu Ji, 101
Lunsford, Andrea, 47, 129
Luria, Alexander, 753
Luther, Martin, 39, 234, 395, 486
Lyceum, 27
Lyco of Troas, 503
Lycurgus, 358
Lysias, 42, 150, 286, 358, 416–417

M

Macauley, Catharine, 771
Machiavelli, 97
MacIntyre, Alasdair, 419
Macrobius, 531, 661
Macrorie, Ken, 420
Magic, 421–422
Magic consciousness, 421
Mailloux, Steven, 47
Malcolm X, 5
Malebranche, Nicolas, 547
Managerial model, 46–47
Manner, 307
Marcus, George, 676
Market research, 567
Marrianus Capella, 313
Martin, Emily, 625
Marvell, Andrew, 73
Marx, Karl, 553, 635
Marxism, 120, 274, 297, 377, 422, 455, 567, 621, 675, 735, 764
Marxist rhetoric, 297, 422–424
Maslow, Abraham, 508
Mass communication, 117, 747
Mass Communication Division, SCA, 693
Mass media, 366
Materialism, 325, 764–765
Mathematical logics, 403
Mathematics, 180, 554
Mathes, J.C., 49
Matthew, Arnold, 333
Maxims, 307
Maximus of Tyre, 663
McKeon, Richard P., 424–428
McKerrow, Raymie, 25
McLuhan, Marshall, 428–429, 480, 737
McNickle, D'Arcy, 9
Mead, Margaret, 241

Meaning, 346, 477, 513, 561, 621, 667
Meaning of Meaning, The (Ogden), 477
Means and ends, 235, 236
Measurement, 120
Media, 118, 172
    electronic, 209–211
    hot and cool, 428
Mediated, 540
Medieval, 39
Medieval aesthetics, 203
Medieval period, 655
Medieval rhetoric, 429–434
Meditation, 448
Medium, *see* Media
Meiosis, 334
Melanchthon, Philip, 153
Mellon, John, 293
Memory, 435–436, 582, 595, 640
Menander of Laodicea, 664
Menander Rhetor, 664
Mencius, 634
Menexenus (Plato), 301, 524, 525
Mental health, 615
Mental illness, 615
Merleau-Ponty, Maurice, 513
Message, 119, 365
Metacommunication, 437
Metadiscourse, 437
Metahistory, 437
Metalanguage, 437
Metalepsis, 438
Metalingual, 365
Metalogicon (John of Salisbury), 651
Metaphor, 74, 102, 123, 268, 298, 343, 386, 438–443, 444, 555, 619, 621, 632, 635, 712–713, 718
Metaphoric, 365
Metaphysics, 425
    of presence, 165, 178
Metaplasm, 270
Metatalk, 437
Metatheory, 118, 437
Metathesis, 270
Method, 112, 180, 427, 559
Metonym, 445
Metonymic, 365
Metonymy, 343, 444–446, 621, 712–713, 718
Metz, Christian, 667
Michigan, University of, 657
Middle Ages, 426, 429–434, 699
    education in, 770–771
Middle style, 698
Mill, John Stuart, 95, 404
Miller, Carolyn, 624
Miller, J. Hillis, 466
Miller, Susan, 132
Mimesis, 635
Mind in Society: The Development of Higher Psychological Processes (Vygotsky), 752
Minoukianos, 224
Minucian, 664
Mnemonics, 435–436

Novel, 64
Novum organum (Bacon), 61
Now Don't Try to Reason with Me (Booth), 82

O

Objection, 592
    stasis of, 694
Objective discourse, 252
Objective narration, 454
Objectivism, 538
Objectivity, 346
Object permanence, 519
Occom, Samson, 8
Odyssey (Homer), 299
Official discourse, 252
Ogden, Charles Kay, 68, 72, 407, 477, 667
O'Hare, Frank, 294
O'Keefe, Daniel Lawrence, 421
Olbrechts-Tyteca, Lucie, 25, 34, 46, 368, 477–478,
    501–502, 736
Oldenburg, Henry, 646
Oliver, Robert T., 478–479
Olson, David R., 314
Olympiacus (Lysias), 416
On Copia (Erasmus), 234
On Figures and Tropes (Bede), 70
Ong, Walter J., 47, 114, 314, 479–480, 480–483,
    718–719
On Ideas of Style (Hermogenes), 304
On Invention (Hermogenes), 304
On-line links, 135
On Staseis (Hermogenes), 304
On Style (Demetrius), 174–175, 303
"On the Crown" (Demosthenes), 175
On the Metrical Art (Bede), 70
On the Sublime ("Longinus"), 303–304, 415,
    530–531
Ontological Argument, 514
Ontology, 118, 517
Operationism, 120
Opposites, 555
    theories of, 553–557
Oral English, 691
Orality, 210, 314, 480–483
Orality-literacy theorems, 480
Oral traditions, 7
Orator (Cicero), 42, 104, 215
Orators, 601–602, 630
Oratory, 53, 163, 176, 484–488, 582
    deliberative, 171–172
    epideictic, 228–231
    forensic, 139
    judicial, 592
    pulpit, 139, 573–575
Order, 139, 455
Ordinary language philosophy, 551
Organization, methods of, 107, 342
Organizational communication, 119, 721
Organizational Communication Division, SCA, 693
Original genius, 204
"Origins of Rhetoric: A Developmental View, The"
    (Emig), 219

Ornament, 168
Orthoepeia, 300
Orthography, 172
Orthological Institute, 68
Orwell, George, 198
Other, the, 488–489
Ought-propositions, 403
Overreacher, 334
Overshootings, 334
Overstatement, 334

P

Paideia, 362, 731
Paired phrases, 207
Palimpsest, 177
Pamphlets, 99
Panathenaicus (Isocrates), 301
Panegyric, 229, 230, 231
Panegyricus (Isocrates), 301, 362
Panhellenism, 485
Parable, 75
Paradiegesis, 191
Paradigm, 378–379
Paradigma, 495
Paradigm shift, 379, 491–492
Paradox, 209
Paradox of substance, 140
Paragogue, 270
Paragraph unity, 63
Paraphrase, 582, 728
Parasceve (Bacon), 62
Parenthesis, 492
Paris, University of, 153
Park, Douglas, 47
Parker, Richard Green, 446
Parliament, British, 89
Parliamentary oratory, 99
Parmenides (Plato), 665
Parmenides of Elea, 299, 488, 556–557, 683
Parole, 654, 665
Participant observation, 222
Partitio, 33, 492, 713
Partition, 107
Partitiones oratoriae (Cicero), 104
Parts of rhetoric, 582
Pascal, Blaise, 546
Passing theories, 160
Passions, 332, 645
Pathos, 29, 332, 492–494, 504, 506, 564
Patriarchy, 264–265
Pazzi, Allesandro de', 533
Peacham, Henry, 216, 494–495, 597
Pearsall, Thomas, 49
Pedagogical grammar, 293–294
Pedagogical strategies, 367
Pedagogy, 495–496, 651
Peer-responding, 420
Peer response groups, 208
Peirce, Charles Sanders, 73, 121, 425, 496–499,
    513, 552, 666–667, 733
Peithô, 299
Peloponnesian War, 359

Schiappa, Edward, 150
Schiller, F.C.S., 552
Schiller, Herbert I., 568
Schiller, Johann, 536
Schlegel, August Wilhelm von, 536
Schleiermacher, Friedrich D.E., 277, 317
Scholarly grammar, 290–291
Scholasticism, 587–588, 655–656
Scholastic method, 183
Science, 121, 373, 403, 426, 617
    normal, 491
    philosophy of, 378, 542–543
    rhetoric of, 622–627
Scientific communication, 647
Scientific discourse, 559
Scientific journal, 646, 647
Scientific method, 62
Scientific revolution, 121, 491
Scientific rhetoric, 62
Scientific writing, 674
Scopes trial, 759
Scotland, 674
Scott, Fred Newton, 657, 696
Scott, Robert L., 463, 517, 658
Scottish education, 367
Scottish Enlightenment, 205, 659–660
Scottish rhetoric, 205
Scottish universities, 59
Screen design, 748
Scriptural exegesis, 96
Scriptures, 74–75
Searle, John, 172, 733
Secondary imagination, 474
Secondary orality, 393, 480
Second persona, 77
Second Sophistic, 661–664, 668
Second Sophistic movement, 630
Second Sophistic period, 430
Secularism, 325
Seldes, George, 568
Selectivity, 447
Select Society, 53
Self, 113, 645, 749
Self-reference, 515
Self-reports, 561
Semantic holism, 580
Semantics, 192, 387–388, 427, 730
Semiotics, 67, 96, 117, 155, 203, 241, 377–378,
    498, 513, 666–667, 733, 748
    structuralist, 550
Seneca, 697
    elder, 163
Seneca the Elder, 661
Seneritas, 697 ·
"Sensible topics," 744
Sensori-motor stage, 520
Sentence combining, 278, 389
Sententia, 345, 562
Sequence, 448
Sermon, 39, 328–329, 573–575, 668–669
Servius, 531
Setting, 455

Sexism, 220, 616
Shannon-Weaver model, 45
Shared consciousness, 260
Shared group fantasy, 259
Shared imagination, 258
Shaughnessy, Mina, 669–670
Shaw, George Bernard, 68
Shaw, Nate, 5
Shelburne, William Fitzmaurice-Patty, second Earl
    of, 559
Shelley, Percy Bysshe, 536, 670–671
Sheridan, Richard Brinsley, 671
Sheridan, Thomas, 53, 213, 671–672
Sherry, Richard, 494, 597
Shor, Ira, 463–464
Sicily, 221, 723
Sidney, Sir Philip, 534, 672–673
Sign, 477, 673
Signified, 513, 666, 673
Signifier, 513, 666, 673
Signifying, 673
Signifying practices, 155
Signs, 50, 96, 136, 447, 498, 654–655, 666
Silence, rhetoric of, 627–628
Similarities, 122
Similes, 123, 343
Situational irony, 356
Situational perspectives for ethical assessment, 238
Situations, 46, 141–143
Sjuzhet, 454
Skinner, Alanson, 7
Slave narratives, 5
Smallwood, Elizabeth Ruth, 89
Smith, Adam, 53, 372, 659–660, 674
Smith, Barbara Herrnstein, 667
Smith, Craig R., 318
Smitherman, Geneva, 78
Social-cognitive theory building, 108
Social construction, 190, 675–677
Social constructionism, 120, 193, 696
Social constructionist theories, 354, 736
Social Construction of Knowledge in Composi-
    tion, 420
Social constructivism, 209
Social harmony, 208
Socialism, 764–765
Social movements, 511, 571
Social mythology, 262
Social science, 117, 757
Social speech, 752
Social structure, 422
Social theory, 23–24
Society, language and, 677–679
Sociolinguistics, 391, 677–679
Socrates, 191, 301, 359, 523, 680–681
Socratic method, 680
Software, 720
Some Thoughts Concerning Education (Locke),
    396
Sonnet sequence, 672
Sopater, 664
Sophist (Plato), 524, 665

Systems theory, 226
System theory, 117

T

Tacit knowing, 538
Tacitus, 216, 581, 661
Tagmemic linguistics, 415, 520–521
Tagmemics, 353, 38–390, 520, 715–718, 750
Talaeus, 587; *see also* Ramus, Peter
Talk-write model, 777
Talon, Omer, 596, 718–719; *see also* Ramus, Peter
Taste, 32, 71–72, 79–80
Taxonomies, 118
Taxonomies of discourse, 576
Teachers of writing, 459
Teaching composition, 113
Teaching practices, 459
Technai, 719
Technê, 116, 198, 301, 319–320, 473, 515, 553, 617, 719
Technical communication, 720–721
Technological criticism, 619–620
Technological environments, 429
Technology, 617
    rhetoric and, 616–620
Teleological, 28
Teleology, 722
Telos, 722
Temporality, 371
Tenor, 343, 439
Terministic screens, 178, 722–723
Tertullian, 668
Tetralogies (Antiphon), 13
Text and Performance Quarterly, 692
Textbooks, 470
Text features, 589
Text linguistics, 193, 415, 715
Text-ownership, 751
Texts, 178, 193, 621, 686, 704
Thales, 554–555
Theater Division, SCA, 693
Themes, 427
Themistius, 664
Theodore of Tarsus, Archbishop of Canterbury, 70
Theodoric, 95
Theodotus, 664
Theogony (Hesiod), 299
Theon, Aelius, 304, 562, 664
Theophrastus, 303, 503
Theoretical knowledge, 28
Theoria, 553
Theory, 120, 141, 559
    of descriptions, 648
Theory of Discourse (Kinneavy), 376
Theramenes, 13
Theses, 315, 427, 642
Thesis, 563, 662
Thick description, 241
Thierry of Chartres, 651
Think-aloud protocols, 572–573
Thinkbook, 369
Thinking, binary, 209

Third Man argument, 514
Third Persona, 341
Thirty, 417
Thomas of Capua, 37
Thonssen, Lester, 63
Thrasybulus, 150
Thrasymachus, 300, 682, 723
Thucydides, 300, 719
Timing, 371
Timotheus, 359
Tisias, 221, 300, 311, 416, 564, 723
Titulus, 96
Tmesis, 723–724
Tone, 748
Tools, 618
"Top-down" approach, 69
Topica (Cicero), 104
Topica Boetii (Boethius), 80
Topics, 6, 116, 354, 427, 724–725
    attack against, 546
Topics (Aristotle), 184, 302
Topic sentence, 63
Topoi, 29, 50, 65, 104, 255, 503–504, 722, 724, 755
Torah, 74
Toulmin, Stephen, 18, 24, 46, 204, 405, 726–727, 736, 756
Toulmin model, 727, 756
Tractatus Coislinianus, 503
Tractatus Logico-philosophicus (Wittgenstein), 477, 769
Traditional criticism, 340
Traditional grammar, 294–295
Trajan, 709
Transactional writing, 84
Transaction theory, 644
Transcendence, 742
Transculturation, 338
Transformational generative grammar, 387
Transformational grammar, 102, 415
Transformations, 73, 102
    cultural, 617
Translation, 580, 728–730
Translation theory, 717
Transparent language, 180
Travel diaries, 369
Trebizond, George of, 595, 730–731
Tria genera causarum, 446
Trial courts, 383
Triangulation, 160
Tribal culture, 7
Trilling, Lionel, 31
Trimbur, John, 463
Trinity College, 648
Trivium, 6, 383, 432, 495, 580, 667, 731
Trivium (John of Salisbury), 651
Tropes, 51, 159, 268, 439, 444, 494, 582, 698, 712, 718
Tropology, 268
True Womanhood, 262
Truman, Margaret, 287
Trust, 647